Current Biography Yearbook

1984

Current Biography Yearbook 1984

EDITOR
Charles Moritz

ASSOCIATE EDITORS
Henry Sloan
Kieran Dugan
Judith Graham
Mary E. Kiffer

ASSISTANT EDITOR
Margaret Brodhead

THE H. W. WILSON COMPANY
NEW YORK

FORTY-FIFTH ANNUAL CUMULATION—1984

PRINTED IN THE UNITED STATES OF AMERICA

International Standard Serial No. (0084-9499)

Library of Congress Catalog Card No. (40-27432)

PREFACE

The aim of CURRENT BIOGRAPHY YEARBOOK 1984, like that of the preceding volumes in this series of annual dictionaries of contemporary biography, now in its fifth decade of publication, is to provide the reference librarian, the student, or any researcher with brief, objective, accurate, and well-documented biographical articles about living leaders in all fields of human accomplishment the world over. Whenever feasible, obituary notices appear for persons whose biographies have been published in CURRENT BIOGRAPHY, and every attempt is made to pick up obituaries that have inadvertently been omitted in previous years.

CURRENT BIOGRAPHY YEARBOOK 1984 carries on the policy of including new and updated biographical sketches that supersede earlier, outdated articles. Sketches have been made as accurate and objective as possible through careful researching by CURRENT BIOGRAPHY writers in newspapers, magazines, authoritative reference books, and news releases of both government and private agencies. Immediately after they are published in the eleven monthly issues, articles are submitted to biographees to give them an opportunity to suggest corrections in time for CURRENT BIOGRAPHY Yearbook. To take account of major changes in the careers of biographees, sketches have also been revised before they are included in the yearbook. With the exception of occasional interviews, the questionnaire filled out by the biographee remains the main source of direct information.

Some persons who are not professional authors but who have written books are included under *Nonfiction* in addition to their vocational fields. The annual bestowal of Nobel Prizes has added articles to the volume. The pages immediately following contain *Explanations; Key to Reference Abbreviations; Key to Pronunciation;* and *Key to Abbreviations.* The indexes at the end of the volume are *Biographical References; Periodicals and Newspapers Consulted; Classification by Profession;* and *Cumulated Index—1981-1984.* The 1940-1950 index can be found in the 1950 yearbook, the 1951-1960 index, in the 1960 yearbook, the 1961-1970 index in the 1970 yearbook, and the 1971-1980 index in the 1980 yearbook.

For their assistance in preparing CURRENT BIOGRAPHY YEARBOOK 1984, I should like to thank the associate and assistant editors.

Charles Moritz

Explanations

Authorities for biographees' full names, with some exceptions, are the bibliographical publications of The Wilson Company. When a biographee prefers a certain name form, that is indicated in the heading of the article: for example, Niemöller, (Friedrich Gustav Emil) Martin means that he is usually referred to as Martin Niemöller. When a professional name is used in the heading, as, for example, Anne Bancroft, the real name (in this case Annemarie Italiano) appears in the article itself.

The heading of each article includes the pronunciation of the name if it is unusual, date of birth (if obtainable), and occupation. The article is supplemented by a list of references to sources of biographical information, in two alphabets: (1) newspapers and periodicals and (2) books. (See the section *Biographical References*, found in the rear of this volume.)

Key to Reference Abbreviations

References to some newspapers and periodicals are listed in abbreviated form; for example, "Sat Eve Post 217:14 S 30 '44 por" means *Saturday Evening Post*, volume 217, page 14, September 30, 1944, with portrait. (For full names, see the section *Periodicals and Newspapers Consulted*, found in the rear of this volume.)

January—Ja	July—Jl	Journal—J
February—F	August—Ag	Magazine—Mag
March—Mr	September—S	Monthly—Mo
April—Ap	October—O	Portrait—por
May—My	November—N	Weekly—W
June—Je	December—D	Review—R

Key to Pronunciation

ā	āle	
â	câre	
a	add	
ä	ärm	
ē	ēve	
e	end	
g	go	
ī	īce	
i	ill	
ᴋ	German *ch* as in *ich* (iᴋ)	
ɴ	Not pronounced, but indicates the nasal tone of the preceding vowel, as in the French *bon* (bôɴ)	

ō	ōld
ô	ôrb
o	odd
oi	oil
o͞o	ooze
o͝o	foot
ou	out
th	then
th	thin
ū	cūbe
û	ûrn; French eu, as in *jeu* zhû), German ö, oe, as in *schön* (shûn), *Goethe* (gû′te)
u	tub

ü Pronounced approximately as ē, with rounded lips: French u, as in *menu* (mə-nü); German ü, as in *grün*

ə the schwa, an unstressed vowel representing the sound that is spelled
a as in sofa
e as in fitted
i as in edible
o as in melon
u as in circus

zh azure
′ = main accent
″ = secondary accent

Key to Abbreviations

AAAA	Amateur Athletic Association of America	ECA	Economic Cooperation Administration
AAU	Amateur Athletic Union	ECOSOC	Economic and Social Council
AAUP	American Association of University Professors	EDC	Economic Defense Community
		EEC	European Economic Community
ABA	American Bar Association	ERA	Equal Rights Amendment
ABC	American Broadcasting Company	E.R.A.	Earned Run Average
ACA	Americans for Constitutional Action	ERP	European Recovery Program
ACLU	American Civil Liberties Union	ESA	Economic Stabilization Administration
ADA	Americans for Democratic Action		
AEC	Atomic Energy Commission		
AEF	American Expeditionary Force	FAO	Food and Agriculture Organization
AFL	American Federation of Labor	FBI	Federal Bureau of Investigation
AFL-CIO	American Federation of Labor and Congress of Industrial Organizations	FCC	Federal Communications Commission
		FEPC	Fair Employment Practice Committee
ALA	American Library Association	FHA	Federal Housing Administration
AMA	American Medical Association	FOA	Foreign Operations Administration
AP	Associated Press	FPC	Federal Power Commission
ASCAP	American Society of Composers, Authors and Publishers	FSA	Federal Security Agency
		FTC	Federal Trade Commission
ASNE	American Society of Newspaper Editors		
		GATT	General Agreement on Tariffs and Trade
B.A.	Bachelor of Arts		
BBC	British Broadcasting Corporation	G.B.E.	Knight or Dame, Grand Cross Order of the British Empire
B.D.	Bachelor of Divinity		
B.L.S.	Bachelor of Library Science	G.C.B.	Knight or Dame, Grand Cross of the Bath
B.S.	Bachelor of Science		
		GOP	Grand Old Party
CAA	Civil Aeronautics Administration	H.M.	His Majesty; Her Majesty
CAB	Civil Aeronautics Board	HUD	Housing and Urban Development
C.B.	Companion of the Bath		
C.B.E.	Commander of (the Order of) the British Empire	IBM	International Business Machines Corporation
CBS	Columbia Broadcasting System		
C.E.	Civil Engineer	ICBM	Intercontinental Ballistic Missile
CEA	Council of Economic Advisers	ICC	Interstate Commerce Commission
CED	Committee for Economic Development	ICFTU	International Confederation of Free Trade Unions
CENTO	Central Treaty Organization	IGY	International Geophysical Year
CIA	Central Intelligence Agency	ILA	International Longshoremen's Association
CIO	Congress of Industrial Organizations		
C.M.G.	Companion of (the Order of) St. Michael and St. George	ILGWU	International Ladies'Garment Workers' Union
Com.	Commodore	ILO	International Labor Organization
CORE	Congress of Racial Equality	IMF	International Monetary Fund
		INS	International News Service
		IRA	Irish Republican Army
DAR	Daughters of the American Revolution	IRO	International Refugee Organization
D.C.L.	Doctor of Civil Law		
D.D.	Doctor of Divinity	J.D.	Doctor of Jurisprudence
D.Eng.	Doctor of Engineering		
DEW	Distant Early Warning Line		
D.F.C.	Distinguished Flying Cross	K.B.E.	Knight of (the Order of) the British Empire
D.J.	Doctor of Jurisprudence		
D.Litt.	Doctor of Literature	K.C.	King's Counsel
D.Mus.	Doctor of Music	K.C.B.	Knight Commander of the Bath
DP	Displaced Person		
D.Pol.Sc.	Doctor of Political Science		
D.S.C.	Distinguished Service Cross	L.H.D.	Doctor of Humane Letters
D.Sc.	Doctor of Science	Litt.D.	Doctor of Letters
D.S.M.	Distinguished Service Medal	LL.B.	Bachelor of Laws
D.S.O.	Distinguished Service Order	LL.D.	Doctor of Laws

M.A.	Master of Arts	RAF	Royal Air Force
M.B.A.	Master of Business Administration	RCA	Radio Corporation of America
MBS	Mutual Broadcasting System	REA	Rural Electrification Administration
M.C.E.	Master of Civil Engineering	RFC	Reconstruction Finance Corporation
M.D.	Doctor of Medicine	RKO	Radio-Keith-Orpheum
M.E.	Master of Engineering	ROTC	Reserve Officers' Training Corps
METO	Middle East Treaty Organization		
MGM	Metro-Goldwyn-Mayer	SAC	Strategic Air Command
M.Lit.	Master of Literature	SALT	Strategic Arms Limitation Talks
M.P.	Member of Parliament	S.J.	Society of Jesus (Jesuit)
MPPDA	Motion Picture Producers and Distributors of America	SCAP	Supreme Command for the Allied Powers
MRP	Mouvement Républicain Populaire	SEATO	Southeast Asia Treaty Organization
MSA	Mutual Security Agency	SEC	Securities and Exchange Commission
M.Sc.	Master of Science		
Msgr.	Monsignor, Monseigneur	SHAEF	Supreme Headquarters, Allied Expeditionary Force
NAACP	National Association for the Advancement of Colored People	SHAPE	Supreme Headquarters, Allied Powers Europe
NAB	National Association of Broadcasters	S.J.D.	Doctor of Juridical Science
		SLA	Special Libraries Association
NAM	National Association of Manufacturers	S.T.B.	Bachelor of Sacred Theology
		S.T.D.	Doctor of Sacred Theology
NASA	National Aeronautics and Space Administration	TVA	Tennessee Valley Authority
NATO	North Atlantic Treaty Organization	TWUA	Textile Workers Union of America
NBC	National Broadcasting Company		
NEA	National Education Association	UAR	United Arab Republic
NLRB	National Labor Relations Board	UAW	United Automobile, Aircraft, and Agricultural Implement Workers of America
N.M.U.	National Maritime Union		
NOW	National Organization for Women		
NRA	National Recovery Administration	UMT	Universal Military Training
NRPB	National Resources Planning Board	UMWA	United Mine Workers of America
NYA	National Youth Administration	UN	United Nations
		UNESCO	United Nations Educational, Scientific, and Cultural Organization
OAS	Organization of American States		
O.B.E.	Officer of (the Order of) the British Empire	UNICEF	United Nations Children's Fund
		UNRRA	United Nations Relief and Rehabilitation Administration
OCD	Office of Civilian Defense		
OEEC	Organization for European Economic Cooperation	UPI	United Press and International News Service
OMB	Office of Management and Budget	USO	United Service Organizations
OPA	Office of Price Administration	U.S.S.R.	Union of Soviet Socialist Republics
OPEC	Organization of Petroleum Exporting Countries	USWA	United Steel Workers of America
OPM	Office of Production Management	VA	Veterans Administration
OWI	Office of War Information	VFW	Veterans of Foreign Wars
PBS	Public Broadcasting Service	WFTU	World Federation of Trade Unions
PEN	Poets, Playwrights, Editors, Essayists and Novelists (International Association)	WHO	World Health Organization
		WMC	War Manpower Commission
		WPA	Work Projects Administration
Ph.B.	Bachelor of Philosophy	WPB	War Production Board
Ph.D.	Doctor of Philosophy		
PLO	Palestine Liberation Organization	YMCA	Young Men's Christian Association
PWA	Public Works Administration	YMHA	Young Men's Hebrew Association
		YWCA	Young Women's Christian Association
Q.C.	Queen's Counsel		

Current Biography Yearbook
1984

Adler, Renata

Oct. 19, 1938– Writer. Address: b. c/o Lynn Nesbitt, International Famous Agency, 1301 Ave. of the Americas, New York City, N. Y. 10019

Although she has only produced four books—two novels and two collections of reportage and film reviews—during a writing career spanning more than twenty years, Renata Adler has attracted the kind of critical attention more often bestowed on a prolific best-selling author. No major reviewing medium failed to comment on her recently published second novel, *Pitch Dark.* Miss Adler's reportage also rarely goes unnoticed: her trenchant articles have been acclaimed and denounced with equal fervor. Even during her tenure as film critic for the *New York Times*, she generated controversy, irritating moviegoers and movie moguls alike with her outspoken, often scathing, reviews of some of the box-office hits of the 1960s. But though she is often the object of media attention, this reclusive, gifted, and award-winning author and journalist manages to preserve an aura of mystery.

Renata Adler was born on October 19, 1938 in Milan, Italy, the third child and only girl of attorney Frederick L. and Erna (Strauss) Adler, German refugees who immigrated to Danbury, Connecticut when Renata was a small child. At the age of seven she was sent to boarding school to learn to speak English without a German accent. Four years later, she returned home and attended the local high school, where she took part in field hockey, the school dramatic club, and other extracurricular activities. Although she disparages her academic achievements there ("If you took the highest average in the class of the person who wasn't going to be a nun, I may have had that"), she actually maintained the highest average of any student in the college preparatory course.

Despite her reluctance to be parted from her family again, Renata Adler enrolled at Bryn Mawr College in Pennsylvania. Finding it difficult to adjust to college, she was punished for infractions of the honor code at least twice, and was unable to submit the required weekly essay. (One of her brothers eventually wrote them all for her.) Nevertheless, by the time she completed work for her A.B. degree in philosophy and German in 1959, she was editor of *The Revue* yearbook, a member of the college arts council, and a popular and indisputably successful student. Graduating *summa cum laude* from Bryn Mawr, she won its highest undergraduate honor, a $1,000 European fellowship. During the next year, Renata Adler studied comparative literature with I. A. Richards at Harvard University, receiving her master's degree in 1960,

Richard Avedon

and then continued her education as a Fulbright scholar in Paris. There she worked with the renowned anthropologist Claude Lévi-Strauss and with the philosopher Jean Wahl at the Sorbonne and obtained a D.d.E.S. degree in 1961.

When Renata Adler returned to New York the following year, the celebrated dramatist S. N. Behrman, for whom she had translated a play, arranged an interview for her at the *New Yorker*, and shortly after that she joined its staff, evaluating unsolicited short stories, reviewing books, and writing pieces for its "Talk of the Town" column. After a short time, she was granted a leave of absence to go to California to visit her fiancé. Her marriage plans fell through, but her connection with the *New Yorker* prospered as she shifted from reviewing books to reporting on such current events as the rise of the New Left, the civil rights march from Selma, Alabama led by Martin Luther King Jr., group therapy, Vietnam, and the Six-Day War. When *Toward a Radical Middle*, a collection of fourteen of her pieces that previously appeared in the *New Yorker*, was published by Random House in 1970, Wilfred Sheed praised it in the *New York Times Book Review* (March 19, 1970) as "a gracefully phrased, ardently intelligent book," and most other critics were equally enthusiastic about her incisive essays.

Her success at the *New Yorker* did not deter Renata Adler from readily accepting an unexpected offer from the *New York Times*, in 1967, to become its new film critic. The selection of someone so young and relatively inexperienced—she had only written five film reviews up to that point—to replace the veteran Bosley Crowther led to speculation about the *Times's* decision. Crowther interpreted it as part of a general trend in newspapers toward hiring "long-haired critics," while the dance and drama critic Clive Barnes, himself a newcomer to the *Times*, viewed it as part of the staid old newspaper's "new generation rejuvenation" pattern. In *Newsweek* (December 4, 1967) Turner Catledge, executive editor of the *Times*, asserted that ability was the major criterion in hiring her. "She's done enough to show us what she can do. We think she has the potential to be a great movie critic." Seemingly less assured, Renata Adler was particularly intimidated by the frequent deadlines she would have to face. "I've never written that much that fast," she said. "It should be fun. But God, it's going to be a lot of movies."

Renata Adler triggered controversy on January 4, 1968 with her very first review, in which she dismissed *The Wicked Dreams of Paula Schultz* as "unrelievedly awful, in such a number of uninteresting ways." In subsequent columns she was an outspoken critic of violence and nudity in film. In her reviews, for example, on January 7, 1968 of *In Cold Blood* and *The Dirty Dozen*, two box-office hits, she argued that "dwelling on pain or damage to the human body in the film's literal terms can [never] be morally or artistically valid." Both film production studios and movie buffs objected to what they considered to be her overly intellectual and moralistic reviews; some readers even questioned whether she liked movies at all. On March 22, 1968 Lopert Pictures Corporation, a subsidiary of United Artists, contended in a full-page ad in the *New York Times* that since she had disparaged so many successful movies, her negative review of its latest release, *Here We Go Round the Mulberry Bush*, amounted to a recommendation. But the management of the *Times* continued to support her, and Miss Adler herself explained in *Newsweek* (April 15, 1968): "I like movies and I like bad movies but that doesn't mean I have to say they're good. I'm not supposed to be drumming up trade for movies that I like or closing down movies that I don't like."

But critical response to Renata Adler's reportage for the *New York Times* was uniformly favorable. It may have been her fearless plainspeaking that won her an invitation to Cuba to report on Cuban films and cultural affairs at a time when the *Times* news staff was barred from entering that country. That trip resulted in a series of three major articles in early 1969. And her pieces on the Cannes Film Festival further added to her growing reputation.

When *A Year in the Dark*, a collection of Miss Adler's articles and reviews, was published by Random House in 1970, one of her colleagues, Christopher Lehmann-Haupt, did not allow their association to temper his candid opinion of the book in the *New York Times* (January 28, 1970). Although he found the book to be of "limited interest" to most readers, he conceded that the reviews seemed "more coherent and graceful than they did when they first appeared," perhaps "because when read in sequence, the pieces modify one another and highlight the subtle shifts in her critical point of view." In *Variety* (February 25, 1970) Robert J. Landry qualified his praise of the film criticism: "Let the record suggest that Renata Adler was awfully good when she was good, but frightfully highbrow and groan-making when she was backing into one of her theories."

After saturating herself in cinema for only fourteen months, Renata Adler announced her resignation from the *New York Times* on February 26, 1969. She explained in *Newsweek* (March 10, 1969) that "frequently, it seemed as though the same movie was coming out again and again under a different title," and in her introduction to *A Year in the Dark*, she commented, "I do not believe in professional criticism anyway, as a way of life." Returning to the *New Yorker*, Miss Adler resumed comment on the world scene, contributing, among other pieces, "Letter from Biafra," which appeared in the October 4, 1969 issue, and an article for the October 3, 1970 "Reporter at Large" section. But she found herself writing more and more short stories, including "Collect Calls" and "Castling," for publication in the *New Yorker*. Recalling in a profile for *New York* magazine (December 12, 1983) why she turned from reporting to fiction writing, she explained, "I think that if you're going to write, after a certain point some of it better be fiction. Unless, as a critic, you're going to be praising everything all the time, it's only fair to take certain risks of your own."

Her decision proved to be a wise one. "Brownstone," a short story first published in the January 27, 1973 issue of the *New Yorker*, won first prize in the 1974 O. Henry Short Stories awards. Of that story, William Abrahams, the editor of the O. Henry Prize Stories series, remarked: "It would be difficult to find a more realistic evocation of the serio-comic tone and detail of metropolitan life in the 1970's in America." He further praised "Brownstone" as "bent upon finding its own form and triumphantly succeeding." Moreover, her first novel, *Speedboat* (Random House, 1976), won the second annual Ernest Hemingway Foundation Award for the best first novel by an American published in the previous year and was included in the *New York Times Book Review's* "Editor's Choice" of the fourteen best books of 1976.

Plotless and virtually without characters except for the narrator, *Speedboat* is composed largely of revised stories and vignettes, including "Brownstone," that had originally appeared in the *New Yorker*. The random and surrealistic snippets of reflection and observation, few of which are even a page long, that make up *Speedboat* trace daily events in the life of a journalist in her mid-thirties who is remarkably like Renata Adler. Peter S. Prescott, who pronounced it the "quintessential New York book" in *Newsweek* (October 11, 1976), judged it to be so representative of its times that he thought *Speedboat* should be stashed away in a time capsule so that future generations would know "how some of us lived and what passed for thought in the '70s."

Like some other critics, Anatole Broyard complained in the *New York Times* (September 23, 1976) that though *Speedboat* was "extremely clever," it was not a true novel and not at all "'important' either, except in a symptomatic sense." Writing in the *New York Times Book Review* (September 26, 1976), Robert Towers agreed that it was improperly labeled but maintained that it was, nevertheless, "a very good book: elegantly written, often funny, vivid in its presentation of the absurdities, the small and great horrors, the booby-traps with which our daily existence is strewn."

Pitch Dark (Knopf, 1983), Renata Adler's latest novel, also consists of a series of brief narratives united only by a sketchy chronology and repeated words and phrases. Through the reflections of Kate Ennis, a journalist-protagonist who again very much resembles Renata Adler, the story of her turbulent eight-year affair with a married lawyer named Jake and its stormy conclusion gradually emerges. Although both her novels are unconventional in structure, Miss Adler insisted in an interview with Samuel Freedman for the *New York Times* (December 27, 1983) that she believes "very much in the traditional form." "I'm always surprised when my writing isn't within it," she continued. "I wouldn't want my book to just be vignettes. I would not set out to break a convention for its own sake." She also made clear in the same interview that she considers reviewers' speculations about whether *Pitch Dark* was actually an autobiographical roman à clef out of place in criticism. (Some thought they discerned thinly disguised portraits of Oriana Fallaci, Janet Cooke, and Claus von Bülow, among others.) "Those are Philistine assumptions," Miss Adler said. "That's talking gossip and not talking fiction. And I think I'm pretty clear on the difference."

But in spite of their quibbles about the book's autobiographical content and its unorthodox structure, most critics held *Pitch Dark* in high esteem. Michiko Kakutani's assessment in the *New York Times* (December 5, 1983) was representative: "Alienated, self-conscious and morally ill-at-ease, Kate Ennis resembles Joan Didion's high-strung heroines—except that she lives in a brownstone in New York. . . . In the end, Kate's personality and voice . . . help *Pitch Dark* transcend the limits of its structure; they make the book not only engaging intellectually, but also emotionally compelling."

During the seven years between the publication of her two novels, Renata Adler was involved in a variety of activities in addition to fiction writing. Through John Doar, a long-time friend who was special counsel for the House Judiciary Committee during its inquiry into the possible impeachment of President Richard M. Nixon, she was appointed speech writer for Peter W. Rodino Jr., Democratic congressman from New Jersey and chairman of that committee. Besides writing his speeches from January to August 1974, she helped to develop in-

vestigative techniques for the committee. Her interest in the subject continued, and she began working on a book about the Nixon impeachment inquiry with the help of an appointment in 1975 as Lucy Martin Donnelly Fellow at Bryn Mawr College, the first Bryn Mawr alumna to be so honored. The book did not materialize, but in December 1976 she published a lengthy article in the *Atlantic*, "Searching for the Real Nixon Scandal," another of her controversial pieces, in which she hypothesized that Nixon might have received contributions during the 1972 presidential campaign from South Vietnamese officials in exchange for prolonging the war and giving them time to line their pockets before fleeing. Her theory polarized her readers. According to Jesse Kornbluth's article in *New York* magazine (December 12, 1983), some Watergate-watchers considered it "a tour de force that verged on being the major scoop" of the investigation, but her friend John Doar, among others, contended that there was "no basis for her hypothesis." Since Miss Adler's experiences while working for Rodino and the flak from the *Atlantic* article convinced her that "you can't be a journalist and not know the law," she enrolled at Yale Law School.

With law school behind her in 1979, Renata Adler returned to writing, and she filled in as film reviewer at the *New Yorker* during Pauline Kael's long autumn vacation that year. She despised the work. "It became almost impossible on anything like a frequent basis to write seriously, with proportion and fidelity, of all this junk," she wrote in her negative review of *The Black Stallion* in the November 5, 1979 issue. She also contributed reviews to other publications. Her attack on Bob Woodward and Scott Armstrong's book about the Supreme Court, *The Brethren*, was featured on the front page of the *New York Times Book Review* (December 16, 1975). A few years later she stirred up a storm with a lengthy and withering review in the *New York Review of Books* (August 14, 1980) of Pauline Kael's collection of film criticism, *When the Lights Go Down*, calling it "jarringly, piece by piece, line by line, and without interruption, worthless." That one *New Yorker* contributor would savage the work of another was considered unthinkable, and Renata Adler remained the focus of literary gossip for some time.

Renata Adler's many honors include a Merit Award from *Mademoiselle* magazine (1964), a Guggenheim fellowship (1973–74), and a literary award from the American Academy of Arts and Letters (1978). She has been a member of the editorial board of the *American Scholar* since 1962 and served on the executive board of P.E.N. from 1964 to 1970. In 1969 Trumbull College, Yale University, appointed her a fellow, an honor she held for three years, and during 1972–73 she was an associate professor of theatre and cinema at Hunter College in New York City under its distinguished professor program.

A tall, slight woman whom Paul Lancaster described as "bird-like" in the *Wall Street Journal* (May 4, 1972), Renata Adler wears her hair in a long salt-and-pepper braid. A very private person whose East Side Manhattan duplex and two-acre country retreat few are privileged to visit, Miss Adler nevertheless has many friends among the famous. She has been the subject of more than one Richard Avedon photographic portrait and her social world includes the likes of Brooke Astor, Drue Heinz, and Jacqueline Onassis rather than fellow writers. She feels that lack. As she explained to Jesse Kornbluth, "It's not my world. As far as I know there isn't a community in the arts of people who wish each other well. It's a temporary and not a good situation."

Renata Adler's work habits may account for her limited production. "I wake up at five or six, I have breakfast," she has said. "I think, 'I should be writ-ing.' And then I think, 'Well, maybe after a little nap.' And that way several years pass. Truly, several years pass." Although the controversies that she has generated might seem to belie it, she is painfully shy. "*Pitch Dark* wouldn't be a personal risk for most writers," Elizabeth Hardwick has observed. "A book this revealing is only a risk for a writer as reserved as Renata." Obviously agreeing, Renata Adler has equated the writing of fiction with "sending a heat-seeking missile at your own life."

References: Guardian p11 Ag 25 '77 por; New York 16:34+ D 12 '83 pors; N Y Times C p11 D 27 '83 por; Contemporary Authors new rev vol 5 (1982); Who's Who in America, 1976-77; Writers' Directory, 1980-82

Alfonsin, Raúl
(äl fōn sēn´ rä ōōl´)

Mar. 12, 1927– President of Argentina. Address: b. Casa Rosada, Buenos Aires, Argentina

On October 30, 1983 Raúl Alfonsín, leader of the middle-of-the-road Unión Cívica Radical (UCR), won election as the forty-fifth president of Argentina, defeating the long dominant Peronist party and ending nearly eight years of military rule. At the time, Alfonsín termed his victory the "beginning of a new era" for his troubled country. Sworn into office on December 10, 1983, Alfonsín immediately faced momentous problems, including runaway inflation, a national debt of some $40 billion, labor discontent, public clamor for an accounting for thousands of missing persons who disappeared un-der military rule, and the disenchantment of the military over their defeat by the British in 1982 in the Falkland Islands. Nevertheless, Argentina's return to the democratic path under Alfonsín was widely regarded as the best means of resolving the nation's difficulties. "The difference between democracy and dictatorship," Alfonsín has asserted repeatedly over the past decade, "is the difference between life and death."

Raúl Ricardo Alfonsín Foulkes, who according to a profile in Time (November 14, 1983) "seems the quintessential Argentine," was born on March 12, 1927 (one source gives March 13, 1926), in the town of Chascomús in Buenos Aires province, seventy-eight miles southeast of the national capital, the oldest of five children of Serafín Alfonsín. His parents ran a moderately prosperous general store founded, according to the Time article, by his great-grandfather, who in 1870 had emigrated from the fertile province of Galicia in northwestern Spain. According to other sources, Alfonsín's father was a native of Galicia who immigrated to Argentina. In any case, Serafín Alfonsín was an ardent champion of the republican cause in the Spanish Civil War and a determined foe of dictator Francisco Franco, as well as a supporter of the moderate Unión Cívica Radical, which dominated Argentine politics until 1930. "I came from a home atmosphere where liberty was not only learned from books," Raúl Alfonsín has recalled. His hero was the Radical leader Hipólito Yrigoyen, who became president of Argentina in 1916.

Alfonsín obtained his early education at the Escuela Normal Regional in his hometown. At thirteen he entered the Liceo Militar General San Martín, where his classmates included Leopoldo Galtieri, who later headed Argentina's military government during the 1982 Falkland Islands war with Great Britain. But after graduating from the military academy at eighteen with a bachelor's degree and the rank of second lieutenant in the army reserve, Alfonsín decided against a military career. From 1945 to 1950 he studied liberal arts and law at the National University of La Plata and obtained a doctorate. While there he became active in the Unión Civica Radical, attracted by its populism, libertarianism, and long-time opposition to the country's landed oligarchy. After he completed his studies, Alfonsin's preoccupation with politics diverted him from the practice of law, though his interest in the humanities remained strong. "If I hadn't followed a political career, I certainly would have pursued philosophy and literature," Alfonsin told an interviewer for the Buenos Aires newspaper La Nación (December 10, 1983).

In the years following the overthrow and exile of dictator Juan Perón in 1955, Argentina alternated between military and civilian governments, with the Peronists remaining a major force in politics. Alfonsin won his first elective office at twenty-four as a representative of the UCR on the local council of Chascomús, and he was from the beginning of his political career outspoken in his support of his party's principles. His views sometimes brought him vitriolic attacks and even death threats from his opponents, and he was arrested on several occasions.

Rising rapidly in Argentine politics, Alfonsin was elected from La Plata to the provincial legislature of Buenos Aires in 1958, and in 1960 he won reelection. With the election of July 1963—Argentina's first under a new system of proportional representation—which brought the UCR leader Arturo Illia to the presidency, Alfonsin entered the arena of national politics as a candidate for the Congreso Nacional, or national parliament, and was elected. In 1967 he was precandidate for the governorship of Buenos Aires province.

Often at odds with the leaders of the UCR, whom he regarded as being too conservative and out of touch with the common people, Alfonsin joined forces in the late 1960s with a small group of fellow party members in an effort to revitalize the UCR into a popular, democratic, rational, and reformist movement capable of winning the masses over from the Peronists and of attaining national power. El Movimiento de Renovación y Cambio (Movement of Renovation and Change), as his faction was known, formally came into being on May 3, 1972. "In my judgment it was essential to accelerate the modernization of the doctrine and practice of Radicalism," Alfonsin said at the time. "We had to put greater stress on social issues and get closer to the people." Unwilling to come into direct conflict with the Peronists, since he agreed with many of their social reform policies, he nevertheless challenged their authoritarianism. "For me any authoritarian component in a popular movement is intolerable," he declared.

In the turbulent UCR convention that was held in Buenos Aires in June 1972, Alfonsin was roundly defeated by the veteran party leader Ricardo Balbin in their bids for nomination as presidential candidate in elections called for 1973 by the military regime of General Alejandro Lanusse. In view of Argentina's growing economic, social, and political problems, Lanusse had decided to allow the country to return to elected civilian government.

But the presidency of Juan Perón that followed his return from exile in Spain in 1973 failed to alleviate the country's ills. Conditions grew steadily worse during the presidency of his widow, Isabel Perón, who succeeded him after his death, and under the succession of military governments that followed her overthrow in March 1976.

Meanwhile, although Alfonsin's stunning defeat by Balbin in his 1972 bid for the UCR leadership led some commentators to suggest that his political career was at an end, he continued to build a solid base of support. During the eclipse of political activity in Argentina after the military takeover in 1976, he remained an outspoken critic of the government, especially in the areas of human rights and economic policy. As cofounder and copresident of Argentina's privately sponsored Permanent Assembly for Human Rights he condemned the arbitrary arrests, murders, and kidnappings of Argentine citizens by paramilitary groups allegedly linked to the government, such as the Argentine Anticommunist Alliance, and demanded an accounting for the thousands of persons who mysteriously disappeared during the last half of the 1970s. He praised the administration of United States President Jimmy Carter for its support of human rights in Argentina and elsewhere but criticized the changes in those policies after Ronald Reagan became president in 1981. As Martin Andersen noted in the New Republic (March 19, 1984), Alfonsin considered Reagan's policies to be "more a defense of capitalism than a defense of democracy." As a lawyer, Alfonsin defended a number of political prisoners.

On the international level, Raúl Alfonsin moved to strengthen ties between the UCR and the social-democratic movements of Europe and to enhance his country's relations with both the United States and the Soviet-bloc countries. At the time of Argentina's invasion of the British-administered Falkland Islands, or Malvinas, in 1982, Alfonsin supported the principle of Argentine sovereignty over the islands but criticized the action of the military government of President Leopoldo Galtieri in enforcing Argentina's claim as "military madness." In 1983 Alfonsin condemned the United States invasion of the troubled West Indian island nation of Grenada.

In what has been described as a political thaw in Argentina following the country's defeat by British forces in the Falkland Islands, President Reynaldo Bignone rescinded a six-year ban on political parties in July 1982 as a step toward returning the country to civilian rule. Alfonsin, who had become the dominant personality in the UCR after the death of Ricardo Balbin in September 1981, lost no time in organizing what he called a "popular mobilization," to wrest power from the military. In his essay La Cuestión Argentina (The Question of Argentina), which was published in 1981, he argued that the country's military establishment had been transformed over the years from a professional force into a body that considered itself the sole guarantor of the nation's political life. While inveighing against leftist terrorism for paving the way for escalating intervention by the armed forces, he also attacked the military for invoking the defense of the national security as a pretext for the suppression of civil liberties and as a coverup for political and economic corruption. Addressing a huge rally in Buenos Aires in July 1982, Alfonsín asserted that democratic rule would be necessary if the armed forces were to be restored to their traditional role of being responsible to civilian authority.

Determined to turn the UCR into a formidable force, Alfonsín toured Argentina, staging rallies from the Andes to Patagonia, and signing up thousands of new party members, many of them young. At the UCR convention, in July 1983, he was elected party leader and nominated presidential candidate for the forthcoming national elections by a margin so wide that it astounded even his supporters. "Only moral force can save us," Alfonsín said at the time. "With it we can create a new political system, a new society." During the election campaign he established himself as a master of consensus and a champion of democracy and social justice. His economic policies resembled those of his party's main rivals, the Peronists, in that he criticized the free market economy, favored high tariffs and centralization of bank deposits, and warned that multinational corporations might be nationalized unless they contributed to the good of the country.

Pledging to eliminate illiteracy and malnutrition, Alfonsín promised voters at campaign rallies that he would suspend the military draft and the purchase of armaments and allocate 30 percent of the national budget to education. "I honestly believe that Argentines at this moment are not divided by deep ideological differences," he said a few weeks before the election. "What we face is the need to address the problems of the unemployed, of child care, of school dropouts, and the destruction of the national economy." Assailing official corruption, he urged Argentines "to overcome this immorality that has seeped into our society and join together in the long march toward peace and prosperity." In an address to a group of American businessmen, Alfonsín called on the United States to "revise its policy toward Latin America" and take a greater interest in "the social condition of the people who produce the wealth, the immense majority of whom live under feudal regimes and governments maintained by force."

Alfonsín's leading opponent in the election was the former Senate president Italo Luder, the lackluster candidate of the Peronist Frente Justicialista de Liberación, or Justicialist Liberation Front, whose mainstay was the powerful Peronist trade union movement. Although long opposed to Peronism, the military clandestinely supported Luder, whom they preferred to Alfonsín, and revelations of collusion between military commanders and Peronist leaders helped to fuel Alfonsín's campaign.

Although opinion polls showed Alfonsín to be Argentina's most popular politician, they also indicated that Luder was the front-runner in the presidential race. It therefore came as a surprise when in the elections of October 30, 1983, in which 80 percent of the eligible voters took part, Alfonsín scored an upset victory, winning 52 percent of the vote against the 40 percent received by Luder, with the remainder divided among seven smaller parties. In the Chamber of Deputies, the lower house of the National Congress, UCR candidates received 129 of the 254 seats, while the Peronists obtained 111. The euphoria experienced by Argentines was expressed by Alfonsín when he said: "We have won, but no one has been defeated. This is a victory for all Argentina." Even Argentina's venerated grand old man of letters Jorge Luis Borges, who in the past had disdained democracy and had said that all he "expected from life was death," now asserted that he had "the duty to go on living." On November 8, Alfonsín named his eight-member cabinet, composed mainly of his close confidants, including the neo-Keynesian Bernardo Grinspun as economics minister.

Alfonsín was formally sworn in as president before the National Congress on December 10, 1983, two months ahead of schedule and five days after Argentina's three-man military junta had disbanded itself. After receiving the sash of office from outgoing president Bignone, he declared himself "the most humble of Argentinians" and pledged to "create national unity . . . , consolidate internal peace, provide common defense, promote social welfare, and strengthen common justice for all." The inaugural was attended by dignitaries and heads of state from Latin America and Europe, including former president Isabel Perón, who had been invited by Alfonsín to return from exile in Spain. The United States was represented by Vice-President George Bush, who said at the time that the "strong commitment to democracy bodes very, very well for Argentina's relations with the United States."

During his first month in office, Alfonsín undertook a series of measures to purge the military and prosecute members for human rights abuses. Courtmartial proceedings began against nine high-ranking military officers, including former presidents Jorge Videla, Roberto Viola, and Leopoldo Galtieri. Responsibility for the national intelligence service and antisubversion agencies was placed under civilian control. A sixteen-member commission was organized under the chairmanship of the distinguished novelist Ernesto Sábato to investigate the disappearances of thousands of people in the 1970s. An amnesty law, passed by the last military government, exempting security personnel from prosecution for human rights violations, was rescinded. In an effort at evenhandedness, the government also started proceedings against seven alleged leftist terrorists of the Montonero guerrilla group.

To alleviate Argentina's economic crisis, Alfonsín's government announced in December a price freeze to help reduce an inflation rate estimated at the time at 400 percent. A budget plan was set up, providing for an increase in fiscal revenues through progressive taxation and calling for a reduction in the overall budget deficit. Alfonsin drew some fire from Peronist labor union officials, who asserted that his proposed emergency wage increases were not enough, and who were incensed by his demands for union reforms, including court-supervised elections and the severing of links between unions and political parties.

Argentina's improved human rights record prompted the United States to lift a ban on military aid that had been imposed in 1978 by the Carter administration, even though an Argentine government spokesman indicated that in view of Alfonsin's declared intention to cut back on armaments, the purchase of weapons was "not a priority of the new government." Alfonsin remained critical of the Reagan administration's foreign policies, especially in Central America, and in early 1984 he declared his government's intention to halt involvement in anti-leftist activities in that area and to cooperate instead with the Contadora group of nations—Mexico, Venezuela, Colombia, and Panama—in seeking a negotiated settlement there. In other areas of foreign policy, Alfonsin, acting through Vatican mediators, negotiated a long-standing conflict with Chile over the disputed Beagle Channel islands, and through Swiss and Brazilian intermediaries conducted talks with Great Britain about the still unresolved status of the Falkland Islands.

Despite continuing inflation, strikes, restiveness within the armed forces, and the parliamentary defeat of the government's labor reform bill, Alfonsin managed to hold his own in the early months of 1984. In late March the United States, in cooperation with Brazil, Mexico, Colombia, and Venezuela, arranged for a stopgap $500-million loan to enable Argentina to avoid defaulting on its foreign debt, while negotiations were being carried on with the International Monetary Fund for a long-term plan that might stabilize the Argentine economy. Because of pressure from the Peronist unions, Alfonsin at first resisted IMF demands for strict austerity measures. But in late September 1984, during a visit to the United States, where he addressed the UN General Assembly, he reached a tentative agreement with IMF officials under which Argentina was to gain access to some $1.42 billion in standby credits while imposing a variety of economic restrictions at home to control runaway inflation. "If he can give Argentines a chance to improve their standard of living," Steve Yolen wrote in U.S. News & World Report (May 7, 1984), "Alfonsin is apt to be around for a long time."

Raúl Alfonsin is married to his childhood sweetheart, the former María Lorenza Barreneche (or Barrenechea), who is of Spanish Basque ancestry. They have six grown children, one of them a resident of the United States, and (as of late 1983) thirteen grandchildren. According to Edward Schumacher, writing in the New York Times (No-

vember 5, 1983), "Alfonsin has somewhat of a hangdog look, with heavy eyelids, a bushy mustache, and bulging jowls. But he has flashing eyes and a spirited manner." His image is seen everywhere in Buenos Aires, on posters, buttons, and T-shirts, and he seems to have become the symbol of Argentina's new-found democracy. Because he founded the newspaper El Imparcial and wrote two books that presented his political ideas, Alfonsin considers himself a frustrated writer. He likes to discuss current issues with the employees of his favorite restaurant, and he enjoys motion pictures, singling out for special praise the French director Alain Resnais' 1959 antiwar film Hiroshima mon Amour. When asked by Stephen Kinzer of the New York Times (November 1, 1983) what qualities he regarded essential for political leaders, he said: "What I admire most is humility. What I cannot stand is arrogance."

References: Christian Sci Mon p4 D 28 '83; La Nación (Buenos Aires) p1+ D 10 '83; N Y Times p14 N 1 '83 por; N Y Times Mag p26+ Je 10 '84 pors; New Repub p18+ Mr 19 '84 por; Time 122:53 N 14 '83 por; International Who's Who, 1984–85

Andersen, Ib
(ēb)

Dec. 14, 1954– Dancer. Address: b. c/o The New York City Ballet, New York State Theatre, Lincoln Center for the Performing Arts, New York City, N.Y. 10023

In 1980 Ib Andersen, then at the height of his career as a principal dancer with the Royal Danish

Ballet, resigned from the company to which he had devoted some eighteen years of his life to sign on with George Balanchine's iconoclastic New York City Ballet, following in the footsteps of fellow Danes Peter Martins, Peter Schaufuss, Adam Lüders, Ulrik Trojaborg, and the Danish-trained Helgi Tomasson. A letter-perfect technician, Andersen has the elegant line, the soaring, light jumps, the seemingly weightless *ballon*, the feathery beats, and the carefree look of effortlessness characteristic of the ideal Bournonville *danseur*, but his musicality and joy in movement also make him a natural for the Balanchine idiom. Since joining City Ballet, Andersen has accepted parts in well over fifty ballets, and he has originated roles in nearly a dozen new works, among them Martins' *Concerto for Two Solo Pianos,* Jerome Robbins' *Piano Pieces,* and the last two major pieces choreographed by the late George Balanchine, *Robert Schumann's "Davidsbündlertänze"* and *Mozartiana.*

The second of the four children of a heating systems contractor and his wife, Ib Andersen was born in Copenhagen, Denmark on December 14, 1954. Neither parent was especially interested in the performing arts, but his mother so enjoyed ballroom dancing that she enrolled her children in social dancing classes when they were little more than toddlers. An energetic child with an inborn appreciation of music, Ib Andersen progressed rapidly. By his seventh birthday, his gift for the dance was undeniable, and at the urging of his instructor, he auditioned for and was accepted by the Royal Danish Ballet School.

Andersen's course of study at the Royal Danish Ballet School included academic lessons as well as a full day of traditional ballet classes and, for the more advanced students, evening performances with the resident opera and ballet companies. "I think I was fourteen when I began to understand that I might as well work as hard as I could, because there's no use in doing all those things and just doing them halfway," Andersen told Marilyn Hunt in an interview for a *Ballet News* (June 1980) profile. "My teachers liked my hard work, rather than my technique or my body. I've *had* to work hard, especially for turnout and for stretch in my feet." The works of August Bournonville, which dominated the Royal Danish Ballet's repertory, required, in addition to strength and stamina, blinding speed and intricate precision footwork, and Andersen willingly put in extra hours under the tutelage of his coaches, Kirsten Ralov, Hans Brenaa, and Flemming Ryberg.

At sixteen, Andersen passed the Royal Danish Ballet's rigorous examinations and was named an "aspirant," a position somewhat comparable to that of an apprentice. His training now included character and mime classes and individual lessons with Edite Frandsen and the legendary Vera Volkova, which, in his words, "really developed my technique and ability to dance." In his second year as an aspirant, Andersen was selected by Rudi van Dantzig, the Dutch choreographer known for his skillful blending of the classical and modern dance idioms, to perform the leading role in the company premiere of *Monument for a Dead Boy,* his psychodrama about the disturbing sexual fantasies of a troubled adolescent. Eager to impress company managers in his first important assignment, the young dancer spent his winter holidays in Amsterdam, working privately with van Dantzig. His hard work paid off, for when he made his debut in the role on April 7, 1973, he stunned critics with his secure technique and with the powerful emotionality of his interpretation.

Officially accepted into the company's corps de ballet in 1973, Andersen began dancing soloist or leading roles almost immediately, among them the Spanish dance in *Swan Lake,* Prince Ivan in *The Firebird,* and solo variations in Harald Lander's technically taxing *Etudes* and in Bournonville's *La Sylphide, Napoli,* and *Lifeguards of Amager.* In addition to being outstanding in the Bournonville repertory, Andersen shone in such contemporary works as Felix Blaska's *Elektro-Bach,* Flemming Flindt's *The Young Man Must Marry,* and Murray Louis' *Hoopla* and *Proximities.* But perhaps his most demanding role as an aspirant was Romeo in John Neumeier's full-length *Romeo and Juliet.* As much theatre as dance, Neumeier's ballets depend heavily on the dancers' characterizations for their impact, and *Romeo and Juliet* is no exception. Although he was at first uncomfortable in his first major dramatic role, Andersen eventually settled down to develop a touching portrait of an impetuous youth consumed by passion.

Largely on the strength of his performance in *Romeo and Juliet,* Andersen was elevated to the rank of principal dancer in 1975, the youngest male dancer to achieve that distinction in the history of the Royal Danish Ballet. American balletomanes got their first look at Neumeier's imaginative *Romeo and Juliet*—and at Ib Andersen—during the company's 1976 North American tour. Despite a few critical brickbats, the ballet proved to be as popular with audiences in the United States as it had been in Denmark, and though Andersen performed Romeo only once in New York City because of a serious injury to his regular partner, Mette-Ida Kirk, he made an unforgettable impression on those lucky enough to have seen him. He and Miss Kirk were "just right—innocent, attractive, not at all neurotic or melodramatic" as the star-crossed lovers, Marilyn Hunt wrote in her review for the dance publication *Eddy* (Winter 1977). "Vulnerable and unsure of everything except love, they rush headlong into each other's arms and those of death. . . . The two never seem to be thinking of their (very fine) technique. Their harmony makes even the complicated lifts seem spontaneous." Andersen also electrified New York audiences with his sparkling virtuosity in such guaranteed showstoppers as *Etudes* and *Napoli.*

Following his promotion to principal dancer, Andersen rapidly expanded his personal repertory, adding to his credits George Balanchine's *Divertimento No. 15* and *Symphony in C*; Jerome

Robbins' *Interplay* and *Fanfare*; the Bridegroom in Lar Lubovitch's version of *Les Noces*; D'Artagnan in Flindt's full-length *The Three Musketeers* and the title role in his idyllic modern revision of Bournonville's *The Toreador*; and the sacrificial victim in Glen Tetley's *Le Sacre du Printemps*—a role he says developed his expressiveness as a dancer as much as Romeo had done. "It had everything," he explained to Kitty Cunningham, who interviewed him for the fall 1981 issue of *Ballet Review*. "You had to use your whole body, from the fingertips to the toenails, and it was a very active ballet. It was difficult for me to express myself that way without doing faces or mime or whatever."

New to Andersen's classical repertory were the parts of the Cavalier in *The Nutcracker*, Prince Siegfried in *Swan Lake*, and Count Albrecht in *Giselle*. Less interested in the so-called "prince roles" because, to use his words, "there's not that much dancing in them," he was perhaps most effective as Albrecht, in Erik Bruhn's staging of *Giselle*, which gives the *danseur* more variations than is customary. Curiously, Andersen did not perform leading roles in many of the great full-length Bournonville ballets until the late 1970s, when the Royal Danish Ballet began preparing programs for the celebration of the centenary of the choreographer's death. That he was more than up to the challenge is evidenced by the thunderous applause that rewarded his performances and by his rave notices. Erik Aschengreen, the noted Danish dance critic and historian, rated Andersen and Lis Jeppesen the outstanding artists of the Bournonville Festival in Copenhagen in 1979. Of all the performers, Andersen most fully personified "Bournonville's *joi de vivre* in [his] allegro dancing," Aschengreen wrote in *Dance* magazine (March 1980), but he also excelled in the mostly mimed roles, offering, for example, a "sensitive and passionate" portrayal of Junker Ove in *A Folk Tale* and of the gentle Carelis in *Kermesse in Bruges*.

After watching Andersen perform with other soloists of the Royal Danish Ballet, augmented on this occasion by guest artists Peter Martins, Peter Schaufuss, and Adam Lüders, in an all-Bournonville program at New York's City Center in the summer of 1979, American critics seconded Aschengreen's opinion. Robert Greskovic, writing in *Ballet News* (September 1979), spoke for the majority of his colleagues when he singled out Andersen for special praise, calling him one of the "most accomplished and pleasurable dancers performing today." The "effortless command of precisely accurate and amazingly articulate technique" that so astounded Greskovic was especially apparent in the humorously competitive "Jockey Dance" from *From Siberia to Moscow* and in the unrelenting combinations of the pas de trois from *Lifeguards at Amager*.

Secure in his position with the Royal Danish Ballet and widely recognized as among the finest Bournonville interpreters in the world, Andersen was, by 1979, nonetheless growing restless. "I had been in the same place from the time I was seven until I was twenty-five," he explained to Kitty Cunningham, "and I came to a point where it was hard to get inspiration and nothing was very surprising." Hungry for artistic challenges, he sounded out his friends in the New York City Ballet about the possibility of his joining the company. With Peter Martins apparently acting as an intermediary, Andersen took a company class under George Balanchine, then City Ballet's artistic director, and shortly thereafter he joined the company, in time for its 1980 spring season at the New York State Theatre.

Andersen made an unscheduled early debut with City Ballet when, gallantly stepping in at the last minute for an injured Daniel Duell, he partnered Heather Watts in a performance of Peter Martins' angular *Calcium Light Night*, which was being taped for broadcast on the PBS program *Dance in America* on February 20, 1980. Having learned the piece—a tongue-in-cheek exercise in pure movement—in just two days, he turned in an intelligent and playful performance that was perfectly suited to the ballet's eccentric style. Evidently taken by the two dancers' instinctive rapport, Martins immediately began choreographing a new piece for the duo: *Lille Suite*, a neoromantic exploration of the vicissitudes of love that was to become one of the biggest hits of the 1980 City Ballet spring season. Andersen's official company debut came on opening night in April 1980, partnering Miss Watts in the intoxicating *allegro vivo* movement of Balanchine's neo-nineteenth-century *Symphony in C*.

Unused to Balanchine's unconventional and experimental classes and to the physical strain of performing nightly, Andersen suffered recurrent bouts of tendonitis during his first few months with the company, but he nonetheless learned, by his own estimate, about two dozen roles in such standard City Ballet offerings as Balanchine's *Divertimento No. 15*, *The Steadfast Tin Soldier*, *Bournonville Divertissements*, *Scotch Symphony*, *Tchaikovsky Suite*, *Ballo della Regina*, and *Apollo*, and in Jerome Robbins' *The Four Seasons*, *Dances at a Gathering*, and *Afternoon of a Faun*. Inspired by his newest dancer's versatility, Balanchine created leading roles for Andersen in *Robert Schumann's "Davidsbündlertänze"*, an affecting and intimate chamber ballet for four couples illustrating incidents in the life of Robert Schumann, and in *Ballade*, an exercise in lyricism designed to extend the expressive capacity of Merrill Ashley, the company's superlative allegro technician.

Continuing to assimilate new roles at an astonishing rate, Andersen danced in no fewer than four world premieres in about as many days during City Ballet's Tchaikovsky Festival in 1981, the most notable being Balanchine's *Mozartiana* and Robbins' *Pas de Deux*, later renamed *Andantino*. *Mozartiana* is, above all, a showcase for Balanchine's principal muse, Suzanne Farrell, but at its heart is a dazzling series of alternating solos that test the principal male and female dancers' agility with tight allegro patterns, off-balance turns, and sudden, unexpected shifts in direction and body alignment. Exploiting Andersen's aerial abilities, Balanchine devised for him a pyrotechnic display of buoyant jumps, double air-turns, and razor-sharp beats. For his lyrical, low-key *Pas de Deux*, set to the second movement of Tchaikovsky's Piano Concerto No. 1, Robbins transformed Andersen and his partner, Darci Kistler, into "ice-skaters" and gave them an Olympics-calibre free-style routine, complete with gliding, skimming steps and coiling turns, that delighted balletgoers and critics alike.

Perhaps because of his extraordinary musicality, Andersen has demonstrated a special affinity for Jerome Robbins' choreography, beginning with his first performance in *Afternoon of a Faun*, in May 1980. His sensitive portrayal of the narcissistic young dance student was particularly striking for the way it emphasized the sensuality of Debussy's music and the thematic relationship between Robbins' conception and Vaslav Nijinsky's erotic original version. He was also unusually effective as the protagonist in the brooding *Opus 19/The Dreamer*, a role Robbins had created especially for Mikhail Baryshnikov. Putting his own imprint on the part, Andersen imposed an "emotional shading" upon each passage, as Anna Kisselgoff reported in her *New York Times* (January 9, 1982) review of his "magnificent" debut in the piece: "All-suffering and vulnerable from the start, he seemed truly in the midst of some nightmare, and the effect was very strong." Andersen also performed in the frothy folk-flavored *Piano Pieces*, which Robbins created for him in 1981, and in the choreographer's exuberant *Gershwin Concerto*.

Peter Martins, too, has frequently turned to Ib Andersen for choreographic inspiration, devising stunning solos and intricate duets for the dancer in the plotless *L'Histoire du Soldat* and, perhaps most memorably, in *Concerto for Two Solo Pianos*. Created for the company's 1982 Stravinsky Festival, *Concerto for Two Solo Pianos* had as its centerpiece a complex, long-spun pas de deux for Andersen and his frequent partner, Heather Watts, that was, in Jennifer Dunning's words, "something like a quirky ballroom dance." "Limbs fit together like interlocking puzzle pieces, tilting off balance and measuring the floor," Miss Dunning wrote in her *New York Times* (February 12, 1984) review of a later performance of the ballet. "Sensuous and tender in its spiky way, the duet extends the limits of expressive partnering." Always an attentive and responsive partner (even though, as Arlene Croce once observed, he "doesn't mate easily" with anyone because of what she called his "stripling asexual quality"), Andersen prefers duets to dancing alone. During his career with City Ballet, he has partnered most of the company's leading ballerinas, but he seems happiest with Miss Watts and Miss Kistler.

As he grew accustomed to the unusual technical demands of the Balanchine repertory, Andersen devoted more of his attention to exploring the subtle emotional shifts and dramatic nuances of the choreography. His headstrong Oberon forcefully subdued Karin von Aroldingen's willful Titania in *A Midsummer Night's Dream* and his fiery gypsy cavalier was more than a match for Suzanne Farrell's sultry temptress in *Tzigane*. Although he is perhaps both physically and temperamentally unsuited to the title role in the lyric theatre piece *Orpheus*, he effectively conveyed the character's desperation and grief. His early training in mime and in the *demi-caractère* style stood him in good stead in his well-rounded portrayals of Franz, the lighthearted country bumpkin in *Coppélia*, and the playful Harlequin in *Harlequinade*, Balanchine's rollicking re-creation of the antics of traditional *commèdia dell'arte* figures. Andersen also brought an unusual dimension to his leading roles in the second section of *Vienna Waltzes*, *Agon*, *Donizetti Variations*, the long-awaited revival of *Liebeslieder Walzer*, *The Magic Flute*, *Stravinsky Violin Concerto*, and in the world premieres of Martins' *A Schubertiad* and the plotless, perpetual-motion extravaganza *Brahms/Handel*, choreographed jointly by Jerome Robbins and Twyla Tharp.

Like most of his City Ballet colleagues, Andersen rarely finds the time to accept guest engagements, but in 1981 he returned to Copenhagen to dance the role of James, opposite Lis Jeppesen's Sylph, in the Royal Danish Ballet's production of *La Sylphide*, which Walter Terry called "one of the most touching performances" of that masterpiece that he had seen in twenty-five years. Andersen "electrified the stage with his soaring leaps and glittering *batterie*," Terry wrote in *Ballet News* (June 1981), "but what is more, suffused that stage with a golden glow with his portrait of the Scots laird, forever young, forever eager, forever doomed by the sweet mockery of dreams."

Slightly built and standing five feet ten inches tall, Ib Andersen is a boyishly handsome man with large, wide-set olive eyes and an expressive face "like a startled fawn's," to quote Tobi Tobias. He has been described by Bart Cook, a New York City Ballet colleague, as "a reserved, modest sort," and his preferred offstage pursuits—listening to music and going to the movies—reflect his nongregarious personality and reticent manner. His busy schedule of daily classes, rehearsals, and performances leaves him little time for recreation, but Ib Andersen has no doubts about having chosen the right profession. "I love to move," he said simply, as quoted in the *Ballet News* profile. "And for me the ballet is the most interesting theatre art because you have to use your fantasy so much and the range of expression is so great." Andersen makes his home in a small apartment near Lincoln Center, the New York City Ballet's headquarters, on Manhattan's Upper West Side.

References: Ballet R 9:28+ Fall '81 pors; Ballet N 1:28+ Je '80 pors; Dance 50:65+ Ag '76 pors; Dance N p1+ Ap '80 por; The Concise Oxford Dictionary of Ballet (1982)

Attenborough, Richard

Aug. 29, 1923– British actor, motion picture
director and producer. Address: h. "Old Friars,"
Richmond Green, Surrey, England

Since the 1940s Sir Richard Attenborough had
been a highly respected character actor, best
known for his finely shaded performances as the
typical "British" survivor in scores of war and adventure films. It was not, however, as an actor but
as the producer and director of the award-winning
epic Gandhi that he finally achieved the worldwide recognition that had so long eluded him. Attenborough, who learned his craft at the Royal
Academy of Dramatic Art and perfected it on the
London stage, differs from his more flamboyant
counterparts behind the camera by emphasizing
narrative rather than visual pyrotechnics. "I work
as an actor works to involve an audience by engaging their emotions . . .," he explained to Barbara
Crossette in an interview for the New York Times
(November 28, 1982). "I have no interest in being
remembered as a great creative filmmaker. I want
to be remembered as a storyteller." He was knighted by Queen Elizabeth II in 1976.

Richard Samuel Attenborough was born on August 29, 1923 in Cambridge, England, the oldest of
the three sons of Frederick Levi Attenborough, an
Anglo-Saxon scholar and the principal of University College, Leicester, and Mary (Clegg) Attenborough. His brother David, the naturalist and
television broadcaster, is the creator of the acclaimed BBC-TV series Life on Earth; John, the
youngest, is in the automotive industry. As a child,
Richard Attenborough "indulged quite frequently
in the creation of [his] own fantasy world," as he
admitted in his book In Search of Gandhi (New
Century, 1982). He also showed an early interest in

painting, music, and theatre—a fascination that
was encouraged by his maternal grandfather, Samuel Clegg, the author of a number of books on art
appreciation. Such frequent dinner guests as Sir
Thomas Beecham, the conductor, Dilys Powell, the
film critic, and Matheson Lang, the actor-manager
and dramatist, further contributed to the boy's
growing interest in the performing arts. By his mid-
teens, Richard Attenborough had decided to become an actor, to his father's chagrin.

From his first formal stage appearance, as a fairy
in an amateur production of Iolanthe, throughout
his years as a pupil at the Wyggeston Grammar
School for Boys in Leicester, Richard Attenborough spent, by his own account, "far more time
than was appropriate" in schoolboy theatrical productions. He also performed regularly with the
Leicester Little Theatre, the local amateur dramatic society, which numbered his mother among its
most active members. In 1940 Attenborough won
the competitive Leverhulme Scholarship to the
Royal Academy of Dramatic Art in London. While
a student at RADA, he made his first professional
stage and screen appearances, as Richard Miller in
a production of Eugene O'Neill's Ah, Wilderness!
at the Intimate Theatre in Palmer's Green and as
the frightened young sailor in Noel Coward's In
Which We Serve (Universal, 1942). In 1942 he was
awarded RADA's Bancroft Medal, given annually
for fine acting.

Shortly after leaving the Royal Academy of Dramatic Art in 1942, Attenborough made his West
End debut at the Arts Theatre, as Ralph Berger in
Clifford Odets' Awake and Sing. Over the next
year, he played important parts in five West End
productions, ranging from Sebastian in Twelfth
Night to Pinkie Brown, the psychopathic teen-age
murderer in a dramatization of Graham Greene's
Brighton Rock. In June 1943 he enlisted in the
RAF. Seconded to its Film Unit, he took the leading
role in the unit's morale booster Journey Together,
then volunteered for the department's operational
arm. For the remainder of World War II, he flew
film reconnaissance missions over Germany.

Following his demobilization in 1946, Attenborough signed a contract with John and Ray Boulting, the twin-brother motion picture production
team. He made a number of films for them in the
late 1940s, most notably, in his view, Brighton Rock
(1947), in which he reprised his stage role of the
cold-blooded hoodlum, and The Guinea Pig (1948),
in which he portrayed a working-class adolescent
on a scholarship to an elite school, where his spirit
is broken by the snobbery of his classmates. Both
films were released in the United States, under the
respective titles Young Scarface and The Outsider.
His other screen assignments amounted to little
more than "simpering baby-faced idiot" roles, to
use his description. Not until the wartime adventure The Gift Horse (British Lion, 1952) did he find,
in the resourceful Cockney seaman "Dripper"
Daniels, another meaty character part.

During the 1950s Attenborough's once promising
film career seemed to come to a dead halt, as he ap-

peared in a series of hackneyed melodramas, among them *Eight O'Clock Walk* (Associated Artists, 1954) and *The Ship That Died of Shame* (Continental, 1955), relieved only by a handful of lifeless comedies, including *Father's Doing Fine* (1952) and *The Baby and the Battleship* (Distributors Corp. of America, 1956). Attenborough fared better on the stage, where he took leading roles in such long-running hits as *To Dorothy, A Son*, the comedy thriller *Double Image*, and Agatha Christie's long-running murder mystery *The Mousetrap*, in which he created the role of Detective Sergeant Trotter.

Increasingly dissatisfied with the caliber of most of his films, Attenborough decided that to achieve any work "of a decent standard" he would have to make his own motion pictures. To that end, he and his friend Bryan Forbes, a former actor turned scriptwriter, formed Beaver Films, with Attenborough as producer and Forbes as screenwriter and director. Their first effort was *The Angry Silence*, an uncompromising look at the human cost of industrial unrest, as seen through the eyes of a worker who is ostracized for refusing to go along with a wildcat strike. Attenborough had a hard time lining up financial backers, but British Lion eventually agreed to put up production funds. To meet the budget restrictions, the technicians and principal players, including Attenborough, waived their usual salaries and agreed to work for a percentage of the profits. When *The Angry Silence* was released in 1960, it was widely praised as one of the best films of the year. Attenborough himself, in the central role, received the best notices of his career to date.

Encouraged by the critical and popular success of *The Angry Silence*, Attenborough and Forbes set up Allied Film Makers in partnership with producers Basil Dearden and Michael Relph, director Guy Green, and actor Jack Hawkins, obtained funds from the Rank Organisation, and over the next few years produced four well-received films: *The League of Gentlemen* (1960), a comedy adventure about a group of down-at-the-heels Army veterans who plan an elaborate bank robbery; the allegorical *Whistle Down the Wind* (1961), in which three North-country children mistake a wounded murderer for Jesus Christ; *The L-Shaped Room* (1962), starring Leslie Caron as a pregnant French girl who takes refuge in a seedy London boarding house; and the eerie psychological thriller *Seance on a Wet Afternoon* (1964), featuring Kim Stanley as a deranged spiritualist and Richard Attenborough as her downtrodden husband.

His portrayal of "the rather sad, pathetic little character" in *Seance on a Wet Afternoon* gave Attenborough the most satisfaction he had ever known as a film actor, and critics agreed. "He had me spellbound," Roald Dahl wrote in his review of the film for *Life* magazine (December 18, 1964). "His is the least menacing of the two parts, yet in everything he does . . . he manages continually in some magical manner to intensify the atmosphere of suspense and doom." Attenborough's perfor-

mance won him a British Academy Award as the best British actor of 1964. The British Film Academy also cited his compelling interpretation of Regimental Sergeant Major Lauderdale, the pompous martinet who puts down a native uprising against his isolated African garrison in *Guns at Batasi* (Twentieth Century-Fox, 1964).

The 1964 British Academy Award was the culmination of a film comeback for Attenborough. The turnaround began in 1956, with the release of the Boulting brothers' *Private's Progress*, the first in a series of satires that poked fun at contemporary British society, from its military regulations to its sexual mores. Perhaps the most popular of the "sequels," which included *Brothers in Law* (1957) and *Only Two Can Play* (1962), was *I'm All Right Jack* (1959), a lampoon of industrial skullduggery that also starred Peter Sellers. Attenborough's other major film roles in the late 1950s and early 1960s were the guilt-ridden scientist who is the anonymous title character in the psychological melodrama *The Man Upstairs* (British Lion, 1958); John Holden, a formerly complacent tradesman who risks his life ferrying Allied troops to safety in the mass evacuation of the Normandy beaches in the documentary-style *Dunkirk* (MGM, 1958); Fowle, the mild-mannered birdseed merchant accused of murdering his wife in the comedy *The Dock Brief* (MGM, 1962); and Bartlett, the steely mastermind behind an Allied breakout from a high-security German POW camp in the all-star World War II adventure *The Great Escape* (United Artists, 1963).

By the mid-1960s, Attenborough had established a reputation as a first-rank character actor who made film critics marvel at his ability to lose himself in his roles. Yet, as Judith Crist observed in an article for the *New York Herald Tribune* Sunday magazine supplement (December 6, 1964), he invariably managed to "[sustain] a certain physical suggestion of everydayness, a certain universal but never quite mundane quality that is uniquely his."

That quality was perhaps never more evident than in Attenborough's first Hollywood feature, *The Flight of the Phoenix* (Twentieth Century-Fox, 1966), Robert Aldrich's edge-of-the-seat adventure about an ill-assorted group of plane crash survivors who patch together a jerry-built flying machine from the remains of their aircraft and pilot it out of the Sahara. As the alcoholic navigator, Attenborough more than held his own with such international stars as James Stewart, Peter Finch, and Hardy Kruger and, by underplaying, made his colorless character the most unforgettable in the movie. Before returning to London, Attenborough played the American sailor Frenchie, the second lead in Robert Wise's sprawling melodrama *The Sand Pebbles* (Twentieth Century-Fox, 1966).

Back in England, Attenborough displayed his versatility in a triad of disparate roles: Silas, the con man who resorts to various disguises to fleece a gullible public in *Only When I Larf* (Paramount, 1968); the unsuspecting Robert Blossom, whose bored wife keeps a lover in the attic in the sex farce *The Bliss of Mrs. Blossom* (Paramount, 1968); and the Pickwickian circus owner in *Doctor Dolittle* (Twentieth Century-Fox, 1967), a musical retelling of Hugh Lofting's children's stories. For his performance in the last-named film, he was awarded a Golden Globe by the Hollywood Foreign Press Association as the best supporting actor of the year.

Throughout the 1960s Attenborough devoted virtually all of his spare time to a project that had become "an obsession": a film of the life of Mohandas K. Gandhi. He first became interested in the Mahatma in 1962, when Motilal Kothari, then on the London staff of the Indian High Commission, asked him to consider making a motion picture about the legendary Indian nationalist and civil rights leader. At the time, Attenborough had no interest in a directing career and little knowledge of Gandhi, but after reading, at Kothari's suggestion, Louis Fischer's mammoth *Life of Mahatma Gandhi* (1950), he was like a man possessed. As he explained to Joseph Gelmis in an interview for *Newsday* (January 18, 1966), "I'd give up anything—cash, any part—to make this film. This sounds trite, but I'm so excited by this man's life, what he was, what he stands for . . . and I'm so fed up with the sick, pointless, despairing films that are being made nowadays."

After his friend, Earl Mountbatten of Burma, the first Governor-General of India, interceded in his behalf, Attenborough won approval for his project from Indian Prime Minister Jawaharlal Nehru in 1963. Over the next few years, he traveled to India repeatedly to talk to people who had known Gandhi, visit places associated with him, and raise production funds. At home and in Hollywood, few investors were willing to risk money on the proposed motion picture, particularly after the box-office failure of *Nine Hours to Rama* (Twentieth Century-Fox, 1962), Mark Robson's political drama about Gandhi's assassination. Undeterred, Attenborough forged ahead until 1967, when he reluctantly shelved the project in deference to David Lean, the Academy Award–winning director who had expressed an interest in making his own film about Gandhi.

At the urging of his longtime friend and colleague, actor John Mills, Attenborough shortly began work on his first venture as a director, *Oh! What a Lovely War* (Paramount, 1969), the film version of Joan Littlewood's musical fantasia on World War I. To get Paramount's financial backing, Attenborough, who also coproduced, agreed to guarantee no fewer than six top stars. In the end, he persuaded thirteen world-famous actors, among them the actor-knights Sir Laurence Olivier, Sir John Gielgud, Sir Ralph Richardson, Sir Michael Redgrave, and Sir John Mills, to join the cast.

Oh! What A Lovely War had its premiere in London on April 10, 1969 to a rapturous response. The critics were especially impressed by the fluidity of the transitions from fantasy palaces to the amusement arcade on Brighton Pier to the battlefields of Flanders. When the film opened in the United States a few months later, the reviews—and box-office business—were nearly as upbeat as

they had been in England. *Oh! What a Lovely War* earned a Golden Globe as the best English-language foreign film of 1969 along with six British Academy Awards, and sixteen international awards.

Because his salary as an untried director had been fairly modest, Attenborough replenished his funds by appearing in several motion pictures, including *David Copperfield* (Twentieth Century-Fox, 1970), the action adventure *The Last Grenade* (Cinerama, 1970), the satirical *The Magic Christian* (Commonwealth United, 1970), *A Severed Head* (Columbia 1971), a faithful but pedestrian adaptation of Iris Murdoch's novel, and Joe Orton's bitter farce *Loot* (EMI, 1970). The best of those films is *10 Rillington Place* (Columbia, 1971), a meticulous reconstruction of the sensational 1950s murder case that led to Britain's abolition of the death penalty. "Resolutely opposed" to capital punishment himself, Attenborough agreed to enact the part of John Reginald Christie, the necrophiliac mass murderer whose testimony in an earlier trial had led to the conviction and execution of an innocent man. Playing Christie was a "deeply disturbing" experience for Attenborough, but his chilling portrayal of "introverted evil," to quote Judith Crist, won him the critics' admiration.

Back behind the camera again, Attenborough directed the epic biographical film *Young Winston* (Columbia, 1972), which covers Churchill's youthful exploits as soldier, journalist, and adventurer. Although a few reviewers quibbled about Carl Foreman's "poorly structured" script, most of them applauded Attenborough's direction of the rousing action sequences and his actor's acute awareness of performance. By all accounts, the acting, from the principals— Simon Ward, Anne Bancroft, and Robert Shaw—to the bit players, was impeccable. The same could not be said for *A Bridge Too Far* (United Artists, 1977), the star-studded re-creation of Cornelius Ryan's best-seller about a botched Allied airborne operation toward the end of World War II. Although Attenborough tried to personalize the key characters with telling details, they were overwhelmed by the "hugeness" of the $25-million movie.

Even while Attenborough was making other motion pictures "Gandhi" was never far from his mind. When in 1972 David Lean abandoned his plans for a film about the Mahatma's life, Attenborough resumed work on his postponed project. "Every career decision I've made since then has been tempered by my love affair with this one project," he admitted to Aljean Harmetz in an interview for the *New York Times* (November 23, 1981). "I've given up forty acting roles and a dozen directing assignments to pursue it." He even turned down an offer to become associate director of Britain's National Theatre because, in his words, "it would have meant giving up 'Gandhi' forever."

In his efforts to raise production funds, Attenborough mortgaged his house, sold his cars, pawned his paintings, and accepted roles in what he has described as "terrible crap." His screen acting credits in the late 1970s included an urbane Scotland Yard detective in the John Wayne vehicle *Brannigan* (United Artists, 1975), a renegade English terrorist in Otto Preminger's inept suspense melodrama *Rosebud* (United Artists, 1975), an arrogant judge in *Ten Little Indians* (Avco Embassy, 1975), an updated and stagey remake of an Agatha Christie mystery, and the genteel Colonel Daintry in *The Human Factor* (Rank, 1979). He also made a guest appearance in the Indian director Satyajit Ray's *The Chess Players* (1977). Hoping to persuade Hollywood mogul Joseph E. Levine to finance "Gandhi," Attenborough agreed to direct Levine's production of *Magic* (Twentieth Century-Fox, 1978), a psychological thriller about a psychotic ventriloquist controlled by his dummy. Despite fine performances from Anthony Hopkins and Ann-Margret, critics complained that the film suffered in comparison to *Dead of Night*, the classic 1945 release with a similar theme.

Toward the end of the decade, Attenborough finally got financial backing for the Gandhi project from Goldcrest Films and Television, Ltd., International Film Investors, and India's National Film Development Corporation, which contributed one-third of the budget. With production funds and a literate script, by John Briley, in hand, Attenborough searched for an actor to play Gandhi. Although he had, over the years, considered such bankable stars as Sir Alec Guinness, Dustin Hoffman, and Robert De Niro, he eventually settled on Ben Kingsley, a little-known but highly respected Anglo-Indian actor with the Royal Shakespeare Company whose screen test as the aged Gandhi was, in Attenborough's words, "absolutely mesmeric." In directing the epic, shot largely on location in India, Attenborough relied on his acting experience to coax from his enormous cast—and perhaps most impressively from Kingsley—astonishingly real portrayals.

Released by Columbia Pictures in 1982, *Gandhi*, which traces the Mahatma's life from his early civil rights activism in South Africa in the 1890s to his assassination in 1948, drew a mixed response. Some critics thought that it was too reverential and "sanitized," to use Gary Arnold's word, but few quarreled with the naturalness of the acting or the emotional impact of Gandhi's message. "Attenborough actually shows us how nonviolence works as a strategy; the contradictions, the dangers, the vanity, and the self-sacrifice of it are still alive for him," David Denby wrote in *New York* magazine (December 6, 1982). "This must be the most emotionally wrenching political movie ever made." One of the top-grossing films of 1983, *Gandhi* won eight Academy Awards, including Oscars for best picture, best director, best actor, and best original screenplay, and many other awards.

Because of *Gandhi*, Richard Attenborough is, in his words, "less of an agnostic" than he was. "Not being able to cope very happily with many of the formalities and constraints of organized religion that in many instances result in the most monstrous examples of man's inhumanity to man, I found it an enormous relief to come across someone who said, 'I am a Hindu and a Christian and a Muslim and a Jew and so are all of you'—meaning that if God is truth, then that is what we are seeking and the manner in which we find truth is to some degree an irrelevancy," he explained to Ernest Leogrande in an interview for the *New York Daily News* (December 5, 1982).

In addition to his work as actor and filmmaker, Attenborough is a director of Goldcrest Films and Television, Ltd., deputy chairman of Channel Four Television, and chairman of Capital Radio, the first commercial station licensed by the Independent Broadcasting Authority. He recently saved Capital Radio from potential bankruptcy by pledging part of his impressive modern art collection against additional financing. The chairman of the Royal Academy of Dramatic Art since 1970, he also serves as the governor and chairman of the British Film Institute, the vice-president of the British Academy of Film and Television Arts, pro-chancellor of the University of Sussex and chairman of its Arts Centre Board, and trustee of the Tate Gallery. Among the most recent of Attenborough's many awards are the Martin Luther King Jr. 1983 Peace Prize, the 1983 Fellowship, the highest accolade of the British Academy of Film and Television Arts, and the 1984 Artist of the Year Award from the Society of the Family of Man. He holds honorary degrees from the universities of Leicester, Kent, and Newcastle.

Once described as having "the face of a melancholy owl and the unruffled ego to match," Richard Attenborough is a stocky five feet eight and one-half inches tall and has a ruddy complexion, blue eyes, and receding white hair. He relaxes by listening to music or attending football matches. (Since 1969, he has been the director of the Chelsea Football Club.) Attenborough's generosity is reflected in his longtime memberships in the Actor's Charitable Trust and Combined Theatrical Charities and his presidency of the Muscular Dystrophy Group of Great Britain. He broke with the Labour party, which he had supported all his life, in 1981 and joined the newly formed Social Democratic party. Attenborough and his wife, the actress Sheila Sim, whom he married on January 22, 1945, have two daughters, Jane and Charlotte, and a son, Michael, who was recently named artistic director of the Hampstead Theatre. The Attenboroughs live in a Queen Anne house in Richmond Green, Surrey.

References: *Film Comment* 19:30+ Ja/F '83 pors; *Horizon* 23:38+ F '80 pors; *London Observer* p7 Ap 17 '83; *N Y Times* II p1+ N 28 '82 por; Castell, David. *Richard Attenborough* (1984); Pettigrew, Terence. *British Film Character Actors* (1982); Thomson, David. *A Biographical Dictionary of Film* (1976); *Who's Who, 1983–84*; *Who's Who in the Theatre* (1981)

Atwood, Margaret (Eleanor)

Nov. 18, 1939– Canadian author. Address: b. c/o Simon & Schuster, Inc., 1230 Ave. of the Americas, New York City, N. Y. 10020

Margaret Atwood, the Canadian poet, novelist, short-story writer, and critic, has been variously—and accurately—described as "the most discussed and widely read writer in Canada," the "national heroine of the arts," and the "high priestess of angst." Since 1966 when she won Canada's highest literary honor for her first book of poetry, *The Circle Game*, her seven poetry collections and five novels have established her as an award-winning writer of international stature. In recent years, her feminist convictions and profound concerns about human rights have figured more prominently in her writing, but her refined style, mythic vision, and carefully wrought images have transformed what might have become tendentious tracts into works of art.

Margaret Eleanor Atwood was born on November 18, 1939 in Ottawa, Ontario, Canada to Carl Edmund and Margaret Dorothy (Killam) Atwood, a dietician. She has a brother, who is a neurophysiologist, and a younger sister. Every year from April to November her family lived in the Quebec wilderness, where her father, a forest entomologist and "a very woodsy man," did research for the government. As a result, Margaret "grew up in and out of the bush, in and out of Ottawa, Sault Ste. Marie and Toronto" and was eleven years old before she attended a full year of school. She began when she was about six to write "morality plays, poems, comic books, and an unfinished novel about an ant." Although she abandoned that pursuit after a couple of years in favor of plans for a career in home economics, in high school she again wrote poetry,

influenced by Edgar Allan Poe, and at sixteen committed herself to a writing career. "It was suddenly the only thing I wanted to do," she explained to Joyce Carol Oates in an interview for the *New York Review of Books* (May 21, 1978).

After graduating from Leaside High School in 1957, Margaret Atwood studied English literature in the honors program at Victoria College of the University of Toronto. There her instructors included the distinguished critic Northrop Frye, the principal of the college, whose mythopoetic theories influenced her poetry. As an undergraduate she reviewed books and wrote articles for *Acta Victoriana*, the college literary magazine, and when she was nineteen she had the gratification of seeing her first poem accepted for publication. In 1961, the year in which she received her B.A. degree, *Double Persephone*, her first volume of poetry, was published in Toronto by Hawkshead Press. In the following year she obtained a Master of Arts degree from Radcliffe College in Cambridge, Massachusetts.

During her year at Radcliffe, Margaret Atwood concentrated on Victorian literature, and after winning a Woodrow Wilson fellowship she continued her study of Victorian literature and of Gothic romances at Harvard University in 1962-63. For the next two years, she worked at such jobs as market researcher, cashier, and waitress, using whatever free time she had at her disposal to write. Although she returned to Harvard in 1965 to continue her doctoral work, she left two years later without completing her dissertation, "The English Metaphysical Romance," a thesis topic that reflected her unabated interest in "the Gothic, the supernatural fantasy, and related forms."

During the 1960s, Margaret Atwood contributed book reviews and articles to *Alphabet*, *Poetry*, and *Canadian Literature*, among other periodicals, and her poems began to appear in such little magazines as *Kayak*, *Quarry*, and the *Tamarack Review*. In addition, four collections of her poetry—*The Circle Game* (1964), *Kaleidoscopes: Baroque* (1965), *Talismans for Children* (1965), and *Speeches for Doctor Frankenstein* (1966)—were published in limited editions by the Cranbrook Academy of Art in Bloomfield Hills, Michigan. It was a revised edition of *The Circle Game* (Contact Press, 1966) that brought her national recognition when it won the Governor General's Award for the year's best book of poetry. In *Canadian Literature* (Spring 1974), Gary Ross saw her use of the wilderness and of the external world in general as symbols of human isolation and congratulated her for resolving the conflict between inner and outer worlds, between individuality and community. The forty spare, free-verse poems in *The Animals in That Country* (Oxford Univ. Pr., 1968; Little, Brown, 1969) are also rooted in Canadian soil, so that it seemed a singularly appropriate gesture when a group of poems from that collection received first prize in Canada's 1967 Centennial Commission poetry competition.

The themes that Margaret Atwood explored in her early collections—a quest for identity, human isolation, love as a power struggle, technology as dehumanizing, and the inefficacy of language—are also motifs in her later verse. In *Procedures for Underground* (Oxford Univ. Pr.; Little, Brown, 1970), images of drowning, journeys, and dreams, a sense of imminent danger, and a lack of personal control over one's fate recur, but those poems are informed with an element of hope, however tentative. Writing in *Canadian Literature* (Autumn 1971), Peter Stevens detected a movement in the book "towards a fundamental belief in the prerogatives of poetry in a threatening, tense world," a view that Melvin Maddocks echoed in his review for *Time* (October 26, 1970). "The Atwood message is beyond formulated pessimism," Maddocks wrote. "It has the rhythmic cycling of hope and despair natural to life itself. A lyricism as honest as a blade of grass in a boulder's crack keeps thrusting through."

In *The Journals of Susanna Moodie* (Oxford Univ. Pr., 1970), Margaret Atwood adopted the persona of an actual historical figure—the nineteenth-century emigrant from England who wrote novels based on her experiences in the Canadian bush. Mrs. Moodie perceives the land as both the source of her sustenance and as the force that destroys her, a form of "paranoid schizophrenia" still endemic among Canadians, according to Miss Atwood. Latter-day Canadians, she contends, also shared for too long the pioneers' attitude that "all literature was written by dead Englishmen," or occasionally by an American, and thus native art was largely ignored until the 1960s, when Canadian nationalism and strong resentment of United States–dictated literary tastes were both in the ascendant. Native authors started several literary magazines as vehicles for Canadian writing, and in support of the movement many writers "also did time as publishers," as Margaret Atwood explained in *World Authors, 1970–75*. From 1971 to 1973 she herself worked for the House of Anansi in Toronto as an editor and member of the board of directors.

During Margaret Atwood's tenure, the House of Anansi published *Power Politics* (1972; Harper, 1973), which many critics rank as the best of her poetry collections. In that series of poems about a failed love affair, she exposed the mutual manipulation inherent in any human relationship and the use of language as weapon. Writing in *Parnassus: Poetry in Review* (Spring/Summer 1974), Rosellen Brown marveled that "Atwood has been able to take those images, which must by now be comfortable to her, nearly domesticated by familiarity, and make them live so fiercely."

Having realized during her years at Harvard that no critical study of the body of Canadian literature had ever been published, Margaret Atwood set out to remedy that deficiency. After making an exhaustive "read-in," she prepared her introductory survey, *Survival: A Thematic Guide to Canadian Literature*, which triggered a controversy on its publication by the House of Anansi in 1972. Canadian literature, she contends in *Survival*, reflects the tendency of Canadians to be willing victims—to the influences of their powerful neighbor to the south, to the land itself, to the still prevalent colonial mentality, among other things—but also mirrors their tendency to be survivalists. Although nationalists liked the attention that the study focused on Canadian literature, some scholars and critics were incensed by her conclusions and asserted that she had chosen to examine only those works that fit her pre-established theories, ignoring, for example, the novels, plays, and criticism of Robertson Davies. The debate made *Survival* "an instant phenomenon," and by 1982 more than 85,-000 copies had been sold, an amazing sales record for a critical study.

The book's overwhelming success also brought its drawbacks. "Largely because of [*Survival*]," Margaret Atwood recounted in *World Authors*, "I became a combination target and cult figure, and began to feel a rather pressing need for privacy." As a result, she moved to a one-hundred-acre farm she had purchased in Alliston, Ontario and left her job with the House of Anansi to become a full-time writer. About the time *Survival* was published, she ended her five-year marriage to an American novelist whom she had met at Harvard and began living with the Canadian novelist Graeme Gibson. Her brightening circumstances may account for the marked change in outlook of the poems in *You Are Happy* (Oxford Univ. Pr.; Harper, 1974). Its four parts map a progression from grief over an abortive love affair to a joyful commitment to a more fulfilling relationship between the sexes. The poems in *You Are Happy* incorporate many of Margaret Atwood's recurring concerns, such as metamorphosis, myth, and landscape as symbol, but in the affirmative, freely given commitment of the lovers in the fourth section, several critics detected a radical shift in her vision. *Selected Poems* (Oxford Univ. Pr., 1976; Simon & Schuster, 1978), consisting of excerpts from *You Are Happy* and her five other major collections, was also acclaimed by critics.

Her increasing involvement during the mid-1970s in human-rights issues, her membership in Amnesty International, and her extensive travels in the southern Caribbean resulted in a considerable expansion of Margaret Atwood's perimeters. She began to explore political as well as personal and sexual violence and the relationships between countries and cultures as well as those between individuals in her most recent books of poetry, *Two-Headed Poems* (Oxford Univ. Pr., 1978; Simon & Schuster, 1981) and *True Stories* (Oxford Univ. Pr., 1981; Simon & Schuster, 1982). In her introduction to *Second Words* (Anansi, 1982; Beacon Pr., 1984), a selection of her critical prose, she explained that widening of vision: "When you begin to write you're in love with the language, with the act of creation, with yourself partly; but as you go on, the writing—if you follow it—will take you places you never intended to go and show you things you would never otherwise have seen. I began as a profoundly apolitical writer, but then I began to do what all novelists and some poets do: I began to describe the world around me."

The poems in *Interlunar* (Oxford Univ. Pr., 1984), her most recent collection, are darker in tone and more muted in imagery than her earlier work, but they deal once again with struggles between the sexes and within each individual, among other topics. Writing in the *Toronto Globe and Mail* (July 7, 1984), John Bemrose detected "a new humanity and depth" in *Interlunar* and considered that collection "an omen that her best may be yet to come."

Despite her established reputation as a poet, Margaret Atwood is more popularly known as a novelist. Even before *The Circle Game* was released, she had written her first, still unpublished, novel. In *The Edible Woman* (McClelland; Deutsch; Little, Brown, 1969), her second novel, the protagonist Marian MacAlpin tries to make a place for herself in society, either by resigning herself to her dead-end career or by escaping through marriage to a lawyer. Since she feels that the men in her life are conspiring to absorb her and to smother her identity, she becomes so obsessed with the ideas of consuming and consumption that she stops eating. When her fiancé refuses to eat a cake in the shape of a woman that she baked for him—symbolic of his attempt to "assimilate" her—she is freed from her anorectic obsession. Critics found her attempt at black humor unsuccessful, her characters bland, and her plot thin, but feminists seized upon it as a "product of the movement," as Margaret Atwood pointed out in her introduction to a 1981 edition. However, she considers it to be "protofeminist," since it was written before the women's movement began.

Another "feminist" novel by Margaret Atwood, *Lady Oracle* (McClelland; Simon & Schuster, 1976; Deutsch, 1977) is also a humorous account of a woman's attempt to escape. This time, however, the heroine is not fleeing the role that others wish to impose on her but the many different roles she herself has assumed—and kept hidden—over the years: fat teenager, author of Gothic romances, mistress of a would-be artist, and a poet whose work is "a cross between Kahlil Gibran and Rod McKuen," among others. Afraid that her multiple identities are about to be exposed and convinced that the woman who underlies them all is essentially unlovable, Joan Foster fakes her own drowning in Lake Ontario and hides out in Italy. Critical response to *Lady Oracle* was mixed. Although several reviewers seconded Linda Sandler's opinion in *Saturday Night* (September 1976) that it was a well-made novel and an "exquisite parody of an obsolete generation," Katha Pollitt maintained in the *New York Times Book Review* (September 26, 1976) that *Lady Oracle*, a "familiar tale of feminist woe," was slow-moving and full of "clumsy contrivances."

Weaving together symbolic landscape, surreal images, transformations, and a poetic prose style, Margaret Atwood won both critical and popular acclaim for *Surfacing* (McClelland, 1972; Deutsch; Simon & Schuster, 1973). Using a modified stream-of-consciousness technique, the unnamed heroine narrates her return to the Canadian bush where she grew up in order to search for her missing father, a scientist working in the North country. That search quickly becomes a quest for her own identity. When she discovers her father's drowned and bloated corpse, she retreats to an island where she depends on nature for sustenance and embarks on a psychic exploration of her suppressed past. She emerges from her experience whole, having come to terms with her barbarous and "civilized" natures, and ready to re-enter society. In his article for *Saturday Review* (April 1973) Benjamin DeMott ventured his opinion that "what is most striking about *Surfacing* is the integrity of the writer's imagination. . . . Everywhere in the language of this story there are dependencies, associative prefigurings, linkages extending and refining meaning. Moments of dramatic crisis evolve from metaphor itself."

The muted humor and intermeshing love triangles in *Life Before Man* (Simon & Schuster, 1979) might have lent themselves to a farcical treatment of contemporary society, but Margaret Atwood molds those elements into a disturbing social-psychological study. Elizabeth, who works at a natural history museum, and Lesje, a female paleontologist also employed there, and Nate, Elizabeth's husband and Lesje's lover, are constantly contemplating extinction of the dinosaurs that Lesje fantasizes living among, of lovers and love affairs, of themselves, and of *homo sapiens*. Paradoxically, the theme of *Life Before Man* is survival, continuing even if life is pointless or even threatening, whether love is realizable or not. "Organisms adapt to their environments," reflects Lesje. "Of necessity, most of the time . . . often with a certain whimsy, you could almost say perversity." Marilyn French declared in the *New York Times Book Review* (February 3, 1980) that in *Life Before Man* Margaret Atwood combined "several talents—powerful introspection, honesty, satire and a taut, limpid style—to create a splendid, fully integrated work."

Bodily Harm (Simon & Schuster, 1982), Margaret Atwood's most recent novel, incorporates her feminist and political concerns. On the pretext of writing a travel article, a young "lifestyles" reporter recovering from the trauma of a mastectomy retreats to a politically unstable Caribbean island that clearly mirrors her own shaky mental and physical state. Unwittingly drawn into a revolution and imprisoned, she emerges a politically aware woman with a sense of her own identity. *Bodily Harm* rivaled *Life Before Man* in the warmth of its critical reception, and the Periodical Distributors of Canada honored it as their 1983 book of the year.

Among Margaret Atwood's other works are two children's books—*Up in the Trees* (McClelland, 1978) and *Anna's Pet* (Lorimer, 1980); two collections of short stories—*Dancing Girls* (1977) and *Bluebeard's Egg* (1983), both published by McClelland; and two anthologies of Canadian poetry, which she edited. Coach House Press published *Murder in the Dark*, a collection of her short pieces in various genres, in 1983. Her many awards include the E. J. Pratt Medal (1961), the Canadian Booksellers' Association Award (1977), the Radcliffe Medal (1980), and two honorary doctorates. She has also been a lecturer in English at the University of British Columbia in Vancouver (1964–65), Sir George Williams University in Montreal (1967–68), and the University of Alberta (1969–70).

Margaret Atwood has blue eyes, dark curly hair, and stands five feet three inches tall. She and Graeme Gibson have moved from Canada to a village near Norwich, England to find some privacy for themselves and their young daughter, Jess.

They planned to live in West Berlin, however, from April to June of 1984, where Margaret Atwood was scheduled to be a writer-in-residence under the auspices of a German arts-council program for foreign artists. Her leisure time interests include gardening and canoeing.

References: Guardian p9 O 14 '70 por, p9 O 23 '82 por; N Y Times Bk Rev p15+ My 21 '78; People 13:69+ My 19 '80 pors; Canadian Who's Who, 1982; Contemporary Authors, new rev vol 3 (1981); World Authors, 1970-75 (1980)

Ax, Emanuel

June 8, 1949– Pianist. Address: b. c/o ICM Artists, Ltd., 40 W. 57th St., New York City, N.Y. 10019

Hailed as "one of the major talents of his generation" by many music critics, the young Polish-born pianist Emanuel Ax has won an impressive array of international awards, including the first Artur Rubinstein International Piano Master Competition, and has played with most of the major orchestras in the United States and Europe. Although Ax is perhaps best known as an interpreter of Chopin, his repertoire ranges from Mozart and Beethoven to such contemporary composers as Igor Stravinsky and Ned Rorem. In spite of his burgeoning reputation as a virtuoso performer and his prodigious musical talent, Ax remains self-effacing and down-to-earth. As he explained to Bob Micklin in a *Newsday* interview (April 11, 1976), he is simply "interested in being a good pianist, in learning a lot of music. . . . Making music is what's important."

Emanuel Ax was born on June 8, 1949 in Lvov, a city that once formed a part of the Austro-Hungarian empire and later became annexed to Poland. After World War II it was incorporated into the Soviet Union, but because, as Ax has said, "it's such a Polish city that nobody admits that it's Russia—at least not the Poles," he considers himself to be "Polish more than anything else." According to Ax, his birth marked the beginning of a "new life" for his parents, Joachim and Hellen Ax, survivors of Nazi concentration camps whose first spouses had both been killed in the Holocaust. When the six-year-old Emanuel heard an Artur Rubinstein recording of a Chopin piano concerto, he immediately decided that he wanted to be a concert pianist, and though he began violin lessons that year, he soon switched to the piano. Joachim Ax, a singer and voice and speech therapist who had studied singing in Vienna and later coached at the Lvov Opera House, was his son's first piano teacher, though he himself was not a proficient pianist.

The Ax family moved to Warsaw when Emanuel was eight, immigrated to Winnipeg, Canada two years later, and in 1961 settled in New York City when the promising young musician won a scholarship to attend the Juilliard School of Music. Admitted to Juilliard's preparatory division, he soon began studying with the Polish-born pianist and educator Mieczyslaw Munz, whose style ("a fine romantic flair supported by an unobtrusive virtuoso technique," according to *Baker's Biographical Dictionary of Musicians*) in the pianistic tradition of Josef Hofmann, Moriz Rosenthal, and Josef Lhévinne, among others, influenced Ax's own manner of playing.

Ax attended public schools on Manhattan's East Side and played basketball and table tennis once or twice a week at the Kips Bay Boys' Club of America. Through the Steven David Epstein Memorial Foundation, the Boys' Club granted him several scholarships, sent him to the University of Maine's summer school to study chamber music, and cosponsored with the State Department's People-to-People program his 1969 concert tour of South America, as a result of which he received invitations from Peru and Bolivia to play with their national symphonies. In 1969 and 1970 he was also a guest soloist with the Chautauqua Symphony conducted by Walter Hendl.

In 1970, the year in which he became a citizen of the United States, Ax received a bachelor's degree in French from Columbia University and after graduation began entering a number of international piano competitions. He placed seventh both in the 1970 Chopin competition in Warsaw and in the 1972 Queen Elisabeth competition in Brussels ("I should have been playing dice," he once quipped), but in 1971 he finished third (no first prize was awarded) in the Vianna da Motta contest in Lisbon. Although first-place honors eluded him, his performance at Brussels won him the not inconsiderable prize of Laureate, and he was among several finalists in the Warsaw contest who were given a twenty-concert tour of Poland. During 1972-73 he also performed at concerts throughout Portugal and at international Chopin festivals in Poland and Czechoslovakia.

His March 12, 1973 New York recital debut at Alice Tully Hall, which was paid for by the Boys' Clubs of America, only enhanced Ax's reputation. According to Donal Henahan in his New York Times review (March 14, 1973), the young pianist proved himself to be a "powerhouse, technically," in his impressive interpretation of Ravel's Gaspard de la Nuit. Although Henahan thought his "hard and cold" tone did not always suit the emotional subtlety of Chopin's Sonata in B minor, Opus 58, he enjoyed Ax's "tasteful" performance of Mozart's Sonata in D and four Schubert songs transcribed by Liszt as well as his "unusually slow and romanticized" interpretation of the Sonata in A by Domenico Scarlatti. Later in 1973 Ax's audition for Young Concert Artists won him a place on the roster of that nonprofit, privately funded organization, thus ensuring him of further concert opportunities. During that same period he also lectured and played informally at various schools during one-to-three-day Young Concert Artists-sponsored "mini-residencies," an activity that, according to Ax, "[is] becoming standard for young artists nowadays."

As part of the thirteenth Young Concert Artists Series, Emanuel Ax performed works by Bach, Schoenberg, Chopin, and Liszt at the Hunter College Playhouse on January 21, 1974 and received an ovation. Writing in the New York Times (January 23, 1974), Robert Sherman applauded his virtuosic mastery and the "temperament, logic and individuality" of his playing. "The sweep is there," he added, "along with complete technical control, but there is also welcome emphasis on a rounded, singing piano tone, on graceful shapings of phrase and line." Ax was also acclaimed for his performance at the May 15, 1974 opening concert of "Three by Three," a series of three concerts, each featuring three artists, at Carnegie Hall. In his New York Times review (May 17, 1974), Allen Hughes congratulated the "highly skilled pianist" on his ability "to achieve any degree of dynamic shading

he wishes," though he had some reservations about Ax's penchant for "rounding off all the corners of his interpretations." Harriet Johnson of the New York Post (May 16, 1974) simply termed him "the best" of the three musicians presented and concluded, "As an artist, Ax is somebody to reckon with."

Although Ax has often been complimented for his technique, he has yet to achieve to his own satisfaction the pianistic artistry of his idol, Artur Rubinstein, to whose recordings he has listened since childhood. He and his wife own a copy of every Rubinstein release, with the exception of a rare (circa 1930) recording of Rachmaninoff's Second Piano Concerto. As he admitted to Paul Hertelendy in an interview for Contemporary Keyboard (February 1980): "I'd like to play in his style! . . . He has the most complete pianism I know: the most powerful, the most emotional, the most aristocratic." Ax must therefore have been particularly pleased when on September 13, 1974 a panel of eminent judges, including Rubinstein himself, awarded him first prize in the first Artur Rubinstein International Piano Master Competition in Tel Aviv, Israel. A "runaway winner" in the contest, according to Paul Hertelendy, Ax received a gold medal, $5,000, and a contract with Sol Hurok Concerts. His first-place honor also included a recording contract with RCA, two appearances at Carnegie Hall, and engagements with such major orchestras as the Berlin Philharmonic, the BBC Orchestra, the Vienna Philharmonic, the Israel Philharmonic, and the Cleveland Orchestra.

But in spite of such a cornucopia of tangible benefits and the impetus that such contests can give a young artist's career, Ax takes a dim view of piano competitions. "They are really lotteries," he has said. "I would stake as much on a bingo game as a piano competition, there are so many variables involved. . . . No one likes contests . . . but that's our only means of getting attention." As a result of all the publicity and engagements that were showered on Ax with the Rubinstein award, he "stopped entering contests right there," as he explained to Donal Henahan in an interview for the New York Times (August 14, 1977), "because there was no point after that." Ten days before he received the Rubinstein prize, Ax had been given the 1974 Michaels Award of Young Concert Artists in recognition of his outstanding achievements as a concert performer. That honor included engagements with the Los Angeles Philharmonic and Rochester Philharmonic and with the symphony orchestras of Atlanta, Chicago, St. Louis, Seattle, and Syracuse, along with appearances as a guest soloist with the Chamber Music Society of Lincoln Center on February 2 and 4, 1975.

His formal New York debut on April 23, 1975 at Alice Tully Hall was also part of the Michaels Award. Reviewing that recital in the New York Times on the following day, Harold C. Schonberg, an expert on pianism, praised Ax's "dream technique" in his performance of compositions by Mozart, Schoenberg, Beethoven, and Chopin, adding that he "has an unusually sonorous tone and is infinitely more of a colorist than most of his contemporaries. A powerful musical impulse—sometimes a bit unformed, to be sure—animates his playing." Speight Jenkins also had some minor reservations in his *New York Post* review of the same date, but he concluded that "at his best," as in his playing of Chopin's Etudes (Nos. 6 and 8), Ax was "glittering, self-assured, finger-light and delightful."

In addition to appearing in solo recitals and with major symphony orchestras, Ax often plays chamber music. "I've always done a lot," he explained to Paul Hertelendy, because "it's my great love, it's the most fun." For about twelve years at the Juilliard School, he studied chamber music "very intensely" with the violinist Felix Galimir because to him it "was simply a natural part of what a musician does." Ax has earned critical acclaim for his performances with such groups as the Galimir String Quartet, the Los Angeles Chamber Music Society, and the Orpheus Chamber Ensemble, among others. Shirley Fleming called his concert with the Tokyo String Quartet on August 16, 1979 at the Mostly Mozart Festival "a successful collaboration" in her review for the *New York Post* (August 17, 1979), and in his March 4, 1979 report for the *New York Times* of the March 2 performance of Ax with the Chamber Music Society of Lincoln Center, Peter G. Davis paid homage to Ax's "superior reading on every count" of Dvořák's Piano Quintet in A, Opus 81, and his "cultured, purling work at the keyboard [that] seemed to inspire the four string players to match his expressive ardor at every turn."

Occasionally Ax has joined forces with Pinchas Zukerman, Lynn Harrell, and Eugenia Zukerman for chamber music performances, but he has collaborated most often with the brilliant young cellist Yo-Yo Ma, whom he met at Juilliard. The onstage personalities of the two men are markedly different—Ma is the "consummate extrovert," while Ax is "more steady and reserved," according to Tim Page in the *New York Times* (October 19, 1982)—but they meld beautifully to produce a memorable performance. During the 1980–81 season, Young-Unk Kim joined Ax and Ma to form a chamber music trio. In an enthusiastic interview for the *New York Times* (July 17, 1981), Ax told Peter G. Davis, "I want to set aside a period every year so that we can continue this association. It's a terrific experience being a part of a permanent group. . . . I think we can only get better the longer we stick together."

In 1979 Emanuel Ax received yet another prestigious award: the Avery Fisher Prize, which is presented every year to an outstanding American instrumentalist and carries with it a $5,000 cash stipend and engagements with the Great Performers Series in Avery Fisher Hall, the New York Philharmonic, the Chamber Music Society of Lincoln Center, and the Mostly Mozart Festival. Although Ax, who has taken part in the yearly Mostly Mozart Festival since 1977, brilliantly plays even the most

demanding scores in the literature, like Brahms's Second Concerto, he finds Mozart's "less grandly scaled scores" equally challenging and satisfying. As he explained to Peter G. Davis in the *New York Times* interview, "You have to concentrate on Mozart especially hard because the margin-of-error range is so small—his scores are so minutely balanced and calculated that every note has to be placed just so and in perfect proportion or the effect will be ruined. It takes tremendous energy and brain work to play Mozart. I have nine or ten of his concertos in my repertory now, but my dream is to play all twenty-five."

Harold C. Schonberg, among other critics, has extolled Ax's interpretations of Mozart. In his *New York Times* review (September 30, 1977) of his performance with the New York Philharmonic on the preceding day, for example, Schonberg was generous in his praise: "Mr. Ax [has] the particular kind of technique that can set Mozart off to best advantage: fluent, yet strongly outlined, with purling scales and lovely tone." Nevertheless, Ax remains more primarily associated with Chopin, having earned a reputation second only to that of Artur Rubinstein as an interpreter of his compositions. Oddly enough, Ax contends that Chopin is not his major interest and feels that he has been typecast because he, too, is Polish by birth and began his recording career with a Chopin album.

Deeply interested in contemporary music, Ax has performed works by Benjamin Lees, Schoenberg, and Shostakovich, and in 1976 he commissioned the Etudes by Ned Rorem for the Bicentennial Piano Series of the Washington Performing Arts Society. In an interview he had with Donald Manildi for *American Record Guide* (January–February 1982), Ax characterized the Etudes as being "terribly difficult. Incredibly difficult. They used so many different techniques—I think it's simply that Rorem knows the piano very, very well—perhaps more so than other composers today." As usual, however, Ax surmounted the difficulties of the score, and Robert Sherman wrote in his *New York Times* review (May 9, 1976) of the premiere of the Etudes on May 6, 1976 at the McMillin Theater: "It would be difficult to overpraise Emanuel Ax."

Under his exclusive contract with RCA, Emanuel Ax has recorded works by Mozart, Ravel, Brahms, and Schumann to critical acclaim. He received a Grammy nomination for his recording of Chopin's F minor Concerto; his all-Beethoven album was included on *Time*'s list of the five best classical albums of 1976; and *Stereo Review* honored Dvořák's Quintet for Piano and Strings in A minor that he recorded with the Cleveland Quartet as its 1977 record of the year. When Donald Manildi asked him why he records the standard repertoire instead of trying to break new ground, Ax explained that it is a matter of playing what he knows best: "The first responsibility in making a record is to make a good one, and the plain fact of the matter is that most pianists study, and then record, works from the standard repertoire. . . .

There's always *another* way of playing a piece, fortunately. With great music there's always room for new ideas." Ax only records works that he has been performing for one or two years, and during a recording session he tries to play as if he were giving a live concert. "It's hard—in many way harder—the business of having to play clearly," he admitted to Paul Hertelendy during the *Contemporary Keyboard* interview. "Sometimes it's hard to let yourself go. It's almost a different form of music-making." He hopes that someday all of his recordings will be of live performances.

Although Ax is meticulous in his preparation of a score, his goal is not so much a note-perfect performance as it is the act itself of "making music." Perhaps for that reason, he prefers the concert hall to the recording studio. "The problem," he once explained to Donal Henahan in an interview for the *New York Times* (August 14, 1977), "is how you make people understand what you understand, make 3,000 people love music the way you love it. Learning to give everything you have at every concert. . . ."

Emanuel Ax loves opera, is an enthusiastic—if less than masterly—tennis player ("my game is mostly picking up the ball"), and, according to Yo-Yo Ma, has "one of the greatest repertoires of jokes since Mel Brooks." Interviewers have often been impressed by his engaging personality and lack of affectation. Weighing in at five feet ten inches and 180 pounds, Ax is admittedly overweight, perhaps because he is a self-confessed "madman for potatoes." "If I ever write an autobiography," he has said, "it will be called *The Sensuous Potato*." Although his demanding concert schedule allows him less time with his wife of ten years, Yoko Nozaki, also a pianist, and their young son, Joseph Akira, than he would like, Ax still enjoys performing. "I'm having a wonderful time," he insists. "Maybe later on I'll get tired of making planes and trains and so on, but right now I'm very happy about it. It's always an adventure."

References: American Record Guide 45:2+ Ja-F '82 por; Clavier 19:12+ Ja '80 por; N Y Times p48 My 20 '75 por; People 18:59+ Ag 9 '82 pors; Who's Who in America, 1984-85

Battle, Kathleen

Aug. 13, 1948– Soprano. Address: b. c/o Columbia Artists Management, Inc., 165 West 57th St., New York City, N.Y. 10019

Universally acclaimed by her peers for what one of them called her "special quality of communicating with the public" as well as for her superlative voice, Kathleen Battle began her professional life teaching elementary school in the inner city in Cincinnati, Ohio. She made her singing debut in 1972 at the Spoleto (Italy) Festival of Two Worlds and went on to earn critical praise in most of the music capitals of the world. Her light lyric coloratura is ideally suited to ingenue and soubrette operatic roles, but, encouraged by her mentor, James Levine, the artistic director of the Metropolitan Opera, she has chosen to develop her recital repertory rather than yield to the temptation of pushing her voice into the high-risk territories of the heavier operatic soprano parts. Her sublime performance in Handel's *Solomon* sent critics into crescendos of superlatives. One of her favorite composers, however, is Mozart, and his work, along with that of Johann Sebastian Bach, Schumann, and Brahms, figures prominently in her list of credits and in her discography, which includes, among other things, Mozart's *Così fan tutte* (Angel), with the Vienna Philharmonic Orchestra under Riccardo Muti, Schumann's *Spanish Love Songs* (Music Masters) and Brahms's *German Requiem* (RCA), with the Chicago Symphony Orchestra under James Levine.

The last of the seven children of Grady Battle, a steelworker, and his wife, Ollie (Lane) Battle, Kathleen Deanne Battle was born on August 13,

1948 in Portsmouth, a small industrial city in southern Ohio. Her siblings—three brothers and three sisters—include a teacher, an accountant, a welder, a secretary, a carpenter, and a personnel supervisor. "It's a wonderfully close family, which gives me strength," Miss Battle told Peter Goodman of *Newsday* (March 25, 1984). "Maybe you don't appreciate it much growing up, when you have to share beds, bedrooms, closets, but you do . . . more later on."

A diligent and hard-working child, Kathleen Battle excelled in all her subjects at the local public school. Consequently, when she began piano lessons at the age of thirteen, her special aptitude for music was not immediately noticed. In high school, she took secretarial courses in typing and shorthand—"I've always been practical," she explained to Heidi Waleson in an interview for Opera News (March 13, 1982)—as well as piano and voice. Despite her love of music and her undeniable singing talent, the idea of a career in the performing arts did not occur to her. "I'm sure that anyone who studies singing hears people saying they have a lovely voice," she told Mark Steinbrink, as quoted in the New York Times (May 2, 1982).

On her graduation from Portsmouth High School in 1966, Miss Battle was awarded a Ford Foundation National Achievement Scholarship. Persuaded by her high school music teacher to major in music instead of mathematics, she enrolled at the College-Conservatory of Music at the University of Cincinnati, but she decided against specializing in performance, opting instead for music education. In addition to her music studies, she registered for courses in art, dance, and languages. When she entered college, Miss Battle, by her own admission, had little knowledge of the classical vocal repertory and even less understanding of the capabilities and limitations of her own voice.

In 1971, her bachelor's and master's degrees in music education from the University of Cincinnati in hand, Miss Battle began teaching fourth-, fifth-, and sixth-graders at the Garfield School in Cincinnati's inner city. In the evenings, she took second-year German in night school and studied voice with Franklin Bens, who focused on the oratorio literature. After studying privately for a year, she auditioned for Thomas Schippers, then the director of the Cincinnati Symphony Orchestra and the co-founder, with Gian-Carlo Menotti, of the Spoleto (Italy) Festival of Two Worlds. Although her previous performing experience consisted of little more than singing in local church choirs, Schippers immediately hired Miss Battle to sing the soprano part in Brahms's Ein Deutsches Requiem, as well as several Handel arias, at the 1972 Spoleto festival. She described her Spoleto debut to Mark Steinbrink as a turning point in her life: "That night was very magical and significant for me. After that experience I knew I wanted to be a singer. . . ."

Returning to Cincinnati in the fall of 1972, Miss Battle continued to teach music at the elementary school level, but she agreed to repeat her performance of Ein Deutsches Requiem for a Cincinnati Symphony Orchestra concert. To prepare for a career as a professional singer, in her spare time she studied opera interpretation, song literature, and acting. Her association with Schippers led to an introduction, in 1973, to the pianist and conductor James Levine, who was then the director of the Cincinnati May Festival. Impressed by the naive young soprano, Levine engaged her to appear with him at the Cincinnati and Ravinia (Illinois) festivals. More important, he oversaw her training and helped her to expand her repertory to include such works as Mozart's Mass in C-Minor, Haydn's The Creation, and Bach's Cantata no. 202, Weichet nur (Wedding Cantata). Levine became, in Miss Battle's words, "the cornerstone of my career—my mentor, coach, adviser and friend."

Miss Battle repaid Levine with strong performances that earned her enthusiastic reviews and several prestigious honors. In March 1974 she placed first in the WGN-Illinois Opera Guild's "Auditions of the Air," winning $3,000 and an appearance as featured soloist in Chicago's annual Grant Park summer concert series. A year later, in April 1975, she took the top prize in the Young Artists Awards, a national operatic competition held at the Kennedy Center for the Performing Arts in Washington, D.C. Later in the same year she received the Martha Baird Rockefeller Fund for Music Award.

Following an engagement at the Ravinia Festival in the summer of 1975, Miss Battle, who had intended to spend the next few months auditioning in Europe, decided instead to accept an invitation to understudy—and eventually succeed—Carmen Balthrop in the title role of Scott Joplin's folk opera Treemonisha on Broadway. "It was a real plunge for me," Miss Battle told Cincinnati Enquirer (November 21, 1975) music critic Nancy Malitz. "Instant initiation. I had no orchestra rehearsal. . . . I was very much on my own. . . ." In his review of her debut in the role for the New York Times (October 23, 1975) John Rockwell complimented Miss Battle on her "perfectly lovely lyric soprano that meets the demands of the role with gracious ease," adding, "There can't be too many instances, on Broadway or in opera, where an understudy has been of this quality." According to Miss Battle, her move to New York City marked the point "when [her] career began in earnest."

The following autumn, Miss Battle won a show-stopping ovation for her interpretation of the aria "Deh vieni, non tardar" in her New York City Opera debut, as Figaro's fiancée, the maid Susanna, in Mozart's opera buffa Le Nozze di Figaro conducted by David Effron. Robert Sherman, writing in the New York Times (September 9, 1976), credited Miss Battle with "some of the loveliest singing" in the production. Moreover, she was "fetchingly at home" on the stage: "Her movements were lithe, her acting natural, and her beguiling sweet tone—though not always forceful enough to soar easily over the orchestra—made her work consistently appealing." One year later, Miss Battle made her Metropolitan Opera debut, as the Shepherd in a new production of Wagner's Tannhäuser. The following season, she essayed the role of Sophie in Jules Massenet's Werther. Her operatic credits for the 1977–78 season also included the parts of Nannetta in Verdi's Falstaff for the Houston Grand Opera and the trouser-role of the page Oscar in the San Francisco Opera's staging of Verdi's Un Ballo in maschera.

By 1980, Miss Battle was able to offer one gauge of her growing confidence in her voice. "The high notes are coming easier now," she reported in an interview for her hometown newspaper, the *Portsmouth Times* (March 22, 1980). "I'll sing a high E in public now, and I don't think I would have said that two years ago." In the 1981-82 Metropolitan Opera season, she was called upon to do just that, as Blonde in Mozart's *Die Entführung aus dem Serail*. Among her other roles that season was Pamina in Mozart's *Die Zauberflöte*. According to Harriett Johnson of the *New York Post* (November 6, 1981), Miss Battle made her Pamina "extraordinarily sympathetic by singing sensitively with bewitching color as if the gods had taught her."

By the 1981-82 season, Miss Battle had clearly found her stride, as the *New York Times*'s John Rockwell, for one, observed. "She is rapidly developing into one of our most valuable artists—a pure, radiant soprano linked to a sensitive interpretive personality," Rockwell wrote in his January 23, 1982 review of her recital of Brahms, Schumann, and Schubert lieder, staged by James Levine at New York City's Alice Tully Hall. Over the past few years, Miss Battle had gradually enlarged her repertory, which had originally been limited mainly to oratorio, to encompass not only opera, but also orchestral concerts and song recitals. Ever cautious, however, she refused to place undue demands on her light, high voice, even if it meant restricting her operatic roles to the soubrettes. "I won't stretch or pull my voice beyond its capacity and capability," she told Heidi Walcson. "Mozart is perfect. There's a clarity of line, a rhythmic thrust, a kind of rhythmic vitality that comes from within, and of course with the color and weight of the voice, he suits me."

Although the critics were unanimous in their praise of Kathleen Battle's voice, some expressed reservations about her acting ability, particularly in the roles of Despina in Mozart's *Così fan tutte*, in which she made her debut at the 1982 Salzburg Festival, and Rosina in the Metropolitan Opera's production of Rossini's *Il Barbiere di Siviglia*. Donal Henahan of the *New York Times* (January 31, 1982) thought that as Despina she was "a bit one-dimensional" and substituted "flouncing activity for wit." While he paid tribute in his *New York Times* review (March 18, 1982) to the "full, lyric richness" of her singing in *Il Barbiere di Siviglia*, John Rockwell, too, found that Miss Battle lacked "that last iota of comic vivacity as an actress."

No such fault, however, could be found with Miss Battle's recital and concert performances. At her Washington, D.C. recital debut in November 1982, the audience responded to her well-chosen program of songs by Purcell, Schubert, Mozart, and Fauré with three standing ovations. Similar enthusiasm greeted her interpretation of the roles of Solomon's Queen and the Queen of Sheba in the Toronto Mendelssohn Choir's presentation of Handel's *Solomon* a few days later. Among the enthusiasts was John Kraglund, the music critic of the

Toronto Globe & Mail. Hailing Miss Battle as "perhaps the greatest young soprano of our time," Kraglund concluded, in his review of November 22, 1982, "In purity of sensuous tone, impeccable phrasing and effortless ornamentation, this was glorious singing beyond anything in my recent experience."

Increasingly confident, Miss Battle undertook the demanding part of Zerbinetta in Richard Strauss's *Ariadne auf Naxos* for the San Francisco Opera in September 1983. In an interview for an *Ovation* profile (March 1984), she conceded that Zerbinetta was "a little risky" for her "because of that [high] E, coming right after Despina, which is so much lower," but she managed the vocal fireworks of the aria "Grossmächtige Prinzessin" with astonishing ease. After hearing her sing the aria in concert with the Lausanne Chamber Orchestra at New York City's Carnegie Hall a month later, Donal Henahan described her voice as "no thin, pennywhistle soprano, but a musical instrument that she used with great subtlety."

During the 1983-84 Metropolitan Opera season, Miss Battle sang the roles of two other Strauss heroines—Zdenka in *Arabella* and Sophie in *Der Rosenkavalier*—for the first time and also added to her growing repertory of Mozartian roles that of Zerlina, the peasant girl in *Don Giovanni*. But perhaps her most ambitious undertaking was the organization of a three-concert recital series at Alice Tully Hall called "Kathleen Battle and Friends." With the assistance of her manager, Sam Niefeld, she chose the music, which ranged from Bach to Duke Ellington and George Gershwin, recruited the "friends," who included James Levine, trumpeter Wynton Marsalis, and flutist Hubert Laws, and scheduled rehearsals. "The combination [of classical music, jazz, and spirituals] could easily have failed," Peter G. Davis maintained in *New York* magazine (January 9, 1984), "but it worked for [Miss] Battle due to the sheer beauty of her soprano and her musical instincts, which are so true and devoid of artifice."

Kathleen Battle's greatest critical triumph of the season, however, came when she again sang the roles of the two queens in Handel's *Solomon*, this time with the Musica Sacra Chorus and Orchestra at New York City's Avery Fisher Hall. "What a liquid, sensuous voice hers has become," wrote a worshipful Donal Henahan in the *New York Times* (March 21, 1984). "With every appearance, the young soprano seems to develop a greater range of expression, a more vibrant voice over her entire range and a new dimension in personality." He went on to praise at length her "gleaming high notes," "ravishing trill," "rich lower range," and musical intelligence. Andrew Porter of the *New Yorker* (April 9, 1984) echoed his colleague's sentiments, calling Miss Battle's interpretation "the most ravishing performance of a Handel air I have ever heard."

Kathleen Battle finished the season "with a sense of accomplishment and relief," to use her words. In the summer of 1984, she traveled to Paris to sing the role of Susanna in *Le Nozze di Figaro* and to Salzburg to reprise her role as Despina in *Così fan tutte*. Miss Battle spends some of her leisure time at her beach house in Quogue, New York, where she tends her flowers and reads biographies. She also maintains an apartment near Lincoln Center on Manhattan's Upper West Side. The fragile-looking soprano, who has large, expressive brown eyes and shoulder-length black hair, often pulled back into a tight bun, puts most of her free time into developing and practising her repertory. She is booked three years in advance, for as many as sixty engagements a year, at $5,000 to $10,000 a performance. Miss Battle discussed her career in a recent interview for *High Fidelity* (February 1984): "Each time I sing, it's a new experience for me. None of the roles I have done has yet reached a pinnacle: they are always evolving and being re-evaluated. . . . I seem to have cycles in what I sing. In the last year, I was in a Strauss cycle. . . . Now I'm starting to concentrate on Handel. . . . And always—always—there is Mozart!"

References: *Hi Fi* 34:4+ *F* '84; *N Y Times* II p23+ *My* 2 '82 por; *Opera N* 46:15+ *Mr* 13 '82 pors; *Ovation* p16+ *Mr* '84 pors; *People* 19:88+ *Mr* 7 '83 pors; *The Negro Almanac: A Reference Work on the Afro-American* (1983); *Who's Who in America 1984-85*

Bird, Rose E(lizabeth)

Nov. 2, 1936– Chief Justice of the California Supreme Court. Address: b. State Bldg., 350 McAllister St., San Francisco, Calif. 94102

When former California Governor Edmund G. ("Jerry") Brown Jr. nominated his Secretary of Agriculture and Services, Rose Bird, to succeed Donald Wright as chief justice of the state supreme court in 1977, it was but the beginning of a public controversy that has intensified since her investiture. An outstanding appellate lawyer with demonstrated administrative ability, Miss Bird, the first woman to serve as chief justice in the state's history, had a reputation as a liberal and, more important, a judicial reformer. Conservative law-and-order advocates, contending that Justice Bird is "soft on crime," have launched repeated recall drives and, in 1978, nearly succeeded in removing her from the bench.

Justice Bird's response to her critics has been to wage a steadfast campaign in behalf of an independent judiciary. "Once special-interest politics begins to undermine the rule of law," she maintained in an opinion piece for the *Los Angeles Times* (June 12, 1983), "it is not hard to imagine a system in which judges put their moistened fingers to the wind, decide what is perceived to be the prevailing view and rule accordingly. Such a system would as surely end the rule of law as would the destruction of our Constitution itself."

The youngest of three children, Rose Elizabeth Bird was born in Tucson, Arizona on November 2, 1936. Her parents, who had operated a chicken farm on the outskirts of the city, separated in 1941, and her father, a former hat supplies salesman who went bankrupt in the Depression, died soon afterward. Faced with the prospect of providing for her family alone, Anne Bird, a trained teacher, took a job installing plexiglass windows on transport planes at nearby David Monthan Air Force Base. In about 1950 Mrs. Bird moved with her family to her home state of New York, where she found work in a plastics factory on Long Island. Rose and her brothers, Jack and Philip, helped out by doing assigned household chores. "We had our responsibilities when we were young, but I really appreciated it," she told Betty Liddick in an interview for the *Los Angeles Times* (April 22, 1977). "I think it builds within children feelings of responsibility not only for themselves but for others."

During her adolescence, Rose Bird began to demonstrate the intelligence, political independence, and ingenuity that were to characterize her career. She easily earned membership in the honor society of the high school she attended in Sea Cliff, Long Island, and though she lived in an area that was, by her estimation, "99 percent Republican," she doggedly canvassed her neighborhood to drum up support for the election of Adlai E. Stevenson, the Democratic presidential nominee in 1952. In her spare time, she contributed to the family finances by taking a series of odd jobs.

Following her high school graduation, Miss Bird accepted a full-tuition scholarship to Long Island

University, where she prepared for a career in journalism by majoring in English, with minors in economics and history. Her extracurricular activities included serving as student director of the *Long Island University Forum of the Air* and editing the college yearbook, *Sound.* The recipient of the Alumni Association Award as the outstanding member of the senior class, she took her B.A. degree, *magna cum laude*, in 1958. She had been granted a fellowship to continue her education at the University of California at Berkeley, but before going on to graduate school, she worked for a year as a secretary to a research scientist at the Polytechnic Institute of New York in order to earn extra money for her living expenses.

In her second year at Berkeley, Miss Bird won a Ford Foundation grant to serve as an intern, or "participating observer," at the California state legislature in Sacramento. Assigned to assist Assemblyman Gordon Whitten, who headed the legislature's public education committee, she helped draft a bill, later adopted into law, establishing a statewide testing program for school children. On the basis of her legislative experience, she decided to switch her course of study from political science to law because it seemed to her that lawyers had the most influence on the development of public policy. Accordingly, in 1962 she entered the Boalt Hall School of Law at the University of California. She received her J.D. degree three years later.

Rose Bird began her professional career in 1965, as clerk to the chief justice of the Nevada Supreme Court. On her return to California the following year, she passed the state bar exam and, in a deliberate effort to disprove the notion that women were emotionally unsuited for trial work, sought a job as a public defender. The first woman ever to be hired by the Santa Clara (California) County Public Defender's Office, Rose Bird began taking on felony cases almost immediately, and within a few months was handling appellate as well as trial work. One of the cases she argued in front of the California Court of Appeals established a precedent in its vindication of the "defense of diminished capacity" in a murder trial. In another textbook case, *People of California vs. Krivda*, Miss Bird, who was by then chief of the appellate division of the Public Defender's Office, successfully argued that the United States Supreme Court had "improvidently" agreed to hear an appeal from the California Supreme Court because the decision of the case in question had been based on an individual's right to privacy as guaranteed under the constitution of California and was therefore an independent state ground.

During her last two years as a deputy public defender, Rose Bird concurrently taught a seminar in criminal defense at Stanford University's School of Law. Although she enjoyed teaching, she turned down Stanford's offer of a non-tenured faculty position. At the end of the 1973–74 academic year she left the university and the Public Defender's Office, with the intention of setting up her own private law practice in the fall. During the intervening summer months, she worked as a volunteer in the Democratic gubernatorial campaign of Edmund G. ("Jerry") Brown Jr. Because she acted as Brown's chauffeur whenever he was barnstorming in her part of the state, she came to know the candidate personally during the course of the campaign, and after his election in November 1974, she became a key member of his transition team.

Governor Brown was so impressed with Rose Bird's work in the transition period that he appointed her secretary of California's Department of Agriculture and Services. She was the first woman to hold a cabinet-level position in the state's history. Miss Bird's appointment broke with tradition in another respect, too, for the nomination had customarily gone to a farmer, even though consumer protection, veterans' affairs, and industrial relations also came within the department's purview. During her tenure as secretary, Miss Bird devoted a considerable amount of her time to upgrading and strengthening the "service" divisions of her department. Under her direction, for instance, the Division of Occupational Safety and Health stepped up its efforts to regulate exposure to hazardous chemicals in the workplace, a problem in which Secretary Bird took a special interest because of the painful aftereffects of her mother's years of employment in plastics factories. But it was her decisions affecting agriculture that generated the most controversy. Concerned about the high incidence of debilitating spinal injuries among farmworkers, she banned the use of the short-handled hoe that forced field hands to spend hours at a time in an uncomfortable stooped position. More important, in fulfillment of a Brown campaign pledge, she drafted a landmark farm labor bill guaranteeing the farmworkers' right to hold secret-ballot union elections and guided its passage through the state legislature.

In February 1977 Governor Brown nominated Rose Bird for the post of chief justice of the California Supreme Court. Her years of "writing legislation and carrying out its intent," he said, as quoted in the *New York Times* (February 14, 1977), had given her "that real world kind of experience that will be valuable in making the judgments a supreme court justice must make." The nomination was immediately attacked by conservatives, among them Pasadena Police Chief Bob McGowen, the president of the Los Angeles County Peace Officers Association, and San Diego Mayor Pete Wilson, who feared that Miss Bird would "champion the criminal defense attorneys" at the expense of the general public. Protesting her lack of judicial experience, a majority of the Republicans in the state legislature urged Attorney General Evelle J. Younger, one of the three-member Commission of Judicial Appointments that has the responsibility of approving or rejecting court appointments, to vote against Miss Bird's confirmation. Perhaps the most potentially damaging criticism of the nomination came from Bishop Roger Mahoney, who, as chairman of the California Agricultural Labor Relations

Board, had worked closely with Miss Bird. In a letter to Attorney General Younger, as quoted in the *New York Times* (March 7, 1977), Bishop Mahoney questioned her "emotional stability" and her "vindictive approach to dealing with all persons under her authority."

Rallying to her defense, Rose Bird's supporters contended that opposition to her nomination was based on partisan politics and sex discrimination. To those who objected to the fact that she had no previous judicial experience, they countered that no fewer than eighteen United States Supreme Court justices, including Chief Justice Earl Warren, had had no previous judicial experience. Among the professional organizations and individuals speaking out in favor of Miss Bird's appointment were the California Women Lawyers Association, the California Bar Association, the California Trial Lawyers Association, California Attorneys for Criminal Justice, all past and current members of the Agriculture Labor Relations Board, excepting Bishop Mahoney, and former California Chief Justice Phil S. Gibson.

With Evelle Younger casting a reluctant vote in her favor, Rose Bird was confirmed and, on March 26, 1977, sworn in as chief justice of the California Supreme Court. In her investiture address, she warned that the judicial system was becoming "more and more removed" from the people whose rights and interests it was supposed to protect. "Our courts are beginning to be perceived as just another example of burgeoning bureaucracy, as places of cold rationality, inaccessible and unaffordable to the average citizen," she said. To restore respect for the courts, she recommended engendering a "sense of participation" in the judicial process. "This sense of participation," she continued, "depends on the willingness of *all* those in our judicial system to deal directly, openly, and compassionately with *all* the people who come before that system—jurors and witnesses, victims and defendants, prosecutors and defenders, corporate entities and the individuals, the persecuted and the privileged alike."

In an attempt to "demystify," to use her word, the judicial process, Chief Justice Bird immediately instituted a number of reforms. Among other things, she appointed special panels to solicit public comment on such problems as court congestion, encouraged the courts of appeals to make their internal procedures public, assigned municipal and superior court judges to fill temporary vacancies on the state supreme court, and gave less experienced and younger judges an opportunity to sit at the appellate level. Miss Bird also prohibited court employees from accepting gratuities from lobbyists, reinstated the use of one-year law clerks in place of central staff members, and named women and representatives from minority groups to the twenty-one-member Judicial Council. Those and other reforms brought her into open conflict with what Gene Blake of the *Los Angeles Times* (August 6, 1978) called the "'good old boys' of the judicial Establishment."

Furthermore, Justice Bird's decisions, on everything from court-mandated busing to achieve racial integration in the schools to the death penalty to the tax-cutting Proposition 13, outraged political conservatives, who launched a "No on Bird" campaign to remove her from the bench. (Under California law, supreme court justices appointed by the governor must be approved by the electorate at the next gubernatorial election, which was, in Rose Bird's case, in November 1978.) Joining forces against Justice Bird were three major groups: the "Law and Order Campaign Committee," led by State Senator Hubert L. ("Bill") Richardson; the "Vote No on Rose Bird Committee," which was funded by wealthy agricultural interests and run by a professional campaign management firm; and the state Republican central committee executive group.

In its issue of August 1978, *California Journal*, a monthly magazine that analyzes the state's government and politics, reviewed eighty-eight of Justice Bird's decisions since she took office. The analysts concluded that although "Senator Richardson may be justified in calling her a liberal . . . , he will have a hard time backing up his contention that she is soft on crime." Nevertheless, her alleged "soft on crime" attitude was the theme of a lurid and inflammatory media blitz that included a graphic television spot depicting a brutal rape followed by the "No on Bird" slogan. The rape image was drawn from a recent, exhaustively reported court case, *People vs. Caudillo*, in which Justice Bird had voted with the majority to declare that, according to California law, rape did not constitute "great bodily injury." In a concurring opinion, Justice Bird wrote, "Personal repugnance toward these crimes cannot be a legitimate basis for rewriting the statute as it was adopted by the legislature."

With the support of the *Los Angeles Times*, the most influential newspaper in the state, which condemned the "malicious attempt" to unseat the chief justice in a pre-election editorial, Rose Bird managed to hold her own against the conservatives' onslaught, winning the election by the slim margin of 52 percent to 48 percent. But before the air cleared, a new storm broke. On November 7, 1978 the *Los Angeles Times* published an article attributed to "well-placed court sources" suggesting that the California Supreme Court had deliberately delayed the issuance of a controversial four-three decision overturning a 1975 state law that had mandated prison sentences for those convicted of using a gun to commit certain crimes so as not to hurt Justice Bird's chances at the polls. The resulting public furor prompted Justice Bird to ask the state Commission on Judicial Performance to look into the allegation. In its investigation, the commission focused on the timing of the disclosure of the predictably unpopular decision and on unethical leaks to the press from within the supreme court itself.

After an initial period of examination and inquiry, the commission opened its televised public hearings in June 1979. Over the next few weeks, five state supreme court justices and a dozen staff members denied all charges of irregularities and improprieties in the handling of cases, but their testimonies presented a rather unflattering picture of the court as an archaic and inefficient institution riven by bitterness, personal conflicts, and infighting. Although the commission's final report, released in November 1979, stated that "no formal charges" of misconduct would be filed against any justice, its inconclusiveness failed to put an end to the controversy. Of the two books about the judicial probe published to date, one, Prebel Stolz's *Judging Judges: The Investigation of Rose Bird and the California Supreme Court* (Free Press, 1981), was highly critical of Justice Bird; the other, Betty Medsger's *Framed: The New Right Attack on Chief Justice Rose Bird and the Courts* (Pilgrim Press, 1983), defended her and denounced the *Los Angeles Times* for shoddy journalistic practices and the "New Right" for questionable tactics.

Tho right-wing attacks on Justice Bird continued into the 1980s, but none of the several conservative-sponsored recall drives has as yet succeeded in placing the issue on the ballot. Justice Bird, who sees the repeated attempts to unseat her as politically rather than personally motivated, has tried to remain above the fray, but in a speech at the annual convention of the California Labor Federation in July 1982, she advised the delegates to be vigilant against the increasing threat to an independent judiciary. "[It is] later than just the eleventh hour," she said. "It is one minute to midnight. We must use our courage to ensure a judiciary not governed by the daily polls but by the rules of law . . . , devoted not to self-preservation but to the preservation of those great constitutional principles which history has bequeathed to us."

In his article assessing the first five years of Chief Justice Bird's tenure for the *Los Angeles Times* (May 21, 1982), Edwin Chen, the newspaper's legal affairs correspondent, described Miss Bird as "a steady champion of individual liberties who is determined to carry on the court's progressive history." As Chen pointed out, she has, among other things, voted to broaden the exclusionary rule, to set rigid guidelines for the admissability of confessions, to abolish the death penalty, and to overturn a guilty verdict based on a past conviction for a similar offense. Lawyers who have argued cases before Justice Bird have invariably found her to be well-prepared, and Laurence H. Tribe, a constitutional law expert from Harvard University, has ranked her opinions "among the most scholarly, thoughtful, intelligent opinions written by any appellate judge in the country." Because she is held in such high esteem by her colleagues, William Warren, the former dean of law of the University of California at Los Angeles, finds it "ironic" that she has been so widely criticized. "She has all those qualities we in society admire," he explained to Chen in the *Los Angeles Times* article. "She's a hard worker, a humanitarian, a champion of the underdog."

Although the constant assaults on her integrity have made her one of the most public figures in California, Rose Bird has nonetheless managed to maintain a private existence. "I've long felt that we debase the political process when we put so much emphasis on people's personalities—the extraneous things about them: what kind of car you drive, what sort of house you live in, what you eat . . . , and what your hobbies are," she told Peggy Lamson in an interview for the book *In the Vanguard: Six American Women in Public Life* (1979). "Sometimes it seems to me we're carrying Hollywood over to politics."

Believing that it is important for a public official to be "as close to an ordinary citizen as possible," as she once put it, Justice Bird does most of her own typing and eschews the chauffeur-driven limousine that comes with her post in favor of her own compact car. For relaxation, she swims, bicycles, roller skates, or plays racquetball. She also enjoys going to the movies and reading nonfiction. A modified radical mastectomy in 1976 and two subsequent operations for cancer forced Miss Bird to reexamine her life. She emerged from the experience, which she has described as "a kind of liberation," with a newfound confidence and serenity. The chief justice lives with her mother in a small house in Palo Alto, California.

References: Los Angeles Times IV p1+ Ap 22 '77 por, I p3+ Ag 6 '78 por, I p3+ My 2 '82 por; N Y Times p48 F 14 '77 por, p12 Je 12 '79 por; Newsweek 89:70+ F 28 '77 por; Time 109:69 F 28 '77 por; Lamson, Peggy. In the Vanguard (1979); Who's Who In America, 1984–85; Who's Who In American Politics, 1983–84; Who's Who of American Women, 1981–82

Bluford, Guion S(tewart), Jr.

(gī´ on)

Nov. 22, 1942– Astronaut. Address: b. c/o National Aeronautics and Space Administration, Lyndon B. Johnson Space Center, Houston, Tex. 77058

When the space shuttle Challenger blasted off for its third flight and the eighth mission of the shuttle program in the dark hours of the early morning of August 30, 1983, there was more than the usual number of members of Congress, entertainers, and other notables gathered at Cape Canaveral, Florida to view the fiery brilliance of the spacecraft's launch. Aboard the STS-8 flight was Guion S. Bluford Jr., then a lieutenant colonel in the Air Force, who became the first black American to fly in space. Not one to consider himself special or heroic, Bluford is a quiet, unassuming person with a lifetime passion for aeronautics. He maintains that he has never encountered obstacles to his development because of racial barriers, and he insists that his greatest fulfillment came from the experience of the flight itself, rather than from being the first black astronaut.

Guion S. Bluford Jr.

But although Bluford may only reluctantly assume the mantle of historical role model, there are others who unhesitatingly affirm his fitness for his position. "If I had to invent the first black astronaut, he would be Guy Bluford," Dr. Curtis M. Graves, deputy director of academic affairs at the National Aeronautics and Space Administration, has said. "He is an all-American black man who is extraordinarily bright, dedicated, and possesses strong values. As a role model, you couldn't ask for a better person."

Guion Stewart Bluford Jr. was born in Philadelphia, Pennsylvania on November 22, 1942, the oldest of the three sons of Guion S. Bluford Sr., a mechanical engineer and inventor, and Lolita Harriet (Brice) Bluford, a special education teacher in the public schools. The Bluford family lived a comfortable middle-class existence in a racially mixed neighborhood of row houses in West Philadelphia, and the parents encouraged their sons to work hard and strive for personal achievement and excellence. Success seemed to be a hallmark on both sides of the family. The Brice side boasted several successful musicians and educators, including the contralto Carol Brice, the pianist Jonathan Brice, and Charlotte Hawkins Brown, the founder of the Palmer Memorial Institute, a black preparatory school in North Carolina. The Bluford family tree included F. D. Bluford, president of the Agricultural and Technical State University in Greensboro, North Carolina, and Lucille Bluford, editor of the *Kansas City* (Missouri) *Call*. Guion Bluford's oldest brother, Eugene, is a computer programmer in Los Angeles; the other brother, Kenneth, is a teacher in Philadelphia.

As a child, Guy Bluford—nicknamed "Bunny" by his family—kept largely to himself, concentrating on crossword puzzles and "mind-twister" games, and building model airplanes. What William J. Broad in the *New York Times* (August 31, 1983) called Bluford's "all-American childhood" included also a paper route and a stint with the Boy Scouts, in which he attained the rank of Eagle Scout. Fascinated from an early age by aviation, Bluford was determined to understand the dynamics of flight. In junior high school his interest was focused on science and mathematics, and by the time he entered high school he had declared his intention to become an aerospace engineer. At the same time he was fascinated with the military and he regularly watched such television shows of the 1950s as *Navy Log* and *West Point Story*.

Bluford's high school physics teacher, Frederick Hofkin, now director of science education for the Philadelphia school system, remembers his young student for his keen interest in science. "He would sit very quietly until I began asking really hard and challenging questions," he told Scott Minerbrook, as quoted in *Newsday* (August 29, 1983). "Then he would come alive." Ironically, Bluford's mother considered her oldest son as the one least likely to succeed, for despite his intellectual curiosity schoolwork did not come easily to him. "Bunny just had to work harder than the rest of us," his brother Kenneth remarked to Bill Prochnau of the *Washington Post* (August 21, 1983). "He put in very long hours. He was always a little behind and trying to catch up." In fact, a guidance counselor from Overbrook High School once visited the Bluford family to advise his parents that Guy was not really "college material" and might be better off as a carpenter or mechanic. But the prospect of a member of the Bluford family not attending college was virtually unheard of, and after Guy Bluford graduated in 1960 from Overbrook High School—where he had been captain of the chess team and a member of the science club, and had worked on the staff of the school yearbook—he enrolled in the aerospace engineering program at Pennsylvania State University.

Bluford embarked on his university studies equipped with a personal drive and determination to fulfill his goals, along with a strong belief in the Protestant work ethic, that he had absorbed from his parents. There was never any question raised in the household that race might be a factor that could hold an individual back. Guion Bluford Sr. and Lolita Bluford were Christian Scientists and "Eisenhower Republicans" who believed that it was not only possible for black children to develop their talents unhindered, but that they had a moral obligation to do so. The civil rights movement of the late 1950s and early 1960s was not considered worthy of family discussion.

One of Bluford's professors at Penn State, Barnes McCormick, who later became head of the university's aerospace engineering department, remembered Bluford as the only black student in the engineering school but did not recall him as "the sort you would expect to be interviewed about twenty years later." Scott Minerbrook quoted McCormick in *Newsday* as describing Bluford as a "very religious person, easygoing, careful in what he said, a late bloomer." Characteristically intense and serious, Bluford studied diligently, enrolled in the Air Force ROTC program, attended meetings of an off-campus Christian Science group, and won the 1962 Phi Delta Kappa leadership award. After submitting a senior thesis in which he investigated the flight of a boomerang, Bluford obtained his B.S. degree in aerospace engineering in 1964, as a distinguished Air Force ROTC graduate.

Following his graduation, Bluford underwent pilot training at Williams Air Force Base in Arizona, receiving his wings in January 1965, and then trained in Arizona and Florida for F-4C combat crew duty. In 1967 he was sent to Vietnam, assigned to the 557th Tactical Fighter Squadron in Cam Ranh Bay, and flew 144 combat missions, including sixty-five over North Vietnam. That same year he received the Vietnam Campaign Medal, the Vietnam Cross of Gallantry with Palm, the Vietnam Service Medal, ten Air Force Air Medals, and the first of three Air Force outstanding unit awards. When his brother Kenneth, then a student antiwar protestor, challenged him with the charge that he was bombing civilians in Vietnam, Guion Bluford's response was typically restrained. "He just blanked out on it," Kenneth Bluford told Bill Prochnau. "To Guy that just didn't compute. He was doing his duty, doing a job he was good at."

Assigned in July 1967 to the 3630th Flying Training Wing at Sheppard Air Force Base in Texas as a T-38A instructor pilot, Bluford served as a standardization-evaluation officer and as an assistant flight commander, teaching cross-country and acrobatic flying. After attending Squadron Officers School in early 1971, Bluford returned to Sheppard Air Force Base as an executive support officer to the deputy commander of operations and as school secretary for the wing. In August 1972 he entered the graduate program at the Air Force Institute of Technology at Wright-Patterson Air Force Base in Ohio, the leading Air Force engineering school in the United States.

After obtaining his M.S. degree with distinction in aerospace engineering in 1974, Bluford continued his studies at the Air Force Institute of Technology while working as a staff development engineer in the Air Force Flight Dynamics Laboratory at the Wright-Patterson Base. He served as deputy for advanced concepts with the aeromechanics division and as branch chief of the aerodynamics and airframe branch in the laboratory. In 1978 he received his Ph.D. degree in aerospace engineering, with a minor in laser physics, after acceptance of his dissertation, entitled "A Numerical Solution of Supersonic and Hypersonic Viscous Flow Fields Around Thin Planar Delta Wings."

In January 1978 Bluford was among the thirty-five astronaut candidates chosen by NASA from a competitive field of some 10,000. The others included Sally K. Ride, who became the first American woman in space, and two other blacks, Ronald McNair and Fred Gregory. When Bluford was asked at the time what he thought of the prospect of being the first black American in space, his reply was low-keyed. "It might be a bad thing, if you stop and think about it," he responded. "It might be better to be second or third because then you can enjoy it and disappear—return to the society you came out of without someone always poking you in the side and saying you were first."

Interviewed in *Ebony* magazine (March 1979) while undergoing training at the Lyndon B. Johnson Space Center in Houston, Bluford commented: "It gives me a chance to use all my skills and do something that is pretty exciting. The job is so fantastic, you don't need a hobby. The hobby is going to work." The astronaut training that Bluford so relished included courses in oceanography, geology, celestial mechanics, space-navigation, powered flight dynamics, spacecraft engineering, and crew station design, as well as a physical fitness program and flights in T-38 jet trainers. In August 1979, on completion of a one-year training and evaluation period, Bluford became eligible for assignment as a mission specialist on space shuttle flights, with responsibility for coordinating activities relating to scientific and engineering experiments.

In April 1982 NASA announced that Bluford had been chosen for the eighth space shuttle mission (STS-8), scheduled for the summer of 1983. The announcement of his selection coincided with that of the choice of Sally K. Ride for the seventh mission. Bluford was happy that Miss Ride was to be the first "first." "She can carry the spear and get the attention," he said. "That relieves me." When he was informed of his selection he returned to his office to finish some work, and did not tell his family until later that night. "I'm very excited about actually flying the shuttle," Bluford emphasized at a press conference at Johnson Space Center on April 29, 1982. "I'm not as hyped up about being the first black." (Bluford became, in fact, not the first black astronaut to fly in space, but the first black American. A black Cuban, Arnaldo Tamayo Méndez, took part in the Soviet Union's *Soyuz 38* flight in 1980.)

Inevitably, whether Bluford wished it or not, the eighth space shuttle mission entered history not alone for its scientific achievements but also for the simple fact of his presence aboard. Before the August 30, 1983 launching, NASA scheduled ceremonies, special banquets, and speeches and brought two planeloads of dignitaries from Washington, D.C. to Cape Canaveral to view the nighttime take-off of the Challenger. The crowd that gathered in those early morning hours included 250 of the nation's top black educators, as well as Congressional Black Caucus members Cardiss Collins and William H. Gray 3d. Also among those present were National Urban League president John Jacob, National Council of Negro Women president Dr. Dorothy Height, jazz musician Lionel Hampton, former basketball star Wilt Chamberlain, and comedian Bill Cosby.

The lift-off at 2:32 A.M. on August 30, 1983 was NASA's first nighttime launching since the *Apollo 17* manned moon flight in December 1972. It presented a magnificent spectacle for the thousands present, with orange flames and billowing white vapor lighting up the sky as far away as Miami, some 200 miles to the south. The timing of the launch was coordinated with the mission's main objective, for which Bluford, as one of the two mission specialists, had primary responsibility—the deployment of a communications and weather satellite for the government of India. That satellite, the Insat-1B, was designed to help Indian meteorologists predict floods and monsoons, to improve the country's telephone systems, and to provide television broadcasts for remote village areas. On the shuttle flight's second day, after the satellite—which had to be ejected above the Pacific precisely at sunset—was successfully launched, Bluford reported to mission control: "The deployment was on time, and the satellite looks good."

In fact, everything was looking good on the successful Challenger flight. While flight commander Richard Truly and pilot Dan Brandenstein maneuvered the craft, Bluford and his fellow mission specialist, Dale Gardner, successfully guided the Challenger's fifty-foot mechanical arm to grasp hold of an 8,500-pound weight of steel, aluminum, and lead in the cargo bay, transport it out into space, and bring it back inside again. That test was conducted in preparation for a scheduled attempted retrieval of a malfunctioning satellite. Bluford and Gardner also conducted experiments with cells from a dog pancreas, a human kidney, and the pituitary gland of a rat. Through a process known as electrophoresis—more effective in a gravity-free environment—they applied an electric field to the cells in an attempt to separate specific cell substances. This type of experiment, begun during previous shuttle flights, was designed to help in the development of drugs to fight such disabilities as diabetes, dwarfism, and cardiovascular disease.

Also present aboard were six rats, fed nutrient bars and raw potatoes by Bluford and Gardner to test their ability to survive in their own "life support module." In addition, a study of the common phenomenon of motion sickness during weightlessness was undertaken by the fifth crew member, Dr. William Thornton, who at fifty-four was the oldest person ever to fly in space. A further accomplishment of the mission was a link-up with NASA's Tracking and Data Relay Satellite, a vital factor in the operation of the European-built Spacelab. Launched in the previous April, the TDRS had been temporarily lost but was brought back into its proper orbit.

For both the takeoff and the landing, Bluford had the additional responsibility of assisting Truly and Brandenstein. The landing—on September 5, 1983 at 3:40 A.M.—was as spectacular as the takeoff had been, with the Challenger swooping down out of the dark sky onto a runway in California's Mojave Desert lit by the world's most powerful floodlights, emitting beams of 4.8 billion candlepower. After the craft landed, within 300 feet of its target, the STS-8 crew was greeted by an enthusiastic crowd, including hundreds of officials of the NAACP and the Urban League, who gave Bluford and his crewmates a standing ovation. "I'm really humbled tonight to see so many people out here . . . to welcome us back," Bluford said. "I feel very proud to be a member of this team, and I think we have a tremendous future with the space shuttle—I mean *all* of us."

That message of pride, confidence, and dedication was the one Bluford carried across the country, as he responded to requests for public appearances. In Washington, D.C. he was given the key to the city by Mayor Marion Barry and was honored with a reception by the Congressional Black Caucus. But undoubtedly the experiences he cherished most were the opportunities he had to address audiences of black youth, to whom he conveyed the message that his parents had inculcated in him. "What I want to pass on to you is that it's very important to set high goals for yourself and realize that if you work hard you will get them," he told a crowd of 600 students in Harlem. "I want you to be the future astronauts flying in space with me."

Guion S. Bluford Jr., who is now a colonel, is the father of two sons, Guion Stewart 3d and James Trevor, who are both science students in college. His wife is the former Linda Tull of Philadelphia, whom he met during his senior year at Penn State and married on April 7, 1964. She works as an accountant with an oil firm. Six feet tall and weighing 180 pounds, Bluford is, according to his own account, "quiet, reserved, and a little on the conservative side." His recreations include jogging, racquetball, handball, and tennis, as well as reading, photography, and working with stereo equipment.

Bluford is a member of the American Institute of Aeronautics and Astronautics, the Air Force Association, and Tau Beta Pi. Among the honors that he has received are the Ebony Black Achievement Award, the NAACP Image Award, the distinguished national scientist award of the National Society of Black Engineers, the NASA space flight medal, and honorary doctorate degrees from several universities. His military decorations, in addition to those he received for his service in Vietnam, include an Air Force Commendation Medal and an Air Force Meritorious Service Award. In August 1984 he was named as one of three mission specialists to take part in a seven-day Spacelab mission sponsored by West Germany, that is scheduled for October 1985.

"I look at my life and I'm amazed that I have had the opportunities to do the things I've done," Bluford has said, as quoted in *Ebony* (November 1983). "From a black perspective, my flight on the shuttle was important because it represented another step forward. . . . Opportunities do exist for black youngsters if they work hard and strive to take advantage of those opportunities."

References: Ebony 34:56+ Mr '79 pors, 39:162+ N '83 pors; N Y Times B p6 Ag 31 '83 pors; Newsday II p4+ Ag 29 '83 pors; Washington Post p1+ Ag 21 '83 por; Who's Who Among Black

Americans 1975–77; Who's Who in America, 1984–85

Bly, Robert (Elwood)

Dec. 23, 1926– Poet; translator. Address; h. 308 First Street, Moose Lake, Minnesota 55767

The rural midwestern poet and translator Robert Bly, arguably the most influential living American poet, is generally regarded as the father of the anti-rhetorical, essentially romantic school of "Deep Imagism" sometimes called "the New Surrealism." Bly and the writers associated with his literary journal *The Eighties* (formerly, in turn, *The Fifties*, *The Sixties*, and *The Seventies*) and with the Eighties Press attempt to breach the intellectual barrier between conscious perception and unconscious reality by, in Bly's words, disregarding "the conscious and the intellectual structure of the mind entirely" and using images "to bring forward another reality from *inward* experience." Their open verse is more in the tradition of the body-centered mysticism of the theosophical philosopher Jakob Böhme and of French Symbolism and Spanish Surrealism than that of Ezra Pound's original Imagism. "Even the Imagists were misnamed," Bly wrote in one of his early theoretical essays; "they did not write images from the unconscious, as Lorca or Neruda, but in simple pictures, such as 'petals on a wet black bough.'"

Among the formative inspirations for Bly's poetic philosophy of "association," or intuitive response to metaphor springing from the unconscious, were Böhme's dictum, "We are all asleep in the outer man," and the ecstatic dynamism that he, as a translator, found in such writers as Federico García Lorca and Pablo Neruda, a "leaping" imagery capable of conveying "new experiences and inner sensations for which there was no precedent in English poetry." Having awakened the inner man and mastered the idiom of serene pastoral ecstasy in the spare, precise verse of his first collection, *Silence in the Snowy Fields* (1962), Bly became passionately political in his National Book Award-winning *The Light Around the Body*, a collection of dissonantly surreal, bitterly satirical barrages against the Vietnam war and the warfare state. His subsequent collections include *The Morning Glory* (1969); *Sleepers Joining Hands* (1973); *This Body Is Made of Camphor and Gopherwood* (1977); *This Tree Will Be Here for a Thousand Years* (1979); and *The Man in the Black Coat Turns* (1981).

The second of two children in a churchgoing Norwegian-American (second generation) Lutheran family, Robert Elwood Bly was born in Madison, Minnesota on December 23, 1926 to Jacob Thomas Bly, a farmer, and Alice (Aws) Bly, who worked in the Lac Qui Parle County Courthouse. Bly's older brother, James, died in an automobile accident in 1971. "My father had two interests," Bly once reminisced. "He read books and he was a farmer. He also had two sons. I read books and my brother became a farmer. When I was a child I used to make myself sick every summer so that I could read books. My father was very understanding. He would say, 'You just take a couple of weeks off and lie in bed and read, and you'll be well again.'"

Bly received his primary education in the Lac Qui Parle County District 94 one-room schoolhouse and his secondary education at Madison High School. "As a Navy recruit in World War II," he recounted in his autobiographical essay "In Search of an American Muse," published in the *New York Times Book Review* (January 22, 1984), "I met for the first time a person who wrote poetry, a man named Marcus Eisenstein, who I think teaches now at a college in Pennsylvania. During a class on radar, he wrote a poem as I watched. I had somehow never understood that poems were written by human beings, and I still remember that moment with delight."

After his discharge from the Navy in 1946 Bly enrolled at St. Olaf's College in Northfield, Minnesota with the intention of pursuing a premedical program. Opting instead for literature, he transferred after a year to Harvard University. As an English major at Harvard he studied with Archibald MacLeish, F. O. Mathiessen, and John Kelleher. Under Kelleher's guidance, he read the prose of Henry David Thoreau, and in poetry he developed a taste not for "the old Auden group" but for William Butler Yeats, Robert Lowell (whose *Lord Weary's Castle* he memorized), and the emerging "new formalists," poets trying to revive the force of rhyme and other formal devices within the context of the experimental gains of the previous several decades. The most prominent of the young new formalists was Richard Wilbur, then a graduate student at Harvard. As he wrote in his *New York Times Book Review* article, Bly, having come to literature "with no tradition at all," considered himself "lucky" to have around him at Harvard "an intense group of beginning writers" that included John Hawkes, Donald Hall, Adrienne Rich, Kenneth Koch, and John Ashbery. "I learned to trust my obsessions. . . . Intensities feed each other."

In retrospect Bly feels that in reading Yeats he was meeting "an old shaman" who "stood for values completely different than those [he, Bly] had understood before that, and one of those was that poetry is written in solitude." Another, as he told Paul Froiland in an interview for an article in *TWA Ambassador* (December 1980), was that "from the ancient point of view" the poet was "connected with the shaman," who was concerned with communicating with spirits and mystic healing and "not with being the spokesman for the moral order." In addition to English literature Bly studied Greek, Latin, and German at Harvard. A member of the staff of the *Harvard Advocate*, he became literary editor of that publication when he was a junior. Taking his B.A. degree *magna cum laude*, he delivered the class poem at the commencement of Harvard's class of 1950. At that time—and for some time thereafter—Bly was writing in iambic pentameter while studying other metrical forms.

Having learned from his reading of Yeats that "in order to write poetry you must be in 'that inner space,'" he retreated into solitude. Struggling to hone his craft, he lived in a cabin in northern Minnesota for half a year and then in New York City for more than two years. Living alone in New York, he supported himself with part-time jobs, including typist, clerk, and house painter.

"When I first encountered poetry," Bly recounted to Paul Froiland, "I assumed that it was . . . words that you see on a page. . . . I failed at writing it. If I read anything aloud . . . it would be completely dead. So I began to memorize the poems, which pulled them back off the page." Bly's "longing for some meter possible in English, yet not iambic" came "from the experience of Pindar's astounding poems," which he read and translated during his sojourn in New York City. His other reading at that time included Horace, Virgil, Jakob Böhme, and Rainer Maria Rilke. Outside of poetry, he read the *Tao Te Ching* of Lao-tsu and the works of Rudolf Steiner, the German occult philosopher whose "anthroposophy" was an attempt to explain the world in spiritual terms, independent of rational thinking.

In 1953 Bly moved to Cambridge, Massachusetts near the Harvard campus, where he continued to live and work in relative isolation, although he directed the first American production of Yeats's *Player Queen* for the Poets' Theatre there. He spent the academic year 1954–55 at the University of Iowa, where he taught freshman composition and the course "Greeks and the Bible" while studying with Paul Engle in the university's Writers' Workshop and working for his master's degree.

The University of Iowa granted Bly his M.A. degree in January 1956 on acceptance of his thesis, "Steps Toward Poverty and Death," a collection of poems. Feeling the academic connection can be a deadly one for poets, he chose not to seek a faculty position at the university. Instead he settled on farmland given him by his father back home in Madison with his first wife, the former Carolyn McLean, whom he had met as an undergraduate at Harvard and married in 1955. On a Fulbright grant in Norway in 1956–57, Bly learned Norwegian and began translating contemporary Scandinavian poetry. It was in the Oslo public library that he read for the first time not only Norwegian poets little known in the United States but also such others as the Chilean poet Pablo Neruda, the Spanish poet Juan Ramón Jiménez, the Swedish poets Gunnar Ekelöf and Harry Martinson, and the Austrian poet Georg Trakl.

After returning to his farm in Minnesota, Bly supported himself and his family for many years by doing occasional teaching and by translating books, including Selma Lagerlöf's novel *Gösta Berlings saga* (*The Story of Gösta Berling*). His reading during that period included R. H. Blyth's *Haiku* and his *Zen in English Literature and Oriental Classics*, D. H. Lawrence's *Fantasia of the Unconscious*, and works by Søren Kierkegaard, Meister Eckhart, Ortega y Gasset, and Federico García Lorca.

In 1957 Bly and William Duffy published the first issue of *The Fifties*. The issue carried an editorial deploring the plethora of "old-fashioned" poetry being published in "isolationist" America and offered translations of poems by Gunnar Ekelöf and the Belgian mystical surrealist Henri Michaux, along with reviews of other poets who were ignored or neglected in the United States. The keystone of the issue was "Looking for Dragon Smoke," Bly's influential essay on the deep image. In response to the first issue of *The Fifties*, James Wright wrote an enthusiastic letter to Bly, the beginning of a long and fecund collaboration. The second issue of the journal featured the first poems by Wright in his "new manner," and after *The Fifties* became *The Sixties*, the Sixties Press issued its first book, *Twenty Poems of Georg Trakl* (1961), translated by Bly and Wright. Its second book, *The Lion's Tail and Eyes: Poems Written Out of Laziness and Silence* (1962), comprised poems by Bly, Wright, and William Duffy.

In the meantime *The Fifties* and *The Sixties* attracted contributions from Louis Simpson and Donald Hall, among other poets working in what Bly called, "for want of a better word, the new imagination." Hall amplified: "This imagination is irrational, yet the poem is usually quiet and the language simple; there is no straining for apocalypse and no conscious pursuit of the unconscious." According to Hall, "there is an inwardness" to the images, "a profound subjectivity," but it is "not the subjectivity of confessional poetry." "This new imagination reveals through images a subjective life which is *general* and which corresponds to an old objective life of shared experience and knowledge."

Out of the serenity of Bly's rural Minnesota solitude came most of the poems of his first collection, *Silence in the Snowy Fields* (Wesleyan University Press, 1962), the haiku-like products of his delight in contact with nature and his awareness of the force of the subconscious in sleep and dreams. As Bly has acknowledged, the poems were influenced by those written by John Millington Synge about the Aran Islands, by Frank O'Connor's translations of medieval Irish writings, and, above all, by the joyful side of the nature poetry of Antonio Machado. In the poems Bly voiced his enjoyment in experiencing the "privacy . . . in this snowy night"; in walking "out at midnight in the moonlight / Dreaming of animals"; and in seeing lamplight falling "on all fours in the grass," "old boards on the ground in early spring," and "The bare trees more dignified than ever, / Like a fierce man on his deathbed."

Reviewing *Silence in the Snowy Fields* in *Poetry* (June 1963), Richard Howard attributed its success to Bly's ability "to confer upon even the simplest words a weight and consequence as of new things" and "to invest his seasons and spectacles, however dull or even dreary, with so much felt life that the simplest monosyllables speak to him and to us." Although a minority of critics faulted the repetition of images, phrasings, and feelings in *Silence in the Snowy Fields*, the collection exerted a subtly revolutionary influence on American poetry in the years following its publication. Writing in the *Hollins Critic* (April 1975), Howard Nelson pointed out that the "artful repetition" enriched the book and held it together "as if it were a single poem." The "snow, fields, barns, lakes, and trees" seemed to Nelson to glow "with some deep, moving mystery," and he considered the book "strikingly original," tapping resources "that had long been turned away from, for the most part, in American poetry: silence, subjectivity, association, the unconscious, a limpid style." As an expression of "a deep marriage between the inner and outer worlds in one man's life," Nelson placed the collection "in the line of *Walden*" and expected "that it will stand, in spite and because of its limitations, as a small (i.e., sixty-page) classic in American poetry."

On an Amy Lowell Fellowship, Bly lived and traveled in England, France, and Spain in 1964 and 1965. Back in the United States, he responded in outrage to the Vietnam war in particular and to what he viewed as the warfare state in general. The philosophy underlying that response was set forth in his essay "Leaping Up into Political Poetry," in which he reconciled the aesthetic and political responsibilities of the poet in a culture that "tries to turn its artists and writers away from political content" and in which poets themselves "do not bother to penetrate the husk around their own personalities and therefore cannot penetrate the husk that has grown around the psyche of the country either." Borrowing Böhme's metaphor encompass-

ing "two worlds," inner and outer, each with its appropriate language, he later developed the notion of the "leaping poem," which springs from the private psyche, flashing light as it moves out into today's public nightmare, where the "death instinct" is rampant.

Accepting the current political situation as a "dark night of the soul" in which "we have been locked up and led blindfold" by "the wise of the world," Bly concluded that to save ourselves we must "see with their eyes." The result was a poetic assault in which his concern, grief, and despair were transmuted with broad wit and quick associative shifts into wildly bursting surreal images mirroring the logic and lies of genocidal oppression. "Let's count the bodies over again," he wrote in "Counting Small-Boned Bodies." "If we could only make the bodies smaller, / The size of skulls, / We could make a whole plain white with skulls in the moonlight!"

Bly read his political poems at colleges and public halls across the United States, often sharing the platform with Lawrence Ferlinghetti, James Wright, Galway Kinnell, Denise Levertov, and other poets belonging to American Writers Against the Vietnam War, an organization that Bly founded with David Ray in 1966. Bly's political poems comprised the bulk of his collection *The Light Around the Body* (Harper & Row, 1967), described by Howard Nelson in his essay in the *Hollins Critic* as "an angry, uneven, powerful book" that contributed to "the growth of an American poetry that is truly political and truly poetry." In the University of Nebraska's *Prairie Schooner* (Summer 1968), Harriet Zinnes wrote: "The poetry that Robert Bly is writing now—[along with that of] such poets as James Wright, Louis Simpson, and W. S. Merwin, for example—is poetry that has finally joined Whitman to a European tradition."

In a gesture of political protest, Bly in 1967 refused to accept a grant of $5,000 to the Sixties Press from the National Endowment for the Arts. When he won the National Book Award for poetry in 1968—for revealing "the invisible but real psyche of our nation" in his writing about "the great events of the spirit and of the day and of the American past"—he turned the $1,000 stipend over to the Resistance, an antidraft organization. At the NBA ceremony he received a standing ovation for his acceptance speech, a bitter attack on America's role in Vietnam. "I know I am speaking for many, many American poets," he said, "when I ask this question: since we are murdering a culture in Vietnam at least as fine as our own, have we the right to congratulate ourselves on our cultural magnificence?"

Bly returned to his pastoral beginnings in the short collection of prose poems, *The Morning Glory: Another Thing That Will Never Be My Friend* (Kayak Books, 1969), which he introduced with the apologia: "Whoever wants to see the invisible must penetrate more deeply into the visible. Everything has a right to exist. If we examine an animal carefully, we see how independent it is of us. The world is complete without us. We feel separated at first; later, joyful."

The political and pastoral were happily merged in the long, loosely cadenced lines of the title poem of *Sleepers Joining Hands* (Harper & Row, 1973). In his essay on Bly in his book *The Fierce Embrace* (1979), Charles Molesworth described the poem as "Bly's celebration of himself, a poem that attempts to reconcile the chanting openness of Whitman with the mythical intensity of Rilke."

In the prose poems of *Sleepers Joining Hands*, Bly moved closer than ever before to a poetry of natural history and what he calls "psychic archeology." In the latter he was influenced by the hypothesis, based on neurological evidence, that Arthur Koestler presented in *The Ghost in the Machine* (1968). According to that hypothesis, the explosive evolution of the human brain resulted in poor coordination between ancient and modern brain structures and a pathological split between emotion and reason. He was also guided by the argument of Carl Jung and others that prehistoric societies were matriarchal and "what we call masculine consciousness is a very recent creation," a "rational" mode maintained at our peril. As he explained in "I Came Out of the Mother Naked," the lone essay among the poems of *Sleepers Joining Hands*, "the Great Mother can best be understood as the union of four 'force fields'" having to do with procreation (the "Good Mother"), ecstasy (the "Ecstatic Mother"), death (the "Death Mother"), and vengeance (the "Teeth Mother"). The most moving poem in *Sleepers Joining Hands* was "The Teeth Mother Naked at Last," a terribly surreal antiwar poem in the prophetic mode, a reminder of the brutal fate automatically in store for a patriarchal society that tramples on humane "feminine" feeling in its greed, ambition, and contempt for spirituality. In 1975 Bly organized a conference on the Great Mother, which has become an annual event, and in 1978 he wrote the play *The Thorn Bush Cock Giant*, which the Great Mother Traveling Troupe took on tour.

In 1975 Bly began using a dulcimer in his poetry readings, to put "a little music underneath the words," and he came to "find it inconceivable to imagine poetry without music." The cosmic religious vision of the prose poems in *This Body is Made of Camphor and Gopherwood* (Harper & Row, 1977) anticipated the mystical neo-pantheism of the verse in *This Tree Will Be Here for a Thousand Years* (Harper & Row, 1979). The latter collection opened with the short essay "The Two Presences" in which Bly contrasted the poet's consciousness, which is "insecure, anxious, . . . cunning," with "the consciousness out there in creatures and plants," a brave melancholy which is "none of these things." In the poems that followed he attempted to bridge the gap between the two consciousnesses, partly by simplification of syntax.

Poems in the same vein by others, including Rilke, were collected by Robert Bly in *News of the Universe: Poems of Twofold Consciousness* (Sierra Club Books, 1980). In his introduction to the anthology, as he later paraphrased it, he said "that most of the harm to the planet has been done by people who believe that they are more intelligent than the planet," and their egotism "has interfered with nature." "The whole ecology movement stands for some of that awareness, that the earth is really more intelligent in its systems than we are." When Frances McCullough, his editor at Harper & Row, moved to the Dial Press, Bly did likewise, and Dial published his collection *The Man in the Dark Coat Turns* in 1981, an intensely personal, introspective book exploring in verse and prose-poems such subjects as the nurturing power of grief, including the neglected area of male grief, and ancestral, familial, and literary relationships. Bly's book-length translations, some issued by his own press, include fiction by Knut Hamsun and poetry by Pablo Neruda, César Vallejo, Georg Trakl, Juan Ramón Jiménez, Göran Sonnevi, Gunnar Ekelöf, Tomas Tranströmer, Vicente Aleixandre, Rainer Maria Rilke, Rolf Jacobsen, Harry Martinson, Bashō, Mirabai, and the Hindu poet Kabir.

Robert Bly is tall, with broad shoulders, bespectacled pale blue eyes, a mane of white hair, usually tousled, and a face that Paul Froiland described as that of "a turbulent poet"—"a kindly, impish face that nonetheless has a driven look about it." When Froiland met him, he was wearing "his garish, half-consciously bohemian outfit, with his bamboo cane hanging from his forearm." Given to extravagant gestures, he is flamboyantly theatrical in his poetry readings (a regular source of income), donning shamanistic masks as he chants to the accompaniment of his dulcimer, which he has never really learned to play properly.

Bly and his first wife, Carolyn, were divorced in 1979. The following year Bly married Ruth Ray, a psychologist, with whom he now lives in Moose Lake, Minnesota. Carolyn Bly lives nearby with her and Robert's four children, Bridget, Mary, Micah, and Noah. Carolyn and Robert share custody of the children, two of whom are in college. The two boys still at home live alternately with each parent. "To augment royalties," Bly wrote in his *New York Times Book Review* article, "I leave my house and family three months a year—January, March, and May. I make most of my living now from teaching small groups of people (some groups are entirely men) who sign up in advance. I teach fairy tales and at times Blake. The memorization of fairy tales helps later writing." With age, he has finally come to "understand the idea that poetry is a form of dance" and to be "able to be nourished more by sorrow and to distinguish it from depression."

References: N Y Times Book R pl+ Ja 22 '84 por; N Y Times Mag p16+ F 3 '80 por; TWA Ambassador p34+ D 9 '80; Bly, Robert. Talking All Morning (1980); Contemporary Authors 1st rev vols 5-8 (1969); World Authors 1950-70 (1975)

Boorstin, Daniel J(oseph)

Oct. 1, 1914– Librarian of Congress; historian.
Address: b. Library of Congress, Washington,
D.C. 20540; h. 3541 Ordway St. N.W.,
Washington, D.C. 20016

NOTE: This biography supersedes the article that
appeared in Current Biography in 1968.

A love of books resolves the paradoxes in the career of Daniel J. Boorstin, who became a renowned historian and the Librarian of Congress even though his professional training had been in law rather than in historical research and writing or in library science. In addition to entertainment, he has said, reading provides "the best direct avenue to the past," preserving the sense of history that he regards as vital to America's well-being. His three-volume masterwork, The Americans (1959–1973), reaped controversy as well as awards with its personal interpretation of United States history as adventure, not a chronology of military and political events, but a confluence of peoples and cultures in an exploration of the unknown. For twenty-five years, beginning in 1944, Boorstin taught American history at the University of Chicago. Moving in 1969 to Washington, D.C., he was associated with the Smithsonian Institution before taking over in 1975 the custodianship, as the Librarian of Congress, of one of the world's foremost cultural centers.

On both sides of his family Daniel Joseph Boorstin is descended from immigrant Russian Jews. He was born to Samuel Aaron Boorstin, a civic-minded, go-getting lawyer, and Dora (Olsan) Boorstin on October 1, 1914 in Atlanta, Georgia. His brother, Robert L. Boorstin, became a California investment counselor. When Daniel was two years old, the family moved to Tulsa, Oklahoma, a burgeoning frontier city where his father prospered. "In the 1920s in that self-styled 'Oil Capital of the World' optimism was the established religion," Boorstin recalled in a first-person sketch for World Authors: 1950–1970 (1975). Growing up in that atmosphere may partly account for the buoyant outlook that helps to make his work exhilarating.

At the age of fifteen, in 1930, Boorstin graduated first in his class from Tulsa Central High School and entered Harvard University. There he came under the influence of F. O. Matthiessen, the noted literary critic and professor of history and English literature, subjects in which Boorstin majored. Besides being elected to Phi Beta Kappa, he distinguished himself as a member of the editorial board of the Harvard Crimson and winner of the Bowdoin Prize for his senior honors essay on Edward Gibbon's The History of the Decline and Fall of the Roman Empire. Awarded his B.A. degree summa cum laude in 1934, he enrolled as a Rhodes scholar in Balliol College, Oxford University, where he studied law and earned first-class honors in two degrees, a B.A. in jurisprudence in 1936 and a Bachelor of Civil Laws in 1937. He also read law at the Inner Temple in London and in 1937 passed the English bar examination to become a barrister-at-law. Living in England and vacationing on the Continent enabled Boorstin to see his homeland from an outsider's perspective. As J. R. Pole pointed out in Pastmasters (1969), "It was during his years at Balliol that he laid—or deepened—the foundation of a twofold interest that has had enduring significance. One of these is in [the] comparative method—the identification of America by comparison and contrast with Europe. The other is in law."

Still inclined toward a legal career, on his return to the United States in 1937 Boorstin studied at the Yale University Law School under a Sterling fellowship. He obtained his Doctor of Juridical Science degree in 1940 and was admitted to the Massachusetts bar in 1942. Meanwhile, at the urging of Matthiessen, he had begun in 1938 to teach American history and literature at Harvard. In 1941 the Harvard University Press published his first book, The Mysterious Science of the Law, a detailed study of the social values implicit in Commentaries on Laws of England by the eighteenth-century British jurist Sir William Blackstone. During the last three of his four years on the Harvard faculty, Boorstin also taught a course in American legal history, an interest that ties in with his editing the three-volume Delaware Cases, 1792–1830 (West, 1943).

Boorstin's actual practice of law seems to have been limited for the most part to a few months of service during World War II in 1942 as a senior attorney in the Lend-Lease Administration. He left the government to become assistant professor of history at Swarthmore College, but after two years moved on to the University of Chicago, where President Robert Maynard Hutchins was setting up an experimental interdisciplinary program in the social sciences. Because the Chicago milieu proved to be so congenial to him, Boorstin remained for twenty-five years, rising through the academic ranks from assistant professor of history to the endowed chair of Preston and Sterling Morton Distinguished Service Professor of American History. While on the Chicago faculty, he also spent considerable time abroad as a researcher, consultant, and, mainly, as a visiting lecturer at the University of Rome, the University of Puerto Rico, the University of Kyoto, the University of Paris, Cambridge University, and elsewhere.

One of the advantages that Boorstin enjoyed at Chicago was the freedom to write. "It was there," Larry Van Dyne noted in the *Washingtonian* (June 1982), "that he developed a reputation as a leading historian of American culture." Boorstin has been described as "an anti-historian historian," and he himself acknowledged in the *World Authors* sketch, "Lacking professional training as a historian, I have been both an amateur (pursuing the subject for the sheer love of it, or more precisely from obsession with it) and an outsider (staying out of some professional ruts simply from not having been instructed in how to stay in them)." His second book, *The Lost World of Thomas Jefferson* (Holt, 1948; Univ. of Chicago Press, 1981), reconstructs the philosophical and scientific sphere of Jefferson and his intellectual contemporaries and introduces Boorstin's perception of the American mind as a product of the experience of a natural environment—geography, landscape—peculiar to the New World.

In *The Genius of American Politics* (Univ. of Chicago Press, 1953) Boorstin expanded his thesis with the proposal that the character of American democracy derives not from ideology but from a unique "combination of historical circumstances." Unlike Europeans, he argued, Americans had "givenness" instead of political theory: "'Givenness' is the belief that values in America are in some way or other automatically defined: *given* by certain facts of geography or history peculiar to us." The elements of "givenness" are the assumptions that America gets its values as "a gift from the past" and as "a gift from the present" and "a belief in the continuity or homogeneity of our history."

The concept of a pragmatic, rather than ideological, foundation of American democracy functions as one of the unifying themes of *The Americans*, in which Boorstin seeks out and analyzes the distinctive character of American institutions and culture. The first volume, subtitled *The Colonial Experience* (Random House, 1958), describes how some settlements, particularly those of the Puritans of Massachusetts and the planters of Virginia, following no preconceived theories, succeeded through their adjustment to the environmental actualities of the New World. The Quakers, on the other hand, partly because of their devotion to a constricting dogma, failed in their pacifist government in Pennsylvania.

With the second volume of his trilogy, *The Americans: The National Experience* (Random House, 1965), Boorstin carried his cultural history of the United States through the period between the Revolutionary War and the Civil War, during which Americans began to change the English language with additions of words and phrases emerging from their own experience. In the westward migration to settle uncharted territory, Boorstin discerned a basic consensus of purpose that has vouchsafed the continuity and homogenization of the nation's development. As he illustrated in *The National Experience*, American resourcefulness in environmental adaptation owes much to technological innovation. His concluding volume, *The Americans: The Democratic Experience* (Random House, 1973), mainly concerns the transformations in lifestyle in the United States brought about during the century since the Civil War by inventors and entrepreneurs like George M. Pullman, Henry Ford, F. W. Woolworth, David Sarnoff, and scores of other well-known, along with lesser-known, "Go-Getters."

For his first volume of *The Americans*, Boorstin won Columbia University's Bancroft Prize in 1959; for his second volume, the Francis Parkman Medal of the American Society of Historians in 1966; and for his third, the Pulitzer Prize for history in 1974. When, in 1981, a French translation of the three books was published as a set in France by Armand Colin under the title *L'histoire des Américains*, it received lavish praise. One reviewer found, "Seize cents pages, et pas un moment d'ennui" (Sixteen hundred pages, and not a moment of boredom). Boorstin has been quoted in *People* (April 19, 1982) as saying, "American history is an exciting story, and a book misrepresents what happened when the story isn't told that way." In the opinion of J. R. Pole, "There is probably no living historian of America who is quite Boorstin's equal in the essential historian's power of bringing the past to life." Pole went on to maintain in *Pastmasters*, "The expert economy of his literary style is an instrument of this power, and his ability to turn a phrase is used not for decorative purposes but to sum up and give point to an explanation. . . . His keen eye for the revealing incident gives his mature writing an anecdotal vitality without detracting from its seriousness of purpose."

Regardless of his accumulation of prestigious awards, Boorstin's work encountered disparagement from some of the more orthodox historians, who felt that he skipped too lightly over the Civil War and Vietnam War and other divisive events. Some also accused him of excessive selectivity in favor of his themes of "givenness" and "consensus" and of oversimplification in his generalizations about European and American cultures. The conservatism, moreover, that Boorstin evinced in his enthusiasm for the ways of an earlier America, his admiration of entrepreneurship, and acceptance of the status quo, for example, aroused the ire of some liberal historians.

In a qualification, however, of his generally rosy view of his country's civilization, Boorstin has repeatedly warned Americans of certain costs of their technological success, one of which is a thinning of the quality of life, a loss of spontaneity and poignancy of experience. He deplored technology's despoiling of Americans' enjoyment of natural things in the final volume of The Americans and in several of his lectures and essays, especially those in The Image: or, What Happened to the American Dream (Atheneum, 1962; published in paperback as The Image: A Guide to Pseudo-Events in America, Harper, 1964), a cautionary attack on the mass media and some aspects of popular culture, and in Democracy and Its Discontents: Reflections on Everyday America (Random House, 1974).

Some of the protest from the left against his work was probably motivated by personal objections to Boorstin himself, who had testified in 1953 before the House Un-American Activities Committee that as a student at Harvard he had been attracted like many other young idealistic intellectuals of his day to Marxism and that he had belonged briefly to the Communist party in 1938–39. Furthermore, he supplied the committee with names of fellow party members. His opponents remembered that testimony when Boorstin lashed out at student anti-Vietnam War demonstrators on the Chicago campus during the 1960s. In one of the essays in his The Decline of Radicalism: Reflections on America Today (Random House, 1969), he distinguished between disagreement, which can reform and strengthen society, and dissent, which tends to block the national tendency toward continuity and consensus.

Boorstin's denunciatory essay, "The New Barbarians," had first appeared in Esquire in October 1968, about a year before he left the University of Chicago to become director of the National Museum of History and Technology of the Smithsonian Institution. The emphasis on technology in the third volume of The Americans, which he completed while in that post, reflects his interest in his work for the museum. In the fall of 1973 he moved on to the duties of senior historian, which included serving as adviser to the secretary on all the projects of the Smithsonian.

Less than two years later, on the retirement of L. Quincy Mumford, the position of Librarian of Congress fell vacant. When President Gerald R. Ford named Boorstin as Mumford's successor, he reportedly hesitated, perhaps because he lacked a background in library science. But, as Van Dyne related in the Washingtonian, he decided in favor of the offer when he came across a 1939 letter from Supreme Court Justice Felix Frankfurter to President Franklin D. Roosevelt advising him to choose as Librarian of Congress someone who "knows books, loves books, and makes books." Although opposed by the American Library Association because he was not a professional librarian and by the Congressional Black Caucus because of his coolness toward affirmative action, Boorstin's nomination was unanimously confirmed by the Senate Committee on Rules and Administration.

Taking his oath of office as the twelfth Librarian of Congress on November 12, 1975, Boorstin became director of a \$200-million-a-year organization that he had called "a multimedia encyclopedia." Its three massive buildings on Capitol Hill, close to Congress, for which the library provides research services, are staffed by some 5,-800 persons. They house 20 million books (the world's largest known collection), 3.5 million maps and charts, motion pictures, photographs, prints, recordings, video cassettes, presidential papers, and a variety of treasures, such as rare manuscripts and Stradivarius violins. As part of his effort to "humanize" the library, to make it "a serious but not a solemn place," Boorstin installed picnic tables around the Neptune Plaza and offered midday concerts. At his direction, and over some objection, the great bronze doors of the Jefferson Building were opened: "They said it would make a draft, and I said that's just what we needed." He also initiated programs, including one on television, to encourage reading. According to the New York Times (July 8, 1983), seven years after his arrival use of the 181-year-old Library of Congress had nearly doubled, with over two million persons flocking to its reading rooms in 1982 and with about 55,000 visiting its buildings and exhibitions.

Although Boorstin's post at the Library of Congress, unlike those he held at the University of Chicago and the Smithsonian, does not allow him free time in his office to work on his books, he has continued to write—on his own at home, mainly in the early morning. His most recent book, The Discoverers (Random House, 1983), compresses into a single volume a wide-ranging history of the many forms of human discovery—man's search for knowledge about all phenomena, time, his own body, plants and animals, the entire earth and its relation to the heavens. His heroes are Herodotus, Ptolemy, Galen, Marco Polo, Gutenberg, Copernicus, Columbus, Newton, Darwin, Schliemann, Freud, and many others, some of them uncelebrated. Like The Americans, The Discoverers is extraordinary for the scope of Boorstin's research, his synthesis of masses of information, and his insight in uncovering unexpected relationships. Reviewing the book for the New York Times (November 16, 1983), Christopher Lehmann-Haupt found it to be a "remarkable history" and called attention to its "dramatic tension," "surprises," "delight," "charm," and "entertainment." Other reviewers compared Boorstin as a popularizer to H. G. Wells and Will and Ariel Durant.

Among Boorstin's earlier books are America and the Image of Europe: Reflections on American Thought (Meridian Bks., 1960); The Sociology of the Absurd: or, The Application of Professor X (Simon & Schuster, 1970), a satiric essay; The Exploring Spirit: America and the World, Then and Now (Random House, 1976), made up of the Reith Lectures that he gave in 1975 over the BBC; and The Republic of Technology: Reflections on Our Future *Community* (Harper, 1978). He is also the author of *The Landmark History of the American People* (Random House), a two-volume work for young readers: *From Plymouth to Appomattox* (1968) and *From Appomattox to the Moon* (1970), and the coauthor with Brooks Kelley of *A History of the United States* (Ginn, 1980), which is being used as a high school textbook. His most important achievement in editing is the thirty-volume *The Chicago History of American Civilization* (Univ. of Chicago Press, 1967-).

Throughout his career Boorstin has undertaken many public service duties. Those that occupy him currently include his responsibilities with the Japan-United States Friendship Commission, the Carl Albert Congressional Research and Studies Center, the Presidential Task Force on the Arts and Humanities, the Gilcrease Museum in Tulsa, and Colonial Williamsburg. Among his awards and tributes are some twenty honorary degrees, including a Litt.D. from Cambridge University.

On a Christmas holiday in 1940 in New York from his teaching post at Harvard, Daniel J. Boorstin met Ruth Carolyn Frankel, who had recently graduated from Wellesley College. They were married on April 9, 1941 and have three sons, Paul

Terry, Jonathan, and David West. Mrs. Boorstin edits all her husband's books. In an article on the Library of Congress for the *Smithsonian* (April 1980) Richard L. Williams described Boorstin as "dapper," noted his "stock of snappy bow ties," and went on to say, "A high-profile man, he likes to do things with style and encourages his staff to do likewise, not to retreat behind anonymity." He seems much at home in the social circles of official Washington, and he and his wife also enjoy outdoor activities, playing tennis, swimming, riding horseback, taking walks, and cultivating a small garden at their country place on the banks of the Potomac in Maryland.

References: *Christian Sci Mon* B p12+ D 5 '78, p19 D 14 '79 por; *N Y Times* B p6 Jl 8 '83 por; *People* 17:95+ Ap 10 '82 pors; *Smithsonian* 11:38+ Ap '80 por; *Washington Post* K p1+ Ja 29 '84 por; *Washingtonian* p128+ Je '82 pors; *Contemporary Authors* new rev vol 1 (1981); Cunliffe, Marcus, and Winks, Robin W., eds. *Pastmasters* (1969); *Dictionary of Literary Biography. Twentieth-Century American Historians* (1983); *Directory of American Scholars* (1982); *Who's Who in America, 1984-85; World Authors: 1950-1970* (1975)

Botha, Roelof F(rederik)

(bwä´tä rōō´ lôf)

Apr. 27, 1932- Minister of Foreign Affairs and Information for the Republic of South Africa. Address: b. House of Assembly, Cape Town, South Africa; c/o Department of Foreign Affairs, Pretoria, South Africa

In a diplomatic career spanning thirty years, Roelof F. ("Pik") Botha, a cautious and pragmatic progressive, has often spurred the white citizens of South Africa to accept limited reform of apartheid, the country's policy of racial segregation, and to achieve accommodation with black African nations. When he addresses the global community, however, Botha staunchly defends South Africa's right to exist as a white nation and its proud intention to pursue its modus vivendi without regard to worldwide disapproval. A master at hardheaded but responsive negotiating as foreign minister since 1977, he has served as a broker for peace, or at least stability, with neighbors whose political programs are anathema—and possibly threats—to segments of South Africa's white rulership. The fragile non-intervention pacts that Foreign Minister Botha was negotiating in 1984 with Angola and Mozambique, after years of hostilities, have been called "Pretoria's most remarkable diplomatic achievement in thirty-five years," and hold some promise of bringing about resolutions of problems in the territory of Namibia/South-West Africa. South Africa's economic, political, and military hegemony

in southern Africa is unquestioned, and Roelof F. Botha plays a paramount policy-making role in maintaining that strength, on which the regime's very survival probably depends.

Roelof Frederik Botha was born on April 27, 1932 in Rustenburg, South Africa, a suburb of the nation's administrative capital, Pretoria. He attended the Volkskool in Potchefstroom, south of Johannesburg, after which he went on to earn his B.A. and Bachelor of Laws degrees at the University of Pretoria. Already a perceptive observer of public affairs, he joined South Africa's Department of Foreign Affairs in 1953, shortly after his graduation, and within three years launched his career as a global diplomat. From 1956 to 1959 he served at the South African legation in Sweden and from 1960 to 1963 acted as a third secretary at its embassy in Cologne, West Germany.

Roelof Botha's diplomatic apprenticeship coincided with a period of nascent political sophistication among Third World nations and of global attention to South Africa's white-supremacist social structure. In 1963, when he joined the team representing the South African government before the International Court of Justice, a judicial organ of the United Nations, the court was in the midst of deliberations on a case brought by Ethiopia and Liberia. Both countries demanded that South Africa surrender to the UN its trusteeship rights over the adjacent territory of South-West Africa, which it had held by League of Nations mandate since 1920. Repudiating charges that it had failed to promote the well-being and social progress of the territory's overwhelmingly black population, the South African government instead threatened direct annexation and imposition of the apartheid system there.

Botha, who was named in 1965 as his country's agent to the court, which is located in The Hague, saw the case through to its formal conclusion in July 1966. In an 8-7 decision, the judges dismissed the charges on technical grounds, remaining silent on the legal merits of the issues. That manifest political sidestepping provoked shock waves and an outcry in many diplomatic circles, but many white South Africans hailed the verdict as a major national victory, and Botha and the entire legal team received a heroes' welcome on their homecoming. When in October 1966 the UN General Assembly issued on its own initiative a resolution abolishing South Africa's jurisdiction over South-West Africa and forming a UN council to administer its development, South Africa nullified the authority of the declaration.

In the late 1960s Roelof Botha continued his legal advisory duties in the Department of Foreign Affairs, acting as its undersecretary from 1968 through 1970 and overseeing its South-West Africa and UN liaison sections. As a candidate of the powerful National party, he became parliamentary representative for the district of Wonderboom in 1970, a seat he held until 1974. That year—in which Botha served as secretary to a foreign affairs study group formed by National party parliamentarians—augured dramatic political shifts in southern Africa, and the former strongholds of friendly powers in Rhodesia, Angola, and Mozambique tottered amid drives for black self-determination.

On the basis of his experience at The Hague, Roelof Botha was assigned membership in the South African delegation to the UN in 1966, a post he held through 1969 and again in 1971, 1973, and 1974. There he gained a reputation as an accessible and conciliatory spokesman for his government, qualities that did not go unnoticed by South Africa's Prime Minister B. J. Vorster, who showed his approval by naming Botha ambassador and permanent representative to the UN in 1974, at the height of an unprecedented campaign to expel South Africa from the international body. In an ambassadorial speech in October 1974 to the UN Security Council, which would have to approve by majority vote the expulsion resolution, Botha defended the "important identity of interests" his nation shared with other states of Africa, pledged that his government would "move away from discrimination based on race or color," and asserted that "one-sided information" about conditions in the country ignored the "great benefits" newly gained by the black population. The United States, United Kingdom, and France vetoed expulsion, but the next month the General Assembly passed a milder measure suspending South Africa's participation in the assembly's current session. As charges flew regarding the act's constitutional legality, Ambassador Botha was called back to Pretoria for consultations. (Since that year, South Africa has been denied the right to participate in General Assembly activities, but still maintains de facto membership and administrative offices at the international headquarters.)

Returning to his country's UN mission in 1975, Botha met Security Council ultimatums on South African withdrawal from South-West Africa (now also called Namibia) and calls for UN-sponsored elections there with agreement in principle to self-determination for the territory. But he conveyed his government's rejection of domination during the transition by the UN or by the South-West Africa People's Organization (SWAPO), whose guerrillas had been skirmishing in an independence struggle with South African troops for a decade. Prime Minister Vorster's pragmatic foreign policy of "détente" with black Africa during that period included efforts to mediate a transfer to black rule in Zimbabwe-Rhodesia, military incursions into Angola, then racked by civil war, and a Namibian constitutional conference restricted to representatives sanctioned by Pretoria. Botha's value as trusted adviser and sensitive advocate for his country's positions received further confirmation in 1975, when he was appointed ambassador to the United States, which maintained generally open and economically fruitful relations with South Africa despite growing impatience with its rigid racism.

Roelof F. Botha served as ambassador to the UN and ambassador to the United States concurrently until 1977, when his cabinet appointment as South Africa's foreign minister raised hopes among progressives ("verligtes") in the National party for effective domestic reforms to address the critical racial situation, as evidenced by the Soweto riots and massacres of 1976. Reporting in the *Christian Science Monitor* (April 29, 1977) on Botha's stumping during a by-election to consolidate his ministry post with a parliamentary seat, Humphrey Tyler quoted Botha's estimation of South Africa's "life-and-death struggle": "We have to be prepared to lose the equivalent of a couple of fingers or an eye or an ear to get through this alive." Botha scored many minor segregation measures as "petty . . . frivolities," and defended his quietly "reformist" stance against Jackie Nel, his hard-liner opponent, who accused the Nationals of "selling out the white man in Africa." But that charge misfired, and Botha won the Johannesburg district election by a landslide of more than 9,000 votes to 652.

To those Afrikaner intellectuals and English-speaking liberals who had come to regard him as a prestigious "glamour boy" and to Botha himself, the successful bid signaled a "powerful mandate to make political changes . . . away from racial discrimination." Nevertheless, Foreign Minister Botha made clear his resistance to the majority rule remedies proposed by the newly installed President Jimmy Carter administration in the United States. Visiting Washington, D.C. in June 1977 for talks with Secretary of State Cyrus R. Vance, Botha asserted that any "one-man, one-vote" plan would be a call for "suicide" leading "to the demise of the white nation" in South Africa. Reports that the United States UN Ambassador Andrew Young viewed South Africa's government as "illegitimate"—a term he later revised to "unrepresentative"—heightened resentment toward the Carter approach.

In August 1977 a Roelof Botha essay on "Why South Africa has a Right to Exist as a White African Nation" appeared in *Intellect* magazine. The foreign minister emphasized his country's historical development, which had produced a society of many nationalist groups, each with it own heritage and right to self-government. Seen from this perspective, Botha claimed, white South Africa's right to preserve its identity had to be respected in working out a just solution to racial antagonism.

Botha defended Vorster's advocacy of some type of federated power-sharing system to prevent domination by the blacks. International sentiment put little stock in that obscure formula, however, and, following a new wave of repression against anti-apartheid leaders, the UN Security Council, with United States approval, imposed a mandatory arms embargo on South Africa in the autumn of 1977, declaring that the flow of weapons to that country formed a "threat to international peace and security." Despite his "moderate" stance on racial issues—judged by some to be more liberal than that of his prime minister—Roelof Botha decried the measure as "transparently dishonest" and based on "selfish political motives." He warned that the UN's "incitement to violence," implicit in its symbolic effort to disarm the South African state in its battle against terrorism and guerrilla raids, would incite a white backlash against any changes seen as concessions to foreign powers. Championing South Africa's sovereign right "to act decisively and in good faith within its borders," Botha denounced the United States as a "faithless friend"

and summed up his countrymen's judgment of the resolution: "War has been declared on us. . . . We are not retreating."

For a short while in 1978 developments within the government of South Africa appeared to hold promise of new leadership roles for Roelof F. Botha. Following news stories that summer about widespread misappropriation of public funds by the Department of Information, Prime Minister Vorster transferred ministerial duties to Botha, who removed the department's secretary and undersecretary and ordered a probe of the charges. When the prime minister announced his retirement in the fall, opinion polls showed Roelof F. Botha to be favored as his successor among South African whites over the other two contenders, Pieter W. Botha, who is no relation, and Cornelius P. Mulder. Experts suggested that Vorster himself wanted the foreign minister to assume the post. Nonetheless, balloting by the National party caucus indicated that many conservatives were deeply skeptical of Roelof Botha's junior status and his mass popularity, and Pieter W. Botha, a strict "party man" and former defense minister, emerged the victor in the runoff.

Regional developments remained in the forefront of Botha's concerns during the late 1970s. Beginning in 1977, he acted as South Africa's negotiator in new efforts led by five major Western powers to achieve the long-awaited UN-backed Namibian independence plan. In July 1978 the international team obtained a preliminary ceasefire agreement from the Angola-based SWAPO guerrillas, accompanied by South Africa's promise to withdraw most of its 18,000 troops from that disputed territory. Once implemented, the truce would pave the way for election of a constituent assembly, followed by governmental elections overseen by a UN taskforce. Foreign Minister Botha quickly hailed the accord as "a new era in southern Africa—something which the people of this subcontinent would all welcome," but the conciliation proved ephemeral. In September 1978 South Africa rejected the UN plan and, with its troops following SWAPO fighters into Angola, sponsored in December elections representing only parties favoring its own plans for the territory. The UN declared the results "null and void," and certainly the unilateral maneuver did nothing to settle the armed conflict over Namibia's status.

South African skittishness over UN intervention increased when final majority-rule elections in Zimbabwe in 1980 chose radical candidate Robert Mugabe as prime minister, leading rightwing Nationals to charge that Namibia would fast become "a second Rhodesia" if the UN had its way. Although Roelof Botha met with Mugabe for what were described as pragmatic and realistic talks, he heeded conservative pressures in his country enough to enter a "holding action" in confrontations with the UN. That policy developed into an outright standstill by September 1980, when a Roelof Botha communiqué to UN Secretary General Kurt Waldheim called the international body the "most ardent protagonist" for the SWAPO guerrillas and, as such, too "prejudiced" to oversee legitimate elections.

The course of events changed dramatically when Ronald Reagan moved into the White House in 1981. Downplaying the human rights emphasis of President Jimmy Carter's international agenda, the Reagan foreign policy team viewed political conflicts in southern Africa in a global context. The new administration was wary of Marxist influences and empathized with anticommunist allies like South Africa, which predicated its low-level military campaigns against Angola and Mozambique and its non-recognition of SWAPO on Soviet influence. According to the Reagan perspective, settlement of the Namibian question depended largely upon whether or not Angola would eject the 25,000 or more Cuban soldiers who had crossed its borders to support its independence struggle. They remained in Angola, purportedly defending it against South African and South African-backed rebel incursions but meanwhile actively aiding the SWAPO fighters.

In April 1981 the United States vetoed a UN proposal for economic sanctions against South Africa. The following month, after spending several days in "friendly" discussions in Washington, D.C. with Secretary of State Alexander M. Haig Jr., Reagan, and other high officials, Roelof F. Botha told reporters he saw "a real possibility of moving ahead" on Namibian independence. Many months of behind-the-scenes talks followed, as mediators tried to coalesce about forty Namibian political factions into an opposition that could effectively face SWAPO in independence elections and as South African military operations against SWAPO bases in southern Angola continued. In December 1982 Angolan and South African representatives held ceasefire parleys. The terms of the discussions, announced by Roelof F. Botha in Cape Town in January, involved an Angolan pledge to keep Cuban, SWAPO, and its own internal forces at least 150 miles from the Namibian border, if, in return, South Africa evacuated Angolan territory. Botha envisaged the truce as a "test period," during which the two countries could ease their mutual mistrust and weigh the benefits of future proceedings on Namibia.

The eventual evacuation of all Cuban troops from Angola was a vague—but, as it turned out, ill-advised—element of the plan. Still on the drawing board in late 1983, diplomatic efforts collapsed when Angolan leaders demanded independence for Namibia before any withdrawal of Cuban troops would take place. The grave international repercussions of the impasse were underlined in early January 1984, when Roelof F. Botha confirmed that South Africa had received a direct order from the Soviet Union to withdraw its troops immediately from Angolan territory, into which they had penetrated about 200 miles.

In mid-January 1984, South Africa began its troop withdrawal from Angola. In February, United States diplomatic footwork, led by Assistant Secretary of State Chester A. Crocker, yielded a breakthrough in the form of direct talks among representatives from the United States, Angola, and South Africa to discuss step-by-step truce procedures and the establishment of a joint monitoring commission to oversee South Africa's withdrawal from Angola and to remove anti–South African insurgents from Namibia. Shortly after the agreement—yet to be fully implemented—Foreign Minister Botha called for a regional peace conference on Namibia, inviting leaders from Angola, the SWAPO insurgents, other Namibian political parties, and anti-Angolan guerrilla forces supported by South Africa. Pretoria's new willingness to bring together all those clashing interests suggested to political experts that South Africans are profoundly weary of war and their huge defense budget, but it also suggested that they may still be searching for a solution in keeping with their own agenda, rather than the UN's.

Prime Minister Pieter Botha and President Samora Machel of Mozambique, on South Africa's northeastern border, signed a joint nonaggression pact in March 1984, in which each side agreed to prevent subversive rebel groups from using its territory to launch attacks against the other. Previously Pretoria had inflicted devastating raids against the bases, harbored by the Marxist Machel regime, of the African National Congress, one of South Africa's oldest revolutionary organizations. But when the Mozambique National Resistance, formerly backed by South Africa, continued its violent anti-Machel activity into late 1984, Machel threatened to cancel his part in the bargain. In response Roelof Botha negotiated a ceasefire declaration between the rebels and the Mozambican government, and he pledged to establish a commission to "work towards early implementation" of the agreement. A nonaggression pact between Pretoria and Swaziland, signed in 1982, was revealed in 1984.

Roelof Frederik Botha is a man of medium height with dark brown hair and a closely trimmed mustache. His earlier image as a boisterous and outspoken statesman, "a dauntless paladin," in the words of John Lelyveld (New York Times, September 21, 1983), willing "to do rhetorical battle with anyone who sullied his country's name," has mellowed into a reserved manner that lacks a combative edge. Botha acknowledged to Lelyveld that he briefly considered retirement from public office in 1982, when it appeared that some of his fellow party members had no intention of exploring more flexible racial policies. That decision was forestalled when hardliners broke ranks to form the National Conservative party.

Observers have noted a decline in Roelof F. Botha's personal influence with the prime minister, but he remains popular with progressive followers of the National party. In late 1983 he lent support to the constitutional referendum that gave Asian and mixed-race, or "colored," citizens a token role in the national Parliament for the first time. Surveying the future which his diplomacy has helped to define, Botha has said, "A policy is now developing in terms of which the governments and leaders of southern Africa seem to realize that they all stand to gain from cooperation and from stability and peace." He has received several awards from his country, including the Grand Cross, the Order of Good Hope, and Decoration for Meritorious Service. In 1953 Roelof Frederik Botha married Helena Susanna Bosman, and the couple have two daughters and two sons. His leisure interests are hunting and fishing.

References: Christian Sci Mon p26 Mr 13 '77 por; Current History 83:105 Mr '84; N Y Times p3 O 29 '77, p3 S 21 '83, IV p3 F 19 '84, p3 O 4 '84 por; International Who's Who, 1984–85; International Yearbook and Statesmen's Who's Who, 1983

Brooks, Louise

Nov. 14, 1906– Actress. Address: b. c/o Alfred A. Knopf, Inc., 201 E. 50th St., New York, NY 10022

Of all the actresses who personified eros in the silent cinema, none was more artless and eloquent than Louise Brooks, a luminous screen siren whom, as the French film archivist Henri Langlois once noted, "the camera seems to have caught . . . by surprise." Even in her earliest films, which were routine flapper comedies made between 1925 and 1927, Miss Brooks animated the stereotype of the capricious coquette with her natural, reserved style, free of the mugging and histrionics surrounding her. She began to give her erotic Hollywood persona true femme fatale shadings in A Girl in

Every Port (1928), but it was only as Lulu, the destructive embodiment of archetypal sexual energy who is finally consumed by her own rapture, in the German director G. W. Pabst's Die Büchse der Pandora/ Pandora's Box (1929) that she became "a dark lady worthy of any poet's devotion," as Kenneth Tynan wrote in a 1979 New Yorker profile that is included in his book Show People (1980).

After making two more films in Europe Miss Brooks returned to Hollywood, where her rebellion against the prevailing star system precipitated her career into an irreversible decline. During sixteen years of oblivion, her haunting screen image remained alive for a devoted cult following, and it enjoyed public revivals in the 1950's and again in recent years. The recent revival, sparked in large measure by Tynan's profile, was given renewed impetus by the publication of Lulu in Hollywood (Knopf, 1982), a collection of the actress' lively memoirs, which has been hailed by critics as a triumph of literary style and anecdotal Hollywood history. That book, along with her contributions to film journals and her interviews, suggests, as Andrew Sarris observed in the Village Voice (September 27, 1983), "a talent that might have been profitably diverted to movie journalism early on," but "here again, Brooks might have been handicapped by a deficiency in cattiness and power-worship."

Louise Brooks was born on November 14, 1906 in Cherryvale, Kansas, the second of the four children of Leonard Porter Brooks and Myra (Rude) Brooks, both of whom came from families of venturesome homesteaders who had settled in Kansas in the late nineteenth century. Her father, a descendant of British farmers, was a lawyer who would eventually become an assistant attorney general of the state of Kansas. In Lulu in Hollywood Miss Brooks recalls growing up in a home that was "literally falling down with books," including the English and American classics, "all of which she read with delight." Her mother, who "always had more creative uses for her energy than disciplining children," pursued "freedom by writing book reviews to present at her women's club, by delivering lectures on Wagner's Ring, and by playing the piano, at which she was extremely talented."

In her mother, Louise Brooks first recognized "the joy of creative effort," and both parents' "resolute pursuit of their own interests" relieved her of "the necessity of lying at home," with the result that she "went into the world with an established habit of truthfulness." That parental pursuit "also accounted for [her] own early autonomy and [her] later inability, when [she] went to work in the Hollywood film factories, to submit to slavery." Regarding her "lifelong curse," her "failure as a social creature," she recalled that her mother "did attempt to make [her] less critical of people's false faces" but she "could not act that way, and so has remained "in cruel pursuit of truth and excellence, an inhumane executioner of the bogus."

From the age of ten, Louise Brooks took dancing lessons and danced at club meetings, fairs, and other gatherings throughout southeastern Kansas, with her mother as accompanist. Photographs taken of her when she was fifteen show, as Kenneth Tynan observed in his *New Yorker* profile, that she was "already a beauty *sui generis* . . . , with her hair, close-cropped at the nape to expose what Christopher Isherwood has called 'that unique imperious neck of hers,' cascading in ebony bangs down the high, intelligent forehead and descending on either side of her eyes in spit curls slicked forward at the cheekbones, like a pair of enameled parentheses."

In 1919 the Brooks family moved to Wichita, Kansas. Two years later, Ruth St. Denis and Ted Shawn's Denishawn Dancers performed in Wichita, and Louise Brooks met Shawn backstage. At his suggestion, she went to New York City the following summer, successfully auditioned for the troupe, and dropped out of school to join it. A fellow member of the troupe, Martha Graham, became her lifelong friend. "I learned to act while watching Graham dance," she said later, "and I learned to move in film from watching Chaplin."

In love with the theatre, Louise Brooks saw all the shows on Broadway, of which one of her favorites was the *Ziegfeld Follies*. Studying the Follies girls, she was repelled by their "fixed" smiles. "I decided right then that onstage I would never smile unless I felt like it," she recalls in her memoirs. "For inside the brat who sweated four hours a day at dancing school lived the secret bride of New York whose goal was the sophisticated grace of the lovely women already seen and studied in the pages of *Harpers Bazaar* and *Vanity Fair*." The secret bride was soon an open one. Replacing her girlish dresses with backless evening gowns worn slashed to the waist, hiding her freckles under what she describes as "decadent black-and-white Aubrey Beardsley makeup," erasing her Kansas accent with the help of a tutor, and learning etiquette from waiters in fine restaurants, Louise Brooks became the darling of Manhattan's cafe society, showered with money, furs, and jewels by the wealthy men who escorted her to nightclubs and parties. "Sexual submission was not a condition of this arrangement," she points out, "though many affairs grew out of it."

Touring the United States with the Denishawn Dancers for two years, Miss Brooks found the discipline oppressive. Dismissed in 1924, she danced in the chorus of *George White's Scandals* for three months, until September 1924, when she left on a whim, and without notice, for London, where she got a job dancing the Charleston at the Café de Paris. On her arrival back in New York in 1925, Florenz Ziegfeld cast her in his musical comedy *Louie the 14th*. The stage director of that show, Teddy Royce, found her erratic conduct, especially her sudden absences, intolerable, but she was one of Flo Ziegfeld's prize beauties, and he hired her again, to do specialty dancing in the 1925–26 edition of the *Ziegfeld Follies*.

That *Ziegfeld Follies* was Louise Brooks's last Broadway show. Meanwhile, she had made her screen debut in a motion picture of which no print is known to exist: *Street of Forgotten Men*, which was filmed at the Famous Players-Lasky studios in Astoria, Long Island in May 1925. Later in the same year she signed a contract with Paramount Pictures, where Walter Wanger, then her best friend, was manager of production. Her first role for Paramount was a bit part as a bathing beauty in *The American Venus* (1925), one of the stills from which inspired John Streibel's syndicated comic strip *Dixie Dugan*, featuring a heroine with a satiny black Dutch-boy bob similar to hers. She subsequently had leading roles in the comedies *Social Celebrity*, (1926), with Adolph Menjou, *It's the Old Army Game* (1926), with W. C. Fields, and *The Show-Off* (1926), with Ford Sterling, all filmed in the Famous Players-Lasky Astoria studios.

On loan to First National Studios, Miss Brooks made *Just Another Blonde* (1926). The first Brooks film of which there is a print in the archives of Eastman House in Rochester, New York is *Love 'Em and Leave 'Em* (1926), a comedy about Manhattan shopgirls in which she displayed, as Kenneth Tynan observed, "that fusion of amorality and innocence which was to become her trademark."

In 1927 Paramount's Astoria facility was closed, and Louise Brooks was, in her words, "sent from its intimate friendliness to the factory coldness of the Hollywood studio." The following year Walter Wanger left Paramount and she "had no sympathetic studio contact whatever." Her 1927 Paramount releases, none of which are represented in the Eastman House vaults, were *Evening Clothes*, *Rolled Stockings*, *The City Gone Wild*, and *Now We're in the Air*.

Under the direction of Howard Hawks in *A Girl in Every Port* (1928), made on loan to the Fox Film Corporation, Louise Brooks deepened, darkened, and made more subtle her erotic screen persona, playing a circus performer whose allure destroys the friendship of two seamen, played by Victor McLaglen and Robert Armstrong. Sexual rivalry is again a motif in *Beggars of Life*, (1928), based on the Jim Tully novel, in which Miss Brooks plays a hobo fugitive from justice disguised as a male urchin—her first notable essay in gender ambiguity. During the filming of S. S. Van Dine's *The Canary Murder Case* (1928), she decided to leave Paramount, when the studio refused to raise her salary in accordance with an escalator clause in her contract. As the actress later explained in an article for the Eastman House magazine *Image*, Paramount, which at that time was preparing to make the transition from silents to talkies, was, like other studios, using the question of unproved vocal talent as an excuse "for breaking contracts, cutting salaries, and taming the stars."

Almost as an afterthought to the salary discussions, B. P. Schulberg, the head of production at Paramount, told her that G. W. Pabst, a master of social realism in the German cinema, had been bombarding him with cables asking to borrow her to play a new screen reincarnation of Lulu, the heroine of "fatal destiny" created at the turn of the century by the proto-expressionist playwright Frank Wedekind. After searching for months for the perfect Lulu, Pabst decided on Miss Brooks after seeing *A Girl in Every Port*, but he was about to settle for Marlene Dietrich when Paramount finally cabled him the news of the American actress' availability. As soon as the shooting of *The Canary Murder Case* was completed, she left for Berlin.

As created by Frank Wedekind in his *Der Erdgeist* (1895; translated as *Earth Spirit*, 1914), a lurid exposé of the sexually depraved pleasures of the German upper classes, and its sequel, the "tragedy of monsters" *Die Büchse der Pandora* (1904; translated as *Pandora's Box*, 1918), Lulu is, in the playwright's words, "the personification of primitive sexuality." She "inspires evil unawares," provoking by her very presence a "rage" of lust "as in a menagerie when the meat appears at the cage," and is herself destroyed by that evil, falling victim to prostitution and a homicidal sexual maniac. Wedekind's plays, condemned as "immoral and inartistic" and banned when first produced, were condensed and somewhat bowdlerized for the screen in Arsen von Czerepy's film *Die Büchse der Pandora* (1922), which had no incest or lesbianism in it and had Asta Nielsen playing Lulu, in Miss Brooks's words, "in the eye-rolling style of European silent acting," devouring her victims and then dropping dead "in an acute attack of indigestion."

In Pabst's *Die Büchse der Pandora/Pandora's Box*, Miss Brooks glided "gracefully and innocently past the overburdened expressionism of German acting and set design," as Andrew Sarris observed in his *Village Voice* article. Of the culminating scene, in which she closes her eyes for a loving kiss and is fatally knifed instead, Kenneth Tynan wrote: "Nowhere in the cinema has the destruction of beauty been conveyed with more eloquent restraint," and David Thomson classes Miss Brooks's performance as a whole as "one of the major female performances in the cinema."

The movie had a quite different reception when it was released by Nero Film in Berlin in 1929. Audiences resented their "German Lulu" being played by "the American girl," and the critics were shocked that Pabst should dare not only to present the prostitute as a victim, an alluring goldfish in a school of piranhas, but to go beyond that, in Miss Brooks's words, "to the final damning immorality of making his Lulu as 'sweetly innocent' as the flowers that adorned her costumes and filled the scenes of the play." Virtually an entire generation of Germans refused to recognize in the film the reflection of Berlin's own decadent reality. "Thus," the actress writes, her "playing the tragic Lulu with no sense of sin remained unacceptable for a quarter of a century."

Next, Miss Brooks starred in Pabst's *Das Tagebuch einer Verlorenen/The Diary of a Lost Girl* (1929), based on Margarethe Böhme's novel about a pharmacist's daughter who is driven by a puritanical society to the reformatory and whorehouse but who blossoms in spite of it all. In discussing that film, Kenneth Tynan agreed with Freddy Buache that Brooks's performances with Pabst celebrated "the victory of innocence and *amour-fou* over the debilitating wisdom imposed on society by the Church, the Fatherland, and the Family."

In the French film *Prix de Beauté/ Beauty Prize* (Sofar Film, 1930), Miss Brooks's last European movie and her first talkie—though her voice was dubbed because she spoke no French—Miss Brooks lent, in Tynan's words, "inimitable flair" to a *film noir* cliché. In that picture, directed by Augusto Genina and co-produced by Pabst, she escapes the humdrum life of a typist by winning a beauty contest and starting a film career, only to be shot dead by the husband she has left behind. Promised a contract by Columbia Pictures, Miss Brooks in 1930 decided to go back to Hollywood, against the advice of Pabst, who wanted her to continue developing her acting under his tutelage. Before they parted, he warned her that her life was "exactly like Lulu's," and that she would "end the same way," discarded "like a used toy" by the rich hedonists with whom she partied. She later confessed to a journalist that Pabst's prophecy had proven to be not far from the mark, that "Lulu's story is as near as you'll get" to hers.

The Columbia contract never materialized, and Louise Brooks's career abruptly declined, partly because she refused to submit to the wiles of the "casting couch" and partly because she was blacklisted in Hollywood as, to use her term, a difficult "flibbertigibbet." Through old friends, she made the grade-C two-reel comedy *Windy Reilly in Hollywood* (Educational Studios, 1931) and had a supporting role in *It Pays to Advertise* (Paramount, 1931) and a small part in *God's Gift to Women* (Warner Brothers, 1931). At age twenty-four, in the prime of her beauty, she made a final return to the theatre in a minor role in the pre-Broadway run of the comedy *Louder Please* in the autumn of 1931. After touring nightclubs in a dance act, she returned to Hollywood, where she made her last film appearances as the ingenue in *Empty Saddles* (Universal, 1936), as a bit player in *King of Gamblers* (Paramount, 1937), as a member of the corps de ballet in *When You're in Love* (Columbia, 1937), and as a feminine adornment in the early John Wayne vehicle *Overland Stage Raiders* (Republic, 1938).

From 1940 to 1943 Miss Brooks ran a dance studio in Wichita. Moving to New York City in 1943, she worked successively in radio soap operas and publicity agencies and as a salesclerk in Saks Fifth Avenue. After quitting her job at Saks, in 1948, she thought she would "earn a little money" by writing "the usual autobiography," but she could not go through with it because she found herself "unwilling to write the sexual truth that would make [her] life worth reading." Between 1948 and 1953, she told Kenneth Tynan, she was "kept" by three rich men, each of whom wanted to marry her. "I had to escape, because I wasn't in love with them." Her escape was into the Roman Catholic

Church, of which she was a member for eleven years, beginning in 1953.

Louise Brooks reached her financial and emotional nadir in 1954, when, she hints, she considered suicide. Her morale was given a boost the following year by Henri Langlois, the French film archivist, who featured her and her work at a huge exhibition in Paris titled "Sixty Years of Cinema." Soon afterward, a group of her old friends pooled their resources to provide her with an annuity, and in 1956 she moved to Rochester at the suggestion of James Card, then the curator of film at Eastman House. In 1958 she flew to Paris as the honored, expenses-paid guest of Henri Langlois at a screening of Die Büchse der Pandora at Langlois's Cinématèque Française. Her last trip away from Rochester was to attend a screening of Prix de Beauté in New York City in 1960.

Louise Brooks was married twice, to the film director Edward Sutherland, from 1926 to 1928, and to Deering Davis for an even briefer time, in 1933, and she was for many years the lover of the millionaire George Preston Marshall. In the sketches in Lulu in Hollywood she writes, sometimes fondly, at others devastatingly, of such old friends and acquaintances as W. C. Fields, Humphrey Bogart, Charlie Chaplin, William Wellman, Constance Bennett, and William Randolph Hearst. Reviewing the book in Esquire, James Wolcott wrote: "Brooks emerges not as a white goddess wreathed in incense but as a sassy companion, wisecracking, knowledgeable, completely free of cant and coy sentiment." Writing in the New York Times Book Review (October 11, 1982), John Lahr described the memoirs as "terse, raffish, authoritative . . . among the best discussions of American film" he had ever read.

After moving to Rochester, Louise Brooks became a scholar of the cinema, privately screening films at Eastman House and writing perceptive articles for such publications as Sight and Sound and Film Culture. Except for her visits to Eastman House, she was a virtual recluse, content to "disintegrate happily in bed with [her] books, gin, cigarettes, coffee, bread, cheese, and apricot jam." Already crippled by osteoarthritis, she was "really walloped" by the disease in 1974, she told Tynan. "That was the end of the booze or any other kind of escape for me. I knew I was in for a bad time, with nothing to face but the absolute meaninglessness of my life." In addition to osteoarthritis, the former actress has acute emphysema. Looking back at her career, Louise Brooks does not think she was "a particularly good actress," that her artlessness was exactly that—an absence of art. Unlike many trained actors and actresses she knew, she was not "frightened of the camera," she recently told a reporter. "In front of the camera, I was just myself. . . . The camera didn't exist."

References: N Y Daily News F p5 S 16 '83 por; C p4 S 18 '83 por; N Y Review of Books 29:27+ O 21 '82 por; N Y Times C p8 S 16 '83 por; New Yorker 55:45+ Je 11 '79 por; Brooks, Louise. Lulu in Hollywood (1982); Katz, Ephraim. Film Encyclopedia (1979); Thomson, David. Biographical Dictionary of Film (1976); Tynan, Kenneth, Show People (1979)

Bruner, Jerome (Seymour)

Oct. 1, 1915– Psychologist; educator. Address: b Graduate Faculty Center, New School for Social Research, 65 Fifth Ave., New York City, N.Y. 10003

For four decades Dr. Jerome Bruner has played a major role in shaping the development of cognitive psychology—that branch of the science that studies human thought processes and the acquisition of knowledge. His ground-breaking work during the 1950s helped to make the concept of mind scientifically respectable and opened new avenues of inquiry into attention, intuition, will, and many other aspects of mental life. Eschewing specialization in favor of interdisciplinary projects, Bruner cofounded, in 1960, the Center for Cognitive Studies at Harvard University, where he investigated, among other things, the growth of cognition in children, including their acquisition and use of language, and its implications for education. His wide range of interests is reflected in his extensive bibliography of well over 200 books, essays, and technical and popular articles.

Jerome Seymour Bruner was born on October 1, 1915, the youngest of the four children of Herman and Rose (Glücksmann) Bruner, Polish immigrants who had settled around the turn of the century in New York City, where Herman Bruner established a thriving business as a watch manufacturer. Blind at birth, Jerome Bruner underwent two successful cataract operations at the age of two. Shortly afterwards, he moved with his family from New York City to the then prosperous middle-class suburb of Far Rockaway, in the borough of Queens. Reared in what he has described as a "nominally observant Jewish" household, he led a "blissfully happy child's life" until the death, in 1927, of his father, with whom he had had a positive if somewhat remote relationship. The loss of his father proved to be an unsettling experience for the boy, both emotionally and literally, for as he explained in *In Search of Mind* (Harper & Row, 1983), "My mother, restless to taste the world as a still youngish widow, moved each year and I with her, shifting schools but failing in confusion to shift allegiances, brooding over a lost world but not quite finding a new one."

During his adolescence, Bruner attended a half-dozen public high schools, none of which challenged him intellectually. "It was too easy," he explained to Maya Pines in an interview for the *New York Times Magazine* (November 29, 1970). "I was always looking for something else. I had a desperate need to read anything I could get hold of." Following his high school graduation in 1933, he enrolled at Duke University in Durham, North Carolina with no specific academic or career goal in mind. He has since attributed his eventual gravitation toward psychology to rather ambiguous general reasons: "partly the place, partly the people, partly the times." At first indifferent to the subject, he gradually became intrigued by the then relatively new Gestalt school of psychology, Freudianism, and cultural anthropology. His "imprinting became irreversible," as he put it, in his senior year, when he collaborated with his instructors on several important research projects, one of which was a study of conditioned helplessness.

After taking his A.B. degree in 1937, Bruner remained at Duke for one year of graduate study under Karl S. Lashley, the experimentalist, then transferred to Harvard University, from which he received his A.M. degree in 1939. At the time, Harvard was home to a diverse group of social science luminaries, including the personality theorists Gordon W. Allport and Henry A. Murray, Kurt Lewin, a Gestalt psychologist, and the behaviorist B. F. Skinner. Bruner, who was beginning his investigations of perception and sensation, worked most closely with Professor Edwin G. Boring, the psychophysicist and historian of modern psychology. But when he came to select a topic to investigate for his doctoral dissertation, Bruner's left-wing and "interventionist," to use his word, political sympathies led him to choose an analysis of the propagandist radio broadcasts beamed at North and South America by Germany, Italy, and Japan during the early months of World War II.

A few weeks after he was awarded his Ph.D. degree in June 1941, Bruner accepted a position with the newly established Foreign Broadcast Monitoring Service of the Federal Communications Commission in Washington, D.C. His job was to analyze the radio broadcasts of the Axis powers and to report the results to the State and War departments. The following year, he was shifted to the program surveys division of the Bureau of Agricultural Economics, where he helped keep tabs on the state of homefront morale. As associate director of the Office of Public Opinion Research in Princeton, New Jersey, a post he took in 1943, he continued to measure popular support of American foreign policy for the Department of State. Some of those surveys were published in *Mandate from the People* (Duell, Sloan & Pearce, 1944), a book he has since dismissed as "naive." Wanting to take a "more direct" part in the war effort, Bruner attempted to enlist in the armed services, but he was turned down because of poor eyesight. He eventually secured an appointment as a so-called "assimilated" major in the Psychological Warfare Division of the Supreme Headquarters Allied Expeditionary Force Europe and spent the last few months of the war reporting on the political and economic situation in areas recently liberated by Allied troops.

Anxious to return to academic life, Bruner accepted a lectureship in psychology at Harvard in 1945. He was promoted to associate professor in 1948 and to professor in 1952. Beginning in 1946, he taught courses in both the Department of Psychology and in its splinter sibling, the Department of Social Relations. Although Bruner had often been frustrated by the narrowness of the original department, he was not entirely happy with the new arrangement, in which the interdisciplinary department concentrated on macrosociological issues while its parent division focused on psychophysics and operant conditioning. As he observed in his autobiographical *In Search of Mind*, "The heart of psychology—the study of the powers of mind and their enablement—fell neglected between the two."

Returning to the study of perception and sensation, which had been his main interest before the war, Bruner, in a series of papers written in collaboration with several of his Harvard colleagues, most notably Leo Postman, formulated a revolutionary theory of perception. He argued, among other things, that constant "errors" of perception were in fact variations of enormous psychological interest and that subjective factors such as values and needs strongly influenced man's perception of his environment. For example, in one of his experiments Bruner asked school-children to adjust a patch of light to correspond to the sizes of various coins. Most of the test subjects exaggerated the sizes of the higher-value coins, but poor children overestimated the sizes to a greater degree than their affluent counterparts. The suprising results of that experiment contradicted the so-called "law of central tendency," which holds that guesses of magnitude err toward the middle. Subsequent experiments along similar lines also suggested that an individual shaped the raw data of perception to conform to his own "model of the universe," to use Bruner's term. The "New Look," as that line of inquiry came to be called, has provided an enduring and flexible methodology for analyzing perception.

In the early 1950s Bruner turned away from the examination of perception toward an investigation of cognitive processes in general. The study of cognition was then in disrepute because it usually involved "mentalistic" concepts beyond the pale of scientific respectability. Dr. Bruner, however, devised a new research technique that not only utilized a minimal conceptual apparatus but also took into account some of his earlier findings about perception. In an experimental setting, test subjects were asked to sort a series of eighty-one cards, each distinguishable by the color, shape, and number of figures enclosed within one or more borders, into common classes. Bruner and his associates observed the subjects while they performed the sorting tasks and identified the types of concept-formation and the various "selection strategies" which they employed.

"Simpleminded though the experiments were . . . ," Bruner wrote years later in *In Search of Mind*, "we managed to gather quite a harvest of interesting findings. We managed to find out the procedures by which ordinary people go about being modestly rational." Bruner and his colleagues, George A. Austin and Jacqueline J. Goodnow, published the test results and an outline of the new experimental technique for analyzing the ways people process information in *A Study in Thinking* (Wiley, 1956). An acceptably "tough-minded" approach to cognition, the book is considered by historians of contemporary psychology to mark the advent of the "cognitive revolution," which over the next generation led to a new acceptance of the study of mental life, with implications for social psychology, the perceptual sciences, learning theory, and other related fields.

One of the underlying dynamics of *A Study of Thinking* was Bruner's desire to create a broader, humanistic context for psychological research. Dissatisfied with the restrictiveness of Skinnerian operant conditioning and also with the sociological cast of the personality theorists, Bruner, together with another Harvard psychologist, George A. Miller, conceived the idea for an interdisciplinary research center devoted to the study of cognition. With a grant from the Carnegie Corporation, the two psychologists opened the Center for Cognitive Studies on the Harvard campus in 1960. Under Bruner and Miller's direction, the center soon became a mecca for specialists from a wide variety of academic disciplines, among them Noam Chomsky, the psycholinguist, developmentalist Bärbel Inhelder, and Roman Jakobson, a specialist in Slavic languages and literature. Experiments conducted under the center's auspices were as diverse as the backgrounds of the experimenters. One research project, in which Bruner himself took part, involved the recognition of blurred pictures.

Concurrent with the establishment of the Center for Cognitive Studies, Bruner became involved in the national debates about American educational reform that were spawned by the Soviet Union's launching of Sputnik, the first artificial earth satellite, and by the escalating Cold War. In the summer of 1959, at the request of the National Academy of Sciences, he chaired a blue-ribbon study group of scientists, scholars, and educators charged with examining the new science curriculum. One of the analytical fruits of that conference was Bruner's seminal *The Process of Education*, a summary of the theories and tentative conclusions of the conferees which was published in 1960 by Harvard University Press. Educators welcomed Bruner's flexible and progressive approach, especially his widely quoted dictum that "Any subject can be taught effectively in some intellectually honest form to any child at any stage of development." In Bruner's view, mastery of "facts and techniques" is ultimately useless because unrelated facts have, as he put it, "a pitiably short half-life in memory." A curriculum ought rather to be constructed "around the great issues, principles, and values that a society deems worthy of the continued concern of its members. . . . The shrewd guess, the fertile hypothesis, the courageous leap to a tentative conclusion—these are the most valuable coin of the thinker at work."

Critical reaction to Bruner's innovative ideas was unanimously favorable, with the radical essayist Paul Goodman, writing in the *New York Herald Tribune* (December 25, 1960), going so far as to predict that *The Process of Education* "will be a classic, comparable for its philosophical centrality and humane concreteness to some of the essays of [John] Dewey." Eventually translated into about twenty languages, *The Process of Education*, which was known as "The Gospel According to St. Jerome" by some of its more devoted adherents, became a worldwide success. Since its publication, Bruner has been a major voice in American educational reform. His later essays on the subject were collected in *Toward a Theory of Instruction* (Belknap Press of Harvard University Press, 1966) and *The Relevance of Education* (Norton, 1971).

A logical outgrowth of Bruner's multifarious activities during the 1960s was his growing interest in the developmental aspects of cognition. Strongly influenced by the Swiss child psychologist Jean Piaget's groundbreaking work on the development of intelligence and by the research of Lev Semyonovich Vygotsky, the Russian psychologist and linguist, Bruner articulated a multistage theory of cognitive development in children in *Studies in Cognitive Growth* (Wiley, 1966), written in collaboration with a number of postdoctoral fellows at the Center for Cognitive Studies. According to that theory, a child successively employs three modes of representation: the enactive (thinking through action, such as riding a bicycle); the iconic (thinking through images); and the symbolic (thinking through language). Bruner dedicated *Studies in Cognitive Growth* to Professor Piaget, who was said to dislike the book. In retrospect, Bruner, too, has found fault with it, contending that it was "too close to Piagetian thought, yet too remote from central issues in his theory, to have much impact."

To get an even more accurate insight into cognitive development, specifically, into the "beginnings of mental life," Bruner decided to concentrate on early infancy. Little research had been done in that area, and the prevailing theories were based largely on inferences about an infant's mental state derived from various physiological measures. Finding the existing methodology inadequate for their purposes, Bruner and several colleagues at the Center for Cognitive Studies devised novel techniques for measuring infants' mental capacities and their readiness to act purposefully. In one of the group's best-known experiments, infants were shown a blurred movie which they could focus by sucking on a pacifier. "And, lo and behold," Bruner told Maya Pines, "these little four-, five-, and six-week-old infants do learn to suck in longer bursts to produce a clear focus." Bruner concluded that a baby was a "hypothesis-generator" from birth, with an embryonic intelligence primed for cultivation. As he explained it in *In Search of Mind*, "The question then is not where or when mind begins. Mind in some operative form is there from the start. . . . The question, rather, is about the conditions that produce human minds that are richer, stronger, more confident."

Bruner's research into the cognitive development of children contributed to the success of the growing movement for the establishment of government-funded daycare centers and early childhood education programs, such as Head Start, in the United States and in Great Britain. Bruner himself took part in the planning of the Head Start program, and after moving to England in 1972, he served as vice-president of the Preschool Playgroup Association of Great Britain. His case study analysis of the British daycare system, *Under Fire in Britain*, was released by the London publishing house Grant McIntyre in 1980.

Weary after a quarter of a century of what he called "Harvard's political squabbles," Bruner had moved to England to accept an appointment as Watts Professor of Psychology and Fellow of Wolfson College, a newly founded graduate institution at Oxford University. There, he reinvigorated his long-standing interest in language acquisition. Inspired by the pragmatic approach of Oxford's language theorists, Bruner undertook an experiment designed to examine the transition from "prelinguistic to linguistic" communication by observing the behavior of toddlers learning to talk. In naturalistic, "homelike" settings, he studied and recorded on videotape the interactions of mothers and their children as they ate meals, played, and read together. The generally accepted view of language acquisition held that it is "untaught," but when Bruner painstakingly analyzed his hours and hours of videotape, he discovered that "a kind of 'tutoring'" was taking place. That tutoring depended on the establishment of a "format," which he defined as "a little microcosm, a task, in which mother and child share an intention to get something done with words," such as book reading. In his view, formats are "little pieces of culture" that not only introduce a child to language but also to the society that created the language. Bruner concluded that formatting, in conjunction with several other factors, comprised what he called the "Language Acquisition Support System," which is analogous on a developmental level to Noam Chomsky's theory of an innate "Language Acquisition Device." He outlined his ideas in *Child's Talk: Learning to Use Language* (Norton, 1983).

After taking a year's sabbatical at the Netherlands Institute for Advanced Study in the Humanities and Social Sciences in Wassenaar, Bruner returned in 1980 to Harvard, where he set to work on his intellectual autobiography *In Search Of Mind* under a program sponsored by the Alfred P. Sloan Foundation. In his review for the *New York Times Book Review* (January 8, 1984), psychologist Howard Gruber called the book "a rare and engrossing picture of a scientist at work, [which] shows how it is that such work can be so immensely enjoyable." In 1981 Bruner accepted the George Herbert Mead Professorship at the New School for Social Research in New York City. Since the beginning of 1984 he has served concurrently as director of the New York Institute for the Humanities.

During the 1960s Bruner served on the education panel of the President's Science Advisory Committee under the administrations of both John F. Kennedy and Lyndon B. Johnson. He has also advised the National Science Foundation, the National Institutes of Health, the Educational Testing Service, and the American Academy of Arts and Sciences. A founding fellow of the National Academy of Education, Dr. Bruner is a fellow of the American Academy of Arts and Sciences and the American Association for the Advancement of Science, and he is a member and past president of the American Psychological Association and the Society for the Psychological Study of Social Issues. Among his many honors and awards are the G. Stanley Hall Medal for contributions to the understanding of human development, the Merrill-Palmer Institute's citation for "service to children," the Distinguished Scientific Award of the American Psychological Association, and honorary doctoral degrees from the Sorbonne, Yale University, Northwestern University, and several other colleges. His memberships in the Cruising Club of America and the Royal Cruising Club reflect his lifelong passion for sailing.

Jerome Bruner has been described as "a man with electric energy and an infectious grin in a leather face." Although his sight was restored in infancy, he has only a narrow range of clear vision, and thus, Howard Gruber has suggested, "For him, seeing is never a simple taking in but always a purposeful turning toward." Dr. Bruner has two children—Whitley, an Arabist diplomat, and Jane, a painter and photographer—from his sixteen-year marriage to Katherine Frost, which ended in divorce in 1956. A second marriage, to Blanche Ames Marshall in 1960, also ended in divorce, in 1983.

References: *Harper's* 229:81+ D '64 por; *N Y Times Mag* p32 N 29 '70 por; *New Repub* 189:31+ D 26 '83; *Psych Today* 16:57+ Ja '82; *Time* 78:78+ O 13 '61, 108:39 Ag 23 '76; *American Men and Women of Science* (1982); *Contemporary Authors* new rev vol 1 (1981); *Who's Who in America,* 1978-79

Callahan, Harry M(orey)

Oct. 22, 1912– Photographer. Address: 153 Benefit Street, Providence, R.I. 02903

During a career of more than forty years, Harry M. Callahan has quietly established himself as one of the most important and influential American photographers of the twentieth century. His classical, precise photographs that transform commonplace objects into images of lyrical beauty combine the principles of "straight" photography (photography of real objects, without manipulation in the darkroom) and formalism and exhibit an amazing range of subject matter along with an impressive command of technique. Nevertheless, he admitted to Valerie Brooks in *Artnews* (October 1983) that "I sort of wish sometimes that I had cared about something else, but I haven't. My whole drive has been to take pictures. It's the only thing I have ever been good at."

Harry Morey Callahan was born in Detroit, Michigan, on October 22, 1912, the only son of Harry Arthur Callahan, a farmer, and Hazel (Mills) Callahan. He had two sisters: Alice, who is no longer living, and Marjorie. After graduating from the public high school in Royal Oak, Michigan in 1931, he enrolled as an engineering major at Michigan State College. Admittedly never studious, he dropped out after three semesters and peddled papers and did odd jobs in Detroit to support himself. In 1934 Callahan began working as a clerk in the accounting department of the Chrysler Motor Parts Corporation, where he remained for seven years. Shortly before he started at Chrysler, Callahan met Eleanor Knapp on a blind date, and on November 25, 1936, the two were married. Their only child, Barbara Mary, was born in 1950.

In 1938 Callahan purchased his first camera, a Rolleicord, and taught himself the rudiments of photography. Growing steadily more involved in his hobby, he joined the Detroit Photo Guild in 1941 and attended a number of its workshops, including one conducted by the celebrated nature photographer Ansel Adams, who first kindled Callahan's interest in photography as an art. As he recalled in an interview with Barbaralee Diamonstein for *Visions and Images* (1982), he was particularly struck by the "beautiful tone and texture" of Adams' work and by those photos shot of the ground nearby, which showed to Callahan that any subject anywhere—not just spectacular landscapes, for example—was suitable material for photographic art. "This was probably the most freeing thing that ever happened to me. From then on, even though I hadn't made a picture, I thought I was a great artist."

Through his lecture at the guild, Adams also introduced Callahan to the work of Alfred Stieglitz, one of the most influential photographers of the twentieth century. Although a founder of both the experimentalist photo-secession movement and the famous avant-garde art gallery "291" at the turn of the century, Stieglitz himself was a purist who refused to tamper with his negatives or prints. Callahan, who also advocated purism, idolized Stieglitz but although they met in 1942 and 1944 at Stieglitz's New York City gallery, An American Place, they failed to strike up any rapport. Nevertheless, Callahan's oeuvre unmistakably reflects the influence of that master photographer.

Although Callahan began his serious work in the early 1940s, the heyday of social documentary photography and the *Life* magazine type of photojournalism, his first notable pictures, taken with a large-format 8 x 10 camera on a tripod, were of grasses and reeds in water (*Detroit, 1941*) or in snow—subjects with no "social relevance" whatsoever. Callahan considered social documentation in art to be important, but when he had tried to take photographs in that vein "they just meant hardly anything to [him]." So, perhaps influenced by both Steiglitz's more than 400 photos of his second wife, Georgia O'Keeffe, and his series of photos of clouds related to emotions, entitled "Equivalents," Callahan instead concentrated on commonplace subjects like landscapes, cityscapes, and seascapes; architecture; strangers on the street; and his family, especially his wife, Eleanor. Those themes would preoccupy Callahan through most of his career, but he varied the photographic means of exploring them. He experimented with different types of cameras and both color and black-and-white film; shot photographic sequences reminiscent of Ansel Adams' famous *Surf Sequence*; and took many camera-confined multiple exposures. In 1950 he even made two films: "People Walking on State Street," which is still unedited, and "Motions."

Early on, Callahan's interest in various modes and techniques and his habit of exhaustively photographing one subject at a time melded to produce a number of important photographic series. One of the best known is his study of passersby, lost in thought, which was shot in 1950 on Chicago's State Street. Using a steep, upward perspective and a camera with a telephoto lens, he walked down the street while holding the camera to his eye; when the head of a pedestrian filled the viewfinder, he snapped the picture. For *Detroit, 1960* and other later photos of pedestrians, however, he shifted the perspective, including more background and shooting from a less exaggerated angle. In another series, he photographed houses in Providence, Rhode Island, and on Cape Cod, Massachusetts, first by using a large 8 x 10 camera, carefully set up on a tripod. "I wanted to take them so that all the lines are straight . . . ," he explained to Barbaralee Diamonstein. "I did that for quite a while, and I thought, 'Well, I can't do this forever. Nobody wants to look at them that way all the time.' So I started doing something else: I started distorting them in [many ways]. I think I've done nearly everything I've photographed in that way."

Callahan's studies of Eleanor are similarly varied. He has photographed her in the nude and clothed, in silhouette, in both black and white and color, alone or with their daughter, and in interior and exterior settings. He also often distorted photographs of her or superimposed them on shots of natural objects or landscapes. One of his most famous photographs, *Eleanor, Chicago, 1949,* is a close-up of her head rising from the lake, with her long hair trailing into the water and the shape of one breast distorted under the lapping waves. The whiteness of her handsome, strong-jawed face sharply contrasts with her black hair. Her closed eyes and the obvious mythic references—to Aphrodite rising from the sea, for example—render it a haunting image, tranquil yet somehow troubling. Her expression is so enigmatic that Robert Hughes, writing in *Time* (December 20, 1976), termed the photograph "Callahan's *Mona Lisa.*"

Eleanor, Chicago, 1949, among other of his masterworks, lends credence to Callahan's assertion that for him "the subject is all-important." "I experiment with various techniques," he explained to Margaret R. Weiss in *Saturday Review* (September 26, 1964), "to help me see things differently from the way I saw them before. That is seeing *photographically,* and when you see photographically you really *see.*" He quickly discovered when he began to photograph nudes, for example, that using just any model "didn't work." In the interview in *Artnews* with Valerie Brooks, he insisted that "[he] wanted to photograph the person for whom [he] had feeling": Eleanor.

Though the subjects of Callahan's work and his means of scrutinizing them varied, a common thread runs through his oeuvre: his obsessive fascination with the most elemental features of photographic art—light, line, and space—and their interplay. That concern is so characteristic of his work that, as Arno Rafael Minkkinen observed in *Contemporary Photographers* (1982), "in almost any Callahan photograph it is possible to see every Callahan photograph." The linearity in his first Detroit nature photographs is repeated in pictures of telephone wires against a white sky and neon lights shot with a moving 35mm camera; the stark, vertical lines in his photographs of building façades in Chicago and New York reappear in a Providence, Rhode Island, photograph of *Weeds in Snow* (1964); and each of these photos, in turn, is reminiscent of *Eleanor, 1947*—a single dark line threading a white background, indicating the cleft between buttocks and thighs. Minkkinen pointed out related examples of Callahan's use of photographic space. In about 1952 Callahan photographed his friend Bob Fine standing in sunlight at the far end of an alley in such a way that "he at first appears as if seen on stage from the very last row of the top balcony. A similar scale illusion takes hold in a 1972 photograph on Cape Cod," Minkkinen continued. "A wind-tussled surf is about to pound a beach like a bedsheet slapped flat for a tight fit. At first, the rushing breaker threatens our toes—we think it so near—then, spying a jogger skirting the surf edge, we grasp where Callahan must be: high on the peak of a sand dune overlooking the whole ocean."

During the latter years of World War II (1944–45), Callahan processed color prints at the General Motors Corporation's photography laboratory. He "hated" that job, so using their savings, he and his wife moved to New York for six months, in the course of which he met with Stieglitz several times as well as with other photographers, including Berenice Abbott, Paul Strand, and Lisette Model. He also became acquainted with Nancy and Beaumont Newhall, who were then establishing the photography department of the Museum of Modern Art. Nancy Newhall arranged the first of the many showings of Callahan's work at the museum, including a number of his color slides lit from behind in the important 1946 "New Photographers" exhibition. Callahan's first one-man show was held in 1946-47 at the 750 Studio Gallery in Chicago, where, in 1948, he met Edward Steichen, a cofounder with Stieglitz of photo-secessionism and the head of MOMA's photography department. Their friendship proved a great support to Callahan's subsequent career.

Returning to the midwest, Callahan unsuccessfully sought work developing prints for photographers at the Institute of Design in Chicago. Instead, Arthur Siegel, a fellow member of the Detroit Photo Guild and chairman of the Institute's Department of Photography, introduced him to the head of that school, László Moholy-Nagy, who hired him as an instructor on the basis of his photography. Moholy-Nagy, a Hungarian-born painter, designer, and experimental photographer, had been a charter member in 1919 of the German Bauhaus movement and later directed the Bauhaus School of Design in Chicago (1937-38) before founding the Institute of Design (1938-46). Callahan's refusal to manipulate his prints and his conviction that photography is a collaboration between himself and the camera—a force with "interesting ideas of its own"—were reinforced by the Bauhaus philosophy, which emphasized the mechanics and technology of art. Moreover, since he was never wholly comfortable with teaching and always found it difficult to explain things verbally, he adapted quite naturally to the Bauhaus method of instruction, which emphasized a solid grounding in the fundamentals of an art—mastering the mechanics of a camera, for example—principally through hands-on experience, and he quickly established a strong rapport with his students. "I'd have my students try everything technical there was to try," he recalled in the Artnews interview. "I made them do what I had never been able to do—take portraits."

Long recognized as one of the most influential photography instructors in the United States, Callahan considers his years at the Institute as "nourishing," although his responsibilities there interfered with his own work. Moreover, he admitted to Barbaralee Diamonstein that "going to the Institute . . . saved [his] life" as an artist. In 1949 he replaced Siegel as head of the department and initiated a master's degree program. In 1950 (a year after the Institute became part of the Illinois Institute of Technology) he hired Aaron Siskind, another important photographer and instructor, to teach documentary photography. In the summer of 1951 Callahan, Siskind, and Siegel all taught at the famous avant-garde school of the arts, Black Mountain College, in North Carolina. Later that year, Callahan was given his first major one-man show at a museum: an exhibition at the Art Institute of Chicago.

As a result of a grant of $10,000 from the Graham Foundation, awarded for advanced study in art, in 1956 Callahan was able to take a fifteen-month leave of absence from teaching for travel to Europe. Despite the change of scene, the subject, mood, and form of his photos remained relatively constant, and in many letters since 1956 to his photographer-friend Todd Webb he expressed his ambivalence about the value of travel and his contentment with staying where he is. Nevertheless, Callahan admitted to Valerie Brooks in the Artnews interview that "going to Europe had a big influence on [him]." "Seeing foreign countries," he recounted, "it struck me that so-called reality was far more powerful and more important to me than multiple exposures and collages and all that stuff." After that first trip, he "no longer cared about the medium in the sense of wanting to see what [he] could do with it." Instead, on his return to the United States he found that he was even more intrigued than before by "subject matter that stands for itself." He has subsequently made several more trips to Europe and has visited Mexico many times.

He has also traveled to Peru and Bolivia (1974), the Middle East (1978), the South Pacific (1979), Morocco (1981), and China and Japan (1983).

Although Callahan enjoyed his work at Chicago's Institute of Design, after fifteen years he sensed that its "spirit" had changed. In 1961 he resigned to become chairman of the photography department of the Rhode Island School of Design in Providence where he developed undergraduate and graduate programs. In 1971, Callahan was able to create a position for Siskind, who also wished to join the faculty at the Rhode Island School of Design. In 1964 Callahan was appointed professor at the school. That year was also marked by the publication of Photographs: Harry Callahan, the first extensive monograph on his work, and by the acquisition by Hallmark Cards, Inc., of the first substantive collection of his photography. During the 1960s and early 1970s he took a sabbatical and several short leaves of absence for photographic field trips or teaching assignments as a visiting professor at schools in the United States and abroad. Callahan finally relinquished the chairmanship of the department of photography of the Rhode Island School of Design in 1973.

He retired from the Rhode Island School of Design in 1977, the same year that he abandoned black-and-white photography. Although he had been taking color photographs since 1941, until 1972 his reputation was based almost entirely on his work in black and white. Part of the reason for that was the high cost of developing color film: in the 1940s, it cost about $150 to have a dye-transfer print made. In 1978 the Light Gallery in New York City mounted a one-man exhibition devoted exclusively to his color photography. Notable among his later color work included in that show is the series of prints of frame houses in Providence he made from 1963 on. He took those photographs with a wide-angle lens, which gives deep perspectives and strange distortions, creating the illusion that the houses are about to collapse on one another or explode. As the critic Janet Malcolm pointed out in the New Yorker (December 4, 1978), those photographs were "marked by a characteristic formalism, deliberation, and singlemindedness, and by a typical continuing obsession with a subject." She was particularly impressed by the "marvelous interplay between the abstract form and the emotional content of the pictures."

Eleanor and Barbara: Photographs by Harry Callahan is his most recent exhibition. Organized by Peter MacGill in New York and circulated by the Center for Creative Photography in Tucson, Arizona, the show began its two-year American tour at the Art Institute of Chicago on January 18, 1984. The seventy-eight photographs in the show provide a twenty-year retrospective on the photographer's devotion to a theme—his family, but almost exclusively his wife—and the variations imposed on it by the camera and by the sensibility behind the camera. Callahan no longer photographs his wife, but Eleanor Callahan told Valerie Brooks in Artnews (October 1983) that photographing her formed part of their daily routine for twenty-five years. "Between four and five was nude-photographing time," she explained. "He took pictures wherever we might be." Callahan has explained that he always wanted to capture her image simply because "there's some beauty that you don't want gone. You want a part of it." In her review of that 1984 exhibition for *Modern Photography* (August 1984), Julia Scully was particularly struck by Callahan's "almost compulsive photographing of a single person" and praised the "spare elegance" and the "exactness of composition combined with masterly technique" evident in every picture, whether a "straight" or technically complex print.

Harry Callahan's many honors include the Rhode Island Governor's Award for Excellence in the Arts (1969); a Guggenheim Fellowship (1972); and the title of Honored Photographer at the eighth Rencontre Internationale de la Photographie in Arles, France (1977). In 1979 he received an honorary Doctor of Fine Arts degree from the Rhode Island School of Design and was elected a Fellow of the American Academy of Arts and Sciences. He has exhibited extensively in the United States and Canada, in Europe, and in Japan. In 1976, the Museum of Modern Art mounted a major retrospective of his work, and in 1978 Callahan, along with Richard Diebenkorn represented the United States at the Venice Biennale. His prints are included in the collections of thirty-three galleries or institutions, among them the International Museum of Photography at the George Eastman House in Rochester, New York; the Hallmark Gallery, the Metropolitan Museum of Art, and the Museum of Modern Art in New York City; the Art Institute of Chicago; and the Victoria and Albert Museum in London. An archival collection of prints, color transparencies, and negatives, as well as his personal papers, was established in 1975 at the Center for Creative Photography at the University of Arizona in Tucson.

Photographs of the artist himself, such as one taken in 1967 by his former student Emmet Gowin, bear out what is known of Callahan's modest, self-effacing manner. In rumpled work clothes and with his five-feet-ten-inch frame slouched against a wall, he seems withdrawn, and his brown eyes are cast down as if to evade the camera. Although like some other photography critics, John Szarkowski, the director of the photography department at the Museum of Modern Art, has detected a similar detached coldness (or a "consistent lack of vulgarity," as Szarkowski phrases it) in Callahan's oeuvre, the artist himself has said he hopes his work "will touch the spirit in people." But as he explained in the *Artnews* interview, the driving force behind his forty-year career has been a desire "to reach the edge of nothingness—the point where you can't go any further. I feel I have come close to that at various times with the Beach Series photographs. A determined single-mindedness and an insistent inner need has led me to that point. That is why I have always kept going back,

and that is what still keeps me going today—keeps me alive."

References: Artnews 82:64+ O '83 por; Contemporary Photographers (1982); Diamonstein, Barbaralee. Visions and Images: American Photographers on Photography (1982); Green, Jonathan. American Photography: A Critical History 1945 to the Present (1984); Szarkowski, John, ed. Callahan (1976); Who's Who in America, 1984-85

Calvino, Italo
(käl-vēn´ō ē´täl-ō)

Oct. 15, 1923– Italian writer. Address: b. Giulio Einaudi Editore, via Umberto Biancamano 1, Turin, Italy

An exceptionally adroit, original, and versatile storyteller, Italo Calvino is acknowledged in the United States as "Italy's best living writer of fiction," to quote Susan Sontag. His international standing derives not merely from a comparison of his work with that of other Italians. A decade ago Gore Vidal found, "During the last quarter century Italo Calvino has advanced far beyond his American and English contemporaries." Calvino's forte is the tale, realistic or fantastic or a blend of the two, which enables him to venture away from the linear narrative development of the conventional novel as he interchanges and combines his short fictional components in sustained and cleverly intricate structures untried by other writers. Especially in his last three novels, *The Castle of the Crossed Destinies, Invisible Cities,* and *If on a Winter's*

Night a Traveler, humanistic themes merge with aesthetic and philosophical questions on literature and its relation to reality. Since 1947 Calvino has been associated, mainly as an editor, with Giulio Einaudi Editore, which publishes his books in Italian.

Italo Calvino was born on October 15, 1923 in Santiago de Las Vegas, Cuba to Italian parents Mario and Eva (Mameli) Calvino, both of whom were tropical agronomists. Soon afterward they returned with their son to San Remo, in Liguria on the Italian Riviera, which he likes to think of as his birthplace. During Italo's childhood in San Remo his father worked as curator of the botanical gardens and experimented with growing tropical fruit on the family farm. "He was raised in a free-thinking family without traditional religious instruction," Frank MacShane wrote of Calvino in the *New York Times Magazine* (July 10, 1983), "[and] was nurtured in an enlightened scientific atmosphere." Like the Italian Nobel Prize winner Eugenio Montale, whom he has called "my poet," he had a strong emotional affinity with nature, especially with the everyday countryside of his early home.

Intending to study agronomy, Calvino enrolled in the Faculty of Science at the University of Turin, where his father was a teacher. In the early 1940s he joined the Italian Resistance to fight against the Nazis and Fascists in the Ligurian mountains. After World War II he reentered the University of Turin, switched his study from science to literature, wrote his thesis on Joseph Conrad, and graduated in 1947. That year he also found employment in the publicity department of the newly formed publishing company Giulio Einaudo Editore, of which he later became an editor. Meanwhile, in 1945, he had joined the Communist party and had begun contributing to *Il Politècnico* and other leftist papers. With the writers Cesare Pavese and Elio Vittorini he shared an involvement both in socialist politics and in the postwar Italian neorealistic literary vogue inspired in part by Ernest Hemingway and other American writers.

In that vein of realism Calvino wrote *Il sentiero dei nidi di ragno* (1947; *The Path to the Nest of Spiders,* Beacon Press, 1957), based on his experiences as a partisan fighter. For his first novel he won the Premio Riccione. The events and characters of the story are seen mainly through the eyes of Pin, a boy from the slums of Genoa who joins the partisans in the hills and, for all his precocious street wisdom, is left astonished and confused by the violent adult world. The perspective of Calvino's early narratives is often that of an innocent, a protagonist with honest but befuddled vision whose mystification in some stories may impose itself on the reader. *The Path to the Nest of Spiders* lacks the grimness of much Italian neorealism, both in fiction and in films, partly because of an exuberant, picaresque flavor for which Calvino is indebted to his boyhood reading of Robert Louis Stevenson's *Kidnapped* and *Treasure Island.*

World War II, as well as the postwar period, also provided the settings for the short stories collected in *Ultimo viene il corvo* (Last Comes the Crow, 1949) and *L'entrata in guerra* (Entry into War, 1954). Some of them were translated in *Adam, One Afternoon and Other Stories* (Collins, 1957), which also included *La formica argentina* (*The Argentine Ant*), a 1952 novella about the struggle of a young couple to cope with the ants that infest their new home. In a survey of Calvino's work for the *New York Review of Books* (May 30, 1974) Gore Vidal maintained, "If 'The Argentine Ant' is not a masterpiece of twentieth-century prose writing, I cannot think of anything better. Certainly it is as minatory and strange as anything by Kafka."

Another allegorical novella of the 1950s reflective of Calvino's concern with contemporary social problems is *La nuvola di smog* (1958, The Cloud of Smog), which appeared in English translation under the title of *Smog* in *The Watcher & Other Stories* (Harcourt Brace Jovanovich, 1971). Also dating from the 1950s are the earliest stories in his gently amusing and satiric *Marcovaldo ovvero le stagioni in città* (1963; *Marcovaldo or The Seasons in the City,* Harcourt, 1983). The title character is a hapless unskilled worker who searches fruitlessly for nature in a dismal industrial city of northern Italy. Anatole Broyard described him in the *New York Times* (November 9, 1983) as "Calvino's Candide, his image of an innocent who survives the 1950s and 1960s in a modern metropolis by willfully misreading reality, as Chaplin did, by opposing his optimism to its negative influences."

Although most of Calvino's narratives with contemporary Italian backgrounds, including *La speculazione edilizia* (1957, Building Speculation), rely generally on straightforward fictional techniques and a more or less realistic approach, fantasy is seldom wholly absent. In his preface to one of the reissues of his first novel Calvino recalled, "It was Pavese who first spoke of a fairy-tale quality in my writing and I, who until then had not realized it, knew it only too well from that moment and tried to confirm the definition." His fondness for fairy tales soon led to an important contribution to Italian literature, *Fiabe italiane* (1956; *Italian Folktales,* Harcourt, 1980), his selection and retelling with annotations of 200 folktales from various regions of his country. "Folktales are real," Calvino wrote in his introduction. "These folk stories are the catalog of the potential destinies of men and women, especially for that stage in life when destiny is formed, i.e. youth."

Again, it was Pavese who discerned in *The Path to the Nest of Spiders* traces of Lodovico Ariosto, author of the Italian Renaissance masterpiece *Orlando Furioso.* During the 1950s, while still writing stories of predominantly matter-of-fact content, Calvino plunged headlong into the realm of improbability with three sharply witty, often funny, and lightly satiric fables that combine elements of Ariosto and folk tales, among others. In *Il visconte dimezzato* (1952; *The Cloven Viscount,* Random House, 1962) Calvino again uses a boy narrator to lend a measure of plausibility to experiences of nature and fantasy. The boy's uncle, Viscount Medardo di Terralba, is split vertically in two by a cannon shot during an Austro-Turkish battle. His too-evil half and his too-good half remain separated for years. Eventually, through the marriages of his rival halves to the winsome peasant girl Pamela and a surgical feat, the viscount regains his wholeness.

Il barone rampante (1957; *The Baron in the Trees*, Random House, 1959), which glows with Calvino's devotion to the eighteenth century, begins in mid-1767, when twelve-year-old Cosimo responds to a family quarrel by climbing a tree. Thereafter the branches of trees in a heavily wooded area of the republic of Genoa remain his home. During the course of his long, comfortable, and enlightened life aloft, he corresponds with Voltaire and once even speaks with Napoleon. The setting of the third *tour de force* of Calvino's trilogy, *Il cavaliere inesistente* (1959; *The Nonexistent Knight*, Random House, 1962), is the time of Charlemagne, one of whose paladins consists only of willpower, discipline, and observance of protocol inside an empty suit of shining white armor. The chronicle of his adventures has been assigned as a penance to a nun, Sister Theodora, who bewails her unfitness: "Apart from religious ceremonies, triduums, novenas, gardening, harvesting, vintaging, whippings, slavery, incest, fires, hangings, invasion, sacking, rape, and pestilence, we have had no experience. What can a poor nun know of the world?" She nevertheless plods through all the mistaken identities, chivalric codes, quests, and challenges, and other trappings of medieval romance. At the end she and the bewitching, love-stricken amazonian heroine Bradamante turn out to be one and the same.

After winning the Viareggio Prize in 1957 for *The Nonexistent Knight*, Calvino won the Salento Prize for his publication in 1960 of all three fantasies under the title of *I nostri antenati* (Our Ancestors). On a visit to New York in March 1983 he said that "the task of the writer is to fight against this plague [of abstract and artificial words], to make a direct, concrete language survive." The fable as a narrative form provided him a way to fulfill that objective, to link philosophical and sociological ideas with the senses. Fables also attracted him because they allow a plurality of interpretations. However remote in time and place Calvino's fables may be and however satisfying simply as tales for their own sakes, they also apply to the dilemmas of modern man. "The problems of our time appear in any story I write," he told Herbert Mitgang in an interview for the *New York Times Book Review* (May 1, 1983).

The same year, 1957, that *The Baron in the Trees* was published, Calvino left the Communist party. He has suggested that the Baron's preference for detachment as a way to deal with mankind represents his own feeling that a writer should be apolitical. The conflicts attending his ideological reassessment and disillusionment about socialist reforms in Italy may be reflected in the most realis-

tic of his books, *La giornata d'uno scrutatore* (1963, The Day of an Inspector), which was published in English as the title story of *The Watcher & Other Stories*. A representative of the Communist party, Amerigo Ormea, is assigned as a poll watcher to the Cottolengo Hospital for Incurables in Turin during the 1953 election. The voting that he oversees by grotesquely maimed and mentally retarded and insane patients may be intended to parody the Italian democratic process itself, while his misgivings and meditations contribute to a satiric barb and directness of social comment uncharacteristic of Calvino.

From somber sociopolitical analyses Calvino returned to fables with *Le cosmicomiche* (1965; *Cosmicomics*, Harcourt, 1968) in a soaring of imagination beyond that of *Our Ancestors*. Each of the twelve chapters, or stories, of *Cosmicomics* begins with a cosmogenic proposition that the narrator, Qfwfq, a sort of whimsical embodiment of the concept of the essential oneness of all forms of life, uses as a springboard to recount his experience of the creation and evolution of the universe. "In spite of recurring influences from varied sources (Borges, de Saussure, Carroll, Barthes, the cartoon strip, semiotics, structuralism, Propp, Lévi-Strauss, Robbe-Grillet, algebra, formal logic, astronomy), the narrative of the *Cosmicomiche* (or *comicosmiche* with convertible terms and parodic play of words) is the expression of a new kind of cosmogenic humor which is unlike anything ever written before," Antonio Illiano observed in *Dictionary of Italian Literature* (1979). *Cosmicomics* was translated into English by William Weaver, who won a National Book Award for his achievement and who has translated Calvino's later work.

Further adventures of Qfwfq appear in *Ti con zero* (1967; *t zero*, Harcourt, 1969; published in England as *Time and the Hunter*, Cape, 1970), which also includes the non-science-fiction tale "The Count of Monte Cristo." Underlying that story as well as those told by Qfwfq in the two collections is the narrator's preoccupation with the nature of his narration—a concern that recalls the trials and tribulations of Sister Theodora in writing her romance of the nonexistent knight and a theme of the three books that followed *t zero*.

Questions of language and interpretation and the relationship of the narrator to the listener abound in the brief and technically ingenious *Il castello dei destini incrociati* (1969, final edition 1973; *The Castle of the Crossed Destinies*, Harcourt, 1976). Calvino's Boccaccio-Chaucerian framing device for his intertwining tales is a gathering of travelers in a castle to tell each other their stories. Struck dumb by magic, they resort to the symbols on tarot cards, traditionally used to predict destinies, as a substitute for words. The same symbols could be used by more than one narrator in new combinations and sequences, thus determining the meaning of the stories that precede and follow. "In a virtuoso passage," Walter Clemons noted in *Newsweek* (February 14, 1977), "[Calvino] finds in the cards not only the stories of Hamlet, Oedipus, Lear and Faust but the writer's own story—a serious player trying to arrange inchoate human experience into coherent patterns."

The semiotic theory of signs, symbols, and codes, which greatly affected aesthetic and sociological thinking in France, where Calvino was living in the late 1960s and the 1970s, as well as Italy, also permeates *Le città invisibili* (1972; *Invisible Cities*, Harcourt, 1974). When an imaginary Marco Polo begins to tell an imaginary Kubla Khan about the imaginary cities of his empire, they communicate in gestures and other signs because Polo has not yet learned the Khan's language. The exquisitely described fifty-five cities, with exotic feminine names like Aglaura, Valdrada, Armilla, and Zobeide, are more truly desires, fears, illusions than places. Perhaps the most beautiful and poetic of Calvino's books, *Invisible Cities* has an enchanting elusiveness in both style and substance. Guided by the Khan, the reader finds his own meaning for the cities, or stories: "Now, from each city Marco described to him, the great Khan's mind set out on its own, and after dismantling the city piece by piece, he reconstructed it in other ways, substituting components, shifting them, inverting them."

In Calvino's next novel, his most popular book in the United States, *Se una notte d'invèrno un viaggiatore* (1979; *If on A Winter's Night a Traveler*, Harcourt, 1981), the protagonist is, in fact, a Reader, or "you," who has a shaping role in the narrative process. Partly a work of metafiction, *If on a Winter's Night* samples and parodies the *nouveau roman* and other contemporary literary styles and techniques through the device of novels—or rather their openings—within a novel. One of his characters, a renowned Irish author, Silas Flannery, also becomes a narrator, through his diary, of chapter eight. "I have had the idea of writing a novel composed only of the beginnings of novels," he discloses. "The protagonist could be a Reader who is continually interrupted." Calvino's framework for his pastiche of ten literary modes involves the efforts of a Reader and an Other Reader, his beloved Ludmilla, to find the continuation of *If on a Winter's Night a Traveler*, which was cut short in their copies of the book by a bindery mixup.

Two delighted American reviewers of *If on a Winter's Night*, Susan Sontag in *Vogue* (May 1981) and, especially, Mary McCarthy in the *New York Review of Books* (June 25, 1981), called attention to the parallel that Calvino draws between reading and making love. Some less-enthusiastic observations that MacShane considered in summarizing comments of various critics may also apply in their tenor to Calvino's other writings: "While admiring Calvino's technical virtuosity, they have dismissed the book as escapist because it is so caught up in its own mechanism that it loses sight of its theme. Because Calvino does not complete the stories he has begun—refusing, for example, to confront and develop the complexity of human love, which is his real theme—Calvino is thought by some critics to by cynical and cold."

Calvino's general reception in the United States has been so favorable that Harcourt Brace Jovanovich followed its 1983 translation of *Marcovaldo* with another collection of his short stories, *Difficult Loves* (*Gli amori difficili*, 1970), which was published in the United States in September 1984. To promote new writers in Italy, Calvino edits a series of short novels, "Cento Pagi" (One Hundred Pages), which is published by Giulio Einaudi. From 1959 to 1966 he and Vittorini coedited *Il Menabò di letteratura*, a journal that also encouraged young writers as part of its interest in broadening the social role of the intellectual. He has edited two volumes of letters and a collection of poetry of Pavese, who died in 1950. Italy's equivalent of the Pulitzer Prize in literature, the Premio Feltrinelli per la Narrativa, was awarded to Calvino in 1972.

On February 19, 1964 Italo Calvino married Argentine-born Chichita Singer, who worked for many years as a translator at UNESCO headquarters in Paris. They have one daughter. Since returning to Italy after a fifteen-year residence in Paris, the Calvinos have lived in a duplex apartment in a palazzo in Rome near the Pantheon. They also have a seaside home not far from Castiglione della Pescaia and keep a small apartment in Paris. In an interview with Francine du Plessix Gray for the *New York Times Book Review* (June 21, 1981) Calvino said that he misses Paris because he is a movie enthusiast and all foreign films there are shown in the original language. As described in that *Times* article, Calvino "is of slight build and medium height. . . . His features are lapidary, as finely chiseled as the profile on a Renaissance medallion. His chestnut eyes are gentle, meditative, withdrawn. . . . His manner is as self-effacing as it is exquisitely courteous. As he raises his head to speak, his usually impassive face is sometimes illuminated by a kind, impish grin."

References: N Y Rev of Books 21:13+ My 30 '74 por, 28:3+ Je 25 '81 por; N Y Times Bk R p1+ Je 21 '81 por, p39 My 1 '83 por; N Y Times Mag p23+ Jl 10 '83 pors; Vogue 171:279+ My '81 por; *Contemporary Authors vols 85–88 (1980); International Who's Who, 1984–85; Trevelyan, Raleigh, ed. Italian Writing Today (1967); World Authors: 1950–1970 (1975)*

Campbell, Joseph

*Mar. 26, 1904– Mythologist; editor; educator.
Address: b. c/o Harper & Row, 10 East 53d St., New York City, N.Y. 10022*

During a long creative life that he has called a "serendipity" but that others have termed a heroic journey, Joseph Campbell has explored the wealth of meanings hoarded in fairy tales, dreams, and the mythologies of virtually the entire world. Now rec-

Joseph Campbell

credit their own senses, honor their own decisions, name their own virtues, and claim their own vision of truth." Although Campbell turned eighty in March 1984, he still sees a journey ahead of him.

Joseph Campbell was born on March 26, 1904 in New York City, the son of Charles William Campbell, a hosiery importer and wholesaler, and Josephine (Lynch) Campbell. He dates his interest in diverse cultures, as he told D. J. R. Bruckner in a *New York Times Book Review* interview (December 18, 1983), from his fascination as a child with Buffalo Bill's Wild West Show, which performed annually at the old Madison Square Garden with cowboys, sharpshooters, and "Indians right off the plains." Trips with his brother Charles and sister Alice to the American Museum of Natural History, according to Donald Newlove in an *Esquire* profile (September 1977), enhanced his attraction to Indian culture. When the Campbells moved to New Rochelle, New York, the nine-year-old boy invaded the public library next door to their house and within a year read all the American Indian books. Already "a good little anthropologist" as a preparatory student at Canterbury School in New Milford, Connecticut, he devoured pioneering studies on the Pacific peoples and succeeded so well in attaining a broad education on his own that, as Newlove put it, by the time he entered Dartmouth College he was "light years" ahead of his classmates.

Dissatisfied with Dartmouth, Joseph Campbell transferred after one year there to Columbia University in New York City, where he exchanged his earlier academic concentration in biology and mathematics for the history of literature, art, and music. After completing work on his A.B. degree in 1925, he embarked on his graduate studies in English at Columbia—partly to keep up his trophy-winning track activities—and concentrated on medieval literature. In 1929 he obtained an M.A. degree for his master's thesis, "The Dolorous Stroke," which analyzed a motif from Sir Thomas Malory's *Le Morte d'Arthur*. On the strength of his thesis, he won a traveling Proudfit fellowship which took him first to the University of Paris in 1927–28, where he studied Old French and Provençal, and then, on scholarship renewal in 1928–29, to the University of Munich where, he told Donald Newlove, "the world opened up."

Ever since his boyhood excursions into folklore and world mythology, Joseph Campbell had been struck by the recurring legends of creation, fire-stealing, death and resurrection, fall and redemption, cosmic floods, virgin births, and mythic heroic journeys. That some of those widely dispersed themes were at the same time held as unique, sacred dogma by the Roman Catholic faith of his upbringing had early on posed "very serious problems" to the young Campbell; when, as a mature student, he encountered the Arthurian Holy Grail narratives, the "problems" took on earnest intellectual dimensions. In Europe, while discovering the art of Picasso and Matisse, reading James Joyce, studying Jung, Freud, Thomas Mann and the

ognized as one of the world's leading mythologists, Campbell has enlightened both scholarly and popular audiences for fifty years in his variegated career as writer, translator, editor, lecturer, and educator. Some admirers have even come to see him as a guru, a designation that Campbell rejects.

In Joseph Campbell's view, myths serve four functions: the psychological centering of the individual; the sociological harmonization of the individual with his community; the cosmological ordering of man's place in the universe; and the relation of the individual to the awesome *mysterium tremendum et fascinans* within himself and all things. For Campbell, articulation of those epic themes in the great stories of all cultures is essential for grasping the spiritual actuality beneath the rationalist dimensions of modern life. He sees that project as carrying us, not back to a longing for the primitive, but into the age of the global village, space exploration, and beyond.

In Campbell's opinion, this epoch holds the promise of a great release for mankind of a magnitude to compare with the development of stable agricultural civilizations thousands of years ago. According to him, the age of scientific research and the power-driven machine has revealed "that aspect of the wonder of the world most appropriate to our contemplation": actual individuals, not a pantheon of beasts or of superhuman celestials. Now "each individual is the center of a mythology of his own. . . . Each and every 'thou' on earth is the center of this world." Twentieth-century artists, poets, and philosophers such as Jung, Yeats, Pound, Eliot, Joyce, Mann, Picasso, Klee, and Spengler bear the fruits of that spirit, each "exploring the same 'dark wood,' each in his own direction." They embody and evoke in their work the modern "heroes" who need the courage "to holy books of Sanskrit, Campbell began to realize the direction that his own voyage would take for the next fifty years. That guiding idea, as he told Charles Leroux of the *Chicago Tribune* (January 19, 1984), is that "the commonality of themes in world myths [indicates] a constant requirement in the human psyche for a centering and a harmonization in terms of deep principles." Conceiving myth as "the pictorial vocabulary of communication from the source zones of our energies to the rational consciousness," Campbell determined to devote himself to its study. Pulled into that investigation by his omnivorous inquiries into the fields of archaeology, philology, philosophy, art history, religion, and psychology, his interest moved "far, far away" from where he was "supposed to be" in his academic pursuits. When Joseph Campbell returned to New York in the fall of 1929, he was "no longer in the Ph.D. bottle." As he told Newlove, "I had *much* more exciting things to do. . . . "

Greeted by the Wall Street financial debacle two weeks after his arrival in the United States, Campbell had "a long season of no jobs" that he used to assimilate his new perspective. He divided the next five years between Woodstock in New York and California. In Carmel he met John Steinbeck and his wife Carol and settled down for several months near them. At the Carmel public library he discovered Oswald Spengler's *Decline of the West*, an encounter that led him to Goethe, Schopenhauer, and Nietzsche. Later he sailed up the Alaskan coast with biologist Ed Ricketts. Campbell looks back upon his West Coast travels as a "glorious" time, during which he learned things that "gave life to [his] life." Although nobody would buy much of the fiction at which he tried his hand during that time, with the profits from one short story he did manage to sell he withdrew to the forest of Woodstock for fifteen months, where he rented "a little shanty, . . . lived on nothing, . . . and read and read and read."

In the academic year of 1932–33 Joseph Campbell taught at his alma mater, the Canterbury School. He next accepted an offer, in 1934, of a teaching post in the literature department of Sarah Lawrence College in Bronxville, New York, where he remained as a faculty member until 1972. His career as a mythologist bloomed in the early 1940s, with his commentaries in *The Complete Grimm's Fairy Tales* (Pantheon, 1944; Random House, 1972) and the first Bollingen Series volume, *Where The Two Came to Their Father; A Navaho War Ceremonial* (Pantheon, 1943), a creation myth text told by Jeff King and recorded by Maud Oakes. During that time Campbell met the noted German indologist Heinrich Zimmer at Columbia; their friendship became so close that, when Zimmer died in 1943, his widow asked Campbell to edit his papers. Beginning in 1946 with *Myths and Symbols in Indian Art and Civilization* (Pantheon; Princeton Univ. Press, 1971), he devoted part of the next twelve years to editing Zimmer's collected works, including *Philosophies of India* (Pantheon, 1951; Princeton Univ. Press, 1969) and *The Art of Indian Asia* (Pantheon, 1955; Princeton Univ. Press, 1960).

The literature of James Joyce had "grabbed" Joseph Campbell during his student days in Paris, where Sylvia Beach of the Shakespeare Book Shop instructed him in the art of reading *Ulysses*. He saw the first work-in-progress publications of *Finnegans Wake* and continued "puttering around" with that work for ten years. When the complete volume appeared in 1939, Campbell accepted the invitation of his Columbia friend Henry Morton Robinson to collaborate on an interpretive text tracing the "skeletal structure" and "majestic logic" within Joyce's great dream-saga. The two were convinced that the surreal, polylingual, unwieldy text of *Finnegans Wake*, largely regarded as a literary curiosity, might be the keystone of the creative arch that gave entrance to Joyce's entire oeuvre. During the four years that Campbell and Robinson spent in "busting" the book, they came to view it as "a mighty allegory of the fall and resurrection of mankind," its language "a compound of fable, symphony, and nightmare" emerging "from the shadowy pits of sleep."

As Campbell and Robinson explain it in *A Skeleton Key to Finnegans Wake* (Harcourt Brace, 1944; Penguin, 1977), Joyce, using Dublin as his world, weaves the legends of Irish and other folk heroes into the tragicomedy of his character H. C. Earwicker, whose public shame, ostracism, and cosmic dissonance exemplify the universal condition of original sin and the neurotic misease of modern man. Earwicker's wife, Anna Livia Plurabelle, is the animating psyche of the book: the circular river of life and Dublin's own river Liffey. In Joyce's telling of that tale, Campbell and Robinson read "a complete and permanent record of our age." Ignored by the prospective publisher until T. S. Eliot personally recommended it, *Skeleton Key* was hailed by critics as a welcome aid to bedeviled readers of *Finnegans Wake*. Joseph Campbell later contributed to *James Joyce: Two Decades of Criticism* (Vanguard, 1948).

Campbell's first book as sole author was *The Hero With a Thousand Faces* (Pantheon, 1949; Princeton Univ. Press, 1980), which seeks "to uncover some of the truths disguised . . . under the figures of religion and mythology." By comparative elucidation of the trials and triumphs of heroic figures found in American Indian, ancient Greek, Hindu, Buddhist, Mayan, Biblical, Nordic, and Arthurian legends—to name a few—Joseph Campbell traces the "monomyth": the classic hero's path of adventure as he or she undergoes the universal rites of passage, experiences which still challenge modern individuals, even as they "stand this afternoon on the corner . . . waiting for the traffic light to change." In such early sections as The Call to Adventure, The Crossing of the First Threshold, and The Belly of the Whale, he describes the hero's retreat from the world scene into the psychic underworld of "unsuspected Aladdin caves." In that night-realm the hero confronts his own deepest self and the obstacles of the ego that distort his own and his society's relation to the cosmic life pulsating within every part of the world. In the trials of such figures as the Buddha, Moses, Prometheus, and Aeneas, Campbell sees the breakthrough to direct experience and assimilation of what C. G. Jung has called "the archetypal images."

The transfigured hero, now a "master of two worlds," must return to workaday society, sharing there the boon he has secured: "visions, ideas, and inspirations . . . [that spring from] the unquenched source through which society is reborn," a new and radical understanding of the authentically human "freedom to live." Campbell's hope for the whole book, as he wrote in his introduction, was that it contribute to "those forces that are working in the present world for unification . . . in the sense of mutual human understanding."

In their mixed reviews, critics betrayed a certain puzzlement about Campbell's goals. While Max Radin of the New York Times (June 26, 1949) found the book to be interesting and stimulating, he deplored "the mystical and pseudo-philosophical fog of Jung" pervading it. The reviewer for the New Yorker (May 7, 1949) felt that Campbell had "fail[ed]" in [his] herculean task" but somewhat grudgingly praised the work as "one of the most fascinating and maddening books of the season." The Hero With a Thousand Faces won the National Institute of Arts and Letters grant in literature in 1949, and went on to become an American campus classic, eventually selling several hundred thousand copies.

While continuing to teach comparative literature at Sarah Lawrence and to write his own books, Joseph Campbell pursued his editorial career. He assisted Swami Nikhilananda in producing a translation of The Gospel of Sri Ramakrishna and oversaw a new edition of The Portable Arabian Nights (Viking, 1952). As editor of the series "Papers from the Eranos Yearbooks" he compiled five volumes, including Spirit and Nature (1954), Spiritual Disciplines (1960), and The Mystic Vision (1969). Campbell also edited The Portable Jung (Viking, 1972) and Rato K. Losang's My Life and Lives: The Story of a Tibetan Incarnation (Dutton, 1977). He became a visiting lecturer at the Foreign Service Institute of the United States Department of State, a function he performed from 1956 to 1973.

In 1959 the first volume of Campbell's magisterial series The Masks of God (Viking) appeared. Volume I: Primitive Mythology discusses the earliest paleolithic and neolithic symbols of the rudimentary repertoire of mythology. Campbell explores the role of the primal factors of experience, such as the cycle of night and day, the polarity of male and female, and the stages of human growth, in legends that set out to order that experience in the primitive hunting and planting societies. "The Birth of Civilization in the Near East (c. 7500–2500 B.C.)" concludes Primitive Mythology and serves as the starting point for Volume II: Oriental Mythology (1962). Here the distinct Eastern myth of eternal return and its goal of the quenched ego embedded in the "still point of eternity" are elaborated in Campbell's consideration of Hindu,

Buddhist, Taoist, and Confucian philosophies. The conflict of man and god or man and cosmos in Western thought appears absurd within those Asian systems—because "God" is "the mystery . . . of the ultimate depth of man's own being," a holy power at once transcendent and immanent. In Volume III: Occidental Mythology (1964) Campbell treats the devaluation of the early mother-goddess cult in the West in favor of a patriarchal myth structure, with important, and perhaps unfortunate, consequences for the conception of man as a responsible, judging individual in Greek philosophy, Judeo-Christianity, and Islam.

On the whole, critical reception of those studies welcomed Campbell's "splendid erudition" and the "intellectual adventurousness" of his "titanic effort" to formulate "the lineaments of a new science, a natural history of man's gods and heroes." Several reviewers, however, echoed one critic's complaint that Campbell's style of presentation, in need of "ruthless editing," "shift [ed] . . . uneasily between the popular-poetic and the scholarly-scientific," so that, according to the London Times Literary Supplement (August 26, 1960), "what precisely is being said is very difficult to grasp." But Campbell himself had acknowledged that his project was necessarily in the way rather of a prospectus than of a definition. Responding to similar criticism about the "vague and shadowy" Hero With a Thousand Faces, he has said, " . . . I wouldn't rewrite a line of the book—it might all come unraveled."

Creative Mythology (1968) forms the capstone of the series, both in its discussion of cultural developments since the Middle Ages and in its summing up of the implications of the mythological complex for modern humanity. In it, Joseph Campbell traces the death knell of the 5,000-year-old "monumental stage" of history—with its opposition of matter and spirit, its universe impelled to motion by superior beings, its Mount Olympuses, pyramids, and cathedral spires yearning up toward gods "out there"—in the new religious, artistic, and scientific spirit first sounded in the twelfth to fourteenth centuries. In theology, Peter Abelard's understanding of the crucifixion of Christ as a moment of mutual approach—crossing over—between God and man paved the way, according to Campbell, for Nicholas of Cusa's recognition of divinity as one's own transcendent essence. The scientific curiosity of Robert Grosseteste, Roger Bacon, and Nicholas Oresme, among others, and their reliance upon experience rather than authority in understanding the world, held out for the future, in Campbell's words, infinite promise. In those developments Campbell sees the dawn of our present period of "world culture," heralding "future against past, individual quest, and the sharp cut of 'proof' into the grip of 'faith.'" Gutenberg's printing press, global navigation, Copernicus' heliocentric universe, and Galileo's telescope were not far behind.

The Masks of God was followed in swift order by The Flight of the Wild Gander: Explorations in the Mythological Dimension (Viking, 1969), a gathering of essays that Campbell had written over the previous twenty-five years. In it he examines the psychological, sociological, and biological explanations of myth's origin and function, and discusses in detail a buffalo legend told by Black Elk, an Oglala Sioux medicine man. Reviewers commended Campbell's insight, graceful narration, and concise scholarship, all of which combined to "make the bones of folklore and anthropology live."

Campbell's editing of the massive *Myths, Dreams, and Religion* (Dutton, 1970) was succeeded by his *Myths to Live By*, which Viking published in 1972, the same year he retired as professor emeritus from Sarah Lawrence. *Myths to Live By* grappled with the apparent cultural impoverishment that attended the demolition by modern science of mythic belief structures. In a vein he would tap in other forums, notably in an interview with Eugene Kennedy for the *New York Times Magazine* (April 15, 1979), Campbell suggests that new myths may replace the old: symbols drawn from the splitting of the atom and, especially, from manned flights to the moon. That space-age adventure, "a re-enactment . . . of Prometheus' stealing fire from the gods," connects us back to a sense of awe and challenges us to go beyond horizons in our own experience: the sight of the "earthrise" over the lunar landscape, as photographed by the astronauts who walked there, showed that "there are no horizons. . . . There is a unity in the universe and a unity in [ourselves]." Widely commented upon, *Myths to Live By* prompted a *Time* essay (January 17, 1972) on "The Need for New Myths."

Joseph Campbell told Donald Newlove, "The day after I quit Sarah Lawrence . . . I boarded a plane to a conference in Iceland on altered states of consciousness and I've been on another course ever since." That course has involved, in part, lecturing at "human potential" institutes in Chicago, at Esalen in California, and elsewhere. Another product of Campbell's active retirement is *The Mythic Image* (Princeton Univ. Press, 1975), a book as much praised for its hundreds of spectacular illustrations as for its eloquent text. It presents the argument that the world's religions are basically one, as demonstrated by a comparison of visual art forms from many civilizations.

In appearance, Joseph Campbell has been described as "handsome . . . in the manner of an aging Shakespearean actor" and "tall as a hero, [with] the pale keen eyes of a hero." In 1938 he married Jean Erdman, a dancer and choreographer, to whom he taught aesthetics during his early years at Sarah Lawrence. Together the couple started the Foundation for the Open Eye, which sponsors lectures and "total theatre" productions combining music, dance, and drama, in New York City in 1972. After living for forty-five years in Manhattan's Greenwich Village, the Campbells have recently established a home in Honolulu, Hawaii.

As a lecturer in the United States and abroad, Joseph Campbell often meets people who tell him that their lives have been touched by his work.

Among them is the "Star Wars" director George Lucas, who has personally thanked him for the philosophical influence of his books. Campbell's current project is *The Historical Atlas of World Mythology* (Alfred van der Marck Editions/Harper & Row). *The Way of the Animal Powers*, the first installment of that proposed four-volume set, was published early in 1984. An "Outline of Everything" that he drew up many years ago in graduate school served as his ground plan for the series. By mapping the stages of culture, the project aims at a bold synthesis of the historical and biological schools of mythological study. Looking forward to its completion, Campbell has said, "I'm eighty . . . but you've got to live as though there were no time limit." His honors include Hofstra University's Distinguished Scholar award, which he received in 1973.

References: *Chicago Tribune* 1 p15+ Ja 19 '84 pors; *Esquire* 88:99+ S '77 pors; *N Y Times Bk R* p25+ D 18 '83 por; *N Y Times Mag* p14+ Ap 15 '79 pors; *Contemporary Authors* new rev vol 3 (1981)

© *1983 Martha Kaplan*

Caro, Robert A.

Oct. 30, 1936– Writer. Address: b. c/o Lynn Nesbit, International Creative Management, 40 W. 57th St., New York City, N.Y. 10019

As a muckraking reporter for *Newsday*, the Long Island, New York daily, in the early 1960s, Robert A. Caro became "interested in how power works." Out of that interest have come two panoramic political sagas, each seven years in the writing and both best-sellers. The first was *The Power Broker: Robert Moses and the Fall of New York* (1974), a biography of the unelected "master builder" who made himself the most powerful figure in the City and State of New York in our time. That work won the Pulitzer Prize for biography and the Society of American Historians' Francis Parkman Prize for the book "which best represents the union of the historian and the artist." The second was *The Path to Power* (1982), the first volume in a projected trilogy about the thirty-sixth president of the United States, *The Years of Lyndon Johnson*. Writing in the *Los Angeles Times*, Richard Eder saw in *The Path to Power* "Gibbon-like dimensions, Gibbon-like thoroughness too, and Gibbon-like passion . . . the base of a monument." The book won the National Book Critics Circle Award as the best nonfiction work of 1982.

Robert A. Caro may, as he believes, be descended from Joseph ben Ephraim Caro, the eminent Spanish-born sixteenth-century rabbinical scholar and codifier of Talmudic law. He was born in the borough of Manhattan, New York City, on October 30, 1936, the first of two sons of Benjamin Caro, a businessman who had emigrated from Lodz, Poland. Caro's American-born mother died when he was eleven. His father considered Caro's venture into non-salaried writing foolhardy and never encouraged him in it, but he was, Caro has said, "very happy" to find himself proved wrong. Benjamin Caro lived just long enough to witness the success of *The Power Broker*.

As a student at P.S. 93 in Manhattan, Caro started a school newspaper, and he spent many of his after-school hours in an Upper West Side branch of the New York Public Library. At Horace Mann High School in the Bronx he edited the school paper, and he was managing editor of the campus newspaper at Princeton University, where he majored in English. R. P. Blackmur, the late literary critic and poet, one of his teachers at Princeton, scolded him for writing too fast and facilely, as Caro recalled in an interview with Leo Seligsohn of *Newsday* (November 21, 1982): "'The trouble with you,' he said, 'is that you think with your fingers.' It struck a chord in me, and after I left the newspaper business, I consciously tried to slow my writing down."

After taking his B.A. degree at Princeton in 1957, Caro worked as a reporter for the *New Brunswick* (New Jersey) *Home News*. He also wrote political speeches for local Democratic candidates, a job that left him "disgusted" with politics. When he joined the staff of *Newsday* in 1959 he was, as he recalls, "very, very shy" and, according to an editor of the paper, "intense, goal-oriented, pegging to be number one." "I thought he would end up as publisher," the editor recounted to Leo Seligsohn. "I never anticipated that he would do what he did."

In his interview with Seligsohn, Caro recalled that his prolixity caused "constant fights" with editors at *Newsday*. To make his line counts look shorter, he tried such devices as narrowing the margins of his copy and leaving out words and in-

serting them later with carets, but the editors always "caught on." While incorrigible in his verbosity, he was otherwise a diligent apprentice in the craft of investigative reporting, taking to heart the admonitions of two successive managing editors, the late Alan Hathway and the late Al Marlens. "Never assume a goddam thing; you have to turn every page," was Hathway's caveat, Caro recalled. While Hathway taught him "what kinds of questions it was essential to ask," Marlens taught him that, despite his shyness, he "*had* to ask them."

Among the exemplary series of investigative reports Caro wrote for *Newsday*, two were especially outstanding: "Suffolk: The Sick Giant," a series about the negligence in county planning that resulted in exploitation of the land; and "Misery Acres," an exposé of interstate fraud in the selling of retirement tracts in Arizona. The latter series, to which Caro devoted a full half-year, won an award from the Society of Silurians, the journalism society composed of elders in the trade, and led to thirty-seven felony indictments and several corrective federal and state laws.

In covering urban issues for *Newsday*, Caro gradually became aware that "all roads led back to" Robert Moses (1888–1981), whose long reign as the unchallenged czar of public works development in the City and State of New York was then drawing to a close. Maneuvering from a variety of quasi-public positions (as many as twelve at one time), Moses controlled public works construction and urban planning in New York State for forty-four years (1924–1968) and in New York City for thirty-four years (1934–1968). Over that time he conceived and carried through an array of public projects without historical precedent, from dams and hydroelectric power plants on the Niagara and St. Lawrence rivers upstate through a state park system covering 2,567,256 acres and linked by 416 miles of broad parkway, to the relandscaping of New York City with eleven great new bridges, six swaths of expressway, and $267-million worth of urban renewal. He cleared slums, approved every inch of the public housing that altered Manhattan's East River skyline, created Jones Beach and hundreds of playgrounds, and was instrumental in the creation of the Coliseum, Shea Stadium, Lincoln Center, and Idlewild (now Kennedy) Airport. By the end of his career, he had been responsible for projects costing a total of $27 billion (1968 value).

While "Moses seemed to be the power behind every issue" that Caro looked into as a reporter, it was difficult for him to "learn much about the decision-making process" because "Moses' empire operated so secretly." He realized that it would be "impossible to show the influence he [Moses] had" except "on the scale of a book." His decision to go ahead with the book jelled when, on a leave of absence from *Newsday* in 1965–66, he was studying urban planning on a Nieman Fellowship at Harvard University. He recalled the moment of decision in an interview with Paul Goldberger for the *New York Times* (August 21, 1974): "I sat in lecture halls and listened to planners explaining how highways or housing was built, and I realized how ridiculous it was. Rational planning considerations have nothing to do with it—decisions were made for reasons far outside the planning process, like the hidden movements of banks, civic authorities, and politicians."

The following year, unable to "rest easy until [he] found out" the real story of "what shaped New York [and] Long Island, and the one man who had done it," Caro quit *Newsday* and began his research on Moses at Columbia University, supported by a one-year Carnegie Foundation fellowship. When he realized that the project was going to take much longer than a year, he and his wife, Ina, sold their house in East Hills, Long Island, she took a job teaching, and they moved into an apartment in the Riverdale section of the Bronx. "Ina worked, we used the money from the house, and I had a small advance," he recounted in the *Newsday* interview with Leo Seligsohn.

The advance, from Simon & Schuster, the first publisher Caro worked with, was minuscule because, as his editor at Simon & Schuster explained to him, "it's a great book but, after all, Robert Moses isn't going to sell because he's not very well known outside New York." After an abortive round with a second publisher, the manuscript finally caught the interest of Robert A. Gottlieb, president of Alfred A. Knopf, who "immediately and unmistakably knew he was in the presence of an extraordinary book," albeit one "that needed a tremendous amount of work."

Assisted by his wife—who tracked down farmers and homeowners dispossessed by Moses' bulldozers in the 1920s and 1930s and who also did the typing—Caro exhaustively researched city, state, and other records. After a long struggle, he gained access to some of the secret files of the Triborough Bridge and Tunnel Authority, which was the seat of Moses' power from 1946 to 1968. Between March 1, 1967 and February 3, 1972, Caro conducted 522 interviews, with persons ranging from Moses' relatives, old friends, and Yale University classmates to politicians and others who had worked with, for, or against him. Reluctantly, Moses himself submitted to seven interviews (actually "monologues," as Caro has described them) and then withdrew his cooperation and, as far as he could, that of his subordinates.

The finished product, published by Knopf in 1974, was *The Power Broker: Robert Moses and the Fall of New York*, a massive (650,000 words, 1,296 pages), colorfully detailed, meticulously documented tome. As told by Caro, the story of Robert Moses began with a young man of "passionate idealism . . . dedicating his life to public service." Entering New York City politics in the teens of the century as a crusader for civil service reform, Moses became a nuisance to the corrupt Tammany Hall machine, which, accordingly, crushed him. "When the curtain rose on the next act of Moses' life, idealism was gone from the stage," replaced by "an understanding that ideas—dreams—were useless without power." According to Caro, "Moses

spent the rest of his life amassing power, bringing to the task imagination, iron will, and determination. And he was successful. . . . With his power he shaped a city and its sprawling suburbs [and] influenced the destiny of all the cities of twentieth-century America."

The base on which Moses built his power, Caro pointed out, was one that had been overlooked by conventional politicians—the public authority ("a fourth arm of government"), which raises its own revenues and operates outside the electoral system. "With his power, Robert Moses built himself an empire . . . a single-headed, tightly administered monarchy [known to initiates as] 'Triborough.' . . . The wealth of that empire enabled Moses to keep many city officials in fear [and thus] to undermine the democratic processes of the largest city in the world, to plan and build its parks, bridges, highways, and housing projects on the basis of his whim alone."

In Caro's view, Moses bulldozed without sensitivity to people and neighborhoods; he rebuilt "with a lavish hand" for the rich and comfortable and "like a miser" for the poor; and he "systematically starved the subways and the suburban commuter railroads" while building his seemingly endless highways. Finally, he "systematically defeated every attempt" by others to create a rational master urban plan, "until it was too late." Thus, the bottom-line bequest of "America's greatest builder" has been Long Island's impossible suburban sprawl, the accelerated deterioration of the rapid transit system in the New York City area, and the glut of automobiles entering the city—a less humane metropolis than it once was, with massive public housing failures and parks and monuments that people are "afraid to travel to or walk around."

The immediate response to *The Power Broker* was heatedly mixed. However, even those critics who considered it "muckraking," "tendentious," "endlessly repetitious," or lacking in "historical perspective" for the most part admitted that Caro's skill at narration and his care in unraveling details from a complicated web of urban politics made it a "fascinating," "engrossing," "extraordinary" work, "uniquely thorough and perceptive in its examination of how power works," a source with which "the scholar who writes the history of American cities in the twentieth century will doubtless begin."

Among the unequivocally positive notices were those of Anthony Wolff in the *Saturday Review* of October 19, 1974 ("certainly the biggest and arguably the best" of "hard-core civics books") and Gore Vidal in the October 17, 1974 *New York Review of Books* ("If Robert Moses had not taken a house at Babylon, Long Island, the history of New York City might have been very different"). Now, with controversy a thing of the past, *The Power Broker* is regarded as a classic in its field. Its sales have steadily increased in the years since its publication, largely because it has become standard required reading in various college courses, from political science, history, and urban planning to psychology. "Nothing, not even getting the Pulitzer, makes me as happy as that," Caro has commented.

When he finished writing *The Power Broker,* Caro "quite logically" decided to begin a book on the late Lyndon Baines Johnson (1908–1973), the Democrat from Texas who rose from poverty to become a member of the United States House of Representatives, the majority leader in the Senate, and, finally, president (1963–1969). Having shown in *The Power Broker* "how power works in one city, with one man," Caro "wanted to show how *national* power works," and "at the national level Lyndon Johnson understood power better than anyone." "Nobody in history," he pointed out to Robert Cassidy in an interview for the *Chicago Tribune* (November 28, 1982), "has controlled the United States Senate—dominated it—the way Johnson did. No one had ever used power the way he did. If I could show exactly how Johnson got power and how he used it—and how it finally brought him to the tragedy that was Vietnam—then I would be showing how power worked at the national level in twentieth-century America."

When Caro began his research, he was an admirer of Johnson's unmatched "genius . . . for using political power for the benefit of poor people." "Sick of dealing with someone like a Robert Moses, who detested people," he thought he would find Johnson more sympathetic, "a man who was shrewd but whose driving motivation was to help the people he grew up with." That perception was to change radically. The more Caro immersed himself in Johnson's life, "the more apparent" it became "that alongside the thread of achievement running through [that] life runs another thread, as dark as the other is bright, and as fraught with consequences for history: a hunger for power in its most naked form." It also became more apparent "not only that this hunger was a constant throughout his life but that it was a hunger so fierce and consuming that no consideration of morality or ethics, no cost to himself—or anyone else—could stand before it."

To research the first volume of the Johnson biography, Caro and his wife moved to Austin, Texas. This time, Ina Jean Caro served as her husband's full-time assistant, helping him pore over the 32-million documents in the Lyndon Johnson Library, doing some of the interviewing, and typing up the notes. Using paper and pencil rather than a tape recorder (which, he found, made people too cautious in their statements), Caro interviewed more than 700 persons, including relatives of Johnson, boyhood friends, college classmates, politicians associated with him in his rise to power, and residents of Johnson's native hill country, a dirt-poor region that had no electricity until Johnson brought it there. To track down elusive details, Caro often crisscrossed the country by airplane. To understand the remote hill country and its people, the Caros lived there for three years.

At first, the subjects of the interviews were telling Caro "the rehearsed stories," the pap already filling other biographies. Within a year, "they opened up" to him, confessing that the complimentary stories about Johnson's childhood and young manhood "never happened." The resulting picture was that of a man "ashamed of his upbringing," running "from something so horrible that he would do anything to be successful." He "never could believe people liked, admired, or respected him," and he was "utterly ruthless in destroying obstacles in his path," with a "seemingly bottomless capacity for deceit, deception, and betrayal." The "qualities of character that emerged later—the credibility gap and so on—were shaped in his youth."

Despite all the work and difficulties, the writing of the first volume of *The Years of Lyndon Johnson* trilogy was for Caro "a thrilling, fascinating . . . adventure." *The Path to Power,* tracing Johnson's life up to 1941, made its debut in excerpts published in the *Atlantic Monthly* in 1981. The excerpts drew widespread cries of "hatchet job," but much of the controversy died down when the entire book, 882 pages long, with full documentation, was issued by Knopf in 1982. Many critics still considered the work a "hostile" and "long-winded" polemic, more a "caricature" than a portrait, but they were outnumbered by those who hailed it as a majestic landmark in American political biography and popular history, awesome in its scope and detail, passionate in its tone, and seamless in its narrative art, evoking an era while making almost palpable the likeness of an American giant. The historian Barbara Tuchman called it "superb and unique . . . meticulous in research, grand in scale," and Merle Miller, the biographer of President Harry S. Truman, described it as "a brilliant and necessary book," with "whole and fascinating areas of Johnson's life no one else discovered."

Poised but intense, Robert A. Caro exudes a restless energy but speaks in a mild, New York–accented voice. With his horned-rim glasses (often removed for photographs), his Ivy League wardrobe, and his carefully groomed dark hair, he is as meticulously neat in his appearance as he is in his writing, and the same is true of his work habits. Because "the only way to keep working all these years was to make believe [he] was going to a real office," he does his writing in a spartan, one-room office he rents on East Forty-first Street in Manhattan, half a block away from the New York Public Library. A fourteen-foot-long outline of work in progress covers one wall of the office, with numbers that refer him to his numbered files. The other walls are lined with some of the books that have influenced him: Edward Gibbon's *The History of the Decline and Fall of the Roman Empire,* Jane Jacobs' *The Death and Life of Great American Cities,* Theodore H. White's *The Making of the President, 1960,* Leo Tolstoy's *War and Peace,* and the works of Herodotus, Thucydides, Shakespeare, and Plutarch, among others. Caro writes his first drafts in longhand (to slow himself down) and types the final versions on one or another of several typewriters. His current work in progress is the second volume of *The Years of Lyndon Johnson.* Another of his books, *The Powers of the Press,* a novel set in Washington and Albany, with an investigative reporter as protagonist, has already been bought by Knopf.

Caro and his wife, who have a grown son, Chase, often entertain writer friends with gourmet meals at their home on Central Park West, and they spend vacations in a house they own in East Hampton. Caro's editor, Robert Gottlieb, describes him as "an obsessive worrier, an obsessive about facts . . . a very old-fashioned person, impassioned and moral, more like an Old Testament prophet." That view is seconded by Lee Koppelman, a Long Island regional planner who introduced him to the mysteries of zoning: "Bob is an idealist. He can seem almost ingenuous at times.

But if something or someone falls short of his expectations, then watch out. He becomes an avenging angel." When Caro unearthed the real Lyndon Johnson, the experience was not an exhilarating one, as he told Curt Suplee of the *Washington Post*: "Actually, it was very depressing. Anyone who thinks I enjoy writing such things doesn't understand me or what I am trying to do."

References: Chicago Tribune VII p1+ N 28 '82 por; *N Y Times* p30 Ag 21 '74 por, p34 My 6 '75 por; *Newsday* A p9 O 25 '74, p11 O 27 '74; *Newsday* mag p23+ N 21 '82 pors; *People* 19:31+ Ja 17 '83 pors; *Washington Post* B p1+ D 9 '82 por; *Contemporary Authors* vol 101 (1981)

Carver, Raymond

May 25, 1938– Short-story writer; poet. Address: b. c/o Alfred A. Knopf Inc., 201 E. 50th St., New York City, N.Y. 10022

When in 1976 Raymond Carver's first collection of short stories, *Will You Please Be Quiet, Please?*, was published, readers and critics were stunned by the power and economy of its prose and the unrelenting, even aggressive, ordinariness of its subject matter, which is strongly rooted in the details of his own life. The world that Carver depicts in his fiction and poetry is populated with inarticulate waitresses, motel managers, salesmen, housewives, and unemployed and drunken husbands unable to voice or even make sense of their anguish over broken marriages and failed lives. His minimalist restraint and searing honesty have brought him

considerable admiration and prestige. *Will You Please Be Quiet, Please?* was nominated for a National Book Award, and his next two collections of fiction, *What We Talk About When We Talk About Love* (1981) and *Cathedral* (1983), were greeted with almost unanimous praise, with the result that Carver has within a few years become one of the best-known short-story writers in the United States. The novelist and critic Robert Towers has hailed him as "one of the true contemporary masters of an exacting genre."

Raymond Clevie Carver Jr. was born on May 25, 1938 in Clatskanie, Oregon to Clevie Raymond and Ella Beatrice (Casey) Carver and grew up with his younger brother in Yakima, Washington, a small town where his father was a saw-filer in a local lumber mill and his mother occasionally worked as a waitress or as a retail clerk. Although his father's periodic bouts of drinking created a "sense of doom and hopelessness in the family," Carver enjoyed his company, especially when he read from the Bible or Zane Grey Westerns or related anecdotes about his grandfather's Civil War adventures. Carver credits those stories, sporting magazines like *Field and Stream*, and his love of hunting with awakening in him a desire to write. While still in high school, he studied writing through a correspondence course and sent his first attempt—a fishing story that his mother tapped out on a rented typewriter—to an outdoor magazine. "The piece came back, finally, but that was fine," Carver has recalled. "It had gone out in the world, that manuscript—it had been places."

After graduating from high school in 1956, Carver worked for six months at a sawmill in Chester, California, where his father was then employed, but he hated the job. He saved up some money, quit, and on June 7, 1957 married sixteen-year-old Maryann Burk, who was then already pregnant with the first of their two children. Since they had no money or marketable skills, the young couple had to struggle constantly to support their small family. "We didn't have any youth," Carver explained to Mona Simpson in an interview for the *Paris Review* (Summer 1983). "We found ourselves in roles we didn't know how to play. But we did the best we could. Better than that, I want to think." Maryann Carver was employed by the telephone company, and he worked nights at odd jobs, including delivery boy, gas station attendant, and janitor. During the day he attended college classes and tried to find the necessary time and privacy to write.

In the fall of 1958 Carver moved with his wife from Washington State to Paradise, California, where he attended nearby Chico State College. There he took an introductory course in fiction-writing with the late author John Gardner, who became one of the strongest influences on Carver's life and career. Gardner introduced him to the "little" literary magazines and patiently helped him to analyze his stories and develop his true voice. "He kept drumming at me the importance of using—I don't know how else to say it—common language, the language of normal discourse, the language we speak to each other in."

Carver transferred to Humboldt State College (now the California State University, Humboldt), where he obtained his B.A. degree in 1963. His work began to be published during his undergraduate years at Humboldt: his short story "Pastoral" appeared in Western Humanities Review, and his poem "The Brass Ring" was printed in Targets, a now defunct literary magazine. At the time of his graduation, he was urged to attend the University of Iowa's prestigious Writer's Workshop, both by Richard Day, an instructor at Humboldt who had himself studied at the workshop, and by John Gardner, who had received his Ph.D. from Iowa. Carver won a small grant from the University of Iowa but, unable to complete his studies because of lack of finances, returned with his family to Sacramento, California after only one year there.

For the next three years, Carver worked nights as a janitor at a Sacramento hospital and continued to write during the day. The year of 1967 proved to be a turning point in his life and career. He was hired as a textbook editor—his first white-collar job—at Science Research Associates, Inc., in Palo Alto; his short story "Will You Please Be Quiet, Please?," originally published in the Chicago-based literary magazine December, was selected for inclusion in Best American Short Stories, an annual anthology edited by Martha Foley; and he began to drink heavily. "There was always a wagonload of frustration to deal with" as a result of the demands of his growing children and the lack of freedom to write, he explained in his interview in the Paris Review. Carver added, in further explanation: "We were still in a state of penury, we had one bankruptcy behind us, and years of hard work with nothing to show for it except an old car, a rented house and new creditors on our backs. It was depressing, and I felt spiritually obliterated. . . . I more or less gave up, threw in the towel, and took to full-time drinking as a serious pursuit."

Despite Carver's alcoholism, his prospects as a writer brightened in the 1970s. He had of course already been published in such little magazines as Midwest Quarterly, but after Gordon Lish, an editor at Esquire, accepted his story "Neighbors" and two poems in 1971 for publication in that magazine, his work began to receive national attention. In 1970 Carver was fired from Science Research Associates, an event that ironically ushered in a "good period," to use his words, for him and his family. Living on his severance pay and unemployment insurance, he at last enjoyed the liberty to write, and his wife was able to complete her requirements for a college degree. His poems and stories continued to appear in literary journals as well as in such popular magazines as Harper's Bazaar. A second small-press edition of his poetry, Winter Insomnia (Kayak Press, 1970), and his first collection of short stories, Put Yourself in My Shoes (Capra Press, 1974), were also published during that time. (Near Klamath, his first volume of poems, had been issued in a limited edition in 1968 by Sacramento State College.) Perhaps most important, his year of enforced "leisure" had given him the necessary time to complete most of the twenty-two short stories included in Will You Please Be Quiet, Please?, the collection that established Carver's reputation as an insightful and powerful writer.

When McGraw-Hill published Will You Please Be Quiet, Please? in 1976, reviewers lavished praise on Carver's stripped-down and muscular prose style reminiscent of Hemingway's and his unsentimental and minimalist depiction of a world where financial problems, uneasy personal relationships, and unemployment are constants—a world very much like that of Carver's own experience. All his writings are grounded in autobiographical details to some extent, he explained to Mona Simpson. "But unless you're a special kind of writer, and a very talented one," he told her, "it's dangerous to write volume after volume on the Story of My Life. . . . A little autobiography and a lot of imagination are best." In "Neighbors," a representative story in the collection, a couple, the Millers, agree to take care of the apartment of their vacationing neighbors, the Stones, whom they envy. As the Millers begin to ape the Stones' lifestyle, going through their possessions, trying on their clothes, drinking their liquor, their lackluster marriage improves. But in their excitement, they leave their only key locked in the Stones' apartment, and in the last scene they hold each other in inarticulate despair at having to return to their own empty existence.

In her appraisal of the collection for Newsweek (April 26, 1967), Margo Johnson voiced the critical consensus: "Carver's stories are filled with glass-sharp details, images and conversations, meticulously arranged to unveil the pain, unhappiness and occasional horror that lie beneath the surface of the ordinary and banal. . . . With painful, funny acuteness, [Carver] captures the electric currents of misery and desperation that shoot through people's lives and singe them indelibly."

Most of Carver's poems also center on that "misery and desperation," especially as reflected in a person's relationships with those he loves. In

"Marriage," for instance, Carver gauges the pressures upon characters in a television show a recently married couple are watching "and the destruction/ they must know lies in store just after/ the next cruel turn of circumstance, and then the next"—facts of life of which, Carver implies, the happy newlyweds are as yet unaware but that will nevertheless inevitably affect them as well. His poems were often published in little magazines, and in 1971 he was a National Endowment for the Arts fellow in poetry. Nevertheless, Carver eventually decided to concentrate his energies on fiction while remaining "an occasional poet."

In the eight brief pieces that make up *Furious Seasons* (Capra Press, 1977) and in *What We Talk About When We Talk About Love* (Knopf, 1981), his next two collections of short stories, Carver was again concerned with the seemingly commonplace events that are actually turning points, often terrifying ones, in people's lives. Again he used a laconic prose style and a paucity of detail in developing his narratives, and again almost all of the reviews were glowing, especially those of the latter volume. Like some other critics, Gary L. Fisketjon in his review for the *Village Voice* (September 18, 1978) commended Carver for being "neither patronizing nor sentimental" in creating characters. Writing in the *San Francisco Review of Books* (May-June 1981), Michael Koepf went even farther in his praise, contending that Carver's distinctive short stories represented a "new wave" in fiction: "He gives us pathos and satire without black humor, simplicity of craft juxtaposed with complexity of emotion." David Kubal, however, complained in the *Hudson Review* (Autumn 1981) that he felt "imposed upon by a monotony of tone, theme, and structure" in the seventeen stories in *What We Talk About When We Talk About Love*, concluding that the collection was "touching, perhaps, but not very moving or cogent—particularly after the seventeenth time."

In spite of his growing literary celebrity, Carver continued to be plagued by alcoholism. Shortly after the publication of *Will You Please Be Quiet, Please?* and *At Night the Salmon Move* (Capra Press, 1976), his third collection of poetry, his drinking nearly killed him. In 1976-77 he moved in and out of alcoholism recovery centers, suffering from blackouts and depression, and was hospitalized several times. His relationship with his family also deteriorated, and by May 1977 he was living alone. (He and Maryann Burk were divorced in October 1982.) But in June of that year, after his fourth hospitalization and with the help of Alcoholics Anonymous, he managed to stop. "If you want the truth," he told Mona Simpson, "I'm prouder of that, that I've quit drinking, than I am of anything in my life."

When *Cathedral*, Carver's fifth volume of stories, was published by Knopf in the fall of 1983, most reviewers noted that with the improvement in his own circumstances Carver seemed to have found a more upbeat, even forgiving, voice than he had previously used in his fiction; true epiphanies

had become possible for his characters, a concession he had never made before. Furthermore, the eighteen stories collected in *Cathedral* were, by Carver's own admission, more "generous": "There was an opening up. . . . I knew I'd gone as far the other way as I could or wanted to go, cutting everything down to the marrow, not just to the bone. Any farther in that direction and I'd be at a dead-end—writing stuff and publishing stuff I wouldn't want to read myself."

Often cited as particularly indicative of the change in Carver's style is "A Small, Good Thing," a revision of an earlier story. In "The Bath," the original version, the child Scotty is hit by a car on his birthday and dies in a few days, though he had been expected to recover fully. The local baker repeatedly phones his shocked and grieving parents, demanding that they pick up Scotty's birthday cake, and the story ends equivocally with one of those nagging, almost taunting, calls. In the revised version the angry parents confront the lonely baker, who was unaware of their son's death. Remorseful and at the same time glad for their company, he gives the couple some rolls, for "eating is a small, good thing in a time like this." Although that simple action does not diminish the tragedy, it offers a measure of comfort, an element rarely found in Carver's earlier stories. In his review of *Cathedral* in the *Washington Post's Book World* (September 20, 1983), Jonathan Yardley concluded that Carver "is a writer of astonishing compassion and honesty, utterly free of pretense and affectation, his eye set only on describing and revealing the world as he sees it. His eye is so clear, it almost breaks your heart." *Cathedral* enjoyed an almost unprecedented level of success for a short-story collection: it sold over 20,000 hardcover copies, was nominated for the National Book Critics Circle award for fiction, and was named one of the best thirteen books of 1983 by the *New York Times*. His most recent book, *Fires* (Capra Press), a collection of previously published essays, poems, and short stories, was also issued in 1983.

In January 1983 Carver became, along with Cynthia Ozick, the first recipient of the Mildred and Harold Strauss Livings award, a renewable, tax-free stipend conferred by the American Academy and Institute of Arts and Letters that provides $35,000 a year for five years. Carver's many other honors and awards include a Wallace Stegner fellowship (1972-73) and fellowships from the National Endowment for the Arts (1971 and 1980) and the Guggenheim Foundation (1979-80). *Will You Please Be Quiet, Please?* was nominated in 1977 for a National Book Award and his short stories, often anthologized, have won O. Henry awards in 1974, 1975, and 1980.

Raymond Carver has been a visiting lecturer at the University of California (Santa Cruz) in 1971-72, the University of Iowa's Writer's Workshop in 1972-73, and the University of Texas (El Paso) in 1978-79. He has also taught on the faculty of Goddard College in Vermont (1977-78) and was a professor of English at Syracuse University for three years. He resigned his professorship in 1983 as a condition for receiving the Strauss Livings award.

According to Mona Simpson, Carver is a "large man who wears simple clothes—flannel shirts, khaki slacks or jeans." He has bushy hair and eyebrows and "a remarkably low and indistinct voice." Carver and Maryann Burk's children, Christine LaRae and Vance Lindsay, are now grown. He shares a home in Port Angeles, Washington with the poet and short-story writer Tess Gallagher. When writing his stories, which are often constructed around chance remarks he overhears or situations he observes, Carver works through many drafts and has said that though finishing the first draft is difficult he thoroughly enjoys the process of revision. He does not believe that fiction has to bring about personal, moral, or social change to be worthwhile: "It just has to be there for the fierce pleasure we take in doing it, and the different kind of pleasure that's taken in reading something that's durable and made to last, as well as beautiful in and of itself. Something that throws off these sparks—a persistent and steady glow, however dim."

References: Paris Review 25:193+ Summer '83 por; Saturday Review 9:21+ O '83; Contemporary Authors 1st rev vols 33-36 (1978); Contemporary Literary Criticism vol 22 (1982); Who's Who in America, 1984-85

Castelli, Leo

Sept. 4, 1907– Art dealer. Address: b. Leo Castelli Gallery, 420 W. Broadway, New York City, N.Y. 10012

"I don't pick painters because they seem to be good, but because they seem to be leaders of a new movement," Leo Castelli has said in articulating the credo that has made him one of the most influential American art dealers of the twentieth century. In the late 1950s Castelli began exhibiting and promoting to international significance avant-garde works that helped to expand the boundaries of late modern art and to define the aesthetics of the post–abstract expressionist period. The Castelli Gallery roster reads like a Who's Who of contemporary artists, and includes such names as Jasper Johns, Robert Rauschenberg, Andy Warhol, Roy Lichtenstein, Ellsworth Kelly, Claes Oldenburg, James Rosenquist, Donald Judd, Sandro Chia, and Robert Morris, among others.

Although he is certainly the dealer-of-choice for any reasonably ambitious painter or sculptor, as well as the prototype for aspiring young dealers, Castelli denies that it lies within his power to "make" an artist. Instead, he views his responsibility, as he told Josh Greenfield in an interview for the *New York Times Magazine* (May 8, 1966), as "the myth-making of myth material. . . . I have to deal with myths from 10 A.M. to 6 P.M. every day. And it becomes harder and harder. We live in an age of such rapid obsolescence."

According to Leo Castelli, he was born on September 4, 1907 in what Josh Greenfield described as "another era—in Trieste under the flag of the old Hapsburg Empire." His name at birth was Leo Krauss, after his father, Ernest Krauss, who had moved to Trieste from Hungary, married into one of that city's oldest families (the Castellis), and risen to the influential position of director of an Austrian bank. But in 1919, when Italy annexed Trieste, he adopted the family name of Krauss-Castelli, and eventually the hyphenated form was dropped in favor of the Latin surname.

The middle child of well-to-do, socially prominent parents, Castelli had a sister, Silvia, and a brother, Giorgio, four years his junior. His mother, though kind and intelligent, was aloof, and Leo felt closer to his sister and to his father, a warm man who, when he had time, involved himself in family affairs. Brilliant and cultivated in the Old World manner, Ernest Krauss was "very bent on giving [his children] a good, solid, disciplined education," as Castelli told Meryle Secrest of *Artnews* (Summer 1982). But despite the high standards his father set for him and the educational advantages of his superior social position, Leo Castelli was in some aspects a poor student, who found mathematics particularly difficult.

As if to compensate for his disappointing scholastic record, Castelli absorbed languages with what Meryle Secrest called "terrifying ease: first

Greek and German, then French." Moreover, he received a thorough education in the history of premodern art and at the age of about fifteen began to read widely in French literature. (He already had been introduced to the German Romantics by his father.) Castelli also began to haunt a Trieste bookshop where he could buy contraband works by contemporary foreign writers, since the fascist government of Benito Mussolini had made such publications virtually unobtainable.

One of the books he got from under the counter was the Bloomsbury critic Clive Bell's *Since Cézanne*, an analysis of postimpressionism that was of crucial importance to Castelli, whose formal study of art had ended at the mid-nineteenth century. "I read helter-skelter, . . . " he told Meryle Secrest. "I read Freud. . . . I wanted to be the perfect Renaissance man." And had Castelli not been inhibited by his father's conventional bourgeois expectations, he might have become a writer or an artist himself. Instead he studied four years at the University of Milan, from which he received a law degree in 1924. He then returned to Trieste where his father found him a job with a large insurance firm. Somewhat ruefully, Castelli has said of those years, "I was adventurous in my spirit, but not in my deeds."

For much of the next decade Castelli enjoyed the life of a "playboy on a limited string," as he admitted during the *New York Times Magazine* interview. To realize his Renaissance-man ideals, and also, perhaps, to overcome the insecurities he seems to have felt in his youth over his slight physical stature, he became an expert mountain climber and skier. It was a "very pleasant" life, Castelli recalled for Calvin Tomkins, author of *Off the Wall: Robert Rauschenberg and the Art World of Our Time* (1980), "with lots of pretty girls, and tennis, and swimming, and things like that."

In 1932 Castelli's insurance company transferred him to Bucharest, Romania, where he fell in love with Ileana Schapira, the eighteen-year-old daughter of Mihail Schapira, one of the country's wealthiest industrialists. Leo Castelli and Ileana Schapira were married in 1933 and, sharing an interest in modern art, they honeymooned in Vienna, where they acquired their first artwork, a Matisse watercolor. In 1937, with the aid of his father and father-in-law, Castelli secured a job in Paris with the Banca d'Italia. There he and Ileana met the leading surrealist painters of the day—Salvador Dali, Max Ernst, and Eugene Berman, among others—and in the spring of 1939 Castelli and René Drouin, an architect and designer of art deco furniture, opened a gallery on the Place Vendôme. Their first exhibition, a surrealist group show, was a spectacular social success that attracted the *beau monde* of Paris. The owners closed the gallery for the summer and went on vacation, but in September France declared war on Germany, and the gallery did not reopen. Drouin joined the army and Leo and Ileana moved to her father's villa in Cannes.

In 1941 the Castellis made their way to New York City, having escaped by means of what Castelli called "very complicated routes through Algeria, Morocco, and Spain" after the German invasion of France in June 1940. They took up residence near Fifth Avenue, at 4 East Seventy-seventh Street in a townhouse owned by Schapira *père*, who had fled Europe ahead of his daughter and son-in-law. Until 1943, when he was drafted into the United States Army, Castelli took graduate-level courses in history at Columbia University. Assigned to military intelligence, in 1944 he returned to Bucharest, where he was responsible for maintaining contact with the anti-Nazi underground. Because of his Army service, he was granted United States citizenship.

After World War II Castelli's father-in-law set him up in the sweater manufacturing business in New York's garment district, but the still restless Castelli now knew that his true passion was collecting modern art. Through contacts with René Drouin, who had reopened his Paris gallery, and Sidney Janis, then one of New York's few dealers in avant-garde painting, he began to dabble cautiously in the risky art market, purchasing works by Jackson Pollock and Willem de Kooning and assisting in the occasional sale of such European masters as Joan Miró and Paul Klee. Castelli began spending most of his time visiting galleries and artists' studios, and at the Museum of Modern Art "gave himself what he considers his real education," to quote Calvin Tomkins.

In 1951 Castelli helped to finance the Ninth Street Show, a landmark exhibition of sixty-one works by sixty-one artists that both documented and celebrated the abstract expressionist achievement. By virtue of his enthusiasm for the new American art, he was elected to membership in the influential Painters' Club, the focal point of activities for the rising New York School. Until then, Leo and Ileana had been mainly regarded as collectors, but artists were beginning to ask more and more frequently, "When is Leo going to open his own gallery?"

Their question was answered in February 1957 when the Castellis quietly opened a small gallery in the living room of their apartment on East Seventy-seventh Street, where they at first dealt in such established masters as Fernand Léger, Pollock, and de Kooning and a few little-known abstract expressionists of the second generation. However, recognizing earlier than most dealers that abstract expressionism had run its course, Castelli was looking for original work that would chart a new course in contemporary art—and in the spring of 1957 he had what he now describes as his "first great epiphany." At a museum show of work by younger artists of the New York School, Castelli was, in his words, "thunderstruck" by a painting titled *Green Target* by an unknown named Jasper Johns.

A few days later, while visiting the loft-studio of Robert Rauschenberg, Castelli chanced upon the twenty-seven-year-old Jasper Johns, who occupied the studio one floor below. There Castelli discovered Johns's now-famous paintings of flags and targets, an experience that the bedazzled art dealer has compared to "seeing the treasures of Tutankhamen." In Johns's coldly representational paintings of commonplace objects, which strongly influenced pop artists of the 1960s, and Rauschenberg's combine-paintings, with their assemblage of such unlikely relics as stuffed goats, car tires, old quilts, and castoff clothing, Castelli had found what he was searching for—work that was, in his words, "entirely fresh and new and not related to anything else."

Johns's exhibition at the Castelli Gallery in January 1958, followed by the attention-getting but much less sensational Rauschenberg show three months later, hit the New York art world like a bombshell. There were sales to the Museum of Modern Art, a reproduction of a Johns painting on the cover of *Artnews*, and general recognition that Rauschenberg and Johns were the first important contemporary artists to break with abstract expressionism. Moreover, Leo Castelli overnight became known, to quote Secrest, as "a prescient spotter of new talent."

In 1959 Castelli moved his gallery to more spacious quarters on the second floor of 4 East Seventy-seventh. That year he also had what he calls "another great epiphany" when he saw the work of Frank Stella, a young unknown fresh out of Princeton who was supporting himself by working as a house painter. Stella, too, was reacting against abstract expressionism, producing austere and impersonal canvases of precisely ruled black stripes that anticipated the minimalist styles of the mid-1960s. Castelli unhesitatingly offered Stella a monthly stipend of $300, which enabled him to devote himself full-time to art. Within a year, Stella was considered the most important young New York painter to emerge since Johns and Rauschenberg.

In 1961 Castelli and his assistant, Ivan Karp, a street-wise young dealer with contacts throughout the underground art circles of lower Manhattan, discovered the work of Roy Lichtenstein. Lichtenstein's canvases were blowups of panels from comic strips—romance comics, with speech balloons narrating the melodrama of love-gone-wrong, and war comics, with exploding fighter planes and "macho" dialogue—that helped to launch the pop art movement. By 1964 Castelli and Karp had taken on such avatars of the pop sensibility as James Rosenquist, whose work was in the style of Times Square billboards, and Andy Warhol, whose unforgivingly realistic paintings of Campbell's soup cans and Coca-Cola bottles made him the art world's first authentic "superstar" since Pablo Picasso and Salvador Dali. As a result, Castelli came to be regarded as a Svengali-like figure responsible for the art movement that eclipsed abstract expressionism.

Although instantly embraced by collectors and gallery-goers, pop was derided by serious critics like Clement Greenberg, who dismissed it as "an episode in the history of taste" rather than of art.

And Castelli himself was belittled in some quarters as an intellectual lightweight whose tenacious obsession with fashion and novelty had short-circuited the careers of second-generation abstract expressionists. (Willem de Kooning, for example, had bitterly complained that "you could give that son of a bitch two beer cans and he could sell them." Inspired by the remark, Jasper Johns made a now-iconic painted sculpture of two Ballantine Ale cans, which Castelli promptly sold to a leading collector of pop art.)

Castelli answered his detractors by arguing that art is to be found in the work of artists, not in the oracular pronouncements of critic-theoreticians. "Painting is what it is," Castelli told Josh Greenfield, "what artists make of it. One has to accept what painters do. One does not have to like it, but one cannot discard it; one can lament a certain fashion, but one . . . just cannot say: 'This is not art, it will go away.' Who decides what is art? . . . Not I. Certainly not I. . . . There are those unsuccessful abstract expressionists who . . . accuse me of killing them; they blame me for their funerals. But they were dead already. I just helped remove the bodies."

By the middle of the decade the art boom of the 1960s was fully underway, and attendance at a Castelli Gallery opening was *de rigueur* for not only trendy art aficionados but critics and museum curators as well. Keeping pace with new developments, in 1965 Castelli added to his stable Donald Judd and Robert Morris, leading minimalist sculptors who carried the spareness of Frank Stella's painting into three dimensions. By the early 1970s the Castelli Gallery had consolidated its preeminence in the field of contemporary art by representing such minimalist innovators as Dan Flavin, Richard Serra, Bruce Nauman, and Richard Artschwager and conceptual artists like Joseph Kosuth and Robert Barry.

In 1971 Castelli opened a new gallery at 420 West Broadway in the downtown Manhattan art district known as SoHo, where, nine years later, he opened at 142 Greene Street a vast (4,500 square feet), white-walled expanse for the exhibition of large-scale work. But in the decade of the 1970s the avant-garde seemed to have run out of ways to titillate or even bewilder a public weaned on a steady succession of ever-newer, more dazzling styles, and the Castelli Gallery appeared to be almost indifferent to the discovery of ground-breaking art. In fact, however, Castelli was waiting for what Secrest called "that indefinable moment when an artist's work will not only look excitingly different, but point in the right direction," and in the early 1980s he took on four new painters. These were Julian Schnabel (who left the Castelli Gallery in 1984), David Salle, Sandro Chia, and Gérard Garouste, leading young artists of the neo-expressionist movement that has revived interest in the painting of the human image and in psychological narrative.

Castelli attracts artists primarily because of his unsurpassed ability to sell their work and to promote it on an international scale. He was one of the first American dealers to insist upon wide European exposure for his artists, a tactic that paid off handsomely in 1964, when Rauschenberg became the first American to win the Venice Biennale's coveted international grand prize in painting. Castelli has also impressed artists by assembling an elite gallery staff that is considered one of the New York art world's best and brightest. (Three former Castelli assistants have founded their own SoHo galleries: Janelle Riering, co-director of Metro Pictures; Ivan Karp, owner of the O.K. Harris Gallery; and David Whitney, who operated the now defunct David Whitney Gallery.)

Castelli's success can also be attributed to his generosity. In addition to the regular monthly stipends he pays his artists (against sales, which he splits on a 50-50 commission basis with some artists and on a 60-for-the-artist, 40-for-the-gallery basis with others) even when their work is not selling, he absorbs all promotional costs and foots the bill for artists' materials. For example, when Castelli discovered Richard Serra in 1967, he offered a guarantee of three years of monthly payments, even though he expected to sell none of the unknown young artist's lead-plate sculptures during that time. "I never expected to find anyone willing to support experimental work," Serra told Meryle Secrest. "It was like getting a Rockefeller grant. Leo has always been generous, supportive, intimate and friendly, a throwback to another century." But, as Josh Greenfield pointed out, "generosity also creates dependency." "Those monthly checks are deadly—and degrading," a former gallery artist confided to Greenfield. "Leo's holding on to you piece by piece."

Despite Castelli's international fame and influence, he is not a wealthy man. He owns valuable early works by Warhol, Rauschenberg, Lichtenstein, and Johns, but can no longer afford the prices his blue-chip artists command, which can range from $30,000 for a large canvas by David Salle to $400,000 for a billboard-sized Rosenquist. From the beginning, Castelli has plowed profits back into what is a formidably expensive operation—two large gallery spaces, a staff of eighteen, and regular stipend disbursements, all of which add up to a monthly overhead of about $200,000. Although the gallery grossed almost $3 million in 1981, it was until very recently a "giant shoe-string operation," according to the gallery's bookkeeper. Moreover, the Castelli Gallery now functions as a quasi-cultural institution with extensive archives that are consulted by art writers, curators, and collectors.

Leo Castelli has been described by Calvin Tomkins as "an engaging blend of European elegance and American enthusiasm." With his seemingly inexhaustible reserves of energy, he has retained the wiry mountain-climber's physique of his youth, and his angular, sharp-featured face "seems, like that of Cocteau, designed to be seen in profile," to quote Secrest. Impeccably dressed, fluent in five languages, possessed of exquisite manners, conversant in music and literature, Castelli is the epitome of Continental sophistication.

It is not surprising, then, that Castelli's charm makes for highly effective salesmanship. "He doesn't want to mention the dirty word 'money,'" painter Freidl Dzubas said of Castelli's soft-sell approach. "People feel he is giving them something special. And he is. Imagine: they come to a man to spend $10,000 and he doesn't want to talk about the $10,000 at all. So they talk around; they talk as layman to layman, as fellow art lover to fellow art lover, as gentleman to gentleman. It's all very flattering—and effective—and deceiving."

Leo and Ileana Castelli were divorced a few years after the opening of their gallery. She then married a Parisian named Michel Sonnabend and in 1962 started her own gallery, the Sonnabend, with branches in Paris and SoHo. After what Ileana termed a brief "cooling-off period," she and Castelli resumed their friendship and became close business partners again. In 1974 they formed Castelli-Sonnabend Tapes and Films, which sells and rents video-art and films by plastic and conceptual artists.

In the early 1960s Leo Castelli wed Antoinette Fraissex du Bost, who in 1969 opened Castelli Graphics, a separate gallery for the exhibition of prints and graphics. Leo and Antoinette ("Toiny") Castelli live in a modest-sized Fifth Avenue apartment overlooking Central Park; the furnishings are eclectic, ranging from a seventeenth-century French chair to a Lichtenstein-designed table and paintings by Johns and Rauschenberg. Their son, Jean-Christophe, who attends Harvard University, has literary ambitions. From his first marriage, Castelli has a daughter, Nina Sundell, who in the late 1960s and early 1970s was copartner of the New Gallery in Cleveland, Ohio.

References: Artnews 81:66+ Summer '82 pors; Life 68:71+ My 1 '70 pors; N Y Times Mag p34+ My 8 '66 pors; Town & Country 129:206 N '75 por; de Coppet, Laura and Jones, Alan. The Art Dealers (1984); Tomkins, Calvin. Off the Wall: Robert Rauschenberg and the Art World of Our Time (1980); Who's Who in America, 1984-85

Chernenko, Konstantin U(stinovich)

(châr nyen´ kō)

Sept. 24, 1911- General Secretary of the Communist Party and Chairman of the Presidium of the Supreme Soviet of the USSR. Address: b. Central Committee of the Communist Party, 4 Staraya Ploshchad, Moscow, USSR

Described in the London Observer (February 19, 1984) as "the first Siberian to lead the Soviet Party and the first true peasant to rule in the kingdom of the proletariat," Konstantin U. Chernenko is the oldest man ever to be elected general secretary of the Communist party of the Soviet Union. For

Konstantin U. Chernenko

years kremlinologists dismissed him as no more than Leonid Brezhnev's "political valet," but Chernenko showed his mettle after his mentor's death. Although he lost both the struggle for party leadership to Yuri Andropov and subsequently his important post in the General Department of the Central Committee, he nevertheless survived to succeed Andropov as head of the Soviet Union. In a country where bureaucrats who have fallen out of favor recede into permanent political oblivion, Chernenko's accession to power is remarkable. Many experts credit his rise not to his administrative abilities, which are lackluster, but to a last-gasp effort by the gerontocracy to retreat from Andropov's somewhat radical reforms before the younger generation of technocrats assumes leadership. That Chernenko will remain only a caretaker leader is not yet certain, however. Soviet expert Dimitri Simes, writing in *Time* (February 27, 1984), warned: "We overestimated Andropov. The danger now is to underestimate Chernenko."

Konstantin Ustinovich Chernenko was born on September 24, 1911 in Bolshaya Tes, a tiny village in the Krasnoyarsk region of Siberia. Although official biographies state that Chernenko is an ethnic Russian, his Ukrainian surname suggests that his parents may have been among the many Ukrainian peasants who settled Siberia in the early 1900s. His family was large and impoverished, and his mother died while he was still a child. In order to earn his living, he had to leave school at the age of twelve to work for a *kulak,* one of the wealthy Siberian peasant farmers soon to be liquidated under Joseph Stalin's collectivization program.

But in spite of his bleak early life, Chernenko's prospects soon improved. As he has recounted in his preface to his *Selected Speeches & Writings* (Pergamon, 1982), when he was a teenager "new

Soviet life was coming into its own," and stirred by "its fresh winds," he joined the district branch of Komsomol, the Young Communist League, in 1926. Although he and his fellow members were very poor, he claims that the promise held out by Communism of "a radiant future for all fascinated [them] and made [them] feel happy." By 1929 he was in charge of the local Komsomol's agitation and propaganda, or "agitprop," activities, which the London *Observer* (February 19, 1984) described as "the crudest form of Communist political education."

In 1930 Chernenko joined the Border Guards, with whom he spent three years fighting anti-Communist rebels and smugglers along the Sino-Siberian border. Although he claims to have volunteered to fight in the front lines, he did not serve in World War II, during which more than twenty million Soviet citizens were killed. Since he is the first Soviet leader not to have fought in that war—a fact that some of his compatriots, especially in the military, hold against him—the Soviet press has recently embroidered upon his service in the Red Guard, praising his expert marksmanship, among other skills. Nevertheless, by Russian standards his military experience is meager.

But if he is to be found wanting in military exploits, Chernenko leaves nothing to be desired as a devoted party member. He joined the Soviet Communist party (CPSU) in 1931 while still in the Guards and was soon appointed secretary of a frontier-post party cell. After his discharge from the army, he was rapidly promoted from head of agitprop activities in the Novoselovo and Uyar districts to director of the Krasnoyarsk regional house for party education and finally to deputy head of the agitprop department of the Krasnoyarsk territory. Further details about his career during the 1930s are scanty, but analysts have speculated that his work consisted of writing propaganda justifying Stalin's campaign to liquidate the *kulaks*. In an article for *Die Zeit* (February 17, 1984), Christian Schmidthäuer reported rumors that Chernenko himself took an active part in that bloody purge.

By the time the Axis countries invaded the Soviet Union in 1941, Chernenko had become secretary of the Krasnoyarsk territorial party committee, and for two years he remained in that post to supervise such home-front activities as the relocation and adaptation of industrial plants for military purposes. In 1943 the CPSU Central Committee sent him to its Higher School for Party Organizers in Moscow, where he spent the remainder of the war, graduating in 1945. That program and a correspondence course from the Kishinev Pedagogical Institute, which he completed in 1953, constitute the sum of his formal higher education.

After the war, Chernenko was elected to the Penza regional party committee, and from 1948 to 1956 he served as chief of the agitprop department of the Moldavian Republic, one of the fifteen republics that make up the Soviet Union. Two years after Chernenko arrived in Moldavia, he met a man who would profoundly change his life: Leonid

I. Brezhnev. Sent to bring that unruly southwest territory firmly under Stalin's control, the handsome and personable Brezhnev would seem to have had little in common with the awkward peasant's son. Yet the two formed a strong bond, and Chernenko is said to have served First Secretary Brezhnev well as propaganda chief. Through Brezhnev, Chernenko first gained a foothold in the Moscow bureaucracy.

The bureaucracy in the Soviet Union is made up of the government and the Communist party. All de facto power resides in the CPSU, which determines official policy on foreign and domestic affairs and the economy. Although within the CPSU the Congress, consisting of elected representatives from all local party organizations, theoretically wields the most authority, the Politburo actually sets policy, and the Secretariat runs day-to-day party affairs. Selected delegates from the Congress constitute the Central Committee, which elects the members of the Secretariat and the Politburo. Membership in both of those top two CPSU bodies is considered a prerequisite for becoming general secretary, the most powerful position in the Soviet Union. The Supreme Soviet of the USSR, the Council of Ministers, and the Presidium of the Supreme Soviet comprise the government, which carries out CPSU-set policy. The Council is the actual executive body of the Supreme Soviet, but the chairman, or president, of the Presidium is the nominal head of state.

Brezhnev, who was transferred back to Moscow in 1952, temporarily fell into disfavor after Stalin's death in 1953. But when he was restored to candidacy membership in the Politburo and to the Secretariat in 1956, he used his influence to help the so-called "Dnepropetrovsk mafia," a group of apparatchiks in Moldavia, including Chernenko, who had linked their careers to Brezhnev's during his tenure there. Brezhnev engineered Chernenko's appointment as chief of the Central Committee's mass agitation work sector, a propaganda position, in Moscow, and when in 1960 Brezhnev became chairman of the Presidium, he promoted Chernenko to chief of staff of that body. In 1965, soon after he replaced the deposed Nikita S. Khrushchev as general secretary, Brezhnev appointed Chernenko head of the important General Department of the Central Committee, the duties of which are to act as a secretariat for the party apparatus, field complaints from citizens, and handle classified documents.

In spite of his increasing prominence in the party hierarchy, Chernenko exercised power primarily by virtue of his closeness to Brezhnev. As chief of the General Department, he kept the general secretary's appointment book, thus controlling access to the head of the party. Moreover, his position in the General Department made him privy to vital information about individuals and events that he used to his and his mentor's advantage. Brezhnev relied heavily on Chernenko's phenomenal memory for detail, referring to him as "my notebook." More ominously, Chernenko's peers dubbed him "the man who never forgets." The two men were personally as well as politically close; they lived in the same Moscow apartment building, where they met nightly in Brezhnev's kitchen for parlays, and even took family vacations together. As Brezhnev's health deteriorated in the late 1970s, he came to depend more and more on his trusted aide. Party members and foreign diplomats grew accustomed to seeing Chernenko at the old man's side, turning up his hearing aid and doling out the daily ration of cigarettes allowed the ailing leader by his doctors. An underground Soviet joke summed up the prevailing view of their relationship: "Brezhnev has been dead for quite some time, but Chernenko hasn't told him."

His role as Brezhnev's political lackey rendered it improbable that Chernenko was being groomed to succeed his mentor, but during the 1970s unmistakable signs clearly indicated that, with Brezhnev's blessing, Chernenko was making a bid for power. After a five-year candidacy, he became a full member of the Central Committee at the Twenty-fourth Party Congress (1971), and in 1976 he was appointed to the CPSU Secretariat. In the following year, he was elected a non-voting, or candidate, member of the Politburo. On his attainment of full membership in the Politburo in 1978, he became not only the youngest person ever to hold full membership in both the Secretariat and the Politburo but also one of just four other men, including Brezhnev, who then held seats in those top two bodies of the CPSU. As a result of his unprecedentedly rapid rise to a position of leadership, foreign diplomats and political analysts asserted that Chernenko was solidly in contention to succeed Brezhnev as general secretary. His increasingly prominent part in such important diplomatic missions as the strategic arms limitation negotiations with the United States, which resulted in the 1979 SALT II Treaty, reinforced that impression.

Nevertheless, Andropov ultimately won the power struggle to become general secretary after Brezhnev's death on November 10, 1982. Chernenko's succession evidently was blocked by a coalition of anti-Brezhnev forces, including the armed services, the KGB, and the diplomatic corps. Dissatisfaction with the Brezhnev regime—whose promised economic and political stability had given way to stagnation—had been growing for years. Fearful that the failing economy and the growing corruption of officials and workers were undermining the nation's defense capabilities, Andropov's backers wanted a new broom that would sweep clean.

In the first few months of his regime, Andropov launched a vigorous attack on inefficiency and corruption. He purged about 20 percent of the provincial party secretaries, most of whom had supported Brezhnev, jailed corrupt officials, and improved worker discipline by cracking down on absenteeism and alcoholism in the nation's factories and offices. Even members of the party elite were subject to Andropov's reforms: Chernenko was dismissed from his strategic position as head of the General Department, although as a sop to the Brezhnevites he was given Andropov's former duties as party ideologist. But Andropov's housecleaning drive soon faltered as his chronic and eventually fatal kidney disease sapped his strength. Also, his "radical" economic policies, which emphasized economic decentralization and monetary incentives for high production, predictably generated enormous uneasiness and resentment among the still powerful party gerontocracy, most of whom had been recruited under his predecessor. In that tense political climate, Konstantin Chernenko's abilities as a capable if unspectacular administrator and his adherence to the traditional party line as exemplified by Brezhnev seemed more and more attractive to the elders of the CPSU. As Andropov weakened, Chernenko became increasingly visible. That he had once again become a force to be reckoned with was confirmed on November 7, 1983, when he stood in for the ailing general secretary at the annual parade commemorating the 1917 Bolshevik Revolution.

On February 13, 1984, four days after the death of Yuri Andropov, Konstantin Chernenko was named general secretary of the Soviet Union, the oldest man ever to win that post. Because of the extreme secrecy that surrounds Kremlin politics, the exact circumstances leading to his election are not known, but Sovietologists reasoned that the entrenched old guard saw in him a welcome opportunity to delay the inevitable rise to power of the young technocrats promoted under Andropov, most notably Mikhail S. Gorbachov and Grigory V. Romanov, and to return to the comfortable stability of the Brezhnev era. Perhaps as a concession to the technocrats for their support of Chernenko, Gorbachov was given the duties of ideologist. As a result, at fifty-three he became the number-two man in the bureaucracy and the most likely successor to the present general secretary. Although Gorbachov's promotion may suggest a new order in the making, at present the Soviet Union under Chernenko seems headed for "a few years of Brezhnevism without Brezhnev," to quote Russell Watson of Newsweek (February 27, 1984). Already signs abound of a return to pre-Andropov moral standards: Moscow policemen once again are openly taking bribes, and several Brezhnevite officials, who under Andropov were imprisoned for corruption, have had the charges against them dropped.

By April 1984, Chernenko had assumed two important additional posts: the chairmanship of both the Presidium and the Defense Council, a highly secretive body that, under the authority of the Politburo, directs the armed forces. Some experts nevertheless asserted that his election to the presidency represented a political convenience for the party—the de facto leader could then take on the protocol duties of head of state—rather than a true consolidation of power. As probably the least experienced general secretary the Soviet Union has ever had, he openly defers to the more seasoned

politicians and diplomats Foreign Minister Andrei Gromyko and Defense Minister Grigory Ustinov. Dusko Doder of the Washington Post (April 15, 1984) described Chernenko's position as a passive "chairman of the board," with Gromyko and Ustinov "being given wide discretion within their own areas."

Chernenko's profound conservatism, as enunciated in his speeches and writings, and his cautious policy statements lend weight to that conclusion. In his major speeches since his election in February, he has launched no radical domestic initiatives and has made clear through implication that Andropov's more drastic reforms, including economic decentralization, monetary incentives, and credit systems, have been abandoned. He has, however, suggested a greater role for unions in economic planning, a trimming of the bureaucracy, better, more productive soviets (local administrative councils), and the use of opinion polls to stay in touch with the public. He also advocated educational reforms that would raise teachers' salaries, extend formal schooling by one year, and upgrade vocational training. While such mild proposals have placated his fellow bureaucrats, some Soviet citizens have expressed to foreign correspondents their concern that with the abandonment of Andropov's anticorruption measures and innovative planning the economy will stall once again. After interviewing a number of Russians, Dusko Doder asserted in the Washington Post (February 19, 1984) that "Chernenko may be the most unpopular man ever elected general secretary."

On foreign policy issues, Chernenko also shows no signs of deviating from previous policies. Although he has made some peaceful overtures to the United States, Chernenko, like the Kremlin leadership generally, is deeply suspicious of the Reagan administration. Reiterating standard Soviet policy, he has refused not only to return to the disarmament talks, broken off in November 1983, until the United States removes its medium-range nuclear weapons from Western Europe, but also to ban chemical weapons or to reduce conventional forces in Europe. He insisted in his first major speech after his election that the Soviet Union advocated "a peaceful settlement of all disputable international problems" through negotiations, but he added that "we will see to it that our country's defense capacity be strengthened, that we should have enough means to cool the hot heads of militarist adventurists." Relations with the United States have remained glacial, and the announcement on May 8, 1984, of a Soviet boycott of the summer Olympic Games to be held in Los Angeles only exacerbated tensions. However, a meeting between Foreign Minister Gromyko and President Reagan on September 28, 1984 and Soviet offers to discuss the limitation of space-based weapons systems may signal the beginnings of a thaw.

Fueling doubts about Chernenko's chances of becoming more than a stopgap chief executive are rumors about his possible illnesses. Although at first he appeared tanned and healthy in public appearances, medical experts, noting his labored breathing, have assumed that he is suffering from emphysema, a chronic lung ailment that causes shortness of breath and often leads to heart disease. Furthermore, his two extended absences from public view in 1983 and a two-month absence in the summer of 1984 are thought to have been imposed by health problems. One source suggested that he had had a lung removed last year. His age is also a cause for concern: at seventy-two, he has already lived ten years beyond the average life expectancy of a Russian man. Since it ordinarily takes a Soviet leader three to four years to secure enough power to launch significant initiatives of his own, Chernenko may not rule long enough to accomplish very much.

No Soviet leader has been so thoroughly dismissed by Western observers as Konstantin Chernenko. Not mincing words, the former United States ambassador to the Soviet Union, Malcolm Toon, has called him a "dullard" and a "colorless bureaucrat," and recent speeches, in which Chernenko has mumbled and stumbled his way through prepared texts, have heightened the West's poor impression of him. Nevertheless, a few analysts insist that he must be taken seriously. Peter Wilsher, writing in the London *Sunday Times* (February 19, 1984), cautioned that "no political weakling ever gets to the top—let alone holds his place—in the brutally competitive Russian political system." Stalin and Khrushchev, he pointed out, were also dismissed as "faceless nonentities" when they first took office. In an article for *Time* (February 27, 1984), William E. Smith concurred, explaining that Chernenko has a "shrewdness, a sort of Soviet equivalent of street smarts," that makes him far from negligible. "The question now," Smith concluded, "is whether a man with so firm a hold on the past will be able to embrace the future."

Chernenko was named to the editorial board of *Agitator* in 1956, and he has written a number of monographs on current issues. His many honors include the Order of Lenin, awarded to him several times; the Order of the Red Banner of Labor, awarded to him three times; the Order of Karl Marx (1979), East Germany's highest honor; the Gold Medal of Hammer and Sickle; and Czechoslovakia's Order of Klement Gottwald. He is also a Lenin Prize laureate.

As with most Soviet leaders, little is known of Chernenko's personal life. His wife, Anna Dmitrievna, is said to love the theatre and cinema, and she arranges private screenings of Soviet movies for the Kremlin wives. Their son Vladimir is an executive in Goskino, the state filmmaking organization. Their daughter, Yelena Konstantinova, has a Ph.D. degree and works for the Institute of Marxist Leninism in Moscow. Sources say Chernenko may have another son, named Albert, from an earlier marriage, who does propaganda work in the Siberian city of Tomsk. The short, stocky Chernenko has bright blue eyes, slanting Asiatic cheekbones, and a shock of white hair. He is invariably seen in dark, baggy suits. Kremlin insiders say he is an even-tempered man who nonetheless cannot abide insincerity or, as he puts it, "barrels with false bottoms."

References: *Christian Science Monitor* p1+ F 15 '84; *London Observer* p9 F 19 '84 por; *N Y Times* p1+ F 14 '84 por; *Newsweek* 103:28+ F 27 '84 por; *Time* 123:28+ F 27 '84 por; Chernenko, Konstantin. *Selected Speeches and Writings* (1982); *International Who's Who, 1984–85*

Childs, Lucinda

June 26, 1940– Choreographer; dancer; actress. Address: b. c/o Performing ArtServices, Inc., 325 Spring St., New York City, N.Y. 10013

Lucinda Childs's spare and orderly dances have both mystified and mesmerized audiences for more than a decade. Like other so-called "post-modern" choreographers, Miss Childs sees dance as pure form. Her dances are mathematical explorations of geometric shapes, and her dancers are expressionless, genderless instruments who etch the intricate patterns on the floor in precisely timed, repetitive sequences of relatively simple steps. The development of Miss Childs's career, from its beginning in the now legendary Judson Dance Theater in 1962, paralleled the development of minimalist art, although the choreographer herself has taken issue with those critics who describe her work as minimalist. In her view, each of her dances is simply "an intense experience of intense looking and listening." In addition to performing with her troupe, the Lucinda Childs Dance

Company, Miss Childs has appeared in the avant-garde opera *Einstein on the Beach,* in two Off-Broadway plays, and in the films *Jeanne d'Iman,* by the South American director Marie Jiménez, and *21:12 Piano Bar.*

Lucinda Childs was born in New York City, New York on June 26, 1940, the daughter of Edward Patterson Childs, a physician, and his wife, Lucinda Eustis (Corcoran) Childs. As a little girl, Miss Childs dreamed of becoming an actress. She appeared regularly in student productions throughout her school years, and when she was about eleven she began to take drama lessons. It was at the suggestion of her acting coach that the youngster, who was, by her own admission, "clumsy, shapeless and on the heavy side," enrolled in a dancing class. Among her early teachers were Hanya Holm, the dancer and choreographer who introduced the Wigman system of modern dance instruction to the United States, and Helen Tamiris, the Broadway choreographer. Pleased with her pupil's progress, Miss Tamiris eventually asked the girl to perform onstage. After that exhilarating experience, as Miss Childs told Sally Banes years later in an interview for the book *Terpsichore in Sneakers: Post-Modern Dance* (1980), she "wasn't sure [she] even wanted to be an actress anymore."

Following her graduation from high school, Lucinda Childs entered Sarah Lawrence College, where she majored in dance. There her dance instructors included Bessie Schonberg, Judith Dunn, and, occasionally, Merce Cunningham, whose experiments in isolated movements so fascinated her that she took additional classes at his New York studio during college vacations. After receiving her B.A. degree in 1962, she continued her modern dance studies with Merce Cunningham and, from 1963 to 1965, with James Waring. She kept up her classical ballet training too, first at the American Ballet Center, then, from 1964 to 1968, with the former ballerina Mia Slavenska.

At Merce Cunningham's studio, Miss Childs met Yvonne Rainer, an iconoclastic choreographer whose work had a strength and simplicity that especially appealed to Miss Childs. Recognizing a kindred spirit, Miss Rainer asked the young dancer to join the fledgling Judson Dance Theater, an experimental troupe, cofounded in 1962 by Miss Rainer and Steve Paxton, dedicated to expanding the dance vocabulary to embrace natural "non-dance" movements. In addition to dancers and choreographers, the group included composers, painters, and sculptors. Within a few months of its establishment, the Judson Dance Theater—so named because it performed at the Judson Memorial Church in Greenwich Village—had become the showcase for experimental dance in New York City.

During her four years with the Judson Dance Theater, Miss Childs performed in dozens of works by Miss Rainer, James Waring, Steve Paxton, and Robert Morris, among others, and created thirteen pieces of her own, most of them solos relating common domestic objects or spoken monologues to movement. In *Pastime* (1963), for example, she sat on a table and manipulated a tube of stretchable fabric with her legs, and in *Geranium* (1964), she physically interpreted and played off the sounds of a taped broadcast of a professional football game.

Street Dance (1964) is probably the most famous of Miss Childs's journeyman compositions. Performed on a street in lower Manhattan, the dance was observable only to the small group of spectators clustered around the windows of an artist's loft overlooking the road. During the course of the six-minute piece, Miss Childs and another dancer alternately blended in with the daily bustle on the street or pointed out shop-window displays or unusual architectural details in the facades of the surrounding buildings. A synchronized taped description of the street-level view explained the two dancers' actions to the audience above. According to Sally Banes, writing in *Terpsichore in Sneakers,* *Street Dance* "extended the definition of dance." In *Vehicle,* a similar but infinitely more complex work created in collaboration with technicians and engineers from Bell Labs for the "Theatre and Engineering" series at the 69th Regiment Armory in New York City in October 1966, Miss Childs and two other performers responded to and interacted with stationary and moving objects, various sound and light sources, and a sonar beam that translated movement into sound.

Toward the end of the decade, Miss Childs, feeling that she had, in her words, "played out [her] ideas," decided to put her "Judson period" behind her and, as she told Ellen Jacobs in an interview for the *SoHo News Weekly* (November 3, 1977), "work outside of a conceptual frame." From 1968 until 1973, she experimented on her own, studied visual arts and education, and polished her classical technique at the Ballet Arts Studio and the Viola Farber Dance Studio. She received her M.S. degree in education from the City College of New York in 1971. To defray expenses during those years, she modeled, taught elementary students in the New York City public school system, conducted workshops in dance technique and composition, served as a guest teacher in choreography at the School of Visual Arts in New York, and contributed articles on dance to such publications as *Dance, Artforum,* and *Drama Review.*

Eventually, Miss Childs discovered in her solitary choreographic explorations a streamlined geometric structure and a bare-bones movement idiom that seemed perfectly suited to her increasing interest in the "time-space" element of a performing art. "I moved into a new world of throwing out all the tricks, getting rid of all the objects and monologues—all the things that aren't dance—and seeing what was left," she explained to David Sterritt of the *Christian Science Monitor* (September 26, 1983). "I started to work with very basic things like walking and turning. I went back to a very simple vocabulary and found a new world opening up for me. It felt infinite." As "a way of dealing with something [she] wanted to keep alive," Miss Childs formed her own company of five dancers, including herself, in 1973.

On December 7, 1973 Miss Childs presented her new company and her new works at a sold-out concert at the Whitney Museum of American Art in New York City. Clad in loose trousers over leotards and wearing sneakers (Miss Childs likes the "plucked feel" of sneakers against a bare wood floor), the dancers executed the four new pieces—Calico Mingling, Particular Reel, Checkered Drift, and Untitled Trio—in silence, their sole accompaniment being the rhythmic patter of their feet. Of those works, the most successful, at least in the eyes of the rather bemused and skeptical critics, were Particular Reel, a solo in which Miss Childs walked and twisted her way through an invisible maze, and Untitled Trio, a three-part dance in which all the performers repeated simple movements over and over again as they traced intricate geometric patterns on the floor. Jennifer Dunning, a dance critic for the New York Times, was especially taken with Untitled Trio. "A relentless intelligence informs Miss Childs's conceptual dances," she wrote in her review of December 11, 1973. "Phrases are repeated in combinations varied by timing, direction, sequence, and the amount of space covered. The combinations are ordered with mathematical precision and, at times, complexity. It is as if dance notation had been turned into dance."

In a handful of recitals over the next few years, Miss Childs attracted a sizable cult following and gained the admiration of the fringe press, whose dance reviewers described and dissected each new work at length. The most influential establishment critics, however, remained largely unimpressed. Arlene Croce, for one, found little to her liking in a 1975 concert featuring, among several new pieces, the walk-duet Duplicate Suite and Reclining Rondo, a flowing, almost lazy exploration of the constantly changing relationships among three dancers as they move along a diagonal. Writing in the April 21, 1975 issue of the New Yorker, Miss Croce remarked, "What made Childs's walk dance interesting (minimally speaking) was nothing organic to the dance itself; it was, rather, that Childs is a striking-looking woman with a beautiful head."

Critics have often commented on Lucinda Childs's transfixing presence on stage. Her uncanny ability to attract and hold an audience's attention undoubtedly contributed to her success as a featured performer in the Robert Wilson–Philip Glass opera Einstein on the Beach, an ambitious, multilayered work built around spectacular visual effects. Miss Childs, who also appeared later in the piece as the droning trial witness, opened Einstein with a riveting walking solo of her own composition that, according to Jennifer Dunning, has taken its place in dance history as "a supreme moment of modernist theatre." Through slight changes in posture and gesture, Miss Childs seemed to assume a variety of characters—a buffoon, a drunk, a pedant, among others—as she advanced and retreated along her diagonal path. For her inspired performance in Einstein on the Beach at the Metropolitan Opera House in November 1976, she won a Creative Artists Public Service Award and an Obie Award.

The following year, Lucinda Childs used physical movements to underline or contradict the emotional tone of her lines in an Off-Broadway production of I Was Sitting on My Patio This Guy Appeared I Thought I Was Hallucinating, Robert Wilson's chamber piece consisting of back-to-back recitations of the same forty-five-minute monologue by two actors, in this case, the author and Miss Childs. Although reviewers disliked the play in general and the "staginess" of Wilson's reading in particular, most of them had kinder words for Miss Childs, whose "refreshing" approach "provided valuable insight into what one could do with a dramatic situation which is subtle almost to the point of extinction," as Richard Philip observed in his comment for Dance (September 1977).

The dancer-actress fared less well when she opened in June 1982 in a Manhattan Theatre Club presentation of The Singular Life of Albert Nobbs, Simone Benmussa's play, based on a short story by George Moore, about two impoverished women who masquerade as men in order to earn a living in mid-nineteenth-century Ireland. The majority of the New York theatre critics thought that Miss Childs's impersonation of the house painter Hubert Page was "unconvincing," primarily because she betrayed her femininity "in every move and gesture," according to the Village Voice's Michael Feingold.

The late 1970s was an especially productive period for Lucinda Childs. In addition to her theatrical appearances, she created a number of new dances, among them Cross Words (1976), a walking solo embellished with pivot turns and hitch kicks; Radial Courses (1976), for a quartet of dancers moving in four overlapping orbits; the intricate straight-line solo Katema (1978); Interior Drama (1977), a buoyant dance for five performers that would have reminded one critic of "a Charlie Chaplin version of a minuet" if it had not been performed so solemnly; and Melody Excerpt, a spiderweb of shifting configurations occasionally reminiscent of an old-fashioned square dance. When Miss Childs introduced some of those new dances in a concert at the Brooklyn Academy of Music's Lepercq Space in November 1977, sharp-eyed critics noticed a more elaborate style and a more complicated "derangement," to use Sally Banes's word, of the carefully ordered movement systems.

For years Lucinda Childs had created her dances to be performed in silence, but after working on Einstein on the Beach, she decided to choreograph to music. Having obtained production funds from the National Endowment for the Arts and the New York State Council on the Arts, she began, in the summer of 1978, collaborating with Philip Glass, the composer, and Sol LeWitt, the conceptual artist, on a full-length piece for ensemble and solo dancer. To complement Glass's mixed instrumental and vocal score, she incorporated into her customary vocabulary of simple movements some more virtuosic steps borrowed from the classical ballet idiom and interspersed spare solos with more intricate group pieces. LeWitt's contribution to the project was a black-and-white film of the dances, which was projected on a scrim at the front of the stage so that the performers, visible through the scrim, seemed to interact with their ghostly, larger-than-life images.

Dance, which had been commissioned by Harvey Lichtenstein, the director of the Brooklyn Academy, had its premiere at the Brooklyn Academy of Music's Opera House on December 1, 1979 before an unusually hostile audience. Many spectators booed loudly or walked out. Although the critics conceded that the piece was "beautifully executed" and "visually ravishing," few could muster any real enthusiasm for it. Most of them agreed with David Sterritt, who concluded in the *Christian Science Monitor* (December 31, 1979), "It was an invigorating evening, yet a vaguely stuffy one. You could sense extremism passing into establishmentarianism, right under your nose."

Lucinda Childs's full-length works are specifically designed for proscenium stages in large theatres because she finds the so-called "alternative spaces" favored by many post-modernists to be limiting. She develops her dances slowly, "by improvisation and inspiration," as she put it, in the studio with her dancers. To keep track of the complicated, precisely timed and counted individual movement sequences and the larger spatial patterns, she carefully notates her dances as she makes them, using colored pencils to plot each dancer's steps and paths on a grid. It may take her a year or more to create a new piece, and collaborative efforts, such as *Relative Calm*, a ninety-five-minute dance that she made with Robert Wilson and the avant-garde composer Jon Gibson, and *Available Light*, the joint work of Lucinda Childs, composer John Adams, and architect Frank O. Gehry, take even longer.

Commissioned for the 1981 Festival D'Automne in Paris, France, where it was wildly applauded, *Relative Calm* was given its American premiere at the Brooklyn Academy of Music's "Next Wave" dance festival in December 1981. Although the basic repetitive movement designs were similar to those Miss Childs had employed in *Dance*, critics and audiences alike found the cool, airy *Relative Calm* to be more accessible than the earlier piece, at least partly because of its myriad variations in steps, timing, and speed. Perhaps its most intriguing section was "Reach," Miss Childs's skipping solo along a diagonal, punctuated by an almost imperceptible increase in the frequency and speed of turns.

A commission of the Museum of Contemporary Art in Los Angeles, California, *Available Light* was an entry in the Brooklyn Academy of Music's "Next Wave" series in October 1983 before it moved on to a standing-room-only engagement at the Théâtre de la Ville in Paris. Taking full advantage of the two-tiered wooden scaffold set Frank Gehry had designed for her, Miss Childs set her dancers moving with and against each other vertically as well as horizontally. According to Anna Kisselgoff of the *New York Times* (November 6, 1983), *Available Light*, which is the least symmetrical and the most balletic of Lucinda Childs's dances, represents "not only a major breakthrough in Miss Childs's career but a major work altogether." The balletic influence can also be seen in Miss Childs's pristine *Mad Rush*, which she recently choreographed for the Paris Opéra Ballet.

A stunning woman with the lean, elongated figure, pale skin, and chiseled bone structure of a high-fashion model, Lucinda Childs has almond-shaped, blue eyes and dark hair, which she usually wears pulled severely back into a tight knot. Interviewers have found her difficult to approach on a personal level, but she willingly discusses her work and the future of the post-modern dance movement. As for her own future plans, she told Alan M. Kriegsman of the *Washington Post* (October 25, 1981), "I'd like to keep dancing for awhile. The truth is, I feel I *must* dance, even if eventually it isn't onstage." Miss Childs is the recipient of several awards and honors, including grants from the Foundation for the Contemporary Performance Arts, in 1968, and the Creative Arts Public Service, in 1974 and 1977, and a fellowship from the National Endowment for the Arts in 1974. The dancer lives in her studio in the SoHo section of New York City.

References: N Y Times C p1+ D 18 '81 por; Sat R 9:34+ Mr '82 por; Washington Post L p1+ O 25 '81 por; Banes, Sally. Terpsichore in Sneakers (1980); Livet, Anne, ed. Contemporary Dance (1978); McDonagh, Don. The Complete Guide to Modern Dance (1976); Who's Who in America, 1984–85

Cleese, John

Oct. 27, 1939– Writer; actor. Address: b. 8 Clarendon Rd. London W.ll, England

Recognized throughout the world as the bureaucratic Minister of Silly Walks, as the frustrated customer in the cheese shop, and for other zany characters from BBC-TV's *Monty Python's Flying Circus*, John Cleese is a prominent member of the six-man team of writers and actors that gave birth to that satiric series in 1969 and, in so doing, overturned the conventions of comedy. With the other *Monty Python* creators, Cleese drew record crowds to the weekly half-hour show on BBC-TV and then on American public television; made several successful films; and recycled material from the shows in spinoff books, records, and personal appearances. With his first wife, Connie Booth, he

John Cleese

Broadway Square East. He remained in New York City to appear briefly in the role of Young Walsingham in the British musical *Half a Sixpence,* which opened at the Broadhurst Theatre on Broadway in April 1965. Returning to England, he made his television debut in 1966 as a writer and performer with David Frost's weekly BBC comedy show, *The Frost Report.* Here Cleese began to shape the character that was described in a profile in *Options* (July 1983) as "the prototype [of the] Englishman—poker-faced yet potentially manic."

Cleese's stint on the Frost show was followed by appearances on commercial television with Frost script editor Marty Feldman, the late comedian, in *At Last the 1948 Show,* and by several minor film roles. He played a public relations man in *Interlude* (Columbia, 1968), a romance starring Oskar Werner; and he appeared in two large-cast comedies of 1970: *The Rise and Rise of Michael Rimmer* (Warner/David Frost), with Peter Cook; and *The Magic Christian* (Commonwealth United/Grand Films), based on the Terry Southern novel and featuring Peter Sellers, Ringo Starr, Spike Mulligan, and Yul Brynner. But Cleese's comic talent hit its stride when he and fellow Cambridge comics Graham Chapman and Eric Idle teamed up with Oxford alumni Michael Palin and Terry Jones and the American cartoonist Terry Gilliam to create *Monty Python's Flying Circus.* A breakneck barrage of satiric skits, surreal cartoons, and antic non-sequiturs, *Monty Python,* directed by Ian MacNaughton, entertained a weekly BBC audience of as many as 10 million for several successful years, beginning in 1969.

Diverting mass audiences by lampooning just about everyone's sacred cows and by profaning many an ikon, the Python sextet extracted its humor from outrage, irreverence, wild exaggeration, and the sort of incongruity exemplified by their depiction of "Hell's Grannies," a terrorist gang of old ladies. As noted in *Image* (February 1975), "the trademark of a Python sketch is a lack of a punch line. Instead of building up to a climax a sketch might simply be dropped in midstream to make room for another." But the show's chaotic style and seemingly gratuitous barbs reflected a dissatisfaction with things as they are. "We all feel strongly that the world is in a mess," Cleese told Scott Thornton of the *Washington Post* (January 14, 1973).

The Monty Python sextet was introduced to the United States in 1972, when episodes from the television series were brought over in the form of a Columbia film, *And Now for Something Completely Different.* The film included such now-classic segments as transvestite lumberjacks breaking into song; an "Upper Class Twit of the Year" competition; the pet shop skit in which an irate Cleese recites a string of euphemisms for death as he returns a dead parrot; and the cheese shop skit in which Cleese's requests for cheeses are answered with ridiculous excuses for why none are available. Although Howard Thompson of the *New York Times* (August 23, 1972) found the Python humor "as dead

wrote and costarred in the BBC-TV comedy series, *Fawlty Towers,* and with the psychotherapist Robin Skynner he collaborated on a book on family relationships. Cleese has staged benefit revues, appeared in several comedy films, produced radio commercials, and created award-winning business training films. A restless comic artist whose manic humor is bound to his conviction of the senselessness of life, Cleese has created a comic persona that mocks the hypocrisy, pomposity, and repressed resentments he finds endemic in his native England.

John Marwood Cleese was born on October 27, 1939, the only child of Reginald and Muriel Cleese, in the Bristol Bay community and seaside resort of Weston-super-Mare, where his father sold insurance. In later years, Cleese would use the name of his birthplace as an adjective denoting the uptight middle-class British manners and assumptions he delights in savaging in his comic sketches. Six feet tall by the time he was twelve, Cleese turned to humor as a weapon of self-defense. "[I was] a weedy, timid kid with no way whatsoever of fading into the background," he told Lee Langley of the *Guardian* (December 19, 1975). "I think I found making people laugh was a way of . . . keeping things going."

Cleese attended Clifton College in Bristol and taught history there for two years, and then went on to Downing College, Cambridge, to study law. He obtained his M.A. degree but abandoned plans for a career in the legal profession after his success with Footlights, the Cambridge performing arts society. He appeared in the Footlights Revue, a campus production that was transferred to London's West End and then, as the *Cambridge Circus,* was presented on Broadway at the Plymouth Theatre in October 1964. It eventually landed at the Off-as the parrot in question," John Simon in that newspaper's Sunday pages (September 10, 1972) applauded its well-aimed "comic vitriol," and Penelope Gilliatt in the *New Yorker* (August 26, 1972) described the show as "battily funny," and marked by "explosions of . . . great talents."

Nevertheless, *Monty Python's Flying Circus* was not seen on American television until 1974, after it had become a weekly habit in Australia, New Zealand, Canada, Pakistan, Yugoslavia, Lebanon, Hong Kong, West Germany, the Netherlands, Switzerland, and the Scandinavian countries. Some public television officials feared that their audiences would not understand the show's medley of British accents, from Cockney to Oxbridge, and its distinctly British humor. But after a season on fifteen public television stations established a cult following among viewers under thirty, the second thirteen-week package of BBC reruns was picked up by sixty-four stations and became the highest-rated series in public television history.

By the mid-1970s the Python crew had produced two books and several record albums, performed live to sellout crowds at London's Drury Lane and New York's City Center, and drawn crowds on both sides of the Atlantic to their second film, *Monty Python and the Holy Grail* (EMI, 1975)—a broad, episodic takeoff on the King Arthur legend that was described in *Halliwell's Film Guide* (1979) as sometimes slow but "often uproariously funny and with a remarkable visual sense of the middle ages."

In the summer of 1975 some enterprising ABC executives bought six Monty Python episodes not previously shown in the United States for two ninety-minute late-night specials to be presented on its *Wide World of Entertainment* series. What followed, as described by Hendrik Hertzberg in the *New Yorker* (March 29, 1976), was an uproar worthy of the *Flying Circus*. The network deleted portions it found offensive; the Python team sued to prevent the broadcast on the charge of artistic mutilation; a viewing of the disputed segments convulsed the court; and an amused judge allowed the broadcast but, as a concession to the performers, ordered an accompanying disclaimer, in which the artists disassociated themselves from the program, asserting that it was edited without their approval. The network then appealed the decision, the concession was disallowed, and the shows were aired with a curt "Edited for television by ABC" tacked on to the credits.

By the time Americans had succumbed to what was described in *Newsweek* (March 31, 1975) as "Pythonmania," the team was no longer producing new shows. Cleese had quit the weekly series during its last year on BBC, maintaining that its demands were driving him "potty." By 1975 he was back on BBC in *Fawlty Towers*, a comedy series he wrote with his wife, the former Connie Booth, an American actress whom he had married on February 20, 1968. She played the waitress Polly in the series, while he was Basil Fawlty, an incompetent, bombastic innkeeper subject to titanic rages and to the shrewish despotism of his wife Sybil, played by Prunella Scales.

The show's first six episodes, which a critic for the *Guardian* (December 19, 1975) called "the hit of the season," were syndicated to PBS in the United States because American commercial broadcasters had rejected them when Cleese refused to make any cuts in the thirty-minute shows to allow time for commercials. Another six episodes, presented on BBC in 1979, were shown on PBS in 1983. Reviewing the first series in the *New York Times* (July 7, 1977), John J. O'Connor found Cleese "hilarious in his daffy antics," and Tom Shales commented on the second series in the *Washington Post* (July 16, 1983) that Cleese was "particularly magnificent when enraged." London's *TV Times* designated Cleese the funniest man on television for the 1978–79 season. Meanwhile Cleese and his wife Connie were divorced in 1978, although they remained on good terms and went on working together on *Fawlty Towers*.

Despite the separate activities of the individual members of the Monty Python troupe and the voluntary demise of the *Flying Circus*, the team continued to make occasional full-length films together. Their *Monty Python's Life of Brian* (Warner/Orion, 1979), a life-of-Christ parody, evoked outraged denunciations from the Catholic Archdiocese of New York, the United States Lutheran Council, and three organizations of Orthodox rabbis. Because of the film's controversial nature, Monty Python at first had difficulty financing it. Eventually the group raised the necessary funds with the help of the former Beatle George Harrison and established HandMade Films to produce it. Over a four-year period, in spite of outcries over its alleged sacrilegiousness and blasphemy, *The Life of Brian* grossed $75 million.

The film is a biography of the fictitious Judean freedom fighter Brian Cohen of Nazareth, a contemporary of Christ who was born in a neighboring stable and is repeatedly mistaken for the Messiah. Vincent Canby commented in the *New York Times* (August 17, 1979) on the film's "delirious offensiveness" and defended it as a lampoon of Biblical epic movies, not the Bible itself, but Gary Arnold of the *Washington Post* (September 21, 1979) criticized it for pulling its punches. "The title leads one to expect a satiric gloss on the Life of Christ," Arnold wrote, but "the troupe evidently lacked the nerve or inspiration" for such a project. But Cleese considers *The Life of Brian* to be Monty Python's best film, and the only one with a sustained theme. The screenplay of *The Life of Brian*, with notes about the making of the film, was published by Grosset & Dunlap in 1979.

It was the absence of a central theme that stymied the team's next movie attempt in 1980. After they had shot several scenes with nothing to tie them together, Cleese suggested that the group "abandon the project for a good lump of time" with the hope of eventually coming up with a plot. Toward the end of 1980 the Monty Python group gave some performances at the Hollywood Bowl, delivering what Michael Palin called "golden oldies," and the crowd roared with laughter in recognition of its old favorite routines. *Monty Python Live at the Hollywood Bowl* was released as a Columbia film in 1982.

Some benefit revues that Cleese staged in London for Amnesty International resulted in the films *The Secret Policeman's Ball* (Document Films, 1979) and *The Secret Policeman's Other Ball* (Miramax Films, 1982). In addition to Cleese and his colleagues on Monty Python, the latter also featured as guest stars Peter Townshend of the rock group The Who, guitarist Eric Clapton, and comedian Peter Cook. In 1981, Cleese appeared as Robin Hood in Terry Gilliam's romp into the past, *Time Bandits* (Embassy). In the 1983 film *Yellowbeard* (Orion Pictures), a slapstick burlesque starring Graham Chapman as a bloodthirsty pirate, Cleese shared billing with an extensive cast that ranged from British comedians Peter Cook, Spike Milligan, and Marty Feldman to the American duo Cheech and Chong. Considered one of the group's lesser efforts, the film received only mixed reviews.

Meanwhile the separate scenes that had dissatisfied Cleese in 1980 were brought together in *Monty Python's The Meaning of Life* (Universal, 1983), presenting the stages of human existence. The opening vignette, written by Cleese and Graham Chapman, depicts birth in a nightmarish hospital. Other scenes include a sketch in which Cleese plays a sex education teacher, performing a demonstration with his nude wife in front of a class of jaded and inattentive adolescents, and a final scene in which the bored inhabitants of heaven watch a numbing television projection of an eternal Christmas.

But by all accounts the show's outstanding skit, achieving Swiftian heights or plumbing the depths of bad taste, depending on the disposition of the viewer, is the restaurant scene in which Cleese plays an obsequious headwaiter and Terry Jones, as the fattest person in the world, engages in an orgy of eating and vomiting. While some critics found the scene gross and obnoxious, Michael Watts of the London *Times* (June 10, 1983) proclaimed it "such savage breach of good taste that it satirizes taste itself." In his *New Republic* review (April 18, 1983), Stanley Kauffmann described the sextet as "significant comic artists" and "the most dangerous madmen at large, ruthlessly perceptive and torrentially gifted, who are angry at everything improvable in human behavior that is not being improved."

Although *Monty Python's The Meaning of Life* won a Special Jury prize at the 1983 Cannes film festival, Cleese hinted that it might be the group's last film together. Frequently impatient with committee work, he maintained that he could have finished the script in half the time had he been working with only one collaborator. Just as he quit the weekly *Flying Circus* early and refused to extend *Fawlty Towers* beyond twelve successful episodes, he emerged from *The Meaning of Life*

feeling the need "to stretch," to "learn a bit," to make his own mistakes, and possibly to write a screen comedy that would have more structure than a group format allows. Meanwhile, he had already embarked on a number of independent enterprises.

Since 1976, when he formed his company Video Arts Ltd., Cleese has produced and acted in business training films with such titles as *Meetings, Bloody Meetings; The Secretary and Her Boss; The Balance Sheet Barrier;* and *Time Management Delegation.* In 1982, the year that Video Arts won the Queen's Award for Exports, he created a series of commercials for American radio, advertising the products of the British candy company Callard & Bowser. The inimitable Cleese touch was evident in the opening ad, a "teaser" that ran five times in sixty-second spots without mentioning the company's name. Other commercials made by Cleese include advertisements for *Asiaweek* magazine in Hong Kong, Lowney's Peanut Butter Cups in Canada, fish fingers in Australia, the Danish Shoe Council, and American Express.

As an actor, Cleese has taken on Shakespeare, playing Petruchio with intelligence and humor in a BBC production of *The Taming of the Shrew*, directed by Jonathan Miller. When the production was seen on American public television in January, 1981, *New York Times* reviewer John J. O'Connor commented on Cleese's conversational delivery, which emphasized textual clarity over mellifluous cadences, and praised his portrait of "a clever man whose outrageous behavior is quite obviously an act designed to woo a woman he admires." George Perry's *The Life of Python*, an examination of the group and its members, was published by Little, Brown in 1984.

In addition to his contributions to such works as *Monty Python's Big Red Book* (Warner Bks., 1975) and *The Strange Case of the End of Civilization as We Know It* (Wyndham Publishers, 1977), Cleese collaborated with his former psychotherapist, Robin Skynner, on the book *Families and How to Survive Them* (1983). A cartoon-illustrated but intrinsically serious discussion of relationships, the book is based on wide-ranging, taped conversations between Skynner and Cleese over a three-and-a-half year period.

Vouching for the serious intent of his book on therapy, Cleese cited his Video Arts films as evidence that he should be seen not simply as a clown but as "an ordinary chap who uses humor to put his points across." Still convinced that "the world is in a mess," Cleese reflected in the London *Times* interview with Michael Watts that "once you get into your forties I think you start to let go of any last lingering thought that life makes any sense, or that society can ever be organized really satisfactorily. Let go of that and almost everything seems to be funny."

John Cleese and his ex-wife, Connie, share custody of their daughter, Cynthia. Since February 15, 1981, he has been married to the former Barbara Trentham, an American actress, film director, and painter. Cleese credits his first wife with having persuaded him to enter psychotherapy. "In the old days, I was very rigid, very Weston-super-Mare," he told Mary Barrett of *Options* (July 1983). After therapy, he felt more capable of self-assertion and better able to express his emotions. He lists his leisure interests as "gluttony" and "sloth." Six feet five inches tall and weighing 200 pounds, with thinning hair and with eyes that he describes as "dirty green," Cleese is, according to Joseph Gelmis of *Newsday* (April 3, 1983), a "mild, courteous, urbane chap." He and his wife make their home near Holland Park in the Kensington section of London. His political affiliation is with the Social Democratic–Liberal alliance. Cleese holds an honorary LL.D. degree from the University of St. Andrews.

References: *Esquire* 101:60+ Ap '84; *Guardian* p10 D 19 '75 por, p11 Je 20 '83 por; *London Times* p12 Je 10 '83 pors; *N Y Times Mag* p34 Ap 18 '76 pors; *Options* p58 Jl '83 pors; *People* 20:83+ S 26 '83 pors; *Washington Post* G p1+ S 4 '83 pors; *International Who's Who*, 1984–85; *Who's Who*, 1984–85; *Who's Who on Television* (1983)

Close, Glenn

Mar. 19, 1947– Actress. Address: b. c/o Creative Artists Agencies, 1888 Century Park E., #1400, Los Angeles, Calif. 90067

In the ten years since her professional debut, Glenn Close has established herself as one of the most gifted actresses of her generation. As versatile as she is talented, Miss Close received a Tony nomination for her role in the hit musical *Barnum* and won a Tony for her portrayal of Annie in the highly acclaimed American premiere of *The Real Thing*; earned an Emmy nomination for her part in one of the most popular made-for-television movies of all time, *Something About Amelia*; and netted Oscar nominations for her roles in *The World According to Garp* and *The Big Chill*. Nevertheless, she shows no signs of slowing down. Because of her recent successes, "there are more possibilities now for interesting projects," she points out. "I'm still very hungry in my profession."

The second child of William and Bettine Close, Glenn Close was born on March 19, 1947 in Greenwich, Connecticut, a town her ancestors had helped found in the late seventeenth century. (Her parents named her after her godmother, Glenn Andrews, a longtime family friend.) She was raised on her grandfather's five-hundred–acre estate in Greenwich with her three siblings: her older sister, Tina, now an artist; Alexander, who is an agronomist and artist; and Jessie, a writer and illustrator of children's books. Although the Closes were members of the Greenwich aristocracy by merit of their wealth and ancestry, her family was "*of* that heritage, but not *in* it," according to Glenn Close. Her parents shunned the country clubs and the activities such as yachting considered characteristic of the upper crust, and they raised their children themselves rather than hiring a nanny. A "wild little tomboy" who enjoyed freely roaming about the estate, she also read extensively and used her imagination to entertain herself, pretending, for example, to be both Lucky (Hopalong Cassidy's sidekick) and Lucky's horse at the same time, or, when in a morbid mood, a terminal cancer patient. By the time she was seven, she was determined to be an actress and fantasized about being "discovered" by Walt Disney.

In 1960 William Close, an eminent Harvard-educated surgeon, opened a clinic in the Belgian Congo (now Zaire), which he ran for sixteen years. During most of that time, the Close children lived alternately in Africa and at boarding schools in Switzerland, but they finally returned to Connecticut to live with their maternal grandmother on Round Hill Road.

Following in the footsteps of her grandmother and mother, Glenn Close attended Rosemary Hall, an exclusive girls' boarding school in Greenwich. Her years there only reinforced her desire to be an actress. She appeared as Romeo in one of the school's annual Shakespearean plays, and with five like-minded friends, she formed "The Fingernails, The Group with Polish," which performed satires of popular songs and staged several short pieces, including a "bizarre skit" entitled "Tarzan and Jane as Played by Charles Bronson and Steve McQueen."

Miss Close has referred to the five years following her high school graduation in 1965 as "the blank period" and her "lost life." A talented lyric soprano, she postponed going to college in order to travel through Europe and the United States as a member of Up With People. But in spite of "some extraordinary experiences" as a singer, she told Judy Klemesrud in an interview for *Cosmopolitan* (August 1984) that she now realizes that she was "extremely manipulated and used." Her marriage in 1969 to rock guitarist Cabot Wade, which ended in divorce after two-and-a-half years, further darkens her memory of that period. Disillusioned with life on the road, she enrolled in 1970 at William and Mary College in Virginia where she majored in drama and minored in anthropology. She received her B.A. degree and Phi Beta Kappa key in 1974. During the spring of her senior year, Howard Scammon, her drama instructor and mentor, arranged for her to take part in the Theater Communications Group's annual auditions for promising young thespians. She made it to the final round, held in Chicago, where she so impressed a representative of the New Phoenix Repertory Company that she was soon asked to audition for small roles and to understudy several female leads, including the part played by Mary Ure in the New Phoenix Repertory Company's production of William Congreve's Restoration comedy *Love for Love*. Just before the last preview at the Helen Hayes Theater on November 11, 1974, Prince informed her that Miss Ure had been dismissed and that she was to assume the role of Angelica, even though she had never had the chance for a rehearsal of the play. In a gracious note, the former leading lady advised her successor to "be strong and brave," and apparently Miss Close heeded that advice, for by her own estimation of her Broadway debut, she "wasn't great, but [she] was pretty damn good." Following the completion of *Love for Love*'s scheduled run, Miss Close went on to appear in two more New Phoenix Repertory Company revivals at the Helen Hayes Theater during the 1974–75 season—Luigi Pirandello's *The Rules of the Game* and Carson McCullers' *The Member of the Wedding*—each of which ran for twelve performances.

After leaving the New Phoenix Repertory Company in 1975, Miss Close won over the next several years a steady succession of roles in a variety of plays, among them regional theatre productions of such classics as *King Lear*, *Uncle Vanya*, *A Streetcar Named Desire*, and *The Rose Tattoo*; Off-Broadway stagings of several works by lesser known playwrights, including the well-received, limited run of Wendy Wasserstein's *Uncommon Women and Others*; and the Broadway musical *Rex*, a box-office failure that closed after forty-one performances. She was luckier with her next Broadway venture. Tried out at the Studio Arena Theater in Buffalo in January 1978, *The Crucifer of Blood*, Paul Giovanni's lighthearted mystery based on Sherlock Holmes and other Arthur Conan Doyle characters, generally pleased critics and theatregoers alike when it began its run of over 200

performances at the Helen Hayes Theater on September 28, 1978. In the supporting role of the villainous Irene St. Claire, the supposedly distressed young lady who comes to Holmes for help, Glenn Close enjoyed a share of the critical accolades and added luster to her growing reputation.

In 1979, in addition to acting in the short-lived Off-Broadway productions of Bjorg Vik's *Wine Untouched* and David Lan's *The Winter Dancers*, Miss Close appeared in two made-for-television movies—*Too Far to Go*, which aired on NBC in March and was subsequently released in 1982 as a theatrical motion picture, and *The Orphan Train*, which CBS broadcast in December. She returned to the Broadway stage in 1980 with a supporting role in *Barnum*, a musical about the life of Phineas T. Barnum, the quintessential American showman. That razzle-dazzle, three-ring-circus show drew rave reviews on opening at the St. James Theatre on April 30, 1980, and critics saw Glenn Close's portrayal of Charity, Barnum's feisty wife, as a unifying mainstay in the diffuse action. Even John Simon, who had had reservations about her performances in the past, acknowledged in *New York* magazine (May 12, 1980) that she was "a splendid Mrs. Barnum, with the ambiguities of a passionate Puritan etched into the wily, pinched prettiness of her face, her very presence exuding the sour-sweet joys of circus lemonade."

Her performance in *Barnum* proved to be a turning point in her career, netting her a Tony nomination as outstanding featured actress in a musical and attracting the attention of director George Roy Hill, who was then casting for the film version of John Irving's novel *The World According to Garp* (Warner Brothers, 1982). "I noticed in Glenn a remarkable quality," Hill explained to Ann Ferrar in a 1984 *Living Anew* interview, "a combination of dignity, warmth and extremely rare serenity." That "charged stillness" led Hill to cast her as Jenny Fields, an imperturbable, lustless nurse who, determined to have a child although she is unmarried, mounts a paraplegic, brain-damaged World War II ball-turret gunner and gives birth to Garp nine months later. As a result of *A Sexual Suspect*, her book about that experience and her raising of Garp, Jenny Fields unwittingly becomes the idol of a group of radical feminists.

In order to begin filming *The World According to Garp*, Glenn Close left the cast of *Barnum* in March 1981 after appearing in well over 300 performances. Aside from the difficulties of a role in which she had to age thirty years over the course of the movie, the demands of the film medium itself were a new challenge for the actress. "To project a character like Jenny in a play, for instance, you'd have to be larger than life," she explained to Ross Wetzsteon in the *American Film* interview. "But to do that in a movie would be too stagy. . . . You have to find a balance between the character's aura and the intimacy of the camera, and it's much harder to work with a camera than a live audience." More than that, she confessed, she was "much more *insecure* in films" because it made her "nervous to have [her] entire performance come out of the editing room."

In spite of her feelings of insecurity, Glenn Close turned in a critically acclaimed performance in her film debut, eclipsing the movie's nominal star, the comedian-actor Robin Williams, who portrayed Garp as an adult. Assessing her "triumph" in the *National Review* (September 3, 1982), the usually acerbic John Simon wrote, "She makes the half-whimsical, half-insufferable Jenny, a sort of intellectualized comic-strip character, into a unified, flesh-and-blood being, believably strange and strangely likable. She looks right: asexually attractive; sounds right: calmly, crisply commanding; and acts right: adamantly wrestling Irving's flightiest fancies down to earth." The vast majority of critics seconded that opinion, and the Academy of Motion Picture Arts and Sciences nominated her for an Oscar for best supporting actress.

Essaying a very different role, Glenn Close next played the androgynous title character in the Manhattan Theater Club's presentation of *The Singular Life of Albert Nobbs*, Simone Benmussa's stage adaptation of a short story by George Moore. Set in Ireland in the 1860s, the drama traces the problems created by a young woman's attempt to escape poverty by disguising herself as a man in order to find work, a deception that remains undetected until her death. Only after seventeen years as a waiter in a Dublin hotel, when she chances to meet another woman similarly disguised, does Albert realize that she cannot escape from that self-imposed limbo: she will always be a "perhaper"—neither a man nor a woman—and thus will always be alone. For her understated, persuasive characterization of Albert Nobbs, Miss Close received unanimous praise in the critics' circle as well as the Obie Award for the best Off-Broadway performance of the season. The play itself, which received laudatory reviews from most critics, ended its limited engagement on July 10, 1982, after a run of four weeks.

Soon after *Albert Nobbs* closed, Glenn Close took on her second motion-picture role. Impressed by her portrayal of Jenny Fields in *The World According to Garp*, writer-director Lawrence Kasdan almost immediately offered her the part of Sarah, another strong, nurturing woman, in *The Big Chill* (Columbia Pictures, 1983). That movie focuses on a group of University of Michigan alumni, political activists in the 1960s, who are brought together again at the funeral of a friend driven to suicide by his inability to adapt his ideals to the changing times. During the course of the weekend reunion, the friends, now mostly affluent members of the "establishment," struggle to come to terms with their friend's death and their own lives. Although critics generally considered *The Big Chill* a shallow, albeit entertaining, examination of the coming-of-age of the baby-boom generation, the cast, which included Kevin Kline, William Hurt, Mary Kay Place, and JoBeth Williams, earned high marks for its ensemble performance, Miss Close netted her second Oscar nomination for her sup-

porting role, and the film was among the top-grossing releases of 1983.

With *Something About Amelia*, Glenn Close scored a hit in yet another medium. In that made-for-television movie, she earned an Emmy nomination for her portrayal of a woman who slowly comes to the devastating realization that her husband (played by Ted Danson) is having sex with their teen-age daughter. Over sixty million people watched that controversial program when ABC aired it on January 9, 1984, making it the second most popular TV film of all time, surpassed only by the same network's *The Day After*. In the interview for *Cosmopolitan*, Miss Close told Judy Klemesrud that she finds the concept of incest so "upsetting and offensive" that at first she refused to even consider the role. After reading the script and discussing it with her parents, she finally agreed to take the part because "people can only benefit by being more aware" of the problem of incest, which is "so damaging and creates such trauma in the children who experience it."

Her next theatrical motion picture also dealt with a family tragedy. In *The Stone Boy* (Twentieth Century-Fox, 1984), a twelve-year-old Montana farm boy (Jason Presson) accidentally kills his older brother (Dean Cain). Shocked and guilt-ridden, the child retreats behind a wall of silence, and his seeming lack of remorse alienates him from his grieving parents, portrayed by Miss Close and Robert Duvall. It is only through the intercession of the kindly, more perceptive grandfather (Wilford Brimley) that parents and son are reconciled. Like most critics, Rex Reed considered the performances of the high-caliber cast "polished and marvelous," but he regretted that the script (Gina Berriault's adaptation of her own short story) gave them so little material to work with. "When Glenn Close describes how her mother just wandered off one day in a soiled dress after feeding the chickens," Reed wrote in the *New York Post* (April 4, 1984), "the film takes on a strange poetry, as though these were characters invented by Eudora Welty. But most of the time this excellent actress finds herself chained to the kitchen stove preparing an endless series of meals nobody ever eats."

Almost immediately after filming *The Stone Boy*, Miss Close had the opportunity to work again with Duvall and, in addition, with another actor she greatly admires, Robert Redford. Although she had already accepted a role in the film version of Henry James's novel *The Bostonians*, Redford was so insistent that she be his co-star and Miss Close was so eager to work with him that extensive negotiations were conducted to release her from that previous contract. Based on the 1952 Bernard Malamud novel of the same name, *The Natural* (Tri-Star, 1984) is the story of the roller-coaster career of a major-league baseball player, Roy Hobbs, portrayed by Redford. Miss Close plays Iris Raines, the childhood sweetheart whom he impregnates and then leaves behind in Nebraska in order to try-out the big leagues and whose mysterious reappearance in his life fifteen years later almost magically ends his slump and helps him hit an all-important home run. (Robert Duvall played the villainous Max Mercy, a famous sports columnist.) Since the movie was Robert Redford's first screen appearance in four years, it received a great deal of press coverage and, like most films in which he appears, was a box-office hit, earning more than $30 million in the first month of its release. Although Vincent Canby complained in his *New York Times* review (May 11,1984) that Iris and the other women in *The Natural* were "little more than functions of the plot," Kathleen Carroll congratulated Glenn Close in the *New York Daily News* (May 11, 1984) for doing "her best to suggest hidden depths in the character of the one decent woman in Hobbs' life."

Since she had played "decent" women in all her films, Miss Close worried about being typecast as "motherly, strong, serene." As a result, she was particularly pleased when she was offered what Ross Wetzsteon described in *American Film* (May 1984) as "the most coveted female stage role of 1984": the part of Annie in the American premiere of Tom Stoppard's *The Real Thing*, directed by Mike Nichols. That scintillating play traces the emotional coming-of-age of Henry, a brilliant but arrogant dramatist played by Jeremy Irons. Through his adulterous affair with Annie, their eventual marriage, and her subsequent faithlessness, Henry painfully searches for what is "real" in human relationships, in social and political commitments, and in art. Since the focus is so clearly on Henry, Miss Close admitted that in some ways Annie was a "thankless role." Nevertheless, she revelled in the chance to portray that highly sexed, funny, idealistic, and boisterous woman, who has a "certain joy and easinesss about her." When the play opened at Broadway's Plymouth Theatre on January 5, 1984, Allan Wallach, among other critics, applauded her interpretation of the role. "[Miss] Close is splendid as Annie," he raved in *Newsday* (January 6, 1984), "giving her a full measure of intelligence, commitment and caring." For her performance, she won the Tony Award for best actress.

On September 1, 1984, Miss Close wed James Marlas, a New York venture capitalist whom she met after the opening of *The Real Thing*, in a ceremony on Nantucket Island, Massachusetts. The five-foot four-inch tall actress, who has gray-blue eyes and blonde hair, enjoys playing tennis, is an accomplished equestrienne, and has sung the national anthem before Mets games at Shea Stadium. She would like to have children someday, but for now the demands of her career continue to absorb most of her attention. Whether preparing a stage, television, or film role, Glenn Close shuns Method acting, preferring instead to rely on her imagination to discover "where [her] character is coming from." "I don't mean in any deep psychological sense," she explained to Ross Wetzsteon, "just where she was a few minutes ago, what's on her mind right now—all in a very precise way. . . . You have to find the emotional center instead [of relying on technique], and that means being open, tak-

ing chances." "When I finally find the character," she continued, "that's the payoff for all the agony. When the character finally begins to crack the shell of her egg, that's the joy."

References: *American Film* 9:16+ My '84 pors; *Chicago Tribune* p5+ F 5 '84 por; *Cosmo* 197:88+ Ag '84 pors; *Living Anew* 1:32+ 1984 pors; *N Y Daily News* (Leisure section) p1+ Ja 1 '84 por; *New York* 15:50+ Ag 2 '82 por

Collins, Joan

May 23, 1933– British actress. Address: b. c/o Aaron Spelling Productions, Inc., 132 S. Rodeo Dr., Beverly Hills, Calif. 90212

"I love playing a villain—it's so very juicy," said actress Joan Collins in the spring of 1982. The introduction of Alexis Carrington, the sexual predator that Miss Collins plays on ABC's weekly prime-time soap opera *Dynasty*, helped to boost the series' sagging ratings above those of its arch-rival, *Dallas*. The role of Alexis, "the woman everyone loves to hate," represents a belated victory for Miss Collins, a veteran of thirty years of undistinguished acting in more than fifty films, many of them forgettable. "*Dynasty* is the highest peak I've had in my life, professionally and in terms of public acceptance," she told Isabel Ellsen in an interview for the British publication *Woman's Own* (May 21, 1983). "It's not *Brideshead Revisited*, in the sense of great television, but what we're doing is what actors used to do in weekly rep—entertain. The series is good for my career, my popularity and for money."

Of English, French, and Dutch ancestry, Joan Henrietta Collins was born in London, England on May 23, 1933, the oldest child of Joseph William and Elsa (Bessant) Collins. Her younger sister, Jackie Collins, is the best-selling author of such soft-core potboilers as *Lovers and Gamblers* and *Lovehead*. As a vaudeville booking agent, Joseph Collins was able to provide his family with a comfortable income and an "interesting upbringing," to quote Joan Collins, since his clients—singers, dancers, and other variety artists—were frequent houseguests. By her own account a "gawky, spotty, shy, boy-hating, and introverted" youngster, Miss Collins idolized those entertainers and dreamed of becoming a glamorous performer herself. She was especially enamored of motion pictures, which she attended as often as three times a day.

While she was a student at the Francis Holland School, a London "public" school for girls, Joan Collins made her stage debut in a West End production of Ibsen's *A Doll's House*. Two years later, she left school to enroll at the Royal Academy of Dramatic Art. Her father's strong objections to her plan collapsed when she reminded him that he had always upheld the benefits of open-mindedness and encouraged her to appreciate opposing viewpoints. Father and daughter struck a bargain: if she showed no progress after two years of dramatic training, she would give up acting and go to secretarial school. During the two years Miss Collins was a student at the Royal Academy of Dramatic Art, she supplemented the subsistence allowance her father gave her by taking an occasional modeling job. One of them led to a contract with the Rank Organisation, Ltd., the huge film production company.

In 1952 Miss Collins made her motion picture debut in a bit part in *Lady Godiva Rides Again* (British Lion, 1951), a satirical comedy she has since dismissed as "wretched." In British films released in the early 1950s, including *Turn the Key Softly* (Astor Pictures, 1954), *The Good Die Young* (Remus, 1954), and *The Square Ring* (Republic, 1953), she invariably played a wayward teenager or a brassy prostitute. The best of those dozen or so movies was *I Believe in You* (Rank, 1952), a *cinéma vérité* treatment of the work of London probation officers that starred Celia Johnson and Cecil Parker. When the film opened in the United States, a reviewer for *Variety* commended Miss Collins for the "strong dramatic" performance she turned in as Norma, a reformed streetwalker. But the good roles were few and far between. "I didn't leave home [for Hollywood] riding the crest," she admitted to Howard Thompson in an interview for the *New York Times* (October 27, 1957). "I had played so many tarts and delinquents I got to be known as a bad bit. People hesitated about hiring me."

Hollywood director-producer Howard Hawks was one of the few important filmmakers willing to take a chance on Miss Collins, casting her as the conniving Queen Nellifer in his epic *Land of the Pharaohs* (Warner Brothers, 1955). It was while she was making *Land of the Pharaohs* that she caught the eye of Darryl F. Zanuck, the chief of production for Twentieth Century-Fox, who bought her contract from the Rank Organisation and signed her up as a studio player. Zanuck gave her star billing in her first assignment for Twentieth Century-Fox—the part of Beth Throgmorton, the hoydenish lady-in-waiting who steals Sir Walter Raleigh from an aging Queen Elizabeth I, portrayed by Bette Davis, in the swashbuckler *The Virgin Queen* (1955). She followed that up with a leading role in *The Girl in the Red Velvet Swing* (1955), in which she played Evelyn Nesbit, the turn-of-the-century showgirl whose jealous husband, Harry K. Thaw, murdered her lover, the celebrated architect Stanford White, in the Madison Square Roof Garden.

For most of the time, however, Miss Collins languished in a succession of what she has since described as "wallpaper parts—the pretty girl who sort of stands there in Susan Hayward's old costumes." She was an ambitious, two-timing chorus girl in *The Opposite Sex* (MGM, 1956), a frothy musical derived from Clare Boothe Luce's satirical comedy *The Women*; a sultry señorita in the adult western *The Bravados* (Twentieth Century-Fox, 1958); a moody alcoholic in *The Wayward Bus* (Twentieth Century-Fox, 1957), an inept adaptation of the John Steinbeck novel; a burlesque queen in the routine caper adventure *Seven Thieves* (Twentieth Century-Fox, 1960); and in a drastic change of pace, a shipwrecked novice nun in the romantic adventure *Sea Wife* (Twentieth Century-Fox, 1957).

Miss Collins fared slightly better in *Island in the Sun* (Twentieth Century-Fox, 1957), Zanuck's big-budget production of Alec Waugh's best-selling novel of interracial passion and murder in the West Indies. The impulsive Jocelyn Fleury, whose life is shattered when her upper-class lover learns of her mixed racial background, was, in Joan Collins' opinion, the "most normal character" she had played to date. Another congenial role was that of Angela Hoffa, the irrepressible siren in Leo McCary's bedroom farce *Rally 'Round the Flag, Boys* (Twentieth Century-Fox, 1959).

Because she was, in her view, so often miscast, Miss Collins frequently clashed with studio executives over her sexpot typecasting. "I think doing stupid parts in stupid pictures can destroy a career," she told Hedda Hopper, the influential Hollywood gossip columnist, as quoted in the *Los Angeles Times* (December 6, 1959). "I'd rather not work in something that's not rewarding, something I find distasteful." One of the film assignments she found especially repugnant was the role of a "nymphomaniac suffragette," to use her description, in a movie version of D. H. Lawrence's *Sons and Lovers*. When she failed to show up on the set, Twentieth Century-Fox suspended her and withheld her salary for eight weeks. Hedda Hopper was among those who sympathized with her "valiant" fight, but the studio executives made her promise to complete two more films before they would release her from her contract. One of those films was Raoul Walsh's tedious Biblical epic

Esther and the King (1960). "It was dreadful," Miss Collins said, as quoted in the *New York World Telegram* (April 7, 1962). "I hope nobody saw it."

According to the Hollywood reporters who seemed to take a voyeuristic glee in recording the details of her private life, including the collapse in 1957 of her five-year marriage to the British actor Maxwell Reed, Miss Collins was as tempestuous and hedonistic off-screen as she was on. In the titillating press accounts of her allegedly scandalous behavior, she was invariably described as a "torrid baggage," a "streamlined vamp," a "voluptuous brunet," or "the British bombshell." A regular of the Hollywood party scene, Miss Collins dated actor Sydney Chaplin, who had worked with her in *Land of the Pharaohs*, Arthur M. Loew, the motion picture executive, hotelier Nicky Hilton, and the son of the Latin American dictator Raphael Trujillo Molina, and for a time she was engaged to Warren Beatty. "I was very immature when I first came to Hollywood," she said years later, as quoted in the *Los Angeles Times* (November 2, 1979). "To a young girl, it was an emotional jungle, and when I looked back I felt I had survived very well." In retrospect, Joan Collins thinks that her reputation as a competent performer survived "very well," too. "As a body of work over the years, it is *not* that fantastic, but I *did* get some not too shabby reviews in some fairly mediocre films," she told Jim Jerome in an interview for *People* (December 20, 1982). "I can cut the mustard as an actress in more ways than people have ever given me credit for."

Unable to find work in Hollywood, she returned to England to play the female lead in the British made Bob Hope-Bing Crosby vehicle *The Road to Hong Kong* (United Artists, 1962), after which she intended to resume her London theatrical career. Instead, she met, and married on May 27, 1963, Anthony Newley, the British actor, composer, singer, and stage director whose credits include the unorthodox musicals *Stop the World—I Want to Get Off* and *The Roar of the Greasepaint—The Smell of the Crowd*. For the next few years she devoted herself to caring for their children, Tara Cynara and Alexander Anthony, known as Sacha, but by 1967 she was ready to accept an occasional film or television assignment. Her credits for the late 1960s include the star-studded mystery film *Warning Shot* (Paramount, 1967), *Can Heironymus Merkin Ever Forgive Mercy Humppe and Find True Happiness?* (Universal, 1969), an insubstantial and, according to the critical consensus, tasteless and self-indulgent personal fantasy written and directed by Anthony Newley, and episodes in a number of television series, among them *The Man From U.N.C.L.E.*, *Star Trek*, *Batman*, *The Virginian*, and *Mission Impossible*.

Following her divorce from Anthony Newley in 1970, Miss Collins settled once again in London. For a time, she "did other things," as she explained to Cheryl Lavin in an interview for a *Chicago Tribune* (October 17, 1982) profile. "I opened a disco, did some interior decorating, TV projects, and I was always working, making some type of movie.

People would say, 'Why did you do a movie like *Empire of the Ants?*' And I'd say, 'Because I have to eat, and that's my job.'" In addition to appearing in the sci-fi thriller *Empire of the Ants* (American International, 1977), Miss Collins played leading roles in the spy adventure *The Executioner* (Columbia, 1970); *Up in the Cellar* (American International, 1970), an innocuous collegiate comedy; *Quest for Love* (Rank, 1971), an offbeat romantic drama; and the horror films *Tales From the Crypt* (Cinerama, 1972), *Tales That Witness Madness* (Paramount, 1973), *Dark Places* (Cinerama, 1974), and *The Devil Within Her* (American International, 1976), a stylish chiller about an infant possessed by Satan.

Under the guidance of Ronald S. Kass, a recording company executive turned motion picture producer whom she married in March 1972, Joan Collins finally emerged as a bankable star in a series of commercially successful "sexploitation" films. The first was *The Stud*, her husband's production of her sister's steamy novel about the sexual athleticism of a young disco manager, in which Joan Collins played Fontaine Khaled, the nymphomaniacal wife of the discothèque's owner. When the film was released in the United States in 1979 by Trans-America Films, American film critics condemned it as "a cheap sex show," but it grossed millions of dollars and made Miss Collins "a household word again," as she put it.

In her interview with Cheryl Lavin, Joan Collins explained her decision to turn to soft-core pornography: "The realization hit me that here I was forty years old—I looked pretty good, I thought I was really a good actress, better than people had given me credit for—and they always noticed my looks more than what I was doing, and I wanted to have it again, have the career. So . . . I appeared all over England playing a very sexy role, taking off all my clothes in an X-rated film. It started my career again." Miss Collins appeared in several other British "skin flicks," among them *Homework*, *Nutcracker*, and *The Bitch*, but she also won supporting roles in Michael Winner's remake of the classic Raymond Chandler whodunit *The Big Sleep* (United Artists, 1978), in the romantic comedy *Sunburn* (Paramount, 1979), and in such popular television series as *Baretta*, *Police Woman*, *Switch*, and *Fantasy Island*.

In August 1981 Joan Collins was hired by Aaron Spelling Productions Inc. to inject some sex and venom into *Dynasty*, the convoluted saga of Denver oil baron Blake Carrington and his scandal-ridden kin, as Alexis Carrington, his scheming and amoral ex-wife. The female counterpart of *Dallas'* vicious J. R. Ewing, Alexis is, in Joan Collins' words, "ruthless, ambitious, pure as the driven slush." Shortly after she arrived on the scene, Alexis began an affair with Blake's business rival, Cecil Colby. In the last episode of the 1981–82 season, Cecil suffered a massive coronary while dallying with Alexis. Faithful viewers had to wait impatiently through the summer's reruns until the show returned in the fall to learn whether Cecil would live or die. As Jim Jerome quipped in *People*, "[It was] a cliffhanger that made Who Shot J. R.? look like Who Killed Cock Robin?" As it turned out, Cecil survived just long enough for a hospital bedside marriage to Alexis, then he quietly expired, making her heir to his fortune and to his rivalry with her former husband. "Roles of this kind are genuinely fun to do . . . ," the actress said, as quoted in the *New York Daily News* (December 17, 1981). "What I'm really trying to do is bring to television the outrageously glamorous women we always saw in films."

Much as the J. R. Ewing character did for actor Larry Hagman, Alexis Carrington has brought Joan Collins international celebrity, but she has no illusions about television stardom. Although she receives some 12,000 love-hate letters weekly, she knows that her position is precarious. "I'm America's brunet flavor-of-the-month," she told one reporter. "That doesn't mean I'm going to be in six months or a year, and I realize that, and it doesn't bother me in the slightest." Recognizing *Dynasty's* limitations, she has continued to accept other assignments. Among other things, she appeared as the wicked witch in Showtime's production of *Hansel and Gretel* and played a leading part in ABC's made-for-television movie *The Wild Women of Chastity Gulch*, and in November 1980 she turned in what one reviewer called an "acceptable performance" in the title role of a London stage production of *The Last of Mrs. Cheyney*. Joan Collins recently signed a three-year, multimillion-dollar contract with Revlon to act as spokeswoman and advertising model for its new fragrance, Scoundrel.

A strikingly beautiful woman, Joan Collins has large, gray-green eyes, dark brown hair, and pale skin. She stands about five feet six inches tall, and she keeps her weight at around 120 pounds by following a healthful diet and exercising regularly in the small gymnasium she had installed in her home. She has outlined her beauty regimen in *The Joan Collins Beauty Book*, which was published in Great Britain by Macmillan in 1980. Since she regularly puts in a fourteen-hour workday while the season's episodes of *Dynasty* are in production, she has little time for sports or for her hobbies of photography and antiques collecting. As she told a reporter for *People* (December 20, 1982), she has even given up "reading crap fiction."

But no matter how busy her schedule, Miss Collins always manages to spend some time each day with her youngest daughter, Katyana ("Katy") Kass. In 1980 Katy, the Kasses' only child, sustained severe brain injuries in a car accident. Miss Collins remained by the comatose child's bedside for six weeks and, after Katy regained consciousness, took an active part in her physical and mental rehabilitation. She has documented her daughter's slow recovery in *Katy; a Fight for Life* (Gollancz, 1982). Committed to improving the care and treatment of brain-damaged children, the actress recently appeared before a congressional committee to urge increased federal funding for neurological re-

search. Since her divorce from Ron Kass, Joan Collins has made her home with Katy in the Coldwater Canyon section of Los Angeles.

Interviewers have found Miss Collins to be outgoing, earthy, and unusually candid about her personal life. Her confessional *Past Imperfect; An Autobiography* (W. H. Allen) was a best-seller within weeks of its publication in Great Britain in 1978, but she now thinks she may have been "too frank." "I was a bit too open about certain events in my romantic life . . . ," she explained to Bob Lardine of the *New York Daily News* (September 18, 1979). "On the other hand, I couldn't write a story about my life without mentioning that I had relationships with men who were instrumental in influencing my life and career. It would have been a total cop-out if I left out the names." Because she had some "regrets" about the book, Miss Collins at first declined to sell the American publication rights, but she has since reconsidered her decision, and *Past Imperfect* was published in the United States in 1984 by Simon & Schuster.

References: Chicago Tribune XII p1+ O 17 '82 por; McCalls 111:20+ N '83 pors; N Y Post mag p3 Je 16 '57 por; People 16:124+ N 16 '81 pors, 18:98+ D 20 '82 pors; Rolling Stone p99+ Mr 29 '84 pors; International Motion Picture Almanac, 1983; Katz, Ephraim. Film Encyclopedia (1979); Who's Who in America, 1984–85; Who's Who on Television, 1983

Conable, Barber B., Jr.

Nov. 2, 1922– U.S. Representative from New York. Address: b. 237 Cannon House Office Bldg, Washington, D.C. 20515; h. 10532 Alexander Rd., Alexander, N.Y. 14005

For twenty years Barber B. Conable Jr. has brought to the deliberations of the United States House of Representatives the traditional Republican values cherished by inhabitants of the small towns of western New York State. During most of that period he has served on the Ways and Means Committee, and he has been the ranking minority member of that powerful body for the past eight years. As a member of the House's longtime minority party, the congressman has not gained much popular recognition, but his announcement, on February 6, 1984, that he would retire that year at the end of the 98th Congress signaled the imminent loss of one of the most important Republican voices and brought forth praise from both parties for a deeply respected ally and adversary. The Republican vice-president George Bush has described his former colleague in the House as "one of the most sane and able men in the United States Congress," and Democratic senator Daniel Patrick Moynihan has said of his fellow New Yorker, "Some men meet standards; others set them. Barber Conable has been one of the others."

Barber B. Conable Jr.

Barber B. Conable Jr. was born in Warsaw, New York, on November 2, 1922 to Barber B. and Agnes (Goulnlock) Conable. His father was a prominent lawyer who served as county judge in Wyoming County, New York. Conable's unusual first name, which he shared with his paternal grandfather as well as with his father, is derived from the surname of one of his great-grandmothers. Conable attended the local schools of his hometown and then enrolled at Cornell University, where he took only three years to complete the requirements for the A.B. degree, which he received in 1942 at the age of nineteen.

After graduating from Cornell, Conable immediately enlisted as a private in the United States Marine Corps. Rising rapidly through the ranks, he was a first lieutenant by February 1945, when he went ashore with an assault wave on the first day of the invasion of Iwo Jima. Conable, who served with the American occupation forces in Japan, was released from the service in 1946, but the outbreak of the Korean war brought him back to active duty from 1950 to 1951. He then remained in the Marine Corps Reserve, from which he retired in 1972 with the rank of colonel.

In 1946 Conable returned to his alma mater to study law. He served as the editor of the *Cornell Law Quarterly* in 1947-1948 and graduated with honors in the latter year. Admitted to the New York Bar in 1948, he then joined a Buffalo law firm. In 1952, after completing his second tour with the Marines, Conable and his father, who had retired from the bench, established a law firm in the Genesee County city of Batavia, New York. The younger man's law practice became only one of his many contributions to the community in the following decade, for he was Republican city chairman in Batavia for five years and also served as

campaign chairman for the Genesee County Republican Committee. The civic-minded Conable also held posts with the Batavia Rotary Club, the Genesee Council of Boy Scouts, the Genesee County United Fund, and the Western New York Hospital Review and Planning Council.

Conable made his first run for public office in 1962 when he won election to the New York State Senate, but he served for only half of his four-year term. The decision of Harold C. Ostertag, a seven-term Republican veteran of the United States House of Representatives, to retire in 1964, at the end of the second session of the 88th Congress, opened the door for the freshman state legislator to step up to the national level. With Ostertag's blessing, Conable won the Republican nomination for the seat from the 37th congressional district, which encompassed all of Genesee, Orleans, and Wyoming counties and parts of Erie, Livingston, and Monroe counties, including a section of the city of Rochester. Then, in November 1964, he successfully withstood the Democratic landslide that swept Lyndon B. Johnson into the White House in the general election. Conable gathered 98,923 votes, or 54.2 percent of the total cast in the congressional race; Neil F. Bubel, the Democratic candidate, took 44.0 percent; and David L. MacAdam, the Liberal nominee, gained 1.8 percent.

During the ten consecutive terms that Conable has served in the House, reapportionment has twice changed his constituency. With the 1972 election his congressional district became the 35th, and with the 1982 race it became the 30th. His domain now includes all of Genesee County and parts of Livingston, Monroe, and Ontario counties, and its boundaries run from Lake Ontario on the north through downtown Rochester to a vast base of small towns and rural communities lying to the south along the New York State Thruway. Those vicissitudes, however, had little impact on Conable's political fortunes. In eight of his nine runs for re-election he won between 64.3 percent and 72.2 percent of the vote. He garnered 119,105 votes, or 68.2 percent of the total in his last bid for office, which pitted him against the Democrats' Bill Benet in 1982.

Congressman Conable's electoral majority fell below 60.0 percent only in 1974 when he captured 56.8 percent of the vote in a race against Rochester's vice-mayor, Margaret ("Midge") Costanza, who later became a top aide to President Jimmy Carter, but in that year Conable and his party were laboring under the shadow of Watergate. The most consistent supporter in the House of Richard M. Nixon's policies, Conable had been slow to abandon the president. Although, late in 1973, he was predicting that Nixon would be exonerated, he gradually yielded to the inevitable. Shortly before the president's resignation in August 1974, Conable acknowledged the overwhelming evidence against Nixon with the comment "I guess we have found the smoking gun" and predicted that a resolution of impeachment would have "overwhelming support in the House."

Although part of Conable's electoral success can be attributed to the traditional affinity of the small towns and rural areas of western New York for Republican candidates, it is also the product of the congressman's solicitous treatment of his constituents, for he has returned to his district for at least forty weekends during each of his years in Congress. In addition, Conable keeps in close touch with the voters through his newsletter, "The Washington Report," that is unusually informative both in its coverage of his activities and in its discussion of his political philosophy.

During his first term in the House, Conable served on its Science and Astronautics Committee, but before the start of the 90th Congress in 1967, he transferred to the Committee on Ways and Means, on which he remained. He is currently also a member of the Joint Committee on Taxation and the Standards of Official Conduct Committee, and, in past sessions, he sat on the Budget Committee, the House Administration Committee, and the Joint Economic Committee.

His intellectual prowess quickly won recognition from members of both parties, and his influence among his fellow Republicans gradually rose. In 1971 Conable was named head of the Republican Research Committee, a largely ceremonial post, but one that strategically placed him in the lower ranks of his party's leadership. Two years later he gained some real power when Representative John J. Rhodes of Arizona gave up the chairmanship of the House Republican Policy Committee in order to succeed Gerald R. Ford of Michigan as minority leader. On December 13, 1973, by a margin of 88 to 77 in a secret ballot, the House Republicans chose to ignore attacks on Conable's membership in the allegedly ultraliberal Council on Foreign Relations and to select him over the archconservative Del Clawson of California as Rhodes's replacement. In doing so, the Republican representatives made Conable the first New Yorker in thirty-five years to hold a top post in their ranks.

Conable remained as chairman of the House Republican Policy Committee until December 1976, when party rules forced him to choose between retaining the leadership of that body and becoming the ranking minority member on Ways and Means. For Conable, who had originally chosen Ways and Means in order "to be astride the great issues," the decision was easy. "The Ways and Means Committee," he assured his constituents, "is a great place for someone interested in legislating, in my mind the reason for being here, and so I made it my preference."

Throughout his score of years in Congress, Conable has maintained a moderate to conservative record. He endorsed American intervention in Southeast Asia, supported spending for the major defense projects of the era, including the antiballistic missile (ABM), the B-1 bomber, and nerve gas; he voted in favor of a constitutional amendment allowing prayer in public schools; and he opposed the establishment of a consumer protection agency and funding for public television. Predictably, his performance has received consistently high ratings from the Ripon Society, the National Alliance of Businessmen, the Americans for Constitutional Action, and the American Security Council. Not surprisingly, he has not fared too well in evaluations by liberal groups such as the Americans for Democratic Action and the Committee on Political Education of the AFL-CIO.

On the other hand, Conable has taken reform positions on a number of important issues. He has, for example, been the Ways and Means Committee's most outspoken critic of trade barriers and of protectionist policies. A firm advocate of campaign finance reforms, he has, since joining the Ways and Means Committee, refused to accept contributions in excess of $50 from any political action committee (PAC) or private donor. Moreover, his support for the Equal Rights Amendment, his acceptance of federal assistance for family planning, and his moderate stance on other "cultural" issues has led New York's Conservative party, which often endorses Republican candidates, to deny him its nomination.

Conable was one of the leading Republican sponsors of the Legislative Reorganization Act of 1970, which was passed thanks to the efforts of liberal Democrats and moderate Republicans like himself. That measure took important steps toward eliminating from the procedures of Congress the element of secrecy which, in Conable's words, "undermines the democratic process and saps public confidence in the House as a responsive and effective legislative body." In particular, the act required the recording of teller votes during consideration of a bill in the Committee of the Whole, if one-fifth of a quorum of House members requested such a count, and it mandated disclosure to the public of roll call votes taken in committee.

In 1970 Conable also played a leading role in changing the process by which Republicans chose their party's ranking members for the various committees of the House. As chairman of a nineteen-member Republican panel on the seniority system, Conable delivered a report in October that called for the elimination of longevity as the sole criterion of leadership, urging instead that the Republicans' Committee on Committees make nominations for the posts and that the Republican conference, a group comprised of all the party members in the House, make the final choices by majority votes on secret ballots. Conable said that his plan would make the party's committee chairmen and ranking members "leaders and not just survivors." The House Republicans adopted it unchanged at the start of the 92d Congress in January 1971.

The passage in 1972 of the State and Local Fiscal Assistance Act, which provided for the distribution of some federal revenues to lower levels of government, ranks as one of Conable's most important legislative accomplishments. The revenue-sharing concept faced formidable opposition from Wilbur D. Mills and John W. Byrnes, respectively the Democratic chairman and the ranking Republican member of the Ways and Means Committee. But it did have the strong support of the Nixon administration and of Conable's old political ally, Governor Nelson A. Rockefeller of New York. After waging a two-year battle, Conable was able to capitalize on the political interests of the committee's urban Democrats and on Mills's presidential ambitions to push the measure through Ways and Means and on to victory in the Congress. "Barber didn't get a lot of credit," Murray L. Weidenbaum, who was the architect of the administration's plan, has recalled, "but there's no doubt he was the prime mover for revenue sharing inside the committee."

Throughout the 1970s Conable devoted much of his attention to tax-related issues. During the presidential administrations of both Gerald R. Ford and Jimmy Carter he supported a series of measures to lower personal income taxes and advocated increasing the depreciation allowances for businesses. In 1978 Conable supported an unsuccessful bill to grant tax credits for tuition paid to private elementary and secondary schools. In that year he also argued in vain in behalf of allowing taxpayers reporting on the standard form to make a special additional deduction for charitable contributions. He claimed that such a benefit would encourage less affluent people to make more donations and would make the general practice of allowing deductions for charitable contributions look less like a loophole for well-to-do taxpayers who submit itemized reports.

With Ronald Reagan's election as president in 1980, it fell to Barber B. Conable Jr., as the ranking Republican on the committee, to guide through Ways and Means the administration's proposal for a three-year series of across-the-board, 10-percent tax reductions. Although skeptical about partisan claims that the plan would by itself revive the economy, he gave it his full support on the ground that an across-the-board cut would maintain a wider and healthier tax base than one aimed at relieving special constituencies. Moreover, Conable believed that he had no choice except to back the president's plan completely, because the Democratic majority in the House had taken 23 of the 36 seats on the Ways and Means Committee, a number disproportionately above the party's overall strength in the chamber. "I tell Danny that he robbed me of my independence," Conable commented in a reference to Ways and Means chairman Daniel D. Rostenkowski. "I tell him that in order to have any impact, the committee Republicans have to stick with the administration." In the end the Economic Recovery Tax Act of 1981 that Conable helped to fashion included most of the president's proposals.

In December 1981 Conable was named to the bipartisan, fifteen-member Social Security Advisory Commission formed by President Reagan to find a solution to the financial troubles of the social security system. The appointment gave Conable an opportunity to work on a problem that had long worried him as he watched the growth of social security benefits and taxes. In 1977 he had charged that the substantial tax hike obtained from Congress by President Jimmy Carter to restore the balance between social benefits and revenues was the "biggest peacetime tax increase in history" and would "soak the middle class." And by the early 1980s he was darkly predicting that the nation was on the verge of a "generational war" in which young Americans would refuse to continue supporting a system that could easily run out of funds before they reached old age. When the committee submitted its final report to the president in January 1983, the members recommended no alteration in the fundamental structure or principles of the social security system. They did, however, call for further increases in social security tax rates, the taxing of some benefits, delays in cost-of-living increases, and the extension of the system to include employees of nonprofit institutions and newly hired federal workers.

The growing federal budget deficits of the 1980s have caused Conable great concern and have led him to modify his positions on certain issues. In 1982 he enthusiastically endorsed the Tax Equity and Fiscal Responsibility Act, which raised revenues by closing some of the business-tax loopholes created in the preceding years. Likewise, in a reversal of a position he took in 1979, Conable pushed unsuccessfully for the adoption of a constitutional amendment requiring a balanced budget. In addition, he has continued to urge reductions in spending, particularly in the areas of military pensions, Medicare, and agricultural price supports.

Barber B. Conable Jr. has been married since September 13, 1952 to the former Charlotte Williams of Buffalo. Mrs. Conable, who was an administrator of the Women's Studies Program and Policy Center of George Washington University in the District of Columbia, has also been a member of the board of trustees of Cornell University and of the advisory council of the State University College at Brockport, New York. The Conables have three daughters, Anne, Jane, and Emily, and a son, Samuel. In Washington, Representative and Mrs. Conable live in a townhouse not far from Capitol Hill. Their permanent home is in the crossroads village of Alexander, New York, where they live in a farmhouse that was built in 1835. Conable has been described as a man who "sees politics in the context of life itself" and whose sense of humor has helped him maintain a perspective on the tumult of national legislative politics.

References: *Congressional Directory*, 1984; *N Y Times* p21 Ja 21 '78; *Wall St J* p10 Jl 9 '73, p26 My 20 '81; *Who's Who in America*, 1984–85

Cox, William Trevor *See* **Trevor, William**

Craft, Robert

Oct. 20, 1923– Conductor; author; music critic.
Address: b. c/o Alfred Knopf, Inc., 201 E. 50th
St., New York City, N.Y. 10022

Although he has established an enviable reputation as a conductor, writer, musicologist, and critic,
Robert Craft is still best known for his close,
twenty-three-year relationship with Igor Stravinsky as his musical assistant and adviser, co-
conductor, amanuensis, intellectual stimulus, and
virtually constant companion. In several articles
published in 1983, Craft has written more intro-
spectively than ever before about the symbiosis between himself and the man who is generally
regarded as this century's greatest composer. In so
doing, he has shed new light on the last decades of
Stravinsky's creativity and on his own controversial role in Stravinsky's career.

Robert Craft was born on October 20, 1923 in
Kingston, New York to Arpha (Lawson) and Raymond Craft, a real estate broker. He admits that his
precocious musicality caused him to lead "a kind
of secret childhood life." At the age of six he was
a boy soprano in an Episcopal church, and as a
thirteen-year-old student at the New York Military
Academy at Cornwall, he was already studying
and collecting such contemporary scores as Stravinsky's Les Noces and Le Sacre du Printemps and
Arnold Schoenberg's Pierrot Lunaire. He continued to pursue his interest in music at Tanglewood,
in Lenox, Massachusetts, Columbia University,
and the Juilliard School of Music, where he studied composition and conducting. As an undergraduate, Craft organized concerts featuring the music
of Stravinsky, Webern, and Schoenberg. After interrupting his studies to serve in the United States
Army Medical Corps in 1943–44, he obtained his
B.A. degree from Juilliard in 1946.

In the next year Craft founded the Chamber Art
Society, with which he made his professional conducting debut at the Hunter College Playhouse on
November 26, 1947. A critic for the New York Herald Tribune (November 27, 1947) was delighted
with his program of "choice works"—Bach's Brandenburg Concerto No. 2 in F, Mozart's Serenade
No. 12 in C, and Stravinsky's "Dumbarton Oaks"
Concerto in E-flat and L'Histoire du Soldat—but
expressed some reservations about his conducting.
Craft's concentration on "beating and cues at the
expense of the vital dynamic contrasts that give
excitement" disappointed the reviewer, who nevertheless concluded that "it was a tribute to so
young and inexperienced a conductor that he got
through such very difficult scores without major
catastrophe."

Over the course of more than thirty-five years on
the podium, Craft has conducted orchestras in
many major American cities and around the world.
He has also presided over many important premieres, including the first American performance
of Stravinsky's Threni (New York, January 4, 1959)
and of Alban Berg's unfinished opera Lulu (Santa
Fe, August 8, 1963), and the world premieres of Edgar Varèse's Nocturnal (New York, May 1, 1961)
and of such Stravinsky compositions as Agon (Los
Angeles, June 17, 1957); Anthem (Los Angeles, February 19, 1962); Abraham and Isaac (Jerusalem, August 23, 1964); Variations (Chicago, April 17, 1956);
and Requiem Canticles (Princeton, October 8,
1966).

Despite his widening experience Craft continued to receive mixed reviews remarkably like the
one that followed his conducting debut. No music
critic impugned his thorough knowledge or painstaking preparation of scores, but some reviewers
were alienated by what they considered his un-
emotional, colorless readings and "dry" style. The
majority of critics, however, share Raymond Eric-
son's opinion that Craft is a "first-rate interpreter
of contemporary scores for recordings." Craft's
credits include over twenty-five pioneering albums for Columbia Records and other companies,
encompassing the complete works of Schoenberg,
Webern, Berg, and Varèse. He has collaborated
with Stravinsky on many recordings of Stravinsky
compositions conducted by the composer himself.
The authority, clarity, and precision that Craft
brings to some of the most complex dodecaphonic
scores have consistently brought him critical acclaim. Writing in the New York Times (April 28,
1957), Edward Downes extolled Anton Webern:
The Complete Works as a "superb album." In his
assessment for the same newspaper (March 25,
1962) of Craft's two-record album of Berg's music,
Eric Salzman termed it "a fine and impressive
achievement."

Through his position as a conductor, Craft eventually met Igor Stravinsky and began a twenty-
three-year relationship that would profoundly affect twentieth-century music. For a Chamber Art
Society concert to be given in New York in April
1948, Craft wanted to conduct Stravinsky's Sym-

phonies of Wind Instruments (1920). Discovering that the score was locally unavailable, he wrote the composer to request a copy of the work, which he happened to be revising at that time. Stravinsky was so struck by the charm and scholarship of Craft's letter that he wrote back offering to conduct the Symphonies and his *Danses Concertantes* himself, free of charge.

Craft first met Stravinsky on March 31, 1948 at the Raleigh Hotel in Washington, D.C. to discuss the scheduled Town Hall concert. Both Stravinsky and his wife Vera, a painter, felt an almost immediate affinity with the much younger man. Impressed by the breadth and depth of Craft's knowledge of even his little-known scores, Stravinsky invited him to spend the summer in his Hollywood home to catalogue his manuscripts and help him with any difficulties that might arise in composing the English-language opera *The Rake's Progress*, for which W. H. Auden and Chester Kallman collaborated on the libretto, since he lacked fluency in English.

From the day he arrived, on June 1, 1949, until the composer's death, Craft was as much a surrogate son or alter ego as he was an assistant. He lived with the Stravinskys as a member of the family, accompanied them on their international travels (which occupied about eight months of each year), conducted more than 150 concerts in conjunction with Stravinsky, and spent every evening in his study, playing records, offering him ideas and criticism, and responding to his work in progress.

Although Craft worked daily with Stravinsky, he received no regular salary but was paid for particular assignments. For example, he received a fee for his selection of texts for *A Sermon, A Narrative and a Prayer* (1962), according to his article in the *Atlantic Monthly* (December 1982). He supplemented his income by directing the Chamber Art Society through 1950 and by conducting and recording (mainly for CBS) the works of a variety of composers ranging from Bach, Gesualdo, Haydn, Monteverdi, and Schütz to the atonalists. He was also a conductor of the Monday Evening Concerts and of the Evening-on-the-Roof series in Los Angeles from 1950 to 1968 and lectured at the Dartington School in England in 1957 and at the Princeton Seminar in Advanced Musical Studies in 1959.

In a reflective piece published in the *New York Review of Books* on June 10, 1982, more than ten years after Stravinsky's death, Craft tried to explain the bond that formed between him and Stravinsky. He suggested that at the time of his 1948 meeting with Stravinsky, the composer stood at a crossroads in his artistic development. Although the Stravinskys had lived for more than ten years in the United States, they still associated chiefly with an émigré community, perhaps because of the Russian-born composer's limited command of English. As Craft pointed out: "Most of his music was not in print, he was not recording, and concert organizations wanted him to conduct only *Firebird* and *Petrushka*. More important, he was becoming increasingly isolated from the developments that

extended from Arnold Schoenberg and attracted the young. Stravinsky . . . wanted to understand this other, unfamiliar music, but did not know how to go about it." Since Craft had known Schoenberg, the father of the twelve-tone school, personally, and was familiar with his scores and those of the other prominent atonalists, he was well equipped to introduce Stravinsky, a staunch supporter of neoclassicism, to dodecaphony.

After Schoenberg's death on July 13, 1951, Stravinsky's attitude toward serial music gradually changed. Encouraged by Craft, he began to listen to recordings of Webern and Schoenberg, among other atonalists. He attended every rehearsal of Schoenberg's *Septet-Suite* that Craft was to conduct on February 24, 1954 and the concert itself. A week after that concert, according to Craft's account in his *Atlantic Monthly* article, Stravinsky broke down weeping, overwhelmed by the impression the concert had made on him, and said he could no longer compose. Craft responded by suggesting that he re-instrumentate his Concertino for String Quartet. Several months later, Stravinsky had completed both that orchestration and the initial section of the *Cantata*. His first cautious ventures into serial composition—the Septet (1953) and parts of the *Cantata*—soon followed.

Stravinsky once wrote, "My young friend . . . is slowly working himself into my music." That Craft conducted rehearsals for Stravinsky's concerts, stood in for him if he could not fulfill his conducting duties, copied scores and checked corrections in them for the composer, and relieved him of other chores was common knowledge. The full extent of Craft's influence on Stravinsky's work, however, has long been a subject of controversy. Writing in the *New Republic* (January 10, 1970), Robert Evett concluded that since Stravinsky's move into the camp of "his old arch-enemies, the modern Viennese school," took place only after his association with Craft, a known proponent of atonalism, "in the marriage of Stravinsky and Dodecaphony, it was Craft who instructed the postulant in the articles of faith, received him into the church, and officiated at the wedding."

Craft confirmed that contention in his piece in the *Atlantic Monthly*, admitting that "to some extent [he] 'directed' and 'controlled' Stravinsky." "In truth," he added, "every Stravinsky opus after and including the Septet and *In Memoriam Dylan Thomas* (1954) was undertaken as a result of discussions between us. . . . I sometimes went so far as to suggest forms that new pieces might take." He concluded that "without [him] Stravinsky would not have taken the path he did."

The 1957 interview that Craft held with Stravinsky on the occasion of his seventy-fifth birthday began a literary collaboration that renewed and perhaps intensified the debate about their relationship. Originally published in several mass-circulation magazines, the interview consisted of brief, leading questions answered at length by the composer. Fleshed out with Stravinsky's correspondence with Claude Debussy, Maurice Ravel,

Dylan Thomas, and others, it formed the basis of *Conversations with Igor Stravinsky* (Doubleday, 1959), the first of six volumes on which he and Craft collaborated. In it, Stravinsky discussed his works and the process of composition, volunteered his opinions of various musicians and other prominent figures, and reminisced about his life. The following two Stravinsky-Craft collaborations, *Memories and Commentaries* (1960) and *Expositions and Developments* (1962), both published by Doubleday, retained the question-answer format. Those books provided more detail about Stravinsky's early years in Russia, especially his studies with Rimsky-Korsakov, the breakdown of his relationship with Diaghilev, and the influence Tchaikovsky had on him. Selections from his correspondence—with Romain Rolland, Serge Diaghilev, Paul Valéry, André Gide, and W. H. Auden—were again included, and a reproduction of the first draft that he and Auden produced for *The Rake's Progress* was inserted in an Appendix to *Memories*.

Most reviewers welcomed the three books for their revelations about Stravinsky and for the virtues of their prose style. Donald Ritchie's appraisal in the *Nation* (June 27, 1959) can be taken as representative: "[The conversations] are wonderful for a number of reasons: they give completely invaluable insight into the process of composition in general, Stravinsky's in particular; they tell more about music and musicians than any other work, and the telling ranges from illuminating commentary to the raciest kind of gossip; and—perhaps most important—they present Stravinsky as he really is."

In the last three collaborations—*Dialogues and a Diary* (Doubleday, 1963), *Themes and Episodes* (Knopf, 1966), and *Retrospectives and Conclusions* (Knopf, 1969)—the "dialogues" with Stravinsky became more like monologues as the interviewer grew less intrusive, and substantial selections from Craft's journal, kept throughout his association with the composer, were included for the first time in the 1963 volume and claimed a larger portion of those that followed, complementing Stravinsky's own account of his life and work. The diary entries discuss every aspect of Craft's life with the Stravinskys, focusing on their home life as well as on their travels, which took the trio around most of the world and often into the company of such luminaries as T. S. Eliot, Isaiah Berlin, Graham Greene, Aldous Huxley, Christopher Isherwood, Stephen Spender, and Ingmar Bergman.

Like a few other critics, John Beckwith, writing in *Canadian Forum* (July 1964), was irritated by the "highly literary and overprecise" language and the "unholy amount of name-dropping and 'in' references" the authors indulged in, but most reviewers warmed to the "spontaneous candor" of the volumes, proclaiming them "an unfailingly profitable mine of fact and insight" and "some of the most lively and intelligent casual reading available." The selections from Craft's diaries were especially well received, and when the complete journals were published as *Stravinsky: Chronicle*

of a Friendship, 1948–71 (Knopf, 1972) one year after Stravinsky's death, Ned Rorem commented in the *New Republic* (June 3, 1972) that Craft "remains aloof, all-knowing, while he involves the reader in the very texture of life. . . . He proves again that he is not only compassionate and sometimes wickedly funny, but the most readable and intelligent living writer on music."

Before *Chronicle* appeared, however, Craft was caught up in a literary-musical scandal fueled by pre-publication publicity for *And Music at the Close: Stravinsky's Last Years* (Norton, 1972) by Lillian Libman, who was Stravinsky's personal manager from 1959 to 1971. As reported in a front-page story by Donal Henahan in the *New York Times* (March 3, 1972), Miss Libman charged that Craft's portrait of Stravinsky as "a dominating, stabbing, extraordinarily witty figure who consorted with the great only" had little relationship to the real Stravinsky, whom she knew as ailing, benevolent, and rather taciturn; that Stravinsky's answers to the questions Craft put to him in interviews were written entirely by Craft; that Craft was not present, as he asserted in his published diary, during an interview between Stravinsky and Yevgeny Yevtushenko; and that several recordings of Stravinsky's work that Columbia had released under the rubric "supervised" or "conducted" by the composer were actually conducted by Craft when Stravinsky was not in the studio. Heralded as "the ideal chronicler of Stravinsky's life, times and ideas" by Simon Karlinsky in the *New York Times Book Review* (July 2, 1972), Craft was now charged by Pierre Boulez in *Time* (June 26, 1972) with "a great falsification of the image of Stravinsky." On the other hand, Ned Rorem maintained in the *New Republic* (June 3, 1972) that Craft's authorship of many interviews credited to Stravinsky "has long been common knowledge to the musical community" and that there was no reason for outrage "when Craft merely interpreted Stravinsky's intellectual thought in communicative English, even as he interpreted the composer's musical thought from the podium."

In articles published in the *New York Review of Books* (April 6, 1972 and June 29, 1972) and the *Guardian* (November 18, 1972), Craft admitted that he should have made it clear from the beginning how the collaboration between him and Stravinsky worked. "Stravinsky spoke, and I put the words together. I don't say they were his words." He also confessed to not having been present during the Yevtushenko interview and to having conducted without Stravinsky's supervision the recordings of *Capriccio for Piano and Orchestra* and *Danses Concertantes* released by Columbia. Nevertheless, he vehemently denied that his portrait of the composer was at all distorted and charged that Miss Libman, in any event, was not close enough to Stravinsky to have had access to the truth. "Only two people know anything about Stravinsky," he asserted. "Only Mrs. Stravinsky and I know. Nobody else can come in now and say what happened."

Since Stravinsky's death, Craft has continued to conduct and record, though in an attempt to break out of Stravinsky's shadow, he generally refuses to appear at all-Stravinsky programs. He writes regularly on music and on contemporary culture for the *New York Review of Books* and other journals, and was a columnist for *World* magazine. Three collections of his pieces have been published by Knopf under the titles *Prejudices in Disguise* (1974), *Current Convictions* (1977), and *Present Perspectives* (1984). Craft is currently editing a multivolume edition of Stravinsky's correspondence. The first two volumes, both published by Knopf, appeared in 1982 and 1984. He also wrote the introduction to *A Stravinsky Scrapbook 1940-1971* (Thames and Hudson, 1984), a collection of nearly 300 photographs of the composer, his wife, and his associates. For his criticism, he received an award in 1976 from the American Academy of Arts and Letters.

Tall, slender, and scholarly in appearance, Robert Craft is a voracious reader and a painstaking as well as prolific writer. He is said to have a photographic memory. Craft claims not to be "a specialist in the music of any particular period. I am a specialist in the music I like. . . . and that certainly includes great portions of the standard repertory." He now makes his home on Manhattan's West Side.

References: Atlan 250:68+ D '82; Herald Tribune IV p5 D 20 '59 por; Hi Fi 14:23+ Jl '64 pors; N Y Rev of Books 29:6+ Je 10 '82; Time 73:70 Ja 19 '59 por; Contemporary Authors new rev vol 7 (1982); New Grove Dictionary of Music and Musicians vols 5 and 18 (1980); Who's Who in America, 1984-85

Craxi, Bettino
(krok´sē bā-tē´nō)

Feb. 24, 1934- Prime Minister of Italy. Address: b. Office of the Prime Minister, Rome, Italy; h. Via Foppo 5, 1-20144 Milan, Italy

When Bettino Craxi took office on August 4, 1983 as Italy's prime minister, he became the youngest person and the first Socialist to hold that post in the republic. As secretary of the Italian Socialist party in the preceding seven years, Craxi had arrested that group's long-term decline and had secured its position as the country's third strongest political force, ranking only behind the Christian Democrats and the Communists. Nevertheless, the Socialists still command the loyalty of only 10 percent

of the electorate, and Craxi must try to govern through a shaky five-party coalition that has repeatedly collapsed in the past few years. Craxi's pragmatic and moderate stance with regard to domestic issues and his pro-Western orientation in foreign affairs will help him maintain control over the majority in his coalition, whose philosophies are more conservative than his. It is not clear, however, that his government will be able to deal more effectively than its many predecessors with Italy's nagging economic problems, including 16 percent inflation, 10 percent unemployment, and a deficit amounting to 15 percent of the country's gross national product.

Bettino Craxi—who was christened Benedetto but has been called by the diminutive version of his name since his infancy—was born on February 24, 1934 in Milan, Italy. His father was a lawyer and a Socialist politician who had migrated from his native Sicily. During World War II the Craxis lived north of Milan in a house where they took refuge from the incessant bombing raids and provided shelter for partisans and for Jews seeking to escape the German occupation. Although Craxi is now an anticlerical, as a thirteen-year-old he once thought of joining the priesthood. Instead, he took the first step toward his own political career by working in his father's unsuccessful 1948 campaign for Parliament on a Popular Front ticket uniting Socialists and Communists.

Craxi enrolled at the University of Milan to study law, but he never completed his degree because he wanted to devote his time to politics and to the Socialist party, which he joined as an eighteen-year-old. Active in the Socialist Youth Movement and on the staffs of a socialist daily and scientific review, he was soon named to the party's committee in the province of Lombardy and, shortly before his twenty-third birthday, was made a member of the national party's central committee. In 1960 he first tasted electoral success when he won a seat on the city council in Milan. Five years later he was named secretary of the Socialist party in Milan and made a member of the national party's executive committee. In 1968 Craxi won election to the Parliament as a delegate from Milan, and he has retained that seat in each of the four succeeding general elections.

During his first years in Parliament Bettino Craxi was an obscure politician who was unknown, according to the public opinion polls, to 90 percent of the Italian people. Obscure or not, the young Milanese became a favorite of Pietro Nenni, the grand old man of the Socialist movement. In 1970 Craxi became a deputy secretary of the Socialist party and gradually began to build his power base within the organization, so that when the Socialists stumbled badly in the 1976 general election, he was ready to make his move. The aging Francesco de Martino stepped aside as the party's general secretary, and on July 16, 1976 the faction-ridden Socialists, in a compromise, selected Craxi to replace him.

Immediately setting to work to revitalize his party, Craxi made his first concern the establishment for Italy's Socialists of an identity distinct from that of the country's Communists. Unlike their counterparts who dominate the political left in France, Spain, Portugal, and Greece, Italy's Socialists have been constantly overshadowed by the Communists, who rank a close second in electoral strength to the right-of-center Christian Democrats. Craxi's strategy has been to purge extreme leftists from the Socialist ranks, to recruit more moderate ones, and to promote younger leaders who are personally loyal to him. In a symbolic gesture, he has changed the party's emblem from the traditional hammer and sickle to a red carnation, and though he has occasionally cooperated with the Communists to preserve left-of-center political control in some locales, he has steadily attacked them at the national level. Craxi and other Socialist spokesmen have accused the Italian Communists of ideological dependence on the Soviet Union, expressing doubt that a party with a Marxist-Leninist philosophy can play a legitimate role in a democratic and pluralist state.

To broaden the Socialists' appeal, Craxi has taken advantage of the inflexibility of the Christian Democrats on the right as well as of the Communists on the left. Aware of the decline of social class background as the determining factor in Italian electoral behavior, he has responded to the rise of issue-oriented politics. Courting Italy's rising new entrepreneurs, managers, and professionals, he has tried to present the Socialist party as a centrist organization capable of providing direction for a country whose governments have too often been immobilized by factionalism. Craxi won a major victory at the forty-second congress of the Socialist party, held in Palermo, Sicily in April 1981, when the delegates adopted a set of "Theses" disavowing the extremism of the past and committing the party to "pragmatism, gradualism, and reform."

The positions taken in recent years by Italy's Socialists have resembled those of Germany's Social Democratic party, for which Craxi has such great admiration. Although the Socialists maintain their allegiance to the welfare state, they reject as goals the nationalization of Italian industry and the introduction of highly centralized economic planning, and express strong opposition to the Soviet Union, which Craxi has scored as "an illiberal society with a few socialist traits." They advocate a series of constitutional reforms, including several that would increase the powers of the executive branch, prevent the parliamentary overthrow of a government unless the supporters of the vote of no confidence have an alternative program with majority backing, and that would establish a minimum percentage of the popular vote that a party must get to qualify for any seats in the legislature. Perhaps the most radical position adopted by Craxi and his followers has been their willingness to negotiate for the release of hostages taken by terrorist groups such as the Red Brigades, which murdered former Prime Minister Aldo Moro in 1978.

Craxi's efforts to revitalize the Socialist party bore results in the local elections held in May 1978, when the Socialists took 13.1 percent of the vote, exceeding by 3.5 percent their performance in the general election of 1976 and almost equaling their share in the local elections of 1974. That improved showing emboldened Craxi shortly after that to nominate eighty-one-year-old Alessandro Pertini to assume the Italian presidency in place of the Christian Democrat Giovanni Leone, who had resigned in response to allegations of corruption. After taking sixteen ballots the Christian Democrats acquiesced in the choice, and on July 9, 1978 the popular and widely respected Pertini began his seven-year term as the first Socialist president of the republic. A year later Pertini was able to return the favor. In the spring of 1979 the Communist party, angered at being excluded from the cabinet, brought down the government of the Christian Democratic Prime Minister Giulio Andreotti. When the Socialists gained 9.8 percent of the votes cast in the June general elections, Pertini asked Craxi to form a government. Hoping to exclude the Communists, who had taken 30.4 percent of the vote, from the cabinet and to build a coalition with the Christian Democrats, the Social Democrats, the Liberals, and the Republicans, Craxi negotiated for seventeen days, but the Christian Democrats, who had gathered 38.3 percent of the vote, wanted a greater share in the government than he was willing to offer. Eventually Pertini had to turn to the Christian Democrat Francesco Cossiga, who formed a government with the Social Democrats and the Liberals but with the tacit agreement of the Socialists to abstain from parliamentary votes.

In March 1980 the Socialists and the Republicans toppled the Cossiga government by withdrawing their passive support. When, in April, Cossiga formed his second administration, the Socialists became part of the governing majority for the first time since 1974 and received nine of the twenty-seven seats in the cabinet. In return, Craxi implicitly promised to cooperate with the Christian Democrats in the future to insure Italy's "governability." The new Cossiga administration lasted until September 1980 when it suffered a vote of no confidence in its economic program.

Four administrations governed Italy between the autumn of 1980 and the spring of 1983. The Socialists took part in each one, and though Craxi chose not to hold a portfolio in any of them, his influence was evident, so much so that commentators have contended that Craxi, whose leadership was endorsed by 70 percent of the Socialist delegates at the forty-second congress in 1981, played the critical role in toppling all four administrations. In May 1981 he signaled the end of the government of Christian Democratic Prime Minister Arnaldo Forlani by boycotting a meeting at which coalition members were to discuss charges that key political figures belonged to a secret Masonic lodge that was linked to corruption and to efforts to undermine the constitution. In August 1982 he withdrew the Socialists from the coalition government headed by Giovanni Spadolini, the Republican party leader who had taken office thirteen months earlier as the first non-Christian Democratic prime minister since 1946. Craxi had been angered by the cooperation of some Christian Democratic members of the majority in defeating a plan to curb tax benefits enjoyed by the oil industry. Nevertheless, he agreed to join a new Spadolini government in return for concessions that gave more power to the office of prime minister and reduced the use of secret votes in parliament.

When, in November 1982, internal bickering brought down Spadolini's regime, the Socialists joined in the new government of Christian Democrat Amintore Fanfani. Craxi, however, soon broke with that administration too, and the seventy-five-year-old Fanfani resigned on April 29, 1983. Craxi claimed to have been distressed by the Fanfani government's turn to the right on economic policies, but observers believed that he primarily wanted to make inevitable the calling of a general election a year ahead of schedule.

The elections precipitated by the fall of the Fanfani government turned out to be a disaster for the Christian Democrats and a disappointment for the Communists. The former took only 32.9 percent of the ballots cast on June 26–27, a figure that amounted to a 5.4 percent decline from their performance in 1979 and marked the first time since 1948 that the party had captured less than 38 percent of the vote. The Communists' share fell by a half-point to 29.9 percent. The Socialists, who failed to make the gains they had expected, were able to increase their hold on the electorate only to 11.4 percent. The arrest, during the campaign, of some Socialist leaders on charges of corruption and some negative reactions to Craxi's drive for power may have been responsible for their relatively poor showing. The neo-fascist Social Movement, with a 1.6 percent increase to 6.8 percent, consolidated its standing as Italy's fourth-largest party; the right-of-center Republicans scored the largest proportional gain with a rise from 3.0 percent to 5.1 percent; and

about one out of every five voters submitted blank or spoiled ballots or threw their support to a splinter group.

Despite the Socialists' modest showing, the party clearly held the balance of power, and President Pertini once again authorized Craxi to form a government. The Communists called on the Socialists to join forces with them, noting that, for the first time since World War II, the left-of-center parties had enough strength to form a government without the Christian Democrats' participation, but Craxi, who rejected the "leftist alternative," set out to build an alliance of Socialists, Christian Democrats, Social Democrats, Republicans, and Liberals that could control 366 of the 630 seats in the parliament. Although he succeeded in creating a government in which three former prime ministers agreed to serve, the Socialists had to pay a price, for they obtained only five cabinet appointments instead of the eight they had held in the previous administration. The lost ministries of defense, which former Prime Minister Spadolini received, and of finance went to the rising Republican party. And in exchange for accepting Craxi as prime minister, the Christian Democrats took the next three highest ranking posts, with former Prime Minister Forlani becoming deputy prime minister, former Prime Minister Andreotti minister of foreign affairs, and Oscar Scalfaro minister of the interior.

Within a little more than a week after taking office on August 4, Craxi's government won important votes of confidence in the Chamber of Deputies and in the Senate, allowing him to pursue the struggle against inflation, which he identified, in a speech on August 9, as the "immediate and dominant objective" of his administration. Since then, the prime minister has introduced an austerity budget that cuts $18.75 billion in expenditures, including $6 billion for health, pension, and social security benefits, and that adds about $6.3 billion in new taxes. Critics on the left have attacked the budget, but Craxi denies that his government has turned to the right and dismisses his opponents as "fourth-rate demagogues."

In foreign affairs Craxi has pursued a strictly pro-American course and, despite the Italian's socialist ideology, he was warmly received by President Ronald Reagan during a visit to Washington in mid-October 1983. At that time the prime minister reaffirmed his country's commitment to accept American Pershing and cruise missiles if the negotiations then taking place in Geneva between the United States and the Soviet Union failed to produce a formula for mutual arms reduction. Craxi and Reagan also announced the formation of a joint Italian-American commission to fight organized crime and to break the drug connection that routes through Sicily as much as 70 percent of the heroin headed for the northeastern United States. Finally, Craxi, whose nation has contributed the largest contingent to the multinational peacekeeping force in Lebanon, suggested to Reagan that the United States, Europe and Saudi Arabia pledge to give money for rebuilding that ravaged land if its warring factions quickly negotiate a settlement. The prime minister later reported that American officials had greeted his plan with "appreciation and interest."

Although his economic policies had provoked the Communists into full-fledged opposition, by mid-1984 Craxi could point with pride to some positive achievements, including the signing, on February 18, of a concordat with the Vatican under the terms of which Roman Catholicism lost its status as the Italian state religion. Other successes were the role of Italian peacekeeping troops in Lebanon; attacks on the crime "families" of Sicily, Calabria, and Naples; attempts at industrial renewal through applying new technology; steps towards welfare and constitutional reform; and a reduction in state spending and a continuing war on inflation.

Bettino Craxi stands six feet three inches tall and has a robust physique. His chubby face, owlish spectacles, and encroaching baldness have made him a favorite butt of political cartoonists. Since his election as prime minister Craxi has dispensed with the blue jeans, open-neck shirts, and other casual attire that he wore in the past in favor of the conservative wardrobe normally associated with national leaders. Craxi is almost as much at home in French and English as he is in Italian and is a gifted public speaker who avoids the oratorical flourishes characteristic of old-style politicians in his country. The prime minister is the author of several volumes of political essays, including *Socialismo e realtà* (1973), *Nove lettere da Praga* (1973), *Socialismo da Santiago a Praga* (1976), and *Construire il futuro* (1977). He is the co-author of *Inequality in the World* (1977).

Prime Minister Bettino Craxi has been described as a man who is more likely to have admirers and enemies than friends, and a public opinion poll taken in 1982 rated only the Pope and Fiat chairman Gianni Agnelli as being more powerful than the Socialist leader. Craxi is said to be drivingly ambitious, ruthless toward opponents even within his own party, and arrogant, but he is also scrupulously honest, and his leadership skills have led some to nickname him "the king." His heroes include the nineteenth-century Italian revolutionary Giuseppe Garibaldi, whose memorabilia he collects, the late American president John F. Kennedy, and Chile's slain Socialist leader Salvador Allende. Craxi, who draws, plays the guitar, and reads in history and politics for his recreation, is an art and film enthusiast who maintains close friendships with a number of writers, actresses, and musicians. Since 1959 Bettino Craxi has been married to Anna Maria Moncini, the daughter of a Socialist railroad worker, whom he met at the University of Milan. Craxi's wife and son and daughter live in Milan, while the prime minister maintains quarters in the Hotel Raphael near the Piazza Navone, in Rome.

References: *Christian Sci Mon* p3 Ag 2 '83 por; *Guardian* p17 My 6 '83; *N Y Times* p3 Ag 5 '83 por; *Toronto Globe and Mail* p8 Ag 5 '83;

International Who's Who, 1984-85; Who's Who in Italy, 1980

Cross, Ben

Dec. 16, 1947– Actor. Address: c/o International Creative Management, Ltd., 22 Grafton St., London W.1, England; Levinson Associates Inc., 927 La Cienega Blvd., Los Angeles, Calif. 90069

The troubled British film industry received a major boost on March 29, 1982, when one of its productions, *Chariots of Fire*, a dramatic account of the victories of two British runners at the 1924 Olympics, won the Oscar award of the Academy of Motion Picture Arts and Sciences for best picture of 1981 over several more elaborate Hollywood films. At the Los Angeles ceremony at which the award was announced, Ben Cross, one of the two stars of *Chariots of Fire*, responded by jumping, according to the man sitting behind him, "out of his seat— about four feet." Cross's jubilation was understandable, because he had previously been virtually unknown despite some success in musicals on London's West End. Since then, his face has become familiar to television viewers on both sides of the Atlantic who have watched him in the miniseries *The Flame Trees of Thika*, *The Citadel*, and *The Far Pavilions*.

Ben Cross, whose given name was originally Bernard, was born into an Irish Roman Catholic family on December 16, 1947 in Paddington, a working-class section of London, England. His father, the doorman of an apartment building, died when Ben was eight of tuberculosis contracted as a member of the Royal Army Medical Corps in

Burma during World War II. Cross's mother worked from dawn to dusk at three separate jobs as a cook and cleaning woman, to support the family, which also included two older sisters. "We weren't ruddy-faced impoverished," Ben Cross told Michael Heaton of *People* (April 5, 1982), "but towards the end of the week we ate potatoes."

Cross's love of the theatre stems from the time he was six or seven, when his father took him to one of London's old music halls. At twelve he made his stage debut, playing Jesus Christ in a pageant at his Roman Catholic secondary school in Streatham. Recalling that experience, he told Edmund Newton of New York City's *Soho Weekly News* (March 2, 1982): "They had me struggling through the school hallways, carrying a big cross on my back, with a crown of thorns and strawberry jam dripping down my forehead. My mother, who had been positioned in the hall to see me, turned to my sister and said, 'My goodness, what's wrong with Bernard?'" Playing Toad of Toad Hall in another school play, based on Kenneth Grahame's *The Wind in the Willows*, Ben Cross discovered that he could make people laugh. "There's a power in that," he told Newton. The talent that he displayed prompted a teacher to suggest that he try drama school. Consequently, he sent in an application to the Royal Academy of Dramatic Art, but when the time came for the audition, he was too timid to make his appearance.

Not as successful in his academic studies as in his theatrical endeavors, fifteen-year-old Ben Cross, to his mother's dismay, left school and home within the same week to work at what he he has described as "a motley ragbag of jobs," including chicken gutter, dishwasher, furniture salesman, and window cleaner. His eye was, however, still on the theatre. While cleaning windows at the Wimbledon Theatre in London, Cross learned of an opening for someone to help build the sets, and he obtained the job. That brought him other backstage work, leading to positions as master carpenter for the Welsh National Opera and stage manager at a theatre in Birmingham. By the time he was twenty-one, Cross faced a dilemma, in which, as he recalled in an interview with Lawrence Van Gelder of the *New York Times* (October 2, 1981), he had to decide either to "make a career of the backstage side of things" or to start over and do what he really wanted to do. Choosing the latter course, he reapplied to the Royal Academy, showed up for the audition this time, and was accepted.

After graduating in 1972 from RADA, where he had appeared in *Oedipus Rex* and *Next Time I'll Sing to You*, among other productions, Cross worked in 1973 and 1974 in provincial repertory. At the Duke's Playhouse in Lancaster he played Algernon in *The Importance of Being Earnest*, and also appeared in *Macbeth* and *Death of a Salesman*, and at the Haymarket Theater in Leicester he was in *Joseph and the Amazing Technicolor Dreamcoat, Equus, Mind Your Head*, and *Irma La Douce*. From 1973 to 1975 he was also a member of the Prospect Theatre, which at that time had no permanent home but toured in Great Britain and abroad. Cross was in the cast of the company's 1973 BBC production of *The Melancholy Hussar of the German Legion*, and he appeared in its stage productions of Shakespeare's *Pericles, Twelfth Night*, and *Henry V* (as the Chorus), and of Peter Shaffer's *The Royal Hunt of the Sun*. He was also in the company's musical *Pilgrim*, based on John Bunyan's *Pilgrim's Progress*, and in a musical version of Dickens' *Great Expectations*.

Cross traveled with the Prospect Theatre Company to West Germany, Italy, and Hong Kong, and also visited the Soviet Union, where he became involved, along with other members of the company, in an effort to obtain freedom for the Jewish ballet dancers Valery and Galina Panov, who were then seeking permission to emigrate. After meeting with the Panovs in Leningrad, Cross was, according to Lawrence Van Gelder of the *New York Times* (October 2, 1981), "punched and kicked by members of the KGB" in what he remembered as his "first real contact with anti-Semitism." Later he managed to smuggle some tape and film back to England for the "Free the Panovs" committee.

The prestigious Royal Shakespeare Company was Cross's next employer. He understudied Alan Howard, who had the lead role of Rover in the RSC's production of the eighteenth-century comedy *Wild Oats*, but Howard never missed a performance. Although Cross managed to obtain a small part of his own, that of Flight Sergeant Kevin Cartwright, in the RSC production of Peter Nichols' *Privates on Parade*, which opened at London's Aldwych Theatre in February 1977, he decided to leave the RSC and seek greater opportunity elsewhere. That opportunity came in London productions of American musicals. He created the role of Wally in *I Love My Wife*, which opened at the Prince of Wales in October 1977 under the direction of Gene Saks, and remained with the show for a year. In Bob Fosse's *Chicago*, which had its London premiere at the Cambridge in April 1979, Cross appeared for nine months as the male lead, Billy Flynn, the lawyer who sings "Razzle Dazzle." In an interview with Pat Lowry in *Women's Wear Daily* (November 16, 1983) Cross described the role as one of his most memorable. "I loved it," he recalled. "It was smutty and irreverent, and [Billy] was a likable rogue." Musicals in general, he told Pat Lowry, are hard work, "but they tend to be comedic and I love comedy."

When a fellow cast member asked what he planned to do after *Chicago* closed, Cross replied facetiously that he wanted to "become a film star." His motion picture experience at that time consisted of a minor role in the all-star war epic *A Bridge Too Far* (United Artists, 1977). Shortly after that, his agent telephoned to suggest that he try out for the part of Harold Abrahams, the 100-meter running champion of the 1924 Olympics in the forthcoming *Chariots of Fire*. Cross's first response was: "You must be joking." Not only did his background greatly differ from that of Abrahams, a wealthy Jew who had attended Cambridge University, but, as he explained to George Vecsey of the *New York Times* (February 28, 1982), his only exercise since leaving school had come from "running to pubs late at night." A run, however, was part of the audition, and so Cross began what proved to be an arduous training process. By the time director Hugh Hudson and producer David Puttnam clocked the candidates for parts in a series of timed runs (Cross and the others refused to race against each other), they were delighted to discover that Cross had finished among the top five out of thirty contenders.

Having won the role of Abrahams, Cross continued to train until he was working out for seven hours daily, doing 600 sit-ups and 500 push-ups as well as jogging several miles a day. The two-and-a-half months of exercise served him and his costar, Ian Charleson, well for the Olympic running scenes of the film, which were shot in one day because of budgetary constraints. After repeating his 100-meter dash several times for different takes, Cross could tell Richard Benyo, as quoted in *Runner's World* (January 1982): "We know absolutely what athletes go through."

In addition to getting into shape physically, Cross immersed himself in the character of Abrahams so thoroughly that his wife exclaimed, "I thought I married a crazy Irish actor. What am I doing living with a crazy Jewish athlete?" In order to be able to copy Abrahams' stride exactly, Cross read textbooks by the athlete and by his coach, Sam Mussabini. In addition, to get an idea of what Abrahams went through as a Jew, he learned some Hebrew and had discussions with a rabbi and with a Jewish financial adviser to the Queen. He also found that his experiences with the Panovs had been helpful in preparing him for that aspect of the role. Cross eventually decided that, despite the obvious differences between himself and Abrahams, he did have something in common with him: what he described to Joyce Wadler in the *Washington Post* (December 3, 1983) as "a mad, driven quality." He added that he was "not driven by a desire for success" but by "a fear of failure."

Released in Great Britain by Twentieth Century-Fox, *Chariots of Fire* had its world premiere in London on March 30, 1981 at the annual royal film performance and met with raves from most critics. David Robinson of the London *Times* (April 3, 1981) called it "the kind of picture for which we have been looking to the British film industry, in vain, for several years, . . . a film of substance and intelligence." The performances of Cross and of Charleson—in the role of Eric Liddell, a devout Scottish Presbyterian—prove, according to Robinson, "how much more exciting it is for the audience to see new talents—extended by the challenge— than the old faces, however well loved."

Those sentiments were echoed by American critics later in the year, when *Chariots of Fire* was released in the United States by Warner Brothers. David Denby of *New York* magazine (October 5, 1981), one of a minority of critics who were unenthusiastic about the film, wrote that it was "vibrantly alive" whenever Cross came on screen.

Another member of that minority, Pauline Kael, referred in her *New Yorker* review (October 26, 1981) to Cross's "performance of unusual dignity."

Many of the American critics had already seen *Chariots of Fire* at the Cannes Film Festival in the spring of 1981. Anticipating that the film would lose in competition for the major prizes, those critics ran their own straw poll, in which *Chariots of Fire* took top honors. Later that year it was the opening attraction at the New York Film Festival, and in March 1982 it won Oscar awards for the best screenplay, costume design, and original soundtrack, as well as best picture of 1981. *Chariots of Fire* became the highest-grossing imported film in American history. Cross only received approximately $10,000 for his performance, but he told Roderick Mann of the *Los Angeles Times* (June 23, 1983): "I'm not complaining. . . . It was certainly the most money I'd ever earned."

Even before *Chariots* opened in London, Cross had resumed his career in the British theatre. He accepted an offer to appear in 1981 in a revival of David Hare's *Knuckle* at the Thorndike Theatre in Leatherhead. That was followed later in the year by another American musical, *I'm Getting My Act Together and Taking It on the Road*, a feminist-oriented, two-character show in which Cross played Joe Epstein, the manager of a singer played by Diane Langton. After that, he costarred with Dorothy Tutin in a BBC-TV version of the play *Life After Death*.

Ben Cross received several film offers following his success in *Chariots of Fire*, but he chose to concentrate on television instead. "Of all the jobs I've been offered, television was the best quality," he told Judy Klemesrud of the *New York Times* (November 20, 1983). "I haven't liked most of the films I've been offered. . . . Film has the greatest international audience, so you have to be very choosy about what you do." Cross's performance in *The Flame Trees of Thika* (1980), made by the British commercial production company Thames Television, was like a vacation for him, not only because of its African location, but also because his supporting role as a big-game hunter was relatively minor, and he did not feel the weight of the production on his shoulders as he had with *Chariots of Fire*. The seven-part saga of a British family in Kenya was shown on American public television's *Masterpiece Theatre* in 1982. Cross took the role of Soviet marshal Mikhail Tukhachevsky in the CBS-TV movie *Coming Out of the Ice* (1982).

After some bargaining with Actors Equity, Ben Cross made his American stage debut in 1982, playing the sinister actor Jeremiah Grady, who returns to America from England to haunt the family of the woman who infected him with syphilis and to avenge his father's murder, in John Guare's Gothic comedy-melodrama *Lydie Breeze*, directed by Louis Malle. The rule at that time was that foreign actors could obtain permission to perform in the United States only if they were members of a repertory company or stars of international stature. Although Cross admittedly did not feel qualified on the second count, he was given special permission to appear in the production. *Lydie Breeze* opened Off Broadway at the American Place Theater to reviews that were mixed for the play, but more generally appreciative of Cross. According to Sylviane Gold, writing in the *Soho Weekly News* (March 9, 1982), "The role is an actor's showpiece, and Cross is sensational, in the true meaning of the word: his acting hits you like a body blow."

Cross returned to television to star in *The Citadel*, BBC's ten-hour adaptation of A. J. Cronin's novel about the idealistic Dr. Andrew Manson and his disillusionment with the corruption of the British medical profession in the 1930s. When *The Citadel* began its *Masterpiece Theatre* run in the United States in November 1983, Cross's performance brought him the critical acclaim with which he was by now familiar. John J. O'Connor wrote in the *New York Times* (November 18, 1983), for example, that he played Manson "to grim and winning perfection."

In the *New York Times* interview with Judy Klemesrud, Cross observed that he tends to play misfits, adding, "I think Ben Cross might like those roles because he's a bit of a misfit himself." That description seems to apply to Ashton Pelham-Martyn, the character portrayed by Cross in the miniseries *The Far Pavilions*, based on a novel by M. M. Kaye. The orphaned son of British parents, Pelham-Martyn was raised in India by an Indian woman. He originally believes himself to be Indian, later discovers that he is English, joins the British army, and falls in love with an Indian princess, played by Amy Irving. In his own words, as he told Steve Wasserman of the *Dial* (November 1983), the character is "a man totally torn between two cultures." The six-hour miniseries, made for the pay-television service Home Box Office, had its premiere in three two-hour segments on successive nights beginning on April 30, 1984.

In the spring of 1984 principal photography was completed on "The Assisi Underground," Ben Cross's first theatrical film since *Chariots of Fire*. James Mason, Maximilian Schell, and Irene Papas are also in the cast of the Cannon Films production, which is based on the real-life efforts of a group of Italian priests to rescue Jews and anti-Nazis from the Gestapo. Cross plays Padre Rufino Niccacci, in whose honor a tree has been planted in Jerusalem.

Ben Cross is five feet eleven inches tall, weighs about 160 pounds, and has brown eyes. In his article for the *Dial*, Steve Wasserman described the actor as fitting almost exactly A. J. Cronin's description of Dr. Andrew Manson: "spare, gawky, dark, rather tensely drawn, with high cheekbones, a fine jaw, and eyes that despite the nervous tensity of the brow are extraordinarily steady and inquiring." Cross was married in 1977 to Penelope Butler, an ex-model, and they have two children, Lauren and Theodore. He divides his time between England and the United States.

In his leisure time, Ben Cross likes to write plays, musicals, stories, and songs, and he enjoys modeling in clay, playing the guitar, and "fooling around on the piano." His film idols include Marlon Brando, Gregory Peck, and Humphrey Bogart. Presenting his views on the acting profession to Edmund Newton in the *Soho Weekly News* interview, Cross described it as "a substitute for going out in a fur skin and clubbing a brontosaurus to death. It's like [the film] *Deliverance*. Why do they go out on that river? It's to get back to that danger, to get the prehistoric juices flowing." A "lapsed Catholic," Ben Cross told David Lewin in an interview for *You; Mail on Sunday Magazine* (April 17, 1983): "Any religion which relies on guilt if you don't adopt certain patterns of behavior has to be dismissed. . . . I happen to believe that basically I am a good person. I am very human, although I can be a pain in the arse sometimes."

References: *Chicago Tribune* VI p17+ O 18 '81 pors; *Dial* 4:12+ N '83 pors; *N Y Daily News* p35 Mr 1 '82 por; *N Y Times* C p10 O 2 '81 por, II p35 N 20 '83 por; *People* 17:83+ Ap 5 '82 pors; *Washington Post* C p1+ D 3 '83 por

Cunningham, Mary (Elizabeth)

Sept. 1, 1951– Business executive. Address: b. c/o Simon & Schuster, Inc., 1230 Ave. of the Americas, New York City, N.Y. 10020

In 1980, Mary Cunningham became one of the youngest high-ranking female corporate executives in the United States, under the mentorship of chairman William Agee at the suburban Detroit-based Bendix Corporation, then the eighty-eighth largest company in the country. Occurring at a time when layoffs were becoming massive in the auto industry and Agee was decentralizing Bendix and divesting it of divisions unrelated to its new high-tech thrust, her meteoric rise to vice-president for strategic planning rankled many of the corporation's grizzled executives and management employees. A smear campaign alleging a boardroom love affair surfaced into sensational news headlines in September 1980, forcing Miss Cunningham's resignation. Following her departure from Bendix, she was for two-and-a-half years a vice-president of Joseph E. Seagram & Sons, the alcoholic-beverage company. Now husband and wife, Agee and Miss Cunningham are, respectively, chairman and president of their own small company, the Semper Corporation. Semper is primarily involved in venture capital and strategy consultation, but Mary Cunningham envisions its becoming also a vehicle for the psychological and legal counseling a professional woman needs "when she goes through the kind of experience" Miss Cunningham did at Bendix.

Mary Cunningham gave her side of the Bendix saga in her autobiography, *Powerplay: What Really Happened at Bendix* (Linden Press/Simon and Schuster, 1984), written with Fran Schumer. Reviewing that book in the *New York Times* (June 24, 1984), Sandra Salmans wrote: "To say that Miss Cunningham does not make the best case for women in business is not to say that she has no case at all. It is hard to imagine a similar furor arising over favoritism, however outrageous, of a young male executive assistant."

Mary Elizabeth Cunningham was born on September 1, 1951 in Falmouth, Maine, where her father's family had built up a prosperous construction business. "We were in the upper echelons of Falmouth society, about as far up as the lace-curtain Irish could go," she recounted in *Powerplay*. "My father had gone to one of the finest preparatory schools in New England and then to Holy Cross College, but he was less interested in books than in having a good time. One of his brothers, the family's favorite child, was killed in a car accident during college, and my father began to drink heavily after that." Ill at ease in Falmouth's country-club, cocktail-party circuit, Mrs. Cunningham rejected her husband's lifestyle. Mary was five and a half when her parents divorced, and she never heard from her father again, except for an annual birthday card. Feeling, like many children in such circumstances, "as if somehow [she] had caused their separation," she "vowed from that day on" to be "so good that it would make up for this terrible thing [she had] done."

With her children—in order of age, John, Shirley, Mary, and Frank—Mrs. Cunningham moved out of the spacious Cunningham house on Casco Bay in Falmouth and into a small rented apartment in Hanover, New Hampshire, where a concerned close relative, Monsignor William Nolan, was pastor of the Roman Catholic parish, which included in its congregation the Catholic students at Dartmouth College. Through Father Bill, as he was known to the family, Mrs. Cunningham found work in Hanover and eventually became secretary at the Dartmouth Catholic Student Center. When she had saved enough money, she bought a modest home for herself and her children in Hanover.

Monsignor Nolan became not only Mary Cunningham's surrogate father but also, in her words, her "conscience . . . teacher . . . friend," and she "drank in every word" he spoke to her about "all those suffering in the world" and the necessity of setting "an example to show others how to overcome the difficult moments." Steeped in the lives of the saints, she found it difficult "to be 'silly' or just fool around with the other kids." As "Father Bill's niece," she was given favored treatment by the nuns at Sacred Heart School in Lebanon, New Hampshire, where she was always the one "chosen to place the crown on the statue of the Blessed Mother." Alarmed at the first signs of a nascent parochial complacency in his spiritual charge, Monsignor Nolan decided she would be better off in the Hanover public-school system, where the achievement-oriented sons and daughters of Dartmouth College faculty members and Hanover professionals mingled with the less sophisticated children of local farmers. At his suggestion, Mary was transferred to the public-school system at the beginning of the fifth grade.

Mary Cunningham's years as an honor student at Hanover High School, from 1966 to 1969, are remembered by her as "difficult ones," because she was "old-fashioned even by fifties standards, let alone in the age of the Rolling Stones." She "started to resent" the "cloistered life" unwittingly inflicted on her by her well-meaning homebody mother, who wanted her to "have fun" but whose "idea of fun was a little out of date." "We weren't part of any social network," she recalled in *Powerplay*. "I tried to put myself in situations where I could 'help' people—volunteer work, hospital work—[but] my 'service' put a distance between us. . . . Mostly I would stay in my room and study." She "found solace" in her work, as she reassured her concerned mother, but she was tempted to tell her also: "There's such a gap between me and other kids because of what you think is 'acceptable' behavior that it's just easier to sit up here and work."

As the end of her senior year at Hanover High School approached, Mary Cunningham received numerous college acceptances, including one to Wellesley (Massachusetts) College. Monsignor Nolan and her mother chose Newton (Massachusetts) College of the Sacred Heart, where her sister, Shirley, had gone and where she, Mary, was given a full scholarship. She dutifully matriculated at Sacred Heart, where she immediately went to the top of her class and became class president, but where the "rough-and-tumble" social life was not to her liking. Without discussing her decision with either her mother or Monsignor Nolan, she applied for a transfer to Wellesley, and the day the transfer came through she knew that her "independence from home had begun."

Planning to become a lawyer, Mary Cunningham chose a combined major of logic and philosophy at Wellesley College. One year of her undergraduate study was done abroad, at Trinity College in Dublin, Ireland. In 1973 she graduated from Wellesley with a B.A. degree *magna cum laude* and a Phi Beta Kappa key and entered the University of Notre Dame law school in South Bend, Indiana. In the meantime, she became engaged to Howard ("Bo") Gray, a black New York City banking executive whom she had met when he was studying at the Harvard University Graduate School of Business Administration. Finding South Bend "not yet ready for an interracial couple," she decided to leave law school after one term in order, as she explained to Lisa Birnbach in an interview for the syndicated Sunday supplement *Parade* (April 25, 1982), "to minimize the difficulty that [her] being in South Bend, Indiana was causing" her fiancé.

Moving to New York City, Mary Cunningham was married there to Bo Gray on December 28, 1974. While working as a paralegal at the New York law firm of Kass, Goodkind, Wechsler and Gerstein, she was told by the firm's partners that she was a "born negotiator" and ought to go into business. Her husband seconded the idea and suggested that she apply to the corporate-credit training program at the Chase Manhattan Bank, where he was then a second vice-president. Accepted as a trainee at Chase Manhattan, she went on to become a corporate lending officer and assistant treasurer. Ambitious to manage more than loans, she saw that the route up the executive ladder would be arduous without a master's degree in business administration since all around her she saw "Harvard MBAs whizzing right by."

In the fall of 1977 Mary Cunningham enrolled in the Harvard Graduate School of Business, where, according to Gail Sheehy in her book *Pathfinders* (1981), she "made few friends" among her male classmates. "If I was a 'hardened, tough-minded broad' my second year of Business School," Miss Cunningham explained in *Powerplay*, "it was because I had been so thoroughly intimidated the first. It took me two-and-a-half months to open my mouth in class the first year." In time she "learned to adapt" to the "competitive environment" and "grew used to living without Bo, perhaps too much so." By the middle of her second year she was accumulating awards and straight "Excellents," and her "thoughts were on the future." In those thoughts was a mixture of religious altruism and worldly ambition. "Her strategic plan," according to Gail Sheehy, "was to jump on the fast track, concentrate her energies exclusively on career advancement, and find a mentor who could take her to the top. . . . She told me [that] there had been no room for love in her early strategic plan."

The religious element was made clearer in the interview with Lisa Birnbach for *Parade*: "At the end of the second year at Harvard Business School, they asked us to write what we expected to be doing for the next thirty years. I saw myself . . . running an orphanage. My dream is to have a ranch for all these talented professionals who would like something more meaningful than going to the Bahamas for another two weeks, where I would also have adopted a significant amount of children. . . . I saw myself, frankly, as a nun of some sort. I have considered the prospect of working with men in a more celibate situation, where I'd be a nun and they'd be priests. Being a member of the Church is a little like being a member of a family—like being a member of that corporation."

When she took her MBA at Harvard in June 1979, Mary Cunningham had many attractive job offers, including one in the corporate finance department of Morgan Stanley & Company, the investment bankers. The one she chose was that which came from William Agee, the president, chairman, and chief executive officer of the Bendix Corporation, a Fortune 500 company with 85,000 employees and sales of $3.9 billion. Once a specialist in supplying parts, especially brakes, to the automobile industry, the Southfield, Michigan-based firm had over a period of several decades expanded into machine tools, aluminum siding, lumber and other wood products, and aerospace and military-weapons components and systems while maintaining its manufacture of auto parts. The brash, aggressive Agee, who became president in 1976, when he was thirty-eight, didn't "mind [Bendix] being called a conglomerate" and pursued diversification "as a strength, not a weakness." In the corporate world he became known for his iconoclasm, his practice of open management, his close-to-the-vest style, and his trading-oriented approach to company growth. "That guy runs Bendix like a stock portfolio," a prominent investment analyst once observed of him.

Mary Cunningham arrived at Bendix on the strong recommendation of J. Leslie Rollins, the former assistant dean of the Harvard Graduate School of Business Administration, who had been Agee's mentor at the school when the Bendix executive was a student there in the early 1960s and his guide when he entered the corporate world. Miss Cunningham joined Bendix as Agee's executive assistant, became vice-president for corporate and public affairs in June 1980, and was promoted to vice-president for strategic planning three months later. From the beginning, he was her mentor and she was his confidante and closest adviser. While they were not yet lovers, as Miss Cunningham vehemently insists, they were, in her words, "kindred spirits."

During her first year at Bendix, Miss Cunningham was "exposed to the nitty-gritty of corporate management," as she recorded in *Powerplay*. During her second year, she was "thrust headlong into far more racy fare: corporate gamesmanship, or, how to play political hardball." The outside setting for that second year was a recession in the automobile industry that was giving the jitters even to upper-level executives. Inside Bendix, the general atmosphere of insecurity was exacerbated by several factors. One was the management shakeup involved in the five-year strategy of decentralization and divestiture on which Agee embarked in 1980, a strategy aimed at repositioning Bendix away from dependence on cyclical automotive and housing markets and toward greater involvement in high technology. Another was a perception that Agee was looking for new ground to conquer, perhaps in politics. In his book *Three Plus One Equals Billions: The Bendix–Martin Marietta War* (1983), Allan Sloan writes, "The perception that Agee planned to leave the company, combined with the departure of a number of high-ranking Bendix executives in 1980, combined to create an unusually high level of corporate politicking, as headquarters employees maneuvered for position in what they perceived as a power vacuum."

In Mary Cunningham's view there were "other motivations, deeper concerns" fueling the politicking, most of which had less "to do with business" than with "jealousy and pride, ego and power." In her *Parade* interview with Lisa Birnbach she attributed the rumors about an Agee-Cunningham romantic liaison to "individuals who were being hurt" by Agee's new five-year strategy for Bendix and who "knew how to utilize the media" to discredit the chairman. More recently, in an interview quoted in the *New York Post* (June 15, 1984), she described herself as a victim of a subtle form of sexual prejudice, "the kind of innuendo and gossip that developed solely because of the stereotypes that women and men had about an attractive woman working beside a mentor" and as "a very convenient pawn in a very powerful game whose objective was ultimately to unseat the chairman of the board."

The game reached its climax at Agee's annual meeting with the 600 employees at Bendix's Southfield, Michigan headquarters, held on September 24, 1980. In keeping with his avowed "democratic" style, Agee addressed all questions raised by the rank and file in a pre-meeting poll. The agenda on that occasion included questions about layoffs, retraining, relocation—and Agee's relationship with Mary Cunningham. "The job she has done is without peer in this company," Agee said. "At the same time, I tell you it is true that we are very, very close friends. . . . " Some members of the press who had been itching to get the story of the alleged romance into print had their hook, and what had been a parochial smear campaign burst into national headlines. Mary Cunningham resigned her position at Bendix two weeks later, on October 8, 1980.

In February 1981 Mary Cunningham accepted the position of vice-president in charge of strategic planning and project development with Joseph E. Seagram & Sons, the United States subsidiary of the Seagram Company Ltd., the world's largest producer and distributor of alcoholic beverages. After she consolidated and formulated a worldwide strategy for the company's diversified wine business, she was promoted to executive vice-president, planning, for the Seagram Wine Companies.

Meanwhile, shared adversity had brought William Agee and Mary Cunningham together emotionally, and their alleged romance became a reality in the months following Miss Cunningham's departure from Bendix. Agee, who divorced his first wife in August 1980, converted to Catholicism and married Miss Cunningham in a Roman Catholic ceremony in San Francisco in June 1982. Miss Cunningham, separated from Bo Gray since 1979, had obtained a divorce from him in January 1981. Both first marriages were annulled by Roman Catholic tribunals.

As Agee's wife, Miss Cunningham was at his side during Bendix Corporation's effort to take over the Martin Marietta Corporation, a manufacturer of missiles and guidance systems for the United States Department of Defense. That effort drew retaliation from Martin Marietta, and the corporate war between the two companies in the fall of 1982 culminated in the takeover of both by the Allied Corporation. On February 8, 1983, Agee resigned his positions at Bendix, effective June 2, 1983. The following October Miss Cunningham resigned from Seagram in order to devote more time to the Semper Corporation, the company she had cofounded with Agee.

Mary Cunningham is an intense person with what she has described as a "melancholy Irish temperament." She has deep blue eyes, shoulder-length strawberry blonde hair, and, in the words of Robert Cross of the *Chicago Tribune* (May 31, 1984), a "pink, scrubbed, and healthy" visage and a smile that "outshines the woodwork." She dresses conservatively, in tailored clothes the severity of which is offset by tasteful jewelry, uses makeup sparingly, and keeps her nails short and unpolished. According to Allan Sloan, the portrait that emerges from the recollections of those who worked with her at Bendix is "of someone who radiates great energy, who is not an original thinker but rather a synthesizer."

Miss Cunningham attends daily Mass and finds "calm" in prayerful visits to the Blessed Sacrament. A longtime friend of William Agee once observed that she seems "driven . . . on a mission from God to reform the corporate world and everyone in it." Her theology has been described as "modern conservative," and her political views are apparently close to those of President Ronald Reagan, for whom she reportedly wrote several speeches before his election to the presidency in 1980. She has played the piano since childhood, and she paints watercolors, some of which she gives as gifts. The Agees make their home in and conduct their business from a large, elegant turn-of-the-century house they own on Cape Cod, Massachusetts. In addition to running Semper, Miss Cunningham draws fees estimated upwards of $5,000 on the lecture circuit, and she devotes some of her time to visiting business schools and, through role-playing psychodramas, showing female students how to deal with some of the problems ignored in their textbooks.

References: *Chicago Tribune* XII p1+ N 14 '82 por, IV p11 Ja 13 '83 por, I p13+ My 31 '84 por; *N Y Post* p71 Je 15 '84 por; *N Y Times* D p1+ O 14 '80; *Parade* p4+ Ap 25 '82 pors; *People* 18:102+ Ja 3 '83 pors; *Washington Post* p1+ S 12 '82 pors

Deighton, Len

(dā´ tən)

Feb. 18, 1929- Writer. Address: b. c/o Anton Felton & Partners, Continuum One, 25 Newman St., London W1, England

With the publication of *The Ipcress File*, his first novel, in 1962, Len Deighton immediately won a place among the foremost writers of spy thrillers. Critics ranked his downbeat saga of international intrigue with the espionage novels of Somerset Maugham and Graham Greene, and it became an international best-seller. Although Deighton's best-selling spy stories earned him a large and devoted following in the course of the next two decades, reviewers often disagreed about their literary merits. Nevertheless, Deighton has made significant contributions to the genre with his reluctant spy-heroes and unusual style and, moreover, seems unconcerned with fluctuations in his critical standing or the number of his books sold. "I am not interested in producing the greatest best-sellers or acquiring a large number of readers," he has said. "I am happy to acquire a strong rapport with a smaller number."

Leonard Cyril Deighton was born on February 18, 1929 in the Marylebone district of London. His father worked as a chauffeur, and his mother, an Irishwoman, was a hotel cook. Deighton enrolled at Marylebone Grammar School, but when World War II broke out and daily classes were disrupted, he became a messenger at his father's first-aid post. His temperament was equally disruptive to his formal education. He maintains that he never passed an exam after entering Marylebone and asserts that his "smartest days" were those in which he played hooky to visit museums or to attend performances of Shakespeare that featured such great actors as Ralph Richardson, Alec Guinness, and Laurence Olivier.

At seventeen, a year after he left school, Deighton joined the Royal Air Force as a photographer in the special investigation branch. Although he failed to qualify as a pilot, he did learn how to fly a plane, and that began his lifelong fascination with aviation. After spending two years in the armed services, he left to become an artist and with the aid of a veteran's grant studied for three years at St. Martin's School of Art. In 1951 he gained admission to the prestigious Royal College of Art, where his friend Joe Tilson, the pop artist, was also studying.

By the time Deighton graduated two-and-a-half years later, he was so accomplished as a commercial artist that he found work as an illustrator for advertising agencies in London and New York. But during the 1950s he also took on a variety of unrelated jobs, including assistant pastry chef at the Royal Festival Hall and steward for the British Overseas Airway Corporation (BOAC). The diversity of his work experiences and the knowledge he picked up from them were later to prove invaluable to him as a writer. His stint in 1956–57 with BOAC, for example, not only gave him the opportunity to stroll through such exotic cities as Calcutta, Hong Kong, and Cairo but also afforded him enough time during layovers to educate himself through reading. Among other disciplines, he became an armchair expert on military history, a subject that he later exploited in his spy novels and several works of nonfiction.

When in 1962 the London *Observer* commissioned Deighton to do a weekly series of "cookstrips"—recipes for French cuisine explained through cartoon drawings—he was able to combine his talent for illustration with his culinary expertise. Their charm and simplicity (Deighton once explained that he wanted to make sure that even a "moron" could follow the directions) made the cookstrips for many years one of the *Observer's* most popular features. His cookstrips were collected in *Action Cook Book: Len Deighton's Guide to Eating* (Cape, 1965; *Cookstrip Cook Book*, Geis, 1967) and *Où Est le Garlic; or, Len Deighton's French Cook Book* (Penguin, 1965; Harper, 1977). He has written several other cookbooks as well.

Deighton's career soon took a more literary turn. While vacationing with his wife in France in 1960, he decided to write a novel "for a giggle," as he explained to Hugh Moffett in an interview for *Life* (March 25, 1966), and he turned out the first half of a spy story before returning to London. Again in France the following year, he finished the novel, and a chance cocktail-party conversation with a London literary agent several months later led to its submission to a publisher.

When *The Ipcress File* (Hodder & Stoughton) was published in 1962, it was warmly received by most critics and became an immediate commercial success. Although the subject—the rescue of top scientists from criminals who plan to sell them to a foreign power—was conventional, readers appreciated Deighton's satiric, if at times wordy, style; his meticulous research, supplemented by appendices and footnotes on the more esoteric points of espionage; and perhaps most of all his unnamed spy-hero. About as unlike Ian Fleming's debonair, upper-class, almost infallible super-agent, James Bond, as is possible, Deighton's sardonic central character is an impudent working-class man, distrustful of his own colleagues as well as of the enemy, and as prone to error as most mortals. Moreover, Deighton's method allows the reader to match wits with the spy-narrator, who, though scrupulously objective in recording his own words and actions, often neglects to reveal how much he has surmised at any given moment. Those elements, combined with a seemingly loose, episodic plot that comes together only towards the end to reveal an intricate and carefully executed design, made *The Ipcress File* a best-seller in England, France, and the United States. It was later serialized in the London *Evening Standard* and made into a film, starring Michael Caine, by Universal Pictures in 1965.

Deighton continued to work that successful vein in his later novels. *Funeral in Berlin* (Cape, 1964; Putnam, 1965) found Deighton's anonymous spy struggling to spirit a Russian scientist out of East Berlin with the aid of Colonel Stok, a KGB masterspy and one of Deighton's more interesting characters. In the *New York Times Book Review* (January 17, 1965) Anthony Boucher, like other critics, compared it favorably to John Le Carré's espionage masterpiece *The Spy Who Came in From the Cold*, and it remained on the *New York Times* best-seller list for twenty weeks. In *Billion Dollar Brain* (Cape; Putnam, 1966), Deighton's secret agent becomes involved in a Texas-based computer espionage ring, and in *An Expensive Place to Die* (Cape; Putnam, 1967) he tries almost single-handedly to avert the detonation of a Chinese hydrogen bomb. Although most critics recommended those novels, only a minority thought they measured up to his earlier productions. In his review of *Billion Dollar Brain* in *Book Week* (May 1, 1966), Richard Schickel complained that the constant flow of technical data and the appendices were "no substitute for sound novelistic observation and, if anything, the scholarly apparatus underscores the writer's failures of purely literary craft." *Horse Under Water* (Cape, 1963; Putnam, 1968) was received even less enthusiastically by the critical fraternity.

Nevertheless, Deighton's innovative espionage novels won him a large and devoted following. By 1966 sales of *The Ipcress File* had topped 2.5 mil-

lion; *Billion Dollar Brain* had gone into its fifth printing in the United States; and *Funeral in Berlin* had sold over 40,000 hardcover copies. In an interview for the *New York Times* (June 21, 1981), Deighton suggested that part of the reason for the success of his novels might be the experiences he brings to them. He learned to scuba dive, for instance, to prepare for writing *Horse Under Water* and mastered helicopter piloting for *Billion Dollar Brain*. "Readers of my books," he theorized, "pay me to do the things they would get a kick out of doing themselves." His "deliciously sharp and flawlessly accurate" dialogue, as H. R. F. Keating described it in the London *Times* (March 12, 1981), is an added strength, but his meticulously delineated settings are perhaps an even more powerful drawing card. Each of his novels contains enough descriptions of exotic places to fill a Sunday travel supplement, and Deighton visits and photographs or sketches every locale before he begins to write to make sure he depicts each with accuracy. Since Deighton's style is so cinematic, his novels are easily transferred to the screen. Michael Caine reprised his role as Harry Palmer in film versions of *Billion Dollar Brain* (United Artists, 1967) and *Funeral in Berlin* (Paramount, 1966), and the screen rights to *An Expensive Place to Die* were also sold.

Still, in *Who's Who in Spy Fiction* Donald McCormick maintained that "technology . . . [is] the first and foremost factor in almost all of Deighton's stories." Although he temporarily abandoned espionage themes after the publication of *An Expensive Place to Die*, Deighton freely indulged his penchant for technological data in several books that focused on his longstanding interests in military history and aviation. *Bomber* (Cape; Harper, 1970)—a lengthy, minutely detailed fictional account of what a bombing run over Germany during World War II was like for the RAF fighter pilots, the Luftwaffe interceptors, and the civilian victims of the raid—and his short stories about soldiers in moments of crisis and confrontation in *Declarations of War* (Cape, 1971; *Eleven Declarations of War*, Harcourt, 1975) received plaudits from reviewers. Although some critics were annoyed by the overwhelming flow of technical information, Edward Weeks, among others, admired Deighton's objective portrayals in *Bomber* of the pilots on both sides.

The mixed reviews of *Declarations of War* reflected its uneven quality. In the *New York Times Book Review* (April 15, 1975) Gene Lyons dismissed most of its short stories as "pompous" and "simplistic and predictable," though he conceded that a few were "fascinating." But in *Books and Bookmen* (December 1971), Peter Elstob ranked Deighton with Stephen Crane in his ability to depict the experiences of men in battle and described several of the stories as being "little short of masterpieces."

More than a decade after the publication of *Declarations of War* Deighton once again tried his hand at a fictional treatment of World War II in

Goodbye, Mickey Mouse (Knopf, 1982), which relates the experiences of two American fighter pilots stationed in Britain. Although its bland love stories and one-dimensional characters drew criticism, most reviewers praised his realistic depiction of aerial warfare. His three factual studies of aircraft and military strategy met with a generally cordial reception. *Airshipwreck* (Cape, 1978; Holt, 1979), on which he collaborated with Arnold Schwartzman, was concerned with the heyday of the disaster-prone dirigibles, and in both *Fighter: The True Story of the Battle of Britain* (Cape, 1977; Knopf, 1978) and *Blitzkrieg: from the Rise of Hitler to the Fall of Dunkirk* (Cape, 1979; Knopf, 1980) he examined the materiel, tactics, and personalities of World War II.

Deighton brought his spy-hero out of mothballs and set him loose again in *Spy Story* (Cape; Harcourt, 1974). Peter Armstrong, a British secret agent who has been hired by a joint Anglo-American naval warfare committee, travels to sundry points of the globe, including the Arctic, while trying to aid a defecting Russian admiral. At one point, he finds himself entangled in a nuclear submarine battle beneath the icepack. Although Pearl K. Bell panned *Spy Story* as "an impenetrable lemon" in *The New Leader* (January 19, 1976), it received complimentary notices from the majority of critics.

Deighton's *Yesterday's Spy* (Cape; Harcourt, 1975) and *Twinkle, Twinkle, Little Spy* (Cape; Catch a Falling Spy*, Harcourt, 1976) followed in quick succession. *Yesterday's Spy* concentrates on Steven Champion, a retired British agent who worked with the French Resistance in World War II and is now suspected by British Intelligence of complicity in an Egyptian plot. Although he considered the characterizations in *Yesterday's Spy* to be typically tenuous, Julian Barnes, writing in the *New Statesman* (May 30, 1975), cited Deighton's effective use of his distinctive technique: "a strong central idea, tough dialogue, narrative fizz, and twists which baffle without making the reader feel like a bubble brain." "It's a good, pacy read," Barnes concluded, "with some splendid bluffs and lots of pleasing violence." In *Twinkle, Twinkle, Little Spy* an American CIA operative and his British secret-agent sidekick rework the usual Deighton ploys to help yet another Soviet scientist to defect. In spite of the growing familiarity of the formula, the book brought Deighton another round of applause.

Adding a further twist to the standard spy yarn, Deighton used quasi-historical events for the focus of his next two thrillers, one of which constructed a scenario for what might have happened had Hitler won the war. A mysterious murder, a plot to rescue an imprisoned George V, and wranglings within the German ruling hierarchy in conquered England failed to salvage *SS-GB: Nazi-Occupied Britain, 1941* (Cape, 1978; Knopf, 1979), a Book-of-the-Month Club alternate selection. Most critics found Deighton's premise interesting, but they agreed with Michael Howard, who in his review for the London *Times Literary Supplement* (Sep-

tember 15, 1978) regretted that Deighton's "almost obsessional care to get the background . . . exactly right" resulted in an overwhelming amount of detail that clogged the narrative.

XPD (Knopf, 1981), a Literary Guild alternate selection, was an even more resounding critical failure. William F. Buckley Jr. joined the critical consensus in excoriating that "most painfully unreadable" fictional account of the unearthing of "the Hitler Minutes"—a transcript of a supposititious meeting between the Führer and Churchill in which the prime minister offered to surrender on almost traitorous terms. That transcript is deemed so sensitive that even forty years after the war any unauthorized person who stumbles upon the secret is subject to "XPD": "expedient demise." John Sutherland, writing in the *London Review of Books* (March 19–April 1, 1981), pronounced it a "routine and nerveless performance" but predicted that "such is the potency of Deighton's name that the novel is bound to sell well." Apparently the publisher agreed, for the first printing of *XPD* ran to 65,000 copies, though only about half that number of *SS-GB* were at first issued. *XPD* became a best-seller on both sides of the Atlantic. Critics were more charitable in their appraisals of *Berlin Game* (Hutchinson, 1983; Knopf, 1984), a "straight" spy story in which the British secret service agent Bernard Sampson braves both the KGB and an unknown mole among his colleagues to rescue a double agent from behind the Iron Curtain. Frederick Busch ranked it among Deighton's best efforts in his *Chicago Tribune* review (December 18, 1983), and the Book-of-the-Month Club picked it as a main selection.

Not limiting himself exclusively to espionage and military history, Deighton has also written *Only When I Larf* (Joseph, 1968), a humorous novel that focuses on a group of con artists rather than spies; the screenplay for that novel (Paramount, 1968); two television plays; and a fictional exposé of the Hollywood movie industry entitled *Close-Up* (Cape; Atheneum, 1972). He was also the travel editor for *Playboy* magazine. The wide range—in both subject matter and quality—of his work and his impressive commercial success have made it difficult to peg Deighton as either a "serious" or "popular" writer. Steering a middle course, in the *Globe and Mail* (October 7, 1971) Leo Simpson dubbed him a "curiously literate hack, a good writer with a sound knowledge of human behavior." Deighton has admitted that his aim is to produce entertainment, not literature, and he once instructed his publisher, to no avail, to label his novels with a disclaimer: "The author guarantees this book has no literary merit whatsoever."

But whatever Deighton's purpose in writing, his spy novels have made significant contributions to the genre. In addition to his innovative use of appendices, his elliptical style, and his heroes in spite of themselves, Deighton has introduced an ambiguous morality into his fictions. Unlike the simplistic world of good pitted against evil where agents suffer no qualms of conscience as, for example, in Ian

Fleming's James Bond series, Deighton's characters are more often than not mired in a morass where no action is clear-cut and the "enemy" as well as the hero may be an upright man. In the interview for *Life* he explained his intention to Hugh Moffett: "All tragedy, which really means all dramatic writing, should have this element that everybody is right in his own sort of way, and it's the fact that all these trains are coming together and breaking, that is the thing that's tragic about it. There's nothing tragic about a villain dying, or something bad being destroyed."

Deighton has regular, sharply sculpted features, short dark hair that is now greying, and wears glasses with angular black frames. In 1960 he married Shirley Thompson, an illustrator. In addition to his literary pursuits, he has opened a London literary agency called Continuum One, established a foundation for offbeat research, and begun a dictionary for words not located in other dictionaries. He now makes his home on an isolated farm near the Mountains of Mourne in Ireland.

References: *Life* 60:84+ Mr 25 '66 pors; *N Y Times Bk R* p34 Je 21 '81 por; *Newsweek* 60:47 D 24 '62; *Contemporary Authors* 1st rev vols 9–12 (1974); *Contemporary Novelists* (1976); *International Who's Who* 1984–85; *Who's Who in the World* (1982); *World Authors* 1950–1970 (1975)

de Kooning, Willem

Apr. 24, 1904– Artist. Address: h. Woodbine Drive, "The Springs," East Hampton, Long Island, N.Y. 11937

NOTE: This biography supersedes the article that appeared in *Current Biography* in 1955.

Perhaps America's leading postwar painter, Willem de Kooning is one of the last surviving members of the original nucleus of the New York School. Along with Jackson Pollock, de Kooning dominated the group of abstract expressionists who revolutionized painting in the late 1940s and made New York City the art capital of the world, and it was to his vigorous, gestural style that the label "action painting" was first applied by his friend and champion, the *New Yorker* art critic Harold Rosenberg. According to another admirer, Thomas

B. Hess, the creative use of ambiguity is central to de Kooning's art: ambiguity can be found in his constant shift between abstraction and representation, and in the obscurity of setting that characterizes his paintings in either style. His forms exist in what de Kooning calls a "no-environment," so that backgrounds and foregrounds are interchangeable.

Willem de Kooning was born in the Netherlands port city of Rotterdam on April 24, 1904, the son of Leendert and Cornelia (Nobel) de Kooning. His father was a wine and beer distributor; his mother presided over a seaman's bar. When Willem was about five they separated and the boy went to live with his father, to whom he was greatly attached. Shortly afterward, his mother took him away with her—a biographical fact to which some critics have attached much significance in assessing the artist's controversial *Woman* series that he painted in the 1950s.

Of more certain significance in de Kooning's career were the four years he spent, starting at the age of twelve, after finishing elementary school, as an employee of the commercial artists and designers Jan and Jaap Gidding. They were so impressed with their young assistant that they enrolled him in evening courses at the Rotterdam Akademie voor Beeldende Kunsten en Wettenschappen, where he received practical training in crafts as well as in academic art instruction. Only one student work by de Kooning survives, a conventional still life in charcoal entitled *Dish with Jugs* (1921), but it displays the masterly draftsmanship, the "virile and elegant line," that remains as the core of his art.

De Kooning's employment between 1920 and 1923 with the art director of a Rotterdam department store not only provided him with practical experience but also introduced him to the achievements of the contemporary Dutch *de Stijl* movement. He spent the year 1924 in Belgium visiting museums, working as a commercial artist, and studying art. Returning to Holland in 1925, he completed his studies at the Rotterdam academy and in 1926 made his decision to leave for the United States, with the intention of becoming an illustrator. After making several aborted attempts, de Kooning finally succeeded in stowing away on a ship bound for America, and he eventually settled in Hoboken, New Jersey, a town that he chose because it had a sizable Dutch community where he could feel at home while learning English. It was not until 1961 that de Kooning became an American citizen.

In Hoboken, de Kooning worked at housepainting and commercial art, meanwhile making forays into New York City, where he visited art museums and galleries. When in 1927 he moved to Manhattan, he began to meet such artists as John Graham, Stuart Davis, and Arshile Gorky, and later, through his friend the poet and dance critic Edwin Denby, made the acquaintance of members of a wider circle of fellow artists, writers, and musicians. Until 1935, when he began to work on easel paintings, he supported himself by doing lettering, sign painting, and carpentry. His employment in 1935 to do murals for the Federal Arts Project gave de Kooning his first chance to paint full-time and transformed him from an artisan into an artist. In 1936 he exhibited a sketch for one of those murals in his first group show, "New Horizons in American Art," which was held at the Museum of Modern Art, and two years later he received his first independent commission to design part of a mural for the Hall of Pharmacy at the New York World's Fair of 1939 and 1940.

In 1937 de Kooning was sharing a studio with Arshile Gorky, who by now was his close friend and a formative influence on his art. He was a member of the Artists Union and belonged to the Greenwich Village art circle that was beginning to change the direction of American painting. His command of classical modeling, combined with traces of Gorky's surrealist style and of Picasso, is apparent in such canvases as *Two Men Standing* (c. 1938) or *Glazier* (c. 1940), two in a series of haunting figures of men, with hints of self-portraiture, who, outlined against featureless backgrounds, stare hollow-eyed at the beholder. The most poignant of that series is *Self-Portrait with Imaginary Brother* (c. 1938).

A number of realistic, Ingres-like portraits of women also date from that period, among them the exquisitely delicate pencil portrait (1940–41) of Elaine Fried, the artist and critic who became de Kooning's wife in December 1943. At the same time, de Kooning was beginning to do such abstracts in high-key colors as *Pink Landscape* (c. 1938) or *The Wave* (1940–41).

Although it is possible to look back over de Kooning's long career and reach the conclusion that he has always painted in "series," the boundaries are not distinct, for one motif or style modulates into another, then returns, with certain transformations. In any case, de Kooning's Men were succeeded by figures of women that were much indebted to Picasso, as is obvious in *Seated Woman* (c. 1940), *Woman* (1944), or the more surreal *Pink Angels* (1945). The muted grays and ochers of the Men were now followed by glowing pinks and greens.

In the 1940s de Kooning was as yet hardly in the public eye, but he had definitely become a kind of subterranean influence upon younger experimental artists. In 1942 he first met and exhibited with Jackson Pollock, to whom he later paid tribute in his laconic eulogy: "Jackson broke the ice" (in paving the way for acceptance of abstract expressionism). In 1949 their group formalized their neighborhood cafeteria get-togethers by establishing the Eighth Street Club, with meetings providing a forum for lectures and general conviviality. Their other favorite gathering place was the old Cedar Bar, then on Tenth Street, which is still remembered for its association with the hard-drinking, often truculent members of the New York School.

It was in 1946 that Willem de Kooning began to undertake the black and white abstractions in oil on paper that many critics consider to be his greatest paintings. Their form followed necessity: the still relatively unknown artist bought commercial black and white enamel paints because they were inexpensive. With them he produced such works as *Light in August* (1946) and *Painting* (1948), densely packed with biomorphic forms—black with white edges or sometimes the reverse—that jostle one another across the picture plane, creating their own ambiguous depths. They were shown at his first one-man show, at New York's Egan Gallery, in 1948 and won the forty-four-year-old artist his first critical acclaim. The culmination of that phase came with the pastel-toned *Attic* (1949) and *Excavation* (1950), both of which were exhibited, along with the work of Arshile Gorky and Jackson Pollock, at the 1950 Venice Biennale. *Excavation*, de Kooning's largest painting (80 x 100 inches), not only introduced monumental scale into contemporary American art but helped to establish abstract expressionism as the major art form of its time.

To the consternation of champions of "pure" abstraction, in 1953 Willem de Kooning burst upon the art world with his next *Woman* series, which was hung in his third one-man show, at the Sidney Janis Gallery in New York City. When observers remarked that it was nowadays impossible to paint faces, the artist nonchalantly replied, "That's right, and it's impossible not to." Begun in 1950, repainted many times over, daily for two years, *Woman, I* was about to be discarded when a visitor, the noted art historian Meyer Schapiro, rescued it and persuaded de Kooning to finish it. "Finish" is perhaps not the correct word, since de Kooning still regards it as incomplete, if not an inexplicable failure. Nevertheless, it was purchased by the Museum of Modern Art and became the most frequently reproduced of any work of art of the 1950s.

"As to [a] painting being finished, I always have a miserable time over that. But it's getting better now—I just stop," de Kooning observed in 1965. Each of his works is a process of starts, eradications, and fresh attacks on the canvas or paper. Typically, traces of painted-over shapes or drawn lines can be detected in many of his works; those pentimenti add to the complexity of the composition. Without taking into account his solid academic training, it seems incongruous that, as spontaneous a painter as de Kooning appears to be, he actually labors over his works for long periods and prepares for them with drawings and smaller painted studies.

In all, there were six of the *Women* in the series that de Kooning painted between 1950 and 1953. Demonic figures, with huge staring eyes and savagely grinning, devouring mouths, and with limbs vaguely moving in all directions, they are painted in thickly impasted, vicious swipes of harsh reds and oranges, slashed with charcoal lines. Although de Kooning once professed to find them humorous, he now admits, "When I look at [them] . . . I get a little scared myself." And he traces them not to a particular woman or even his concept of women, but to Mesopotamian and Cycladic idols, with an admixture of a modern touch: the sensuous mouths of cigarette ad models. De Kooning's obsession with one image was a precursor of such 1960s pop art as Andy Warhol's *Marilyn* [Monroe] paintings.

Figural work gave way to abstraction again in the later 1950s as Willem de Kooning began to paint large (70 x 80-inch) urban and highway landscapes such as *Gotham News* (1955-56), *Backyard on Tenth Street* (1956), and *Montauk Highway* (1958). Incorporating swift visual impressions, they exemplify his observation that "content is a glimpse of something, an encounter like a flash. I guess you could call me a slipping glimpser."

In 1961 de Kooning started working on a group of country landscapes done with summery colors—*Rosy-Fingered Dawn at Louse Point* (1963) and *Pastorale* (1963), the latter of which was the last canvas he painted as a Manhattan loft-dweller. In that year he moved permanently to East Hampton, Long Island, which since the early 1950s has been a popular vacation spot for New York artists and writers. There in 1962 he started to design and build a studio and adjoining house, changing the plans with the same frequency and methodical attention to detail that characterize all his creative activity. The impressively large, functional studio, with its glass walls and white terrazzo floors that admit and reflect back the steely shore light so similar to that of his native Holland, was finally completed in 1969. There de Kooning works with his neat array of tools, including housepainter's brushes, spackle knives, and scrapers, and with large numbers of salad bowls in which he mixes his unique compound of tube oils beaten with water, kerosene, and safflower oil. He has never used acrylics, preferring slower drying paints; often he covers his paintings with newspaper, ostensibly to keep them from drying, but actually, the process of pulling the paper off adds tactile complexity to the painted surface. Two or three studio assistants help him to stretch canvases and mix paints.

Toward the mid-1960s de Kooning's Women reappeared in his work, but now merged with abstract landscape forms, just as his earlier abstractions had often embodied parts of human figures. The Women inhabit ambiguous suggestions of beach scenery: often there are effects of shimmering reflections of water. Sprawling in a matrix of "seductive and juicy" tones of pinks, lipstick reds, and whites, the sun-drenched *Clam Diggers* (1964) or *Singing Woman* (1965) are lasciviously frolicking "girlies." Although those paintings did not arouse the fury provoked by the 1950s "bitch goddesses," they were dismissed by many critics for their "mushy" softness. Their reaction seemed to confirm the artist's self-observation: "Art never makes me peaceable or pure. I always seem to be wrapped in the melodrama of vulgarity."

By the 1970s de Kooning's pendulum had swung once more to the abstract, with the figure of the woman engulfed by its surrounding landscape. Those paintings convey the effect of water, figures on the dunes, air, and motion—sense impressions caught by the "slipping glimpser" as he pedaled along the beach roads. Most successful of the works of that period are, perhaps, a group of untitled canvases: expanses of bold, brilliantly colored slashes of paint. That impulse has continued up to the present. *Pirate* (1981), for example, possesses a "lyric intensity" of pinks and golds, but with an important change. From about 1981 on, de Kooning's paintings have loosened and lightened. Graffiti-like scrawls of fresh, unmixed colors over large areas of white evoke air and water, but those wide swashes of color, thinner in texture than formerly, still reveal the artist's powerful gestural brushwork. In de Kooning's latest creations, executed in his favorite 70 x 80-inch dimensions, all is reduced to color and light, and nothing is titled. The artist's figurative impulse continues, however, for his drawings, whether in pencil, charcoal, or sepia, are almost wholly devoted to shapes of women, with occasional forms that suggest marine creatures, another kind of evocation of water that has always constituted a part of his physical and creative environment.

Among the many honors that have been bestowed upon Willem de Kooning are Holland's Order of Orange-Nassau, which was awarded him on his seventy-fifth birthday in a ceremony at the Solomon R. Guggenheim Museum in New York. In 1964 President Lyndon B. Johnson presented him with the Presidential Medal of Freedom. He has been a member of the American Institute of Arts and Letters since 1960. His work is represented in the holdings of major museums all over the world. Sought since 1954 by collectors, they now command enormous prices: *Two Women* (1955) was sold by Christie's, the art auction house, in 1982 for $1.2 million, the highest price yet paid for a work by a living American artist.

Willem de Kooning's influence upon the later generation of New York School artists and some of their pop art successors has been prodigious, even greater perhaps than that of Jackson Pollock. He has also shaped the outlook of many others through such published lectures as "What Abstract Art Means to Me," which he delivered at a Museum of Modern Art seminar in 1951, with its credo: "Painting is a way of living." De Kooning taught at

Black Mountain College in North Carolina in 1948, at Yale University in 1950-51, and at Smith College in a series of lectures in 1965. Nevertheless, the painter protested early in his career that he represents no particular movement or style, and he has remained anti-ideological, with no reductive "message."

In his later years de Kooning has become more and more reclusive. No longer in touch with the New York art world, he was distinctly unimpressed with the two most recent retrospectives of his work, "Willem de Kooning in East Hampton" at the Guggenheim Museum in 1978 and, the most comprehensive to date, that held at the Whitney Museum of American Art in 1983-84. Museum retrospectives, he once declared, "treat the artist . . . as if you are dead and they own you." Although de Kooning has left his New York environs relatively seldom, he did visit Paris in 1968, where he made his first visit to the Louvre, and in the same year returned for the first time to Holland to see the installation at the Stedelijk Museum in Amsterdam of his 1968-69 touring retrospective. In 1969 he went to Japan, where his encounters with printmaking inspired his own experiments and profoundly influenced his "freely calligraphic" black and white lithographs.

It was also in 1969 that, on a trip to Rome, he met a friend who persuaded him to do some small clay figures, despite de Kooning's dislike of the medium, and have them cast in bronze. The following year, the English sculptor Henry Moore suggested that de Kooning increase the size of those figures; work on a series of large-scale bronze figural sculpture occupied him over the next decade. With their flickering, "kneaded and pummeled surfaces," works such as Seated Woman (1969) or Clam Digger (1972) remind critics of the kind of sculpture created by Degas or Matisse.

De Kooning has always been attractive to women, with his blond hair, now white, still cut somewhat like the typical little Dutch boy, his keen blue eyes, and his wide, sensual mouth. His imposing head with its dominating nose and high cheekbones belies his relatively short and slight build. His hands are long and supple, and during the act of painting his fierce concentration is revealed by the tensing of his facial muscles. His conversation reveals his lively intelligence, his sense of humor, and his humility at his own success.

Temporarily separated in 1955, Willem and Elaine de Kooning have continued to live together since 1978. De Kooning maintains close ties with Joan Ward, the mother of his beloved daughter, Lisa, both of whom live very near him. His studio is not far from the cemetery where his old friends Stuart Davis, Jackson Pollock, Frank O'Hara, and Harold Rosenberg are buried. "It would be very hard for me now to paint anywhere else," he has said. At eighty, Willem de Kooning is still vitally engaged with his medium on a daily basis, still open to new impulses, choices, and decisions as he continues to work long hours in his studio.

References: Art N 71:54+ S '72; N Y Times Mag p43+ N 20 '83 pors; Newsday p3+ S 5 '76 por; Contemporary Artists (1977); Hess, Thomas B. Willem de Kooning (1959), Willem de Kooning (1968); Waldman, Diane. Willem de Kooning in East Hampton (1978); Who's Who in America, 1984-85

Ershad, Hussain Muhammad
(er shäd´)

Feb. 1, 1930- President of the People's Republic of Bangladesh; army officer. Address: b. Government House, Dhaka, Bangladesh

The People's Republic of Bangladesh, which gained its independence from Pakistan in 1971, has from the beginning been plagued with seemingly insurmountable problems, notably grinding poverty, overpopulation, corruption, and political chaos that resulted in the violent deaths of two of its heads of state—Sheik Mujibur Rahman in 1975 and General Ziaur Rahman in 1981. But in recent years, political observers have seen some hope for Bangladesh's 95-million people in the administration of Lieutenant General Muhammad Ershad, a political moderate who attained power in a bloodless coup in March 1982 and assumed the presidency in December 1983.

Ershad, who regards the function of the army as "combining the role of nation-building and national defense into one concept," while stressing his commitment to democracy, has achieved some success with his reforms, in particular his efforts to decentralize the country's administrative and legal systems, his crusade against corruption, his drive to increase agricultural output, his implementation of population-control measures, and his promotion of a free-market economy. According to Rodney Tasker, writing in the *Far Eastern Economic Review* (December 22, 1983), "Ershad . . . is credited by almost every diplomatic and political observer, even those among the opposition parties, with being a sincere man with an honest desire to pull one of the world's poorest countries out of its economic, political, and social mire."

Hussain Muhammad Ershad, the son of Makbul Hussain and his wife, Mojida Begum, was born into a family of jurists on February 1, 1930, in Rangpur, North Bengal, then a part of British India. His father was one of the principal lawyers of the Rangpur district bar. Ershad obtained his early schooling in his home community. He attended Carmichael College in Rangpur and then entered the University of Dhaka, from which he graduated with a B.A. degree in the first division in 1950, some three years after the region that is now Bangladesh became the eastern part of the newly established Islamic Republic of Pakistan.

After completing his studies at the officers' training school at Kohut, West Pakistan, Ershad was commissioned in September 1952 as an infantry officer in the Pakistani army and assigned to an East Bengal regiment. From 1953 to 1958 he was in infantry regimental service, and from 1960 to 1962 he was adjutant of the East Bengal Regimental Center at Chittagong. He served with the East Pakistan Rifles from 1962 to 1965 and saw combat duty in the 1965 India-Pakistan war as a company commander in the Chuadanga-Meherpur sector of the Kushtia district of East Pakistan.

On completing the staff course at the Command and Staff College at Quetta, West Pakistan, Ershad served in 1967–68 as deputy assistant adjutant and quartermaster general. Promoted to lieutenant colonel, he then served as commanding officer of an infantry battalion in the 3d East Bengal Regiment in 1969–70. While Bangladesh, in alliance with India, was waging its struggle for independence from Pakistan in 1971, Ershad was in command of an infantry battalion of the 7th East Bengal Regiment in the West Pakistan province of Sind. After the establishment of the newly independent People's Republic of Bangladesh, under the Prime Ministership of Sheik Mujibur Rahman, Ershad, along with other Bengali officers, chose repatriation. Promoted to colonel, he was appointed in December 1973 as the first adjutant general of the new Bangladesh army.

In June 1975, Ershad, by then a brigadier general, was sent to New Delhi, India to study at the National Defense College there. On his return later in the year, he was promoted to major general and appointed deputy chief of staff of the Bangladesh army by Major General Ziaur Rahman ("General Zia"), who had become army chief of staff after the assassination of Sheik Mujibur Rahman. Ershad also served, from 1975 to 1978, as chairman of the coordination and control cell for national security. In December 1978, General Zia—who had as-

sumed the national presidency in April of the previous year and was leading the country back to civilian rule—appointed Ershad chief of staff of the army. In November 1979, Ershad was promoted to lieutenant general.

Despite President Zia's popularity and the relative success of his political and economic reform efforts, there was strong opposition to him within his own army, and on May 30, 1981 he was assassinated at Chittagong in an attempted coup by mutinous army officers. In the aftermath of the assassination, the armed forces under the command of General Ershad, who had remained loyal to President Zia, played a key role in upholding the country's fragile democratic institutions and preserving the constitutional process.

Although officially the military remained "absolutely neutral" in the campaign for the presidential election, scheduled for November 1981, and Ershad denied that he had political ambitions, the army under his leadership became actively involved in the political process. Ershad was convinced that a return to power of the Awami League, founded by the late Sheik Mujibur Rahman, would be a disaster for the nation. Consequently, he worked energetically for the late President Zia's Bangladesh National party (BNP) and personally persuaded the aged Abdus Sattar, who had been Zia's vice-president and had served as acting president since the assassination, to run for the presidency as the BNP candidate. Although Ershad could have declared martial law, he wanted to give the constitutional process a fair chance. "I had been asked several times to take over," he later said, as quoted in the *New York Times* (March 25, 1982). "It would have been appropriate in the context of the situation prevailing then. But I rejected the suggestion because we have faith in democratic values and wanted to serve the country in the positions we are occupying." On the other hand, Ershad insisted on an active role for the military to prevent further coups and to promote the country's stability.

Some 21.6-million Bangladeshis went to the polls on November 15, 1981 to cast their votes for eighty-three registered presidential candidates. With 65.8 percent of the vote, Sattar, backed by Ershad, won a landslide victory over his nearest opponent, Awami League candidate Kamal Hossein, who received 26.3 percent. After an abortive protest by Awami League spokesmen, who charged that the vote was rigged, Abdus Sattar was sworn in as president on November 20, 1981. But the failure of the Sattar government to bring about political and economic stability prompted Ershad to demand a more significant role for the military in the decision-making process. Consequently, on January 1, 1982, Sattar, under pressure from Ershad, established a powerful National Security Council consisting of the top leaders of the government and the military. Six weeks later, on February 11, Ershad and other top military officers assumed virtual control of the presidential palace. Sattar was ordered to dissolve his forty-two-member cabinet and replace it with a new panel of eighteen members taken from a list approved by the military, and the National Security Council was reduced in size to increase the power of the military within it. American observers saw the move as confirmation of the army's dominance, short of an actual military takeover.

Finally, on March 24, 1982, Ershad ousted President Sattar in a bloodless coup, imposed martial law, and established himself as martial law administrator, ending the three years of civilian rule that had been instituted by the late President Zia in 1979. He suspended the constitution, dissolved Parliament, imposed a dusk-to-dawn curfew, and placed troops in control of all key points. In a nationwide radio broadcast, Ershad declared that the military takeover had been necessary to weed out "corruption in public life." He declared that his "whole and sole aim" was to "reestablish democracy in accordance with the hopes and aspirations of the people" and promised to allow elections as soon as feasible. The deposed President Sattar voiced his agreement with Ershad.

In the days that followed, Ershad announced the formation of special military tribunals to try persons accused of corrupt practices and named a council of advisers to help him govern. New martial law regulations provided for the death penalty or long terms of imprisonment for such economic crimes as smuggling, tax evasion, hoarding, profiteering, or black-market operations. In what Ershad described as a "total jihad," or holy war, against corruption, hundreds of persons, including several former government ministers, were arrested and prosecuted.

In the beginning, Ershad assumed all executive and legislative powers, granting only ceremonial functions to the new president, A. F. M. Ahsanuddin Choudhury, whom he had appointed shortly after the coup. But, believing that democratic institutions had never been given a fair trial in his country, he pledged to restore popular rule within two years. Meanwhile, a faltering economy, brought on in part by crop failures resulting from drought and pest attacks, prompted Ershad to impose austerity measures in accordance with demands from the World Bank and other sources of foreign aid. Development projects that had been initiated under a 1980 five-year plan were reduced by about one-third.

Convinced that a free-market economy was more efficient than government control, the Ershad administration began in June 1982 to denationalize some 70 percent of the nation's main industries, including jute and textile mills. Private management contractors were to be hired to supervise the 30 percent that remained in the public sector. In addition, local industries were to be protected by a ban on imports of goods that could be produced at home, while at the same time, incentives were introduced to stimulate foreign investment. In the interest of more efficient agricultural production, the government facilitated the distribution of irrigation equipment, fertilizer, pesticides, and agricultural credits to local farmers. Land reforms were introduced to safeguard the interests of small farmers and the security of tenure of sharecroppers, and agricultural laborers were for the first time guaranteed a minimum wage. Furthermore, population control, an issue of vital importance in Bangladesh, was effectively dealt with by such measures as house-to-house "motivational campaigns" for family planning.

To promote greater popular participation in government administration on a grass-roots level, while at the same time ensuring the continued dominance of the military, the Ershad government in the months following the coup initiated a system under which administration and implementation of regional development programs was vested in several hundred local units known as upazillas, or sub-districts, governed by popularly elected local councils. For more efficient dispensation of justice, the Ershad government established civil and criminal courts on the upazilla level, under simplified procedure codes.

Despite rumors of friction within the top ranks of the military, Ershad managed to consolidate his position of leadership during his first few months in power. "Obviously, Ershad heads the military government in the country. But it is in effect a joint effort by the armed forces for implementing an agreed socio-economic program," S. Kamaluddin wrote in the Far Eastern Economic Review (October 29, 1982). "Ershad, by virtue of his position as the army chief of staff and his seniority, has emerged as a 'godfather' figure." Confident enough that he could travel abroad without jeopardizing his position at home, Ershad went to New York City in June 1982 to attend the United Nations disarmament conference, at which he declared that the billions of dollars spent around the world on armaments should be reduced and the savings used for the benefit of "the teeming masses of global underprivileged."

After a pilgrimage to Mecca, the holy city of Islam, in September 1982, Ershad went to India in October for two days of talks with Prime Minister Indira Gandhi, resulting in agreement on a number of long-standing disputes, including accords on sharing the waters of the Ganges River and extending bilateral trade. Later that month, Ershad, having assumed the title of prime minister or president of the Council of Ministers, attended the Commonwealth heads-of-government regional meeting at Suva, Fiji. In December 1982 Ershad visited the People's Republic of China to strengthen cooperation in such areas as agriculture, and in January and February of 1983 he discussed his country's relations with Islamic nations on official visits to Kuwait and Morocco. In May 1983, the Bangladesh government formed a joint investment company with Saudi Arabia, a major contributor of foreign aid.

During 1983, Bangladesh experienced some economic improvement, partly as a result of increased foreign investment and greater food production. An eighteen-point development program, announced by Ershad early in the year, was designed to promote agricultural self-sufficiency and full employment. The military regime remained rather low key, and its continued imposition of martial law along with press censorship and other restrictions did not prevent stirrings of political activity among the still circumscribed parties of the opposition. In February, riots broke out at Dhaka University and elsewhere, when secular-minded students and members of the opposition protested a plan by Ershad to "turn Bangladesh into an Islamic state" and require the study of Arabic and the Koran in the nation's schools. The disturbance resulted in a number of arrests and the closing of universities for several months, and prompted Ershad to rescind his proposals.

In an effort at conciliation, in March 1983 Ershad eased the ban on political activities and called for a national dialogue with opposition leaders. In response, the opposition parties, including a fifteen-party coalition headed by Hasina Wajed, the daughter of Sheik Mujibur Rahman, and a more conservative grouping of seven parties, led by Khaleda Zia, the widow of Ziaur Rahman, put forth a series of demands, including an end to martial law and to various restrictions on civil liberties. Although Ershad rejected most of the demands, he made some concessions, such as a relaxation of press censorship and an end to the ban on indoor political rallies. In response to opposition demands for a parliamentary system, which he denounced as "simply a farce," he set forth plans for a presidential system of government.

Ershad attended a meeting of nonaligned nations at New Delhi in March 1983 and visited Yugoslavia for talks on economic cooperation in June. In August he was host to a meeting of South Asian foreign ministers at Dhaka, at which a program for regional cooperation was launched. On a visit to Washington, D.C. in October 1983, Ershad had a friendly meeting with President Ronald Reagan, who praised his efforts to promote democratic institutions and economic growth and his emphasis on private enterprise. On his return home, he was visited in November, successively, by Queen Elizabeth II, President Kenneth Kaunda of Zambia, and Canadian Prime Minister Pierre Elliott Trudeau. Between Bangladesh and the Soviet Union, friction had been mounting in recent years, and in November 1983 eighteen Soviet diplomats suspected of interfering in Bangladesh politics were expelled from Dhaka. There was also some ill feeling between Bangladesh and India during the year because of India's plan to build a strong fence along the India-Bangladesh frontier to keep out Bangladeshi refugees.

Ershad further relaxed political restrictions on November 14, 1983 and announced that presidential elections would be held in May 1984. But opposition leaders were dissatisfied and demanded that parliamentary elections be held first. On November 28, after violent demonstrations against the government had erupted in Dhaka and elsewhere, Ershad promptly reimposed restrictions and placed opposition leaders Hasina Wajed and Khaleda Zia under "protective custody." On December 11, 1983, shortly after the conclusion of an Islamic Conference foreign ministers' meeting in Dhaka, Ershad proclaimed himself president and dissolved his cabinet in what was seen as an effort to consolidate his power before the forthcoming presidential election. In a television address to the nation he declared that the move was a necessary step "paving the way of transition to democracy from martial law." Political restrictions were further eased on March 26, 1984, the thirteenth anniversary of Bangladesh's independence from Pakistan, and over 200 prisoners, including the leaders of the opposition, were released. But amid continued unrest and failure of the government and the opposition to reach an accord, the May elections were canceled and tentatively rescheduled for December 1984.

Ershad explained his view of his political leadership to Mary Anne Weaver of the *Christian Science Monitor* (March 1, 1984): "You cannot rule Bangladesh from a pedestal. You must be one of them, a man from amongst the people, a simple man, with a heart, a good mind. Then, and only then, can you win over the people. . . . "

Hussain Muhammad Ershad and Begum Roushan, who married in 1956, have a son and an adopted daughter. Observers have referred to Ershad as "soft-spoken," with a "cool, modest manner," a wry sense of humor, and a "somewhat lackluster personal image among the masses" despite his frequent visits by helicopter to the remote regions of his country. Active in athletics since his youth, Ershad was a star soccer player during his student years. He enjoys playing golf and tennis, and he has served as chairman of the National Sports Control Board and president of the Bangladesh Lawn Tennis Federation. A champion of quality education, he was for five years chairman of the governing board of cadet colleges. Ershad has also served as chief adviser of Bangladesh Muktijodda Sangshad, the freedom fighters' association, and as a member of the board of trustees of Sena Kalyan Sangstha, a social welfare organization.

Fond of art, literature, and oriental music—especially the songs of Rabindranath Tagore and Nazrul Islam—Ershad writes Bengali poetry, which he has occasionally contributed to literary journals. "I'm a Bengali. I have poetry in my blood," Ershad told Mary Anne Weaver in an interview in the *Christian Science Monitor* (March 1, 1984). "I began as the typical undergraduate poet—emotional, romantic, poems of sentiment. But now they're mostly about my country and my people."

References: *Christian Sci Mon* p7+ Mr 1 '84 por; *Washington Post* A p11 O 25 '83 por; *International Who's Who, 1984–85*; *Who's Who, 1984*; *Who's Who in the World, 1982–83*

Evren, Kenan

Jan. 1918– President of the Republic of Turkey; army officer. Address: b. The Office of the President, Ankara, Turkey

In the predawn hours of Friday, September 12, 1980, General Kenan Evren, a career military officer and armed forces chief of staff of the Republic of Turkey, led the military in a bloodless coup. By fiat, he immediately took the title of head of state and with his National Security Council sought to restore peace and order to his strife-ridden country by restricting political activity, strengthening antiterrorist provisions, and most important, by restoring limited democracy through a new constitution that was approved by referendum in 1982 and that automatically installed him as president for a seven-year term. General elections in November 1983 returned a civil government to power, but President Evren, his country's "loyal and stubborn son," remains a force to be reckoned with in Turkey's political future.

Kenan Evren, born in January of 1918 in Alaşehir near the Aegean city of Manisa, grew up during a period of radical change in Turkey. In 1923 Mustafa Kemal, who later took the name of Atatürk ("father of the Turks"), won independence for Turkey after the dissolution of the Ottoman Empire in the wake of World War I and instituted a series of sweeping changes that transformed the country from a backward, Islamic-theocratic state to a more modern, pro-Western, secular one, in which members of the armed forces were progressive, highly respected, and stalwart defenders of his code, which is known as Kemalism.

Like most Turkish young men of his generation, Evren viewed military service not only as an honorable profession but also as a means of social ad-

vancement. He began his training at the Maltepe Military High School and went on to attend the Turkish War College in Ankara, from which he graduated in 1938, the year of Atatürk's death. Commissioned as a third lieutenant in the artillery, he underwent further training at the School of Artillery and the Army Staff College. Advancing rapidly, he became chief of staff of the Turkish brigade of the NATO forces during the Korean war and later served as chief of staff of the Army schools (1959–60) and chief of Army operations (1960–61). He was promoted to the rank of general in 1964.

During that period, Turkey was troubled by almost constant civil unrest. Although an expanding industrialized economy benefited the country during the early 1950s, the combination of too rapid expansion and poor harvests precipitated an economic crisis. The government responded to increasing discontent by wooing the large rural population with a partial return of some religious and cultural practices banned by Atatürk and by simultaneously suppressing student demonstrations, dissident newspapers, and rival political parties. Nevertheless, it failed to address the underlying socio-economic problems. Calling for a return to Kemalism, the armed forces staged a coup in May 1961. A civilian government was soon installed, and it drew up a new constitution in July that established a bicameral Parliament and a weakened executive.

That constitution made matters worse, however, since its system of proportional representation virtually guaranteed that no majority government would emerge. Over the next twenty years, the Republican People's party and the new Justice party (a re-formation of the now outlawed Democratic party) vied for power by forming one shaky coalition after another with small extremist factions, and the resulting political instability paralyzed the country. In 1971 high military officials again staged a coup. Although they soon approved a new civilian administration, the 1961 constitution continued to block effective legislative action. Süleyman Demirel, leader of the center-right Justice party, and main opposition leader Bülent Ecevit of the social democratic Republican People's party virtually shared the prime minister's responsibilities in the decade of the 1970s as their stalemated coalitions alternately rose and fell.

With the Parliament's authority rapidly declining, political extremism flourished. By July 1980, martial law had been imposed in twenty of Turkey's sixty-seven provinces, but bombings, assassinations, and the taking of hostages (sometimes of whole villages) continued unabated, with the dead numbering twenty and more a day. Inflation had soared to 125 percent and unemployment had reached 30 percent; the gross national product plunged from a remarkable 7.7 percent in the early 1970s to near zero in 1979; the increasingly unfavorable balance of trade was driving the country to the verge of bankruptcy; and shortages were constantly worsening. As if that were not enough, the

Soviet invasion of Afghanistan and the assumption of power by the Ayatollah Ruholla Khomeini in Iran were exacerbating fears about Turkish national security.

In the midst of all the upheaval, General Evren continued to rise in the military hierarchy. Westerners came to know him as a reliable moderate. He was promoted to the rank of full general in 1974 and became chief of the Turkish General Staff in 1978. In that post, he gained popular recognition for his public exhortations to elected officials, urging them to rein in social disorder. His was the voice of stern but benevolent patriotism in the Kemalist tradition amid the internecine wranglings of the weak Parliament, unable after five months of balloting to elect a president.

After his warnings to the government went unheeded for six months, General Evren led the armed forces in a coup on September 12, 1980. He firmly reminded the people of the prevailing conditions that led to the coup in his predawn speech on that morning. "All citizens with some common sense . . . will accept that the vitally important political, economic, and social problems have reached threatening proportions. . . . " He pledged that the new regime would end Turkey's political violence, restore political and economic stability, protect the nation from external threat, and swiftly rebuild the foundations of democracy. Within twenty-four hours, the ruling five-man junta or National Security Council suspended the constitution, dissolved Parliament, extended martial law to the entire country, banned most labor union activity, and placed in custody hundreds of political leaders from the left and right, including ousted Prime Minister Süleyman Demirel, Bülent Ecevit, Necmettin Erbakan of the fundamentalist Moslem National Salvation party, and ultra-right National Action party ("Grey Wolves") leader Alpaslan Turkes. General Evren moved quickly to revamp the government. Ranking civil servants were told to return to the routine management of their ministries, but extremist provincial officials were replaced by moderates. On September 20 retired naval commander Admiral Bülent Usulu was appointed interim prime minister, and the next day the junta announced a twenty-six–member civilian cabinet, few of whom were affiliated with any Turkish political party. Writing in *Current History* (January 1981), Morris Singer described the cabinet as "technocratic," that is, geared toward solid bureaucratic administration. Six weeks after taking charge, the National Security Council approved a provisional constitution that granted itself all the powers and authority previously exercised by the bicameral parliament. It also announced its intention to strengthen the court system in order to "combat and prevent anarchy and terrorism."

After the coup, political killings declined sharply and civil peace prevailed. Political observers at first conjectured that the junta's administration would last only a few months, but General Evren refused to commit himself to a definite timetable. At a press conference five days after the coup, he said the armed forces wanted to return to their primary duty of external defense as soon as possible, but, he insisted, "We will not leave our present duty until we . . . clean up all the country." He rejected calls for hurried elections lest the military "be humiliated" by failing to achieve its goals by the time the voters went to the polls. Nevertheless, he reiterated his promise to return Turkey to democratic rule: "As good soldiers, we always keep our word."

Reactions in the West to Evren's takeover were tempered by Turkey's important geographic and strategic position: it guards the entrance to the Black Sea to the north, shares a 370-mile border with the Soviet Union to the east, and has committed 600,000 men to NATO's armed forces. But, when under Ecevit's administration Turkey invaded Cyprus in 1974 on behalf of the minority population of Turkish Cypriots, Greece withdrew from NATO, and the United States Congress halted its military aid to Turkey. Without American aid, Turkey was hobbled in upgrading its antiquated military hardware with the state-of-the-art equipment necessary to make it a credible deterrent to Soviet aggression in the region. Turkey's shutdown of American bases in the country and mounting problems in Afghanistan and Iran made Western powers all the more eager to work with Evren's regime in an effort to mend holes in the NATO alliance.

As a result, Evren's administration met with approval from western allies for lifting in October 1980 Turkey's veto on Greece's reentry to NATO's military cadre. With the rapprochement, which diplomatically sidestepped the issues of Turkey's presence in Cyprus and its disputed airspace and water rights in the Aegean Sea, a NATO airforce command base was established in Larissa, Greece, improving the cohesion of NATO's easternmost reaches. (In April 1984 Evren's government became the first to recognize the self-proclaimed secessionist Turkish Cypriot Government on Cyprus. That action was met with "great concern" by Javier Pérez de Cuéllar, the UN secretary general.) Relations with the United States had begun to warm in the late 1970s, and American economic and military aid to Turkey steadily increased after Evren's takeover. In December 1981 two visits to Ankara by Secretary of Defense Caspar W. Weinberger and Secretary of State Alexander M. Haig Jr. conclusively demonstrated the American commitment to "enlarge and improve defense cooperation" with General Evren's government. Weinberger gave the Reagan administration's generally positive view of the junta: "They have many of those principles [of democracy] in effect now and are working very diligently to secure a new constitution . . . , and we feel it is entirely proper to be of such assistance as we can during this proceeding." At the same time, NATO mounted a $900 million resupply effort for the Turkish armed forces. Steadfastly refusing to be manipulated by the West, Evren vigorously rejected interference in Turkish affairs from the Council of Europe and the European Parliament.

In late 1981, Evren began to restore democracy. In November of that year the junta appointed a consultative assembly to draw up a new constitution for popular vote as the first step toward general parliamentary elections. General Evren announced the charter's main points in April 1982 and made clear that ratification of the document would automatically constitute his own election as president for a seven-year term. He told the people that the new constitution would "prohibit communism, fascism, and a theocratic regime," and warned Süleyman Demirel and Bülent Ecevit to end their opposition to the military authorities. "The nation has liberated itself from them," the general declared, "and does not want to be led by the same persons." The full text of the charter, made public in October of that year just weeks before the vote, banned from politics all major political figures for up to ten years. Other key sections provided that no new political party could be formed with a majority membership from an abolished party; that the president could appoint high-level ministers, dissolve Parliament and call new elections, and preside over the armed forces general staff; and that, on the advice of his council, he could declare an emergency and rule by decree.

The charter dismayed some of Turkey's intellectuals, labor unionists, and religious adherents, who charged that it simply gave a formal stamp of approval to a militaristic regime, but business leaders gave the plan their wholehearted backing. Although former foreign minister Hasan Isik described the proposals as "an imperial edict rather than a constitution," General Evren defended his role as "constitutional guarantor" and responded to the negative reactions with a clampdown on criticism of the text's key provisions "in any shape, form, or manner." Making himself highly visible during a national campaign tour to promote the new constitution, Evren made the most of his great personal popularity among his countrymen and urged: "If you don't want to relive those dark days of terrorism and anarchy, then vote yes to the constitution; I am vouching for it."

On Sunday, November 7, 1982 approximately 90 percent of Turkey's 20.7 million registered voters gave the constitution their approval in what was seen more as a vote of confidence in Evren's paternalistic rule and his dramatically successful antiterror campaign than for the constitution, which many voters had not even read. Using color-coded ballots placed, according to a New York Times report (November 8, 1982), in nearly transparent envelopes, the citizenry paved the way for the establishment of new political parties and for the parliamentary elections, scheduled for late 1983. There had been some concern, even within Evren's administration, that the vote might be used to protest the economic austerity measures imposed by the regime, but General Evren interpreted the successful referendum as Turkey's irrevocable "condemn[ation of] anarchy, terrorism, and separatism." Within the week he was sworn in to begin his formal seven-year term as president of the republic.

Two years after their coup, the Turkish military leaders could claim that several of their initial goals had been accomplished. Their major focus had been on improving Turkey's balance of trade, and exports had doubled in 1981 and increased another impressive 30 percent in 1982. Pursuing a "multidimensional" foreign policy, the government negotiated trade agreements with Eastern bloc nations, and President Evren toured China and Korea to firm up economic cooperation. The gross national product had risen 4.4 percent, the highest increase in Europe for that period. Consumer items and enough petroleum and other industrial raw materials could now be imported, and the inflation rate fell 100 points, to about 25 percent. The $14.5 billion foreign debt had been stabilized, in part with eased payment terms and new investments and in part, analyst Sari Gilbert suggested in the International Herald Tribune (March 10, 1983), by "reversing old state socialism policies and strengthening the private sector."

The domestic sphere, however, did not show the same dynamic upturn as the trade economy. The already high unemployment was rising in the early 1980s. Cash flow problems and the de facto devaluation of the Turkish lira made for low profit margins, forcing many small firms out of business. Addressing the concerns of the manufacturing classes in late November 1982, General Evren's government agreed to adjust prices and, in a move to discourage black market operations, to revise standards of wealth assessment. A broad reform of the country's antiquated banking system also came under discussion.

The priorities of General Evren's regime alarmed some observers and allies concerned about human and civic rights. Although the death penalty was not meted out to convicted terrorists to the extent some had feared, martial law allowed police to shoot to kill fleeing suspects and to hold prisoners for ninety days without formal charges. By 1982 up to 100,000 alleged extremists had been detained, with 25,000 jailed at any one time. Amnesty International reported that torture and degrading treatment of prisoners, "widespread and systematic" before the coup, were now increasing. In spring 1982 the government acknowledged the deaths of fifteen persons as a result of torture, publicly condemned such practices, and punished several members of the police force. Nevertheless, some Western allies withheld aid and brought complaints to the Council of Europe to protest infringement of human rights. Officials in Ankara argued that the worst offenses against rights occurred before the coup. "Then the most elementary human right—the right to live and work—was violated," said a government minister.

In the months following the constitutional plebescite, partial preparation for the parliamentary elections was accomplished by a purge of key public institutions: press censorship was tightened, trials of political suspects stepped up, and leftist university professors were dismissed. In April 1983 officials lifted the twenty-two–month ban on political parties, but new rules for party formation required National Security Council approval of party manifestoes (and thus, indirectly, of candidates) and continued the ban on old parties and their former leaders. A source close to Evren reported that his "main worry" was the return of the "old, sterile, and harmful political party spirit." When attempts to revive under new names the Justice and Republican People's parties came to light in May of that year, the National Security Council ordered Süleyman Demirel into "forced residence" in the western city of Canakkale and abolished the new Great Turkey party established by his associates.

The military lent its tacit support to the Nationalist Democratic party led by retired general Turgut Sunalp, former Turkish representative to NATO headquarters in Brussels. His party was joined in the race by the Motherland party, headed by Turgut Özal, who had resigned as deputy prime minister in 1982, and by the officially sanctioned opposition party, the Populists. Political experts noted a lack of interest among the electorate, perhaps because all three party leaders pledged markedly similar programs to uphold the "spirit of September 12" and to continue Evren's pro-Western orientation. But when public opinion polls showed Özal leading the other candidates in popularity by early November, the government banned further publication of polling results, and on election eve President Evren broadcast to the country an understated endorsement of the Nationalist Democrats.

In spite of Evren's speech (some observers say because of it), the Motherland party won a clear majority of parliamentary seats in the November 5, 1983 election, automatically making Turgut Özal the new prime minister. Dispelling some fears that he would reject an outcome unfavorable to his candidate, President Evren immediately called on all Turks to accept the results and embraced Özal in a meeting at the presidential palace. Although before stepping down the junta adopted a law forbidding criticism of its past actions and continuing martial law for an indefinite period, Evren told Özal the armed forces would return to their barracks "confident that democracy will be safeguarded," and on December 14, 1983 he approved, with minor changes, Özal's chosen cabinet, most of whose members were engineers. The new prime minister swiftly instituted reforms to streamline bureaucracy and centralize economic decision-making, and the Turkish nation, "glad to get back to democracy," began a new political life under the watchful eyes of President Kenan Evren, who retains his say in matters of defense, foreign policy, and internal security.

The handsome, silver-haired Kenan Evren is married and has three grown daughters. In spite of his high office, he maintains a modest way of life, and it has been said that the Turkish people cherish him more than any leader since Atatürk. "All freedoms provided by democracy are for those who believe in it," he has said. "Can the rights and freedoms of millions of virtuous people believing in democracy be safeguarded if those who seek to destroy [democracy] abuse rights and freedoms to achieve their goals? To my mind this is the crux of the matter."

References: Current History 80:27+ Ja '81; International Herald Tribune S p7+ Mr 10 '83; Nation 235:616+ D 11 '82; N Y Times p1+, p4 S 13 '80 por, IV p4 S 21 '80; Newsweek 47:62+ Ap 6 '81 pors; International Yearbook and Statesmen's Who's Who, 1983; Who's Who in the World, 1980–81

Ferraro, Geraldine A(nne)

Aug. 26, 1935– U.S. Representative from New York. Address: b. 312 Cannon House Office Bldg., Washington, D.C. 20515; h. Forest Hills, N.Y. 11375

The Honorable Geraldine A. Ferraro, Democratic congresswoman from Queens, New York City, is no ordinary member of the United States House of Representatives. Since her election as the first female representative from the conservative 9th Congressional District in New York in 1978, she has shown herself to have the political savvy and ambition that vice-presidential dreams are made of. Her talent, willingness to work hard, and party loyalty have made her the "favored daughter" of the Democratic establishment. More important, Walter F. Mondale, the Democratic presidential contender, recognized that as an Italian-American Roman Catholic from a large Northeastern state, a happily married wife and mother of three, and a shrewd politician, Ms. Ferraro had plenty of ticket-balancing charms, and as a result he selected her as his running mate, the first woman ever to be nominated by a major party for that office. The congresswoman freely admits that her selection had a lot to do with her gender, but she consistently emphasized that she was qualified for the position. Her past performance suggested that Geraldine Ferraro would help give the Reagan-Bush ticket a real run for its money.

Geraldine Anne Ferraro was born on August 26, 1935 in Newburgh, New York, the fourth child and only daughter of Dominick Ferraro, an Italian immigrant who owned a lucrative restaurant and a five-and-dime store, and Antonetta L. (Corrieri) Ferraro. Of her siblings, only one, Carl, survived. His twin brother died at birth, and Gerard, his younger brother, was killed in an automobile accident at three years of age. The Ferraros named their daughter in his memory. The little girl was pampered and showered with affection—especially by her father, who gave her an abundance of toys and often left work early to take his "princess" to a movie matinee. His sudden death from a heart attack on May 29, 1943 abruptly ended that fairy-tale existence. Geraldine never wept for her father but internalized her grief, which led to a serious bout of anemia that kept her out of school for a year.

Subsequent poor investments left Antonetta Ferraro with little money. She was forced to move the family to a small apartment in the Bronx and later to Queens, and she worked crocheting beads on dresses to support Geraldine and Carl. Nevertheless, by scrimping and saving she managed to send her bright daughter to fashionable Catholic schools for girls, first to Marymount School in Tarrytown, New York, and then on scholarship to Marymount College in Manhattan, where she majored in English. After graduating with a B.A. degree in 1956, Geraldine Ferraro taught grade school in the Queens public school system for four years while, with additional financial aid from her mother, she attended night classes at Fordham University Law School, from which she received a J.D. degree in 1960. On July 16, 1960, about a week after she passed her bar exam, she wed Manhattan real-estate developer John Zaccaro, but she chose to retain her maiden name for professional use in recognition of her mother's support and devotion. She was admitted to the New York State Bar the following year and to the United States Supreme Court Bar in 1978.

As the couple had agreed before their marriage, Ms. Ferraro (as she prefers to be called) settled down to raise a family before pursuing her own career. While caring for their three children during the next fourteen years, she occasionally worked part-time as a civil lawyer for her husband's real-estate business and for other clients. To provide an outlet for her energy and ambition, she spent much of her time at local Democratic clubs, which gave her the opportunity to establish and maintain contacts within the legal profession, and she became increasingly involved in local politics. She helped

her cousin Nicholas Ferraro in his successful bid for the state senate and worked on other local campaigns. In the process, she developed ties with civic groups, schools, and churches that would later help her own political career in Queens.

Finally in 1974 Ms. Ferraro accepted a full-time position as an assistant district attorney in the Investigations Bureau, a job she obtained with the help of her cousin, by then the popular district attorney of Queens. In 1975 she was assigned to the new Special Victims Bureau, which she helped create to handle cases of child abuse, domestic violence, and rape, and two years later she became its head. Dealing with victims of rape and child abuse every day was emotionally and professionally demanding: what she saw at work often kept her from sleeping at night. Although she sympathized with her clients, Geraldine Ferraro acquired a reputation as a tough prosecutor. Attorney Stephen J. Singer recalled in a *New York Times* article (July 21, 1984) that "she was a difficult opponent who did her job and didn't show any mercy," but colleagues also praised her fairness in plea negotiations, her persuasive courtroom presentations, and her overall professionalism.

But during her four years with the Special Victims Bureau, Geraldine Ferraro's political philosophy underwent a radical change. Her growing conviction that the root of many of the crimes with which she dealt was poverty and social injustice transformed her from a "a small-'c' conservative," as she used to describe herself, to a confirmed liberal. Moreover, her inability as an assistant district attorney to do more than treat the symptoms of those problems, the emotional drain of her work, and her dissatisfaction with a boss who paid her less than her male colleagues because she was married led her to quit the D.A.'s office in 1978 and to look for a political berth.

Even before James J. Delaney, the Democratic representative from the 9th Congressional District, announced his retirement, Geraldine Ferraro had eyed that predominantly working class, ethnic section of Queens. Such bastions of Archie Bunkerism as Astoria and Ridgewood would seem to be unlikely power bases for a liberal feminist, and to make matters worse, local Democratic leaders failed to support her. But her cousin's political clout, her husband's financial backing, and her Italian heritage in a district with ethnic neighborhoods gave Ms. Ferraro a running start. Putting together an appealing package of support for law and order, the elderly, and neighborhood preservation, she won the three-way Democratic primary with 53 percent of the vote and went on in the general election to defeat conservative Republican Alfred A. DelliBovi by a ten-point margin in spite of his mudslinging campaign, the memory of which still infuriates her. In 1980 and 1982 she handily won reelection to the House in campaigns that were heavily financed by political action committees (PACs).

Putting her difficult campaign behind her, Congresswoman Ferraro arrived in Washington in 1979 and applied herself to learning the political ropes on Capitol Hill. Like all freshmen in Congress, Representative Ferraro served at first on rather unglamorous committees, but she took full advantage of her assignments. On the Post Office and Civil Service Committee she fulfilled a campaign pledge to get a zip code in her district changed, and on the Public Works and Transportation Committee she pushed for more funding for mass transit around congested airports such as LaGuardia adjoining her district. She admitted in an interview for *New York* magazine (July 16, 1984) that she would have loved to sit on a prestigious committee like Foreign Affairs but, she observed pragmatically, "if you don't do for your district, you don't get reelected."

Thomas ("Tip") O'Neill, the influential Speaker of the House, took an immediate liking to Geraldine Ferraro because of her ingratiating manner, her diligence, and her pro-labor, liberal stand. (During her three terms in Congress, the Americans for Democratic Action gave her an average approval rating of 76 percent, while the AFL-CIO Committee on Political Education gave her an average approval rating of 91 percent.) As a "team player," she also scored points with the Democratic leadership by voting with the party 78 percent of the time during her first term in the House and by adhering even more closely to the party line in her second and third congressional terms. Like most of her fellow Democrats, Geraldine Ferraro opposes cuts in funding for social programs and the deployment of the MX missile (though she consistently supported its development during the Carter administration) and favors aid to Israel and a mutually verifiable nuclear freeze. On issues of importance to her constituents, however, Representative Ferraro has not hesitated to cross party lines, voting against mandatory busing and for tuition tax credits. She also advocates a strong defense, is less adamant than other party members on the need to cut military spending drastically, and has backed funding for the Trident nuclear submarine and the Pershing II nuclear missile. Nevertheless, she draws the line at production of the B-1 bomber, nerve gas, and President Ronald Reagan's proposal for a space-based defense system.

As a strong proponent of women's rights, Congresswoman Ferraro also supports federal funding for abortions, especially in cases of rape or incest. When questioned about the contradiction between that stand and the tenets of her Roman Catholic faith, she has repeatedly asserted that she cannot justify imposing her personal moral views on others. That position is obviously unpopular in her predominantly Catholic district, and the archbishop of New York, John J. O'Connor, has also criticized that stand in September 1984 as irrational and as a misrepresentation of the Church's teaching on abortion. As a result, she has emphasized instead the fight that she and other feminists have waged to achieve financial parity for women. In 1981 she cosponsored the bipartisan "Economic Equity Act," which is supposed to accomplish many of the aims of the defeated Equal Rights Amendment, and originated two of its sections: one that lowers the age at which employees can be vested in private pension plans and protects the rights of widows and divorcées to share in that portion of their husbands' pensions accumulated during marriage, among other provisions; and another that increases to $2,000 the amount that a woman, whether a homemaker or full-time employee, can deposit in a joint Individual Retirement Account. But unlike some of her more intransigent and abrasive feminist predecessors in the legislature, such as Bella Abzug and Shirley Chisholm, Geraldine Ferraro demonstrated her willingness to "play by boys' rules" while pushing women's issues. Consequently, she has been able to take strong stands without alienating her male colleagues. As Barney Frank, a Democratic congressman from Massachusetts, explained in the *Chicago Tribune* (March 15, 1984), "She manages to be threatening on issues without being threatening personally."

Her pragmatism, closeness to the Democratic leadership, and ability to be "one of the boys" quickly brought Geraldine Ferraro political rewards. With Tip O'Neill's backing, she was elected secretary of the Democratic caucus in 1980 and 1982, a post that entitled her to sit on the important House Steering and Policy Committee, which controls committee assignments. In 1981 she served as a House representative on the Hunt Commission, which was charged with rewriting the delegate selection rules for the 1984 Democratic convention. By all accounts, she did an excellent job of winning a 14 percent share of the delegate pool for uncommitted, appointed "superdelegates" (governors, big-city mayors, congressmen, and party officials), a change that her mentor, Tip O'Neill, had pushed for. Her superior performance on that commission helped her to win yet another political plum when in 1983 the Speaker passed over party members with more seniority to appoint her to the powerful Budget Committee. There Geraldine Ferraro received a crash course in economics.

But it was Geraldine Ferraro's appointment as chairman of the 1984 Democratic platform committee, a position she had sought, that won her almost instant party prominence. As the first woman to hold that post, she enjoyed the added benefit of free media exposure, and she admitted to Robert W. Merry in a *Wall Street Journal* interview (May 29, 1984) that she was "taking full advantage of it." Representative Ferraro was determined to make the platform a "thematic" document broad enough for anyone in the party—especially Walter F. Mondale, the leading contender for the party's presidential nomination—to run on. She strove to keep out any references to specific legislation, such as the controversial bipartisan Simpson-Mazzoli immigration bill, in order to unite the party behind the platform. Pressure from women's groups, who insisted on including an ERA plank in the document, and from other lobbies as well as from Gary Hart and Jesse Jackson, made that virtually impossible, but Representative Ferraro handled the special interests and the sometimes heated committee meetings with skill and aplomb. The platform that her committee submitted for ratification at the Democratic convention on July 17, 1984 pleased most party members, and Geraldine Ferraro emerged as an even brighter political star.

Since throughout the Democratic primary campaigns, political analysts and party leaders had mentioned the possibility of a woman as the vice-presidential nominee, Representative Ferraro's appointment to the platform committee made her a top contender for that honor. The first nomination by a major party of a woman for vice-president, according to political experts, was sure to create excitement, generate media exposure, and, perhaps most important, entice women to support the Democratic ticket in November 1984. Those factors influenced Walter Mondale to include Representative Ferraro and Dianne Feinstein, the mayor of San Francisco, on his "short list" of possible running mates, but few thought he would buck tradition to nominate one of the two. On July 12, 1984, however, Mondale announced that Geraldine Ferrraro had agreed to run with him in the fall elections. The barrage of publicity and the additional women's votes that a sexually balanced ticket would win were not the only motives in Mondale's decision. Although in some quarters Representative Ferraro was seen as a potential liability, or at best a neutral factor, in the Democrats' campaign in the South, she was expected to draw votes from Italian-Americans, Roman Catholics, and the heavily populated northeastern industrial states.

Although the congresswoman from Queens freely acknowledged that she would not have been considered for the vice-presidency if she were not a woman, she insisted that her selection was based on her qualifications for the position, not on political strategy. Nevertheless, critics of Representative Ferraro's rapid rise to national leadership lost no time in pointing out her deficiencies, citing her limited experience in foreign affairs and military matters, a lack she had tried to remedy through fact-finding trips in 1983 and 1984 to Central America, the Middle East, Cyprus, and East Asia. Others judged her legislative experience as too meager for someone who would be second in line for the presidency of the most powerful nation in the world. "Because she's the darling of the leadership, we've handed her every prize in the book. She hasn't been tested here [in the capital]," contended a congressman in *Time* (June 4, 1984). In summing up the opinion of her critics, Elisabeth Bumiller reported in the *Washington Post* (April 29, 1984) that some of Representative Ferraro's colleagues "see her as too compromising, too ambitious, too close to the leadership, . . . and too much of a traditional pork barrelist who merely gets money for pet projects back home." Yet even her detractors, Elisabeth Bumiller added, recognize her as "one of the best instinctive politicians, man or woman, on Capitol Hill."

After their nominations were confirmed by the Democratic convention, Walter Mondale and Geraldine Ferraro immediately began campaigning in earnest. But when Ms. Ferraro initially backed down from a promise to release her husband's tax returns for public scrutiny, the resulting controversy over her finances slowed the campaign's post-convention momentum. During a two-hour press conference on August 21, 1984 in which she did release her and her husband's returns, she admitted that she had underpaid her taxes, a mistake she attributed to an accountant's error, but added that she had that week paid the Internal Revenue Service the $53,459 she owed in back taxes and interest. Reporters also questioned her about the $134,-000 contribution her family made to her 1978 congressional campaign (the legal limit is $1,000 per person) that she had later refunded under orders from the Federal Election Commission. The financial disclosures she made also showed that she and her husband had assets of $3.78 million.

Her confident, relaxed manner during that press conference helped her to weather that storm and the subsequent tempest stirred up by her husband's questionable handling of the finances of an elderly woman, whose assets he managed as the court-appointed conservator of her estate. (Although his borrowing of $175,000 from the woman's estate was not illegal, the court removed him as custodian.) Nevertheless, the House Ethics Committee continued to investigate whether she violated the Ethics in Government Act by failing to list her husband's assets on the standard disclosure form required of all House members.

Although Representative Ferraro admitted that she was somewhat awed by the possibility of becoming the nation's first female vice-president, she maintained that she is "truly most concerned with one thing, and that's beating Ronald Reagan." But in spite of her best efforts during the hard-fought campaign and an impressive showing in a mid-October debate against Vice President George Bush, the Democratic presidential ticket suffered a devastating defeat at the polls on November 6, 1984 as President Reagan won forty-nine states and 525 electoral votes, the highest electoral vote total in the nation's history. In sharp contrast, the Democratic ticket garnered only thirteen electoral votes (ten from Mondale's home state of Minnesota and three from the District of Columbia), but it took 36,930,923 (41 percent) of the popular vote.

Studies by political analysts showed that, although Representative Ferraro by no means hurt the Democrats' chances of capturing the White House, she had not attracted as many votes from women and Italian-Americans as had been expected. Nevertheless, she considered her candidacy important because it opened new opportunities for women and encouraged them to be more politically active. "Over $4 million came in from women contributors," she noted during a post-election news conference. " . . . We have reached out and women have reached to us as a result of my candidacy." And, she added, "No one ever said we would win an election because there is a woman on the ticket." Despite the disappointing election results, the congresswoman has no intention of retiring from politics. She may make a bid for the Senate seat of New York Republican Alfonse D'Amato in the 1986 election.

Geraldine Ferraro is a short, slim, attractive, and fashionably dressed woman with streaked blond hair and hazel eyes. The Zaccaros have a large Tudor-style home in the Forest Hills Gardens section of Queens, a beach house on Fire Island, and a winter home in St. Croix. A full-time housekeeper-cook relieves Representative Ferraro of domestic chores, but when time allows she still likes to do the weekly shopping and fix meals for her husband and children: Donna, a financial analyst with Salomon Brothers of New York City; John, Jr., a student at Middlebury College in Vermont; and Laura, who postponed her freshman year at Brown University to join the rest of the family in helping with the campaign.

Geraldine Ferraro tends to be impatient and highstrung, according to Elisabeth Bumiller in the *Washington Post* article, and is as demanding of others as she is of herself. When stumping on the campaign trail and fulfilling her family obligations, she has little time for leisure, but she seems to thrive on the pressure. In fact, she cultivates her image as a tough politician. "I haven't gone through life having things given to me," she insists. "I had to work for it. So if that makes you tough, yeah, I guess I'm tough." Political analysts suggested that she would need that stamina and all the tenacity she could muster to weather the rigors of the uphill 1984 Democratic campaign.

References: *N Y Times* p1+ Jl 13 '84; *Newsweek* 104:16+ Jl 23 '84 pors; *Time* 124:10+ Jl 23 '84 pors; *Washington Post* K p1+ Ap 29 '84 por; *Who's Who in America, 1984–85*; *Who's Who in American Politics, 1983–84*

Fierstein, Harvey

(fĭr´stēn)

June 6, 1954– Playwright; actor. Address: b. c/o George Lane, William Morris Agency, Inc., 1350 Ave. of the Americas, New York City, N.Y. 10019

The talented and flamboyant playwright and actor Harvey Fierstein, who began his career as a transvestite diva in the homosexual underground, made American theatrical history in 1982 when, in his words, he became the first "real live, out-of-the-closet queer on Broadway." The vehicle of Fierstein's epiphany was his own partly autobiographi-

cal *Torch Song Trilogy,* a seriocomic drama about the life, loves, and growth to maturity of a "drag queen," the first successful "crossover" work in American theatre. For it, Fierstein won two Tony awards, one for best playwright and the other for best actor, and he followed up that grand slam by writing the book for the spectacular "gay" musical *La Cage aux Folles,* one of Broadway's biggest hits in years.

The gay sensibility has long been a covert influence in the theatre. Even after it began to surface in the late 1960s, it remained distorted and unfocused, usually taking the form of anger or self-deprecating camp, which, as Fierstein has said, "is not going to open anyone's heart up." The secret of Fierstein's success, aside from his bravado, has been his instinct for balancing laughter with tears and his ability to put the homosexual experience in universal terms understandable to a mainstream audience. He is able to do that because his deviant subject matter is at its core conservative: he focuses not on sex but on love, not on promiscuity but on commitment and domesticity.

Harvey Forbes Fierstein pronounces his last name differently than the other members of his family, who pronounce the name's first syllable as if it were spelled "fear," not "fire." The actor-playwright was born in Brooklyn, New York on June 6, 1954 to Jewish parents who had emigrated from Eastern Europe. His father, a handkerchief manufacturer, died in 1976. His mother, Jacqueline Fierstein, is a librarian at the Jackie Robinson Intermediate School in Brooklyn. Fierstein has an older brother, Ronald, a Park Avenue lawyer. Ronald, a heterosexual, played a crucial supportive role when Harvey was embarking on his career. "You have a vision," Ronald counseled him when Harvey was unsure of himself. "Go for it."

When they were growing up in the Bensonhurst section of Brooklyn, the Fierstein brothers, at the urging of their parents, took advantage of New York City's cultural opportunities, especially the Saturday matinee performances of Broadway shows. Partly because he thought he might become a painter and partly to please his parents, Harvey studied art at Pratt Institute in Brooklyn after he graduated from high school. When he "came out" at age thirteen, his parents took the news in stoic stride. "We were brought up with the feeling that the family unit was everything," Fierstein explained to Michiko Kakutani of the New York Times (July 14, 1982), "and something as minuscule as my being gay was not going to disrupt that." He was lucky in his role models, he told Jack Kroll of Newsweek (June 20, 1983): "The very first gay couple that I knew . . . had been together about thirty years. . . . My formative years were spent seeing that gays were just like straight people. Except we had a better sense of humor."

Fierstein was, in his words, "a fat kid," ballooning to more than 240 pounds as a teenager. Comfortable with his sexual orientation but not with his girth, he turned to cross-dressing for self-protection as well as self-expression. "In drag, I could completely become someone else," he recounted to Ross Wetzsteon in an interview for New York (August 22, 1983). "And guess what? I liked it." When he was sixteen he began performing as a female impersonator at a homosexual nightclub in Manhattan's East Village, using names like Virginia Hamm and specializing in impressions of Ethel Merman singing such songs as "Rose's Turn" and "You Can't Get a Man With a Gun." Even then, he knew that he "didn't want to stay in that world of gays doing things for other gays," that he had "to make [his] own place."

Fierstein's nightclub work led in 1971 to his theatrical debut as an asthmatic lesbian cleaning woman in Andy Warhol's play Pork at La Mama Experimental Theatre Club, Ellen Stewart's avant-garde East Village company. During the following year, while studying days at Pratt Institute, he acted nights in a score of plays at La Mama, Theatre Genesis, and other Off-Off Broadway houses. His voice, already a little hoarse, became the gravel pit it now is, he claims, through the damage done his vocal cords in his second show, Xircus, the Private Life of Jesus Christ, in which he had to shout a monologue over a recording of Kate Smith singing "God Bless America." Among his subsequent shows were an all-male version of The Trojan Women, a sadomasochistic play about Vietnam titled Vinyl Visits an FM Station, and what he remembers as a "just awful" play that Harry Koutoukas, a celebrated Sheridan Square literary dandy, wrote for him in exchange for his cleaning Koutoukas' apartment, an unbelievably cluttered pack-rat's heaven. In the course of his busy commuting between his home in Brooklyn, Pratt Institute, and Off Off Broadway, Fierstein lost eighty pounds.

Emboldened by Koutoukas' example, Fierstein began writing his own "raunchy chic" Off-Off-Broadway vehicles around the time he graduated from Pratt Institute with a fine arts degree in 1973. The first of those outrageously campy plays, a work inspired by the cleaning of Koutoukas' apartment, was In Search of the Cobra Jewels, produced at the Playwrights' Workshop Club. It was followed by Freaky Pussy—in which Fierstein played a transvestite prostitute working out of a subway men's room—and Cannibals Just Don't Know Better. Flatbush Tosca, an updated, transvestite version of the Puccini opera, was produced by the New York Theatre Ensemble in 1975.

In 1976 the breakup of a two-year love affair left Fierstein almost suicidally depressed. At the suggestion of a therapist, he exorcised his heartbreak by writing about it. The ultimate result was Torch Song Trilogy, consisting of three one-act plays chronicling six years in the life of Arnold Beckoff, "a kvetch," in Fierstein's words, "of great wit and want," seeking self-identity and self-respect. Narrated by the sardonic but vulnerable protagonist with a pathos couched in Jewish humor and bitchy wisecracks, the trilogy is a mixture of melodrama and stand-up comedy. Arnold recounts, and philosophizes about, his progress from promiscuous, self-centered gay "drag queen" entertainer to settled, solid "family" person. From the beginning he is a fatalistic romantic at heart, with a sensibility akin to that expressed in the torch songs of his beloved 1920s. The basic theme, according to Fierstein, is "the realization that homosexuals can be just as normal as heterosexuals." "By the end, you're rooting for him because, really, everyone wants what Arnold wants—an apartment they can afford, a job they don't hate too much, a chance to go to the store once in a while and someone to share it all with."

With Fierstein playing Arnold Beckoff, the first play in the trilogy, The International Stud, had its premiere at the Theatre for the New City in the East Village in 1976 and had a second production at La Mama in 1978. In that play, Arnold falls in love with Ed, a bisexual schoolteacher, loses him to a woman, Laurel, and takes up with a handsome male model, Alan. The cleverest of the three plays is the second, Fugue in a Nursery, in which Arnold and Alan visit Ed and Laurel at their Vermont farmhouse. A dazzling crossfire of colloquies and couplings ensues (to the music of a fugue written by Ada Janik), wounding egos all around. That play had its first performance in 1979, moving from La Mama to Off Broadway within the year. Five years have elapsed when the action begins in the third play, the best of the three, Widows and Children First!, which also had its premiere at La Mama in 1979. Alan has been killed by a gang of homophobes, but Arnold is proceeding with his and Alan's plan to adopt David, a homosexual street urchin, and Ed has left Laurel and is sleeping on Arnold's couch. Into this scene intrudes Arnold's repressive mother (one of the trilogy's departures from autobiography), with whom Arnold has a showdown. "[My mother] thinks I hate her and everything she stands for," Arnold says in the course of his intense final monologue. "And I don't, for the life of me, know how to tell her that what I want more than anything is to have exactly the life she had. With a few minor alterations."

With the moral and financial support of John Glines and Lawrence Lane—whose nonprofit corporation, The Glines, is devoted to helping cultural projects with homosexual themes—Fierstein brought the three plays together into a single package. When the consolidated *Torch Song Trilogy* opened Off Off Broadway at the Richard Allen Center in the autumn of 1981, audiences shunned it. "We couldn't give tickets away," Fierstein recalled in an interview with Loren King for *After Dark* (September 1982), explaining that part of the problem was the program's length (then four and a half hours, later reduced to three hours and forty minutes, with much of the homosexual special pleading removed) and part was that "many of the critics had seen *Stud* and *Fugue* at La Mama and didn't like them." "But those same critics came back and said they misjudged. . . . This gave me a new respect for critics."

The turning point came with glowing reviews by Michael Feingold in the *Village Voice* (September 26–October 3, 1981) and by Mel Gussow in the *New York Times* (October 1, 1981). Gussow, who had felt that the 1978 production of *The International Stud* was "a sincere but sentimentalized view of a transvestite *in extremis*," now found himself enjoying Arnold's wit ("the pithy humor of a Fran Lebowitz") at the same time that he was "moved by his dilemma." The story, Gussow wrote, becomes "richer as it unfolds," and "the cumulative event is one to be experienced and savored." "Mr. Fierstein's self-incarnation," he concluded, "is an act of compelling virtuosity." Even the redoubtable John Simon of *New York* (December 14, 1981) was beguiled by *Torch Song Trilogy*'s "bittersweet harmony" and what it has "to tell us about the way we live now."

In January 1982 *Torch Song Trilogy* moved to Off Broadway, beginning its regular commercial run at the Actors Playhouse in Greenwich Village. The production won the *Village Voice*'s Obie award for best Off-Broadway play of the season and drew such notices as that of Jack Kroll in *Newsweek* (March 15, 1982): "Without one dirty word, with no nudity, and not a single leer or smirk, *Torch Song Trilogy* tells us a great deal about the absurd but anguished shifts in our sexual and emotional arrangements. Fierstein's ability to combine almost nonstop humor with a complex texture of emotional levels is remarkable. . . . And [as an actor] Fierstein is a living breathing theatre all by himself." Stanley Kaufmann, writing in the *Saturday Review* (March 1982), thought the production had too much of a "gag-tainted" Neil Simon touch but nevertheless agreed with James Leverett's introduction to the book of *Torch Song Trilogy* (Gay Presses of New York, 1982): "[The trilogy's] radical accomplishment is . . . to accord homosexuality absolutely equal, undeniable status within the entire range of human experience."

After five months at the Actors Playhouse, *Torch Song Trilogy* moved uptown to the Little Theatre on June 10, 1982. The sold-out performances and the rave notices continued, and the play won *Newsday*'s George Oppenheimer Playwriting Award in addition to the Tony awards for best play and best actor. In presenting the Oppy, *Newsday* publisher David Laventhol said, "Harvey Fierstein not only writes with perception, but for almost two hours he holds center stage as the leading character in this moving and entertaining play." Writing in the *Village Voice* (October 12, 1982), Anna Mayo reported that *Torch Song Trilogy*'s deficiencies "in the probability department" didn't matter as long as Fierstein was "up there hoofing," wiping them out with his "inspired" dialogue and "luminous . . . utterly whacked out performance." "Somewhere along in the middle of this prolonged hermaphroditic/ Jewish joke the audience gets its heart broken," she wrote "but (almost) before they boo-hoo he switches them to euphoria."

Ironically, controversy over *Torch Song Trilogy* was mostly confined to the homosexual community, where advocates of promiscuity objected to Fierstein's espousal of "middle-class" fidelity and monogamy. "We had gotten all this praise," Fierstein recounted to Jack Kroll in the *Newsweek* interview, "and we were just about to get hit with the homosexual backlash. Suddenly the AIDS (Acquired Immune Deficiency Syndrome) thing hit and the backlash withered away." The AIDS epidemic drew attention to the rampantly wanton lifestyle of many homosexuals, especially in such centers of gay culture as San Francisco, which Fierstein described as a "sexual Disneyland." "Gay liberation should not be a license to be a permanent adolescent," he observed to Kroll. "If you deny yourself commitment, then what can you do with your life?"

While starring in *Torch Song Trilogy*, Fierstein was signed by the producer Alan Carr to write the book for a musical stage version of *La Cage aux Folles*, the popular French play by Jean Poiret that had spawned two popular motion pictures. (Carr had already signed Jerry Herman to write the music for the show and Arthur Laurents to direct it.) *La Cage aux Folles*, in Fierstein's perception, is "a musical about a marriage"—the enduring union of two men in their fifties. One is Albin, a transvestite who performs as Zaza, "the queen of the Riviera." The other, the "plain" partner, is Georges, Albin's impresario-lover. The two share an apartment behind their St. Tropez nightclub, *La Cage aux Folles*, which can be translated literally as Cage of Crazies or loosely, reflecting French slang, as Cage of Queers. Their ménage includes Jean-Michel, the young man they have raised, the offspring of Georges's one heterosexual experiment. "Basically it's the same plot as *You Can't Take It With You*, *The Munsters*, *Mame*—a classic farce plot about a weird family with a normal kid," Fierstein pointed out to Ross Wetzsteon in the *New York* interview.

The plot becomes turbulent when Jean-Michel finds the young woman he wants to marry, the daughter of a puritanical politician famous for his moral crusading, and the prospective parents-in-law are coming to meet Jean-Michel's "parents." Fierstein and his collaborators decided not only to tone down the crude farce of the original play, to "make the characters more human," but also to change the theme to "a marriage of twenty years almost ruined by a son's thoughtlessness." Fierstein explained to Ross Wetzsteon: "The villain of the original play is the father of the girl, this very uptight man. But in our version he's a paper tiger, and the one who does villainous deeds is the son—like asking Albin not to be there when the parents of the girl come. He cannot see that this man who raised him is his mother. And once we had that angle, I felt we had something very important to say. The original play was a farce—extremly funny, but the heart was not there. Our version is blatantly romantic, and hopefully very funny."

In June 1983 Fierstein turned his role in *Torch Song Trilogy* over to David Garrison in order to put the finishing touches on *La Cage aux Folles*, which was beginning its pre-Broadway tryout in Boston, with George Hearn in the role of Albin and Gene Barry in that of Georges. The production was an extravaganza in the old-fashioned tradition, with a quiet, sentimental love story counterpointed by lavish sets (by David Mitchell), a flashily costumed (by Theoni V. Aldredge) transvestite chorus line (with two real women added to keep the audience guessing), and generous amounts of schmaltz in Jerry Herman's score. The combination of glamour and compassion kept sold-out audiences in Boston's Colonial Theater at a fever pitch, to a degree that amazed even the show's principals. "I'm not surprised that they like it," Arthur Laurents told a reporter, "but this is something bordering on mass hysteria."

After breaking box-office records at the Colonial in Boston, the $5-million production moved to the Palace Theatre in New York City in August 1983 with an advance sale estimated between $4 and $6 million. As in Boston, the audiences in New York were ecstatic, and critics hailed the show as, in Fierstein's paraphrase, "a Ziegfeld Follies with heart"—with some reservations. "The near-frenzy that tingled through the huge auditorium during the show, the rapture with which the audience responded to every purportedly comic or emotional line, to every musical number, even to the costumes and scenery," Stanley Kauffmann wrote in the *Saturday Review* (November–December 1983), "gave me a great deal more pleasure than the show itself." Kauffmann, who considered *Torch Song Trilogy* "the truest and most enlightening American play about homosexuality" he knew, contrasted it with *La Cage aux Folles*: "*Trilogy* dramatized the difference of the homosexual from the heterosexual, the rights and benefits of that difference. [Fierstein's] book [for *La Cage aux Folles*], abetted by Jerry Herman's lyrics, tells us over and over that basically we're all alike. . . . This isn't equality; this is mush."

In a similar vein, Frank Rich of the *New York Times* (August 22, 1983) enjoyed "the glitz, showmanship, good cheer, and almost unflagging tunefulness" but found that "in its eagerness to please all comers, this musical is sometimes as shamelessly calculating as a candidate for public office." Glossing Frank Rich, Robert Brustein concluded his review in the *New Republic* (September 19–26, 1983) with the observation that "it is the homosexual community who will ultimately have to determine whether it is better served by 'positive' and pretty evasions or by the unadorned and possibly 'bleak' truth." Among the many more positive reviews of *La Cage aux Folles* was that of Jack Kroll in *Newsweek* (August 29, 1983): "This is a feat of showbiz smarts that must be saluted. . . . Fierstein's brashness, Herman's apple-pie lyricism, Laurents's clear-eyed realism all meshed to make a success out of a project that many showbiz savants thought would never work."

Fierstein's play *Spookhouse* has been described by him as "a very black comedy" about a well-meaning homosexual social worker whose efforts to help a lower-class Coney Island family only add to the family's problems. That play ran Off Broadway for fifty-one previews and six performances during the 1983–84 season. Fierstein has also written a television drama, *Kaddish and Old Men*, about two octogenarians who have been secret lovers for half a century. Among his other projects are a London production of *Torch Song Trilogy* and, possibly, a motion picture adaptation of the trilogy and a television situation comedy. The NBC network has shown an interest in Fierstein's idea for a TV series about a New York homosexual that would entertain and at the same time help to dispel homophobia.

Although lower-keyed and softer-spoken, the private Harvey Fierstein does not much differ from his public persona. Al Goldstein, who interviewed him for *Hustler* (January 1984), found him to be "personable and funny," with a "relaxed attitude," and others have described him as "direct," "unassuming," "compassionate," and "immune" to homophobic bigotry—a man who insists "on being himself." According to Jerry Herman, "He's such a warm, caring person, he's the perfect collaborator. The key word is 'instinctive.'" In an interview with Leslie Bennetts for the *New York Times* (June 26, 1983), Fierstein revealed that he is "slightly dyslexic," that he reads "at a snail's pace" and "can't write a decent sentence grammatically." His wonted diet of junk food and Southern Comfort has not diminished his robustness, but his heavy cigarette smoking has probably enhanced—if that is the word—the extraordinary huskiness of his voice. The actor-playwright shares his apartment in Park Slope, Brooklyn with two dogs, a rabbit, and pillows, slippers, and various other items with a bunny motif. After a two-and-a-half-year retreat into celibacy, he recently began dating again, but his lover, another actor-writer, does not "live in" because Fierstein prefers to live alone.

Fierstein does not share the views of those who look down on such earlier plays dealing with the homosexual milieu as *The Boys in the Band* as "dated" and "over-serious." "*Torch Song Trilogy* will be dated soon as well . . . ," he said in an interview for *Plays and Players* (July 1983). "For myself, I greatly appreciated *Boys in the Band* for doing what had never been done before. . . . It was an honest piece of work beautifully written and well constructed. It was of its time." "The single most important thing I'm saying," Fierstein told Ross Wetzsteon in the *New York* interview, "is that we have to get the concept out of our minds that love and commitment and family are heterosexual rights. They're not. They're *people's* rights. Hetero-

sexuals [or] gays can adopt or reject them, but everyone has the right to choose. . . . The way I look at it, I'm a human being first and gorgeous second." The tall and now only slightly beefy actor and playwright explained, with a smile, that to him female impersonation is "total fantasy": "Even though I know I look like a football player wearing a dress, in my mind's eye I'm beautiful."

References: After Dark 14:24+ S '82 pors; Guardian p14 Je 9 '83 por; N Y Times C p17 Jl 14 '82 por, II p3 Je 26 '83 por; Newsday II p23 Je 22 '83 por; Newsweek 101:71 Je 20 '83 pors; New York 6:30+ Ag 22 '83 pors; People 19:82+ Je 6 '83 por; Plays & Players p12+ Jl '83 pors

FitzGerald, Garret

Feb. 9, 1926– Prime Minister of Ireland. Address: b. Dáil Éireann, Leinster House, Kildare St., Dublin 2, Ireland; Department of the Taoiseach, Government Buildings, Upper Merrion St., Dublin 2, Ireland

Under the realistic leadership of Prime Minister Garret FitzGerald, the government of the Republic of Ireland has put aside the thorny question of Irish unity and has at long last apparently begun to make progress in an Anglo-Irish dialogue. That exchange of opinions is aimed at bringing about an accommodation between the Protestant majority and the Roman Catholic minority in strife-torn Northern Ireland, which comprises the six (out of thirty-two) historic Irish counties that remained under British rule when overwhelmingly Catholic Southern Ire-

land (as the republic was then known) became independent in 1922. With the distant possibility of reunification in mind, FitzGerald is also hoping to secularize the Irish republic, so that denominational differences will no longer be an obstacle. At the same time, he has to cope with an economic crisis marked by 14 percent unemployment, rampant inflation, and a large budget deficit covered by foreign loans.

The scholarly FitzGerald was trained as a barrister and an educator and is expert in political economy, which he taught at University College, Dublin and on which he has written several books. A member of the moderate Fine Gael, Ireland's second-strongest party, he served as foreign minister in the government of Liam Cosgrave (1973–77) and succeeded Cosgrave as party leader in 1977. As the head of a precarious Fine Gael–Labour coalition, he first served as prime minister, or *taoiseach* ("chief" in the Irish language) from June 1981 to March 1982. Unseating Charles J. Haughey, the leader of the dominant Fianna Fáil party, with a stronger Fine Gael–Labour coalition, he formed his present government in December 1982.

Garret FitzGerald has said that one of the principal reasons he entered politics was "to work for the resolution of the conflict between [his] father's and [his] mother's peoples." He was born in Dublin, Ireland on February 9, 1926 to the nationalist poet and statesman Desmond FitzGerald, a Catholic, and Mabel (McConnell) FitzGerald, a Presbyterian from Ulster. Both parents fought in the uprising against British rule in Dublin in 1916. That insurrection was brutally suppressed in the British "Black and Tan" reign of terror, but guerrilla warfare resumed in 1919 and culminated in Britain's granting dominion status to the twenty-six counties of Southern Ireland in 1921. Those counties became the Irish Free State, a self-governing member of the British Commonwealth, and the six counties in the north with Protestant majorities, which remained part of the United Kingdom, were partitioned off. As J. C. Beckett, a professor of history at Queen's University in Belfast has pointed out, the partitioning was "an expedient imposed on the country by a hard-pressed British cabinet," and it has never been fully accepted as permanent by southern or Catholic Irishmen, including such conciliators as Garret FitzGerald.

Desmond FitzGerald served in the Free State government as minister for external affairs (1922-27) and as minister for defense (1927-32). With the entry into force of Ireland's present constitution in 1937, the Free State became the Republic of Ireland, and the republic gradually attenuated its association with Britain, withdrawing completely from the Commonwealth in 1949.

Garret FitzGerald was raised in the Catholicism of his father. He grew up in Bray, County Wicklow, where he received his elementary education at St. Brigid's School; in Dungarvan, County Waterford, where he began his secondary education at Coláiste na Rinne (Ring College), an Irish-language boarding school; and in Dublin, where he completed his secondary education at another boarding school, Belvedere College. Majoring in education and economics, he did his university studies at University College, Dublin, a constituent college of the National University of Ireland, where he earned a Ph.D. degree. In addition, he took a law degree at King's Inn, Dublin, and he was called to the bar in 1946.

FitzGerald was research and schedules manager for Aer Lingus (Irish Air Lines) from 1947 to 1958. At University College, Dublin, he was a Rockefeller research assistant in 1958-59 and a lecturer in political economy from 1959 to 1973. For many years, beginning in 1954, he also worked in journalism, as Irish correspondent for BBC radio and for the British publications the *Economist* and the *Financial Times* and as economic correspondent for the *Irish Times*. During the same period he wrote the books *State-Sponsored Bodies* (1959) and *Planning in Ireland* (1968), published by the Institute of Public Administration in Dublin.

Ireland's parliament, the Oireachtas, is a bicameral legislature composed of a sixty-member Seanad (senate) and a 144-member house of representatives, the Dáil. The members of the Dáil are directly elected by proportional adult suffrage. Those of the Seanad, representing not popular constituencies but, for the most part, a vocational cross-section of the country, are nominated by the prime minister, the universities, and several vocational panels, and they are elected by an electoral college. The Fianna Fáil, or Republican party, founded by Éamon de Valera, dominates the Dáil, consistently holding about half of the seats. Next in power is the business-oriented Fine Gael party, with approximately a third of the seats. The Labour party trails with less than a fifth of the seats, and smaller parties and independents together hold but several. FitzGerald served the Seanad from 1965 to 1969, when he was elected to the Dáil from Dublin South-East, the constituency he has represented ever since.

FitzGerald was the Fine Gael opposition frontbench spokesman on education from 1969 until 1972, when he became the spokesman on finance.

It was in 1972 that Charles Knight & Company Ltd. published his most acclaimed book, *Towards a New Ireland*. In his column in the London *Observer* (June 10, 1973), the pseudonymous Pendennis wrote: "*Towards a New Ireland* . . . should help to dispel the popular British illusion that the Irish have only one academic politician of international standing, Conor Cruise O'Brien. In ability and intellect, FitzGerald is definitely world class. Now that Ireland is part of the European Economic Community, it ought to show."

In the parliamentary election of February 1973 Fianna Fáil, which had been in power for sixteen years, failed to retain its absolute majority, and Liam Cosgrave, the leader of Fine Gael, formed a government in coalition with the Labour party. FitzGerald was appointed minister for foreign affairs in the Cosgrave government, and he served with that portfolio until Fianna Fáil returned to power four years later. During that term in the cabinet, he served as president of the Council of Ministers of the European Economic Community, from January to June 1975.

Following the electoral defeat of 1977, FitzGerald replaced Cosgrave as the leader of Fine Gael, and with his characteristic energy and drive proceeded to rebuild the party. Under his leadership, Fine Gael, once solidly conservative, became more liberal in social policy without abandoning its economic orthodoxy, and in four years it increased its parliamentary representation from forty-three seats to sixty-five, the total with which it emerged from the election of June 1981. Fianna Fáil held seventy-eight seats coming out of that election, but FitzGerald outwitted Charles Haughey, the incumbent Fianna Fáil prime minister, in the race to form a new government; with the support of one independent deputy and the abstention of two others, he formed a coalition with Labour that was approved by an 81-78 vote of the Dáil.

In his first statement as prime minister, FitzGerald said he would immediately address himself to Ireland's faltering economy and the "urgent" situation in Northern Ireland. The economic ills included inflation (which was approaching 20 percent), unemployment (approaching 11 percent), a mounting foreign debt, and the highest per capita budget deficit in Western Europe (more than $1 billion). Public tension in the south over the sectarian strife and terrorism in Northern Ireland had reached an emotional peak in reaction to a hunger strike by the Irish Republican Army militants demanding political-prisoner status at the Maze prison in Belfast. Ten of the protesting prisoners died of starvation during the seven-month strike, which began in March 1981.

Totally antipathetic to the use of guerrilla warfare as a means toward the reunification of Ireland and fearing the possibility of the spirit of violence in Northern Ireland spilling over the border and infecting unemployed young people in the Republic of Ireland, FitzGerald continued the dialogue Haughey had begun with the government of British Prime Minister Margaret Thatcher with a more cooperative and less militantly nationalistic attitude than Haughey's. Meeting on November 6, 1981, a month after the hunger strike at the Maze prison ended, he and Mrs. Thatcher agreed on establishing an Anglo-Irish intergovernmental council to discuss a range of mutual concerns, the most urgent of which was the situation in Northern Ireland.

In addressing "an economic and financial crisis more grave than any this state has previously faced," FitzGerald early in his first term increased sales taxes, announced spending cuts, and allowed interest rates to rise. As unpopular as those moves were, FitzGerald knew they were too moderate to halt the continuing growth of the balance-of-payments deficit, the government debt, and the unemployment and inflation rates. His first full budget, presented to the Dáil in January 1982, was the harshest in independent Ireland's sixty-year history. Aimed at reducing the budget deficit by $400 million despite social welfare concessions to the Labour party coalition partners, the budget proposed a 30 percent increase in taxes. The "old reliable" pleasure penalties, the special taxes on cigarettes, beer, and spirits, would be escalated; the price of petrol would rise to $2.30 a gallon; and the value-added tax on general merchandise would be raised from 15 to 18 percent and be applied for the first time to clothing and shoes, including children's wear. The subsidy for butter would be reduced and that for milk would be eliminated.

Following the defeat of the budget by one vote, parliament was dissolved on January 27, 1982. In the ensuing election campaign, FitzGerald went to the voters with virtually the same budget that had brought his government down. The only important change was deletion of the politically sensitive value-added tax on children's clothing and shoes. Charles Haughey, the leader of the opposition, while basically in agreement with FitzGerald on the budget, objected to the application of the value-added tax to any clothing and shoes. In addition, he criticized FitzGerald for trying to raise taxes and cut services too hastily for the purpose of reducing foreign borrowing. Haughey favored more such borrowing, arguing that its use in investment and production would make possible more social spending with less economic austerity. Regarding Irish reunification, both candidates favored continuation of Dublin's talks with Westminster and acknowledged the need for the republic to make unification more attractive to the North's Protestants by allaying their fear of immersion in a Catholic state, but Haughey took a harder line, pressing above all for the withdrawal of British troops from the North. As for secularization in the South, a beginning had been made with the 1972 repeal of a constitutional provision according the Catholic church a privileged position in the republic, but a Catholic bias was still implicit in such laws as those banning divorce and the sale of contraceptives (other than by prescription). FitzGerald called for amendments to relax those laws.

As in the previous election, Fianna Fáil fell short of an absolute majority in the voting on February

8, 1982 and the balance of power was again left in the hands of minority parties or independents. On March 9 Haughey returned to office with the backing of three deputies from the leftist Workers' party and two independents. His initial budget reflected deference to his Workers' party partners, but a deepening of the recession and a budget deficit conservatively estimated at 10 percent of the gross national product forced Haughey to face up to the need for a comprehensive restructuring of the economy. On October 21, 1982 the Haughey government issued a five-year plan proposing reductions in public spending and employment and ceilings on the wages of public employees. Viewing the plan within the context of 13 percent unemployment and double-digit inflation, the three Workers' party deputies joined the opposition in voting against it. The vote of no-confidence brought down the Haughey government on November 4, 1982.

Haughey's party came out of the November 24, 1982 election with seventy-five seats. Fine Gael, with seventy, and Labour, with sixteen, in tandem had a clear majority, making possible a coalition with full-term prospects. The chief obstacles to a coalition were economic differences, with FitzGerald giving priority to public finances and Dirk Spring, the new Labour leader, concentrating on unemployment. On December 12, 1982 the differences were worked out in a pact calling for the creation of an unemployment task force and a national development corporation; a review of the welfare system; higher taxes on the financial sector and luxury real estate; civil service reform; and changes in the marriage laws and a constitutional review designed to remove obstacles to North-South reconciliation.

As the leader of the new Fine Gael–Labour coalition, FitzGerald assumed office for the second time on December 14, 1982. Faced with the prospect of a 16.5 percent budget deficit, his government on February 9, 1983 put forward an austerity budget bringing that estimate down to 13.5 percent, or $2.35 billion. The budget incorporated substantial tax increases and reductions in government spending. The latter included a pay freeze on government wages and cuts in capital spending on telecommunications, housing, and roads. Among the proposed tax increases were hikes in the value-added tax, from 18 to 23 percent for most goods and from 30 to 35 percent for electrical appliances; a new tax rate of 65 percent for top-bracket earnings and a new 1 percent surcharge on all incomes; and an increase in worker contributions to social security. In addition, the budget ruled out adjustments of tax brackets to inflation. Some 100,000 workers marched in demonstrations against the budget in Dublin and other cities on April 13, 1983.

A national referendum on abortion was held in the Republic of Ireland in September 1983. Abortion was already outlawed by statute, except in cases where childbirth clearly threatened the life of the mother. The question up for referendum was whether to enshrine the prohibition in the constitution, by amendment, so as, in the words of one of the pro-lifers, "to close the [abortion] door before it can be opened." FitzGerald, who had once favored such an amendment, now urged voters to reject it, arguing that the word "unborn" as used in the referendum was legally vulnerable. The electorate, however, turned out overwhelmingly in favor of the amendment, by a vote of 66 to 33 percent.

During a seven-day visit to the United States in March 1984, FitzGerald conferred in the White House with President Ronald Reagan (who visited Ireland three months later) and addressed a joint session of Congress. The purpose of his visit was, as he explained it, threefold: "to communicate . . . the attraction [of Ireland] as a location for American companies' industrial investment"; "to communicate the continuing message to America of offering no aid to those engaged in violence in Northern Ireland—violence which affects us in the republic indirectly"; and "to highlight the positive steps which the constitutional nationalist parties [in Ireland] are taking to create conditions for progress toward removing the causes of violence."

His mention of "positive steps" alluded to the New Ireland Forum, a study group concerned with "the manner in which lasting peace and stability can be achieved in a new Ireland through the democratic process." Leaders of Ireland's three major parties and Northern Ireland's moderate Catholic party, the Social Democratic and Labour party, held the opening meeting of the forum in Dublin on May 30, 1903. After eleven months of debate and research the forum issued a report on the future of Ireland on May 2, 1984. The report was nationalist in tone but conciliatory in language, stressing "consent" and "accommodation." In the section on immediate action, Irish unity was not even mentioned, and when it was considered as a remote possibility, the report made the first acknowledgment ever that those in Northern Ireland who favor continued unity with Great Britain ("Unionists") are British citizens and that any all-Irish reunification framework would require a new, nondenominational constitution protective of their cultural heritage and their civil and religious liberties.

The report put forward three options for achieving permanent peace and stability in Northern Ireland: a single Irish state, joint authority between London and Dublin, and a federal system. After the publication of the report, FitzGerald made clear that while he viewed a united Ireland as the "preferred option," power-sharing in Belfast was the immediately practical option, the one that could form a meaningful basis for discussion of the report at an Anglo-Irish summit meeting later in 1984—a meeting in which he hoped to win British cooperation in bringing the Northern parties to the conference table. British officials had already shown interest in the power-sharing idea, and James Prior, the secretary of Northern Ireland, was reported to favor some such an initiative.

Seeing a unitary Irish state as a definite goal and not a preferred option, Charles Haughey furiously accused FitzGerald of "walking away from the forum report." In response, FitzGerald remarked that "it is easy to make speeches about Irish unity—if you ignore the facts." One of the facts was that the growing support for Sinn Fein, the political arm of the Irish Republican Army, was well on its way to making the Social Democratic and Labour party the minority nationalist party in Ulster. Describing the report as "an agenda, not a blueprint," he set May 1985 as the deadline for setting up an institution for governing Northern Ireland that will take account of both the Unionist and nationalist traditions and accommodate "the two identities in a way [in] which neither can be subordinate to the other." Damage to an emerging British-Irish rapprochement regarding Northern Ireland was apparently a major aim of the Irish Republican Army's terrorist bombing of a hotel in Brighton, England in October 1984, a month before FitzGerald and British Prime Minister Margaret Thatcher were scheduled to confer on the matter. The bombing killed two persons, injured thirty-four, and came dangerously close to wiping out Mrs. Thatcher and her entire cabinet.

FitzGerald is strongly pro-European, partly because he looks to Europe for support in Ireland's dealings with Britain regarding Northern Ireland. He was director of the Irish Council of the European Movement in the 1960s and a member of the international executive committee of the movement in 1972-73, and he is a vice-president of the European People's party, the Christian Democratic group in the European Parliament. Among other memberships are those on the governing board of University College, Dublin and in the senate of the National University of Ireland.

Garret FitzGerald and Joan O'Farrell were married on October 10, 1947. They have three grown children, Mary, John, and Mark. FitzGerald is a gentle, low-keyed, affable man with a common touch and what one reporter has called "a rumpled air." Irish political wags cynical of his idealistic, "no blarney" approach to the world's second-oldest profession have facetiously dubbed him "Garret the Good," a title that nonetheless befits someone consistently described by interviewers as thoughtful, self-deprecating, and "totally honest." FitzGerald's knowledge of world affairs is as wide as it is keen, and it combines with a passion for mathematics that helps keep his search for political solutions within logical parameters. "He is a great hope," Victor Griffen, Dublin's leading Protestant minister, has remarked, as quoted by Fred Hauptfuhrer in *People* (March 19, 1984). "If the Northern Protestants can trust anybody, they'll trust Garret FitzGerald."

References: Current World Leaders 21:8 *Ja '78 por; London Observer* p44 *Je* 10 '73 *por; London Sunday Times* p16 *My* 6 '84 *por; N Y Times* p4 *Jl* 1 '81 *por; Wall St J* p26 *Mr* 15 '83 *por; International Yearbook and Statesmen's Who's Who,* 1983; *International Who's Who,* 1984–85, *Who's Who,* 1984

Ford, Harrison

*July 13, 1942– Motion picture actor. Address: b.
c/o Lucasfilm, Ltd., P.O. Box 2009, San Rafael,
Calif. 94912*

Harrison Ford, today's most popular screen hero,
is the top-grossing actor in motion-picture history,
personifying the spirit of adventure in films of derring-do that have earned more than a billion dollars at the box office. Although the epithet "the new
Humphrey Bogart," as some have called him,
somehow misses the mark, Ford represents a return to the Hollywood tough-guy tradition that the
director Ridley Scott calls "laconic realism," portraying cool, straight-talking, quick-witted men of
action. Ford first encountered popular success in
the ensemble role of the hot-rodder Bob Falfa in
George Lucas' *American Graffiti* (1973); he rose
from relative obscurity to celebrity as Han Solo, the
roguish but likable space buccaneer in Lucas' *Star
Wars* fantasy trilogy (1977-1983); and he achieved
certifiable stardom as Indiana Jones, the archeological soldier of fortune in Steven Spielberg's
Raiders of the Lost Ark (1981) and *Indiana Jones
and the Temple of Doom* (1984). Among Ford's other major credits is Rick Deckard, the antiheroic,
bedraggled policeman stalking errant androids in
a society of the future in Ridley Scott's science-
fiction thriller *Blade Runner* (1982).

Of mixed Irish-Catholic and Russian-Jewish descent, Harrison Ford was born in Chicago, Illinois
on July 13, 1942. With his brother, he grew up in
suburban Park Ridge and Morton Grove, Illinois.
Although he did not immediately aspire to acting,
there was, as he has put it, "circus" in his family:
his grandfather was a vaudevillian, and his father,
an advertising executive and producer of television commercials, did some radio acting and still
does voiceovers for commercials.

As a boy, Ford was little interested in sports and
afflicted with, in his words, "a real fear of facing
people." Scholastically, he achieved good grades in
elementary school, but he lost interest in academic
subjects in high school because he had no goal to
relate them to. "I thought of education only as a tool
for success," he explained to Edwin Miller in an interview for *Seventeen* (July 1983). "I didn't have
the proper respect for education for its own sake."
As a philosophy major at Ripon College in Ripon,
Wisconsin, he was, according to David Harris, its
dean of men, "certainly bright enough to do a fine
job" scholastically but "didn't have his heart in it."

Ford put in four years at Ripon without taking a
degree. He did, however, finally find a subject that
interested him: drama, which he took when he
needed an elective in his junior year. While acting
in student productions, he discovered in his stage
personae a freedom from shyness, a sense of responsibility, and his "first experience of working
with a group of people on a clearly defined goal."
He threw himself wholeheartedly into dramatics,
doing a season of summer stock in Williams Bay,
Wisconsin and then heading for Hollywood.

A scout for Columbia Pictures discovered Ford
when he was appearing in a production of *John
Brown's Body* at a playhouse in Laguna Beach, California. Signed to a $150-a-week contract, he
joined eleven other good-looking young actors and
actresses in Columbia's New Talent program, an
attempt to revivify the old star-building system.
Under that system, the neophytes on the payroll
took acting classes and were tried out in bit parts
while the studio groomed them for possible stardom. It was a grind that went against Ford's grain.
"They gave me enough to pay my rent," he explained to Edwin Miller in the *Seventeen* interview, "but the attitude that they could manufacture
a star from raw material was silly. Styling your
hair, dressing you—it was all so deadly wrong, calculated to remove all those particularities which
made you interesting in the first place."

Ford made his motion-picture debut with a one-
line appearance as a bellboy in *Dead Heat on a
Merry-Go-Round* (1966) and followed it with bit
parts in *Luv* (1967) and *A Time for Killing* (1967),
also known as *The Long Road Home*. Finding him,
in his words, "too difficult," Columbia dropped
Ford after eighteen months. Three days after he
left Columbia, he was under contract to Universal
Pictures, which cast him in small roles in the motion picture *Journey to Shiloh* (1968) and episodes
of the television shows *The Virginian*, *The F.B.I.*,
Gunsmoke, and *Ironside*.

Universal loaned Ford out to Michelangelo An-
tonioni for *Zabriskie Point* (1969) and back to Columbia for *Getting Straight* (1970). Ford's roles in
those films about student revolutionaries were minor, and his part in *Zabriskie Point* ended up on
the cutting room floor. Disillusioned with the studio system and fearful of over-exposure in de-
meaning television roles, he decided "not to do any
more acting unless the job had a clear career
advantage." Without renouncing acting, he turned

for a living to carpentry, which he had taught himself from books and from the experience of remodeling a home he bought in the Hollywood hills for his then growing family. Not only was the manual craftsmanship—remodeling houses and building cabinets and furniture—"a relief from what he had been doing before"; it also affected his auditioning for roles, giving him a pride, perspective, and feeling of security transcending that of unemployed actor.

While Ford was plying his carpenter's craft, his one good friend from Columbia days, Fred Roos, an associate of Francis Ford Coppola, was engaged by director George Lucas to cast his low-budget film *American Graffiti* (Universal, 1973), to which Coppola lent his name as producer in order to attract major studio backing. That motion picture, a slice of nostalgia co-written by Lucas in evocation of his own coming-of-age in Modesto, California, was set on a summer night in Modesto circa 1962 and focused on four teenagers (Richard Dreyfuss, Ron Howard, Paul Le Mat, and Charles Martin Smith) restlessly experiencing the bitter-sweet end of summer and of adolescence. Recommended by Roos and assured by him that *American Graffiti* had hit potential, Ford tested for and got the supporting role of Bob Falfa, a slightly older hot rodder from out of town who challenges the local auto-cruising champion, Big John (Le Mat) to a drag race that provides the comic-melancholy story with a violent climax. As Roos had predicted, *American Graffiti* was a huge commercial success, eventually grossing $117 million, fifty times the amount Universal had invested in it. It also drew critical raves, but Ford did not stand out in the notices and, playing safe, continued with his carpentry.

Again through Fred Roos, Ford was tapped for Francis Ford Coppola's crime thriller *The Conversation* (Paramount, 1974), set in the grim netherworld of electronic surveillance. That film starred Gene Hackman as Harry Caul, a sleazy wiretapping expert-for-hire with self-destructive qualms of conscience. Ford was cast as Martin Stett, a corporate hatchet man trying to pry from Caul tapes that Caul knows will lead to murder. "There was no role there," Ford has recalled, as quoted by Alan McKenzie in *The Harrison Ford Story* (1984), "until I decided to make him [Stett] a homosexual."

The Conversation won the grand prize at the Cannes Film Festival, among other awards, but critical appreciation continued to elude Ford. In his next role, the walk-on part of a tearful witness in the television movie *The Trial of Lieutenant Calley* (1974), he was, in the view of Stanley Kramer, the producer-director of the film, "absolutely wonderful . . . intense, tremendously sensitive." More substantial was his role as the eldest son of Jennifer Blackwood (Sarah Miles) in the TV movie *Dynasty* (1976), based on James Michener's novel about a family of early-nineteenth-century Ohio pioneers.

Ford's principal occupation remained carpentry until his first major role in a major motion picture,

that of Han Solo, the cocky pirate starship captain in George Lucas' space adventure *Star Wars* (Twentieth Century-Fox, 1977). Set "a long time ago in a galaxy far, far away," *Stars Wars* concerns Princess Leia Organa of Alderraan, the leader of the Alliance to Restore the Republic, and her effort to mount a rebellion against the evil Galactic Empire, which has destroyed her planet and precipitated the collapse of the noble republic of planets. Her principal enemies are the power-mad emperor Grand Moff Tarkin (Peter Cushing) and the sinister magician Darth Vader (played under dark armor by David Prowse), a fallen knight of the Jedi, who had been the righteous guardians of the republic. Her chief allies are the young Luke Skywalker (Mark Hamill), the wise old Jedi wizard-warrior Ben Obi-Wan Kenobi (Alec Guiness), and Solo, an intergalactic soldier-of-fortune with a heart of gold beneath his flip, wry cynicism. Ford's seemingly effortless swashbuckling performance won him the admiration of fellow actors as well as critics. Mark Hamill found him to be "a very strong person, sure of what he's doing." "He really gets right to the meat of the scene," Hamill told Edwin Miller when Miller was preparing his *Seventeen* article. "More than any other actor I've worked with, he adds shading to a character and improvises bits of action that aren't in the script."

The enthusiastic response of public and critics to the visual splendor and rip-roaring adventure of *Star Wars* swept across most of the usual barriers of opinion, taste, and age and brought overnight celebrity and financial security to its ensemble of stars (who had profit-sharing clauses in their contracts). It was the first film ever to gross more than $10 million in one weekend, and in its first year of distribution it grossed $300 million, by far the largest box-office take in motion-picture history up until that time.

The first film Ford was "happy with" when seeing himself on the screen was *The Empire Strikes Back* (Lucasfilm, 1980). Another box-office blockbuster, that stunning sequel to *Star Wars* was produced by Lucas and directed by Irvin Kershner. Although *The Empire Strikes Back* is virtually one long high-tech battle, the personalities and relationships of the protagonists are given more depth and finer shading, and there is the first inkling of romance between Han Solo and Princess Leia. The film is a cliffhanger, ending with Darth Vader putting Solo into a carbon freezing chamber. It was Ford who suggested the audience-pleasing dialogue that takes place as Solo is about to become a human ice cube: grief-stricken, Princess Leia finally confesses, "I love you"; Solo, his arrogant wit intact, responds, "I know."

In *Return of the Jedi* (Lucasfilm, 1983), the last motion picture in the *Stars Wars* trilogy, produced by Lucas and directed by Richard Marquand, Princess Leia frees Han Solo from the carbon freezing chamber and Darth Vader, who turns out to be Luke Skywalker's father, regains control of his true identity and hurls the Emperor to his death. The film ends in unabashed sentimentality, with Luke at peace with the memory of his father and Han and Leia all but walking off into the sunset together. In the view of many critics, the revving-up of dazzling special effects—the "flash and hardware," as Ford calls it—slapstick, and parodic allusions to other works of fantasy and science fiction in *Return of the Jedi* overwhelmed the human and dramatic elements, including the Han Solo character. Audiences had a different response, making the film the third-ranking box-office grosser of all time as of the beginning of 1984.

Meanwhile, Ford deliberately widened his range, in the small but significant roles of a psychically shattered Vietnam veteran in Jeremy Paul Kagan's *Heroes* (Turman-Foster, 1977) and an intellectual, inscrutable army colonel in Francis Ford Coppola's Vietnam epic *Apocalypse Now* (United Artists, 1979); in the supporting role of a commando officer in *Force Ten from Navarone* (Navarone Productions, 1978); in the starring role of the American World War II pilot involved in an adulterous romance with a classy British Red Cross worker (Lesley-Anne Down) in *Hanover Street* (Columbia, 1979); and as a bandit who chums up with a Polish rabbi (Gene Wilder) in Robert Aldrich's sentimental, offbeat western *The Frisco Kid* (Warner Brothers, 1979). Ford perhaps best demonstrated his versatility as well as his ability to sustain a virtuoso starring role as Rick Deckard, the glumly reluctant twenty-first century cop tracking and gunning down rebellious replicants (genetically engineered humanoid robot slaves) in the commercially unsuccessful but widely appreciated *Blade Runner* (The Blade Runner Partnership, 1982), an adaptation of Philip K. Dick's novel *Do Androids Dream of Electric Sheep?*

Ridley Scott, the director of *Blade Runner*, credited Ford with "an immense understanding of the entire movie-making process" and a "tremendous" input into "the story level as well as . . . his own character." As Scott pointed out, Ford had become a star not with *Star Wars* but with *Raiders of the Lost Ark*: "Before that, Ford was not a well-known actor, but the man who played Han Solo." Conceived by George Lucas and directed by Steven Spielberg, *Raiders of the Lost Ark* (Lucasfilm, 1981) has as its protagonist Professor Indiana Jones, an intellectual but tough globe-trotting archaeologist (reminiscent of the pulp heroes of the 1930s and 1940s) in a battered fedora competing with the Nazis for occult digs in the 1930s. The film, widely regarded as a masterpiece of pop cinema, was one of the biggest box-office draws in history, with a gross exceeding $231 million. "The spirit of the piece is beautifully captured in Harrison Ford's performance," David Ansen wrote in *Newsweek* (June 15, 1981). "He's a wry hero, but he's a real one—exuding just that quiet, sardonic masculinity that made stars like Bogart and Gable at once larger than life and down to earth."

Indiana Jones and the Temple of Doom (Lucasfilm, 1984), the sequel to *Raiders of the Lost Ark*, has been doing even better at the box office, by 25 percent, despite an outcry of criticism that it is too

luridly violent for children's viewing. Kathleen Carroll of the *New York Daily News* (May 23, 1984) described it as a "rousing piece of entertainment," and Vincent Canby of the *New York Times* (May 23, 1984) called Ford's "an exceptionally skillful comic performance, demonstrating easy charm and timing." During the summer of 1984 Ford was on location in the Amish community of Lancaster, Pennsylvania, filming "Witness," a topical suspense story that begins with a murder on a train. In it, Ford departs from stereotype in his portrayal of a police detective.

Ford approaches acting as he does carpentry. "If you know your craft," he has explained, as quoted by Alan McKenzie in *The Harrison Ford Story*, "you can figure out the logic of a particular job and submit yourself to it. It all comes down to detail." When he is acting, his "job is to be Indiana Jones, or whoever," and personal information about Harrison Ford the private person "can only water down the illusion." Jealous of and reticent about his private life, he has become elusive with interviewers, asserting, "The most interesting thing about me is the work that I do. That's what I am." He also keeps a low profile because, having "never liked being stared at," he hates "the hassle of being famous." He feels fortunate to have been "a late bloomer," as he told George Haddad-Garcia in an interview for *Genesis* (June 1982): "Ten years ago I couldn't have handled this degree of success and money. Now I simply ask for a certain amount of money and I get it. I'm not complicated or mysterious. I just do my job and am lucky to be in efficient, entertaining pictures. We have fun making them, but we never thought they'd be monster hits."

Harrison Ford is six feet one inch tall and has a strong physique, piercing blue eyes, a soft, take-it-or-leave-it voice, and a scar beneath his lower lip, the result of an automobile accident he was in a few years ago. Easygoing, he still fits the description given of him by his college dean of men, David Harris—"very likable, a fellow with a good sense of humor, usually courteous, with an underlying seriousness." Edwin Miller, the *Seventeen* interviewer, who sensed in him a "wary, self-contained strength," observed that Ford "doesn't sound off on politics or social issues," and he quoted him as complaining, "I'm only willing to talk about a certain part of myself—and that part is taken as the whole person." Ford's relationship with such associates as George Lucas, Steven Spielberg, and Francis Ford Coppola is one of mutual affection and respect. Well-read and well-spoken, the actor eschews buzz words in conversation and lives "in fear of being stuck at some Hollywood party for an eternity," listening to people "talk shop or . . . trivia."

Ford and his former wife, Mary, an honor graduate of Ripon College, were divorced in 1978. Their two teenaged sons, Benjamin and Willard, live with their mother, and Ford shares his home in a Beverly Hills canyon with Melissa Mathison, the screenwriter, whom he married in March 1983. Much of the furniture in the house was built by him, and he finds in the odd jobs of carpentry and the gardening he does at home "an escape from the mind-wrestling; something simple, direct, visible, palpable, possible." Ford confessed to George Hadad-Garcia that he is not easy to live with, partly because he keeps his own counsel. "I just don't go to anyone for advice or for a shoulder to lean on. My questions are for me to answer out of my own experience. The Buddha said, 'Work out your salvation with diligence.'"

References: Chicago Tribune VI p8+ Je 20 '82 pors; Films Illustrated 7:291+ Ap '78 pors; N Y Times C p13 Jl 1 '77 por; People 16:86 Ja 4 '82 por; Rolling Stone p33+ Jl 24 '80 por; Seventeen 42:114+ Jl '83 pors; McKenzie, Alan. The Harrison Ford Story (1984); Who's Who in America, 1984–85

Gibson, Mel

Dec. 1955(?)– Actor. Address: b. c/o Paramount Pictures Corp., 1 Gulf & Western Plaza, New York City, N.Y. 10023

In recent years, the budding Australian film industry has not only produced several motion pictures of distinction, but it also has discovered, in Mel Gibson, a dynamic new star to rank with the great Hollywood male sex symbols from Errol Flynn to Robert Redford. A graduate of Australia's National Institute of Dramatic Art, Gibson has tested his acting talent in a wide variety of films, with an emphasis on action-adventure movies, most notably Gallipoli and The Year of Living Dangerously. His star quality has not been lost on Hollywood executives, one of whom described him as having "the magical charisma of the greats. He walks on the screen and sizzles."

An American by nationality, Mel Gibson was born in Peekskill, New York, in December 1955. (Some sources give his year of birth as 1956.) The sixth of eleven children, he spent his boyhood in Peekskill and in Mount Vision, a small town in rural upstate New York, near Oneonta. Fearing that his older sons would soon be drafted into the United States Army and sent to fight in the Vietnam war, Gibson's father, a brakeman for the New York Central Railroad, decided to immigrate with his wife and children to Australia, the homeland of his mother, Eva Mylott, an opera singer. With the proceeds from a settlement the father had received after an on-the-job injury, the family took up residence in Sydney, on Australia's eastern coast. As Mel Gibson told an interviewer for Cosmopolitan (May 1983), he found it hard to adjust to his new country: "The kids made fun of me and called me Yank, and I had a fairly rough time of it."

After graduating from a local Catholic high school, Gibson considered becoming a chef or a journalist, but when his sister submitted an application in his name to the National Institute of Dramatic Art at the University of New South Wales, he decided to go through with the required audition, even though he had never thought about acting as a career. "They made me do all these silly things— improvise, sing, dance—and I got in," he recalled to Dan Yakir in an interview for an After Dark profile (November 1981). "I know it was terrible, but it seemed good then. I guess they saw something raw in me." When the auditioning committee asked him why he wanted to become an actor, he replied, "I've been goofing off all my life. I thought I might as well get paid for that."

While he was a student at the National Institute of Dramatic Art, Gibson made his film debut in what he later described in the interview for Cosmopolitan as "a cheap, nasty flick, an abomination" called Summer City (Intertropic Films, 1977). In that low-budget film about four young men on a weekend surfing holiday, he played the nineteen-year-old Scollop, who, in his words, "simply surfed and acted dumb, which was all I could possibly handle at the time." David Stratton, the Australian film historian and the author of The Last New Wave: The Australian Film Revival (1980), shared Gibson's disparaging opinion of Summer City. In his view, the motion picture was interesting only for the "excellent" performances of Gibson and costar Steve Bisley.

On his graduation from the National Institute of Dramatic Art in 1977, Gibson joined the State Theatre Company of South Australia and played small parts in a variety of classical and contemporary plays, including Oedipus, The Les Darcey Show, and Cedoona. Shortly after that, George Miller, who had been impressed by Gibson's magnetic screen presence in Summer City, invited him to try out for the title role in Mad Max, a futuristic "chase-and-crash" adventure that was to be Miller's first feature-length effort as a director. On the night before the audition, Gibson was badly beaten in a barroom brawl. He showed up at the studio nonetheless, his face looking "like a busted grapefruit," as he put it. Fortunately, his bruised and battered appearance turned out to be just what was required for the part of Max Rockatansky, the embittered leader of a special police unit who avenges the deaths of his wife and son at the hands of a marauding motorcycle gang.

Described by its star in an interview for the British periodical *Films & Filming* (June 1983) as "probably the classiest B grade trash ever made," *Mad Max* (Roadshow, 1979; American International, 1980) became the biggest commercial success of any Australian film to that date, reportedly grossing over $100 million worldwide. It made an especially big hit in Germany and Japan, where it broke attendance records, but in the United States its box-office receipts were disappointing. Before its American release, *Mad Max* was dubbed from its impenetrable Australian dialect into what one critic called "country-and-western English," and the ineptly synchronized dubbing was, according to some reviewers, among the film's cinematic flaws. Critics also found fault with the "flimsy plot line," the "rudimentary dialogue," and the "sadism." Although he had only a handful of lines, Gibson managed to project a strength that, as Andrew Sarris noted, helped "give the frenetic action some psychological coherence."

Gibson followed *Mad Max* with a very different type of film: *Tim* (Pisces, 1979; Satori Productions, 1981), an adaptation of Colleen McCullough's novel about the sexual awakening of the middle-aged Mary Horton, played by Piper Laurie, and the belated coming-of-age of young Tim Melville, the handsome but mentally retarded day laborer she hires to do her gardening. Challenged by the role of the ingenuous and loving Tim, Gibson found his "key" to the character early in the filming. "It wasn't so much playing someone retarded but rather stressing the innocence aspect of it—as if he were someone normal who has a link missing somewhere," he explained to Dan Yakir. "I couldn't have played him drooling—it would've been a turn-off." Gibson acquitted himself well enough to win the Australian Film Institute Award for best actor and a "Sammy," given by *TV Times* magazine, as the year's best new talent. American critics and audiences were, on the whole, less favorably disposed toward the film than their Australian counterparts, but they generally exempted Gibson from their negative comments. Archer Winsten, who reviewed *Tim* for the *New York Post* (September 17, 1981), was perhaps Gibson's most enthusiastic admirer. The young actor's portrayal was, in Winsten's view, "a thing of beauty, in its subtle shading of an adult with a very young mind," and his "command of simplicity" was nothing short of "astounding."

Gibson's next effort, *The Z Men*, a predictable World War II adventure that was, in his words,

"ruined by hack direction," dropped out of sight shortly after its Australian release, by John McCallum Productions in 1980. He was luckier in his next assignment—the role of Frank Dunne in Peter Weir's *Gallipoli* (R & R Films, 1981; Paramount, 1981). Set during World War I, *Gallipoli* follows the lives of Frank and his friend Archy from their initial encounter as competitors in a provincial track meet through their enlistment in the Australian light cavalry and their subsequent training in Egypt to their participation in the disastrous campaign to take control of the Dardanelles that gives the film its title. *Gallipoli* derives much of its power from the contrast between its two young heroes. Archy is an eager, patriotic idealist; Frank, a cocky, cynical realist. "Peter [Weir] wanted my character to be the new Australian," Gibson explained to Dan Yakir, "the survivor, the one who lives to talk about it—as opposed to Archy, who was the cream of the Australian youth that got slaughtered by the thousands."

The strong "mateship" that developed between Frank and Archy over the course of the film required an unusual degree of teamwork from its two leading players. According to Weir, Gibson and Mark Lee, in his first important film role, played off each other like seasoned veterans. The "chemistry" between the young actors was, in Weir's word, "electrifying" and contributed greatly to the credibility of the narrative. Both a popular and a critical success in its homeland, *Gallipoli* swept the Australian Film Institute Awards for 1981, winning top honors in nine categories, and brought Gibson his second best actor nod. When the film was released in the United States in the autumn of 1981, it set house records during its first weekend at the Baronet Theater in New York City, despite its mixed notices. Some critics contended that its pictorial beauty diluted its effectiveness as an antiwar statement; others argued that its sentimentality turned it into what Gary Arnold called "a somber, dovish Art Object." Gibson, however, was universally praised for the "wit," "ingenuity," and "sensitivity" that he showed as Frank.

After the phenomenal international success of *Mad Max*, it was inevitable that Gibson would be called upon to reprise his characterization of Max Rockatansky in a sequel. Director George Miller deliberately fashioned the plot of *Mad Max 2* (Roadshow, 1981) after such classic American westerns as *Shane*. In the film, Max, an apathetic and sullen loner as a result of his earlier experiences, regains his self-respect and "learns to live again" when he defends a colony of postnuclear homesteaders who are besieged by a rampaging band of outlaw bikers. Technically far superior to its predecessor, *Mad Max 2* scored an even bigger hit with audiences, and unlike the first *Max*, it attracted considerable critical support in the United States, where it was released by Warner Brothers in 1982 under the title *The Road Warrior*. Gibson's authoritative portrayal of the laconic hero won the endorsement of Vincent Canby, the *New York Times*'s influential film critic, who now numbered himself among the actor's widening circle of American admirers. "Here is a major league film personality . . .," Canby wrote in the *Times* of August 29, 1982. "It has something to do with his looks, which are more clean-cut than the character he plays in the Miller film, and also with the kind of cool, infinitely pragmatic manner with which he deals with his existential situation. . . . I can't define 'star quality,' but whatever it is, Mr. Gibson has it."

One indication of Mel Gibson's growing reputation as a bankable international star was MGM's decision to underwrite the production of his next film, *The Year of Living Dangerously*, the first time an Australian feature had been fully financed by a major American studio. Gibson accepted the central role because of his admiration for Peter Weir, the director, and in spite of reservations about his character, Guy Hamilton, an ambitious but untried Australian broadcast journalist on his first overseas assignment. In an attempt to make a name for himself, Hamilton is drawn into events leading up to the overthrow, in 1965, of Indonesian President Sukarno by the mysterious Australasian he hires as his cameraman. As Gibson explained in the interview for *Films & Filming*, it was "the most difficult film role" of his career because he had to develop "an initially unsympathetic hero into a character of depth and emotion."

In building his characters, Gibson finds that the important physical details—what he calls the "externals"—come easily; the "internal stuff" requires days of thinking and pulling "bits and pieces" together. "I believe in using my imagination," he told Dan Yakir in the *After Dark* interview. "I don't think actors lose themselves completely when they play. They use a certain aspect of themselves, whether recessive or dominant. They simply change the proportion, stress one or the other. . . . [Acting] forces you to look at yourself and other people and observe what makes them behave the way they do," he continued. It "adds to one's self-awareness."

The location shooting of *The Year of Living Dangerously* in the Philippines was repeatedly disrupted by threats of violence against cast and crew from Moslem militants, who may have been provoked by persistent rumors that the film took a decidedly anti-Moslem stance, and Gibson himself received several frightening phone calls. Unnerved by the continual intimidation, Weir packed up and completed the filming in Australia without incident. But following its premiere in 1982, *The Year of Living Dangerously* fell victim to another sort of curse: a general feeling among critics that the film raised expectations that it failed to fulfill. Many thought that the complicated plot line was poorly developed. Even Gibson admitted that he had to see the movie twice in order to figure everything out. The performances of the leading players, however, were generally applauded. Reviewers were especially taken by the "spunky, romantic-comedy quality," to use Pauline Kael's words, Gibson brought to his role. As Vincent Canby observed in his *New York Times* (January 21, 1983) review,

"If this film doesn't make an international star out of Mr. Gibson . . . , then nothing will. He possesses both the necessary talent and the screen presence."

After completing work on *The Year of Living Dangerously*, Gibson turned down starring roles in several motion pictures in order to take the part of Biff, the older son of Willy Loman, in Arthur Miller's American classic *Death of a Salesman* at the Nimrod Theatre in Sydney. Over the years, the actor has intermixed appearances on the Australian stage with his film roles. "It's more rewarding for me than any other form of acting," he has said, as quoted in *Films & Filming*. "I can go on the stage and get completely lost in a role. There's a constant flow to the character in those two hours." His most recent stage credits include the roles of Rebel, an American deserter during World War II in the long-running Australian play *No Names, No Pack Drill*, Romeo in *Romeo and Juliet*, and Estragon in Samuel Beckett's tragicomedy *Waiting for Godot*. Gibson has also appeared in episodes of the Australian television series *The Sullivans*, *Tickled Pink*, and *The Hero*.

Lately, however, film assignments have kept Gibson, whose salary has jumped to a reported $1 million or more per picture, so busy that he has had little time for other projects. His most recent film release is *The Bounty* (Orion, 1984), Dino De Laurentiis' remake of *Mutiny On the Bounty*, with Gibson as Fletcher Christian and Anthony Hopkins as Captain Bligh. Based on Richard Hough's history *Captain Bligh and Mr. Christian* rather than on Nordhoff and Hall's fictionalized "Bounty" trilogy, as its two predecessors had been, *The Bounty* was more of a character study than an adventure on the high seas. Unlike Clark Gable and Marlon Brando, who had essayed the role of Fletcher Christian in the earlier film versions, Gibson, according to a *Chicago Tribune* (April 22, 1984) interview, saw Christian not as a romantic hero, but as "just a loyal office boy, immature, about twenty-two, who just 'did his nut' [went crazy] one day and was very sorry afterward." Gibson has also completed work on "Mrs. Soffel," a romantic thriller costarring Diane Keaton, and "The River," his first American-made feature, which the trade magazine *Variety* has described as "a 1980s *Grapes of Wrath*."

The dark-haired, blue-eyed Mel Gibson keeps his five-foot-ten-inch, 160-pound body in shape by running regularly and eating sensibly. To relax, he goes to parties with fellow actors or attends sports events. Acquaintances describe him as a shy, modest man who scoffs at the "international star" tag and appears determined not to let his newfound fame go to his head. As he told Lewis Archibald of *The Aquarian* (February 2, 1983), "Everything's just been happening too fast. . . . I've gotta put the brakes on here. Or I'll smack into something." Gibson and his wife, Robyn, a former nurse, have a daughter, Hannah, and three sons, including the twins, Edward and Christian. The family lives in a converted seaside boarding house in Sydney, which "still has numbers on the doors." Although he retains his American citizenship, Gibson insists that he does not want to move from Australia. "It's beautiful where I live," he explained in one recent interview, "and slow, and I never feel endangered."

References: After Dark 14:46+ N '81 por; Films & Filming p20+ Je '83 pors; N Y Sunday News Leisure p3 Ja 23 '83 por; Newsweek 99:67 My 31 '82 por; People 19:99+ F 14 '83 pors; International Motion Picture Almanac, 1983

Gielgud, John
(gĕl′gŏŏd)

Apr. 14, 1904– British actor and director.
Address: b. c/o International Famous Agency, 22 Grafton St., London, W. 1, England; h. South Pavilion, Wotton Underwood, Aylesbury, Bucks, HP 18 OSB, England

NOTE: This biography supersedes the article that appeared in Current Biography in 1947.

Few actors have been favored with speaking voices as musical as that of Sir John Gielgud. Yet, in the course of a long and illustrious career, he has repeatedly demonstrated that the mellifluous, instantly recognizable Gielgud sound is but a single component of a multifarious talent—the big gun, as it were, in what has been described as "an extraordinary arsenal of acting skills." Along with Lord Olivier and the late Sir Ralph Richardson, he has dominated the English stage for more than sixty years, and of the three, he has been generally ac-

knowledged to be "the supreme and most sensitive Shakespearean of his day." In recent years, through his incisive handling of character parts in films and on television, Gielgud has broadened his appeal immeasurably, attaining late in life the sort of "visibility" that only the mass media can confer. Gielgud was knighted by Queen Elizabeth II in 1953 and named a Companion of Honour in 1977.

The third of the four children of Frank Gielgud, a stockbroker, and his wife, the former Kate Terry-Lewis, Arthur John Gielgud was born in London, England on April 14, 1904. On his mother's side Gielgud is descended from the famous Terry family, which had given nineteenth-century English playgoers three of their favorite leading ladies: Kate Terry, his grandmother, and his great-aunts Marion Terry and Ellen Terry, who is one of the most celebrated Shakespearean actresses in British theatrical history. Paternally, too, Gielgud is descended from histrionic stock of the highest caliber, for his great-grandparents were among the leading actors in Poland in the late eighteenth century. In his book of reminiscences, An Actor and His Time (Sidgwick & Jackson, 1979), Gielgud suggests that his "Slav side" helped to make him "more original as a performer." "If I had been a pure Terry, with the emotional facility of that family," he wrote, "my acting talent might have developed in a more conventional way."

Gielgud's most treasured toy throughout his boyhood was a model theatre, for which he designed and painted scenery and, with his siblings, invented plays. Especially good at drawing, he spent hours sketching costumes and illustrating stories and poems. For a time, he considered a career as a theatrical set designer, but when he learned that he would have to study architecture and technical drawing and would have to master mathematics, he gave up the idea.

Gielgud began his formal education in 1913 at Hillside, a boarding school in Godalming. An indifferent student, he excelled only in English and religion, but as an actor in extracurricular stage productions, he easily outshone his classmates. His marks were nonetheless good enough to earn him a nonresident scholarship to the Westminster School in London in 1917. Upon completion of his studies there three years later, Gielgud decided to forego a university education and try his luck on the stage. With the permission of his reluctant parents, he auditioned for a place in Lady Constance Bennett's drama school. To his delight, he was promptly awarded a year of tuition-free instruction. During school holidays, he made his first professional appearance, as an unpaid walk-on in a production of Henry V at the Old Vic Theatre.

In 1922, after spending several terms at Lady Bennett's school, Gielgud secured his first salaried job in the theatre "entirely through influence," to use his words. At the invitation of his cousin, the actress Phyllis Neilson-Terry, he served as an assistant stage manager and a general understudy in a touring production of J. B. Fagan's The Wheel. On his return to London, the young actor, realizing that he was woefully ill-prepared for his chosen craft, applied for and won a scholarship to the Royal Academy of Dramatic Art. It was after seeing him in a RADA showcase presentation that Nigel Playfair, the producer, engaged him to portray the Poet Butterfly in Karel and Josef Capek's imaginative satire The Insect Play. Although Gielgud believes that he "created a very bad impression" in the piece, Playfair immediately entrusted him with a supporting role in Robert E. Lee, John Drinkwater's critically acclaimed but commercially calamitous historical drama.

Gielgud left RADA in 1923 and, over the next few years, tested his talents in a variety of roles, ranging from Charley in a West End revival of the farce Charley's Aunt to Romeo, opposite Gwen Ffrangcon-Davies' Juliet. His first attempt at Romeo was, by his own admission, a "great failure." "I was too self-conscious," he explained years later, as quoted in Lillian and Helen Ross's The Player (1962). "I sang all the verse; I posed a lot, instead of finding the real animal knowledge of a young man in love." During three successive repertory seasons at the Oxford Playhouse in the mid-1920s, he learned how to create a character "from the inside out," to use his words. It was while he was playing the bumbling student Trofimov in an Oxford Playhouse production of Chekhov's The Cherry Orchard that he "began to see for the first time that it was possible to project a personality completely different from one's own, rather than just showing off."

In between seasons in Oxford, Gielgud understudied and, ultimately, replaced Noel Coward in West End productions of the latter's controversial The Vortex and of the sentimental melodrama The Constant Nymph. After making a disastrous Broadway debut as the Tsarevitch in the short-lived costume drama The Patriot in 1928, he returned to London, where he portrayed "nervous, hysterical young men," as he once put it, in a series of mostly ephemeral contemporary plays. His only notable acting assignment in the late 1920s was that of Oswald in a limited run of Ibsen's Ghosts, starring the legendary Mrs. Patrick Campbell.

Eager to meet the challenge of great classical roles, Gielgud joined the Old Vic company in 1929. In two consecutive seasons with that ensemble, he took on a staggering variety of Shakespearean roles: Romeo; Antonio in The Merchant of Venice; Richard II; Oberon in A Midsummer Night's Dream; Mark Antony in Julius Caesar; Orlando in As You Like It; Macbeth; Hamlet; Hotspur in Henry IV, Part I; Prospero in The Tempest; Antony in Antony and Cleopatra; Malvolio in Twelfth Night; Benedick in Much Ado About Nothing; and King Lear. Gielgud's training at the Old Vic was crucial to his continuing development as an artist. Besides teaching him "the value of teamwork," his years there instilled in him a desire to explore further the diverse characters he had portrayed on the Old Vic's stage. Over the next four decades, he welcomed virtually every chance he got to reinterpret those roles, frequently in productions that he himself directed.

Among the Shakespearean heroes that Gielgud played at the Old Vic and refined in subsequent performances was Romeo. In the actor's 1935 staging of Romeo and Juliet, he and Laurence Olivier created much excitement by appearing alternately as Romeo and Mercutio. Two years later, Gielgud directed and starred in a West End production of Richard II, winning praise for the depth and subtlety of his characterization of the poet king. During the same 1937-38 season, he also directed himself in an acclaimed production of The Merchant of Venice. His interpretation of Shylock was so compelling that, as one reviewer reported, "the whole house [was] motionless under the painful weight of his realism."

In 1940 Gielgud tackled the role of King Lear for the second time. Shakespeare scholar Harley Granville-Barker functioned as the architect of the Old Vic production and helped the actor chart "with brilliant exactness Lear's progress from worldly to spiritual authority," according to the London Times's drama critic. Gielgud took two further stabs at playing the tragic king: in a production that he and Anthony Quayle directed at Stratford-upon-Avon during a busy 1950-51 season—to which the actor also contributed a chillingly repressed Angelo in Measure for Measure and an unusually strong Cassius in Julius Caesar—and in a boldly stylized 1955 staging designed by the sculptor Isamu Noguchi. For his second attempt at Prospero, at the Old Vic in 1940, Gielgud altered his conception of the character to make him a much more vigorous figure. Returning to the part for the third time, under Peter Brook's direction in 1957, he stressed Prospero's vindictive nature. The validity of his novel approach to The Tempest was borne out when the production transferred from Stratford-upon-Avon to London's West End and chalked up capacity business for the duration of its run. Gielgud played his last—and, perhaps, his best—Prospero at the Old Vic in 1974.

It was not until 1942 that Gielgud once again turned his attention to the title role in Macbeth, a part many considered to be outside his natural range. That he was more than equal to the task was attested to by James Agate, the influential British drama critic, who commended the actor's "magnificent virtuosity," particularly in the banquet and apparition scenes. Other characters from the Shakespeare canon whom Gielgud has portrayed—often to stunning effect—include the obsessed Leontes in Peter Brook's memorable 1951 revival of The Winter's Tale, Cardinal Wolsey in Henry VIII at the Old Vic in 1958, and Othello in Franco Zeffirelli's operatic staging of the tragedy for the Royal Shakespeare Company at Stratford in 1961. But of all Gielgud's Shakespearean characterizations, Hamlet was perhaps the most memorable. James Agate proclaimed Gielgud in 1944, "the best Hamlet of our time." Theatregoers on both sides of the Atlantic flocked to his understated and cerebral performances, making Hamlet one of the most successful productions of the seasons in London in 1934-35 and in New York City in 1936-37.

From its modest beginning in 1957 as a solo recital prepared at the behest of the British Arts Council and scheduled for presentation before a select few, *The Ages of Man*, John Gielgud's program of excerpts from the writings of Shakespeare, evolved into a one-man show with which, off and on over the next ten years, he enthralled audiences around the world. In each of its several limited runs on Broadway in the late 1950s and 1960s, Gielgud was regularly accorded a standing ovation. The American theatrical establishment expressed its appreciation of the Shakespearean tour de force by giving the actor a special 1959 Tony Award. A televised version of *The Ages of Man*, broadcast in two hour-long segments by CBS-TV, earned an Emmy Award as the outstanding dramatic program of the 1965-66 season.

John Gielgud has been equally effective as an interpreter of the English comedy of manners and of Chekhov's naturalistic dramas. Over the years, his impeccable performances as Mirabell and Valentine in his own productions of, respectively, Congreve's *The Way of the World* and *Love for Love* delighted audiences, and his precise delineation of the sardonic Joseph Surface in Sheridan's *The School for Scandal*, in a long-running 1963 production that he himself staged, was judged by critics to be the standard against which future portrayals of the pious hypocrite would have to be measured. Equally definitive was Gielgud's interpretation of the role of John Worthing in Oscar Wilde's *The Importance of Being Earnest*. Always aware of "the delicate subtlety of character," as he put it, in Chekhov's plays, Gielgud returned again and again to the dramatist's works, both as actor and director. He has appeared as the befuddled old actor in *Swan Song*, the foolish Gaev in *The Cherry Orchard*, Konstantin in *The Seagull*, the world-weary title character in his own colloquial adaptation of *Ivanov*, and as Tusenbach and, later, Vershinin in *The Three Sisters*.

Because his fame rests largely on the talent he has shown for infusing new life into the classics, relatively little attention has been paid to Gielgud's continued encouragement of contemporary dramatists, especially talented unknowns. Shortly after signing a three-play contract with producer Bronson Albery in 1931, Gielgud, exercising the pick-and-choose prerogative implicit in their pact, selected for his first vehicle Richard Mackenzie's *Musical Chairs*, a script that had been rejected by five other producers. That the actor's taste matched his daring was confirmed by the play's lucrative nine-month run in the West End. Two years later, Gielgud persuaded Albery to stage *Richard of Bordeaux*, a historical drama written by the theatrical novice "Gordon Daviot," a pseudonym of mystery writer Elizabeth Mackintosh. Again his instinct was infallible. The play, in a lavish production directed by the actor, was the smash hit of the 1933-34 London season, and Gielgud's sensitive portrayal of the title character drew rave notices.

Among the better-known contemporary playwrights whose careers were advanced by Gielgud's astute theatrical sense and his enormous drawing power at the box office are Rodney Ackland and Christopher Fry. The former was no stranger, Gielgud having coproduced and directed his adaptation of the Hugh Walpole novel *The Old Ladies* in 1935, but their collaborative project eleven years later was infinitely more ambitious: the dramatization of Dostoevsky's *Crime and Punishment*. With Gielgud turning in a riveting performance as the impoverished student Raskolnikov, the play fared well in England (Agate rated Gielgud's portrayal of the central character "the best thing after Hamlet he has ever given us"). In New York, however, the actors were forced to take salary cuts in order to eke out a short run in the winter of 1947-48. Christopher Fry's *The Lady's Not for Burning* was, on the other hand, a winner in both its West End and Broadway incarnations, in 1949 and 1951, respectively. That romantic comedy in verse, which captured the New York Drama Critics Circle Award for best foreign play of the season, owed much of its success to Gielgud's affecting portrayal of Thomas Mendip, an itinerant soldier in fifteenth-century England, and to his deft direction of Fry's animated and intricate verse.

Gielgud's reputation as a director with an uncommon and sensitive understanding of the text soared in the mid-1950s with the extravagantly praised production of Enid Bagnold's offbeat comedy *The Chalk Garden*, featuring Edith Evans and Peggy Ashcroft. To achieve a comparable change of pace in his acting career, he persuaded Hugh ("Binkie") Beaumont, the theatrical impresario, to entrust him with the twin chores of staging and starring in Noel Coward's *Nude with Violin*. Gielgud relished the opportunity to play the "very broad" and somewhat "vulgar" part of Sebastian, the shrewd valet—a role for which he was, by his own estimation, unsuited. Critically, the gamble backfired, but notwithstanding the savage notices, the play enjoyed a healthy run, thanks to Gielgud's presence. The actor deviated from type again in 1958 when he portrayed the spiritually troubled James Callifer in Graham Greene's metaphysical melodrama *The Potting Shed*. The following year, he directed his longtime friend Ralph Richardson in a production of Greene's comedy *The Complaisant Lover*, which was thought to owe its huge commercial success to the "extremely touching performance" that Gielgud had coaxed out of Richardson. In recognition of his inspired guidance of Jason Robards, Hume Cronyn, and George Grizzard in Hugh Wheeler's *Big Fish, Little Fish*, his American colleagues awarded him a Tony for the best direction of a play during the 1960-61 Broadway season.

For Gielgud, to whom the stage had "not only been his work, but also his passion and his refuge," as Michiko Kakutani observed in the *New York Times* (September 23, 1980), the next few years comprised a period of rather drastic readjustment. The advent of iconoclastic young playwrights, including the so-called "Angry Young Men" and the Absurdists, dismayed him. His fear that the parade might be passing him by was fortified in 1964 when his highly publicized Broadway production of *Hamlet* with Richard Burton in the title role drew a daunting number of unfavorable notices. "I don't think I brought enough theatricality to my conception of it," Gielgud said later of his attempt to stage the tragedy as a "rehearsal piece." "I think Peter Brook could have done it better." Later in the year the actor, who was eager to try his hand in an avant-garde piece, accepted a role in Edward Albee's *Tiny Alice*, and though he found it difficult to get a handle on his ill-defined character, his performance as the victimized Brother Julian earned him a 1965 Tony Award nomination as best actor. Returning to the classical repertory, Gielgud joined the National Theatre in 1967 to play Orgon in Sir Tyron Guthrie's broadly comic staging of Molière's *Tartuffe* and the title role in Peter Brook's ritualistic mounting of Seneca's *Oedipus*, but he failed to achieve the sort of transcendent breakthrough that he had hoped for.

The unlikely vehicle that restored John Gielgud to his eminence was *40 Years On*, an allegorical comedy by Alan Bennett, one of the quartet of irreverent young comedians whose satirical revue *Beyond the Fringe* had captivated both English and American audiences in the early 1960s. *40 Years On* chronicled Britain's decline as a world power in a series of skits, ostensibly being performed by a group of public-school boys as an anarchic end-of-term entertainment. Gielgud's portrayal of the ultraconservative headmaster who presides over the outrageous goings-on marked the introduction into his acting of a disarming new element—self-parody—and brought him his best reviews since *The Ages of Man*.

The actor's next contemporary role was Sir Gideon Petrie, the saintly pacifist philosopher in *The Battle of Shrivings*, a short-lived didactic drama by Peter Shaffer, whose maiden theatrical effort, *Five Finger Exercise*, had—under Gielgud's apt direction—been a big hit a decade before in the West End and on Broadway. He followed that up with David Storey's *Home*, in which he and Ralph Richardson portrayed, respectively, Harry and Jack, a pair of addled senior citizens who reside in what the author identifies vaguely as "some form of institution." Following a sold-out limited engagement at the experiment-oriented Royal Court Theatre in London, *Home* transferred to the Morosco Theatre in New York City for an equally successful commercial engagement that stretched from November 17, 1970 to February 20, 1971. The co-starred knights were not only neck-and-neck contenders for the Drama Desk's annual "outstanding performance" accolade, with Richardson ultimately capturing a slightly higher percentage of the votes, but were also Tony Award nominees. Much less gratifying was Gielgud's experience on Broadway later that season as the director of Albee's grandiloquent disquisition on death, *All Over*, a resounding flop.

Back in London for the 1971–72 London theatre season, Gielgud portrayed the revered stage-and-screen star Sir Geoffrey Kendle in *Veterans*, Charles Wood's comedy about the shooting of a film epic on location in Turkey. The critics perceived that he was playing himself in the Royal Court offering but granted that he "did so surpassingly well." Next, in what was for him a traumatic "first," Gielgud suffered the ignomiy of being sacked from his job as director of the Broadway-bound revival of the musical comedy *Irene*, starring Debbie Reynolds. Although he had two lavish productions (*The Trojans* by Hector Berlioz and Benjamin Britten's operatic treatment of *A Midsummer Night's Dream*) at the Royal Opera House, Covent Garden, to his credit, Gielgud had never before attempted to command the disparate creative talents behind a Broadway musical, and the discovery that he was not up to the task left him feeling, in his word, "miserable."

Gielgud returned to the Royal Court Theatre in the summer of 1974 to appear as Shakespeare in Edward Bond's parable *Bingo*, which traced the last days in the Bard's life. In 1975 at the National Theatre he gave another superb performance—this time as an articulate, down-at-the-heels poet in Harold Pinter's enigmatic *No Man's Land*. Ralph Richardson was once again his costar, and they worked together as harmoniously as they had in *Home*. Repeating their roles on Broadway in 1976, the duo jointly won an Outer Critics Circle Award "for distinctive achievement in the theatre" and a Drama Desk Award for providing audiences with the "outstanding theatrical experience of the season." Gielgud has not appeared on the New York stage since *No Man's Land*, but his incomparable performances as the doltish Sir Politic in Peter Hall's 1977 National Theatre presentation of Ben Jonson's classic farce *Volpone* and as Sir Noel Cunliffe, the waspish, retired Oxford don in Julian Mitchell's *Half-Life*, will long be remembered by London playgoers. During the past decade, Gielgud has also chosen to phase out his career as a stage director, the last assignments he undertook having been revivals in 1974 and 1975 of Coward's *Private Lives* starring Maggie Smith, Somerset Maugham's *The Constant Wife* with Ingrid Bergman heading the cast, and *The Gay Lord Quex* by Arthur Wing Pinero.

While he has never been a "movie star" in the conventional sense, John Gielgud can lay claim to an impressive list of motion picture credits dating back to 1924, when he appeared as an opium-addicted sculptor in the melodramatic silent film *Who Is the Man?* His first substantial film part was Inigo Jollifant in the 1932 movie version of J. B. Priestley's novel *The Good Companions*. For several years Gielgud struggled to find the cinematic equivalent of his theatrical technique. Fearful of overacting, he underplayed to the point of near-catatonia the lead role of Ashenden, the reluctant spy in Alfred Hitchcock's thriller based on a Somerset Maugham novel, *The Secret Agent* (Gaumont-British, 1936); he went to the other extreme in the low-budget biography *The Prime Minister* (Warner Brothers, 1941), giving what for him was an unusually "busy" performance as Benjamin Disraeli. It was not until he portrayed Cassius in Joseph L. Mankeiwicz's production of *Julius Caesar* (MGM, 1953) that Gielgud finally shed his self-consciousness in front of the camera and began to enjoy filmmaking. His characterization of Cassius was widely praised and earned him a British Academy Award as best British actor of the year. Other congenial roles in the 1950s were Clarence in Laurence Olivier's production of *Richard III* (Lopert, 1955), the sanctimonious Edward Barrett in MGM's reverential remake of *The Barretts of Wimpole Street* (1934), and the Earl of Warwick in Otto Preminger's *Saint Joan* (United Artists, 1957).

After an absence of seven years Gielgud returned to the screen at Richard Burton's request to play the cunning Louis VII of France in the movie version of Jean Anouilh's *Becket* (Paramount, 1964), which costarred Burton as Thomas à Becket and Peter O'Toole as Henry II. His skillful impersonation of the French king won him a 1964 Oscar nomination in the category of best supporting actor. Whether it was his association for the first time with a critical and box-office hit such as *Becket*, or whether it was merely the result of the motion-picture industry's belated realization that Gielgud's persona conferred a degree of class—a kind of cultural credibility—on virtually every enterprise, the actor's screen services have been in almost constant demand since the mid-1960s. A few of the films in which he has appeared—MGM's inept cinematization of the popular Morris L. West novel *The Shoes of the Fisherman* (1968), Columbia's musical remake of *Lost Horizon* (1973), and *Penthouse* publisher Bob Guccione's sensational *Caligula* (PAC, 1980)—are considered by most critics to be unworthy of an artist of his stature. But as Gielgud pointed out to Wendy Smith in an interview for *Publishers Weekly* (August 15, 1980), movies are "great fun to do," and after years of physically taxing and only moderately remunerative theatre work, he finds it a pleasure to be "handsomely paid" and a relief to be spared "the responsibility of a very big thing to sustain." He welcomes the opportunity to work with new film directors, and has remarked that his only fear is that "they'll be so respectful they won't have the courage to tell you what's wrong with your acting."

Among the dozens of films that have heightened rather than dimmed the luster of Gielgud's reputation are Orson Welles's flawed yet fascinating *Chimes at Midnight* (Peppercorn-Wormser, 1966), retitled *Falstaff* for its American release, in which he played the conscience-stricken, dying King Henry IV; Tony Richardson's antiwar polemic *The Charge of the Light Brigade* (United Artists, 1968), wherein he portrayed Lord Raglan, the doddering incompetent who gave the order for the suicidal attack; and American International's star-studded version of *Julius Caesar* (1970). He was a "sheer joy to watch," too, as the wily Lord Sissal in *Eagle in a Cage* (National General, 1972); as the autocratic Victorian hospital administrator in *The Elephant Man* (Paramount, 1980); and as Beddoes, the quintessential gentleman's gentleman in Paramount's all-star whodunit *Murder on the Orient Express*, the role that brought him his second British Academy Award, as the best supporting actor of 1974. He turned in another award-winning performance as the dying novelist who is the pivotal character in Alain Resnais' convoluted *Providence* (Cinema V, 1977), for which he was named best actor of the year by the New York Film Critics. But it was not until 1982 that he won his first American Academy Award, for his supporting role as the hero's sharp-tongued butler in *Arthur* (Warner Brothers). Gielgud was prominently featured in both *Chariots of Fire* (Warner Brothers, 1981) and *Gandhi* (Columbia, 1982), successive winners of the best-picture-of-the-year Oscar.

Besides recreating for the small screen his stage roles in *Ivanov*, *Home*, and *No Man's Land*, Gielgud has starred in the television adaptation of Terence Rattigan's *The Browning Version*, which was aired by CBS-TV in 1959; *From Chekhov with Love*, a CBS-TV special production in 1968; and the *NET Playhouse* presentation of *The Mayfly and the Frog*, also in 1968, but most American viewers know the actor for his striking portrayal of supporting characters. Among the many made-for-television movies and miniseries enriched by his presence are *The Love Song of Barney Kempinsky* (ABC, 1966); *Probe* (NBC, 1972); *Frankenstein: The True Story* (NBC, 1973); *QB VII* (ABC, 1974); *Les Misérables* (CBS, 1978); *Brideshead Revisited* (PBS, 1982); and *The Scarlet and the Black* (CBS, 1983). In the ongoing PBS series *The Shakespeare Plays*, coproduced by the BBC and Time-Life, Gielgud has thus far appeared as the Chorus in *Romeo and Juliet* and as John of Gaunt in *Richard II*. He is also familiar to TV watchers as the supercilious butler in the commercials for Paul Masson wines.

In addition to *An Actor and His Time*, Gielgud is the author of the autobiography *Early Stages* (Macmillan, 1939), *Distinguished Company* (Heinemann, 1972; Doubleday, 1973), a volume of recollections of some of the famous theatrical personages he has known over the years, and *Stage Directions* (Heinemann, 1963; Random House, 1964), a collection of essays and speeches. For a man of his remarkable accomplishments, he is, according to most interviewers, refreshingly humble—"a rare combination of splendor and modesty," as William Peper of the *New York World Telegram and Sun* put it in 1965. Away from the theatre or the sound stage, he is, by his own account, "a very timid, shy, cowardly man." "I'm very helpless as a person," he admitted to Michiko Kakutani, who interviewed the actor for a *New York Times* (September 23, 1980) profile. "I've never understood politics. I was never any good at games or sports. I can't drive a car. Except for reading and doing puzzles and going to picture galleries, I've never even had any hobbies. I love to have everything done for me. Until I get to the theatre—and then I want to do everything myself."

An impeccably tailored man of courtly behavior, Sir John Gielgud is a trim five feet eleven inches tall and has pale blue eyes and the Roman profile of a silent film era matinee idol. In his spare time he reads "trashy American novels," putters around the garden of his eighteenth-century carriage house in Wotton Underwood, near Oxford, or watches television so that he can keep up with new performers "without the embarrassment of having to go round and say what I thought of the play," as he explained to Miss Kakutani. In the past few years, he has husbanded his energies more carefully, and although he is not adverse to doing another stage production, he clearly enjoys playing cameo film and television roles. "If one plays them with taste and sensitivity, one can be quite useful," he

told Miss Kakutani. "I think that's how I should like to be remembered. As an actor—a somehow useful actor."

References: Guardian p10 S 19 '73 pors; N Y Post p15+ F 6 '71 por; N Y Times C p7 S 23 '80 por; Newsday II p4+ N 14 '76 por; Pub W 218:10+ Ag 15 '80 por; Time 122:70+ Ag 15 '83 pors; Franke, Lewis and Booth, John E. Actors Talk About Acting (1961); Harwood, Ronald. The Ages of Gielgud (1984); International Who's Who, 1984–1985; Who's Who, 1984–85; Who's Who in America, 1984–85; Who's Who in the Theatre (1981)

Golub, Leon (Albert)

(gä´ lub)

Jan. 23, 1922– Painter. Address: b. c/o Susan Caldwell, Inc., 383 W. Broadway, New York City, N. Y. 10012; h. 530 La Guardia Pl., New York City, N.Y. 10012

In the early 1950s—a period when the art world celebrated abstract expressionism—the artist Leon Golub began to make his mark as a figurative painter, but it was not until the 1980s that his works, with their strong political overtones, achieved their widest recognition. His outsize depictions of assassins, mercenaries, and political inquisitors, subjects that he had begun to paint in 1976, were likened by Michael Brenson, writing in the New York Times (February 10, 1984), to "violent news images that fill our living rooms from continents away." Critic Peter Schjeldahl, in the Village Voice

(October 22, 1982), compared Golub to "an alarm clock set to go off in the early '80s and wake everybody up," and wrote of him: "A fringe figure for most of his long career—one of those artists who, though far from unknown, might be termed 'famous for being ignored'—Golub has rather suddenly become a major artist of our cultural moment, which he is helping to define."

Leon Albert Golub was born in Chicago, Illinois on January 23, 1922, the son of Samuel and Sara (Sussman) Golub. He received his formal training in his chosen field at the University of Chicago, where he majored in art history and obtained a B.A. degree in art in 1942. After World War II service in the United States Army from 1943 to 1946, he enrolled at the Art Institute of Chicago, where he studied with Paul Wieghardt, Kathleen Blackshear, and Robert Lifuendahl. He received his bachelor of fine arts degree there in 1949 and became a master of fine arts in 1950.

As a student at the Chicago Art Institute, Golub joined with other art students who were war veterans to produce a new kind of painting and sculpture that, in the words of Franz Schulze in the Christian Science Monitor (April 9, 1960), "bore the mark of a violent, desiccated expressionism and a surreal fancy both obsessive and disturbed." The young postwar rebels rejected most of the art of the post-medieval Western tradition. Instead they drew inspiration from earlier history and more primitive cultures, such as pre-Columbian America, Africa, Oceania, ancient Greece, Etruria, and the Romanesque. They were also inspired by such modern influences as the Belgian avant-garde painter James Ensor, the dadaist movement, and the German expressionists. Emphasis was on the subconscious, reflecting the influence of Freudian theory, and the group was facetiously referred to as the "pre-rationalites," an allusion to the nineteenth-century British Pre-Raphaelite school. They also became known as the Chicago "monster" school, a title with which Golub was closely identified.

On graduating from the Chicago Art Institute in 1950, Golub began teaching art at Chicago's Wright Junior College. He continued to be identified with the "monster" school, represented at Chicago's vanguard "Momentum," which became the forum for the battle between the "monsters," who focused on dramatic images of the human condition, and the purist-abstractionist painters, who eschewed all reference to the human figure or the real object. The latter came chiefly from the Bauhaus-oriented Institute of Design in Chicago.

After exhibiting at the Contemporary Gallery in Chicago in 1950, at Purdue University in 1951, and with Wittenborn & Company in New York City in 1952, Golub began to receive major attention with his solo show at New York's Artist's Gallery in 1954. In a statement accompanying that exhibition, Golub wrote: "I think we live in an age of creative degeneracy wherein only the unknowing—the naive and the primitive . . . speak simply and well." In a largely negative review, a critic for the *New York Herald Tribune* (May 29, 1954) wrote: "The most interesting thing about Leon Golub's . . . show . . . is that it has virtually sold out. Clearly this young man from Chicago is to be the art world's new darling. Nothing else is very clear about him, however." The critic found one picture in the show, *Recurrent Image*, "interesting and poetic." The rest he regarded as "murky in idea, boring in execution, altogether heavy-handed and witless, and absurdly pretentious." Two years later, however, a review in the *New York Herald Tribune* (May 26, 1956) said of Golub's solo show at the Feigl Gallery: "It is impossible not to feel in his work the impression of a deeply imaginative, intense and serious artist of our time."

Golub's work was warmly received when he exhibited at a 1954 Guggenheim show in New York City entitled "Younger American Painters" that later toured the country. Of his 1955 show at the Feigl Gallery a critic for the *New York Times* (March 26, 1955) wrote: "Feelings of pity and terror are aroused by the grossly strong semi-abstract figures in Leon Golub's paintings. . . . But the brutal expressionism of his painting style goes even beyond the distraught character of his subjects, fabulous as a Siamese-twin sphinx, tragic as his entombed couple, and symbolic as his *Flight*."

Golub's style has been compared to the *art brut* of the French painter Jean Dubuffet and even more directly to the style of the British post-World War II painter Francis Bacon, with whom he shared a dedication to the human figure and a rejection of the currently dominant abstract expressionism. Golub's article titled "A Critique of Abstract Expressionism" in the *College Art Journal* (Winter 1955) aroused considerable ire at a time when Franz Kline, Willem de Kooning, Jackson Pollock, and Mark Rothko were popular heroes. In it he claimed that "abstract expressionism had discarded the individualist of the Renaissance," and he stressed his credentials not only as a painter but also as a scholar. In later opinions he suggested that both minimal art and abstract art were offshoots of modern technology.

With his 1956 exhibition at the Feigl Gallery in New York City, Golub seemed to have reached the culmination of his early primitive style. A critic for the *New York Times* (May 22, 1956) wrote of that show: "A forceful and committed personality emerges in the expressionist paintings of Leon Golub. . . . His paintings are consistently symbolic, reaching back into history at times for occult tribal myth. . . . Golub is an introverted, quiet expressionist. His colors are geared to ascetic, contemplative moods. With mauves, blacks, dull reds, the artist creates amalgams of ears, bones, half-hidden heads and signs, building up a personal iconography for such themes as mother and child, the family group, sphinxes, priests and princes."

Although abstract expressionism continued to be the prevailing tendency in American art during the 1950s, the prestigious Museum of Modern Art in New York City bucked that trend with a group exhibition in 1959 called "New Images of Man," and Golub's figure-oriented work was prominently featured in the show. As a critic for *Time* (September 7, 1959) described his work, "Leon Golub paints men in pain. His views are frontal and direct: lumpish, lacerated heads with dull yellow catlike eyes. His technique—layer on layer of colored lacquer, chipped, gouged and pumiced—gives the effect of eroded sculpture come hauntingly to life." The critic noted that Golub's work seemed to be influenced by Romanesque statues that he saw during his stay in Italy in 1956 and 1957. In his own statement for the catalogue of "New Images of Man," Golub observed: "Man is seen as having undergone a holocaust or mutation. The ambiguities of these huge forms indicate the stress of their vulnerability versus their capacities for endurance."

By the time the "New Images of Man" show was presented, Golub's style had already been undergoing a change from the primitive and symbolic to one that was more centered on his own "images of man," some of them evoked by the sculptures of Hellenistic Greece. Writing in *Leon Golub: A Retrospective Exhibition of Paintings from 1947 to 1973* (1974), Lawrence Alloway described the artist's work in the period from 1947 to 1958 as representing the time of the "dervish principle," which was based on the perception, as Carter Ratcliff noted in *Art in America* (January 1984), that the artist, "whirling in a painterly panic, . . . tried to force his inward demons into big-scale visibility."

With his painting *Damaged Man* (1955), resembling statues of the Hellenistic period, Golub made one of his first ventures into what Carter Ratcliff has called the "entropic classicism" of his "Ozymandias phase"—a term suggested by Shelley's famous poem. He continued that style into the 1960s with two series of paintings called, respectively, *Gigantomachies* and *Combats*. Outstanding as an example of the former period is the huge oil painting titled *Burnt Man*, or *Fallen Warrior*, completed in 1960 and compared by critics with the sculpture *Giant*, a part of the Great Altar of Zeus at Pergamon from about 150 B.C. Both the marble statue and the painting show a giant figure fallen to his knees. The statue, which is in the Pergamon Museum in East Berlin, is broken in several places and the face is completely eroded. Posed in roughly the same position, Golub's painting shows a giant whose skin is almost entirely pitted and seared as by fire. That image later became a symbol of the artist's protest against the war in Vietnam.

During the years from 1959 to 1964, while he and his wife, the artist Nancy Spero, lived in Paris, Golub's work was considered by critics to have "mellowed" somewhat. In a review of a solo exhibition of his paintings held at the Allan Frumkin Gallery in New York in November 1963, John Canaday of the *New York Times* (November 24, 1963) wrote: "The Golub men are of the same breed as before—heavy-limbed, square-headed, chunky-muscled—but they differ from their predecessors in being intact. . . . Mr. Golub is now able to paint in a spirit of affirmation rather than of doubt and accusation." The new works were part of the series called *Combats*, and featured fresco-like paintings, compared by Canaday to "fragments of some mural that might have decorated an ancient arena." Instead of being passive victims, the men are shown engaged in combat with each other. Golub's own comments on the exhibition referred to "what is violent, violated and pathetic," but he concluded that his "combats" show a retention of "belief in classic art and man as mediator in his own destiny."

At the time that Golub returned to the United States to settle in New York City in 1964, the war in Vietnam was beginning to involve the energies of a large group of artists who eventually formed a united protest group. Golub's work entered a new phase, characterized by paintings that were more vehement in expression than those of his previous "combats" period. Charged with anger provoked by the war, they were the first of his works to be overtly political. Golub created what was described by Peter Schjeldahl in the *Village Voice* as "huge paintings, on torn canvas, of American soldiers shooting civilians," that were reminiscent of Picasso's 1951 *Massacre in Korea*.

Along with some 600 other artists, Golub took part in the New York City demonstration known as "Angry Arts Against the War in Vietnam." As Golub wrote in *Arts Magazine* (April 1967), the artists expressed themselves "through their work to dissociate themselves from the U.S. policy in Vietnam." During the week from January 29 to February 4, 1967, an enormous collage of paintings, drawings, paper dolls, barbed wire, and other items was installed at the Loeb Student Center at New York University. Golub's own contribution was a display of photostats from his *Burnt Man* series of 1960, mounted with a handwritten message against the war. "Its success as art is problematic," Golub wrote of the collage in his *Arts Magazine* article. "But its public success was remarkable."

Golub's anti–Vietnam War paintings, which he continued to produce into the 1970s, had evolved from his earlier *Gigantomachies* and *Combats* series depicting men in battle, but in the later works the scenes of struggle became more specific. "It's clear for the first time who are the victims and who the aggressors," Carter Ratcliff wrote in *Art in America* (January 1984). He noted that Golub's only non-figurative works were the *Napalm Gates* series (1970-71) but pointed out that "even here the body is to be seen . . . if one is up to it. On these large strips of canvas, paint mimics incinerated skin."

But despite the obvious antiwar sentiment expressed in his Vietnam-era paintings, Golub did not view those works specifically as protest. "I am struggling to get a reading on what's going on in the giganticized time-space of the twentieth century," he told Irving Sandler in an interview conducted under the auspices of the Archives of American Art that was reprinted in part in *Arts Magazine* (February 1970). The figures that constitute the subjects of his work are, in his words, "conceptualized in abstract terms as personifications of force. . . . These figures, whether giants, Roman athletes, contemporary men, heroes, humanoid monsters—call them what you will—express power relations in the world, relations torn asunder and clashing. Power is expressed in terms of violence and conflict; this is my subject matter."

A retrospective exhibition of Golub's work of the period from 1947 through 1974 was shown in the Museum of Contemporary Art in Chicago in 1974 and at the New York Cultural Center in 1975. Reviewing that show and one of Francis Bacon's work at the Metropolitan Museum of Art, Harold Rosenberg observed in the *New Yorker* (May 12, 1975) that the aim of both artists was to "report . . . on the postwar world in its physically menacing and psychologically deranging aspects." For such a profound and broad theme, Rosenberg noted, "it was necessary, in their view, to restore the human figure to its traditional place at the top of the hierarchy of artistic subjects." He pointed out, however, that neither Golub nor Bacon ever merely copied things in the manner of the photo-realists, but instead, "report contemporary facts by converting them into metaphors of art."

Golub continued his preoccupation with symbols of "power" during the late 1970s with a series of about 100 small portraits, done from photographs, of such world leaders as Mao Zedong, Nelson Rockefeller, General Franco, and Ho Chi Minh. The paintings were considered a transitional stage for Golub. According to Peter Schjeldahl, "These crude, bland little pictures, their paint scraped down into the tooth of the canvas, suggested no political intent, but rather a simple, mindless fascination with the 'look' of powerful men."

In his early works, Golub had been painting largely with lacquer, but since the 1960s he has been using mainly acrylics. With acrylic paint, he developed a scraping technique used for the delicately colored backgrounds of what is considered by critics to be the strongest and best work of his career. Golub's enormous paintings of the early 1980s, painted on the floor of his studio on unstretched canvas, are first covered with acrylic paint, which is allowed to dry, then dissolved with solvent, and scraped into the canvas with a meat cleaver.

Golub's paintings of the 1980s, bearing such thematic titles as *Mercenaries, Interrogations, Riots and White Squads,* and *Horsing Around,* are, in the words of Peter Schjeldahl, "political art" that is "stunning in its sophistication and courage" in that it gives "the political criminal, not the victim, full and particular humanity." The artist "confronts power where it is both dark and vulnerable, in dirty work done out of sight and out of mind." As Golub told Carter Ratcliff, "I'm trying to make transparent what are the effects of power in our society. . . . Of course my work is also opaque. You almost can't get past the moment of the painting. But that difficulty is intended to lead you past the moment, to an inference of what these brutal images signify."

The huge, unframed paintings—most of them about ten feet high and twelve feet wide—have been praised for their uncanny capacity for drawing the viewer into the scene to complete the work by examining it. Michael Brenson, writing in the *New York Times* (February 10, 1984), commented on Golub's "larger than life-sized political thugs, sometimes stripped to the waist, sometimes dressed in dungarees or battle fatigues, [who] chat, fondle their guns or women, pose while torturing or look at us with annoyance just after they have put a gun to a victim's head," and concluded that they "do not so much stick in the mind as take it over."

But despite the apparent authenticity of his images, Golub does not generally obtain them at first hand. His inspirations include such contemporary sources as newspaper photos, television programs, and erotic magazines, as well as such influences out of the past as Goya, Picasso, Orozco, Jacques-Louis David, and the nineteenth-century French academic painters. As Carter Ratcliff pointed out in his 1984 *Art in America* article, Golub's work also betrays the influence of modern abstract art, which seems to be the source of his relatively flat figures and of the "color field" backgrounds against which his subjects emphasize the artist's view that "power and stress" begin and end in "the human body and human actions."

Since he began exhibiting in 1948, Golub has shown his paintings in many major cities in the United States, as well as in Toronto, London, Paris, and Melbourne. His work has been included in many group shows, some of which were presented in conjunction with antiwar benefits. Among the many collections that include his paintings are those of the Museum of Modern Art, the Art Institute of Chicago, the Corcoran Gallery of Washington, D.C., the Museum of Tel Aviv, and a number of universities. Awards and honors that he has received include a Florsheim Memorial Prize in 1954, a Ford Foundation grant in 1960, and a Guggenheim Foundation grant in 1968. Golub was elected to the American Academy of Arts and Letters in 1973 and was awarded an honorary doctor of fine arts degree by the school of the Art Institute of Chicago in 1982. Golub taught at Wright Junior College in Chicago from 1950 to 1955, at University College of Northwestern University in Chicago

from 1953 to 1956, at Indiana University in Bloomington from 1957 to 1959, at the Tyler School of Art at Temple University in Philadelphia in 1965, and at the School of Visual Arts in New York City from 1966 to 1969. Since 1970, he has been professor of art at Rutgers University, where he was appointed John C. Van Dyke Professor of Visual Arts in 1983.

Leon Golub, a slender man with thinning gray hair, has been characterized as being "articulate" and "ferociously amiable." He and his wife, the artist Nancy Spero, whom he married on December 15, 1951, make their home in New York City. They are the parents of three sons, Stephen S., Philip S., and Paul S. Golub. Over the years, Leon Golub and Nancy Spero have on occasion held joint exhibitions of their work, the most recent at the Sarkis Galleries of the College of Art and Design in Detroit in 1983. In commenting on a retrospective exhibition of Golub's work that was presented at the New Museum of Contemporary Art in the fall of 1984, Michael Brenson noted in the *New York Times* (September 28, 1984) that Golub's "pictorial investigations of political terror . . . are the culmination not only of sustained political concern, but also of a lifelong journey into the human heart."

References: Art in America 72:74+ Ja '84 por; N Y Times p20 F 10 '84; Village Voice p96+ O 22 '82; Contemporary Artists (1983); Dictionary of Contemporary American Artists (1982); Who's Who in America, 1984–85; Who's Who in American Art (1984)

Gossage, Rich

July 5, 1951– Baseball player. Address: b. San Diego Padres, P.O. Box 2000, San Diego, Calif. 92120

The relief pitcher, who for a long time was professional baseball's unsung hero, has finally come into his own. The most fearsome of the major-league salvage artists enjoying the new recognition of their importance and the increased income accruing from it is the San Diego Padres' short reliever Rich Gossage, a hulking, mean-looking righthander who intimidates opposing batters with his ninety-four-mph jumping fastball and what he calls his "slurve," a combination slider-curve. The Padres, denizens of the cellar of the National League West throughout their previous fifteen-year history, signed Gossage to a multimillion-dollar contract in January 1984 in the hope that he would help make them serious title contenders— which indeed they became, taking the National League championship in 1984. Gossage, an eight-time All-Star, came to the Padres from the New York Yankees of the American League, for whom he saved 150 games over six years. Before becom-

Rich Gossage

ing the big stopper in the Yankee bullpen, he pitched short relief for the Chicago White Sox (1972-76) and the Pittsburgh Pirates (1977). At the time of his signing with San Diego his major league career saves totaled 206.

Although baseball fans know him as Rich and "Goose," Gossage has always been known as Rick to his family and friends. The second son and the fifth of six children of Jack Andrew Gossage Sr. and Susanne (Radich) Gossage, he was born Richard Michael Gossage on July 5, 1951 in Colorado Springs, Colorado, at the foot of Pike's Peak in the Colorado Rockies. Jack Gossage Sr., who had almost struck it rich in the gold fields of Cripple Creek, on the other side of Pike's Peak, in the 1940s, was a landscaper who, according to Gossage, "liked the outdoors a lot more than he liked to work." "We didn't have much money, but I had a fun childhood," the pitcher told Phil Pepe in an interview for the *Sporting News* (August 22, 1981). "If I wasn't hunting and fishing with my dad, I was playing ball with him or watching the *Game of the Week* with him. There was no professional baseball in our area, so the only major league games I ever saw before I became a pro were on television."

As a child, Gossage threw baseballs as often and as long as anyone would catch them. His chief receiver was his older brother Jack Jr. (who once tried out for the New York Yankees, unsuccessfully). As Gossage recalled in his interview with Phil Pepe, Jack Jr. pretended never to be satisfied with the strength of his pitches. "He'd keep telling me, 'Can't you throw any harder than that?' And I'd be busting my gut trying to throw the ball harder, trying to hurt him." Thus goaded, Gossage became the fastest hurler in the local Little League, and at Wasson High School in Colorado Springs he was, ac-

cording to one of his coaches, "a whale of a competitor" in both basketball and baseball, with the same "grim determination . . . that you see now."

As a lanky high school senior, already six feet two inches tall, Gossage drew numerous college basketball scholarship offers with his scrappy play at forward and his spectacular corner jump shot. Forsaking those offers—as well as a prospective major in forestry at Colorado State University—he decided to sign with the Chicago White Sox, who picked him in the ninth round of professional baseball's free-agent draft in June 1970. His father did not live to see Gossage become a pro; Jack Gossage Sr. died in 1969.

At Sarasota, Florida and Appleton, Wisconsin in the White Sox farm system in 1970, Gossage pitched in thirteen games and went 0-3. Pitching for Appleton in 1971, he led the Midwest League with an 18-2 record and a 1.83 earned-run average. Witnessing one of Gossage's performances in 1971, Chuck Tanner, then the manager of the White Sox, was struck with the idea of bringing him up to Chicago as a relief pitcher, because Gossage had not only the necessary ready strength, with or without rest, but also the "proper mental makeup: if somebody got a hit off him, he'd get so ticked he'd want to throw the ball through the backstop." Having been brought up with the old view of the bullpen as the place where superannuated starting pitchers went into semi-retirement, eking out their terminal keep by mopping up other people's messes, Gossage misunderstood Tanner's decision to make him a reliever, considering it a "slap in the face" and a "demotion." As he told Harry Stein in an interview for *Sport* (April 1978), it took him several years to accept being in the bullpen. "But, I tell you, now there's no greater satisfaction than going in with no outs, bases loaded, and a one-run lead and keeping that lead. In a situation like that, it's all on the line. . . . That's what relief pitching is all about."

Terry Forster, Gossage's roommate at Appleton, was called up to the Chicago bullpen at the same time as he. "Two of the hardest young throwers I ever saw in baseball," Chuck Tanner later said of Forster and Gossage. "You know what I liked about Gossage? I liked his face. People laugh when I tell them that. But it's true. I can't describe what I mean. You don't recognize it till you see it, but he's got a *winning* face." Under Johnny Sain, the Chicago pitching coach, Gossage added finesse to his raw power, developing his slider-curve. While working on that breaking ball, however, he lost his fastball temporarily, for several years. From a 7-1 record in Chicago in 1972 he went to 0-4 in 1973, and he finished the 1973 season pitching 5-4 with Iowa in the American Association. After a 0-2 start with Appleton in 1974, he returned to Chicago, where he went 4-6 the rest of the season. Recovering his fastball, he had a banner bullpen year in 1975, with a 9-8 record, a 1.84 earned-run average, and a league-leading twenty-six saves. The *Sporting News* named him American League Fireman of the Year, and he played in his first All-Star game.

When Chuck Tanner went to Oakland in 1976, Paul Richards, Tanner's successor as manager in Chicago, moved Gossage out of the bullpen and into the starting rotation, with disappointing results: a 9-17 record and a 3.94 earned-run average. In November 1976 Chuck Tanner moved from Oakland and the American League to the Pittsburgh Pirates of the National League, and at the winter meetings the following month he obtained both Gossage and Forster in a trade for two Pirates, outfielder Richie Zisk and pitcher Silvio Martinez. Working out of the bullpen again, Gossage stunned National League batters with his performance with the Pirates in 1977: an 11-9 record, twenty-six saves, the second-best earned-run average in the league (1.62), and the league record for most strikeouts by a relief pitcher (151). In his honor a mascot goose was let loose on the playing field before each game, and when he struck out his first batter in a game the Pittsburgh scoreboard beamed, "The Goose is loose."

Kent Tekulve, a fellow reliever in Pittsburgh, told William Nack of Sports Illustrated that he learned a mental attitude from Gossage: how to "be laid back," to "go with the flow," because "you're going to get your brains knocked out once in a while, but you just have to come back and throw again." "He's the kind of guy who could leave the park when the game was over, and go out for a couple of beers, and sitting out there at the bar, you couldn't tell whether he won or lost. . . . He was always on an even keel."

Gossage earned $46,800 in Pittsburgh, but his performance there led to much more money, attracting as it did the eye of George Steinbrenner, the owner of the New York Yankees and the biggest spender in the free-agent market. Granted free agency on October 28, 1977, Gossage a month later signed a six-year Yankee contract worth $3.6 million. "I was hoping the Yankees would draft me," Gossage, an admirer of the New York team since childhood, later said. "I loved the Yankees. When they did pick me . . . , I went there with the most positive of feelings."

Steinbrenner now felt that he had the best bullpen in the majors, a two-man system, with the veteran lefthander Sparky Lyle providing long relief and Gossage short relief. Lyle, however, felt that there was not room for both him and Gossage in the Yankee pen, and that he, Lyle, would be the one to go. "If we split the work," Lyle (with Peter Golenbock) wrote in The Bronx Zoo (1979), his chronicle of the 1978 Yankee season, "neither of us will be able to stay sharp . . . [and] between a guy who throws a 100-mile-an-hour heater, as Goose does, and an eighty-mile-an-hour slider, you'll see, it'll be Goose in there, not me." Lyle began asking out in March 1978, and he was finally traded to the Texas Rangers the following November.

After a miserable first few weeks in New York, Gossage hit his stride. In mid-season 1978 he again played in the All-Star game (his fourth), and he finished the season with a 10-11 record, a 2.01 ERA, and a league-leading twenty-seven saves. The greatest thrill of his career was his narrow save of the divisional playoff game against the Boston Red Sox in Fenway Park, Boston on October 2, 1978. Facing Carl Yastrzemski in the last half of the ninth inning, with two men on and two out and the Yankees leading 5-4, he found himself literally shaking with unwonted dread. In an interview with Joe Donnelly of Newsday (April 3, 1983), he remembered his thoughts as he tried to calm himself: "I felt like I was facing a firing squad. Then it came to me. I asked myself, 'What's the worst thing that can happen to me?' I had an answer. I'll be in the mountains of Colorado tomorrow. I guess to some it might sound silly, but it was like the weight of the world came off my shoulders. . . . Suddenly I could breathe. That last pitch I threw to Yaz, the one he popped up foul to [Graig] Nettles, that ball had a foot more on it than any other pitch I threw that day."

Gossage went on to pitch the victory over the Kansas City Royals that clinched the American League pennant for the Yankees, and in the World Series he blocked rallies by the Los Angeles Dodgers, giving up one hit and no runs in three games and winning the decisive game for the world championship. In 1978 Gossage was for the second time named the American League's Fireman of the Year. In addition, he was chosen Rolaids Relief Man of the Year.

In a clubhouse scuffle with Cliff Johnson on April 19, 1979, Gossage tore a joint ligament in his right thumb. With their ace reliever disabled for twelve weeks, the Yankees slumped, ultimately to fourth place in the American League East. The following year the team rebounded to first place in the division and Gossage tied for the league lead in saves, with thirty-three, and finished third in the voting for both the Cy Young Award and the Most Valuable Player in the American League. His biggest disappointment of the year came in the league championship series against the Kansas City Royals, in the third and final game of which George Brett turned one of his pitches into a game-winning three-run homer.

The Yankees took the American League championship in the strike-shortened 1981 season with the help of the one-two relief punch of Ron Davis, who would be sent in to hold a lead in the middle innings of a game, and Gossage, who would usually relieve Davis in the eighth or ninth inning. Many New York players not already alienated by George Steinbrenner's win-or-else attitude became so during the 1981 World Series, which the Yankees lost 6-2 to the Los Angeles Dodgers after winning the first two games. Following the second game, which Gossage saved, Steinbrenner's inopportune ranting in the clubhouse roiled the relief hurler, who sent a shoe flying angrily across the room. "We were two games up and it felt like we were two down," Gossage later recounted. "I was upset all winter. Believe me, we did not lose that World Series." The team as a whole was angered and demoralized when, following the final game of the series, Steinbrenner publicly apologized to the

New York fans for the loss of the world championship.

In a largely unprintable outburst caught on tape by a reporter and circulated privately among sports writers in 1982, Gossage excoriated "the Fat Man upstairs." In Steinbrenner's vain attempt to turn New York into a speed-based team, the Yankees went through three managers and forty-five players in 1982, and they plummeted to fifth place in the American League East. Gossage saved thirty games that year, and he had a 2.23 ERA. As of the end of the 1982 season his major-league career earned-run average was 2.90.

One of the oddest episodes in baseball history began on July 24, 1983, in a game between the Yankees and the Kansas City Royals in Yankee Stadium. The Yankees were leading 4-3 in the top of the ninth, with two outs, when George Brett of Kansas City hit a two-run homer off Gossage, putting the Royals in the lead, 5-4. The umpires nullified the home run, however, on the ground that Brett's bat had been doctored with pine oil to improve Brett's grip. Kansas City protested the umpires' ruling, and on July 28, 1983 Lee MacPhail, the president of the American League, restored the homer and ordered that the game be resumed where it had left off, in the top of the ninth with two outs and the Royals leading 5-4. The resumption, which took place on August 18, 1983, was a twelve-minute, sixteen-pitch affair in which no more scoring was done by either side. Mike Armstrong, the Kansas City starter, was credited with the win and Gossage with the loss. The Yankees finished the season in third place in the American League East, and Gossage had a 13-5 record, a 2.27 ERA, and twenty-two saves. His six-year Yankee statistics included 506 strikeouts in 518 innings and a 41-28 record.

Meanwhile, what he termed "the Steinbrenner show" had drained "all of the fun" out of baseball for Gossage. "There was never any room for the human element money can't buy," he later explained. "Why did he [Steinbrenner] have to remind us how much money we make . . . [to] shove it down our throats at meetings all the time?" Adding to his demoralization was the temperamental way that Yankee manager Billy Martin was using him, often issuing summonses in the middle of an enemy rally. (Gossage was accustomed to entering a game at the beginning of an inning; calling him in at mid-inning gave him neither time for settling down nor room for making errors.)

Wanting "to enjoy playing again," Gossage announced his decision to look elsewhere for employment in November 1983. Of the many offers that came to him from both leagues, the most attractive was that of the National League's San Diego Padres, with whom he signed a contract on January 6, 1984. The contract was a $6 million package covering five years, an option for a fifth year, and deferred compensation guaranteeing Gossage an annual income beyond his playing years, through the year 2016. Dick Williams, the San Diego manager, knowing that Gossage "throws harder when he's not pitching from the stretch,"

told the press that he would, with possible rare exceptions, call on the reliever only at the beginning of innings and that he would try never to use him before the eighth inning. "He's going to be one of our big, big men," Williams said. "And I certainly have no intention of abusing him."

In the middle of April 1984, when the Padres were already playing above .500, catcher Terry Kennedy told a reporter: "There is a feeling of finality when Goose goes out there, and you know he's going to win 80 percent of the time. You can't overstate what he means to this club. I knew he was going to have an impact, but, psychologically, I didn't think it would be like this." Later in the season the Padres took and kept the lead in the National League West, thanks in part to Gossage's saves, which totaled twenty-five in 102 innings by the end of the season. "It's the way I remember baseball from before I got to New York," Gossage said of his playing with the Padres. "Fun."

Abysmal performances by San Diego's starting pitchers in the postseason games in 1984 put an excessive burden on the bullpen. The middle-distance relievers and wrap-up king Gossage came through nonetheless in the five-game league championship series against the Chicago Cubs, in which Gossage pitched four innings and saved two games for the victorious Padres. Their heroics were insufficient to stop the Detroit Tigers in the World Series, however. Gossage was called to the mound twice in the world championship games, in a minor one-inning role in game four and as the "goat" in game five. Going into the latter game, the Tigers were leading the series three games to one. In the seventh inning of that game Gossage gave up a solo homer to Lance Parrish that advanced Detroit to a two-run lead. In the eighth, with men on second and third, Gossage faced the Detroit power hitter Kirk Gibson. San Diego manager Dick Williams instructed him to walk Gibson, but Gossage talked Williams into letting him pitch to the slugger. The result was a home run and the loss of the series to the Tigers.

Rich Gossage and Cornelia Lukaszewicz, his high-school girlfriend, were married on October 28, 1972. With their two sons, Jeffrey Carlton and Keith Michael, the Gossages live in Colorado Springs, near the mountain lakes and trails where Gossage spends much of his leisure time fishing and hunting. His other recreations include golf, racquetball, watching western movies, and listening to country music (Willie Nelson is a favorite). The pitcher is six feet three inches tall and has, in the description of Thomas Boswell of the *Washington Post* (May 18, 1981), a "puffy, pussycat face, which has a wispy, playful, almost zonked-out serenity." Mild-mannered, he himself finds "scary" the "meanness that comes out" of him on the mound. "It's a violent feeling," he has said, "and I'm not a violent person."

References: *Christian Sci Mon* p1+ O 20 '81 por; *Los Angeles Times* III p1+ Ja 7 '84 por, III p3 F 13 '84; *N Y Times* B p7 N 23 '77 por, C p1+ Je 4

'79 pors, C p1+ S 22 '80 pors; Newsday p120 O 1
'80 por; Sport 66:22+ Ap '78 por, 72:25 Jl '81 por;
Sporting News 192:2+ Ag 22 '81 por, 197:3 Mr 9
'84 por; Sports Ill 53:45+ S 29 '80 por, 55:64+ S 28
'81 pors; Washington Post E p1+ My 18 '81 pors;
Thorn, John. The Relief Pitcher (1979); Who's
Who in America, 1984–85

Hall, Donald

Sept. 20, 1928– Writer. Address: h. Eagle Pond
Farm, Danbury, N. H. 03230

Since the publication, almost three decades ago, of
Exiles and Marriages, his first book of poetry, Donald Hall has established a sterling reputation as
poet, prose stylist, and editor. Critics have savored
his musicality, humor, and lyricism, while his colleagues have admired the versatility of his technique, which has ranged widely over the years
from classical meters to syllabics, free verse, and
surrealism.

Although Hall is not by strict definition a "New
England poet" like Robert Frost, he has dealt in
much of his recent work with his childhood experiences in that region and in 1975 gave up his ten-
ured position as an English professor at the
University of Michigan to move back to the family
homestead in New Hampshire, the source for a
great deal of his inspiration. In addition to writing
and to giving hundreds of poetry readings, Hall
was associated with several BBC radio shows from
1959 to 1980; served as host, in 1974–75, of a series
of television interviews called Poets Talking; and
has recorded albums of poetry by Longfellow and
Whittier, among others.

Donald Andrew Hall Jr. was born in New Haven, Connecticut on September 20, 1928 to Donald
Andrew and Lucy (Wells) Hall. He grew up in the
nearby town of Hamden, where his father was the
treasurer for the family dairy business. Surrounded by books as a child, he quickly became en-
grossed in them, with the encouragement of both
his parents. He recalled in an autobiographical article for the New York Times Book Review (January 16, 1983) that his mother often read poetry to
him, including his childhood favorite, "The Moon's
the North Wind's Cooky," by Vachel Lindsay. An
only child, he turned to books for companionship
and entertainment. At first he read such staples of
juvenile fiction as The Hardy Boys and Bobbsey
Twins series, but he soon discovered the works of
Edgar Allan Poe, who became his literary idol: "I
wanted to grow up and be like Poe; I wanted to be
mad, addicted, obsessed, haunted and cursed; I
wanted to have eyes that burned like coals, profoundly melancholy, profoundly attractive." Not
surprisingly, his early short stories and poems,
which he began to write when he was twelve, were
rather morbid and in the Gothic tradition. The subject of his first poem, which he wrote to impress a
baby-sitter, was death, for example, and his later
juvenilia bore such chilling titles as "Blood" and
"Night-Walker."

From the time he was six, Hall spent at least part
of every summer vacation at Eagle Pond, his maternal grandparents' farm in New Hampshire.
During the mornings he read or wrote and helped
his grandfather, Wesley Wells, with the haying or
other chores later in the day. He preferred the farm
to his lonely life in Hamden and especially enjoyed listening to his grandfather talk about his ancestors or recite poems like "Casey at the Bat" or
"What the Deacon Said" from his seemingly inexhaustible repertoire. "I sat in the tie-up on a three-
legged stool," he reminisced in the New York
Times Book Review article, "watching him milk his
Holsteins as his dear voice kept time with his
hands and he crooned wonderful bad poems with
the elocutionary zeal of another century."

Although he continued to write fiction until he
was twenty, Hall concentrated on writing poetry,
and gradually T. S. Eliot and H. D. dethroned Poe
in his idolatry. During his two years at Hamden
High School, he began submitting his poems to major magazines, including The New Yorker, The
Nation, and The Atlantic, but with no success. But
"Wind-in-Storm," his imagistic poem patterned on
the work of H. D., was published in the high
school's annual literary magazine, The Cupola,
and won its first prize for poetry, and several obscure little magazines published some of his poems
in 1944. That fall he transferred to the Phillips Exeter Academy in New Hampshire, and the next
summer his parents sent him at his request to the
Bread Loaf Writers Conference, sponsored by
Middlebury College in Vermont.

Because "an undiagnosed illness" forced him to
miss a total of about a half-year's schooling that he
had to make up, Hall graduated from Exeter in

1947 after two and a half "grueling but intellectually useful" years of study and entered Harvard that fall. As a staff member on the *Harvard Advocate*, the university's prestigious literary magazine, he was associated with undergraduates who would later become some of the country's most renowned poets. As a tribute to the magazine on its eighty-fifth anniversary, he edited in 1950 an anthology of forty-eight items, mostly poetry and fiction, previously printed in the *Advocate* that had been written by Harvard undergraduates who later became famous. Published by Twayne, *The Harvard Advocate Anthology* included contributions by the historian Arthur M. Schlesinger Jr., the poets Wallace Stevens and T. S. Eliot, and the twenty-sixth and thirty-second presidents of the United States, Theodore and Franklin D. Roosevelt. The poet and translator Dudley Fitts, himself a Harvard alumnus, observed in the *New York Times Book Review* (April 8, 1951) that "no more fitting commemoration could be imagined than Mr. Hall's admirably chosen anthology."

During his years at Harvard, Hall was influenced by his friendships with other undergraduate poets—Robert Bly, John Ashbery, and Adrienne Rich, among others. Their discussions of poetry went further toward shaping his work and convincing him that he was a "writer," for good or ill, than, perhaps, his association with Robert Frost and other distinguished "elders," as he called them, including Archibald MacLeish and Richard Eberhart. "My early poetry concentrated on form entirely," he explained in *World Authors, 1950–1970*. "I was concerned that poetry should be only technique, and perfectly finite." His honors thesis, entitled "Yeats' Stylistic Development as Seen Through a Consideration of His Published Revisions of 'The Rose,'" reflected that interest; moreover, the Lloyd McKim Garrison prize that he received for his poetry collection "A Single Look," for which he used the pseudonym of Rhadamanthus Gall, reflected the growing mastery of his craft. In 1951 Hall also received Harvard's John Osborne Sergeant prize for Latin translation.

After graduating from Harvard with a B.A. degree in 1951, Hall was given a Henry fellowship to attend Oxford University. He studied "theoretical prosody, typical of [his] interests at that time," as he recalled in *World Authors*, and in 1953 obtained a B. Litt. degree. While at Oxford, he was secretary and later president of the Oxford Poetry Society, and in 1952 for his long poem "Exiles" he won an honor rarely accorded an American: the Newdigate Prize for narrative poetry. Returning to the United States in 1953, he studied in 1953–54 at Stanford University as a Creative Writing Fellow under the eminent poet and critic Yvor Winters.

As a Junior Fellow in the Society of Fellows at Harvard for the next three years, Hall enjoyed a "long episode of freedom" during which he "did nothing but read and write." He made good use of that opportunity: *Exiles and Marriages* (Viking, 1955), which included his Newdigate Prize–winning poem, was completed at that time

and was named the 1955 Lamont Poetry Selection by the American Academy of Poets. The poems in that autobiographical collection concerned his own early experiences and his marriage but, according to Hall, were primarily "keens over the dead, glorifying him [his grandfather Wesley Wells] as a saint of a destroyed civilization." *Exiles and Marriages* won praise from most reviewers for its wit, lyricism, and technique. According to the critic for *Time* (December 5, 1955), it was distinctive for "its own true tone composed in almost equal parts of intelligence and imagination."

In 1957 Hall joined the faculty of the University of Michigan at Ann Arbor as an assistant professor of English. A year after he moved to Michigan, Viking published his second book of poetry, *The Dark Houses* (1958), which consisted of two sections, "Houses on Residential Streets" and "Men Alone." Hall described it as "the book of [his] father's death, [which] largely examined the outward details of the life of the American suburbs" but also explored "an alternative to that life." Critical reaction was mixed. Although several reviewers expressed disappointment in what they considered to be his shallow but witty treatment of his subject, they once again singled out his technique for special praise. "Perhaps the principal achievement of the book," concluded the poet Thom Gunn in the *Yale Review* (December 1958), "is in Hall's use of syllabics and a kind of syllabic blank verse, two techniques by which he produces an effect where the deliberate flatness of a certain type of free verse is combined with the emotional control of regular meter."

A Roof of Tiger Lilies (Viking, 1964) evinced a marked change in Hall's style and thematic emphasis. He recalled in *World Authors* that as early as 1954 he "had begun to distrust the vanity of technique" and gradually envisioned "poetry as exploration of the inward continent of the spirit." Consequently, the verse in his third collection, much of which had been published previously in periodicals, often had a surrealistic, dream-like tendency. "Many of these poems," the writer of the dust jacket explained, "seem to consist wholly of direct actions and sensuous images; they often deal with magical transfiguration or metamorphosis, with the experience of *breaking out*." The critics generally welcomed Hall's shift of direction. In *Encounter* (March 1965), Martin Dodsworth rated *A Roof of Tiger Lilies* as an "excellent," if at times perplexing, book and though Robert Mazzocco complained that "psychologically, these poems do not fulfill themselves," he concluded in the *New York Review of Books* (April 8, 1965) that "aesthetically, [they are] Hall's most impressive achievement." The new poems in *The Alligator Bride* (Harper & Row, 1969)—revisions of poems from earlier collections constituted two-thirds of the volume—were cast from the same matrix, and the critic for the *Virginia Quarterly Review* (Spring 1970) discerned in them evidence of Hall's "continually deepening poetic awareness."

Hall continued his exploration of "the inward continent of the spirit" in his next three poetry collections—*The Yellow Room* (Harper & Row, 1971), *The Town of Hill* (David R. Godine, 1975), and *A Blue Wing Tilts at the Edge of the Sea* (Secker & Warburg, 1975). Of the three, *The Yellow Room*, a recounting of a failed love affair, was accorded the warmest critical reception. In her review for *Poetry* (January 1972), Phoebe Pettingell extolled Hall's imagery, which "create[s] a sensual picture conveying an emotion," and found his use of surrealism in the poems to be apt. She concluded, "Keeping his vision personal, without straining for generalities about love and loss, he writes honestly. . . . [This] is a commendable attainment."

Hall's teaching position at the University of Michigan had not made overwhelming demands on his time, and money he earned from giving poetry readings enabled him to take frequent leaves of absence. Nevertheless, in 1975 he "jettisoned tenure to live the improvised day," to use his words, and moved to Eagle Pond Farm, which he had bought on the death of his grandmother, Kate Wells. His return to the farm, which his family had owned for over a century, allowed him to concentrate full-time on his writing, but, perhaps more important, in going back to his origins, it gave him a sense of his personal and familial past. The poems in *Kicking the Leaves* (Harper & Row, 1978), all of which focus on death, grew out of his reflections on his ancestors and on his own place in the "continuum [of] the decades" that were spurred by his move to New Hampshire. The book was generously praised by the majority of critics. The noted poet Hayden Carruth, writing in *Harper's* (November 1978), found the collection "both excellent and deeply moving." *The Toy Bone* (Boa Editions), his most recent volume of poetry, was published in 1979.

Donald Hall has not limited his writing to poetry, however. He has edited several highly regarded poetry anthologies, including *The New Poets of England and America* (Meridian, 1957) with fellow poets Louis Simpson and Robert Pack and *A Choice of Whitman's Verse* (Faber, 1968). Two of his plays have been staged—*An Evening's Frost*, a tribute to Robert Frost that starred Will Geer and was first produced at the University of Michigan at Ann Arbor in 1965 and later Off Broadway at the Theatre De Lys; and *Bread and Roses*, which opened at the Power Center in Ann Arbor, Michigan in February 1975. His two biographies—*Henry Moore: The Life and Work of a Great Sculptor* (Harper & Row, 1966) and *Dock Ellis in the Country of Baseball* (Coward McCann, 1976)—were highly regarded by reviewers. His critical study *Marianne Moore: The Cage and the Animal* (Faber, 1970) was also warmly received. However, perhaps his best-known—and certainly his best-selling—work is his textbook *Writing Well* (Little Brown, 1973), which has sold over 400,000 copies. Mr. Hall is presently completing work on its fifth edition. From 1953 to 1962 Hall was the poetry editor of the *Paris Review*, and he has published three collections of essays about poetry.

One of Hall's most critically acclaimed prose works, *Remembering Poets: Reminiscences and Opinions* (Harper & Row, 1978), examines the last years of four great twentieth-century poets: Ezra Pound, Dylan Thomas, T. S. Eliot, and Robert Frost, all of whom he knew personally. A kind of latter-day Boswell, Hall modestly termed his work "literary gossip," but according to Seamus Cooney in his review for *Library Journal* (February 15, 1978), "his book blends well-honed anecdotes with amateur psychologizing and intelligent criticism in an agreeably readable fashion. . . . Interpretation, whether plausible or strained, is properly subordinated to the vivid sense of the living presence of the four poets." He has also published three collections of his essays on poetry. The critical consensus on his children's books, *Andrew the Lion Farmer* (Methuen, 1959; 1961), *Riddle Rat* (Warne, 1977), and *Ox-Cart Man* (Viking, 1979), was also favorable. In the *Horn Book* (February 1980), M. M. Burns described *Ox-Cart Man* as "a pastoral symphony translated into picture book format [in which] the stunning combination of text and illustrations re-creates the mood of nineteenth-century rural New England. . . . Quiet but not static, the book celebrates the peacefulness of a time now past but one which is still, nevertheless, an irrefutable part of the American consciousness." The American Library Association honored *Ox-Cart Man* with the 1980 Caldecott Medal.

The love of New England and "the peacefulness of a time now past" that informed *Ox-Cart Man* originated in the summers Hall spent as a child at Eagle Pond Farm, the stories with which Wesley Wells regaled him, and the experiences they shared. *String Too Short to be Saved* (Viking, 1961), a series of autobiographical essays in which he retails anecdotes about his ancestors and Eagle Pond Farm, and re-creates days of haying and blueberry-picking, paid tribute to his grandparents and a way of life he thought had died with them. In a chapter Hall appended to a later edition (Godine, 1979), he discussed his move back to the farm in 1975 and a significant discovery he made then. "The people remain, we belong among them, and they are not dead but endure. The dead are dead enough, and their descendants occupy new bodies, but *everything is the same*." "The people who live here . . . ," he continued, "take from the dead, and from the enduring land, qualities of frankness, wit, honesty, and goodness." Rural New England of the nineteenth century was also *his* rural New England, and in *String Too Short* and other recent articles and poems, Hall celebrates its timelessness. *Ragged Mountain Elegies*, a play he adapted from *String Too Short*, was commissioned by the Peterborough (New Hampshire) Players and ran for two weeks in the summer of 1983. That year, he was honored for his writings about New England with the Sarah Josepha Hale award.

Donald Hall shares his Eagle Pond home with his second wife, Jane Kenyon, a poet and lexicographer, whom he married on April 17, 1972. By his marriage to Kirby Thompson, which ended in divorce in 1969, he has two grown children, Andrew and Philippa. Among the many honors he has received are the Edna St. Vincent Millay Award of the Poetry Society of America (1955), the Longview Foundation award (1960), and two Guggenheim fellowships (1963-64, 1972-73). Since moving to the farm, he divides his time among a variety of writing projects, reading, and such chores as fueling the wood-burning stoves. For recreation, he plays table tennis, takes walks, and watches baseball on television.

Hall so much enjoys giving poetry readings that in recent years he has concentrated on writing poetry "in which the sound itself keeps the listeners intent." "The listener doesn't have to understand this poem intellectually," he has explained, "but to enjoy it as a sensual object, to take it into the ears and be moved by it." In his article in the New York Times Book Review he summed up the course his career as a poet has taken so far and his constant goals: "What began perhaps as the north wind's cooky—what continued variously as affectation and self-love; what zaps crazily up and down in public recognition—finds repose only in love of the art, and in the desire, if not precisely the hope, that you may make something fit to endure with the old ones."

References: Esquire 101:68+ Ja '84 por; N Y Times C p1 Ap 1 '81; N Y Times Book Rev p7+ Ja 16 '83 por; Contemporary Authors, new rev vol 2 (1981); Who's Who in America, 1984-85; World Authors, 1950-1970 (1975)

Hatfield, Mark O(dom)

July 12, 1922– United States Senator from Oregon. Address: b. Rm. 463, Russell Senate Office Bldg., Washington, D.C. 20510

NOTE: This biography supersedes the article that appeared in Current Biography in 1959.

"I pray for the integrity, justice, and courage to vote the correct vote, not the political vote," Republican Senator Mark O. Hatfield said in a recent interview for the publication Christianity Today. "It's a reckless style of politics, but it's the only style I know." Hatfield has been practicing his "reckless style of politics"—an amalgam of conservative theology and liberal philosophy—since his election to the Oregon state legislature in 1950. After sixteen years of experience in state government culminating in two terms as governor, he was elected in 1966 to the United States Senate where he has continued to support the policies of social responsibility and fiscal restraint that distinguished his gubernatorial tenure. Hatfield is, by his own admission, "fiercely independent," and he has frequently found himself standing virtually alone, most often as a critic of military adventurism, unwarranted and, in his view, immoral increases in defense spending, and "arrogant" and "dangerous" foreign policy initiatives.

Mark Odom Hatfield was born in the small town of Dallas, Oregon on July 12, 1922, the only child of Charles Dolen Hatfield, a railroad construction blacksmith, and Dovie (Odom) Hatfield, a schoolteacher. In the early 1930s the Hatfields moved to nearby Salem, the state capital, where Mark Hatfield completed his elementary and secondary education in the public schools. Precociously introduced to politics in 1932 by his mother, a staunch Republican, he made the rounds of his neighborhood, distributing handbills calling for the reelection of President Herbert Hoover. By the time he was in high school he was taking part in local Republican political campaigns either as a full-time volunteer or as a paid employee.

Following his graduation from Salem High School in 1940, Hatfield enrolled at Willamette University, a Methodist-affiliated college in Salem, as a political science major. His defeat in a bid to become student body president there is the only electoral setback of his career. Shortly after obtaining his B.A. degree in 1943, he joined the United States Navy. Assigned to a landing craft in the Pacific, he took part in the battles at Iwo Jima and Okinawa, and he was among the first Americans to see at firsthand the devastation caused by the atomic bombing of Hiroshima. Toward the end of his thirty-one-month tour of duty, he was engaged in the postwar transport of Chiang Kai-shek's troops from Vietnam to northern China. That experience had a profound influence on his personal and political philosophy. "I went into the Navy a small-town boy and a convinced isolationist," he said, as quoted in the *Saturday Evening Post* (May 9, 1959). "That was before I saw the want and waste in the world, before I saw men and women in Asian streets literally dying of hunger. I knew I could never be an isolationist again, and it was a painful awakening."

On his discharge from military service in 1945 with the rank of lieutenant (j.g.), Hatfield reenrolled at Willamette University, this time to study law. Deciding to study for an advanced degree in political science instead, he transferred to Stanford University in 1947. For his M.A. degree, which he received the following year, he submitted a thesis on the labor policies of President Hoover, whom he greatly admired. "I identified strongly with Herbert Hoover and his ideas," he explained in his autobiography *Not Quite So Simple* (Harper & Row, 1968). "I became a Republican for a composite of reasons—environmental, parental influences, and conviction, gained particularly during my studies at Stanford."

Returning to Salem, Hatfield joined the faculty of Willamette University as a political science instructor in 1949. Within a year, he was promoted to associate professor and was appointed dean of students, positions that he held until 1956. Meanwhile, he plunged into Republican party politics, becoming in short order state chairman of the Young Republican Policy Committee, an "action organization," a precinct committeeman, and vice-chairman of the party's county central committee. Eager to put his progressive political theories to the test, he announced in 1950 his candidacy for the state legislature. Running on the slogan "No Vote-Bait Promises, but Sound Legislative Action," he easily won a seat in the Oregon legislature. Hatfield served as a state representative from 1950 to 1954 and as a state senator from 1954 to 1956.

Since Willamette is located conveniently across the road from the Oregon statehouse, Hatfield continued to teach, though on a reduced schedule, while he served his three terms in the legislature, but on his election in 1956 to the post of secretary of state, the second-ranking elective office in the executive branch of Oregon's government, he resigned from the faculty. Two years later Hatfield decided that he was strong enough politically to risk a run for the governorship in the traditionally Democratic state. By capitalizing on the political errors of his opponent, incumbent Governor Robert D. Holmes, Hatfield withstood a nationwide Democratic landslide in the off-year election to become the youngest governor in the history of Oregon. He was reelected to a second term in 1962.

Fulfilling a campaign pledge to revitalize Oregon's moribund economy, Hatfield soon launched an aggressive promotional campaign to encourage exports, expand trade with the Far East, and lure new industry to the state. The fruits of his labors were a new all-time high in employment, the greatest economic expansion in the state's history to that date, and a substantial diversification of industry.

The economic development of Oregon was Hatfield's chief goal as governor, but he also devoted considerable time and effort to reorganizing and simplifying the state's cumbersome administrative structure and to lobbying for the human rights, education, labor relations, and environmental programs that he had so vigorously supported as a state legislator. In what was for him an agonizing decision, he refused to commute the sentence of a person condemned to death, though he is personally opposed to capital punishment. His view that an elected official must uphold the law of the land was also reflected in his stand against civil disobedience. While he believes in the individual citizen's right of public protest, he has always drawn the line at flagrant violation of the law because, in his view, it inevitably results in "a disorderly society . . . in which no one's rights can be guaranteed or protected."

Hatfield's personable appearance, considerable charm, and demonstrable success as governor of Oregon made him a popular figure with Republican bigwigs, who tapped him to nominate Richard Nixon for president at the party's national convention in 1960 and to deliver the keynote address in 1964. Yet Hatfield remained very much his own man. At annual National Governors' Conferences throughout his tenure as Oregon's chief executive, he tried repeatedly to persuade his counterparts to go on record in support of civil rights, and in 1965 and 1966 he stood alone in his refusal to endorse President Lyndon B. Johnson's Vietnam war policy. He was especially appalled by the American bombing of North Vietnam. "Terroristic or indiscriminate bombing must involve the deaths of noncombatant men, women, and children and merits the general condemnation of humanity," he explained, as quoted in the *New York Times* (November 9, 1966). "It cannot be justified as an instrument for the fulfillment of United States foreign policy."

Hatfield's opposition to the escalating war in Indochina became the key issue in his 1966 campaign for the United States Senate seat being vacated by Maurine B. Neuberger, since his Democratic rival, two-term Congressman Robert B. Duncan, was a staunch supporter of President Lyndon B. Johnson's Southeast Asian policies. To bring the wider impact of the war home, Hatfield reminded Oregonians in his stump speeches that the downturn in the state's lumber industry was in some degree an economic side effect of the war. Overcoming the built-in handicap of a Democratic registration edge of some 100,000 voters, Hatfield narrowly defeated Duncan by about 25,000 ballots. Partly because of his careful attention to the interests of his constituents (his office handles some 200 constituent cases each week), he fared considerably better in his reelection bids. In 1972 he surpassed former Senator Wayne Morse, a Republican turned Democrat and an even more vocal dove, by a plurality of 70,000 votes, and in 1978 he won election to a third term by an overwhelming majority against weak Democratic opposition.

Although he could have taken his Senate seat on January 3, 1967, Hatfield honored his commitment to complete his term as governor, which ended on January 9. Consequently, he was the last of the freshman senators to be sworn in and thus ranked 100th in seniority. But because the Republicans had done well at the polls that year, having made a net gain of four seats in the Senate, more committee assignments were open to Republican freshmen. Hatfield was assigned to the Senate Interior Committee, his first choice, to the Agriculture and Forestry Committee, and to the Select Committee on Small Business.

Hatfield's primary concern as a freshman legislator was the "de-Americanization" of the war in Vietnam. During his first term in office he supported or submitted many "end-the-war" bills, the most famous being the so-called Hatfield-McGovern Amendment that he and Senator George S. McGovern of South Dakota cosponsored in 1970. (That measure, which set a deadline of December 31, 1971 for the withdrawal of all United States troops from Indochina, was defeated in a 55-39 roll-call vote.) Undaunted by repeated legislative setbacks, Hatfield continued to press his case on the Senate floor and in public appearances across the country. By emphasizing the long-term domestic and international effects of continued participation in what was, in his view, "clearly a civil war," the senator hoped to persuade his fellow citizens that American involvement in the conflict was as politically misguided as it was morally wrong. His outspoken opposition to the war, which he described in 1973 as "a sin that scarred the national soul," cost him the support of Republican hardliners and earned him a place on President Richard Nixon's infamous "enemies list."

Throughout his senatorial career Hatfield has argued against the "negative" and "defensive" philosophy of anti-Communism as the determining factor in the formulation of American foreign policy. As he explained in his 1968 autobiography, the greatest threat to world peace is not untrammeled Communist aggression, but the "food-population crisis." To prevent Communist countries from successfully exploiting "the unmet hope of hungry and oppressed peoples in Africa, Asia, and Latin America," he has recommended that the United States adopt a "positive," "offensive" foreign policy based on a recognition of "the interests of the *people* of the world—not their governments." To that end he generally opposed large-scale foreign military assistance, including, most recently, the sale of sophisticated surveillance aircraft to Saudi Arabia, preferring to rechannel the funds into aid programs that directly benefit people.

For similar reasons Hatfield has regularly turned down increases in military appropriations earmarked by the Pentagon for the development and deployment of the B-1 bomber, the MX missile, the neutron bomb, and binary nerve gas, among other things. "There is to me a direct ratio between the increase of our arsenals and the diminishing sense of national security . . . ," he ex-

plained to Louise Sweeney in a *Christian Science Monitor* (June 17, 1982) profile. "There comes a time in a nation's life when additional money spent for rockets and bombs, far from strengthening national security, will actually weaken national security—when there are people who are hungry and not fed, people who are cold and not clothed." In keeping with that view, every year since 1977 Senator Hatfield has introduced the so-called World Peace Tax Fund Bill, which would allow conscientious objectors opposed to military spending to channel their tax dollars into "nonmilitary programs and special peacemaking projects" whereas the current system forces such citizens to either evade their taxes or compromise their moral or religious principles. The bill has never passed but continues to gain support each year.

Although he has consistently voted for the so-called "safety-net" social welfare programs, Hatfield advocates turning over the administration of those programs to local social welfare institutions and agencies, including private ones. In his commitment to improving the quality of life for all Americans, he has called for comprehensive environmental planning on all levels to "integrate our economy and our ecology" in ways that "demonstrate loving stewardship of the whole of creation," as he puts it. His legislative efforts in behalf of environmental protection include votes in favor of water pollution control, the reforestation of public lands, and the development of alternative energy sources.

A dedicated and responsible libertarian, Senator Hatfield has waged war on increasing governmental intrusions into the lives of individual citizens throughout his political career. At the height of the Vietnam war, for instance, he introduced a bill to abolish the draft, arguing that it constituted "a total governmental invasion of the liberties of America's young men." In order to give the individual more of a voice in his own government, Hatfield has proposed eliminating the electoral college in favor of direct election of the president, vice-president, and some cabinet secretaries, limiting the terms of senators and congressmen to twelve consecutive years, and perhaps most important, decentralizing government. His "neighborhood government" bill, which would return funds and power to local communities, was specifically designed to stimulate participatory democracy.

When the Republicans won control of the Senate in the 1980 election, Hatfield at last found himself in a position of some power, as the new chairman of the Appropriations Committee. Interpreting the results of the election as a mandate to rein in federal spending, he went along with President Ronald Reagan's budget- and tax-cutting proposals at first, but by 1982 he had modified his stance to retain needed social programs and to fund a public-works jobs bill. In September of that year he and Senator William Proxmire of Wisconsin joined forces to orchestrate an override of Reagan's veto of a $14.1 billion appropriations bill, handing the president his first major legislative defeat. The following year Hatfield, who favors a constitutional amendment requiring a balanced federal budget, tried to broker a lean fiscal 1984 budget that included sizable cuts in defense allocations, judicious trimming of social spending, and increased taxes to reduce the swollen deficit.

Determined to apply the same fiscal scrutiny to military spending proposals as the White House applied to social programs, Hatfield prodded the Pentagon to find ways to "get more security out of the same dollars," as he expressed it. A self-styled "nuclear pacifist, not a pacifist in general," he strongly objected to requests for funds to increase the United States' nuclear stockpile on economic as well as moral grounds. "It weakens America to commit over $200 billion over the next six years to nuclear weaponry at a time when the economy needs capital to modernize its production capability and channel more manpower and womanpower toward scientific and engineering fields so that we can better compete in the international marketplace," he explained, as quoted in U.S. News & World Report (April 5, 1982). "This, too, is a matter of national security."

As a first step toward raising the threshold for nuclear war, Hatfield cosponsored with Senator Edward M. Kennedy of Massachusetts a bipartisan resolution for a freeze on the testing, production, and deployment of nuclear weapons by the two superpowers. In his opinion, such a freeze could serve as the moral basis for extending a nuclear moratorium to the rest of the world. The two senators have donated the profits from sales of their citizens' handbook Freeze! How You Can Help Prevent Nuclear War (Bantam, 1982) to the national nuclear-freeze movement.

Early in his career as a public servant, Mark Hatfield, who had grown away from the institutional Protestant church of his youth, experienced a rebirth of his Christian faith. His religious reaffirmation was to affect profoundly his philosophy of government. Applying what he has described as the "Christ ideal" to politics, he insists that evangelicalism cannot be separated from social commitment. "You can't see merely the soul of man," he has said, as quoted in Time (September 19, 1969). "There is also the hunger of man, the sickness of man, the indecent, obscene poverty of man." Hatfield nevertheless dislikes the notion of Christians seizing the "levers of power" through sectarian political organizations. "When we try to form a new force," he has observed, "we're imitating the world and its means of exercising power. We have a greater power . . . expressed in love, compassion, and the other fruits of the Spirit." According to some longtime Washington observers, several prominent conservative Protestants came to espouse liberal political causes largely because of Hatfield's earnest and persuasive arguments.

Hatfield's religious beliefs recently became a political issue because he opposes abortion. In many interviews, however, the senator has explained that he bases his objection on constitutional grounds and on scientific research that, in his opinion, proves that life begins at conception. A strong supporter of federally funded family-planning programs, the senator himself favors prohibiting abortions except to save the mother's life, but in his legislative efforts he has preferred to leave the matter up to the individual states. His proposed 1983 amendment to the Constitution, which would have allowed the states to outlaw or restrict access to abortions, was rejected by the Senate in a 50–49 roll-call vote.

In July 1984, while running for a fourth term in the Senate, Hatfield came under fire when syndicated columnist Jack Anderson disclosed that Mrs. Hatfield had accepted $40,000 from the Greek entrepreneur Basil A. Tsakos, the founder and chairman of Trans-African Pipeline Corporation, of whose $10-billion oil-pipeline project Senator Hatfield had been a firm supporter. Tsakos and the Hatfields contended that the sum was a payment for Mrs. Hatfield's services; a real estate agent, she had helped Tsakos look for a residence and office in Washington, D.C., had given Mrs. Tsakos advice about redecorating it, and had counseled the couple about possible investments in Europe and the United States. But since the senator had written letters endorsing the pipeline proposal and had supported it in conversations with Secretary of Energy Donald P. Hodel and Senator James A. McClure, the chairman of the Senate Committee on Energy and Natural Resources, among others, some critics saw the checks given Mrs. Hatfield as a thinly disguised payment to the senator for using his influence to advance Tsakos' project. That view was reinforced by former employees of Tsakos who maintained that Mrs. Hatfield had rendered him no services and by the senator's financial-disclosure forms that revealed several large, outstanding debts of the Hatfields. Hatfield freely acknowledged his support of the pipeline but maintained that it was unjust to assume a connection between his career and that of his wife.

Later that month, he and his wife told a press conference that she had actually received a total of $55,000 from Tsakos and that they were donating the entire sum to charity. While admitting that he made "an error in judgment" by not asking his wife to disassociate herself from Tsakos once he himself became involved in the pipeline proposal, he denied any wrongdoing but added that as a public official he "should avoid even the appearance of impropriety." The Justice Department launched an inquiry into the matter, and Senator Hatfield also requested an investigation by the Senate Ethics Committee. That committee found insufficient grounds to warrant a further investigation into the charges of unethical conduct but reserved the right to reopen the case if the Justice Department were to find any incriminating evidence against him.

A slim, ruggedly handsome six-footer with blue eyes and graying brown hair, Mark Hatfield has "an aura of old-fashioned goodness as palpable as pine soap," according to Louise Sweeney. He is, by his colleagues' accounts, unpretentious and amiable, and his wide circle of friends includes a number of legislators and government officials, among them Senator John C. Stennis of Mississippi, a notorious hawk whose views are diametrically opposed to his own. In his rare free moments the senator gardens, studies theology and philosophy, or reads political biographies and novels. Married since July 8, 1958, Hatfield and his wife, the former Antoinette Marie Kuzmanich, a real estate broker and the author of several cookbooks, have four children: Elizabeth, Mark Odom Jr., Theresa, and Charles Vincent. Senator Hatfield has lectured extensively, and he has written many articles and several books, among them *Conflict and Conscience* (Word, Inc., 1971) and *Between a Rock and a Hard Place* (Word, Inc., 1976), about his evangelical faith and its relationship to his political life.

Once, when on a trip to India, Hatfield was assured by Mother Teresa of Calcutta that in struggling against the abysmal poverty around her, the Lord had not called her to be successful, only to be faithful. Hatfield has said: "I'm not Mother Teresa, but I take a pragmatic view and can recall that to my own role." On November 6, 1984 he was elected to a fourth term in the Senate, defeating the Democratic challenger, Oregon State Senator Margie Hendricksen.

References: Christian Sci Mon B p1+ Je 17 '82 por; Christianity Today p18+ O 22 '82 por; N Y Times B p10 Ap 1 '82 por, IV p4 S 30 '84; Newsweek 78:21 Jl 19 '71, 88:75 O 25 '76, 104:43 Ag 20 '84 por; Time 94:60 S 19 '69; Contemporary Authors vols 77-80 (1979); Douth, George. Leaders in Profile (1975); Eels, Robert and Nyberg, Bartell. Lonely Walk (1979); Who's Who in America, 1984-85; Who's Who in American Politics, 1983-84

Hawking, Stephen W(illiam)

Jan. 8, 1942– British physicist. Address: h. 5 West Rd., Cambridge, England.

Stephen W. Hawking, the Lucasian professor of mathematics at Cambridge University, is widely regarded as the most brilliant theoretical physicist since Albert Einstein. Hawking is, in his own words, "primarily interested in gravity—on all scales," from the galactic vistas of Einstein's general theory of relativity, where stars live and die with predictability, to the subatomic world of quantum mechanics, where elementary particles behave unexpectedly. He is best known for his calculations of the physics of the hypothetical apertures in the fabric of space-time known as black holes. Those calculations have advanced the prospect of a unified field theory reconciling the varying laws of general relativity, quantum mechanics, and classical thermodynamics in its description of how our universe began and how it works. Hawking's ability to soar creatively in cosmological thought has been abetted by a severe physical disability: since 1963 he has been afflicted with the slow, wasting neuromuscular disorder popularly known as Lou Gehrig's disease, for which there is no known cure.

The oldest of four children of Frank Hawking, M.D., a prominent research biologist, Stephen William Hawking was born on January 8, 1942 in Oxford, England. He grew up in London, where his father headed the division of parasitology at the National Institute for Medical Research, and in the London suburb of St. Albins, where he was a good but not outstanding student at St. Albins School. "I always wanted to know how everything worked," he told Dennis Overbye in an interview for a profile in *Omni* (February 1979). "I would take things apart to see how they worked, but they didn't often go back together."

Hawking was drawn to science from his earliest years, but he decided not to follow his father into medicine and biology because he felt that "the biological subjects were too inexact, too descriptive," as he explained to Overbye. "It is only with molecular biology that the basic interactions have come to be studied." In 1959-60, his first year at University College, Oxford University, he read mathematics, and he took up physics the following year. "He did very little work, really, because anything that was do-able he could do," Robert Berman, his physics tutor, recalled, as quoted by Michael Harwood in the *New York Times Magazine* (January 23, 1983). "It was only necessary for him to know that something could be done, and he could do it without looking to see how other people did it. . . . He didn't have very many [books], and he didn't take notes. Of course, his mind was completely different from all of his contemporaries', and he did, I think, positively make an effort to come down to their level and, you know, be one of the boys. . . . He coxed the college second eight, and he was very popular." Hawking's independent ways and casual study habits resulted in a final examination score that put him on the borderline between first and second class honors, necessitating, as Berman recounted, an oral exam. "And of course the examiners then were intelligent enough to realize they were talking to someone far cleverer than most of themselves."

Before receiving his B.A. degree at Oxford, in 1962, Hawking considered staying on at the university for graduate work in astronomy, but the observatory there was equipped only for the observation of sunspots, "and, anyway," as he explained to Dennis Overbye in the Omni interview, he "was always more interested in theory than in observation." He decided he had "better go to Cambridge, where they did have work on theoretical astronomy" and cosmology, which applies creative thinking as well as scientific knowledge to the study of the character of the universe. Hawking found cosmology "exciting, because it really did seem to involve the big question: Where did the universe come from?"

No sooner had Hawking installed himself under the tutelage of the cosmologist Dennis W. Sciama at Cambridge University than he was struck by what he calls "that terrible thing"—amyotrophic lateral sclerosis, an incurable deterioration of the motor neurons of the spinal cord, medulla, and cortex. It disables skeletal muscles, affecting speech, swallowing, limbs, and shoulders and usually ending in fatal atrophy of the chest muscles. On the bright side, if it may be called that, it is, according to its victims, painless, and, fortunately for a thinker such as Hawking, it does not affect the brain or the senses.

Depressed by the prospect of progressive physical atrophy and, perhaps, early death, he made little progress in research during his first two years at Cambridge. Then the disease began to stabilize, and it appeared that he would survive, albeit disabled. With the encouragement of Sciama, he summoned his natural buoyancy and returned to work on his Ph.D. degree. The real "turning point," in his view, was his marriage to Jane Wilde, a student of languages, in 1965. "It made me determined to live," he recalled, as quoted by John Boslough in Science '81 (November 1981), "and it was about that time that I began making professional progress."

Hawking made that initial progress in collaboration with his friend and Cambridge colleague Roger Penrose. He and Penrose applied a new, intricate mathematical method of their own devising to the general theory of relativity, developed by Albert Einstein to explain how gravity affects the behavior of the universe and its large systems. Out of Einstein's predictions came the concept now known as the black hole, a term coined by the Princeton cosmologist John A. Wheeler to denote a cosmological mystery that has fascinated astrophysicists for decades. As explained by Karl Schwartzschild, Robert J. Oppenheimer, and others, one of the ways a black hole might be created is by the gravitational collapse of a star of sufficient mass (ten times that of our sun). When the dying star exhausts its thermonuclear fuel, it succumbs to the pressure of its own gravity and collapses inward, shrinking to a point of such density that not even light can escape to infinity. The star is obliterated from the observable universe, and in its place is left a ghostlike pocket of gravity sucking any object within its "event horizon" toward its vortex, known as a "singularity," a particle of infinite density, zero volume, and infinite gravitational field.

In such a particle, space is "bent" and time as we know it ends. "Because all known laws of physics are formulated on a classical space-time background, they will all break at a singularity," Hawking has pointed out. "This is a great crisis for physics because it means one cannot predict the future. One does not know what will come out of a singularity." Most astrophysicists assumed that singularities would prove to be only mathematical artifacts, because, according to Newtonian principles, such a contraction to infinite density could not happen in the real universe. In a paper he published in 1965, however, Penrose demonstrated that, for a singularity to occur, the gravitational collapse of a star need not proceed in a smooth, symmetrical manner and could thus actually occur if certain conditions were met in the physical universe.

In effect, Penrose proved that, if general relativity is correct, space-time can reach a singularity. The following year, Hawking adapted the same method to show, inversely, that "time has a beginning," that our universe need not be perfectly smooth in its evolution to have come out of a singularity. Taking into account the theory of general relativity and the observable asymmetry of our universe, he demonstrated that one could run the cosmic clock backward to the singularity in which the "Big Bang" occurred, sixteen or seventeen billion years ago. "The big question," he later explained, "was, Was there a beginning or not? Roger Penrose and I discovered that, if general relativity is correct, there did have to be a beginning."

Hawking's theorem was first argued in the last chapter of his "Properties of the Expanding Universe," the thesis for his Ph.D. degree, which he received in 1966. Remaining at Cambridge as a fellow of Gonville and Caius College, as a member of the graduate staff of the Institute of Theoretical Astronomy, and as a member of the department of applied mathematics, he, together with Penrose, refined his mathematical techniques and further developed his predictions about singularities, the space-time continuum, and the fate of matter in the path of that continuum. "This work," he later recounted, "culminated in a general all-purpose singularity theorem of Hawking and Penrose in 1970." Included in that theorem was the prediction that while singularities cannot be observed, because they violate the manifold of space and time, the black holes in which they occur can be detected by their surface boundaries, the event horizons, which would be calculable as wave-fronts of light.

"The first hint that there might be a connection between black holes and thermodynamics," Hawking recounted in his paper "The Quantum Mechanics of Black Holes," published in the January 1977 *Scientific American*, "came with the mathematical discovery in 1970 that the surface area of the event horizon, the boundary of a black hole, has the property that it always increases when additional matter or radiation falls into the black hole." Moreover, he went on, if two black holes merge, the resulting black hole has an event horizon area greater than the sum of those of both. This suggested an analogy to the concept of entropy—a measure of the disorder of a system—in thermodynamics, the second law of which is that entropy always increases with time.

The analogy between the properties of black holes and the laws of thermodynamics was extended by Hawking, James M. Burdeen, and Brandon Carter when they related the change in mass of a black hole to a change in the area of the hole's event horizon, a temperature-proportionality in keeping with the first law of thermodynamics, which says that a small change in the entropy of a system is accompanied by a proportional change in the energy of the system. Seeking a clearer understanding of the entropy of a black hole, Hawking, Carter, and others, following a suggestion put forth by Jacob D. Bekenstein in 1972, arrived at the "no-hair" theorem, so called because it predicts that a black hole preserves no details of its pre-collapse entity other than the parameters of mass, angular momentum, and electric charge. The apparent "fatal flaw" in Bekenstein's suggestion, as Hawking explained in his *Scientific American* article, was "that if a black hole has a finite entropy that is proportional to the area of its event horizon, it ought to have a finite temperature, which would be proportional to its surface gravity," and "this would imply that a black hole could be in equilibrium with thermal radiation at some temperature other than zero." According to classical concepts, "no such equilibrium is possible because the black hole would absorb any thermal radiation that fell on it but by definition would not be able to emit anything in return."

Hawking resolved the paradox encountered in large black holes, where only general relativity was assumed to apply, only after turning to the study of minuscule black holes, the scale of which is that of subatomic particles, the domain of quantum mechanics, a theory Einstein did not fully accept because of its intrinsic uncertainty. Quantum theory supposes that space is not empty but, rather, full, teeming with pairs of particles and antiparticles that are forever materializing and canceling each other out. Using quantum theory, Hawking reasoned that there could be black holes other than those formed in the death throes of stars and that millions of such holes, the size of subatomic protons, could have been thrust into existence by the force of the primordial Big Bang.

Carrying quantum mechanics over into his investigation of what the behavior of matter in the vicinity of a black hole would be, Hawking found, to his great surprise, and consternation, that "the black hole seemed to emit particles at a steady rate." At first reluctant to believe his own finding, he finally became convinced that "it was a real physical process" because "the outgoing particles have a spectrum that is precisely thermal." While large black holes emit particles slowly, he predicted, mini-holes, emitting at a much higher temperature, eventually explode, becoming "white" holes from which energy and particles gush.

The prediction that "the black hole creates and emits particles just as if it were an ordinary hot body with a temperature that is proportional to the surface gravity and inversely proportional to the mass" made fully consistent Bekenstein's suggestion that a black hole had a finite entropy, because the prediction implied that a black hole could be in thermal equilibrium at some finite temperature other than zero. Hawking's mini–black hole calculations also provided an answer to the puzzle of the "missing mass" necessary to close the universe. According to those calculations, the unpredictability of the particles at the frontier of a black hole was even greater than that which was usually associated with quantum mechanics. Usually, either the position or the velocity of particles was unpredictable. In this instance, neither one was predictable. As Hawking observed in the *Scientific American*, "It therefore seems that Einstein was doubly wrong when he said, 'God does not play dice.' Consideration of particle emission from black holes would seem to suggest that God not only plays dice but also sometimes throws them where they cannot be seen."

Hawking presented his mathematical evidence that a black hole could emit thermally in the paper "Black Hole Explosions?," delivered at an Oxford University symposium in February 1974. Most of his startled colleagues at first rejected the evidence. Even after the evidence was confirmed by others using various different approaches, it continued to represent perhaps the greatest challenge ever presented to theoretical physics. In unreconstructed general relativity theory, black holes could only get larger and could not emit anything. But, from the point of view of quantum mechanics, black holes could literally evaporate and explode, causing entropic disorder. The "Hawking radiation," as emissions from black holes came to be known, demonstrated dramatically that black holes did not exist apart from the rest of the universe but, despite severance from the space-time continuum, affected it in important ways. Additionally, for cosmologists, the possibility that black holes emit matter strengthened their link to the Big Bang theory of the origin of the universe.

Named a research assistant in the department of applied mathematics and theoretical physics at Cambridge in 1973, Hawking was promoted to professor of gravitational physics in 1977. Because of his physical handicaps he was exempted from arduous lecturing and teaching duties and was thus given the freedom to concentrate singlemindedly on his research. The most far-reaching result of Hawking's black hole research has been its contribution to the advancement of the nascent theory of "supergravity," the most likely unifier of the quantum and general relativity theories. In the lecture Hawking gave on the occasion of his inauguration as Lucasian professor of mathematics at Cambridge on April 29, 1980, he pointed out that a unified field theory would have to reconcile four kinds of interaction known to physics: "In order of strength they are the strong nuclear force, which works only at the atomic level; electromagnetism; the weak nuclear force, which controls radioactive decay; and finally, the weakest by far, gravity, which interacts with everything. . . . At the moment the only candidate to unify all four forces is supergravity, which relates particles with vastly different characteristics through a theory called supersymmetry. . . . If the theory survives testing, it will probably be some years before we develop computational methods that will enable us to make predictions and before we can account for the initial conditions of the universe as well as local physical laws."

With G. R. R. Ellis, Hawking wrote *The Large Scale Structure of Space-Time*, published by Cambridge University Press in 1973, and he collaborated in the editing of the Cambridge University Press volumes *General Relativity: An Einstein Centenary Survey* (with Werner W. Israel, 1979) and *Superspace and Supergravity* (with M. Roč̌ek, 1981), the proceedings of the 1980 Nuffield Workshop at Cambridge. He is a member of the prestigious Royal Society of London, and his many honors include the Albert Einstein Award, the Maxwell Medal, and several honorary degrees.

Stephen W. Hawking is slight, weighing no more than 120 pounds, and boyish looking, except for the wrinkles around his eyes. In his waking hours he is confined to a motorized wheelchair, the operation of which is one of the few things he can do physically. He controls the movement of the wheelchair by the pressure of his left hand, the only limb that retains a vestige of power. Unable to hold a book, he reads with the aid of an automatic page-turner. While he can use a computer especially adapted for him, he cannot write, and his indistinct speech is understandable only to those who know him well, who interpret for visitors. His writing is done in his head and dictated to a secretary.

Blessed with a superior memory, Hawking uses his brain as a mental blackboard. "I tend to avoid equations as much as possible," he told Michael Harwood in the *New York Times Magazine* interview. "I simply can't manage very complicated equations, so I have developed geometrical ways of thinking instead. I choose to concentrate on problems that can be given a geometrical, diagrammatic interpretation. I can manage equations so long as they don't involve too many terms. . . . Often I work in collaboration with someone else, and that is a great help, because they can do all the equations."

Don Page, one of the favored few of Hawking's protégés (he lived with the Hawking family during three years of post-doctoral work at Cambridge), explained to Harwood that the necessity of working in his head forces Hawking to "get really to the heart of the matter and try to eliminate inessential details." This gives his papers "a great deal of elegance and beauty, because they really speak of the essential things, although sometimes it does have the unfortunate aspect that those of us who don't understand all the details may find some connecting arguments missing." Hawking's necessity is theoretical physics' gain, because the *sine qua non* of the expansion of the frontiers of the science is not precise calculation but great organizational ideas from which such calculation can issue. Hawking comes up with the overview principles and leaves the working-out of technical details and the comparison with practical experimentation to his collaborators. He arrives at new ideas by an intuitive leap and then tries to justify it by filling in the intermediate steps. If the intermediate steps do not work, he gives the idea up.

Hawking and his wife, Jane, have two sons, Timothy and Robert, and a daughter, Lucy. The Hawkings live on the ground floor of a Victorian mansion owned by Cambridge University, a ten-minute wheelchair ride from Hawking's office. "I think Stephen has achieved an important ambition—to extend the bounds of human knowledge by just one step," Mrs. Hawking said when Dennis Overbye interviewed her for the *Omni* article. "Not many of us are in a position to do it. . . . He hasn't wasted any of his talents at all. In fact, he's intensified them." Hawking himself told Overbye that he is "happier now" than he was before the onset of his illness: "I was very bored with life. I drank a fair bit, I guess; I didn't do any work. . . . When one's expectations are reduced to zero, one really appreciates everything that one does have." In his *Science '81* article, John Boslough described his first encounter with Hawking as "shocking." "His condition seems far worse than one expected," Boslough wrote. "But after a short time with this gentle, witty man, one forgets the illness." Hawking told Boslough: "My goal is simple. It is complete understanding of the universe."

References: N Y Times Mag p16+ J 23 '83 pors; Omni 1:44+ F '79 por; Science '81 2:66+ N '81 pors; Boslough, John. Stephen Hawking's Universe (1984); McGraw-Hill Modern Scientists and Engineers (1980); Who's Who, 1984-85

Hersh, Seymour (Myron)

Apr. 8, 1937– Investigative reporter; author.
Address: b. 1236 National Press Bldg.,
Washington, D.C. 20045; h. 3214 Newark St.
NW, Washington, D.C. 20008

During the 1960s and 1970s when frequent disclosures in the press about governmental covert activities at home and abroad raised the status of investigative reporters to that of cultural heroes, Seymour Hersh was labeled "an almost unrivaled master of the governmental exposé." His articles on the massacre at My Lai won him instant celebrity, which was reinforced by his later "scoops" on CIA domestic spying and the wiretaps of Henry Kissinger's aides, among others. Although critics charge that Hersh uses "dirty tricks" to get information, his extensive investigations have resulted in award-winning articles, a 1970 Pulitzer Prize, and four controversial books. In 1968 Hersh made a brief excursion into politics, when he served as Senator Eugene J. McCarthy's press secretary during the New Hampshire presidential primary. When asked what drives him to continue his journalistic inquiries, he responds, "I just want people to know the truth."

Seymour Myron Hersh, who was born on April 8, 1937 in Chicago, Illinois to Isadore and Dorothy (Margolis) Hersh, enjoyed a "very happy childhood" while growing up with his twin brother and older sisters, also twins, on Chicago's South Side. His father ran a dry-cleaning plant where Seymour sometimes worked. Raised like "a Jewish prince," to use his words, he had "no idea what [he] wanted to be." After attending the University of Chicago for three-and-a-half years, he received his B.A. degree in history in 1958. He then entered the university's law school but left after one year because of poor grades.

Hersh began his journalism career in 1959 as a copy boy and later as a police reporter for the Chicago City News Bureau, which has served as a proving ground for several prominent newspapermen early in their careers. He quit that "torture chamber," as he called it, after half a year and worked for the next six months as a public information officer at Fort Riley, Kansas. Returning to Chicago in 1961, Hersh and a former City News Bureau colleague founded a suburban newspaper, but he left the partnership after a year. Turning next to the wire services, he signed on in 1962 as a reporter for United Press International in Pierre, South Dakota, but when he was refused a transfer to UPI's Washington bureau he went to work in Chicago for the Associated Press in 1963, joined its Washington press corps in 1965, and was promoted to Pentagon correspondent in 1966.

Working at the Pentagon, Hersh learned to be skeptical when he discovered attempts by the military to manipulate the news and to cover up operations that would evoke an explosive public response if they were ever revealed. He wrote an article for the *New Republic* about one such operation: the stockpiling of nerve gas by the Army at its overseas command posts. Some of his pieces also portrayed his fellow reporters at the Pentagon in less than complimentary terms. However, it was a lengthy article by him on chemical and biological warfare (CBW) that AP "butchered," to use his term, by cutting it by 80 percent that spurred Hersh to quit that wire service in June 1967 to become a free-lance investigative reporter.

In spite of the problems he faced at the City News Bureau, UPI, and AP, Hersh believes that the reportorial positions he held early in his career provided him with excellent training. In a February 23, 1975 interview with Rone Tempest for the *Detroit Free Press*, Hersh explained: "I learned the business from the bottom up and I think it had a terrific impact. I think I had a great background. I spent four years with AP and learned how to write, re-write and edit. I feel that a lot of that stuff was invaluable in the shaping of my career."

After leaving AP, Hersh continued his probings into chemical and biological warfare and published several articles on the subject in the *New Republic*, the *New York Times*, and the *New York Times Magazine*. He expanded his investigations into his first book, *Chemical and Biological Warfare: America's Hidden Arsenal* (Bobbs-Merrill, 1968), in which he detailed the history of CBW, the development of American policy on it, the effects of chemical and biological agents, and their use in the Vietnam war. He also catalogued the military and civil organizations in the United States conducting classified research in the field and described the extent of similar programs in other countries. Although the London *Times* labeled him "the Ralph Nader of America's chemical and biological armory," his work had less of an initial impact than that of the well-known consumer crusader. In an interview with Richard Lee in the *Washington Post* (July 12, 1970), Hersh recalled,

"Somehow it failed to make much of a mark at first. The public and the press simply did not want to believe that the United States was stockpiling nerve gas at Army commands overseas."

Most reviewers lauded Hersh's book as a painstaking and thorough study of a controversial subject, but C. J. Thoman, writing in *Best Sellers* (July 15, 1968), complained about his anti-CBW bias. "Obviously sincere attempts to explain the rationale behind CBW research and development are almost sneeringly brushed aside. . . . On the other hand, facts and statements that support the author's thesis are greeted with rapture." Information from Hersh's work was subsequently used in a congressional inquiry into CBW, and many credit his book with influencing President Nixon's decision to stop the production of biological weaponry.

On October 22, 1969 a telephone call from Geoffrey Cowan, a Washington, D.C. lawyer, set Hersh on the trail of the facts about the My Lai massacre, as it came to be known, another story that the American public at first refused to believe. Cowan explained that a lieutenant was to be secretly court-martialed at Fort Benning, Georgia for the murder of seventy-five civilians in Vietnam. (The number eventually reached more than 450.) Noted for his doggedness, Hersh spent about two days and made more than twenty-five telephone calls to his contacts at the Pentagon before he came up with some "sketchy details" about the incident. More phone calls revealed the name of the accused: Lieutenant William L. Calley Jr. Using the "standard newspaperman's bluffing operation," that is, "pretending to know more than [he] did," he further prodded his sources, discovering in the process that the military considered the My Lai tragedy to be a freak occurrence perpetrated by war-weary soldiers "gone berserk." Through his perseverance and with the support of a $2,000 grant from the Philip Stern Family Fund for Investigative Journalism, Hersh tracked down and conferred with Calley's lawyer, George Latimer, who formerly had sat on the Court of Military Appeals; he ferreted out Calley, who had been hidden by the military; and he conducted an interview with the twenty-six-year-old lieutenant. The resulting article, the first of five stories in Hersh's award-winning series, was written during the flight back to Washington.

Both *Life* and *Look* had refused the story, but David Obst, a neighbor of Hersh in Washington, agreed to try to sell it through his small syndicate, the Dispatch News Service, which had placed articles by correspondents in Vietnam and Asia. Offered to fifty newspapers for $100, the My Lai story was bought by thirty-six. Such newspapers as the London *Times*, the *Boston Globe*, and the *San Francisco Chronicle* featured it on their front pages. Hersh and Obst also reportedly collected $10,000 from CBS for arranging an exclusive interview with Paul Meadlo, a private in Calley's platoon who had admitted taking part in the atrocity.

For the next five months Hersh traveled around the country, gathering information through inter-

views with more than fifty GIs who were with Calley at My Lai for his four later articles and his second book, *My Lai 4; A Report on the Massacre and Its Aftermath* (Random House, 1970). For his coverage of the incident Hersh received the Pulitzer Prize for international reporting in 1970, the Long Island University Department of Journalism's George Polk Memorial Award, the Worth Bingham Prize, and the Sigma Delta Chi Distinguished Service Award and Bronze Medallion. His reportage also brought him instant fame, including appearances on talk shows and on *60 Minutes*. When asked by Rone Tempest during the *Detroit Free Press* interview whether the personal publicity hurt his effectiveness as a reporter, Hersh replied, "No, it doesn't hurt your effectiveness. It's just a pain in the neck. If anything, it's probably a plus for your effectiveness. Let's face facts, people like dealing with a celeb."

Not everyone welcomed Hersh's disclosures about the massacre. He received a lot of hate mail, including one letter in which he was excoriated as a "sleazy goon" and as a "heinous hack," his favorites among all the abusive epithets. The reviewers, however, approved both of his investigation and the book *My Lai 4*. Voicing the critical consensus in the *Saturday Review* (May 30, 1970), Tran Van Dinh extolled the book as an "eloquent testimony to the high quality, vigor, and vigilance of American journalism and reporting. Mr. Hersh richly deserved his Pulitzer Prize."

Cover-Up: The Army's Secret Investigation of the Massacre at My Lai (Random House, 1972) discussed the Army hearings on My Lai, which were conducted by a panel headed by General William R. Peers, and the prosecution of Calley. Like Hersh's other two books about his investigations, *Cover-Up* was commended by reviewers. In *Book World* (April 2, 1972), Robert Sherrill hailed *Cover-Up* as "another of Hersh's awesome reporting achievements," and Arthur Prager informed his *Saturday Review* (April 1, 1972) readers that Hersh had done a "masterful job of investigative reporting, raking back into the light a number of facts the American public would rather forget."

Several interviewers have questioned Hersh about his reasons for conducting such exhaustive and exhausting inquiries. Although he admits that he is "big on scoops," he contends that neither publicity nor money is his primary motivation: he simply "hate[s] secrets." As he explained to Robert Lee in an interview for the *Washington Post's Potomac* magazine (July 12, 1970), "There was a story people needed to know about. I had this *total outrage* that this stuff goes unreported."

In 1972, to "accomplish more and reach more people" than he could as an independent reporter, Hersh joined the staff of the *New York Times*—the newspaper that had turned him down for a job in 1967. During the seven years that he spent as an investigative reporter for the *Times* in New York (1975–78) and at its Washington bureau (1972–75, 1978–79), Hersh added to his impressive list of "scoops": Secretary of State Henry A. Kissinger's authorization of wiretaps on seventeen National Security Council aides; President Richard Nixon's secret war in Cambodia; the theft of secret documents from Kissinger's office by Pentagon agents; the CIA's unsuccessful, covert attempt to raise a sunken Soviet submarine from the Pacific with the *Glomar Explorer*; and the CIA's domestic surveillance operations in violation of its charter.

A. M. Rosenthal, the executive editor of the *New York Times*, once "proudly refer[red] to . . . Hersh as the most valuable journalism property in the country," according to Joe Eszterhas, writing in *Rolling Stone* (April 10, 1975). Hersh annexed more honors for his reporting during his tenure at the *Times*, confirming "Abe" Rosenthal's estimation of his abilities. In 1973 he won the Front Page and Scripps-Howard awards and his second George Polk Memorial plaque for his exposé of the secret and unauthorized bombings of North Vietnam ordered by Air Force General John D. Lavelle. His stories on domestic spying by the CIA brought him a Sidney Hillman prize and another Polk award in 1974, and he earned a Drew Pearson prize in 1976 for his report on the CIA's involvement in the toppling of President Salvador Allende's regime in Chile. In 1975 he received a John Peter Zenger Freedom of the Press Award.

In 1979 Seymour Hersh left the *New York Times* to write another book. Although he has described working there as a "form of bondage," he admits that he "enjoyed" it. "It's a very, very good place to write stories," Hersh has said. "It's credible, the editing is very good. It's a love-hate relationship." In recent years several pieces by Hersh have appeared in the *New York Times*, including a two-part article, "The Qaddafi Connection," about a group of ex-CIA agents and military men who sold their expertise and restricted materials to Libyan terrorists.

After his departure from the *New York Times* Hersh engaged in extensive research and conducted over 1,000 interviews to produce his "densely detailed" exposé of Henry A. Kissinger, *The Price of Power; Kissinger in the Nixon White House* (Summit Books, 1983). Its thesis is that in his drive for self-aggrandizement and power Kissinger was willing to undertake anything, regardless of the human cost. One of the book's more controversial allegations is that during the 1968 presidential race Kissinger provided secret information on the Vietnam peace talks in Paris, which he had gathered through his close association with President Lyndon B. Johnson, to members of Nixon's campaign staff in order to win admission to Nixon's inner circle. Hersh also charges that, at the same time, Kissinger tried to ingratiate himself with the Democratic contender, Hubert H. Humphrey, by giving his aides Nelson A. Rockefeller's personal files on Nixon. *The Price of Power* also discusses the Nixon administration's supposed role in the overthrow of Chilean president Salvador Allende and of Norodom Sihanouk, ruler of Cambodia, and suggests a connection between SALT negotiations and the sale of wheat by the United States to the Soviet Union in 1972.

Although Hersh also took the press to task in his latest book for its failure to discover and disclose covert operations during the Nixon presidency, the focus of debate has been his accusations against Kissinger. The former Secretary of State has labeled Hersh's account of his alleged machinations during the 1968 campaign as a "slimy lie" and has asserted that on the subject of himself and Nixon *The Price of Power* is full of "sly innuendoes" and "fairly contemptible gossip." As Hersh explained to Bruce Manuel in the *Christian Science Monitor* (June 24, 1983): "It all boils down to Kissinger's version of the truth or mine. I'm going to stick with mine and pray that critics questioning it will call up the people I asked and make their own effort to find out."

In his review for the *New York Times* (June 9, 1983), Christopher Lehmann-Haupt congratulated Hersh for "avoid[ing] the typically hectoring tone of the investigative reporter or the ideologue with an ax to grind. Indeed, [he] manages to sound like a historian, a morally objective one at that." In January 1984, Hersh received a general nonfiction award from the National Book Critics Circle for *The Price of Power*.

"Being an investigative reporter is like being a freak," Hersh has said. "You're trying to get information other people don't want you to have. I don't make deals, I don't party and drink with sources, and I don't play a game of leaks. I read, I listen, I squirrel information. It's fun." Although Hersh has been characterized as a modern-day Clark Kent of *Superman* fame, he is not a mild-mannered reporter. One government official, complaining to *Time* (January 6, 1975), described his modus operandi: "He wheedles, cajoles, pleads, threatens, asks a leading question, uses little tidbits as if he knew the whole story. When he finishes you feel like a wet rag." His colleagues, however, admire his persistence. Having worked on the *Glomar Explorer* story in competition with Hersh, syndicated columnist Jack Anderson told *Newsweek* (March 31, 1975), "Every place we went, Hersh had been there." A *New York Times* reporter added, "When Sy starts on a story, he just goes and goes and goes." His persistence is fueled by his belief that the journalistic corps must still learn how to tackle the "hard questions," how to "go beyond the surface."

Despite, or because of, his longtime focus on the political sphere, Hersh has said that he is "not a political person." The brevity of his stint as Eugene McCarthy's press secretary in 1968 was due to the fact that he "couldn't stand . . . the power struggles" among his fellow campaigners. "I don't like politics. I'm suspicious of it," he told Rone Tempest.

Seymour Hersh, who avoids the Washington social circuit, likes to play tennis when his schedule permits. He and the former Elizabeth Sarah Klein, whom he met at the University of Chicago, were married on May 30, 1964 and have three children: Melissa, Matthew, and Joshua. Hersh likes spending quiet evenings with his family at home where, reportedly, it is forbidden to mention Henry Kissinger's name at the dinner table.

References: *Chicago Tribune I p15+ Je 14 '83 por; Rolling Stone p48+ Ap 10 '75 por; Washington Post Potomac mag p13+ Jl 12 '70 pors; Contemporary Authors vols 73-76 (1978); Who's Who, 1982-83; Who's Who in America, 1984-85*

Hirsch, John (Stephen)

May 1, 1930– Canadian Director. Address: b. Stratford Festival Theatre, P.O. Box 520, Stratford, Ontario, Canada N5A 6V2

North America's most illustrious classical repertory theatre, the Stratford Festival, is also claimed by a large part of its audience as Canada's national theatre, despite taints of colonialism in its thirty-two-year history. Since 1981 the festival's artistic director has been a dynamic, flamboyant, avowed "Canadian Culture-Monger," John Hirsch, who believes in staging the world's great plays "in a Canadian way with a Canadian sensibility." But having for many years directed plays in New York and on the United States West Coast, as well as throughout Canada, Hungarian-born Hirsch is an international artist who imports non-Canadian actors and directors when needed and who wants to pay increased attention in the festival's repertory to the less-familiar Shakespearean plays and lesser-known European classics, along with more American plays. "What distinguishes Hirsch from most superstar directors," Mark Czarnecki wrote in *Maclean's* (June 29, 1981), "is his total commitment to a role for theatre in a society's struggle to define itself and maintain lasting human values."

The older of two sons in a middle-class Jewish family, John Stephen Hirsch was born to Joseph and Ilona (Horvath) Hirsch on May 1, 1930 in Siófok, Hungary, a resort town on Balaton Lake. His father owned a hardware store. As a boy, John Hirsch became acquainted with many forms of theatrical entertainment, variety shows, drama, opera, and ballet. He remembers that the city of Budapest had at that time twenty professional theatres. When he was six years old, he fashioned puppets from wood, cork, wires, and strings and staged shows for the delight of other children and his family. He dates his directorial career from that enterprise.

At the age of ten Hirsch went to live in Budapest and attend the Israel Gymnasium. Thereby he escaped the Nazi transportation a few years later of Siófok Jews to Auschwitz, where his parents and younger brother, Stephen, perished. He also survived the Soviet and American bombings of Budapest. Interned in a United Nations refugee camp in Germany after World War II, he earned his way by putting on puppet shows for other displaced persons. In 1947 in Paris, where he applied at several embassies for a visa to some other country, he was accepted in a program funded by the Canadian Jewish Congress to settle Jewish orphans in Canada.

During the Atlantic crossing the young refugees were shown a map of Canada and asked to choose where they wanted to live. Hirsch pointed to Winnipeg, reasoning that its central location guaranteed plenty of action and promised safety from invasion. On Thanksgiving Day (which in Canada is celebrated on the second Monday in October) in 1947 he arrived in Winnipeg and soon afterward became the adopted member of the family of Mrs. Pauline Shack. His home life bolstered his self-esteem. "I became very Jewish," he has recalled, as quoted in the *Maclean's* article. "I had a huge self-hatred as a child; with the whole world collapsing I was constantly being told I was guilty. But in Winnipeg you declared your Jewishness."

Encouraged by Mrs. Shack's daughter, Sybil Shack, an elementary school principal, Hirsch attended night classes to learn English and later entered the University of Manitoba, which in 1952 awarded him the B.A. degree with honors. Meanwhile, he had worked at an assortment of jobs, including those of office boy at Aronovitch & Leipsic Ltd. and porter on the Canadian National Railway. Throughout his changing experiences, the theatre remained an overriding interest in his life, and he was disappointed that in Winnipeg there was no professional theatre and that there were, in fact, few opportunities at that time for a professional actor anywhere in Canada. But he joined an amateur group, the Winnipeg Little Theatre, for which in 1951 he directed his first play, William Saroyan's *The Time of Your Life*, and of which he served from 1953 to 1957 as production stage manager.

In collaboration with Tom Hendry, whom he met in college, and a few other drama enthusiasts, Hirsch set up a puppet theatre called the Muddy

Water Puppets. The troupe toured Winnipeg schools and community clubs in subzero temperatures in 1952 presenting *Peter and the Snowman*, a revised version of a play that he had written for his puppet theatre in the refugee camp in Germany. With $300 from the Junior League, an earlier contributor to the Muddy Water Puppets, Hirsch and his friends organized a theatre for children, which produced *Sour Kringle* and other plays of his authorship. For a time he was also artistic director of Winnipeg's Rainbow Stage, an outdoor summer theatre for musical comedies.

Hirsch's work with the amateur stage and the response of Winnipeg audiences convinced him that the potential existed for a professional theatre, which he hoped would also be indigenous, a reflection of community interests and talents. In 1957 he and Hendry therefore invested their savings in a project they called Theatre 77 because their rented playhouse was exactly seventy-seven steps from Winnipeg's busiest street corner. By its second season Theatre 77 had become a professional group, paying everyone who worked for it. And it remained professional after merging in 1958 with the Winnipeg Little Theatre to form the Manitoba Theatre Centre, whose name indicates its founders' intention that it serve the entire province. To promote appreciation of theatre and encourage new talent, the company began a theatre school and a studio theatre workshop.

The Manitoba Theatre Centre, with its resident stock troupe, became the cradle of regional theatre throughout Canada. In its seventh season Shirley Mair described it in *Maclean's* (March 6, 1965) as "one of the liveliest resident playhouses in North America." She noted that in its first season it had an audience of 32,000 for its eight plays and sixty-three performances, as compared to the 135,000 theatregoers who attended its eight plays and 286 performances in 1964. During the last two years, 1964 and 1965, that Hirsch was its artistic director, the MTC's productions included Tennessee Williams' *Cat on a Hot Tin Roof*, Brendan Behan's *The Hostage*, his own play for children, *Box of Smiles*, Shaw's *Heartbreak House*, Shakespeare's *The Taming of the Shrew*, and Bertolt Brecht's *Mother Courage*, a French production of which, *Mère Courage*, he also directed at Le Théâtre du Nouveau Monde in Montreal in 1964.

For their inspiration Hirsch and his associates in Winnipeg looked to the Stratford Shakespearean Festival, founded in large part by the British director Tyrone Guthrie, who directed Alec Guinness in the title role of *Richard III* when the festival opened on July 13, 1953. "This theatre, at the time when we started [the Manitoba Theatre Centre], was the hope, the hub, the generating plan for this country's theatre," Hirsch said in a talk that he gave in 1981 to the Stratford company's actors and production staff. "Stratford made it possible for all of us, in those days, to know what standards are and what really fine, great work in the theatre meant."

In the summer of 1965 Hirsch went to Stratford as the guest director of Chekhov's *The Cherry Orchard*, in which Kate Reid played Madame Ranevskaya. That Russian classic was a favorite of Hirsch, who once said, as quoted in the Toronto *Globe and Mail* (August 27, 1976), "I think it is especially necessary to do Chekhov in Canada because he dealt with people in a remote and isolated world that is very close to our own." He undertook the staging of *The Cherry Orchard* with much preparation, which included, as it turned out, his experience of having directed Miss Reid in a production of Edward Albee's *Who's Afraid of Virginia Woolf?* in Winnipeg during the preceding winter.

Invited back to Stratford in 1966, Hirsch directed *Henry VI*, and in 1967 he opened the season with a presentation of *Richard III* that incited controversy because of his contemporary approach to Shakespeare's historical play. Over some opposition, during the summer of 1967 at Stratford he also directed *Colours in the Dark*, which the Canadian playwright James Reaney had been commissioned to write for Canada's Centennial (1967) and which was of particular interest to Hirsch because of his conviction that Canadian theatre should promote Canadianism. "When I talk about Canadianism, I'm not talking about chauvinism," Czarnecki quoted him in *Maclean's* as explaining. "I'm not talking about nationalism. I'm talking about self-actualization. I'm talking about self-awareness."

Canadianism, it would seem, moved a step forward at the end of the 1967 season when John Hirsch and Jean Gascon, head of Le Théâtre du Nouveau Monde, took over the artistic direction of the Stratford Festival from England's Michael Langham, who retired. During his two years as Gascon's associate Hirsch staged in 1968 *A Midsummer Night's Dream*, giving it a contemporary flavor, and *The Three Musketeers*, a dazzling, action-packed, and highly praised adaptation of the Dumas novel, and in 1969 *Hamlet* and a musical version of Petronius' *The Satyricon*.

By mid-August 1969 Hirsch had left his position with the Stratford Festival, partly because he wanted more time to work in theatre outside Canada. He was in considerable demand for the New York stage, where he made his directorial debut in December 1966 with the Repertory Company of Lincoln Center at the Vivian Beaumont Theatre in a production of Federico Garcia Lorca's *Yerma*. For the same company in April 1967 he directed Brecht's *Galileo*, which New York critics agreed was the best play of the season at the Beaumont—with one reviewer, Emory Lewis of *Cue* (April 22, 1967), hailing it as "the best drama of the season, on or off Broadway"—and credited the subtle and imaginative staging of Hirsch as much as the performance of Anthony Quayle in the title role. His work in *Galileo* earned Hirsch the Outer Critics Circle Award for 1966-67.

Joseph Heller's satiric indictment of war, *We Bombed in New Haven*, which Hirsch directed at Broadway's Ambassador Theater in October 1968, failed to draw a similar unanimous approval from the critics, who debated Heller's merits as a playwright. But Hirsch himself received generally good notices: Walter Kerr of the New York Times (October 27, 1968) admired his "swift, polished staging job," and George Oppenheimer of Newsday (October 17, 1968) commented on his "impeccable direction." Also on Broadway, at the Longacre Theater in March 1969, he directed Tyger! Tyger! and Other Burnings, a program in the repertory of the National Theatre for the Deaf.

Making New York his temporary base after he had ended his partnership with Gascon at Stratford, Hirsch worked mainly with the Lincoln Center Repertory company, for which he directed, among other major productions, The Time of Your Life in November 1969, John Millington Synge's The Playboy of the Western World in January 1971, and Sophocles' Antigone in May 1971. But since his association with that theatre was not restrictive, he was free to direct Chekhov's The Seagull in early 1970 at the Habimah National Theatre in Tel Aviv, Israel; Brecht's A Man's a Man in August 1970 with the Guthrie Theatre Company in Minneapolis, where he returned in July 1972 for A Midsummer Night's Dream; and Heathcote Williams' AC/DC, a satirically venturesome and technically difficult British import, in February 1971 at the Chelsea Theatre Center of Brooklyn, for which he won an Obie award for distinguished direction.

On one of his several visits back to the Manitoba Theatre Center, Hirsch staged, in January 1974, Shloime Ansky's The Dybbuk, a Yiddish play about demonic possession that he himself translated and adapted—an achievement that brought him a Canadian Authors Association award. He presented The Dybbuk later in 1974 at the St. Lawrence Arts Centre in Toronto and again, in 1975, at the Mark Taper Forum in Los Angeles.

Because of his commitment to produce The Dybbuk, among other obligations, Hirsch had to delay for some months his full-time occupancy of the post of head of television drama of the Canadian Broadcasting Corporation, to which he had been appointed for a four-year term beginning in early 1974. Television was not an unfamiliar medium to him. In the mid-1950s he had worked as a director for CBWT, CBC's Winnipeg TV station. Later he was especially proud of his production of Tom Hendry's drama about a Canadian teenage air cadet during World War II, Fifteen Miles of Broken Glass, which CBC presented in 1966. He also directed for CBC a television version of The Three Musketeers, adapted from his 1968 Stratford Festival production.

At the CBC headquarters in Toronto, Hirsch's goal was to revitalize the ailing TV drama department by transfusions of new actors and playwrights, developing native drama while not neglecting the classics. But because his objectives required long-term planning, the government's budget cuts and policy of one-year financing for the CBC network frustrated many of his efforts. Some of his dramatic presentations had disturbing or controversial elements, and, as Blaik Kirby suggested in the Toronto Globe and Mail (February 19, 1975), "The MP's may well prefer to see the CBC remain safe and bland." Among the programs with which he left his mark on the network were A Gift to Last, For the Record, and King of Kensington.

The magnetism of live theatre for Hirsch had led to his making provision in his contract with the CBC for time off for stage engagements. In the summer of 1976, for instance, he directed Maggie Smith in Chekhov's The Three Sisters at the Stratford Festival. When he left the CBC, he welcomed an opportunity he had long hoped for, to work on Shakespeare's The Tempest. His direction of Anthony Hopkins as Prospero at the Mark Taper Forum in May 1979 favorably impressed Richard Eder of the New York Times (May 28, 1979), who thought the production "extraordinary" and Hirsch "original and wise" in the aspects of the play that he chose to emphasize. In 1979 Hirsch became consulting artistic director of the Seattle Repertory Theatre, where in October of that year he directed Shaw's Saint Joan, which he had first staged more than a decade earlier at Lincoln Center. Among his other productions in Seattle were Rodgers and Hart's Pal Joey in April 1980 and American Dreams: Lost and Found, an entertainment by Studs Terkel, in March 1981.

Meanwhile, in December 1980, the board of governors of the Stratford Festival had chosen Hirsch for a three-year term as artistic director of Canada's principal theatre. His appointment ended a prolonged crisis of indecision and dispute over leadership following the resignation of Robin Phillips, an English director whose reliance on non-Canadian stars had incurred some displeasure. In order to fulfill his contract with the Seattle company, Hirsch could serve only as consultant at Stratford during the first six months of 1981, but with the help of the producer Muriel Sherrin, he assured the opening of the threatened twenty-ninth season. He did not direct any of the festival's plays in 1981, but in 1982 was responsible for the staging of The Tempest and, in 1983, of As You Like It and Molière's Tartuffe.

As head of the Stratford Festival, Hirsch is concerned not only with aesthetic standards, but with a training program for actors and with funding and financial planning. Although he very much enjoyed the 1983 season, Czarnecki observed in Maclean's (June 20, 1983), "Hirsch's own inspiration seems shackled by the educational mandate he has set for the festival and by his tireless lobbying on its behalf." Soon after Hirsch had signed a two-year extension of his contract in mid-1983, Leslie Bennetts interviewed him for the New York Times (July 31, 1983) and quoted him as saying, "I came in in the middle of the sinking of the Titanic. . . . In the last three years, we started to build a new company. And to build a company takes time." A year earlier, nevertheless, Clive Barnes, the drama critic for the New York Post (July 19, 1982), had reported on Hirsch's first full season with the festival: "The good news is that Ontario's Stratford Festival is itself again, and seemingly as splendid as ever." Nevertheless, some critics who attended the 1984 season complained of the conservatism of the repertory and a lack of young directors.

To Michael Billington, the drama critic of the *Guardian* (August 12, 1984), the most significant and lasting achievement of John Hirsch is his establishment of the Young Company at the Third Stage. The group consists of a dozen younger actors of exceptional promise who master classical acting techniques under the tutelage of Michael Langham, and who also learn from working with senior actors. That, according to Billington, will be the most important legacy that Hirsch can possibly pass on to his successor.

Hirsch is a member of the board of the Theatre Communications Group, U.S.A., a service organization for nonprofit professional theatres, has been a consultant to many Canadian cultural groups, and has lectured at the National Theatre School of Canada, Columbia University, and New York University. In 1967 he was awarded the Service Medal of the Order of Canada and in 1976, the Molson Prize. He has also received, among other tributes, an honorary D.Litt. degree from the University of Manitoba and L.L.D. degree from the University of Toronto.

Referring to Hirsch's description of himself as one of Canada's "vagabonds" and "exotic birds," Czarnecki wrote in *Maclean's* (June 29, 1981), "Nothing can adequately prepare for the first encounter with Hirsch—the infinitely extended limbs, the piercing nasal voice emanating from the dark bush of a face, the absurd, stork-like gawkiness of this theatrical prophet." Home for Hirsch is a house in Toronto on the edge of a ravine. Away from the theatre he spends some of his time cooking, painting, and writing poetry.

References: Macleans 78:16+ Mr 6 '65 por, 86:39+ Ap '73 por, 94:48+ Je 29 '81 pors; N Y Post p31 Ja 25 '68 por; N Y Times II p1+ Jl 31 '83 por; Toronto Globe and Mail p15 N 24 '73 por, E p5 Ja 5 '80 por, p15 N 28 '83 por; Canadian Who's Who, 1983; Notable Names in the American Theatre (1976); Oxford Companion to the Theatre (1983); Who's Who in America, 1984-85; Who's Who in the Theatre (1981)

Hirsch, Judd

Mar. 15, 1935– Actor. Address: b. c/o Artists Agency, 190 N. Canyon Dr., Beverly Hills, Calif. 90210.

Judd Hirsch considers himself to be an "inside out actor"—one who, like his contemporaries Dustin Hoffman and Richard Dreyfuss, built a successful career on the strength and depth of his talent rather than on physical attractiveness. A professional actor for twenty years, Hirsch is perhaps best known for his Emmy Award-winning portrayal of the grumpy Alex Rieger in the popular television situation comedy *Taxi*, but he is equally adept as a dramatic actor. His sensitive interpretations of such varied characters as the exuberant Matt Friedman in the Pulitzer Prize-winning play *Talley's Folly* and as Berger, the warmhearted psychiatrist in the highly praised film *Ordinary People*, won him, respectively, Tony and Oscar nominations.

A native of New York City, Judd Hirsch was born on March 15, 1935, the younger son of Joseph Sidney Hirsch, an electrician, and his wife, the former Sally Kitzis. He has one brother, Rolland. For a time the family led an itinerant existence, moving some thirteen times within the city before Judd entered the second grade. "I don't know what it was," he told an interviewer for *Redbook* magazine (November 1981). "Probably inner family turmoil of a sort that I was too young to understand. But I never really felt permanent." The Hirsches finally settled in the West Bronx, where Judd Hirsch attended DeWitt Clinton High School. He was, by his own admission, "a troublesome kid" not much given to studying, but he earned respectable grades in mathematics and science.

Following his high school graduation in 1952, Hirsch enrolled at the City College of New York as a physics major. At some point during the 1950s, he also studied architecture at the Cooper Union for the Advancement of Science and Art. He received a B.S. degree from City College in 1960. Unable to hold a job as a junior engineer, he eventually turned to acting, a craft that had intrigued him since his freshman year in college. "I'd started to look around me, to read, to go to plays, and actors *fascinated* me," he told Tom Burke of *TV Guide*

(March 28, 1979). "Wow! Guys who could, through their work, have some kind of an *effect* on society! The instant I enrolled in acting school and stepped on a stage to do a scene in front of people, I knew I'd found a home."

Over the next few years, Hirsch attended a succession of acting schools, among them the American Academy of Dramatic Arts, and studied independently with such noted acting coaches as Herbert Berghof, Uta Hagen, Gene Frankel, and Viveca Lindfors. Throughout that period, he supported himself by working as a hospital bill collector, a busboy, a driver at a summer camp, a library page, and a clerk at a law office. In about 1963 he was hired to play the lead in a summer stock production of Herb Gardner's comedy *A Thousand Clowns*. At the end of the run, he joined a theatrical troupe that specialized in revivals of old melodramas. "I played all the villains in a cape and sneakers," he quipped years later, as quoted in the *New York Daily News* (December 6, 1977). He also appeared in, by his own count, "hundreds" of television commercials.

Hirsch landed his first Broadway role in 1966, when he took over the part of the Telephone Repairman in Neil Simon's long-running comedy *Barefoot in the Park*. The following year, he snared the supporting role of the Thief in *Scuba Duba*, Bruce Jay Friedman's black comedy about a neurotic Jewish tourist whose wife has run off with a black scuba diver. In August 1968 Hirsch assumed the part of the hapless, cuckolded hero. His unorthodox interpretation of the volatile Harold Wonder captured the attention of the *New York Times*'s Clive Barnes, who found him to be a "more serious, less zany" Harold than his predecessor, Jerry Orbach.

Following a season with the experimental Theatre of the Living Arts in Philadelphia, Pennsylvania in 1969–70, Hirsch returned to New York City, where he appeared in several Off-Broadway productions, including a short-lived staging of Jean-Claude van Itallie's farce *Mystery Play* at the Cherry Lane Theater in January 1973. Shortly after that, he joined the Circle Repertory Company, a group of actors, directors, playwrights, and designers dedicated to creating "living" plays. He made his company debut within weeks in *The Hot l Baltimore*, Lanford Wilson's Saroyanesque drama about social misfits living in a condemned Baltimore hotel. As Bill, the feisty night manager, Hirsch blended smoothly into what *Newsweek*'s Jack Kroll, in his review of February 26, 1973, called "one of the best ensemble efforts I've ever seen in an Off-Off-Broadway company."

The circle repertory's critically acclaimed production of *The Hot l Baltimore* transferred in March 1973 to Off-Broadway's Circle in the Square Theater, where it ran for more than 1,100 performances. Toward the end of the year, Hirsch left the cast to take the part of Saul Nathan in the company's staging of Richard Lortz's family melodrama *Prodigal*. In his appraisal of the play for the *New York Times* (December 18, 1973), Clive Barnes singled out for special praise Judd Hirsch's portrayal of the "baffled, puzzled, and bullying eldest brother, clumsily dealing with life's most unfair proposition, that good guys finish last." To broaden his experience, Hirsch also directed a production of *Not Enough Rope*, Elaine May's one-act play about a suicidal young woman whose only solace is popular music, which was presented by the Circle Repertory Company in a twin bill with Sheila Quitten's *Busy Dyin'* in June 1974.

After seeing Hirsch in *The Hot l Baltimore*, an executive with Universal Studios recommended the actor for the leading role in the company's upcoming television special *The Law*. First broadcast by NBC-TV on October 22, 1974, *The Law*, a penetrating, cinéma-vérité examination of the American criminal justice system built around a sensational murder trial, was both a critical and a popular success and brought Hirsch, who played Murray Stone, the fast-talking public defender, the best notices of his career to that date. In the words of a reviewer for the trade paper *Variety* (October 30, 1974), Hirsch "emerged full-blown as a performer to be reckoned with—gutsy, brainy and compassionate beneath his brash, streetwise veneer, and utterly convincing in every aspect of the script. He seems to be one of those actors who has already trimmed all the fat off his technique, and he deftly plumbed every facet of his demanding role in almost flawless fashion, sans tricks or gimmicks." A three-episode miniseries derived from *The Law* that aired in the spring of 1975 was, in Hirsch's view, only a "slick, pale" imitation of the hard-hitting original, but it won an Emmy nomination as the outstanding limited series of the season.

For a time Hirsch remained in California, where he found work in a number of television projects, including the made-for-television movies *The Keegans*, *The Legend of Valentino*, and *Fear on Trial*, and episodes of the series *Two Brothers* and *Medical Story*. He returned to the New York stage in January 1976 in the Circle Repertory Company's production of Jules Feiffer's sardonic fable *Knock Knock*. As Mel Gussow observed in his *New York Times* (January 19, 1976) review, Hirsch played Wiseman, the smart-alecky genie who takes on a variety of guises, "with a Sid Caesarean virtuosity." That technical skill earned him a Drama Desk Award as best supporting actor in a play after the production moved to Broadway in February.

Hirsch left *Knock Knock* two months later to accept the title role in *Delvecchio*, a CBS-TV dramatic series about a tough big-city detective studying to be a lawyer. Although it received respectable ratings, *Delvecchio* was axed by the network after the 1976–77 season. Hirsch, who had envisioned something similar to *The Law*, blamed "hack writers and directors" for failing to make the series more than standard cops-and-robbers fare. His performance in the series, however, did not go unnoticed. Soon after *Delvecchio* was canceled, he was chosen to play the embittered and brutal Groffo Stepanowicz, who is passed over as leader of his clan in favor of his more capable son, in *King of the Gypsies* (Paramount, 1978), the film version of Peter Maas's nonfiction best seller about generational conflict in the gypsy subculture. His wry portrayal of a more likable character in "Rhoda Loves Mike," an episode of the television sitcom *Rhoda*, led to his first Emmy nomination, as outstanding lead actor for a single appearance in a series during the 1977–78 season.

Because he liked Hirsch's "New York sound" and his ability to project, at the same time, strength and vulnerability, Neil Simon wrote the central role of his autobiographical play *Chapter Two* with the actor in mind. After some initial hedging, Hirsch accepted the part, thinking that it might serve as "a kind of image breaker," as he put it, after a succession of tough-guy roles on television. *Chapter Two*, which had its world premiere at the Ahmanson Theater in Los Angeles, California on October 7, 1977 and then two months later settled in for a long run on Broadway, is the bittersweet story of George Schneider, an emotionally shattered recent widower who is tormented by guilt when he finds happiness with his second wife, a young actress. By all accounts, Hirsch accomplished Schneider's mood swings with impressive skill. As Richard Eder reported in the *New York Times* (December 5, 1977), he began the play "in dazed misery, his eyes fixed, his face swollen, his mouth dry, his stomach pumping wretchedness," but he was "quite transformed in courtship; his eyes literally [lighted] up."

Judd Hirsch remained with *Chapter Two* until the summer of 1978 when he withdrew from the cast to take a leading role in the new television situation comedy series *Taxi*, which focused on an ill-assorted group of New York City cabdrivers, most of them claiming to be just temporary hackers, biding their time until something better turned up. Only Alex Rieger—Hirsch's character—was resigned to a life behind the wheel.

Often compared to the award-winning sitcoms *All in the Family*, *Barney Miller*, and *The Mary Tyler Moore Show* because of its witty, literate scripts and the expert ensemble playing of its well-matched cast, *Taxi*, an ABC entry, was one of the few programs among the new series to finish the 1978–79 season in the top ten. According to television critics, Hirsch's solid performance was a key ingredient in the series' success. Reviewing the show for *TV Guide* (December 23, 1978), Robert Mackenzie praised the actor's cool, understated delivery, adding, "He gets more out of a morose stare than some comics milk from a whole repertoire of mugging." During *Taxi*'s five-year run on the ABC and NBC networks, Hirsch was twice awarded, in 1981 and 1983, an Emmy as the outstanding actor in a comedy series. The second award came after NBC had canceled the show—an irony that was not lost on Hirsch. In his acceptance speech, which he later dismissed as an attempt to have "fun," he publicly scolded the network executives responsible for prematurely removing the series from the program roster.

Hungry for the "discipline" of rehearsals and daily performances, Hirsch took advantage of the annual break in *Taxi*'s shooting schedule to return to the stage in a role tailored specifically for him by Lanford Wilson. In writing *Talley's Folly*, Wilson had deliberately set out to construct a piece around a character as "many-faceted" as Hirsch, a longtime friend. The character was the charming, ebullient Matt Friedman, an immigrant Jewish accountant who, in Mel Gussow's words, habitually "dramatizes himself with jokes, games, and imitations." During the course of the offbeat comedy, which is set in a ramshackle boathouse—the "folly" of the title—in 1944, Matt woos and wins Sally Talley, the wellborn nurse's aide on the verge of spinsterhood whom he has been courting by letter since the two had their week-long idyll the previous summer.

When *Talley's Folly* opened for a limited Off-Broadway engagement at the Circle Repertory Company's Circle Theater on May 1, 1979, reviewers chorused their praise of Hirsch's characterization of the irrepressibly romantic Matt Friedman. "Judd Hirsch has never been better," Clive Barnes remarked in the *New York Post* (May 4, 1979). "Warm, ironic, nervily cocky, full of self-doubt yet also self-awareness, he brings the complex, fascinating man completely to life." If anything, the critics' enthusiasm for Hirsch's performance increased after *Talley's Folly* moved to Broadway in February 1980. For Brendan Gill, writing in the *New Yorker* (March 3, 1980), it was "a feat of acting that one doesn't fear to call memorable: at some moments he threatens to become all four Marx Brothers at once; at other moments, he threatens to break our hearts." Hirsch's work in *Talley's Folly* won him an Obie Award in 1979 and a Tony nomination for best actor in a play in 1980.

Hirsch's stagnating motion picture career finally took off with the release in 1980 of *Ordinary People* (Paramount), the domestic drama directed by Robert Redford that took four major Academy Awards, including best picture of the year. A compelling examination of an affluent couple's struggle to come to terms with their emotionally disturbed adolescent son, *Ordinary People* featured Hirsch in the pivotal role of the compassionate psychiatrist who pokes, pulls, and prods the boy back to reality. For his contribution to *Ordinary People*, Hirsch earned an Academy Award nomination as best supporting actor. (He lost in the balloting to his young costar, Timothy Hutton.) Hirsch's film credits also include *Without a Trace* (Twentieth Century-Fox, 1983), in which he played a sympathetic detective searching for a missing child, the film version of Herb Gardner's comedy *The Goodbye People* (Embassy, 1984), and *Teachers* (United Artists, 1984), which Rex Reed described as "a cross between *Blackboard Jungle* and *Grease*."

Fulfilling a longheld dream, Hirsch returned to New York in the fall of 1983 to play Trigorin in the Circle Repertory Company's limited-run production of Chekhov's *The Seagull*. "I love the play, and

I love the part," he explained to Patricia O'Haire of the *New York Daily News* (November 6, 1983). "Trigorin is a writer, just like Chekhov, and he's about as close to Chekhov as he could be. These are very human people. They seem to have everything, but tap just below the skin of any character, and you see someone who is desperately unhappy, or feels inadequate." Although he is an admirer of Hirsch's work, Frank Rich was disappointed by the actor's portrayal of Trigorin. "[He] merely strolls disconsolately about, reciting his lines blandly in a jarring New York accent," Rich complained in reviewing the production for the *New York Times* (November 25, 1983). "It's impossible to accept him as any kind of writer, let alone one who expresses Chekhov's esthetic views."

A broad-shouldered six-footer weighing 175 pounds, Judd Hirsch has green eyes, unruly dark brown hair, and, according to one interviewer, a rugged "street face, a face of interchangeable ethnicities and professions." To keep fit, he jogs regularly, swims, and plays tennis. He is an animated conversationalist and seems to enjoy talking to reporters. Speaking rapidly in his raspy voice, he is unusually candid about the problems of his unpredictable profession. Among the handful of successful actors whose careers are divided between the New York stage and the Hollywood soundstage,

Hirsch maintains an apartment in Manhattan's Greenwich Village and a house, which he is remodeling himself, in the San Fernando Valley of California. During his infrequent vacations, he usually tries to spend some time at the cabin that he designed and built in the Catskill Mountains. Hirsch is the father of a teenage son, Alexander, from the second of his two marriages, both of which ended in divorce.

Despite his success in films and television, Hirsch's enduring passion is the stage. He reportedly turned down the chance to star in a television miniseries for an estimated six-figure salary, in order to appear in *Talley's Folly*. "If turning down a bad part means it's all over for me tomorrow, as far as fame, riches and all those bad reasons for being an actor," he told David Elliott of *USA Today* (February 7, 1983), "well, you'll find me back at the Circle Rep, doing some unknown play by an unknown writer. And enjoying it. I don't care what it is, or how big it is, I just want a thing to be good."

References: *NY Daily News* p44 D 6 '77 por; *N Y Sunday News* mag p6+ F 24 '80 pors; *N Y Times* II p4+ Ja 29 '78 por, C p19 My 15 '80 por; *Newsday* mag p22+ Ap 13 '80 pors; *Redbook* 158:59+ N '81 pors; *TV Guide* 27:27+ Mr 28 '79 por; *Who's Who in America*, 1984-85; *Who's Who in the Theatre* (1981)

Houseman, John

Sept. 22, 1902– Director; actor; writer; educator. Address: b. c/o Simon and Schuster, Inc., The Simon and Schuster Bldg., 1230 Ave. of The Americas, New York City, N.Y. 10020

NOTE: This biography supersedes the article that appeared in *Current Biography* in 1959.

Despite four decades of distinguished work in theatre, films, and television as a writer, producer, director, and teacher, John Houseman remained largely unknown outside the theatrical profession until he won an Academy Award as best supporting actor of 1973 for his portrayal of the imperious law professor in *The Paper Chase*. Houseman, who began his career as a grain merchant, revitalized the American theatre over the years by founding no less than eight repertory companies, including the legendary Mercury Theatre in the 1930s and, most recently, the acclaimed Acting Company. His contributions to motion pictures and television, mostly as a producer of quality films and performing arts series, were no less important. Nonetheless, the energetic and versatile Houseman is justifiably proud of what he has described as his "professional transformation from a respected but neglected veteran in the theatre to one of the most sought after and highly paid aging male performers in the mass media."

Born Jacques Haussmann in Bucharest, Romania on September 22, 1902, John Houseman was the only child of Georges Haussmann, a Jewish-Alsatian grain speculator, and May (Davies) Haussmann, who was of Welsh-Irish descent. (He officially Anglicized his name in the early 1930s.)

Because of the precarious nature of Georges Haussmann's career, the family fortunes rose and fell in rollercoaster fashion, and Houseman spent his nomadic but culturally rich childhood in a series of palatial hotel suites or furnished rooms on the Continent, depending on the state of the family bank account. Although his early schooling was erratic, he quickly picked up the native languages of the countries he visited, and by the time he was ready to begin his formal education, he could speak Romanian, French, German, and English.

When Houseman was seven, his parents sent him to live with a public school master, near Bristol, England. Two years later, in 1911, he enrolled as a day boy at the Clifton Preparatory School, an exclusive public school where he was virtually ostracized by his classmates. He progressed to Clifton College Junior School in 1913 and, finally, to Clifton College in 1916. An apt student, he concentrated on modern languages and, in his spare time, edited the *Cliftonian* and headed the Clifton College Dramatic Society, which he had founded. In 1918 he won a senior scholarship in modern languages to Trinity College, Cambridge University, but because of what he has described as "financial reverses and family problems," he turned it down.

At the invitation of a merchant friend of his family, Houseman set sail, in 1919, for Argentina, where he planned to study Spanish and learn the grain business. He stayed on for eighteen months, working as a "dude gaucho" on a cattle ranch and then as a junior clerk in the foreign exchange department of the Dutch Bank in Buenos Aires. On his return to England in 1921, he signed on as an apprentice in an international wheat brokerage firm. In the evenings and on weekends, he wrote short stories about his experiences in Argentina, some of which were published in the *New Statesman*. In 1924 he moved to New York City to accept a job with the Continental Grain Corporation, a post he held until he formed his own exporting company, the Oceanic Grain Corporation, in 1929. At some point in the late 1920s, he began to translate and adapt French and German plays into English as a hobby. When the stock market collapsed, he decided to go into theatrical production and direction, even though, by his own admission, he had "no training, no craft, no special skill or experience of any sort" in theatre.

Houseman first achieved theatrical recognition in 1934, as the director of a Broadway production of the Gertrude Stein–Virgil Thomson opera *Four Saints in Three Acts*, with an all-black cast. Later in the same year, he collaborated with the poet Countee Cullen on a black *Medea* and directed two productions, Ibsen's *The Lady From the Sea* and Maxwell Anderson's *Valley Forge*, for the Theatre Guild. Ready to try his hand as a producer, he cofounded, with Nathan Zatkin, the short-lived Phoenix Theatre Group, whose opening presentation, in 1935, was Archibald MacLeish's verse play *Panic*, featuring Orson Welles in the leading role.

At least partly because of his success in working with black actors on the highly acclaimed *Four Saints*, Houseman was named head of the Negro Theatre Project, a subdivision of the WPA's Federal Theatre Project, in 1935. Unwilling to mount pointless black revivals of past Broadway hits, he drew up a bold program that alternated the presentation of contemporary works by black playwrights with innovative stagings of the classics. The most famous and commercially successful of the Negro Theatre Project's productions was the "voodoo" *Macbeth*, so-called because Houseman and Orson Welles, who directed, switched the setting of the tragedy from Scotland to nineteenth-century Haiti and hired authentic witch doctors to portray Shakespeare's "weird sisters."

In 1936, still under the auspices of the Federal Theatre Project, Houseman and Welles set up a classical theatre unit at Maxine Elliott's Theatre, where their productions included Marlowe's *Doctor Faustus*, with Welles in the title role, and *The Cradle Will Rock*, Marc Blitzstein's controversial anticapitalist opera. Houseman took time out from his duties as managing producer to direct Leslie Howard in a Broadway revival of *Hamlet* and to head, briefly, Vassar College's theatre department, where he staged several student productions.

Late in 1937 the two men withdrew from the Federal Theatre Project, leased a theatre on Broadway, and launched the Mercury Theatre with a modern-dress version of *Julius Caesar*, which played to packed houses throughout its run. It was followed by critically praised productions of George Bernard Shaw's *Heartbreak House*, Thomas Dekker's rarely staged domestic comedy *The Shoemakers' Holiday*, and Georg Büchner's *Danton's Death*. Although none of them equaled the success of *Julius Caesar*, those productions confirmed the Mercury Theatre's place in the history of the American stage. Meanwhile, Houseman and Welles collaborated on the writing and production of the radio series *The Mercury Theatre of the Air*, which broadcast versions of such literary classics as *Dracula*, *A Tale of Two Cities*, *Jane Eyre*, *The Heart of Darkness*, and most notably, H.G. Wells's *The War of the Worlds*. The authenticity of the last-named program, presented as a series of news bulletins, panicked some listeners into believing that the United States had actually been invaded by Martians.

Following the financial collapse of the Mercury Theatre, Houseman directed the American Lyric Theatre's production of *The Devil and Daniel Webster*, a musical folk play by Stephen Vincent Benét and Douglas Moore, and the Theatre Guild's staging of Philip Barry's allegory *Liberty Jones*, worked with Richard Wright on a dramatic adaptation of Wright's novel *Native Son*, which he and Welles produced on Broadway in 1941, and produced or wrote scripts for several radio shows. At about that time, he also collaborated with Herman Mankiewicz on the screenplay that later came to be called *Citizen Kane*. Named vice-president of David O. Selznick productions in 1941, he worked on the preparation of the films *Jane Eyre* (1944) and *Saboteur* (1942) and produced a summer repertory season at the Lobero Theatre, featuring Selznick contract players in Eugene O'Neill's *Anna Christie*, Shaw's *The Devil's Disciple*, and the premiere of William Saroyan's *Hello, Out There*.

After the United States entered World War II, Houseman resigned from Selznick's production company to join the Office of War Information, where he put his flair for languages and his radio experience to good use as chief of programming for overseas radio operations. For the next eighteen months, he supervised the production of news programs and features in twenty-seven languages for the "Voice of America" broadcasts. He also produced *Tuesday in November*, a documentary short subject about the American electoral process, which was widely distributed overseas.

Returning to Hollywood in late 1943, Houseman became a producer for Paramount Pictures and, later, for MGM, RKO, and Universal. During the next twenty years, he produced a score of motion pictures, among them the moody *The Unseen* (1945); *The Blue Dahlia* (1946), a compelling mystery written by Raymond Chandler; Max Ophüls' sentimental classic *Letter From an Unknown Woman* (1948); *The Bad and the Beautiful* (1952), a penetrating behind-the-scenes look at Hollywood; and the star-studded *Executive Suite* (1954). His screen credits also include a critically lauded *Julius Caesar* (1953), with a first-rate cast headed by John Gielgud, James Mason, and Marlon Brando; *Her Twelve Men* (1954) a saccharine vehicle for Greer Garson; *Lust For Life* (1956), a biography of the artist Vincent Van Gogh starring Kirk Douglas; and Tennessee Williams' *This Property is Condemned* (1966).

Over the years, Houseman's films garnered twenty Academy Award nominations and seven Oscars, five of them for *The Bad and the Beautiful*. Commenting on Houseman's contributions to the art of filmmaking in a piece for the *Saturday Review* that was published shortly after the release of the *The Bad and the Beautiful*, Arthur Knight, the film critic and historian, observed: "Quite apart from matters of taste and discrimination Houseman is becoming prized and respected as a man who knows what he wants and—at least as important—who understands the proper mechanism for getting it."

Between motion picture assignments, Houseman worked on television projects, mainly for CBS. He was, among other things, responsible for conceiving, preparing, and producing each of the twenty-six segments of the ambitious Sunday-afternoon omnibus *The Seven Lively Arts* in the 1957–58 season, and from 1958 to 1960, he served as executive producer of the legendary *Playhouse 90*, generally regarded as the best dramatic anthology series of television's so-called "golden age." The two series earned Houseman three Emmy Awards, and *Playhouse 90* also received a prestigious Peabody Award for outstanding achievement in dramatic entertainment.

From time to time during the 1940s and 1950s, Houseman indulged his love of live theatre by directing or producing stage presentations in New York and California. On Broadway in the late 1940s, for example, he directed the enchanting fantasy *The Lute Song*, starring Mary Martin and Yul Brynner, and *Beggar's Holiday*, an updating of John Gay's *The Beggar's Opera* with an integrated cast and music by Duke Ellington, and produced Allan Scott's comedy *Joy to the World*.

Convinced that there was an audience for serious drama in southern California, Houseman founded, in 1947, Pelican Productions, whose first season included stagings of Thornton Wilder's *The Skin of Our Teeth*, Jean-Paul Sartre's *No Exit*, the North American premiere of Garcia Lorca's *The House of Bernarda Alba*, and the world premiere of Bertolt Brecht's provocative *Galileo*, with Charles Laughton in the title role. Although each of the plays, presented in limited runs, attracted large and enthusiastic audiences, the company was hard-pressed to recoup its production costs, largely because of Houseman's policy of keeping ticket prices low, and in 1948 Pelican Productions went out of business.

Until Houseman's production of *King Lear* opened on Broadway in December 1950, Brooks Atkinson, the dean of New York's drama critics, had agreed with Charles Lamb's contention that the tragedy could not be acted. But in his *New York Times* column of December 26, 1950 Atkinson confessed that Houseman and Louis Calhern, who portrayed the king, had forced him to change his mind. In their hands, he wrote, "[Lear] came alive as an original work of art in the theatre. . . . Houseman had molded all the details of the performance in the shape of a trenchant, somber, stormy drama. This is what Shakespeare intended." Similar praise greeted his direction, four years later, of Robert Ryan and Mildred Natwick in *Coriolanus*.

Houseman's unquestioned skill as an interpreter of Shakespeare led to his appointment, in 1956, as artistic director of the American Shakespeare Festival Theatre and Academy in Stratford, Connecticut. Realizing that he could not hope to attract established stars after the Festival Theatre's disastrous first season in the summer of 1955, Houseman decided to showcase the company's young performers in what he has described as "bold, imaginative productions of unfamiliar, contrasting plays"—*King John*, *Measure For Measure*, and as "a concession to conventional programming," *The Taming of the Shrew*. To solve staging problems, he asked Rouben Ter-Arutunian, the set designer, to build an open, steeply raked, platform stage with the functional flexibility of an Elizabethan theatre. The gambit paid off in full houses and excellent critical notices, especially for *Measure For Measure* and *Shrew*, which eventually transferred to Broadway for limited runs.

After his prosperous initial season at the helm of the American Shakespeare Festival Theatre, Houseman agreed to stay on for three more years. Having proved the troupe's viability as a classical repertory company, he was free to concentrate on planning more challenging programs and on training his actors. To that end, he established an acting school in New York City, under the general administration of his associate, Jack Landau, and persuaded such theatrical luminaries as John Gielgud, Michael Redgrave, Harold Clurman, and Michel Saint-Denis to serve as guest lecturers.

With the directing chores divided between Houseman and Landau, the Festival Theatre Company presented, over the next three seasons, productions of *Othello, The Merchant of Venice, Romeo and Juliet, All's Well That Ends Well, A Midsummer Night's Dream, The Merry Wives of Windsor, The Winter's Tale,* and *Much Ado About Nothing.* The company's version of *Much Ado,* set on a nineteenth-century Texas ranch and starring Katharine Hepburn and Alfred Drake as Beatrice and Benedick, scored such a hit with audiences that, after a sold-out Broadway engagement, it toured the country for months under the sponsorship of the Theatre Guild. Houseman and Landau described the growth and development of the American Shakespeare Festival Theatre in their book *American Shakespeare Festival: The Birth of a Theatre* (Simon & Schuster, 1959).

By the end of the decade, John Gassner, the influential critic and drama anthologist, was hailing the American Shakespeare Festival Theatre company as "the best repertory company we have had in the United States since 1926 when the Theatre Guild had its short-lived Acting Company." But in spite of the critical garlands and the audience acclaim, Houseman, whose hopes for the troupe's future included year-round employment for the actors and support staff, the expansion of the repertory to include non-Shakespearean plays, and a regular season in New York City, among other things, was hamstrung in his efforts by the conservatism of the Festival Theatre's executive committee. Unable to reach an agreement with the committee, Houseman resigned in August 1959, citing "divergences" over artistic policy. He returned to Stratford briefly in the mid-1960s to direct T. S. Eliot's *Murder in the Cathedral,* with Joseph Wiseman as the Archbishop, and *Macbeth.*

For the next half-dozen years or so, Houseman pursued unrelated projects which, in his words, gave him "no consistent sense of accomplishment or satisfaction." His professional credits for that "unsettled" period include directing productions of *Otello* and *Tosca* for the Dallas (Texas) Civic Opera, creating the short documentary film *Voyage to America* for the 1964 New York World's Fair, and producing the CBS-TV American historical anthology series *The Great Adventure.* He seems to have found the most gratification in his work as the artistic director of the Los Angeles–based Professional Theatre Group, a company of stage-trained film and television actors and directors who put on limited runs of classic and contemporary plays. Houseman himself directed *Antigone, King Lear, Measure For Measure,* Pirandello's *Six Characters in Search of an Author,* O'Neill's *The Iceman Cometh,* and the West Coast premiere of Chekhov's *The Three Sisters.*

In January 1967 Houseman became director of the drama division of the Juilliard School of the Performing Arts in New York City. Charged with formulating the philosophy and drawing up the curriculum for an actor-training program specifically designed to meet the needs of American actors required to work in a variety of styles and forms, Houseman decided to focus on teaching actors how best to convey "the author's intent to the audience," as he explained in an interview for the *Christian Science Monitor* (September 8, 1972). With the help of Michel Saint-Denis, he devised a comprehensive four-year course of study that included classes in everything from speech to circus acrobatics to theatre history. Over the next eighteen months, he recruited the faculty, many of them veteran professional actors, and selected, by audition, the first class of three dozen students from some six hundred applicants.

While overseeing the artistic development of successive classes at Juilliard, until he relinquished his post in 1976, Houseman kept his hand in as a professional director. Among other things, he mounted productions of the contemporary operas *Antigone, The Losers, The Mines of Sulphur,* and Ernest Bloch's *Macbeth* for the Juilliard Opera Theatre; served, from 1967 to 1970, as producing director of the Association of Producing Artists (APA-Phoenix) Repertory Company, for which he staged several plays, including Michel de Ghelderode's *The Chronicles of Hell* and *Pantagleize;* and directed Henry Fonda in David W. Rintels' one-man biographical drama *Clarence Darrow* and Jason Robards and Maureen Stapleton in Clifford Odets' *The Country Girl.*

Perhaps most important in his view, Houseman established, in 1972, for Juilliard's drama graduates a permanent repertory troupe, known as the Acting Company. Beginning with limited seasons at the City Center in New York, the group soon progressed to national tours. During the first four years of its existence, the Acting Company performed its varied and demanding repertory of classical and contemporary plays before more than 500,000 people in over ninety cities to virtually unanimous approval. Critics nationwide were impressed by the versatility and range, the feeling for style, the clarity of diction, and most of all, the seamless ensemble playing of the young actors. Some of the performers who got their start in the Acting Company are Tony Award winners Kevin Kline and Patti LuPone and motion picture stars William Hurt and Christopher Reeve. Since 1979 Houseman has shared the artistic management of the Acting Company with Michael Kahn and the late Alan Schneider.

Although Houseman had appeared briefly, as Admiral Barnswell, in the 1964 political thriller *Seven Days in May* (Seven Arts), his acting career did not begin in earnest until 1973, when he agreed to portray the irascible, autocratic Professor Kingsfield in *The Paper Chase* (Twentieth Century-Fox), a film about the trials and triumphs of a bright young law student directed by James Bridges, a colleague from his days with the Professional Theatre Group. Playing his role with "magisterial jowliness" and "patrician crustiness," Houseman embodied "every nuance of the quintessence of scholarly teaching," to quote Judith Crist, writing in New York (October 22, 1973). His brilliant debut performance was followed by appearances as a corporate despot in the futuristic moral fable Rollerball (United Artists, 1975); the enigmatic head of the CIA in Three Days of the Condor (Paramount, 1975), Sydney Pollack's cerebral thriller; a wealthy dilettante in the crime drama St. Ives (Warner Brothers, 1976); and a stern psychiatrist in Joan Tewkesbury's Old Boyfriends (Avco-Embassy, 1979). He also played supporting roles in the supernatural chillers The Fog (Avco-Embassy, 1980) and Ghost Story (Universal, 1981).

Included among Houseman's numerous television acting credits are a reprisal of his Professor Kingsfield role in the critically praised but short-lived CBS series The Paper Chase and appearances in the miniseries Washington-Behind Closed Doors, Marco Polo, and The Winds of War and in the special presentations Fear On Trial, Gideon's Trumpet, and Truman at Potsdam, in which he took the part of Sir Winston Churchill. He has also become familiar to TV viewers as the courtly spokesman for Smith Barney, the investment counseling firm, Puritan oil, the Chrysler Corporation, Seawatch Condominiums, and the fastfood chain McDonald's. "I have fun making [commercials]," he admitted in a recent interview. "They are very, very lucrative."

John Houseman, who is six feet tall and usually weighs around 200 pounds, has blue eyes and thinning white hair. He has been described by interviewers as being charming, unpretentious, and "warmer" than his onscreen persona. A compulsive worker, he claims to be "absolutely incapable" of relaxing. "Fear is the spur that drives you to a great deal of activity," he told Allan Wallach in an interview for Newsday (October 19, 1975). "Originally, I did so many things . . . as a sort of insurance, because I didn't want to have all my eggs in one basket. One is always terrified of a flop, of a disaster, and I always felt it was nice to have a couple of other paths to take in case something went wrong in one of them."

Houseman traced the history of his multiple careers in his autobiographies Run-Through, (1972), Front and Center (1979), and Final Dress (1983), published by Simon & Schuster. The first two volumes were nominated for a National Book Award. Houseman and his wife, the former Joan Courtney, whom he married in 1950, have two sons: Michael, an anthropologist, and Charles Sebastian, a painter. An earlier marriage to the actress Zita Johann ended in divorce. The Housemans divide their time between a seaside home in Malibu, California and a New York City apartment overlooking Central Park.

References: Chicago Tribune I p17+ D 20 '79 pors; N Y Times II p1+ Ap 21 '74 por; Newsday I p3+ O 19 '75, mag p2+ Mr 16 '80 pors; People 19:57+ Ja 17 '83 pors; TV Guide 26:31+ N 18 '78 por; Washington Post K p1+ O 7 '79 pors; Who's Who in America, 1984–85; Who's Who in Theatre (1981)

Iglesias, Julio

(ē glä syäs hoo lyō)

Sept. 23, 1943– Spanish popular singer; songwriter. Address: b. c/o Rogers & Cowan, 9665 Wilshire Blvd., Beverly Hills, Calif. 90212; c/o CBS Records International, 51 W. 52d St., New York City, N.Y. 10019

According to Newsweek (July 11, 1983), "The most popular singer in the world today isn't Mick Jagger or Kenny Rogers or Paul McCartney or even Frank Sinatra. He's a . . . Spaniard named Julio Iglesias, a master of the love song." Reputed to be the best-selling musical artist in the history of recording, Iglesias has sold over 100 million albums, a feat that earned him a place in the Guinness Book of World Records. Although it was not until 1983 that he made his United States debut, hard-working Julio Iglesias has won stardom in more than sixty countries, accomplishing that impressive climb to international fame in a little over a decade after winning acclaim at the 1970 Eurovision song contest, with notable good taste and a lack of the raucous sensationalism that characterizes some pop singers.

Julio José Iglesias de la Cueva was born in Madrid, Spain on September 23, 1943 (some sources give the year erroneously as 1944) to Dr. Julio Iglesias Puga, a prominent gynecologist, and Maria del

Rosario de la Cueva Perignat, who are now separated. He has a younger brother, Carlos, who gave up a promising career as a surgeon to act as Julio's financial manager. On his father's side of the family, Julio Iglesias' ancestors came from Galicia in northwestern Spain, while his mother, a native of Madrid, traces her family roots to Puerto Rico, Cuba, and Andalusia. Iglesias considers himself profoundly Galician and has recorded "Un Canto a Galicia" in tribute to the land of his paternal forebears.

The Iglesias family, comfortably settled in Madrid's elite Argüelles district, which is an upper-middle-class neighborhood near the Parque del Oeste, sent Julio and his brother to the nearby Colegio de los Sagrados Corazones, a Roman Catholic school. There, the singer recalled in his 1981 autobiography *Entre el cielo y el infierno* (Between Heaven and Hell), his grades were poor and he did not qualify for the choir, but he became an enthusiastic soccer player. During those early years, Julio Iglesias spent his summer vacations with his family at Cangas in Galicia, and later in Peñiscola, on the Mediterranean coast.

On completion of his secondary education, Julio Iglesias embarked on the study of law, with the idea of eventually entering the Spanish diplomatic service. He also continued to play soccer, serving on the junior reserve squad of the famous Real Madrid Club de Fútbol as goalkeeper, and some experts predicted a bright career for him in that sport. His family insisted, however, that he finish his studies.

A crippling auto accident, while he was driving with friends on the outskirts of Madrid in the late summer of 1963, temporarily put an end to his studies and cut off his promising career as a soccer player. Only the help of his family, the patient loyalty of their chauffeur, José Luis, who accompanied him through the long therapy towards recovery, and his own strength of will and determination managed to pull Iglesias through that painful convalescence. His weight dropped to less than 100 pounds. But the sight of his father entering the sickroom with a wheelchair moved him to vow never to use it, and he became determined to recover the use of his limbs.

It was during that trying period that a nurse gave Julio Iglesias an inexpensive guitar to occupy his time and take his mind off his near-fatal accident. By listening to singers on the radio and trying to accompany them on his guitar, he became familiar with the world of music for the first time and discovered that he had a musical talent of which he had been unaware. He played along with song competitions broadcast in 1967 over the radio from San Remo and Benidorm and announced to his father and mother, much to their surprise, that someday they would hear him in such festivals.

Not long afterwards, during postconvalescence, Iglesias was sent to Cambridge, England by his parents to improve his English. While there, he wrote his first song, entitled "La Vida sigue igual" ("Life Goes on as Usual"). With it he won the competition at the Benidorm Song Festival held on Spain's Mediterranean coast on July 18, 1968, launching him on his way to international recognition as a singer. At first, however, Iglesias yielded to his family's wish that he continue his law studies. "I promised my father I would finish one career before I began another," he told an interviewer for the *Las Vegas Review-Journal* (March 18, 1983), "so for one and a half years after I won the contest I didn't do a lot of singing. I stayed with the law work and kept my promise to my father."

Meanwhile, Iglesias began writing songs in quick succession, including "El Viejo Pablo," "No llores, mi amor," "Yo canto," "Lágrimas tiene al camino," and "Alguien en algún lugar." For the 1970 Eurovision Festival in Holland, he wrote the song "Guendoline," and although he did not win that competition, the song became one of the major hits of the year and made his name well known throughout Europe. With his singing career in Europe well under way, Iglesias crossed the Atlantic for the first time with an invitation to take part in the Viña del Mar festival in Chile, where he had already been heard over the air. That trip, followed by a visit to Guatemala, began a remarkable career in Latin America that has kept his records at the top of the charts in many Spanish-speaking countries year after year, and has led to scores of personal appearances from the Rio Grande to Patagonia and throughout the Caribbean. Extending his activities to Eastern Europe, Iglesias taped a television program in Romania in the early 1970s. About that time he also began to appear in Spanish-language motion pictures but, admittedly not an actor, he was unsuccessful at the box office and his film performances failed to win critical acclaim. By the time he won the 1972 Eurovision song contest, Iglesias' records were selling in the Arab countries and in Japan, as well as in Europe and Latin America.

Among Iglesias' early LP albums, recorded under the Alhambra label, are *Como el Alamo al camino* (1972), *Julio Iglesias* (1972), *Soy* (1973), *A Mexico* (1975), *El Amor* (1975), *America* (1976), *A mis 33 años* (1977), and *Emociónes* (1978). He then signed an exclusive contract with Richard Asher, the head of the New York–based CBS Records International division, who had been impressed by his Benidorm Festival performance. His albums under the CBS International label include *De niña a mujer* (1981), of which the title song was inspired by and dedicated to his daughter. Others are *Hoy* (1980), *El Disco de oro* (1981), and *Momentos* (1982). By the early 1980s Iglesias had racked up sales of 100 million albums that have earned him several hundred gold records and some 100 platinum ones. His output averages about eight new albums a year.

Under contract to CBS, Iglesias was sent on frequent tours to Italy, Germany, and France, with records being cut in the languages of those countries, as well as in Portuguese, Japanese, and his native Spanish. Jim Miller and Mac Margolis noted in their story about Iglesias in *Newsweek* (July 11, 1983): "It is reckoned that every thirty seconds in some corner of the world another one of his songs is played." The *Newsweek* writers added that "Behind Iglesias's undeniable mystique lies an astounding amount of sheer hard work." His record-making procedure starts with the selection of some three dozen songs, many of which are wholly or partly Iglesias creations, as part of the upcoming albums to be released worldwide in the following season. Iglesias makes that painstaking choice in close collaboration with his producer of long standing, Ramón Arcusa, a former member of the popular Spanish vocal team "Duo Dinámico." Arcusa then flies to Madrid to supervise the orchestral track production, a vital factor in every Iglesias disc. Once that has been satisfactorily achieved, Iglesias and Arcusa review and remix the tracks, deciding what backup vocals are to be added and to which market each will be directed.

It is then that the most taxing phase, Iglesias' actual recorded addition of his own vocals, can begin. Since he is a perfectionist, Iglesias may cut one take after another for hours on end, making up to forty takes of a single song until he is convinced that the finished product is impeccable. "The result is records that shimmer in the mind like the memory of a Mediterranean sunset," the *Newsweek* writers observed. Inglesias told *Los Angeles Times* society editor Jody Jacobs (January 24, 1983) that for the past five years he spent as much as seven, eight, or nine months a year in the recording studio. He prefers to record in the evenings and is prepared to work into the small hours of the morning for several months straight.

Although Julio Iglesias had for some time been popular among millions of Hispanics in the United States, it took him a number of years to break into the English-speaking market. British tourists who had been fascinated by his songs while vacationing in Spain began taking his records back home. In 1981 he became the first Hispanic singer to soar to the top of the British charts with a number-one song hit, his own Spanish version of the Cole Porter classic "Begin the Beguine." He followed up that success with another best-selling single in the British isles, a rendition of "Yours," which had been made popular by Vera Lynn some years earlier.

Encouraged by what British writer Donald McLachlan of *Woman* magazine (August 21, 1982) termed "his stunning success" in Britain, Julio Iglesias and CBS Records began to prepare his first album in English for British and American audiences. The planning of his entry into the top ranks of United States show business, designed and carried out with consummate finesse by the public relations firm of Rogers & Cowan, was considered a classic of its kind in the trade. In a story about "hype" in today's marketplace, *U.S. News & World Report* (December 5, 1983) quoted a Hollywood writer as calling that public relations campaign "simply brilliant," though the fact that Iglesias was already a major singing star abroad gave the campaign a huge impetus from the start.

Despite the "Julio Who?" joke started by some talk-show hosts, such as Johnny Carson and David

Letterman, when the singer's name first began to be mentioned widely in the United States, before long Iglesias was appearing on their programs and singing at some of the outstanding celebrity events around the country. In January 1983 he made a guest appearance in California at a dinner given by the American Society for Technion-Israel Institute of Technology honoring Kirk Douglas, and in March of that year, Douglas and his wife were hosts of a star-studded party at Chasen's restaurant to present Iglesias to the Hollywood establishment. That same month, the singer gave sold-out performances at the Radio City Music Hall in New York, the Universal Amphitheatre in Los Angeles and the MGM Grand Hotel in Las Vegas.

In September 1983 parties to celebrate Iglesias' fortieth birthday were given in Paris and New York City, with invitation lists that featured many of the reigning celebrities from several continents. During his visit to Paris, Iglesias was presented with the Medaille de Vermeil de la Ville de Paris by Mayor Jacques Chirac and received the first Diamond Disc Award of the *Guinness Book of World Records* as the world's best-selling recording artist, with over 100 million LP albums sold. That year, Iglesias was himself the guest singer at a gala birthday party for Frank Sinatra, which was sponsored by NBC, and he was featured at the Country Music Award ceremonies.

President and Mrs. Ronald Reagan were so impressed by his performance at an outdoor concert at Wolf Trap, near the nation's capital, that Iglesias was invited to the White House on several occasions. He took part in a 1982 White House salute to Bob Hope and was featured with Andy Williams, Leslie Uggams, and the Reagans on an NBC "Christmas in Washington" special in December 1983. In the spring of 1984 Iglesias sang at a White House gala benefit for the Princess Grace of Monaco Foundation and at a state dinner for French President François Mitterrand.

The first American-made, all-English Julio Iglesias album, *1100 Bel Air Place*, recorded under the supervision of producer Richard Perry, sold over a million copies within five days of its release by CBS, in August 1984. It features something to please everyone, including Iglesias duets with Diana Ross, Stan Getz, the Beach Boys, the Pointer Sisters, and country music star Willie Nelson. That multifaceted approach prompted pop music critic Lynn Van Matre of the *Chicago Tribune* (February 26, 1984) to suggest that a good title for the album might be "Julio Iglesias Covers All Bases," since it obviously sought to maximize his appeal to very different kinds of listeners. The song Iglesias recorded with Willie Nelson for that album, "To All the Girls I've Loved Before," released as a single before the album appeared, reached the top ten on *Billboard* magazine's listing of hits in March 1984.

In the spring of 1984 Iglesias concluded a multimillion-dollar contract with the Coca-Cola Company that may well be the most spectacular deal of its kind in show business history. Under its provisions, he is to promote the merits of Coca-Cola and

Diet Coke in commercials to be presented in 155 countries. The Coca-Cola Company, in turn, agreed to sponsor Iglesias' seven-month world-wide concert tour that was scheduled to begin in June 1984 with a benefit at the United Nations and included concerts that summer at New York's Jones Beach Theater and Radio City Music Hall. The contract was viewed as a response to singer Michael Jackson's advertising campaign for Pepsi-Cola.

In accordance with a provision in his CBS contract that he must be in the United States several months each year, Iglesias spends much of his time at the $3 million mansion he bought in 1978 on an island off Miami Beach, not far from the Criteria studio where he has cut many of his hit records, or at the Bel Air, California residence he bought in late 1983 to be used during his frequent West Coast visits. He owns property in Tahiti, Majorca, and Madrid, and he has a yacht, a private jet plane, and a fleet of luxury cars. Both his parents have spent a great deal of time with him in Florida since the elder Iglesias was rescued from Basque terrorists who had kidnapped him and held him prisoner in Spain for nineteen days in late 1981.

Julio Iglesias' marriage to Philippine-born Isabel Preisler (Hispanicized to Preysler) on January 20, 1971 ended in annulment in 1979. The couple had two sons, Julio José and Enrique, and a daughter, Chaveli. Iglesias, who remains devoted to his children, has not married again, despite the endless list of romances attributed to him by gossip columnists. He has been romantically linked to Priscilla Presley and actress Sydne Rome, among others. His close friends have included the late President Anwar Sadat of Egypt.

Described by reporters as elegant, debonair, "breeze-thin and dream-handsome," and the "sexiest male singer of the century," Julio Iglesias dresses in conservative, tailor-made Caraceni suits for his personal appearances and avoids extravagant mannerisms or gyrations on stage. His own description of himself as "just a skinny guy in a pair of baggy pants and a T-shirt" refers to the simple garb he favors in private. Dark-eyed and perpetually suntanned, Iglesias weights 158 pounds and is about six feet tall. He still walks with a slight limp as a consequence of his accident. His favorite recreations are swimming, sailing, bicycling, and relaxing with his beloved dogs.

Among the influences on him, Iglesias acknowledges Paul Anka, Neil Sedaka, Barbra Streisand, and Frank Sinatra, who in his words "all have a Mediterranean feel." He has never learned to read music because he believes that it might inhibit his interpretation of songs. According to the *Newsweek* profile, "His appeal, in the end, is simple. Using every technique of the modern recording studio and his own diaphanous voice, he has taken the Mediterranean pop ballad and raised it to a spectacular new pitch of melodramatic grandeur. It is an achievement that even skeptics grudgingly admire."

References: *Chicago Tribune* XIII p18 F 26 '84 pors; *Newsweek* 102:69 Jl 11 '83 por; *Washington Post* D p1+ D 15 '83 pors; Iglesias, Julio. *Entre el Cielo y el Infierno* (1981)

Irons, Jeremy

Sept. 19, 1948– British actor Address: b. c/o Hutton Management, 200 Fulham Rd., London SW10 9PN, England; c/o Cowan Bellow Associates, 45 Poland St., London W1V 4AU, England

Jeremy Irons' bravura performance as the witty and flippant but ultimately vulnerable dramatist hero of Tom Stoppard's play *The Real Thing*—in which he made his New York debut—not only earned him the Tony and Drama League awards as best actor of the 1983–84 Broadway season but also brought him the kind of public adulation usually bestowed on the great matinee idols of the past. Although he was trained at the Bristol Old Vic Theatre School and perfected his craft in the unparalleled British repertory system, Irons first made his name as a film and television actor in such mature and probing productions as *The French Lieutenant's Woman*, *Betrayal*, and *Brideshead Revisited*. "I like to do things which are difficult for me," he explained to Michael Bygrave in an interview for a profile in *Film Comment* (March/April 1983). "I'm very frightened of starting to live off the fat of the land, of doing work which pays me a lot but which doesn't really keep me alive as a person or as an actor." Irons' many honors include the Variety Club of Great Britain's award for best film actor of 1982 and, in the same year, nominations in both the film and television categories for a British Academy of Film and Television Arts best actor award.

The third child of Paul Dugan Irons, a chartered accountant, and his wife, Barbara Anne (Sharpe) Irons, Jeremy John Irons was born on September 19, 1948 in Cowes, a yachting resort town on the Isle of Wight, off the south coast of England. His parents separated when he was thirteen, and shortly afterwards, he enrolled at the Sherborne School, a public school in Dorset that he has described as "philistine." "My school turned out a very good bank manager, it was on that sort of level; a very good sort of middle ranking military officer," Irons told Lewis Archibald in an interview for *Arts Weekly* (October 27, 1982). "It taught you to keep a stiff upper lip, hold in your emotions, not to cry, to be respectable, to fit in. All the things which are . . . *useless* if you want to be an artist of any sort." Throughout his years at Sherborne, he indulged his own artistic bent by playing the drums in a rock music group and by acting in schoolboy productions of such classics as Sheridan's *The Critic*.

As a boy, Irons dreamed of becoming a veterinarian, probably because, as he acknowledged years later in a conversation with Leslie Bennett of the *New York Times* (January 9, 1984), he wanted "the way of life of my childhood—of living in the country with dogs and horses—to continue forever." His hopes of a veterinary career dashed by his failure to pass the required physics and chemistry exams, he moved to London following his graduation in 1965 and found employment as a social worker at a youth club in the economically depressed Camberwell area. To eke out his meager salary, Irons became a parttime busker, singing and playing his guitar outside the movie houses in Leicester Square. He took such pleasure in performing that he decided to try his luck in the theatre. Through a newspaper advertisement, he got a job as an assistant stage manager and general factotum at the Marlowe Theatre, a repertory company in Canterbury. Eventually, he was accepted for training at the Bristol Old Vic Theatre School. On completion of the two-year course of study, he was asked to join the Bristol Old Vic Company. In his three years with the troupe, Irons progressed from minor parts to central characters in the company's variegated repertory. His roles included Florizel in Shakespeare's *The Winter's Tale*, Simon in Noel Coward's *Hay Fever*, and Nick in Joe Orton's *What the Butler Saw*.

In 1971 Irons left the Bristol Old Vic to take his chances in the commercial theatre in London's West End. Determined to wait for the right part, he supported himself by working as a house cleaner and gardener for the firm Domestics Unlimited. Finally, late in the year, Irons landed the role of John the Baptist in *Godspell*, the rock musical based upon the Gospel according to St. Matthew, even though, as he told *New York* magazine's Rhoda Koenig (January 23, 1984), "I sing like an actor and dance like a duck." *Godspell* opened at the Round

House on November 17, 1971 and eventually transferred to Wyndham's Theatre in the West End, where it enjoyed a long run. Irons has worked steadily in his chosen profession ever since, expanding his range by accepting a wide variety of roles, from Don Pedro in *Much Ado About Nothing* to the devious Mick in Harold Pinter's enigmatic *The Caretaker* to the title character in the one-man tour-de-force *Diary of a Madman*, an adaptation of Nikolai Gogol's short story. He also appeared as Petruchio in the New Shakespeare Company's staging of *The Taming of the Shrew* and as Harry Thunder in the Royal Shakespeare Company's production of John O'Keefe's eighteenth-century comedy *Wild Oats*, one of the biggest hits of the 1976–77 London season.

Irons got the best notices of his career to that date for his portrayal of James Jameson, the gentle civilian artist who is trapped with the remnant of British colonial forces left behind to guard an isolated jungle base camp in the Congo in Simon Gray's short-lived *The Rear Column*. In the play, Gray describes, in grisly detail, the gradual physical and moral disintegration of the men as the months pass without the arrival of the promised relief contingent. Under Harold Pinter's direction, Irons was especially convincing in the climactic scene, when Jameson finally breaks down and arranges an act of cannibalism so that he can record it in his sketchbook. His gentleman-painter "has both the unaffected saintliness the others ascribe to him and that coolness, that detachment, which eventually allows him to procure victims for sacrifice," Benedict Nightingale wrote in a review for the *New York Times* (March 5, 1978). "What sticks in the mind afterward is his offhand, anecdotal confession of evil." Irons' interpretation earned him the Clarence Derwent Award as the most promising newcomer of the year.

Between stage assignments, Irons often appeared in television series for the BBC and London Weekend Television International, among them *The Voysey Inheritance*, *Langrishe Go Down*, *Notorious Woman*, *Love for Lydia*, and *The Pallisers*. (The last three series were eventually telecast in the United States on the Public Broadcasting Service.) Irons also impersonated a "silly ass Bertie Wooster type" in a sherry commercial. To avoid being typecast, he turned down the foolish roles his popular sherry commercials were bringing him, and in fact, declined a lucrative offer to appear in three more commercials. "I thought in the end it would harm me more than it would help me," he explained, as quoted in the *New York Times* (September 18, 1981). "I mean, as an actor, your aroma is made up of all the work you've done. And you have to be very careful."

Taking matters into his own hands, Irons determinedly sought the role of the hedonistic and self-absorbed Charles Ryder in Granada Television's adaptation of *Brideshead Revisited*, Evelyn Waugh's novel about the decline of the March-mains, an aristocratic English Catholic family, between the two world wars. The producers at first intended to cast the actor as Sebastian Flyte, the Marchmain family's prodigal son, but Irons was adamant. "I knew I could do that flashy, lovable thing. But also I couldn't think of anyone else who would do Charles right," he told Rhoda Koenig. "Charles Ryder is actually almost the man that I was educated to be—an Englishman who kept his emotions bottled up and who swam through life using his creamy English charm, as Waugh described it."

Irons eventually prevailed and, in mid-1979, joined Brideshead Revisited's brilliant cast, headed by such luminaries as Sir John Gielgud, Sir Laurence Olivier, and Claire Bloom. Filming of the lavishly produced series, which began on location in Malta, continued for nearly two years, as one delay—a prolonged strike, production difficulties, Irons' prior movie commitment—followed another. When the eleven-episode series finally reached the home screen in England late in 1981 and in the United States a few months later, critics hailed it as a "sumptuous dramaturgic feast" unequaled in television history. Viewers responded with comparable enthusiasm, making it the highest rated dramatic series ever broadcast by PBS. As for Jeremy Irons' performance as Charles Ryder, reviewers called it "brilliant" and "virtually flawless." John J. O'Connor, who appraised the production for the New York Times (January 18, 1982), was especially impressed by Irons' ability to "[avoid] excesses while making every nuance blazingly clear."

In the midst of making Brideshead Revisited, Irons began work on Karel Reisz's film adaptation of John Fowles's best-selling Victorian romance The French Lieutenant's Woman (United Artists, 1981). He had been recommended for the leading male role—that of Charles Smithson, the gentleman geologist whose obsessive interest in the mysterious woman of the title brings about his downfall—by Harold Pinter. At Pinter's urging, Reisz had screened Irons' sherry commercials and Langrishe Go Down, in which the actor had portrayed a predatory, arrogant German. The range he displayed in the two parts convinced Reisz that the actor was up to the task. Fowles's convoluted novel revolves around the relationship between Smithson and the enigmatic Sarah Woodruff, a governess ostracized by the community because of her scandalous affair with a visiting French naval officer. Written in the Victorian style, with Thackeray-like editorial intrusions by the omniscient author, the book had defeated screenwriters for years, but Pinter, who served as Reisz's scenarist, came up with the idea of using the film-within-a-film device to suggest the modern narrative voice and multiple endings of the novel. His ingenious solution set the romance of Charles and Sarah within the on-location dalliance of Mike and Anna, the actors portraying the Victorian lovers.

Fired by the challenge of playing not two characters but one character (Charles) as interpreted by the other (Mike), Irons more than held his own opposite the Academy Award–winning actress Meryl Streep, who was Sarah/Anna. Miss Streep's

"slightly chilly passion is beautifully complemented by Jeremy Irons as Charles—ardent, anguished, a figure of gentlemanly steadfastness that is touchingly inadequate to the situation," David Ansen observed in his Newsweek (July 21, 1981) review of The French Lieutenant's Woman. "As Mike, a slicker, glibber man, he's effortlessly charming at first, but as his involvement with Anna intensifies, perhaps fed by his identification with the role he's playing, Mike's eyes take on Charles's haunted look."

The release of The French Lieutenant's Woman, coupled with the virtually simultaneous telecast of Brideshead Revisited, made Irons, whose only previous screen credit was the minor role of the choreographer Michel Fokine in Herbert Ross's opulent soap opera Nijinsky (Paramount, 1980), an international star. To "break the mold" those two productions had begun to make for him, as he put it, he eagerly accepted when Jerzy Skolimowski, the expatriate Polish director, approached him with the idea for a film about Polish laborers working illegally in England. After a few months respite, during which time he contributed several scenes from Shakespeare to All the World's a Stage, Ronald Harwood's ambitious BBC series on theatre history, Irons went back before the cameras to play Nowak, the protagonist, narrator, and "central consciousness," to use Joy Gould Boyum's term, of Skolimowski's cinematic black comedy Moonlighting (Universal, 1982). Sent to London in December 1981 to oversee the cut-rate renovation of his Polish employer's London townhouse, Nowak becomes increasingly isolated and desperate as he tries to conceal the news about the imposition of martial law in their homeland from his non-English-speaking charges, resorts to shoplifting and petty thievery to make ends meet, and employs dictatorial tactics to complete the job in record time.

When Moonlighting opened at the New York Film Festival in September 1982, critics noticed a parallel between Nowak's authoritarianism and the recent Communist crackdown on Solidarity, Poland's powerful independent trade union movement. In an interview with Gene Siskel of the Chicago Tribune (April 10, 1983), Irons conceded that the film was indeed "about repression everywhere and about how power does corrupt," but it was also about "how an alien feels living in a strange society." That the actor succeeded in suggesting Nowak's loneliness and anxiety is evident in his glowing notices. Reviewers were especially impressed by his subtle use of body language. "The way we communicate is not with dialogue," the actor once insisted, as quoted in the New York Daily News (September 28, 1982). "We communicate by the way we sit, the way we're silent, the way we move, whatever. I am aware as an actor that half or three-quarters of my instrument of communication is that."

That mastery of nonverbal communication was crucial to Irons' next venture: the film version of Betrayal, Harold Pinter's dissection of adultery, in which the actor took the role of Jerry, the impulsively romantic literary agent whose long-standing affair with his best friend's wife spawns a series of lies and deceptions. Told in reverse, the minimalist tale of multiple infidelities depends as much on what Irons has called the "small . . . signs" of deceit as on dialogue for its stunning impact. Irons and his costars, Ben Kingsley and Patricia Hodge, were so expert at conveying the nuances of Pinter's subtext that many critics preferred the film, which was released by Twentieth Century-Fox in 1983, to the original stage production.

After completing Betrayal, Irons went on to portray the captain in a BBC made-for-television movie of D. H. Lawrence's short story The Captain's Doll; Harold Ackland in a film version of Ibsen's The Wild Duck opposite Liv Ullmann; and the title character in Un amour de Swann/Swann in Love (Orion Classics, 1984), Volker Schlöndorff's motion-picture adaptation of the first volume of Marcel Proust's A la recherche du temps perdu. With those commitments out of the way, Irons jumped at the chance to play the leading role in the American premiere of The Real Thing, Tom Stoppard's scintillating play about the emotional coming-of-age of a brilliant but arrogant dramatist named Henry. "I think Tom's soul and my soul must be quite similar . . . ," the actor told Leslie Bennetts. "I think his love of England, of exact language, of manners, of style, of clothes, all are a lot like me. . . . And I sort of instinctively knew Henry. I like his lack of self-consciousness, and the way he has a craft that he's good at. I like his boyishness; there's a lot of the child in Henry, and I've always believed that in every man there's a little boy trying to get out."

At the heart of The Real Thing, the most autobiographical of Stoppard's works, is the search for what is "real" in human relationships, in social and political commitments, and in art. When the play opened at the Plymouth Theatre on Broadway on January 5, 1984, Irons' touching transformation from the glib artificer of words to the inarticulate lover wounded by his wife's infidelity was applauded by New York critics as a triumph of naturalistic acting. "Early on, one senses a yearning beneath the smart banter; later, something melancholy, even somber; and before the end that long willowy figure has drooped, blanched and vocally crumpled . . . ," Benedict Nightingale wrote in his encomium for the New York Times (January 15, 1984). Even John Simon, never an admirer of the actor's work, was impressed. "There is throughout a fine blend of shrewdness and fatuity, irony and vulnerability . . . ," Simon remarked in his New York magazine (January 16, 1984) review. "This man, in Irons' hands, makes you believe that he is an artist of talent, and that under the flippancies . . . , he cares about something."

An uncommonly handsome man, Jeremy Irons stands six feet one inch tall and has light brown hair, classically chiseled features, and rather sorrowful brown eyes. Like many others in his gregarious profession, he turns to such solitary pursuits as boating (he occasionally weekends on his vintage sailing punt), horseback riding, and walking his mongrel dog, Speed, for relaxation. Although he has claimed to be "lazy, selfish, and too self-obsessed," he devoted some of his free time during the New York run of The Real Thing to organizing and promoting a benefit in behalf of a shelter for homeless mothers and their children in the Bronx, explaining simply that he "thought it would be nice to put a bit back in the pot."

Irons has been married since March 18, 1978 to Sinead Cusack, an associate artist of the Royal Shakespeare Company. They have one son, Samuel. An earlier marriage to Julie Hallam, an actress, ended in divorce. Home for Irons and his family is a Victorian house, which he renovated himself, near Hampstead Heath in northwest London. Totally dedicated to his career, the actor has formulated long-range objectives that include playing more Shakespearean roles, "because of the way Shakespeare stretches you," and directing, "when acting is no longer enough and when I've learned more." Until then, he told Leslie Bennetts, "I just want to keep myself in a position where all the good parts I would want to play are offered to me. I'd like to be big box office all over the world, just so that I would get offered the roles and could pull people into the theatre."

References: Chicago Tribune VI p5+ Ap 10 '83 pors, II p1+ Jl 17 '84 pors; Films in R 32:532+ N '81 pors; Gentlemans Q p270+ Ap '84 pors; New York 17:32+ Ja 23 '84 pors; N Y Times C p8 S 18 '81, C p13 Ja 9 '84 por; Newsweek 98:98 S 21 '81 pors; Washington Post E p1+ Mr 22 '84 pors; International Who's Who, 1984–85; International Motion Picture Almanac, 1984; Who's Who, 1984–85; Who's Who in America, 1984–85; Who's Who on Television, 1982

James, Clive (Vivian Leopold)

Oct. 7, 1939– British journalist; critic; broadcaster. Address: b. c/o The Observer, 8 St. Andrews Hill, London EC 4, England

The writer and broadcaster Clive James, once described by a peer as "a highly verbal misfit," is one of the most scintillating figures in contemporary British intellectual journalism. A polymath with an antic wit and an undisguised delight in his own virtuosity, James has been at his most serious in his literary criticism, collected in The Metropolitan Critic (1974), At the Pillars of Hercules (1977), and From the Land of Shadows (1982). He found a vent for his self-described "impulse to shock" and his shrewd eye for the ridiculous in his weekly television columns for the London Observer, which regaled more than a million readers from 1972 to 1982 and which may be sampled in the collections Visions Before Midnight (1977), The Crystal Bucket (1981), and Glued to the Box (1983).

Clive James

Since 1982 James's gadfly intelligence and sense of humor, which can be outrageously rude but is seldom unamiable, have been given wider cultural rein in feature articles for the *Observer* and steady employment as a top-billed cultural commentator on television itself. In his farewell television column in the *Observer* he wrote: "After ten years of writing this column I still face the gleaming tube with undiminished enthusiasm, but with increasing frequency I find my own face looking back at me. . . . Creativity and criticism, in my view, are more continuous than opposed, but there is such a thing as conflict of interest. . . . By standing up and moving aside for my gifted successor, Julian Barnes, I avoid the possibility of finding him suddenly sitting in my lap. No doubt he will slag one of my programmes first chance he gets, but by then I will be in the habit of damning all critics as fools."

Clive Vivian Leopold James was born in the Sydney suburb of Kogarah in New South Wales, Australia on October 7, 1939. His baptismal name was simply Vivian Leopold, and he first answered to the name Vivian. Clive was his own choice, allowed him in childhood by his mother when she realized the embarrassment the sexual ambiguity of the name Vivian was causing him. James's father was Albert Arthur James, described by him as a mechanic "of humble birth and restricted education." His mother, Minora May (Darke) James, had quit school at fourteen to go to work as an automobile upholsterer at General Motors Holden. "The Depression kept them so poor," James writes of his parents in his *Unreliable Memoirs* (Knopf, 1981), "that they had to wait years to get married and have me." Although the parents were communicants of the Church of England, out of peer influence James gravitated to the local Presbyterian church, its Sunday school, and its Boys' Brigade.

James has no memory of his father, who volunteered to go off to fight the Japanese at the beginning of World War II, never to return. On the advice of her departing husband, who mistakenly anticipated the Japanese bombing of greater Sydney, Mrs. James left the modest family home at 6 Margaret Street in Kogarah and with her son went to live in Jannali, a whistle stop half-an-hour farther down into the bush on the Illawarra railway line from Sydney. "A hard case called Mrs. Turnbull" made infants' school in Jannali "unbearable" for James, who was then, and well into adulthood, he says, "unable to cope with authority . . . tending to oscillate between nervous flippancy and overly solicitous respect."

Captured by the Japanese, Albert Arthur James survived the war only to die in the crash of an American plane transporting prisoners-of-war out of Japan in August 1945. His mother's traumatic bereavement ("It was several days before she could control herself") "marked" James "for life," contributing, he says, to "a tiresomely protracted adolescence" during which he wasted "a lot of other people's time, patience and love." In *Unreliable Memoirs* he confesses: "I know now that until recent years I was never quite all there—that I was play-acting instead of living and that nothing except my own unrelenting fever of self-consciousness seemed quite real. Eventually, in my middle thirties, I got a grip on myself."

After the war James moved with his mother back to 6 Margaret Street in Kogarah, where Mrs. James eked out a supplementary income to her meager War Widow's pension by doing piecework smocking babies' dresses at home, into the small hours of the night. In Kogarah, infants' school was "still a nightmare" for James, but "things marginally improved" when he was promoted, a year early, to primary school. He achieved the early promotion on the strength of his reading ability, which he had acquired at his aunt's house in Jannali, pouring over heaps of back issues of the magazines *Wide World, National Geographic, Picture Post, Lilliput, Collier's, Saturday Evening Post, Life,* and *Reader's Digest.* He "can't remember what it was like not to be able to read English fluently," and to this day when he is learning to read a new language he tries "to savor the moment that separates not knowing how from now knowing how not to."

Inheriting the few hundred magazines he discovered in Jannali, James read them over and over for several years, "until the covers pulled away from the staples." He felt about them "the way Turgenev felt about the emblem book he wrote of to Bakunin and made a part of Laretsky's childhood in *A Nest of Gentlefolk.*" Later he became addicted to comic books and boys' adventure stories, especially those featuring air aces, ignoring even into his teens the "better class of reading matter"—cheap sets of Dickens, Thackeray, and the Brontës—stacked away in his mother's hall cupboard. "I always had an automatic aversion to the set books," he confesses. "Reading off the course was my nature."

The masked heroes of Saturday matinee movie serials fired James's early fantasy life, and his taste in motion pictures only gradually improved after he and his mother began attending every change of program at the Ramsgate and Rockdale odeons in Sydney. Passionate about aviation, he spent many of his weekends at the aerodrome at Mascot, a few miles from Kogarah, watching the DC-3s and other planes take off and land. Through that experience, the reading of books and aviation magazines, and the study of charts, he became as expert at aircraft recognition as a professional. Also fascinated by motor vehicles, he virtually memorized whole weekly issues of *Autocar* and *Motorcycle* magazines.

Small for his age, not very good at sports (except swimming), and accused of being the teacher's pet because of his high grades, James in primary school took refuge in a comic persona, becoming, in his words, "the class smart-alec"—"a solitary's way of being gregarious." He finished elementary school in classes for the gifted in Hurtsville, near Kogarah, and his marks won him a bursary to the Sydney Boys' High School, the best secondary school in the city. To what he describes as his mother's "torrential" distress, he rejected the bursary and instead chose to go to Sydney Technical High School, a "tumbledown" vocational school, partly because his closest chum was going there and partly because he mistakenly thought that Sydney Tech would turn him into an aeronautical engineer.

Demoralized by the workshop orientation of Sydney Tech, James did poorly in all subjects except German and English, and he shone only in the latter. Luckily, just about the time that he graduated from high school, the Australian government took mercy on war "orphans" and granted them a free university education without the prerequisite of meeting Commonwealth scholarship standards. As an arts student majoring in English at Sydney University, James skipped lectures and, while haunting the university library, he was always careful "not to read anything on the course." If the syllabus called for Beaumont and Fletcher, he read Mencken and Nathan, and he went "mad on the Americans generally." He gained admission to the third year of the honors school, he boasts, only through his "ability to conjure an essay out of thin air . . . that and the incidental benefit of reading Shakespeare morning, noon, and night."

James's first published poems and essays appeared in *honi soit*, the literary weekly at Sydney University, which he edited in his senior year. Also as a senior, he was the assistant producer and chief sketch writer for the annual Union Revue. During an hiatus in his studies, he did his term of conscription in the Australian National Service. Before taking his honors degree in English, he began reviewing books for the *Sydney Morning Herald* as well as a new Australian journal of opinion called the *Nation*. After taking the degree, he joined the staff of the *Morning Herald* as assistant to the editor of the Saturday magazine page, a rewriting job in which he began to become convinced that "writing is essentially a matter of saying things in the right order."

Vaguely feeling that it was "time to move," James drew his severance pay from the *Morning Herald* and booked passage for England on the steamship *Bretagne*, which sailed from Sydney on December 31, 1961. After a good deal of getting nowhere in London, in 1964 he began his graduate work at Pembroke College, Cambridge University, where he was president of Footlights, the dramatic society. He continued to direct Footlights revues throughout the 1960s. Toward the end of the decade he read Kenneth Tynan's first book, *He That Plays the King*, "night after night, wondering how to make what was happening on stage half as thrilling as what the prodigious young critic had made happen in print." Later, it was Tynan, by then a personal friend, who placed in James's head the idea "that the presumptuousness of publishing a television column in book form was the very reason why it should be done."

When James entered the English literary scene in the late 1960s, the fashion among younger critics was abrasively countercultural, a "doggedly cultivated" stance that he came to see as "a waste of time" because "in Great Britain there was no direct involvement with the Vietnam war and hence no political reinforcement for the social pretensions of the counterculture." His own first professionally published critical essay of any length, "An Instrument to Measure Spring With" (1969), on E. E. Cummings, was written with a bravura that would nowadays, he has said, cause him "to go somewhere dark and sleep off the fever." "But at the time, when beatnik poets who could hardly string ten words together were being hailed as geniuses, it seemed important to convey something of the excitement contained in the collected works of an old bohemian who, for all his protestations of spiritual liberty, belonged firmly in the eternal tradition of schooled art."

The essay on E. E. Cummings was among those brought together in James's first collection, *The Metropolitan Critic* (Faber, 1974), consisting of literary criticism first published in the *Review*, the London *Times Literary Supplement*, and the *Listener* in the late 1960s and early 1970s. In reassessing the judgments expressed in that book, James later said that he thought that in the title essay of the collection he "was right in tracing Edmund Wilson's early radicalism to the American past rather than to the Soviet present" but "probably wrong to make light of it." Regarding "A Dinosaur at Sunset," he acknowledged that George Bernard Shaw's "imagination failed catastrophically in later life, so that he became a promoter for the totalitarian regimes whose evil he should have been the first to see," but "moral qualities" were predominant in the second volume of Shaw's collected letters, the book James had reviewed, and he persisted "in believing them to be great ones."

A more straightforward style and more tranquil mood were evident in the essays in James's second collection of literary criticism, *At the Pillars of*

Hercules (Faber, 1977), some of which were first published in Encounter, Commentary, and the New York Review of Books. The essays included mixed evaluations of Lillian Hellman ("a pioneer women's liberationist" and "an unrepentant Stalinist") and Norman Mailer ("He has gazed too long into the abyss, and now the abyss is gazing into him"); an appreciation of Raymond Chandler's detection of "incipient permanence in what sounded superficially like ephemera"; an encomium of W. H. Auden; and a positive assessment of Alexander Solzhenitsyn ("a creative artist of the very first order").

"Solzhenitsyn, like Shaw, is a master spirit who has the limitations of a master spirit," James later wrote, after Solzhenitsyn's messianic rage against Western complacency regarding Communism made him a darling of the reactionary right. "He wants the free world to have an integrated sense of ethical purpose, such as he himself has. The free world can't have that, but if he were not the man who thought it could, then he would never have given us his analysis and evocation of what an unfree world is actually like." The "magnitude of the cultural tragedy" in the Soviet Union, the official obliteration of an "inventive, forward-looking, past-respecting, liberal-minded pre-revolutionary culture" and the repression of "the deliberate poetry of talented people" rooted in that culture became clearer to James after he began studying Russian in 1975 (because he could "no longer bear not to know something about how Pushkin actually sounded"). In that study he first came fully to realize, "For all its energy and achievement, the Soviet post-revolutionary decade was already a stunted parody of what might have been . . . what must have been. Almost the entire mental life of a whole great nation was destroyed."

The first fruits of James's Russian studies appeared in some of the essays in his third collection of literary criticism, From the Land of Shadows (Cape, 1982). In his introduction to that book he wrote: "The West's best chance to endure is in staying true to its liberal heritage. . . . If the West is ever in doubt as to what that liberal heritage actually consists of, all it has to do is take a long look at the Soviet Union, and ask how the alleged giant, which undoubtedly possesses a strapping pair of hairy thighs, ever came to have such a pin head. . . . There is some point to the contention that the totalitarian states came into being specifically to remind us that there is such a thing as liberty after all."

Meanwhile, the pyrotechnics that James suppressed in his literary criticism were being released in his television criticism. When he became the Observer's TV critic in 1972 he found "not just an excuse, but a demand, for every elliptical trick in the bag," because "quiddities, quibbles, and riddles were the only means of keeping up with the requirements for comment that came gushing out of the screen." As he sat down on Friday mornings to compose his column for the following Sunday's paper, he was aware of "a million sharp-witted readers . . . waiting to test [his] responses against theirs." In such a situation, "the condition of elementary adequacy" was "to leave no phrase unturned."

His television criticism was first brought between covers in Visions Before Midnight (Cape, 1977). Sifted with an eye to what might interest an American audience, Visions Before Midnight, along with The Metropolitan Critic and At the Pillars of Hercules, was published in the United States in the one volume First Reactions by Alfred A. Knopf in 1980. In his preface to First Reactions James wrote, regarding the Visions Before Midnight section of the book: "American readers who wonder why there is nothing about Upstairs, Downstairs will not, I hope, feel insulted if they are told that some of the British programmes which are screened on Masterpiece Theatre in the U.S.A. are regarded as run-of-the-mill fantasy in their land of origin [and that] The Rockford Files is admired not just for its qualities of story and character but James Garner's miraculous social ease and the way the California air looks so warm."

American reviewers described First Reactions as "packed with aggressive learning, wit and flash" and James as a "perceptive critic," a "superb reader of poetry," and a "madly funny" and "deft" discerner of "degrees of badness" in television, able to make of Princess Anne's wedding, for example, "a brilliant deadpan comedy." In the Saturday Review (September 1980), John Fludas observed: "The schooled intelligence, the love of language, and the knowledge of human ways that you sense in the giggle pieces [about television] flower eloquently in [the literary] studies."

Reviewing James's second volume of television criticism, The Crystal Bucket (Cape, 1981), a critic for Publishers Weekly (March 13, 1981) wrote: "Devotees of James . . . regard him as a cross between Shakespeare and Noel Coward. . . . Taking the measure of American and British programs, James displays startling insights that he expresses in incomparably witty wrapups." British reviewers called James "far and away the funniest critic in regular Fleet Street employment," "one of the few columnists who make you laugh aloud."

James's introduction to his farewell volume of television criticism, Glued to the Box (Cape, 1983), was a conscientious twenty-page essay summing up what he had learned from the ten-year experience. He began facetiously, talking about the occupational hazards of the television critic ("The present writer once spilled a tray of ice-cubes into his lap when he saw Barbara Woodhouse kissing a horse") and then proceeded to more serious matters, such as the folly of deploring television's artistic limitations and its "distortion" of life. "Television is a medium only in the sense that a window is a medium," he pointed out. "A window might limit our perception of the world. . . . But [we] know the world for what it is. That is how we know the window for what it is: because we know that it does not very much shape the world—only, temporarily, what we see. . . . From the reviews given this volume's two predecessors I have grown used to finding out that I don't take the real achievements of television seriously—the real achievements being plays devoted to what their authors conceive as the decaying social fabric of contemporary Britain. On the other hand I take such meretricious, commercially motivated travesties as *Holocaust* far too seriously. . . . There is some prestige to be won by pointing out how the original works of art produced by the box are very few and that even those are not up to much. But to see the originality and truth in what was never meant to be art at all is the television critic's real task. To see the inadequacy and bogusness of much that claims the status of quality is the same task from a different aspect."

Even James's lightest prose is heavy in comparison with his mock-epic verse. *The Fate of Felicity Fark in the Land of the Media: A Moral Poem in Rhyming Couplets* (Cape, 1975) had among its characters one Ross Kenwell, a controversial film director, and Harold Half-Pint, "an elliptical playwright." That work was followed by the "tragic poem" *The Improved Version of Peregrine Prykke's Pilgrimage through the London Literary World* (Cape, 1976); the "political poem" *Britannia Bright's Bewilderment in the Wilderness of Westminster* (Cape, 1976); *Fan-Mail* (Faber, 1977), consisting of seven verse letters; and *Charles Charming's Challenges on the Pathway to the Throne* (New York Review, 1981), a guide to the royal wedding and such guests as Prime Minister Margo Hatbox and historian A. J. P. Tailspin.

James wrote the lyrics that were set to music and sung by Pete Atkin on several RCA record albums, including *Driving Through Mythical America* and *Live Libel*. Warner Brothers Music, Ltd. has published some of the songs under the title *A First Folio*. James's television credits include the series *Cinema, Up Sunday, Saturday Night People, Clive James on Television*, and *The Late Clive James* and the documentaries "Shakespeare in Perspective: Hamlet" (1980), "The Clive James Paris Fashion Show" (1981), and "Clive James Live in Las Vegas" (1982).

Clive James is taller and heavier than average, and he is more hirsute in the eyebrows than he is at the hairline. When he was a television critic he acknowledged that his wife abetted his task "with scholarly precision as well as infinite patience" while his daughters "grew increasingly valuable as an early warning system: they were the first to spot the vital importance of *Tiswas* and if it had not been for their keen eyes [he] might have been much slower to notice that Lucy in *Dallas* had no neck." He summed up his political worldview in the introduction to *From the Land of Shadows*: "I spent a good number of my young years being scared witless by the foreign policy of the United States, which seemed specifically designed to yield the moral advantage to the Eastern powers. . . . The Carter administration, which it is fashionable at the moment to laugh at, did something to reverse this policy and is thus likely to gain credit in the long view, especially now that President Reagan seems as determined to misunderstand the world he is living in as all his predecessors put together." James knows that changes need to be made in the Western democracies, but he is "of the wrong generation, and [has] the wrong education, to believe in his heart that they should be radical changes."

References: *Contemporary Authors* vol 105 (1982); James, Clive. *Unreliable Memoirs* (1981); *Who's Who, 1984-85*

Jayewardene, J(unius) R(ichard)

(jā-ə-wär´də-nä)

Sept. 17, 1906– Executive President of the Democratic Socialist Republic of Sri Lanka. Address: b. President's House, 66 Ward Place, Colombo 7, Sri Lanka

Under the leadership of Junius Richard Jayewardene, who took office as executive president in February 1977, the Indian Ocean island nation of Sri Lanka, known until 1972 as Ceylon, has provided much encouragement for those who believe that Third World countries can modernize without resorting to authoritarian government. Firmly committed to Western-style democracy and to the free-enterprise system, Jayewardene has implemented economic and social reforms that have won widespread admiration and support. But the nation is torn by intercommunal strife between its Sinhalese majority and its Tamil minority that threatens to impede further progress, and although Jayewardene's forty years in politics have sensitized him to the Tamil problem, a peaceful resolution of the conflict has thus far eluded him.

Junius Richard Jayewardene (the name is spelled Jayawardene in some sources), the son of Justice E. W. and Mrs. A. H. (Wijewardene) Jayewardene, was born in Colombo, the capital of what was then the British crown colony of Ceylon, on September 17, 1906. His younger brother, Harry W. Jayewardene, is chairman of the board of management of the Sri Lanka Foundation Institute. Jayewardene's family was part of the prosperous and influential native middle class that rose to prominence under British rule. Many of his relatives were lawyers, active in the country's nascent political life, and his parents apparently intended that he too would someday enter politics, as indicated by their decision to name him "Junius" after the renowned, pseudonymous Englishman who wrote a vitriolic series of polemical political letters during the reign of King George III.

Like more than two-thirds of his compatriots, Jayewardene was reared in the Theravada form of Buddhism. As a child, he often played at his grandmother's home, a white stone seaside mansion that now houses the American Embassy. Educated at the Royal College in Colombo, where he was a member of the school's cricket eleven, he then went on for higher studies to the Ceylon University College and the Ceylon Law College, both in Colombo, and graduated from the latter in 1932.

After practicing law for several years as an advocate of the Supreme Court of Ceylon, Jayewardene joined the Ceylon National Congress party, and from 1940 to 1947 he was its honorary general secretary. Elected in 1940 to the Colombo Municipal Council, he served on it until 1943 when he won a by-election for the seat representing the constituency of Kelaniya in the State Council, Ceylon's highest legislative body.

In 1947, when Ceylon's political life underwent a series of transformations preparatory to its becoming an independent republic with full dominion status within the British Commonwealth in February of the following year, the National Congress, led by D. S. Senanayake, merged with several smaller parties to form the moderate United National party (UNP). A new constitution was adopted in 1948 in which the State Council became the House of Representatives within a bicameral legislature. It remained in effect until 1972, when under another new constitution a unicameral legislature, called the National State Assembly, was established. Jayewardene served as the UNP's treasurer in 1947 and 1948 and occupied the seat for Kelaniya in the House of Representatives from 1947 to 1956. Elected in July 1960 to the seat for the constituency of Colombo South, he retained it until 1977, when he won election to the seat for Colombo West.

Meanwhile, the UNP had won an easy victory in February 1948 in Ceylon's first post-independence election, and D. S. Senanayake, the party's leader, became the new nation's first prime minister. Jayewardene served as minister of finance in Senanayake's cabinet until 1953, and in that post he headed Ceylon's delegation to the 1948 Sterling Talks in London. He also regularly represented Sri Lanka in London at the annual Commonwealth Prime Ministers' Conferences from 1948 to 1953 and at the annual Commonwealth Finance Ministers' Conferences from 1948 to 1952.

From 1947 to 1952 Jayewardene was a governor of the World Bank and International Monetary Fund. In 1950 he collaborated with Percy Spender of Australia on the Colombo Plan, an international program for providing financial and technical assistance to developing Asian nations. In 1951 he led Sri Lanka's delegation to the Japanese Peace Treaty Conference in San Francisco. The outspoken hostility to the Soviet Union that he voiced while there won him the approval of John Foster Dulles and other Western diplomats but led his political opponents at home to dub him, derisively, "Yankee Dick."

In 1953 Jayewardene became minister of food and agriculture as well as leader of the House of Representatives under Dudley Senanayake, who had succeeded to the prime ministership after the death in March 1952 of his father, D. S. Senanayake. Now widely recognized as the party's second-ranking leader, Jayewardene held both posts until 1956 when the UNP was defeated by the leftist Sri Lanka Freedom Party (SLFP). From March to July 1960, while the UNP was briefly again in power, Jayewardene served simultaneously as minister of finance, information, broadcasting, local government, and housing in Dudley Senanayake's Cabinet.

In the election of July 1960, the UNP was once more defeated by the SLFP, whose leader, Mrs. Sirimavo Bandaranaike—the widow of former Prime Minister Solomon W. R. D. Bandaranaike, who had been assassinated the year before—became the world's first woman prime minister. Serving as leader of the parliamentary opposition, Jayewardene headed Sri Lanka's delegation to the fiftieth convocation of the Royal Commonwealth Society in London in 1961. When the UNP returned to power in March 1965 and Dudley Senanayake again formed a government, Jayewardene became minister of state as well as parliamentary secretary to the prime minister, who also served as minister of defense and external affairs. In 1967 he chaired the ministerial meeting at Algiers of the Group of 77, an ad hoc organization of developing nations. Elected its vice-president, he led the group's ministerial mission to Great Britain and the Scandinavian countries in November of that year. In 1968 he led the Sri Lanka delegation to the United Nations Conference on Trade and Development (UNCTAD) in New Delhi, India. When after the general election of May 1970 Mrs. Bandaranaike returned to the prime ministership as head of a United Front that combined the SLFP with a Moscow-oriented Communist party and a Trotskyite party, Jayewardene again led the parliamentary opposition during a period marked by much political violence. After Dudley Senanayake died in April 1973, he became the leader of the UNP.

Although Ceylon had long been renowned for its favorable climate, natural beauty, and agricultural plenitude, the country had entered upon difficult times by the 1970s. Despite the fact that its governmental system, patterned on that of Great Britain, was one of the few functioning parliamentary democracies in the Third World, its primarily agrarian economy was gravely troubled as a result of fluctuations in the demand for tea, rubber, and copra, its main products. Simultaneously, the SLFP's policy of nationalizing large estates, accompanied by inept management, had slackened initiative, efficiency, and productivity throughout the country. As a result, unemployment became rampant, reaching 20 percent by the mid-1970s, and social welfare measures stretched the government's finances to the breaking point, while shortages were commonplace and prices soared. Furthermore, the SLFP government was riddled with corruption and nepotism. Many of its highest officials were members of Mrs. Bandaranaike's family who had remained in their posts despite evidence of incompetence and efforts to enrich themselves.

By contrast, Jayewardene was widely regarded as a *dharmishta*, or "righteous one," and as the general election of July 1977 approached, he made those issues the focus of his campaign. To attract poorer voters to his essentially middle-class party, he gave the UNP's program the gloss of a socialist veneer, but at the same time he emphasized that Sri Lanka's economic salvation could only come through the cultivation of capitalism and the development of the private sector. That goal would be accomplished by, among other means, the establishment of a vast free-trade zone near Colombo to make the island more inviting to foreign investors and by restructuring its government along French lines, with an executive president serving a fixed term rather than a prime minister continually dependent on parliamentary support, because—in Jayewardene's view—only a strong executive could initiate the needed reforms. Convinced that Sri Lanka's emergency was beyond partisan solution, Jaywardene promised that if elected he would form a coalition government representing all of the country's political parties.

The election returns surpassed all expectations. The UNP, which had held nineteen seats previously, won 139 seats in the 168-member Parliament, with a clear majority of the popular vote, while the SLFP, which formerly held ninety-one seats, retained only eight, and both Marxist parties were excluded. As a long-standing exponent of the democratic process, Jayewardene was, ironically, not completely happy about the scale of his victory, since it meant that his government, which obviously could no longer be the coalition that he had promised, would be deprived of the constructive criticism and moderating influence provided by a strong opposition. Furthermore, he feared that the radical parties, now lacking a parliamentary outlet, might turn to violence to attain their goals.

On the other hand, Sri Lanka's voters had given him an overwhelming mandate. Since the governmental changes he had called for would provide the means of implementing the rest of his program, Jayewardene turned to those measures first. With the necessary two-thirds majority in Parliament assured, the existing constitution was amended to create an executive presidency, and on February 4, 1978, after resigning his parliamentary seat in order to be eligible, Jayewardene was inaugurated into the new office in a festive ceremony held in Kandy, the island's ancient capital, that included a *raja perehera*, or royal procession, of 141 elephants. A new constitution for what was now known as the Democratic Socialist Republic of Sri Lanka went into effect on September 7, 1978. Its features included direct election of the president for a six-year term and proportional representation in parliamentary elections to ensure that the distribution of seats would conform with the popular vote.

Jayewardene's reforms and innovations in the nonpolitical sphere proceeded with equal dispatch. Animated by the realization that high-technology solutions are often too sophisticated for the needs of a developing country, he retained a West German engineering organization to design an improved version of the bullock cart, the primary means of transportation in Sri Lanka's rural areas and even in many of its towns. To improve worker morale, he introduced such measures as posting on street signs the names of the personnel responsible for keeping the street clean and paying traffic officers a percentage of the fines they collected.

In order to have funds available for developmental purposes without further imbalancing the government's budget, Jayewardene trimmed Sri Lanka's bloated civil service to about a quarter the size it had been during the SLFP regime. Moreover, taking a drastic step that all parties recognized as necessary but one that had been impossible before the adoption of the new constitution, he revised the nation's social welfare system to ensure that food and fuel aid went only to the poor and not to the hundreds of thousands of others, including most of the country's richest families, who had also been regularly receiving subsidies.

Emphasizing the need for economic diversification, foreign investment, and free enterprise as the keys to Sri Lanka's development, Jayewardene repeatedly indicated, often in veiled terms, that his government was not hostile to the United States and would follow a "genuinely nonaligned" foreign policy rather than "leaning more to some states than to others," as the SLFP government had done. Although he was circumspect about "naming names," he made it abundantly clear that his sympathies lay with the West by adding, "I am very much devoted to the democratic principle, so wherever there are free elections and democratic freedoms, I am closer to them than to those who haven't got those freedoms."

The most important features of Jayewardene's program, partly financed by funding from the World Bank and other foreign sources, included the massive Mahaweli River Development Plan and the free trade zone north of Colombo. The former, which entailed the construction of five major dams and reservoirs at a cost estimated at $1.2 billion, was to bring 900,000 acres of virgin land into cultivation, improve the irrigation of much other farm land, and provide hydroelectric energy needed to power new industries and electrify backward rural areas. It was originally designed as a thirty-year plan, but Jayewardene insisted that it could be completed within six years. Many experts disagreed. The 200-square-mile free trade zone north of Colombo was well established by mid-1979, with several factories in operation and more expected to follow, since it offered foreign firms an inviting combination of a free-enterprise climate and an industrious, well-educated work force coupled with lavish direct subsidies, tax exemptions, and low wage rates.

Progress on both of those projects and also on the urban renewal of Greater Colombo was significant, and the Sri Lankan economy, as a result, displayed signs of improved health. For example, although traffic in Colombo harbor increased substantially, waiting time for ships dropped from an average of two or three months to less than a week by the early 1980s. Nonetheless, inflation remained unchecked, partly as a result of the devaluation of the rupee, and unemployment hovered around 20 percent, requiring continued huge welfare expenditures that the nation could ill afford.

Hoping that those difficulties would disappear as the development plans proceeded, Sri Lanka's voters endorsed Jayewardene's program by re-electing him, with 52.4 percent of the vote, for a six-year term as president in October 1982. The contest was widely regarded as a referendum that posed a clear-cut choice between what William K. Stevens described in the *New York Times* (October 20, 1982) as "free-wheeling, high-growth capitalism" and "something very near to a classic form of welfare socialism."

But despite Jayewardene's election victory, the nation's tranquility was soon shattered by the renewal of a racial-ethnic conflict dating back to pre-colonial times. The majority of the Sri Lankan populace of some 14.8 million are members of the predominantly Buddhist Sinhalese ethnic group, but there is also a sizable Tamil minority, mostly Hindu and amounting to about 20 percent of the total population. Prejudice against the Tamils has been widespread, and since most of them are concentrated in one region, the Jaffna Peninsula, they have developed a strong separatist sentiment. In 1977 Jayewardene promised to meet some of the demands of the Tamils but apparently failed to recognize the potential gravity of the problem and postponed action on it while devoting himself to economic development. By the early 1980s the country was increasingly disturbed by terrorist actions perpetrated by the Tamil Tigers, a nationalist group that was believed to have Communist backing. The Sri Lankan army and police, dominated by Sinhalese, responded with brutal reprisals, and

in the summer of 1983 anti-Tamil riots resulted in several hundred deaths and much loss of property.

Despite his declared intention to find means of alleviating the grievances of the Tamils, Jayewardene has, according to Amnesty International, countenanced serious violations of human rights in the effort to suppress Tamil terrorism. Moreover, maintaining that secession would be absolutely unacceptable, he has, through legislation, effectively deprived the Tamils of legal representation by refusing to permit members of the two Tamil political parties, which both have separatist platforms, to be seated in Parliament. The situation reminded some observers of that in Cyprus, for just as Turkey became militarily involved in Cyprus to protect that island's Turkish minority, India has taken an interest in the well-being of its ethnic kin in Sri Lanka, even though India's Prime Minister Indira Gandhi, with whom Jayewardene has cordial relations, had thus far resisted demands from some of her compatriots for intervention in Sri Lanka.

In the months that followed the summer riots, Jayewardene removed some of the restrictions on civil liberties, ending censorship, easing the curfew, and freeing a number of political detainees. By October 1983 conditions had calmed down enough to enable Jayewardene to meet in a conference with opposition parties. Although still adamantly opposed to secession for the Tamils, he was now willing to discuss federalism as a possible solution.

But national reconciliation talks, convened by Jayewardene in January 1984, failed to end the strife, and in April the government temporarily imposed a state of emergency. In May, amid continuing violence, an American engineer and his wife were kidnapped and briefly held by Tamil separatists in Jaffna. Meanwhile, loan negotiations between Sri Lanka and the International Monetary Fund were suspended after the Jayewardene government rejected IMF demands for strict economic measures including currency devaluation. During June and early July 1984, Jayewardene visited the United States, Great Britain, and India to discuss means of alleviating his country's ethnic conflict and to propose international initiatives in the struggle against terrorism.

Interested in sports since his youth, Jayewardene was president of the Ceylon Cricket Association from 1952 to 1954. He has also been active as a Buddhist lay worker, serving as managing trustee of the Anagarika Dharmapala Trust since 1935 and as secretary of the Buddhist Congress Tri Pitaka Trust from 1940 to 1947. Fluent in both Sinhalese and English, he has published several books, including *Some Sermons of the Buddha* (1940), *Buddhism and Marxism and Other Buddhist Essays* (1957), *Selected Speeches, 1944–1973* (1974), *A Better Life for the People* (1978), and *A New Path* (1978).

Junius Richard Jayewardene—who is popularly known as "J. R."—was married in 1935 to Eleena Rupasinghe, a wealthy heiress. They live in his family's colonial-style home in Colombo, which they find more comfortable than Government House, the official presidential residence. They have one son, a Buddhist monk. A tall, slender man of impresssive appearance and charismatic appeal, whose physical energy belies his age, Jayewardene usually appears in public in a spotlessly white traditional native garment. According to Denzil Peiris, writing in the *Guardian* (June 11, 1980), his "political speeches and writings are urbane, and self-possessed even under scurrilous criticism. Ice water runs through his veins."

References: *Cur World Leaders* 21:19 Mr '78, 24:40+ Ja '81; *Guardian* p7 Je 11 '80 por; *N Y Times* A p7 Ag 31 '77; *International Who's Who*, 1983-84; *International Year Book and Statesmen's Who's Who*, 1984; *Who's Who*, 1984-85

Johanson, Donald C(arl)

June 28, 1943- Anthropologist. Address: b. Institute of Human Origins, 2453 Ridge Rd., Berkeley, Calif. 94709

With the results of his remarkable discoveries of hominid fossil remains in Ethiopia's Afar triangle in the 1970s, the American paleoanthropologist Donald C. Johanson has challenged prevailing views on human evolution. Excavating at Hadar in Africa's Great Rift Valley in 1974, Johanson unearthed "Lucy," the 3-million-year-old skeleton of a small-brained but erect-walking anthropoid, the oldest relatively intact skeleton of any bipedal human ancestor ever found. On the basis of that and other finds, he proposed for consideration as the

oldest known ancestor of *Homo sapiens* a new species of primate, which he named *Australopithecus afarensis* (the Afar Ape-man), a species more primitive than the previously known *Australopithecus africanus*.

Johanson's analysis of his fossil finds, formally published in 1979, dealt a major blow to the belief that fully erect posture evolved concurrently with the freeing of hands for toolmaking and the enlargement of the brain. "Lucy proved that what we call bipedalism was *the* thing that separated us from the apes," he has explained. "It's the primal character. When we stood up and walked on two legs, we were on the road to man. For more than a century we've believed that big brains, stone tools, and bipedal posture all went together. But Lucy preceded the big-brained toolmakers by almost two million years." Johanson, formerly the curator of physical anthropology at the Cleveland Museum of Natural History, is now director of the Institute of Human Origins in Berkeley, California. The excitement he experienced in his scientific detective work comes across in his account of that work, written with Maitland A. Edey, *Lucy: The Beginnings of Humankind* (Simon & Schuster, 1981), the recipient of an American Book Award.

Donald Carl Johanson was born on June 28, 1943 in Chicago, Illinois to Carl Torsten Johanson, a barber, and Sally Eugenia (Johnson) Johanson, both immigrants from Sweden. Two years later the father died, and eventually mother and son moved to Hartford, Connecticut where Mrs. Johanson went to work as a domestic. Johanson became interested in anthropology through Paul Leser, a neighbor in Hartford who taught the subject at the Hartford Seminary Foundation and who became a surrogate father to him. His specific interest in paleoanthropology, the study of fossils of human ancestors, was sparked by the finds of Louis and Mary Leakey in Tanzania, which he read about in high school. Using a new potassium-argon dating method, the Leakeys in 1959 identified their *Australopithecus boisei* skull as a 1.8-million-year-old hominid fossil—the first to be reliably dated—and three years later they discovered a true human fossil, *Homo habilis* (handy man, or toolmaking man), of similar age. Other early influences on Johanson were the works of Charles Darwin and Thomas Huxley.

Paul Leser tried to dissuade Johanson from going into anthropology because, he argued, the career opportunities were better in chemistry, which Johanson was good at in high school. Temporarily bowing to Leser's advice, Johanson entered the University of Illinois as a chemistry major, but the subject "bored" him, and, besides, the Leakeys were proving that "a man could make a career out of digging up fossils." Switching his major, he took his B.A. degree with honors in anthropology in 1966. In the course of his undergraduate study he gained archeological field experience at various midwestern sites.

Primarily concerned with human paleontology, Johanson successfully applied to the University of

Chicago to do graduate work there under F. Clark Howell, the paleoanthropologist credited with instituting the multidisciplinary approach to archeological site development. In 1970 he took his M.A. degree at Chicago, with the thesis *Morphological and Metrical Variability in the Chimpanzee Molar Dentition*, and four years later he took his Ph.D., with the dissertation *An Odontological Study of the Chimpanzee with Some Implications for Hominoid Evolution*. Johanson's graduate research took him to museums in England, France, Belgium, Kenya, South Africa, and Germany and on field expeditions in Ethiopia.

Johanson began his professional career in 1972 as an assistant professor in the department of anthropology at Case Western Reserve University in Cleveland, Ohio and as associate curator of anthropology at the Cleveland Museum of Natural History. He remained attached to both institutions for nine years, during the last several of which he was adjunct professor at the university and curator of physical anthropology and director of scientific research at the museum.

Most of the early-man and near-man discoveries in eastern Africa in the first three-quarters of this century were made in Tanzania, notably by Louis and Mary Leakey; in Kenya, notably by the Leakeys' son, Richard; and on the Lower Omo River in southwest Ethiopia, notably by F. Clark Howell and Yves Coppens. In 1972 the French geologist Maurice Taieb introduced Johanson to a new fossil rich region, the Hadar Valley in northeastern Ethiopia, the home of the Afar people. Six weeks of preliminary reconnaissance there convinced Johanson that it was a paleontological hot spot. Taieb organized the International Afar Research Expedition, and Johanson, assisted by Yves Coppens, raised funds, some from the National Science Foundation, and assembled a small team of scientists and students.

In October 1973 the team set up camp near the Awash River in the Hadar Valley. The 1973 season produced no teeth or jaws, usually the best-preserved fossils, but Johanson did find a three-million-year-old knee joint, the oldest anatomical evidence of bipedal stature and locomotion, the hallmark of hominids. When the team returned to Hadar in October 1974 it located fragments of four hominid skeletons. Then, at noon on November 30, 1974, Johanson and Tom Gray, a graduate student, made the grand discovery: a 3-million-year-old, three-foot-six-inch female hominid skeleton, 40-percent complete. The camp rocked with excitement following the discovery, as Johanson recounts in *Lucy*: "That first night we never went to bed at all. We talked and talked. We drank beer after beer. There was a tape recorder, and a tape of the Beatles' song 'Lucy in the Sky with Diamonds' went belting out into the night sky. . . . At some point . . . the new fossil picked up the name of Lucy. . . . We were sky-high, you must remember, from finding her."

Johanson went on to place Lucy in the scheme of human evolution. "We can picture human evolution as starting with a primitive ape-like type that gradually [became] more man-like. . . . The handiest way of separating the newer types from their ape ancestors is to lump together all those that stood up on their hind legs [as] hominids. I am a hominid [of] the genus *Homo* and [of] the species *sapiens*: thinking man. . . . I consider Neanderthal [Man] conspecific with *sapiens*, with myself. . . . Before him in time was a less advanced type: *homo erectus*. Put him on the subway and people would probably take a suspicious look at him. Before *Homo erectus* was . . . *Homo habilis*; put him on the subway and people would probably move to the other end of the car. . . . Back of *homo habilis*, might be something like Lucy . . . out of the human range entirely." Lucy, he concluded, is in the category of hominids who are "too primitive to be called humans," who "must be given another name." The name he ultimately decided on was *Australopithecus* (for southern apes) *afarensis* (for the region where Lucy was found).

Back in the United States in 1975 with probably the most electrifying fossil in the world, Johanson suddenly found himself beseiged by scientists eager to work with him, and money ceased to be a problem. Having just been appointed curator of physical anthropology at the Cleveland Museum of Natural History, he began phasing the best of his students graduating from Case into postgraduate work with him there. With additional funding from the National Science Foundation, the L. S. B. Leakey Foundation, the National Geographic Society, and other patrons, Johanson returned to Hadar with an expanded team in the fall of 1975. That season the team made a great fossil discovery: "the First Family." On a slope beside the ancient lake at Hadar (designated Afar Locality 333) Johanson and his associates unearthed a cluster of 200 bones and teeth, the fossil remains of an *Australopithecus afarensis* band of at least thirteen individuals who had met sudden death together, probably by drowning in a flash flood. From a scientific viewpoint, the 333 collection brought the promise of new insights into the anatomy of early hominids. In philosophical terms, as Johanson observed in an article in the *National Geographic* (December 1976), the assemblage confirmed his personal belief "that man as an intelligent being has his origins in cooperative behavior."

With generous grants from a number of foundations, Johanson developed a major laboratory of physical anthropology at the Cleveland Museum of Natural History, beginning in 1976. Scholars from all over the world were attracted to the lab to join Johanson and his associate Timothy White in their study of the fossils from Hadar as well as similar specimens found by Mary Leakey at Laetoli in Tanzania. His decision to classify the fossils as those of a distinct, previously unnamed species ancestral to both the *Homo* line and the now long extinct *Australopithecus africanus* was announced in 1978, and he and White published an interpretative paper on the subject in the January 26, 1979 issue of *Science*.

Neither Johanson nor White was prepared for the explosion of interest that followed the formal disclosure of *afarensis* in print. Along with enthusiasm, there was criticism in the response, mostly on the ground that his invention of the species *Australopithecus afarensis* was precipitate and perhaps unnecessary. Beyond the nominalist issue of species designation, *Australopithecus afarensis* raised substantial questions concerning the time-frame of human evolution and the relationship of the acquisition of upright gait to the development of a recognizably human brain. Since the fossils had been dated at over three million years but were not of the *Homo* lineage, it followed that humankind had emerged later than had been supposed. Another jolt to received wisdom was the conclusion that bipedalism had come about not in tandem with, but prior to, an enlarged brain; it was an adaptive development that could account for pair-bonding, separation of sexual receptivity from the estrus cycle, rapid child-bearing, and adequate nurturance. What this led to, as Johanson pointed out, was "mosaic evolution," the idea that "man did not become man through an evolutionary process that operated uniformly over the body," that "some parts of the body became human before others."

Among Johanson's challengers were Mary Leakey, who declined public comment except to say that she was "utterly shocked," and her son Richard, who disputed Johanson—without severing their friendship—in professional journals and symposia during 1979. "The reason we have received so much criticism from the Leakeys," Johanson guessed, "is that this is the first time a major viable alternative to their way of thinking has been proposed in thirty-five or forty years." He explained to Peter Gorner of the *Chicago Tribune* (April 2, 1981): "The Leakeys seemed locked into tradition. Louis Leakey never could accept the idea that man descended from the australopithecines—creatures like Lucy. He found them 'too brutish,' too apelike. . . . Richard and Mary are just upholding the family tradition." The Leakeys, positing a *Homo* lineage going back four or five million years (two million further back than Johanson's estimate), discounted Johanson's *afarensis* as not a separate human ancestor but rather a curious offshoot from the evolutionary tree, an unusual *Australopithecus africanus*. While disagreeing with Johanson over the identity of the fossilized footprints she found at Olduvai Gorge in Tanzania (whether they were early *Homo* or relatives of Lucy), Mary Leakey did agree that the footprints established bipedal walking approximately 1.5 million years earlier than previously thought.

After the 1976 archeological season, the annual expeditions to Hadar were suspended for two years because of political unrest in Ethiopia. During those years Johanson conducted preliminary field research surveys in Yemen and Saudi Arabia. He returned to Ethiopia briefly in 1978 and resumed direction of the Hadar expedition in 1982. Early in 1982 he left his position as curator of physical anthropology and director of scientific research at the Cleveland Museum of Natural History to become director of the newly founded Institute of Human Origins in Berkeley, California in 1981. In addition to the book *Lucy*, Johanson has written some seventy-five articles for professional and popular journals, and he collaborated on the PBS television productions *First Family* (1981) and *Lucy in Disguise* (1982). He hosted the BBC/Partridge Television series *Nature* (1982) and narrated the National Geographic Society film *Fossils: Clues to the Past* (1983).

Donald C. Johanson, a sturdy six-footer with brown eyes and brown hair, speaks German and Swedish in addition to English. First married, and divorced, when he was a graduate student, he married his second and present wife, the former Susan Rannigan, on May 16, 1981. The couple has two children, Colleen and Matthew. Johanson's recreations include tennis and photography. In politics, he is a Democrat.

In his broader philosophical views Johanson focuses on the commonality shared by human beings with all living things by virtue of DNA, the organic life-code that marks all of nature as one family. "This whole world of nature," he observed in one of the many speeches he gives to scientific and humanities groups, "is an incredibly intricate web, which is so interconnected that no matter where we touch it the response is felt in every other part of that web." He sees human evolution as a novel experience that culminated "in a species capable of exploring and unraveling its own beginning" and thus of making understandable the mystery of the cosmos.

From his paleoanthropological platform, Johanson has on occasion spoken out on such issues as urban social disintegration. In an interview with an editor of *U.S. News and World Report* (April 13, 1981), he addressed the dangerous possibility that we "have moved so far away from our natural environment that we are no longer in tune with the world around us." "If we are interested in seeing that humankind survives," he said, "it's going to be up to us to overcome such problems as nuclear holocaust." In his acceptance speech when presented with a 1983 Distinguished Service Award by the American Humanist Association, he stated his view that the "one goal" of education is "to enlighten people, to get them away from relying on religious dogma" and his fear that "we are going to return very quickly to something that people like our president and his sidekick, Jerry Falwell, are so interested in developing—that is, ignorance." "Ignorance leads . . . to prejudice [and] prejudice to repression," he said, adding: "I am terribly worried about the future. . . . We are at an important evolutionary juncture . . . and if we want our descendants to one day look back on their ancestry and ask where they came from, we've got to prevent someone from pushing the button."

References: *Chicago Tribune* p14+ Ap 2 '81; N Y *Times* C p2+ Ja 30 '79 por, p1+ F 18 '79 por, B p15 D 16 '82; *People* 13:80+ Mr 3 '80 pors;

Johanson, Donald C. and Edey, Maitland A. Lucy (1981); Reader, John. Missing Links (1981)

Kelly, Petra (Karin)

Nov. 29, 1947– West German political leader; social activist. Address: b. c/o Die Grünen im Bundestag, Bundeshaus, 5300 Bonn 1, Federal Republic of Germany; h. Leuchsstrasse 5/1, 8500 Nuremberg, Federal Republic of Germany

Described variously as an "antiparty party," as "an amalgam of people with grievances," and as "a lobby for people without lobbies," West Germany's environmentalist and antinuclear Green party, which first entered the Bundestag in March 1983, has as its most visible and articulate representative Petra Kelly. A former civil servant with the European Community, Miss Kelly helped to found the Green party in 1979 and serves as a speaker for its parliamentary faction. Inspired by Thoreau, Gandhi, and Martin Luther King Jr., rather than by Marx and Lenin, Miss Kelly served her apprenticeship in social activism as a student in the United States during the turbulent 1960s and has since devoted herself to the struggle against nuclear weapons installations, against pollution of the environment, and for peace and human rights.

Petra Karin Kelly—whose family name was originally Lehmann—was born in Günzberg, Bavaria on November 29, 1947. Her father, a journalist, abandoned the family when she was about seven, and after divorcing him, her mother, the former Marianne Birle, married Lieutenant Colonel John E. Kelly, a United States Army officer stationed in West Germany, who adopted her. A frail and sickly child, Petra Kelly often had to forgo sports and physical education classes at the Roman Catholic girls' boarding school in Günzburg that she attended until the age of thirteen. About three years of her early life were spent in hospitals, where she underwent several kidney operations. It was perhaps her own vulnerable physical condition that inspired her idealistic desire to help the less fortunate, and for a time she had the ambition to become a nun or a missionary.

In 1960 Lieutenant Colonel Kelly brought his family to Columbus, Georgia, where Petra soon mastered the English language. Later, as a high school student in Hampton, Virginia, she took part in school debates in which she criticized United States military involvement in Vietnam. In 1966 she enrolled in the School of International Service at American University in Washington, D.C. where she studied political science, international relations, and world politics, and served for a year as a teaching assistant. Among other distictions, she received a Woodrow Wilson fellowship. Motivated by the writings of Henry David Thoreau and by the activities of the Rev. Martin Luther King Jr., she took part in civil rights and antiwar demonstrations. In 1968 she was a volunteer in the presidential campaign of Robert F. Kennedy and founded Students for Kennedy in Washington. After Kennedy's assassination she worked as a volunteer in the office of Hubert H. Humphrey, whom she had met on a television talk show featuring foreign students, during which she challenged his support of the Vietnam war. Later, after talking with him, she came to respect Humphrey as a man with "socially just ethics and deep political feeling" and "one of the very few uncorrupted politicians in America," as she told Clive Freeman of People (November 22, 1982). Voted "outstanding woman of the year" by her fellow students, Petra Kelly graduated cum laude from American University in 1970 with a B.A. degree.

Perhaps the most traumatic experience in Petra Kelly's life was the death in 1970 of her ten-year-old half-sister, Grace Patricia Kelly, after a three-year bout with eye cancer. Her belief that overdoses of radiation treatment at a clinic in Heidelberg contributed to her sister's death later may have helped to motivate her opposition to nuclear armaments and power plants. In 1973, in her sister's memory, Petra Kelly founded at Nuremberg the Grace P. Kelly Association for the Promotion of Cancer Research for Children. To help achieve its goals Petra Kelly planned to establish the "Heidelberg Children's Planet," described in Scala magazine (No. 10, 1981) as a model of "an autonomous children's world" in which "children with cancer and other chronic illnesses can play and learn and . . . express their most fundamental needs." Designed to "offer a natural alternative to the cold, intimidating, sterile world of the conventional hospital," the Children's Planet garnered widespread international support but must await the availability of the necessary funds to be put into operation.

Meanwhile, after graduating from American University Miss Kelly went to the Netherlands for a year to study political science at the University of Amsterdam, working at the same time, until October 1971, as a research assistant in the Europa Institut. She obtained her M.A. degree from the university after submitting a thesis in which she criticized the Marshall Plan and the right-wing pro-Europe forces, contending that their real aim was to place conservative Christian Democrats into power in post-World War II western Europe.

Joining the staff of the European Community (EC) in Brussels in late 1971, Petra Kelly served as an assistant in its general secretariat. In 1972 she was for a year on the staff of the Bourse de Recherche and worked under a grant on a study of the political orientation and goals of various European organizations and movements in the years from 1945 to 1970. During 1972–73 she joined the administration of the EC's economic and social committee on questions involving vocational training, migratory workers, salary levels, and general problems concerning labor. In October 1973 she became administrative counselor in the secretariat of the EC, with responsibility for social problems, environmental protection, health, and consumer interests. She remained in that post until 1982, even though, as she told the *People* interviewer, she considered the EC in part "a corrupt organization, squandering a lot of the taxpayers' money."

Concurrently with her employment with the EC in Brussels, Petra Kelly engaged in West Germany and abroad in a variety of environmentalist, women's rights, and peace activities. Impressed by the idealism of West German Chancellor Willy Brandt, she joined his Social Democratic party in 1972. That year she became active in the Bundesverband Bürgerinitiativen Umweltschutz (BBU), or Federal Association of Citizens for Environmental Protection, an umbrella organization of West German environmentalist groups, and she often contributed to its periodical, the *BBU-Umweltmagazin*. In 1979 she was elected to the BBU executive board, with responsibility for promoting international contacts. After resigning in late 1978 from the Social Democrats because of what she regarded as a betrayal of the party's principles on defense and energy policy by Brandt's successor as chancellor, Helmut Schmidt, she helped to found Die Grünen (the Greens) as a formal, though loosely organized, political party. In the July 1979 elections for the largely ceremonial European Parliament in Strasbourg, Petra Kelly headed the list of candidates for the Greens, who obtained 3.2 percent of the vote.

At first the Greens were little more than a motley organization of pacifists, feminists, former Marxists, and ecologists who were opposed to such projects as the extension of the Frankfurt airport and who were concerned about the environmental effects of chemical pollution and nuclear power plants. When in December 1979 the Schmidt government accepted a NATO plan for the stationing on West German soil of a new generation of American-built intermediate-range nuclear missiles aimed at the Soviet Union, the Greens found a unifying issue in their opposition to that plan.

In March 1980 Petra Kelly was elected to the three-member executive of the Greens and became its speaker. Although in the federal elections in October of that year the Green party obtained only 1.5 percent of the vote—far short of the 5 percent needed to enter the Bundestag—it soon met with some success in state and local elections. Its 1980 entry into the Landtag of Baden-Württemberg with 5.3 percent of the vote was followed by similar breakthroughs in West Berlin, Lower Saxony, Hamburg, Bremen, Hesse, and Schleswig-Holstein, and in some states the Greens replaced the Free Democrats as the third-strongest party.

Reelected to the party executive at the Greens' congress at Offenbach in October 1981, Petra Kelly obtained an unpaid leave of absence from her duties with the EC in early 1982 to devote herself more fully to national politics. In the Bavarian Landtag elections later that year she headed the list of Green candidates, and though the party's 4.6 percent of the vote was not enough to qualify it for representation in parliament, it exceeded that of the Free Democrats. In keeping with a rule mandating the rotation of the Greens' party leadership every two years, Miss Kelly relinquished her position on the executive at the party congress at Hagen in November 1982 and was succeeded by Rainer Trampert.

Meanwhile, on October 1, 1982, following the defection of the Free Democrats from his coalition and his defeat in a vote of confidence in the Bundestag, Schmidt was replaced as chancellor by Helmut Kohl, whose Christian Democratic-Free Democratic coalition ended thirteen years of Social Democratic government. The scheduling of federal elections for March 6, 1983, in which Kohl was pitted against the Social Democratic standard-bearer Hans-Jochen Vogel, provided the Greens with a new opportunity to enter the Bundestag.

In their discussion concerning election strategy at the Hagen congress, the Greens failed to reach an agreement on a coherent economic policy. There were differences of opinion between those, like Rainer Trampert, who favored working with labor and the Social Democrats to alleviate the nation's economic ills, and those who, like the East German exile Rudolf Bahro, foresaw in the arms race the possible end of civilization and therefore considered such issues as unemployment to be of secondary importance. Like the British economist E. F. Schumacher, they believed that "small is beautiful" and favored grassroots democracy, decentralization of government, and the rejection of "mammoth technologies" and "mammoth social structures." There was, however, general agreement within the party on opposition to the stationing of NATO missiles in West Germany, and at a Greens' convention at Sindelfingen near Stuttgart in January 1983 that issue was made the central plank of the party's election platform.

Campaigning for as many as twenty hours a day, often to the point of exhaustion, Petra Kelly held late-night press conferences, took part in campaign meetings, seminars, and television debates, and personally answered hundreds of letters a week. "We are immediately prepared to take over responsibility," she said on a television broadcast, "but we are not prepared to agree to projects that represent a threat to our survival merely for the sake of gaining power." She ruled out a coalition with the Social Democratic party unless it were willing to meet the fundamental demands of the Greens and noted that although the Social Democrats under Vogel had moved to some extent toward the Greens' position on missile deployment and environmental protection, they did not go far enough. "There are some things on which we will simply not compromise," she told an interviewer for *U.S. News & World Report* (November 1, 1982). "These are questions of peace and energy and ecology. In those areas, you cannot talk about the lesser of evils. There is no such thing as small death. . . . There must be no Pershing II or Cruise missiles here. . . . Then we must move out of the NATO power bloc. And there must be a shutdown of all German nuclear power plants."

In February 1983 Petra Kelly and retired Bundeswehr General Gert Bastian, a fellow Green candidate, staged a three-day "war crimes tribunal" at Nuremberg's Meistersingerhalle, during which survivors of Nazi concentration camps and of the Hiroshima atom bomb attack were invited to testify. Its purpose was to indict the world's five nuclear weapons nations, in particular, the United States and the Soviet Union. "What we are trying to do," Petra Kelly said at the time, "is to show that the very possession of nuclear weapons is a crime of immense proportions."

In the elections of March 6, 1983, which resulted in a victory for Kohl's Christian Democratic–Free Democratic coalition and a defeat for Vogel's Social Democrats, the Greens received 2,164,988, or 5.6 percent, of the 38,937,573 votes, moving into the 498-member Bundestag for the first time, with twenty-seven representatives. "The entry of the Greens into parliament has far-reaching consequences for the whole country," Michael Binyon wrote in the London *Times* (March 8, 1983). "It enfranchises a generation of disaffected youth. . . . It brings to fruition the student revolt that began in Berlin in 1968 against the accepted norms and values. It symbolizes the power and influence throughout the whole country now of the 'Alternatives,' of those who previously opted out but have now been coopted in. It has broadened the framework of Western democracy."

Elected along with Otto Schily and Marieluise Beck-Oberndorf to the three-member speakers' council of the Greens, Petra Kelly declared her intention to practice acts of civil disobedience within the parliamentary framework, such as, for example, disclosure of secret documents that might be considered of interest to the public. In a political program drafted shortly after the elections, the Greens indicated that though their voting power in the Bundestag was limited, they would make a major impact with such actions as a boycott of the forthcoming national census, revealing defense secrets, peace marches in Moscow, Washington, and Geneva, and investigations of alleged financial irregularities involving the major political parties.

In keeping with her declared intention to be active "on the street" as well as in the Bundestag, Miss Kelly along with four fellow members of the Greens went to East Berlin in May 1983, where they demonstrated against nuclear arms and unfurled a banner that read "Swords into Plowshares"—the slogan of the East German peace movement. Arrested and briefly held by East German police, the group was then released and returned to West Berlin. When at the time of a massive peace rally in Krefeld in June some violence broke out in protest against a visit to West Germany by United States Vice-President George Bush, Miss Kelly asserted that the violent demonstrators "had nothing to do with the peace movement."

On a visit to the United States in July 1983, Petra Kelly met with members of the State Department and other officials in Washington but did not succeed in obtaining an audience with President Ronald Reagan. Interviewed on NBC News' *Meet the Press*, she spoke out in favor of unilateral disarmament in view of the "overkill capacity on both sides," denounced all forms of violence, and criticized United States intervention in Central America and what she considers to be the Reagan administration's "double standard" on human rights, as well as the Soviet occupation of Afghanistan and the suppression of the Solidarity movement in Poland. Philip Geyelin wrote in the *Washington Post* (July 24, 1983) about his encounter with her during her visit: "There is no arguing with Petra Kelly. To talk to her is to open a floodgate. She has done her homework and can talk the jargon of nuclear weapons and arms control. . . . Petra Kelly represents the main guard of a serious movement with a prevailing dedication to nonviolent protest." He concluded that the Greens "constitute a potent and"—with their "battle plan" mentality—"potentially dangerous force" but "a force to be treated with some measure of respect."

In September 1983 Petra Kelly was joined by the Nobel Prize–winning author Heinrich Böll and by American activists Daniel Ellsberg and Philip Berrigan, among others, in a peaceful three-day blockade of a United States military base at Mutlangen in Baden-Württemberg, and in October she spoke alongside Willy Brandt in a peace rally in Bonn that was attended by some 200,000 people. After a visit in November to East Berlin and then to Moscow, where they startled spectators by staging an antinuclear rally in Red Square aimed against both NATO and the Warsaw Pact, Miss Kelly and six of her party colleagues returned to Bonn to map out strategy to influence the forthcoming Bundestag vote on deployment of the NATO missiles. But their efforts failed when on November 22, 1983 deployment was approved by a vote of 286 to 226.

The difficulty faced by the Greens in their efforts to maintain party unity among their disparate factions was demonstrated by the resignation in February 1984 of General Gert Bastian from the parliamentary party. Bastian, who like Petra Kelly represented the "fundamentalist" faction of the Greens, seeking to maintain their independence as an "antiparty party," had been increasingly critical of their internal power struggles and of the growing tendency toward Marxism-Leninism and anti-Americanism within their ranks. Then, in April 1984, apparently to prevent development of a leadership cult, the Greens's Bundestag faction removed Petra Kelly along with the other two floor leaders and three business managers from the party's parliamentary leadership, replacing them with a new six-member all-female committee.

A member of the editorial board of *Forum Europa*, Petra Kelly has also contributed many articles, both in German and in English, to *Gandhi Journal*, *The Ecologist*, *Neue Politik*, and other periodicals, and with Jo Leinen she published in 1983 the book *Prinzip Leben. Ökopax—Die Neue Kraft* (Life Principle: Ökopax—The New Strength) and *Um Hoffnung Kämpfen* (To Fight for Hope). Among the honors that she has received are a 1982 "Alternative Nobel Prize," sponsored by the Swedish stamp dealer Jakob von Uxküll, and the 1983 peace prize of Women Strike for Peace.

Petra Kelly, who is unmarried, is the sponsor of a Tibetan orphan girl living in India whom she supports financially. While working for the EC, she contributed 50 percent of her salary to the Greens. As described by Ronald Steel in *Vanity Fair* (October 1983), "She is certainly photogenic, with her short-cropped blond hair, her intense blue eyes, her sharp cheekbones, and her sense of style. . . . [She] has the frame of an incipiently anorectic adolescent: wiry energy covering over deep fatigue. . . . She is so absolutely sure of herself, the way you imagine Joan of Arc to have been. And like the Maid of Orleans, she is a hard cross to bear: shrill, humorless, dogmatic." Morley Safer, who presented a segment on Miss Kelly on *60 Minutes* in February 1983, was at first hostile to what he called her "ragtag party" but concluded that she was "a fresh and provocative voice in a nation dominated by some of the most boring politicians in the Free World." Petra Kelly's closest companion is her maternal grandmother, Kunigunde Birle, now in her late seventies, who accompanies her frequently to meetings and demonstrations.

References: Aufbau p15 S 3 '82 por; Esquire 102:53+ S '84 por; Frankfurter Allgemeine Zeitung p12 Mr 8 '83 por; German Tribune p4 Mr 6 '83 por; N Y Times p8 Mr 7 '83 por; N Y Times Mag p37+ F 13 '83 por; People 18:136+ N 22 '82 pors; Time 121:32 Mr 21 '83 por; Vanity Fair 46:70+ O '83 por; Wall St J p1 Ja 30 '84 por; Washington Post C p3 Mr 6 '83 por; International Who's Who, 1984–85

Kelman, Charles D(avid)

May 23, 1930– Ophthalmologist; musician.
Address: b. c/o The Media Shop Inc., 29
Maplelawn Dr., Commack, N.Y. 11725

Once hailed by the professional journal *Cataract* as "the man who started the cataract revolution," Dr. Charles Kelman, one of America's foremost ophthalmologists, has given an entirely new direction to the field of eye surgery. Before Kelman invented what is called the "phacoemulsification and aspiration process," patients with cataracts had to undergo risky surgery requiring a ten-day hospitalization, followed by a convalescence period lasting up to six weeks. In striking contrast, Kelman's revolutionary invention permits cataract surgery under local anesthetic in the doctor's office, with the patient often able to walk out, ready to resume normal activity the next day. He has also developed the "Kelman lenses," which can be inserted in the eye after cataract surgery, often eliminating the need for additional corrective lenses. In 1981, the American Society of Contemporary Ophthalmology honored Kelman with its first award for outstanding achievement in cataract surgery.

But such medical breakthroughs represent only one facet of Kelman's many talents. A jazz saxophonist and songwriter, he has played at Carnegie

Hall, the Concord Hotel in the Catskills, and the Fontainebleau in Miami Beach—sometimes accompanied by the great jazz vibraphonist Lionel Hampton, who is one of his most grateful patients.

In addition, he has written a book for the layman about cataract surgery and "Through My Eyes," his autobiography, scheduled for publication by Crown in 1985. Currently, he is at work on a Broadway play and a novel. A twenty-minute film about his techniques for cataract surgery, which he wrote, scored, directed, and produced, won first prize in the 1969 Barcelona Medical Film Competition. On November 30, 1982 Senator Alfonse D'Amato requested that his colleagues in Congress join in a salute to Kelman "for giving so many people the gift of sight, the sound of music, and the benefits of his outstanding intellectual skills."

Charles David Kelman was born on May 23, 1930 in Brooklyn, New York to David Joseph and Eva (Gelles) Kelman. He began playing the harmonica at the age of six, soon performed over the radio on the Horn & Hardart Children's Hour, and by the time he was nine had mastered the clarinet and the saxophone. Jimmy Dorsey was his idol. As a student at Forest Hills High School, Kelman won a citywide competition to become first clarinetist in the New York All-City Symphony Orchestra, but since he was so involved in his extracurricular musical activities, his studies suffered. "Maybe you should go to trade school," Kelman remembers the high school principal saying. "I won't give you a recommendation for college."

Although Kelman himself did not have his sights set on college and wanted to be a musician, he took to heart the advice of his father, an inventor and a vice-president of a manufacturing firm: "Do what you want. Be a singer, saxophone player, comedian, band leader—but first—be a doctor." Intending to enter the medical profession, he enrolled at Tufts University in Medford, Massachusetts, and, by attending day and night classes and taking courses in the summer, completed the four-year premed program in just two years. Since several American medical schools had rejected the applications he had submitted as an undergraduate, with the suggestion that he reapply at a later date, on his graduation with a B.S. degree in 1950, he decided to attend the medical school of the University of Geneva, in Switzerland.

Nevertheless, a musical career still strongly appealed to Kelman, who partly paid his way through medical school by playing the saxophone for the Swiss Broadcasting System and the Swiss Jazz Quartet and by composing for the Theater of Geneva. Together with the pianist François Charpin, he wrote "Le Petit Déjeuner," which, when recorded by the popular French singer Jean Sablon, became a hit. Music, in fact, led him to choose ophthalmology as his specialty. Returning by ocean liner to Europe for his third year of medical school, he began jamming with the ship's band and some fellow passengers, one of whom turned out to be a saxophonist and ophthalmologist from Poughkeepsie, New York. The following summer Kelman spent a few weeks watching his newfound friend operate and as a result became fascinated by ophthalmic surgery. After obtaining his M.D. degree with honors in 1956, he returned to New York City and com-

pleted his internship at Kings County Hospital in 1956–57 and then did postgraduate work in ophthalmology at Bellevue Hospital in 1958, the same year in which he began his ophthalmic residency at the prestigious Wills Eye Hospital in Philadelphia.

During his internship and residency, Kelman spent his lunch hours visiting music publishers and pulling out of his black doctor's bag songs he had written. "I was still hoping I could make a hit record," Kelman explained in a cover story for *Medical World News* (December 8, 1980). "I figured that if I did, I would just put my M.D. in my pocket and go into music." He did, indeed, almost do that after he wrote and recorded, under the pseudonym of Kerry Adams, a song called "Telephone Numbers." It was awarded four stars by *Cashbox* and *Billboard* magazines and became the "pick of the week" on radio stations in fifty cities. But two weeks after "Telephone Numbers" started to climb the charts, Chubby Checker came out with "Twist," starting a trend that eclipsed "Telephone Numbers" along with other artists and works. Today Kelman speaks of his sudden rise and fall good-humoredly, wryly noting that if "Telephone Numbers" had been a success and he had abandoned medicine, he would "be a broken-down songwriter right now, looking for another hit." When he met Chubby Checker, he shook his hand and thanked him.

With no hit record forthcoming and with his residency completed, Kelman settled down into his new profession. At first he fitted people for eyeglasses under the Health Insurance Plan of Greater New York, but the work presented no challenge, and he hated it. He wanted to go into surgery—that ambition was what had drawn him to ophthalmology in the first place—but an aspirant first had to spend years building up a practice. Kelman's restless mind searched for new and more creative outlets within his specialty. One evening while reading the July 17, 1962 issue of *Look* magazine, Kelman was struck by its cover story on the New York neurosurgeon Dr. Irving S. Cooper, who was pioneering cryogenic surgical techniques, that is, the use of steel probes, supercooled by liquid nitrogen, to treat tumors and Parkinson's disease. The possible applications of cryosurgery in ophthalmology immediately intrigued Kelman, and he tried the next day to contact Dr. Cooper. After two months of persistent telephoning and writing, he reached Dr. Cooper, who agreed that cryogenics might be useful in ophthalmic surgery. He allowed Kelman to use his laboratory, technicians, lab animals, and unique freezing equipment, and Kelman worked there one day a week for a year with the goal of making a cryoprobe small enough for use in removing cataracts.

A cataract, whether "senile"—that is, associated with the process of aging—or congenital, is a clouding of the lens of the eye, and cataract surgery consists of the removal of the clouded lens. There had been few advances in cataract surgery over the centuries. The ancient Egyptians removed cataracts by inserting a hollow reed into the eye and then sucking out the opaque lens. By the early 1960s, the instruments were more advanced, but the procedure was similar: the surgeon made a 180° incision on the cornea through which he grasped and pulled out the lens with forceps. If the lens were ruptured by the forceps, a toxic fluid would be released that could cause irritation, inflammation, and sometimes blindness.

Kelman's first breakthrough came in 1963 when he refined Cooper's probe for the exigencies of eye surgery. In addition to reducing the size of the probe, he obtained the necessary low temperature by substituting ordinary water—cooled to -40° F by an electric current passed through two different metals—for the expensive liquid nitrogen. The new probe, called a "cryostylet," made the surgery safer, for when the probe touched the lens, a portion of the lens would freeze and form an "ice ball" that would act as a kind of handle for easier removal of the lens, greatly reducing the danger of a rupture. The cryostylet also worked well in repairing detached retinas.

After his discovery, Kelman learned to his dismay that the same technique had been invented by a Polish eye surgeon about two years earlier. Nevertheless, it was not the lack of originality but the reactionary stance of the medical profession that at first created obstacles to the acceptance of the cryostylet, even after Kelman had developed a portable probe. "I was treated as a heretic," he recalled in the *Medical World News* article. "Medicine is a very conservative profession, and here they were doing the cataract operation with a little $4 forceps, and I came along with a machine costing several hundred dollars. I was ridiculed. It was called a gimmick and a lot of other things. [When the technical advance was reported in the popular press,] the hostility from establishment ophthalmologists grew worse." Yet within a year the application of cryosurgery to ophthalmology began to spread, and by 1965 the American Academy of Ophthalmology devoted an entire morning session during its convention to the subject—giving full credit to the Polish surgeon and none at all to Kelman.

Undeterred, Kelman was already at work on something new. The cryostylet had improved the success rate of cataract surgery, but the operation still required a stay of four to seven days in the hospital followed by four to six weeks of convalescence, and the surgeon still had to make a 180° incision, closed by six to eight sutures. Kelman was searching for a process that would allow for a much smaller incision in the cornea, making the procedure simpler for the surgeon and less painful for the patient. In order to fund his project, he submitted a $14,000 grant proposal to the John A. Hartford Foundation, which had supported Cooper's cryosurgery research. He detailed his proposed investigation of the effects of freezing on other parts of the eye, and as an afterthought, added an off-the-cuff paragraph, explaining that he also intended to explore ways of breaking up a cataract and removing

it through a needle puncture. That last paragraph caught the Foundation's attention, and when Kelman rewrote his proposal to fit the Foundation's funding provisions—its grants were never less than $280,000—he received $299,000 to support his research from 1963 to 1966. He spent the first $90,000 of the grant to set up a research laboratory at the Manhattan Eye, Ear and Throat Hospital.

The first two and a half years of experimentation turned out to be discouraging. Obsessed with the project, Kelman worked long hours every day with no tangible results, and he spent $250,000 with nothing to show for it. Then a serendipitous occurrence brought his long-sought breakthrough. While he was having his teeth cleaned with an ultrasonic drill, his dentist explained how the drill dissolved tartar with high-frequency sound. Suddenly Kelman reasoned that since the drill could break up tartar it would probably also break up a jelly-like cataract. He rushed out of the dentist's chair, across town to his laboratory, and then back to the dentist's office, bringing with him a cataract he had removed from a cat's eye. When he applied the drill to the cataract, nothing seemed to happen, but when he returned to his lab to examine the cataract under the microscope, he saw that the drill had successfully dissolved the clouded lens.

Kelman immediately commissioned Cavitron Surgical Systems, the manufacturer of the dental drill, to produce an ultrasonic drill adapted to his specifications. Four weeks before his Hartford grant expired, he successfully removed a cataract from a dog with his new drill. On the basis of that promising and innovative new technique, called "phacoemulsification and aspiration," he received a three-year extension from the foundation to continue his work. In 1967, when his first paper on the process was published, the medical establishment again responded to Kelman with hostility, at least partly because of the $40,000 price tag on the new device. But he continued to perfect his instrument, developing a sharp-tipped drill that vibrates at 40,-000 strokes per second, dissolves the lens, and sucks it out with a precisely regulated vacuum needle. Only a two- to three-millimeter incision and one suture are needed, and the patient is able to resume normal activity by the next day. Finally Kelman received professional recognition for his work. His paper presented to the 1968 AMA meeting was widely praised, and in 1969 he won the American Academy of Achievement Golden Plate award for outstanding achievement in medicine.

Although his professional credentials were now well established, Kelman continued to strive for further improvements in cataract surgery. By 1982 he had perfected two "Kelman lenses," which are easily removable post-operative artificial intraocular lens (IOL) implants. One can be inserted in the anterior chamber of the eye; a second can be inserted in the posterior chamber. Often patients who have cataracts removed and one of those lenses inserted do not require either contact lenses or eyeglasses to correct their vision further. In 1982 he had about a dozen patents granted or pending for different aspects of the phacoemulsification and aspiration process. To explain cataracts to the layman, Kelman wrote *Cataracts: What You Must Know About Them* (Crown, 1982).

Since 1963 Kelman has lectured extensively and conducted seminars and demonstrations on the uses of phacoemulsification and aspiration and on the Kelman lenses. He is currently the chief of ophthalmology at the Lydia E. Hall Hospital in Freeport, New York, which built an operating suite for him in which he performs between 800 and 1,000 cataract operations a year. He also maintains a staff of eighteen—including four ophthalmologists and two optometrists—at his Empire State Building office, which occupies half of an entire floor. Kelman is a consulting ophthalmologist to many hospitals in the New York area as well as to the Charing Cross Hospital in London, England and the Ichilov Hospital in Tel Aviv, Israel. He is also a fellow of the American Academy of Ophthalmology and Otolaryngology and a member of the American Medical Association, the American Society for Contemporary Ophthalmology, and several international medical associations. In addition, Kelman is an associate professor of ophthalmology at New York Medical College in Valhalla, New York and a professor of Ophthalmology at the Hahnemann Medical College and Hospital in Philadelphia. Kelman insists on personally training every surgeon who wants to use the phacoemulsification device and has traveled around the world for this purpose. Instead of charging a fee for his instruction, he requests that his students make a donation to the David J. Kelman Research Foundation, which he established in 1970 in honor of his father and over which he presides.

Although he continued to strive to expand the frontiers of ophthalmology, Kelman was becoming restive. "I was an accepted part of the establishment and the old challenge was gone," he has explained. "I no longer had a cause." As a result, he again felt drawn towards the world of music. Returning from the 1974 American Academy of Surgeons convention, he passed Carnegie Hall and impulsively determined to perform there. He not only booked Carnegie Hall for a date in the following year but also contacted a charity to let it know it would receive the proceeds. Kelman immediately began taking singing and drama lessons from a well-known vocal coach in preparation for his highly successful March 1, 1975 concert debut. Backed by a thirty-piece orchestra, he sang his own songs and several standards, played the sax, clarinet, and piano, and joked with the audience. But the performances of guest stars Lionel Hampton and opera singer Jan Peerce, two of his former patients, stole the show. For Kelman, it was the realization of a lifelong dream. "The happiness I had from performing on a stage where all those great performers had stood was indescribable," he has recalled.

Since then, Kelman has delighted audiences of friends, patients, and strangers at concerts that have raised more than two million dollars for char-

ities related to eye disease and blindness. He is in his element on the stage, poking fun at the medical profession both in one-liners and in songs he writes such as "Big Bad Cataract," "My Business is Eye Business," and "Chuck the Knife." All who hear him play testify that he is an accomplished saxophonist. He has also appeared on Johnny Carson's "Tonight Show," the "Today Show," and "Real People," among other television programs.

Charles D. Kelman has dark hair, a warm smile, and dresses stylishly. By his marriage on April 15, 1962 to Joan Schechtman, he has three children: David Joseph, Lesley Ann, and Jennifer Leigh. He is a golfer of professional calibre and pilots his own jet helicopter. Although affluent enough to own a penthouse at North Shore Towers on Long Island and a palatial home in Boca Raton, Florida, Kelman insists that he does not define his goals in monetary terms and that he has yet to attain everything he wants from life. "In 1963 I set ten goals for myself," he told one interviewer. "They included being at the top of my profession; getting married and having children; being involved in some kind of show business venture; being in good physical condition; and having an international flavor to my activities. I've achieved all of those things and I'm working on a new list." Kelman has performed surgery on the very young, including a four-month-old Italian infant with cataracts and other children with congenital eye defects, and on such celebrities as Hedy Lamarr, Joe Frazier, and Ann Miller. The New York City disc jockey William B. Williams, another former patient and the master of ceremonies at his Carnegie Hall debut, has joked, "You haven't lived until you're lying there, waiting for an operation to begin on your eyes, and Dr. Kelman is standing over you humming a couple of bars of 'Stardust.'"

References: Medical World News 21:57+ D 8 '80 *por; Newsday* p7+ Jl 25 '76 *pors; Sat R* 55:45+ Ap 15 '72 *pors; Who's Who in America, 1980–81*

Kennedy, Donald

*Aug. 18, 1931– President, Stanford University.
Address: b. Office of the President, Stanford
University, Stanford, Calif. 94305; h. 623 Mirada,
Stanford, Calif. 94305*

With his appointment as commissioner of the federal Food and Drug Administration (FDA) in 1977, Donald Kennedy, who had already established himself as a brilliant academic researcher and gifted educator, became the focus of public attention. During his two-year tenure at the FDA, he won the respect of consumer groups as well as medical and drug lobbies for his adroit, if not always successful, handling of such emotionally charged issues as the proposed bans on saccharin and Laetrile. Since becoming president of Stanford University in 1980,

Donald Kennedy

journals as *The Biological Bulletin*, the *Journal of General Physiology*, and the *American Journal of Ophthalmology*. In 1960 he accepted the offer of an assistant professorship at Stanford University where his brilliant work as both a researcher and a teacher led to his rapid promotion to full professor and chairman of the biological sciences department by 1965.

During a sabbatical in 1972–73, Kennedy did research at Stanford's Center for Advanced Study in the Behavioral Sciences and also chaired a committee on pest-control strategies for the National Academy of Sciences (NAS) in Washington, D.C. The NAS serves as an objective adviser on science and technology to the federal government, among other duties, and Kennedy's work for that organization may have first sparked his interest in the relationship between science and government policy. On his return to Stanford, he had the opportunity to explore that connection in more depth as chairman of the new interdisciplinary Human Biology Program. According to a Stanford press release, the physicians, biologists, and social scientists in the program investigate "the institutional and scientific basis of public policy problems, including human health and environmental quality."

While continuing to teach and conduct research at Stanford, Kennedy once again commuted to Washington in 1976–77 to serve as senior consultant to the White House Office of Science and Technology Policy (OSTP). He enjoyed helping to shape policy on food and nutrition, focusing attention in the nation's capital on the life sciences, and taking part as well in the establishment of a new program within the Department of Agriculture to increase its support for basic research. Nevertheless, as Kennedy recalled in an interview with Karen J. Winkler for *The Chronicle of Higher Education* (October 29, 1979), he had decided that "at the close of the [Ford] Administration, [he] was going to bring all that to a close" to return full-time to academe.

But Kennedy's high standing among his colleagues and his many contributions to OSTP, particularly his knowledgeable and articulate testimony on behalf of that office before the House and Senate appropriations committees, brought him to the attention of Joseph A. Califano Jr., the secretary of Health, Education and Welfare in the newly inaugurated Carter Administration. David A. Hamburg, president of the Institute of Medicine of the NAS, proposed to Califano that Kennedy be appointed assistant secretary for health, but Califano and Kennedy agreed that the post would be best filled by a physician. Kennedy, however, gladly accepted Califano's offer of the post of commissioner of the Food and Drug Administration (FDA), and he took a leave of absence from Stanford to do so. Having long insisted that scientists should consider government service as a standard part of their careers, Kennedy had decided that the FDA "was exactly the sort of place you should go if you want to put your money where your mouth is." Although

he has remained embroiled in controversy, including an effort by several major universities to limit the Defense Department's power to censor the publication of government-sponsored research findings. Reflecting on his varied roles as professor, researcher, and administrator, Kennedy modestly claimed that he had "stumbled and staggered through [his] career," yet he has earned nothing but the highest praise for his achievements along every step of the way.

Donald Kennedy was born in New York City on August 18, 1931, the son of William Dorsey Kennedy and Barbara (Bean) Kennedy. He has one brother, Dorsey Kennedy. Donald Kennedy was raised primarily in New York City, but for his secondary education he attended Dublin School, a private boarding school in Dublin, New Hampshire, from which he graduated in 1948. Because of his longstanding interest in natural history, he first planned to study ecology when he entered Harvard University, but he soon decided to major in biological sciences. In spite of his rigorous academic program, he found time to become a member of Harvard's downhill ski racing team and later its coach. After receiving an A.B. degree, *cum laude*, in 1952, he continued his studies at Harvard, specializing in neurophysiology. The university awarded him master's and doctorate degrees in 1954 and 1956, respectively, and he was honored with a National Science Foundation fellowship for the 1955–56 academic year.

In 1956 Kennedy started his professional career as an assistant professor of biology at Syracuse University, and by 1959 he had been promoted to associate professor. During that time, he wrote or collaborated on several articles dealing with various aspects of neurophysiology, especially vision, that were published in such respected scientific scientists often give advice to and exert influence on government through advisory committees, he maintained that it is "unfortunately less common [for] the academic scientist [to take] time to lend policy leadership to organizations that are involved in regulatory decision-making. That, I think, is where a whole critical set of decisions has to be made, and where the contributions of people with the kinds of training that academic scientists have are much needed." He was sworn in as commissioner on April 7, 1977.

Kennedy's appointment as FDA commissioner came at a critical juncture in the agency's history. The top post had been vacant since the resignation of the previous commissioner, Dr. Alexander M. Schmidt, in July 1976, and there were about seventy additional vacancies in essential professional positions. Over the previous three years, the FDA, which then had a budget of $242 million and a staff of 7,200, had been the object of more than one hundred congressional inquiries, fifty critical reports by the General Accounting Office, and a number of internal investigations as well. In a *New York Times* article (March 14, 1977), Richard D. Lyons described the FDA as "the Federal Government's most criticized, demoralized and fractionalized agency."

In trying to solve those problems, however, the new commissioner had several advantages over his most recent predecessors, among them that he was the first non-physician to hold that post since 1965. That fact delighted several FDA critics, including the consumer-oriented Health Research Group, which believed that an academic would be less easily swayed than a medical doctor by lobbying groups for manufacturers of drugs and medical devices. The Pharmaceutical Manufacturers Association, for its part, declared itself "hopeful about developing a decent working relationship" with Kennedy, and the American Medical Association pronounced him a good choice. In addition, as Peter Barton Hutt, former chief counsel to the FDA, pointed out in *Science* (March 25, 1977), Kennedy's solid professional standing and important academic and scientific connections alone immediately "upgrade[d] the FDA beyond anyone's wildest hopes." The commissioner intended to make the most of that tenuous grace period to achieve as quickly as possible his chief goal: restoring public confidence in the agency. One means to that end was to attract more scientists of high calibre to the FDA, and although every other commissioner had also tried to do that, observers believed that because of his outstanding reputation, Kennedy would succeed where the others had failed.

The first test of Kennedy's abilities involved one of the biggest controversies ever to hit the FDA. On March 9, about a month before he took over, the agency moved to ban saccharin, an artificial sweetener, after Canadian studies linked it to a high incidence of bladder cancer in laboratory rats. The 1958 Delaney Clause mandates that the FDA must ban any food ingredient that causes cancer in humans or animals. Since cyclamates, another sugar substitute, had been banned in 1969, no other practical artificial sweetener would be available. Dieters and diabetics, among others, were outraged over the agency's proposal, and the manufacturers of diet foods and drinks, represented by the Calorie Control Council, mobilized immediately against the ban and conducted a massive, well-financed publicity campaign. The council urged the public to send the detachable slips protesting the ban that were included in its ads to the FDA, and over 150,000 people did just that. The furor continued unabated even after Kennedy reclassified saccharin as an over-the-counter drug and permitted bulk sale of it for table-top use. Although that move allowed the FDA to circumvent the Delaney Clause, it presented problems for manufacturers who, according to law, then had to prove that the "drug" was not only a safe but also an effective treatment for obesity and diabetes, for example, in order to keep it on the market. Congress responded to the heated debate by imposing an eighteen-month moratorium on the proposed ban and later extending it when it was due to expire. The legislators, however, did allow warning labels to be placed on products containing saccharin. Throughout the controversy and even years later, Kennedy insisted on the scientific merit of the Canadian studies, confirmed through research by the NAS and others, and defended the agency's action.

Even before the saccharin controversy was temporarily resolved by Congress, another explosive issue confronted the FDA. Laetrile, a drug extracted from crushed apricot pits that releases minute amounts of cyanide into the body, had been highly touted as a kind of panacea for cancer. No valid research supported that claim, and therefore the FDA began an intensive drive to take the harmless but ineffective drug off the market. Nevertheless, some terminally ill cancer victims and their families viewed Laetrile as their last hope for a cure, and others, including California governor Jerry Brown, reasoned that if the drug could do no harm those people should not be denied access to it. Kennedy, however, maintained that it was indeed potentially dangerous in that patients using it might neglect more conventional, effective treatments: in fact, the FDA reported cases of cancer victims who had died after refusing life-saving surgery in favor of that drug.

Consequently, the debate over Laetrile quickly evolved into a battle over the government's right to restrict a person's freedom of choice. Since the FDA can only regulate products that cross state lines, lobbying groups pressured state legislators to legalize the manufacture, distribution, and sale of Laetrile within state boundaries. The legislatures in several states were disposed to comply, but Kennedy refused to let the emotionally charged issue rest. Struggling to resolve the problem by leading the public and its representatives to a sober assessment of the effects of the drug, he maintained that "really free choices are informed choices. The function of regulation is to give consumers accurate signals to shape free choices." Accordingly, he dispatched a four-man task force to present the FDA's findings on Laetrile before state legislatures, but he also ordered the agency's attorneys to prepare to contest its legalization in court. Nevertheless, about a dozen states had legalized Laetrile by July 1977.

Other controversial issues followed in quick succession. Kennedy had to battle not only agricultural lobbies but the Carter administration and Congress, which were sensitive to the demands of the farming interests, when he moved to phase out the use of sodium nitrate, a carcinogen, as a meat preservative. In spite of varying degrees of opposition from partisan groups, he also sought to ban the use of fluorocarbon sprays, which were depleting the earth's protective ozone layer; the advertising and sale of over-the-counter daytime sedatives, which induced drowsiness rather than lessening anxiety; and a liquid protein diet regimen, which was implicated in the deaths of at least thirty-one persons. Perhaps Kennedy's most important effort was to update the pharmaceutical laws, which govern, among other things, testing procedures for new drugs. The revisions were designed to decrease the time between the invention of a drug and its sale, make more information available to the public about drugs, foster competition—partly through the publication of a list of equivalent generic drugs—between drug manufacturers, and facilitate the FDA's efforts to quickly remove dangerous products from store shelves. In September 1979 a modified version of the proposal passed the Senate, but it stalled in the House of Representatives.

As commissioner of the FDA, Kennedy had soon realized that because of the political realities in the capital the "ratio of science to policy" in Washington was not very high. Yet it was not because of frustration at repeated defeats that Kennedy tendered his resignation in April 1979. On the contrary, he made clear that he was sorry to leave but had accepted the post of vice-president and provost at Stanford, which had to be filled immediately. During his tenure, his ability to explain drug testing results with clarity and candor to laymen, his affability, and his amicable press relations had won high marks from all quarters. Voicing the consensus of opinion, a New York Times editorial (July 2, 1979) asserted that with Kennedy's departure the FDA "lost its best commissioner in a long time."

A host of new challenges opened up for Kennedy with his return to Stanford. As provost, he moved quickly to improve faculty and staff salaries, took charge of faculty affirmative action programs, and created task forces to attract women professors. In June 1980, to the surprise of no one, Kennedy was appointed as Stanford's eighth president, succeeding Richard W. Lyman, who was leaving to head the Rockefeller Foundation.

Although the high-pressured whirlwind of Washington had been left behind, Kennedy's outspokenness and engagement with pressing public concerns thrust him into the center of debate on more than one occasion, often on issues concerning the conduct and funding of scientific research. In June 1981 he testified before the House of Representatives Committee on Science and Technology about the growth of commercial sponsorship of basic academic research. While Kennedy acknowledged that such sponsorship shortened the "lag time" between research innovations and their application, he also pointed out the need to be wary of introducing commercial motivations to academia and potential conflicts of interest on the part of faculty members. In March 1982 he hosted a conference at Pajaro Dunes, California, at which he and the leaders of four other universities joined with the heads of ten corporations to explore the practice of and conflicts involved in commercially funded research, especially in the field of genetic engineering.

Another conflict-of-interest question concerned government regulation. In the fall of 1981, a Russian specialist in robotics was invited to visit Stanford as the guest of the National Academy of Sciences. Before his arrival, the U.S. Commerce Department told Stanford officials not to allow the Soviet expert even normal access to research facilities at the university, which were sites of much government-sponsored, though unclassified, work. The university found the conditions unacceptable, and the visit was canceled. In addition, in April 1984 Kennedy joined with Marvin L. Goldberger, president of the California Institute of Technology, and Paul Gray, president of the Massachusetts Institute of Technology, to protest new Defense Department restrictions on the publication of unclassified military-related research. The three presidents insisted that their institutions would refuse research contracts subject to the proposed Defense Department veto power.

Stanford University clashed with the Reagan Administration over other issues as well. The one that received the most press coverage was the drawn-out negotiations for the establishment of a Reagan Library at Stanford to house the presidential papers. Kennedy made clear that the university would welcome the papers and a special library to house them, but it rejected the concept of a Ronald Reagan Center for Public Affairs that would be under the governance of the independent Hoover Institution of War, Revolution, and Peace, the conservative "think tank" located on the campus, rather than under the university's control.

Meanwhile, public service assignments outside the university have also received Kennedy's attention. In 1981 he joined the board of directors of the Health Effects Institute, which investigates the impact of automotive emissions on human health, and he participated in November 1983 in a scientific conference on the probable environmental aftereffects of nuclear war.

Donald Kennedy has been a member of the Institute of Medicine of the National Academy of Sciences since its founding in 1970, and in 1972 he was elected to the academy itself. The American Association for the Advancement of Science, the

California Academy of Sciences, and the American Academy of Arts and Sciences have also elected him to membership. From 1970 to 1976, he served on the Harvard Board of Overseers. Kennedy has published over sixty articles in major scientific journals, collaborated on a textbook, *The Biology of Organisms* (John Wiley, 1965), and served on the editorial boards of such publications for laymen or professionals as *Science* and *Journal of Neurophysiology*. Since its establishment in 1974, he has held the endowed Benjamin Scott Crocker professorship in Human Biology at Stanford, and in 1976 he received Stanford's Dinkelspiel Award for outstanding service to undergraduate education. He has also been awarded several honorary degrees.

Donald Kennedy, who is six feet tall and weighs 170 pounds, maintains his lean physique by running, skiing, and playing volleyball. On June 11, 1953, he married Barbara Jeanette Dewey, who is now the director of community relations at Stanford Hospital. The couple has two daughters, Laura Page and Julia Hale. Known for his warmth and sincerity, Kennedy shared his optimistic philosophy with Stanford's class of 1982. "Work hard, stay healthy, and have some fun," he advised. "Be committed to things in an unembarrassed and enthusiastic way."

References: Chronicle of Higher Education 19:3 O 29 '79 por; Science 195:1307 Mr 25 '77 por, 205:173+ Jl 13 '79; Washington Post E p1+ D 15 '77 por; Who's Who in America, 1984–85; Who's Who in American Politics, 1979–80

King, Don

Dec. 6, 1932– Boxing promoter. Address: b. c/o Don King Productions, 32 E. 69th St., New York City, N.Y. 10021

"There ain't no others like me," booms Don King, who bills himself as "The World's Greatest Promoter," and with good reason, since he is indisputably the most powerful promoter in boxing today. King's flamboyant public image is marked by his wild hairdo, flashy jewelry, and evangelical monologues embellished with quotations from Shakespeare and other literary immortals. A former numbers czar from Cleveland, Ohio, who was once convicted for manslaughter, he suddenly became a millionaire about two years after his release

from prison. Beginning in 1974 with the George Foreman-Ken Norton fight in Caracas, Venezuela, King set the scene for such pugilistic extravaganzas as the Ali-Foreman "Rumble in the Jungle," the Ali-Frazier "Thrilla in Manila," the Larry Holmes-Gerry Cooney "The Pride and the Glory," and the doubleheader "The Crown Affair." In his ten-year career as a boxing entrepreneur, Don King has shifted control of the power structure from the traditional white brokers to black entrepreneurs, has expanded the perimeters of the sport to the Third World, and has raised many millions for prizefighters.

Since the days when he promoted the career of Muhammad Ali, Don King has signed up "almost as many world champions and contenders," as one sportswriter has noted, "as the rest of the world combined." His stable has included Greg Page, Michael Dokes, Victor Galindez, Sugar Ray Leonard, Roberto Durán, Wilfredo Gómez, Leon Spinks, Aaron Pryor, and Larry Holmes. Most of the major fights in the last decade have been promoted by King and his closest competitor, Robert Arum. When asked in a Penthouse interview (January 1984) whether it is true that he and Arum control boxing promotion in the United States, the controversial King, whose operations are constantly under investigation, responded: "We put on the most promotions because we work hard at what we do. . . . You have to deliver. I'll deliver, Bob Arum will deliver. And the rest of them will fall short."

Donald King was born in Cleveland, Ohio on December 6, 1932, the fifth of seven children of Clarence and Hattie King. While the boy was still attending Lafayette Elementary School, his father, a steelworker, died on Pearl Harbor Day in an explosion at the Jones and Laughlin plant. With the $10,000 double indemnity money ("tragedy money," as King has called it), his mother moved the family to an area called Mount Pleasant, bordering the black ghetto. There he found his first job, as a chicken runner for Hymie's Chicken Shack, swiftly delivering live chickens to the slaughterer's knife, and he also became a hustler who sold peanuts and fruit pies, baked by his mother and his sister Evelyn, to gamblers in the policy houses. His mother roasted hundreds of pounds of peanuts every weekend and Donald and his enterprising brothers stuffed so-called "lucky numbers" into the small sacks of peanuts, so that when their numbers happened to match the winners, the boys could claim a tip. While attending John Adams High School, Donald became caught up in stories about such great lawyers as Clarence Darrow, and considered taking a pre-law course in college.

To finance his freshman year at Kent State University, King took over part of his older brother Tony's numbers route during the summer. Going from house to house, he collected daily bets and stowed away the policy slips in a window box at home, but when he forgot to turn in one winning slip to his boss, he had to pay the winner out of the bulk of his savings. The bookie refused to give him a loan for his tuition. "So I stayed," Don King recalled in an interview with Michael Katz for *Sport* magazine (July 1982), "and I took my little $200-a-week business and in a year and a half's time, I had my brother working for me, and the bookie . . . he was working for me." Nonetheless, Don King spent a year at Western Reserve University in Cleveland before resuming his thriving numbers career. "I made the irrational realization," he recalled, "that you go to school in order to get educated, you get educated so you can get some money, but I already was making money, so why should I go to the school."

During his twenties, King, now known as Donald the Kid to his intimates, forged ahead to become one of the chief numbers racketeers in Cleveland. "I was a respected man in the community," he related in an article in *Sepia* (October 1975), "because I always paid off. And because I was so damn honest the white mobs came after me with machine guns. Wanted to blow my house down, kidnap my kids." His front porch was blown off in 1957. When Muhammad Ali, an eighteen-year-old Olympic medalist then known as Cassius Clay, visited King's supper club in 1960, they struck up a friendship. King had taken up boxing himself at the same age, but after being knocked out cold in his first fight, he never sparred again. By Cadillac car or by plane, King followed Ali to all his fights across the country, until the boxer was forced into professional exile in the late 1960s because of his refusal to fight in Vietnam, and King was sentenced to prison for manslaughter.

King contends that after an argument with Sam Garrett, one of his numbers runners, over an unpaid debt, the runner attacked him from behind. In the fistfight that ensued, the man's head hit the pavement, and he later died. Sentenced to a term of one to twenty years, King did not appeal because he feared his reputation as a numbers overlord would be prejudicial. After hauling hog manure in the work gang by day, King found a haven in the prison library in the evenings. There he immersed himself in world literature and philosophy and now liberally quotes (or misquotes, as the media like to point out) the classics, especially the plays of William Shakespeare, who in *As You Like It* taught him the "sweet uses of adversity." King also took university correspondence courses, but though he had proved his academic mettle by earning an A average in freshman English, business law, economics, and political science, he declined an offer of a scholarship to the Harvard School of Business. After serving three years and eleven months at the Marion, Ohio Correctional Institution, to which he refers as "one of my alma maters," King was paroled on September 30, 1971, and in 1983 Governor James Rhodes of Ohio granted him a full pardon. "I came out armed and dangerous," King observed in an article in *TV Guide* (March 29, 1980). "Armed with wisdom and knowledge."

Involving himself in community service work after his release, Don King organized a benefit to raise funds for Cleveland's Forest City Hospital, Ohio's only black hospital, which was about to close its doors. By persuading Muhammad Ali to fight in a ten-round exhibition with four different opponents on August 28, 1972, he raised $82,500 and saved the hospital. Spurred on by Ali, King soon became a full-scale boxing manager, with Richie Giachetti as his trainer. He signed Jeff Merritt, whom he had discovered while in prison, Ray Anderson, a light heavyweight who used to work with Ali, and finally Ernie Shavers. At Madison Square Garden on June 8, 1973 Shavers scored a first-round knockout of Jimmy Ellis, but much to King's chagrin, he did not have the next world champion, for on returning to Madison Square Garden in December, Shavers was downed by Jerry Quarry in the first round.

Turning to the more profitable career of promoting, King joined forces with Henry Schwartz of Video Techniques, a new firm that handled closed circuit television for title bouts. Schwartz had just ended his association with Top Rank, a closed circuit firm run by Robert Arum, a Harvard Law School graduate and former member of the Attorney General's staff, who had become Muhammad Ali's lawyer and promoter. The notorious feud between Arum and King began when Arum garnisheed the purse from the Shavers-Quarry fight to assure payment of a small debt and ignored King's bid for the rights to the second Ali-Frazier fight on January 28, 1974. Although King asserted that Schwartz brought him into the arrangements for George Foreman's title defense against Ken Norton in Caracas, Venezuela on March 26, 1974 "as a black interface to deal with blacks only," that first heavyweight bout between two Americans to be held outside the United States started King on the road to professional glory.

The firm of Don King Productions, Inc., was born with the "Rumble in the Jungle," which was also named "The Fight of the Century." In a dramatic coup that identified him as the most fabled boxing promoter in the world, King, in association with Video Techniques, charted the Ali-Foreman bout in Kinshasa, Zaire, Africa, with the unheard-of purse of $5 million for each contender. Without any money of his own, but with a reliance on his ghetto jive and spellbinding grandiloquence, King succeeded in gaining the trust of Muhammad Ali, George Foreman, and officials in the government of Zaire (formerly the Belgian Congo), who put up $12.1 million to underwrite the match. "I worked very hard," King told Red Smith in a profile for the *New York Times Magazine* (September 28, 1975), "and had an odyssey that goes from Chicago to New York, from Chicago to San Francisco, from San Francisco to New York again and back to Paris, London . . . to get the extensive financing that was necessary for a poor product of the black ghetto in Cleveland to come up with $10 million. I wanted to bring something more astronomical in figures to the fighters than hitherto had been done." On October 30, 1974 Muhammad Ali ripped away the heavyweight title from Foreman with an eighth-round knockout.

By staging six more of Muhammad Ali's title fights, King raised unprecedented millions for him before he returned to Bob Arum's fold. Ali faced Chuck Wepner in Cleveland for $1.5 million and Ronnie Lyle in Las Vegas for $1.2 million. In international arenas, he fought Joe Bugner in Kuala Lumpur in Malaysia for $2.2 million and Joe Frazier in the Philippines for $0 million. Dubbed "the thrilla of Manila, the saga of our lifetime," the last-named fight took place on the fourth anniversary of King's release from prison, September 30, 1975, and was viewed over television by nearly one billion people. Ali's fight with Jean Pierre Coopman in San Juan, Puerto Rico brought him $1.5 million. On April 30, 1976 Ali sparred with Jimmy Young at the Capital Center in Landover, Maryland for $1.5 million. "Ali, Herbert [Muhammad, son of the late leader of the Black Muslims and Ali's manager], and I formed the triumvirate that truly shocked the world," King proclaimed, as quoted in *Encore American & Worldwide News* (July 6, 1976). "We were an all-Black business making Black decisions. Never had the business world seen a situation that powerful. It behooved my white counterparts to try to break this chain because as it grew in strength and vibrancy, it began to become symbolic."

But King was "angry, terribly hurt and confused," as he expressed it, when he lost the Muhammad Ali–Ken Norton fight, scheduled for the fall of 1976, to Arum in a deal that gave the bid to Madison Square Garden for $2 million less than the $8 million that King had raised. Although that deprived him of his grip on Ali, King still held a commanding position in the overall control of boxing's heavyweight division. For example, because he promoted the Ken Foreman–Jimmy Young fight in Puerto Rico in March 1976, King possessed commitments for the future matches of *both* pugilists. The lightweight champion Roberto Durán and the welterweight Sugar Ray Leonard also came under the aegis of Don King.

With the renewed popularity of boxing on home television, Don King orchestrated an ambitious series of tournaments that were planned to set up an American champion in each of eight boxing weight classes. In a contract with ABC-TV, he launched the *U.S. Boxing Championships* on January 16, 1977 on the flight deck of the United States Navy aircraft carrier *Lexington*, which was anchored off Pensacola, Florida. Other unusual sites were the United States Naval Academy at Annapolis, the Marion, Ohio Correctional Institution, and the Randolph Air Force Base in San Antonio, Texas.

Following charges of fixed bouts, kickbacks, exaggerated rankings, and misrepresentation of contenders' credentials leveled by *Ring* magazine, the so-called "Bible of Boxing," ABC suspended the tournament in April 1977 and retained attorney Michael Armstrong to investigate. A federal grand jury and the FBI also instituted probes of their own. In the 327-page Michael Armstrong report, which was released in September 1977, Don King Productions, Inc., was castigated for "a good deal of unethical behavior," and though charges of illegal conduct were not brought against King, his business was adversely affected. Passionately defending himself, he contended that he was slandered because of his race. In the *Penthouse* interview he asserted: "I became the scapegoat of the situation because I was the captain of the ship."

After the reverse in his fortunes, King discovered a new heavyweight champion in the person of a former sparring partner of Muhammad Ali, Larry Holmes, who had won all twenty-eight of his professional fights but did not go against top competition until 1978. In a spectacular showing watched by the audience at Caesar's Palace Sports Pavilion in Las Vegas, Nevada and by some forty million television viewers, Holmes battered Ken Norton for the World Boxing Council Championship on June 9, 1978, winning on a split decision after a stormy fifteenth round. On October 2, 1980 Holmes racked up his eighth consecutive knockout, shattering the heavyweight record of seven that had been set by Joe Louis four decades ago. In that event, which King billed as "The Last Hurrah," the struggle of Muhammad Ali, the only three-time heavyweight champion in history (1964, 1974, 1978), to gain a fourth title ended when his trainer stopped the uneven contest after the tenth round. In another spectacular King outing, billed as "The Pride and the Glory," which grossed a record $42–45 million, Larry Holmes scored a technical knockout over Gerry Cooney on June 11, 1982, to retain his title. In what was promoted as "The Crown Affair," the first heavyweight championship double-header, on May 20, 1983 at the Dunes Hotel in Las Vegas, Larry Holmes defeated Tim Witherspoon by a split twelve-round decision for the World Boxing Council title, and Michael Doakes gained the World Boxing Association title in his match with Mike Weaver.

Although he continued to be the target of ongoing investigations on certain aspects of corruption in boxing and on possible links to organized crime,

Don King scrambled back to the front ranks of boxing promotion, surpassing his arch-rival, Bob Arum. Each has supported opposing sanctioning bodies that determine how many titles there should be and the ratings of the boxers: King backs the World Boxing Council and Arum endorses the World Boxing Association. Because they increased the separate slates of champions, by 1980 the number of world boxing finalists rose to twenty-six, in fourteen categories. By 1982 King could take pride in his promotional ties to some 100 fighters.

In the midst of his setbacks, King had recognized the potential of pay television, and in 1981 he established the Don King Sports and Entertainment Network, a cable system which is modeled after Home Box Office and operates once a month. In 1982 he closed a deal with ABC Video Enterprises to produce fifteen monthly title shows on his own network, for about $400,000 for each event, and in 1983 he promoted twenty-three world title matches. His business empire, including D. K. Chemicals, is estimated to be worth about $50 million. An entirely new, but typically grandiose, promotional venture for Don King was a concert tour in the late spring of 1984 by the Jackson Brothers, the music group led by superstar Michael Jackson. When the Jackson brothers became unhappy with King's management, they reduced his authority by hiring two more managers, though King shared 15 percent of the profits with the Jacksons' parents, who originally hired him.

In the boxing world, fears of encroaching monopoly have been expressed by Don King's riled and uneasy peers. In the New York Times (May 15, 1983), Michael Katz wrote: "In this corner, a Don King fighter. In that corner, a Don King fighter. Frequently they are both managed by the promoter's adopted son, Carl." That stifling of competition is further confirmed by Katz's report that six of the top heavyweight contenders owe allegiance to King, that he is the promoter of record of thirteen of twenty-seven current world champions, and that he has almost cornered the market on the lightweight class of fighters. Moreover, because of his new alliance with Pepe Cordero of the WBA, and his long-standing friendship with President José Sulaiman of the WBC, King has become a major force in both governing bodies, wielding still greater power to influence ratings. Citing the example of Lou and Dan Duva, Katz notes that King is not the only promoter in boxing to hire a family member as a manager in order to avoid an illegal conflict of interest. As for the possibility of antitrust violation, King told Katz in the interview in Sport: "If the fighter asks me, I sign him up. They've been asking because they know I perform."

Never indicted for any crime relating to his boxing operations, Don King tenaciously denies any wrongdoing. "All I'm doing is working in the tradition of America. I am a pioneer, a trailblazer. I'm tired of chasing rumors," he told Michael Katz, who characterized him as "a tough, hard-boiled businessman, a master salesman and shrewd politician." Although King and Arum have both

been described as "master arm twisters," King's associates admit to a grudging affection for him and note his sense of humor, his readiness to compromise, and his loyalty to his fighters. He has long been acknowledged as a "legend" and a "genius" by friends and foes alike, and he amazes even himself. "The first step in all my operations," he informed Michael Katz, "is to pray and get God's blessing and guidance. Because of that I can make moves that sometimes they're so phenomenal, they really enthrall me, they mesmerize me. When I look back at them, I say, 'Wow!'"

Although he once declared that he sometimes feels that he is "selling insanity," Don King plumes himself on having revolutionized the pay scale in boxing. During the Sport interview he explained: "Where I don't have an individual I am paying, just my presence in the bidding arena makes them get more money by going to their promoter and saying, 'You know I was talking to Don King,' and they never even have to talk to me on the phone. The guy'll say, 'Don't go to King, don't go to King.'" Believing that boxing is "the last vestige of the free enterprise system," King opposes government regulations, but advocates schedules, pension plans, and continuity for the sport.

The headquarters for Don King's wheeling and dealing is a penthouse suite of offices on the sixty-seventh floor of the RCA Building in Rockefeller Center in New York City, instead of the proverbial cramped back rooms of Madison Square Garden. At his East Side Manhattan townhouse, King has welcomed such guests as President Julius Nyerere of Tanzania, whom he customarily greets with his smiling "How's m'man?" Since his assault in a Bahamas hotel room by James Cornelius, promoter of the Muhammad Ali–Trevor Berbick fight, King has hired bodyguards to accompany him on his travels. "I must go where the wild goose goes" is one of his favorite sayings. He escapes from the madding crowds of the boxing game at his 400-acre farm in Orwell, Ohio, where his wife Henrietta, who raises Black Angus cattle, and his daughter Deborah and sons Carl and Eric live. There, King's fighters receive full medical care, including dental work and regular CAT scans. Golf is the only other sports activity that King enjoys apart from boxing.

Don King has received such honors as the 1976 Urban Justice Award and the Heritage Award for the individual who has best promoted racial harmony through sports. A former member of the Democratic party's executive finance committee, he has contributed funds to groups that include the NAACP, the Congressional Black Caucus, the United Negro College Fund, and UNICEF. A hulking, cigar-chomping man with a small moustache and twinkling eyes, King stands about six feet three inches and weighs around 250 pounds. At noon conferences in his office, he may wear a velvet-trimmed tuxedo and a ruffled shirt. Reporters use vivid figures of speech to describe his very visible jewelry and his black-gray springing-up hair. In a question-and-answer column in the Los Angeles Herald Examiner (February 24, 1984) Don King explained his hair style as "an aura of God. I don't treat it, I don't take care of it, it just pops up. So I feel it's indicative of my being ordained and anointed by He who sits high and keeps his eyes on the sparrow. My hair just keeps standing up every morning, and I know I have to keep carrying the cross and producing my extravaganzas. I want the people to see my hair in all its crowning glory."

References: Black Enterprise 6:22+ Jl '76; Encore American & Worldwide News 5:28+ Jl 6 '76 pors; Esquire 84:65+ N '75; N Y Daily News mag p6+ Ja 4 '76 pors; N Y Times V p1+ My 15 '83 pors; N Y Times Mag p15+ S 28 '75 pors; Newsday p118+ Mr 4 '77 por; Penthouse p131+ Ja '84 por; Sepia 24:26+ O '75 pors; Sport 73:12+ Jl '82 pors; Sports Illus 41:30+ S 2 '74 por, 43:33+ S 15 '75 por, 46:22+ My 2 '77 por; Toronto Globe & Mail pS1 O 6 '84 por; TV Guide 105:55+ Je 30 '75 por; Washington Post B p1+ Ap 30 '76 pors

Kinnock, Neil (Gordon)

Mar. 28, 1942– British politician. Address: b. House of Commons, SW1, London, England

On October 2, 1983, the British Labour party elected the forty-one-year-old Welshman Neil Kinnock to head its beleaguered ranks. Chastened by the defection of the party's conservatives in 1981 to form the Social Democratic party and embarrassed by a resounding defeat in the June 9, 1983 general elections, the majority of Labourites determined that only Kinnock was charismatic enough to unify the party's warring factions and revive its flagging political fortunes. Kinnock, the youngest man ever

to head the party, brings to the post little governmental experience beyond his thirteen years as MP for Bedwellty in Wales, but he nevertheless possesses formidable political assets: a rare gift for oratory, a charmed way with the press, and an attractive, politically astute wife. Alternately dubbed the "Welsh windbag" and "the golden boy with the silver tongue," Kinnock has enjoyed a truly meteoric rise to political influence.

Neil Gordon Kinnock was born on March 28, 1942 in the Welsh coal mining town of Tredegar, a Labour party stronghold, the only son of Gordon and Mary (Howells) Kinnock. His father, a collier, was forced to leave the mines because of dermatitis on his hands and he subsequently took a job at the Ebbw Vale steel mill. Kinnock remembers that as a child he watched every morning as his mother bandaged his father's chronically inflamed hands before he went off to the mill. Although the Kinnocks were relatively well-to-do for a blue-collar family, they made a point of acquainting their son with the widespread poverty and hardship in the depressed coal-mining regions. For example, having returned to work as a district nurse after her husband left the mines, Mary Kinnock took Neil during his holidays from Georgetown, the local junior school, along with her on her rounds to see the impoverished patients she attended.

Both of Neil Kinnock's parents were socialists, and his father, an active member of the Labour party, introduced the boy to politics at the age of ten by taking him to hear the fiery orator Aneurin Bevan, a native son of Tredegar who served as health minister from 1945 to 1951 in the Labour government led by Prime Minister Attlee and helped to design the National Health Service; from that day on, Bevan has been one of Kinnock's greatest heroes. By the time he was fourteen, he told Caroline Moorehead in an interview for the London *Times* (July 28, 1980), he had "socialist convictions" based on his first-hand knowledge of financial hardships and other problems in the mining valleys of Wales. His acquaintance with those difficulties, "translated by two very intelligent parents, backed up by attendance at meetings addressed by Bevan, [and] cemented by reading Orwell and Sinclair Lewis," impelled him to join the Labour party, though he had to lie about his age to do so.

An indifferent student, Kinnock nevertheless did well enough in the lower forms to win a place in the Lewis School, a selective state institution in nearby Pengam. Neither an outstanding scholar nor a first-class athlete, he hated the school's rigid curriculum and public-school pretensions. After repeatedly trying to get his parents to remove him, Kinnock eventually settled down and managed to get into the university, but his experience at the Lewis School scarred him with a deeply felt aversion to the education of the privileged classes.

At University College, Cardiff, where Kinnock went in 1961 to study industrial relations and history, he found himself in a much more congenial atmosphere. Although his scholarship did not improve—he failed the degree exam on his first attempt and barely passed on his second—Kinnock quickly established himself as a campus leader. From 1962 to 1965 he was chairman of the Socialist Society, and from 1965 to 1966 he served as president of the Students' Union. As a college pol, Kinnock organized a successful boycott of South African oranges in the student cafeteria and protests against the imprisonment in 1963 of the South African black political activist Nelson Mandela; took part in Friday night debates at the canteen; and worked as a volunteer for Labourite James Callaghan (a man whom he would later oppose vociferously) in the 1966 election.

After graduating from the university with a B.A. degree in 1966, Kinnock became a tutor-organizer for the Industrial and Trade Union Studies division of the Workers' Educational Association (WEA). Despite his own lackluster educational career, he proved to be an exceptional teacher. Lecturing on the economic background of current events to packed classrooms, he won many supporters through his four years of WEA work. Nothing in his life before or since, he said in the London Times interview, has been as "enlightening and entertaining."

In 1967 Kinnock moved to Pontllanfraith in Bedwellty (now Islwyn), a South Wales constituency composed of two depressed mining valleys. Through his WEA work there, he soon developed a youthful circle of followers within the local Labour party. Early in 1969 he learned that local Labour MP Harold Finch did not intend to run again. (Some of his detractors contend that the ambitious Kinnock moved to Bedwellty primarily because of that possibility.) Kinnock's allies immediately urged him to stand for Bedwellty, one of the safest Labour seats in the country. His opponent was a popular middle-aged miner's agent named Lance Rogers, who had the backing of the powerful National Union of Mineworkers. At the nomination meeting, which in Bedwellty is tantamount to the election, the first vote following the candidates' speeches was tied, 75 to 75, and they were asked to speak again. While Rogers simply repeated his speech, Kinnock returned with a new and grandiloquent piece of oratory and won on the second vote, 76 to 74.

Taking his seat in Parliament in 1970, Kinnock devoted most of his energy to his constituency work and spent long hours traveling between London and Wales to keep in constant touch with his district. His first and only administrative experience at the national level came in 1974–75 when he served as private parliamentary secretary to Michael Foot, then secretary of state for employment. After the moderate James Callaghan became prime minister in 1976, he offered the young Welsh MP a junior ministerial post in either Industry or in Prices and Consumer Protection, hoping to gain credibility with the party's left wing; but Kinnock, who strongly disapproved of Callaghan's support for nuclear deterrence, cuts in public spending, and tough income policies, refused both offers.

Having completely disassociated himself from Callaghan, he was in a strategic position to assume a more prominent leadership role after the Labour government's humiliating loss on May 3, 1979 to the Conservative party, led by Margaret Thatcher.

In 1978 Kinnock was made a member of the Labour party's policy-forming body, the National Executive Committee, and began to attract national recognition the following year when he accepted a position on the opposition's front bench as shadow minister of education. His first major speech railing against the Tory cuts in education drew a standing ovation and national media coverage. Speaking at schools, colleges, and political rallies across the country, Kinnock enunciated his own educational philosophy, which combines a violent dislike of public schools with a passionate commitment to education as an "inalienable human right." In the 1980 London Times interview he said that the function of education should be "to be useful and to promote equality and enlightenment . . . not [to] produce a leader class." For all the favorable publicity he received, Kinnock's initiation into national politics was not exactly painless. His lack of experience and tendency to overstatement occasionally caused him embarrassment, as when in June 1980 he claimed without substantiation that Tory education cuts had forced school children to raffle off their books. The Conservatives delighted in such gaffes; nevertheless, Kinnock built strong grass-roots support among the nation's teachers and gained national attention for his flamboyant oratory. According to Peter Gilman, writing in the Sunday Times (July 17, 1983), as shadow education minister he was "generally held to have made a success of one of the less glamorous portfolios."

The devolution issue brought another important test of Kinnock's national leadership potential. In a special referendum on March 1, 1979, Welsh voters were asked whether they wanted limited self-rule through a regional assembly to be located at Cardiff, a plan that set the Welsh nationalists against the more assimilated Welsh who think of themselves primarily as British. Although proud of his heritage, Kinnock opposed devolution vigorously, breaking with his mentor Michael Foot, whom he had known since 1963, and with party leader Callaghan over the issue and exacerbating the already marked contempt felt for him by the Welsh nationalists. Yet his willingness to buck his own political faction within the Labour party convinced some skeptics that he was not simply a political opportunist, and the resounding 3 to 1 defeat of devolution at the national polls—the vote against it was 9 to 1 in his own constituency of Bedwellty—vindicated Kinnock's political judgment.

After the defeat of Callaghan's conservative Labour government in 1979, the "hard Left," or Marxist, faction led by Anthony Wedgwood Benn pushed through an important procedural change for electing the party's leader. Previously, the party's MPs had decided who among them would be leader, but now the electoral body was widened to include the more radical trade unionists and the local constituency parties. The MPs and the local constituency parties were each allotted 30 percent of the vote, while the trade unions were granted a 40 percent share. Since that innovation swung the party decidedly more to the left, many conservatives, finding the new procedure and the apportionment of votes unacceptable, seceded to form the new Social Democratic Party in 1981. Although he approved of a broadened electorate, Kinnock felt the Bennites' views were too extreme for the party regulars and bitterly opposed Benn's bid for the post of deputy leader in 1981, for which many leftists in the party have yet to forgive him. He also helped to elect Michael Foot as party leader in 1980, an action that many Labourites came to resent once the aging Foot proved ineffectual, leading the party in the June 9, 1983 election to its worst defeat at the polls since 1918.

Neil Kinnock survived those chronic and often fierce intraparty squabbles to emerge as the leader of the party's "soft," or non-Marxist, left. Although an admirer of Marx, he endorsed "radical gradualism" over class warfare and preferred to stress how "practical, modern, up-to-date microchip socialism really is" rather than the correctness of the party's political theories. His realistic tendency was exhibited in a willingness to compromise and a greater sensitivity to the party's rank-and-file, whose views are usually more conservative than those of their leaders. "I enjoy the spark of idealism. I warm myself on it," he has declared. "But you can't live in it, you can't eat it, you can't lie in it, you can't cure diseases with it, and it's these tangibles we are about."

His combination of political pragmatism and fierce idealism, in addition to his popular following and excellent relations with the media, made Kinnock a front-runner for the party leadership when Foot resigned after the disastrous 1983 elections. Against three older and more experienced contenders—the centrist Roy Hattersley, Eric Heffer, a "hard" leftist, and Peter Shore—on October 2, he won on the first ballot with 71 percent of the vote, receiving majority support from all three sections of the party's new electoral college. In a subsequent vote, Roy Hattersley was elected his deputy secretary, thus creating a "dream ticket" that united the party's fractious left and right.

Although he has repeatedly stressed that the "packaging" of the party's policies, rather than those policies themselves, is largely responsible for Labour's poor showings at the polls, since his election Kinnock has also taken some steps to woo popular support. Purging its extreme left, he dismissed five members of the Militant Tendency from the party in October and has tried to align its views more closely with British public opinion. He has softened his stance on Britain's membership in the European Economic Community, convinced that the country should withdraw from it only as "a last resort," and he has backed a popular Conservative policy that would allow public-housing tenants to buy the property they rent. Nevertheless, he continues to follow the party line in his fundamental

opposition to an income policy (an agreement between unions and government setting the level of yearly wage increases) and in his support of massive government spending. The major stumbling block he faces is the Labour party's firm allegiance to the cause of unilateral nuclear disarmament, an unpopular stand with many British voters. Although he himself has long advocated that policy, immediately after his election he supported a compromise resolution favoring multilateral disarmament, only to have the party's voting membership defeat it by a large majority. Accordingly, he has since reaffirmed the party's commitment to scrap the Polaris missile and abandon the Trident if the Labourites are brought to power in the next election. (At its annual conference in October 1984, the Labour party firmly committed itself to unilateral disarmament and to the expulsion of all U.S. nuclear weapons from Britain.) The alternative that Kinnock offers is a buildup of Britain's conventional defenses, such as an "effective anti-invasion technique, electronic equipment, [and] mines [in] both land and sea," although he concedes that such measures might prove even more expensive than the present nuclear armament. In a trip to the United States in February 1984, his first in nine years, Kinnock explained those positions during meetings with President Ronald Reagan, Secretary of Defense Caspar W. Weinberger, and other political and labor leaders.

By focusing the party's attention on the common "enemy," Prime Minister Margaret Thatcher's Conservative government, Kinnock has also tried to quell the Labourites' divisive in-fighting. The Tories have supplied Kinnock with some good ammunition in the last few months: a steamy sex scandal involving a Cabinet minister, persistently high unemployment, and the installation of American cruise missiles at Greenham Common. Kinnock has made the most of the Conservatives' faltering confidence, eloquently protesting recent cuts in the National Health Service and lambasting what he sees as British knuckling under to United States foreign policy. Some observers of the British political scene, however, feel that Kinnock's best chance lies in stressing personality over policies, in the contrast between his witty, eloquent style and Margaret Thatcher's stiff and glacial manner. As he recently quipped, "She used to be conceited, but now she thinks she's perfect." Evidently Kinnock's strategy is working, for after his election the Labour party had pulled within one percentage point of the Tories in public opinion polls. That development highlights "the already noticeable drift of British politics toward the American presidential model," according to R. W. Apple Jr. in his sketch of Kinnock in the New York Times (October 5, 1983).

But according to a poll conducted in September 1984, popular support for the Labour party had dropped to 36 percent, six points lower than that for the Conservatives. Kinnock's personal standing had slipped even more drastically: the percentage of those polled who were satisfied with his performance fell from 43 percent in February to 29 percent in September. Political analysts speculated that the violence during the protracted strikes by the National Union of Mineworkers, and other unions with which the Labourites are associated, may be partly responsible for the souring of the public's opinion of Kinnock and his party. In addition, his position within his party was weakened at the annual Labour party conference, which opened on October 1, 1984, when over his opposition the party, spurred by Arthur Scargill, the leader of the National Union of Mineworkers, gave a vote of support for the striking mineworkers. He backed the union's six-month strike but wanted to distance the party from the violent acts committed by some of the strikers. He suffered another setback with the resounding defeat of a proposal to revise the process for "reselecting," or nominating, Labour MPs. Although he did not expect it to be adopted, Kinnock supported the so-called Evans amendment that sought to broaden the electorate to include the members of the constituency of a district, not just the often left-leaning executive committees, because many of the more conservative Labour MPs worried that such committees would not accept them as candidates for their seats. However, with his rousing, well-received speech on the second day of the conference, Kinnock managed to rally more support for his leadership.

Kinnock faces enormous obstacles in his drive to rebuild the Labour party, not the least of which is the Social Democratic/Liberal Party Alliance. If the Labourites continue to split moderate votes with the Alliance, it will be impossible for either to unseat the Conservatives. Kinnock must also overcome his lack of experience in government. He has always preferred speech-making to committee work, and some of his critics feel that he will never master the complexities of national policy-making. Clearly, the Welshman, the youngest Labour leader ever, must belie his reputation for being a political "lightweight" and outsider if he is to become a serious contender for the prime ministry.

The personable Neil Kinnock stands five feet nine inches tall and has red hair and freckles. A devoted family man, he prefers to spend his evenings at home in Ealing, West London with his wife, the former Glenys Elizabeth Perry, and their children, Stephen and Rachel. Since their marriage in March 1967, Kinnock has relied heavily on the support and political expertise of Glenys, a specialist in reading disorders, and their friends credit her with helping him to overcome his greatest political liabilities: a tendency to exaggerate and to speak out strongly on an issue without knowing the facts. Kinnock is an avid sports fan who follows soccer, rugby, and cricket. A devotee of both classical and rock music, he has a fine bass voice and loves to sing hymns. He has edited a compilation of Aneurin Bevan's writings and speeches (As Nye Said, 1980) and would someday like to write a novel, which he considers to be "the most direct and painless way of telling the truth for politicians." In the interview with Caroline Moorehead for the

London Times, Kinnock said: "I want to retire at fifty. I want to play cricket in summer, geriatric football in winter, and sing in the choir." Given his ambition and enormous appeal, however, there seems little likelihood that England's newest Labour leader will get his wish for an early retirement.

References: London Observer S 26 '82 por; London Observer Mag p28+ F 24 '80 por, p17+ O 2 '83 pors; London Times Jl 28 '80; Sunday Times p17 Jl 7 '83 por; International Who's Who, 1984–85; Who's Who (1984)

Kinski, Nastassja
(nä stä´ shä)

Jan. 24, 1961– Motion picture actress. Address: b. c/o Smith & Siegal, 1650 Broadway, New York City, N.Y. 10019

The hauntingly photogenic German-born actress Nastassja Kinski is, as the Chicago Tribune's Gene Siskel has so shrewdly discerned, "the Isadora Duncan of the movies." An intuitive perfectionist, she is, in her own words, "ready to die for a moment of emotion." Miss Kinski began her career as a sultry adolescent in German films of the mid-1970s. She began to take herself seriously as an actress with her brooding portrayal of the tragic heroine of Tess (1978), Roman Polanski's adaptation of Thomas Hardy's novel Tess of the D'Urbervilles, which was filmed in France. Always willing to take risks in roles that defy convention, she made her American debut as an exotic circus gamine in Francis Ford Coppola's experimental musical fantasy *One from the Heart* (1982), and she followed up that portrayal with starring parts in Paul Schrader's horror film *Cat People* (1983) and James Toback's romantic thriller *Exposed* (1983). Venturing into farce, Miss Kinski played the comic foil for Dudley Moore in Howard Zieff's *Unfaithfully Yours* (1984) and Susie the Bear in Tony Richardson's *The Hotel New Hampshire* (1984) with a talent that "tells us," as Julie Salamon of the *Wall Street Journal* observed, "that this is someone to watch—and not only for her European good looks."

Nastassja Kinski was born Nastassja Nakszynski in West Berlin on January 24, 1961 to the Polish-German stage and film actor Klaus Kinski and the German poet and writer Ruth Brigitte, two of the more colorful members of West Germany's jet-set bohemia. Although she was raised as an only child, she has an older half-sister, Pola, also an actress, and a younger half-brother, Nanhoi, both Klaus Kinski's children by other wives. A free spirit closer to the Slavic than to the German temperament, she has never gotten "along with Germans very well" because, in her view, "they're not tolerant" and that is "a mentality [she] can't deal with."

Miss Kinski remembers her early homelife as stormy but "wonderful," full of "fights and tears, happiness and sweetness and breakdowns where we would destroy the house and then make up." Her parents treated children as "whole human beings," and "everything was always talked out." Following Klaus Kinski's film-making itinerary to locations in France, England, Italy, and Spain, the Kinskis lived like nomads, and Natassja learned to speak English, French, and Italian in addition to her native German. She also learned Spanish, but over the years she has let it lapse.

Her parents separated when Natassja was eight years old. A year later she moved with her mother to Caracas, Venezuela, where a painter boyfriend of the mother's was living, and she rarely saw her father after that. "My father always wrote us love letters . . . ," she recalled in an interview with Gene Siskel of the *Chicago Tribune* (April 4, 1982). "Then he got strange, and we had a period where we wouldn't talk, and I didn't understand. But now we're sort of back together in our minds, and I love him dearly."

On the other hand, Miss Kinski grew closer to her mother, whom she has often described as her "closest friend" and most trusted confidante and professional adviser. "I love her because she always gave me freedom," she explained to Robert Lindsey when he interviewed her for the *New York Times* (January 18, 1981). "She was like a mother cat [who] watches the little kittens go off and learn to run and hunt and all the other things you must learn [but who,] if the kittens are threatened, . . . is fierce." She led "a very conventional life" until puberty, when she became "like an animal running wild, tasting all the honeys." "My mother let me do it, and I think she was right; I think it's important for everyone to be able to go through that; now I don't have to."

"One of the things that still makes [her] angry," Miss Kinski confided to Pete Hamill when he interviewed her for the *New York Daily News* (April 17, 1983), is that she "wanted to play the piano when [she] was young, and . . . didn't." Loving music and dance of all kinds, she originally aspired to become a ballerina, and after she and her mother returned to Germany she regularly went dancing with girlfriends on Sundays at a rock 'n' roll club in Munich. It was there one Sunday in 1974 that the film director Wim Wenders discovered her, as she recounted to Gene Siskel. "He did not know who I was then. My name was not Kinski, it was Nakszynski. He asked if I wanted to be in a movie and took my number. I forgot about it, but his people kept calling and calling. So I did the part, mainly for the money. It wasn't much money, but it was a lot to me, and my mother and I needed it."

The Wenders film in which Miss Kinski made her debut was *Falsche Bewegung/The Wrong Move* (1975), Peter Handke's adaptation of Goethe's *Bildungsroman*, *Wilhelm Meisters Lehrjahre*, which traces the odyssey of a young writer in quest of self-discovery and vocation. In that film she played Mignon, the roving deaf-mute juggler in love with the itinerant hero, who sees her for the child she really is. *Falsche Bewegung* was well received by German critics, including Siegfried Schober of *Der Spiegel*, who considered it "one of the most important German films since Lubitsch, Lang, and Murnau."

Among Miss Kinski's subsequent screen credits was the leading role of the boarding school vamp in *Hotel der leidenschaftlichen Blumen/Passion Flower Hotel*, produced by Arthur Brauner and directed by Andre Farwagi, a film she dislikes "so much" she wishes she "had the money to buy it up and burn it." She remembers Tator Krimi's *Reifezeugnis* ("Diploma") as a "flop," but her portrayal in that made-for-television motion picture of a schoolgirl whose seductiveness unsettles a teacher brought her more national attention than her theatrical features had up to that point. In the Anglo-German feature film *To the Devil a Daughter* (1976), a lackluster adaptation of Dennis Wheatley's witchcraft thriller, she played the titular vestal rescued from the clutches of a satanist (Christopher Lee) by a good occultist (Richard Widmark).

In Italy Miss Kinski made *Stay As You Are* (1978) under the direction of Alberto Lattuada, who described her as "a mixture of poison and nectar." In the film she played a college student, an illegitimate child with a father complex, who seduces a married landscaper (Marcello Mastroianni), a man, it turns out, who may be her father. When *Stay As Your Are* was released in the United States by New Line Cinema in 1979, critics were generally more impressed with her "pert and provocative" beauty than her manner and bearing. Miss Kinski was nonplussed when *Playboy* magazine published nude stills from the film with Mastroianni cropped out. "I was brought up to believe that there is nothing shameful about the naked human body," she explained to an anonymous interviewer for *American Film* (October 1979). "Nudity does not bother me as such. It's beautiful and quite natural. But when pictures are taken out of films, and the context is lost, it's perhaps a different thing."

In the beginning, Miss Kinski felt movie acting to be a "strange" profession in which "you earn a lot of money for nothing," for pretending "to be somebody else." Then, "all of a sudden," as she recounted to Pete Hamill in the *New York Daily News* interview, "it got to [her] . . . like a drug." The turning point was the making of *Tess* under the direction of Roman Polanski, whom she had met in Munich in October 1976, when she was fifteen and he was a fugitive from a conviction for the statutory rape of a thirteen-year-old girl in the United States. After a brief love affair, the two settled into a platonic relationship in which Polanski was her professional mentor, for several years, and close friend, which he remains. "He introduced me to beautiful books, plays, movies," she told Peter Lester of *People* (April 13, 1981). "He educated me." Polanski used her as the model in a pictorial spread he edited for the December 1976 issue of the French *Vogue* and then sent her to the United States and England to study acting and perfect her English. She spent part of her sojourn in England living and working on a farm in Dorsetshire in preparation for her role as Tess, one with which she personally identified.

Dorset was Thomas Hardy's native shire, fictionalized as "Wessex" in his novels about country people tyrannized by rigid Victorian codes of behavior and caught in the collision of the industrial revolution with old rural ways. In *Tess of the d'Urbervilles* (1891), the victim is a selfless and courageous nonconformist whose love of life and of others is exploited, thwarted, and punished with social ostracism. Forced onto an upward social course by her impoverished, avaricious family, Tess is seduced by a pseudo-aristocrat, abandoned by the man she later marries when he learns of the seduction, shunned by the church, and ultimately pushed to vengeful murder and her own death.

Because of his legal problems, Polanski shot *Tess* not in England, which has an extradition treaty with the United States, but in France, which does not. At great expense, he transformed locations in Normandy into replicas of Dorset and painstakingly evoked life as it was lived in Hardy's "Wessex." With newfound taste and admirable restraint, he departed from the macabre perversity of his previous entertainments and hewed faithfully to Hardy's leisurely and fluid pace, profound compassion, and muted rage at injustice.

Tess was roundly panned when released in Germany in 1978 but well received in France the following year. Major studios in the United States were at first unanimously reluctant to market the film, partly because they considered it too literary and too long (almost three hours) for commercial success and partly, perhaps, because Polanski was anathema. After successful previews in New York

and Los Angeles in December 1980, however, Columbia Pictures elected to distribute *Tess* nationwide, where it made a profit at the box office and received generally good reviews. Some critics had reservations about the film's lack of "passion" and "tone" as well as Miss Kinski's "prosaic" acting, but most raved about *Tess*'s "sheer physical beauty" and the actress's dark sensuality and "luminous" and "sultry-sweet" presence, at once "patrician and earthy." The Hollywood Foreign Press Association awarded Golden Globes to both *Tess*, as best foreign film of the year, and Miss Kinski, as best new female star. The National Academy of Motion Picture Arts and Sciences honored the opulent cinematography of Ghistain Cloquet and the late Geoffrey Unsworth with an Oscar and nominated both Polanski and the film itself for awards.

Francis Ford Coppola cast Miss Kinski as Leila, the exotic young circus acrobat who briefly lures the hero (Frederic Forrest) away from the heroine (Terri Garr) in the musical romantic fantasy *One From the Heart* (Columbia, 1982), Coppola's first experiment in "electronic cinema," set in a surreal, studio-built Las Vegas. With little substance beneath its glitzy dazzle, that tour de force from Coppola's Zoetrope Studios was, in the critical consensus, a boring waste of acting talent.

In *Cat People* (Universal, 1982), Paul Schrader's grade-A eroticization of Jacques Tourneur's legendary 1942 grade-B horror quickie of the same name, Schrader coupled, in his words, "incest with fear of loss of virginity, with bestiality, with bondage." The "whole notion" of his *Cat People*, according to Schrader, was "one of incestuous people who become animals if they have sex outside their own family." Schrader chose Miss Kinski to play the female lead in the movie because he wanted to "go back to that pre-World War II sensibility of the screen goddess," someone who could be projected as "ethereal," and he surmised in her "a sex-goddess kind of beauty." He designed the film "so that she could be bigger than life," a "magical character."

Cat People, with its state-of-the-art special effects, was widely welcomed as a classic of the *cinéma fantastique* in its own right—uneven, perhaps, and disjointed and excessively gory, but nevertheless feverishly poetic in its dramatization of the beast lurking within sexual obsession. Some critics saw as "a brilliant stroke" the director's bringing together in the film's incestuous brother-sister relationship "those strange staring eyes" of Malcolm McDowell with "the edgy feral presence" of Nastassja Kinski.

Others found Miss Kinski's voice "flat," except in her shifts of dramatic and emotional gears, when it became a "literal screech." "It strikes me in retrospect," Andrew Sarris wrote in his review of *Cat People* in the *Village Voice* (April 13, 1982), "that she was ideally cast in *Tess* because the part called for an unvarying intensity and oxlike obduracy." In her review in the *New Yorker* (May 3, 1982), Pauline Kael described Miss Kinski's voice as having "no music," as sounding "dubbed."

"Is it simply that she speaks English inexpressively? Or is it from that slightly twisted openmouthed look, as if a toad had just leaped out? She never quite seems to be inside the story, even when she's prowling about in the moonlight, naked and sinuously clumsy, with blood drooling from her mouth." Miss Kinski herself "would have loved" Cat People "to be less slick."

During the filming of Cat People the actress, who has exceptionally good rapport with animals in real life, was photographed by Richard Avedon with several of the animals from the film. The controversial definitive photograph from that session showed the actress with a python coiled around her nude body. First published in Vogue, it became the best-selling poster in the United States and has been reproduced in more magazines than any other photo Avedon has taken. The photographer considered Miss Kinski "without a doubt, the most beautiful, sensitive, intelligent and sensuous actress" he had worked with "since the days of Marilyn Monroe and Audrey Hepburn," and he was certain that "we are going to watch her career evolve just as we have lived through the screen lifetimes of those movie heroines Ingrid Bergman, Vivien Leigh and Garbo."

Miss Kinski went against the advice of her agent and others around her in agreeing to make her third American film role that of the female lead in Exposed (MGM/United Artists, 1983), an existentialist adventure dreamed up in the id of its director, James Toback, the American cinema's subterranean Walter Mitty. "When I sensed Jimmy's obsessions, his enthusiasm," she recounted to Pete Hamill in the New York Daily News interview, "I felt I had to do it. I had to trust him." In this instance, described by Jack Kroll in Newsweek (May 2, 1983) as "not so much a movie as . . . a torrential wet dream," Toback's obsession was with chic violence and with Kinski herself, cast as a college dropout from Minnesota who becomes a top model in New York and is drawn into a web of international intrigue. Such scenes as an autoerotic dance were saved by the actress's "sunflower sensuality," to use the words of Kroll, who advised that she "break loose from the fantasy-mongers, of whom nobody mongs better than Toback."

As Richard Corliss observed in Time (May 2, 1983), the story line of Exposed "functions as a metaphor" for Miss Kinski's "dangerous need to be used by directors whose eccentricity overwhelms their artistry." In his profile of her in the Chicago Tribune Gene Siskel noted that each of the directors of her first three American films had used her "as an object of intense desire" who exists "mostly in closeups and reaction shots." Siskel quoted her as complaining that all of her directors had portrayed her as "this strange girl who hardly talks and yet has a great effect on people" and not given her the chance "to let that bloom out that is inside" her. In her interview with Richard Corliss, however, she confessed her willingness to be "a creature of the director's imagination." "I want to get a glimpse of his eyes searching out things inside of me," she said. "I want to go to heaven and hell for him. I want to make his dreams come true." Corliss thought that she deserved "credit for daring to embody the disturbed visions of directors like Schrader and Toback."

The lurid romantic excesses of Jean-Jacques Beineix's Moon in the Gutter (Gaumont) drew boos and hisses as the French entry at the Cannes Film Festival in 1983. Miss Kinski, who felt at home in her role in that film as a playgirl who drowns her emotional pain in compulsive lovemaking with a man in similar pain, regarded the display of antipathy to the movie as an indication that it "touches something they don't want to have touched." In contrast to the reception given Moon in the Gutter at Cannes, Miss Kinski herself was welcomed with a mass adulation rarely equaled in the history of the festival.

Also screened at Cannes in 1983 was Peter Schamoni's Spring Symphony, which was titled Symphony of Love when it was released by Warner Brothers and Columbia Pictures. Miss Kinski's portrayal in that film of Clara (Wieck) Schumann, the pianist, composer, and wife of the composer Robert Schumann, brought her the Bundespreis, the German equivalent of the Oscar, one of several German film awards she won in 1983. In September 1983 the actress went to the Pennsylvania mining town of Brownsville to begin work in the yet to be released "Maria's Lovers," a melodrama of triangular passion directed by Andrei Konchalovsky and costarring Robert Mitchum.

Nastassja Kinski showed more flexibility than ever before as the wife of the orchestra conductor (Dudley Moore) unhinged by jealous suspicion in Unfaithfully Yours (Twentieth Century-Fox, 1984), Howard Zieff's slapstick remake of Preston Sturges' 1948 farce. That film, Miss Kinski's first major commercial success since Tess, was also a fair success with most critics other than Sturges aficionados. Pauline Kael, previously so derisive of Miss Kinski's acting, observed that she was "becoming more striking and assured—muskier, too." It was in the credits for Unfaithfully Yours that the actress reverted to the original spelling of her first name, which she had anglicized to Nastassia at Roman Polanski's suggestion in 1978.

The release of Unfaithfully Yours was quickly followed by that of the zany tragicomedy The Hotel New Hampshire (Orion Pictures, 1984), Tony Richardson's screen adaptation of John Irving's fast-paced novel about the jaunts and jollities of the eccentric and disaster-prone Berry family as they establish one hotel after another, from New Hampshire to Vienna. Among the multitude of characters in Irving's absurdist three-ring circus is Susie, an ugly young lesbian known as Susie the Bear because she lives her life hidden from reality inside a bear suit—until the love of her family heals her of her depression and disorientation. That difficult role was movingly performed in the movie by a deglamorized Nastassja Kinski. As if in answer to those critics who could not accept her as stringy-haired and plain-looking, Miss Kinski explained in her interview with Carol Krucoff of the *Washington Post* that one reason she had accepted so many projects in so short a time was that "they all touched something deep" in her, and none did so more than Susie the Bear. "What is reality and what she [Susie] sees about herself are two different things," she explained. "Something melts inside Susie so she can take off the bear suit. This happened to me. There is a beauty about myself that I never saw, or I rejected, until recently." Subsequently, Miss Kinski had roles in *Paris, Texas*, which won the grand prize at the Cannes Film Festival in May 1984, and *Maria's Lovers*, which was being readied for release in October 1984.

Physically, Nastassja Kinski, who usually wears no makeup off camera, projects both fragility and strength, poise and gawkiness. She is tall (five feet seven and a half inches) and angular, with a mobile face, a full mouth, and gray-green flashing eyes. As Richard Corliss remarked in his *Time* cover story, she is a "true camera animal" because it is only in her special, direct rapport with the lens that "these disparate, classically mismatched" physical parts mysteriously combine with her energy and intelligence to enthrall the viewer with an image at once wary and seductive.

The actress maintains homes in Paris, the Bahamas, and New York City (which she prefers to Los Angeles because of its European-like vitality and diversity). Her chief recreations are reading (including the German, Russian, and French classics and, in recent years, the Bible), movie-going (*Frances* and *Viva Zapata* are favorites), and listening to music (from classical to jazz, Elvis Presley, and the Beatles). While appreciating the personal freedoms won for her and other women by the feminist movement, and acknowledging that "women are still not treated equally," Miss Kinski adheres to the "old-fashioned" belief that "men and women are different." "I'm free," she explained in the *Washington Post* interview, "but I also want to love a man, have many children, have a real life too." Following reported romantic liaisons with Dudley Moore and Gerard Depardieu, among others, Miss Kinski married Ibrahim Moussa, the Egyptian talent agent, film producer, and jewelry company representative, on September 12, 1984, ten weeks after the birth of her son by Moussa, Aljohsa.

Nastassja Kinski's often aloof screen persona belies a real-life warmth and accessibility. Democratic, she socializes as easily with technicians on the set as with celebrities. Open and direct, she is willing to be candid on almost any subject in interviews. Those who know her describe her as "modest," "realistic," and the possessor of a "light and sunny" personality. With her precocious sophistication and her unique, lilting accent, she is, as Pete Hamill observed, twenty-three years old "but seems as old as Europe."

References: American Film 5:64+ O '79 pors; Chicago Tribune VI p18+ Ap 4 '82 pors; N Y Daily News mag p6+ Ap 17 '83 pors; N Y Times

p13+ Ja 18 '81 pors; Newsweek 97:60 F 23 '81 pors; Parade p8+ Ag 8 '82 pors; Time 121:44+ My 2 '83 pors; Washington Post B pl+ S 8 '83 pors

Kolvenbach, Peter-Hans

1928– Roman Catholic priest; Superior General of the Society of Jesus. Address: b. Borgo Santo Spirito, 5, Rome, Italy

With the election of the Very Reverend Peter-Hans Kolvenbach as superior general of the Society of Jesus in September 1983, the largest (26,000 members) and most influential Roman Catholic religious order of men regained its internal autonomy after two years under a caretaker administration imposed by Pope John Paul II. From the beginning of his reign, in 1978, the Pope made clear his determination to curb what he viewed as an unwarranted and dangerous permissiveness in faith and discipline rampant in the church since Vatican Council II. John Paul was especially displeased with alleged leftist theological revisionism and worldly activism, particularly in political causes in the Third World, on the part of Jesuit priests, who take a special vow of fealty to the pope in addition to the vows of poverty, chastity, and obedience common to all Roman Catholic religious orders.

Father Kolvenbach is the twenty-eighth successor to St. Ignatius Loyola, the former Spanish military officer who founded the Company of Jesus (the society's original name) during the Counter Reformation of the sixteenth century as an intellectually and spiritually disciplined elite corps devoted to serving the papacy with military-like obedience wherever the faith was weak or challenged. The new superior general is a linguistic scholar and teacher whose background in Orientalism amply suits him for the ecumenical aspect of the Jesuits' work as front-line missionaries and educators worldwide. Although Dutch-born, Kolvenbach is a member of the church's Armenian rite. For seventeen years he worked in Lebanon, and at the time of his election he was rector of the Pontifical Oriental Institute in Rome, where he taught linguistics and Armenian. In addition, he was a member of the Curia commission for theological dialogue between the Roman Catholic church and the Orthodox churches. As superior general, he does not repudiate the progressive policies of his predecessor, Father Pedro Arrupe y Gondra—who resigned after suffering a paralyzing brain hemorrhage in 1981—but he does not intend to allow Vatican grievances against the Jesuits ever again to accumulate without obediently looking into their merits. "The Society of Jesus has no meaning and loses its very reason to exist," he has said, "if it lacks distinctive fidelity to the Holy Father."

Peter-Hans Kolvenbach, born in the village of Druten, the Netherlands in 1928, entered the Society of Jesus in the nearby university city of Nijmegan when he was twenty years old. After undergoing two years of cloistered spiritual training at the Jesuit novitiate in Nijmegan, he took the vows of poverty, chastity, and obedience. Following three years of philosophy at the University of Nijmegan and four years of theology at St. Joseph University in Beirut, Lebanon, he began working for his doctorate in Armenian and Oriental linguistics. Concurrently, he began teaching. His training was rounded off with a year-long second novitiate in a Jesuit retreat house in Pomfret, Connecticut. In 1961 he was ordained and took the Jesuits' distinctive fourth vow.

After his ordination, Kolvenbach completed his doctoral studies and returned to Beirut as a professor of general linguistics at St. Joseph University. In addition, he administered the Jesuits' Near East vice-province, which encompasses Syria and Egypt as well as Lebanon. In Lebanon, he left the church's Latin rite and joined the Armenian, one of several Eastern rites that are in union with Rome but have a language, liturgy, and spiritual tradition close to those of Orthodox Christianity. Some of his time in Lebanon was spent working with Palestinian refugees in their camps.

In 1981 Kolvenbach was appointed to the faculty of the Gregorian University in Rome. In addition to running the university's Pontifical Oriental Institute and teaching linguistics and Armenian there, he was an adviser to Wladyslaw Cardinal Rubin, the prefect of the Sacred Congregation of the Oriental Churches, the Curia department that supervises the church's Eastern rites, and a member of the Secretariat for Promoting Christian Unity, where his work was in the dialogue with the Eastern Orthodox churches.

Meanwhile Kolvenbach's long assignment in the Near East had distanced him from the ecclesiastical turbulence, generated by the reformative decrees of Vatican Council II (1962–65), that created a crisis of authority in the Western church, especially in the Netherlands, where liturgical experimentation and theological reappraisal had a head start. Before the gravity of the crisis became apparent, Pedro Arrupe, elected superior general of the Jesuits in 1965, told his priests that, in the spirit of the council, they must become "more Ignatian than Ignatius" in adapting to new times. He exhorted them to stop speaking a language "men no longer understand" and to make amends for the Christian divisiveness to which Jesuits, among others, contributed in the past through "an exaggerated sense of loyalty to one's own church at the expense of charity" and "a too-rigid concept of the truth."

Arrupe soon realized that he was preaching to the already converted and that the task of promoting change was not going to be as difficult as that of keeping it within bounds acceptable to the Vatican. As early as 1966, Pope Paul VI expressed to Arrupe his "surprise and grief" over "news and rumors about your society as well as other religious orders" moving away from "venerable customs" toward "more free and personal expression." Three years later, under pressure from Rome, Arrupe regretfully expelled from the Society of Jesus two prominent Dutch priests who publicly advocated an end to compulsory clerical celibacy. In protest, the Jesuit administrator for northern Europe and the provincial of the Dutch Jesuits both left the order.

Pope Paul had mixed feelings about the fervor of Arrupe's encouragement of American Jesuit civil rights activism, and he was concerned about the interpretation that might be put on the Superior General's prison visit to Daniel Berrigan, the Jesuit peace radical convicted of destroying United States 1A Selective Service files in 1968. Berrigan's rationale for his action was the antithesis of the Vatican position on the proper role of priests in contemporary society. "One simply cannot announce the Gospel from his pedestal . . . ," he explained in court, "when he was not down there sharing the risks and burdens and the anguish of his students."

Following the thirty-second general congregation of the Society of Jesus (1974–75), Pope Paul VI sharply questioned some "puzzling" points in the decrees of the congregation, including an apparent departure from Thomism in Jesuit training, wider latitude for theologians vis-à-vis the church's magisterium, or teaching authority, and the "excessive emphasis, at a temporal level, on human advancement and social progress to the detriment of . . . evangelization." During his brief reign, in 1978, Pope John Paul I reiterated Paul VI's complaint, but the issue was soft-pedaled until the installation of Pope John Paul II in the chair of St. Peter in October 1978. From the beginning, John Paul II minced no words in rebuking Jesuit priests who had become "social directors, political leaders, or functionaries of a temporal power" and those who bucked the "traditional" teaching on such matters as clerical celibacy, women in the priesthood, and artificial birth control. While priests must help "to promote justice connected with world peace," he said, they, unlike the laity, are not free to assume roles not intrinsic to the priestly function, nor should they give in "to the temptation to reduce the mission of the church to the dimensions of a simply temporal project."

Addressing a Jesuit audience in September 1979, Pope John Paul II warned against "secularizing tendencies" and urged a striving for greater "doctrinal orthodoxy." Cracking down on the American Jesuits, the Pope had Arrupe silence William J. Callahan, an outspoken advocate of women in the priesthood, in 1979, and forbade Representative Robert F. Drinan of Massachusetts, the only priest in the United States Congress, to seek reelection, in 1980. At the Pope's request, Arrupe in December 1979 sent a letter to all Jesuit superiors calling for "appropriate firmness in seeking a remedy for regrettable shortcomings" in their work for the church. As for the priests who had become partisans in revolutionary movements in Latin America, the Philippines, and Africa, the message relayed from the Vatican appeared to be: desist, or defrock.

When he suffered a stroke in August 1981, Father Arrupe named the American Jesuit Vincent O'Keefe his vicar general, to administer the affairs of the order until an election could be held. Two months later, Pope John Paul II, suspending the rules under which the Society of Jesus operates, removed O'Keefe, postponed the election of a new superior general indefinitely, and appointed the octogenarian Paolo Dezza, a conservative Vatican bureaucrat, to administer the order. As associate administrator, the Pope named a younger conservative, Giuseppe Pittau, whom he described as "a real Jesuit."

In February and March 1982, Jesuit provincial leaders from around the world met in Rome for discussions in which Paolo Dezza acted as go-between with the Pope. A moderate participant in the discussions gave a reporter the gist of the Pope's argument: "There has been so much emphasis on 'being relevant' that many Jesuits are theologically illiterate. What the Holy Father is saying is that Jesuits should know something about what happened between Jesus and Vatican II." Apparently satisfied that his message was heard, John Paul personally ended the conclave on a conciliatory note, praising the Jesuits as "the vanguard of renewal" in the church and telling them they now had his permission to prepare for electing a new superior general.

The papal interregnum ended and the Jesuits regained their autonomy with their thirty-third general congregation, held in Rome in September and October 1983. On September 13, the tenth day of the congregation, the 220 delegates elected their new superior general, passing over Giuseppe Pittau, the perceived papal favorite, to select Peter-Hans Kolvenbach by an overwhelming majority on the first ballot. "I am going to do a lot of listening," Kolvenbach said after his election. "I'm not going to make any statements about Latin America or anywhere else until I find out the facts from people who have been there firsthand."

The American Jesuit Timothy S. Healey, the president of Georgetown University, saw Kolvenbach's election as symbolic of a change in the Society of Jesus that reflects a change in the church as a whole. "The church and the society are newly focused on the works of peace," Healy said in a speech in New York City in November 1983. Like Father Arrupe, Kolvenbach is a man "bred in the first world but experienced in the Third," he pointed out. "Father Kolvenbach is a Dutchman with long years in the Middle East. The fact points up a change as profound, as full of grace and hope as any I have known in my forty-three Jesuit years." With the "major land shift" of Vatican II, Healey went on, the church's mission work changed from direct evangelization to "work on the quality of life, the growth of Christian laity, the care and feeding of a church body [that] is as new as the springtime. The role of the society has seen that same kind of change. The last general congregation reached deep into the roots of Jesuitry and legitimated advocacy . . . on the side of justice, with a new kind of preoccupation with men's lives on earth."

In the fall of 1984 Kolvenbach visited New York City, where his generally positive comments about liberation theology drew press attention. While there he met for discussion with Fr. Ernesto Cardenal, Nicaragua's minister of culture.

Tall and silver-haired, with beard and hornrimmed glasses, Peter-Hans Kolvenbach looks as ascetic as he is reported to be in fact. According to colleagues, he sleeps on the floor of his bedroom in the Jesuit world headquarters (an impressive stone building one block from St. Peter's Square), rises at 4:30, joins in such menial chores as clearing the table and carrying the luggage of guests, and makes it his practice to traverse Rome and its environs on foot rather than by car or bus, even when the distance that duty takes him is five or six miles. Gentle in manner, laconic in speech, and shy of publicity, he yet has what priests who have worked with him in Rome describe as "an enormous suaveness" and "a charm in dealing with people." A professor at Fordham University who knew him in Lebanon told a reporter for Catholic New York (November 10, 1983): "He is a very capable man [whose] major expertise is his calm, behind-the-scenes encouragement of people under very trying circumstances. His intelligence, moderation, and courage are very much respected." In addition to Dutch and Armenian, Kolvenbach speaks fluent English, German, French, Russian, Italian, and Spanish.

References: Catholic New York p23 N 10 '83; Guardian p12 O 9 '83 por; Macleans 96:42+ S 26 '83 por; N Y Times O 30 '83, p9 N 26 '83 por; Newsweek 102:67 S 26 '83 por; Time 122:59 S 26 '83 por; U S News 95:16 S 26 '83 por

Komar, Vitaly

Sept. 11, 1943– Artist.

Melamid, Aleksandr

July 14, 1945– Artist.

Address: b. c/o Ronald Feldman Fine Arts Inc.,
31 Mercer St., New York City, N.Y. 10013

Occupying a unique position in the contemporary art world, Vitaly Komar and Aleksandr Melamid are Soviet Jewish émigrés and longtime partners who were once described by Grace Glueck, a critic for the *New York Times*, as a "two-man art collective." Since their days as art students in Moscow in the mid-1960s, they have collaborated so closely on their works that it is impossible to distinguish between their contributions. Although their heavy emphasis on socialist realism has led some critics to label them as political artists, their work defies easy categorization. Melamid and Komar, who originated "sots art," a Russian version of pop art, have appropriated every style from seventeenth-century classicism to abstraction and have created their own political and religious systems in other works. They insist, however, that a common thread runs through their oeuvre: "We don't believe in anything," Melamid has explained. "We are not against Communism, or against capitalism, or *for* either. Irony is above everything because nothing is taken seriously. Some of our works can be funny and some tragic, but they are always ironic."

Born in Moscow on September 11, 1943, Vitaly Komar is older than Aleksandr Melamid, also a Muscovite, who was born on July 14, 1945. Information about their early lives is hard to come by, but it is known that from the ages of thirteen to fifteen each boy attended an art school in the capital. The two finally met in the mid-1960s in an anatomy class at Moscow's Stroganov Institute for Art and Design. Becoming close friends, they almost immediately began to work together on artistic projects. In 1965, two years before their graduation from the Institute, they held the first of their "one-men" shows, as they call them, "Joint Works on the Theory of Art."

After joining the officially sanctioned Artists Union (a necessity for any Soviet artist wishing to earn a living), Komar and Melamid each received a few official commissions, which they dutifully executed in the approved socialist-realism style. But "finding in each other a secret subversive," according to a *World Artists* profile, they began to explore different techniques and styles and, like other dissident artists, showed their avant-garde paintings in secret or sometimes had them smuggled into the West. They continued to collaborate so closely—one man often completing a canvas the other had started—that it was often impossible to determine what each artist had painted. They cultivated that practice because it helped to ensure the objectivity of their works. "We want to present reality with the maximum precision," they explained in *New York* magazine (February 9, 1976), "and to do that, we have to reject our individual perceptions. Working as a team is one of our tools to overcome our personal styles. The self-expression of an artist is detrimental to true realism."

Strongly influenced by the American pop-art movement of the 1960s, Komar and Melamid created their own version of it in 1972, christening it "sots art," a term they derived from *sotsialisty*, the Russian word for socialist realism. Just as Robert Rauschenberg, Andy Warhol, and other American pop artists used advertising symbols—celebrities such as Marilyn Monroe or commonplace objects such as Campbell soup cans and Brillo-pad boxes—as subjects of their art in order to satirize the pervasive commercialism and materialism of their consumerist culture, Komar and Melamid likewise focused on the omnipresent element in all aspects of their society—socialism. Komar and Melamid say that their work is really "anti-pop-art," in which they transform "the great, the heroic . . . into the small and insignificant. Warhol did the opposite . . . ," according to Melamid. "We take a significant subject—Stalin, Communism—and sign it Komar and Melamid. We are inconsequential beings tangling with heroes."

Exploiting the socialist-realism poster style, they produced witty but bitingly ironic comments on "the ideological thrust of Soviet propaganda art," to quote Grace Glueck. In the same article for the *New York Times Magazine* (May 8, 1977), she described the subject matter of their jointly executed, experimental works as "the strapping, heroic workers, the charts of production achievement and the mosaicized heads of Lenin and other Soviet idols found on billboards and façades all over the

Aleksandr Melamid

country." In less subtle paintings, they depicted a medallion featuring their own profiles instead of those of the standard Soviet heroes and Melamid's wife and son as idealized collective-farm workers. With *Post-Art #1 (Andy Warhol)* (1973), which consists of a print of Warhol's celebrated painting of a Campbell soup can that they "aged" with a blowtorch and mounted on canvas, and other similarly treated American pop-art prints, they blatantly lampooned the Soviet government's practice of fabricating historical documents to support politically expedient assertions. When they showed some of their least radical works in the sots-art style to the Artists Union in order to get permission for a public exhibition, their memberships were immediately revoked because of the "distortion of Soviet reality and departure from Soviet realism" evident in the paintings.

In order to support themselves, Komar and Melamid then joined the Soviet Union of Graphic Artists, designed book dust jackets and record covers, and taught art at night school. They continued painting together, without entertaining any hope of public showings, though some of their work was circulated privately among Moscow intellectuals. On September 15, 1974, the two men "went public" by joining twenty-five other dissident avant-garde artists in an unsanctioned outdoor exhibition in Belijaevo, a suburb of Moscow, but KGB agents roughed up the spectators and some foreign journalists and confiscated the art works (including some by Komar and Melamid). Finally, trucks bulldozed the exhibition. The international outcry against such flagrant censorship resulted in lenient treatment of the artists, several of whom had been arrested, return of the confiscated art on September 17, and an officially approved exhibition on September 29 in Moscow's Ismailovo Park.

As their own works attracted increasing attention in the West, chiefly through the efforts of Melamid's cousin Aleksandr Goldfarb and through articles in 1974 by Hendrick Smith in the *New York Times* and by Herbert Gold in the *Los Angeles Times*, Komar and Melamid found a degree of protection from irate Soviet officials. "A reputation is necessary for our creative work," Melamid explained in *Newsweek* (February 16, 1976). "The more we are heard, the more we can say." Indeed, when David K. Shipler interviewed Komar and Melamid for the *New York Times* (February 7, 1976), they claimed to be "conversationalists," not artists, whose paintings—consisting of conversations rendered concrete—should spur the viewer into talking. As an additional aid, they cut off the upper left-hand corners of a series of paintings. A more fundamental purpose of the series, they explained, was to demonstrate "the right of the artist to an anti-individual style. The cut-off corner is 'we' or our position with respect to the history of art."

While remaining faithful to the purpose of sots art, in the mid-1970s Komar and Melamid began employing a wide range of styles in their "cut-corner" paintings and other works, from the traditional ones of the European Old Masters, which in fact had been endorsed in Stalinist Russia as a means of dressing up and legitimating socialist art, to abstraction and literalism, in part as a further demonstration of their "anti-individual style." In *Double Self-Portrait* (1976), they depicted themselves as religious figures in a Baroque painting. Writing in *Artforum* (January 1978), Marc Fields described another cut-corner painting as "a scabrous mixed-media canvas painted by the random application of a variety of acids and dyes." *Biography,* one of their most intriguing works outside of that series, also best illustrates their eclecticism. In a minutely detailed series of 197 small (one-and-three-quarter-inch) square panels, each in a different style, they illustrated the life of a Soviet man, showing his birth, education, loves, and concerns, and in the process recapitulated the history of twentieth-century Russia. But, as Aleksandr Goldfarb pointed out in an article for *New York* magazine (February 9, 1976), their various styles constituted more than merely academic technical exercises: "the style in which each small panel is painted is as important as what the panel shows. *Biography* is a life story written in the language of art history."

Also influenced by conceptual art, a movement that emphasized the artist's message rather than his medium, in 1975 Komar and Melamid staged in Moscow several "happenings"—somewhat theatrical artistic presentations akin to performance art— in which they wore masks of Stalin and Roosevelt and robes covered with exotic markings, or, in another instance, built a "nest" with the help of their students and sat in it hatching their "art eggs" until Soviet officials forced them off with fire hoses. Other of their conceptual art–inspired works satirized Western culture, especially its materialism.

In *A Catalogue of Superobjects—Supercomforts for Superpeople* (1977), a printed text with photographs issued in a limited edition of one hundred copies, they advertised thirty-six "elegant little fetish objects," as Marc Fields described them in *Artforum* (January 1978), "that could slip unobtrusively into the ads in the margins of the *New Yorker*." They included a gold or pearl ball that a user places in his mouth to make his every word golden or a pearl; a gold-plated grill that ensures pure thoughts when one wears it over his face; and a precious-wood pedestal that purportedly relieves one of "the vain desire to scramble up the ladder of social success."

Like many other conceptual artists, Komar and Melamid were also interested in language. In an intriguing work entitled *Color Writing: Ideological Abstraction #1* (1974), they assigned a separate color to each character in the Cyrillic alphabet and then used that color code to encipher Article 129 of the Soviet constitution, which ensures freedom of speech, assembly, and religion. To celebrate their first exhibition outside the U.S.S.R., which opened at Ronald Feldman Fine Arts Inc. in New York City on February 7, 1976, they again combined art and cryptography in *Music Writing: Passport*. Komar and Melamid created that atonal composition, which was performed simultaneously in Moscow, New York, and many other cities around the world, by assigning a musical value to each Cyrillic character and then transcribing articles from a Soviet internal passport in that "alphabet."

With *Biography* and several sots-art works smuggled out of Russia featured at that Feldman gallery exhibition, the show attracted international attention. But their gibes at socialism and the U.S.S.R. in their compositions made Komar and Melamid *personae non gratae* in the Soviet Union. Their subsequent applications for exit visas brought about their dismissal from the Graphic Artists union and the impossibility of their finding other work. The visas were not approved for some time, but in October 1977 Melamid and his family were permitted to immigrate to Israel, and Komar was allowed to join his partner there in December. The next year they immigrated to the United States.

Since applicants for exit visas must relinquish their Soviet passports, for a while both Komar and Melamid were stateless persons. Partly to dramatize that fact, they created TransState, an intricate system in which each person is his own state and therefore empowered to enter into alliances, issue his own currency and passports, and so on. The impish artists even made their own portable border posts to mark the boundaries of their TransStates. Not surprisingly, they took as their motto the famous statement attributed to Louis XIV: "*L'état, c'est moi.*"

When they were reunited in Israel, Komar and Melamid staged a pseudo-religious rite that consisted of constructing a temple and "sacrificing" Komar's suitcase and other symbols of their ties with Russia in a kind of exorcism of the "evil angel"

that had hung over them in their homeland. The "temple" was then smashed, the pieces collected as relics, and then reassembled at the Feldman gallery as *Temple to the Third*. They went on to create a religion, complete with text, icons, and relics and together served as its "Thirteenth Prophet." Continuing in that irreverent vein, in *Excavations on Crete* (1978) Komar and Melamid "discovered" the bones of the Minotaur. (The bones were actually obtained from a mail-order house in India.) From 1978 to 1981 they conducted a sporadic "happening" they called *Komar and Melamid Inc., We Buy and Sell Souls*, in which they bought souls—including that of Andy Warhol—and then auctioned them in New York and Moscow, thus "ensuring the immortality of the original owners," as critic Jamey Gambrell explained in *Artforum* (April 1982). In 1984 the duo staged a "Close-Out Sale" of souls neither successfully auctioned nor reclaimed, which the Feldman gallery billed as "a testament to the failure of their first capitalist venture," adding that "souls not reclaimed or sold will be donated to a worthy cause."

Even after Komar and Melamid settled in the United States, Soviet culture and its heroes and socialist realism still figured predominantly in their work. Although the *Superobjects* catalogue, some sots-art works featuring American advertising symbols, and a portrait of Ronald Reagan as a centaur were included in the sold out 1982 exhibition at Ronald Feldman Fine Arts, the paintings that focused almost exclusively on Stalin and Lenin and that were uniformly rendered in the classic seventeenth-century style appropriated by Soviet socialist realists in the late 1940s and 1950s drew the most attention. Most art critics, though charmed by the obvious wit of the paintings, interpreted them as little more than well-executed, ironic comments on Soviet socialism. For example, writing in *Time* (October 25, 1982), Robert Hughes described *Stalin and the Muses*, which showed Clio, the muse of history, offering a volume to that leader, as "'objectively' a hilarious spoof" of Soviet revisionist history but on another level a jab at "official art" of any origin; and in her review for *New York* magazine (October 11, 1982) Kay Larson perceived "an indictment of the fairy-tale yearnings of official Soviet society" in *View of the Kremlin in a Romantic Landscape*. As Thomas Lawson pointed out in an interview with Komar and Melamid for *Real Life Magazine* (Winter 1983), the result was that they were increasingly "taken up as prime examples of 'good' political artists."

Although Komar and Melamid agree that their 1982 exhibit at the Feldman gallery was humorous and highly ironic, they insisted in an interview with Jamey Gambrell in the *East Village Eye* (February 1983) that it "wasn't devoted to ironies at the expense of Soviet power, but irony in regard to any and every kind of painting. . . . The paintings . . . didn't caricature Stalin, but Poussin." That is, their art is not only anti-individualistic but also anti-artistic, an expression of their own radical nihilism. To clarify their intention, they drew on the

German philosopher Hegel's theory of a pyramid, or hierarchy, of the arts, which placed comedy at the apex. "Hegel wrote that comedy is higher, greater, than tragedy because it destroys art altogether . . . ," they explained. "You can't build anything on comedy because everything crumbles beneath you." In their own works, they continued, "We can feel how everything is continually being destroyed—every exhibit is another destruction."

In addition to mounting their seven shows at Ronald Feldman Fine Arts Inc. (the most recent of which ran from January 7 through February 11, 1984), Komar and Melamid took part in "The Monumental Show" in Brooklyn in 1981, where their life-size portrait of Hitler was slashed by an onlooker "tired of irony," and they have lectured, performed, and exhibited at museums and colleges across the United States. Their works are included in the collections of the Museum of Modern Art, the Metropolitan Museum of Art, and the Guggenheim Museum in New York City; the Israel Museum in Jerusalem; and the Australian National Gallery in Canberra. In 1982 they received a $25,000 grant from the National Endowment for the Arts, the first Russian artists to be so honored.

Vitaly Komar lives in New York City, the only place, he says, "where you can be a professional foreigner, because everyone here is so used to hearing English spoken badly that they understand." Aleksandr Melamid, a slight man who has dark, curly hair, lives in a Russian émigré community in Jersey City, New Jersey with his wife and their two children. The two artists share a "small, seedy studio," as Grace Glueck described it in the New York Times (January 29, 1984), on East 33rd Street in New York City. Komar, who is heavy-set with a round face, long black hair, a mustache, and goatee, is divorced from his Russian wife but is inseparable in his work from his partner. They talk over all their projects and make sketches before setting down to work. They start out with two paintings, and as they get bored they switch from one to the other. Discussing their unique partnership with Grace Glueck in the latter article, Komar admitted that it is not always smooth sailing: "Sometimes our relationship reminds me of old couples. We argue about something, and we say that's the end, no more collaboration. Then the next day we're back together again."

References: Artforum 16:38+ Ja '78, 20:58+ Ap '82 por; N Y Times II p25+ Ja 29 '84 por; N Y Times Mag p33+ My 8 '77 pors; Newsweek 87:89 F 16 '76 por; World Artists 1950–80 (1984)

Koppel, Ted

(kop´əl)

Feb. 8, 1940– Broadcast journalist. Address: b. c/o ABC News, 1717 De Sales Ave., N.W., Washington, D.C. 20036

"Fame is only an offshoot of what I've always really wanted: to be one of the best," Ted Koppel has said. Now regarded as probably the most outstanding of the serious-minded interviewers on commercial American television, Koppel honed his craft in twenty years of broadcast journalism, during which time he has dedicated himself to ministering to the public's right to know. His career as foreign and diplomatic correspondent for ABC News, which brought him four Overseas Press Club awards from his colleagues, peaked in 1980 with the launching of his much-praised live interview program, *ABC News Nightline*. With *Nightline*, Koppel has acquired a loyal audience who appreciate the plainspeaking, articulateness, and topical urgency of his interviews with celebrity guests.

The phenomenal success of *ABC News Nightline*, the first regular extension of network news time since NBC and CBS expanded their evening updates from fifteen to thirty minutes in 1963, has astonished media experts. The gamble that ABC producers took in showcasing a late-night, in-depth news forum five times a week has paid off by creating an audience of some seven

million viewers that "nobody knew was there," as Judith Adler Hennessee pointed out in her profile of Koppel for *Esquire* (January 1984). With its state-of-the-art satellite technology and with what its former executive producer, William Lord, has called "an embarrassingly generous budget," *Nightline* is a paramount instance of "'pure television,'" according to *Newsweek* (February 16,

1981): "global in perspective, intimate in presentation, and always rivetingly spontaneous." Backed by his energetic, dedicated staff, Ted Koppel orchestrates a show that represents a coup for ABC News and serves as a model of quality journalism on a commercial television network.

Edward James Koppel was born on February 8, 1940 in Lancashire, England, the only child of well-to-do parents who had fled Nazi Germany in 1938, shortly after the father served a prison term there for the crime of being Jewish. A rubber-tire industrialist, Koppel's father had been officially invited to open a factory in Lancashire, but instead he was interned for a year at an enemy-alien prison camp on the Isle of Man. Ted Koppel has recalled his mother as "very artistic, a piano player and beautiful singer" who found those first years in England "extraordinarily difficult." As a boy Koppel attended boarding school in Great Britain, where he added a proficiency in French to his bilingual fluency in English and German. When he was thirteen, the Koppels immigrated again, this time to the United States, partly to offer their son richer career opportunities. They settled in New York City, where Ted Koppel attended the McBurney School, a private prep school. Although he told an interviewer for People (January 3, 1983) that he was a procrastinator as a child, exasperating his "parents and teachers . . . by the fact that [he] would wait until the last minute," he completed the four-year curriculum of high school in three years.

According to Bob Reiss, who interviewed him for the Washington Post Magazine (September 6, 1983), even as a boy Koppel had his sights on a journalistic career, and Edward R. Murrow, the legendary radio broadcaster whose reports from London during the Blitz set new standards for hard-hitting, factual reportage, was his childhood hero. Koppel took his B.A. degree in speech at Syracuse University (where the campus radio station provided his first live broadcasting experience) and then transferred to Stanford University in California, where he obtained his master's degree in journalism in 1962. Upon flunking the Associated Press broadcasters' test, he taught English at the McBurney School for a short while and then landed a job as a "glorified copy boy," as he put it, for the New York City radio station WMCA. In 1963, the year in which he became a United States citizen, he joined the staff of WABC radio, also in New York.

His hardworking professionalism soon received such recognition at WABC that Ted Koppel started doing general assignment news commentaries, becoming, as he told William Henry 3d of the New York Daily News (November 11, 1980), the "youngest network correspondent ever." Known as "sidebars," his brief analyses formed part of the radio program Flare Reports. A major break, in terms of exposure and a chance to demonstrate his unflappable, concise style, came when he was in Washington, D.C. just after the assassination of President John F. Kennedy. He was scheduled to do a short report when the newly installed President Lyndon B. Johnson drove by, but the motorcade was delayed and Koppel instead had to ad-lib for one-and-a-half hours. In 1964 he reported on the first of many presidential nominating conventions he would cover, and he became the anchorman for a nightly ABC Radio newscast in New York City the following year. During the same period Ted Koppel covered the burgeoning civil rights movement as a correspondent in Selma, Alabama and helped to compile The Wit and Wisdom of Adlai Stevenson, which was published in 1965.

Impressed by Koppel's talent for clarifying issues, ABC News officials transferred him to Vietnam in 1967, and it was there that he made the changeover from radio to television journalism. For about a year he reported from the network's Saigon Bureau, bringing to that beat along with his other qualifications a working knowledge of the Vietnamese language. He was next promoted to the post of Miami bureau chief, where his duties included reporting on Richard M. Nixon's 1968 presidential campaign and coverage of political developments in Latin America. Returning to the Far East as Hong Kong bureau chief starting in January 1969, Koppel traveled throughout the entire Pacific region, from Vietnam to Australia, for a year and a half. His work there won him his first Overseas Press Club award for best television commentary on foreign news, in 1971.

His promotion to the position of ABC News' chief diplomatic correspondent in July 1971 signaled Ted Koppel's ascension as a major national network correspondent. Using Washington, D.C. as his home base and the Department of State as his main beat, Koppel continued his global travels while covering diplomatic affairs. He accompanied President Richard Nixon on his historic visit to the People's Republic of China in 1972 and returned there for a two-month stay the following year. One result of his fact-gathering tours was the 1973 documentary program "The People of People's China," for which he served as co-correspondent. In 1975 he returned to China with President Gerald R. Ford. When the shuttle diplomacy of Secretary of State Henry A. Kissinger took Koppel some quarter-million miles around the world during the mid-1970s, the two men developed a close and lasting rapport, although Koppel declined an offer to become Kissinger's State Department spokesman. One of the byproducts of that association was "Kissinger: Action Biography," a special documentary that was telecast over ABC-TV in June 1974 with Koppel as producer and correspondent. He also acted as correspondent for some segments of the monthly ABC News Close-Up, the network's critically praised, award-winning journalistic series that began in 1973. As if all those assignments were not enough, in July 1975 Koppel accepted the post of anchorman for the evening ABC Saturday Night News, while still serving as head diplomatic correspondent.

When his wife, the former Grace Anne Dorney, enrolled as a law student at Georgetown University in the fall of 1976, Ted Koppel took a year's leave of absence from his State Department post, with the blessing of ABC News president William Sheehan. During that time he served as a daily commentator from his home in the Washington area and flew to New York City once a week to continue his Saturday news anchorman duties. With Marvin Kalb, the CBS newsman, Koppel spent some of his year's leave in writing the thriller *In the National Interest* (Simon & Schuster, 1977), the story of an American secretary of state whose discovery of an explosive political secret during Mideast negotiations is known only to a star television reporter. The book became a minor best-seller, with mixed reviews that acknowledged its "possible popular appeal" and "clean . . . brisk" writing, but Koppel told Judith Adler Hennessee during the *Esquire* interview that, in his present view, " . . . it ended up being terrible."

Although during the 1970s Ted Koppel was cementing his reputation as a journalist whose grasp of the issues went beyond mere familiarity to dependable authority, the image of his employer, ABC News, enjoyed far less prestige than the news divisions of the other two national networks. As Barbara Matusow has reviewed ABC's credibility problems in her incisive study *The Evening Stars; The Making of the Network News Anchor* (1983), in the late 1960s and early 1970s ABC was something of an orphan in the communications industry. Its operating budget was only a fraction of those at NBC and CBS, and a reputation for spotty coverage of fast-breaking news stories yielded it only a low 15 percent of the television-viewing audience. Describing an unfortunate syndrome that helped to perpetuate the network's difficulties at that time, ABC correspondent Sam Donaldson told Miss Matusow: "People [involved in news events] realized there was no point in staying around because they would never get on the air with their information, so they went home." Soon after Harry Reasoner, the highly respected newscaster, bade farewell to CBS in late 1970 to anchor the *ABC Evening News*, the situation improved. ABC's share of the viewing audience rose to 22 percent, and advertising revenues for news programs increased fivefold.

Nevertheless, in the mid-1970s reliable, first-rate reportage from ABC News was still, in Barbara Matusow's term, a "precarious" undertaking. In May 1977 network moguls moved to overhaul the lackluster division by decreeing a 25 percent across-the-board budget increase and by recruiting ABC Sports head Roone Arledge as the new president of ABC News. Celebrated in the television industry for his high-tech innovations in live sports programming and for masterminding in-depth sports features of high quality, Arledge had secured for ABC the lion's share of the sports-oriented public, but since he could lay no claim to any exposure as a news producer, many ABC news staffers looked askance at what they feared would be his glitzy handling of their division, already laboring under its frivolous image. Making rapid personnel changes in the news departments, Arledge some months after his accession fired the ex-

ecutive producer of the *Saturday Night News* while Ted Koppel, its anchorman, was on a Bermuda vacation, unaware of the decision. Angered because "the executive producer is the key person in the broadcast" and because he sensed the new president's intention to ease him out of the program as well, Koppel tendered his resignation from ABC News. But Arledge refused it, and slowly the working relationship between the two men improved, along with the visibility of ABC's news coverage under Roone Arledge. Although Koppel told Barbara Matusow that ABC News "was already a first-class operation in the early seventies," he now credits Arledge with overcoming old perceptions of the network and giving it a first-class reputation.

Edged out of the anchor spot, Ted Koppel continued as State Department correspondent when his sabbatical year ended. His star again ascended in April 1979, when he acted as lead reporter for an eleven-segment series, "Second to None?", which examined the strategic nuclear balance. Koppel researched the story himself and presented it, as he told an interviewer for the *Christian Science Monitor* (April 13, 1979), to convey "complex material to an audience that hasn't paid much attention in the past but must in the future . . . *if* there is to be a future." Shown over a two-and-a-half week period as part of the network's eleven o'clock broadcast, *World News Tonight*, the series might not, Koppel admitted, help the ratings, but he hoped the review of military preparedness would "help a larger segment of the American public understand the SALT [II] debates." His work was rewarded with an Alfred I. duPont–Columbia University Award in broadcast journalism.

On November 4, 1979 a militant cadre of Iranian students, acting in the spirit of their new revolutionary leader, the Ayatollah Ruholla Khomeini, besieged the United States embassy in Teheran and took fifty-two diplomatic staff members as hostages. The hostage crisis gripped the American consciousness, and fear for the diplomats' lives and concern about global repercussions ran high. As it happened, among all the major networks—whose reporters the Iranian government had expelled that summer—only ABC managed to land a lesser-known London correspondent in Teheran on the day of the seizure. Taking advantage of its early monopoly on news of the immediate situation, on November 8 ABC News premiered its "temporarily permanent" series *The Iran Crisis: America Held Hostage*, annexing it to *World News Tonight* in the eleven-thirty evening slot that Roone Arledge already had under option for program development.

Frank Reynolds, the eleven o'clock anchorman, gave each night's update, as prepared by Ted Koppel at the State Department, Sam Donaldson, and their producers, with reports ranging from factual bulletins to in-depth discussions of the Mideast's diplomatic scene and the Islamic revolution. When, later that month, Reynolds took a night off, Koppel filled the anchor spot, and he became an increasingly familiar figure as the hostage impasse dragged on and Reynolds took other news assignments. Counting on success, in late March 1980, with no end in sight to their "temporary" coverage, ABC producers transformed the series into *ABC News Nightline*, regularly slotted for a twenty-minute segment four nights a week and with its format broadened to treat other issues. When Dan Rather and Roger Mudd, among other early candidates for the long-term anchorman post, turned out to be unavailable, Ted Koppel was given the nod. Roone Arledge has explained: "We discovered Ted had this wonderful ability to keep the conversation going in a way that everyone could follow."

Favorably compared to public television's *MacNeil-Lehrer Report*, the quintessential "thinking-man's" news series, *Nightline* carries the advantage of a vast high-finance news organization. Ted Koppel and the production staff brainstorm each night's program that same morning, using long-distance conference calls to explore possible issues and approaches. About ten feature stories may be in the works at any one time, but *Nightline*'s flexible planning allows for virtually last-minute scheduling to focus on late-breaking stories. With ABC News' expanded team of correspondents and with its access to global satellite transmission, interviewees from anywhere in the world may be called upon to comment. The length of the program, which has been officially one-half hour since January 1981, may also be adapted to the issue: on the night of the November 1980 elections, for example, network producers allotted *Nightline* almost two hours of airtime, so that Ted Koppel could lead a variety of candidates and commentators on a broad review of the voting. Special editions are sometimes scheduled, such as a recreation of D-Day events on the fortieth anniversary of that Allied force invasion.

Thoroughly briefed for the show, Ted Koppel prefers to prepare no questions before the actual interview begins. Koppel enjoys the unpredictability and spontaneity of the live interviews—and thinks that his audience does also—but nevertheless believes that he exercises an editorial control in that setting that is unavailable in taped discussions. His deft style of inquiry, learned in the diplomatic arena—where, he says, the manipulation of language by the powerful is a high art—cuts through bombast without browbeating. Although his private views are said to lean to the conservative—for example, he calls himself a "pragmatist" in the area of foreign policy, the necessities of which he sees as "basically, amoral"—he takes care not to impose a blanket interpretation on any topic. Koppel believes that he commands audience respect precisely because of his professional neutrality: "If viewers come to the conclusion that I'm pronuke or anti-Reagan and I am using the program as a soapbox, I'm lost," he told one interviewer.

ABC News Nightline often begins with a short filmed correspondent report providing an overview of that night's topic. The range of stories is as broad as Koppel's own spectrum of interest: domestic issues such as urban homelessness, stock market fluctuations, the Ku Klux Klan, or the judicial system, and international questions involving political defectors to the United States, ecological destruction, Central America, or the arms race. Both the famous and the unknown may appear to present their sides in matters of controversy. Koppel has sparred with the likes of the Reverend Jerry Falwell, Sugar Ray Leonard, President Marcos of the Philippines, Yassir Arafat of the Palestine Liberation Organization, and Mikhail Baryshnikov, to name a few of his guests on the show. That catholic embrace of issues and celebrities is dictated less by headlines than by his own inquisitiveness and his creative production ideas. "And I do these shows to educate me as much as anyone else," he told William Henry 3d. "Our standard is if it interests those of us who produce the show, then it will interest [others]."

Koppel insists upon a non-condescending but informative tone for the program, thereby winning viewers from all walks of life. Reflecting his roots, he favors foreign policy stories, and has wanted to cover human rights violations regularly, but he says that an unrelentingly bleak presentation would lead viewers to turn the dial and sponsors to jettison their advertising. He balances news values with business values: "The networks have a right to know their product is salable. We have to be responsive to what causes people to watch." Since spring 1981 *Nightline* has been broadcast five nights a week.

While continuing to discharge his *Nightline* responsibilities, Ted Koppel also takes on assignments in election coverage. He coanchored Ronald Reagan's inauguration in 1981 and joined the president on his trip to China in 1984, has hosted special programs on urgent political issues, and in January 1984 presided with Phil Donahue over a televised forum of debate among the eight Democratic presidential aspirants. As a regular moderator for ABC News' six yearly telecasts of *Viewpoint*, a forum for analysis of television news, he was called upon to take charge of a special edition of that program that was televised live after the network's 1983 premiere of *The Day After*, a made-for-TV movie about the aftermath of nuclear war in a midwestern city. That week he also presided over the four segments of "The Crisis Game," a simulation of National Security Council planning during a superpower confrontation.

In a high-rolling industry where, Koppel says, the guarantee of clout in decision-making circles depends on "how you are perceived to be perceived by the powers that be," Ted Koppel's salary is reported to be considerably over $500,000 a year. "I think the salaries are outrageous. . . . I feel very guilty about having so much when there are so many people who have so little," he told Tom Shales of the *Washington Post* (January 8, 1981). But he accepts that remuneration in order to retain his negotiable influence. As he remarked to Shales, "I do have a great interest in exercising power—I hope for the good."

When Frank Reynolds died in July 1983, Roone Arledge approached Koppel about taking over as *ABC Evening News* anchorman, but Koppel declined, explaining that, compared to the gratification of making *Nightline* his own show with his own imprint, early evening newscasts, where the anchorman usually reads a staff-prepared script, "seem terribly boring." A ten-month experiment in expanding *Nightline*'s half-hour length to an hour was ended in early 1984, partly because the longer version seemed to lack sharp focus, and with renewed affiliate-station interest Koppel's late-night future looks bright.

Ted Koppel is a short man with thick reddish hair and broad facial features. His sober professional air belies the humor for which he is known among friends, which sometimes leads to impersonations of William F. Buckley Jr., Richard Nixon, Adlai Stevenson, and Cary Grant. In 1963 he married Grace Anne Dorney, whom he met at Stanford University and who, according to Koppel, has been one of the strongest influences in his life. Mrs. Koppel now practises law with a Virginia firm. The couple live in Potomac, Maryland with their four children: Andrea, Deirdre, Andrew, and Tara. Koppel lists his recreations as reading, skiing, running, and playing tennis, and his faults as "a certain pomposity and intellectual arrogance." Among his honors are an Emmy award for his April 1981 *Nightline* analysis of Reagan's election victory and a George Polk Award in 1982 for best television reporting.

References: *Esquire* 101:50+ Ja '84 por; *New York* 17:22+ Ag 13 '84 pors; *NY Times* II p22 D 7 '80 por; *People* 7:83+ Ja 10 '77 pors, 18:84+ Ja 3 '83 pors; *TV Guide* 29:26+ Ap 18 '81 por; *Wash Post Mag* p14+ S 6 '83 por; Matusow, Barbara. *The Evening Stars*; *Who's Who in America*, 1984-85

Laurents, Arthur

(lo'rents)

July 14, 1918– Playwright; screenwriter; director. Address: b. c/o Shirley Bernstein, Paramuse Artists Asssociates, 1414 Ave. of the Americas, New York City, N.Y. 10019

Although he is little known to the general public, Arthur Laurents has been a dominant figure in the theatre for more than thirty years. His accomplishments include the librettos for two of Broadway's musical classics, *West Side Story* and *Gypsy*, the groundbreaking psychological dramas *Home of the Brave* and *A Clearing in the Woods*, the screenplays for such popular films as *The Way We Were* and *The Turning Point*, and the direction of the acclaimed Broadway productions *I Can Get It For You Wholesale*, *Gypsy*, and, most recently, *La Cage Aux Folles*. Laurents is considered to be one of the few American masters of high comedy and of writing for the musical stage, yet he thinks of himself primarily as a "social playwright." A deep interest in what he has called the "fundamentals of human behavior" and in the individual's struggle against hypocrisy and conformity are among the recurring themes of his work.

Arthur Laurents was born in Brooklyn, New York on July 14, 1918, the son of Irving Laurents, a lawyer, and Ada (Robbins) Laurents, a teacher. Reared in the Flatbush section of Brooklyn, he got his first taste of the theatre at summer camp, where he was picked for a part in the play *The Crow's Nest* because, as he told Leslie Bennetts in an interview for the *New York Times* (August 21, 1983), he was "agile enough to climb up the mast of a ship and bright enough to remember some lines." The experience left him "wildly stagestruck," to use his words, and he became an avid theatregoer, regularly attending the performances of a neighborhood stock company and occasionally venturing into Manhattan to see the latest Broadway productions. It was "the moment of the curtain going up" that enchanted him, Laurents explained to Leslie Bennetts. "You never knew what you were going to see. . . . Theatre is a fantasy, and you can make it all come true."

Following his graduation from Erasmus Hall High School, Laurents continued his education at Cornell University in Ithaca, New York, where he majored in English. After receiving his B.A. degree in 1937, he performed for a time in a satirical nightclub revue that he had put together with several friends, then devoted himself to writing radio plays, including episodes of the popular series *Hollywood Playhouse*, *Dr. Christian*, and *The Thin Man*. When the United States entered World War II in 1941, he immediately enlisted in the United States Army. Initially assigned to a paratroop unit at Fort Benning, Georgia, he eventually ended up working on military training films. He also wrote the scripts for the radio programs *The Man Behind the Gun*, *Army Service Forces Present*, and *Assignment Home*. Developed to educate the public about the problems of returning servicemen, *Assignment Home* won a Variety Radio Award as "one of the outstanding shows" of 1945. One of Laurents' scripts for the series—"The Face," about a maimed veteran's rehabilitation—was selected for inclusion in the volume *The Best One-Act Plays of 1945-46*.

In the course of his research for *Assignment Home*, Laurents visited veterans hospitals and talked with a number of soldiers whose physical disabilities had been triggered by a psychic trauma. Drawing on those interviews, he began working on a psychological drama about a battle-scarred ex-soldier. In *Home of the Brave*, an Army psychiatrist discovers the cause of a young Jewish veteran's amnesia and partial paralysis to be subconscious guilt over the death of his buddy, whom he had suspected of anti-Semitism. The play, which opened to mixed reviews at the Belasco Theatre on Broadway in December 1945, closed after only sixty-nine performances, but it was belatedly recognized by the majority of New York critics as a bold and important contribution to the postwar American theatre. The play won for Laurents a grant from the American Academy of Arts and Letters and a share in the annual Sidney Howard Memorial Award for new playwriting talent. A film version of *Home of the Brave*, rewritten by Carl Foreman as a story of racial rather than religious prejudice, was released by United Artists in 1949.

After his next dramatic effort, *Heartsong*, failed to win over either critics or audiences during its pre-Broadway trial in 1947, Laurents reluctantly left New York for Hollywood, where he hoped to find the high-paying screenwriting job that would "pay off debts," as he told Glenn Loney in an interview for *After Dark* (November 1973). In short order he turned out the screenplay for Alfred Hitchcock's technically innovative chiller *Rope* (Warner Brothers, 1948), which he adapted from Patrick Hamilton's melodrama *Rope's End*; the final version of the script for *The Snake Pit* (Twentieth Century-Fox, 1948), Anatole Litvak's shockingly realistic film about life in a state mental hospital; the scenario for *Caught* (MGM, 1949), a contrived tearjerker directed by Max Ophuls; and, with Philip Yordan, the film adaptation of Yordan's Broadway hit *Anna Lucasta* (Columbia, 1949).

Laurents returned to Broadway in February 1950 with *The Bird Cage*, a melodrama detailing the backstage troubles of a ruthless and tyrannical cabaret owner. Despite the efforts of an able cast,

headed by Melvyn Douglas and Maureen Stapleton, and a top-flight director, Harold Clurman, the play disappointed critics, who had expected more from the author of *Home of the Brave*. The *New York Times*'s Brooks Atkinson spoke for most of his colleagues when he dismissed *The Bird Cage* as "pretty hackneyed stuff." Hobbled by the largely unfavorable critical response, the play survived for just three weeks.

The playwright fared better with *The Time of the Cuckoo*, a rueful comedy about a lonely and guileless American spinster, brilliantly played by Shirley Booth, who finds romance with a married Italian shopkeeper during a summer holiday in Venice. Writing in what Brooks Atkinson described as the "leisurely, fluid style" of "a mature artist," Laurents enriched his rather shopworn tale with witty dialogue and unusually well-rounded characterizations. Arthur Laurents "has one most fundamental gift of a writer: he is interested in people . . . ," Atkinson observed in his thoughtful analysis of the play for the *New York Times* (November 2, 1952). "In view of the effortlessness of his style, the amount of insight he conveys is remarkable. Every character is a full-length portrait. . . . By never sacrificing human truths for showmanship Mr. Laurents has written a literate, unpretentious modern play that is alive in every detail." One of the unquestioned hits of the 1952-53 Broadway season, *The Time of the Cuckoo* was the basis for the motion picture *Summertime* (United Artists, 1955), starring Katharine Hepburn, and for the moderately successful 1965 musical comedy *Do I Hear A Waltz?* with music and lyrics by, respectively, Richard Rodgers and Stephen Sondheim.

In the mid-1950s, Laurents divided his time between New York and Hollywood, where he earned a reputation for his skillful adaptations of plays and novels. His screen credits for those years include *Bonjour Tristesse* (Columbia, 1958), Otto Preminger's film version of Françoise Sagan's bestseller about a self-centered teen-age girl who tries to prevent her widowed father's remarriage, and the romantic melodrama *Anastasia*, in which an exiled White Russian general persuades an amnesia victim that she is the only surviving child of the last czar and, as such, the sole heir to the Romanov fortune. When *Anastasia*, directed by Anatole Litvak and starring Ingrid Bergman, was released by Twentieth Century-Fox in 1956, Bosley Crowther, writing in the *New York Times* (December 14, 1956), commended Laurents for adding "strong scenes" that Marcelle Maurette's play "barely suggested" and for expanding "the conflicts within the heroine." Miss Bergman's interpretation of the character won her an Academy Award.

Meanwhile, back on Broadway, Laurents offered the offbeat drama *A Clearing in the Woods*. The psychological fantasy, which opened at the Belasco Theatre on January 10, 1957, starred Kim Stanley as a neurotic woman who confronts her past selves (played by three different actresses) at her old home in a forest glade. Critics generally found the play to be ambitious and original, but also "pretentious," "labored," and "curiously unstimulating." Closed after a run of only three-and-a-half weeks, *A Clearing in the Woods* was revived to critical acclaim in 1961 as a presentation of *The Play of the Week*, the televised dramatic anthology series.

In the mid-1950s Laurents began working on a contemporary musical version of *Romeo and Juliet*, with the feuds of rival New York City street gangs replacing the conflict between the Capulets and the Montagues. The concept originated with choreographer Jerome Robbins, who first suggested it to Laurents and Leonard Bernstein, the composer, in 1949. The trio eventually brought in Stephen Sondheim to write the lyrics. When *West Side Story* finally opened at the Winter Garden on September 26, 1957, its raw vitality electrified audiences. While Bernstein's score and Robbins' high-voltage choreography and innovative staging were given much of the credit for this smash hit, Laurents' "lean and wiry" book, to quote the *New York Daily Mirror*'s Robert Coleman, also came in for its share of the praise. For example, John McClain, in his opening night review for the *New York Journal American*, complimented Laurents for having "captured the talk of the juveniles, or a reasonable facsimile, and woven it into a magic fabric." The *New York Times*'s Brooks Atkinson went even further, calling the playwright's contribution "the essential one."

After a triumphant Broadway run of about two years, *West Side Story* was made into a hit film that garnered eleven 1961 Academy Awards, including best picture, and it has been resurrected on the New York stage several times. While viewing the most recent Broadway revival, at the Minskoff Theatre in 1980, critics were struck by the fact that Laurents' book seemed to have aged while the music and the dances were as fresh and vital as ever. Among other things, the reviewers felt that the book was dated by its "preachy liberal pieties," its unrealistic dialogue, which, to Walter Kerr's mind, was "never as authentic as the switchblades that come whipping out of dirty pockets," and the "arbitrariness of its plotting"—a fault that Brendan Gill blamed not on Laurents but on Shakespeare.

Assured further Broadway assignments by the spectacular success of *West Side Story*, Laurents went on to collaborate with Stephen Sondheim and Jule Styne on *Gypsy*, a musical based on the memoirs of the stripper Gypsy Rose Lee. The play, which focused on Gypsy's ambitious, larger-than-life stage mother, portrayed by Ethel Merman, opened in May 1959 to a critical fanfare. With few exceptions, New York critics lined up behind Kenneth Tynan, who, in his review for the *New Yorker* (May 30, 1959), hailed Laurents' libretto as "an exemplary mixture of gaiety, warmth, and critical intelligence." Like *West Side Story*, *Gypsy* achieved a two-year Broadway run, spawned a successful motion picture, and became one of the most frequently staged musicals on the strawhat circuit. In 1973 Laurents himself directed a somewhat altered version of the show, with Angela Lansbury in the role of Mama Rose, at the Piccadilly Theatre in London. Following its sold-out British stand, the production toured Canada and the United States before settling in at the Winter Garden, where it was welcomed by Martin Gottfried of the *New York Post* (September 24, 1974) as "one of the landmarks in the American musical's growth to maturity." The revival of *Gypsy* earned Laurents a Tony nomination and a Drama Desk Award for best direction of a musical.

Laurents' first experience as a director had come in 1960, when the Theatre Guild mounted his play *Invitation to a March* at the Music Box Theatre on Broadway. Described by Laurents as a "high comedy" about conventionality versus nonconformity, the play boasted a first-rate cast, including Celeste Holm, Jane Fonda, and Eileen Heckart, and a crisp, literate script with "close-Shavian"—to use Walter Kerr's term—repartee. But despite those advantages, *Invitation to a March* failed to attract a wide audience, possibly because, as Frank Aston observed in the *New York World-Telegram and Sun* (October 31, 1960), it was "more cerebration than dramatics."

In 1962, at the invitation of David Merrick, the producer, Laurents tackled the direction of the musical comedy version of Jerome Weidman's *I Can Get It For You Wholesale*, about the trials and tribulations of the garment trade in New York City. For many critics, the most entertaining things about the production were the well-staged comic contrast between the frantic, behind-the-scenes activity in the models' changing rooms and the composure of the fashion show and Barbra Streisand, making her Broadway debut as the unnoticed and overworked secretary, Miss Marmelstein. Two years later, Laurents did double duty as the librettist and director of *Anyone Can Whistle*, a wholly original musical, with music and lyrics by Stephen Sondheim, describing the efforts of a small-town mayor to create a tourist industry around the alleged curative powers of a local "miracle" rock. Years later, in an interview for the *New York Daily News* (February 15, 1980), Laurents admitted that the show was "kind of mad." "The musical techniques were a bit of everything," he explained. "We used forms that had been done in musical comedy, cabaret, operetta." When *Anyone Can Whistle* opened in April 1964, it drew a few appreciative notices as "the first avant-garde Broadway musical comedy," to quote John Chapman, but it lasted for only nine performances.

In his second original musical libretto, for *Hallelujah, Baby!* Laurents traced the progress of a young black couple, played by Leslie Uggams and Robert Hooks, through the shifting social practices and attitudes of twentieth-century America. Directed by Burt Shevelove, with music by Jule Styne and lyrics by Betty Comden and Adolph Green, the show opened at the Martin Beck Theatre in April 1967 to generally lackluster reviews, but it nonetheless picked up four Tony Awards, including one for Laurents as the author of the best musical of the year, and enjoyed a respectable nine-month run.

Returning to a favorite theme—hypocrisy in modern society—Laurents, in his high comedy *The Enclave,* focused on a close-knit group of well-to-do, liberal friends whose plans to create an island of security in a block of renovated townhouses are shattered when the only bachelor of their number announces that his young male lover will be sharing his home. "In this case," Laurents told Glenn Loney in the *After Dark* interview, "homosexuality is a metaphor for all the things we claim to accept in society but don't really want to look at. In friendships particularly, where we pretend we love our friends for what they are but it's really for what we want them to be for us." Following its world premiere at the Washington (D.C.) Theater Club in February 1973, *The Enclave* moved to an Off-Broadway playhouse in New York City. Edith Oliver, who commented on the production for the *New Yorker* (December 3, 1973), found little to admire in the "stagy" script but she appreciated Laurents' "ingenious and original" direction and the ensemble work of his actors. In the mid-1970s, Laurents achieved his greatest commercial success to that date with the release of two motion pictures—*The Way We Were* (Columbia, 1973) and *The Turning Point* (Twentieth Century-Fox, 1977)—for which he had written the original screenplays. Although flawed by what some critics considered to be its shallow treatment of the Hollywood witch hunt of the 1950s, *The Way We Were,* which paired Barbra Streisand as a leftwing Jewish intellectual and Robert Redford as an ambitious WASP novelist, was entertaining because of the sexual chemistry between its costars. *The Turning Point,* too, was notable for the performances of its costars, Anne Bancroft and Shirley MacLaine. Written at the suggestion of Nora Kaye, a former principal dancer with the American Ballet Theatre, and directed by Miss Kaye's husband, Herbert Ross, *The Turning Point* depicted the effects of choice and change on the lives of two middle-aged women—one a fading prima ballerina agonizing over her approaching retirement, the other a former dancer who had given up a promising career to raise a family. Widely hailed for the powerful performances of its two stars, the film also won acclaim for Laurents' "literate, mature, and compelling" script, to quote the trade paper *Variety.* For his efforts, Laurents earned the Writer's Guild Award for best drama written for the screen and an Academy Award nomination—one of the eleven accorded the motion picture—for best screenplay of the year.

The phenomenal popularity of the two films solidified Laurents' reputation as a writer of uncommonly well-rounded roles for women. "I think men and women have similar fears, doubts, jealousies—all the dark colors," he explained, as quoted in the *New York Daily News* (December 14, 1973), after the release of *The Way We Were,* "but . . . women are more open, and men more covered. It's our culture." He continued his string of strong female characters with *The Madwoman of Central Park West,* a one-woman musical show that he wrote in collaboration with Phyllis Newman. Built around the character of a woman trying to resume her career after marriage, the 1979 show, which Laurents also directed, featured original songs by Leonard Bernstein, Stephen Sondheim, Jule Styne, and Betty Comden and Adolph Green.

Laurents' most recent theatrical venture was the staging of *La Cage Aux Folles,* the lavish Broadway musical version of the long-running French farce about a pair of aging homosexuals who are the owners and transvestite stars of a bawdy night club in St. Tropez. Having signed on because he was eager to work with playwright Harvey Fierstein, who supplied the libretto, and Jerry Herman, who composed the score, Laurents, as director, took pleasure in devising theatrical "tricks," as he described them to Leslie Bennetts, to heighten the impact of the story, as well as in assuring that "people and emotions"—which he felt had "been missing from musical theater, badly" in recent years—remained at the heart of the play. An immediate box-office hit, *La Cage Aux Folles* won six Tony Awards, including best musical of 1983.

Short and lithe, Arthur Laurents has been described as "a smallish, compact man who [looks] like a cross between a Roman senator and a gym instructor." Despite the admiration and respect of his colleagues, he is, by his own admission, unusually self-critical. "I never thought I was good enough, by my own standards, and I still don't," he told Leslie Bennetts. "My goal has never changed. I want to write or direct something that will make me say, 'Yes, that's really great.' I like a lot of things I have done, but they haven't been good enough for me. So you keep going. . . . I may surprise myself, and finally pull it off!" Laurents, whose recreations include tennis and water and snow skiing, makes his home in Quogue, New York, on the south shore of Long Island.

References: After Dark 6:34+ N '73 por; Guardian p3 D 6 '58; N Y Times II p1 Ag 21 '83; Biographical Encyclopedia and Who's Who of the American Theatre (1966); Contemporary Dramatists (1977); McGraw-Hill Encyclopedia of World Drama (1984); Who's Who in America, 1982–83; Who's Who in the Theatre (1981)

Lawe, John (Edward)

Feb. 26, 1922– Labor union official. Address: b. Transport Workers' Union, 1980 Broadway, New York City, N.Y. 10023

On January 3, 1977 John Lawe took office as president of Local 100, the New York chapter of the Transit Workers of America, which is better known to the public as the TWU. Although Lawe has led the union's contract negotiations only twice, each settlement has turned out to be highly controversial. In 1980 the TWU struck for eleven days before

John Lawe

it finally came to terms with the Metropolitan Transportation Authority (MTA), the administrative arm of New York City's transportation system, and in 1982 the TWU opted for binding arbitration, long anathema to organized labor. Despite public criticism and dissension within the TWU, Lawe has twice been reelected president.

John Edward Lawe was born on February 26, 1922, in Kilass, Ireland and was reared in Strokestown, County Roscommon, Ireland. His father, Luke Lawe, was a cattle farmer, and his mother, Katherine Duffy Lawe, was a housewife. One of ten children, John Lawe spent his formative years on the farm where, he remembers, "we made our butter and killed our own bacon." Lawe graduated from high school in 1936. Four years later he left his family's farm to work in the peat fields, where his natural leadership was recognized by his being made foreman in charge of 100 men digging peat moss for fuel. He remained there for almost a decade before he decided to immigrate to the United States, against the advice of his family. "The Irish have an inbred wanderlust," he once confided to a reporter, adding, "I think I wanted to see the world and develop my potential."

In 1949 Lawe arrived in New York City, where he soon discovered how painful the transition from a small town in rural Ireland to a metropolis could be. Finding work as an elevator operator in the Barbizon-Plaza Hotel, he found himself placed on a grueling split shift. In an interview with the *New York Daily News* (March 16, 1980) Lawe lamented, "They didn't have a union and I was very unhappy." After quitting his job at the Barbizon-Plaza, Lawe became a bus cleaner for the Fifth Avenue Coach Company, a private bus line that featured luxurious double-decker buses.

Lawe's union career began in 1953 when he was made shop steward at the Fifth Avenue Coach Company's 132d Street garage. That year the TWU went out on strike against the private bus lines to attain a forty-hour week for its workers. His wife was pregnant, he was picket captain from midnight to 8 A.M., and he then went to his daily job for $1.00 an hour in the laundry at Columbia Presbyterian Hospital. After a month-long strike, the union won its shortened work week and Lawe was promoted from maintenance worker to bus driver. He also advanced his union standing by becoming Section Chairman in 1954 and chairman of Fifth Avenue's entire division in 1958. His ascension continued after the Fifth Avenue Bus Line was absorbed into a new city bureaucracy called the Manhattan and Bronx Surface Transit Operating Authority (MBS-TOA), the result of a merger of public and private bus lines in Manhattan and the Bronx. In 1964 he became recording secretary for his union local.

One of New York City's more memorable labor rebellions began on January 1, 1966—the day that John V. Lindsay took office as mayor—when the members of Local 100 walked off their jobs. The transit workers, under the leadership of the fiery Michael J. Quill, immobilized the buses and subways for twelve days, ultimately winning wage and benefit increases more than double what the city had offered them when the strike began. Although Quill occupied center stage and was conspicuous on local television, Lawe was deeply involved in union activities during the strike, and his rapid rise following the work stoppage reflected the quality of his leadership. In succession, Lawe advanced to chairman of the MBSTOA bus workers in 1966, vice-president of Local 100 in 1968, and member of the TWU's international executive board in 1969. Lawe began working for the TWU full time in 1971, the year that he successfully negotiated a contract between the MTA and the private bus lines.

After Michael Quill's death, in 1966, Matthew Guinan became head of the TWU, and Lawe developed a close personal relationship with Guinan, who began to groom Lawe to succeed him. When Guinan advanced to the presidency of the international union in 1977, Lawe was elected president of Local 100, with Guinan's full backing.

Lawe took over the TWU during a transitional period in its history, when the Irish Americans who had once dominated the union were being displaced by black and Hispanic workers, who were pressuring the union's hierarchy to obtain wage and benefit packages that would not be eroded by the rampant inflation of the 1970s. For a time, the leadership was successful, but when the TWU contracts came up for negotiations in 1976, Guinan was only able to win a cost of living adjustment, which provides for periodic salary increments as the cost of living rises, for his membership. Two years later, when the transit union squared off for another round of contract talks, Lawe was president of Local 100, while Guinan continued to direct the union's bargaining team. The TWU fared much better than any of the other municipal unions, but its increases were less substantial than they had been in the past.

Running in a field of four candidates in December 1979, Lawe became the first head of Local 100 to win election with a plurality, rather than a majority, of the votes. The divisions in the union became even more evident during the 1980 contract talks, when the TWU demanded a 30 percent wage increment over two years. The new MTA chairman, Richard Ravitch, not only maintained that there was no money available to meet that demand but also insisted on "considerable improvement in productivity and changes in the work rules," as he put it.

By the end of March 1980 negotiations between the union and the MTA had stalled. According to reporter William Serrin of the New York Times (May 7, 1980), Lawe and Ravitch, with the help of a panel of mediators, arranged a scenario to avert a strike. On March 31, only hours before the strike deadline, Ravitch offered the TWU a 6 percent wage increase. As planned, Lawe went back to the union's executive board and proposed a 7 percent salary increment for each year, with a cost of living adjustment for the last six months of the pact, but the executive board shouted Lawe's proposition down, and the scenario projected by Lawe and Ravitch came to nothing.

After the strike deadline had passed, a mediation panel offered a contract proposal that Ravitch and Lawe were willing to accept, calling for eight percent wage increases each year and a cost of living differential as well. The TWU's executive board rejected that proposition, making a strike inevitable. In Lawe's words, as quoted in the New Yorker (May 25, 1980): "Michael J. Quill . . . had a saying that every 10 to 15 years the members get restless and have to have a strike to get the restlessness out of their system."

The strike began on Tuesday, April 1, 1980. Because the first two days of the walkout coincided with the Jewish feast of Passover, the full impact of the transit workers' action was not felt until April 3, when the huge influx of automobiles entering and leaving the city created massive traffic tieups. Nevertheless, the city's ebullient mayor, Edward I. Koch, refused to give in. He cheered on people walking across the Brooklyn Bridge and, in the words of United Federation of Teachers president Albert Shanker, turned the strike into a "moral crusade."

Lawe had other troubles on his hands besides Mayor Koch. The union's rank and file workers, especially the blacks and the Hispanics, were angry that Lawe seemed unconcerned about improving the lot of semi-skilled workers. Arnold Cherry, one of the dissident leaders on Local 100's forty-six-man executive board, was quoted by the New York Times (April 7, 1980) as saying: "Since minorities came on the job, we feel that the system—that's union and management—has been working more against us than for us." That attitude exerted even greater pressure on Lawe to obtain an impressive contract for his members, and he was,

moreover, forced to deal with the issue of "givebacks," or the cancellation of contractual gains won by the TWU in the past. The MTA would not remove those demands from the bargaining table, despite Lawe's assertion that if the "giveback" issues had been resolved, the union might have accepted the 8 percent pay raise proposed by the MTA panel.

As the strike entered its eighth day, Lawe received more bad news. Justice John A. Monteleone fined the TWU and the Amalgamated Transit Union $1 million for violations of New York State's Taylor Law, which prohibits strikes by public employees. In addition, Lawe and six other union officers were each fined $250 for what the judge termed "criminal contempt" of his injunction barring a strike. Monteleone also imposed the Taylor Law penalty of deducting two days of an employee's wage for each day he was out on strike. Nevertheless refusing to order his people back to their jobs, Lawe admitted that the judge's decision might bankrupt the TWU, but he asserted that "Our union was not built on money, but on backbone."

On Friday afternoon April 11, 1980 with the walkout in its eleventh day, Lawe abruptly ended the strike in a most unusual way. An executive board meeting was called to discuss the MTA's most recent salary offer: a 9 percent wage increment in the first year, 8 percent in the second year, in addition to a cost of living adjustment. Despite the fact that there was a tie vote by the union's executive board on the proposed pact, Lawe almost unilaterally called off the strike and submitted the agreement to the 31,000 TWU members for a mail-ballot referendum.

TWU insurgents were outraged by Lawe's action. Calling the agreement a "sellout," Arnold Cherry said that the settlement was "way below what they expected after being off the job for eleven days." Lawe's opponents tried to mount a campaign to defeat the ratification of the contract, citing the "givebacks" as further justification to renegotiate. On May 12, however, the contract was approved by more than a three to one margin. Gratified by the election results, Lawe assured the press that "the so-called dissidents in reality were only a handful of members."

Toward the end of 1981 Lawe was involved in a bitter campaign for reelection as president of Local 100. In addition to charges that he had ignored democratic principles by administering the union in an autocratic manner, he was accused of misappropriating strike benefits estimated at $350,000. Lawe countered by filing a libel suit against one of his opponents, Michael Warren, and against the New York Post, which had supported many of Warren's accusations.

The major issue in the campaign was how members of the union would conduct their bargaining when their contract expired on March 31, 1982. Lawe favored abandoning the union's long-standing policy of "no contract, no work" and expressed a willingness to accept binding arbitration if contract talks stalled. Another presidential hopeful, Arnold Cherry, feared that binding arbitration would result in the loss of benefits that the union had won over the years. The candidates traded charges and countercharges, with Lawe ultimately emerging as the winner by 11,782 votes to 5,439 for Cherry, 3,225 for Warren, and 127 for Edward Kartsen. Lawe interpreted the outcome of the election as a mandate to submit contract disputes to a mediation panel rather than to resort to a strike. Along those lines, Lawe successfully pushed for his union to be placed under the jurisdiction of the Office of Collective Bargaining.

Although the 1982 contract talks did indeed go down to the wire, Lawe submitted the entire pact to arbitration. In early April 1982 the impartial panel awarded members of Local 100 salary increments of 21½ percent over three years. In view of the fact that the cost of living adjustment was locked into the workers' wage structure before the increases were granted, the real gain amounted to nearly 26 percent, a figure that Lawe predicted would not be matched by the other city unions.

Testifying in Washington, D.C. on June 7, 1984 before the investigations and oversight subcommittee of the House Public Works and Transportation Committee, Lawe maintained that he had not been consulted by officials of the New York City Transit Authority about their decision to take a fleet of 851 Grumman "Flxible" buses off the streets. If his advice had been sought, he said, he would have recommended mechanical repairs rather than their removal. He also made clear that he felt that relations between his union and the new management of the Transit Authority had deteriorated.

John Lawe is a man of average height, who weighs about 195 pounds and has brown eyes and an abundance of gray hair. He and his wife, the former Mary Heaney, live in Mount Vernon, a suburb of New York City. They have three children: Deirdre, a nurse in charge of cardiac care at Montefiore Hospital in the Bronx, Patricia, a nuclear technician, and Desmond, who heads an accounting division for Rockefeller Center, Inc. A Roman Catholic, Lawe is deeply committed to the Catholic cause in Northern Ireland. He relaxes by reading, working around the house, and playing what he terms "a lousy game of golf."

References: The Chief Jl '81 por; N Y Daily News Mr 16 '80 por; N Y Times B p8 Mr 20 '80 por, p27 Mr 6 '82 por

---

Lendl, Ivan

(len´ dəl ē vän´)

Mar. 7, 1960- Czech tennis player. Address: b. c/o ProServ, Inc., 888 17th St., N.W., Washington, D.C. 20006; c/o United States Tennis Association, 51 E. 42nd St., New York City, N.Y. 10017

With his stunning, come-from-behind victory over John McEnroe, currently top-ranked internationally, in the final of the 1984 French Open, Ivan Lendl overcame a major hurdle in his bid to become the world's finest tennis player. Twice the winner of the prestigious Volvo Grand Prix Masters tournament and the victor in countless lesser events over the past four years, the moody Czech right-hander had failed in every previous attempt to capture a title in the French, British, American, or Australian national championships—the four tournaments that comprise tennis's "Grand Slam." Despite his having led his country to its only Davis Cup championship, his string of forty-four consecutive victories in match play, and his domination of McEnroe, Lendl was not satisfied until his victory in Paris. "I've won I don't know how many tournaments in my career," he said in an interview in mid-1983, "and I would give them all away for a Wimbledon, French, or United States Open."

An only child, Ivan Lendl was born in Ostrava, an industrial city in northern Czechoslovakia near the Polish border, on March 7, 1960. His father, Jiri Lendl, a lawyer, was once numbered among the top fifteen tennis players in the country; his moth-

er, Olga (Jenistova) Lendlova, who now works as a secretary, was an even more distinguished player, having once been ranked second nationally in women's singles. Olga Lendlova began taking her son along to her daily practice sessions when he was just three years old. By the time he was four, the little boy was hitting balls against a wall with a wooden paddle. Ivan also played basketball and soccer, but most afternoons he headed for the tennis courts and played whoever was there or, if he could not find an opponent, practised against a wall—a recourse he disliked, as he explained to a reporter for *Sports Illustrated* (January 12, 1981), because "I could not beat the wall."

Recognizing their son's aptitude, the Lendls enrolled him at their local sports club, one of some 650 such clubs in Czechoslovakia. His first coach there was Oldrich Lerch, a veteran instructor who taught him to play aggressively, to "jump on the ball," as he put it. Lendl also picked up pointers from playing matches against his parents and, as one of the club's regular ball boys, from observing the techniques and tactics of the more experienced tournament players. When Lendl made his own tournament debut at eight, he was eliminated in straight sets, 6-0, 6-1, in the opening round. Undaunted, he continued to play in tennis meets, and by his early teens was a regular entrant in the nation-wide round of summer tournaments organized by the sports clubs.

Lendl began entering the major international junior tournaments in 1975, when he made it to the quarterfinals of the prestigious Orange Bowl in Florida. The following year, he survived to the final of the singles competition in the Banana Bowl in Santos City, Brazil before falling victim to the up-and-coming John McEnroe. Two years later, Lendl was the world's number-one player on the junior circuit, having won the Orange Bowl championship and the Wimbledon, French, and Italian junior titles. Turning professional in 1979, he played so well during his first twelve months on the men's singles tour that he advanced his Association of Tennis Professionals' computer ranking from seventy-fourth to twentieth. In recognition of his achievements, *Tennis* magazine named him Rookie of the Year.

Of the thirty-five events he entered in 1980, Lendl won seven, including five consecutive Volvo Grand Prix championships in just six weeks. Among his victims were such established professionals as Guillermo Vilas, Eliot Teltscher, and Brian Teacher. But perhaps his most impressive victories were over Björn Borg, then top-ranked in the world, in the finals of the Canadian Open and of the Swiss international indoor tennis tournament. In the latter, Lendl stalled a Borg comeback effort to take the match in five sets, 6-3, 6-2, 5-7, 0-6, 6-4. He closed out the year by leading the Czech Davis Cup squad to its first Davis Cup championship, contributing two singles-match triumphs and, with Tomas Smid, a doubles win to his crew's 4-1 mastery of the Italian team.

Ranked sixth in the world going into 1981, Lendl joined seven other top players in the Volvo Grand Prix Masters round-robin tournament at New York City's Madison Square Garden in January. In the opening round of his Masters debut, Lendl routed veteran Harold Solomon, 6-3, 6-1. His defeat of Guillermo Vilas, 7-5, 6-4, in his second match guaranteed him a berth in the semifinals and rendered the outcome of his third scheduled round-robin match, against Jimmy Connors, meaningful only insofar as it determined the semifinal match-ups. After besting Lendl, 7-6, 6-1, in that third round match, Connors publicly accused the Czech of "tanking," or intentionally losing, in order to gain a more favorable pairing in the semifinals. (Lendl shrugged off the charge at first, but he eventually admitted that he had indeed deliberately dropped the second set.) Lendl disposed of his semifinal opponent, Gene Mayer, rather easily in straight sets, while Connors, in the other semifinal bout, fell to the redoubtable Björn Borg. Although Lendl had upset Borg in their two previous meetings, in the Masters final he, too, crumbled under the Swede's relentless pressure from the backcourt. In a match marked by extended baseline rallies of forty or more shots, Lendl, visibly tiring, double faulted on several crucial points and committed thirty-seven unforced errors on his usually reliable forehand to lose the championship, 6-4, 6-2, 6-2.

Six months later, Lendl had a chance to avenge his Masters defeat when he came up against Borg in the final of the French Open, but Borg, on his way to his sixth French Open singles title, turned back the Czech's challenge, 6-1, 4-6, 6-2, 3-6, 6-1. Wiped out in the first round of Wimbledon play by the unheralded Australian Charlie Fancutt, Lendl took advantage of the free time to prepare for Czechoslovakia's upcoming Davis Cup meet against the United States. He opened the series brilliantly, trouncing John McEnroe in straight sets, but Connors won his first singles match, and the next day the experienced American duo of Bob Lutz and Stan Smith overwhelmed Lendl and his partner, Tomas Smid, in doubles to give the United States a two-to-one lead. McEnroe sealed the victory for the American team by whipping Smid, and Connors, playing for "personal pride," subdued Lendl, 7-5, 6-4. Lendl's next major tournament was the United States Open at the National Tennis Center in the Flushing Meadow section of Queens, New York. Seeded third, he made it as far as the fourth round, where he was stopped by Vitas Gerulaitis. Wisely playing to the Czech's comparatively weak backhand, Gerulaitis forced Lendl out of his best game to eke out a five-set victory, 6-3, 6-4, 3-6, 3-6, 6-4. Recovering quickly, Lendl finished the year in high style, taking the crown in his last six Grand Prix events. Overall, he reached the final in fifteen of the tournaments he entered during 1981 and won nine titles.

Extending his winning ways into the new year, Lendl, who had moved up to second place in the computer rankings, captured the Volvo Grand Prix Masters championship, crushing an unusually erratic John McEnroe in the semifinals, 6-4, 6-2, and outlasting Vitas Gerulaitis in a hotly contested, four-hour five-set final. Riding high on a winning streak of thirty-five consecutive Grand Prix matches, Lendl went on to victories in the WCT Gold Coast Cup Classic in Delray Beach, Florida and the Molson Tennis Challenge in Toronto, Canada, where his final victim was once again John McEnroe. Lendl's string was snapped at forty-four matches by Yannick Noah of France in the final of the Congoleum Classic in La Quinta, California on February 22, 1982, but it remains the second-longest winning streak in the history of open tennis. (Guillermo Vilas racked up fifty victories in a row in 1977.)

In May 1982 Lendl pulled out of a long-scheduled World Team Cup tournament in Germany in order to take part in the more lucrative so-called Tournament of Champions in Forest Hills, New York. His withdrawal from the international competition, in which he was to have played for Czechoslovakia, cost him suspension of his membership in the Association of Tennis Professionals and a reported $10,000 in fines, but he more than recouped that financial loss by taking the Tournament of Champions' $100,000 first prize. On his way to the final, he dropped only nineteen games in five matches, and in the final itself, he routed Eddie Dibbs, 6-1, 6-1, in just forty-nine minutes.

After watching Lendl perform in the Tournament of Champions, the veteran tennis writer Neil Amdur rated him the tour's "most consistent" competitor. "The only players who seem capable of reaching Lendl's level are McEnroe, because of his serve-and-volley style; Guillermo Vilas, because of his superb conditioning and similar baseline style; Jimmy Connors, because of his equally weighty ground strokes; and Yannick Noah, because of his style on faster surfaces," Amdur observed in the New York Times (May 10, 1982). In fact, since the 1981 United States Open, Lendl had lost only three times—once to Noah and twice to Vilas—in ninety-two matches against sixty-four different opponents, but he still lacked the Grand Slam victory deemed necessary for a number-one ranking.

Because the slow clay surface of the Roland Garros Stadium in Paris favors baseliners with strong ground strokes, most tennis experts felt that Lendl, who was seeded second, had a good chance to capture his first Grand Slam title at the 1982 French Open, but he was ousted in the fourth round by the unseeded Swede, Mats Wilander, an equally steady baseliner, 4-6, 7-5, 3-6, 6-4, 6-2. "I just wasn't hitting the ball," Lendl said afterwards, as quoted in the New York Times (May 31, 1982). "My timing was off, especially in my forehand. That's why he was outplaying me from the baseline. I can't do much without my forehand."

Exhausted by his grueling tournament schedule and admittedly disappointed by his defeat in the French Open, Lendl decided to skip Wimbledon and take a few weeks off to rest. Rejoining the tour in August, he was turned back in his bid for a third straight Canadian Open title by a determined Gerulaitis, who recovered after a shaky first set to win the final, 4-6, 6-1, 6-3. Lendl fared better in the ATP championships, a warmup to the United States Open. Relying on his powerful and accurate forehand, he tamed Connors in the semifinal and Steve Denton, one of the fastest-rising young American players, in the final. The United States Open's third seed, behind McEnroe and Connors, Lendl got off to a slow start. He was uncharacteristically erratic in his first-round match against

Ramesh Krishnan, and he barely survived a second-round challenge from Tim Mayotte, who extended the Czech to five sets, but he eventually settled down, routing both Mats Wilander and Kim Warwick in straight sets to win a spot in the semifinals. After prevailing over McEnroe in his semifinal contest, also in straight sets, Lendl came up against his longtime nemesis, Jimmy Connors. By effectively neutralizing Lendl's kicking serve, Connors immediately took control of the match, and before Lendl knew it, he was two sets down. He fought back gamely to retrieve the third set, but he could not sustain the momentum, and Connors went on to win his fourth United States Open title, 6-3, 6-2, 4-6, 6-4. It was the ninth time Connors had defeated Lendl in their ten meetings.

Lendl avenged his humiliation at the hands of Jimmy Connors in the United States Open when he crushed the American, 6-3, 6-1, in the semifinal of the Volvo Grand Prix Masters tournament in January 1983. In the final of that event, in what was one of the best matches of his career to that date, he completely dominated John McEnroe. Playing confidently and cagily, he held serve throughout the match and kept his opponent offbalance with deep and sharply angled shots to take the contest and the title by the impressive score of 6-4, 6-4, 6-2. Despite his heartbreaking losses in the Grand Slam tournaments, 1982—which, in tennis, officially ended with the Masters—was another banner year for Lendl. He had tied a record for total tournament victories with fifteen, and he won $2,028,850 in prize money, exclusive of his reported seven-figure income from exhibition matches and endorsement contracts.

McEnroe got his own back a few weeks later in the final of the United States Pro Indoor Tennis Championship, where he broke Lendl's sixty-six-match indoor winning streak. By attacking Lendl's second serve and repeatedly rushing the net, McEnroe so unsettled the Czech that he blew a 3-1 lead in the crucial second-set tiebreaker. He never regained his self-confidence and fell to McEnroe, 4-6, 7-6, 6-4, 6-3. A badly inflamed tricep muscle kept Lendl off the courts for most of the spring, but by the time Wimbledon rolled around, he was in fighting trim. The grass courts at the All England Lawn Tennis and Croquet Club in Wimbledon are the fastest in the world and, in general, are more congenial to serve-and-volley players than to those who rely on powerful ground strokes, like Lendl. Quickly adjusting to the unfamiliar surface, Lendl made it as far as the semifinals before succumbing to McEnroe, a master of the serve-and-volley technique, in straight sets.

After losing at Wimbledon, Lendl badly wanted a victory in the United States Open. More at home on the rubberized asphalt surface at the National Tennis Center, he sailed through to the semifinals without losing a single set. Of his first five opponents, only Mats Wilander, whom he defeated 6-4, 7-6 in the quarterfinals, was ever really in the match. Lendl's relatively easy three-set semifinal victory over Jimmy Arias set up a rematch of the

1982 Open final against Connors, and once again, the feisty Connors prevailed. Apparently unnerved by Connors' tenacity and by his uncanny ability to adjust his game to the swirling winds and changing court conditions, Lendl hit several returns long, and he seemed to have trouble controlling his flat, booming serve. Only 47 percent of his first serves were good, and he twice double-faulted at set point. After double-faulting when serving for a two-sets-to-one lead, a demoralized Lendl lost ten straight games and the match, 6-3, 6-7, 7-5, 6-0.

Although Lendl had once again failed to capture a single Grand Slam title, he was nonetheless the winner of a 1983 Seagram's Seven Crowns of Sport Award as Men's Tennis Player of the Year, on the strength of his impressive overall record. He had reached the finals in fourteen of the twenty-two tournaments he had entered, and he had won six-ty-eight of eighty-one matches. The Czech was especially effective against the top twenty players, taking twenty-three of twenty-nine matches for a winning percentage of .793—the highest on the circuit.

Throughout the year, Lendl had worked hard at improving his game. With the help of Wojtek Fibak, the Polish pro who acts as his unofficial coach, he learned to topspin his backhand and to give more depth and spin to his second serve. He also perfected his already formidable first serve. Tossing the ball unusually high and slightly to the right, Lendl drills it home at speeds approaching 140 m.p.h. According to the general consensus, Lendl, who strings his composite Adidas racquet at seventy-two pounds of tension, hits the ball harder than anyone on the circuit, and he has been known to hit it directly at an opponent. Lendl has outlined his strategy and technique in a series of instructional columns for the *Washington Post* and in the book *Ivan Lendl's Power Tennis* (Simon & Schuster, 1983), which he wrote in collaboration with Eugene L. Scott.

Troubled by a pulled hamstring, Lendl won only one tournament—the Luxembourg Open—in the first five months of 1984, although he managed to reach the finals in three other Grand Prix events. Back on top of his game by June, he powered his way past the likes of Paul McNamee, Anders Jarryd, Andrés Gómez, and Wilander in the early rounds of the French Open, but his prospects for a title seemed dim, for his opponent in the final was John McEnroe, who had swept their last five battles and was then riding a forty-two-match winning streak. With his scorching first serve and his aggressive serve-and-volley game McEnroe jumped out to an early lead, but when he lost control of his service in the third set, Lendl pounced. Cashing in on the American's mistakes, Lendl used lobs and passing shots to confound McEnroe and, having found his own devastating first serve, took command of the match. His 3-6, 2-6, 6-4, 7-5, 7-5 triumph gave him his first Grand Slam crown and silenced those tennis buffs who had dubbed him "the champion loser," a reference to his defeats in four previous Grand Slam finals. Lendl's jubilation

was perhaps tempered somewhat by his subsequent losses to Jimmy Connors in the Wimbledon semifinals a few weeks later and to John McEnroe in the final of the United States Open in September.

Ivan Lendl's world-class success at a relatively youthful age augurs well for even greater championship play in the years to come. "He's too good a player not to win the major titles," tennis master Arthur Ashe has observed. "By the time he's [Jimmy] Connors' age, I think he will have won quite a few of the big tournaments."

Lean and angular, Ivan Lendl stands six feet two inches tall and weighs 175 pounds. He has a sharp-featured face with prominent cheekbones, deep-set hazel eyes, and brown hair. Because of his no-nonsense attitude and sullen demeanor on the tennis court, Lendl has been labelled "the Tin Man" and "the Grim Reaper" by the press, but according to his friends, he is an engaging and witty man with a mischievous sense of humor. Wary of reporters, he has steadfastly refused to discuss his private life, though he will talk at length about his profession. In addition to his native tongue, he speaks Russian, German, Polish, Slovak, and English.

Between tournaments, Lendl relaxes by golfing, skiing, or playing tennis on roller skates. His preferred sedentary pursuits are going to movies, watching athletic events on television (he enjoys most sports, with the exceptions of boxing and American football), and reading modern history. To keep fit, he runs regularly, and he invariably practises his tennis game daily, even when he is on vacation. Lendl also devotes a considerable amount of his free time to working as a volunteer for the Foundation for Children with Learning Disabilities.

Reportedly uninterested in material possessions, Lendl has invested most of his yearly seven-figure income—less the 20 percent he pays annually to the Czech Tennis Federation—in real estate in the United States, France, and Czechoslovakia. His one indulgence is his collection of expensive cars. As of January 1984, he owned a Porsche, two Volvos, and three Mercedes-Benzes. Lendl owns a house in Greenwich, Connecticut, an apartment in Paris, France, and a condominium in Boca West, Florida, but he considers Ostrava, which he visits several times a year, to be his home and his legal residence. To preserve his nonresident status in the United States, he spends fewer than 163 days a year there.

References: New York 16:42+ Ag 29 '83 pors; N Y Times C p9 Ja 4 '82 por, C p1+ Ag 27 '84 pors; N Y Times Mag p34+ My 16 '82 pors; Newsweek 99:81 F 22 '82 pors; Sport 74:37+ Jl '83 pors; Sports Illus 54:47+ Ja 12 '81 pors; Washington Post C p1+ F 15 '82 por; Who's Who in America, 1984-85

Le Roy Ladurie, Emmanuel (Bernard)

July 19, 1929– French historian. Address: b. c/o Collège de France, 11 place Marcelin-Berthelot, 75231 Paris, France; h. 88 rue d'Alleray, 75015 Paris, France

Since the publication in 1966 of his now classic study of the peasants of Languedoc—*Les Paysans de Languedoc*—Emmanuel Le Roy Ladurie has acquired an enviable reputation not only among his fellow historians but also among a mass audience of lay readers for his ingenious re-creations of medieval society in such best-sellers as *Montaillou; the Promised Land of Error*, first published in France in 1978. Le Roy Ladurie is one of the leading disciples of the *Annales* school of historiography, which draws upon an amazing range of academic disciplines from climatology to literary analysis in an effort to depict the way of life and impact upon history of commoners who lived many centuries ago. Not without some justification, Lawrence Stone, an eminent colleague, has called Le Roy Ladurie "one of the most—if not the most—original, versatile, and imaginative historians in the world."

A native of the predominantly rural area of Normandy in northwestern France, Emmanuel Bernard Le Roy Ladurie was born on July 19, 1929 in the tiny village of Les Moutiers-en-Cinglais, which is located in the Calvados department. The son of Jacques and Léontine (Dauger) Le Roy Ladurie, he was raised in a conservative, strongly religious environment that he has described as having changed very little since before the French Revolution. Le Roy Ladurie's father, a wealthy landowner who has been prominent in public life for many years, served in the Vichy government for a few months during World War II as Minister of Agriculture.

Later he joined the Resistance movement and actively fought against the Germans. Since 1929, when he was first elected mayor of Moutiers-en-Cinglais, Jacques Le Roy Ladurie has held several posts in that town and in Normandy. Emmanuel Le Roy Ladurie has two sisters, Marie, who is an author, and Cécile. His brother, François, was killed in 1950 in an airplane crash.

An introverted child, Le Roy Ladurie quickly developed a taste for reading, which he indulged in his father's large library. By the time he was eight, he had decided to become a naval officer, but he gave up that ambition because of his nearsightedness and thought briefly of joining the priesthood. For several years before the outbreak of World War II, he lived with his grandmother in the departmental capital of Caen, where he attended the Collège Sainte-Marie. After war broke out, he transferred to the Collège Saint-Joseph in Caen, a school run by the Christian Brothers. He recalls being happy there, even though there was no instruction in history.

When he was sixteen, Le Roy Ladurie was sent to the Lycée Henri-IV in Paris to prepare for the Ecole Normale Supérieure. After a year and a half there, he was expelled by the headmaster for a prank. Because no *lycée* in Paris was likely to accept him after his expulsion, he enrolled in the Lycée Lakanal in Sceaux, a suburb of Paris. His interest in the politics of the extreme left had been piqued at the Lycée Lakanal by his fellow students, by such current events as Mao Zedong's victory in China, and by his exposure to Marxism in the history classes of Jean Bruhat. When in September 1949 he entered the Ecole Normale Supérieure where the majority of students were Communists, he immediately joined the French Communist party (PCF), according to Bertrand Poirot-Depech in the *Guardian* (March 28, 1982), "with the same abject devotion which very nearly took him into holy orders."

At the Ecole Normale Supérieure on the rue d'Ulm in Paris, much of Le Roy Ladurie's time was devoted to militant activities on behalf of the PCF, including violently provocative acts against rival Titoist and Trotskyite groups. He was also involved in the Fédération d'Education Nationale, the Union Nationale des Etudiants Français, and other union organizations. After completing his undergraduate degree in 1951, Le Roy Ladurie continued to work for the PCF, devoting himself to such tasks as a statistical analysis of the Paris working class. He also continued his own studies, and after completing a research paper entitled "L'Opinion publique français et la guerre du Tonkin sous Jules Ferry, vers 1880," an analysis of French policy in Indochina, he was awarded the *diplôme des études supérieures*. In 1952 he received France's most prestigious teaching diploma, the *agrégé d'histoire*.

Soon after his appointment as *professeur* at the Lycée Montpellier in 1953, Le Roy Ladurie left that school to fulfill his military obligation. As a result of his two years in the army of occupation in the German Federal Republic, his enthusiasm for

Communism, waning since the death of Joseph Stalin in 1953, diminished further, and the 1956 exposé of that Soviet leader by Nikita Khrushchev and the Russian invasion of Hungary obliterated it. He resigned in 1956 from the Communist party, though he was active for a while in the French Socialist party (PSU). By 1963 he had "slipped into [his] old skin," as he recounted in his autobiography, *Paris-Montpellier, PC-PSU, 1945-63* (Gallimard, 1983), and put his "political conscience on a back-burner."

Instead he turned his attention to history, and when he resumed his duties at the Lycée Montpellier he began an exhaustive study of the region in southern France that was formerly known as Languedoc. Through tax records and other documents, he reconstructed and explored the peasant society of that region over the course of more than two hundred years, from the late fifteenth to early eighteenth centuries, or roughly from the end of the Hundred Years' War through the reign of Louis XIV. After seven years of research, his brief survey, *Histoire du Languedoc* (History of Languedoc), was published by Presses Universitaires de France in 1962, and for his 1,037-page expansion of that study, *Les Paysans de Languedoc* (SEVPEN, 1966; *The Peasants of Languedoc*, Univ. of Illinois Pr., 1974), he was granted a doctoral degree in letters by the Sorbonne in 1963.

Les Paysans de Languedoc was hailed as one of the masterpieces of the *Annales* school of historiography, which takes its name from *Annales: Economies, Sociétés, Civilisations*, a journal founded in 1929 by the school's two originators and principal figures, Lucien Febvre and Marc Bloch. *Annales* historians reject as inadequate the *histoire événementielle*, or straightforward chronicle of events, that was characteristic of nineteenth-century historiography. Since no event occurs in a vacuum but results from an extremely complex concatenation of factors, the *Annalistes* recreate as far as possible whole cultures in an attempt to understand a certain event or era. As a result, anthropology, theology, demography, sociology, and psychology, among many distinct disciplines, all fall within the purview of the *Annalistes*. Their focus on the common people rather than on the ruling class is another hallmark of the *Annales* school.

Climatology is yet another tool Le Roy Ladurie exploited in his researches. While studying such phenomena as crop failures and famines in Languedoc, he began to appreciate the crucial importance of climate in agrarian history. By using grape-harvest dates, parish records, and even dendrochronological analysis of tree trunks embedded in French glaciers, he was able to chart fluctuations in temperature and climate in Europe, principally in France, since the year 1000 A.D. The result was his pioneering study *Histoire du climat depuis l'an mil* (Flammarion, 1967; *Times of Feast, Times of Famine: A History of Climate Since the Year 1000*, Doubleday, 1971). In his review of the English edition for *Scientific American* (February 1972), Philip Morrison praised Le Roy Ladurie's effort "to restore the historian's interest in climate for itself, in a document-based history of climate; not overstated, not crudely cyclical and not ignorant of the physical clues." Although *Times of Feast, Times of Famine* may be rough going for the layman, the majority of critics agreed with Morrison that for historians and experts in other fields it is a useful and authoritative treatment of the impact of climate on history.

Montaillou: village occitan de 1294 à 1324 (Gallimard, 1975; *Montaillou: The Promised Land of Error*, Braziller, 1978), Le Roy Ladurie's next major study, is not only much more accessible to the general reader but also one of the best-selling historical works ever published in France. He based that book on a unique document that had been preserved in the Vatican Library for over six hundred years: an amazingly exact, early fourteenth-century transcript of an inquisition of ninety-eight Cathars, twenty-seven of whom lived in Montaillou. (The Cathars, a heretical sect, maintained that all matter is evil and that since Jesus Christ was angelic, he never underwent the carnal experiences of birth and death.) The chief inquisitor, the bishop of Pamiers (who later became Pope Benedict XII), grilled the accused and other villagers on every aspect of their lives, both personal and social, as well as on their beliefs about magic, religion, fate, and a wide variety of other topics. In the course of the investigation, commonplace customs like the village grooming sessions—during which the women deloused both themselves and the men while gossip and intimate secrets were often exchanged—as well as the notorious lechery of the local priest, Pierre Clergue, were discussed with equal candor.

The transcript had long been known to exist, and excerpts had in fact been published by 1965, but through his careful sifting of facts, immense erudition, and informed judgments, Le Roy Ladurie extracted from the manuscript a description of late medieval village life unrivaled in its accuracy, sense of immediacy, and depth of detail. In her appraisal of *Montaillou* for the *Christian Science Monitor* (September 20, 1978), Jane Majeski expressed reservations about his method of culling information from the document and his manner of presentation. However, D. H. Fischer voiced the critical consensus in the *New Republic* (December 9, 1978), when he lauded the study as "a virtuoso performance, which brings its subjects to life with remarkable success. No other book I can think of," he continued, "communicates so clearly the nature of the new history as this one." Quick to recognize the importance of *Montaillou*, Le Roy Ladurie's colleagues were especially enthusiastic about its revelations of the *mentalité*, or psychology, of the village's inhabitants. The drama that came alive in the manuscript, the sexual frankness of much of the testimony, including disclosures of homosexuality, and its appeal to the strong sense of regionalism in southern France made *Montaillou* a bestseller, and almost 200,000 copies of it were bought within a few months of its publication.

In *Le Carnaval de Romans: De la Chandeleur au mercredi de Cendres, 1579-1580* (Gallimard; *Carnival in Romans*, Braziller, 1979), Le Roy Ladurie moved ahead two centuries to the town of Romans in the Dauphiné region of France. The focus of the narrative is an abortive uprising by peasants and craftsmen against the ruling elite that ended with the brutal massacre of the leaders of the insurgents during the town's annual Mardi Gras festival in 1580. Le Roy Ladurie saw the uprising in Romans, triggered by high taxes, an oppressive government, and other problems, as symptomatic of the growing political, social, religious, and cultural turbulence in France at that time. He hoped that a close examination of that microcosm—through available official documents and manuscript accounts by eyewitnesses and direct participants—might provide some insight into the state of affairs in the country in general. Like many other critics, Lawrence Stone, writing in the *New York Review of Books* (November 8, 1979), greeted *Carnival in Romans* as a "dazzling psychodrama," but he took issue with what he thought to be Le Roy Ladurie's too ingenious interpretations of the symbolism of the parades, costumes, and feasts of the carnival and his biased portraits of its principal figures. Nevertheless, he asserted that "what matters is the fascination of the story, and the author's dextrous interweaving of a brilliant analysis of social conflicts . . . with a more dubious but intriguing reading of the various elements of that historic carnival in Romans."

Next, Le Roy Ladurie scrutinized marriage and village life in eighteenth-century southern France, a region also known as the Pays d'Oc. Expanding his arsenal of investigative skills to include such techniques as structuralist literary analysis, linguistics, and comparative folklore, he based his study on the short tale *Jean-l'ont-pris*, a masterpiece of Occitan literature written by Jean-Baptiste Castor Fabre, and its relationship to the old, well-known folk tale "Godfather Death." Written between 1756 and 1760, *Jean-l'ont-pris* narrates the attempts of the wily title character to marry the daughter of a certain wealthy landowner, and it was also long considered a faithful portrait of peasant society. "Godfather Death" also centers on a crafty young man. Asked to be the godfather of a poor couple's son, in gratitude Death gives the child when he turns eighteen the ability to predict whether a sick person will live or die. Because of that gift, the young man wins renown, a fortune, and in some versions the hand of the king's daughter. In the end, of course, Death, whom the gentleman had tricked more than once, evens the score by claiming his godson's life. Le Roy Ladurie's resulting treatise, *L'Argent, l'amour et la mort en Pays d'Oc* (Seuil, 1980; *Love, Death and Money in the Pays d'Oc*, Braziller, 1982), clarifies the relationship, according to the Occitan commoners' way of thinking, between marriage, money, mortality, and the supernatural. The book met with a lukewarm critical reception. Although most reviewers found it intriguing, John Bossy, for one, considered it to be

repetitious and overloaded with diagrams and lists. However, Bossy conceded in *Encounter* (April 1983) that "it is a worthy effort and ought to provoke a good deal of constructive thought." Le Roy Ladurie's adeptness at combining literary analysis with historical anthropology is also apparent in *La Sorcière de Jasmin* (Seuil, 1983), a study of peasant beliefs about witchcraft.

Over the years, Le Roy Ladurie has explored various means of compiling historical data, including for a short time the computer. That interest as well as the breadth of his studies—birth control methods in medieval France, the global spread of disease, the rise of the nation-state, the role of the modern historian, to name a few—are reflected in his articles and essays. Many of those originally printed between 1964 and 1973 were published in *Le Territoire de l'Historien* (Gallimard, 1973), a two-volume work. Selections from it comprised *The Territory of the Historian* (1979) and *The Mind and Method of the Historian* (1981), both published by the University of Chicago Press. *Parmi les Historiens* (Among the Historians, Seuil, 1983) is his most recent collection. He has also collaborated with others on several studies and has contributed to many reference works.

During his twenty-year career, Le Roy Ladurie has been honored with many prestigious academic appointments. He taught at the Sorbonne (1970-71) and at the University of Paris VII (1971-73) before he accepted his present position at the Collège de France. His appointment there to the chair of the history of modern civilization in 1973 was regarded as especially significant since his two predecessors had been among the most distinguished *Annales* historians, Lucien Febvre and Fernand Braudel. Since 1965 he has also held the position of the director of studies at L'Ecole des Hautes Etudes en Sciences Sociales, the major research center for *Annales* historians. The French historian has taught at Princeton University and at the University of Michigan, where he holds the rank of adjunct professor of history. The universities of Leeds, England and Geneva, Switzerland have awarded him honorary degrees.

Emmanuel Le Roy Ladurie was married on July 9, 1955 to Madeleine Pupponi, whom he met during his student days while both he and his future wife were active in the Communist party. The couple have two children, Anne and François. Besides cycling and swimming for recreation, Le Roy Ladurie devotes much of his spare time to movies, opera, ballet, and theatre. He speaks English fluently and has been "fascinated" by American culture ever since his first visit to the United States. A popular figure in the French media, Le Roy Ladurie often appears on state television and contributes articles and book reviews to publications such as *Le Monde*, *L'Express*, and *Le Nouvel Observateur*. In 1979 he collaborated with film director Daniel Vigne on a six-hour television documentary on French peasant life entitled "Inventaire des Campagnes" (Téléproductions Gaumont) that was awarded the Prix de la Critique and was later published in book form (Editions Jean Claude-Lattès, 1980). Le Roy Ladurie is a *chevalier* of the French Legion of Honor.

References: *Guardian* p14 Mr 28 '82; *Historia* p83+ Mar '80; *International Who's Who, 1984–85*; *Le Roy Ladurie, Emmanuel. Paris-Montpellier: P.C.-P.S.U. 1945–63 (1982); Who's Who in France, 1983–84*

Lewis, Carl

July 1, 1961– Track and field athlete. Address: b. c/o Tom Tellez, Athletic Dept., University of Houston, 4800 Calhoun Blvd., Houston, Texas 77004

Since 1981 American track and field has been dominated by the sprinter and jumper Carl Lewis, who ranks number one in the world in the 100-meter race and the long jump and number two in the 200 meters. Lewis' best in the 100 meters is 9.97 seconds, the third fastest time ever, .04 seconds short of the international record, and in the 200 it is 19.75, the second fastest, .03 seconds behind the world mark. In his "home event," the long jump, Lewis has registered 28 feet 10¼ inches both indoors and out, for world records at low altitude and just 4¼ inches short of the record set by Bob Beamon in Mexico City, a mile-and-a-half above sea level, in 1968. At the Olympic Games in Los Angeles in the summer of 1984 Lewis won four gold medals, in the 100 meters, the 200 meters, the long jump, and the 4x400-meter relay, duplicating Jesse Owens' feat at the 1936 Berlin Olympics.

"The support and stability of Carl's home life is why he handles winning and losing so well," Tom Tellez, the University of Houston coach who has been Lewis' mentor since 1979, told Hank Nuer in an interview for *Inside Sports* (August 1984). Frederick Carlton Lewis was born on July 1, 1961 in Birmingham, Alabama to Bill Lewis, who ran track and starred in football at Tuskegee Institute, and Evelyn (Lawler) Lewis, a fellow Tuskegee graduate, who represented the United States as a hurdler in the 1951 Pan-American Games. Lewis' oldest brother, Mack, was a high-school sprinter and Cleve, the next oldest, has played professional soccer. His sister, Carol, two years Carl's junior, is currently the top-ranked American woman long jumper and an outstanding sprinter, hurdler, and high jumper. She is Carl's closest friend and confidante.

Early in Carl Lewis' childhood the Lewises moved to the middle-class Philadelphia suburb of Willingboro, New Jersey, where Bill and Evelyn Lewis became high-school teachers and founded the Willingboro Track Club. Growing up in Willingboro, Carl showed an interest in music, learning to play the cello and drums. Physically, he was for many years the family runt, regularly losing to his younger sister in track events. "I didn't mature until high school," he recounted to Hank Nuer, "while others began maturing in the seventh, eighth grade. There was talent there all the time, but it was only when I got older that I really blossomed." In the meantime, he "really worked hard," trying "to be perfect . . . like they [his siblings] were when they were good."

Lewis began running for his parents' track club when he was eight. At twelve, in 1973, he won the long jump at a Jesse Owens Youth Program meet in Philadelphia with a leap of 17 feet 6 inches. On that occasion Owens counseled the other boys in the meet to "take a lesson" from "this spunky little guy." Between his sophomore and junior years at Willingboro High School, Lewis suddenly began sprouting physically, and in his junior year his mark in the long jump shot from less than 23 feet to more than 25. In the 1978 national junior championships in Memphis, Tennessee he ran the 100 yards in 9.3 seconds and long-jumped 25 feet 9 inches, a national high-school record. As a senior in high school he was All-American in the 200 meters as well as the long jump, and by the time he graduated he was the top-ranked high-school track athlete in the United States.

Bill and Evelyn Lewis were, along with Paul Mimore, the track coach at Willingboro High School, Carl Lewis' athletic mentors until, in 1979, he went on to an athletic scholarship to the University of Houston (where he majored in communications). At the university he came under the tutelage of Tom Tellez, and he has remained under Tellez's guidance since. Tellez, expert in applying the laws of physics and kinesiology to track and field, immediately saw several flaws in Lewis' long-jump style. He observed that Lewis was inconsistent in his approach, with the result that his last four strides were too long. This caused him to stop at the point of takeoff and thus to lose velocity and go into flexion that put stress on his patella tendon. The net result was a swelling of the knee every time he jumped. Once his approach run was corrected, Lewis gained maximum horizontal velocity from his great sprinting speed and the knee problem disappeared.

Under Tom Tellez's guidance, Carl Lewis increased the length of his approach run from under 150 feet, the conventional distance, to more than 170, a distance he covers in precisely twenty-three strides, building to a momentum of twenty-seven miles an hour. Knowing that run-up speed is useless without follow-up control, Tellez taught Lewis not to "hang" in his takeoff, but to use a "hitch kick," a pedaling motion of legs and arms that came naturally to Lewis.

In an interview with Charles Siebert for *Esquire* (April 1983), Tellez explained why he disagrees with the prevalent emphasis on height, or lift, in long jumping and stresses instead the velocity of the approach run and the importance of not losing that velocity at the point of takeoff: "[Height is] dramatic, but you don't go anywhere. You're taking away from the most important thing, which is horizontal velocity. When you break contact with the board, your hips, which are your center of mass, form a perfect parabolic curve throughout the jump. We know this; research tells us. You cannot alter the parabolic curve. And . . . horizontal velocity is a two-to-one ratio to vertical velocity, so I'm not interested in getting that much height in a long jump."

Tellez told Siebert of his amazement at Lewis' ability to translate the physical laws into the workings of his own body. "The basic mechanics have been around for years. I know how to take these mechanics and put them in an athlete. And when you get an athlete like Carl, hey, that's what you dream about. . . . In the long jump, he has a great physical sensation of what he's supposed to do. Once he gets that going, then it all unfolds. Everything he's done has not been by accident; it has been planned."

The jump Lewis developed departs from the old theory that a long jump is really a high jump at the end of a run, as the athlete explained to Frank Litsky of the *New York Times* (June 6, 1982): "What I do is totally unnatural. I leave the board going almost forward. Most people go up and look beautiful in the air, but they come straight down. When I'm in the air, I rotate forward, and I have to fight to keep my balance or I'll fall flat on my face. That's why I use a hitch kick to swing my balance forward. Bob Beamon jumped this way. Ralph Boston did too. My best attribute is my balance in the air. I was always a terrible basketball shooter, but I could double pump and triple pump in the air because I had balance."

Lewis qualified for the 1980 Olympics, but American participation in the Moscow Olympiad was canceled by President Jimmy Carter as a gesture of protest against the Soviet invasion of Af-

ghanistan. Representing the University of Houston at the National Collegiate Athletic Association indoor championships in Baton Rouge, Louisiana in the spring of 1981, Lewis finished first in the 100 meters with a time of 9.99 seconds—just .04 seconds behind Jim Hines's world record—and in the long jump with a leap of 27 feet 3/4 inch. It was the first time in the seventeen-year history of the meet that any athlete had ever won events in both track and field. Two weeks later he repeated his double feat in the United States outdoor track and field championships in Sacramento, California, taking the 100 meters in 10.13 seconds and the long jump with a leap of 28 feet 3½ inches. From that point on, Lewis would consistently do the long jump in 28 feet or more, coming ever closer to Beamon's magnitude of 29-plus (which was widely regarded as a fluke when Beamon achieved it). None of his contenders would break out of the 27-plus magnitude, save Larry Myricks of the United States (28-1) and L. Dombrowski of East Germany (28-0¼).

As the best amateur athlete of 1981, Lewis received the Amateur Athletic Union's Sullivan Award. At the national outdoor championships in Knoxville, Tennessee in 1982 Lewis achieved his third major double. In the 100 meters he made his usual, calculated slow start, trailing the field for the first fifty meters before accelerating. "The reason I'm so powerful the last forty or fifty meters," he explained to a reporter, "is because I can relax very well and when you relax you don't decelerate as much. Everybody decelerates from about sixty meters to the finish line—everybody! But the one who decelerates the least has the strongest finish."

Disqualified for academic reasons during the 1981–82 scholastic year, Lewis has since that time competed not under the auspices of the University of Houston but rather under those of the Santa Monica (California) Track Club. At Modesto, California in May 1982 Lewis again registered a double, taking the long jump with a leap of 28 feet 1 inch and the 100 meters in 9.97 seconds, a low-altitude record and a whisker away from the world record. At the National Sports Festival in Indianapolis, Indiana two months later he made a long jump estimated at 30 feet, but that leap was disqualified on a technicality and he came away from the festival with an official mark of 28-9.

A year later, at The Athletics Congress (TAC) outdoor championships in Indianapolis, Lewis gave his most memorable performance to that date, scoring a triple. In addition to registering 28 feet 10¼ inches, the world's best mark at low altitude, in the long jump, he won the 100 meters in 10.27 seconds and the 200 in 19.75. His 200-meter time was just .03 seconds short of Pietro Minnea's world record, and in the opinion of many seasoned observers he might have broken that record had he not raised his arms in a premature victory wave—a gesture viewed by some of his rivals as an example of what they consider his "showboating."

Lewis won three gold medals at the world championships in Helsinki, Finland in August 1983. One medal was for the 100 meters (10.07 seconds), another for the long jump (a fraction over 28 feet), and the third for the 400-meter relay, in which the Americans set a world record of 37.86 seconds. Lewis ran the last 100 meters of the relay in 8.9 seconds. After the Helsinki meet, allegations surfaced in the Scandinavian press to the effect that Lewis was using the strength-building male hormone testosterone. Because he felt it important "to help younger athletes realize you don't need steroids," Lewis subsequently submitted to, and passed, drug tests administered by the United States Olympic Committee. Other rumors circulating in Europe questioned Lewis' heterosexuality. In his interview with Hank Nuer for *Inside Sports*, Lewis labeled those reports as "insanity" conjured up out of "jealousy" by "three athletes." "I know exactly who they are, but I'm not going to mention names, because that's not really fair." He said that homosexuality is "a touchy subject for most people," but for him "it isn't." "One way to attack a man is by attacking his masculinity. But if you are very masculine and believe in yourself, it is very hard to attack your masculinity."

In 1984 Lewis increased his approach run in the long jump from 168 to 170 feet. His strides, stronger and faster than before, remained the same in number—precisely twenty-three. He opened the 1984 season with a 20.01 in the 200 meters and a flat 10 in the 100 meters, and in the Millrose Games in Madison Square Garden in New York City in January 1984 he made a long jump of 28 feet 10¼ inches, an indoor world record.

In anticipation of Olympiad XXIII, Lewis wrote, in collaboration with the composer Narada Michael Walden, the song "Going for the Gold," which he sang on a recording released in June 1984. In the Olympic trials he qualified with finishes of 10.06 in the 100 meters, 19.86 in the 200, and 28 feet 7 inches in the long jump. In the Olympic Games themselves, in Los Angeles in August 1984, he began his golden sweep with a 9.99-second victory in the 100 meters. The crowd was disappointed when, in the long jump, he leaped only 28 feet 1/4 inch in his first attempt, fouled in his second, and passed on the last four (because, as he later explained, he "got a little sore after the second jump" and "didn't want to risk a chance of injury"). Nevertheless, his initial leap sufficed to bring him his second gold medal. For his third, he ran the 200 meters in 19.80 seconds, an Olympic record, and for his fourth he anchored a United States team that took the 400-meter relay in 37.83 seconds, another Olympic record. As in 1980, the Olympics in 1984 were tarnished and devalued by politics. This time, the Soviet Union and some of its satellites, tit for America's 1980 tat, failed to participate.

Following the Olympics, Lewis competed in five European countries, pleasing the crowds more than he had those at the Olympics. He found Europeans to be more "knowledgeable" than Americans, he told Randy Harvey in an interview in Brussels for the *Washington Post* (September 11, 1984). Once "shy and unsure of himself," Lewis was now, Harvey observed, "a man who wears dark glasses even indoors . . . remains aloof from all but a small circle . . . and has a separate bus with a police escort to take him to and from hotels" but who is "less obsessed with himself than many lesser athletes."

Because he is not competing under National Collegiate Athletic Association regulations, Lewis is permitted, within current amateur guidelines, to earn money from meets, personal appearances, endorsement contracts (chiefly with Nike, the athletic gear manufacturer), and other deals negotiated for him by his business manager, Joe Douglas, who is also the general manager of the Santa Monica Track Club. (The money must be put into a trust fund, from which he may withdraw annually "training expenses" of $7,200, or a larger amount if approved by the International Amateur Athletic Federation.) His current yearly earnings have been estimated at $600,000, and Douglas predicts that the figure will grow to seven or eight digits within another year. Lewis, who plans to compete until 1986, has been grooming himself for a second career, taking acting lessons at Warren Robertson's Studio Workshop in New York City and doing part-time television broadcasting at the ABC affiliate in Houston. The Dallas Cowboys drafted Lewis in the twelfth round of the 1984 National Football League draft and the Chicago Bulls hold the National Basketball Association rights to him, but he is not interested in playing either football or basketball.

Lewis, a flashy dresser with an extensive wardrobe, lives in an elegantly appointed four-bedroom Victorian-style house in suburban Houston with his pet dog Natasha, a Samoyed. His table is set with Baccarat crystal and Christofle silver, and he drives a BMW 745 (which carries on its rear bumper the slogan, "Life has no finish line") and a Jeep Scrambler. Broad-shouldered and lean-waisted, the track and field star is six feet two inches tall and weighs 180 pounds, the bulk of which fill out his smooth but muscular upper torso and legs. "In his silver tights and high-strung manner of prancing about the track infield during a workout," Hank Nuer observed in his *Inside Sports* article, "Carl Lewis resembles a professional dancer more than he does a world-class athlete. . . . His youthful exuberance is fun to watch." Gentle and soft-spoken, not given to talking shop, and possessing a sardonic sense of humor, he comes across to many of his fellow athletes as laconic and aloof, and his enemies among them consider him "rude" or "arrogant." To that criticism Coach Tellez has countered, "Confident, yes; arrogant, no." According to Tellez, Lewis is "compassionate," "friendly," "steady," "very coachable," "thinking all the time," and unspoiled by celebrity—"the same type of kid who walked in here as a freshman." Lewis is elusive with the press, but when cornered he is a good interviewee, articulate and forthright.

"God makes Carl Lewis what he is," Bob Sevene, a coach at Athletics West, has observed. "I mean, he doesn't even train hard. He is genetically made to do what he does." Lewis' grace in performance, what he calls his "relaxed speed," carries over into an easygoing attitude toward life in general. A professed born-again Christian, he refrains from responding in kind to the sometimes vicious gossip about him, attributing it to "frustration," and he believes that his faith, like that of his close friend and fellow sprinter Calvin Smith, has "helped us to relax in competition" and to avoid crippling injuries. "Competition . . . has hurt a lot of athletes," he told Hank Nuer in the *Inside Sports* interview. "They compete *too* much, and that's where they get injuries. My faith has given me strength so that I don't feel I have to prove myself or win every race."

References: *Chicago Tribune* III p1+ Je 10 '84 pors; *N Y Times Mag* p13+ Je 17 '84 pors; *Newsday* O p1+ Jl 22 '84 pors; *Newsweek* 104:26+ Ag 20 '84 por; *Sport* 15:17+ Ag '84 pors; *Sporting News* 198:3+ Jl 30 '84 por; *Washington Post mag* p22+ Jl 22 '84 pors

Loudon, Dorothy

Sept. 17, 1933– Actress; singer. Address: b. c/o Lionel Larner, Ltd., 850 7th Ave., New York City, N.Y. 10019

After twenty-five years in show business, Dorothy Loudon finally achieved the recognition that had so long eluded her when she received the 1977 Tony Award for her performance in the smash hit musical *Annie*. Miss Loudon, who had begun her career in the early 1950s as a singer and comedienne in New York City cocktail lounges and smart supper clubs, perfected her craft on television variety shows, in countless strawhat and touring pro-

ductions, and in a series of Broadway flops, beginning in 1962 with the ephemeral *Nowhere To Go But Up*. Although she was trained at the American Academy of Dramatic Arts, Dorothy Loudon is basically an instinctive actress. "I reach back and get it from somewhere," she told Judy Klemesrud in an interview for the *New York Times* (April 28, 1977), "but I don't know where. . . . It just comes from somewhere. Something's working up in my head." In recognition of Miss Loudon's outstanding performances over the years and her contribution to the theatre, the Lambs theatrical club honored her with its 1984 Shepherd award. She is the first woman to receive the prestigious award in the 110-year history of the organization.

Dorothy Loudon was born on September 17, 1933 in Boston, Massachusetts, the only child of James E. Loudon Jr., the advertising manager for a machine company, and Dorothy Helen (Shaw) Loudon, who played the piano in the sheet music department of Filene's department store. It was from her mother that Miss Loudon learned the 1,-500-odd "awful old songs," to use her words, that comprised her nightclub repertory. In about 1936 the Loudons moved to Indianapolis, Indiana. They returned to New England in the mid-1940s, settling in Claremont, New Hampshire, where Dorothy continued the dancing and piano lessons she had begun in the midwest. "I wanted to be Eleanor Powell . . . , in a turban, dancing through hoops of fire," she told Gerritt Henry in an interview for *After Dark* magazine (October 1977).

Putting her lessons to practical use, Dorothy Loudon often appeared in student theatrical productions at Stevens High School. Her performances were good enough to win her a drama scholarship to Syracuse University, where she studied under Sawyer Falk. During summer vacations, she took acting lessons from Gertrude Binley Kay, a drama coach at Emerson College in Boston. After several semesters, Miss Loudon left Syracuse to pursue her training at the American Academy of Dramatic Arts in New York City. She supported herself throughout those years by singing in neighborhood nightspots, making "cover" records for RCA of song hits recorded on other labels by better-known artists, and appearing occasionally on radio and television programs, among them, the short-lived situation comedy series *It's a Business*, which had its premiere on the Dumont television network in March 1952.

Dorothy Loudon got her proverbial "big break" in 1954, when she auditioned for Julius Monk, the enterprising owner of the chic Ruban Bleu nightclub in New York City. Recognizing her talent for comedy, Monk advised the young singer to scrap her tired routine of torch songs and standards and put together an act satirizing the "chanteuse" style. Her new show, in which she caricatured popular song stylists, including Ella Fitzgerald, Anita O'Day, and Chris Connor, made such a hit with Ruban Bleu patrons that she became a regular featured performer there. Over the next few years, in engagements at the Ruban Bleu, the Blue Angel,

Mister Kelly's, and other nightclubs around the country, she polished and revised her repertory, adding, among other things, a devastating takeoff on Shirley Temple and songs lampooning "anything I could think of," as she once put it, from Rachel Carson's best-seller The Sea Around Us to contemporary American theatre ("I've Got Those Tennessee Williams Southern Decadence Blues").

By the early 1960s, Dorothy Loudon was considered to be one of the top comediennes on the cabaret circuit. She found an even wider audience with her recordings, among them the album Dorothy Loudon at the Blue Angel (Decca, 1960), and her frequent guest appearances on such television variety series as The Perry Como Show, The Ed Sullivan Show, The Kraft Music Hall, and The Dinah Shore Show. She also performed on the variety specials Those Ragtime Years (1960), Music of the Thirties (1961), and Regards to George M. Cohan (1962), and in 1959 she served as a regular celebrity panelist on the transient NBC game show Laugh Line. But she is perhaps best known to viewers as the successor to Carol Burnett on The Garry Moore Show. After her first appearance on the program in December 1962, New York Post television columnist Bob Williams wrote, "Dorothy Loudon arrived like a doctor's prescription with all the essential ingredients—a sweet and saucy flair for humor, a versatile vocal style, an ability to 'move around' without stepping on the dancers and a fine fast-draw, slow-take sense of sketch comedy. Suddenly, the Moore show looked young again." Garry Moore apparently agreed, for he signed Miss Loudon for the remainder of the 1962-63 television season and took a one-year lien on her services for the following season.

Dorothy Loudon made her debut on the legitimate stage in 1962, in the pre-Broadway tryout of The World of Jules Feiffer, a trio of skits directed by Mike Nichols. The play folded on the road, but her amusing portrayal of the Chaplinesque chimney sweep turned sexpot in "Passionella," Feiffer's skewed version of Cinderella, brought the actress to the attention of New York producers, and shortly thereafter, she went into rehearsal for the Broadway-bound musical comedy Nowhere To Go But Up. Cast as Wilma Risque, a brassy nightclub singer, she was, as one reviewer remarked, "the sole authentic jewel" in "a collection of rhinestones and paste." Although the show survived in New York for less than two weeks, Miss Loudon was rewarded for her efforts when Theatre World, the annual survey of American drama, named her the season's most promising newcomer.

During her summer holidays from The Garry Moore Show in 1963, Miss Loudon starred in a touring production of Meredith Willson's energetic musical comedy The Unsinkable Molly Brown, and the following summer, she appeared in a strawhat revival of Cole Porter's Anything Goes. In September 1965 the actress signed on to play the brainy, frustrated housewife Ellen Manville in the national company of Luv, Murray Schisgal's first full-length comedy. She finally returned to Broad-

way in September 1968, in the Noel Coward revue Sweet Potato. The show opened to generally unfavorable reviews, but both Clive Barnes of the New York Times and George Oppenheimer of Newsday appreciated Miss Loudon's ability to "belt out a song with the best of them," to use Barnes's words.

A few days after Sweet Potato closed in November, Miss Loudon was tapped for the part of Lillian Stone, whose philandering, middle-aged husband is the central character in The Fig Leaves Are Falling, a musical comedy about the impact of the sexual revolution on domestic life in suburbia by Allan Sherman, the late parodist, and Albert Hague. When the George Abbott production opened on Broadway on January 2, 1969, it was savaged by the critics, and only Dorothy Loudon, who managed to transcend her one-dimensional role, escaped unscathed. Her performance saved the evening for Clive Barnes. "She gives herself to the audience like a bride, whether she is pertly putting forward the wronged wife's viewpoint, or whether she is swinging into a vaudeville routine . . . ," he wrote in the New York Times (January 3, 1969). "The important thing about her is that she is both lovable and vulnerable, so much so that I feel personally affronted at the way this show wastes her." Although Fig Leaves expired after just four performances, Miss Loudon came away with a Drama Desk Award and a Tony nomination as best actress in a musical.

Dorothy Loudon and George Abbott teamed up again later in the year in an acclaimed revival of the 1935 comedy hit Three Men on a Horse. Capitalizing on the opportunity to appear in a first-rate farce, she made the most of the peripheral role of Mabel, the dizzy ex-chorine, and won her second consecutive Drama Desk Award. Its excellent notices notwithstanding, Three Men on a Horse closed after 100 performances, and by January 1970 Dorothy Loudon was back on the road again, playing the female leads in The Apple Tree, a collection of three loosely related one-act musicals by Sheldon Harnick and Jerry Bock, and, later, in You Know I Can't Hear You When the Water's Running, Robert Anderson's program of four one-acts dealing humorously with various sexual matters.

The following year, after the ignominious pre-Broadway failure of the highly touted Lolita, My Love, Alan Jay Lerner and John Barry's misbegotten musical adaptation of Vladimir Nabokov's novel, in which she had played Charlotte Haze, the nymphet's mother, Dorothy Loudon took to the road again in touring productions of popular contemporary plays. Her stage credits for the early 1970s include the central female characters in each of the three one-act comedies that comprise Neil Simon's smash hit Plaza Suite, the leading role in the revue The Trouble With People . . . and Other Things, also by Neil Simon, and perhaps most notably, the embittered Beatrice Hunsdorfer in Paul Zindel's Pulitzer Prize-winning drama The Effect of Gamma Rays on Man-in-the-Moon Marigolds. Her lone Broadway credit during those years was the role of Edith Potter, the perpetually pregnant gossip, in a 1973 all-star revival of *The Women*, Clare Boothe Luce's brittle comedy.

Her triumphant return to Broadway, as Miss Hannigan in the 1977 blockbuster *Annie*, was the result of a happy accident. A few months earlier, she had chanced to run into Mike Nichols, a friend from her days at the Blue Angel, in a Manhattan rehearsal hall. Nichols, who had taken over as producer of the musical during its out-of-town tryouts, offered her the plum role of Aggie Hannigan, the mean-spirited manager of the Dickensian orphanage that is "home" to Annie. "At first, I didn't want to do the part," Miss Loudon admitted to Judy Klemesrud in the *New York Times* interview. "There's an old saying, 'Never be in a show with kids, dogs, or an Irish tenor,' and this show had all three. But the main reason was that there was no humor in Miss Hannigan." She finally agreed to join the cast, on the condition that her character be made "more vulnerable" and "believable."

Working instinctively, Miss Loudon, in collaboration with Martin Charnin, the play's lyricist and director, virtually rewrote her part during rehearsals. By the time *Annie* reached New York, in April 1977, Miss Hanningan was, in Jack Kroll's words, "a manic descendant of Cinderella's stepmother." "Dorothy Loudon raises mugging to a high art," Kroll continued in his panegyric for *Newsweek* (May 2, 1977). "She mugs with her face, her voice, her body—I swear she mugs with her very mind." Her campy portrayal won her a cornucopia of honors, including the Tony, Drama Desk, and Outer Critics' Circle awards for best performance by an actress in a musical.

Dorothy Loudon was supposed to have begun work on her first film, tentatively titled "Good Times/Bad Times," in the spring of 1978, but the project never materialized, and before the year was out, she was back on Broadway, starring in Michael Bennett's autumnal musical *Ballroom*. After years of playing comedy, she found the role of Bea Asher, the lonely middle-aged widow who falls in love with an unhappily married man she meets at the Stardust Ballroom, to be a welcome change. "She's a real woman as opposed to a musical-comedy lady. . . . ," the actress explained to Richard Alleman in an interview for the theatrical publication *Playbill* (December 1978). "Bea Asher doesn't sit back after her husband dies and let life consume her. She goes out and makes a new life. She's a survivor."

Ballroom opened on December 14, 1978 to mixed notices from the critics, most of whom felt that Bennett had failed to give his essentially sound concept "enough support in the book and music," as Jack Kroll remarked in his review for *Newsweek* (January 1, 1979). Dorothy Loudon, however, was universally praised. Even the notoriously hard-to-please John Simon was enchanted by her portrayal. "Has anyone ever gotten more out of shyness, tentativeness, even a self-effacing way of bending the body this way and that, as though a straight posture were an unexampled piece of

ostentation?" he asked in his appraisal for *New York* magazine (January 8, 1979). "She delivers not only dialogue and songs to unassuming perfection, but also silences, thoughts, changes of heart. Thanks to her, you feel as well oriented inside Bea Asher as inside your own skin, and quite a bit safer, as one always does inside true artistic creation." For her performance, Dorothy Loudon earned Tony and Drama Desk award nominations as best actress in a musical and the Woman of the Year award from Yeshiva University's Albert Einstein College of Medicine.

After *Ballroom* ended its run in late March 1979, Dorothy Loudon flew to Los Angeles to begin work on her own situation comedy series for CBS-TV. Slotted into the network's late-summer preview schedule, *Dorothy* followed the adventures of a divorced former showgirl who wangles a job teaching music and drama at an exclusive girls' boarding school. Miss Loudon had turned down several earlier sitcom proposals, but she had high hopes for *Dorothy*, primarily because of its uncontrived situations. Shortly after its disappointing debut in August 1979, however, the series was axed by ratings-conscious CBS executives. "I'm just not good on television," Miss Loudon had told Judy Klemesrud two years earlier. "I belong in the theatre. I need body contact. I have to work off the instant reactions of the audience. I cannot work off the red light; I freeze."

Early in 1980 Dorothy Loudon was chosen to succeed Angela Lansbury as Mrs. Lovett, the depraved accomplice of the "demon barber of Fleet Street" in Stephen Sondheim's Tony Award–winning and quasi-operatic musical *Sweeney Todd*. It was the first time she had not had to audition for a part. The interpretations of Dorothy Loudon and her costar, George Hearn, who succeeded Len Cariou in the title role, subtly altered the perspective of *Sweeney Todd*, deflecting it from Grand Guignol and directing it "toward demented domestic comedy," according to John Corry of the *New York Times* (March 21, 1980). Miss Loudon's comic characterization of Mrs. Lovett, who obligingly disposed of her lover's victims by baking them into meat pies, had a human dimension that had been wanting in Angela Lansbury's more outrageous portrayal. To quote Clive Barnes, writing in the *New York Post* (March 17, 1980), "[She] made this blowsy, corruptible, amoral harridan into a funny figure of pity."

In her next venture, Ernest Thompson's *West Side Waltz*, Dorothy Loudon shared the spotlight with the legendary Katharine Hepburn. Following a year-long national tour, the comedy opened at the Ethel Barrymore Theatre in New York on November 19, 1981 for a limited run. A rather insubstantial story about the tentative friendship between Margaret Mary Elderdice, a strongwilled, sharp-tongued widow, and her solicitous, dimwitted neighbor, Cara Varnum, who pass the lonely afternoons by playing piano-violin duets, *West Side Waltz* owed its commercial success largely to Miss Hepburn's drawing power at the box office.

Dorothy Loudon managed to mine some humor out of the under-realized character of Cara, but she was, as Walter Kerr observed in the *New York Times* (November 29, 1981), "essentially the victim of an unattractive role."

In December 1983, Dorothy Loudon opened in what was to be her second Broadway hit, *Noises Off*, Michael Frayn's "farce within a farce" about a down-at-the-heels British repertory company touring the provinces in a production of the tacky sex comedy "Nothing On." As a washed-up television comedienne assigned the role of a Cockney housemaid, Miss Loudon played her part with her customary brio. In the course of mastering the carefully choreographed slapstick routines and the precisely timed entrances and exits that are the hallmarks of the clockwork-like farce, she sustained two bruised ribs, two broken toes, and a sprained ankle, among other injuries. Although *Noises Off* is the quintessential ensemble piece, the *New York Times*'s Frank Rich singled out Dorothy Loudon for special praise. "She gets every laugh . . . ," he wrote in his column of December 12, 1983. "Watching the glee with which [she] attacks her role, one imagines that she's recollecting every bomb that blighted her own theatrical career during those long years before *Annie* brought her in from the wilderness."

Slim and petite, Dorothy Loudon has short blond hair, blue eyes, and a mobile face. Because exercise "bores" her, she does not follow any prescribed workout routine, and she shuns active sports. For relaxation, she plays the piano, paints, writes, or sews. An accomplished seamstress, she makes most of her own clothes. Interviewers have found her to be rather shy in comparison with her onstage persona. "I'm happiest when I'm onstage," she admitted to Richard Alleman. "I think that's probably why most people act: it's because they get to be somebody else. I find a strength onstage that I don't have offstage. It's when I have my confidence." Dorothy Loudon married Norman Paris, the Emmy Award–winning composer and her longtime musical arranger, on December 18, 1971. Since her husband's death in 1977, the actress has lived alone in an apartment overlooking Central Park on Manhattan's Upper West Side. Her home is decorated with the early American antiques she has collected over the years and with family and theatrical mementos.

References: After Dark 10:64+ O '77 pors; Chicago Tribune p8 S 12 '82 por; N Y Times C p23 Ap 28 '77 por; Sat Eve Post 236:70+ Ap 6 '63 por; Washington Post C p1+ Mr 15 '82; Notable Names in the American Theatre (1976); Who's Who in America, 1984–85; Who's Who in the Theatre (1981)

Louganis, Greg

(lōō gän´ əs)

1960(?)– Diver. Address: b. c/o William Morris Agency, 151 El Camino Dr., Beverly Hills, Calif. 90212

Even before the 1984 Olympic Games, at which he became the first man in fifty-six years to capture the gold medals in both the springboard and platform diving competitions, Greg Louganis was considered by his fellow divers to be about as close to perfection as it is possible to be. Since taking the silver medal in the platform event at the 1976 Olympics, he has so dominated his sport, particularly on the springboard, that he has been virtually without rivals. The only diver ever to score straight perfect tens in an international competition, Louganis owns three World and four Pan American championships, and he recently won his twenty-ninth national crown, setting a record for most national diving titles.

Of Samoan and northern European ancestry, Gregory Efthimios Louganis was adopted shortly after his birth, in 1960, by Peter and Frances Louganis. His adoptive father, then a bookkeeper for the Fisherman Marine Company in San Diego, California, eventually became a tuna-boat controller for the American TunaBoats Association. Reared in El Cajon, a suburb of San Diego, Greg Louganis,

as he prefers to be known, and his older sister, Despina, who is also adopted, began taking dancing lessons when they were little more than toddlers because, as Louganis explained to Anita Verschoth years later in an interview for *Sports Illustrated* (May 11, 1981), "Mom didn't want any klutzes."

The pair were soon doing song-and-dance routines in dance studio recitals and local talent competitions. It was in his dance classes that Louganis learned the concentration technique that later proved crucial to his development as a championship diver. To help her students memorize the steps in a new dance number, Louganis' teacher would lower the lights in the studio, turn up the volume of the recorded musical accompaniment, and ask the children to visualize the routine from beginning to end. "I didn't leave the room until I could do the routine flawlessly in my head," Louganis told Derrick Jackson of Newsday (August 12, 1984).

Teased by his classmates at the local public school because of an early reading disability, Louganis spent most of his free time in the dance studio or the gymnasium. He had added gymnastics to his extracurricular activities on the advice of a physician, who thought that the vigorous exercise, by increasing his lung capacity, would cure his asthma. When the boy began practising his acrobatic tumbling routines off the diving board into the family's backyard pool, Peter Louganis decided it was time to enroll his son in diving classes at the Parks and Recreation Center in nearby La Mesa. Within two years, Greg Louganis was accomplished enough to score a perfect ten in the diving at the 1971 AAU Junior Olympics in Colorado Springs, Colorado. Among the spectators at that meet was Dr. Sammy Lee, the gold medalist in the ten-meter platform diving event in the 1948 and 1952 Olympic Games. "When I first watched him, I said to myself, 'My God, that's the greatest talent I've ever seen!' Lee told Anita Verschoth. "He was on the springboard, and his spring was so much higher than that of any other child his age, or even thirteen- and fourteen-year-olds. He was years ahead of his age group."

Four years later, in 1975, Peter Louganis asked Lee to coach his son in preparation for the upcoming 1976 Summer Olympics in Montreal, Canada. Readily agreeing, the veteran diver, who refused to accept payment for his services, imposed upon his young charge a strict training regimen, which included prohibitions against smoking and drinking. Under Lee's guidance, Greg Louganis mastered the most difficult of the required dives off both the ten-meter platform and the three-meter springboard, but he was unexpectedly cautious, and Lee occasionally had to goad him into attempting a new dive.

During the six months before the Summer Games, Louganis lived at Lee's home and spent most of his working hours at the pool. Having earned a berth on the United States Olympic diving team with relative ease, he went on to qualify for both the springboard and platform diving events. Perhaps because of his inexperience in international competition, Louganis was unable to concentrate on the day of the springboard final, which he has since described as "one of those days when you don't want to get wet," but he nonetheless earned a respectable sixth-place finish. Rested and relaxed after the three-day break between the

springboard and tower contests, he edged out the favorite, two-time gold medalist Klaus Dibiasi, in the platform preliminaries to win the prized last slot in the diving order for the final. In the championship match, however, Dibiasi reasserted his supremacy over the field to take his third successive gold medal. Louganis finished in second place, just 23.52 points behind the leader—a remarkable achievement for a sixteen-year-old athlete at his first Olympic Games, as Dibiasi himself acknowledged when he told his young rival, according to Sports Illustrated (May 11, 1981), "Next Olympics, I watch you."

Returning to his daily routine in September 1976, Louganis suffered from temporary post-Olympic depression. "The Olympics are the highest any amateur athlete can go, and when you get back home, it's hard to adjust," he explained to Bruce Newman of Sports Illustrated (May 8, 1978). "When I came back from Montreal, a lot of my friends at high school wouldn't talk to me because they thought I had changed. It was very hard on me at the time." His depression was compounded by a bout with mononucleosis and a series of debilitating injuries. Over the next eighteen months, he gradually regained both his health and his confidence, and by the spring of 1978 he was collecting more than his share of national and international diving crowns, including both the one-meter springboard and ten-meter platform titles at the National AAU Indoor Diving Championships, the platform titles at the Hall of Fame International Diving Meet, and, perhaps most important, the World Aquatic Championships, where he succeeded Dibiasi as the gold medalist.

Louganis made his name primarily as a platform specialist, but in the fall of 1978 he began to concentrate on springboard diving, not so much as a matter of choice but as a matter of circumstance. He had accepted a scholarship from the University of Miami in Miami, Florida, and collegiate diving consists only of one-meter and three-meter springboard events. In his freshman year, he won his first national three-meter crown. He has taken the one-meter and three-meter national springboard titles at both the Indoor and Outdoor Diving Championships ever since.

Equally successful at international meets, Louganis captured first place in the springboard and platform competitions at the Pan-American Games in 1979. Later in the year, he was well on his way to a victory in a head-to-head duel against the Soviet Union in Tbilisi when, in the course of attempting a reverse dive in the pike position off the unpredictably bouncy plywood surface of the ten-meter tower, he misjudged his takeoff and, as he descended, struck his head against the edge of the platform. Knocked unconscious, Louganis plummeted the thirty-three feet to the pool below. He suffered a concussion and a badly bruised back, but within a few days he was well enough to resume his daily practice sessions. Back in top form before the year was out, Louganis was heavily favored to win two gold medals at the upcoming 1980

Olympics. He was denied that opportunity by the United States government's decision to boycott the Summer Games in Moscow in protest of the recent Soviet invasion of Afghanistan.

In January 1981 Louganis transferred from the University of Miami to the University of California at Irvine in order to train year-round under Ron O'Brien, the head diving coach at the famed Mission Viejo Nadadores swim club. Taking a much needed break from competitive diving, he signed up for an unusually heavy course load during his first semester at Irvine. A drama major, with a minor in dance, Louganis also appeared in several campus theatrical productions, occasionally serving as assistant choreographer and dance captain as well. He received his bachelor's degree in theatre from the University of California in 1983.

Meanwhile, Louganis continued to perfect his diving skills. Under Coach O'Brien's watchful eye, he usually makes between seventy-five and 100 dives a day, but except for an occasional workout on the spotting apparatus, he follows no set exercise routine, relying instead on his dance training to keep in shape. "I'd much rather be in a studio and dance my heart out than go to a gym and pump iron," he explained to Lawrie Mifflin in an interview for the New York Times (July 11, 1983). Thanks to his years of regular ballet classes, he has perfect body alignment and an extraordinary flexibility that allows him to curl and bend into much tighter tucks and pikes than his rivals. Moreover, because of his leg strength (he can do a thirty-inch standing vertical jump), Louganis achieves more height off both the platform and the springboard, which he depresses considerably further than most divers. The extra height gives him more time to perform his dives so that he seems to be moving with what one awed sportswriter called "a majestic slowness."

"When Greg dives well, I don't think there's anyone who can beat him," Phil Boggs, the CBS sports commentator and the 1976 Olympics gold medalist on the springboard, told Lawrie Mifflin. "There are people who get into the water cleaner, with less splash, and there are people who spin faster, like some of the acrobatic Chinese divers. But there's nobody who combines all the elements like Greg does—power, grace, and that catlike awareness of his body that enables him to stay almost always straight up and down in the air. He's the state of the art in diving." Virtually unchallenged on the springboard, Louganis has taken first place in every major national and international event since 1981, often by a wide margin of victory. In the 1982 World Aquatic Championships in Guayaquil, Ecuador, for example, he won by a staggering 116 points. As if to confirm his preeminence in the sport, on his way to the platform title at the same meet he racked up tens across the board for his execution of an inward one-and-one-half somersault. He was the first diver in history to earn a perfect score from all seven judges in an international competition.

Perhaps because he views diving as an art form and considers himself to be more of a performer than a competitor, Louganis seems to be motivated more by the artist's constant quest for perfection than by the combative "killer instinct" of the world-class athlete. "I suppose it's possible that you can improve some way—positioning, height, strength," he said recently, as quoted by John Husar in a Chicago Tribune (April 15, 1984) profile. "So it pushes you. You have to have someone or something pushing you." Over the past several years, at least on the platform, that "someone" has been Bruce Kimball, an apparently fearless diver with an unusually clean, almost splashless entry that invariably earns him high marks from the judges. "It's kind of unnerving, the way Bruce disappears on his entries," Louganis told Lawrie Mifflin. "He's pulling nine-and-a-halfs and tens, and I had to find an edge to keep ahead of him."

In national and international diving competitions, seven judges rate each entrant's execution of a specified number of required and optional dives on a scale of one to ten, considering his approach, takeoff, action in midair, and entry. The diver's point total for each dive is calculated by dividing the judges' scores, minus the highest and lowest ratings, by three-fifths and then multiplying the result by the so-called degree of difficulty (ranging from 1.3 to 3.5) of the dive. Louganis, the self-described "biggest chicken in [his] sport," has managed to maintain an edge over Kimball by adding to his competitive repertory dives with higher degrees of difficulty, such as a back three-and-a-half somersault in the tuck position, which has a difficulty factor of 3.3.

Louganis unveiled some of his new dives at the National AAU Indoor Diving Championships in April 1983, but because he was not yet in full control of them, Kimball prevailed. A month later, at the Fédération Internationale de Natation Amateur (FINA) Diving World Cup competition, it was a different story, as Louganis came from behind on his last dive—a reverse three-and-one-half somersault tuck worth 3.4 on the difficulty scale—to take the cup by 4.11 points. When the two men met again later in the year at the Pan American Games in Caracas, Venezuela, they traded the lead until the final dive. Out in front by only 16.92 points, Louganis tossed off a nearly perfect reverse three-and-a-half, earning five nines, a ten, and an eight from the judges for a score of 91.80 points—one of the highest totals ever recorded for a single dive. It was more than enough to put him safely out of Kimball's reach.

As the reigning platform and springboard world champion, Louganis went into the 1984 Olympic Summer Games in Los Angeles, California under enormous pressure. "[The judges] have seen probably the best dives that I've ever done in my entire life," he explained to John Husar. "Now they want to see something better. They don't want to see the same dives because their expectations are higher." Despite his misgivings, Louganis simply overwhelmed the opposition in the Olympic springboard competition, surpassing the second-place finisher, Tan Liangde of the People's Republic of China, by an astonishing 92.10 points.

Two days later, in the Olympic platform preliminaries, Louganis turned in six nearly flawless optional dives to roll up a world best total point effort of 688.05. His superlative showing in the qualifying contest, which earned him the right to dive last in the final, set the stage for a dramatic conclusion to the medal round. Second to teammate Bruce Kimball after the compulsory dives, Louganis came into his own in the optional dives portion of the event. Having edged into the lead with a score of 91.20 for his execution of a three-and-a-half somersault tuck, he had the chance, with his tenth and final dive, to become the first diver to exceed 700 points in the history of the sport. "I was scared going into the last dive . . . ," he admitted afterwards, as quoted in the *New York Times* (August 13, 1984). "You're up there thirty-three feet above the water, with not a whole lot on, and seven people judging you, and it's a very vulnerable position. You've got to have a lot of confidence in yourself." While waiting his turn on the platform, he psyched himself up, as he customarily does, by singing the song "Believe In Yourself" from the musical *The Wiz*. Stepping to the edge of the platform, he leapt high into the air, curled his body into a tight ball, spun through three-and-a-half somersaults, straightened, and arrowed into the water. The judges awarded him a score of 92.82, making his total for the platform competition an unprecedented 710.91. Kimball, in the best showing of his career, came in second, nearly seventy points behind.

Favored with the ideal build for a diver, Greg Louganis stands five feet nine inches tall and weighs a lithe and muscular 160 pounds. His uncommonly low percentage of body fat (it was recently measured at 7 percent) is comparable to that of a world-class sprinter. Perhaps his sole physical defect is a slight bowleggedness, but he has characteristically turned that flaw to his advantage: while spinning in the pike position, he "spots" the water through his legs. A soft-spoken and shy man, Louganis is, by his own admission, "not a social person," and he prefers to spend his free time with close friends or at his apartment near Mission Viejo. "There are other things outside diving," he told Lawrie Mifflin. "Relationships, friendships. Quality friendships, not just going to meets and bumming around with people because you're there. A lot of people get very one-dimensional in competitive sports, and three years ago, I was in the same boat. If you'd asked me what I would do when I stopped diving, I'd have been lost. I would have really floundered. Now, I'm actually looking forward to my retirement from diving." He recently signed with the William Morris Agency and has announced that he will pursue a career in acting.

References: *Chicago Tribune* IV p4 Ap 15 '84 pors; *Los Angeles Times* III p1+ Ja 10 '84 pors; *N Y Times* C p1+ Jl 11 '83 pors; *Sports Illus*

54:32+ My 11 '81 pors, 58:60+ My 9 '83 pors, 59:10+ Ag 29 '83 pors

Lustiger, Jean-Marie
(lü´´stē-zhä´)

Sept. 17, 1926– Roman Catholic prelate. Address: Maison diocéine, 8 rue de la Ville-l'Evêque, 75008 Paris, France

Jean-Marie Cardinal Lustiger, the Archbishop of Paris, a convert to Catholicism, resents being regarded as an ecclesiastical "exhibition," but there is no gainsaying his anomalous position in ecumenical history: he, the ranking Roman Catholic churchman in France, was, in his words, as quoted in *Time* (February 16, 1981), "born Jewish and will remain so, even if that is unacceptable to some." Consecrated a bishop (of Orléans) in 1979, Lustiger was appointed Archbishop of Paris by Pope John Paul II in 1981 and elevated to the cardinalate the following year. Like the Pope, Cardinal Lustiger, though French-born, is of Polish extraction, and in matters of faith and morals as well as style he is a man after the Pontiff's own heart—a staunch traditionalist who is open to and adept at discourse with religious dissenters and secular humanists.

Intellectually and politically, Lustiger's conservatism combines with a socialist (albeit non-Marxist and anti-Soviet) orientation, creating a point of view that defies easy classification. He himself describes his world view as that of "a modern man" who addresses issues in terms of "reality," not "ideology." Georges Suffert, a French magazine editor who is an old friend of Lustiger's, when interviewed by John Vinocur, the *New York*

Times's bureau chief in Paris, in 1983 pointed out that the Cardinal's real singularity is that in an age of unbelief "he believes in God." Lustiger favors a greater role for lay people, both men and women, in the church. While opposing the ordination of women and married men as priests, he advocates the admission of married men to the deaconate to alleviate the shortage of priests.

The son of Charles and Gisèle Lustiger, nonpracticing Jews who had emigrated from Poland, Jean-Marie Lustiger was born Aaron Lustiger on September 17, 1926 in Paris, where his parents ran a small textile business. The process of his conversion to Christianity dates from the day in 1937 when, as a ten-year-old, he surreptitiously unlocked a forbidden cabinet in the family library and discovered a Protestant Bible. Partly because he considers it a private matter and partly because the subject has proved to be a sensitive one for some Jews, he now avoids public discussion of his conversion, or, as he views it, his religious "crystalization." He dealt with the subject at length on only one occasion, an interview with two editors of the Israeli newspaper *Yediot Ahronot* that he considers definitive. "There was this interior road," he explained, "and at the end was the figure of Christ as the Messiah and a figure of the Jewish people—that was the key to my thinking." He went on to tell the Israeli editors that his deepest wish was twofold: "that the Christians don't forget they were grafted onto a single root . . . Israel" and that "Judaism could perhaps recognize in Christianity a consanguinity given by God."

Lustiger recalled how he tried to explain his conversion to his parents, who "seemed" to find it "revolting": "I told them, 'I am not leaving you. I am not passing into the enemy camp. I'm becoming what I am. I am not stopping being a Jew—just the opposite. I'm discovering a way of living it.' I know that's scandalous for some Jews to hear. . . . But I lived it." His parents finally accepted his conversion in 1940 when the Nazis occupied France and the conversion became, in their eyes, a means of survival. "For me, no," Lustiger told the editors of *Yediot Ahronot*. "It was something else." Sent to live with a Roman Catholic family in Orléans, Lustiger was baptized there on August 25, 1940, taking the Christian name Jean-Marie. (Although he includes the name Aaron on legal documents, such as his passport, only his baptismal name appears on church records.) Later, his sister, Arlette, followed him into the Catholic church.

Back in Paris, Lustiger's father survived the Nazi pogrom by going underground. (He died in 1982.) His mother, who tried to keep the family business going, was arrested and deported back to Poland, where she died in the death camp at Auschwitz in 1943. While acknowledging that the Catholic hierarchy might have done more to stop or impede the Holocaust, Lustiger, as quoted by John Vinocur in the *New York Times Magazine* (March 20, 1983), maintains that it is "cheap" to hold the church culpable when the real issue, in his view, was, and remains, the breakdown of European spiritual values.

Following his graduation from a lycée in Orléans, Lustiger worked in a factory in Decazeville for a year. Already drawn to the priesthood, he wanted to begin his religious studies as soon as France was liberated, but out of deference to the wishes of his father he first studied literature at the University of Paris instead. During the course of his secular studies, he was active in the Jeunesse Etudiantes Chretiennes (Young Christian Students) movement. Finally entering the Carmelite Seminary in Paris after the war in 1946, he took degrees in philosophy and theology at the Institut Catholique de Paris and was ordained a priest on April 17, 1954.

For fifteen years following his ordination Lustiger was Catholic chaplain at the University of Paris, and during his chaplaincy he regularly led student pilgrimages to the Holy Land and to Rome. In 1963 he wrote what he later described as an "insolent" letter to Pope John XXIII, which led to an intense student audience with the Pope. According to John Vinocur in his *New York Times Magazine* article, that Vatican visit of Lustiger and his students "became a small legend because the dying Pontiff is said to have asked about the students on his deathbed."

From 1969 to 1979 Lustiger was assigned to the parish of Ste. Jeanne de Chantal in Paris. Toward the end of his tenure as a parish priest, Lustiger underwent a *crise de foi*, or crisis of faith, as he later recounted to a reporter for the Jewish Telegraphic Service. In that crisis, he said, he was considering leaving France for Israel. "I began to learn Hebrew, by myself, with cassette tapes. Does that seem absurd, making your *aliyah* [a Jew's return to his ancestral land]? At that time I thought that I had finished what I had to do here, that I was at a crossroads, and that one of the possibilities was to be in Israel. I didn't have any precise plans. I thought I could find my place there."

Meanwhile Lustiger's work as a parish priest had not gone unnoticed by Paolo Cardinal Bertoli, then the papal nuncio in Paris. After becoming Pope John Paul II's chamberlain in 1978, Bertoli recommended Lustiger to the Pope as an ecclesiastic in the Pontiff's own grain: a modern intellectual, able to hold his own in debate with secular humanists and their fellow travelers within the church while remaining firmly inimical to the further erosion of ecclesiastical faith and discipline. Like the Pope, Lustiger viewed the community of true believers as a minority in the world, but a sanguine minority, representing not the sunset of Christianity but its new dawn. In 1979 the Pope was looking for a calmative successor to Bishop Guy Riobé of Orléans, who had stirred unrest in the diocese by his championing of a married clergy and his activism against the buildup of nuclear weapons in Europe. John Paul settled on Lustiger, in whom he would not be disappointed.

Lustiger's first major act after his episcopal consecration on December 8, 1979 was a letter to the priests of the Orléans diocese supporting the Pope's conservative position regarding an exclusively male clergy. During his tenure in Orléans, the enrollment in the diocesan seminary doubled, at a time of diminishing priestly vocations in France generally. After a terrorist bomb killed four people outside a synagogue on Rue Copernic in Paris in the fall of 1980, Lustiger wrote a long article for the weekly *Le Nouvel Observateur* reminding Christians that Jesus was a Jew and that anti-Semitism is a betrayal of their Lord.

When Pope John Paul II named him to succeed the aging François Cardinal Marty as Archbishop of Paris in February 1981, it was to Lustiger "as if all of a sudden the crucifix began to wear a yellow star." The day after his nomination he told the reporter for the Jewish Telegraphic Service: "I've always considered myself a Jew, even if that's not the opinion of some rabbis. . . . For me, the vocation of Israel is bringing light to the *goyim*. That's my hope and I believe that Christianity is the means for achieving it. I think that in being a disciple of Christ in my way, I enter into God's design, a part of a promise made good." As quoted in *Newsweek* (February 16, 1981), he also talked about France's spiritual crisis, which "other nations cannot understand": "We have gone through paganism, libertinism, rationalism, [Marxist] socialism—all of them opposed to Christianity. It is not surprising we are a divided people."

Lustiger's straddling of Judaism and Christianity drew criticism from French conservatives of both faiths. Father Noël Barbera, a leader of the right-wing Catholic movement in France that had been headed by Archbishop Marcel Lefebvre before Lefebvre's apostasy, told John Vinocur, "The fact that he is a Jew doesn't bother me because I'm not a racist. But what upsets me is someone who says, 'I'm a Jew and I intend to remain one.' The Apostles broke with the synagogue." Michael Williams, the rabbi at the synagogue on Rue Copernic where the terrorist bombing occurred in 1980, took a more moderate view: "Morally he [Lustiger] is most certainly not a Jew, and yet he is obviously a sensitive, intelligent man who . . . has a great understanding and affection for it [the Jewish world]." Meyer Jais, the former chief rabbi of Paris, said: "The faith of Israel and the Christian faith are not reconcilable. To claim both is to sentence yourself to live in a perpetual denial of one and the other."

In addition to his pastorship of the Archdiocese of Paris, Lustiger is the ordinary for Eastern Rite faithful without ordinaries. (An ordinary is a prelate who has official jurisdiction over the public welfare in a specified territory.) In the Roman Curia he is a member of the Council for the Public Affairs of the Church, which handles the Vatican's relations with civil governments, and of two congregations, those concerned with the worldwide episcopate and with sacraments and divine worship. When Lustiger was made archbishop, one Curia member was quoted in the *Time* report as grousing, "Is the Pope going to pack the episcopate with Poles?" When he became a cardinal, the Curia's ultraconservative faction was markedly reticent regarding his selection, concerned as it was

about his "newness in the Roman Catholic tradition." According to John Vinocur, those feelings have "given way to expressions suggesting he was not only an interesting choice, but an intelligent one."

In talking to Vinocur, Cardinal Lustiger pushed aside the *Times*'s Paris bureau chief's attempts to classify him intellectually and politically. "You're confusing a modern man with an American liberal," he said. "An American liberal isn't necessarily a modern man. The essential role of people who think is being able to reflect, and, precisely, not to give in to whatever waves are rising." While he deplores the pouring of social resources into nuclear weapons, he went on to say he considers the advocacy by American clergymen of unilateral disarmament "excessive" and "presumptuous." "What's being proposed is turning a country into a prophetic subject. If it's Belgium or Holland or Switzerland, O.K., perhaps, because they risk nothing, and in any case, they don't take care of their own defense no matter what happens. But if the prophetic subject is the United States, you've got to think twice. A whole people has got to want it . . . and not by a feeling of fear or defeat, but by a positive choice. The whole nation has to be ready to offer itself as a martyr, and who's ready for that?"

Regarding the West's feeling of guilt about the third world, Lustiger told Vinocur that he considered the feeling justified in view of the "super-rich" position of the advanced industrialized countries. But he went on to reject "gigantic, almost mythic explanations," such as the multinational conspiracy theory, which he views as inflated, more "ideological" than "real." Ideologies, as he sees them, produce not solutions to world problems, but "messianic subjects." "And if the messianic subject is called '*ein Volk, ein Reich*,' or when it's called the proletariat, that's very dangerous. Even when it's called the third world." The root problem, as he sees it, is the breakdown of religious values. "The West is born of Christianity, and the crisis of the West is that it isn't Christian anymore. Period. The West was born of Christianity, and that's the whole story." At a rally of Catholics demonstrating in defense of church schools in April 1984, Lustiger stressed compromise with the government, but the following month he publicly objected to the government's plan to require private-school teachers to be civil servants.

A stocky, ruddy man, robust but tending to short-windedness, Jean-Marie Cardinal Lustiger wears not a heavy pectoral cross, but a small silver one designed by a sculptor he knows. Working six days a week—he spends Thursdays at a Jesuit retreat house—he drives his Peugot from his residence to his cathedral, Notre Dame, and to masses, catechism classes, and other gatherings at the 105 parishes under his jurisdiction. John Vinocur, who accompanied him on his itinerary, quoted his most salient message as, "As things stand now, to say you believe Jesus is the son of God is going to become an enormous act of courage for little kids. That's the situation we're in."

French television viewers are well acquainted with the intelligence, clarity and sense of conviction that Lustiger conveys on the public platform. Privately, he is quick and somewhat intransigent in decision-making, more interested in human contact than paper work, and unusually retentive in remembering the many people he meets. According to Robert Sole in *Le Monde* (April 19, 1984), he can be "impatient" in his hyperactivity, "curt and on occasion cutting" in his manner, "caustic" in his humor, and "somewhat risqué" in his language. Not a conspicuous ascetic, the Archbishop enjoys gourmet meals, including good wine, when he returns to his residence in the evening. One of his regrets is that his busy schedule leaves him little time for reading and listening to music. Sermons by Lustiger were collected in *Sermons d'un curé de Paris* (1978). The Archbishop has also written *Pain de vie, Peuple de Dieu* (1981).

References: N Y Times p4 F 2 '81, p1+ Ja 6 '82 por; N Y Times Mag p29 Mr 20 '83 pors; Newsweek 97:57 F 16 '81 por; Time 117:77 F 16 '81 por; U S News 94:14 Ja 17 '83; International Who's Who, 1984-85; National Catholic Almanac, 1983

© 1984 Fred W. McDarrugh

MacDermot, Galt

1928- Composer. Address: b. c/o RCA Records, 1133 Ave. of the Americas, New York City, N.Y. 10022

The Canadian-born composer Galt MacDermot, a white musician strongly influenced by African rhythms, has written thirteen musicals, ranging from the reggae score for Derek Walcott's *The Charlatan* to the music for five Broadway shows. Among the latter were the innovative *Hair*, the first pop-rock musical, which had a Broadway run of 1,750 performances beginning in 1968 and became a worldwide stage and recording sensation; the more quietly successful *Two Gentlemen of Verona* (1971-72), originally scored for the New York Shakespeare Festival; and *The Human Comedy* (1984), a short-lived musical version of William Saroyan's screenplay and novel. Outside of his work for the stage, most of MacDermot's creative energy goes into instrumental compositions, especially those for his own combo, the New Pulse Jazz Band.

Of Protestant Irish descent, Galt MacDermot was born in Montreal, Canada in 1928 to Terence W. L. MacDermot, an educator and diplomat, and Elizabeth (Savage) MacDermot. Previously assistant professor of history at McGill University and principal and teacher of history at Upper Canada College, a Montreal secondary school, Terence W. L. MacDermot joined the Canadian Department of External Affairs in 1944. He was high commissioner to South Africa from 1950 to 1954, ambassador to Greece and Israel from 1954 to 1957, and high commissioner to Australia from 1957 to 1961.

Music pervaded the MacDermot home. Terence W. L. MacDermot played the piano mornings before going off to his university and high school duties, and Mrs. MacDermot was interested in dance. Galt MacDermot was a young child when he learned to play, first, the violin and, then, the piano, but he did not become obsessed with music until, when he was fifteen or sixteen, he discovered the boogie woogie and jazz of Pete Johnson, Duke Ellington, and Meade Lux Lewis. When he moved to South Africa with his family he enrolled at the University of Capetown, and he took a B.A. degree in music composition and organ there.

The education that "turned him completely around," however, was that which he picked up in the black African neighborhoods. "They'd be playing what was really rock and roll," he recounted to Robert Berkvist in an interview for the *New York Times* (May 11, 1969). "What they called *quaylas*—like a South African version of High Life—very characteristic beat, very similar to rock. Much deeper, though, much more to it. It's just got a fantastic feel to it. Africans, when they get a beat going, it's just something. You don't hear it anywhere else." While in South Africa he tried his hand at writing opera. One of his efforts was based on an African folk tale, another on Joyce Cary's novel *Mister Johnson* and a third on H. G. Wells's short story "The Country of the Blind."

Having married in South Africa, MacDermot returned to Montreal with his Dutch-born wife, Marlene, a clarinetist, in 1954. For seven years he was employed by the Westmount Baptist Church in

Montreal as organist and choirmaster; weekends, he played piano with a jazz trio. In 1961 he moved with his growing family to England, where a jazz composition of his, "African Waltz," recorded by Johnny Dankworth, had become a best-seller. Released in the United States on the Roulette label in 1961, "African Waltz" won Grammy awards in two categories, best original jazz composition and best instrumental theme or instrumental version of a song. During the two-and-a-half years he spent in London, MacDermot supported himself and his family by playing piano.

From England, the MacDermots came to the United States. Settling in New York City, they bought a house on Staten Island, where they still live. For several years MacDermot supported himself and his family by making demonstration records for music publishers, all the while hankering to write a stage show.

In 1967 one of the music publishers, Nat Shapiro, introduced MacDermot to Gerome Ragni and James Rado, two actors who had written the book and lyrics for a musical and were looking for someone to write the music. Joseph Papp, the head of the New York Shakespeare Festival, had shown interest in their script, which was about the hippie "flower children," the flourishing counterculture of the time, typified by a sexually liberated lifestyle, a celebration of psychedelic drugs, and a message of "peace" and "love" in addition to unleashed hairiness and unconventional dress. Unlike Ragni and Rado, who were, in MacDermot's words, "into the hippie thing," he "didn't even know about it." But "there was something nice" about the script, and he found it "amusing," not "boring the way most scripts are." With delight, he took the book home, sat down at his piano, and began to turn the lyrics into the songs that would become Hair.

The songs came easily, according to MacDermot, because the lyrics, and their rhythms, were "so natural." "This was my kind of music," he told Betty Flynn of the Chicago Tribune in an interview datelined October 4, 1968. "I never really wrote straight jazz, and I hated Broadway. I was always a pop-rock writer, and now everything started to come together. The hymn-type music, the folk music I had heard in Africa."

The only song that gave MacDermot any trouble was "Aquarius," which "took a little while" because his "original setting was a little stiff and they didn't like it." Nevertheless, "Aquarius" turned out to be one of his personal favorites among the songs in Hair. He also particularly liked "Good Morning, Star Shine" and "What a Piece of Work is Man." The best song of all, in his opinion, was part of the war sequence "Ripped Open by a Metal Explosion."

Hair was first produced Off Broadway, at the New York Shakespeare Festival's Public Theatre, in the fall of 1967. There, it attracted the producer Michael Butler, who moved it first to the Cheetah, a midtown Manhattan discotheque, and finally to the Biltmore Theatre on Broadway. En route, it was constantly revised. "If we stopped with what we had at Cheetah," MacDermot told Blaik Kirby of the Toronto Globe and Mail (September 27, 1969), "you wouldn't have heard much more about it. It was a more conventional musical, and putting it on wasn't much fun. By the time we got to Broadway, it was just like a picnic."

The revisions made in Hair along the way to the Biltmore included the elimination of most of the original book, so that the show moved from one song to the next in the operatic manner that MacDermot prefers to the Broadway musical theatre's traditional reliance on nonmusical links. The result was a dynamic, impressionistic "tribal" portrait, set in a junkyard hippie commune and sympathetically limning the Dionysian values and rituals of the shaggy, barefoot, rag-tag communards—"turned-on, tuned-in" dropouts from middle-class American society. The portrait was more a frenetic, haphazard "happening" than a story, although a plot of sorts emerged in the plight of one of the long-haired characters, Claude (played by James Rado), a member of a menage a trois (the other members of which were played by Gerome Ragni and Lynn Kellogg). In the plot's dénouement, a shorn, uniformed Claude is, in spite of his opposition to the war, on his way to Vietnam—an outcome lamented by the disheveled tribe he leaves behind as they hold hands all around in the show's antipatriotic finale.

Under Tom O'Horgan's direction, Hair opened at the Biltmore on April 29, 1968. (On opening night—and for a month thereafter—MacDermot was in the pit, playing piano with the band. "It was my kick to play with them," he later said.) The show was an immediate smash hit critically as well as commercially, eliciting predictions that it would revolutionize the Broadway musical with its multisensual theatricalization of rock music.

The New York critics hailed it as a "joyous" "hippie Hellzapoppin" thrumming "with vitality," a show "fresh" and "unassuming even its pretensions," with the season's "best" and "most varied" score, one that "precisely serves its purpose." Brendan Gill of the New Yorker (May 11, 1968) considered Hair an "exhilaratingly frantic jumble," more medium than message, but he was unable not to "consent to this merry mind-blowing exercise in gibberish." Jack Kroll of Newsweek (May 13, 1968), who had described the Off-Broadway production as "a vivid uproar that has more wit, feeling, and musicality than anything since West Side Story," thought that something had "been lost" in the "fantastically convoluted patterns" the show accrued in its trek uptown but that there was "no denying the sheer kinetic drive of this new Hair." The reviewer for Time (May 10, 1968), wrote: "What holds it together is the score, which pulses with an insistent, primitive beat. With gleeful impertinence, the music...and the lyrics... release the pent-up yelps of the sons and daughters of the affluent society."

Going into its second season in September 1969, the Broadway production of Hair had grossed almost $4 million. Los Angeles and London productions had grossed more than $2 million each, and later productions opened to big advances in Chicago, San Francisco, and Toronto. Abroad, the show did as well at box offices in Munich, Stockholm, Copenhagen, Sydney, Paris, Tokyo, and Rio de Janeiro. In addition to the box-office proceeds, large sums came in from records and film rights.

Recordings of "Aquarius," "Good Morning, Star Shine," "Hair," and "Ain't Got No" swept the pop charts, and the original Broadway cast album of *Hair* (RCA Victor) won the Grammy award for best Broadway-show LP of 1968. But by the time Milos Forman's motion-picture version of *Hair* was released, in 1979, the celebration of the 1960s as the dawning of the age of Aquarius had become what critics called a "period musical," with a blunted impact on post-Vietnam audiences. Stage revivals of *Hair* suffered the same fate. When the show returned to the Biltmore Theatre for seventy-nine preview performances and fifteen regular-run performances in the fall of 1977, critics described it as an "artifact" from a "lost youth culture" and a "notion whose time has gone," because "many a '60s rebel has discovered that iconoclasm, graffiti, drugs, and sloganeering were not the answer to pollution, confusion, and the bomb." The show's "single saving grace" was MacDermot's music, with its "resilient, tuneful tenacity."

"Although many theatrical elements that were original with *Hair* have since been absorbed by Broadway," Marilyn Stasio wrote in *Cue* (November 11, 1977), "this revival reminds us how distinctive and vital the real thing was. . . . For all its enthusiastic adoption of such *Hair* hallmarks as nudity, strong language, and total-theatre staging, Broadway never did manage to recapture the show's biggest contribution—its electrifying presentation of the rock musical idiom. Hearing Galt MacDermot's music again certainly recharges one's musical batteries, and also stirs up regrets for the revolution it promised but never delivered."

Meanwhile, MacDermot had written several liturgical pieces, including the masses "Take This Bread" (1971) and "Mass in Our Time" (1975); the music for a 1969 New York Shakespeare Festival production of *Twelfth Night*; and, in the early 1970s, two London flops, two Broadway flops, and a Broadway success. The London stage failures were *Isabel's a Jezebel*, a 1970 rock opera ending tragically, with, in MacDermot's words, "an abortion, the murder of a child," and *Who the Murderer Was*. The Broadway hit was *Two Gentlemen of Verona*, a free-form musical adaptation of Shakespeare's play on which MacDermot collaborated with lyricist John Guare and librettist Mel Shapiro. Produced by Joseph Papp and directed by Shapiro, *Two Gentlemen of Verona* won a Tony award in its pre-Broadway run at the New York Shakespeare Festival, in the summer of 1971, and a New York Drama Critics Circle award after it moved to the St. James Theatre, the following December. The Broadway flops, both produced in 1972, were *Dude*, a confused and confusing religious allegory, with book and lyrics by Gerome Ragni, and *Via*

Galactica, a futuristic opera about an outer-space colonial revolution, with book by Christopher Gore and lyrics by Gore and Judith Ross.

Temporarily withdrawing from theatrical work, MacDermot concentrated on writing instrumental music, especially for his own group, eventually named the New Pulse Jazz Band, which began as a family ensemble that played his tone poems at home on Staten Island in the mid-1970s. His twin daughters Iolanthe and Sarah, then eleven years old, played flute; his daughter Elizabeth, fifteen, played alto saxophone; his son, Vincent, nineteen, played trombone; his wife, Marlene, played clarinet; and he played piano. Later Vincent took over the band and revamped it, bringing in a professional trumpet player and several woodwind players to replace the other family members.

"I like music with a pulse," MacDermot explained to John S. Wilson of the *New York Times* (May 8, 1981). "I've always been an Ellington fan. I'd been influenced by West Indian music, and Larry Marshall, a singer, has called my music 'pulse music.' But the name New Pulse Jazz Band actually came from the fact that two of the musicians in the band are from New Paltz, New York." The New Pulse Jazz Band made its public debut in a concert given by the singer Nell Carter in 1979. It performed at the annual "All Nite Soul" program at St. Peter's Lutheran Church in the Citicorp Building in Manhattan in 1980, and it was part of "An Evening of New Music by Galt MacDermot" at Symphony Space, another Manhattan location, in 1981. The evening included "O Babylon," a reggae musical written by MacDermot to the words of a play by the Caribbean poet Derek Walcott.

"MacDermot's music for his band can be related to Alec Wilder's light and witty octets, which Mr. MacDermot said he has never heard, or the work of the Raymond Scott Quintet in the 1940's," John S. Wilson observed. "It developed out of compositions he was writing for a wind quintet. That, he remembered, started him writing for a bass with four horns over it." MacDermot told Wilson that writing for the New Pulse Jazz Band was a new experience for him: "I write very quickly when I write songs, setting a lyric to music. But these instrumental things take more time than anything I've ever done. When you're writing a show, you're following words. But here, there's nothing but musical ideas. I'm trying to take several strains and 'jam' with them to create something that holds your interest for three or four minutes."

Returning to the theatre, MacDermot, in collaboration with librettist William Dumaresq, wrote *The Human Comedy*, an operatic musical based on William Saroyan's sentimental screenplay and novel about smalltown homefront life during World War II. First produced at the New York Shakespeare Festival's Public-Anspacher Theatre beginning in December 1983, *The Human Comedy* began its brief Broadway run at the Royale Theatre on April 5, 1984. Reviewing the Off-Broadway production in *New York* (January 9, 1984), John Simon, while faulting Dumaresq's lyrics ("not in

MacDermot's but, rather, in Saroyan's league"), rated MacDermot's music as coming "closest to matching that" of *Hair*. "The music, especially when purely orchestral," Simon wrote, "actually surpasses that of *Hair*, managing to be unlike anybody else's without sacrificing melodiousness. Moreover, it is inventively orchestrated by the composer, and handsomely played by a dozen knowing musicians." In his review of the Broadway production for *Newsday* (April 6, 1984), Allan Wallach described it as a "gentle pop-folk opera" with a "sweetness" flowing from MacDermot's "lovely" score, "a clear stream of melody." "Drawing upon various kinds of American music, from hymns to 1940s pop, MacDermot has composed music that intensifies the uncomplicated feelings."

In recent years MacDermot has rejected many Broadway scripts, most of which, in his words, "sound like they were written in the '30s by men in their '80s," and "'80s orchestrations in the '30s theatres don't work." "Broadway musicals are not to my taste," MacDermot told Blaik Kirby of the *Toronto Globe and Mail*. "I'm into folk music and jazz and African music—into rhythm generally, whereas Broadway is not that. It's pretty schmaltzy. To achieve feeling by rhythm takes work." For MacDermot, "the play's the thing" and the composer is the "servant of the librettist." He likes "setting the words of another person's life, which is like painting a picture—you wouldn't paint a picture of yourself over and over." On the other hand, as he told Betty Flynn of the *Chicago Tribune*, he wants the "whole show sung, or at least motivated by music" because he "always gets bored when the talk starts."

Galt MacDermot is of medium height and has blue eyes, graying brown hair, a soft voice, and a gentle, unpretentious manner. With his family, he lives in the modest wooden house he bought on Staten Island in 1964. One of his masses was written for his local church, St. Mary's Episcopal. So as not to disturb his family, MacDermot has bought a second house, next door to his home, where he plays his piano and does his work. Most of his music is written mornings, between nine o'clock and noon. Treasuring anonymity, he shuns publicity that might disturb his quiet life as a Staten Island local, and he enjoys playing the piano inconspicuously in some of the borough's hideaway night spots. In classical music MacDermot is partial to "guys like Stravinsky, Haydn, and Beethoven."

References: N Y Post p15 S 9 '72 pors; N Y Times II p1+ My 11 '69, C p4 My 8 '81 por; Newsday II p3 Ap 8 por; Toronto Globe and Mail p9 S 27 '69 por, p10 Ja 22 '73 por; Washington Post p9 O 6 '69

Machel, Samora Moises
(mä-shel´)

Sept. 29, 1933– President of the People's Republic of Mozambique. Address: b. Office of the President, Maputo, Mozambique

Determined to bring about the revolutionary transformation of the People's Republic of Mozambique and to make it the first genuinely Marxist state in Africa, Samora Moises Machel is serving concurrently as the president of its government and of its one political party. Before taking over the reins of political authority, Machel commanded Mozambique's guerrilla fighters in a war of liberation that lasted for a decade. Although he has softpedaled his ideology and made compromises when necessary in order to achieve the goals he has set for his backward, impoverished, and divided country, he remains committed to the basic principles of his long-term political program, which has already achieved the integration of the top leadership of both the party and the state apparatus.

Samora Moises Machel was born on September 29, 1933 in the village of Chilembene (sometimes spelled Xilembene) in the fertile Limpopo Valley of Gaza Province in southern Mozambique. A member of the Shangana subgroup of the Tsonga, the second-largest of the country's ten ethnic groups, he comes from a peasant family whose

holding was expropriated by the colonial government in the early 1950s as part of a program to make farmland available to white settlers from Portugal.

Machel's memories of his childhood under the Portuguese colonial regime are uniformly bitter.

His parents' ability to eke out a living from the soil was hampered by governmental regulations requiring them to grow cotton rather than food crops for their own sustenance and to sell their produce at arbitrarily low prices. In order to ward off starvation his older brother and many other relatives were forced to work as contract laborers in the Witwatersrand mining and industrial region of South Africa under conditions verging on slavery. When his brother died in a mining accident his parents received only a pittance in compensation, and several other members of his family were also killed or seriously injured.

Despite the grinding poverty and oppression of his early years, Machel took pride in the fact that his grandparents and great-grandparents had fought against the Portuguese in the nineteenth century. His paternal grandfather had been a troop commander in the army of Gungunhana (sometimes spelled Maguiguana), a Shangana chieftain who dominated much of southern Mozambique until his defeat in November 1895. His maternal grandparents, because of their resistance activities, were exiled to Angola and then to São Tomé e Príncipe.

Machel was raised as a Presbyterian, but because the only educational opportunities available to Mozambicans in the colonial period were to be found in Roman Catholic mission schools, he had himself baptized as a Catholic to qualify for admission. Life at the mission, where he had to toil in the fields when not attending classes, was far from idyllic, and he once recalled for an interviewer from the London Observer (March 28, 1976) that the "white priests used to say that God was white and that blacks did not go to heaven when they died." But his teachers apparently recognized his ability and tried to cultivate it, for when he completed the six years of the primary grades they sought to persuade him to enter a seminary for further study.

Machel refused, however, and found himself a job instead, using his earnings to pay for a nursing course that he attended nights. He then became a nurse and later a medical assistant at the Miguel Bombarda Hospital in Maputo (formerly Lourenço Marques), the capital city of Mozambique. The hospital post, where he was paid less than whites for the same work, played an important role in raising his political consciousness, for it made him painfully aware, as he later told a British reporter, that in Mozambique "the rich man's dog gets more in the way of vaccination, medicine, and medical care than do the workers upon whom the rich man's wealth is built." In the context of the social stratification of Mozambique in the colonial period, when virtually all of the African populace was illiterate and few jobs above the menial level were open to nonwhites, it also made him a member of the country's tiny but potentially influential urban black elite.

In the late 1950s the Portuguese regime stepped up its already repressive security measures in response to an upsurge in anticolonialist feeling that had been stimulated by events in Algeria, Indochina, and the Congo, and later by the outbreak of an armed revolt in Portuguese Angola in 1961. As a result several nationalist groups coalesced among Mozambican expatriates living in other African countries. None of those groups amounted to very much at first, but in June 1962 they merged into a single organization, the Front for the Liberation of Mozambique (Frente de Libertação de Moçambique), known as FRELIMO. Their leader was Eduardo Chivambu Mondlane, a Mozambican intellectual émigré who is usually but incorrectly described as a non-Marxist because he had personal ties to the West and stood for a policy of nonalignment.

In 1960, traveling without Portuguese interference because he held a United Nations passport, Mondlane made a fact-finding trip through Mozambique. It was apparently at that time that he and Machel first met, although some reports place the date of their meeting in 1961. The two men became close friends, and as a British reporter later remarked, "[Machel] observed the way the colonial system worked from inside a hospital; he learned what to do about it from Eduardo Mondlane." Adopting Mondlane's political philosophy, Machel cast his lot with FRELIMO when the new body was founded, and sometime in 1962 or early 1963 he left Mozambique for its headquarters in Dar es Salaam, the capital city of Tanzania.

Later in 1963 Machel was sent to Algeria for military training, and on his return to Tanzania he was appointed the head of FRELIMO's first military camp, charged with organizing a guerrilla force to fight the Portuguese. He also became one of the movement's chief tactical planners. In September 1964, when the Mozambique People's Liberation Forces (FPLM) began their armed struggle against the Portuguese by sending a raiding party of about 250 men across the Rovuma River into Cabo Delgado, Mozambique's northernmost province, Machel was in command and shortly afterward personally led the first major attack against a Portuguese army post. When the war spread to the adjacent Niassa Province in 1965, Machel took command of the forces in that region. Later in 1965 he organized FRELIMO's preparation center at Nichingwea, Tanzania, where FPLM cadres received their political and military training before serving, as his official biographical statement puts it, as "active agents for the transformation of society."

Unlike most black African leaders, during that period Machel spent most of his time in the field with his men, leading them in combat and sharing their dangers and hardships. In 1966 when Felipe Samuel Magaia, the secretary of FRELIMO's defense department, was assassinated, Machel replaced him, thus becoming a member of the party's central committee. Meanwhile, FRELIMO had gained control of large portions of the Mozambican interior as Portuguese forces pulled back to areas more easily defended against guerrilla incursions. In that "liberated zone," under his jurisdiction as defense secretary, Machel began to create the nucleus of a new social order, organizing people's committees to administer the civilian populace and rural farming cooperatives as a first step toward the ultimate goal of collectivizing agriculture. Ironically, he used the existing *aldeamentos*, or centralized villages, formerly condemned by FRELIMO as "concentration camps," which the Portuguese army had set up in order to cut off contacts between the rural peasantry and FRELIMO agents. Around the same time he accelerated the program of ideological indoctrination of FPLM personnel, assigning political commissars to all larger units and regional commands.

While fighting the Portuguese in the bush and struggling to win the hearts and minds of the peasants in the liberated zones, the members of FRELIMO were also waging a bitter and sometimes bloody ideological war behind the scenes. Even today the conflict is known only in the barest outlines because what little information is available is couched in opaque Marxist jargon. In any case, the dispute came to a head at FRELIMO's Second National Congress in 1969, the party's first convocation in Mozambique. Representing the FPLM and associated with the movement's most radical (i.e., Chinese-oriented) faction, Machel played a major role in the confrontation between what his official biographical statement refers to as "the revolutionary position" and "the reactionaries and new exploiters . . . [who] openly allied themselves with colonialism"—dissidents within the party, including pro-Western elements, moderates who sought a negotiated settlement with Portugal, Soviet-oriented Communists who opposed FRELIMO's tilt toward the Chinese, and ethnic and tribal factions.

The radical wing emerged victorious from the party congress, as reflected by the fact that Machel was appointed supreme commander of FRELIMO's armed forces even though he was a southerner and virtually all of the FPLM fighters, who until then had been commanded by one of their own, were Maconde warriors from the north. Although the radicals now dominated the FRELIMO apparatus, dissatisfaction was widespread and a wave of assassinations and counter-assassinations ensued.

The internecine war within FRELIMO culminated in February 1969 with the letter-bomb murder of Mondlane. The vacancy at the top was temporarily filled by its vice-president, Uria Simango, a Protestant minister, but in April 1969 the central committee decided to invest the party's leadership in a three-man directorate made up of Simango, Machel, and Marcelino dos Santos, FRELIMO's foremost political theoretician. Six months later Simango broke with the other two and was expelled from the party. He then joined a rival group based in Zambia. In May 1970, "after the desertion of the reactionaries," as the official biography puts it, the central committee elected Machel the president of FRELIMO, "thus acclaiming the triumph of the people's interests and positions."

Over the next few years the war in Mozambique widened its scope and increased its intensity, but from a military standpoint it had reached an impasse. Although FRELIMO dominated the country's interior, the Portuguese remained in firm control of the towns and coastal regions as well as the vital area around the huge Cabora Bassa dam and hydroelectric project on the Zambesi River in Tete Province. While each side was able to harry the other, neither could muster enough strength to win a decisive victory.

The key to victory, however, was not the military situation so much as the colonial power's will to fight, and Portugal, one of Western Europe's smallest and poorest countries, trying unsuccessfully to cope with revolts in both Mozambique and Angola, was being drained in a cause that few of its people were willing to support. Thus the issue was finally decided in Lisbon, the capital of Portugal, where on April 24, 1974, in a bloodless coup that was later dubbed "the happy revolution," military officers overthrew the existing regime and instituted a democratic government committed, as its first order of business, to ending its colonial conflicts.

Proclaiming their willingness to grant Mozambique its independence, the new rulers of Portugal called for a ceasefire to be followed by a referendum on the country's future. Although most political observers were convinced that the people of Mozambique would have overwhelmingly cast their ballots not only for independence but also for FRELIMO as their new government, Machel was unwilling to trust the matter to a vote and demanded immediate independence with no strings or conditions attached. Some sporadic fighting continued along with the negotiations, but in September 1974 the Portuguese yielded to Machel. A transitional government with a FRELIMO majority and a Portuguese minority was set up, and it was agreed that Mozambique would become independent as of June 25, 1975, the thirteenth anniversary of the founding of FRELIMO.

Reluctant to associate himself directly with the transitional government because of its cooperation with the former colonial authorities, Machel remained in Tanzania until the end of May 1975. Then, crossing the border at Mueda, he made a triumphal tour of Mozambique, arriving in Maputo around June 24. The next day, in a gala ceremony held in the city's football stadium, he officially proclaimed the People's Republic of Mozambique as an independent state "based on the alliance of the worker-peasants" and declared the nationalization of all land, economic enterprises, property, and public services, such as medicine and education. That night FRELIMO's central committee unanimously chose him as the new country's president, and on July 1 he selected and swore in his cabinet, formally known as the Council of Ministers. The fact that about half of its members were whites, Asians, or persons of mixed ancestry aroused some resentment but was tangible proof of Machel's frequent assertions that FRELIMO was class- rather than race-oriented and that opportunity was open to all who shared its philosophy and who merited advancement.

Despite the jubilation that attended the assumption of power by FRELIMO, the new state was ill-prepared for independence. In an address on July 1, 1975 Machel warned: "We need to be conscious of the great difficulty we shall face. In the phase of people's democracy in which we are now engaged as a phase of the Mozambican revolutionary process, our aim is to lay the material, ideological, administrative, and social foundations of the state."

Machel's government and party intend to establish a society governed by the principles of "scientific socialism" and to help eliminate white minority regimes in southern Africa. Both goals have posed perhaps insurmountable difficulties. Mozambicans were proud of their government's ability to help the independence movement in Southern Rhodesia during the final phases of the struggle that led to the birth of the new state of Zimbabwe, but their country's relationship with South Africa has been an ongoing source of embarrassing contradictions. Possessing almost no industry and producing few agricultural exports, Mozambique earns most of its foreign exchange from South Africa, serving as a transit link for the shipment of its goods, selling it electricity from Cabora Bassa, and, most painful of all, supplying large numbers of contract laborers under the agreement originally negotiated by the Portuguese. Unable to find a way out, Machel's government has had to follow the "pragmatic" course of restraining its opposition to the apartheid regime.

Pragmatic readjustment and ideological retreat have also characterized developments in regard to the country's other goals. Machel insists that he wants to make Mozambique "the first fully Marxist state in Africa." Originally he tried to follow the Chinese model rather than the Soviet since his country, like China, is predominantly agrarian and traditional, but during the war and even more so afterward he had to moderate his predilection in order to obtain Russian economic aid and political support.

An army mutiny in December 1975, after Machel announced that the troops, in light of their revolutionary function, would not be paid, was the first of many indicators that the Mozambican people, because of their lack of education and the persistence of tribalism, were not ready to play the social role he envisioned for them. As a result, at FRELIMO's Third National Congress in February 1977 Machel had to abandon his conception of the party as a mass movement encompassing all classes and interests. Instead he transformed it into a tiny and closely knit group of the ideological elite, "the vanguard of the proletariat," which would run a highly centralized and authoritarian governmental apparatus patterned on that created by the Portuguese, while creating class consciousness among the people.

The reorganization of the party enabled Machel to make important short-term compromises. In the early 1980s, for example, recognizing the country's ongoing economic stagnation, he temporarily opened many spheres of activity to private enterprise and took steps to make Mozambique more inviting to Western capital. Visiting Western Europe for that purpose, he made special efforts to effect a reconciliation with Portugal that would make it possible for the two countries to work together in pursuit of their mutual economic interests.

Poverty, ignorance, and lack of development comprise Mozambique's colonial heritage because the orientation of its economy and infrastructure to Portugal's needs gave it almost nothing to build on. The mass exodus of whites in 1975–76 left it almost entirely without such skilled workers as mechanics and technicians, not to mention managers and administrators, so that there are few persons capable of running things, much less of training others. The diversity of the country's ethnic elements, combined with the lack of an adequate internal transportation system, has facilitated sectionalism and impeded the growth of a national consciousness.

The enthusiasm that greeted the dawning of independence has become diluted, and Machel has had to introduce forced "reeducation" and other repressive measures to counteract corruption and a general restiveness that could prove dangerous to his regime if politicized. Moreover, in the country's interior provinces, which he has found as difficult to control effectively as did the Portuguese before him, he has been striving for the past few years with no success to contain a growing guerrilla insurgency backed by South Africa, which in its mode of operation resembles the one he commanded during the war with Portugal. Mozambique's ethnic diversity works to his advantage, since it makes it difficult for his opponents to find a basis for uniting against him. The insecurity of his regime is underscored by the fact that his personal bodyguard is made up not of Africans but of East German and Portuguese mercenaries.

On the banks of the Nkomati River on March 16, 1984 Mozambique signed a nonaggression treaty with South Africa, in which both parties pledged to deny support to each other's internal enemies. Shortly after that, a commission was set up to guarantee that terms of the treaty would be enforced. Most political observers agreed that given the disastrous conditions obtaining in Mozambique at the time, the Mozambicans had no other choice than to sign the pact, the first to be signed between an independent African black country and South Africa.

Samora Moises Machel's first wife, by whom he has a teenage son, died while he was living in Tanzania. His second wife, Graça Simbine, whom he married on September 7, 1975, is Minister of Education and Culture in his cabinet and a member of FRELIMO's Central Committee. A dark-skinned, bearded man of average height, Machel has been described by reporters as warm, intense, genuine, and articulate. His decorations include Mongolia's Order of Sujebator, the Lenin Centenary Medal (1970), and the Joliot Curie Gold Medal (1976). His prolific Marxist writings on political and economic problems have not yet been translated into English.

References: *Christian Sci Mon* p8 *Jl* 9 '74 por; *London Observer* p11 *Jn* 22 '75 por; *N Y Times* p3 *Jn* 25 '75; *Who's Who in the World*, 1984–85

Mandela, Nelson (Rolihlahla)
(män-dä´lä)

*1918– South African political activist; lawyer.
Address: Pollsmoor Prison, near Cape Town,
Republic of South Africa*

In June 1964 the South African Supreme Court sentenced Nelson Mandela, a lawyer and a leader of the African National Congress (ANC), to life in prison on charges of sabotage and conspiracy to overthrow the government by violence. Nevertheless, Nelson Mandela remains one of the most prominent figures in the black nationalist struggle against South Africa's white minority rule. In August 1983, at a mass antigovernment rally in Capetown, a new multiracial movement called the United Democratic Front was launched to protest constitutional proposals that would give a role in the white-dominated government to Indians and persons of mixed race—commonly known as "coloreds"—while continuing to exclude blacks. The new movement formally named Nelson Mandela as its patron. At the rally, Dr. Allan Boesak, a young colored clergyman, declared, "South Africa belongs to all its people"—echoing the words of Mandela.

Nelson Rolihlahla Mandela was born in 1918 at Umtata, in the Transkei territory of the Eastern Cape, where his father, Henry Mandela, was chief of the Xhosa-speaking Tembu tribe. Renouncing his hereditary right as successor to the tribal chief-

dom, Mandela decided to prepare for a legal career, leading to politics, which he regarded as the best way to help his people. He attended school at the Methodist Mission Center in Healdtown and studied at University College at Fort Hare but was expelled after two years for his role in a 1940 student strike. He then worked as a policeman in the Transvaal mines while studying law by correspondence at Witwatersrand University and obtained his law degree from the University of South Africa in 1942.

Two years later, Mandela joined the African National Congress, South Africa's oldest liberation group, founded in 1912, which led the early struggle for civil rights and, inspired by Mohandas K. Gandhi, sought the redress in injustice through nonviolent direct action. Influenced by Anton M. Lembede, who opposed participation by Africans in World War II and demanded a declaration of South Africa's aims for black people, in 1944 Mandela, along with Oliver Tambo, Walter Sisulu, and others, founded the Congress Youth League, which eventually dominated the ANC. Although the League and its members maintained a strong stand in the 1940s against multiracial cooperation and collaboration with the Communist party and emphasized African self-reliance, Mandela maintained the friendly relations he had formed with radical whites and Indians as a law student. As a result of his contacts with Communists, his early political views were well to the left, although he never fully espoused the Marxist line and gradually moved toward classic African nationalist socialism. In his view, the withdrawal of labor was the most decisive nonviolent weapon.

When the National party—which came to power in South Africa in 1948 with a political platform legalizing the extant system of racial segregation known as apartheid—adopted and enforced such legislation as the Prohibition Against Mixed Marriages Act and the Population Registration Act, the Youth League responded with a nationwide call for civil disobedience. For the next dozen years, Mandela and the Youth League led the struggle to unite various antigovernment forces.

In 1950 a mass labor strike was broken by police, resulting in the deaths of eighteen blacks. That year the government passed the Group Areas Act, legalizing strict racial segregation by occupation of an area, and the Suppression of Communism Act, which defined a Communist as any person who aimed at "bringing about any political, industrial, social or economic change within the Union . . . by unlawful acts"—a definition so broad that it enabled authorities to ban any person they considered dangerous to the state.

The legislation created an uneasy partnership between the Communist party and the ANC, resulting in a schism that eventually split the latter organization. African leaders justified the alliance by appealing for united action against a common threat but avoided the question of black unity. In his December 1951 presidential address to the Youth League, Mandela declared, "I do not think we differ concerning our ideas of the aims of African nationalism . . . , a free, independent, united, democratic and prosperous South Africa. . . . The problem of the Youth League and Congress today is the maintenance of full dynamic contact with the masses." While recognizing the existence of internal conflicts, he regarded differences of opinion to be those of tactics rather than of policy. But to maintain its mass appeal, the aims of the ANC were kept ambiguous, and Mandela concentrated his efforts on the organization of resistance protests and the coordination of individual efforts under the leadership of the ANC.

After serving in 1951–52 as president of the ANC Youth League, Mandela became president of the Transvaal branch of the ANC as well as deputy national president under Albert Luthuli. As volunteer-in-chief in the 1952 Defiance Against Unjust Laws Campaign, led jointly by the ANC and the Indian Congress, Mandela controlled the entire volunteer organization, leading those prepared to risk prison terms by breaking apartheid laws in a series of planned demonstrations that resulted in some 8,000 arrrests and left fourteen people dead and thirty-five wounded. Although Albert Luthuli, then president of the ANC, was nominally in charge, Mandela was the key figure in implementing the campaign.

Banned in December 1952 for his part in the Defiance Campaign, Mandela was prohibited from attending all gatherings for six months and confined to the magisterial district of Johannesburg under the terms of the 1950 Suppression of Communism Act. That same month, he and Oliver Tambo set up a legal practice in Johannesburg, establishing the first black law partnership in South Africa. Mandela also organized a nucleus of leadership in the African reserves that eventually carried on the work of the ANC after it was banned by the government.

In 1953 Mandela was given a suspended jail sentence of nine months for his leadership of the Defiance Campaign. After the ban was renewed that September for a two-year period and he was ordered to resign from the ANC, Mandela remained for a time behind the scenes. Meanwhile, in a move to complete segregation in all public spheres, the government had obtained passage of the Reservation and Separate Amenities Act and the Bantu Education Act, setting off some public protests.

Mandela reappeared in public in 1955, after the lifting of his bans. In June of that year he spoke at the Congress of the People, held in Kliptown near Johannesburg, in support of the formation of the Congress Alliance which united the ANC and other nonparliamentary political organizations. Spurred by a vision of an egalitarian South Africa, representatives of the organizations adopted a Freedom Charter, which called for a nonracial state, the division of land among those who work it, and restoration of the national wealth to the people. That charter has remained the credo of the ANC and of Nelson Mandela. Following the con-

gress, a multiracial committee was established to coordinate the activities of the different organizations.

South Africa's epic treason trial began in 1956, a year of riots, boycotts, and demonstrations against government proposals to create seven reserves in which blacks would be segregated. When, in December, 156 leaders of the Congress Alliance organizations were arrested, Mandela was among the many Africans charged under the Suppression of Communism Act with advocating revolution to fight apartheid and with seeking to establish a "people's democracy" modeled on Soviet bloc nations. The trial dragged on until March 1961, when all the defendants were acquitted because of insufficient evidence. During the trial, Mandela divorced his first wife, and in 1958 he married Winifred Nomzamo, a medical social worker. Since it was normal practice for defendants to be freed on bail during the lengthy recesses, Nelson and Winnie Mandela set up their household in a Johannesburg suburb.

Meanwhile, the trial had caused some rifts among the leadership of the Congress Alliance. In 1959 Robert Sobukwe formed the Pan Africanist Congress (PAC), which stressed black nationalism and took many young members away from the ANC. When the government extended existing pass laws, requiring women as well as men to carry pass books, the ANC organized an ineffectual demonstration. Then Sobukwe announced a nationwide campaign of nonviolent resistance against the pass laws, and on March 21, 1960, in Sharpeville, near Johannesburg, thousands of unarmed Africans gathered outside the police station without their passes. Police turned their guns on the protesters, killing sixty-nine and wounding eighty-six. Many demonstrators were reportedly shot in the back as they ran from the police.

Following the Sharpeville massacre, the government declared a state of emergency, and instituted a detention law under which anyone could be held for ninety days without trial. All nonparliamentary political organizations and public meetings were banned, and more than 2,000 persons were arrested. Mandela, who was detained for several months without charges or trial, apparently became convinced as a result of Sharpeville that the days of nonviolent resistance were over.

Following his acquittal, Mandela was appointed honorary secretary of the All-African National Action Council, founded on March 25, 1961 at the All-African Conference at Pietermaritzburg. The semiunderground movement called for mass demonstrations throughout the country against the proclamation of the white supremacist Republic of South Africa on May 31, 1961. After the conference, Mandela was hunted by the police and was for some eighteen months a fugitive, disguised at times as a laborer, janitor, or garage worker. He became head of *Umkonto we Sizwe* (Spear of the Nation), an underground paramilitary branch of the ANC, founded to commit acts of sabotage and attack targets symbolizing apartheid or having economic value, but he ruled out terrorist acts against persons. Over an eighteen-month period *Umkonto we Sizwe* claimed credit for more than seventy acts of sabotage. During that time Mandela traveled through Africa, speaking before a pan-African conference in Ethiopia in January 1962, raising funds, and taking part in military training in Algeria. At one point he was even reported to be in England. His ability to elude the South African authorities caused him to be widely known as the "Black Pimpernel."

On August 4, 1962 Mandela was apprehended by South African security police in Natal while disguised as a chauffeur and driving a car. Conducting his own defense, he turned his trial into an indictment of white domination. He challenged the right of the court to hear his case, asserting that he was not bound legally or morally to obey laws made by a government in which he had no voice. In the end, the court sentenced him to three years imprisonment for incitement of a strike and an additional two years for leaving the country without valid travel documents. He began to serve his sentence in Pretoria central prison, most of it in solitary confinement.

After police, on June 11, 1963, raided the underground ANC headquarters in Rivonia, a Johannesburg suburb, Mandela was brought from the Pretoria prison to join other leaders of *Umkonto we Sizwe* in standing trial for sabotage, high treason, and conspirary to overthrow the government. In the non-jury Rivonia trial, which began in October 1963, the defendants—six Africans, two whites, and one Indian—were indicted for Communist activities and for responsibility for 192 acts of sabotage between June 1962 and July 1963. Opening his defense on April 20, 1964, Mandela admitted that he had been one of the founders of *Umkonto we Sizwe* and that he planned sabotage to combat oppression, but he denied that the struggle was Communist-inspired. He went on to emphasize that his paramilitary group rejected terrorism, but warned that more militant leaders would resort to terrorism if the government continued its oppressive policies. "It would be unrealistic and wrong for African leaders to continue preaching peace and nonviolence at a time when the government met our peaceful demands with force," he asserted.

The seven-month trial ended in June 1964, when eight of the defendants were convicted of sabotage and treason and sentenced to life in prison. A Union party spokeman expressed regret at the time that Mandela had not been charged with high treason, which could have brought him a death sentence. After appeals from abroad for clemency were rejected by Prime Minister Hendrik F. Verwoerd, the defendants were sent to Robben Island, seven miles offshore from Cape Town, to begin their prison terms.

In the two decades since his conviction, Nelson Mandela has been officially considered as a "non-person," who in the eyes of the authorities does not legally exist in South Africa, and whose views may not be discussed or printed. Neverthe-

less, he remains very much alive in the memories of South Africa's nonwhite majority, and occasionally there have been articles about Mandela in the foreign press and in *Sechaba,* the official publication of the ANC, now published in various locations outside South Africa.

David McNicoll, an Australian journalist, wrote in the London *Observer* (April 22, 1973) about visits with several prisoners on Robben Island, including Mandela, who was then taking law courses by correspondence with London University. McNicoll found that discipline in the prison was strict and work consisted mainly of brick-making, laboring in the bamboo factory, digging in the lime quarries, and collecting seaweed. Talking about his own experiences, Mandela told McNicoll: "Things have improved. Diet and clothing are better. . . . In 1965 I used to work in the quarry, where I could only see the sky. . . . Then in November 1971, I was put on collecting seaweed. This is the most popular job—you can see the sea, feel it, and watch the ships coming and going." Commenting about the lack of communication with the outside world, he said: "We get no information. . . . But we are intelligent people, and we manage to keep in touch with world affairs. . . . On this island we abound in hope. . . . I know that my cause will triumph."

Despite his isolation, Mandela has remained a symbol for the aspirations of South Africa's nonwhite majority. In January, 1980, three black nationalists, armed with rifles, took twenty-five persons hostage in a Pretoria bank in an ill-fated attempt to obtain Mandela's release. At Witwatersrand University a "free Mandela campaign" was launched on March 20, 1980, receiving almost simultaneous overseas support. Within two months, over 58,000 black and white South Africans had signed petitions calling for the release of Mandela and all political prisoners throughout the country. An article in *Sechaba* (July 1980) described Mandela's influence as derived "from the fact that he stands at the meeting point of two irreconcilable world-outlooks or ideologies. . . . He is advocating the new, revolutionary outlook of a future South Africa. Important visitors from overseas visit him. . . . Universities honor him. . . . An atomic particle has been named after him at Leeds University in Britain. . . . Mandela's release is a prerequisite for a democratically elected government."

Mandela left Robben Island on April 1, 1982, when he and five other prisoners were secretly transferred to the maximum security Pollsmoor Prison, outside Cape Town. The transfer was ostensibly made for administrative reasons, but friends of Mandela have suggested that prison officials found that he was exerting too strong an influence among the approximately 400 political prisoners on Robben Island, where he had organized a large-scale educational program for the inmates.

In March 1984 the South African government offered to release Mandela on condition that he would agree to settle in the nominally independent black tribal "homeland" of Transkei, of which his cousin, Chief Kaiser Matanzima, was president. But Mandela emphatically rejected the offer, asserting that he would accept nothing less than unconditional release and that he would have nothing to do with the "homelands" policy, through which South Africa's white supremacist government, in accordance with its practice of *apartheid*, was resettling over 3.5 million black people. At the same time, Mandela affirmed his allegiance to the still outlawed African National Congress.

No Easy Walk to Freedom, a collection of Mandela's articles and speeches from the years 1953 to 1963, was published by an American firm, Basic Books, in 1965. Among the honors that he has received are the Jawaharlal Nehru award from the Indian government, the Bruno Kreisky prize for human rights, the Freedom of the city of Glasgow, honorary citizenship of Rome, and honorary degrees from the National University of Lesotho and City College of New York.

By his first marriage, which ended in divorce in 1957, Nelson Mandela had three children, of whom one, a son, died in an automobile accident. He and Winnie Mandela have two daughters, Zindziswa (Zindzi), who works for the Institute of Race Relations in Johannesburg, and Zenani (Zeni), who is married and lives in Swaziland. Known as the "first lady" of black South Africa, Winnie Mandela was among seven black leaders banned for activities in connection with the 1976 Soweto riots and was sent to Brandfort in the Orange Free State, where she runs a mobile clinic and a feeding program for infants and the elderly. She must ask special permission and travel 650 miles by air each time that she pays her monthly thirty-minute visit to her husband, which is all that is allowed her.

An amateur heavyweight boxer and long-distance runner in his younger years, Mandela stands at six feet four inches and exudes what a friend, quoted in the *New York Times* (April 21, 1964) described as "an animal magnetism that attracts the masses like pollen attracts bees." Mrs. Helen Suzman, a member of South Africa's parliamentary opposition, who visited him in July 1983 at Pollsmoor Prison, found him to be in good health and spirits. And Winnie Mandela has said of him, as quoted in the *New York Times* (July 19, 1978): "Don't believe those stories about a tottering old man you read in some of the pro-government newspapers. . . . He's as upright and proud as the day he was arrested."

References: *Africa South of the Sahara, 1982–83*; Carlson, Joel. *No Neutral Ground (1973)*; *From Protest to Challenge vol 4 (1977)*; Gerhart, Gail M. *Black Power in South Africa (1978)*; *International Who's Who, 1984–85*; Lipschutz, Mark R. and Rasmussen, R. K. *Dictionary of African Historical Biography (1978)*; *McGraw-Hill Encyclopedia of World Biography vol 7 (1973)*; Segal, Ronald. *Political Africa (1961)*

Marsalis, Wynton
(mär sel´ is)

Oct. 18, 1961– Musician. Address: b. c/o ICM Artists, Ltd., 40 W. 57th St., New York City, N.Y. 10019

Extolled by the renowned French trumpeter Maurice André as "potentially the greatest horn player of all time," the twenty-three-year-old trumpet virtuoso Wynton Marsalis has quickly established himself as not only a first-rate jazz artist but also as an equally talented classical musician. Since the age of seventeen, when he won an award at the prestigious Berkshire Music Center, the gifted Marsalis has continued to garner prizes, including Grammy Awards in 1984 for his classical and jazz albums, making him the first artist ever to win in both categories in one year. Even more impressive is the belief of most critics that Marsalis has yet to reach the peak of his abilities.

Wynton Marsalis, the second of the six sons of Dolores and Ellis Marsalis, was born on October 18, 1961, in New Orleans, Louisiana and raised in Kenner, a nearby town. Both his parents are musically talented: an alumnus of Dillard University, Ellis Marsalis is an instructor in jazz improvisation at the New Orleans Center for the Creative Arts who was once touted by Larry Kart in the *Chicago Tribune* (February 28, 1982) as "New Orleans' premiere jazz pianist"; Dolores Marsalis, a graduate of Grambling College, sang for a time with jazz groups and later worked as a substitute teacher before devoting herself to raising their musically gifted children. Branford, their oldest child, was playing clarinet and piano by the time he reached second grade and is now an accomplished tenor and soprano saxophonist. Encouraged by Branford's musical prowess, Ellis Marsalis approached

Al Hirt, the celebrated trumpet player and leader of the band in which he was then playing, for an advance to buy six-year-old Wynton a trumpet. The advance was not forthcoming; instead, Hirt gave the boy one of his own old horns. Although he made his debut the next year, playing "The Marine Hymn" at the Xavier Junior School of Music, Wynton was too interested in his basketball and Boy Scout activities to practise very often.

But when Wynton Marsalis was twelve, a recording by the great jazz trumpet player Clifford Brown fired his enthusiasm. As a youth who always set high goals for himself, Wynton Marsalis found the challenge of mastering so difficult an instrument and so demanding an idiom as jazz irresistible. His rivalry with another young trumpet player, a fellow student at Benjamin Franklin High School, and his studies with John Longo, a trumpet player schooled in both classics and jazz, also inspired him to use every free moment to practise or to listen to countless recordings featuring the trumpet. One of them, a classical album performed by Maurice André, also piqued his interest in the classical trumpet repertoire.

His lessons with Longo, his classes in theory and harmony at the New Orleans Center for the Creative Arts, and his hard work soon began to pay off. As a result of winning a statewide youth competition, at fourteen Marsalis was a featured soloist with the New Orleans Philharmonic Orchestra, playing Franz Joseph Haydn's Trumpet Concerto. Appearing with that orchestra again two years later, he performed Johann Sebastian Bach's Brandenburg Concerto No. 2 in F Major. During most of his high school years, Marsalis also played first trumpet with the New Orleans Civic Orchestra, performed with the New Orleans Brass Quintet and other local bands, and was one of eight members of the "Creators," a teenage funk rock group in which Branford Marsalis played the saxophone.

When he was seventeen, Marsalis studied at the Berkshire Music Center at Tanglewood in Massachusetts, which waived its age requirement to allow him to attend, and he won its Harvey Shapiro Award as the outstanding brass player. There he astounded his musical elders with his versatility. "You see," he explained to Whitney Balliett in the New Yorker (June 20, 1983), "I knew they couldn't believe that a seventeen-year-old who could play the hell out of classical music also knew a lot about jazz." Similarly, his 1979 recital at the New Orleans Center for Creative Arts, in which he moved effortlessly from Johann Hummel's E-flat major Trumpet Concerto to jazz numbers, amazed even seasoned professionals. "It wasn't so much his daring," the trumpet player Ronald Benko explained in People (February 20, 1984), "but that each half of his program was equally wonderful."

In spite of the long hours he devoted to his music, Wynton Marsalis maintained a 3.98 grade point average (on a scale of 4.0), was a National Merit Scholarship finalist, and received scholarship offers from Yale University and other Ivy League schools. He turned all of them down. "I had been

going to white schools for a long time," he told Leonard Feather in an interview for Newsday (May 23, 1982). "The education is better, but the problem is the racial vibes you have to deal with." In 1979 he accepted a full scholarship from the Juilliard School of Music in New York City, and he played with the Brooklyn Philharmonia and in the pit band for Sweeney Todd on Broadway to support himself. But after about a year at the famed music school, he was chafing at the bias against jazz he perceived there. "When you play jazz at Juilliard, people laugh; it's like the darkies cracking jokes, man," he contended in an interview with Annalyn Swan for Newsweek (May 17, 1982). So when the famous drummer Art Blakey, impressed by Marsalis' performance with him during a Manhattan club date, asked him to spend his 1980 summer vacation with his Jazz Messengers, Marsalis accepted with alacrity. At nineteen, he also became the band's musical director. It was on the road with Blakey ("a truly educational experience," according to Marsalis) that he began to attract national attention. Jon Pareles recounted in his New York Times Magazine article (June 17, 1984) that his "pure, pealing tone and mercurial solos" during his stint with Blakey "caused the jazz press to declare him a prodigy."

In 1981 Marsalis left Juilliard without taking a degree. Although he continued to play with Blakey from time to time, he spent that summer touring Japan and the United States with another great jazz group: pianist Herbie Hancock's V.S.O.P. quartet, which also included bassist Ron Carter and drummer Tony Williams, all three of whom had made up the rhythm section of Miles Davis' band in the 1960s. He joined V.S.O.P. for the double album Quartet (Columbia, 1981) and was featured as a sideman or soloist on several other albums, all released in 1982: the Jazz Messengers' A La Mode (Concord); the in-concert double album Jazz at the Opera House (Columbia), in which he played several numbers with saxophonist Wayne Shorter; The Young Lions (Elektra), a recording of the 1982 Kool Jazz Festival that includes his performance of "B 'n' W" with vocalist Bobby McFerrin; and saxophonist-composer Chico Freeman's Destiny's Dance (Contemporary). For Fathers and Sons (Columbia, 1982) Wynton, Branford, and Ellis Marsalis joined Freeman and his father, the saxophonist Von Freeman, in an unusual and well-received tribute to traditional jazz, with each family recording one side of the album.

His undeniable and ever-increasing virtuosity prompted critics to vote Wynton Marsalis "the talent most deserving of wider recognition" in a 1981 Down Beat poll. Similarly impressed, Columbia Records awarded him a contract that year under the terms of which he was to record both jazz and classical music—an unprecedented stipulation for a jazz artist. But some jazz cognoscenti criticized Marsalis "for sounding like an encyclopedia of jazz trumpet styles," as Jon Pareles phrased it in the New York Times Magazine article. Responding in the course of the interview for that article to those charges, Marsalis asserted that "if you play trumpet and you *don't* sound like Miles [Davis] or Dizzy [Gillespie] or Clifford [Brown] or Fats [Navarro], you're probably not playing jazz. If you don't sound like somebody else, you sound like nothing."

Nevertheless, Marsalis' own distinctive style has been evolving slowly. The stabbing phrases and coolly swinging beat he displayed while he was with Art Blakey—evoking comparisons with the late Lee Morgan, a trumpeter who broke into the jazz scene with Blakey in the late 1950s—gradually gave way during his stint with V.S.O.P. to a sound closer to that which Miles Davis pioneered in his recordings for the Blue Note label in the 1960s. The rhythms were tensely expectant, harmonies and statements of theme became more complex, and the listener was frequently caught off guard by shifts in key, tempo, and mood. In an article for the *Chicago Tribune* (September 18, 1983), Larry Kart pointed out that in Marsalis' fascination with technique, ability to "play around corners," and tendency to indulge in "flamboyant fantasy and serio-comic wit" in solos, he revealed an even closer kinship with Wayne Shorter, the tenor and soprano saxophonist for Davis' band. "Marsalis obviously feels that the innovations of that group have yet to be superseded," Kart asserted, "because almost every performance on the two albums he has made under his own name pays homage to the style of the mid-'60s Davis Quintet."

The stylistic affinity with Davis' group that Kart detected in *Wynton Marsalis* (Columbia, 1981), his debut album as a leader, may have been partly due to the fact that Herbie Hancock produced it at Marsalis' request and that he and the other V.S.O.P. members, along with Branford Marsalis, were featured sidemen on four cuts, made in a Tokyo studio. On the remaining three selections, the Marsalis brothers were joined by drummer Jeff Watts and pianist Kenny Kirkland. In an attempt to reach an audience not restricted to jazz aficionados, Columbia Records mounted a marketing campaign that was unusually aggressive for a jazz release, sending out sample covers and cassettes and arranging press interviews. New Orleans' mayor Ernest Morial even proclaimed a "Wynton Marsalis Day" in February 1982 to honor him. But it was Marsalis' incisive playing that impressed critics and fans alike. In *Stereo Review* (May 1982) Chris Albertson was effusive in his praise of "the assurance, articulation, and self-possessed originality" that the twenty-year-old Marsalis displayed. "As for the album itself," he concluded, "there is not a blemish on it." Spurred by widespread interest in Marsalis' sudden appearance on the jazz scene, his association with prestigious artists, CBS' promotional muscle, and such glowing reviews, sales of *Wynton Marsalis* topped 125,-000—a figure considered remarkably robust for a jazz release. In the annual *Down Beat* poll, the album was voted the best jazz LP of 1982, and Marsalis was named both musician of the year and best trumpeter, winning over Miles Davis and Dizzy Gillespie, the perennial favorites in those categories. (Davis, it should be noted, had been ailing in the past year.)

In 1981 Marsalis formed his own jazz band with Branford Marsalis, Kenny Kirkland, Jeff Watts, and bassists Phil Bowler and Ray Drummond. Released in 1983, *Think of One* (Columbia) marked his debut as a producer and the recording debut of his quintet. More eclectic and adventurous than his first album, it included such jazz classics as the title track, a piece by Thelonious Monk; Duke Ellington's little-known composition "Melancholia"; the ballad "My Ideal"; and five original compositions, three by Marsalis, including his wittily titled "Knozz-Moe-King." *Think of One* demonstrated that Marsalis was continuing to develop his own style. In his complimentary review of the album for the *New York Times* (June 19, 1983), Jon Pareles noted that even on the title track, for example, where the band members are "clearly indebted to the 1960's Blue Note stable," they are also "working to make their time sense as open and flexible (and well coordinated) as their harmonies." "The theme keeps coming back in different arrangements," Pareles explained, "and at one point in a different tempo, as if Mr. Marsalis were toying with all the implications of its odd spaces." Dissenting from the generally enthusiastic reviews of that album, Whitney Balliett wrote in the *New Yorker* (June 20, 1983) that the five original compositions on the album were "overarranged, melodically weak, and full of niggling devices like Mingus tempo changes and fadeout endings."

Wynton Marsalis made his classical album debut with *Trumpet Concertos*, which he recorded in London with Raymond Leppard and the National Philharmonic Orchestra. Released simultaneously with *Think of One*, the CBS Masterworks digital album featured concertos in E-flat major by Haydn and Hummel and one in D major by Leopold Mozart. In an interview with Eric V. Copage for the *Daily News* (June 30, 1983), Marsalis pointed out that he had chosen those standard pieces with a great deal of care: "In jazz, if you can't play bebop, then you can't play. In classical music, you have to show that you can play music from the established repertoire if you want to be taken seriously."

Critics did indeed take Marsalis seriously and were nearly unanimous in their praise of his pure tone and impeccable phrasing. Chris Albertson especially admired the originality of his interpretations. "Marsalis's own cadenza ends the first movement [of the Haydn concerto]," Albertson noted in *Stereo Review* (September 1983), "and, unless my ears deceive me, there is a salient smidge of New Orleans in it." Marsalis' embellishment of the second movement of the Mozart concerto also aroused the enthusiasm of that critic, who concluded that his "recording debut as a classical artist is every bit as impressive as his extraordinary jazz debut was." *Think of One* and *Trumpet Concertos* each sold over 100,000 copies. Moreover, for those albums Marsalis won Grammy awards in February 1984 for the best solo jazz instrumental performance and for the best classical performance with an orchestra by an instrumental soloist, becoming the first artist ever to receive—or even be nominated for—awards in both jazz and classical categories in a single year.

Nevertheless, while no one has ever faulted Marsalis' tone or technical facility, several jazz critics have questioned the depth of his musical statements. Gregory Ironman Tate of the *Village Voice* (June 8, 1982) deemed Marsalis "an intelligent but unfocused young improviser, substituting technical braggadocio for his lack of Miles' incisive, shaping omniscience," and in the London *Times* (October 27, 1982) Richard Williams, an early promoter of Marsalis, charged that at a 1982 engagement of his quintet Marsalis "in particular ran through his bag of tricks without much thought for anything save flabbergasting the bourgeoisie." But Marsalis is quick to concede that he still has a lot to learn. "I know I can play fast and high, but that's not what jazz is all about," he admitted to Larry Kart in a *Chicago Tribune* interview (September 18, 1983). "Take Don Cherry, who is a phenomenal trumpet player," Marsalis continued. "He can't really play the trumpet technically, but that makes him get down to the essence of the music, whereas I have so much technique that it gets in my way. I'll just be playing stuff because I can play it, which distracts me from what I should be playing."

Marsalis has excited controversy within the usually laid-back world of jazz with his words as well as his music. In two interviews published by *Down Beat* magazine, one in tandem with Branford Marsalis in December 1982 and a second in July 1984, he dismissed as defectors from true jazz those musicians who blend jazz with rock or with rhythm 'n' blues. He also sniped at another wing of contemporary jazz, which promotes experimentation with free-form or "avant-garde" approaches. "We need young musicians trying to really learn how to play their instruments," Marsalis said. "Not all these little sort of pop-type cult figures, talking-all-the-time heroes, who have these spur-of-the-moment, out-of-their-mind, left-bank, off-the-wall theories about music which make no sense at all to anybody who knows anything about music." Those put-downs were qualified on other occasions, and advisedly so, since many of Marsalis' heroes—Miles Davis, Wayne Shorter, Freddie Hubbard, Herbie Hancock, and others—have used electrified and synthesized instrumentation and have dabbled with open musical structures. The remarks have served, however, to highlight his belief that jazz is a "precise language" representing a tradition that must be studied and mastered before it can be improved upon. In the London *Sunday Times Magazine* (June 17, 1983), Brian Case noted that the young trumpeter practises what he preaches, having returned stylistically to the mid-1960s, "to the height of artistry modern jazz attained before it was displaced." "He commands the spectrum from lashing top notes to the neglected depths of register," Case continued. "His tone is distinctive, properly full and burnished, and his flights of imagination are sometimes so complex that the mind tires, gapes, and hooks on again."

A slim young man, Wynton Marsalis has a round face and a brush mustache and wears wire-rimmed glasses. He neither drinks nor smokes and lives in a Brooklyn brownstone with his brother Branford. A dapper dresser, he favors expertly tailored dark suits, especially when performing. Marsalis maintains a heavy playing schedule. In addition to working on both his latest jazz release, *Wynton Marsalis: Hot House Flowers* (Columbia, 1984), and an album of baroque music with Raymond Leppard and the English Chamber Orchestra, he also performed in 1984 with Sarah Vaughan at the season opening of the Boston Pops; traded enthusiastically received solos with trumpet player Maynard Ferguson at the Kool Jazz Festival; gave a triumphant performance at the Mostly Mozart Festival; and toured extensively with his quintet. But in spite of his successes in classical music, Marsalis plans to devote himself exclusively to jazz, "the ultimate twentieth-century music." As Nicholas Jennings pointed out in *Maclean's* (March 26, 1984), Marsalis can afford to limit himself because he "has the gifts to grow in whatever direction he wants."

References: Ebony 38:29+ Mr '83 pors; Macleans 97:49 Mr 26 '84 por; Newsday II p19 My 23 '82 por; Newsweek 99:104 My 17 '84 por; Time 122:94 N 7 '83 por

---

Mayr, Ernst

(mīr)

July 5, 1904– Biologist; educator. Address: b. Museum of Comparative Zoology, Harvard University, Cambridge, Mass. 02138; h. 11 Chauncy St., Cambridge, Mass. 02138

Through such incisive, ground-breaking studies as *Systematics and the Origin of Species* (1942) and *Animal Species and Evolution* (1963) Ernst Mayr revolutionized the standard definition of species and theories of speciation and established himself in the process as one of the most influential evolutionary biologists of the twentieth century. He was also a principal catalyst in the important modern evolutionary synthesis, which united the contentious forces of the naturalist and the geneticist for a more effective study of evolution within the Darwinian framework. The eighty-year-old scientist has most recently turned his unbounded energy and genius to an exhaustive history of the controversies and key figures in his field. The first volume of that study, *The Growth of Biological Thought* (1982), has already been hailed as a modern classic.

Ernst (Walter) Mayr was born on July 5, 1904 in Kempten, Germany (a Bavarian city now part of West Germany) to Otto Mayr, a judge, and Helene (Pusinelli) Mayr. He has two brothers, one of whom is a judge and the other an engineer. During

Ernst Mayr

his youth, Mayr received a broad general education, studying Latin for nine years and Greek for seven, and he also developed a wide range of interests, including birdwatching. When he was eighteen, he spotted on a lake near his home the first pair of red-crested pochards seen in central Europe in seventy-seven years. As a result of that discovery, he eventually met Erwin Stresemann, Germany's leading ornithologist, who influenced him greatly.

Although in compliance with family tradition Mayr enrolled in 1923 as a medical student at the University of Greifswald, Stresemann persuaded him to pursue his avian interests by working during his summer vacations at the University of Berlin's Zoological Museum. By 1925, Mayr has recounted, he had become "so enchanted with the work and with the idea of following in the footsteps of Darwin and other great explorers of the tropics" that he abandoned his medical studies to devote himself to zoology. After completing his dissertation ("Die Ausbreitung des Girlitz") on the zoogeographic problem presented by the sudden immigration of the serin finch into large parts of Europe, he received his doctoral degree in zoology, *summa cum laude*, from the University of Berlin in 1926.

Named assistant curator to the University of Berlin's Zoological Museum on July 1, 1926, Mayr remained in that post until 1932 while at the same time pursuing his own field research. But "to study the life of the tropics," he recounted in the introduction to his selected essays, *Evolution and the Diversity of Life* (Belknap Press, 1976), " . . . was the greatest ambition of [his] youth." He soon had the opportunity to fulfill his dream, for in 1927 Mayr met Lord Walter Rothschild, a distinguished British zoologist, who asked him to undertake an ornithological expedition to Dutch New Guinea,

one of the world's remotest outposts. He arrived in Dutch New Guinea in April 1928 and explored successively the bird fauna of three mountain ranges, the Arfak, Wandammen, and Cycloop mountains. Despite various tribulations (he wrote that at one point "[his] camp really resembled a hospital more than a collecting station"), he decided to stay in New Guinea, and undertook in 1928-29 a University of Berlin-sponsored expedition to the Saruwaged mountains (Huon Peninsula) and Herzog mountains in the Mandated Territory of New Guinea. In 1929-30, as a member of the American Museum of Natural History's ambitious, long-term Whitney South Sea Expedition, Mayr explored the Solomon Islands. As he explained in *Evolution and the Diversity of Life*, those early field experiences "had an impact on [his] thinking that cannot be exaggerated," and he spent the next several decades exploring the full implications of his Pacific studies.

Following his Solomon Islands expedition, Mayr worked in 1931-32 as a Whitney research associate in ornithology at the American Museum of Natural History in New York City. When he was named associate curator of the museum's Whitney-Rothschild Collection in 1932, he settled permanently in the United States and became a naturalized citizen. For the next ten years, he devoted himself to the natural history subdisciplines of taxonomy (the system of classification of plants and animals) and to systematics (a more general study of the diversity of organic life) in order to compile his exhaustive and definitive *List of New Guinea Birds* (American Museum of Natural History, 1941), which Mayr considers his finest taxonomic work. In an article for *Science* (January 20, 1984), Harvard paleontologist Stephen Jay Gould, who has worked with Mayr, was careful to point out that although laymen might be misled by the title of that work Mayr's *List* was much more than "a simple compilation" of facts that demanded more diligence than intellectual acumen to assemble. Rather, Gould explained, "each species is a separate puzzle, a little exemplar of scientific methodology requiring hypothesis, test, and comparison for a resolution of range and a definition of content." Before the end of the decade, Mayr had also completed two well-received field guides to the avian life of the South Seas: *Birds of the Southwest Pacific* (1945) and, with Jean Delacour, *Birds of the Philippines* (1946), both of which were published by the Macmillan Company.

While preparing his *List of New Guinea Birds*, Mayr became acutely aware of the inadequacy of the usual methods of distinguishing between separate but closely related species and marked variations within a single species. By the 1930s, there were two predominant taxonomic schools of thought. The traditional taxonomic method established by the eighteenth-century Swedish botanist Carolus Linnaeus emphasized morphological differences; but in the twentieth century, some scientists began to rely on genetic makeup to differentiate between species. Both methods had obvious shortcomings. Using the Linnaean method, for example, scientists had for years considered the blue goose and the snow goose of the northern United States to be separate species since they looked so different, but biologists later determined that they merely represented color variations within one species. The greatest problem with the genetic system was that, if taken to its extremes, every individual plant and animal would have to be labeled as a distinct species since no two are genetically identical.

In a series of lectures and articles in the 1930s and 1940s, Mayr offered a more logical definition of species. He proposed in his 1940 paper "Speciation Phenomena in Birds" that "species are groups of actually or potentially interbreeding natural populations which are reproductively isolated from other such groups." The blue goose and the snow goose, therefore, were of a single species since they freely interbred. One immediate benefit of such a definition was that it transformed "species" from a rather arbitrary taxonomic convenience into a real unit in nature. It also led to the discovery of many cryptic or sibling species.

During this time, Mayr also developed his theory about how a new species evolves, a topic that was hotly debated by biologists in the 1930s. The famous nineteenth-century British naturalist Charles Darwin based his theory of evolution, published as On the Origin of Species (1859), on his observation that a certain degree of variation exists among the members of any given species. His hypothesis, simply stated, proposed that those individuals whose characteristics were best suited to their environment were most likely to survive long enough to reproduce, thus passing on those beneficial characteristics to their offspring. Eventually, those traits would be disseminated through the entire population. He therefore concluded, according to The New Columbia Encyclopedia (1975), that "the origin and diversification of species results from the gradual accumulation of individual modifications." With the qualification that only genetic, not acquired, characteristics could be transmitted from one generation to another, that theory of "natural selection" became widely accepted. Darwin, however, had taken for granted that variations exist within a population: he did not even attempt to determine how those variations occurred. Since the question of how those modifications are produced is of critical importance in any evolutionary theory, that problem became the pivotal point of the ensuing controversy.

According to the theory advanced by geneticist Richard Goldschmidt and other eminent scientists, the multiplication of species is due entirely to a certain type of genetic mutation called "systemic mutation." The adventitious intrusion of these "hopeful monsters," as he termed such mutants, into nature's pantheon implied that new species emerge instantaneously rather than gradually and are a product of individuals rather than groups, that geographic factors are relatively unimportant, and that natural selection's only use is to weed out

harmful mutants. All those ideas offended Mayr. In articles that began appearing in 1940, Mayr argued that new species emerge over long periods of time in geographic isolation, not from individual mutations that could occur within a single generation and within the parent population. That theory of "geographic speciation," which had been advanced as early as 1825 but whose popularity had lapsed, suggested that species evolve when owing to environmental changes or geographic obstacles part of a species population becomes isolated in a reduced range. For example, the original woodlands of Australia slowly broke up into separate forests near the coast as the climate grew more arid. The vast steppe lands that separated them made it increasingly difficult for members of single species of birds to interbreed. Since those small, isolated populations would have a distinctly limited gene pool, the stage would be set for new and relatively rapid combinations of inherited characteristics. In addition, the environment might vary in important ways from that in the usual species range. As a result, in the context of that uniquely demanding natural and genetic environment, in time new daughter species would emerge, complete with genetic "isolating mechanisms," as Mayr called them, that would prevent their members from breeding with other species, including members of the parent population, when the geographic or environmental barrier were eventually removed or surmounted. Mayr's ideas about species and speciation were widely accepted upon their publication in his landmark study Systematics and the Origin of Species (Columbia Univ. Pr., 1942). As the author later observed, "That geographic speciation is the prevailing process of speciation, at least in animals, was no longer questioned after this date."

As a consequence of his work in systematics, Mayr became an important force in the "modern evolutionary synthesis." As he explained to Carol A. Johmann in an interview for Omni (February 1983), previously within the Darwinian framework there had been "two main branches of evolutionary biologist—the laboratory geneticist and the field naturalist—and each was highly ignorant of what the other knew and of the kinds of ideas, concepts, and evidence the other had. As a result, they were both one-sided in their explanations" of evolutionary phenomena. By equating speciation with the acquisition of genetically based isolating mechanisms, a process facilitated by geographic and environmental factors, however, he proved the interdependence of the two branches of study. Mayr's interest in evolution and evolutionary theory increased steadily during the 1940s. In 1946 he founded the Society for the Study of Evolution and a year later he established its journal, Evolution, which he edited until 1949. He was the society's first secretary and served as its president in 1950.

Promoted in 1944 to curator of the Whitney-Rothschild Collection of the American Museum of Natural History, Mayr held that post for nearly a decade. In addition to his curatorial duties and work for the exhibition halls of the museum, he wrote numerous articles for scientific journals and popular magazines and collaborated on important scholarly works, coediting with G. L. Jepsen and G. G. Simpson *Genetics, Paleontology, and Evolution* (Princeton Univ. Pr., 1949) and writing the textbook *Methods and Principles of Systematic Zoology* (McGraw-Hill, 1953) with E. G. Linsley and R. L. Usinger. Mayr resigned his curatorship in 1953 in order to accept a position at Harvard University as the Alexander Agassiz Professor of Zoology, and from 1961 to 1970 he also served as director of Harvard's Museum of Comparative Zoology.

Continuing his work in evolutionary theory at Harvard, Mayr refined what he considers to be "perhaps the most original theory [he has] ever proposed." Although he had been a strong proponent of geographic speciation, further study convinced him that there were two forms of such speciation. As early as the 1920s and 1930s, while examining specimens collected on his South Seas expeditions, Mayr had noticed that the most physically distinctive variations within a species occurred in members living on the edge of the species range. When he later became more interested in evolution and explored the full significance of that finding, he concluded that "the evolutionarily most important events take place in such peripherally isolated populations." That concept of "peripatric speciation" suggested that a distinct species may arise when a few adults—even a single fertilized female—wander beyond the periphery of the species range and establish a new colony or "founder population." If the colony survived, the different environment and limited gene pool would exert great pressure for relatively quick evolutionary change. Such rapid emergence of new daughter species through peripatric speciation, he conjectured, might explain the gaps in the fossil record (that is, the theoretical "missing links") that had long puzzled paleontologists. As Stephen Jay Gould noted in *Science* (January 20, 1984), even after almost four decades of continued research and scientific discoveries, the theory of peripatric speciation "has not only held up remarkably well as by far the major mode of speciation in nature, but has also been unusually fruitful in extension and implication."

Published by Harvard University's Belknap Press in 1963, *Animal Species and Evolution* expounded his peripatric speciation theory in the context of a thorough, detailed synthesis of advances made in taxonomy, population genetics, zoogeography, and other fields of evolutionary study since the publication in 1942 of *Systematics and the Origin of Species*. Writing in *Science* (May 10, 1963), L. H. Throckmorton and J. L. Hubby praised the treatise as "an eminently readable and thoroughly absorbing description of one of the most fascinating areas of biological investigation." In an even more enthusiastic review, the eminent evolutionary biologist Sir Julian Huxley hailed it as "a magistral book . . . certainly the most important study of evolution that has appeared in many

years—perhaps since the publication of *The Origin of Species.*"

In the chapter on human evolution in that treatise and later in several newspaper and magazine interviews, Mayr expressed little hope for the future of mankind. Like Sir Julian Huxley and other scientists, Mayr believes that the human brain reached approximately its modern size over 100,-000 years ago. There is no evidence for further improvement but danger of retrogression. He has speculated that as men grew more intelligent and banded together, below-average individuals were given a greater degree of protection and thus a better chance of surviving to reproduce. As a result, natural selection was excluded. An obvious means to stem the decline, Mayr has suggested, would be positive eugenics: allowing only the "best" of mankind to reproduce. Since that method is "totally intolerable," Mayr has repeatedly emphasized the importance of education as a means of improving the species. He warns, however, that all such efforts will be futile unless the population explosion and destruction of the environment are soon checked, for on his present course man faces almost certain extinction.

Having served as a driving force in the successful establishment by late mid-century of the "new systematics" (of which his definition of species was the centerpiece) and neo-Darwinism as fundamental principles of evolutionary biology, Mayr began to explore in the late 1950s the historical and philosophical aspects of biological thought in celebrated papers on the establishment of Darwinism; on Darwin's development of the concept of natural selection; and on the thought of the Chevalier de Lamarck (1744–1829), one of the first men to conceive of the possibility of gradual evolution. Since his appointment as professor emeritus at Harvard in 1975, Mayr has concentrated even more vigorously on that field. His extensive studies culminated in yet another scientific tour de force: *The Growth of Biological Thought* (Belknap Press, 1982), the first volume in a projected two-volume, exhaustive history.

Almost a thousand pages long, the tome is divided into three sections: "the diversity of life," "evolution," and "variation and inheritance." In each, Mayr traces the centuries-long struggle between the "essentialists," who believe that every species has a distinct "essence" that is present without variation in every member, and the "population thinkers," whose emphasis on the uniqueness of each individual and thus a degree of variation within each species cleared the way for Darwinism. The theories of each school and its major thinkers are applied in turn to Mayr's three topics rather than presented as a coherent whole, but "Mayr is so effective in this mode of analysis," Frederic L. Holmes wrote in the *Washington Post's Book World* (June 20, 1982), "that he is amply justified in his choice of organization." The scientist's dual role, as participant in those controversies and historian of them, resulted in a very personal, perhaps biased, presentation, but like most critics

Holmes concluded that "in spite of this major limitation, *The Growth of Biological Thought* will be a richly rewarding experience for all who take the trouble to grapple seriously with it. Mayr's vivid manner, his clear analytical distinctions, his candor in meeting controversies head on, make his discussions as stimulating as they are valuable." The second volume will discuss the other half of the biological sciences: "functional biology," an umbrella term for subdisciplines such as embryology, physiology, and biochemistry.

A member of numerous professional societies, Mayr has received nine honorary degrees from universities around the world and he has also been honored with many awards and prizes, including the Wallace Darwin Medal (1958) and the Linnean Medal (1977) from the Linnean Society of London, the National Medal of Science (1970), and the prestigious Balzan Prize (1984), the equivalent in the biological sciences of the Nobel Prize. On May 4, 1935 Ernst Mayr married Margarete Simon. They have two children, Christa Elisabeth and Susanne. In his leisure time, Mayr, who is five feet ten inches tall and has white hair and brown eyes, is a naturalist, gardener, and traveler. He has no political or church affiliation.

References: Omni 5:73+ F '83; Science 223:255+ Ja 20 '84 por; Science 84 5:40+ Je '84 por; Contemporary Authors new rev vol 2 (1981); McGraw-Hill Modern Men of Science vol II (1968); Who's Who in America, 1984-85

McClintock, Barbara

June 16, 1902– Geneticist. Address: b. Cold Spring Harbor Laboratory, Cold Spring Harbor, N.Y. 11724

When eighty-one-year-old Barbara McClintock was awarded the 1983 Nobel Prize for Medicine or Physiology for her pioneering work in the mechanisms of genetic inheritance, her colleagues were unanimous in applauding her achievement. "It is not a controversial award," remarked James Watson, the discoverer, with Francis Crick, of the molecular structure of DNA and the director of the Cold Spring Harbor Laboratory in New York, where Dr. McClintock has lived and conducted her often solitary research since 1941. "No one thinks of genetics now without the implications of her work." Yet this recognition was a long time coming, for the work cited by the Nobel committee—her discovery of movable genetic elements in the maize plant—was first published in 1951. At the time, scientific orthodoxy scorned the notion that genes could "jump" around on a chromosome, and Dr. McClintock was left to continue her work in isolation. It was not until the advent of molecular biology that others independently confirmed her research. In a public statement issued a few hours after she was named a Nobel laureate, Barbara McClintock, who is only the third woman to be awarded an individual rather than a shared prize in the sciences (the others were Marie Curie, in 1911, and Dorothy Crowfoot Hodgkins, in 1964), told reporters: "The prize is such an extraordinary honor. It might seem unfair, however, to reward a person for having so much pleasure, over the years, asking the maize plant to solve specific problems and then watching its responses."

Barbara McClintock was born in Hartford, Connecticut on June 16, 1902, the third of the four children of Thomas Henry McClintock, a physician, and his wife, Sara (Handy) McClintock. After the birth of her only brother in 1904, she was periodically sent to live with her paternal aunt and uncle in rural Massachusetts so that her mother could better care for him. As she recalled to her biographer, Evelyn Fox Keller, in an interview for Miss Keller's book *A Feeling For the Organism: The Life and Work of Barbara McClintock* (1983), she "immensely" enjoyed the months she spent in the country with her relatives on and off until she attained school age. In 1908 the McClintocks moved from Hartford to what was then the semirural Flatbush section of Brooklyn, New York, where Thomas McClintock took a job as company doctor for Standard Oil's tanker crews. Once more back with her family, Barbara McClintock attended the local public elementary school, but she was more interested in ice skating or playing baseball, football, and volleyball with the neighborhood boys than in studying. In retrospect, however, her most valued experiences as a child were solitary ones—reading and "thinking about things," as she put it.

In her science classes at Erasmus Hall High School in Brooklyn, Barbara McClintock put her passion for "thinking about things" to practical use. "I loved information," she told Miss Keller. "I loved to know things. I would solve some of the problems in ways that weren't the answers the instructor expected. . . . It was a tremendous joy, the whole process of finding that answer, just pure joy." Dr. and Mrs. McClintock had always encouraged their children to be independent and individualistic, but when Barbara failed to develop appropriate "feminine" behavior and concerns during her adolescence, Mrs. McClintock worried that her daughter might become, in Miss McClintock's words, "a strange person, a person that didn't belong to society," or, worse, "a college professor."

Partly because of her mother's opposition to her attending college, Miss McClintock went to work as an interviewer in an employment agency after her graduation from high school in 1918. Determined "to educate [herself] some way or other," she spent her evenings and weekends reading at the library. Her dedication and singlemindedness so impressed her parents that they eventually gave in, and in 1919 Barbara McClintock enrolled at Cornell University in Ithaca, New York as a biology major in the College of Agriculture.

From the first day of classes she was enthralled by her courses, but she somehow found the time to lead an active social life. Among other things, she played the banjo with a jazz group and served as president of the freshman women's class. She even considered pledging a sorority, but when she discovered that none of her Jewish friends had been asked to join, she rejected the invitation. As she became more and more absorbed in her studies, she gradually withdrew from the collegiate social whirl. It was during that time that she consciously chose the solitary life. "I was just not adjusted, never had been, to being closely associated with anybody, even members of my family . . . ," she explained to Miss Keller. "There was not that strong necessity for a personal attachment to anybody. I just didn't feel it."

In her junior year Miss McClintock began taking graduate courses in genetics, and on receiving her B.S. degree in 1923 she registered as a graduate student in the botany department, with a major in cytology and minors in genetics and zoology. She took her M.A. degree in 1925 and her Ph.D. degree two years later. The decade of the 1920s was a stimulating time for students at Cornell's College of Agriculture, for members of the college's faculty were breaking new ground in the investigation of plant genetics, particularly in the breeding and study of maize, or Indian corn, whose multicolored kernels provide visible evidence of genetic changes from one generation to the next. In her first year of graduate school, Miss McClintock found that she could identify individual maize chromosomes under the microscope by their distinctive morphological features. Her discovery opened the door to the integration of plant-breeding experiments with chromosomal analysis.

Together with two fellow graduate students, Marcus M. Rhoades and George W. Beadle (both of whom were to become renowned geneticists), Barbara McClintock pursued her study of the morphology of maize chromosomes and the correlation between visible genetic traits and the newly discovered cytological markers. She published no fewer than nine papers outlining her research between 1929 and 1931. In collaboration with another young colleague, Harriet Creighton, she conducted an experiment that conclusively proved the widely held assumption that chromosomes exchange genetic information and physical material when they cross over in the early stages of meiosis, or cell division for reproduction.

When the famed geneticist Thomas Hunt Morgan visited Cornell in the spring of 1931, he was so excited by the McClintock-Creighton findings, which the two scientists themselves considered to be preliminary, that he immediately wrote a letter to the editor of the *Proceedings of the National Academy of Sciences* announcing a forthcoming article on the subject. Thus encouraged, Dr. McClintock and Miss Creighton submitted their trailblazing paper, "A Correlation of Cytological and Genetical Crossing-Over in *Zea mays*," which has been described as the cornerstone of experimental genetics. Published in August 1931, it preceded by several months the publication of the results of Curt Stern's parallel study of the fruit fly *Drosophila*.

In 1931 Dr. McClintock was awarded a two-year fellowship by the National Research Council. Over the next twenty-four months, she divided her time between Cornell, the University of Missouri in Columbia, and the California Institute of Technology in Pasadena, making the frequent cross-country trips in her Model A Ford roadster. She first went to the University of Missouri at the invitation of Lewis Stadler, a former colleague at Cornell and a pioneer in the use of X-rays to induce genetic mutations. The deliberate creation of mutations in the maize plant greatly facilitated the investigation of its genetic structure and composition, and in the summer of 1931 Miss McClintock undertook the task of identifying the nature of the chromosomal alterations that showed up as dramatic changes in the color and texture of the maize kernels. Her examination of mutant circular or ring chromosomes, which often produced variegated kernels, was crucial to her later work. Other important discoveries followed, among them the detection of what she named the "nucleolar organizer"—that region of a particular chromosome responsible for the formation and organization of a functional nucleolus, the small, round mass in the metabolic nucleus involved in the synthesis of ribosomes.

The recipient of a Guggenheim Fellowship, Dr. McClintock traveled to Berlin, Germany in 1933 to study with Richard B. Goldschmidt, the controversial geneticist who headed the Kaiser Wilhelm Institute. Partly because of her admitted political naivete, the trip was a traumatic experience. "Disturbed and utterly panicked," to use her words, by the rise of Nazism, she abruptly returned to Cornell. There, Dr. McClintock was forced to confront the reality that the avenues of professional advancement open to women were severely limited. Despite the acclaim she had received for her work, Cornell would not give her a faculty appointment. (According to Miss Keller, it was not until 1947 that Cornell hired its first woman assistant professor in a discipline other than home economics.) Although she could easily have obtained a teaching position at a women's college, Dr. McClintock was determined to carry on her genetic investigations as a research scientist.

For two years the Rockefeller Foundation funded a research position for Dr. McClintock in Rollins A. Emerson's genetics laboratory at Cornell, but the uncertainty of the arrangement irritated the young scientist, especially since less qualified male colleagues were being offered more stable appointments. She was not interested in prestige or a high salary, but she did want to be evaluated on her merits and not her gender. Finally, in 1936 she was asked to join the faculty of the University of Missouri as an assistant professor. Over the next few years, in addition to teaching, she continued to probe the cytogenetics of maize and published a series of papers explaining the process by which broken chromosomes reanneal. Despite her election in 1939 to the vice-presidency of the Genetics Society of America, Dr. McClintock's status at the University of Missouri remained marginal. Her independence and maverick behavior, coupled with the prevailing prejudices against women academics, precluded any chance of promotion. By 1941 she had decided to leave the university.

Dr. McClintock spent the summer of 1941 working with her old friend Marcus Rhoades at the Cold Spring Harbor Laboratory on Long Island. Toward the end of the year, Milislav Demerec, a geneticist she had known for several years, became director of the department of genetics of the Carnegie Institution of Washington at Cold Spring Harbor. He immediately offered Dr. McClintock a one-year and then a permanent position. She has been working at the Cold Spring Harbor Laboratory ever since. After a shaky start, the 1940s turned out to be not only an unusually productive decade for her but also one in which she at last received some recognition for her pioneering work: in 1944 she was elected president of the Genetics Society of America, listed among the 1,000 top scientists in the United States by the new edition of *American Men of Science*, and perhaps most important, she became only the third woman to be named to the National Academy of Sciences.

It was also during the 1940s that Barbara McClintock performed the experiments that led to her discovery of transposable genetic elements, or "jumping genes," as they are sometimes called. Observing succeeding generations of maize, Dr. McClintock noticed in the leaves and kernels of some plants color changes that failed to follow a predictable hereditary pattern. When she compared the variant specimens with their parent plants under the microscope, she found that parts of the chromosomes had changed position. She eventually concluded, after six years of painstaking research and documentation, that the genes that determine such characteristics as color are manipulated by genetic "controlling elements," whose locations on the chromosomes are not fixed. One controlling element, which she named the dissociator, is responsible for suppressing the activity of the pigment gene; another, the activator, controls the dissociator—in effect, summons it to "jump" into action alongside a particular structural gene. The discovery of transposable elements, or transposition, had far-reaching implications for the understanding of cell differentiation in the growth and development of an organism.

Dr. McClintock's theory of movable genetic elements was at total variance with the predominant view of genes as immovable beads on a string. When she presented her findings at a Cold Spring Harbor symposium in the summer of 1951, virtually no one understood—let alone accepted—the significance and implications of her work. "They called me crazy, absolutely mad at times," she recalled years later. Disappointed by the scientific community's repeated dismissals of her work, Dr. McClintock stopped publishing the results of her experiments a few years later, although she continued her research.

In the 1950s advances in the relatively new field of molecular biology, including discovery in 1953 of the "double helix" structure of DNA, the molecular basis of heredity, lent a measure of support to Dr. McClintock's theory of genetic transposition; yet at the same time it served to isolate her even more from the scientific mainstream. Fascinated by the mechanistic aspects of molecular biology, young researchers generally disdained her "old-fashioned" approach based on observation over time, documentation, and microscopic analysis. From 1958 to 1960 Dr. McClintock, at the invitation of the National Academy of Sciences, took time out from her research to train Latin American cytologists to collect and identify indigenous strains of maize, and in 1965 she was appointed Andrew White Professor-at-Large by Cornell University, a chair she held for ten years.

Fittingly, it was the sophisticated techniques of molecular biology that eventually vindicated Barbara McClintock's 1951 discovery of transposable genetic elements in maize. In a series of genetic engineering experiments in the 1970s, molecular biologists found that pieces of bacterial DNA do indeed "jump around" on the chromosomes. The implications of those findings are enormous, affecting everything from genetic engineering to cancer research to the study of evolution. Finally recognized as a scientific visionary, Dr. McClintock was showered with honors and awards, including the Kimber Genetics Award from the National Academy of Sciences in 1967, the National Medal of Science in 1970, the Albert Lasker Basic Medical Research Award—the highest honor of its kind in the United States—and Israel's Wolf

Foundation Prize in 1981, and Columbia University's Horwitz Prize, which she shared with Susumu Tonegawa, in 1982. She was also awarded in 1981 a lifetime, tax-free annual fellowship of $60,000 from the MacArthur Foundation. When asked by a reporter if she was bitter about the long years of neglect, Dr. McClintock replied, as quoted in *Newsday* (October 11, 1983), "If you know you're right, you don't care. You know that sooner or later, it will come out in the wash."

The title of Evelyn Fox Keller's biography of Barbara McClintock—*A Feeling for the Organism*—reflects the geneticist's holistic approach to science as well as her reverence for nature. "[An organism] isn't just a piece of plastic, it's something that is constantly being affected by the environment, constantly showing attributes and disabilities in its growth . . . ," Dr. McClintock explained in an interview for the book. "You need to know those plants well enough so that if anything changes . . . , you [can] look at the plant and right away you know what the damage you see is from—something that scraped across it or something that bit it or something that the wind did."

Many of Dr. McClintock's key discoveries came to her through her almost intuitive grasp of the nature of the organism she was examining. "I found that the more I worked with [chromosomes] the bigger and bigger [they] got, and when I was really working with them I wasn't outside, I was down there," she told Miss Keller. "I was part of the system. . . . I even was able to see the internal parts of the chromosomes—actually everything was there. It surprised me because I actually felt as if I were right down there and these were my friends."

Barbara McClintock, who stands five feet tall and weighs about 100 pounds, has graying brown hair worn in a short, cropped style and bright, alert eyes. Uninterested in what she has called "decorating the torso," she dresses simply and casually, usually in dungarees, shirt, cardigan, and oxfords. She reads omnivorously and, according to her colleagues, can converse on a wide variety of subjects, ranging from insect evolution to Tibetan Buddhism. Her fascination with Tibetan Buddhism is a reflection of her conviction that the Western "scientific method" is but one path to a fuller understanding of the nature of life.

Dr. McClintock regularly spends as many as sixteen hours a day working in her cornfield or laboratory, but when she takes the time to relax she is most likely to go for a long walk in the woods, armed with field guides on birds, insects, or plants. An intensely private person, she has shunned publicity throughout her career. Characteristically, on the morning she learned that she had been awarded the Nobel Prize, she dodged the anticipated reporters and went for a walk to gather black walnuts to use in baking brownies for friends. Dr. McClintock lives alone in a small apartment in Cold Spring Harbor within easy walking distance of her laboratory.

References: N Y Daily News p26 O 16 '83 pors; N Y Rev of Books 31:3+ Mr 29 '84; N Y Times B p3 N 18 '81; New Scientist p78+ O 13 '83 pors; Newsweek 98:74 N 30 '81 por, 102:97 O 24 '83 por; Time 122:53+ O 24 '83 pors; American Men and Women of Science (1982); International Who's Who, 1984-85; Who's Who in America, 1984-85; Who's Who of American Women, 1983-84

McFarlane, Robert C(arl)

July 12, 1937- United States government official. Address: b. National Security Council, the White House, 1600 Pennsylvania Avenue, N.W., Washington, D.C. 20500

Robert C. McFarlane, Ronald Reagan's national security adviser since October 1983, is responsible for helping the president make and advance the crucial policy decisions, often involving issues of war and peace as well as long-term national goals and interests, that determine America's relations with other countries. Coincidentally, McFarlane's presence in the White House helped to blur the perceived edges of the Reagan world view as the Republicans geared for the presidential elections of 1984, when they hoped to appeal to a wider constituency than the "New Right" that credited itself with generating the momentum for Reagan's victory at the polls in 1980. Unlike his predecessor in the post of assistant to the president for national security affairs (his exact job title), William P. Clark, McFarlane, a former Marine lieutenant colonel, is not a conservative ideologue but a pragmatic technocrat whose only hard line is the importance of a strong military presence as the bolster of international diplomacy. He has defended "covert action" in such regions as Central America as an "intermediate option of policy," giving the United States an alternative between doing nothing and going to war on the side of allies under attack.

Like Alexander Haig before him, McFarlane made the transition from military to foreign affairs under the guidance of Henry A. Kissinger, the New Right's "liberal internationalist" bête noir, in the Republican administrations of Richard Nixon and Gerald R. Ford. After the Democratic interregnum of President Jimmy Carter, he returned to the executive branch in 1981 as counselor to Haig, President Reagan's first secretary of state.

Robert Carl McFarlane (who is known to his friends and associates as "Bud") was born in Washington, D.C. on July 12, 1937 to William Doddrige McFarlane, a New Deal Democratic Congressman from Texas, and Alma (Carl) McFarlane. He grew up in Graham, Texas, and after graduating from high school there he entered the United States Naval Academy in Annapolis, Maryland. In 1958 he received his B.S. degree in electrical engineering at Annapolis and was commissioned a second lieutenant in the United States Marine Corps.

McFarlane spent most of the following seven-year period on duty in the Far East. In 1965 he was sent to the Graduate Institute of International Studies at the University of Geneva in Switzerland, where he received his M.S. degree in strategic studies magna cum laude two years later. After tours of duty in Japan, Korea, and Vietnam, McFarlane joined the administration of President Richard Nixon in 1971 as a White House fellow, a capacity in which he served as executive assistant to the president's counsel for legislative affairs.

In 1973 McFarlane became the military assistant to Henry A. Kissinger in the Nixon White House, where Kissinger held the two posts of national security adviser and head of the National Security Council in addition to his duties at the Department of State. Following the resignation of President Nixon in 1974, Kissinger and his staff, untainted by the Watergate scandal, survived the transition to the Ford administration. When Kissinger left his White House positions in 1975, Lieutenant General Brent Scowcroft, his deputy at the National Security Council, resigned his military commission in order to accept promotion to national security adviser. McFarlane remained military assistant under Scowcroft, with the upgraded title of special assistant to the president for national security affairs.

When the Democratic administration of Jimmy Carter displaced the Ford presidency in January 1977, the Marine Corps assigned McFarlane to the National Defense University, in Washington, D.C. As a senior research fellow there, he wrote the papers "The Political Potential of Parity" and "At Sea, Where We Belong," both of which were published in the U.S. Naval Institute Proceedings.

In addition, McFarlane wrote Crisis Resolution: Presidential Decision Making in the "Mayaguez"

and Korean Confrontations (Westview Press, 1979) in collaboration with Colonel Richard G. Head of the Air Force and Frisco W. Short, a retired army colonel. The book analyzed two incidents that occurred during the Ford presidency: the Cambodian seizure of the United States merchant vessel Mayaguez and the killing of two American officers in the demilitarized zone between North and South Korea. Balancing the danger of small-scale crises escalating into major conflicts against America's need to defend its fundamental interests and maintain its credibility as a superpower, McFarlane and his coauthors gave the Ford administration high marks for its response to the two incidents. Examining the decision-making process and the political, moral, military, and other criteria involved, they concluded: "The United States paid a high price to recover the Mayaguez and her crew, but the military actions achieved results, demonstrated firmness, and restored confidence in the ability of the United States to act and protect its interests. On the Korean DMZ, the response achieved the immediate results of obtaining a North Korean apology and enhanced long-term American security interests. Thus, the importance of successful crisis management stems not simply from the immediate crisis situation, but from the significance of international crises as tests of stability, national character, will, and resolve."

According to friends, McFarlane's superiors in the Marine Corps did not fully appreciate the value of his work in the White House and at the National Defense University. Deciding he had been away from military life long enough, they sent him on a tour of duty in Okinawa. Unhappy in that situation, and troubled as well by the course of President Carter's foreign policy, he resigned from the Marines in 1979 and joined the professional staff of the Senate Armed Services Committee. Working closely for two years with Senator John Tower, a fellow Texan and the committee's ranking Republican member, he gained experience on Capitol Hill that would soon serve him well as an advocate with Congress for the Reagan administration's foreign policy legislative agenda.

Alexander M. Haig Jr., then President Reagan's secretary of state, knowing McFarlane from their service together in the Nixon and Ford administrations, brought him into the Reagan administration as a counselor in the Department of State in January 1981. As counselor, McFarlane worked with Pentagon officials on contingency plans for dealing with problems in Cuba and Central America, secretly visited Pakistan in an unsuccessful effort to persuade President Mohammed Zia ul-Haq to abandon his nuclear weapons program; in testimony before the House Foreign Affairs Committee, strongly criticized Israel for failing to consult the United States before using American-supplied warplanes in an air strike that destroyed a nuclear reactor nearing completion in Iraq; and personally carried to Israeli Prime Minister Menachem Begin the Reagan administration's nonplused reaction to the unilateral preemptive strike.

Haig's undersecretary at the Department of State was William P. Clark, a career-long political cohort of President Reagan's whose sketchy knowledge of foreign affairs had caused him embarrassment during his Senate confirmation hearings. When Clark became national security adviser in January 1982, he did so on the strength of his Reaganist ideological purity, not his expertise in foreign policy. As his expert, Clark took along to the White House with him Robert C. McFarlane, in the position of deputy assistant for national security affairs.

As Clark's deputy, McFarlane ran the day-to-day operations of the National Security Council and its staff, coordinated the activities of all relevant agencies, and digested the complex mass of information from those agencies into formulations that could be understood and used by Clark and President Reagan. He was, for example, a principal writer of the September 1982 speech in which President Reagan boldly but unsuccessfully tried to resuscitate the Camp David accords by asking Israel to stop its building of settlements in occupied Arab lands and Jordan to cooperate in the creation of a Palestinian homeland on the West Bank.

As a liaison with the Department of State, McFarlane was, in the words of one official at the department, "the facilitator, the one you could talk sense to." It was as a lobbyist on Capital Hill, however, that McFarlane proved most effective, running interference for the president and lowering Congressional hackles raised by Clark's hard line. Willing to compromise to achieve a bipartisan foreign policy, he was instrumental in saving several administration initiatives from defeat in Congress. One was the MX missile, which Congress voted against funding in December 1982. Working with Brent Scrowcroft, who had been appointed chairman of the Commission on Strategic Forces, McFarlane helped to reverse the vote the following spring by rallying the support of moderate Democrats for an omnibus bill approving not only the building of the MX but also the development of a small, single-warhead missile and the adoption of a more flexible strategic arms control offer to the Soviet Union, including the "build-down concept," which became the Reagan administration's answer to the nuclear freeze movement. "More than anyone else in this administration," Democratic Representative Les Aspin of Wisconsin observed, "Bud McFarlane is the guy who has the confidence of members of Congress."

In July 1983 President Reagan named McFarlane to succeed Philip C. Habib as his special envoy to the Middle East, where the overlapping of the Arab-Israeli conflict and the civil war in Lebanon had turned that country into an international powder keg. The mission was a frustrating one for McFarlane, as it had been for Habib before him. The Israelis, who occupied a quarter of Lebanese territory, would agree to a timetable for the complete withdrawal of their troops only if Syria, which occupied half the country, did likewise. Syrian Presient Hafez al-Assad refused to comply un-

less and until Lebanon had a government that did not in his view threaten Syrian interests—a government that would, presumably, be incapable of reaching an accord with Israel.

When President Reagan named McFarlane to succeed William Clark (who had moved to the Department of the Interior) as national security adviser in October 1983, the appointment was deplored by the Republican party's New Right but warmly welcomed in the Department of State and the diplomatic community, which trusted the steadiness of his hand in foreign affairs and appreciated how he had virtually singlehandedly brought to the National Security Council staff an awareness of the importance of a flexible arms control policy in international as well as congressional relations.

Among the international danger spots to which the new national security adviser gave his close attention were the Persian Gulf, where the Ayatollah Ruhollah Khomeini threatened to block the oil route; Europe, where the Soviets warned of a showdown over the deployment of United States medium-range nuclear missiles; and Nicaragua, where the administration's anticommunist strategy was jeopardized by congressional overtures to cut off "covert" aid to the anti-Sandinista rebels. In a television interview on November 14, 1983 McFarlane said that President Reagan favored the recent revival of the Central American Defense Council to consider the possibility of mounting a military alliance for the overthrow of the Nicaraguan government but that "to suggest that they are plotting some kind of invasion is a little overdrawn."

Meanwhile, American strategy in the Middle East was progressing toward seemingly total disarray, along a route that began with the October 1983 kamikaze truck-bombing of the United States Marine base in Beirut, Lebanon in which 241 American servicemen were killed. Following that massacre, areas around Beirut suspected of harboring hostile forces were subjected to American air strikes. In the United States the Department of Justice launched an investigation into leakage of information about the strikes from the White House to the press. "The information in [published] articles led the public to believe that Bud [McFarlane] himself had made recommendations relating to particular military actions," White House counselor Edwin Meese 3d explained, as quoted in the *Washington Post* (November 24, 1983), "and this would make him a more prominent target while he was going from country to country."

Siding with Secretary of State George Shultz and against brass in the Pentagon, McFarlane warned that a "precipitate and unilateral" withdrawal of the American Marines from Lebanon would severely damage United States security interests in the Middle East and "contradict the ideals and values which underwrite our position of leadership." Heeding that warning, President Reagan in January 1984 approved a plan for the gradual redeployment of the Marines. Following the collapse of Lebanese President Amin Gemayel's factionalized cabinet and victories of Muslim militias over government troops in west Beirut and the city's southern environs, however, virtually complete withdrawal of the international peacekeeping force was accelerated. As McFarlane had feared, President Gemayal then abrogated the Israeli-Lebanese security pact and turned to Soviet-leaning Syria to help him maintain his government and resolve the rivalries that had been tearing Lebanon apart for nine years.

The National Security Council—consisting of the president, the vice-president, the secretaries of state and defense, the director of the Central Intelligence Agency, and the chairman of the joint chiefs of staff—meets at the discretion of the president to discuss domestic, foreign, and military policies as they relate to national security. According to a senior administration official quoted by Leslie H. Gelb in the *New York Times* (March 28, 1984), President Reagan deals with differences of opinion in the council "only on the broadest macro terms, and that still leaves basic differences between Shultz and [Secretary of Defense Caspar W.] Weinberger unresolved and prevents the adoption of consistent policies." Gelb commented: "With a few exceptions, the National Security Council staff is still widely regarded as weak [in strategy], but now much better run than before. . . . McFarlane has been trying . . . to gain agreement on a set of priorities for Mr. Reagan, such as orienting policy more toward Asia than Europe, starting a visible dialogue with Moscow, and making a hard push on Arab-Israeli negotiations, [but] at this point [he] is said to be focusing on more modest goals, including some action on Soviet-American relations . . . , preventing further erosion of Washington's position in Central America, and avoiding a war in the Middle East." Most of the decision memoranda are prepared for the president's signature by McFarlane and his staff without formal National Security Council meetings.

According to White House and other administration officials cited by Leslie H. Gelb, McFarlane has made his staff into "a more powerful bureaucratic instrument in day-to-day affairs," but he remains "far less powerful personally on major policy issues" than his predecessor, William P. Clark. "The source of McFarlane's power is knowledge of substance and an understanding of how the bureaucracy works," Gelb wrote, "not a personal relationship with President Reagan. . . . Mr. McFarlane is known to feel that his ability [in major policy decisions] is sharply circumscribed by Mr. Reagan's continuing insistence on cabinet-style government. . . . But, without exception, officials say he has substantially upgraded the professional quality of formulating and coordinating policy on routine matters such as deciding on aid levels and preparing for the president's trip to China." On major issues the best that McFarlane can do, usually, is to reconcile conflicting points of view without offering clear strategies. An example was the study on possible Soviet arms-control violations sent to Congress by the administration. The study juggled at least three points of view: that of

the Department of State (cautious but open to negotiation with the Soviets), that of the civilian leadership at the Pentagon (accusatory), and that of President Reagan (non-accusatory).

Occasionally, McFarlane has been able to join with George Shultz in making recommendations, such as tougher options in Central America, that prevailed over those made by Secretary of Defense Weinberger or others. Also, on the other hand, McFarlane was the person primarily responsible for persuading President Reagan not to fire Richard Perle, Weinberger's assistant for security aspects of high-tech trade with the Soviet Union. Weinberger did not want to lose Perle, whose firing was, if reports were correct, suggested by Malcolm Baldrige and the business-minded liberal internationalists at the Department of Commerce.

In preparation for President Reagan's trip to China in April 1984, McFarlane was involved in a completely different trade issue—overcoming the opposition of congressional conservatives to high-tech trade with China. The amendment to the Export Administration Act written by Senator Jesse Helms applying to China trade restrictions similar to those already in effect against the Soviet Union contradicted the Reagan administration's "differentiation" policy regarding the two countries.

Robert C. McFarlane and Jonda Riley were married on June 7, 1959. They have three children: Lauren Leigh, Scott Patrick, and Melissa Anne. McFarlane is in his office six and sometimes seven days a week, generally arriving by seven in the morning and staying until late at night. A methodical worker, he always has on his person a batch of three-by-five note cards, and his hand-typed memos are military-like in their precision as well as their style and jargon. McFarlane is as tough-minded as he is soft-spoken, and he is a model of discretion and caution. His solemn public face and somewhat wooden public manner belie, according to friends, a mischievous sense of humor ranging from dry wit to zaniness, in the proper social circumstances. In addition to numerous military honors, McFarlane received the Alfred Thayer Mahan Award for literary achievement in 1979.

References: N Y Times p12 O 18 '82 por, p3 Jl 23 '83, p14 O 18 '83 por; Newsweek 102:25+ O 24 '83 por; U S News 5:28+ O 31 '83 por

---

McGinniss, Joe

Dec. 9, 1942– Writer. Address: b. c/o Sterling Lord, 660 Madison Ave., New York City, N.Y. 10021

"For me the only valid kind of writing is simply one guy telling you where he's been, what he knows and feels," Joe McGinniss said in an interview in 1970. His first book, *The Selling of the President*

Joe McGinniss

1968, a biting indictment of the manipulation of the American electorate by sophisticated mass-marketing techniques, was riding high on the national best-seller lists at the time. McGinnis has been meeting that self-imposed criterion in his column for the *Philadelphia Inquirer*, in his free-lance magazine pieces, and in such books as *Heroes*, since he began his journalistic career nearly twenty years ago. But in the books many critics consider to be his best—*Going to Extremes* and *Fatal Vision*—he let others do the talking, reporting their words with a journalist's detachment and revealing their moods and "tell-tale snippets of character," to use critic William Brashler's words, with a short-story writer's economy and eye for detail.

Joe McGinniss was born on December 9, 1942 in New York City, the only child of Joseph Aloysius and Mary (Leonard) McGinniss. His father, a construction specifications engineer, left that field in the late 1940s to open his own travel agency in a Manhattan hotel. Reared in Rye, a prosperous bedroom suburb of New York, Joe McGinnis attended Resurrection School, an elementary school run by the Sisters of Charity. He was, by his own admission, a "skinny, awkward, weak, and physically uncourageous" youngster, who had few friends. To compensate, he read a great deal and invented dozens of "complicated sports games played with dice." "I lived a splendid fantasy life through those games: I was quarterback, goalie, high-scoring center, brilliant relief pitcher, champion miler," he recalled in his book *Heroes* (Viking, 1976).

As a boy, McGinniss planned to enter the priesthood, like his paternal great-uncle. Instead, following his graduation from Archbishop Stepinac High School in 1960, he enrolled at the College of the Holy Cross, in Worcester, Massachusetts, where he became interested in journalism. "I thought writing would be a neat way to be involved with sports," he explained to Timothy Moore in an interview for the *Washington Post* (December 2, 1980). Turned down by the Columbia Graduate School of Journalism and armed only with a B.S. degree, which he received from Holy Cross in 1964, McGinniss talked his way into a reporting job with the *Port Chester* (New York) *Daily Item*. Nine months later, in 1965, he moved on to a night reporter's berth on the *Worcester* (Massachusetts) *Telegram*. The following year he finally reached his goal of becoming a sportswriter, when he joined the staff of the *Philadelphia Bulletin*.

McGinniss proved to be so adept at sports reporting that the rival *Philadelphia Inquirer* offered him a position as a sports columnist. Instead, to broaden his range, he asked for a general column, and to his surprise, the *Inquirer's* editors agreed. When he inaugurated his triweekly column for the *Philadelphia Inquirer* in 1966, he was, as far as he knew, the youngest regular columnist for a major American newspaper. Tailoring his pieces for the *Inquirer's* younger readers, he wrote mainly about subjects of local interest at first, but within a year, he decided to range further afield. Over the next few months, he covered and commented on the escalating American military involvement in Vietnam, the 1968 presidential primary contests, and the assassinations of the Rev. Martin Luther King Jr., the civil rights leader, and Senator Robert F. Kennedy, a candidate for the Democratic presidential nomination.

Although generally popular with the *Inquirer's* readers, McGinniss did not always see eye to eye with the newspaper's conservative publisher, Walter H. Annenberg. One column, in which McGinniss blamed the violence inherent in American society for Senator Kennedy's assassination, so infuriated Annenberg that he published an editorial in apology. Stung by his employer's public rebuke, McGinniss took a week off to conduct a long-delayed interview with sportscaster Howard Cosell for *TV Guide* magazine. It was from one of Cosell's acquaintances that he first heard about the involvement of high-powered Madison Avenue advertising agencies in the 1968 presidential election campaigns. According to McGinniss' informant, an advertising executive, the staffs of the front-running contenders of both major parties had hired experienced advertisers familiar with television marketing techniques to create and "sell" attractively packaged images of their respective candidates.

McGinniss was so intrigued by the belief that a presidential candidate would ultimately be measured "not against his predecessors—not against a standard of performance established by two centuries of democracy—but against [talk show host] Mike Douglas," as he put it, that he decided to investigate that relatively new political phenomenon in depth. He had at first intended to examine the television strategies of both standard-bearers—Vice-President Hubert H. Humphrey, the Democratic nominee, and his Republican party counterpart, former Vice-President Richard Nixon—but after he was rebuffed by the Humphrey camp, he focused his attention on the more cooperative Nixon organization. Although some of his critics contended that he deliberately misled Nixon staffers in order to win their confidence, McGinniss insists that he made his aims clear from the beginning. "My great advantage was that I wasn't considered press," McGinniss explained later, in an article for Life (October 10, 1969). "I was the guy writing a book."

Unable to obtain a leave of absence from the Inquirer, McGinniss resigned from the newspaper in June 1968 to follow the Nixon campaign around the country. Over the next five months, he observed the Republican candidate in action in stump speeches, sat in on top-level brainstorming sessions, attended tapings of spot commercials and of the carefully orchestrated one-hour "man in the arena" panel shows, and repeatedly interviewed Nixon's closest media advisers, including Frank Shakespeare, who had been with CBS Television, Harry Treleaven, a former account executive for the giant advertising agency J. Walter Thompson, and Roger Ailes, who had once been executive producer of The Mike Douglas Show.

In The Selling of the President 1968 (Trident, 1969), McGinniss contended that the highly touted "new" Nixon, the winner of the 1968 presidential election, was not much different from the Nixon who had lost the 1960 contest to John F. Kennedy. It was Nixon's image, redesigned in keeping with the McLuhanesque realities of a television-addicted electorate, that had changed. As McGinniss explained in his book, Nixon's media consultants created an image of the Republican candidate as "the leader, returning from exile. Perhaps not beloved, but respected. Firm but not harsh, just but compassionate. With flashes of warmth spaced evenly throughout." To buttress his argument that in an electronic-age election, "the medium is the massage and the masseur gets the votes," McGinniss devoted one-third of his book to reprinting notes and memoranda from Nixon's media advisers. Reviewers were generally divided along political lines. Those to the left of the political spectrum hailed The Selling of the President 1968 as witty and insightful, if "a bit frightening," reportage; those to the right denounced it as a one-sided "hatchet job."

Shortly after its publication in October 1969, The Selling of the President 1968 hit the New York Times's best-seller list, where it remained for seven months. For four of those months, it topped the chart. The phenomenal success of his first book made Joe McGinniss, at twenty-seven, a national celebrity and a "hot" property. Publishers asked him to write a book about the so-called "Chappaquiddick incident," in which Senator Edward M. Kennedy had been involved in an automobile accident that resulted in the death of his young woman passenger; broadcast executives dangled offers of a talk show or a job with the network news; and theatrical producers begged him to write a Broadway play. McGinniss turned them all down. "What this book has brought me is the first time I've had a chance to think in five years," he told Kay Bartlett in a May 1970 interview for The Associated Press. "It will also make up in advance for all the better books I hope to write that won't sell."

Over the next few years McGinniss devoted himself to completing a novel, The Dream Team (Random House, 1972), a thinly disguised autobiographical tale about the adventures of a young author on a national tour to promote his best seller. The book sold 25,000 copies in hard cover—an unusually high number for a first novel—and was chosen as an alternate selection by the Literary Guild. During the early 1970s, McGinniss continued to contribute free-lance articles on a wide variety of subjects to such publications as the Saturday Evening Post, Harper's, Sports Illustrated, Sport, Look, and the New York Times Magazine. His series of articles about the deteriorating situation in Vietnam, which was syndicated nationwide by the Philadelphia Inquirer in April 1971, was admired for its unsparing honesty and for its splendid writing.

Depressed by what seemed to him to be the erosion of the ideals and values that had once determined the course of American society, McGinniss set out, late in 1972, to look for individuals who still personified those ideals and values. He conducted in-depth interviews with a number of prominent Americans who, in another time, might have been recognized and honored as national heroes: Senator Edward M. Kennedy, the political heir apparent to the Kennedy Camelot; General William C. Westmoreland, who commanded American forces in Vietnam; Pulitzer Prize winners Arthur Miller, the dramatist, and William Styron, the novelist; Joe R. Hooper, a Congressional Medal of Honor winner and the most decorated soldier of the Vietnam war; and antiwar activist Daniel J. Berrigan, among others.

While rummaging through "the debris of America's shattered illusions," as he expressed it, McGinniss came face to face with the bits and pieces of his own broken dreams: his failed marriage, his stalled career as a writer, and his emotional instability. Heroes is as much a chronicle of McGinniss' personal search for meaning in his life as it is of his public search for "the vanished American hero." Some critics thought that McGinniss had perhaps "gone too far in identifying his personal disillusionment with the decline of heroes," as Christopher Lehmann-Haupt observed in his New York Times (April 27, 1976) review; others objected to his "glib" theories on the demise of heroes, but virtually all of them agreed that Heroes was, at least in parts, a brilliant piece of journalism.

Having spent the better part of two arduous years in the soul-wrenching experience of writing Heroes, McGinniss was, by mid-1975, "hungry for something different," as he put it, "something big, something fresh, something new." On impulse, he traveled to Alaska later in the year and remained there for about eighteen months. For much of that time, he lived in Anchorage, where he struck up friendships with high-rolling oilriggers, transplanted "flower children" and "hippies with Rotarian hearts," whiskey-sodden Eskimos, and assorted fast-buck artists. On his occasional forays into the Alaskan wilderness, he explored, among other places, Prudhoe Bay, a high-tech colony of pampered oil pipeline workers; the isolated settlement of Barrow, the "caboose of the world"; and the breathtakingly beautiful Brooks Range, where he and several fellow campers stumbled upon an exquisite hidden valley that was, in McGinniss' awestruck eyes, a "remnant of paradise." "I've never been anywhere where the extremes stand out so much," McGinniss told Timothy Moore.

Because it followed hard on the heels of Coming Into the Country, John McPhee's best-selling account of his Alaskan sojourn, McGinniss' Going to Extremes (Knopf, 1980) was inevitably compared to the earlier book, even though the paths of the two writers had rarely crossed. As Paul Theroux, for one, noted in his evaluation for the New York Times Book Review (September 14, 1980), McGinniss lacks McPhee's "high style" and metaphysical intensity, but in Going to Extremes, he proved to be an "unflappable" and "thorough" reporter—a "Studs Terkel on snowshoes." Moreover, his wry detachment perfectly suited his examination of Alaska's seamy underside. In a series of brilliantly drawn vignettes, whose subjects are the get-rich-quick adventurers lured north by the discovery of oil, he managed to describe "the destruction of nature and culture by exploitative invaders" without "a sentence of preaching," much to the admiration of Mark Kramer, who reviewed the book for the Nation (September 27, 1980). "Again and again, with an elegant journalistic jujitsu, McGinniss has his people do themselves in, announce their own poignance, crassness, lostness and, now and then, nobility."

McGinniss' gift for revealing character has perhaps never been more apparent than in Fatal Vision (Putnam, 1983), his meticulously researched account of the bizarre case of Dr. Jeffrey R. MacDonald, a respected physician and Green Beret officer whose pregnant wife and two young daughters were brutally bludgeoned and stabbed to death—by a quartet of drug-crazed, chanting hippies, according to MacDonald—in their Fort Bragg, North Carolina residence in 1970. (MacDonald himself suffered numerous superficial wounds in the alleged assault.) Largely because of his "All-American Boy" character, MacDonald was cleared of any complicity in the gruesome crimes in pre-trial military hearings in 1970, but nine years later, he was tried and convicted of three counts of murder, based on a detailed analysis of circumstantial evidence at the crime scene.

It was shortly before his trial that the publicity-conscious MacDonald, who was at the time of his arrest the director of emergency services at St. Mary's Hospital in Long Beach, California and a

nationally known lecturer on child abuse, asked McGinniss to write a book about his case—a book that he hoped would exonerate him. Fascinated by MacDonald, whom he described as having "something of the aura of Robert Redford in The Candidate—with, perhaps, faint, distant echoes of Gatsby," the writer readily accepted. McGinniss went into the project assuming that MacDonald was innocent, but five weeks of damning testimony convinced him otherwise. Unable "simply to accept the jury's verdict," he spent the next three years trying to "get a fuller picture." His thorough investigation uncovered, if not a motive, at least a possible cause of MacDonald's murderous rampage in his "pathological narcissism" and his abuse of psychosis-inducing amphetamines.

Fatal Vision brought McGinniss his best notices to date. Most critics agreed that the exhaustively detailed chronological reconstruction holds the reader's attention for some 700 pages because McGinniss had ingeniously combined the elements of a cracklingly good mystery story, a tense courtroom drama, and a dispassionate in-depth investigative report. More than one reviewer complimented the author for his skill in memorably sketching the major figures in the case, particularly the enigmatic MacDonald, and they were virtually unanimous in applauding his scrupulous research and "unobtrusive" and "precise" writing. "Fatal Vision smells of integrity," Christopher Lehmann-Haupt concluded in his review for the New York Times (September 21, 1983), "and that's one of the many things about it that make it irresistible to read, even if its vision of the human soul is somewhat bleak and frightening."

A lanky six-footer with thick brown hair and with sorrowful eyes that belie his boyish grin, Joe McGinniss looks years younger than his chronological age. He took up marathon running in the 1970s and finished the New York City Marathon in 1978, 1979, and 1980, but he has since given up the sport because of an injury to his knee. His preferred sedentary pursuit is reading, particularly fiction. He has "a powerful aversion," to use his words, to television. Although he has described writing as a "lonely, awful, terrible, frustrating and depressing and just arduous and just endless" process, he is, by his own admission, a compulsive writer. "It's like looking for the perfect wave," he told Timothy Moore. "You can't quit until you write the perfect book." On November 20, 1976 McGinniss married the former Nancy Doherty, a writer and photographer. They have a son, Matthew. He also has three children, Christine, Suzanne, and Joe, from an earlier marriage to Christine Cook that ended in divorce. The McGinnisses make their home in a rambling house in Williamstown, Massachusetts, a location he chose because "there is nothing else to do but write."

References: N Y Post p55 O 8 '69 por; Washington Post B pl+ D 2 '80 por, D pl+ O 20 '83 por; Writers Digest 56:15+ Mr 1976; Contemporary Authors vol 25 (1971); Who's Who in America, 1984–85

McKellen, Ian

May 25, 1939– British actor. Address: b. c/o Fraser and Dunlop Ltd., 91 Regent St., London W1R 8RU, England

In a theatrical era marked by intensely individual acting styles, British actor Ian McKellen remains stubbornly committed to the playwright's words—to "their meaning, their sound, their tone, their limitless possibilities, equivocations and conciseness," as he explained in a 1980 interview for the *Washington Post*. His dedication to and uncommon understanding of the words of classical and contemporary dramatists have made him, in the eyes of many observers, the most likely successor to Laurence Olivier as Britain's preeminent actor.

A professional performer for nearly a quarter of a century, McKellen earned his credentials as a classical actor of unusual weight and intelligence in 1969 when he doubled, to universal acclaim, in the roles of *Edward II* and *Richard II*. Since then, his performances in dozens of productions in Great Britain, principally for the Royal Shakespeare Company, and, less frequently, in the United States have earned him a basketful of "best actor" honors, including a 1981 Tony for *Amadeus* and an unprecedented three consecutive Society of West End Theatre awards for *Pillars of the Community* in 1977, *The Alchemist* in 1978, and *Bent* in 1979. McKellen was named a Commander of the British Empire in 1979.

The younger of the two children of Denis Murray and Margery (Sutcliffe) McKellen, Ian Murray McKellen was born in Burnley in the industrial north of England on May 25, 1939. He spent his earliest years in the Lancashire town of Wigan, then, at the age of twelve, he moved with his family to nearby Bolton, where his father was borough engineer and surveyor. Introduced to the magic of make-believe at an early age by the performers in the traveling fairs that occasionally visited his hometown, McKellen has been, by his own admission, "daft about the theatre" all his life. As a boy, he haunted the wings of the local variety theatre, attended performances by the Bolton repertory company, and during summer school camps at Stratford-upon-Avon often slept overnight in the ticket line in order to see productions at the Shakespeare Memorial Theatre.

McKellen's own "stumblings about the amateur stage," as he put it, began in the mid-1940s, when he appeared in end-of-term plays at Wigan Grammar School. Later, at the Bolton School, a "public" school with a flourishing drama society, he took leading roles in dozens of schoolboy productions. Nevertheless, when he enrolled at St. Catharine's College, Cambridge University, it was with the intention of becoming an English teacher or a journalist. He even went so far as to apply for a reporting job with the *Bolton Evening News*, to which he regularly contributed short "chit-chat" pieces. Not until the critical accolades came pouring in for his performances as Justice Shallow in *Henry IV Part II* and Baron Tusenbach in Chekhov's *The Three Sisters*, among others, did he consider a career as a professional actor. "It was like being told you were beautiful when you always thought you had big ears," he said, as quoted in *Woman's Journal* (May 1976).

During his three years at Cambridge, McKellen served as president of the Marlowe Dramatic Society, which is noted for its fine Shakespearean verse speaking, and appeared in twenty-one undergraduate productions, many of them directed by John Barton, then a don at the university. In an autobiographical article for the *New York Times* (September 27, 1981), McKellen credited Barton, George Rylands, and F. R. Leavis, his English literature tutors, with instilling in him "a respect for the written word," which he carried into the rehearsal room.

Shortly after taking his B.A. degree in 1961, McKellen made his professional debut, as Roper in Robert Bolt's historical drama *A Man for All Seasons*. Over the next three years in repertory seasons at the Arts Theatre in Ipswich and at the Nottingham Playhouse, he played, among other parts, the title roles in *Henry V*, *Luther*, and *Sir Thomas More*, Arthur Seaton in the working-class melodrama *Saturday Night and Sunday Morning*, and Aufidius in Tyrone Guthrie's production of *Coriolanus*. His affecting portrayal of Godfrey in James Saunders' *A Scent of Flowers* at the Duke of York's Theatre in London's West End in the fall of 1964 earned him a Clarence Derwent Award for most promising newcomer of the year and brought him a tempting offer from the National Theatre. He agreed to take the part of Claudio in *Much Ado About Nothing* for the National's 1965 spring season, but he declined to accept a three-year contract with the company, preferring to try his luck as a free-lance artist.

McKellen's bravura acting in a wide variety of roles, ranging from Napoleon in Shaw's *The Man of Destiny* in 1966 to the effeminate Harold Goringe in Peter Shaffer's *Black Comedy* in 1968, soon secured him a place among the ranks of the best of the young British actors. Reviewers found his interpretations of the visionary Andrew Cobham in Arnold Wesker's *Their Very Own and Golden City* and the voluble Alvin in *A Lily in Little India*, Donald Howarth's drama about loneliness, to be especially effective. For his performance in the latter, he was named most promising actor of 1966 by *Plays & Players*. American audiences got their first look at McKellen in November 1967 when he opened on Broadway as Leonidik, the goodhearted but irritatingly dull writer, in Aleksei Arbuzov's sentimental drama *The Promise*. A critical success in London, the play fared less well in New York City and closed after only twenty-three performances.

For the 1969 Edinburgh Festival, McKellen accepted his most daunting challenge to that date— the title roles in the Prospect Theatre Company's productions of *Richard II* and *Edward II*. It was the first time an actor had doubled as the two deposed kings in repertory since 1903. Critics and theatregoers alike marveled at the way in which McKellen's characterizations subtly pointed out the thematic similarities of the two plays while at the same time dramatically emphasizing the differences between the Shakespearean and Marlovian monarchs. His Edward was a headstrong, temperamental neurotic; his Richard, a rather innocent ascetic who seemed to embody the medieval concept of the divine right of kings. McKellen's command of the characters was such that reviewers differed only in choosing the better of the two interpretations.

By 1970 Ian McKellen was generally considered to be the most gifted and versatile actor of his generation. As if to underscore his multifaceted capabilities, he took on, in fairly rapid succession, the roles of Darkly, the meddling busybody in Barry Hines's two-character play *Billy's Last Stand* at the Royal Court Theatre Upstairs; Captain Plume in Farquhar's Restoration comedy *The Recruiting Officer* and Corporal Hill in Wesker's *Chips With Everything* for a Cambridge Theatre Company tour; the drunken and lonely old actor Svetlovidov in Chekhov's one-act play *Swan Song*, the inaugural production of the Crucible Theatre in Sheffield; and the title character in *Hamlet* for the Prospect Theatre Company. Critics, who had eagerly awaited McKellen's debut as Hamlet, were on the whole disappointed by the actor's flamboyant and idiosyncratic interpretation, which was, in the eyes of several reviewers, as eccentric and mannered as those of the great nineteenth-century tragedians.

Partly in an effort to counter what he has called his "tendency to act in an overly individual way," Ian McKellen cofounded, with fellow actor Edward Petherbridge and director David Williams, the Actors Company in October 1971. Designed to function as a kind of cooperative, with its members involved in every aspect of pre-production planning, from choosing the scripts to recruiting the directors, the Actors Company stressed equality in casting and in salary. "We wanted to form a company which *was* a company, where everyone would be the same, and everyone would play the big parts and the small," McKellen explained to Pat Garrett of *Woman's Journal* (May 1976). "It wasn't just a scheme to fulfill a theory of democracy, but to try and raise the standards as high as possible."

For their first touring season, which included a stand at the 1972 Edinburgh Festival, the seventeen members of the Actors Company chose Ford's Jacobean bloodbath *'Tis Pity She's a Whore*, Feydeau's farce *Le Dindon*, under the translated title *Ruling the Roost*, and *The Three Arrows*, Iris Murdoch's melodrama set in medieval Japan. In keeping with company policy, McKellen balanced the plum role of Giovanni, the protagonist in *'Tis Pity*, with the bit part of the emotionally disturbed bellhop in *Ruling the Roost*. The following year, on tour in England and at an engagement at the Brooklyn (New York) Academy of Music, he appeared in Actors Company productions of Chekhov's *The Wood Demon*, Congreve's *The Way of the World*, *King Lear*, and *Knots*, a series of sketches adapted by Edward Petherbridge from R. D. Laing's book of the same name.

At the invitation of John Barton, McKellen left the Actors Company in 1974 to join the Royal Shakespeare Company. Barton, an associate director of the RSC, immediately cast his former student in the title role of his unorthodox staging of Marlowe's *Doctor Faustus*. Although a few critics had some "intellectual objections" to Barton's radical revisions or to McKellen's occasionally "incantatory" or "histrionic" style, the majority were completely won over by the actor's extraordinary portrayal of "a naked soul raked in torment," to quote Frank Marcus, the drama critic of the London *Sunday Telegraph*. During his first season with the Royal Shakespeare Company, McKellen also undertook the roles of Faulconbridge in Barton's somewhat free version of *King John* and of the unscrupulous bogus marquis in Frank Wedekind's satirical comedy *The Marquis of Keith*.

In the spring of 1975 McKellen took time off from the RSC to direct a West End revival of *The Clandestine Marriage*, the eighteenth-century social comedy by David Garrick and George Colman. It was his fourth directorial effort, his previous productions being Jay Allen's adaptation of the Muriel Spark novel *The Prime of Miss Jean Brodie* at the Liverpool Playhouse in 1969, Joe Orton's *The Erpingham Camp* at the Watford Palace Theatre in 1972, and Ronald Mavor's *A Private Matter* at the Vaudeville Theatre in London in 1973. McKellen generally elicited above average performances from his actors, notably from Alastair Sim as Lord Ogleby in *The Clandestine Marriage*. As McKellen told Gordon Gow in an interview for *Plays & Players* (October 1974), his experiences as a director helped him "enormously" as an actor because directing "requires objectivity" and an ability to "see the whole," to find "the significance of the entire play."

Before returning to the largely classical repertory of the RSC, McKellen tried his hand at a role in contemporary drama—that of Colin, the guilt-ridden young husband, in the Young Vic's production of *Ashes*, David Rudkin's study of a childless marriage. Back with the RSC in time for its 1975 fall season at the Aldwych, he triumphed as Aubrey, the disillusioned clergyman turned burglar, in the company's first-rate revival of Shaw's *Too True To Be Good*. The eloquence and conviction with which he delivered the climactic closing monologue—Shaw's scathing attack on "the horrors of the naked mind"—electrified even the most jaded critics.

McKellen's assignments for the 1976 Stratford season were Romeo in *Romeo and Juliet*, Leontes in *The Winter's Tale*, and the title role in Trevor Nunn's studio production of *Macbeth*. His antic Romeo was almost universally condemned as melodramatic and mannered, and McKellen himself admitted that he had come to the part "too late." He proved more successful as Leontes, one of his favorite roles and, as Michael Coveney noted in *Plays & Players* (August 1976), one "ideally suited to his temperament and verse-speaking abilities." The actor's transformation from "hot-headed avenger to penitent recluse" was, by all accounts, tremendously moving.

McKellen believes that his interpretation of Leontes would have been "vastly better" on a smaller stage. Like Trevor Nunn, the RSC's joint artistic director, McKellen favors scaled-down productions of the classics, particularly of Shakespeare's works, primarily because, as he explained in an interview in April 1980, "it's easier to convey [Shakespeare's] subtleties if you're not having to strain over acreage of empty space to reach the back of the gods at Stratford." In the almost claustrophobic atmosphere of The Other Place and, later, the Warehouse, the RSC's studio theatres in, respectively, Stratford and London, the actor gave what many critics consider to be his finest performance, as Macbeth.

Capitalizing on the audience's closeness, McKellen enriched his characterization of Macbeth as a courtly "golden boy" poisoned by ambition with physical details that would have gone unnoticed in a larger theatre. When he stumbled from the murder chamber, horrified at his own treachery, the bloody daggers rattled audibly—"a sound I shall remember till my death," wrote Michael Billington—in his trembling hands. He also risked unconventional readings of the familiar soliloquies, thus making "connections where none before had been apparent," according to Robert Cushman. But perhaps most important, he created "a stifling intimacy," to use Hersh Zeifman's words, by maintaining a rapidly shifting eye contact with all members of the audience, drawing them into the action and making them, in effect, accomplices to Macbeth's crimes.

When Malcolm Macalister Hall asked McKellen to define the appeal of his craft in an interview for the British publication *Honey* (March 1982), McKellen replied, "As an actor one is allowed to get in touch with all the things that human beings are capable of—very deep emotion, or murder, or suicide—and step over that dangerous line which most of us pull away from." In his performance as Macbeth, for which he was named best actor of 1976 by *Plays & Players*, McKellen stepped boldly over that line and pulled his audiences after him.

McKellen played Macbeth in repertory in Stratford and London for nearly two years, alternating that part with the roles of Romeo, the liberal Langevin in *The Days of the Commune*, Brecht's play about the populist uprising in Paris in 1871, Alexander Ivanov, the political dissident who shares his cell with a lunatic in Tom Stoppard's *Every Good Boy Deserves Favour*, and the fraudulent hypocrite Karsten Bernick in an acclaimed production of Henrik Ibsen's *Pillars of the Community*. McKellen accomplished Bernick's transformations from affable, public spirited town consul to indifferent husband with a facility worthy of Face, the master of deceit and disguise whom he portrayed with such virtuosity in Nunn's breakneck-paced staging of Ben Jonson's *The Alchemist*.

McKellen has always subscribed to the concept of actors as "traditional rogues, peasant slaves and vagabonds, traveling where their audiences live and work," as he once wrote in an article for the London *Times* (October 9, 1976). It was not surprising, then, that he jumped at the chance when Trevor Nunn asked him, late in 1977, to plan and lead a small-scale regional tour of towns and villages not regularly visited by touring theatrical troupes. Realizing that the fifteen actors who comprised the company would be performing in less than ideal conditions, McKellen, Nunn, and John Napier, the set designer, devised a portable stage that could be easily adapted to suit any location, and with minimal scenery changes could accommodate each of the three pieces McKellen had chosen for the group's repertory: *Twelfth Night*, *The Three Sisters*, and the anthology *And Is There Honey Still For Tea?*, a "celebration of Englishness" compiled by Roger Rees, a member of the touring company. McKellen himself took the parts of the self-effacing Andrei in *The Three Sisters* and, in *Twelfth Night*, Sir Toby Belch, whom he portrayed unconventionally as a dissipated, middle-aged country gentleman. Because of the actors' commitment to the goals of the enterprise, the challenge of adapting to a succession of "theatres," and the obvious gratitude of the audiences, McKellen has rated the three-month tour as the "best job" he has ever had.

During his tenure with the Royal Shakespeare Company, McKellen, by his own admission, shed many of the mannerisms that had occasionally marred his earlier performances. To discover how his experiences with the RSC would affect his other work, the actor left the company at the close of the small-scale tour in October 1978 to accept the leading role in the Royal Court's production of *Bent*, Martin Sherman's harrowing play about a homosexual who tries to survive in a Nazi concentration camp by pretending he is a Jew. Drama critic Ned Chaillet spoke for the majority of his colleagues in his review for *Plays & Players* (June 1979): "McKellen's performance . . . is a further demonstration of his mastery of the stage. In this play alone, his range is immense. He swoops through Coward-like control of comedy to all the pain of a destroyed human being. It should now be clear that McKellen is a great actor."

When *Bent* closed following a six-month run in November 1979, McKellen took his widely praised one-man show *Acting Shakespeare* on a British Council-sponsored tour of Israel, Scandinavia, and the United States. He conceived the show, which reflects his own feelings about Shakespeare as "a craftsman" and a "man of the theatre," for the 1976 Edinburgh Festival. In subsequent performances, including wildly acclaimed appearances in the United States and Canada in 1983 and 1984, he continually revised and refined it, with the primary aim of making the characters he portrayed, among them Falstaff, Prince Hal, Mistress Quickly, and both Romeo and Juliet, "come alive," to use his words, for his audiences. For most viewers, the highlight of the evening was his perceptive line-by-line textual analysis of the "tomorrow" soliloquy from the last act of *Macbeth*.

Ian McKellen Acting Shakespeare was first televised in the United States by the Public Broadcasting Service in April 1982. Among McKellen's other television credits are Sir Terence Rattigan's *Ross*, Ibsen's *Hedda Gabler*, *David Copperfield*, and most recently, *The Scarlet Pimpernel*, *Dying Day*, a psychological thriller that was broadcast in the United States in 1982 as an episode in the PBS series *Mystery!*, and *Walter*, about a mentally handicapped adult. His film work includes *Alfred the Great* (MGM, 1969), *Thank You All Very Much* (Columbia, 1969), *Priest of Love* (Filmways, 1981), in which he overcame the handicap of a shapeless and superficial screenplay to turn in a solid performance as D. H. Lawrence, and the thriller *The Keep* (Paramount, 1983).

After an absence of thirteen years, McKellen returned to the Broadway stage in December 1980 to play the prolific eighteenth-century Viennese court composer Antonio Salieri in *Amadeus*, Peter Shaffer's drama based on the legend that Mozart may have been poisoned by his envious older rival. Because it required frequent switching from the persona of the decrepit and cantankerous Salieri to that of his dapper, younger self, the role was among the most challenging of McKellen's career. In keeping with his usual practice when playing a historical figure, McKellen did little research. "I had a script," he explained to Harold C. Schonberg of the *New York Times* (December 19, 1980). "My job was to portray the character, not to rival the author's scholarship."

Unlike Paul Scofield, the originator of the role, who concentrated on the elderly Salieri, McKellen focused on the younger and on his realization of his own mediocrity as a composer in the face of Mozart's genius. His bravura performance sent critics to their thesauruses in search of superlatives and brought cheering spectators to their feet. For his portrayal, McKellen was honored with the Tony, Drama Desk, and Outer Critics Circle awards as the best actor of the 1980–81 Broadway season. Since returning to the London stage, he has appeared in the ill-fated West End production of Sean Mathias' *Cowardice*, in 1983, and in *Coriolanus*, Thomas Otway's Restoration tragedy *Venice Preserv'd*, and *Wild Honey*, Michael Frayn's translation of Chekhov's *Platonov*, in repertory at the National Theatre in 1984. In the last-named play, McKellen turned in what Sheridan Morley, writing in *Plays & Players* (September 1984) described as a "marvellously comic" performance in the chaotic central role of the schoolmaster "forever falling over his own promises."

A solidly built six-footer, Ian McKellen has mesmerizing blue eyes and light brown hair. Offstage, he is modest, shy, and unpretentious. He enjoys interviews, especially when the conversation turns to the relationship between art and society in general, and art and politics in particular. Politically left-wing himself, he believes that art should be radical, in the sense that it should be an instrument for change. Ian McKellen sees a dynamic relationship existing between the theatre and society. "It is not the purpose of theatre to leave things as they are," he once remarked. McKellen has participated numerous times in benefit performances for groups like the Save the Children Fund and in theatre workshops for young people, and has helped to raise support for the Shakespeare Globe Theatre Centre of London.

McKellen's acting career leaves little time for anything else. He has no hobbies per se, although he enjoys cooking and writing. Over the years, he has contributed articles and book reviews to such publications as *Plays & Players*, the *Guardian*, the London *Observer*, and the *New York Times*. On his rare days off, he may go to the theatre or to a concert, but he is as likely to spend his free hours puttering around his eighteenth-century London house, which he has filled with books and contemporary paintings (he is especially fond of the modern industrial scenes of northern England by the artist L. S. Lowry), or watching the Thames river traffic passing just a few yards from his back door.

References: Guardian p9 F 10 '69 por; London Observer mag p17+ Ja 29 '78 pors; N Y Sunday News Leisure sec p3+ Ja 25 '81 pors; N Y Times II p1+ S 27 '81; Newsday II p4+ Jl 12 '81 pors; Plays & Players p15+ O '74 pors, p21+ Ap '84 pors; Time 117:94 Mr 2 '81 por; Who's Who, 1984–85; Who's Who in the Theatre, 1981

McMurtry, Larry (Jeff)

June 3, 1936- Writer. Address: b. Booked Up
Book Store, 1214 31st St., N.W., Washington,
D.C. 20007; c/o Simon & Schuster, 1230 Ave. of
the Americas, New York City, N.Y. 10020

As a Southwest regional novelist whose themes,
characters, and dialogue emerged from a Texas in
transition from an old order to a new disorder, Larry McMurtry was credited with having revitalized
the western genre by an introduction of realism,
satire, and what one reviewer called "a Rabelai-
sian comic wit." After his sixth novel with a Texas
setting, Terms of Endearment (1975), he wrote
about Hollywood in Somebody's Darling (1978),
about Washington, D.C. in Cadillac Jack (1982),
and then about Las Vegas in The Desert Rose
(1983). His break with Texas as the scene of his stories of clashing relationships followed his change
of residence from Houston to Washington, but
rather than cutting his ties with his home state, in
Cadillac Jack, for example, he made his title character and narrator a former Texas rodeo cowboy.
The best known of McMurtry's novels are those
that have been adapted for the screen, especially
The Last Picture Show and Terms of Endearment.
Three of the women he created have been Oscar-
winning vehicles, most recently for Shirley Mac-
Laine as best actress in Terms of Endearment,
which in 1984 the Academy of Motion Picture Arts
and Sciences also chose as the best picture.

The son of a Texas rancher, Larry Jeff Mc-
Murtry was born to William Jefferson and Hazel
Ruth (McIver) McMurtry on June 3, 1936 in Wichita Falls, north central Texas. There were another
son and two daughters in the family. Having settled
in Archer County, just south of Wichita County, in
the 1880s, his paternal grandfather was a frontiers-

man and cattleman who cherished the myth of the
cowboy, a romantic and perhaps somewhat tragic
figure committed to "a heroic concept of life" on
the vast and lonely plains, as McMurtry pictured
the type in his book of essays on Texas, In a Narrow Grave (Encino Press, 1968; Univ. of New Mexico Press, 1983). Remnants of the old West were
vanishing when Larry was growing up on the family ranch near Archer City. That small town became
the home of his adolescence and is the model for
Thalia, the setting of The Last Picture Show, which
McMurtry, with irony, "lovingly dedicated" to his
hometown.

Although McMurtry had been riding horseback
from the age of three, he did not feel inclined to
follow the family occupation of cattle raising. Rather, he was a bookish boy who discovered Don
Quixote when he was twelve and "was permanently altered by it." In his essay "Texas: Good Times
Gone, Or Here Again?" (Holiday, September 1965),
he wrote, "A part of my generation may keep something of the frontier spirit even though the frontier
is lost. What they may keep is a sense of daring and
independence, transferred from the life of action
to the life of the mind." He graduated from Archer
City High School with honors in 1954, studied for
a semester at Rice University in Houston, and in
early 1955 enrolled in North Texas State University in Denton to major in English. There he wrote
verse, stories, and essays for the student literary
magazine, Avesta. One of his pieces, "Journey to
the End of the Road," was a critical study of the
"beat" movement, particularly of the contributions
of Jack Kerouac, Allen Ginsberg, and Kenneth
Rexroth. Several fragments of his undergraduate
fiction later appeared in altered form in his novels.

Returning to Rice University after he had
earned his B.A. degree from North Texas State in
1958, McMurtry divided his time between studying
English and writing his first two novels. In 1960
Rice University granted him an M.A. degree and
Stanford University a Wallace Stegner Fellowship
in fiction for 1960 and 1961. Following his two
years of graduate work in California he pursued an
intermittent teaching career, at Texas Christian
University in Fort Worth in 1961–62 and Rice University in 1963–64 and from 1965 to about 1969.
Temporary monetary relief from teaching came in
the form of a Guggenheim award for creative writing in 1964.

During the 1960s Larry McMurtry wrote scores
of book reviews for the Houston Post and many articles, mainly about Texas, for various periodicals.
Nine of his essays were collected in In a Narrow
Grave, which, according to Jonathan Yardley, book
columnist for the Washington Post (October 13,
1982), is "arguably the best book ever written about
Texas." Some of the themes that he explored in
nonfiction concerned him also in his early novels.
Of the inconsistencies, moreover, in his attitude toward Texas that appear in his essays, he wrote in
"A Handful of Roses," which is included in In a
Narrow Grave, "a very deep ambivalence it is, as
deep as the bone. Such ambivalence is not helpful

in a discursive book, but it can be the very blood of a novel."

McMurtry's first novel, *Horseman, Pass By* (Harper, 1961), makes considerable use of symbols and of the myths and legends of the cowboy, but is essentially a realistic treatment of life on a west Texas ranch in the early 1950s. The narrator is seventeen-year-old Lonnie, the grandson of Homer Bannon, whose herd of cattle has become afflicted with hoof-and-mouth disease. Bannon resists the urging of his stepson, Hud, that he hurriedly sell the cattle to some "dumb" rancher. The destruction of the herd by government agents and the subsequent death of Bannon represent the loss of the old way of ranching, while Hud, the Cadillac-driving cowboy, personifies the diminution of the values of his stepfather's generation.

In retrospect, *Horseman, Pass By* has seemed to its author an immature work, incorporating "at best" his vision at the age of twenty-two, or, as he said in an interview for the *Washington Post* (December 12, 1971), "a very sentimental first novel." Among its fictive elements that Larry McMurtry continued to work with were the earth mother figure—here, the family Negro cook, Halmea, whom Lonnie adores and Hud rapes; the admirable older man, or father model; and the rite-of-passage theme. Charles D. Peavy pointed out, furthermore, in his invaluable Twayne study, *Larry McMurtry* (1977), "The lonely restlessness Lonnie exhibits at the end of the novel heralds the aimless quests of the rootless males in [some of] McMurtry's later novels." The title *Horseman, Pass By*, borrowed from William Butler Yeats's epitaph, exemplifies McMurtry's preference for elegiac titles for his early books. *Horseman, Pass By* was changed to *Hud* in the film version, which starred Paul Newman in the title role and Patricia Neal, who as Alma (Halmea) won an Oscar. The movie, directed by Martin Ritt, was released by Paramount in 1963.

Like *Horseman, Pass By*, McMurtry's second novel, *Leaving Cheyenne* (Harper, 1963), has a setting near the town with the fictitious name of Thalia in the ranch countryside of his boyhood. As the author has explained, its title, which he took from the cowboy ballad "Goodbye, Old Paint," imports not a departure from Wyoming's capital city, but the passage of youth. The story deals with Molly's lifelong love for Gideon, a rancher, and Johnny, a cowboy. Unwilling to break up the close friendship of Gideon and Johnny by choosing between them, Molly marries a third man, Eddie. During the course of that failed marriage, she has a son by Gideon and a son by Johnny. Each of the three principal characters narrates a section of the novel, thereby enriching what McMurtry would regard as the textural quality implicit in the complexities of the triangular relationship. The film adaptation of *Leaving Cheyenne*, renamed *Lovin' Molly* (Columbia, 1963) and directed by Sidney Lumet, starred Blythe Danner in the title role.

For *The Last Picture Show* (Dial, 1966), Larry McMurtry moved his Texas locale from a rural area to a small town in the early 1950s. Its title,

again elegiac, refers to the closing of the town's movie theatre upon the advent of television. A critic for the London *Times Literary Supplement* (March 23, 1973) wrote that *The Last Picture Show* "is best known for its fetching and very effective nostalgia." If so, it is a nostalgia permeated by the resentment and bitterness that McMurtry felt toward the town of his adolescence. Some of the author's own emotional experiences are probably also reflected in the anguished coming-of-age gropings of teenage Sonny and his friend Duane in a stifling community. Much of the interest centers on Sonny's shabby affair with Ruth Popper, the neglected wife of the latently homosexual high school coach. Her feelings toward Sonny are both motherly and sexual. So explicit is McMurtry's treatment of adolescent sexuality in Thalia and so black his humor that the novel was banned in Australia in 1967 on the grounds of indecency. As Peavy observed, however, "McMurtry's use of black humor in *The Last Picture Show* should not be overemphasized, for the novel is a highly symbolic and complex work, as well as a scathing denunciation of the spiritual stagnation of a small town."

McMurtry had taken no part in the preparation of the screenplays of his first two novels, but when *The Last Picture Show* was translated into film, he collaborated with the director Peter Bogdanovich on the script. The movie, which was filmed in Archer City and released by Columbia in 1971, won a Motion Picture Academy of Arts and Sciences nomination for best screenplay, and Cloris Leachman won an Oscar for best supporting actress as Ruth Popper. As a change from writing novels, McMurtry has since then worked intermittently on scripts, scenarios, and drafts of film stories. Scriptwriting is for him "an interesting craft," secondary in appeal to the creative art of writing fiction. He has also made important contributions to film criticism, mainly through a monthly column he wrote for *American Film*, which in 1975–76 published his series of articles on screenwriting.

It was largely because of the intellectual inadequacy of Archer City that McMurtry became a bookman. "I grew up in a bookless town in a bookless part of the state," he explained to Richard Lee, who interviewed him for the *Washington Post Magazine* (December 5, 1982), "and I assumed that I would always be in Archer City, and books would be my only escape from life as it was lived there." To buy new books when he was in college, he sometimes had to sell old books from his collection and thereby began to gain experience as a book dealer. While a graduate student at Stanford University, he worked as a book scout for several San Francisco stores. On his return to Texas in 1965, he became a scout and dealer with the Houston firm The Bookman, acquiring an expertise in rare books.

In 1969 Larry McMurtry moved from Houston to the Washington, D.C. area. After giving a few courses in creative writing at George Mason University in Fairfax, Virginia and at American University, in 1971 he abandoned teaching to spend his time on writing and helping to operate a bookstore that he opened in Washington's Georgetown with John Curtis and Marcia Carter. "The bookstore is a good balance to my writing. It's intellectually challenging but not emotionally demanding," David McCullough quoted McMurtry as saying in the *Book-of-the-Month Club News* (February 1976). He has remarked elsewhere, moreover, that constant reading is essential to writing, that he has worked simultaneously at both reading and writing. Among the books he read after settling in Washington were those that he reviewed weekly, on Mondays, over a period of several years for the *Washington Post*.

When questioned by press interviewers about why he chose to live in Washington, McMurtry replied with the ostensible reason that he had heard the city was a good place to finish a book. The novel on which he was then working—and had been writing and revising for some years—was the nearly 800-page *Moving On* (Simon & Schuster, 1970). For that novel, the first in a trilogy of the urban Southwest, he drew on his familiarity with the environment he was leaving, mainly in and around Houston, and on some aspects of his own life there. The unifying force in a story of many characters, places, and subplots is Patsy Carpenter, who is initiated into self-awareness and maturity through the ordeal of a disintegrating marriage. McMurtry's sure grasp of the language of rootless young men and women passing through both the rodeo circuit and the frustrating academic community has been praised as among the merits of the book.

Failure of marriage is a recurrent theme of McMurtry's work, including *All My Friends Are Going to Be Strangers* (Simon & Schuster, 1972), an episodic and picaresque novel narrated by its protagonist, Danny Deck, who had appeared briefly in *Moving On*. At the beginning of the story Danny is a Rice University graduate student whose first novel is soon to be published. Never expecting his dreams to come true, he finds that he does not know how to handle his feelings when one of them does. He rushes into a foredoomed marriage, moves to California, and after his breakup with his wife and several sexual encounters with other women, makes his way back to Texas. *All My Friends* ends with the hero's wandering into the Rio Grande River to destroy the manuscript of his second book and presumably himself. The aimlessness of the characters of McMurtry's on-the-road novel is matched by its meandering structure. Martha Duffy complained in *Time* (April 3, 1972) that McMurtry's "books are constructed like tumbleweed . . . with no discernible direction," but she acknowledged that he did "create indelible people and brilliant set-piece scenes."

Martha Duffy's description of *All My Friends* as "acute, elegiac, funny and dangerously tender" may apply also to *Terms of Endearment* (Simon & Schuster, 1975). In that last volume of Larry McMurtry's trilogy of intertwined relationships, Emma Horton, one of the women to whom Danny made love, suffers through her own troubled marriage. Her story is told from the point of view, though not in first-person narration, of her mother, a Houstonian from New England, Aurora Greenway. The irrepressible forty-nine-year-old widow, in fact, takes over the greater part of the novel as she tries to dominate her daughter and reproves, teases, confuses, and beguiles her train of assorted "suitors," as she calls them. But the comedy of manners turns to tragedy in the relatively brief final section when Emma dies of cancer. Even some of the reviewers who found *Terms of Endearment* thoroughly readable and delightful objected that the parts of the novel did not hold together. "I like funny books that turn sad," McMurtry told McCullough as if in reply. "It's a trick Thackeray liked to use." The film version of *Terms of Endearment,* a Paramount release of 1983, brought Oscars to James L. Brooks for direction and scriptwriting, to Shirley MacLaine for her portrayal of Aurora Greenway, and to Jack Nicholson for best supporting actor.

Just as the ending of *Terms of Endearment* and, indeed, of the other Texas novels may be Thackerayan, the names of McMurtry's characters sometimes have a Dickensian ring. Bo Brimmer, Pete Sweet, Swan Bunting, Mercy Merker, and Raven Dexter, among others, contribute to the synthetic atmosphere of his disenchanted novel about Hollywood, *Somebody's Darling* (Simon & Schuster, 1978). The title character, Jill Peel, is a film director searching for self-realization and coping with her first success and with misgivings about her career. To tell her story McMurtry returned to the device of triple perspective, employing as narrators Jill and the two men she loves, Joe Percy, a protective older man who writes second-rate TV scripts, and Owen Oarson, a foul-mouthed boor from Texas who wants to duplicate as a producer the celebrity he had once enjoyed as a football star. In one of his essays for *American Film* McMurtry wrote that in Hollywood he had only pleasant experiences. But most of his amusing portraits of the people who constitute the mainstay of the motion picture industry are less affectionate than mordantly satiric.

When, after his long residence in Washington, McMurtry chose that city as the principal setting of a novel, *Cadillac Jack* (Simon & Schuster, 1982), he presented the nation's capital through the skeptical eyes of an out-of-towner, a Texan. "Cadillac Jack" is his trade name because as a footloose antiques scout he crisscrosses the country in his pearl-colored Cadillac in search of "exceptional objects" of every description. Since Jack responds as eagerly to beautiful women as to rare antiques, much of his story focuses on his erotic vicissitudes. To Jonathan Yardley of the *Washington Post* (October 13, 1982) *Cadillac Jack* was "a real mess of a book," but McMurtry had his defenders, including Aaron Latham, who in the *Chicago Tribune* (October 17, 1982) appraised the novel as a "hard-to-find treasure." Agreeing with Latham, evidently, in 1984 MGM/United Artists bought the film rights to *Cadillac Jack* for a reported $250,000.

One of the strengths of McMurtry's fiction, as a reviewer for the London *Times Literary Supplement* (March 23, 1973) has noted, derives from his "talent for characterization and the evocation of place—together with his ability to blend them convincingly, so that they seem almost to interdepend." That observation holds true even for his novel with a background not based on long familiarity—for *The Desert Rose* (Simon & Schuster, 1983), whose locale is Las Vegas. "The Las Vegas book came out of a two-day visit. I wrote it very quickly," McMurtry told Richard Lee in the *Washington Post Magazine* interview. Its persistently optimistic and romantic heroine, Harmony, is a beautiful, but aging, topless dancer in a Las Vegas casino. When things go awry for her, as they often seem to do, she consoles herself with the companionship of her pet peacocks. The crisis that threatens her happiness even more than her blighted love affairs is the decision of the floorshow's manager to supplant her with her just as beautiful, though not so goodhearted, sixteen-year-old daughter, Pepper. McMurtry's hilarious grim humor, at times reminiscent of Erskine Caldwell, is tempered in *The Desert Rose* by wistfulness.

While in graduate school at Rice University, on July 15, 1959 Larry McMurtry married Josephine Ballard. He is the father of one son, James Law-

rence. The marriage ended in divorce in August 1966. In interviews for the press McMurtry prefers not to talk about his private life, though he does discuss his writing habits, telling Louise Sweeney of the *Christian Science Monitor* (February 6, 1976), for example, "The great secret of producing for a fiction writer is regularity . . . being in the same place at the same time every day." When he travels, he takes along a duplicate typewriter to preserve as much of his routine as possible. "McMurtry is not, for all his maverick ways, a formidable or forbidding person," Richard Lee wrote in the *Washington Post Magazine*. "He's rather amiable in a low-key way. . . . He's about 6 feet tall, a thoughtful, bookish-looking man [with] unruly black hair with touches of gray at the temples. . . . Only the twang in his voice tells you he's from Hud country."

References: *Book-of-the-Month Club N* p6 F '76; *Christian Sci Mon* p17 F 6 '76 por; *New Yorker* 52:86+ Je 14 '76; *Washington Post* E p1 D 12 '71 por; *Washington Post Mag* p12+ D 5 '82 por; *Contemporary Authors* 1st rev vols 5–8 (1969); *Contemporary Novelists* (1976); *Dictionary of Literary Biography; American Novelists since World War II* (1978); Peavy, Charles D. *Larry McMurtry* (1977)

Medvedev, Roy (Aleksandrovich)

(med vād´ yef)

Nov. 14, 1925– Soviet historian; dissident. Address: c/o Zhores A. Medvedev, National Institute for Medical Research, "The Ridgeway," Mill Hill, London NW7 1AA, England; Abonnement Post Box 45, Moscow G-19, USSR

When in early 1983 the dissident historian Roy Medvedev was harassed by Soviet authorities, the veteran American journalist and social critic I. F. Stone compared him to Peter Abelard, the twelfth-century French philosopher who was twice condemned by the medieval Roman Catholic Church because he challenged its theology from within. "Both merit a similar place in the history of the ever continuing human struggle for freedom of thought," Stone wrote in the *New York Times* (January 28, 1983).

Described in a *Nation* editorial (June 4, 1983) as "one of the few sources for intelligent and accurate analysis of Soviet current events," Medvedev differs from such other dissidents as Aleksandr I. Solzhenitsyn or Andrei D. Sakharov: he continues to subscribe to socialism and believes that any changes in the direction of democratization must come from within Soviet society itself. Although none of his major works has been published in the Soviet Union, Medvedev has won recognition in the West with such books as his comprehensive in-

vestigation of Stalinism, *Let History Judge* (1971); his guardedly optimistic *On Socialist Democracy* (1975); his critical but sympathetic biography *Khrushchev* (1983); and his study of the men who comprised Joseph Stalin's inner circle, *All Stalin's Men* (1984).

Roy Medvedev and his identical twin brother, Zhores—who became a biologist and now lives in England—were born on November 14, 1925 in Tblisi, the capital of the Soviet Socialist Republic of Georgia. Their father, Aleksandr Romanovich Medvedev, a descendant of a family of craftsmen and traders from Ashtrakan on the Caspian Sea, served as a political commissar with the Red Army in the civil war that followed the Russian Revolution and later taught philosophy at the Leningrad State University and at Tolmachev Military-Political Academy. Their mother, Yulia Isaakovna Medvedeva, whose maiden name was Reiman, was a cellist from a Jewish professional family.

Aleksandr Romanovich Medvedev, whom his sons idolized, was arrested during the Stalin purges in 1938 and died in an Arctic labor camp in 1941. For a time the Medvedev brothers were stigmatized as sons of an "enemy of the people," but in 1956 the father was posthumously rehabilitated as a result of letters that Roy and Zhores Medvedev and their mother sent to the Communist party's Central Committee after Stalin's death in 1953. "The fact that my father was arrested was something frightening and completely incomprehensible, completely out of accord with the ideas of Leninism or Marxism or socialism," Roy Medvedev has been quoted as saying. "I understood that our lives had been visited by a great evil, but the extent of that evil I could not then understand. But I wanted to figure it out even then, so I decided in my earliest years to busy myself with politics, with social science, to examine what is good and what is bad in our society."

After his World War II service in the Red Army, Roy Medvedev studied at Leningrad State University, where he obtained a B.S. degree in philosophy in 1951. He was awarded the equivalent of a Ph.D. degree in 1958 by the Academy of Pedagogical Sciences of the USSR in Moscow. During the early 1950s he taught history at the Ural Secondary School in Sverdlovsk, and then served as director of a secondary school in the Leningrad region. In the late 1950s, Medvedev worked for the Publishing House of Pedagogical Literature in Moscow as deputy to the editor in chief. During most of the 1960s he was a senior research associate and department head at the Research Institute of Vocational Education in the Academy of Pedagogical Sciences, and in 1970-71 he was one of its senior scientists.

Roy Medvedev became a member of the Communist party after the twentieth party congress in February 1956, at which Nikita S. Khrushchev in his famous speech denounced Stalin's crimes and misrule. Following a renewed call for de-Stalinization at the twenty-second party congress in 1961, Medvedev began to write his first major work, an exposé of Stalinism, hoping that the congress had signaled an orientation towards democracy. He completed the preliminary version in 1965 and submitted the manuscript to the Central Committee of the party, but it was not approved, and his final version, completed in 1968, fared no better,

although it eventually circulated underground as *samizdat.*

When in 1968 the party's theoretical journal, *Kommunist,* published an article defending Stalin, Medvedev replied with a letter of protest. The letter was never published by *Kommunist,* but it appeared in the émigré journal *Posev* without Medvedev's permission. It has been suggested that the letter was forwarded to *Posev* by the KGB, or secret police, to discredit Medvedev. In any case, as a consequence of his letter and of the publication, in Paris that year, of his essay *Faut-il réhabiliter Staline?* (Need We Rehabilitate Stalin?), Medvedev was expelled from the Communist party in 1969.

Translated into English by Colleen Taylor and edited by David Joravsky and Georges Haupt, in 1971 Medvedev's *samizdat* manuscript was published in the United States by Alfred A. Knopf and in Great Britain by Macmillan with the title *Let History Judge: The Origins and Consequences of Stalinism.* The work is a comprehensive historical study and analysis of Stalinism, based on a wide variety of sources, including unpublished archival material dating back to 1917, as well as interviews with persons directly involved in the events described.

Medvedev concluded that Stalin was not actually a madman, even though a certain streak of paranoia was present in his makeup. He viewed the dictator as a man obsessed with absolute power and regarded Stalinism as the evil force that corrupted Communism. In his opinion, an understanding of its origin and of how it could be avoided in the future was an essential step on the road towards democracy. According to Edward Crankshaw, writing in the London *Observer* (March 26, 1972), *Let History Judge* "is nothing less than a one-man attempt to rescue the history of the Soviet Union from the party hacks and . . . to salvage the honor of the revolution."

Meanwhile, during the years that Roy Medvedev was working on *Let History Judge,* he and his brother, Zhores, were also occupied with putting out a monthly typewritten anti-Stalinist underground magazine, *Politicheskii Dnevnik* (Political Diary), seventy-nine issues of which appeared in the years from 1964 to 1971. The journal focused mainly on the analysis of political developments within the Soviet Union, and materials used included private as well as official sources, and the products of the underground press. Typewritten copies were circulated among a selected group of intellectuals and dissidents whom the Medvedev brothers felt they could trust. To avoid direct intervention by the KGB, they had to use caution; they refrained from making explicitly anti-Soviet statements and toned down the level of criticism so that there would not be excessive publicity. "Our approach was more professional," Zhores Medvedev has said. "We wanted to study things—socialist democracy, criticism of censorship, confiscation of mail, exchanges in science. . . . "

Because Roy Medvedev knew that after publication of *Let History Judge* in the United States he would not be able to continue his *Political Diary*, he decided in 1971 to send part of the journal to the Herzen Foundation in Amsterdam. At the same time, he resigned from his position at the Academy of Pedagogical Sciences and since then has concentrated on free-lance writing. Shortly afterward, his archives were raided, and for a time he went into hiding. The Herzen Foundation published nineteen issues of the *Political Diary* in the original Russian in two volumes, in 1972 and 1975, and it was in the latter volume that Roy Medvedev was for the first time identified as the editor. A representative selection of the contents of the *Political Diary*, translated into English by George Saunders and edited by Stephen F. Cohen, was published by W. W. Norton in 1982 with the title *An End to Silence: Uncensored Opinion in the Soviet Union; From Roy Medvedev's Underground Magazine, Political Diary*.

When in 1970 Zhores Medvedev was forcibly committed to a mental hospital for what medical authorities called his "incipient schizophrenia" and "paranoid delusions of reforming society," Roy Medvedev helped to obtain his release by organizing a protest group of twenty prominent scientists, including Andrei D. Sakharov and Igor Tamm. To inform the public of Zhores Medvedev's ordeal and of the official use of psychiatry to put the damper on dissidents, the brothers wrote a book to which each contributed alternating chapters. When it was published in Russian by Macmillan in London in 1971, and in English, with the title *A Question of Madness*, by Alfred A. Knopf in New York later that year, the book evoked much sympathy from its readers in the West. Stripped of his Soviet citizenship, Zhores Medvedev has been living in exile in London since 1973.

In 1971 Roy Medvedev completed a draft of a book tentatively titled "Socialism and Democracy," which focused on Soviet eonomic and social problems and the then current trends within the Communist party. Circulated in *samizdat* format, it was smuggled out of the Soviet Union by Zhores Medvedev and published in Russian in Amsterdam in 1972. It was translated into English by Ellen de Kadt and published in the United States in 1975 by Knopf with the title *On Socialist Democracy*.

In *On Socialist Democracy* Roy Medvedev identified himself with the "party democrats" within the ruling Communist organization, though he was careful to point out that the two numerically strongest and most influential groups were the neo-Stalinists, who had thrived under the partial rehabilitation of Stalin following the downfall of Khrushchev, and the centrist majority of moderate conservatives, including the "law-and-order" politicians with little interest in social problems, who condone large military budgets and strong internal security systems. On the other hand, the aims of the party democrats are, in Medvedev's words, a "thoroughgoing, comprehensive democratization of Soviet society," including a decentralization of authority, an emphasis on civil rights and the rule of law, free elections, and even a multiparty system. Quoting Lenin's statement that "the victory of socialism is impossible without the realization of democracy," Medvedev insists that the repressive features of Soviet politics are not inherent in Marxism-Leninism but result from exceptional historic circumstances and may be corrected without a return to capitalism. Writing in the *New York Times Book Review* (July 13, 1975), Stephen F. Cohen classed *On Socialist Democracy* with such other landmarks of socialist literature as the German revisionist theoretician Eduard Bernstein's *Evolutionary Socialism* and Lenin's *What Is to Be Done?*

Roy Medvedev's insistence that democratic reforms in Soviet society must come from within is the theme of his 7,000-word essay "The Problem of Democratization and the Problem of Détente," which widely circulated in the West in late 1973. In it he took issue with the views of such fellow dissenters as Andrei D. Sakharov and Aleksandr I. Solzhenitsyn who maintained that pressure from the West was needed if freer emigration and liberalization were to be achieved in the Soviet Union. In early 1974 he praised Solzhenitsyn's exposé of Stalin's prison camps, *The Gulag Archipelago, 1918-1956*, as "mercilessly truthful" and condemned the enforced exile of the noted author as a "moral defeat" for the Soviet government. But after Solzhenitsyn issued a letter from exile, demanding, among other things, an abandonment of Communist ideology and a return to the Orthodox religion, Medvedev accused him of having "retrograde opinions."

In 1975 Roy Medvedev founded a new underground political journal called *Dvadtsaty vek* (Twentieth Century) and became its editor. Ten issues were published before the Moscow city prosecutor forced the journal to close down in 1976. A collection of essays from that journal appeared in two volumes as the *Samizdat Register* (Norton, 1977-81). A volume of Medvedev's *Political Essays* was published by Spokesman Books, a British firm, in 1976.

In collaboration with his brother, Zhores, Roy Medvedev published *Khrushchev: The Years in Power* (Columbia Univ. Press, 1976), dealing with the Soviet leader's rise, the implementation and failure of his agricultural policies, and his downfall. In *Problems in the Literary Biography of Mikhail Sholokhov* (Cambridge Univ. Press, 1977), Medvedev discussed questions that had been raised about the author of *And Quiet Flows the Don*. *Philip Mirinov and the Russian Civil War* (Knopf, 1978), which Medvedev wrote with Sergei Starikov, deals with a Cossack leader and Red Army commander whose challenge to the revolutionary regime's peasant policies proved to be his undoing. In *The Last Years of Nikolai Bukharin* (Norton, 1980), Medvedev paid homage to an old Bolshevik who fell victim to Stalin's purges. A series of interviews with Medvedev conducted by the Italian journalist Piero Ostellino was published as *On Soviet Dissent* (Columbia Univ. Press, 1980). Other books by Roy Medvedev available in English translation are *The October Revolution* (Columbia Univ. Press, 1979), *On Stalin and Stalinism* (Oxford Univ. Press, 1979), and *Lenin and Western Socialism* (Schocken, 1981).

Medvedev's biographical study *Khrushchev* (Anchor/Doubleday, 1983) is the first comprehensive book about the Soviet leader. Written with the help of the Khrushchev family, its publication was regarded as an act of political courage because of its sympathetic treatment of a man who is still looked upon with disfavor by the Soviet establishment. Although Medvedev never denied that Khrushchev was a totalitarian dictator or that he committed serious blunders, he views him as, in effect, something of a hero who put an end to Stalin's atrocities. Harlow Robinson, who reviewed *Khrushchev* for the *Christian Science Monitor* (May 13, 1983), called Medvedev's book "a magnificent piece of work, especially considering that he wrote it . . . under surveillance."

In his book *All Stalin's Men; Six Who Carried Out the Bloody Policies* (Doubleday, 1984), Roy Medvedev presents biographies of six members of the dictator's "inner circle" who survived the Stalin era: Kliment Y. Voroshilov, Anastas I. Mikoyan, Mikhail I. Suslov, Vyacheslav M. Molotov, Lazar M. Kaganovich, and Georgi M. Malenkov. Medvedev depicts those men as being for the most part ruthless, inept, and wholly subservient to Stalin and concludes that democratic institutions must be established to improve the quality of Soviet leadership. In reviewing *All Stalin's Men* for the *Toronto Globe and Mail* (July 7, 1984), John Gellner wrote: "Reading Roy Medvedev's remarkable book . . . one feels increasing admiration for those Soviet dissidents who in the face of insurmountable obstacles keep up their spirits in the hope for a better future for their homeland."

Roy Medvedev has been equally unsparing toward what he considers to be abuses in the Western world. He and his brother, Zhores, published a lengthy article in the *Nation* (January 16, 1982) entitled "A Nuclear *Samizdat* on America's Arms Race," in which they condemned the "primitive" cold war attitude of Americans toward the Soviet Union and their tendency to "greatly oversimplify complex social and historical processes." When in the fall of 1983 President Ronald Reagan referred to the Soviet Union as an "empire of evil," Roy Medvedev asserted that the president had "stepped over the boundaries of rhetoric," and that his statement was a "direct insult."

Although Roy Medvedev has managed to avoid imprisonment or exile, he has occasionally been harassed by Soviet authorities. After he was interviewed in 1981 by Walter Cronkite for American television, his apartment was ransacked and some research data were confiscated. In January 1983 he was summoned to appear before the Soviet prosecutor general, accused of having produced "mockingly hostile scribblings that have slandered the Soviet Union," and threatened with imprisonment. Refusing to sign a statement in which his writings were referred to as political "lampoons," he issued a statement of his own, describing his works as those of "a citizen struggling to see his country live at peace with the world, flourishing in democracy and socialism."

According to Zhores Medvedev, his brother has been able to avoid arrest because the authorities under the Russian legal system were unable to cope with his kind of writing. "To prove somebody's guilt," he pointed out, "they have to find facts which they can specify as slander of the Soviet state. . . . The prosecutor general could not give an example of slander in Roy's work."

After the death of Yuri Andropov, Roy Medvedev wrote a relatively sympathetic article for the *New York Times* Op-Ed page (February 15, 1984), in which he asserted that the late Communist party general secretary had "accomplished much in his brief time," including a crackdown on the corruption that had flourished under Leonid I. Brezhnev. Shortly afterward, the authorities stationed police at Medvedev's apartment door, to turn away foreigners and journalists. No explanation was given for the move.

Roy Medvedev was married in September 1956 to Galina A. Gaidina, a physiologist, and they have a son, Aleksandr. Medvedev makes his home in a fifth-floor walkup apartment in northwestern Moscow. Joseph Kraft, after meeting with Medvedev, described him in the *New Yorker* (January 31, 1983) as a "white-haired, rubicund man . . . with eyes of azure blue and a benign aspect that makes him resemble Boris Pasternak in his last years." Medvedev has been described as soft-spoken but able to convince by force of argument.

References: Book World p11+ S 7 '80 por; N Y Times p7 F 23 '79 por; Contemporary Authors vols 81–84 (1979); International Who's Who, 1984–85

Mintoff, Dom

Aug. 6, 1916– Prime Minister of Malta. Address: b. Auberge de Castille, Valletta, Malta; h. "The Olives," Xintill St., Tarxien, Malta

Under the socialist Prime Minister Dom Mintoff, the nature of economic and political life in the tiny island nation of Malta has changed drastically in the ten years since the former British crown colony became a republic. Strategically located in the central Mediterranean, midway between Europe and North Africa and between Suez and Gibraltar, Malta was for centuries a military base for seafaring world powers. With the loss of military rent (viewed as "the wages of sin" by Mintoff), the 122-square-mile archipelago, having little arable land and few natural resources on its rocky terrain, was left with ship repair, small industry, and tourism

Dom Mintoff

for its livelihood. While building a welfare state and diversifying industry at home, Mintoff has internationally sought economic ties that will underwrite his country's neutrality and lead the way to a demilitarized Mediterranean independent of superpower influence.

Malta's population of 326,178 is predominantly Roman Catholic and of Phoenician and Carthaginian descent, with a mixture of Arabic and European traditions and two languages: English and the indigenous Maltese, an Arabic dialect. Fierce in his pursuit of national dignity and self-reliance, the revival of Maltese civic spirit, and the repair of the damage done by European imperialistic incursions, Mintoff is a confrontational politician both abroad, in his relations with more powerful nations, and at home, with his foes in the conservative Nationalist party and in the church, which he regards as the traditional ally of a power structure inimical to the interests of the working class. A fiery orator, he is hailed by his followers as the charismatic "great one." His critics, on the other hand, consider him an authoritarian with totalitarian tendencies and accuse him of undermining democratic institutions through patronage, measures of doubtful constitutionality, gerrymandering, and even physical bullying, including the use of electoral goon squads. "His political failings, if not particularly original, are magnified by his characteristic drive," E. A. Mallia, a Maltese intellectual, has observed. "And his failings are in some measure our own writ large."

One of nine children of Lawrence Mintoff, a cook with the Royal Navy in Malta, and Concetta (Farrugia) Mintoff, Dom Mintoff was born Dominic Mintoff (he has never used the full given name) in Cospicua, Malta on August 6, 1916. Cospicua was so named by the Knights of Malta to signify the part that the town played in the defense against Turkish invaders in the sixteenth century. The Knights, now a Roman Catholic charitable organization especially devoted to the care of the sick and the wounded, were originally religious-military crusaders. Once called the Friars of the Hospital of St. John of Jerusalem, the order was founded in the twelfth century to aid pilgrims to the Holy Land and protect them from Turkish assaults. After the fall of Jerusalem, the Hospitalers moved to Cyprus, Rhodes, and Malta. Given sovereignty over Malta by the Holy Roman Emperor Charles V in 1530, they ruled the archipelago until 1798, when Napoleon Bonaparte conquered it. With British Royal Navy support, the islanders soon drove out the French, and Malta was annexed to the British Crown in 1814. A "garrison" colony, it was ruled by British military governors throughout the nineteenth century and into the twentieth. Following World War I, it was granted partial autonomy, but in 1933 that was withdrawn and Malta reverted to the status of crown colony.

One of Mintoff's brothers became a priest and a sister became a nun, and Mintoff himself studied briefly as an adolescent in a Roman Catholic seminary. At the University of Malta, he took a bachelor of science degree in 1937 and an additional degree in engineering and architecture two years later. On a Rhodes scholarship he did further study at Oxford University in England, where he became acquainted with members of the radical establishment, including the late Hugh Dalton. While he liked England, he was struck by the contrast between the ideals presented at Oxford and the realities of the colonial regime in Malta.

After taking an M.A. degree in engineering at Oxford in 1941, Mintoff worked as a civil engineer in the United Kingdom on a War Office appointment for two years. In 1944 he returned to Malta where, as an architect and engineer, he helped to begin the rebuilding of an infrastructure devastated by Axis aerial bombardment early in World War II. Situated in the narrows between Sicily and Libya, Malta played a crucial role in the Allied victory in the Mediterranean. For its heroic collective wartime resistance, King George VI bestowed on the "Island Fortress" the George Cross, Britain's highest civilian award for bravery.

In 1945 Mintoff became a member of the council of government and the executive council of the Malta Labour party, which was then in opposition. Two years later, the first elections were held under a new constitution giving Malta limited self-rule. Supported by industrial and dockyard workers, Mintoff was elected to the legislative assembly in a Labour rout of the Nationalist party, a Christian Democratic coalition. In the Labour government he was named deputy prime minister and minister of works and reconstruction. In 1949 he resigned those posts in a dispute with the party's leadership over its stance vis-à-vis the British government on the issue of aid in the ongoing reconstruction of Malta. The party split, with Mintoff heading the group of dissidents who considered the leadership weak-kneed in not demanding British and Marshall Plan funding sufficient for the job of reconstruction.

With the party in disarray, the Labour government fell. In the ensuing years Mintoff wrested control of the party from the old guard, and he led the Labourites back to power in 1955. As prime minister, he for three years sought in vain to obtain Malta's integration into the United Kingdom, with all the benefits accruing therefrom, including representation in the British parliament and participation in the U.K. welfare system. Fearing to set a precedent that might lead to its being "eaten up" by its former colonies, England balked. After negotiations broke down, Mintoff resigned as prime minister on April 26, 1958 and, doing an about-face, turned his energies to advocacy of full independence from England. When civil disturbances broke out following his resignation, the British declared a state of emergency, revoked the 1947 constitution, and returned Malta to colonial administration. At Mintoff's instigation, the Maltese staged a general strike in protest, and in England the British Labour party leader Aneurin Bevan, Mintoff's chief role model, condemned Britain's Conservative government for resorting to authoritarian colonial rule.

An acrimonious feud between Mintoff—who regards the Church as an ally, however unwitting, of reactionary political and social forces—and Malta's Roman Catholic Archbishop Michael Gonzi culminated in a 1961 interdict temporarily barring Mintoff from the sacraments. In the 1962 electoral campaign the Archbishop's opposition, and that of the priests under him, exerted what Mintoff called "the most barefaced moral pressure on an all-Catholic population." That opposition cost him the 1962 election, and the 1966 election as well. In the late 1960s there was a rapprochement between Mintoff and the church, easing his return to power in 1971 and his reelection in 1976.

Meanwhile, Britain had finally granted Malta independent status within the British Commonwealth in 1964. Mintoff boycotted the parliamentary ceremony marking the inauguration of independence to demonstrate his scorn for the terms on which independence was won. "In 1971, when we took office, we had an English governor-general, an English queen, English currency, a Bank of England man as the head of our central bank," he recalled with residual anger in an interview with James M. Markham of the New York Times (October 14, 1979). "The biggest commercial bank was English entirely, Barclays; our drydocks were run by a British firm, Swan Hunter; our development corporaton was run by a chairman who was English. We had a police force which was run by a commissioner who stated openly that his loyalty was to the British crown and nobody else. We had an army which was run by a brigadier general as an appendage of the British Army. Think of anything we had—telecommunications, entirely in British hands, for instance. We had an agreement with Britain, imposed by Britain before the so-called independence of 1964, whereby the British had the right to acquire any land on the island for defense purposes. This was only eight years ago. Now Malta is a republic. Everything has changed, nothing is British anymore—in eight years."

Shortly after he took office in 1971, Mintoff expelled the Italian commander of the NATO base on Malta and withdrew the American fleet's stopover privileges, thus sacrificing, in his words, "a lot of dollars . . . the wages of sin." When the last British military forces departed in 1979, the NATO base closed and Mintoff was left with "an $80-million hole" in his budget. To fill that hole he set about obtaining foreign aid, preferably grants, and investments, "money for enterprises that will replace these sinful activities" and at the same time guarantee Malta's nonalignment. Mintoff turned first to Libya, but he soon had a falling-out with Colonel Muammar el-Qaddafi over oil-drilling rights in the waters between Malta and Libya. (The dispute ended when the matter was referred to the International Court in The Hague.) Italy, recognizing Malta's neutral status, signed an agreement pledging grants and loans worth $95 million over five years and promising to consider military assistance should Malta be attacked. China agreed to a $40-million loan and a long-term aid program aimed at keeping the Soviet Union out of Malta. Not to be outdone, the Soviet Union then officially recognized Maltese neutrality and bought the right to store naval fuel in the former NATO bunkering facilities. Of all the countries with which he entered into agreements, China impressed him the most because of the dedication of its people to the belief that "common safety is in common action." "I've been to other Communist countries . . . ," he told a reporter, "and in none of these countries have I felt that Communism is a deeply felt conviction. In China it is."

The American response to Mintoff's effort to neutralize Malta and demilitarize the Mediterranean was "very ambiguous," as the Prime Minister pointed out to James D. Markham of the New York Times. "You [Americans] don't know whether it is better for the United States to support a free Mediterranean or to remain here and oppose directly Soviet influence and Soviet penetration. Are you really stopping the Soviets from having a big interest in the Mediterranean? You haven't. You're the losers. . . . You've put in the NATO and so on . . . a Maginot Line, and they've come in the back like this. We don't want you to dismantle without the other side dismantling. We want you to second this move [for a free Mediterranean] but you don't. Neither you nor the Soviets want this."

Mintoff's proclaimed policy of nonalignment was the major issue in the parliamentary elections of 1981, with the opposition leader, Eddi Fenech-Adami, describing as "unacceptable" the deal with the Soviet Union and calling for closer economic and defense ties with the West. Amid charges of gerrymandering and reports of violence by partisans of both sides, the Labour party held onto its three-seat majority while actually losing the popular vote, with 49 percent as opposed to the Nationalists' 51 percent.

In his campaign to socialize medicine in Malta, Mintoff has brought in foreign physicians to replace striking private doctors. That campaign merged with his resumed confrontation with the church when his government closed Malta's two church-run hospitals—the last remaining places where private physicians could still practice—after the government was refused 50 percent of the bed facilities for free hospitalization. After losing its two teacher colleges and the theology department at the University of Malta (the charter core of the university), the church fought to preserve its elementary and secondary schools (which educate one-fourth of Malta's pupils) in the face of Mintoff's plans to make the church use its wealth to subsidize free education in those schools. According to press reports early in 1983, Mintoff and Archbishop Joseph Mercieca, the successor to Archbishop Gonzi, were no longer on speaking terms. The government accused the Archbishop of aborting a 1980 agreement between the state and the association representing private schools. In October 1984 Mintoff went to the Vatican to seek a concordat.

Stocky and compact, Dom Mintoff is five feet five inches tall. On the stump, he is at his most peppery in Maltese. In private conversation, where he often uses a cultivated English, he is usually amiable and soft-spoken, but he abhors small talk and time-wasting socializing. He puts in as many as sixteen hours a day in his office in the Auberge de Castille, an ornate building in Valletta, the Maltese capital, constructed centuries ago by the Knights of Malta. His home, the villa "The Olives," is in Tarxien, five miles away. He also owns a cottage by the sea on the Delimara peninsula, where he retreats to swim, water-ski, and converse with cronies from the local fishing and farming communities. Among his other recreations are bocci and horseback riding. In 1947 Mintoff married Moyra de Vere Bentinck, an upper-middle-class Englishwoman, by whom he has two daughters. Because she prefers to live in England, he and his wife have lived apart for many years while maintaining "good relations," according to a family friend.

Prime Minister Mintoff is "not an easy man to deal with" politically, as an anonymous profile writer noted in the London *Observer* (January 16, 1972). "He has vast charm but he is quick to rage. He leaps about, physically and mentally; he is intolerant and slow to forgive. He is impatient of protocol. His proposals in negotiation tend for him to represent the final settlement. Few Western politicians can have swept out of so many conferences; conflict is the condition of his life. He is as stubborn as Mr. [Edward] Heath. And, despite his almost paranoic behavior, his purpose has always been clear and it has been informed by his love for his island and for its tough, kindly, and highly excitable people."

References: *Guardian* p13 Ja 23 '73; London *Observer* p8 Ja 16 '72; N Y Times p4 Ja 12 '72

por, p4 O 14 '79; *Current World Leaders* 23:365 My '80; *Who's Who in the World* (1982–83)

Morgan, Joe

Sept. 19, 1943– Baseball player. Address: b. Oakland A's, Oakland-Alameda County Coliseum, Oakland, Calif. 94621

The second baseman Joe Morgan has been a welcome anachronism in an age of increasing specialization in major-league baseball. One of the game's underappreciated greats, Morgan established himself as a stellar all-round second baseman in the years following his arrival in the majors in 1964. At his peak, in the 1970s, he was widely considered the most complete player in the National League, and he has continued to excel over the whole range of fielding, hitting, running, and stealing bases even in the twilight of his career. The speed and power that contribute to his prowess are, remarkably, packed into a five-foot-seven, 155-pound body—diminutive by major-league standards.

In addition to his playing skills, Morgan brings morale to a club: since reaching his prime with the Cincinnati Reds, perennial National League contenders in the 1970s, Morgan has only once played for a team that has finished below third place, and every team he has joined has improved upon his arrival and declined after his departure. After completing the 1983 season with the Philadelphia Phillies, Morgan retired, because he felt that it was time for him to be at home with his family in Oakland, California. Then the Oakland A's approached him, and he signed a one-year contract. When he started the 1984 season with the A's, he was among the top ten base stealers in baseball history, with 681 steals, and he held the major-league record for most consecutive errorless games by a second baseman (ninety-one) and the National League records for most games (2,190), seasons (nineteen), and putouts (5,056) by a second baseman. In the 1984 season Morgan broke the record for most career home runs by a major-league second baseman, with 268.

Joseph Leonard Morgan was born on September 19, 1943 in Bonham, Texas. In the late 1940s the Morgans moved to Oakland, California, where Joe, by his own account, "had a very ordinary childhood." His father nurtured his interest in baseball, taking him to Pacific Coast League games, giving him his first lessons in batting and fielding, and encouraging his aspiration to play in the major leagues. Jackie Robinson, the second baseman who broke the major-league color barrier, was his first hero. A later major source of inspiration for him was another second baseman, Nellie Fox, who proved that one did not have to be a giant to excel in the majors. As a left-handed batter, Morgan sought to emulate Ted Williams' quick swing and keen strike-zone judgment. In his early days on the sandlots, Morgan had trouble hitting, because he was smaller than the other boys, but he swung as if he had their heft, gripping the bat at the end of the handle. When he learned to choke up, his batting improved.

By the time Morgan joined Oakland's Little League his position of choice was second base. He led the Young American League in Oakland in home runs, and he began trying out for the major leagues while playing for Castlemont High School in Oakland. Because of his slight physique, scouts were unimpressed, and after graduating from high school Morgan enrolled in Oakland City College. In the spring of his freshman year there, Bill Wight, a scout for the National League's Houston Astros (then called the Houston Colt .45's) noticed him. "He was small, and there wasn't much he could do about that," Wight told Wells Twombly for Sport (January 1967). "But. . . . I liked his aggressiveness. He was self-assured without being cocky."

Signed by the Astros, Morgan began his professional career with the team's California League Class A farm club at Modesto, where he batted .263 and hit five home runs early in the 1963 season. Later in the same season he was transferred to Durham in the North Carolina League, where he went .332 and hit thirteen homers in ninety-five games. Called up to Houston for the final eight games of the season, he hit .240 in his first twenty-five major league at-bats.

Morgan was returned the next year for further experience with the Astros' farm club at San Antonio, Texas. The statistics he racked up there—a league-leading 106 double plays, a .967 fielding percentage, a .323 batting average, ninety runs batted in, and forty-two double-base hits that tied for league lead—earned him the Texas League's Most Valuable Player award. Once again he was summoned to Houston toward season's end, and this time he remained.

As a rookie second baseman in 1965, Morgan, knowing that his fielding needed improvement, rehearsed double-plays for hours before official practice sessions and profited from the coaching of Nellie Fox, who retired from active play that same year. "Fox drove one point home very hard," Morgan recalled in an interview with Maury Allen of the New York Post (July 15, 1976). "He said when you lay down the bat and pick up the glove, forget about hitting. When you pick up the bat, forget about everything bad that's happened in the field." That season Morgan batted .271, hit fourteen home runs, drove in forty RBIs, led the club in at-bats, hits, triples, and fewest times grounded into double plays, and tied a league record for most hits in a game, with six. In the Sporting News poll of National League players he was voted rookie player of the year.

Along with his other totals for 1965, Morgan led the league with ninety-seven unintentional walks—a product of his almost oracular strike-zone sense. With one of the quickest swings in baseball, he was already able to watch a pitch a split-second longer than other hitters before committing himself. "Whatever you throw up there," Jon Matlack, the pitcher, once remarked, "the umpire calls a ball unless Morgan swings at it. Morgan knows the strike zone and the umpires give him everything close." And once he had walked to first base, he was in a position to advance—by hook or by crook.

Also evident from the beginning of Morgan's tenure with the Astros was his enthusiastic team spirit and contagious confidence. He recalled in an interview with Larry Linderman for Sport (June 1984): "I used to tell people that when you get Joe Morgan you're not just getting a ball player—you're getting a guy who's going to do whatever he can to help the organization. . . . You help your team win by doing more than just playing baseball; you [also] help your team win in the clubhouse." Regarding Morgan's exhortatory stance vis-à-vis his teammates, the Astro outfielder Jimmy Wynn explained to a reporter in 1967: "He's the most earnest man I ever met. He means every word he says and he means to do everything he says he will. He's no braggart."

In the first half of the 1966 baseball season Morgan charted a .315 batting average, and in June he became the first Houston player ever named to the National League All-Star team. But later that month he suffered a broken kneecap during infield practice, forcing him onto the bench for five weeks. During that hiatus, the club began to slide from a hopeful fourth place in the league, and it ended the season eighth. Morgan hit .285 for the year while walking eighty-nine times, scoring sixty runs, increasing his stolen base total from eleven to twenty-nine, and going 133 games with only fourteen errors on the field. The following year he improved his balance at the plate, and at Nellie Fox's suggestion devised a characteristic style of flapping his left elbow while standing for a pitch in order to keep the arm up and free of the body for hitting stronger line-drive balls.

An injury during an early game against the New York Mets in 1968 required surgery on Morgan's knee ligaments and kept him out of all but ten games that season. The following year, his .236 batting average was a career low, but he reached career high marks with 110 walks, forty-nine stolen bases, and fifteen homers. In 1970 Morgan played in the All-Star game for the first time, and in 1971 he led the league in triples, with eleven. Then, following an argument with the Astro management over fielding errors and the usefulness of his unique compact swing, Morgan was labeled a "troublemaker" and traded to the Cincinnati Reds in an eight-man deal, in November 1971.

The Reds' acquisition of Morgan signaled a major overhaul of their playing strategy in 1972, from reliance on power-hitting to a speed-based effort. "Quickness is my game—at bat, in the field and on bases . . . ," he later explained to Phil Elderkin for the *Christian Science Monitor* (August 11, 1975), "Because of it, there isn't a rival pitcher who can consistently throw the ball by me." Placed in the second slot of the club's batting lineup, Morgan joined the swatting masters Pete Rose, Johnny Bench, and Tony Perez in setting up scoring situations. In 1972 he reached base safely 40 percent of his times at bat, averaging .292. He belted sixteen homers, led the league with 115 walks and 122 runs, and finished second in stolen bases, with fifty-eight. The Reds trounced the Pittsburgh Pirates in the league championship series, three games to two, with the help of two Morgan homers. In the World Series—in which Morgan scored four runs—the Reds lost to the Oakland A's. In the All-Star game that year Morgan drove in the winning run for the National League and was named the game's Most Valuable Player.

Nineteen seventy-three proved an even better year for Morgan, as he finished with a .290 batting average, 111 walks, 116 runs, sixty-seven stolen bases, and twenty-six home runs and became the first player ever to hit twenty-five or more home runs and steal sixty or more bases in the same season. He also led the National League in double plays turned at his position, with 106, and won his first Gold Glove award as the league's finest defensive player at his position. Morgan reprised his appearance at that season's All-Star game (he would play in the next six All-Star meetings), and the Reds once again battled for the league championship, but they lost the playoff series to the New York Mets, three games to two. In 1974 Morgan hit .293, drew 120 walks, socked twenty-two home runs, scored 107 runs, stole fifty-eight bases, and received his second straight Gold Glove.

A redundancy of superlatives marked the 1975 season for both the Reds and Joe Morgan. After adjusting to a "promotional" move from second to third place in the batting lineup, Morgan finished the season with a .327 batting average, blasting in ninety-four runs with seventeen homers and collecting a league-leading 132 walks. He won another Gold Glove, leading National League second basemen with only eleven fielding errors. Cincin-

nati went 108-54 that year, capturing the West Division title by twenty games.

Sixty-seven base thefts were among Morgan's contributions to Cincinnati's 1975 championship season. A self-proclaimed "student of the game," Morgan later analysed his stealing technique for a reporter: "Most people think a man steals because he's *fast*. . . . but I have a *quickness*. I mean, I'm going at top speed when I have taken one step. But more than that, I know exactly how much of a lead to get against every pitcher in the league. This is because I study them all." That Morgan's liberties on the bases can demolish a pitcher's concentrated rhythm was demonstrated in the first league playoff game against the Pittsburgh Pirates. After wangling a walk from pitcher Jerry Reuss, Morgan methodically stole second and third bases on the next two pitches and ran home on a fly ball, and the rattled Reuss allowed hits for four more Reds runs in the inning. Cincinnati won that game, 8-3, and rolled over the Pirates in the next two meetings, 6-1 and 5-3, to take the league crown.

The Reds defeated the Boston Red Sox in the 1975 World Series, thanks in part to Morgan's dancing off base—he goaded pitcher Reggie Cleveland into throwing to first base sixteen times in the space of three pitches at one point in the fifth game—and to his bloop single in the ninth inning of the seventh game that brought in the winning run. His winning the National League's Most Valuable Player award by a record margin in November 1975 was a reaffirmation of his reputation for all-round prowess. Writing in *Sports Illustrated* (March 1, 1976), Roy Blount Jr. observed that Morgan was the only man in baseball who could "do all the following things extremely well: Field, hit for average, hit the long ball, steal bases, . . . draw walks, . . . avoid strike-outs, maintain a lively, sunny disposition, and think."

In 1976 Morgan became only the second player in the league's history to be named MVP twice consecutively. The accolade recognized his high season totals (a .320 batting average, a career-high twenty-seven homers, sixty stolen bases, a league-leading .576 slugging percentage) and his team effort for the Reds, who humiliated the New York Yankees in the 1976 World Series in four straight games with some help from Morgan's first-game, first-inning home run and two RBIs. Morgan also took his third Gold Glove for fielding excellence in 1976.

In 1976 major league baseball switched from what has been called an "indentured servitude" system to the free agent system. One side effect of that change was pressure for higher salaries, and by the winter of 1977 many Cincinnati players, including Morgan, grew frustrated with the reluctance of the team's front office to acknowledge the new salary structures. After arousing some suspense about his future plans, Morgan signed a new, three-year contract with the Reds in 1977 for a reported $1 million, a raise of approximately $100,000 over his previous year's earnings. The 1977 season marked a decline for both the Reds

and Morgan. He hit twenty-eight homers, stole forty-nine bases, had seventy-eight RBIs and 117
walks, and hit .288, an average that disappointed
him. Cincinnati lost the West Division title to the
Los Angeles Dodgers by ten games in 1977 and by
three in 1978. Playing part of the 1978 season with
a torn stomach muscle, Morgan's batting average
fell to .236, and he posted his fewest runs, hits, and
walks in a decade. Hampered by an ankle sprain,
he did not improve significantly the next season. In
late 1979 he declared for free agency and shortly
thereafter signed with the Houston Astros. He later
suggested that the Cincinnati management's fiscal
conservatism had broken the team's spirit: "My
philosophy is that if you don't change with the
times you die—and that's what happened with the
Reds."

During a personal and team slump in 1980, Morgan held a pep meeting with his Houston teammates. In the weeks following the meeting Morgan
corrected a flaw in his batting stance, and he ended
the 1980 season hitting .243 with eleven homers
and forty-nine RBIs. The Astros captured the West
Division title, but lost the league playoff series to
the Philadelphia Phillies. Moving to the San Francisco Giants in the strike-shortened 1981 season,
Morgan hit .240 with eight homers and thirty-one
RBIs and stole twenty-four bases. It was during
that season that he began to take restorative breaks,
sitting out of games occasionally.

In 1982 Morgan hit his 1,000th career RBI, batted
.289, and hit fourteen homers, helping the Giants
stay in the West Division race until the final week
of seasonal play. "You can't overemphasize what
he meant to us," Giants manager Frank Robinson
attested to Dan McGrath of the Sporting News (December 20, 1983). "He was our leader on and off the
field." The Giants voted him their Most Valuable
Player and the Sporting News named him the
league's Comeback Player of the Year for 1982.

Turning down an offer to manage the Houston
Astros after the 1982 season, Morgan signed with
the Philadelphia Phillies. With the Phillies in 1983
he went .230, with sixteen homers, seventy-two
runs, fifty-nine RBIs, and eighty-nine walks, and
the team reached the 1983 World Series, which
they lost to the Baltimore Orioles. Knowing that he
was tiring, Morgan considered the 1983 season his
last, until his friend Roy Eisenhardt, president of
the American League's Oakland A's, persuaded
him to play one year with Oakland. "I happen to
love Oakland," he has explained. "I grew up there,
I got a great education there and I feel a debt to the
city." The A's finished the 1984 season in fourth
place in the league's West Division, with Morgan
turning in a .244 batting average, forty-four RBIs,
twenty-one doubles, six homers, sixty-six walks,
and eight stolen bases. On July 23, 1984 Joe Morgan
hit his 2,500th baseball in professional play.

Joe Morgan and his wife, the former Gloria
Stewart, his childhood sweetheart, live in Oakland
with their daughters, Lisa and Angela. Robert
Ward of Sport (August 1976) has described Morgan's demeanor as "cool and cocky, [as he moves]

through the air as if he had a special understanding
with space. He fills it beautifully, elegantly, like a
dancer." Morgan, a righthander when not in the
batter's box, wears a trim mustache and shows a
touch of gray in his black hair. His favorite recreations are golf and billiards.

References: Sport 43:46+ Ja '67 pors, 56:45+ Ag
'73 pors, 75:19+ Je '84 pors; Washington Post F p2
O 5 '80; Baseball Register (1982); Burchard,
Marshall. Joe Morgan (1978); Cohen, Joel H. Joe
Morgan: Great Little Big Man (1978)

Morley, Malcolm A.

1931- Painter. Address: b. Xavier Fourcade Inc.,
36 E. 75th St., New York City, N. Y. 10021

Although considered a "legendary bad boy" with a
pugnacious temperament, Malcolm Morley has
generated controversy more often for his trend-
setting artistic developments than for his occasionally surly behavior. He has been labeled the father
of two very different and very important movements in art—photorealism and neo-
expresssionism—but has only recently been accorded substantial recognition as a major
contemporary artist. "I played underdog longer
than I needed to," he explained in the New York
Times (February 12, 1984). "But the art was getting
stronger and I didn't want to blow it. It's like I've
been holding a poker hand for twenty-five years.
Now I'm showing my cards."

Malcolm A. Morley was born in 1931 in the
Highgate section of London, England. He did not
know his father and recalls only that "he had an

Italian name" and "was a bad egg." On his mother's remarriage in about 1937, he adopted his stepfather's surname, Evans, which he retained until he left England for the United States in 1958. Morley spent most of World War II in London, but he was forced to evacuate after his home was destroyed by a V-bomb.

As a child, Morley was fascinated by the sea, an interest that would carry over into many of his paintings. He carved wooden ships, constructed models of sailing vessels, and several times ran away from home with the hope of becoming a seafarer. When he was ten, he attended a naval academy but was soon expelled. Eventually he obtained a berth as a galley boy on a tug towing a bucket dredger to Newfoundland, Canada, and later he worked on barges in the North Sea. Morley's obsession with sailing waned after the war. Returning to London, he committed several misdemeanors for which he spent two terms in "borstal"—that is, a juvenile reformatory—by the time he was seventeen. His release only led to further attempts at larceny and more arrests until he finally was sentenced to a three-year term at Wormwood Scrubs prison in West London.

That prison term proved a turning point in Morley's life. Influenced by the visiting instructor of his prison art class, by a correspondence course in illustration through which he mastered painting in water colors, and by his intensive reading, Morley decided by the time he was released on probation after serving two years of his sentence that he would become an artist. He visited St. Ives in Cornwall, then a popular artists' colony, where he managed to paint enough to gain some attention from the resident artists. His work also impressed his probation officer, who engineered his admission to London's Camberwell School of Arts and Crafts in 1952. One day while painting a landscape in Richmond Park, the young Morley was "discovered" again, this time by the famous actor Sir John Mills, who not only bought the painting but arranged for Morley's transfer to the prestigious Royal College of Art, which waived its usual academic requirements and admitted him in 1954 on the strength of his obvious talent.

During his three years at the Royal College of Art, Morley generally restricted his paintings to landscapes, cityscapes, and figurative compositions. Although many of his fellow students, including Richard Smith and Joe Tilson, gravitated toward pop art, Morley remained aloof from them and from that trend. "I was an Angry Young Man, really," he recalled in a New York magazine interview (February 20, 1984). "A classic case. A chip on my shoulder, smoldering, the whole trip. The only thing I liked about art school was the women." But as a result of his viewing "Modern Art in the United States," an exhibition mounted by the Tate Gallery in London in 1956, he found a congenial form for his art. He was so struck by the paintings there of such noted American abstract expressionists as Willem de Kooning and Mark Rothko that he visited New York City, the home of that movement, be-

fore his graduation from the Royal College of Art in 1957 and immigrated to New York in 1958.

When Morley was not working as a waiter in the city or on Long Island, he continued to paint some landscapes and views of Brooklyn, where he was then living, but he experimented more and more with abstract painting. Barnett Newman, the famed abstract painter whom he met by chance when serving him in a restaurant, also was an important influence on Morley's early career, and he encouraged the young artist by praising the "sense of light" in his works. Most of Morley's early abstract paintings were done in black and white, reminiscent of de Kooning's work in the 1940s, and revealed his intense interest in the texture of a painting's surface and in the paint itself. In such works as High July (1964), he used such unusual implements as a pastry gun to apply the paint in flat, horizontal bands interrupted by impastoed lines. His abstract paintings and some later stylized landscapes and seascapes were exhibited at his first one-man show, held at the Kornblee Gallery in 1964. Reviewing that exhibition in the New York Times (November 7, 1964), Stuart Preston commented that "semaphoric incidents are laid out in parallel strips and layers. The results make interesting pictorial reading."

By 1964, however, Morley was already moving away from abstraction. His childhood interest in ships, perhaps unconsciously suppressed after a model ship he planned to paint was destroyed by the bomb that struck his home, was reasserting itself. Friends detected in his abstract paintings the configurations of ships, and to the bottom of his last abstract painting he attached four strips cut from a photograph of a sailing vessel. The structural sculptor Mark di Suvero suggested that he exploit his preoccupation by using the ocean liners passing his studio window as subjects. Instead, Morley began to paint realistic monochromes of battleships and sailors, sometimes tracing them from photographs and then applying a grey ink wash to produce a hazy image like a newspaper photograph.

Although Morley once tried to paint an ocean liner from dockside, he utterly failed because in order to grasp visually the entire ship he was forced to shift his perspective, thus destroying the picture plane. His solution to that problem was twofold: he turned to using postcard and travel-brochure photos of ships and cruise passengers, which gave him models on a more reasonable scale; and he then divided the photo into a sixty-four-square grid by which he could transfer and enlarge the image, square by square, on to his similarly marked canvas. In his introduction to Malcolm Morley: Paintings 1965–82 (London: Whitechapel Art Gallery, 1983), Michael Compton, keeper of exhibitions and education at the Tate Gallery, pointed out that "this practice has become a central component of Morley's technique and is not only a convenient device but is embedded in the purpose and meaning of his work." The grid allowed Morley to produce completely objective paintings by forcing him to concentrate on each block singly without reference to the entire picture. As a result, he was less likely to paint interpretively or to inject his feelings into the work. To ensure objectivity to an even greater degree, he would often cut the gridded photo into strips, turn his canvas and one strip at a time upside down, and paint it in that manner. The resulting painstakingly detailed acrylic pictures, including *Empire Monarch* (1965), *SS Amsterdam in Front of Rotterdam* (1966), and *Ship's Dinner Party* (1966), were such exact reproductions that critics labeled them "photorealistic" and hailed Morley as the father of the ensuing photorealistic movement.

Morley himself prefers to term those works "superrealistic," perhaps because his purpose, unlike that of Howard Kanovitz and some other photorealists, was not simply to create the illusion of a photograph and his method was more painterly. Although not visible from a distance, his brushstrokes become obvious on close examination, and the white border around most of his paintings from that period further emphasizes the artificiality of the painted image and its two-dimensionality. Moreover, as Michael Compton explained, "the margin may also be an image of the paper or card on which the model is printed and is just as much an illusion as the ship, the sea, or anything else represented in the picture." An additional indication of Morley's insistence on that point is his unwillingness to make corrections on his paintings. When, for an extreme example, he misjudged the canvas size needed for *Empire Monarch*, he painted the excess canvas black instead of trimming it. During that period, he also occasionally used art masterpieces as his models, transferring them to his canvas in the same manner. The most notable of those paintings is *Vermeer, Portrait of the Artist in his Studio* (1968).

Art critics read even deeper meanings into Morley's superrealistic compositions. A reviewer for *Life* (June 27, 1969) contended that the combination of Morley's "commonplace" subjects, "garish" colors, and execution resulted in "an ironic comment on the commercial images that saturate our culture." In his appraisal in the *New York Times* (March 2, 1969) of Morley's third one-man show at the Kornblee Gallery, Peter Schjeldahl agreed that through those elements Morley was attempting to convey a satiric message, but he considered the artist's method too heavy-handed. Nevertheless, he conceded that "at its best, this art makes contact with a modern form of 'nature'—photo-reality, reproduction-reality—whose mystery, charm and occasional horror affect us daily."

With *Race Track* (1970), Morley signaled an abrupt break with realistic painting at the height of its popularity. He spent months faithfully reproducing by his usual method a poster photo of the Greyville Race Course in South Africa, and he even painted each of the thousands of spectators individually. But after completing the remarkably detailed painting, he imposed a large red X across the entire canvas. Many critics interpreted the X as not only a denunciation of photorealism—a style he considered "wasted" by most artists of that

school—but also as a reference to Malcolm X and the civil rights movement, a reading strengthened by the South African setting of the work and the obvious pun in its title.

In an interview with William Zimmer for the *New York Times* (February 12, 1984), Morley characterized his superrealistic paintings as the "heights of repression," perhaps because of the self-imposed restrictions of the grid method, the banality of his chosen images, and the studied emotionlessness of his brushwork and the finished composition. Although he used the grid throughout the 1970s, he soon abandoned the photographic model and the device of the white border. More important, his choice of subject and his freer brush allowed him to release his repressed violent feelings on canvas. According to Paul Richard, writing in the *Washington Post* (September 10, 1983), "Almost all the Morleys made since *Race Track* seem admissions of old rage." For his reintroduction of emotion to painting, cognoscenti have dubbed him the father of neo-expressionism.

Perhaps influenced by the then popular conceptual art movement, Morley's behavior also reflected a freeing of suppressed emotion. In one particularly well-known incident, he tried to deface his satiric *Buckingham Palace with First Prize* (1970) when it was presented for sale by Florists' Transworld Delivery (FTD) at a 1974 Paris auction. Arriving with a TV camera crew he had hired and a water gun filled with red paint, he tried to write "faux" (false) across the canvas, but the forewarned auction house had covered the picture with plastic sheets. Morley managed, however, to nail the water gun to the painting as it was being removed, and some of the paint bled on to the canvas. The gun and paint stains have never been removed. Also, at a time when he found it difficult to sell his work, he once destroyed a painting just after it had been sold, slashing the canvas and returning the $40,000 check to the shocked buyer. "I was kind of a little bit off my head—I would have to be," Morley recalled with some embarrassment in the *New York* interview. "I was motivated by a desire for recognition of some kind."

One of the earliest and most celebrated paintings that reflected his new style and attitude is *Los Angeles Yellow Pages* (1971), which depicts a cover of a telephone directory, featuring a photo of downtown Los Angeles, that Morley had used as a palette. Once again, he rendered it as realistically as possible, but the deceptively accurate reproduction of the cityscape is undercut by the typography on the cover, the paint smears, and the worn patches, among other elements, that he also reproduced. Furthermore, the illusion of the cover's reality is in turn destroyed by both the painter's obvious brushstrokes and the flat, opaque black "rent" painted in the middle, itself an illusion. Critics praised *Yellow Pages* for its skillful rendering of emotion as well as for the images of earthquakes and other natural catastrophes that it called to mind. Mark Stevens described it in *Newsweek* (January 9, 1984) as "a brilliant bit of visual poetry: nothing brings out horror better than something ordinary."

Turning to oils, a more emotive medium, with *Piccadilly Circus* (1973), Morley gave even freer rein to his emotions. Originally intended to be a pastiche of abstract expressionism in the late-1940s style of de Kooning, it became, to use Michael Compton's words, "deliberately a mess." A vastly enlarged image of a postcard of Piccadilly Circus was largely obscured by splashes and generous strokes of paint with the result that at first glance it looked like "a vast traffic accident." In an ambiguous final touch, he attached a bag of grey paint at the top of the canvas into which friends shot arrows, thus allowing the paint to drip over the surface of the picture. (The bag and arrows are permanent parts of the painting.)

In 1973 the artist started to experiment with freestanding, three-dimensional paintings, such as *New York City Postcard Fold-Out* (1973) and *Hollywood Film Stars and Homes Postcard Fold-Out* (1974). The latter consisted of painted pieces of crumpled metal and has been destroyed. Gradually, he employed three-dimensional models for his works. Often they were tableaux of toys—boats, soldiers, trains, and planes—in a box. Morley used a framed, string grid placed over the open end of the box to transfer the image, including the box itself, to his canvas. He used that technique for *Train Wreck* (1975), *Age of Catastrophe* (1976), *Little Corner of Plane-Ship Catastrophe and Central Park* (1976), and other of his early nightmarish "catastrophe" paintings, which Kay Larson described in *New York* magazine (March 5, 1984) as "trains and planes (and a few ships) crashed in a storm of paint, a wild van Gogh-like hail of brushstrokes." For later catastrophe paintings he constructed tableaux that included small reproductions of some of his own completed works or preliminary drawings and water colors. One of the most important of those paintings, *The Day of the Locust* (1977), incorporates *Los Angeles Yellow Pages* and *SS Amsterdam in Front of Rotterdam* and is an overtly political composition inspired by his trip to the Berlin Wall.

In *The Ultimate Anxiety* (1978), Morley reproduced in his superrealistic style a postcard of a Francesco Guardi painting that depicts the ancient Venetian ceremony of the Doge wedding the sea. Over this he superimposed at a diagonal a painting of a toy train as if it were crashing on the Doge's ship. Like *Race Track*, *The Ultimate Anxiety* seems to be a disavowal of his previous styles and the beginning of a new phase. Since 1978 Morley has relied less on three-dimensional models for his works, turning instead to his own drawings and watercolors, especially his landscapes, which he then adapts and renders in oils. His brushstroke is even more liberated; his subject matter, far more varied; and his palette, sensuous and vibrant. Full of rich symbolism and references to myth and art history, such recent works as *Out Dark Spot* (1978) and *Christmas Tree (The Lonely Ranger Lost in the Jungle of Erotic Desire)* (1979) are clearly deeply personal, psychological allegories. Critic Michael Brenson, writing in the *New York Times*

(April 13, 1984), interpreted one such picture, *Day Fishing at Heraklion* (1983), as "a metaphor for the artistic ship in which he sets sail each time he embarks on a new artistic journey." Brenson also pointed out in his work the influence of Picasso, Van Gogh, Robert Delaunay, Jackson Pollock, de Kooning, and Edouard Manet. Far from being insulted by implications that he is derivative, Morley told William Zimmer in the *New York Times* interview that he would rather be labeled "the child of something" than be known as the father of photorealism or neo-expressionism. "I'd rather be the child of Cézanne. . . . Cézanne, Manet, Velázquez—I think about them all the time in my studio."

Morley's works have been presented in many individual exhibitions over the past twenty years and in nearly one hundred group exhibitions since 1955, both in the United States—principally in New York City—and in Cologne, Paris, London, Amsterdam, and other major European cities. The most important of his one-man shows was a major retrospective of his works from 1965 to 1982 mounted by the Whitechapel Art Gallery in London. During 1983 the exhibition traveled from Basel, Switzerland, to Rotterdam, the Netherlands, and then to London before opening at the Corcoran Gallery in Washington, D.C. It was also shown at the Museum of Contemporary Art in Chicago and the Brooklyn Museum in New York City, where it ran until April 1984. As a result of that retrospective, which was reviewed by most major art critics, Morley's reputation as an important contemporary artist was firmly established.

During his career, Morley has also taken time to teach art. He was at first involved in the adult program of the New York City Board of Education (1961–64), and in 1965, through the recommendation of artist Roy Lichtenstein, he was invited to teach at Ohio State University. He also taught for extended periods at the School of Visual Arts, New York (1967–69) and the State University of New York at Stonybrook (1972–74), and he has given lectures and seminars at a variety of educational institutions. He also took part in the German Academic Exchange Program in 1977, but after seven months was forced to cut short his visit to Berlin when he became ill.

Malcolm A. Morley, a stocky man with a bald pate and grey beard, maintains a studio in the SoHo district of Manhattan and a home in Bridgehampton, Long Island. He married an American woman soon after he immigrated to New York but is now divorced. When asked during the *New York* interview about the radical changes in his painting style over the years, Morley claimed they resulted from "self-radicalization" and eleven years of psychoanalysis. So wrenching was the process of discovering himself and his style that he described it as "literally a matter of life and death."

References: Newsday II p15 Mr 18 '84; New York 17:40+ F 20 '84 pors; Contemporary Artists 2d ed (1983); Malcolm Morley: Paintings 1965–82

(1983); Who's Who in America, 1984–85; Who's Who in American Art (1978)

Mulroney, (Martin) Brian

March 20, 1939– Prime Minister of Canada.
Address: Office of the Prime Minister, Langevin Block, Parliamentary Buildings, Ottawa, Ontario K1A 0A2, Canada

Few Canadians coming directly from the private sector have made such rapid strides on their way to public prominence as Brian Mulroney, who became the eighteenth prime minister of Canada on September 17, 1984. Only as recently as June 1983 the former president of the Iron Ore Company of Canada had been elected leader of the Progressive Conservative party and as such, had automatically become a member of the Parliament. The first Conservative leader to come from the province of Quebec in almost a century, Mulroney is also the first Tory ever to come to Conservative leadership without having previously run for public office.

Mulroney succeeded the Liberal party leader John Turner, whose tenure as prime minister was one of the briefest in Canadian history. Turner, whose pro-American and fiscally conservative ideology does not differ markedly from Mulroney's, became prime minister at the end of June 1984, after the departure of Pierre Elliott Trudeau, but in the general election called for September 4, the Liberals went down to defeat, and Turner with them.

The third of six children, Martin Brian Mulroney was born on March 20, 1939 to Benedict and Irene (O'Shea) Mulroney in Baie Comeau, a pulp and paper manufacturing town on the St. Lawrence River north of Quebec City. The Roman Catholic Mulroney and O'Shea families had come to Canada from Ireland during the great potato famine in the mid-nineteenth century, and Benedict and Irene Mulroney had come to Baie Comeau in search of work during the Great Depression. During the day Benedict Mulroney toiled at the mill that dominated the town's economy, and at night he worked independently as an electrician. The times were tough, but Brian Mulroney, who grew up speaking English at home and French on the streets, remembers them fondly. "It was almost, in some ways, an idyllic community," he says, "except for the fact that nobody had any money; but nobody needed very much."

Convinced that education was the only hope for Brian to get out of Baie Comeau, the Mulroneys scrimped enough money together to send him, at fourteen, to St. Thomas College, a boys' boarding school in Chatham, New Brunswick. In 1955 he enrolled at St. Francis-Xavier University in Antigonish, Nova Scotia, and after graduating with a B.A. degree with honors in political science, he studied law for one year at Dalhousie University in Halifax, Nova Scotia. He then transferred to Laval University in Quebec City, where he became one of the first anglophone students to take all of his courses in French.

At St. Francis-Xavier University, Brian Mulroney came into contact with the famed Reverend Moses Coady, who founded the Antigonish Movement of social activism, and he also became entranced with politics. Although his family had been Liberals, Mulroney gravitated to the Progressive Conservatives. Impressed by Robert Stanfield, the leader of Nova Scotia's Tory Opposition, he had decided that the Liberals were a closed operation "with no place for a boy like me." As a freshman, he was recruited for the campus Conservative club by Lowell Murray, who is now a member of the Canadian Senate. In 1956 Mulroney made a long and arduous train trip from Antigonish to Ottawa to serve as a youth delegate at the PC convention that chose John Diefenbaker as its national leader. In serving as national vice-president of the Youth for Diefenbaker movement, he seized the opportunity to make himself known to as many Tory politicians as possible, and he later continued the practice of boldly making contact with national leaders. By the time he was a student at Laval University, Mulroney was on speaking terms with Prime Minister Diefenbaker and had built a network of political connections that was the envy of his friends.

On completing law school, Brian Mulroney joined the prestigious Montreal firm of Ogilvy, Cope, Porteous, Montgomery, Renault, Clarke, and Kirkpatrick. Remaining there as a partner until 1976, he developed into an excellent labor lawyer with a deserved reputation as a skilled negotiator and conciliator. Although his clients included such business giants as the Power Corporation of Montreal and the Iron Ore Company of Canada, he continued to consider himself a friend of the workers. "My father was a unionized man, a member of the QFL [Quebec Federation of Labor] in fact," he has said. And he has recalled with reference to the summer jobs that he took in order to pay for his schooling, "I spent eleven years as a laborer in Baie Comeau, so I know a worker when I see one."

Although Mulroney was actively engaged behind the scenes in Tory politics during his years with the Montreal law firm, he remained unknown to most Canadians until March 1974, when rebellious workers caused $35 million in damages to a construction site for a hydroelectric dam on James Bay. That rampage, which climaxed several years of labor unrest in Quebec, prompted Robert Bourassa, the premier of the province, to appoint Mulroney along with Guy Chevrette to a three-man Royal Commission of Inquiry into Union Freedom, which was headed by Robert Cliche, associate chief justice of the provincial court. On the politically balanced tribunal, Cliche unofficially represented the socialist New Democratic party; Mulroney, who was once his student at Laval, the PC; and Chevrette, the Parti Quebecois. The Cliche commission uncovered a network of corruption reaching all the way from the lowest ranks of the QFL to one of Bourassa's former aides who sought electoral support from the union in return for giving it a monopoly over the labor force at James Bay. In the midst of much publicity, including telecasts of its hearings, the commission issued a 600-page report that offered scores of recommendations for the reform of labor relations and union practices in Quebec.

Mulroney remembers his tenure on the Cliche commission as "an exciting, tumultuous time," and though his role left him open to death threats, it also kept his name constantly in the media. As the Tory leadership convention scheduled for February 1976 approached, friends urged Mulroney to test his new political fame and vie for control of the party. Acceding to their wishes, he did extremely well on the first ballot, finishing second behind the pre-convention favorite, Claude Wagner of Quebec. Mulroney's hopes faded quickly, however, as alliances were made and allegiances transferred between the rounds of voting. By the fourth ballot another young Tory, Joe Clark of Alberta, swept past both Wagner and Mulroney to capture the leadership.

Four months after his unsuccessful campaign, Mulroney accepted the post of executive vice-president for corporate affairs in the Iron Ore Company of Canada, and one year later he became its president. Mulroney calmed the restive labor force at the Iron Ore Company and, toward the end of his seven-year tenure, the business, which had not paid dividends during most of the 1970s, once again became profitable. In November 1982, however, the declining international demand for steel and falling iron ore prices forced Mulroney to announce that, by July 1983, the company would close one mine in Schefferville, near the Labrador border, and to suspend operations at another one, in Labrador City. The Schefferville closing put 285 miners out of work and virtually shut down the town, while the Labrador City suspension idled 2,000 employees temporarily and 500 permanently.

Some of Mulroney's critics predicted that his actions would finish him politically, and in February 1983 Mulroney had to go to Schefferville to face questioning by four Parti Quebecois provincial cabinet ministers and eleven Parti Quebecois and Liberal backbenchers. But by using the occasion to offer a generous compensation package to the affected workers and to present his own plan for the development of northern Canada, in the end Mulroney managed to win sympathy and media approval for his handling of the problem.

During his years at the Iron Ore Company, Mulroney devoted himself to service endeavors that enhanced his civic stature and added to his long list of influential contacts. He helped collect money for several universities and chaired a drive that brought St. Francis-Xavier $4 million more than its fund-raising goal of $7 million. Although he continued to be involved in PC affairs, he received no post during the short-lived Clark administration, which held power in Canada between the Tories' victory in the general election of May 1979 and Prime Minister Pierre Trudeau's return to office after the Liberals recaptured parliament in the general election of February 1980.

Before the general meeting of the Progressive Conservatives that was held in January 1983 in Winnipeg, Brian Mulroney had expressed his support for the party's incumbent leader, Joe Clark, but Clark subsequently won the endorsement of only 67 percent of the 2,000 delegates for his leadership. The disappointed Clark on January 28 called for a convention to choose a new leader and on February 2 stepped down as the head of the parliamentary opposition. On March 21, at a press conference in Ottawa, Mulroney announced his resignation from the Iron Ore Company and declared himself a candidate for the leadership. He later spoke of his mixed emotions about giving up his business career for the risks of public life. "You know," he said, "there's a certain amount of ambition in these things, and there's also a certain belief that you can do something to change it. . . . And if I make it, fine. And if I don't, at least I'll be able to say when they put me down, I didn't sit on the goddamn sidelines, I tried. That's all I can do."

Commentators noted that Mulroney offered the PC a combination of youth and vigor that reminded many Canadians of the late John F. Kennedy. Mulroney pleased the more conservative or "blue" Tories dissatisfied with the moderate or "red" look of the party under Clark, but perhaps equally important, he could provide the predominantly English-speaking Tories with a bilingual leader and with a base in Quebec, where their party held only one parliamentary seat to the Liberals' seventy-four seats. In all, Mulroney appealed to many Tories hungry for a winner and embittered by the brief regime of Joe Clark.

At first Mulroney tried to capitalize on his advantages with a low-keyed campaign that was designed to erase memories of the slick and expensive one he had conducted in 1976. But he became more aggressive when on May 16 the Carleton University School of Journalism released the results of a pre-convention poll of Tory delegates that indicated that he not only trailed Clark by 35 percent to 19 percent as a first-ballot choice but also fell behind a third candidate, John Crosbie of Newfoundland, as a second-ballot preference. Mulroney spoke out more frequently, became more available to the media, and supplied every delegate with a copy of Where I Stand, a 103-page summary of his recent speeches. Nevertheless, by the time the PC convention opened in Ottawa's Civic Centre on June 9, up to half of the 3,140 delegates were still uncommitted.

The main candidates for the leadership handled themselves well at the policy sessions held on the first day of the convention. When they presented speeches on the second night, the unilingual Crosbie won sympathy with his faltering efforts to say a few words in French; Clark was uninspiring; and Mulroney played it safe. On Saturday, June 11, as expected, Clark seized the first-ballot lead with 1,091 votes; Mulroney's 874 votes were somewhat more than had been forecast; and Crosbie's 639 were lower than he had hoped. Clark lost six votes on the second ballot, while Mulroney and Crosbie gained 147 and 142 respectively from candidates eliminated by their low totals in the previous round. Crosbie, who had been finance minister during Clark's brief term as prime minister, hoped to join forces with the front runner to stop Mulroney on the third ballot, but the negotiations faltered. When Crosbie finished third and last on that tally, he was eliminated, and the stage was set for the fourth and final ballot, on which Mulroney surged past Clark and defeated him by 1,584 to 1,325.

After Mulroney's victory his defeated rivals rallied to his support. The new leader's next objective became that of winning a safe seat in the House of Commons, without which he could neither lead the Opposition nor hope to succeed Trudeau as prime minister. He wanted to represent a Quebec riding, or parliamentary district, eventually, but that choice was not available to him at first, since Roch La Salle, who holds the only Tory seat in Quebec, was unwilling to resign. Instead, when Elmer MacKay, a veteran of twelve years in parliament, stepped down as the representative from the northeastern Nova Scotia riding of Central Nova, Mulroney announced his candidacy on June 15 to continue the Tories' long-established control of the sprawling, economically depressed district of 64,-000 people. Mulroney, who knows the province well because of his university days at St. Francis-Xavier and Dalhousie, soon moved his family to a three-bedroom log cabin in Northumberland Strait, Nova Scotia, to prepare for the by-election set by Prime Minister Trudeau for August 29, 1983.

Trading his elegant business attire for a wardrobe of old sweaters, unpressed pants, and moccasins, Mulroney campaigned vigorously against Alvin Sinclair and the Reverend Roy De Marsh, his Liberal and New Democratic opponents respectively. Despite the efforts of eleven of Trudeau's cabinet members who trekked to Nova Scotia to oppose the new Tory leader, Mulroney scored an impressive victory of 18,882 to 7,828 over the second place finisher on election day. Moreover, in another by-election that was held on August 29 across the continent in British Columbia, the Tory candidate, in whose behalf Mulroney had personally appeared and campaigned, recaptured a riding from the NDP. Public opinion polls taken in the wake of Mulroney's victory in Nova Scotia suggested that the Tories might be ready to gain the support of a majority of Canadians for the first time since the late nineteenth century.

Meanwhile, Mulroney began to assemble a team of advisers to help him prepare for Canada's next general election and for the possible formation of a Progressive Conservative government. Although his inner circle has consistently included a core of friends from his days at St. Francis-Xavier and at Laval, he denies charges of cronyism. He showed a remarkable sense of political balance in his selection, in September, of a shadow cabinet, whose thirty-four members bear the responsibility for keeping a vigilant eye on the activities of their counterparts in the Trudeau administration, whom they would replace in the event of a Tory victory. Mulroney's choice of Sinclair Stevens, a favorite of the right wing and one of his early supporters, for external affairs offset his earlier selection of the moderate Norman Atkins of Toronto as national campaign chairman. He managed to find slots for three of his rivals for the leader's post—John Crosbie, Michael Wilson, and David Crombie—who became finance, trade, and communications advisers, respectively. Overall, Mulroney appointed to his shadow cabinet twenty members of parliament who had backed Joe Clark in the preceding June.

The Tories eagerly awaited Mulroney's debut in parliament, which was scheduled for mid-September, but the new leader of the Opposition stumbled several times during his first few days in the House of Commons. The Liberals exposed inaccuracies in his negative reading of an International Monetary Fund report on the Canadian economy, and he created embarrassment for himself one afternoon by failing to have information about a government decision made that morning on transportation subsidies for his constituents in the Maritime Provinces. But Mulroney quickly rallied to deliver an attack on the government for its alleged abandonment of the country's two-million unemployed and, in the following months, his performance continued to improve. In October, for example, Mulroney, Trudeau, and NDP leader Ed Broadbent negotiated an all-party resolution encouraging Manitoba to change its constitution to extend the range of its French-language services. The resolution's conciliatory language helped to save Mulroney from alienating Manitoba's Tories hostile to bilingualism, and the parliament's decision not to put the agreement to a vote likewise spared him the public display of deep divisions on the language issue among his followers in the House.

Because of his party's strong standing in the polls and of his own efforts to draw together its ideological wings, Mulroney avoided spelling out the specifics of his program before Turner set the date for the next general election, though it seemed likely that his brand of conservatism would be pragmatic rather than reactionary. In foreign affairs, Mulroney staunchly supports the North Atlantic Treaty Organization and the United States. He chided the Trudeau government for sniping at Washington and endorsed both the American intervention in Grenada and the American plan to test the guidance system for the cruise missile in Canada. Not surprisingly, he is a vocal critic of the Soviets and a champion of Israel. In the domestic sphere, Mulroney advocates a balanced budget, spending cuts, and incentives for businessmen and investors. Nevertheless, he maintains that he stands firmly behind medicare and Canada's other social programs and, unlike many Tories, he does not advocate the placing of public enterprises in private hands.

At his first press conference, held on September 28, 1984, within less than two weeks after taking office as prime minister, Mulroney lived up to general expectations by making clear that his first priority was the improvement of the Canadian economy, including an attack on the country's high rate of unemployment. With that in mind, he announced that he had set the date of November 13 for an informal meeting with the premiers of Canada's ten provinces, at which time a date would be established and an agenda prepared for a later meeting on the economic problems bedeviling the country. Among his other high priorities were a renewal of Canada's "special relationship" with the United States; an encouragement of foreign investment; parliamentary reform; and the prevention of nuclear war.

Since May 26, 1973 Brian Mulroney has been married to the former Mila Pivnicki, the daughter of a prominent Montreal psychiatrist. The couple met, a year before their marriage, at the swimming pool of the Mount Royal tennis club in Montreal. They have three children—Caroline Ann, Benedict Martin, and Robert Mark.

Well equipped for politics in the age of television, Mulroney stands 6 feet, 1 inch tall, is strikingly handsome, speaks in a rich baritone, and favors fashionable clothes. He has shunned alcohol for several years, but is said to "live" on cigarettes and coffee. He spends so much time in telephoning that Canadian cartoonists have incorporated telephones in their caricatures of him. His principal recreation is tennis.

References: Macleans 96:10+ Je 20 '83 por; Toronto Globe and Mail p10 Je 29 '83 por; Canadian Who's Who, 1981

Naisbitt, John
(nes´ bit)

1929(?)- Social analyst. Address: b. c/o The Naisbitt Group, Suite 301, 1101 30th St., N.W., Washington, D.C. 20007

Since the late 1960s, social analyst John Naisbitt has been writing and lecturing about what he believes to be major shifts on the American scene, notably the decline of the so-called "smokestack industries" and the emergence of a society characterized by the exchange of service and information, global economic interdependence, and increased reliance on computers. But until 1982, Naisbitt was little known outside the United States corporate community. With the publication of his best-selling Megatrends: Ten New Directions Transforming Our Lives (1982), an easy-to-read book in which he presents his optimistic view of the future, Naisbitt suddenly became one of the most sought-after interpreters of the contemporary scene. The subscriber list for his Trend Report—which contains his analysis of developing social and economic trends and of how such trends interrelate—has swelled, despite criticism that some of his conclusions seem obvious and that his reports are often repetitious. "I would subscribe to the Trend Report just to find out what John Naisbitt is thinking," one typical Naisbitt partisan has said, as quoted in Advertising Age (October 11, 1982).

John Naisbitt, the son of a bus driver, was born in Salt Lake City about 1929 and grew up in a strict Mormon family, on a sugar-beet farm near Glenwood, Utah. "My grandfather Sorenson, from Denmark, was a disciple of Brigham Young," Naisbitt told Paul Hendrickson of the Washington Post (May 3, 1983). "Brigham sent him down to start the town of Glenwood. . . . Three-hundred people, incredibly isolated, incredibly rigid, incredibly loving." Although the Mormon elders of his home community wanted him to become a missionary, Naisbitt decided at an early age that he "had to get out." At fifteen he left high school, and in 1946 he joined the United States Marine Corps. It was during his stint with the Marines that Naisbitt first came upon the idea of reading for pleasure.

Upon his discharge two years later, Naisbitt enrolled at the University of Utah as a political science major. After further studies at Cornell and Harvard universities, he went to work for the public relations department of the Eastman Kodak Company, writing speeches for the company chairman. His career odyssey then took him, successively, to the Unitarian Service Committee, the Great Books Foundation, the public relations department of Montgomery Ward and Company, and the National Safety Council in Chicago, where he was director of information.

In the mid-1960s, Naisbitt moved to Washington, D.C. and obtained a post as a special assistant to Francis Keppel, the United States commissioner of education. His work with Keppel led to a position as a top aide to John W. Gardner, secretary of what was then the Department of Health, Education, and Welfare. Naisbitt also served for a time as a special assistant to President Lyndon B. Johnson. He then returned to the private sector as assistant to the president of Science Research Associates (SRA), an educational firm, later absorbed by IBM, that produced examinations and other curriculum materials and promoted the use of computers as educational tools. During his tenure at SRA, Naisbitt, whose responsibilities included obtaining federal contracts for the firm, was featured in a story in the Washington Post (July 3, 1966) about the rising stars of the fledgling computer and electronic technology industries.

In 1968 Naisbitt set up his own company, the Chicago-based Urban Research Corporation (URC), to keep business informed about city affairs. "It started out as an effort to develop a manual for companies who wanted to provide job training for the hard-core unemployed," Naisbitt told a reporter for Advertising Age. But 1968 was also a year of increasing urban unrest and inner-city riots, and Naisbitt soon directed his energies toward trying to determine "what was really going on in this country," so that major disasters might be avoided. In 1970, Bantam Books published Right On! A Documentary on Student Protest, compiled by Naisbitt and Maryl Levine.

The method that Naisbitt adopted for putting his finger on the public pulse was content analysis, an intelligence gathering technique used by the Office of Strategic Services in World War II that involved observing public behavior and events through their coverage by local newspapers. His immediate inspiration for the adoption of that technique was the work of the historian Bruce Catton, who used daily newspapers to reconstruct the American Civil War era with a high degree of accuracy.

In Naisbitt's view, new ideas often originate in smaller communities. "Ours is a profoundly bottoms-up society," he has said. "We look at the local events reported in newspapers because, collectively, what's happening in cities and towns is what's happening in America." Content analysis, as applied by Naisbitt, is based on the assumption that the news "hole," or space devoted to current news stories, in a newspaper is relatively constant in size. Thus, when new issues and problems are brought to the public's attention, some existing concerns must be edged out. By monitoring changes in the amount of coverage given to various topics, Naisbitt believes that he can spot shifts in the public's expectations, values, and preoccupations.

In 1970 Naisbitt began to publish the results of his studies, supplying his clients—who by 1972 included the Chase Manhattan Bank, Eastman Kodak, Harvard University, the Illinois Department of Labor, and the Ford and Rockefeller foundations, among many others—with information culled from over 20,000 newspaper articles per month. At the time, data from some 200 newspapers was clipped, evaluated, cross-indexed, and recorded on microfiche by a staff of a dozen analysts, who then filed it under housing and urban renewal, employment, poverty, and other categories. Emerging patterns were highlighted in a monthly report called NewsBank. Other URC publications included the bimonthly Urban Crisis Monitor, aimed at urban specialists, research organizations, and libraries, and the Urban Reporter, a newsletter for executives.

Naisbitt began publishing the Trend Report, a thick loose-leaf publication, in 1973. Included in that quarterly periodical are the summaries and "trend alerts" that have helped Naisbitt to establish his reputation as a top-flight prognosticator. He forecast, for example, the end of mandatory retirement a year before it was legislated by Congress, the problems involved in the use of nuclear power well before the accident at the Three Mile Island nuclear reactor, and the failure of the Equal Rights Amendment to win ratification four years before the fact. In 1978 he predicted that "acid rain" resulting from industrial pollution would become a national issue, as it later did. On the other hand, Naisbitt's forecasts have on occasion been wrong, as was the case with his prediction that President Jimmy Carter would be reelected in 1980.

About 1975, Naisbitt moved to Washington, D.C., where he established the Center for Policy Process. In 1981 the Center became the Naisbitt Group, a research institute that focuses on national issues. By 1982, Naisbitt had pinpointed ten social shifts that, in his words, typify "the directions in which we are restructuring America." He identified those "major transformations taking place right now in our society" in Megatrends: Ten New Directions Transforming Our Lives (Warner Books, 1982). Discounting the influence of such national power centers as New York City and Washington, D.C., he based his analysis on local patterns, particularly those in five bellwether states—California, Florida, Washington, Colorado, and Texas—in which, according to Naisbitt, "most social invention occurs in this country."

Megatrends begins with Naisbitt's observation that the industrial era is over and the American economy is now based on "the creation and distribution of information." The key reason for this shift, Naisbitt believes, is the development of the computer. Citing an estimate that by 1985, 75 percent of all jobs will in some way involve computers, Naisbitt notes that "schools around the nation are beginning to realize that in the information society the two required languages will be English and computer."

Balancing the trend toward increased technology, Naisbitt sees a human response that he labels "high touch"—the need for people to interact with one another. Accordingly, he expresses doubt that so-called "electronic cottages"—computer-equipped homes that double as workplaces—will catch on, because "people want to go to the office. People want to be with people." As one example of "high touch," Naisbitt cites the growing "hospice" movement to promote medical self-help by, among other things, establishing a network of supportive services that enable the terminally ill to be cared for at home and replacing some hospital delivery rooms with homelike "birthing rooms." Naisbitt sees the development of hospices as evidence that people are developing their own antidotes to the complex and often dehumanizing advances in medical technology.

Analyzing world economic trends, Naisbitt observes that Japan has emerged as a formidable industrial power, and that Americans no longer enjoy the world's highest standard of living, being exceeded in that respect by Sweden, Denmark, West Germany, Switzerland, the Netherlands, and Norway. He notes that the United States is shifting from "an isolated, virtually self-sufficient *national* economy to being part of an interdependent *global* economy" marked by increased trade, production sharing the manufacture of products that utilize components from many nations—and barter agreements with countries like those of the Eastern bloc or the Third World that lack hard currency. Naisbitt envisions worldwide interdependence as the hope for world peace. "If we get sufficiently interlaced economically," he claims, "we will most probably *not* bomb each other off the face of the planet."

Another theme of *Megatrends* is Naisbitt's unorthodox view that "it does not really matter anymore who is President, and Congress has become obsolete." He believes that social change does not originate with established leaders but is sparked by the citizenry. "Real political power," he argues, "that is, the ability to get things done, has shifted away from Congress and the presidency to the states, cities, towns, and neighborhoods." In business, Naisbitt asserts, "employees and the corporations that employ them are in the process of redefining the worker's role in the institution," with the resulting emergence of "a new theory of

workers' rights and worker participation" and the decline of the corporate hierarchy system. The wave of the future, he believes, is the development of horizontal "networks" that allow for the free exchange of ideas, the sharing of resources and information, and the establishment of "linkages between people and clusters of people."

We are, Naisbitt maintains, living in a "time of parenthesis," between the waning era of hierarchies, centralization, and industrialization and the emerging era of horizontal decision sharing and the use of brainpower instead of physical power to create. He concludes: "Although the time between eras is uncertain, it is a great and yeasty time, filled with opportunity. If we can learn to make uncertainty our friend, we can achieve much more than in stable eras." *Megatrends* ends with the exultation: "My God, what a fantastic time to be alive!"

Warner Books launched *Megatrends* in October 1982 with a $75,000 advertising budget and a twenty-three-city tour by the author. Initial sales were brisk, sparked by the decision of the Book of the Month Club to offer *Megatrends* as a featured selection. By the fall of 1983 *Megatrends* had gone through nineteen printings and sold over half-a-million hardcover copies. As of late 1984, the book had been on the *New York Times* best-seller list for 102 weeks, and worldwide sales, in seventeen languages, including Japanese, had passed the 5-million mark.

Reviewers, however, were not universally enthusiastic. Although *Library Journal* (October 1, 1982) labeled *Megatrends* "timely and fascinating reading," Karl E. Meyer noted in the *New York Times Book Review* (December 26, 1982): "Mr. Naisbitt has produced the literary equivalent of a good after-dinner speech." Meyer quarreled with Naisbitt's contention that the current trends in American society were virtually irreversible, and he took issue with the author's claim that political power was being defused. "If local governments are resurgent," Meyer wrote, "why are they pleading with an obsolete Congress for relief from an unimportant President's New Federalism?" Sounding a similar note, Bill Abrams of the *Wall Street Journal* (September 30, 1982) expressed doubt that Naisbitt had enough evidence to support his claims, and Emily Yoffe, writing in *Harper's* (September 1983), criticized Naisbitt's content analysis methodology as too casual and his judgments as too intuitive.

Few reviewers could resist commenting on what a writer for the *Washington Monthly* (January 1983) termed Naisbitt's "relentlessly optimistic look at the future." A critic for *New Realities* (August 1983), while praising Naisbitt for the "aptness and subtlety" of his judgments, nevertheless felt that the author tended to be "overly optimistic" and to "gloss over some of the problems that threaten the planet's future," such as nuclear war and political unrest. Andrew Hacker of *Fortune* (December 27, 1982) noted that *Megatrends* contained no analysis of what the future holds for the poor or for the growing population of senior citizens. Nevertheless, much of the public evidently agreed with a long-time client of Naisbitt, who said, as quoted in *Advertising Age,* "John is invaluable as a catalyst for your own thoughts. His overview provides a starting point, gives you a backdrop that you can use to better understand why things are happening."

With the success of *Megatrends,* the Naisbitt Group's revenues increased from $450,000 in 1981 to an estimated $1.6 million in 1983. The national *Trend Report* is now supplemented by the *Bellwether Report* and the *Year Ahead* service, as well as a newsletter for the general public called *John Naisbitt's Trend Letter.* In addition, Naisbitt has been working with the economist Michael Evans on a series of regional stock market indexes. Corporate clients of the Naisbitt Group pay up to $20,000 per year for a package of seminars, full-day workshops, and written reports. Naisbitt, who reportedly receives about two dozen requests for speaking engagements and opinions each day, commands as much as $10,000 to $15,000 per speech. His advice has been sought by many public officials, including President Ronald Reagan.

The paperback edition of *Megatrends,* released by Warner Books in February 1984, immediately climbed to the top of the nonfiction charts. Naisbitt made no changes in the soft-cover incarnation of his book except for a revision of the introduction and an updating of some of the figures. He added no discussion of what he reportedly believes to be the eleventh megatrend: the shift "from sex roles to synergy." Despite the failure of the Equal Rights Amendment, Naisbitt believes, as reported in *Esquire* (May 1983), that "women's values are reshaping society from the grassroots," resulting in "a reconciliation between the sexes at a deep level, a greater harmony between qualities we used to consider either masculine or feminine." According to Naisbitt, competition between men and women is beginning to give way to a new kind of cooperation based on individual contribution that "could well mean the end of the battle of the sexes."

Naisbitt is a governor-at-large of the National Association of Security Dealers; a director of the Houston-based CRS/Sirrine Group, an architectural and engineering firm; and a past public director of the American Institute of Architects. Honors that he has received include the 1980 Benjamin Y. Morrison award for promoting understanding, and two honorary doctorates in the humanities.

Trim and blond, John Naisbitt sports a full beard that makes him look, as described in *Advertising Age,* "like a cross between a bank president and an Old Testament prophet." In recognition of his newfound celebrity status, he was engaged to appear with the broadcasting tycoon and sportsman Ted Turner and other achievers in a recent advertising campaign for shirts. During his years in Chicago he was occasionally seen jogging along the shore of Lake Michigan in the company of former world heavyweight boxing champion Muhammad Ali.

Naisbitt, who has been married twice and is the father of five children, is helped in his work by his daughter Claire, an artist, and by his present wife, the writer Patricia Aburdene, with whom he coauthored a book tentatively titled "Reinventing the World We Live In," which was scheduled for publication in 1985. According to Naisbitt, the book offers "new models and guidelines for what really works for people and institutions in the information society."

References: Advertising Age 53:M4+ 0 11 '82 por; Christian Sci Mon p13 O 30 '72 por, p21+ Ap 3 '84 pors; Harper's 267:16+ S '83; N Y Times D p16 O 11 '83; Omni 7:108+ O '84 por; Wall St J p56 S 30 '82 por; Washington Post B p1+ My 3 '83 por

Nettles, Graig

Aug. 20, 1944– Baseball player. Address: c/o The San Diego Padres, P.O. Box 200, San Diego, Cal. 92120

Belying third baseman Graig Nettles' equanimity on major-league baseball's playing fields and his detachment from clubhouse politics are a prickly temperament, a glib tongue, and an often devastating sense of humor—traits that brought him in the 1970s into an adversarial relationship with George Steinbrenner, the ostentatious owner of the New York Yankees, a man widely perceived as the American League's fickle spendthrift. The last straw for Steinbrenner, apparently, was *Balls* (Putnam, 1984), a memoir of Nettles' baseball career, written in collaboration with Peter Golenbock, in which the owner comes across, for the most part, as an egomaniacal Simon Legree. When the book's advance promotion came to Steinbrenner's attention in March 1983, Nettles was summarily traded to the San Diego Padres of the National League.

With Nettles' departure, New York lost its team captain, one of its best lefthanded power hitters, and one of the best defensive third basemen of all time. The agile infielder, who began his major-league career in 1967 and joined the Yankees seven years later, holds the major-league seasonal records for assists and double plays by a third baseman (412 and fifty-four in 1971) and the American League career record for home runs by a third baseman (333). He led the American League in chances per game, the best indicator of a player's range, in 1971, 1973, and 1976, and he had a league career fielding average of .964, exceptional for the hot corner. With San Diego during the 1984 season he batted .228, hit eleven doubles, one triple, and twenty home runs, and drove in sixty-five runs, eight of them game-winners. In the league championship series against the Chicago Cubs he contributed two runs-batted-in to the Padres' victory; he also had two RBIs in the World Series, which San Diego lost to the Detroit Tigers.

Graig Nettles was born in San Diego, California on August 20, 1944. As he explains in *Balls*, his given name, a combination of Greg and Craig, was his mother's idea. "My dad was away at war, so he didn't have any say. I never knew I had a strange name until I got to high school, when everyone kept misspelling and mispronouncing it." To this day, one of Nettles' "pet peeves" is "people who think they know [him] real well but who call [him] Craig."

Nettles' father, Wayne Nettles, was a Dust Bowl Okie who migrated to San Diego during the Depression. His mother came from the mining town of Bisbee, Arizona. After starring in football at San Diego State University (then San Diego State College), Wayne Nettles was a San Diego police officer for ten years before becoming a high school teacher. "My dad started me playing ball when I was four or five," Nettles recalls. "He encouraged me to play at the playground, and I was always outdoors, playing ball. From him I learned the joy of playing baseball. Especially when there's sunshine every day." Nettles' younger brother, Jim, also learned that joy, and he too went on to become a professional baseball player.

Small for his age, Nettles showed little professional potential when he played second base and shortstop at San Diego High School. Better at basketball, he won a San Diego State University scholarship in that sport. In college he started putting on weight, which slowed him down in basketball but made him a power hitter in baseball. While in college, he played semipro baseball summers in Alaska, where he was spotted by a scout for the Minnesota Twins of the American League. Dropping out of college at the end of his junior year, he was picked by the Twins in the fourth round of the 1965 free-agent draft. They offered him a $15,000 bonus; at first he held out for $20,000 but finally he relented.

Starting out in the Minnesota farm system at Wisconsin Rapids in the single-A Midwest League, Nettles led the league in home runs, with twenty-eight, in 1966. Promoted to Charlotte in the AA Southern League in 1967, he tied for most homers in that league, with nineteen. Called up to the Twins for the last month of the 1967 season, he hit safely in one of his three times at bat. During that brief stint in Minnesota he had his first contact with Billy Martin, who was then a coach there.

In 1968 Martin became manager of the Twins' Denver franchise in the AAA American Association and Nettles became a infielder with the same club. In Denver, Nettles, who had been playing second base, switched to third, a position in which he would have a better chance of moving permanently up to the majors, since the Twins already had an excellent young second baseman in Rod Carew. Nettles "hated" Martin until he "began to understand that the reason Billy did all that screaming and yelling was so you wouldn't make the same mistake again." "He took that team, which was in last place," Nettles recounts in *Balls*, "and he made us into pennant winners. When I saw the results, I stopped hating Billy Martin and [saw] him for what he was: an extraordinary leader."

Again temporarily called up to the Twins toward the end of the 1968 season, Nettles batted .224 in twenty-two games. In 1969, when Martin was promoted to manager of the Twins, Nettles played with Minnesota on and off from the beginning of the season. With Harmon Killebrew tending the hot corner, he filled in at third base in only fifteen games, platooning the rest of the time with Cesar Tovar in left field. Because he had not yet realized his defensive potential, much was expected of him at the plate, and he was not hitting up to that expectation. When Billy Martin was fired the following winter, Nettles was traded to the Cleveland Indians. When he arrived in Cleveland, he recalls, the first thing he read about himself was, "He's a good hitter, but he can't play third base."

That image began to change in Cleveland, where, playing full-time in a major-league starting lineup for the first time, he developed into both a superior power hitter and a superior fielder and demonstrated durability even when in pain. At the plate in 1970 he blasted twenty-six home runs and had a slugging average of .404, and in the field he led American League third basemen with a .967 average. During that season he witnessed first baseman Tony Horton's nervous breakdown during a slump, an incident that intensified his own determination "to relax during a game" and "to forget a bad game and not dwell too long on a good one."

Whenever Cleveland played the Baltimore Orioles, Nettles closely watched Brooks Robinson, the Baltimore third baseman, especially in infield practice. Observing the way that Robinson would maintain his grace of movement while making off-balance throws, Nettles practiced at doing the same. Ever since, in spring training he goes from ten minutes of normal infield practice to twenty minutes in which he throws from awkward positions at or near the bag. "It helps my coordination," he has explained, "and is very useful when I'm confronted with that particular situation during a game."

His second season in Cleveland was even better than his first: batting .261, he hit eighteen doubles and twenty-eight homers and drove in eighty-six runs; distilled, his record-setting statistics in the field represented a saving of 4.2 games above the average—the best defensive performance in the majors since those of Bill Mazeroski in the 1960s. Playing almost as well in 1972, he attracted the eye of the New York Yankees, a team that could use his fielding skill at third base and expected that his home-run output would increase in Yankee Stadium, the structure of which favors lefthanded distance hitters. On November 27, 1972 the Yankees gave up four players in a trade for Nettles and Cleveland catcher Jerry Moses. One month after the trade the Yankees were bought by the multimillionaire shipbuilder George Steinbrenner, the man who would turn the New York franchise from "a fun team" (as Nettles first knew it) into the flamboyant but grim "best team that money can buy" and whose lavish shopping sprees in baseball's free-agent market would, in the words of Baseball Commissioner Bowie Kuhn, threaten the "competitive balance" of the game.

After a typical slow start at the plate in New York, Nettles finished the 1973 season with eighteen doubles, twenty-two home runs, and eighty-one runs-batted-in; in the field, he led American League third basemen in assists, with 410, and total chances, with 553. By contrast, he began the 1974 season with a flourish, hitting eleven home runs during one month (April)—a record he shares with Willie Stargell and Mike Schmidt—and then slowed down to an average of two homers a month. Fielding, he led league third basemen in 1974 in putouts, with 147, and total chances, with 545.

As the 1974 season was ending, New York and Baltimore were nip and tuck for first place in the east division of the American League. On the next-to-last day of the season, a Saturday, Baltimore clinched the pennant by defeating Detroit. "We still had a meaningless final day to play on Sunday," Nettles recounts in Balls, "and George Steinbrenner came into the clubhouse that Sunday and gave us another of his rah rah speeches. . . . Instead of his saying, 'You guys gave everything you had. Nice going . . . ,' he told us, 'Today's game is the most important of your career.' We looked at one another; thinking, 'What the hell is he talking about?' We had just battled 161 games and lost by one. . . . For some reason he thought the fans would hate us if we lost that last game. . . . He doesn't give the average fan much credit."

Nettles hit his stride in 1975, batting .267, slugging twenty-four doubles, four triples, and twenty-one home runs, driving in ninety-one runs, and leading league third basemen in assists (379). In his first All-Star game, he hit safely once in four times at bat. He was reunited with the man who "taught

[him] how to win" on August 1, 1975, when Billy Martin replaced Bill Virdon as Yankee manager. Martin remained manager for three years, and he returned to the position periodically thereafter, in between fallings-out with Steinbrenner.

The Yankees won their first pennant in twelve years in 1976, thanks in part to Nettles' league-leading thirty-two home runs. He also contributed in the field, leading league third basemen in double plays (thirty), assists (383), and total chances (539). In the league championship win over the Kansas City Royals, he hit two homers, and he drove in two runs in the World Series, which New York lost to the Cincinnati Reds.

Nettles, a private person at heart, quiet and good-humored even in his irascibility, has always shied away from publicity and locker-room fracases. (His nickname "Puff" derives from his habit of suddenly disappearing from scenes of commotion.) His feud with George Steinbrenner did not begin, or begin to emerge, until spring training in 1977, when, following the signing of Reggie Jackson for an astronomical sum (approximately $2.8 million), half the New York roster was holding out or demanding contract renegotiation. The Jackson affair was the latest development in a trend that had begun with the first free-agent draft, in 1976. "When I saw the contracts George offered the free agents," Nettles relates in Balls, "it made my stomach upset. We were the guys who had made the Yankees an attractive team, the ones who had turned them into a winner, and he gives the new players all the money."

For his part, Nettles wasn't demanding more money (his salary was then $120,000 a year) but merely a restructuring of his contract for better income-tax advantage. Steinbrenner refused to change the contract, and Nettles walked out of camp. "Before George would allow him to come back," Ed Linn chronicles in Steinbrenner's Yankees (1982), "he had not only humiliated his All-Star third baseman but had boasted, publicly, about how he had humiliated him. Nettles doesn't forget. . . . When the boss came flying in to raise a little hell with the club after they had gotten off to such an atrocious start that same season, it was Nettles . . . who said . . . , 'The more he flies, the better the chance will be of the plane crashing.'"

The 1977 season was Nettles' most powerful ever at the plate, marked by thirty-seven home runs (for a 6.3 percentage) and 107 runs-batted-in. He was again named to the American League All-Star team, the Sporting News picked him for the league all-defensive team, and he won the American League Gold Glove as best defensive third baseman. After defeating Kansas City in the league championship series, the Yankees won the world championship by downing the Los Angeles Dodgers in the World Series, four games to two.

Nettles batted .276, the highest average of his career, in 1978. That year the Yankees again beat the Royals in the championship series. In the World Series against the Los Angeles Dodgers they lost the first two games and were holding a slim lead in the third when Nettles turned the tide with four spectacular plays that deprived the Dodgers of at least six runs and allowed the Yankees to win, 5-1. The New York team rolled on from there without a loss to take the series, four games to two.

On August 2, 1979 catcher Thurman Munson, the Yankee team captain and Nettles' closest friend, was killed in a plane crash, a tragedy that affected Nettles deeply. The Yankees finished the 1979 season in fourth place in the American League East, and Nettles' statistics for the season included a .253 batting average, twenty homers, and seventy-three RBIs. Felled by hepatitis on July 23, 1980, he was out of action for the rest of the 1980 season. He returned to the lineup for the league playoffs, which the Yankees lost to the Kansas City Royals.

In an American League East mini-playoff during the strike-shortened 1981 season, New York defeated Milwaukee in the first two games and lost the next two. Before the decisive fifth game, Steinbrenner went into the clubhouse and read the Yankees "the riot act," as Nettles recounts in Balls. "That's when the fun stopped. . . . Here was this big shipbuilder about to lose in the playoffs to a used-car salesman. He couldn't abide that. So right before the final game, he gave us a chewing out. We won that game, and to this day he thinks he rallied us."

New York defeated Oakland in the 1981 American League championship series, and Nettles, who had nine RBIs in three games, was voted the series' Most Valuable Player. In the one game he played in the World Series against the Los Angeles Dodgers he performed well in general and made one particularly spectacular diving catch on a ball Steve Garvey hit off Rich ("Goose") Gossage. Breaking his thumb in diving for a ball in the second game, he was sidelined during the three games that the Yankees lost in Los Angeles. Although his thumb was still throbbing, he played six innings of the final game, in New York. The Yankees lost that game, and with it the series, prompting George Steinbrenner to make a public apology to the New York fans that mortified and riled Nettles and his teammates.

George Steinbrenner named Nettles the Yankees' team captain in January 1982. During the following season the Yankees went through three managers and forty-five players in Steinbrenner's futile attempt to turn the Bronx Bombers into a team based on speed, a move not well suited to their home park. The Yankees finished in fifth place in the American League East, with a miserable 79-83 record, and Nettles' batting average (.232) was the lowest of his Yankee career and his slugging, in decline since 1979, was, by his standards, merely respectable (eleven doubles, two triples, eighteen homers).

Throughout the winter following the 1982 season Nettles' right shoulder, which he apparently jammed in a dive for a ball during the season, bothered him, and as spring training approached in 1983 it was not any better. "I was really worried . . . ," he revealed to Bill Madden of the New York Daily News (June 10, 1983). "If I couldn't throw, I was finished." He went to Dr. K. C. Chin, the San Diego acupuncturist whom he had consulted about his hepatitis. "It sounds like voodoo, I know," he told Madden, "but it worked. My shoulder feels fine—as good as ever."

With the return of Billy Martin as manager of the Yankees in 1983, Nettles improved in batting (.266) and slugging (seventeen doubles, three triples, and twenty home runs); the Yankees improved in record (91-71) and standing (third in the American League East); and attendance at Yankee stadium increased by 300,000. When Steinbrenner fired Martin again, Nettles could not think of any reason other than "George got tired of having to take a back seat to Billy."

In his final feuding with Steinbrenner over money, Nettles demanded only what he regarded as his rightful place within the salary structure Steinbrenner himself had set up in New York. In the chapter of Balls written (or dictated) the day after the 1983 season ended, Nettles said: "I've been one of his [Steinbrenner's] top players. I'm third in RBIs and third in home runs, so pay me right behind Winfield and Kemp. . . . I play offense and defense, whereas he pays some guys just to play defense or offense. And then there are a lot of guys he pays a lot just to sit on the bench [or] at home." Opting for free agency at the end of the 1983 season, Nettles began talking to representatives of other teams and "had thoughts of coming home to San Diego to play." He knew that "the Padres were looking for a power-hitting third baseman" and that he "would have fit perfectly into their plans for a couple of years."

In a contract meeting with Nettles on November 1, 1983, Steinbrenner argued that he, Nettles, would never get the kind of money he was asking for anywhere else. Nettles agreed: "I don't expect Baltimore or Boston to pay me the money I'm asking from you. But if I'm going to stay here, I'm going to fit in with your salary structure. If I go to another club, I'll be willing to fit in with their salary structure." Steinbrenner finally relented, and on November 4, 1983, the free-agent draft deadline, Nettles was signed to a new, two-year contract worth $1 million a year. Less than five months later, however, Nettles was suddenly traded to the San Diego Padres. Public speculation about the reason for the trade included Nettles' objection to a Yankee plan to platoon him with Toby Harrah in 1984. The common wisdom, however, was that the trade would probably never have taken place were it not for the effect of Balls's advance billing on George Steinbrenner's ego. At the time of his departure from the Yankees, Nettles' major-league career statistics included a .251 batting average, 1,-707 putouts, 4,642 assists, 396 double plays, and 239 errors.

Unlike third basemen who guard the foul line against doubles, Nettles stays closer to the shortstop, stopping hits through the hole and helping the rest of the infield. This dangerous tactic is possible in his case because he moves to his right easily, cutting off balls hit down the line without giving up additional singles. "I'm amazed at his quickness," Al Rosen, then president of the Yankees, and a former star third baseman himself, said of Nettles in 1978. "He's got a great body. . . . Very supple. . . . He gets to the ball faster than any third baseman I've ever seen. He has a great ability to dive for balls and recover. . . . His positioning is almost uncanny. He knows what to do at all times."

Gene Michael, who was the Yankee shortstop when Nettles joined the team in 1973 and who later became a Yankee coach, was "impressed with his thinking right away." Michaels told Joe Donnelly of Newsday (October 8, 1978): "He always wanted to help out. . . . He's a real good base runner with below average speed. He does all the little things right. . . . Fans should really respect him because he's giving them baseball and third base like they've never seen it." Bob Lemon, one of the succession of Yankee managers in the late 1970s, viewed Nettles as a team "stabilizer." "No matter how he's hitting, it never affects his fielding," Lemon said in his interview with Joe Donnelly. "And

when he gets hot, he can practically carry a ball-club. He's [emotionally] almost even keel all the time. You just write him in on your lineup card and . . . you know you're not going to be hurting there."

Graig Nettles and Virginia Meckling, better known as Ginger, met at San Diego State University, and they were married on November 25, 1965. They have three sons, Mike, Tim, and Jeff, and a daughter, Barrie. The Nettles live in a $150,000 suburban home in El Toro, California. Thomas Boswell of the Washington Post (October 15, 1978) described the third baseman as "lean, supple, sardonic [and] fair-haired," with a "mischievous face." The inscription on the back of Nettles' glove reads "e5," meaning "error by third baseman," and the license plate of his Mercedes reads "PUFF E5." Nettles, who is six feet tall and weighs 185 pounds, is righthanded except when hitting a baseball.

References: N Y Daily News mag p6+ Ap 8 '79 pors, p47 Je 10 '83 por; Newsday S p10+ O 8 '78 pors; N Y Times p3 Ja 31 '82 por; Nettles, Graig and Golenbock, Peter. Balls (1984)

Norman, Marsha

Sept. 21, 1947– Playwright. Address: b. c/o Samuel Liff, William Morris Agency, 1350 Ave. of the Americas, New York City, N.Y. 10019

Marsha Norman, whose 'night, Mother was awarded the 1983 Pulitzer Prize for drama, is one of a growing number of young women playwrights who are currently revitalizing American theatre with the range of their subject matter and the depth of their characterizations. Like Beth Henley, the 1981 Pulitzer Prize winner, she is a product of the Actors Theatre of Louisville, which produced her first play, Getting Out, in 1977. Miss Norman is known for her searing honesty, naturalistic dialogue, and preoccupation with the broken dreams of "folks you wouldn't even notice in life," as she once expressed it. "I grieve so for people who do not have the power of language, and what I want to be able to do in my work is to make my language skills available to them," she said recently, as quoted in Ms. magazine (July 1983). "In a sense Arlene [in Getting Out] agrees, Jessie [in 'night, Mother] agrees to trust me to present them fairly, and I agree to grant them a voice."

Marsha Norman was born Marsha Williams in Louisville, Kentucky on September 21, 1947, the oldest of the four children of Billie Williams, an insurance salesman, and his wife, Bertha Williams. (She takes her professional name from the surname of her first husband.) Reared in Audubon Park, a middle-class neighborhood in Louisville, she was, by her own account, a lonely child, primarily because her mother, an uncompromising fundamentalist Methodist, did not think the other

neighborhood children were "good enough" to play with her daughter. Marsha passed her solitary hours practicing the piano, reading, playing with her imaginary friend, Bettering, and writing stories.

Among the best students in her class at Durrett High School, where she was a member of the National Honor Society, Marsha Norman worked on the editorial staffs of the school newspaper and yearbook. In her junior year, her essay "Why Do Good Men Suffer?" won first prize in a local literary contest and was later published in the *Kentucky English Bulletin,* a professional education publication. The subject of that essay still fascinates her. "What else is there to know in the world?" she asked Mel Gussow in an interview for a *New York Times Magazine* (May 1, 1983) profile.

Following her graduation from high school, Miss Norman enrolled at Agnes Scott College, a distinguished small liberal arts college for women in Decatur, Georgia, to which she had been awarded a scholarship. Because the school did not have a creative writing department, she majored in philosophy. In her spare time, she worked as a volunteer in the pediatric burn unit at Grady General Hospital in nearby Atlanta. Shortly after taking her B.A. degree in 1969, she returned to Louisville and married Michael Norman, her former English teacher. For the next two years, she took graduate courses at the University of Louisville, earning her master's degree in 1971. (She has since completed most of the requirements for a second master's degree at the Center for Understanding Media in New York City.)

Having decided to "put in some time saving the world," as she once put it, Marsha Norman took a job teaching disturbed adolescents at the Kentucky Central State Hospital. "What we had there were children who never talked at all, as well as ones who would just as soon stab you in the back as talk to you," she told Judy Klemesrud of the *New York Times* (May 27, 1979). "There were lots of violent kids there." One thirteen-year-old girl in particular was "absolutely terrifying," she continued. "People got bruises when this kid walked in the room, she was so vicious. . . . When I began to think about writing my first play, I thought back to that experience because it was so terrifying to me."

In 1973 Marsha Norman joined the staff of the Brown School for gifted children, where she taught filmmaking to adolescents and drew up a humanities curriculum for children of middle-school age. Although she had never considered a career as a writer, mainly because she had no role models, she began submitting occasional pieces—which were, in her words, invariably "whimsical" and "very positive"—to local newspapers. She wrote a play, too—a musical for children about Thomas Edison and other American inventors. By 1976 she was writing full-time, contributing articles and book reviews to the *Louisville Times,* for which she also created the weekend children's supplement "The Jelly Bean Journal."

At about that time, Marsha Norman met with Jon Jory, the artistic director of the Actors Theatre of Louisville, to ask his advice about a program she was developing with the aim of involving local youngsters in the performing arts. In the course of their wide-ranging conversation, Jory encouraged her to try writing a play about "a painful subject." Recalling the violent and abusive teenage inmate who had terrified her while she was working at the Kentucky Central State Hospital, Miss Norman decided to make the young woman the focal point of a drama that examined the effects of long-term in-

carceration on the human psyche. Before she sat down to write, she interviewed fifteen women prisoners about their family backgrounds, social lives, hopes and dreams, and experiences behind bars. "They were very generous with their stories," she told Judy Klemesrud, "and very willing to tell me exactly what it was like to be in prison and exactly what it was like to be out."

In *Getting Out,* Arlene Holsclaw, a jittery and only marginally rehabilitated parolee who has just been released from prison after having served eight years for robbery, kidnapping, and manslaughter, tries to come to terms with her past as embodied in the character of Arlie, her younger self, and to adjust to her uncertain future. While she fixes up her shabby apartment on her first day of freedom, she is tormented by reminders of the savage, foulmouthed girl she once was as several unwelcome guests—a lecherous ex-guard, her selfish mother, and her strung out former pimp—invade her privacy. Most disturbing, however, is Arlie herself, who, summoned by a fleeting memory or a visitor's thoughtless word, threatens to destroy Arlene's hard-won emotional stability and jeopardize her chance for a new life. "That person locked up was me," Miss Norman admitted to Judy Klemesrud. "My whole life I felt locked up. I felt in isolation. . . . I think the writing of *Getting Out* for me was my own opening of the door."

Stunned by the play's impact, Jon Jory decided to stage *Getting Out* as part of the 1977 Festival of New Plays at the Actors Theatre of Louisville, from which it emerged as cowinner of the top playwriting prize. In the following year *Getting Out* was voted the best new play produced in a regional theatre by the American Theatre Critics Association, and it was later published in the volume *The Best Plays of 1977-78* (1980), the first non–New York production ever to be so honored.

After a limited run at the Mark Taper Forum in Los Angeles in February 1978, *Getting Out* moved to New York City, where it opened the Phoenix Theatre's Off-Broadway season at the Marymount Manhattan Theatre in October 1978. The response of critics and audiences was so overwhelmingly favorable that the company mounted a revival at the Theatre De Lys in May 1979. There, its eight-month run netted Marsha Norman the John Gassner New Playwrights Medallion from the Outer Critics Circle and the first annual George Oppenheimer *Newsday* Playwriting Award, given to the "best new American playwright" whose work is produced in New York City or on Long Island. In a statement announcing the Oppenheimer award, a spokesman for the selection committee singled out for special praise Miss Norman's "sharp, clearly defined characters" and the skill with which she dovetailed the overlapping scenes involving Arlene and Arlie. "Instead of becoming intrusive," he said, as quoted in *Newsday* (September 16, 1979), "the memory-images of Arlie add depth to the scenes of Arlene's difficult passage."

An occasional demurrer to the "jarring" and "tired" theatrical device of using two actresses to portray the protagonist at different ages in her life was virtually the only objection lodged against *Getting Out* by the New York critics. In an unusual show of unanimity, the majority agreed that the drama was "American theatre at its honest best, with no phony glamour, just great talent, commitment, and intelligence," as Jack Kroll observed in his review for *Newsweek* (May 28, 1979). The incandescent performances of Susan Kingsley, as the curiously passive Arlene, and Pamela Reed, who portrayed the raging Arlie, contributed immeasurably to the play's success, but it was Marsha Norman's affecting delineation of Arlene's plight that most impressed the critics. "*Getting Out*'s central premise—the fragility of conversion and the need to accept the evil inside one—is not, of course, a new one," Richard Eder wrote in his review for the *New York Times* (May 17, 1979], "and sometimes it is set down a trifle schematically. The play's achievement is not intellectual; it is dramatic and emotional, and as such, it is a triumph of the season."

The recipient of a playwright-in-residence grant from the National Endowment for the Arts, Marsha Norman spent most of 1978 and 1979 working with the Actors Theatre of Louisville. Her contributions to the company included *Third and Oak*, a twin-bill comprised of the one-act plays "The Laundromat," about two women—one recently widowed, the other trapped in a loveless marriage—who meet by chance in a neighborhood laundromat, and "The Pool Hall," a dialogue between the establishment's proprietor and the son of a famous pool shark; and *Circus Valentine*, in which a woman aerialist dares a triple somersault in order to drum up business for a faltering family circus. *Third and Oak* was one of the biggest hits of the company's 1978 season, but *Circus Valentine*, staged in 1979, turned out to be a disappointment. "It was devastating," Miss Norman told Allan Wallach of *Newsday* (May 8, 1983). "It took me about two years to recover from it and regain my confidence. . . . But the wonderful result of failure was that ultimately I felt strengthened by it—that they [the critics] had hated the play and I survived. That they had said everything awful that could ever be said. And I *still* wanted to write. It was *still* what I wanted to do at ten o'clock in the morning."

Over the next few years, Marsha Norman continued to collaborate from time to time with the Actors Theatre of Louisville, most notably on a 1980 workshop production of *The Hold-up*, a western comedy based on her grandfather's tall tales. (A revised version, in a production by the American Conservatory Theatre, opened to generally favorable reviews in San Francisco in 1983.) She also worked with the resident company at the Mark Taper Forum, on a 1979–80 Rockefeller playwright-in-residence grant. To "buy back writing time" for herself, she contributed the teleplays "It's the Willingness" to the PBS series *Visions* and "In Trouble at Fifteen" to the NBC series *Skag* and wrote the as yet unproduced screenplays "The

Children With Emerald Eyes" for Columbia Pictures, "Thy Neighbor's Wife" for United Artists, and "The Bridge" for the producer Joseph E. Levine.

In November 1978 Marsha Norman, whose marriage to Michael Norman ended in divorce in 1974, married Dann C. Byck Jr., a prominent Louisville businessman with an interest in the theatre. About two years later, the couple moved to New York City, where Byck established himself as a theatrical producer. Marsha Norman had feared that the frenzied pace of Manhattan would be detrimental to her work, but she found instead, in the city's close-knit community of playwrights, a source of inspiration and support. "We benefit from watching each other walk down the path . . . ," she explained to Paula Span, who interviewed her for the *Washington Post* (April 30, 1983). "We all understand that we don't always have to be good, but we have to keep trying."

During the summer of 1981, Miss Norman wrote *'night, Mother*, a wrenching two-character drama in which she probes an individual's right to control his own life and, if necessary, end it. As the curtain rises, Jessie, a frumpy, middle-aged woman who has been drained of hope by years of disappointment, matter-of-factly announces to her elderly mother, Thelma, that she intends to commit suicide later that evening. Over the next ninety minutes, Thelma moves through disbelief, anger, resentment, and, finally, resignation as she tries, with increasing desperation, to dissuade her daughter. Forced to justify her decision, Jessie says simply: "I'm just not having a very good time and I don't have any reason to think it'll get anything but worse. I'm tired. I'm hurt. I'm sad. I feel used. . . . I'm what was worth waiting for, and I didn't make it. Me, who might have made a difference to me. . . . I'm not going to show up, so there's no reason to stay, except to keep you company, and that's not reason enough because I'm not very good company." After drinking a cup of cocoa and leaving some last-minute instructions about managing the household in her absence, Jessie goes to her room, closes the door, and pulls the trigger. "Suicide for Jessie is not an act of cowardice, giving up or despair," Marsha Norman has said, as quoted in *People* magazine (May 16, 1983). "It is her answer to the problem of her life, what she feels will fix it."

First staged by Robert Brustein's American Repertory Theatre in Boston, Massachusetts in January 1983, *'night, Mother* opened at the Golden Theatre on Broadway on March 31, 1983, with Kathy Bates as Jessie and Anne Pitoniak as Thelma. Miss Norman had written the play with the actresses, friends from her days at the Actors Theatre of Louisville, in mind, and their beautifully balanced performances went a long way toward explaining the mass appeal of the play in spite of its depressing subject. Stanley Kauffmann of the *Saturday Review*, Michael Feingold, who covers theatre for the *Village Voice*, and the *New York Post*'s Clive Barnes were among those reviewers who found faults—most of them minor—in the play, Kauffmann going so far as to suggest, in his review of January 1983, that 'night, Mother was fatally flawed by "the author's tyrannical governance of characters in order to flesh out a gimmicky framework: the suicide announcement at the start and the pistol shot at the finish." For most critics, however, the play was "not an inflated abstract argument about life versus death," as Frank Rich noted in his New York Times review of January 12, 1983, "but an intimate eavesdropping on two people."

Even before its Broadway opening, 'night, Mother had earned Miss Norman the Susan Smith Blackburn Prize, which is awarded annually to a woman playwright for "a work of outstanding quality in the English-speaking theatre." The Pulitzer Prize and a handful of Tony Award nominations boosted flagging ticket sales in the late spring, and by the summer of 1983, 'night, Mother had settled in for what was to be a respectable ten-month run. Nevertheless, because of the enormous ongoing costs of a Broadway production, Miss Norman was forced to waive 50 percent of her royalties for most of the engagement to help meet the weekly budget. 'night, Mother, with the original cast, reopened for a brief run at the Off-Broadway Westside Arts Theatre on April 18, 1984.

Marsha Norman has found the inspiration for each of her plays in "an emotional memory." "It always begins with a memory of a moment of extraordinary intensity," she explained to Paula Span, "a moment I was in great pain, or a moment when I was desperately afraid, or a moment when I was in awe of an act of courage." Eventually, she went on, the characters take over. "It's like having house guests. . . . It's quite possible to be having supper with your husband and be interrupted by these imaginary people. I sit there at the table and hear lines of dialogue or suddenly understand why something is so." When she is ready to commit her thoughts to paper, she usually writes the sensitive, emotional scenes in longhand and the "mean, nasty stuff," to use her term, on a typewriter, although she has recently begun to rely more heavily on her personal computer.

Because she feels it's "impossible" to present new works commercially, Miss Norman prefers to take her plays first to a regional theatre, where she can see each piece onstage and polish and refine it without premature press coverage. In February 1984 she tried out her most recent work, Traveler in the Dark, at the American Repertory Theatre in Boston. The "traveler" of the title is a guilt-ridden, disillusioned cancer researcher, played by Sam Waterston, who suffers a crisis of faith after failing to save the life of a stricken colleague. In searching for an answer, he returns to his boyhood home and a confrontation with his father, a revivalist preacher, portrayed by Hume Cronyn. The consensus of early reviews was that Traveler in the Dark was "less an effective drama than a didactic argument between opposing points of view," as Hilary DeVries pointed out in the Christian Science Monitor (February 22, 1984): "The writing here is forced and

self-conscious, as if the playwright knows she is addressing 'Big Themes' and 'Real Psychic Pain.' She is so earnest in telling us the point of her play that she doesn't trust her characters. It's a tremendous barrier, over which the audience's emotions never quite leap."

A slim woman standing five feet four inches tall, Marsha Norman has chin-length dark brown hair, blue-green eyes, and delicately chiseled features. Although she does not follow a formal exercise routine, she maintains her trim figure by regularly taking long walks. For relaxation, she knits or joins her husband in performing chamber works for piano and clarinet. Their apartment near Central Park on Manhattan's Upper West Side is decorated with Marsha Norman's collections of American Indian rugs, antique quilts, and ceramics.

References: Ms 12:56+ J1 '83 por; N Y Times II p4+ My 27 '79 por, C p13 Ap 19 '83 por; N Y Times Mag p22+ My 1 '83 por; Sat R 9:28+ O '83 por; Contemporary Authors vol 105 (1982)

O'Connor, John J(oseph)

Jan. 15, 1920– American Roman Catholic prelate. Address: b. Chancery Office, Archdiocese of New York, 451 Madison Ave., New York City, N.Y. 10022

John J. O'Connor, a prelate after Pope John Paul II's own traditionalist heart, was appointed by the Pope to succeed the late Terence Cardinal Cooke as archbishop of New York, America's most prestigious Roman Catholic see, in January 1984. O'Connor developed his brisk disciplinary style in the United States Navy, in which he served for twenty-seven years before retiring as chief of chaplains and in the rank of rear admiral in 1979. As a member of the committee that drafted the American bishops' 1983 pastoral letter on war and peace, he took some of the bite out of that document's criticism of United States nuclear-arms policy and strategy. At the time of his appointment to New York, he was bishop of Scranton, Pennsylvania, where he proved himself to be a take-charge, no-nonsense administrator. In Scranton he also won the affection of his flock with the warm and easy manner, self-deprecatory sense of humor, ecumenical spirit, willingness to listen, and sensitivity to individuals—especially the disadvantaged— that soften the edge of his assertive orthodoxy in doctrine and discipline. While a hard-liner against artificial birth control, a married priesthood, the ordination of women, and, above all, abortion (which he regards as "murder"), O'Connor considers himself "progressive, even—heaven forbid!—liberal on social issues."

John Joseph O'Connor is one of five children of the late Thomas J. O'Connor, whose parents were immigrants from County Cork and County Roscommon in Ireland, and Dorothy M. (Gomple) O'Connor, whose ancestry was German. He was born in Philadelphia, Pennsylvania on January 15, 1920. The birth took place with the aid of a midwife in the brick row house in which the O'Connors were then living on Carroll Street, in a West Philadelphia working-class neighborhood. John Joseph was baptized in St. Clement's Church, a block away. Later the O'Connors moved to 2631 South Holbrook Street and became parishioners of St. Brendan's Church. The Archbishop has two younger sisters, Mrs. Dorothy Hamilton of St. Petersburg, Florida and Mrs. Mary Theresa Ward of Chadds Ford, Pennsylvania. His older brother, Thomas J. O'Connor, lives in Sea Isle City, New Jersey. Another brother, Joseph O'Connor, is no longer living.

Thomas J. O'Connor was a goldleafer, a craft passed on to him by his father. He earned a comfortable living restoring antique furniture and gilding the ceilings and walls of churches and other buildings, but when Mrs. O'Connor was blinded by glaucoma, much of his income was drained by the search for a medical cure. After a year Mrs. O'Connor's sight returned, apparently spontaneously. She regarded her recovery as a miraculous response to novenas she had made to St. Rita, the patroness of the blind.

O'Connor received his schooling at four Philadelphia schools, two of them public and two parochial. He owes his vocation, he says, to the Christian Brothers who taught him at West Catholic High School. Teachers remember him as a "shy and frail" boy, nicknamed "Shadow" because he was small for his age, but "versatile and very intelligent," with "a great memory" and an impressive speaking voice in recitation. His sister Dorothy was quoted by Charles Lackman, Patrick Smith, and Philip Messing in the *New York Post* (February 1, 1984): "I thought my brother was average. Then, all of a sudden, he showed remarkable signs of an enormous intelligence, a brilliance. It just seemed to come out of nowhere." He also "always had a dry wit," she said, and "a strong sense of values."

Growing up, O'Connor worked at a succession of after-school jobs, including street hawker of vegetables for a truck farmer, stock boy in a department store, and Western Union delivery boy. As a teenager he ran his own bicycle-repair business. For recreation, he devoured the Horatio Alger books and other boys' adventure stories, played sandlot football and roller-skate hockey, watched air-mail pilots drop off and pick up postal sacks at the National Guard airfield on the outskirts of Philadelphia, and sang around the player piano with the family on Sunday nights. His boyhood hero was the football player Red Grange.

In 1936 O'Connor entered St. Charles Borromeo Seminary in the Overbrook section of Philadelphia, where, according to some classmates, he "never really stood out from the crowd" and "wasn't what you would call a plugger." According to others, however, he wasn't happy unless he was engaged in multiple activity that "would give another person a nervous breakdown." Classmates quoted in the special edition of *Catholic New York* (March 15, 1984) published on his arrival in New York City remembered him as "a pretty good artist," as "pretty exacting as a director" of musicals and plays, and as never studying from the class text but "from St. Thomas Aquinas himself, reading the *Summa Theologica*."

O'Connor was ordained a priest of the Archdiocese of Philadelphia on December 15, 1945. After his ordination he was assigned to St. James High School in Chester, Pennsylvania, where he taught English, civics, literature, and religion and directed dramatic productions. While teaching, he performed curate's duties at St. Gabriel's parish in Norwood, Pennsylvania and began work on the first of his three graduate degrees, an M.A. in advanced ethics, at Villanova University. He later earned an M.A. degree in clinical psychology at the Catholic University of America and a Ph.D. in political science.

Father O'Connor's "first love" was work with mentally handicapped children. In the early 1950s he began working with the Pennsylvania Association for Retarded Children and, at the request of John Cardinal O'Hara of Philadelphia, became involved in establishing an archdiocesan center for retarded children. "I really thought that was how I'd be spending my life," he told Tricia Gallagher, one of the contributors to the special March 15, 1984 edition of *Catholic New York*.

The direction of his vocation was changed by the Korean war. While professing "no desire or affinity for the military," O'Connor requested permission to volunteer for service in the military chaplain corps soon after the outbreak of the war in 1950. The request was at first denied, but in 1952 Cardinal O'Hara did an about-face and notified

O'Connor of his approval. "I signed up for two years, stayed for one more year, moved to work in the chief of chaplain's office and stayed on for another year," he recounted, as quoted by Tricia Gallagher in *Catholic New York*. "Bishop Bryan McEntegart asked me to teach at Catholic University, but there was a letter from Cardinal O'Hara asking me to stay on for one more year, and at that point, I went regular Navy."

As a chaplain, O'Connor ministered to Marines as well as Navy men in combat in both Korea and Vietnam. He recounted his experiences in Vietnam and what they meant to him in *A Chaplain Looks at Vietnam* (World, 1968). That book, written in O'Connor's usual easy, flowing style, expressed both a defense of American policy and a loathing of war as it affects combatants and innocent civilians in the battle zone. "No priest can ever watch the blood pouring from the wounds of the dying . . . without anguish and a sense of desperate frustration and futility," he wrote. "The clergy back home, the academicians in their universities, the protestors on their marches are not the only ones who cry out, 'Why?'"

O'Connor has had second thoughts about the book, as he told Dick Ryan when the latter interviewed him for a series of biographical articles in the *New York Post* (March 12–17, 1984): "I think that, on balance, I would not . . . write that book . . . now that I have a greater sense of my ignorance in the situation. I sincerely tried to be knowledgeable about the war but from hindsight I recognize that I hardly even scratched the surface. It would be foolish to say that I did not write from a prejudiced perspective no matter how hard I tried." One passage he did not regret and would not rewrite, he said, was one near the end of the book: "Every war is the wrong war in the wrong place, and at the wrong time."

Chaplain O'Connor also did tours of duty aboard destroyers, cruisers, and submarines in the North Atlantic, the Mediterranean, the Caribbean, and Antarctica, and he served ashore at Marine and Navy bases in the United States and abroad. At the United States Naval Academy at Annapolis he was the first Roman Catholic priest to become senior chaplain, and he was Navy chief of chaplains from 1975 to 1979.

During his career in the Navy, O'Connor instituted drug and alcohol rehabilitation workshops for Navy personnel in San Diego, California and Norfolk, Virginia; was instrumental in the introduction of closed-circuit television to many ships and the designing of religious programming for that television worldwide; and helped set up moral guidance programs for Navy personnel and their families. For those programs he wrote several manuals on character education, on the philosophy and ethics of military leadership, and on family coping with the problems peculiar to Navy life.

When O'Connor retired from the Navy in the rank of rear admiral in 1979, he carried away with him the Legion of Merit with Combat V, the Meritorious Service Medal, and the Distinguished Service Medal, among other decorations. Consecrated a bishop by Pope John Paul II in Rome on May 27, 1979, he was assigned as auxiliary in charge of military chaplains to Terence Cardinal Cooke, the Archbishop of New York. At that time occupancy of the New York see still carried with it the spiritual leadership of Roman Catholics in the United States armed forces. That tradition, begun with Patrick Joseph Cardinal Hayes in 1919, would end early in 1984, when Pope John Paul II separated the New York archepiscopacy from the military ordinariate.

During his term as military vicar general, O'Connor wrote *In Defense of Life* (Daughters of St. Paul, 1981), an analysis of the church's teachings on issues relating to war and peace. In that book he acknowledged that "the conditions for a just war may have changed" but concluded that it would not "be honest to aver that the Church has come down overwhelmingly on the side of conscientious objection as the norm and military service as the exception."

O'Connor attracted national attention as one of the five members of the drafting committee of the American bishops' 1983 pastoral "The Challenge of Peace: God's Promise and Our Response." That controversial statement challenging some of the most fundamental aspects of United States nuclear-arms policy and strategy, was two grueling years in the making. Arguing against the nuclear-arms freeze and for the American right to first use of small-scale nuclear weapons, O'Connor had what some have viewed as a "hawkish" influence on the committee, but the other, more dovish committee members apparently welcomed his traditional "just war" input. In an interview published in *Catholic New York* in December 1981 O'Connor rhetorically asked, "Who doesn't want to stop war? Who doesn't want to speak out? I'd love to experience that feeling of euphoria that seems to come with a call to dismantle all arms, to shout out 'I'm free at last!' But would the country, would the free world thank me for this? We'd be completely vulnerable."

Arguing for a delay in a statement by the American bishops on Central America, O'Connor told a meeting of the National Conference of Catholic Bishops in Washington, D.C. in November 1981: "I ask not that we turn our backs on our brothers and sisters in Central America, nor do I ask that we delay a statement until it achieves the distinctions worthy of a Duns Scotus and the rhetoric of Dante or Shakespeare. I shudder and tremble at my own presumption in standing here before you and urging delay when I have to live with my conscience and dream of the deaths of our modern martyrs or hear during my own sleepless nights the cries of those who call agonizingly for our help. It is because I want to honor those deaths and answer those cries that I plead that we do what is best for those people over the course of 10,000 tomorrows. I do not believe this statement to be demonstrably best for these people merely because it could be issued today."

In like manner, O'Connor later cautioned the bishops regarding their in-progress pastoral letter on capitalism, intimations of which have inflamed the powers that be in America and multinational finance. As quoted by Dick Ryan in the *New York Post*, O'Connor said: "The business and industrial community of New York has obviously contributed enormously to the general welfare by providing jobs and income. The degree to which this has been done justly is something that, from a distance, I've never been able to evaluate. But . . . just to take potshots at the business community or else try to pull down the whole house of cards would be terribly self-defeating. The reality is that we have some enormously rich people and some very, very poor people. And there's no question that the cycle of poverty has to be broken. How we do that will be the concern of the bishops in that pastoral. But I cannot imagine the bishops attacking the concept of capitalism."

Appointed bishop of Scranton, Pennsylvania in May 1983, O'Connor was installed in the post the following month. In Scranton, he lost no time in visiting all parishes and high schools of the diocese, appearing on television as often as possible, convening the first diocesan synod in 115 years, opening Scranton's first shelters for the homeless, raising parochial school teachers' pay, and engaging in ecumenical activity. When asked to name his greatest accomplishment in Scranton, he said, according to Charles W. Bell of the *New York Daily News* (March 18, 1984), "When I got here, women weren't allowed to wear slacks in the chancery. I told them they could."

Pope John Paul II's appointment of O'Connor to the see of New York was announced on January 31, 1984 and became effective on March 19, 1984. The new archbishop signaled the style he would bring to America's richest and most influential archdiocese in the formal installation ceremony on March 20, 1984, when, in the pulpit of St. Patrick's Cathedral, he jocularly placed his mitre on the head of a surprised and delighted namesake, altar boy John J. O'Connor. He followed up that debut by barnstorming the parishes of his new jurisdiction, meeting as many as possible of the 1.8 million people under his spiritual care, quipping all the while. During those pastoral peregrinations he temporarily left the details of archdiocesan administration to his vicar general, Bishop Joseph T. O'Keefe. As O'Keefe told Charles W. Bell of the *New York Daily News*, Archbishop O'Connor is "concerned about the homeless, the hungry, the crippled, and especially the retarded" and "totally repelled by the possibility of nuclear war." He is "even more repelled," he said, "by the actuality of war against the unborn. Any society that permits the destruction of its own unborn is doomed."

O'Connor's absolute stand on abortion has put him at odds with "pro-choice" Catholic politicians, notably Geraldine Ferraro, the Democratic vice-presidential candidate, and Mario Cuomo, the governor of New York. In September 1984, the Archbishop criticized Ms. Ferraro for giving "the world to understand that Catholic teaching is divided on the subject of abortion," when in fact that teaching is monolithic. He was alluding to a 1982 letter signed by Ms. Ferraro and other Catholic members of Congress asserting that "there can be a range of personal and political responses to the issue." Also in 1984, O'Connor stirred controversy when he refused to sign a New York City mayoral executive order banning discrimination in employment or hiring because of "sexual orientation or affectional preference." While the church does not condemn chaste homosexual "inclination," it does not condone the promotion or practice of homosexuality, and the Archbishop felt that the distinction was not clear in the executive order. "We would rather close our child welfare agencies than violate church teaching," he said. In a suit brought in behalf of O'Connor, the Salvation Army, and Agudath Israel of America, state Supreme Court Justice Alvin Klein on September 5, 1984 ruled Mayor Edward I. Koch's executive order unconstitutional on the ground that in issuing it Koch had usurped the powers of the New York City Council.

Unlike his immediate predecessors in the New York archepiscopacy, O'Connor does not bear the title of military vicar. With the title of apostolic administrator, he is temporarily overseeing the United States military vicariate, a worldwide archepiscopal jurisdiction comprising 2.3 million American Catholics in the armed forces, Veterans' Administration hospitals, and diplomatic offices. The day-to-day operation of the vicariate is being administered by Archbishop Joseph T. Ryan until Pope John Paul II names an archbishop as permanent head. The informed speculation is that the vicariate headquarters will be transferred to Washington, D.C.

Archbishop John J. O'Connor is a robust six-footer of ramrod stature and commanding bearing. A polished speaker, he has a spontaneous wit, a warm, gentle manner, an arm-around-the-shoulder geniality, and a scorn for the pomp and trappings of office that disarm the fiercest of his ideological opponents. He is the "best politician" Mayor James McNulty of Scranton has "ever met." A seemingly tireless man with strict work habits, Archbishop O'Connor has been described by Bishop O'Keefe as "almost a workaholic." When he does seek recreation, it is usually in a book, music, golf, cross-country skiing, or swimming. In New York, the Archbishop has become the collector of myriad caps, the gifts of his fans, from baseball players to Mayor Edward I. Koch.

References: *Catholic New York* p1+ F 2 '84 pors, p1+ F 9 '84 pors, p1+ Mr 15 '84 pors; *N Y Daily News* p5+ F 5 '84 pors, p1+ Mr 13 '84 pors; *N Y Daily News mag* p1+ Mr 18 '84 pors; *N Y Post* p38+ F 1 '84 pors; *N Y Times* E p6 F 5 '84 por; *Newsday* II p4+ F 27 '84 pors; *Who's Who in America,* 1984–85

Ortega, Daniel

*Nov. 11, 1945- Coordinator of the Junta of
National Reconstruction of Nicaragua. Address:
b. Casa del Gobierno, Managua, Nicaragua*

In Nicaragua in 1979 the guerrilla avengers of the
martyred nationalist hero Augusto César Sandino
(1895-1934) brought to an end the American-
backed Somoza dynasty, the longest and, in the
eyes of many, the most corrupt dictatorship in Latin
American history. The first among equals in the
victorious Sandinista leadership was Comandante
Daniel Ortega, a patriotic pragmatist without
whose wide popular following the otherwise doctrinaire leftist revolution might never have succeeded. Confronting the gargantuan task of
rebuilding an impoverished country devastated by
the civil war and bled bankrupt by the Somoza oligarchy, the Sandinista junta, as coordinated by Ortega, set up a Government of National
Reconstruction that was originally pluralistic as
well as socialistic. Ironically, that government's efforts to maintain its diversity and to nurture a
mixed economy domestically and remain nonaligned internationally have been hampered by
economic sabotage and cross-border military raids
carried out by United States–supported "freedom
fighters." Ortega saw hope for a change in the
American perception of Nicaragua as an epicenter
of Communist influence in Central America in bilateral discussions held partly under Mexican auspices in the summer of 1984. The Reagan
administration's hostility to the Sandinistas remained implacable, however. After Nicaragua
agreed to sign a regional peace treaty drafted by
the Contadora group (Colombia, Mexico, Panama,
and Venezuela) in September 1984, Representative
Michael Barnes of Maryland, the chairman of the

House subcommittee on hemispheric affairs, said,
"The administration's objections to the treaty reinforce my belief that it's never had any real interest
in a negotiated settlement."

Daniel Ortega Saavedra was born on November
11, 1945 into a lower middle-class family in the
town of La Libertad, Nicaragua. He has a younger
brother, Humberto, now the minister of defense in
the Sandinista government. Another younger
brother, Camilo, who was also a leader in the
Sandinista revolution, was reported killed in 1978.
One of the Ortega brothers' chief revolutionary
role models was their father, a veteran of the peasant army of Augusto César Sandino, after whom
the Sandinistas are named. After United States
Marines occupied Nicaragua (for the third time in
seventeen years) in 1926, Sandino and his men
waged protracted guerrilla warfare against the invaders. Stalemated, the American force withdrew
in 1933, leaving behind as surrogate the infamous
National Guard (Guardia Nacional), native mercenaries trained and supplied by them and headed
by Anastasio Somoza Garcia, a graduate of West
Point military academy. After the American withdrawal, Sandino laid down his arms and accepted
an invitation for "peace talks" with Somoza. Following one of the talks, he was seized and assassinated. Thus began the Somoza dynasty, which,
with American support, for more than four decades
would rule Nicaragua as if it were a family estate,
taking as its own up to 30 percent of the arable
land, exercising a monopoly control of the economy, protecting American interests, and repressing
political opposition. After Anastasio Somoza
Garcia was assassinated in 1956, his older son, Luis,
became president. Luis' rule was almost benevolent in comparison with those of his father and his
younger brother, Anastasio Somoza Debayle, who
succeeded to the presidency in 1967.

After graduating from secondary school, Daniel
Ortega entered the Jesuit-run Central American
University (Universidad Centro-Americana) in
Managua to study law, but he dropped out after a
few months and went underground, joining the
Frente Sandinista de Liberación Nacional (FSLN)
in 1963. Organized two years before by Carlos Fonseca Amador, Silvio Mayorga, and Tómas Borge
Martínez (now the minister of the interior in the
Sandinista government), the FSLN was a nationalist guerrilla army of students, peasants, and workers seeking to avenge Augusto César Sandino. Its
immediate goals were, in the words of Amador,
first, the overthrow of "the Somozaist clique" that
had "reduced Nicaragua to the status of a neo-
colony exploited by the Yankee monopolies and
the country's oligarchic groups" and, second, the
establishment of "a revolutionary government
based on the worker-peasant alliance and the con-
vergence of all the patriotic, anti-imperialist, and
anti-oligarchic forces in the country." Its long-term
goal was "a social system that wipes out the exploitation and poverty that our people have been subjected to."

Although at least ten years younger than most of the FSLN's leaders, Daniel Ortega won rapid promotion in the organization. He was in charge of the FSLN's urban resistance campaign by 1967, when he was captured and jailed by the National Guard. He remained incarcerated for seven years, until December 30, 1974, when he and some dozen other Sandinista prisoners were released in exchange for high-level Somocista hostages. Ortega and the other released prisoners were flown into exile in Cuba, where he received military training under veterans of Fidel Castro's guerrilla campaigns. After a few months, he secretly returned to Nicaragua and rejoined the FSLN's guerrilla war against Somoza.

There were three "tendencies," or factions, within the FSLN, held together under Carlos Fonseca Amador's strong leadership. The two smaller factions, one of which was led by Tómas Borge Martínez, were doctrinaire Marxist-Leninist. The Terceristas, or Third Party, led by Daniel Ortega and his brothers, was the least extreme and least ideological, and it succeeded in winning a wide spectrum of support, from peasants to wealthy upper-class intellectuals.

Following Carlos Fonseca Amador's death in combat in 1976, the differences between the hard-line factions and the Terceristas developed into an open rift. The chief point of contention was the participation of the Terceristas—under the cover of the Movimiento de los Doce, or the Group of Twelve, an organization of businessmen, academics, and clergy led by the Roman Catholic priest Father Ernesto Cardenal (now the minister of culture in the Sandinista government)—in the Frente Amplio de Oposicion (FAO), a bourgeois-dominated popular alliance of anti-Somoza forces. (Even the middle and upper classes, apart from the oligarchs, had been politicized when, following the earthquakes that devastated Managua in 1972, Somoza's scandalous mismanagement of relief and reconstruction funds demoralized the country's industrial sector in addition to enraging the displaced, starving poor.) Under the leadership of the liberal bourgeoisie, the FAO sought not a radical change (which even the petit bourgeoisie wanted) but only a modification of the status quo—"Somozism without Somoza." Obstinately rejecting even that moderate demand, Anastasio Somoza Debayle set about bloodily repressing the popular movement. He succeeded only in disintegrating the FAO and discrediting its leadership, leaving in its place an insurrectional mass movement in desperate need of new guidance.

The Terceristas moved into the leadership breach. "We could not oppose this torrent-like movement," Humberto Ortega explained to an interviewer at the time. "All we could do was stand at its head . . . and give it some direction. . . . If we had not given form to this mass movement, it would have lapsed into general anarchy." With the breakup of the FAO and the discarding of a bourgeois solution to the national crisis, the major obstacle to the unification of the FSLN was removed.

The three FSLN factions set up a unified command structure on December 9, 1978, and they fused into a single organization on March 26, 1979.

Numbering only in the hundreds, the FSLN was militarily vastly inferior to the 15,000-strong Somocista armed forces. To compensate, it adopted a strategy, borrowed from the Vietnamese, that forced the National Guard to disperse its technico-military capacity. That strategy combined military action with total mobilization at the social, economic, and political levels. Thus, when the Sandinista guerrillas launched their "final offensive" in the spring of 1979, they did so with the support of a dense network of mass organizations that used the frontal offensive as a prop for a general strike (widely supported by employers) and a nationwide uprising. At the same time, support for the Somoza dictatorship from abroad had crumbled: the Organization of American States almost unanimously opposed any North American intervention in the civil war in Nicaragua; the dictatorship had been condemned by the Andean Pact countries, some of which were openly aiding the Sandinistas, who also had the support of Mexico; and United States backing of the dictatorship, previously unconditional, had become ambivalent under the human rights-oriented administration of President Jimmy Carter.

Seeing that the game was up, Anastasio Somoza Debayle pursued a scorched-earth policy during his final months in power. Partly in revenge against the oppositional bourgeoisie, the National Guard systematically bombed industrial areas, destroying factories, hospitals, schools, and housing as well as people. (A total of more than 40,000 died during the civil war, and tens of thousands more were wounded, orphaned, and left homeless.) Two-and-a-half million head of cattle from Somoza's vast ranches were slaughtered and shipped as beef to cold storage in Miami, Florida for later sale. By double-mortgaging his businesses, borrowing heavily from foreign private banks and the International Monetary Fund, and running up bills with multinational corporations, Somoza saw to it that any government succeeding his would be deluged with debt and handicapped by an abysmal international credit rating. Incredibly, the International Monetary Fund, with American approval and over the protests of respected Nicaraguan economists, gave the lame-duck dictator a loan installment of $33.2 million, which was deposited in the Central Bank of Managua in May 1979 and mysteriously disappeared after the bank closed down during the Battle of Managua the following month. In addition, Somoza looted the national treasury before fleeing to Miami with his retinue, including the National Guard high command, on July 17, 1979. He later moved to Paraguay, where he was assassinated on September 17, 1980.

The victorious Sandinista rebels marched triumphantly into Managua on July 19, 1979. To avoid the traditional Latin American pitfall of one strongman usurping the spoils, they had already decided on a collective, pluralistic Government of National

Reconstruction. Pending elections (originally promised by 1985), executive power was invested in a Tercerista-dominated junta of five men (later reduced to three) coordinated by Daniel Ortega under a nine-person directorate equally representing the three FSLN factions. A range of anti-Somoza groups, including conservatives, were represented in the Cabinet and the Council of State, a vocationally diverse assembly sharing legislative power with an eleven-member consultative body, the Council of Government. Domestically, the Government of National Reconstruction promulgated a mixed economy and boasted of confiscating as few properties and enterprises as possible outside of those that had been owned or controlled by the Somoza oligarchy. Among the measures introduced were trade controls and the nationalization of local banks and insurance companies. Abolishing the death penalty, the government credited itself with relatively humane treatment of captured National Guardsmen. Internationally, it professed a policy of nonalignment.

"Somoza left us in ruins," Tomás Borge Martínez recounted to Claudia Dreyfus in a group interview for Playboy (September 1983). "Thousands dead. Backwardness. Illiteracy. Incredible poverty. He left us old factories that could not compete in the market. He left us no money in the national treasury. . . . Everything but the debts, billions in debts, went abroad. Beyond all that, beyond many deaths, the torture, the poverty, Somoza left us bad taste—mal gusto. He wanted . . . to turn Nicaragua into a kind of Miami, which is not the best cultural tradition of North America."

With every sector of the economy in a state of crisis and much of the population of 2.5 million in imminent danger of starvation, Ortega sought foreign help in relief and reconstruction while remaining wary of strings that would compromise Nicaragua's international neutrality. Among the countries responding to his pleas were Mexico and Venezuela, both of which began shipping oil to Nicaragua in 1980 on a 70 percent cash–30 percent credit basis; Italy, which provided the bulk of the money for the building of a geothermic electric plant at La Paz Central; the Soviet Union, which gave economic support and help in the development of hydroelectric and other projects; Cuba, which sent teachers and technical, medical, and military experts as well as materiel; and France, which supplied economic aid and military equipment. Later, when the counterrevolutionaries began their hit-and-run forays into northern Nicaragua from havens in Honduras, Libya also offered military aid. Almost half of the economic assistance received by Nicaragua since the civil war has come from Latin America and the countries of Western Europe, including the Netherlands and Belgium; 20 percent has come from Communist countries.

Seeking United States aid, Ortega visited President Jimmy Carter in the White House in September 1979 and came away with a commitment for a $75-million loan and an additional $40 million in other forms of aid. American policy shifted abruptly when Carter was succeeded in the presidency in January 1981 by Ronald Reagan. Accusing Nicaragua of acting as a conduit of arms from Cuba to leftist guerrillas in El Salvador and "inviting alien influences and philosophies" into the hemisphere, the Reagan administration sought to "destabilize" the Sandinistas before they could "consolidate" their power. Soon after President Reagan took office, the United States government began tightening the economic screws on Nicaragua, canceling the last $15-million payment of the loan approved by the Carter administration, halting credits for the purchase of $9.6-million worth of United States wheat, and slashing by nearly 90 percent the amount of sugar Nicaragua could sell to the United States.

By September 1981 the economic crisis in Nicaragua had worsened to such a point that the Government of National Reconstruction enacted the Measures of Economic and Social Emergency. In October 1981, when the United States and Honduras held joint naval maneuvers in territorial waters of Honduras, the Sandinistas became fearful of another threat, one to Nicaragua's national security. That fear grew in November and December 1981, when the CIA's financing, training, and supplying of ex-Somocista National Guardsmen and other anti-Sandinistas on the Honduran border became public knowledge. In response to the threat of invasion, the Sandinistas began beefing up their defensive forces, and in March 1982 the Government of National Reconstruction decreed a state of national emergency, tightening censorship of the press and curtailing the civil liberties of the domestic opposition. The Reagan administration, which differentiated between "totalitarianism" (bad and unacceptable) and "authoritarianism" (bad but acceptable), interpreted the "state of siege" reflected in the September 1981 and March 1982 emergency measures in Nicaragua as a "drifting toward totalitarianism" that confirmed the rightness of Reagan's hard-line policy toward the Sandinistas.

By February 1983 several thousand American-backed Nicaraguan counterrevolutionaries were massed along the Honduran side of the Honduran-Nicaraguan border, and for the first time the contras, as they are called, were joined by Honduran military units prepared to provide artillery support. At the same time the United States increased its military presence on sea and land and in the air around Nicaragua. Early in March, cross-border raids by the contras reached a new magnitude. In the view of Robert E. White, the former American ambassador to El Salvador, the "true intent" of the incursions was "neither to overthrow the Sandinistas nor, as Mr. Reagan claimed, to interdict the negligible trickle of arms from Nicaragua to El Salvador" but rather "to provoke the Sandinistas to cross the Honduran border and attack the counterrevolutionaries' base camps." "Washington is determined to create an ill-starred, region-wide military battle," White wrote in the New York Times (May 2, 1983), "hoping in the end to negotiate a region-wide solution on its own terms. . . . But even the hot-headed and inexperienced Sandinistas refused to fall into so obvious a trap. They ordered their troops to stay well clear of the Honduran border and reiterated their offer to negotiate with Honduras or the United States."

While the ex-Somocistas were attacking from the north, the Sandinista defector Edén Pastora Gómez was leading incursions in the south, from Costa Rica. The raiders, north and south, failing to elicit significant popular support (except among the historically isolated Miskitu Indians, who have charged the Sandinistas with human-rights violations), took not a single town and established no permanent bases within Nicaragua, but they wreaked havoc nonetheless, destroying infrastructure (including oil facilities and bridges) and taking 1,000 lives, bringing the two-year total of Nicaraguan dead to more than 5,000. Ortega estimated the economic damage for 1983 at $128 million. The national security crisis forced the Sandinista government to raise its defense spending to 25 percent of its budget and to institute an unpopular military draft, at a time when the populace was increasingly grumbling about the prices and shortages of foods, medicine, and other basic goods and the rationing of soap, sugar, cooking oil, and gasoline.

Following the invasion of Grenada by the United States in October 1983, Ortega took steps to dispel the negative American perception of Nicaragua. That November he announced that his government was prepared to stop buying arms from abroad and to ask Cuban and other foreign military advisers to leave, and he promised the presidents of the friendly Contadora countries (Mexico, Venezuela, Colombia, and Panama) that the restraints on the domestic opposition in Nicaragua would be loosened. In overtures to that opposition as well as in response to the pressure of the Sandinistas' democratic friends in Latin America and Europe, he proclaimed an amnesty for exiles in December 1983, and announced in February 1984 the scheduling of "democratic" elections.

The amnesty, offering land or compensation to "landowners who have abandoned their property or whose property has been occupied," was directed chiefly at peasants and excluded "oligarchs" seeking restoration of "the old privileges." The elections, for president, vice-president, and a ninety-member constituent assembly, were scheduled for November 1984. At a meeting of the eighty-one-member Sandinista Assembly, Ortega was named the party's presidential candidate and Sergio Ramírez Mercado its vice-presidential candidate.

Aside from six small parties, including fragments of the traditional Liberal and Conservative parties, the chief civilian opposition was a coalition of three political parties allied with two labor federations and the organized business community. The unofficial presidential candidate of the coalition was Arturo José Cruz, an opposition leader who had been a member of the ruling junta and ambassador to the United States before resigning in protest of Sandinista policies. To encourage the participation of Cruz in the electoral campaign, the Sandinistas made some concessions, including relaxed censorship of the opposition newspaper La Prensa, but they refused to allow the monitoring of the elections by foreign observers. The Cruz backers let the deadline pass without registering their candidate, in the hope of discrediting the elections and forcing the Sandinistas to make more political concessions, including the release of scores of prisoners and major changes in the government. After a long period of grace, election officials announced on August 22, 1984 that no further extensions for registration could be made because such extensions would hold up the printing of ballots. In accordance with the Nicaraguan law applying to parties not participating in elections, the three coalition parties lost their legal recognition. "They did not provide conditions for a fair election," Luis Rivas Leiva, the head of the opposition coalition, told the press, "so we are staying out."

A new anti-Sandinista military offensive, begun in March 1984, reached its climax the following month in the mining of Nicaragua's ports, an operation reportedly involving American vessels offshore. The fifteen-judge International Court of Justice in the Hague condemned American involvement in the harassment of Nicaragua in May 1984. Subsequent to an agreement reached between Ortega and United States Secretary of State George P. Shultz, talks between representatives of the United States and Nicaragua finally began in June 1984 and continued through the summer. Most of the discussions, described as "substantive" by the Mexican foreign ministry, were held in Manzanillo, Mexico.

The bilateral talks had mostly to do with the regional peace plan then being mediated by the four-nation Contadora group. That plan was aimed at insuring free, internationally inspected elections, the withdrawal of foreign military forces, and the halting of support for guerrilla movements in Central America. There was disagreement among American officials on some points of the treaty that was approved by the Contadora negotiators on September 7, 1984, but, as one official explained later, "no one expected the Nicaraguans to accept it, so we didn't really worry about the treaty." Only after Nicaragua, in a surprise move on September 21, 1984, announced that it was prepared to sign the draft treaty, did nonplussed State Department and White House officials begin marshalling objections to the document. "I'm not sure what there's left to talk about at Manzanillo," one State Department official said, as quoted by Philip Taubman in the New York Times (September 24, 1984). "The whole point was to get the Nicaraguans to accept the Contadora proposals. Now they have, but we say we aren't satisfied. I'm not sure I would blame the Nicaraguans if they were confused."

In a speech before the United Nations General Assembly on October 2, 1984, Ortega charged that "intelligence information from various sources" indicated that the United States was planning a two-stage invasion of Nicaragua timed to force the

Sandinistas to cancel the national balloting scheduled for November 4. The first-phase strategy, he said, was for contras to invade from the north "with full logistical support from the United States." The second phase was for a Grenada-style operation, in which some Central American countries would request "aid" from the United States "to eradicate the 'Sandinista threat.'" Thus, as he later told editors of *Newsweek* (October 15, 1984), United States troops would take part in the invasion once the contras had made inroads. "We have been making gestures to different countries, [including] Western countries, in a search for interceptor planes. . . . Nicaragua is the only country [in the area] that doesn't possess this type of plane. And yet Nicaragua is the one country that needs it. . . . The best thing would be that the Central American countries that have this type of airplane get rid of them, so that those of us that don't have them won't be forced into seeking them."

A short man who wears rose-tinted glasses, Daniel Ortega has the reputation of being the most in-

tense of the Sandinista leaders. (He surprised observers with his smiling cordiality when he met with President Jimmy Carter in the White House in 1979.) While not an especially dynamic speaker or brilliant theorist, Ortega is an adroit, patient mediator and a shrewd strategist, respected by Nicaraguan conservatives as well as radical leftists. When in prison, he took to writing poetry, some of it angry and heavy with four letter words, and some on the order of "I Never Saw Managua When Miniskirts Were in Fashion." Ever flexible, he still believes, ideally, in political pluralism and a mixed economy despite some of the turns the revolutionary government has been forced to take. The Comandante is a bachelor.

References: NY Times p7 Mr 26 '83; Newsweek 101:38 Mr 21 '83 por; Playboy 30:57+ S '83 por; Time 121:18 Je 6 '83 por; U S News 90:25+ Mr 23 '81 por; Ridolf, James D., ed. Nicaragua: A Country Study (1982); Russel, Peter und Vandermeer, John, eds. The Nicaragua Reader (1983)

Paterno, Joe

Dec. 21, 1926– Football coach. Address: b. The Pennsylvania State University, University Park, Penn. 16802

Shortly after he became head football mentor at The Pennsylvania State University two decades ago, Joe Paterno, the thinking man's coach, announced his "grand experiment," aimed at proving that a major college football program can emphasize academic credibility over winning and still

produce a national champion. The national championship was more of a goad than a goal to Paterno—who believes that "it is the striving to be number one that's important"—but he achieved it anyway, when Penn State defeated Georgia in the Sugar Bowl on New Year's night 1903, following a 10-1 season in 1982. A year later, Penn State's victory over the University of Washington in the Aloha Bowl brought Paterno's career record as head coach to 170 wins, thirty-eight losses, and two ties—the best winning percentage among major college coaches with tenures of ten years or more.

The remarkableness of Paterno's record can be appreciated only in light of his priorities, which cut him off from the widespread, scandalous practice of recruiting physically superior but marginally literate athletes and maintaining them as "students." The "Penn State way," as his players call Paterno's approach, rests on two tenets: there is more to college than football, and there is more to football than winning. Ninety percent of Paterno's scholarship players have left college with degrees, a record unmatched among major college teams with the exception of the Fighting Irish of Notre Dame.

Joseph Vincent Paterno was born in Brooklyn, New York, on December 21, 1926, the firstborn son of Angelo Lafayette and Florence (de Salle) Paterno, both native Brooklynites of Italian descent. His father, an appellate court clerk, was a late aspirant to a legal career, working his way through law school and passing the bar when he was in his forties. Growing up in the Flatbush section of Brooklyn with his brother, George, and his sister, Florence, Paterno never had "an unhappy day as a child" that he can recall. His father encouraged his and his brother's participation in sports in a manner that Paterno feels "was probably responsible for . . . the way [he] turned out": "He used to say first, 'Did you have a good time?' and second, 'Who won?'" Paterno also became interested in politics through his father, who did legwork and speechwriting for local Democratic candidates. In addition, the Paterno children were exposed to recorded opera at home and to live opera at the Brooklyn Academy of Music.

After completing their elementary schooling at St. Edmund's parochial school, Paterno and his brother went on to Brooklyn Preparatory, a Jesuit school, where they played baseball and basketball as well as football. Although older, Joe made the varsity football team after George because he was too light at first (125 pounds). Playing in the same backfield, the skinny-legged but brainy Joe called signals while the heavier and faster George attracted more attention as a running back. Academically, Joe was most inspired at Brooklyn Prep by a teacher named Father Birmingham, the model for the priest confessor in The Exorcist, the novel and screenplay written by William Blatty, who was in the class just behind Joe Paterno's at the school. "Father Birmingham was the guy who got Bill Blatty to write The Exorcist," Paterno revealed to Paul Hendrickson of the Washington Post (January 1, 1979), "and me to read Vergil."

Everett M. ("Busy") Arnold, a New York businessman who privately recruited for Brown University, his alma mater, was a friend of Zev Graham, the football coach at Brooklyn Prep. It was Arnold who arranged for the Paternos to attend Brown University with private scholarship assistance after they graduated from Brooklyn Prep. Joe arrived at Brown in the summer of 1945, was inducted into the United States Army six weeks later, and returned to Brown after a year's military service. With his brother as his backfield mate, Joe Paterno quarterbacked two winning seasons for coach Charles A. ("Rip") Engle at Brown, 7-2 in 1948 and 8-1 in 1949. On the Brown basketball team, his forte was defense.

George Paterno went on to become the football coach at the United States Merchant Marine Academy at Kings Point, New York. Joe, an English major at Brown, was planning to go on to Boston University Law School and perhaps eventually into politics. Just before he took his B.A. degree in June 1950, however, he helped Coach Engle with the quarterbacks in spring practice. Engle, who had already accepted the position of head football coach at The Pennsylvania State University, asked him to go along as offensive backfield coach. Paterno, who needed money for law school—he had contemplated prep-school coaching in the Boston area, decided he "had nothing to lose but a little time" and agreed to go to Penn State long enough to help Engle convert Penn State's offense from a single wing to a double T. The "little time" is yet to run out.

The Pennsylvania State University is an unlikely football giant, a former agricultural college nestled in rustic Nittany Valley in mountainous central Pennsylvania. The winning tradition begun there by Coach Bob Higgins in 1939 was continued by Rip Engle, who coached the Nittany Lions for sixteen years without a losing season and with only one .500 campaign. As Engle's chief assistant, Paterno was responsible for the development of such quarterbacks as Galen Hall, Dick Hoak, Pete Liske, Milt Plum, Al Jacks, Jack White, Tony Rados, and the All-American Richie Lucas. The All-American halfbacks Lenny Moore and Roger Kochman also played under his tutelage.

Knowing that Engle planned to retire after the 1965 season and that he, Paterno, was slated to replace him as head coach, Paterno turned down six offers to coach elsewhere during his final two years as assistant to Engle. The transition from Engle to Paterno was exceptionally smooth because Penn State, unlike most schools, gives tenure to assistant coaches (after three years) and Paterno thus did not have the problem of hiring a new staff when he took over in March 1966. "The university president said I could get anyone I wanted," he told the press the following August, "but I felt I already had the best." (The "best" included the veteran assistant coach Jim O'Hora, at whose home Paterno boarded during his early years at Penn State.) He said he hoped to continue Engle's winning streak without being "a carbon copy," that he would replace his predecessor's winged T with the I formation and that he thought he would "gamble a bit more than Rip."

The closest Paterno would come to a losing season was his first, when the Nittany Lions went 5-5, duplicating their 1965 record. The following year, an 8-2 record in the regular season took the team to the Gator Bowl where Paterno's willingness to "gamble a bit" against Florida State lost him a win but projected him into national prominence as a daringly heretical tactician. For years afterwards he would be remembered among analysts of bowl games as the coach who elected to try for a first down on fourth-and-one at his own fifteen-yard line when he was ahead 17-0. The Seminoles' defense held, their offense scored, and the game ended in a 17-17 tie. As Paterno later explained, he knew that orthodoxy called for a punt in that situation, but "there [he] was on the bench with a very tired defensive team." "I had told the players time after time, you have to take chances to win. It was a moment to put up or shut up."

"We had fun, what the heck," Paterno said, recalling the backfired play against Florida State in an interview with Dan Jenkins for Sports Illustrated the following year (November 11, 1968). He explained his attitude in the context of his "grand experiment": "We're trying to win football games . . . but I don't want it to ruin our lives if we lose. . . . I tell the kids who come here to play, enjoy yourselves. There's so much besides football. [There's] art, history, literature, politics."

The greatest disappointments of Paterno's career were to see his undefeated, untied teams of 1968, 1969, and 1973 ranked lower than first in the national polls. He was "the most annoyed" in 1969 when Penn State had the longest winning and unbeaten streaks in the country and President Richard Nixon "took something away from my kids before the bowls." (In a locker-room appearance, Nixon had told the Texas Longhorns they were the number-one team in the nation.) In his 1973 commencement address at Penn State, Paterno asked, "How could the President know so little about Watergate in 1973 and so much about football in 1969?"

That invitation to give the commencement address was among the many demonstrations of campus affection shown Paterno after he finally decided, agonizingly, to decline the most lucrative of the several pro contracts offered him, a six-year contract from the Boston Patriots estimated at $1.3 million or $1,268,000 more than his annual salary at Penn State. "In the end," he told Sandy Padwe of Newsday (January 8, 1973), "I didn't feel I should leave a job where I had been happy, where I had made so many friends. It's a good atmosphere. I have what I need materially. I'm not rich, but I'm not lacking anything. I have five kids and this is the perfect place to raise them. . . . I know all my players don't love me, but I've enjoyed working with the people we've had here." With less agonized deliberation, Paterno declined a political bid in 1974, when Pennsylvania gubernatorial candidate Drew Lewis wanted him as his running mate.

Paterno coached his next four teams to a combined 37-11 record, and his 1978 squad went through the regular season undefeated and achieved Penn State's first-ever weekly number-one ranking. However, the Lions lost to Alabama 14-7 in the Sugar Bowl and finished the 1978 season ranked fourth. After the bowl game, Paterno was named College Football Coach of the Year by the American Football Coaches Association. He had received similar awards previously from the Walter Camp Football Foundation and the Washington Touchdown Club, but he considered the 1978 award "the most meaningful" of his career, coming as it did "from [his] fellow coaches."

In 1979 when Paterno temporarily took on the burden of university athletic director in addition to his coaching chores, his team got out of control, not so much on the field—where it went 8-4—as off. Penn State lost three starters because of academic ineligibility and three others for arrests on charges ranging from drunken driving to first-degree burglary. Regaining its morale, the team had records of 10-2 in 1980 and 10-1 in 1981.

Over the years, Paterno's preferred form of offense has been a conservative "grunt 'n' grind" attack, mostly on the ground. In 1982, having the stellar combination of ace passer Todd Blackledge at quarterback and All-American Curt Warner at tailback, he opened up his offense. With Blackledge throwing for twenty-two touchdowns, Penn State rallied for seven straight wins after losing to Alabama, posted a 10-1 regular season mark and a number-two ranking, and earned a Sugar Bowl date with the number-one-ranked University of Georgia. In the Sugar Bowl, Warner outgained the

Bulldogs' Heisman Trophy winner, Hershel Walker, 117 yards to 103 on ten fewer carries, and scored twice to spearhead a 27-23 victory that brought Penn State its first national championship. Paterno was named Coach of the Year by United Press International and the Football Writers of America as well as the American Football Coaches Association. Todd Blackledge, a born-again Christian, told Thomas Granger in an interview for an article in the Saturday Evening Post (October 1983), that he "learned discipline" from Paterno. "You learn to adjust to him and his style and to do things his way, or you have a miserable time. He's a very upright, moral person, and he did a good job of pushing his values."

The Penn State team that won the national championship was decimated by graduation the following June, leaving Paterno with the task of shaping up a raw varsity for the next season, a coaching challenge that gave him more "fun," as he put it, than he had had in years. As Paterno knew, the team was not ready for the first game of the 1983 season, the newly sanctioned Kickoff Classic, against the University of Nebraska (which would go on to second ranking nationally), and the Corn Huskers humiliated the Nittany Lions, 44-6—the widest margin of defeat suffered by Penn State since Paterno's first year as head coach. The Lions lost their next two games as well, giving them the worst start by a defending national champion in more than forty years. Under quarterback Doug Strang, the team regrouped sufficiently to finish the regular season 7-4-1, and in the Aloha Bowl in Hawaii on December 26, 1983 it won a close defensive game against the University of Washington, 13-10.

Meanwhile, the prestige of the 1982 national championship had amplified Paterno's voice as a longtime crusader for the restoration of sanity to mainstream college football, which too often, in some schools, was resorting to questionable recruiting and curriculum-rigging practices, including under-the-table payments and special soft classes for minimally literate athletes—practices that Paterno viewed as an exploitation of and disservice to the athletes themselves. On the lecture circuit and on television talk shows he spoke about the moral conflicts of coaches and the problems of student athletes, both exacerbated by the pros' treatment of college teams as breeding farms for talent and by the new bonanza of television money.

A speech Paterno made at the National Collegiate Athletic Association on January 17, 1983 embroiled him in national controversy. The key controversial point was his support of NCAA's Proposition 48, which is to take effect in 1986. Designed to raise academic standards for athletes, the proposition lays down new eligibility requirements: a high school senior, in order to be eligible to play varsity sports as a college freshman, has to earn a combined score of 700 on the Scholastic Aptitude Test or 15 on the American College Testing exam and graduate from high school with a grade-point average of 2.0 out of a possible 4.0 In addition, English, math, and nine other designated core subjects must be part of the high school curriculum. Paterno's advocacy of Proposition 48 brought critical reaction from leaders at black universities who feel the new eligibility rules are racially biased.

Actually, Paterno was not as vehement about Proposition 48 as he was about Proposition 49B, which allows an athlete to receive a grant-in-aid as a college freshman while not allowing him to compete as a freshman. "I've always been opposed to freshman eligibility for varsity sports, anyway," he said, as quoted by Ira Berkow in the New York Times (February 28, 1983). "I think a student needs his first year as a period of adjustment to college life. With Proposition 49B, the student who doesn't reach the academic standards before entering college can, with diligence, get his grades up so that he can be eligible for sports during his following years in school."

The NCAA reforms will go down easily at Penn State. Paterno recruits shrewdly, but none of his recruits are marginal students. There is no special dormitory for athletes on campus, and varsity members must attend to their studies—including classes on the weekends of games—or be demoted or dismissed. They are encouraged to take part in other extracurricular activities, including minor sports, as part of a full college life—even, sometimes, when that means absence from a practice session or a game.

Joe Paterno and Suzanne Pohland, a Penn State graduate, were married on May 12, 1962. The Paternos, who have two daughters and three sons, live in a modest home they own on McKee Street in State College, Pennsylvania, the town surrounding the campus area called University Park. The house is a couple of blocks from the campus and a little over a mile from Beaver Stadium, the home of the Nittany Lions. Paterno walks to the stadium when he has time, and he drives in his station wagon when he does not. Brisk walks and handball games are his chief forms of exercise, along with his constant pacing back and forth along the sideline during games. His game-time wardrobe is an incongruous, Ivy League-jock combination, beginning with a tie at the neck and ending with white socks and athletic shoes.

Paterno's players refer to him among themselves, not always affectionately, as "the Rat." He has black, slicked-back hair, a prominent nose topped by thick bifocals that tint in sunlight, and a Brooklyn-accented voice that becomes ever shriller as he harangues his men. According to his wife, he is not quite as "volcanic" as he used to be, and a friend attests he is not as "abrasively" cocksure or as "terribly" intense. While temperamentally reclusive, he is a ready, fast-talking conversationalist, enjoying small talk and humorous asides as well as literary discussions, and with the press is an accessible, lively jouster.

When working on his game plans, Paterno often has Beethoven, Verdi, or Puccini playing on the stereo, and his favorite recreation is going to symphony concerts in Pittsburgh. A registered Republican ("My father would roll over in his grave if he knew"), Paterno still harbors an attraction to politics, which would allow him to continue in a different way the role in which he sees himself, that of an educator. Proud of the status of full professor that The Pennsylvania State University gives him, he considers it "a tragic waste, for both of us" if "after four years a kid leaves and he hasn't learned anything" from him. He does not want to be remembered by his children as just "a good football coach [who] won a lot of games."

References: Sat Eve Post 225:61+ O '83 pors; Sport 50:50+ N '70 pors; Sports Ill 29:19+ N 11 '68, 39:46+ N 19 '73 pors, 52:43+ Mr 17 '80; Washington Post C p3 Ja 1 '79 pors; Riley, Ridge. Road to Number One (1977)

Pendleton, Clarence M(cLane), Jr.

Nov. 10, 1930– Chairman, United States Commission on Civil Rights. Address: b. Commission on Civil Rights, 1121 Vermont Ave., N.W., Washington, D.C. 20425; Pendleton & Associates, 233 A St., Suite 905, San Diego, Calif. 92101

Since November 16, 1981, when President Ronald Reagan appointed him chairman of the United States Commission on Civil Rights, Clarence M. Pendleton has been at the center of a political storm, for the conservative Republican has taken a number of stands that most observers would not have expected from the first black to hold that sensitive post. He has, for example, opposed desegregation through busing, because he believes it violates the principle of neighborhood schools and because he doubts that predominantly white schools are necessarily better than predominantly black ones. Moreover, he has denounced affirmative action as a "bankrupt policy" that detracts from the legitimate achievements of those who would have succeeded in any case. Such controversial statements have alienated Pendleton from the majority of black spokesmen, and some leaders of minority and women's groups have even urged Congress to cancel funding for the commission. Pendleton, however, is undaunted. "The black leaders are just killing themselves by abandoning me," he charges. "I was one of their only links to the administration, and they've blown it."

Clarence McLane Pendleton Jr. was born on November 10, 1930 in Louisville, Kentucky to Clarence McLane Pendleton Sr. and his wife, Edna Marie (Ramsaur) Pendleton. He grew up in Washington, D.C., where his father was the first swimming coach at Howard University, an assistant director in the District of Columbia recreation department, and a lifeguard at the Banneker recreation center in the black community. Until Clarence was six, the Pendletons lived in the black neighborhood known as Deanwood, and he attended the city's public schools. Washington's policy of segregation kept Pendleton from displaying his considerable talents as a swimmer in school meets, but he looks back upon his youth without bitterness and notes that "a lot of us didn't do too badly when we got out in the world."

Pendleton had the good fortune of belonging to a family that was so well-established in the black community that it was able to expose him to excellence despite the segregated environment of Washington. His paternal grandfather, who had finished Howard University Law School in 1896, was a lawyer in Baltimore. "He never had any money," Pendleton has remarked, "but he was a helluva lawyer." His maternal grandfather was a graduate of St. Augustine College, and a granduncle was a rector at St. Luke's Episcopal Church, where Pendleton served for fifteen years as an altar boy. Clarence Pendleton Sr. instilled a strong sense of discipline in his son, who remembers doing "a lot of hanging around on street corners when [he] was a kid," but adds that he "didn't get into trouble because the guys knew they'd catch hell from [his] father if [he] messed up."

After graduating from Dunbar High School, where many children of the black middle-class were educated, Pendleton followed in the steps of his grandfather and father by enrolling at Howard University. He earned his B.S. degree in 1954 and worked briefly for the District of Columbia recreation department before joining the United States Army. He served with a medical unit at Fort Monmouth, New Jersey and was released from active duty in 1957 with the rank of specialist third class. He then returned to Howard, where he had excelled as a swimmer and as a football player, to take a post as a physical education instructor while working on a master's degree in education, which he obtained in 1961. Taking over Dr. Thomas F. Johnson's duties as swimming coach, he earned the reputation of being demanding, but his team won ten championships in eleven years and gained berths in national competitions. In the summers of 1964 and 1965 Pendleton also coached Egyptian swimming teams that won national championships. He also served at Howard as head baseball coach, head rowing coach, and assistant football coach.

By 1968 Clarence M. Pendleton was the divorced father of two children, and his straitened financial situation forced him to leave Howard for a post as a recreation coordinator with the Model Cities program in Baltimore. The new job offered Pendleton, who received no pay for coaching, double the annual salary of $7,500 that he had received as a teacher. "I really enjoyed the molding of people," he recalls, "but I was starving." In 1970 he returned to Washington to become the director of the urban affairs department of the National Recreation and Parks Association, where he worked to increase community involvement in the establishment of recreation programs and to persuade the federal government of the need for year-round planning rather than short-term undertakings aimed at preventing summer riots. He also promoted an idea he developed in Baltimore for the construction of well-lighted, multilevel open-air athletic and recreational facilities in inner cities where real estate costs were high. The design of his model structure, which, in a play of words on his nickname, he called "Penny's Pavilion," resembled that of a parking ramp.

In 1972 Mayor Pete Wilson of San Diego recruited Pendleton, who had been looking around for a chance to do something entirely his own, to direct the Model Cities program in his rapidly expanding southern California city. After spending three-and-one-half years in that job, Pendleton succeeded John Jacob as executive director of the San Diego Urban League, an important post that was once held by Vernon E. Jordan before he became head of the National Urban League. Under his direction the city's Urban League pursued its normal agenda in behalf of the civil and social rights of San Diego's population of 90,000 blacks. He marshaled support for the black Marines who had been subjected to attacks by the Ku Klux Klan at nearby Camp Pendleton and sponsored, for its annual fund-raiser, a $5.00 soup-and-cornbread night that San Diego's senior citizens could afford. But, as president of the Urban League's federally subsidized subsidiaries, the nonprofit San Diego County Local Development Corporation and the profit-oriented Building for Equal Opportunity, Pendleton also shepherded the organization into such innovative enterprises as packaging loans for small businesses and upgrading and managing small apartment units.

Opinion is divided over Clarence M. Pendleton's accomplishments as head of the San Diego Urban League. He maintains that, under his direction, the league negotiated $24 million in business loans, created 8,000 nonsubsidized jobs, increased its real estate holdings from $218,000 to $3 million, and returned $17 for every single dollar invested in it by the city. Some critics complain, however, that members of minority groups received too small a share of the loans dispersed, and Hope Logan, the chairman of the league's board, denied in 1982 that Pendleton's profit-making ventures had returned any money to the organization. Nevertheless, Pendleton, whose credo is "the best social program I know of is a job," defends the Urban League's support of private business as "certainly better than affirmative action" and offers to match his record against "anyone else's rhetoric any day."

Working in San Diego was a revelation for Pendleton, whose previous experience had been restricted to cities where Democrats were the "movers and shakers." Pendleton, who says that he arrived as Model Cities director with the conviction that the government owed blacks "every damn thing," was soon convinced that the progress underway in San Diego "was taking place in the private, unsubsidized, free-market sector." Under the influence of Mayor Pete Wilson and of Edwin Meese 3d, the San Diego confidante of Ronald Reagan, Pendleton reevaluated his political stance as a self-described "bleeding-heart liberal" and switched his allegiance to the Republican party. He cast his first vote for the GOP in 1975, in support of Wilson's candidacy for governor of California, and by 1980, when Pendleton was the only one out of more than 150 officers in the Urban League to support Ronald Reagan's bid for the presidency, his commitment to the party was solid. He dislikes, however, being described as a "black Republican." "I am a Republican who happens to be black. I didn't become part of the party to be in the auxiliary."

Pendleton's switch in political allegiance did not lead him to renounce his belief that government intervention may sometimes be necessary to protect human rights and to advance equal opportunity. For example, he remained a staunch supporter of the Voting Rights Act and a somewhat lukewarm supporter of the Equal Rights Amendment and continued to advocate welfare for those "who don't have the means to cope." He nevertheless deplored the idea that "all minority progress comes out of a civil rights or social service gun," convinced that heavy reliance on the government would sap the self-reliance of black Americans. "If minorities and blacks expect everything from the government," he has argued, "then I think we stay on the plantation." Likewise, he decided that affirmative action in the form of racial quotas for hiring and promoting can mislead young members of minority groups into neglecting to prepare themselves properly for the world of work. "The only way for blacks to get a real piece of the action," according to Pendleton, "is to get out there and compete in the marketplace and not rely solely on handouts or political favoritism."

Clarence M. Pendleton gained national attention for the first time when President Ronald Rea-

gan, on November 16, 1981, named him to replace Arthur S. Flemming as the chairman of the United States Commission on Civil Rights. Foes of the administration complained that the White House had dismissed the septuagenarian Flemming because the moderate Republican was openly critical of Reagan's resistance to busing and affirmative action. They also feared that the simultaneous removals of Flemming and of another moderate Republican, Stephen Horn, boded ill for the six-member commission that had been established in 1957 to advise Congress on the enactment and enforcement of legislation pertaining to civil rights and equal opportunity. The only previous presidential dismissal had occurred in 1974, when Richard M. Nixon requested and received the resignation of Flemming's predecessor, Father Theodore M. Hesburgh, who also had advocated greater reliance on busing as a means of school desegregation. The Reagan White House issued a statement, however, that it was only pursuing a normal course of appointing officials compatible with the administration's philosophy and denied any intention to alter the independent and bipartisan nature of the commission.

Controversy clouded the selection of Clarence M. Pendleton, who believes that his conservative views make him "an outcast among black leaders." The National Urban League gave him only a qualified endorsement, and the *New York Times* editorialized that he did "not come close to the distinguished appointees of past presidents." Critics from San Diego questioned his recent actions, as vice-chairman of the San Diego Coalition Dedicated to Economic and Environmental Development, in opposing the construction of a military hospital on the site of a cemetery in a black neighborhood, because the new facility would have provided jobs. Instead, Pendleton had argued that the area should be reserved for industrial or residential development and had supported building the hospital at a Balboa Park site favored by Edwin Meese, the founder of the coalition. The Federal Bureau of Investigation cleared Pendleton of allegations concerning his payment of income taxes and his management of a $94,000 grant from the Department of Health, Education, and Welfare, and the Senate Judiciary Committee took the unusual step of using the meeting scheduled for a vote on Pendleton's confirmation to ask him last-minute questions about his taxes and political views. On March 17, 1982, however, the committee recommended the nomination without apparent opposition, and the full Senate soon gave its approval.

The new chairman frequently found himself politically isolated from the other members of the commission, including vice-chairman Mary Louise Smith, the former Republican national chairman, who had been appointed by Reagan to replace Stephen Horn. Pendleton's first official act was to issue, on May 27, 1982, with dissenting comments, a previously prepared report charging that Reagan had cut real federal spending for civil rights enforcement. Later in the year he abstained from a vote in favor of busing, reduced the responsibilities of the state advisory committees, and advised thirty-three state commission chairmen who had written a critical letter to Reagan to resign.

Pendleton's main clashes within the commission stemmed from his support of President Reagan's actions to limit the scope of affirmative action. In January 1983 he opposed the commission's condemnation of the administration's requests that federal appeals courts throw out, on grounds of reverse discrimination, affirmative action plans devised to increase promotions among minority group members in the New Orleans police department and to prevent layoffs among them in the Boston police and fire departments. In August 1983 he dissented from another attack by the commission on the administration's position on the case of *Firefighters v. Stotts*, which was headed for the Supreme Court. In doing so, he agreed with the administration's contention that the justices should overturn a lower court decision directing the financially troubled city of Memphis to lay off senior white firemen rather than recently hired black ones.

During his first year as head of the Commission on Civil Rights, Pendleton emerged, in the view of one of his colleagues, as a "wild card," despite his defense of President Reagan. "Even though I am a presidential appointee, I understand my independence," he asserted. "I am not over here to impede the work of the agency or the progress of civil rights." In 1982 Pendleton chided Reagan when the chief executive considered granting tax exemptions to racially discriminatory schools and when he was slow to endorse renewal of the Voting Rights Act. He also warned William French Smith, the attorney general, that a ruling by the Fourth U.S. Circuit Court of Appeals exempting the University of Richmond from Title IX requirements for equal treatment of female athletes because the school's intercollegiate sports program did not directly receive federal aid "would decimate civil rights protection" guaranteed by the Education Amendments of 1972.

Early in 1983 Pendleton wrote to Reagan to complain about the "lack of cooperation" and "intolerable delays" suffered by the commission in its efforts to collect data on the race, ethnic origins, and sex of high-level presidential appointees. And in July of that year he charged that the administration's proposed budget for 1984 entailed "substantial cuts and revisions in programs that have been effective in improving the quality of education for the disadvantaged, minorities, and women." Perhaps most important, Pendleton has expressed doubts that the president has a clear civil rights policy and has tried to convince him of the need to demonstrate to minorities that "there's a racial safety net so that they don't perish in moving from a color-conscious to a color-blind society."

Throughout the first year and a half of Pendleton's tenure on the civil rights panel, President Reagan sought to reinforce the embattled chairman by replacing three Democratic commissioners with appointees more sympathetic to the thinking of the administration. A financial scandal forced one White House nominee to withdraw, and the Senate rejected another and delayed action on two more. The Congress and Reagan finally reached a compromise after the president, in October 1983, announced that he would unilaterally replace the three incumbents with three appointees who were more conservative. Under the terms of legislation signed into law on November 30, 1983 a new commission was established with eight members who would serve fixed terms and would be subject to dismissal only for neglect or malfeasance. Pendleton was named to a six-year term as chairman, and Reagan's three choices received appointments. One of the president's Democratic nemeses and Mary Louise Smith, whose votes had brought her into disfavor with the administration, lost their seats, but the three other incumbents were retained.

The new commission, which held its first two days of meetings in mid-January 1984 in the affluent Baltimore suburb of Hunt Valley, quickly sought to assert its independence. On the first day it criticized both an unnamed White House official for saying that the new agency was "on our side" and Democratic presidential hopeful Walter F. Mondale for promising to "fire everybody Reagan has hired" and "to hire everybody he fired." Soon, however, the impact of the new majority, which Pendleton described as being held together by a "neoconservative" attitude, became evident. On January 16 the commissioners voted 5-3 to cancel a study of the effects of budget cuts on colleges where most students were black or Hispanic. Pendleton led the majority, which argued that since budget cuts were not inherently discriminatory, they were beyond the purview of the commission. That same day the commissioners voted to continue a study of the adverse consequences of affirmative action on Americans of southern or eastern European descent and to reexamine the validity of discrimination as a single explanation for inequality in income and education. And on January 17 the commissioners, by a vote of 6-2, denounced the use of quotas to increase the number of blacks promoted from sergeant to lieutenant in the Detroit police department. "This is not a commission for minorities but a commission for Americans," Pendleton commented. "We believe everybody is to be protected, not just minorities and women."

In spite of its general political orientation, the new commission has not always been in complete agreement with the Reagan administration. In particular, the commission has differed with the White House on the 1984 decision by the Supreme Court in *Grove City College v. Bell*. In that case the justices concluded that federal laws which prohibit sex discrimination by schools and colleges receiving federal funds apply only to the specific, offending departments and not to the whole institution. Pendleton has urged Congress to adopt legislation that would overturn the ruling by making clear

Congress's intent to have broad, recipient-wide coverage both under Title IX of the Education Amendments of 1972 and under Title VI of the Age Discrimination Act.

Clarence M. Pendleton comes to Washington for meetings of the Civil Rights Commission but continues to live on the West Coast. Although he resigned in April 1982 from his position with the Urban League, he remains active in business and public affairs around San Diego, as chairman of San Diego Transit, as president of Pendleton and Associates, a business development and investment firm, and as chairman and president of the San Diego Local Development Corporation. He is a trustee of the Scripps Clinic and Research Foundation and serves on the boards of the Greater American Federal Savings and Loan Association and of the San Diego Coalition for Economic and Environmental Balance.

With his wife, the former Margrit Krause, whom he married in 1970, Clarence Pendleton makes his home in Bay No. 4 Park, a neighborhood of San Diego. Pendleton, who has run every day since recovering from a heart attack that he suffered in 1976, says that the birth of their daughter, Paula, in 1979 was "the greatest thing" that ever happened to him. "She reduces my daily stress," Pendleton has explained. "When I hold her, all the tension goes out." By his earlier marriage Pendleton has two grown children, George and Susan, who live in Washington, D.C.

References: Nation 238:1+ F 4 '84; People 17:71+ Ja 11 '82 pors; Washington Post p1+ N 14 '82 pors; Who's Who in American Politics, 1983–84

Peters, Bernadette

Feb. 28, 1948- Actress; singer. Address: b. c/o Richard Grant, Lippin & Grant, Inc., 8124 W. 3d St., Suite 204, Los Angeles, Calif. 90048

The actress, comedienne, singer, and dancer Bernadette Peters is fond of saying, "I've done it all—everything but circus acrobatics," and in just about every medium in which she has appeared—theatre, motion pictures, television, recordings, and nightclubs—she has excelled. Among the distinctions that she has earned along the way are a Drama Desk award, a Theatre World citation, a Best of Las Vegas award, the Hollywood Foreign Press Association's Golden Globe award, and several Tony award nominations. Yet many of the productions in which she has appeared have failed critically or floundered commercially, and her performances have often been the only thing singled out for praise in projects that were otherwise panned. Even the much heralded Stephen Sondheim musical Sunday in the Park with George, in which she opened on Broadway in May 1984, received only lukewarm reviews from critics, while her own contribution was widely acclaimed.

Bernadette Peters was born Bernadette Lazzara in Ozone Park, Queens, in New York City, on February 28, 1948. Her father, Peter Lazzara, a first-generation Italian-American, drove a bread truck. Her sister, Donna De Seta, who is nine years older than she, became a show business casting agent. She also has a brother, Joseph, three years her senior. Bernadette's mother, Marguerite (Maltese) Lazzara, who died in 1982, was a stagestruck housewife who arranged for her youngest child to receive tap-dancing lessons at the age of three and her singing lessons soon after that. "Mom . . . always wanted to become an actress herself," Miss Peters told Bob Lardine, as quoted in the New York Sunday News (October 24, 1976). "When I was a kid, she fulfilled herself through me."

At five, while attending kindergarten at Public School 58 near the two-family shingle house in which she grew up, Bernadette made her professional debut as a regular on television's Horn and Hardart Children's Hour and won $800 on Name That Tune. She was nine when she joined Actors Equity, ten when she changed her name to Peters (after her father's first name) to avoid being typecast in ethnic roles, and eleven when she appeared as Tessie in a New York City Center revival of Frank Loesser's musical The Most Happy Fella in February 1959. At thirteen she appeared in her first major role, as Baby June, on an eight-month road tour of Gypsy, on which she was accompanied by her mother. But as a teenager she was interested more in her social than in her professional life. "I had my attention on friends at school. I didn't want to be different," she told an interviewer for *Women's Wear Daily* (May 29, 1984). She attended Quintano's School for Young Professionals on Manhattan's West Side, graduating in 1966, and studied acting with David LeGrant, tap dancing with Oliver McCool 3d, and singing with Jim Gregory, but she did not perform during most of her high school years. "When you're a teenager you're too aware of yourself," she explained to Kay Gardella of the *New York Sunday News* (September 19, 1976). "The words were sticking in my mouth and all I could think about was how I looked."

Nevertheless, Bernadette Peters knew what she wanted to be when she grew up, and an aptitude test that she took in high school confirmed her belief that her main talent was in the performing arts. "I used to get home from high school in time for the 4:30 movie, and I got to see all those great old pictures," she told Peter Reilly in an interview for *Stereo Review* (December 1981). "I developed a real love for Ruby Keeler and Rita Hayworth and Mary Martin. . . . I have a photographic mind, and I remember exactly how they were sometimes when I sing." But Miss Peters' road back into show business was not made smooth by the shaky vehicles in which she appeared. Cast in the Off-Broadway Stage 73 production of *The Penny Friend*, a musical adaptation of Sir James Barrie's *A Kiss for Cinderella*, she had "her moments as Cinders," Dan Sullivan grudgingly acknowledged in his *New York Times* review (December 27, 1966), but the production was roundly denounced as unbearably saccharine and "icky-sticky-goo."

In May 1967 Bernadette Peters was an understudy in the short-lived Broadway production of *The Girl in the Freudian Slip*. In October of that year she played Bettina in *Johnny No-Trump*, which expired after only one performance at the Cort Theatre, and in November she was featured in *Curley McDimple*, a musical parody of Shirley Temple movies, at the Off-Broadway Bert Wheeler Theater. "It isn't too difficult to collect moth-eaten clichés and put them into a loose-jointed musical like this one," Richard P. Cooke wrote in the *Wall Street Journal* (November 24, 1967). He added, however, that Bernadette Peters, in the role of Alice, an out-of-work entertainer who befriends Curley, "has an excellent voice and as an actress fits a parody role the best of the adults on stage."

The pattern of being cast in mediocre shows was briefly broken for Bernadette Peters when she appeared as songwriter George M. Cohan's sister Josie in the hit Broadway musical biography *George M!*, which opened at the Palace Theater on April 10, 1968. John S. Wilson in his review in the *New York Times* (June 9, 1968) called *George M!* "the one flicker of light in a drab Broadway season," and though Clive Barnes in the *New York Times* (April 11, 1968) found the book to be "scrappy, ill-prepared, mediocrely written," he extolled Joel Grey in the title role and praised the entire cast. For her superior performance in her relatively minor role, Miss Peters was given a Theatre World citation.

Miss Peters' short lucky streak peaked at the end of the year, when she was cast as Ruby, an ambitious hayseed from Utah who hoofs her way to stardom, in a spoof of 1930s Busby Berkeley musicals called *Dames at Sea*, with book and lyrics by George Haimsohn and Robin Miller and score by Jim Wise, which opened five days before Christmas 1968 at the Off-Broadway Bouwerie Lane Theater. Writing in the *New York Post* (December 21, 1968), Jerry Tallmer proclaimed the show "indisputably the best musical of the year or maybe several years," and hailed Miss Peters' "super-perfect" Ruby, "whose every break-step and glide-away and intonation . . . is sheer delight." Clive Barnes revealed in the *New York Times* (December 22, 1968) that he had been steeling himself for something coy or cute and was surprised to find "a real winner, a little gem of a musical." Bernadette Peters, he concluded, was "adorable." Walter Kerr wrote in the *New York Times* (January 5, 1969) that he was captivated by Miss Peters, whom he found "especially interesting in relation to her feet: she dances as if they'd stuck to her and she were frantically trying to get rid of them."

Dames at Sea and its female lead attracted nationwide attention, a phenomenon then unusual for an Off-Broadway production. The reviewer for *Time* (January 3, 1969) called Bernadette Peters "the comic delight of the show," and Edith Oliver in the *New Yorker* (January 4, 1969) termed it "a joy to watch any expression, whatever it is, spread over her blank, wide-eyed face, and to watch her sudden, strenuous tap dancing." Miss Peters won the 1968 Drama Desk Award for her performance, which was immortalized by the Columbia original cast recording.

Unfortunately, success did not ensure more good material. By the end of 1969, Miss Peters was cast as the ingenuous waif Gelsomina in a stage musical adaptation of Federico Fellini's film classic *La Strada*, presented at Broadway's Lunt-Fontanne Theatre. "The book is weak, and the music and lyrics by Lionel Bart are undistinguished to the point of Muzak-like oblivion. This really is music to forget to," Clive Barnes wrote in the *New York Times* (December 15, 1969). Citing the cast as a saving grace, he continued: "In a different show the birdlike and croaky Bernadette Peters would have become a star overnight." Brendan Gill, writing in the *New Yorker* (December 20, 1969), found "nothing to praise in this bizarrely misbegotten enterprise" except "the touching presence of Bernadette Peters," who was "adorably gallant and woebegone."

Miss Peters was again cast in a nostalgic vehicle in 1971, in a revival at New York's Imperial Theater of the 1944 hit musical *On the Town*, with a score by Leonard Bernstein. "Unfortunely, the revival is a dud," T. E. Kalem lamented in *Time* (November 15, 1971). Other reviewers were more charitable, pointing out the difficulty of retaining the freshness and novelty of the wartime original and praising Miss Peters as Hildy, the man-hungry taxi driver who chauffeurs three sailors on leave in New York City. Applauding her performance in the *New York Times* (November 1, 1971), Clive Barnes wrote: "Miss Peters sings, acts, and dances with a saucer-eyed naughtiness and wide-voweled drawl that is totally enchanting." Miss Peters was nominated for a Tony award for her portrayal of Hildy, though the show closed after only seventy-three performances.

In the summer of 1971 Bernadette Peters toured with a production of *W. C.*, in which she played to Mickey Rooney's W. C. Fields, and in 1972 she appeared as Dorine in a Philadelphia production of Molière's *Tartuffe*. Scarcity of good material forced her to turn to Hollywood, but her favorable notices from stage performances did little to help her to obtain good film roles. She acted in such films as director John Erman's *Ace Eli and Rodger of the Skies* (Twentieth Century-Fox, 1973), about barnstorming air aces, described in *Variety* (April 25, 1973) as a "dreary nostalgia drama," and director Robert Aldrich's prison comedy-melodrama *The Longest Yard* (Paramount, 1974), starring Burt Reynolds, in which her small role as the warden's secretary was barely noticed.

Her dismal encounters with the movies were partly compensated by television guest spots—on CBS-TV's *Carol Burnett Show,* where Bernadette Peters was an "unofficial regular" beginning in 1969, and on a Bing Crosby special (CBS-TV, 1970) —and by her performances as Josie in *George M!* (NBC-TV, 1970), as Lady Larkin in *Once Upon a Mattress* (CBS-TV, 1972), and as Doris in the made-for-television film *The Owl and the Pussycat* (Screen Gems, 1974). During the 1970s she began to appear in a solo act as a nightclub entertainer, for which her technical mastery and energetic stage presence brought her frequent engagements from coast to coast.

Returning to the Broadway stage, Bernadette Peters was cast as the female lead, opposite Robert Preston, in David Merrick's costly production of *Mack and Mabel,* the Jerry Herman musical about Mack Sennett, the director and producer of slapstick silent films, and his leading lady, Mabel Normand. But although a reviewer for *Variety* (July 3, 1974) bet on *Mack and Mabel* as "an almost sure hit" when it opened at the Los Angeles Civic Light Opera, it failed to captivate the critics when it began its New York run at the Majestic Theater in October 1974. Brendan Gill of the *New Yorker* (October 14, 1974), noted that Miss Peters' performance as Mabel "prompts the dread word 'adorable' to leap up unbidden off the typewriter keys," but Jack Kroll of *Newsweek* (October 21, 1974) argued that "she can sing, dance, and act, but . . . she hasn't learned how to express an entire personality through the 'cuteness' which is her leading trait." Once more, Bernadette Peters was nominated for a Tony award and again was featured in the original ABC cast recording.

Back in Hollywood, Bernadette Peters appeared with Rod Steiger in a minor role, as the comedian's two-timing girlfriend, in the unanimously panned *W. C. Fields and Me* (Universal, 1976), which promised only to "trap her further in screen cameo-clichés," according to a *Variety* reviewer (March 31, 1976). Vamp roles in the action movie *Vigilante Force* (United Artists, 1976) and in Mel Brooks's slapstick *Silent Movie* (Twentieth Century-Fox, 1976), in which she played the torch singer Vilma Kaplan, did little to enhance her career. Then the innovative Norman Lear invited her to costar in his CBS-TV situation comedy series *All's Fair* as Charlotte, or "Charley," an ultraliberal photographer who falls in love with an archconservative newspaper columnist, played by Richard Crenna. It was a significant departure for the young actress: no nostalgia, no music, no dancing. Early reviews were encouraging, and the critic for *Time* (September 20, 1976) called Bernadette Peters' role a "long-overdue opportunity to close in on an identifiable personality," but he shrewdly predicted that the show was too sophisticated and cerebral to succeed in the ratings. It was canceled in the spring of 1977.

In 1977 Miss Peters was introduced to comedian Steve Martin by the agent Marty Klein. The two paired up professionally as well as privately for some four years, costarring in Martin's first movie, *The Jerk* (Universal, 1979), a farce directed by Carl Reiner. Martin, who wrote the screenplay, starred as Navin Johnson, the doltish white adopted son of black sharecroppers, and Miss Peters portrayed his cornet-playing cosmetologist girlfriend, a role that Martin created for her. Reviewing the film in the *Chicago Tribune* (December 14, 1979), Gene Siskel expressed the views of many when he complained that *The Jerk* was "too much of a dumb thing," but most critics were kinder to Bernadette Peters.

Her first album of pop songs, called *Bernadette Peters,* was issued by MCA records in 1980. Her sexiness made news when she engaged *Playboy* magazine illustrator Alberto Varga to come out of retirement to design the jacket of her second MCA pop album, *Now Playing* (1981). Maintaining a career-long practice of shunning nudity, she wore a short negligée. Although some reviewers focused more on the visual than on the audio aspects of *Now Playing,* those who really listened to her interpretation of such oldies as "Dedicated to the One I Love" and "Don't Say Don't" were impressed. Bill Carlton of the *New York Daily News* (September 7, 1981) found that Bernadette Peters "has perfect pipes for pop, a very supple, wide-ranging pitch that often surprises the listener with sudden, delightful twists and leaps," and Peter Reilly in *Stereo Review* (December 1981) hailed her as "perhaps the finest singing actress since Streisand."

Bernadette Peters and Steve Martin again collaborated as costars in *Pennies from Heaven,* the controversial $20-million MGM musical directed by Herbert Ross which was based on a successful 1978 British television miniseries. Released during the Christmas holiday season of 1981, the film perplexed reviewers by presenting a bleak Depression-era melodrama within the framework of a brassy musical. Martin played Arthur, an unemployed sheet-music salesman who deserts his frigid wife and seduces, impregnates, then abandons Eileen, a virginal grade-school teacher, portrayed by Bernadette Peters. Eileen eventually has an abortion and becomes a prostitute. The wistful fantasies of the luckless characters are enacted in lip-synched production numbers copied from 1930s musicals. In the context of "so expertly stylized" a movie, these "classic 'quotes' become profoundly stirring," Gary Arnold wrote in the *Washington Post* (December 18, 1981). Arnold called *Pennies from Heaven* "the finest American movie of 1981" and credited Miss Peters with "the strongest performance in the film." But few critics shared his enthusiasm, and *Pennies from Heaven* languished at the box office. Nevertheless, her performance earned Miss Peters the Hollywood Foreign Press Association's Golden Globe Award for best actress.

Also in 1981, Bernadette Peters played a "kooky" would-be suicide in the Canadian film *Tulips* (Avco-Embassy), and she appeared in *Heartbeeps* (Universal), director Allan Arkush's $10-million critical and commercial failure, as a robot enamored of her fellow robot, Andy Kaufman. In November of that year, she hosted a *Saturday Night Live* show on NBC-TV, and in December she appeared on the cover of *Playboy*, along with an interview and four pages of photos featuring her in lingerie.

After appearing in a small part, as the villainous Lily, in the film version of the musical *Annie* (Columbia, 1982), Miss Peters returned to the New York stage, accepting $210 a week to costar with Christine Baranski in a production at the Off-Broadway Manhattan Theater Club of playwright Sybille Pearson's *Sally and Marsha*. In that distaff "Odd Couple," directed by Lynne Meadow, she portrayed Sally, a homespun South Dakota housewife who makes friends with her neighbor, Marsha, a discontented New York sophisticate. Although critics found flaws in the play itself, praise ran high for its two-woman cast. "Miss Peters has become a virtuoso actress, with flying saucer eyes, a sincerity as tangible as her nose, and a transparent inner range for feeling made all the more poignant by her manic doll-like exterior," Clive Barnes informed the readers of his *New York Post* column (February 22, 1982).

In 1983 Bernadette Peters appeared in a pre-Broadway workshop production of Stephen Sondheim's new musical *Sunday in the Park with George*, centered upon the French neoimpressionist painter Georges Seurat's pointillist masterpiece *Un Dimanche Apres-Midi a l'Ile de la Grande Jatte* (A Sunday Afternoon on the Island of La Grande Jatte). When the iconoclastic and danceless musical opened at Broadway's Booth Theatre on May 2, 1984 with a budget reported to be $2.1 million and advance sales of about $1.2 million, critics were made aware of the overwhelming problems involved in presenting a musical based on a painting. Opinion about Sondheim's score, which was almost overpowered by the show's stunning visual

effects, was divided, and criticism of writer-director James Lapine's book was widespread.

Bernadette Peters, who did not let her initial ignorance of the identity of Georges Seurat get in the way of her performance, was cast in the role of Dot, the model and mistress of the artist, who was played by Mandy Patinkin. She also appeared in the second act, which was set in an avant-garde art exhibition of the present, as his now aged daughter, Marie. Brendan Gill in his *New Yorker* column (May 14, 1984) found Miss Peters "perkily charming"; Frank Rich rhapsodized in the *New York Times* (May 3, 1984) that "wonderful Miss Peters overflows with . . . warmth and humor"; and a reviewer for *Variety* (May 9, 1984) reported that she displayed "charm, flash, and an utterly winning way with an audience" in an "impressively self-effacing performance by an actress of genuine star magnitude." Critics applauded her contributions to RCA's original cast album of the show.

"I've never worked with anyone I like working with more than Bernadette," Stephen Sondheim has said, as quoted in *Life* (July 1984). "She tells you exactly what's on her mind." Other professionals agree on her directness, efficiency, and competence. Norman Lear told an interviewer for *TV Guide* (October 9, 1976) that even without rehearsal "her readings and timing were automatically almost perfect." Bernadette Peters' seriousness about her craft borders on piety. "A lot of people think acting is something you do for yourself," she has said, as quoted in the *New York Post* (May 29, 1980). "I like to think it is something you do for the people who come to see you."

Originally not especially religious, Bernadette Peters experienced a "spiritual awakening" in 1974 and has become a nonsmoking, nondrinking, meditating vegetarian without "a single vice," as she once assured Bob Lardine. "You gotta eliminate the flaws: become a clean piece of clay you can mold into anything," she was quoted in *TV Guide* (October 9, 1976) as saying. "You gotta maintain your instrument in perfect condition, and for an actor, the instrument's yourself." Her leisure-time activities include tennis, painting, yoga, playing the piano and guitar, and collecting old songs and antique jewelry.

Five feet three inches tall and voluptuous, Bernadette Peters has brown eyes and curly, dark hair that has since childhood been lightened to blonde. Kay Gardella described her in the *New York Sunday News* (September 19, 1976) as looking "like the whipped cream on top of a sundae," and elsewhere she has been compared to a "Kewpie doll." Her physical appearance, along with her vocal flexibility and range, and her skill as a dancer seem to have typecast her for musical productions. In 1984 she was chosen by *Harper's Bazaar* as one of America's ten most beautiful women.

Her coast-to-coast shuttle in her quest for good roles has kept Bernadette Peters from settling down geographically or romantically, and she usually lives modestly in rented apartments. Commenting on her failure, thus far, to attain the superstardom that she merits, she has said, as quoted in *Happenings* (September 1983): "It's important not to become discouraged, and very, very important to be individual. . . . If you're like someone else, then what do they need you for?"

References: *After Dark* 7:40+ N '74 pors; *Esquire* 97:96+ Ja '82 pors; *N Y Daily News* p6 O 28 '84 por; *People* 17:70+ Mr 29 '82 pors; *The Illustrated Who's Who of the Cinema* (1983); *Who's Who in America*, 1984-85; *Who's Who in the Theatre* (1981)

Phillips, William

1906(?)- Editor; writer. Address: b. c/o *Partisan Review*, 121 Bay State Rd., Boston, Mass. 02215; h. 101 West 12th St., New York City, N.Y. 10011

When William Phillips and Philip Rahv launched *Partisan Review* as an independent journal in 1937, it was the voice of a small, embattled band of New York intellectuals who sought to fuse their radical, but aggressively anti-Stalinist, politics with literary modernism. Early contributors included, among others, Delmore Schwartz, a gifted writer of poetry, fiction, and criticism; the novelist and critic Mary McCarthy; the literary essayist Lionel Trilling; Dwight Macdonald, an ideological firebrand and acerbic political journalist; and Meyer Schapiro, Clement Greenberg, and Harold Rosenberg, all of whom addressed central questions pertaining to modern culture as well as modern art. But by the decade of the 1950s those little-known mavericks and rebels had entered the mainstream of American high culture, and *Partisan Review*

was the nation's most influential literary-political magazine.

Although William Phillips is himself an accomplished literary and cultural critic whose forte is evaluating subjects in their historical context, he has never been a prolific writer, and it is his editorship of *PR*, as his journal was popularly known in its heyday, that has established his importance in American letters. And in his memoir, *A Partisan View: Five Decades of the Literary Life* (Stein and Day, 1983), Phillips records the lives and the often fractious ideological battles of the intellectuals who formed the charmed circle of *Partisan Review*.

Just as the "story" of William Phillips' life is inseparable from the history of *Partisan Review*, his origins are in key respects typical of those of the first generation of writers who were the nucleus of his magazine: his birth to Jewish emigrants from Eastern Europe; his growing up in the Bronx, which earlier in this century, as Phillips notes in his memoir, was "the dumping ground . . . for European immigrants, as it is now for blacks and Puerto Ricans"; and his escape to Manhattan via matriculation at City College, the "poor boy's steppingstone to the world," to quote Phillips. It is typical, too, that Phillips' cultural attitudes should have been formed in the 1920s, the decade when the modernist movement in the arts solidified, and that his views matured in the 1930s, when, in the depths of the Depression, he was swept into the Communist movement (although he never joined the Communist party).

Phillips, who refuses to divulge his date of birth, was born in Manhattan to Russian immigrants, his mother, Marie Berman, having come from Kiev and his father, Edward Litvinsky, from Odessa. His father took the name "Phillips" on the advice of fellow immigrants, who felt "Litvinsky" was an unsuitable surname in America, and who also persuaded him to become an attorney—the profession for which he was, as Phillips said, "least suited." When Phillips was one year old his parents separated, and his mother returned with her only child to Kiev, where they lived for three years with her large extended family. On returning to the Bronx, they were reunited with Phillips' father, who, a few years later, moved the family to Rockaway, Long Island, where he entertained fantasies of becoming a judge. However, as Phillips recalled in *A Partisan View*, "All that happened was that my father lost what little law practice he had in the Bronx." The family moved back to that borough and eventually settled into a fourth-floor walkup apartment on Crotona Park East, where they stayed "precariously, often unable to pay the rent, until [Phillips] got out of college."

Attending the then predominantly Jewish P.S. 40 and, later, Morris High School, Phillips was an "A" student until his senior year, when he lapsed into a period of intellectual languor. Substituting sports and daydreams of inordinate athletic and sexual prowess for books and ideas, Phillips seems to have sought escape from an unpleasant, even bizarre, home life. His father, having failed utterly as a "provider," dabbled superficially in philosophies ranging from Yoga and Christian Science to "dematerialization"—all of which had the effect of keeping reality at bay. Phillips' mother, too, suffered from a lack of a sense of reality, with her "search for another world," as Phillips termed it, taking the form of hypochondria (though she was to live to the age of ninety-six). Nor was the presence of Phillips' maternal grandmother in the household a stabilizing force. A cunning, strong-willed, cantankerous woman, she viewed her son-in-law with contempt and passed up no opportunity to turn her daughter against him.

Nevertheless, in his senior year at City College Phillips discovered T. S. Eliot's *The Sacred Wood*, a collection of essays that introduced him to modernism and dispelled his malaise. While studying for his master's degree and also teaching English on a part-time basis, at New York University he began to read the seminal modernists, from Baudelaire and Yeats through Joyce, Pound, and Mann, to educate his eyes with Picasso, Mondrian, and Kandinsky, and "to [soak] up all the criticism and aesthetics [he] could lay [his] hands on." Also at NYU, Phillips encountered the still flourishing bohemian subculture of Greenwich Village, and in the first years of the Great Depression he became politicized—significantly, not by a visceral response to the blighting of lives caused by hard times, but by reading such liberal journals of opinion as the *Nation* and the *New Republic*.

By 1933 Phillips had begun to attend meetings of the John Reed Club, a left-wing organization of writers and painters, and soon became secretary of the New York branch. It was about this time that he met Philip Rahv, a Jewish emigrant from Eastern Europe who was also absorbed in militant politics and was receptive to avant-garde culture. Both Rahv and Phillips had begun to write for *The New Masses*, a sectarian left-wing magazine, but, appalled by its crude party-line and agitprop aesthetics, they decided to start their own, more sophisticated journal. "We were cocky kids," Phillips recalled, "driven by a grandiose idea of launching a new literary movement, combining . . . the best of the new radicalism with the innovative energy of modernism."

The first issue of *Partisan Review* appeared in February 1934, and this, its "Stalinist phase," as Phillips calls it, lasted through eight more issues, until the fall of 1936. In those intervening two-and-a-half years, however, Phillips and Rahv had become disillusioned with Communism in all its forms. As the official organ of the John Reed Club, *Partisan Review* was under constant pressure to subordinate literary standards to the expediencies of the Soviet-dictated party line—and Phillips and Rahv could not stomach the vulgarity of condemning T. S. Eliot as a "reactionary" who wrote on behalf of ruling-class interests while inflating the reputations of "proletarian" novelists like Mike Gold and Jack Conroy. And in addition to seeing Communism—especially Stalinist Communism—

as inimical to the concept of the autonomy of art, *Partisan's* editors now realized that democratic socialist ideals were also incompatible with orthodox Marxism.

The first issue of the new *Partisan Review* came out in December 1937. With Phillips and Rahv serving as founding fathers and chief theoreticians, the renovated editorial board included such independent spirits as F. W. Dupee, Dwight Macdonald, Mary McCarthy, and George L. K. Morris, a talented abstract painter of independent means who helped finance what was a shoestring, issue-to-issue operation. With a "debut" number containing pieces by, among others, Delmore Schwartz, Lionel Trilling, and Edmund Wilson, *PR* announced itself as unique among the "little magazines," inasmuch as its allegiances went to both experimentalism in the arts and social and political thought that was uncompromisingly radical. As Phillips later observed, *Partisan Review* stood for "purity in politics and impurity in literature."

Because the revival of *Partisan Review* coincided with the Popular Front's peak of influence among New York intellectuals, the Communist press mounted a campaign of abuse against Phillips and Rahv, slandering them as "Trotskyites, counterrevolutionaries, literary snakes, [and] agents of imperialism," to quote Phillips. In that atmosphere of violent polemics, Phillips and Rahv, who were not political virgins, responded in kind. According to social historian Christopher Lasch, the two editors "earned from American intellectuals a lasting debt of gratitude by exposing the totalitarian character of Soviet Communism . . . at a time when not only radicals but many liberals still looked to [Stalinist Russia] as the hope of the world."

In those years the Marxist-influenced *PR* intellectuals interpreted their experience in terms of their "alienation," and his skirmishes with the sectarian left seem to have reinforced Phillips' sense of himself as an outsider. "I was," he reflected in *A Partisan View*, "a disaffected writer and an editor of an against-the-grain publication. I was a Jew. I believed in modernism, which at that time was outside the dominant culture. I had become an anti-Communist after a brief flirtation with the party, [and that shift] was not very fashionable."

Besides exposing the brutality of Stalinism, in the late 1930s and early 1940s Phillips and his editorial confreres battled tirelessly against provincial and philistine currents in American culture. To oppose the undercurrent of populistic nationalism in the American character, they opened their pages to European and English modernists like Ignazio Silone, George Orwell, Franz Kafka, Nicola Chiaromonte, and Stephen Spender, and, after World War II, to Jean-Paul Sartre, Simone de Beauvoir, Arthur Koestler, and Albert Camus. Thus, *PR* contributed to the "internationalization" of American culture and kept alive the idea of an artistic avant-garde at a time when both left and right trumpeted the virtues of cultural "Americanism."

In 1943 disagreements among the editorial board led to the resignation of Dwight Macdonald, who wanted *PR* to become more political and less "literary," and who did not support an American victory in World War II. Strongly influenced at that time by Trotskyism, Macdonald argued that the war was a conflict between rival capitalist states, a struggle for worldwide economic supremacy, whereas Rahv maintained that fascism must be defeated, notwithstanding the systemic flaws of the Allied powers. Despite Phillips' ambivalence—he was wary of any postwar settlement that would enhance the power of the Soviet Union and leave American capitalism intact—he, too, offered passive support of the war effort. Phillips now views the taking of that position as marking the end of his traditional Marxism, for the realization that he and other radical intellectuals had a personal as well as a political stake in an American victory was to lead to the partial endorsement of nationalist impulses.

By the late 1940s, *Partisan Review* had "clawed its way to cultural strength," as Irving Howe put it in his autobiography *A Margin of Hope* (1982). "The magazine could now hoist reputations, push a young writer into prominence, and deal out punishment to philistines, middlebrows, and fellow travelers. Because it stood for something, *Partisan Review* gained influence." In those years *PR* published important new European writers like Hannah Arendt, Sartre, and Camus. William Barrett, a young philosopher who became an associate editor in 1945, introduced contemporary existentialism to North American readers, and talented young Americans like Robert Lowell, Saul Bellow, Norman Mailer, Elizabeth Hardwick, James Baldwin, Bernard Malamud, and Norman Podhoretz began to appear in its pages. The review also helped to disseminate the ideas of the New Criticism by publishing such Southern writers as Allen Tate and Robert Penn Warren, and in the art criticism of Clement Greenberg abstract expressionism received its first serious attention outside of the then tiny New York art world.

In the postwar years of the Cold War, Phillips and his associates also stood for support of the United States government's policy of containment of Communism. Phillips believed that large segments of the American liberal establishment harbored attitudes that amounted to appeasement of the Soviet Union, and he even feared that the progressives' blindness to the totalitarian character and expansionist aims of the U.S.S.R. threatened to produce what Lionel Trilling decried as "the Stalinization of the liberal mind." Accordingly, Phillips was a charter member of the American Committee for Cultural Freedom, which was founded in 1951 and did not disband until 1963, and he served for many years on the executive board of that association of prominent anti-Communists.

Although consistently a left-wing anti-Communist, Phillips, decades later, was harshly criticized by Lillian Hellman for his activities during the 1950s. In her book *Scoundrel Time* (1976),

Hellman accused *PR* anti-Communists of having failed to defend her and others who were victimized by congressional investigations of alleged Communists, and of having failed to speak out against Senator Joe McCarthy, the demagogic leader of the so-called witch hunts. In his memoir, though, Phillips pointed out that his journal *had* editorialized against McCarthy and had published numerous anti-McCarthy articles as well. Phillips admitted that his anti-Communism may have carried him, on occasion, too far to the right, but he asserted that he did not come to the aid of Communists because "what one was asked to defend was their right to lie about it. . . . It was not just a case of defending people with whom we disagreed but who had similar aims. The Communists . . . had betrayed the principles socialists, liberals, and humanists of any kind shared."

By the early 1960s, when the avant-garde was becoming institutionalized, the circle of vanguard writers around *PR* had, as Phillips said, "moved out of their intellectual ghetto and become more worldly." In 1963 *Partisan Review* became affiliated with Rutgers University in New Jersey. Despite its cultural influence, the quarterly review had existed precariously, operating with a small staff and, often, a budget deficit. Because Rahv was uninterested in the less glamorous aspects of publishing and feigned total incompetence in practical matters, administrative responsibilities had fallen on Phillips' shoulders. Consequently, the move from Greenwich Village to Rutgers gave Phillips more free time (he became professor of English with release time for magazine work) and strengthened his hand in editorial quarrels with Rahv. Their disagreements had become increasingly rancorous over the years and were exacerbated by the upheavals of the 1960s.

A brilliant editor and polemicist and a gifted literary critic, Rahv nevertheless was, William Barrett has claimed, "a dark and faintly menacing character" who schemed and maneuvered constantly to increase his "power" in the intellectual community. Since the late 1950s, however, he had been devoting less and less of his time to *PR*, leaving Phillips as de facto editor in chief. But in 1965, when Rahv returned with a vengeance to the radicalism of his youth, he initiated a lawsuit, challenging the editorial board's recent election of Phillips to the position of chief editor. A legal settlement was reached that ratified the editorial rights of both men, but they ceased to collaborate, for as Rahv moved left—"No one else was radical enough or [pure] enough to meet his revolutionary standards," Phillips trenchantly observed—his literary views became more conservative. In 1969, three years before his death, Rahv started a new journal, and Phillips was designated editor of *Partisan Review*, the position he continues to hold.

According to Phillips, the turbulent decade of the 1960s was "a trying period for me, for *Partisan Review*, for those of us who had our roots in earlier eras and traditions." In literature the journal continued to publish up-and-coming writers, including

Susan Sontag, whose influential essay "Notes on 'Camp'" first appeared in PR, Christopher Lasch, Morris Dickstein, and Richard Poirier, all of whom joined Phillips' editorial board. All of those writers possessed the feeling for older traditions that were central to the spirit and substance of PR, but each in varying degrees—and often to Phillips' discomfort—flirted with the nascent counterculture and the New Left, which challenged assumptions held dear by earlier culture critics.

Added to those pressures from the left was the swing to the right of former liberals, many of whom, especially William Barrett, Norman Podhoretz, and Diana Trilling, had been core members of the Partisan Review "family." As the decade wore on, political life became more polarized, and Phillips found himself and his magazine under attack from both flanks—from the left, because PR allegedly went too far in accommodating itself to American values, and from the new conservatives, who accused Phillips of kowtowing to the fashionable radicalism of the New Left. Phillips occasionally tried to act as a mediator between those two warring factions, but his efforts failed. And although he succeeded in steering a middle course between the two extremes, the schismatic decade aggravated what Phillips called his "feelings of loneliness and uprootedness, of being an outsider."

Partisan Review's association with Rutgers came to a stormy end when a new university administration, in a budget-tightening move, ordered the journal off the campus by mid-1978. Phillips quickly found a new sponsor, Boston University, but when Rutgers officials discovered that PR's valuable files would accompany the journal to its new home, a flurry of court orders ensued and the magazine's office was padlocked and occupied by police. Phillips moved his staff to Boston, but Rutgers had the files impounded, contending that they had been "donated" to its library. In December 1979, as the result of court proceedings that Phillips likened to a "theater of the absurd," the files were returned to Phillips after Rutgers had been allowed to microfilm them.

Unlike many of his past colleagues, Phillips has not embraced neoconservatism, and in A Partisan View he sharply responds to Norman Podhoretz and William Barrett, whose recent memoirs, according to Phillips, distort aspects of his own and his magazine's history. In Breaking Ranks (1979) Podhoretz accused Phillips of betraying the anti-Communist faith, speculating that the editor's motives were fear of ostracism—or even of criticism—by the left. In The Truants (1982) Barrett argued that Phillips had simply failed to follow the logic of his anti-Communism to its inevitable conclusion—neoconservatism. But, according to Phillips, he was "never afraid of becoming a neoconservative. What was there to be afraid of? We were always being criticized by the left. And now, after all, the neoconservatives have been riding high." More important, Phillips maintains that the neoconservative position is fraught with contradictions. In their opposition to "alienation, . . . bohemians,

. . . affirmative action, the women's movement, homosexuals, [and] abortion," the neoconservatives have, in Phillips' view, idealized "the norms of respectability" in a way that solves nothing. Moreover, in their celebration of the virtues of American free enterprise, the neoconservatives seem blind to the role of unrestrained American consumerism in disrupting what Phillips calls "a sense of order and purpose and moral values."

Phillips believes that, in the 1980s, "we are all living out the unsolved problems—intellectual as well as political—first posed [in the 1930s]," and in his memoir he darkly meditates on current trends and their implications. His pessimism stems from the fact that seemingly implacable forces have "tended to break down the very notion of intellectual authority" and to undermine traditional humanist values as well. "In the Communist countries," he writes, "the channels of dissidence, political idealism, revolt, even the normal channels of reform as well as disaffection have been bottled up. In the West, the traditional forms of protest and change have been distorted [in part by] the insatiable appetites of the market. . . . Hence the incessant demand for novelty, the lack of interest in the past, and the confusion of quantity with quality." Phillips thinks that it is perhaps realistic now only to hope that "things do not get worse—that the status quo is maintained. What a contradiction one has arrived at: to have been brought up on the necessities of history and now to be drawn psychologically and politically to the stability that exists only outside of history."

His convictions have from time to time taken Phillips to the fringes of the world of electoral politics. He actively supported the New York City mayoral campaign of the liberal John V. Lindsay in 1966; set up, with George Plimpton, a committee of writers for Robert F. Kennedy during the late senator's 1968 run for the Democratic party's presidential nomination; and in 1976, again with Plimpton, cochaired a writers' committee for Jimmy Carter. In 1967 he took part in discussions that led to the founding of the Coordinating Council of Literary Magazines, serving as chairman of the organization from 1967 to 1975, when, as he put it, he was "kicked upstairs" and given the title of honorary president.

Despite his criticism of Phillips' liberalism, in The Truants William Barrett portrays his former editor as a warm and brilliant man whose "conversation flow[s] like a radiant and sparkling stream." According to Barrett, a writer's block descended on Phillips when he was a young man and never relinquished its grip. However, that "tragedy," as Barrett calls it, "may have been the self-defeating fruition of [Phillips'] own powers of intelligence." He was a formidable dialectician who could "enter into a discussion, even when he had not read the materials at issue . . . and soon be directing the flow of argument, skipping nimbly from one side or the other as it pleased him. But this brilliance to argue either side of a question exacted its toll; it brought with it a . . . quality of detachment and sterile skepticism that had more hold over him than he was aware."

In addition to writing *A Partisan View*, Phillips is the author of *A Sense of the Present* (Chilmark Press, 1967), a collection of his essays, most of which had appeared in *Partisan Review* and *Commentary* magazine. He has edited numerous volumes of short fiction and, with Rahv, three anthologies of writings from *PR*. He has taught at several leading universities, including the New School for Social Research, the University of Minnesota, and Sarah Lawrence College, and has held the rank of professor at Boston University since 1978. His wife is the former Edna M. Greenblatt, whom he married when he was a graduate student.

References: Commentary N '68; N Y Rev of Books p14+ S 12 '68; N Y Times C p17 Ag 9 '78, C p17 D 26 '83; Gilbert, James Burkhart. Writers and Partisans: A History of Literary Radicalism in America (1968); Who's Who in America, 1982–83

Ponnamperuma, Cyril (Andrew)

Oct. 16, 1923– Chemist; educator. Address: b. Laboratory of Chemical Evolution, University of Maryland, College Park, Md. 20742

In the course of two decades of research, the world-renowned exobiologist and chemist Cyril Ponnamperuma has explored the challenging and multifaceted mystery of the origin of life. Exploiting dramatic advances in molecular biology, astrophysics, and micropaleontology, among other disciplines, Ponnamperuma has constructed a convincing theory about the series of chemical reactions that gave rise to the precursors of life on this planet and, even more important, has duplicated those reactions in the laboratory through experiments that recreate the atmosphere of the primordial earth. His analyses of meteorites and the atmospheres of other planets have led him to conclude that the process of chemical evolution that generated life on earth might have occurred elsewhere in the universe as well. How life has begun,

Ponnamperuma has noted, "is a question which has been for ages in the mind of the philosopher and the theologian. But today we dare to approach this subject in a strictly scientific and experimental manner."

Cyril Andrew Ponnamperuma was born on October 16, 1923 in Galle, Ceylon, the tiny island country, now called Sri Lanka, that lies off the coast of India, to Andrew and Grace (Siriwardene) Ponnamperuma. His parents were both educators who, he recalled in an interview with John Langone for *Discover* magazine (November 1983), believed that "what really matters are things of the mind." His curiosity about science and the natural world may have been awakened by a scientist-uncle who solved differential calculus problems as a pastime and "drove home the fun of doing science" by performing such simple chemical feats as producing a silver coin by dipping a copper one in mercury.

Following his parents' wishes, Ponnamperuma studied philosophy at the University of Madras in India, where he received his B.A. degree in 1948. Returning to Galle, he taught science at St. Aloysius' College until 1951, when he determined to seek a more lucrative career as a chemist. While crediting his background in philosophy with giving him a viewpoint different from that of most organic chemists, Ponnamperuma has also said: "It's nice to think I couldn't find the answers in philosophy, so I turned to science, but that isn't really the case. I've always been interested in chemistry."

Pursuing that interest at the University of London's Birkbeck College, Ponnamperuma studied under the renowned crystallographer J. D. Bernal, a pioneer in the study of the origins of life. While working there for his B.Sc. degree, which he received with honors in 1959, he was employed from 1952 to 1954 as a research chemist for B. X. Plastics, Ltd., and at Bunzy & Biach, and from 1955 to 1959 as a radiochemist in the radioisotope laboratory at London Hospital. His involvement in the field of chemical evolution, spurred by his studies with Bernal, intensified during his years at the University of California at Berkeley as a research associate at the Lawrence Radiation Laboratory and as a graduate student under the Nobel laureate Melvin Calvin, who conducted experiments simulating the primordial atmosphere of the earth in an attempt to discover how the chemical bases necessary for life were created.

In 1962 Ponnamperuma obtained his Ph.D. degree and, as a result of a National Academy of Sciences award, began a one-year resident associateship at the Ames Research Center of the National Aeronautics and Space Administration (NASA), located at Moffett Field, California. He continued to work at the Ames Research Center as a research scientist in its exobiology division through 1963 and was promoted in 1965 to chief of its chemical evolution branch, the primary purpose of which is the study of the origin of life.

In an article for *Nature* (January 25, 1964), Ponnamperuma wrote that the centuries-old concept of the biological unity of all life, strengthened by Darwin's studies in the nineteenth century, forms the "cornerstone of modern biology." Taken one step further, that logically points to a common chemical basis for all life as well, since the two primary components of organic matter, nucleic acid and protein, are chemical compounds. Scientists had long known that if the mystery of the origin of life on this planet were to be solved they had to discover how the chemical components of those two basic molecules were formed, how they linked together to produce nucleic acid and protein, and how, in turn, those molecules joined to create self-replicating—that is, organic or living—molecules. Two scientific breakthroughs in 1953 gave enormous impetus to practical research in chemical evolution. At the University of Chicago, Stanley L. Miller and Harold C. Urey subjected for several days a "primordial soup"—a mixture of methane, ammonia, hydrogen, and water vapor supposed to have comprised the atmosphere of pre-biotic earth—to electric sparks that simulated the energy of lightning. Analyzing the result, they detected traces of amino acids, the building blocks of protein. The discovery by Francis Crick and James Watson of the structure of deoxyribonucleic acid (DNA), a component of nucleic acid, gave a further clue in the search for life's precursors. According to Watson and Crick, DNA consists of a double helix chain of nucleotides; a phosphate, a sugar, and one of four bases—adenine, cytosine, guanine, or thymine—make up each nucleotide. Those findings formed the basis of the experiments of Melvin Calvin and of Ponnamperuma himself.

Stimulating and important results from Ponnamperuma's researches were not slow in coming. In 1963 he and his colleagues reported that adenine had been created in the laboratory under the pre-biotic "primordial soup" conditions. Ponnamperuma's team had adjusted the Miller-Urey formula somewhat, decreasing the amount of hydrogen and bombarding the mixture with high-energy electrons that approximated the energy of cosmic rays striking the primitive earth. Later that year, they subjected that hydrogen-poor mixture to ultraviolet light, such as the sun emits, and produced adenosine triphosphate (ATP), the major source of energy for cells. ATP, the most complex molecule synthesized in a lab up to that time, was produced

so abundantly during the experiment that Ponnamperuma considered it the likely source of energy for all life forms before the development of photosynthesis. The larger implications of that and similar research hardly escaped Ponnamperuma. "Such experiments," he explained, "are lending significant support to the theory that biological molecules, which are the prerequisites of life, could have appeared by the interaction of forces and materials which existed on earth before life did."

Ponnamperuma announced further advances in 1965. Still working with primordial soup, he had produced at separate times all five nucleotides that comprise nucleic acid: the four that constitute DNA as well as the uracil-based nucleotide found in nucleic acid's other component, ribonucleic acid (RNA). In addition, he and his colleague Ruth Mack had bonded together up to three uracil-based nucleotides during the experiment. The team achieved best results when they used a bed of clay like that which probably formed as tidal flats dried up on earth billions of years ago.

A significant rationale for basic research into chemical evolution during the 1960s was provided by NASA's interest in possible forms of life, or potentially life-generating environments, to be found in outer space. As an exobiologist—a scientist who investigates extraterrestrial life systems—Ponnamperuma had goals in studying primitive atmospheres that were linked to the broader aspects of space research. Consequently, as a principal scientific investigator for NASA, Ponnamperuma analyzed samples of lunar soil returned by the 1969 Apollo 12 space mission and data relayed to earth from Mars by the Viking 1 and 2 spacecraft in 1976. While neither of those studies indicated the existence of precursors or remnants of life on the moon or Mars, Ponnamperuma remained optimistic about the possibility of extraterrestrial life.

In preparation for an exploration of Jupiter in the 1970s by NASA's Pioneer and Voyager space probes, Ponnamperuma and his team conducted experiments whose results lent weight to his hypothesis that chemical evolution and the generation of life were not necessarily limited to earth. In articles that appeared in the scientific and popular press as early as 1967, he reported that by directing an electrical charge into a mixture of methane and ammonia, supposed to be the principal components of Jupiter's upper atmosphere, his team had produced nineteen precursors of amino acids. Furthermore, with the addition of water, which the scientists thought was available in a lower layer of the giant planet's deep atmosphere, various amino acids were formed. As additional support for the contention that life could arise in Jupiter's seemingly hostile environment, they exposed bacteria and yeast to the pressures of a simulated Jovian atmosphere; most of those microorganisms survived. In an article entitled "Life on Jupiter?" written with Peter Molton for *New Scientist* (December 6, 1973), Ponnamperuma concluded: "If ordinary terrestrial organisms can survive the rigors of the Jovian climate, life evolved under such conditions should find Jupiter a comfortable haven."

Ponnamperuma's suppositions about the make-up of Jupiter's atmosphere and the organic compounds it might contain were supported by photographs taken by Voyager 1 and 2 in 1979 that showed that the colors of the clouds surrounding the planet closely resembled the browns and yellows produced in his experiments with the Jovian primordial soup. He also conjectured that Jupiter's long-studied and controversial red spot might be similar to the red polymers formed in those laboratory tests.

Another long-term project presented itself to Ponnamperuma in the shape of a meteorite that fell to earth on September 28, 1969, landing in Murchison, Australia. Scientists had been intrigued for over a century by "carbonaceous chondrites"—rare meteorites containing traces of carbon, the element common to all life and the basis of organic chemistry—and some had even claimed to have found spore coats, lignite-like matter, or other signs of life or its precursors in various meteorites, but critics contended they were only terrestrial contaminants. The Murchison meteorite, however, was a prime specimen for study, especially since it was retrieved by scientists while still lukewarm and therefore unlikely to have been contaminated by terrestrial organic matter. Ponnamperuma and other scientists subjected fragments to various tests such as gas chromatography and mass spectrometry in order to reveal its chemical composition. At least sixteen amino acids were found at first, including five of the twenty existing on earth in living matter.

More important, the properties of those amino acids, eleven of which had no known function in earthly organisms, ruled out the possibility that they were contaminants. Although amino acids in terrestrial life forms are "left-handed," that is, in solution they will deflect a beam of polarized light to the left, the samples from the 4.5 billion-year-old meteorite showed an even distribution of left-handed and rare right-handed molecules. "We don't know why nature's like this," Ponnamperuma admitted in a New York Times profile (February 23, 1982). "It may have something to do with conditions back at the time life first emerged, something about the primordial chemistry that favored left-handedness. Who knows?" he added with a smile, "God may be left-handed." The optical properties of the molecules as well as the unusually high proportion of carbon-13 isotopes detected in them led him to conclude that the Murchison meteorite provided "the first conclusive proof of extraterrestrial chemical evolution." In addition, the age of the meteorite indicated that chemical precursors of life have existed since the creation of the solar system. Using the same methods to screen for contaminants, Ponnamperuma and his team at the Ames Research Center detected in the Murray meteorite, which had fallen at Murray, Kentucky on September 20, 1950, the very same amino acids. "This identical pattern of amino

acids and pyrimidines in two meteorites," he explained, "could mean that this is a basic phase in the chemical process leading to life."

In 1971 Ponnamperuma joined the faculty of the University of Maryland as professor of chemistry and director of its new Laboratory of Chemical Evolution, which had been established with the support of NASA and the National Science Foundation (NSF). While continuing his study of the Murchison meteorite, in 1977 he began to take part in a NASA-NSF-sponsored project to collect meteorites from the contaminant-free environment of Antarctica. Samples of such meteorites also contained amino acids of extraterrestrial origin. A more controversial discovery concerned 3.83-billion-year-old rocks, recovered from a remote part of Greenland, that were found to contain hydrocarbons. Tests conducted by Ponnamperuma indicated that those hydrocarbons, also 3.83-billion years old, had been produced by photosynthesis. That dating suggests that forms of life existed on earth 400-million years earlier than had been previously thought and is disputed by some scientists, who believe that the fossils found in the Greenland rocks were more recent contaminants.

At a meeting of the American Chemical Society in the summer of 1983, Ponnamperuma reported that the Murchison meteorite had yielded further remarkable results. According to an article that appeared in the New York Times (August 30, 1983), Ponnamperuma asserted that through sophisticated procedures he had been able to identify in samples of the meteorite all five bases that comprise DNA and RNA. He also announced what he considered an even more significant breakthrough: in further experiments with primordial soup at the Laboratory of Chemical Evolution, he had synthesized "in one fell swoop" the same five nucleotides. Those results, according to Ponnamperuma, further supported the theory that the steps from nonlife to life were relatively simple and might have been made wherever conditions in the universe were right. However, he cautioned, according to the New York Times, "We found only the precursors of life. We have not found life elsewhere. We have not made life in the laboratory."

The author of several hundred articles that have appeared in professional journals in the United States and abroad, Ponnamperuma has also written or edited, alone or in collaboration, about a dozen books. In addition, in 1970–72 he edited the journal Molecular Evolution, and from 1973 to 1982 he was editor of Origins of Life. He has received many honorary degrees and awards, including in 1980 the first A. I. Oparin Gold Medal of the International Society for the Study of the Origin of Life, of which society he was named president in 1983. He belongs to other professional organizations, among them the American Association for the Advancement of Science and the American Chemical Society. In addition to fulfilling his duties as director of the chemical evolution laboratory, he teaches graduate and undergraduate courses at the University of Maryland and lectures extensively to scientific and lay audiences on chemical evolution.

Cyril Ponnamperuma maintains an interest in his native land, traveling there four times a year and serving as a science adviser to Sri Lanka's president, J. R. Jayewardene. Concerned about world hunger, he belongs to the International Dambala Institute, which advocates wider cultivation in the tropics of the winged bean, a plant rich in vitamins, minerals, and protein that flourishes in Sri Lanka. Ponnamperuma, who became a naturalized United States citizen in 1967, married the former Valli Pal, a native of India, on March 19, 1955.

They have one daughter, Roshini Manel. Ponnamperuma is a voracious reader. "My wife tells me I'm married to chemistry," he explained to Bart Barnes of the *Washington Post* (February 15, 1979), "but I am interested in art and I do a little gardening." A Fellow of the Explorers Club, he is also a member of the Cosmos Club near his home in northwest Washington, D.C.

References: Discover 4:51+ N '83 pors; N Y Times p4 F 23 '82 por; Washington Post G p1+ F 15 '79 por; American Men and Women of Science (1982); Who's Who in America, 1984-85

Price, George (Cadle)

Jan. 15, 1919 Prime Minister of Belize. Address: b. Office of the Prime Minister, Belmopan, Belize

On September 21, 1981 the small tropical Central American nation of Belize—formerly the Crown colony of British Honduras—attained its independence within the British Commonwealth. The man most closely identified with Belize's quest for sovereignty is its prime minister, George Price, who helped to found the country's dominant People's United party in 1950 and served as its premier since 1964, when Great Britain granted internal self-government to the colony. Over the years, the main obstacle to Belizean independence has been the hostility of neighboring Guatemala, which claims Belize as part of its Spanish heritage and maintains that Great Britain had violated a treaty concluded in 1859 by failing to provide a transpor-

tation route through the colony from Guatemala City to the Caribbean Sea. Nevertheless, Price has managed to bring his 150,000 people into the family of nations, steering a "middle course" within the framework of what he calls a "peaceful, constructive Belizean revolution."

Of Scottish and Maya Indian ancestry, George Cadle Price was born on January 15, 1919, the third of the eleven children of William Cadle Price, an auctioneer, and of Irene Cecelia Escalante de Price, in the family's ramshackle wooden house in Belize City, in what was then British Honduras. Educated at the Holy Redeemer primary school and at St. John's College in his native city, Price also studied for a time in the United States, where he attended the St. Augustine Seminary in Bay St. Louis, Mississippi with the intention of becoming a Roman Catholic priest. When his father became ill in 1942 and was no longer able to work, Price ended his studies and took a job as a private secretary to Robert S. Turton, a local businessman, to support the family.

Entering politics in 1944, as a twenty-five-year-old candidate for the Belize City Council, Price was at first defeated, but he won election to the council in 1947 and remained on it for seventeen years. Also in 1947 he was elected president of the General Workers' Union, a post he held until 1952. When the British authorities devalued the British Honduras dollar in 1950 over the objections of local officials, Price helped to found the People's United party (PUP), which called for complete independence from Great Britain. He served as its secretary from 1950 until 1956, when he became party leader. In 1954 he was elected to the legislative assembly of British Honduras and became a member of the colony's executive council; from 1958 to 1962 he was mayor of Belize City.

In the elections of March 1957 Price led his PUP to victory over the colony's two other parties, winning all nine of the elected seats in the fifteen-member legislative assembly. Calling himself the head of the "liberation movement from the shackles of colonialism," Price opposed proposals that British Honduras join a West Indies federation and rejected the idea of economic integration, on the ground that such a move could lead to political incorporation. "The people are aware of the fact that this country is part and parcel of Central America, upon which its economic hopes depend," he told reporters after the elections.

Later in 1957 Price led a delegation to London to discuss economic aid and constitutional reforms with British officials. But the talks were broken off by Alan Lennox-Boyd, the British colonial secretary, because Price had allegedly held secret talks with the Guatemalan minister in London, who was said to have proposed that British Honduras sever its ties with the British Crown and become associated with Guatemala in a Central American federation. Although Price had reportedly insisted that the Guatemalan minister's proposals be made through the proper channels, and that any final decisions were up to the people, in December 1957 he was summarily dismissed from the executive council by Governor Colin Hardwick Thornby for "breaking his oath of loyalty to the Queen." Some 700 British troops were flown in to British Honduras from Bermuda about that time, to forestall a possible Guatemalan-inspired coup. Shortly after that, the legislative assembly of British Honduras passed a resolution reaffirming the colony's loyalty to Queen Elizabeth II and approved a motion of confidence in Price as leader of the majority party. In April 1958 Price was tried on charges of having made seditious statements about the British Crown, but he was acquitted.

In the elections of March 1, 1961—the first under a new constitution designed to give British Honduras eventual independence within the Commonwealth—the PUP won all eighteen elective seats in the newly expanded twenty-five-member legislative assembly, and Price took on the title of first minister. By that time he had come to reject Guatemala's claims outright, so that when the Guatemalan consul in Belize suggested in August 1961 that Guatemalan president Miguel Ydigoras Fuentes be invited for an official visit, Price turned him down.

In July 1963 Price headed a delegation to London for a constitutional conference with the Colonial Office. The resulting document provided for internal self-government for British Honduras effective in January of the following year, under a ministerial system headed by a premier, and a national assembly consisting of an elected eighteen-member House of Representatives and an appointed eight-member Senate. When Price took over as premier on January 1, 1964, British Honduras was faced with many problems, not the least of which was a deficit in foreign trade. A recent hurricane, which had destroyed much of Belize City, had also devastated about one-third of the mahogany reserves, a major factor in the economy. Furthermore, there was the persistent claim of Guatemala to sovereignty over British Honduras, prompting Great Britain to continue to station troops there. Nevertheless, Price insisted that independence as a member of the Commonwealth was within reach. He even suggested that the country might become part of a Central American federation, "but never as a dependency of Guatemala."

In the campaign for the first election under the new constitution, scheduled for March 1, 1965, Price pledged to bring the country to independence within two or three years. He was opposed by Philip Goldson, head of the National Independence party (NIP), which despite its name favored indefinite postponement of independence, pending the establishment of a more solid economic base. Interviewed shortly before the election, Price emphasized his commitment to his party's Christian Democratic ideology of evolutionary economic and social reforms. Contrasting conditions in British Honduras with those that had prevailed in British Guiana under Marxist premier Cheddi Jagan, Price asserted: "We are obtaining our objective peacefully. . . . We do not have race problems here." Taking 57 percent of the popular vote, Price's PUP won sixteen of the eighteen seats in the House of Representatives. He was formally sworn in as premier on March 3, 1965. Predicting an economic upturn despite continued economic adversity, Price negotiated for private capital investment to implement a seven-year development plan, begun in 1964. Because of his concern about the possible effects of Cuban propaganda broadcasts on his compatriots, he asserted in early 1966: "We have to show the people that what Communism can do for the country Christian Democracy can do better."

In May 1968 Price rejected a plan for an association between Guatemala and British Honduras on the ground that it would limit the country's freedom. Worked out over a three-year period by Bethuel M. Webster, a United States authority on international law, the program called for an independent British Honduras by 1971, and for collaboration between it and Guatemala in matters of defense, foreign affairs, communications, and economic development, with Guatemala assuming the "big brother" role. The proposal was abandoned both by Great Britain and by Guatemala, which continued to claim sovereignty over the colony.

By the early 1970s, British Honduras—or Belize, as it became formally known in June 1973—seemed to have all the prerequisites for independence, including a flag, a national anthem, and the institutions that go along with a stable government. In August 1970 the new Mayan-styled capital city of Belmopan, located some fifty miles inland to safeguard it from hurricanes, went into operation, and in May 1971 Belize became the twelfth member of the Caribbean Free Trade Association. But continuing friction with Guatemala forced a postponement of Price's plans for early independence.

Responding to a buildup of Guatemala's troops along its border with Belize in 1972, the British augmented their military forces there, while Price doubled the size of the territory's special paramilitary forces in its police department. Under pressure from the Organization of American States, Great Britain agreed to withdraw its troops and accept OAS mediation. In the view of Price, the Guatemalan action underscored the need for an international guarantee of his country's independence. "An independent Belize can't stand up against any Central American country," Price was quoted in the *Wall Street Journal* (June 22, 1972) as saying. "What we are trying to do is work up an independent agreement on an international basis, so that not only the United Kingdom would come to our defense, but also the United States, Canada, Mexico, and Jamaica."

Reports in the mid-1970s of possible petroleum deposits in Belize prompted Guatemala to step up its diplomatic efforts among Latin American nations for its claims on the country, which it equated with Argentine claims to the British-held Falkland Islands. Meanwhile, Price gained some backing for his demands from the nonaligned movement, whose representatives, meeting in Lima, Peru in August 1975, resolved to support Belizean independence, and from the United Nations General Assembly, which in December passed a resolution reaffirming "the inalienable right of the people of Belize to self-determination and independence." Support also came from the Cuban government of Fidel Castro, and from the Panamanian military leader, Brigadier General Omar Torrijos.

On the domestic scene, Price suffered setbacks as the opposition, now organized into a coalition known as the United Democratic party (UDP), under the lawyer Dean Lindo, made considerable headway in national assembly elections and won control of the Belize City Council. Government spokesmen charged the UDP with playing into the hands of the Guatemalans by maintaining that Belizeans did not want independence, while UDP spokesmen expressed concern that Price might suspend elections, institute a one-party system, and bring Belize into an alliance with Cuba. Defying a government ban, hundreds of UDP backers staged an anti-independence rally in Belize City in July 1977, bearing placards that read: "God Bless Our Queen," "Referendum Before Independence," or "To Hell With George Price."

In January 1978 Price went to London for discussions with Foreign Secretary David Owen, during which it was proposed that Belize cede to Guatemala 300 square miles of land and 700 square miles of sea at its southern end in return for a pledge by Guatemala that it would relinquish its previous claim to sovereignty over all of Belize. Price flatly rejected the proposal, asserting that Great Britain, with the support of the United States, wanted Belize to divest itself of an area larger than that of some independent Caribbean countries. He noted that under the arrangement Belize would be giving up territory with potentially valuable resources in return for vague promises.

In the local election of December 1978 the UDP won control of six of Belize's eight town councils, a result that UDP spokesmen attributed to popular dissatisfaction with the government's neglect of domestic issues. In the 1979 campaign for national elections, the PUP affirmed its demand for independence under security guarantees from Great Britain and the United States and called for social improvements, agrarian reform, and income redis-

tribution. Campaigning under the slogan "It's Time for a Change," the UDP advocated ambitious economic projects under a free-enterprise system and repeated earlier charges that the PUP had Communist tendencies. Meanwhile, government leaders at a Commonwealth conference held in Zambia in August 1979 declared their support for the "legitimate aspirations of the people of Belize for early and secure independence." The elections, in November 1979, resulted in a victory for Price's PUP, which won thirteen of the eighteen seats in the House of Representatives.

During 1980, there appeared to be some progress in negotiations between Guatemala and Great Britain concerning the future of Belize, but within the country, the opposition continued to criticize the government's aspirations for independence. When in early 1981 Price's PUP presented a draft constitution known as the White Paper, the UDP refused to take part in an effort by the government to canvass citizens for comments on the document.

In March 1981 representatives of Guatemala, Great Britain, and Belize signed the outlines of an agreement in London that was to give independence to Belize by the end of the year. Under its provisions, Guatemala was to be assured of access to the Caribbean and to Belize's two southernmost island groups, with mutual free port facilities and seabed mining rights, in return for recognition of Belize's existing frontiers. But the arrangement aroused violent protests in Belize, with UDP spokesmen charging that it constituted a "sellout" to Guatemala and demanding an immediate referendum on the question of independence. Continuing violence prompted Price to declare a state of emergency.

Nevertheless, independence talks were carried on in London during April 1981 by British and Belizean officials, who agreed on a constitution based largely on existing democratic institutions in Belize. But though it appeared for a time that an agreement was possible, negotiations collapsed in July after Guatemala demanded the right to establish military bases on the Belizean islands. When in early September 1981 Guatemala broke off consular relations with Great Britain and closed its border with Belize, the British government decided to go ahead unilaterally with independence, agreeing to maintain a defense force of some 1,600 men and a squadron of fighter planes on Belizean territory "for an appropriate time."

At midnight on September 21, 1981, to the accompaniment of parades, fireworks, reggae music, dancing, and a twenty-one gun salute, Belize formally became an independent nation within the British Commonwealth, ending more than three centuries of British colonial presence on the American mainland. After the lowering of the Union Jack and the raising of Belize's new red, white, and blue flag, Prince Michael of Kent, representing Queen Elizabeth II, handed the instruments of government over to Price, who in addition to the prime ministership also retained the portfolios of foreign affairs and of finance and development.

Dr. Minita Gordon, a Belizean sociologist, was appointed governor general of the new nation. Price's "middle course" in foreign affairs was emphasized by the fact that among the sixty-three countries that sent representatives to the ceremonies were Marxist Cuba, Nicaragua, and the Soviet Union, as well as the United States, whose fifteen-member delegation was headed by Assistant Secretary of State Thomas Enders. The ceremonies were boycotted by the UDC, and by Guatemala, which cast the only negative vote when Belize was admitted to the United Nations as the 156th member on September 25, 1981. Price offered a "hand of friendship" to Guatemala, declaring at a news conference that normalization of relations with its neighbor was his government's number-one priority.

Since independence, Belize's relations with Guatemala have not improved, despite continuing negotiation efforts, and membership for Belize in the Organization of American States must await resolution of its conflict with its neighbor. On the domestic scene, Price's PUP has continued to be challenged by the UDP, which in January 1984 won all nine seats on the Belize City Council. In response, Price shifted his cabinet to the left, at the same time relinquishing his economic development and foreign affairs portfolios.

Nevertheless, despite its poverty, Belize has comparatively favorable social and economic conditions. An effective church-state school system that Price helped to introduce has brought adult literacy up to about 90 percent. Religious and ethnic diversity has not resulted in much sectarian strife, and extremist political groups have little following. Although its once lucrative timber resources have been largely depleted, the country's modest economy—based to a large extent on sugar, citrus fruits, and other food crops, with some light industry—has been able to sustain the population and, with economic help from Great Britain, to generate a 5 percent annual growth rate. Moreover, the prospect of oil production has generated some guarded optimism among Belizeans.

A tall, slender bachelor who looks much younger than his years, George Price leads an austere lifestyle. He lives alone in a small bungalow similar to those occupied by junior civil servants, on a salary reported in 1981 to be only $8,000 a year. His gentle, soft-spoken, and unpretentious manner belies the energy with which he operates: he rises at five, attends mass daily, and travels extensively around the country in his old Land Rover. Over the years he has learned to know many of his compatriots by name. Price reads voraciously, writes poetry, listens to classical music, and plays the electric organ. In 1982 he was appointed to Great Britain's Privy Council.

References: N Y Times p3 S 23 '81 por; Washington Post p27 F 16 '81; International Who's Who, 1984–85; Who's Who, 1984–85; Who's Who in the World, 1982–83

Quennell, Peter (Courtney)

(kwĭn´ ′l)

Mar. 9, 1905– English writer. Address: 26 Cheyne Row, London, SW3, England

The gift that the English biographer and literary historian Peter Quennell values most highly in the creative individuals that he writes about—especially Hogarth, Byron, Ruskin, and Proust—is probably the capacity for seeing that enabled them to expand the vision of others. "A passionate observer," like those men, he has opened his readers' eyes in scores of books, as author and editor, and in several magazines, including *History Today*, of which he was coeditor for many years. Quennell's work as a whole imparts his enjoyment of art and literature and of art in literature with charm and wit and with what Harold Nicolson once praised as "an unobtrusive style which has all the elasticity and strength of silk."

Peter Courtney Quennell was born on March 9, 1905 to Charles Henry Bourne and Marjorie (Courtney) Quennell near Bromley, a borough of London, England. The oldest of three children, he had a sister, Gillian, and a brother, Paul. Their father was an architect and their mother a painter, but they are best known as social historians—the

joint authors and illustrators of a series of educational books, the most popular of which is *A History of Everyday Things in England* (1918–34). "My father was a man who loved quality—the quality of really sound workmanship," Peter Quennell wrote in *The Marble Foot: an Autobiography, 1905–1938* (Collins; Viking, 1976). He also had a drive for hard work that he transmitted to his son.

Soon after Peter's birth the family moved to the Bickley suburb of London, into a house of neo-Georgian façade, "Four Beeches," which his father had designed. There he spent an "extremely happy" early childhood, he has recalled, enjoying the garden and the tree house his father made for him. But his sensitivity to his surroundings was not entirely joyful. "Imagination, then as now, was both my Heaven and my Hell," he related in *The Marble Foot*; "and, once I had learned to read, at the age of four or five, not only its enchanting pleasures but its excruciating pains acquired, of course, a double strength." When he was about ten years old, a visit with his mother to France, where Rouen especially impressed him, led to his decision to become a writer.

His architectural practice having been diminished by the outbreak of World War I, C. H. B. Quennell had to sell "Four Beeches." By 1917 he had moved his family to the Hertfordshire town of Berkhamsted, eventually designing and building a not so comfortable house, "Crabtrees." Shortly before the war ended, Peter was transferred from his first school, St. Alfred's in London's Chislehurst, to Berkhamsted Grammar School, which he attended as a day student and whose headmaster was Charles Greene, father of Graham Greene.

Because he was alleged to be "highly strung" and "unduly sensitive," Quennell enjoyed several privileges at Berkhamsted, such as an exemption from sports. Fascinated with antiquity and brass-rubbing, he spent much of his spare time bicycling to old parish churches in the vicinity. He also wrote poetry in free verse, some of which appeared in the anthologies *Public School Verse* for 1920 and 1921. His work was included, moreover, along with pieces by Walter de la Mare, Robert Graves, D. H. Lawrence, and others, in Edward March's *Georgian Poetry, 1920–1922* (1922), the last in a then-famous series of poetry collections. Of his own contributions, all in free verse, to the volume, Quennell observed in *The Marble Foot*, "In each I was endeavouring to record a moment of visionary exaltation. . . . The result I aimed at was not an exact description of something I had felt or seen, but its symbolic equivalent, realized by the powers of language." A privately printed collection of his verse, illustrated with his own drawings, *Masques and Poems* (1922), added to his glory.

"An established protégé" at seventeen, to quote his phrase, Quennell was also in 1922 accepted at Oxford University and awarded an English literature scholarship. But on the advice of the authorities, he waited until October 1923, when he was eighteen, to enroll in Balliol College. In his recent memoir, *Customs and Characters: Contemporary Portraits* (Weidenfeld; Little, Brown, 1983), he described himself as having had "many of the silliest faults of a conceited Oxford aesthete." He attended only one lecture and limited his academic efforts to the composition of a weekly essay. But on his own, he read widely, began work on a biography of William Blake, and became friendly with or acquainted with Evelyn Waugh, Cyril Connolly, Anthony Powell, Kenneth Clark, and Edward Sackville-West, among other undergraduates who later contributed to England's intellectual wealth. His hedonistic diversions, however, involved him in a brief affair with a campus seductress that led to a term's suspension. He left Oxford forever in October 1925.

As if to console him for that disgrace, kind notices greeted Quennell's *Poems*, published by Chatto & Windus the following year. His only other book of adult verse, titled *Inscription on a Fountain-Head* (Ariel Series), followed in 1929. Perhaps it was the symbolic nature of his own poetry that made him receptive to a suggestion of T. S. Eliot that he write a book on the Symbolist Movement. When *Baudelaire and the Symbolists* (Chatto) appeared in 1929, a reviewer for the *Spectator* (December 28, 1929) judged it "a valuable series of studies" and praised Quennell's "delicacy of discrimination and interpretation" in his portraits of eight poets, but deplored his "artificial and clumsy style."

Quennell has acknowledged that the book was not well written, but he was determined to improve. As the excitement that had been his incentive for writing poetry began to fade, he turned his energy in the late 1920s to a mastery of prose and entered his apprenticeship as a literary reviewer for the *New Statesman*, whose editor, Desmond MacCarthy, usually assigned him books of verse and occasionally a novel or a biography. Quennell also contributed to *Life and Letters* and the *Criterion*. At a time of socially conscious writing, as he explained in *The Marble Foot*, he did not share the "puritanical distaste for style" of many young authors: "My main preoccupation was always with words and with their proper literary use. It was only through evolving a style, I thought, that I could discover what I had to say, and give any discoveries I made the necessary shape and substance."

In 1930 Quennell accepted an appointment as professor of English literature and language at the Tokyo Bunrika Diagaku, a Japanese government university primarily for teachers. He agreed to remain for three years, but, dissatisfied with the response of his students and with his constricted lifestyle at the university, he resigned in 1931. His travel book, *A Superficial Journey through Tokyo and Peking* (Faber, 1932), is an admittedly rather unsympathetic record of his Japanese experiences, along with a contrasting account of his visit to China.

While in Tokyo, Quennell worked on an "ambitious but ill-fated novel," as he described it. *The Phoenix-Kind* (Chatto, 1931), according to E. B. C. Jones in the *Adelphi* (August 1931), is an "extremely clever, sophisticated," and deliberately flat presentation of the futile triangular relationship of Virginia, Julian, and Paul, on which Quennell's talents had been "thrown away." He also published a collection of smoothly crafted tales, *Sympathy and Other Stories* (Faber, 1933). To earn a living, on his return to London he had resumed his flow of essays and literary reviews to the *New Statesman* and *Life and Letters*.

The work, meanwhile, that satisfied Quennell's need for more durable achievement involved his deep, almost compulsive, preoccupation with the life of George Gordon, Lord Byron. In the study that he regards as his first truly mature book, *Byron: the Years of Fame* (Faber; Viking, 1935; 3d revised edition, 1967), he covered the poet's stay in England from the summer of 1811 to the spring of 1816. Quennell's access to unpublished private papers and his sympathy with his subject account for some of the freshness in the penetrating analysis of character that earned his book favorable attention in both England and the United States. In its sequel, *Byron in Italy* (Collins; Viking, 1941), Quennell again brought a light touch to his scholarship as he engaged his readers in his vigorous and fluid narrative. The enduring quality of his interest in Byron is evident in his editing of *Byron: Selections from Poetry, Letters and Journals* (Nonesuch, 1949); *Byron, a Self-Portrait: Letters and Diaries, 1789 to 1824* (Murray; Scribner, 1950); and *Byronic Thoughts* (Murray, 1960). He also collaborated with Emily Morse Symonds on the editing of *To Lord Byron; Feminine Profiles Based upon Unpublished Letters* (Murray; Scribner, 1939).

With the publication of *Byron: the Years of Fame*, or soon afterward, Quennell exchanged literary journalism for the less-meager monetary rewards of advertising. One of the clients of the London agency that employed him was the temperamental cosmetician Elizabeth Arden, for whom he undertook several exacting visits to New York City. Demonstrating his ability to handle two jobs at once, he edited, with a biographical foreword, *The Private Letters of Princess Lieven to Prince Metternich* (Murray, 1937; Dutton, 1938) and wrote *Victorian Panorama: A Survey of Life and Fashions from Contemporary Photographs* (Batsford; Scribner, 1937).

Just before the onset of World War II, Quennell completed *Caroline of England; an Augustan Portrait* (Collins, 1939; Viking, 1940), a study of the consort of King George II and other personages, many of them writers, of the early Hanoverian court. In his lively blending of biography with history he captured the ethos of an age that he explored repeatedly in later books. During the war he tried not to let his assignments with the Ministry of Information, the Ministry of Economic Warfare, and the London Fire Service overshadow his literary concerns. At the height of the war he wrote the commentary and captions for Cecil Beaton's collection of photographs in *Time Exposure* (Batsford; Scribner, 1941). In 1943 he became book critic for the *Daily Mail*, a post that he held until 1956, and in 1944 accepted the editorship of the *Cornhill Magazine*, a greatly respected literary periodical that had published the work of such eminent writers as Thackeray, Dickens, George Eliot, Thomas Hardy, and Henry James. During Quennell's seven years as editor the *Cornhill Magazine's* contributors included Clive Bell, John Betjeman, Elizabeth Bowen, Truman Capote, André Gide, Rose Macaulay, Somerset Maugham, Evelyn Waugh, and H. G. Wells.

By the end of the war Quennell also had finished *Four Portraits* (Collins, 1945), published in the United States under the title of *Profane Virtues; Four Studies of the Eighteenth Century* (Viking, 1945), which centered on the epoch following that of his book on Caroline of Anspach. "I endeavoured to unite my four heroes [James Boswell, Edward Gibbon, Laurence Sterne, and John Wilkes] in a single literary pattern, which would serve to illustrate the broader pattern of the age," he explained in *The Wanton Chase: an Autobiography from 1939* (Collins; Atheneum, 1980). As they had done in connection with his treatment of Byron, critics commended Quennell for entertaining as well as informing his readers while avoiding the current tendency toward fictionized, or novelistic, biography.

Relating his subject to the times in which he lived continued to be one of Quennell's techniques in a succession of biographies: *John Ruskin; the Portrait of a Prophet* (Viking, 1949; Collins, 1952); *Hogarth's Progress* (Collins; Viking, 1955); *Shakespeare; the Poet and his Background* (Weidenfeld; World, 1963) *Alexander Pope; the Education of Genius, 1688-1728* (Weidenfeld; Stein and Day, 1968); and *Samuel Johnson; his Friends and Enemies* (American Heritage Press, 1972). Although characterized as popular works, the biographies for the most part demand close reader attention and assume considerable knowledge of literature. Critics generally appraised Quennell as a factually reliable biographer, though not infallible.

In his digressions from biography Quennell usually remains within the bounds of literature and art: *The Singular Preference; Portraits and Essays* (Collins, 1952; Viking, 1953); *Spring in Sicily* (Weidenfeld, 1952); *Romantic England; Writing and Painting* (Weidenfeld; Macmillan, 1970); and *Casanova in London and Other Essays* (Stein and Day, 1970; Weidenfeld, 1971). He collaborated with Hamish Johnson on *Who's Who in Shakespeare* (Weidenfeld; Morrow, 1973) and *A History of English Literature* (Merriam, 1973).

As early as 1933, with the publication of *Aspects of Seventeenth Century Verse* (J. Cape), Quennell had been intermittently occupied with editing aside from his work in journalism. From 1951 to 1967 William Kimber and Company brought out a string of his editions of extracts from Henry Mayhew's books about London. Other books that he edited include George Borrow's *The Bible in Spain* (MacDonald, 1959); Henry de Montherlant's *Selected Essays* (Weidenfeld, 1960; Macmillan, 1961); William Hickey's *Memoirs* (Hutchinson, 1960); *Marcel Proust, 1871-1922: a Centenary Volume* (Weidenfeld; Simon & Schuster, 1971);

Vladimir Nabokov; his Life, his Work, his World (Weidenfeld, 1979); A Lonely Business; a Self-Portrait of James Pope-Hennessy (Weidenfeld, 1981); and The Selected Essays of Cyril Connolly (Stanley Moss/Persea, 1984).

Together with the professional historian Alan Hodge, Quennell also edited The Past We Share; an Illustrated History of the British and American Peoples (Weidenfeld; Prometheus, 1960). In January 1951 he and Hodge had become coeditors of a new historical monthly magazine, History Today, which combined high standards of scholarship with readability. A. L. Rowse, who often sent articles to that journal, wrote in "A Tribute to P. Q. and A. H." (History Today, November 1979) that Quennell "has the eye and the knowledge of an artist, and this must have contributed most valuably to one of the special distinctions of History Today, its illustrations." Quennell, in fact, did select most of the covers as well as the illustrations and was largely responsible also for the literary excellence of the articles. Hodge's editorship ended with his death in the spring of 1979; Quennell served as sole editor until October of that year.

As a biographer Quennell often surrounds his subjects with the cultural leaders of the age. Similarly, in his books of recollections, The Sign of the Fish (Collins; Viking, 1960) and Customs and Characters, and in his autobiographies of 1976 and 1980, he himself becomes the focus for surveying the twentieth century's intellectual and, marginally, social scene in England and to a lesser degree France. Even as a teenager, when he entered the good graces of the Sitwells—Edith, Osbert, and Sacheverell—he gravitated to the literati. But the range of his portraits is fairly broad, including such disparate personalities as Greta Garbo, Teilhard de Chardin, and the double agents Donald Maclean and Guy Burgess. As V. S. Pritchett remarked in the New Statesman (September 25, 1970), Quennell "is a master of the rapid sketch from life." His perception, moreover, of the London stage and its people was deepened by his reading of Proust, whom he long admired.

Peter Quennell is a tall, trim, and well-groomed man, as urbane as the books he writes. When he was seventeen he had a pet owl and all his life he has been fond of dogs and cats. He has been married three times and has a son, Alexander Quennell, born on June 23, 1967. In his autobiographies he declines to give the names of his wives, but is frank about many aspects of his marriages and his affairs with women other than his wives. On another personal matter, he writes openly about the "moments of panic, spells of deep melancholy and long bouts of atrabilious gloom" that plagued him much of his life. And in The Wanton Chase he sums up his religious views: "I have always lacked faith and, since I grew up, have ceased to believe either in a Christian God or in the possibility of a future life. . . . Today, now that a personal God has receded, Art, which has strengthened and enriched the legend, and surrounded it with splendid images, seems more and more to take its place. At

seventy-five, my own belief in Art remains as passionate as fifty years ago."

References: History Today 29:701+ N '79 pors; N Y Times p35 Ap 24 '83 por; N Y Times Bk R p13+ Ap 10 '77 por; International Who's Who, 1983–84; Quennell, Peter. The Sign of the Fish (1960), The Marble Foot (1976), The Wanton Chase (1980), Customs and Characters (1982); Twentieth Century Authors (1942; First Supplement, 1955); Who's Who, 1984–85

Rangel, Charles B(ernard)

June 11, 1930– United States Representative from New York. Address: b. 2330 Rayburn House Office Bldg., Washington, D.C. 20515

The most influential black politician in New York State and a member of the Democratic leadership group in the House of Representatives, Charles B. Rangel represents the 16th Congressional District in Manhattan, which includes his native Harlem, Washington Heights, and part of the Upper West Side. A liberal who understands the delicate art of compromise, Rangel is an adept behind-the-scenes negotiator who pursues his legislative goals not with ideological adamancy but with a combination of diligence, charm, and astute assessments of the interests of his colleagues. In recognition of Rangel's political skills, House Speaker Thomas P. ("Tip") O'Neill, Jr., appointed him a deputy whip in February 1983, and he is also the third-ranking member of the powerful House Ways and Means Committee. Although contentedly ensconced in Congress, Rangel has not ruled out the possibility of challenging the incumbent New York City mayor, Edward I. Koch, in 1985.

Charles Bernard Rangel was born in New York City on June 11, 1930, the second of Ralph and Blanche (Wharton) Rangel's three children. His parents separated when he was very young, and he was raised in Harlem by his mother, a seamstress in New York's garment district, and his maternal grandfather, an elevator operator. He dropped out of DeWitt Clinton High School in the Bronx in his junior year and then, after holding a few dead-end jobs, enlisted in the United States Army in 1948. During the Korean war, Rangel won a Bronze Star after being wounded while bringing some forty men out from behind Chinese lines.

Although he by no means glorifies army life, Rangel feels that his experience in the armed services represented a major turning point for him because it revealed the existence of alternatives to the poverty-ridden environment in which he had grown up. "When I was exposed to a different life, even if that life was just the army, I knew damn well I couldn't get back to the same life I had left," he told Emile Milne during an interview for the *New York Post* (April 3, 1971). Discharged from the army in 1952, Rangel earned his high school diploma the following year by completing two years of work in one. In 1957 he obtained a B.S. degree from New York University's School of Commerce. He then won a full scholarship to the law school at St. John's University in Brooklyn, where he obtained his J.D. degree in 1960.

Admitted to the New York State bar in 1960, Rangel began practicing law with little financial success, though he did achieve a favorable reputation among black civil rights activists for his willingness to provide them with legal assistance. In 1961 he was appointed an assistant U.S. attorney in the Southern District of New York by Attorney General Robert F. Kennedy but remained in that post for only one year. In 1964 the young lawyer joined Percy Sutton, the Manhattan Borough president, who is widely regarded as Rangel's political mentor, in establishing the John F. Kennedy Democratic Club on West 130th Street in Harlem.

In 1966 Rangel was elected to the first of his two consecutive two-year terms in the New York State assembly from Harlem's 72d assembly district. In Albany, where he emerged as a leader among the state's black legislators, he supported the liberalization of the abortion law and opposed the imposition of stiffer jail terms on prostitutes on the ground that it would have little impact. Favoring legalization of the numbers game, he argued, as quoted in *Ebony* (February 1971), that "for the average Harlemite, playing numbers is moral and a way of life." Rangel eventually became a political friend of the liberal Republican Governor Nelson A. Rockefeller, who secured the Republican line on the ballot for him in his 1968 reelection campaign. Branching out into national issues, he endorsed the first nationwide protest day against the Vietnam war in 1969.

In a gesture of self-confidence, in June 1970 Rangel challenged Harlem's charismatic and nationally known United States representative, Adam Clayton Powell, in the Democratic congressional primary. Although Rangel had considerable regard for Powell's accomplishments, he ran against the incumbent because of his poor attendance record in Congress during the previous year. Running in a crowded field of five, he edged out Powell by a razor-thin margin of 150 votes out of about 25,000 cast. In the general election Rangel won 88 percent of the vote, with both Democratic and Republican backing.

During his first term in the House of Representatives, Rangel concentrated on efforts to stem the flow of heroin into the United States from abroad, asserting that residents of black slums are the primary victims of drug-related crime. (In the early 1970s Harlem was estimated to have some 30,000 heroin addicts.) In February 1971 he condemned the Nixon administration for not dealing firmly enough with Turkey, where most heroin originated in the form of opium poppies, and with France, where the heroin was illegally manufactured. Later that year he unsuccessfully offered a proposal requiring congressional action to stop a cutoff of foreign aid to any country not cooperating in the effort to halt drug trafficking, but his efforts helped to secure House adoption in 1971 of a bill authorizing the president to reduce aid to any such country.

Within New York City, the freshman representative also came down hard on the drug issue. He created considerable controversy by accusing some members of the New York Police Department of working with drug pushers and by denouncing a recommendation of Mayor John V. Lindsay's narcotics control council for a rehabilitation experiment under which some addicts would be given maintenance doses of heroin. Describing the plan as a "colonialist type of thinking," he charged, as quoted by Paul L. Montgomery of the *New York Times* (May 31, 1971), that "they just want to go into Bedford-Stuyvesant and Harlem and pick up 500 black and Puerto Rican guinea pigs. The philosophy is 'Keep them high, write them off, forget it.' It's a cruel hoax to play on people." He added: "They want to get a foot in the door to legalize heroin. . . . " Rangel favored research to discover a nonaddictive substitute for heroin.

When he ran for reelection in 1972, Rangel faced a significant Democratic primary challenge from Livingston Wingate, who in the 1960s had been the director of Haryou-Act, Harlem's antipoverty agency. Although Rangel had the backing of most Democratic organizations in the district, Wingate derived support from the old Powell organization and some community-oriented groups, including the black nationalist-oriented Congress of Racial Equality, which Rangel denounced for advocating "a separatist racial policy destined to bring about tragic polarization of the races." Because of reapportionment following the 1970 census, the district had been reorganized, so that while it was still located mostly in Harlem, it was now only 65 percent black. Rangel won the primary by a margin of more than three to one. Since then, he has not faced a serious electoral challenge and has received Democratic, Republican, and Liberal party backing in every general election.

During the 1970s Rangel compiled a markedly liberal voting record. According to the *Congressional Quarterly Almanac*, he never voted with the House's Republican–Southern Democratic conservative coalition on more than 6 percent of key roll call votes in any year from 1971 through 1979. As a stern critic of an interventionist foreign policy and astronomical military expenditures, he voted to end the United States bombing of Cambodia in the early 1970s and against funding the B-1 bomber in 1975 and nuclear carriers in 1977. On domestic issues, Rangel cast votes in favor of busing for school integration in 1974 and government financial assistance for abortions in 1975. He opposed the deregulation of natural gas in 1976 and 1977 and backed auto pollution controls in 1977 and the creation of a consumer protection agency in 1978. In the following year he opposed the continuation of a lid on food stamp expenditures.

At the time, Rangel was expanding his power and influence in the House and in 1974 was elected chairman of the Congressional Black Caucus. During that year, Rangel, as a member of the House Judiciary Committee, received much publicity and considerable respect for his well-informed questioning of witnesses during the panel's consideration of impeachment articles against President Richard M. Nixon. In 1975 he became the first black ever to be appointed to the powerful Ways and Means Committee, whose jurisdiction extends to such crucial areas as tax policy and welfare legislation, in 1976 he was appointed to the Select Committee on Narcotics Abuse and Control, and in 1977 his House colleagues from the New York congressional delegation selected him as majority regional whip for New York State. Two years later, Rangel ascended to the chairmanship of the important health subcommittee of the Ways and Means panel. By the end of the decade he was a member of the Democratic Steering and Policy Committee, which nominates committee chairmen and proposes the party's legislative priorities.

Rangel's rapid rise within the ranks of the House of Representatives can be attributed to his impressive political skills as a hard worker with a profound knowledge of legislative issues and with a flair for the art of persuasion. Genial and eminently sociable, he is able to win friends and influence people with his charm, his repertory of jokes, and his ingratiating candor. In making his opinions known he may sometimes use strong language, but never with personal animosity, and he is a careful listener who is able to size up the needs of his colleagues. Those assets make him a masterly practitioner of politics as the art of compromise, and despite his liberal record, he often works effectively behind the scenes to accomplish what he considers possible, even if the package may not include everything he wants. Aware of the dangers of excessive pragmatism, he said during an interview with Sheila Rule for the *New York Times* (November 12, 1979): "I guess I'm practical, but you have to live with yourself and make sure you are not so practical that you sell out a part of yourself."

His political adroitness enabled Rangel to obtain results that might have eluded less able legislators. As chairman of the Ways and Means health subcommittee in 1979 and 1980, he had to deal with a number of conservatives on that panel. Dispensing with ideological labels, Rangel kept in mind that, as he put it, "there was no way in hell" that the conservatives could not be concerned about the senior citizens and low-income people in their districts. By using that approach of studying the interests of other legislators, he was able to secure more of the legislation he wanted than by being a hardline, inflexible liberal. High tribute to Rangel's expertise came from Guy Vander Jagt, a Republican representative from Michigan, who collaborated with him on welfare reform legislation during the late 1970s. In Sheila Rule's *New York Times* piece on Rangel, Vander Jagt was quoted as saying: "He's given a little and I've given a lot. He has persuaded me with a tremendous grasp of subject matter and an ability to explain his position in a very winning way."

During the early 1980s Rangel's star continued to be in the ascendant. In 1981 he gave up his health subcommittee chairmanship to become chairman of the Ways and Means oversight subcommittee, a position that gave him control over probes into Reagan administration cuts in such programs as Social Security, Medicare, Medicaid, and welfare. By 1983 he had become the third-ranking member of the thirty-five-member Ways and Means Committee, enjoying a good working relationship with its chairman, Dan Rostenkowski, Democrat of Illinois. Perhaps even more important, he found favor with House Speaker "Tip" O'Neill, who made him a deputy whip in February 1983, a move that brought him into the House's inner leadership circle. That year O'Neill also appointed Rangel chairman of the Select Committee on Narcotics, which placed him in a strategic position to deal with the drug problem that plagued his district.

Because of his strong political base in Washington, Rangel is in a favorable position to help his home state. During a 1982 House-Senate conference on the Tax Equity and Fiscal Responsibility Act, he won for New York continuation of leasing arrangements for the Metropolitan Transit Authority, authority to make wider use of mortgage revenue bonds for housing, and extensions of industrial development bonds on which the state depends for funding industrial projects. Early in 1983 he successfully steered through the House an additional $45 million in federal revenue as reimbursement for its Medicare expenses. At the same time, Rangel began pressing for $155 million in federal expenditures for constructing and operating shelters for the homeless, an issue of growing urgency in New York City.

As the most important black politician in New York City by the late 1970s, Rangel inevitably became involved in the ongoing dispute between the city's black communities and Mayor Edward I. Koch. In 1977 Rangel endorsed Koch in the Democratic mayoral runoff primary against Mario Cuomo, who is now governor of New York State. Soon many blacks, along with their political leaders, came to regard Koch as unfriendly to their interests. Rangel challenged Koch on such matters as his plans to shut down municipal hospitals in minority neighborhoods and his budget cuts in programs benefiting blacks and Puerto Ricans. But as a practical politician, he tried to work with the Koch administration to secure the best possible city services for his constituents instead of seeking a confrontation with the mayor.

Although Rangel endorsed Koch for reelection in 1981, within two years he had become as sharply critical of the mayor as most other black leaders in New York City. "I don't know anybody in politics that I dislike enough that I would recommend that he sit down with the mayor," Rangel told Frank Lombardi of the New York Daily News (July 24, 1983). "Is the man ill? . . . Tragically, there's something about him that he cannot reach out to the black community."

The deterioration of relations between Rangel and Koch led to speculation that the congressman might run for mayor in 1985. Observers pointed out that if an alliance of the over three million blacks and Hispanics in the city could be formed and if those minorities turned out to vote in large numbers, as blacks had recently done for black mayoral candidates in Chicago and Philadelphia, a black candidate could win. Rangel indicated in 1983 that, since he feels "partly responsible" for Koch's electoral victories in 1977 and 1981, he would feel obligated to consider running only under certain conditions: if there were significant grass-roots support for a black candidate; if blacks forged an effective citywide coalition; and if they could not form a consensus around another candidate. But it seems clear that Rangel would prefer to remain in Congress, where he might eventually become Ways and Means chairman, or even, eventually, House Speaker, a possibility he admits to "fantasizing" about.

By their marriage on July 26, 1964 Charles B. Rangel and Alma (Carter) Rangel have two teen-aged children, Steven and Alicia. He and his family live in Washington, but he returns to New York City on weekends. Rangel owns and occupies the building on West 132nd Street in Manhattan in which he grew up. The stocky, five-foot eleven-inch Rangel carries into his personal life the ingratiating personality that characterizes his public image, for his wife describes him as a "soft touch" and his friends view him as a "nice guy."

References: N Y Daily News p50 Je 16 '71 por; N Y Post p22 Ap 3 '71 por; N Y Times p38 D 12 '74 por; Who's Who in America, 1984-85; Who's Who in Black America, 1977-78

Rawls, Lou

Dec. 1, 1936– Singer. Address: b. c/o The Brokaw Company, Suite 411, 9255 Sunset Blvd., Los Angeles, Calif. 90069

The easy baritone of the "fusion" soul stylist Lou Rawls is one of the most recognizable voices in contemporary pop music. While the voice is unmistakable, it is not easy to categorize. Rawls began his career as a gospel singer with the late Sam Cooke and the Pilgrim Travelers in the late 1950s, but he was identified by some as a jazz singer after he scored his first commercial success. As Rawls told Edward J. Fay of the New York Daily News (October 1, 1982): "Then I cut another record and they said, 'Oh, no. He's a blues singer.' Then I was a pop singer, and now they have a new word—fusion. I guess that's what I am, since I do all of that." That does not mean he has compromised his art, as some purists have charged. "I wouldn't do a song if it weren't me. . . . I fuse my own style with a song," Rawls has said. That style is, as Fay observed, "sweet as sugar, soft as velvet, strong as steel, smooth as butter."

Rawls has recorded forty-six albums, including the platinum LP All Things in Time and the gold albums Lou Rawls Live, Soulin', Unmistakably Lou, and When You've Heard Lou. Among his classic singles are "Breaking My Back" and "Mean Black Snake." The National Academy of Recording Arts and Sciences has honored him with three Grammy Awards for best male rhythm and blues vocalist. The recordings that earned him the Grammys were *Unmistakably Lou* and the singles "Dead End Street," an evocation of his ghetto childhood, and "A Natural Man." Among his Grammy nominations was one for his gold single "You'll Never Find (Another Love Like Mine)."

In recent years Lou Rawls has perhaps become best known as the chief fundraiser for the United Negro College Fund, for which he hosts an annual telethon, and as the chief commercial spokesman for Anheuser-Busch, the brewers of Budweiser beer. The handsome, elegantly groomed Rawls establishes a warm rapport with mainstream audiences, thanks in part to the lyrical and dramatic "rap" with which he frames his songs, a flow of wry patter that gives his listeners insight into life on the mean ghetto streets from which he came. Rawls's many television credits include the singing of "The Alphabet Song" on *Sesame Street* and the voice-over for Garfield the Cat in an animated version of the comic strip.

Louis Allen Rawls was born on the South Side of Chicago on December 1, 1936. The birth date of 1935 given by some sources can probably be attributed to the fact that as a teenager Rawls lied about his age in order to join the National Guard. His father, the late Virgil Rawls, a Baptist minister who also worked as a clothes presser, left the family ménage shortly after Lou's birth. (The singer had a reunion with Virgil Rawls just before his death in 1975.) Not long afterward, his mother, Evelyn Rawls, left for the West Coast, where she worked in defense plants and later became a talent agent. From that time on Rawls was raised by his grandmother, Eliza Rawls, in a succession of South Side apartments. "I was raised on 35th and South Park when it was tough," he has recounted. "I went to Forrestville Elementary and Dunbar High. In between I learned about life. Everything happened in my neighborhood. I learned about people. I just sing about them, that's all."

With his grandmother, Rawls attended the Greater Mount Olive Baptist Church, where he joined the junior choir when he was seven. At the South Side's Regal Theatre Rawls witnessed performances by Billy Eckstine, Arthur Prysock, and other popular black singers, and his childhood neighborhood peers included such future pop vocal celebrities as Sam Cooke, Curtis Mayfield, and members of the Staple Singers, the Flamingos, the Dells, and the Impressions. When he was fourteen he joined a gospel quintet, the Chosen Gospel Singers, which competed with other local groups at Friday night gatherings.

After his grandmother died, Rawls, then in his mid-teens, upped his age and joined the National Guard to supplement the meager pass-the-hat earnings of the Chosen Gospel Singers. Later he was drafted into the United States Army, in which he served for two years with the 82d Airborne Division, based at Fort Bragg, North Carolina. After his discharge from the army, he toured churches and gospel programs across the United States with the Pilgrim Travelers, a gospel group whose other members were Sam Cooke, Eddie Cunningham, and Cliff White. Driving in a Cadillac from St. Louis to Memphis one rainy night in 1958, the quartet collided with an eighteen-wheeler truck. Cunningham was killed, Cooke suffered minor eye injuries, White broke his collarbone, and Rawls received a brain concussion. "Had they taken me to a public hospital, I probably wouldn't have lived," Rawls told Louie Robinson of *Ebony* (October 1978), "but they took me to the Memphis VA hospital." Showing no vital signs, he was "actually pronounced dead in the ambulance on the way to the hospital," and he remained in a coma for five-and-a-half days. He sustained a loss of memory for about three months, and it was a year before he fully recovered.

The Pilgrim Travelers regrouped just long enough to reach Los Angeles. Rawls "just laid around in L.A." until he "recovered pretty good," as he related to Louie Robinson. He added: "Then I started hanging around in the little coffeehouses and things like that. Even though I was in the religious field, I still knew all the dudes who were in the blues-jazz field—Bobby Blue Bland, Junior Parker, B. B. King. We all traveled the same circuit down through the South. We were traveling the Bible belt and they were traveling the blues belt, which was the same belt, same people."

Rawls made the transition from gospel halls to nightclubs by concentrating on such songs in his repertoire as "Every Day I Have the Blues," with which he felt comfortable when performing in either milieu. He began doing solo gigs in coffeehouses and other small clubs in 1959, and within that year he performed in a Dick Clark show at the Hollywood Bowl and had non-singing roles in episodes of the ABC network television series *Bourbon Street Beat* and *77 Sunset Strip*. His most important early television credits were guest performances on Steve Allen's late-night show on ABC.

Capitol Records signed Rawls in 1961, apparently with some thought to grooming him as a possible successor to Nat King Cole, then the Capitol superstar. His first album for Capitol was *Stormy Monday* (1962), a collaboration with the blues pianist Les McCann. It was followed by *Soulin'* and *Tobacco Road* (which included the cut "In the Evening When the Sun Goes Down"). After hearing Rawls sing selections from *Tobacco Road* in person, John Pagones of the *Washington Post* (November 20, 1964) described him as a "vibrant, handsome personality" with a "big and bluesy" voice that makes up in "elasticity" what "it lacks in richness."

In an interview with Leonard Feather published in the *New York World Journal Tribune* (January 15, 1967), Rawls observed that his early Capitol recordings "sold pretty well, but strictly on the chitlin' circuit." The problem, largely, was the absence on vinyl of Rawls's live rapport with audiences, which was enhanced by his patter and monologues. Early on, he had learned to overcome the noisy distractions in clubs and capture the attention of the customers by rapping out extemporaneous introductions to his songs. He carried the strategy into the studio for the first time with *Lou Rawls Live* (1966), which was recorded before a live audience. All of the songs on the album were reprises (including "St. James Infirmary" and "World of Trouble"), except for three, including "Streetcorner Hustler's Blues," about a two-timing South Side dandy confronted by his knife-wielding wife as he waits for his mistress on the street.

With *Lou Rawls Live* Rawls crossed over into the mainstream pop market. The LP sold out in its first week and ultimately went gold, selling more than a million copies. The single "Love Is a Hurtin' Thing" became his biggest hit to date after "You'll Never Find Another Love Like Mine," and "Dead End Street" hit the Top 40 in 1966 and brought him his first Grammy Award in 1967.

In 1966 Rawls stopped the show at the Randall's Island (Manhattan) Jazz Festival and broke attendance records at the Village Gate in Greenwich Village. Reviewing Rawls in concert at Carnegie Hall in January 1967, Robert Salmaggi wrote in the *New York World Journal Tribune* (January 16, 1967): "He is loose, exuberant, aware . . . The Rawls sound is born of the blues, of gospel halls, of drafty, musty one-room apartments, of being kicked and kicked again, of anguish, servility, protest ("Stormy Monday"), of hope ("On Broadway"), of losers, loners, and lovers. He strays into the pop-ballad field on occasion, but blues are his baby and soulin' is his bag." The Carnegie Hall concert kicked off a tour of major clubs and concert halls country-wide.

The following year Rawls won the *Downbeat* poll for favorite male vocalist, displacing the then perennial winner of that poll, Frank Sinatra, and in 1970 he was nominated for a Grammy for his single "Your Good Thing (Is About to End)." When Capitol Records failed to renew his contract in 1971, Rawls signed with MGM Records. Mike Curb, the president of MGM, tried to fit Rawls into a "bubble gum" format, but the singer managed to make the blues song "A Natural Man" the B side of his first MGM single and that cut brought him his second Grammy, in 1972. Unhappy with MGM, Rawls lost no time in moving out. His first, brief stop was with Bell Records, for which he cut one single, "She's Gone," a commercially unsuccessful collaboration with Darryl Hall and John Oates. Leonard Maltin, reviewing a performance by Rawls at the Manhattan Club in the *Village Voice* (February 21, 1974) wrote: "Lou Rawls is not a jazz singer, yet he shares with very few other contemporary vocalists the kind of honesty and musical assuredness that makes his sound appealing for devotees of pop, soul, or jazz. . . . His voice has developed an individual style that projects strength but never loses its mellowness. . . . there is an innate integrity in everything he sings: nothing is fluffed off, not even reprises of hit records which he must have sung hundreds of times."

Assessing his career during the recording sabbatical he took following "She's Gone," Rawls decided to aim at the tuxedo set. "There are people who like to dress up and go out," he later told a reporter, "and I'm gonna be the flamboyant, finger-poppin', uptown goodtime Charlie to sing to them." In 1975 he signed with Philadelphia International Records, a CBS subsidiary, thus placing himself under the guidance of two masters of what is known in the trade as MOR (middle of the road), Kenny Gamble and Leon Huff. His 1976 Philadelphia International release "You'll Never Find (Another Love Like Mine)," a ballad with a light salsa beat, became his first gold single and won an American Music Award. It was also nominated for a Grammy, along with the singer's "Groovy People." Out of Rawls's collaboration with Gamble and Huff also came the jukebox nuggets "Lady Love" and "See You When I Git There" and the 1977 albums *All Things in Time* and *Unmistakably Lou*. *All Things in Time* reached third place on the soul charts and became Rawls's first platinum LP, selling a million copies. With *Unmistakably Lou*, Rawls won his third Grammy.

By the mid-1970s Rawls was a familiar figure on the television shows of Johnny Carson, Mike Douglas, Merv Griffin, Don Kirshner, Dinah Shore, and others, and his concert and club engagements were in the class circuit, comprising such venues as the Newport Jazz Festival, the Astrodome Festival, the Palmer House, the Maisonette, Mr. Kelly's, and the MGM Grand Hotel. His career moved into high gear in 1976 when he linked up with his present agent, Norman Brokaw, who negotiated the singer's contract with Anheuser-Busch. Rawls's voice and face became identified with Budweiser beer in television and radio spots and print and display advertising.

Anheuser-Busch joined with CBS in promoting *Lou Rawls on Broadway*, a musical showcase that ran for ten days at the Mark Hellinger Theatre in the autumn of 1977 to mixed reviews. "Mr. Rawls manages to touch so many bases with such a smoothly homogenized style that he emerges as a prototypical middle-of-the-road singer . . .," John S. Wilson observed in the *New York Times* (November 25, 1977). "He is most effective, however, simply as Lou Rawls, recalling the songs that took him from the 'chitlin' circuit' to Broadway in a friendly, engaging manner that reaches easily across the footlights." According to the critic for *Variety* (November 30, 1977), Rawls did "many things well" but his attempt at MOR "all but" eliminated "interest in the things he does best." But purist criticism of Rawls's "compromising" did not conspicuously slacken the momentum he was building up in the mainstream. He went on the road with the formula developed for his Broadway show, a mixture of his own R & B hits, such show tunes as "Send in the Clowns" and selections from *Porgy and Bess*, and tributes to Nat King Cole, Duke Ellington, and Louis Armstrong. With his new format he performed to standing ovations at the Sahara Hotel in Lake Tahoe, Nevada in July 1978 and at the Greek Theatre in Los Angeles the following month. Later in the year he made a tour of Australia—his second—where the correspondent for *Variety* (December 27, 1978) reported on his engagement at the Hilton Hotel in Sydney: "Polished to a high gloss, . . . Rawls's act was warmly received by his first Sydney audience since his 1972 tour. His smooth line of chatter immediately caught the right tone and for the whole ninety-minute show he performed flawlessly." The energetic Sydney singer Brenda Kristen, who opened for him, was "a perfect complement" to the laid-back Rawls, and the largely Australian twenty-four-piece orchestra "blended" well. "Rawls's skill with standards was much in evidence, particularly on 'Sophisticated Lady.'"

Back in the United States Rawls toured with Natalie Cole, the daughter of Nat King Cole, and with A Taste of Honey (Janice Marie Johnson and Hazel Payne). With the financial underwriting of Anheuser-Busch, Rawls in 1979 launched *The Lou Rawls Parade of Stars*, his annual telethon for the United Negro College Fund. The three-hour nationally syndicated show, featuring Rawls and cohost Ed McMahon and such performers as Miss Cole, Bill Cosby, Charlie Pride, Dionne Warwick, Tony Bennett, Norm Crosby, Glen Campbell, and Lola Falana, generated contributions of $15 million to UNCF through 1982. The money goes to forty-two historically black private colleges with a combined enrollment of some 50,000 students, half of whom come from homes with annual incomes of less than $12,000.

Early in 1982 Rawls moved from Philadelphia International to Epic Records, another CBS subsidiary. His debut Epic album, *Now Is the Time*, produced by the estimable Thom Bell, included the song "This Love," written by Clyde Orange of the Commodores. That LP was followed within the year by *When the Night Comes*, among the tracks of which was "Wind Beneath My Wing." Recorded in Nashville, *When the Night Comes* was Rawls's first collaboration with John Haffkine, the creator/producer of the group Dr. Hook and the Medicine Show.

In *Rhythm & Rawls*, a CBS television special aired in June 1982, the singer explored his roots as a soul singer while serving as a host to musicians representing the very latest in black pop: A Taste of Honey, Richard ("Dimples") Field, the funk act Cameo, gospel singer Andrae Crouch, Patti Austin, James Ingram, and Kool & the Gang. Rawls sang a gospel duet with Crouch and reminisced about the Apollo Theater, in between singing "Stormy Monday Blues," Duke Ellington's "Take the A Train," and Sam Cooke's "Having A Party." Wayne Robins of *Newsday* (June 18, 1982) considered "running with that contemporary crowd" a "step in the right direction for Rawls."

During the summer of 1982 Rawls had engagements at the Resorts International Hotel in Atlantic City and the Sahara Hotel in Lake Tahoe. For the USO, he put together a show of music, dance, and comedy that he took to Norfolk Naval Base, McGuire Air Force Base, and Fort Hood Army Base in the United States. During the holiday season at the end of 1982 Rawls's variety troupe entertained American servicemen on military bases in Japan, Korea, and the Philippines.

Among the stars joining Rawls in his 1983 telethon for the United Negro College Fund were Natalie Cole, Marilyn McCoo, Stevie Wonder, Paul McCartney, Roberta Flack, Stephanie Mills, and Sister Sledge. During the summer of 1983 he entertained troops at Fort Bragg, North Carolina, performed with the North Carolina School of the Arts Jazz Band and the Atlanta Symphony Orchestra, and sang the national anthem before an Atlanta Braves baseball game in the Atlanta-Fulton County Stadium in Georgia.

In October 1983 Rawls was in Memphis, Tennessee for the week-long festivities celebrating the renovation, then in progress, of Beale Street, which had been declared the "Home of the Blues" by an act of Congress in 1977. Rawls, the national spokesman for the project returning a 1920s atmosphere to the historic street, was preparing to open his own nightclub there, Lou's Place, adjoining the country singer Charlie Rich's restaurant, the Silver Fox. "I've always wanted a club, and this opportunity just fell into place," he told a reporter. "I want to offer class entertainment. Fifty percent of a performance is the way you look. People don't want to spend money to watch someone who looks worse than they do. I won't let anyone on my stage in jeans and a T-shirt."

Conforming to his own rule, Rawls is superbly tailored in his appearances before audiences. Concentrating on vocals, he does no dancing during his performances, and while he likes a big-band accompaniment, he will have nothing to do with monitors, amplifiers, and other electronic gimmickry. Regarding disco and hard rock, he told Edward J. Fay in the *New York Daily News* interview: "I don't regret seeing any of those fads leave. They had half the kids of the '60s going deaf. Today it's changing. People want to be able to sit down and listen to music—not sit down and listen for half an hour and have someone tell you that was 'Blue Moon' and you didn't know it." In selecting songs, he looks for a beat and, above all, for a love theme that suits him. "First of all, I look at the lyrics . . . even before I know what the melody is. It has to mean something to me, something that has happened to me. I try to look for songs people can relate to."

Lou Rawls's strong resonant voice belies his slight build and short stature. Younger-looking than his years, the singer has a manner in which a hint of shy diffidence is combined with suave confidence. After an eleven-year marriage, he and Lana Jean Rawls were divorced in 1973. Rawls spends ten months of each year on the road, doing much of his traveling in rented cars. The other two months he lives in a house he owns in central Los Angeles with his two children, Lou and Louana, and a full-time housekeeper. One of his recreations is playing table tennis with the children. To "reestablish the things (he) already knew but had let slip," Rawls has been a participant in Scientology, the partly religious self-help program founded by L. Ron Hubbard.

References: Ebony 22:140+ Nov '66, 33:112+ Oct '78 pors; People 7:95+ May 30 '77 pors; Time 89:68 Ja 27 '67 por; Today B p15 N 1 '76; Harris, Sheldon. Blues Who's Who (1979); Who's Who in America, 1984–85

Redpath, Jean

Apr. 28, 1937– Scottish folksinger; recording artist. Address: b. c/o Iddy Olson, 5 Craft Pl., Jamaica Plain, Mass. 02130; Philo Records, 70 Court St., Middlebury, Vt. 05753

An energizing force on the American folk music scene since 1961, the Scottish performer and scholar Jean Redpath is the leading purveyor of the musical legacy of her country. Miss Redpath, who lectured on folk music at Wesleyan University in Connecticut in the early and mid-1970s, has been a member of the faculty of Stirling University in Scotland since 1979. The repertoire on her record albums—of which there were twenty by 1984—encompasses traditional Scottish ballads, songs of Robert Burns and Franz Joseph Haydn, and such contemporary classics as "Song of the Seals." Commenting on Jean Redpath's album Lowlands in Stereo Review (May 1982), Noel Coppage paid tribute to the rare quality of the artist's untrained voice. "'Music' is personal," he wrote, "but, whatever your lineage, if you like beautiful sounds you've got to like the voice of Jean Redpath. . . . As in the case of a woodwind instrument, you can hear just a hint of air escaping around the vocal

cords, and like a clarinet in the hands of a master, Redpath's instrument covers a considerable range so smoothly that there's no hint of strain. Talk about art concealing art and you are talking about the way Jean Redpath sings."

Because of her name, some people assume that Jean Redpath is an American Indian, but, as she pointed out, with a somewhat exaggerated burr, in an interview with Susan Wilson of the Boston Globe (January 20, 1983), her name is "sherr-ly Scottish." Born in Edinburgh, Scotland on April 28, 1937, she grew up in Leven, in the county of Fife, not far from Edinburgh. She has an older brother, Alexander Redpath. Both of her parents came from musical families. Her father, James Redpath, is no longer living, and her mother, whose maiden name is Dall, still makes her home in Leven. Singing was part of her everyday environment, and as a child Jean Redpath absorbed many of the old Scottish songs. By the time she was ten, she was "already recognized as 'having a voice,'" she has recalled. Increasingly, she came to prefer traditional music to the other types that she heard on the radio or in performance by traveling concert groups. Her formal musical training was limited to one singing lesson. "When I was sixteen . . . I went to this chap," she told Eleanor Blau, as quoted in the New York Times (January 25, 1980). "He played the piano, the guitar, and the flute, and sold sheet music, and when I arrived, he disappeared and came back with music for me to sing: 'When the Heather Gleams Like Stardust on the Hills'—the kind of music I abhor." It was not until she was about nineteen that Miss Redpath first heard the term "folk music."

Following her graduation from Buckhaven High School in Fife in 1954, Jean Redpath entered Edinburgh University to major in medieval studies. Her discovery of its School of Scottish Studies helped her to decide on her lifework. A department of the faculty of arts, the school gathers oral and written sources for customs and beliefs, traditional tales, songs and music, and social organization. Its research facilities maintain an extensive archive of tape and disc recordings of the oral tradition of both the Gaelic and the Scottish-speaking areas. The classic Scottish ballad became Jean Redpath's chief interest, and she served as president of the university's Folk Song Society. During that period, she supported herself as a secondary school teacher and also was, at various times, "major-domo of a boarding house, driving instructor, and odd-time hosteler," as Robert Shelton noted in the New York Times (November 15, 1961).

Impelled by wanderlust, Jean Redpath made her first trip to the United States in March 1961 with only eleven dollars to her name. She visited the family of a fellow student in San Francisco, and her performance at a hootenanny there launched her on her career as a "wandering minstrel." The route by which she arrived in New York City, where she encountered almost instant success in Greenwich Village, was circuitous and accidental. The veteran Scottish singer Hamish Henderson had contacted an agent in Michigan in her behalf for a booking in Philadelphia. She recounted her experiences to Kristin Baggelaar and Donald Milton, as quoted in their book *Folk Music: More Than a Song* (Crowell, 1976): "Well, being very green and never having done anything so special, I begged, borrowed, and stole my fare across country, and when I landed in Philly I discovered that the club owner had skipped out of town three weeks before and hadn't paid his last performer." She then accepted an offer of a ride to New York City with some new friends who took her to an apartment in Greenwich Village where a hootenanny was in progress. The participants included Bob Dylan, Jack Elliott, and the Greenbriar Boys, who were then performing at Gerde's Folk City. With her first performance at Gerde's six weeks later, Jean Redpath became part of the folk music renaissance of the early 1960s.

In his review of her Gerde's performance, Robert Shelton wrote in the *New York Times* that Jean Redpath "would charm an audience with her repertoire alone." Her selections from the approximately 250 songs that she knew included dramatic classic ballads, down-to-earth "bothy" ballads from plowmen's shacks, songs by Robert Burns, drinking songs, childhood songs, and "mouth music"—a kind of improvised accompaniment for dancing. Shelton described the voice of this "big-boned, apple-cheeked, radiantly healthy girl" as "a clear, rich, beautiful mezzo-soprano, sure-pitched enough to sustain long unaccompanied numbers." With her witty banter, flavored with "glottal stops and a thick burr," she transmitted her love of her country's history, customs, and language to her audience between numbers. "Getting a review in the *New York Times* gave me a good hard push off the road of starvation because I had been living on peanut butter and jelly up until then," Miss Redpath has said.

According to a *Variety* reviewer (October 31, 1962) who caught her fourth performance at Gerde's Folk City, Jean Redpath soon began to "command a remarkable audience reverence." After making more appearances with other artists at cabarets and at folk festivals, Jean Redpath gave her first solo recital in the United States at the arts festival of the New School for Social Research in New York City on July 19, 1963. Robert Shelton, who found it "a compelling evening of music and talk," attested that her untrained voice "was always full in tone, right on pitch, and projected in a way that put her head and shoulders above most women folk singers to be heard today." He volunteered a piece of advice: "Some of our singers who draw huge crowds with a gag and a fast beat would do well to study Miss Redpath's art." The sizes of her audiences were necessarily small—"ideally, a group of fifty people or less," Jean Redpath has pointed out—because, she said, "the kind of music I sing tends to be highly personal and dependent on an intimate situation." That is "almost self-destructive in terms of making a living," she added, "because you can't ask a big fee from a place that doesn't hold many people."

The first recording that Jean Redpath cut was *Skipping Barefoot Through the Heather* for Prestige/International, but its release followed that of her *Scottish Ballad Book* (1962) on Elektra. The artist wrote liner notes about her sources, and texts of the ballads were inserted in the album. Elektra next issued Miss Redpath's *Songs of Love, Lilt and Laughter* and *Laddie Lie Near Me*. Her album *Frae My Ain Countrie*, for Folk Legacy, appeared in 1973. It was reviewed in the 1983 catalog of Cahill & Company of Dobbs Ferry, New York with the following comment: "The unadorned honesty of her presentation only heightens the plangent delicacy hidden in each song. Here in sixteen bands is something like the very soul of Scotland."

In 1972, the peripatetic troubadour settled down in Middletown, Connecticut as artist in residence at Wesleyan University. Appointed a full-time lecturer on folklore in the music department of the university two years later, she also taught classes in the Middletown secondary schools on Robert Burns, the classic ballad, and folk music. In the interview in *Folk Music: More Than a Song*, Miss Redpath commented on her academic appointment: "It's a chance to stay in one place, with all the books and all the records, and I can really sink my teeth into the things that I'm singing." With reference to her ongoing research and her method of learning songs, she added: "I'm also acquiring all sorts of repertoires as well because classic ballads, with which I'm most involved, need a lot of living with before you can sing them." In 1975 Miss Redpath began recording for Philo Records in Vermont. In her album *Jean Redpath*, a collection of quiet songs with stories whose poignancy she found produced "catharsis rather than melancholy," she performed some of the selections without accompaniment and was joined in others by Abby Newton on the cello. The album includes several ballads from the five-volume collection *The English and Scottish Popular Ballads* (1883–98), compiled by the American scholar Francis James Child, as well as a song written by Ewan McColl for the BBC in the late 1960s.

After living in the United States for fifteen years, during which she made periodic visits to Scotland, Jean Redpath returned to her own country on a permanent basis in 1976. Now a recognized interpreter of Scottish traditional music, Miss Redpath was one of only four performers commanded to appear at the banquet and entertainment for Queen Elizabeth II and the royal family at Edinburgh Castle during the Queen's jubilee year, 1977. She has led several tours for the Scottish Arts Council, and she has often been heard on the radio. Miss Redpath has also served as host of the BBC television series *Ballad Folk*, and with other singers she performed on the recording of the same title. At the annual Edinburgh International Festival, her flute-like voice has been heard in concerts for the Saltire Society. In 1979 Jean Redpath became the first artist in residence at the University of Stirling where she tutored in traditional Scottish song and ballad as part of the Heritage of Scotland summer school program.

Following her recording for Highway/Trailer Records in Redditch, Worcestershire of *There Were Minstrels* (1977), a collection of traditional songs including the stirring "Dumbarton's Drums," Jean Redpath produced her next group of albums under Philo's auspices in the United States: *Song of the Seals* (1978), *Father Adam* (1979), and *Lowlands* (1980). The unforgettable title song of *Song of the Seals* is a modern classic, with music by Granville Bantock and lyrics by Harold Boulton. "A sea maid sings on yonder reef," the song begins. "The spell-bound seals draw near / A lilt that lures beyond belief / Mortals enchanted hear / Coir an oir an oir an oir O. . . . " The haunting refrain of "this rather arty song," Miss Redpath observed in the liner notes, "touches something so close to the heart that it has been 'recognized' by those born as far from the Hebrides as the Calabrian Hills of Italy." Revealing her typical mode of adding to her repertoire, she wrote: "I learned it from the singing of Father [now Canon] Sidney McEwan." Regarding other songs in the album, she noted, similarly, of "Davy Faa": "I think I learned this from the singing of Arthur Argo"; of "Poor Rovin' Lassie": "I heard it sung by Marg Sinclair of Thurso"; and of "Birnie Bouzle/Johnny Lad": "I learned it from the singing of Hamish Henderson."

Jean Redpath's extensive liner notes afford further clues to her manner of working. She reveals how she deals with historical sources and lines of transmission, both written and oral, as well as the varied versions and intricate connections of both lyrics and melodies from as early as the seventeenth century. For example, an early recording of "Father Adam" by Rory and Alex McEwan stayed in her "inactive" mental file for many years, until in 1977 she was reminded of it by hearing a seventeenth-century recorder piece with the melody of "a much traveled English dance tune" on a radio program in Boston. Her reference materials have included such collections as John Forbes's *Cantus, Songs and Fancies* (1662), James Johnson's six-volume *Scots Musical Museum* (1787-1803), Alexander Campbell's two-volume *Albyn's Anthology* (1816-18), William Motherwell's *Minstrelsy Ancient and Modern* (1827), Peter Buchan's *Gleanings of Scarce Old Ballads* (1825), Gavin Greig's *Folksong of the North East* (1909-14), and Francis James Child's *The English and Scottish Popular Ballads* (1883-98). Miss Redpath notes that three of the Child ballads on the *Father Adam* disc, "Sir Patrick Spens," "The Twa Brothers," and "The Trooper and the Maid," crossed the ocean directly from Scotland to America. The *Lowlands* album includes three Child ballads, the eerie "Clerk Saunders," the haunting "Mary Hamilton," and the mystical "Riddles Wisely Expounded," as well as such contemporary pieces as Dave Goulder's "Far-Away Tom" and Rosemary Hardman's "Who Shall Count for Thee." Texts are often collated from various sources, and some melodies are common to several ballads.

Since the mid-1970s Jean Redpath has focused much of her attention on recording the songs of Robert Burns, the national poet of Scotland. In addition to his better known poems, Burns wrote song lyrics of varying quality and mood for traditional melodies, which he collected from tune books, street ballads, and broadsides of the time. "He always started with a tune before he wrote a song," commented Miss Redpath. Except for a few, such as "Auld Lange Syne," most of those songs were forgotten. The American composer Serge Hovey began to research and produce all 323 Burns songs in a planned series of twenty record albums, all to be sung by Miss Redpath in authentic mode, backed by a small instrumental ensemble. Funded in part by the National Endowment for the Arts, the scholarly volume I of the huge undertaking was issued by Philo in 1976. Its songs include "Charlie, He's My Darling," "The De'il's awa wi th' Exciseman," "A Red Red Rose," and "Logan Water"—which has a traditional melody similar to that of the American cowboy ballad "Oh, Bury me not on the Lone Prairie."

In his review of volume II of *The Songs of Robert Burns* in *Stereo Review* (June 1981), Paul Kresh described it as "mostly sweet but sometimes salty"—an album that "bursts with infectious music"—and found Jean Redpath "quite simply, wonderful." Superlatives continued, with the comment of a reviewer of volume III (1981) in the *Los Angeles Times*: "Once again, Redpath proves that no one else can sing the traditional songs of Scotland as she can; she is a wonder." Volume IV of *The Songs of Robert Burns* was also released in 1981 by Philo. The pianist and composer Keith Jarrett provides the instrumental accompaniment to Miss Redpath's vocal renditions on Volume V of the series, scheduled for release in 1985. Jean Redpath's repertoire was further enlarged by the Scottish songs of the Austrian composer Franz Joseph Haydn (1732-1809), who over a period of sixteen years had composed arrangements for several volumes of Scottish songs at the request of publishers who selected the melodies and arbitrarily fitted them to the words. Miss Redpath's *Haydn: Scottish Songs* was slated for 1984 release, along with still another album, *Lady Nairne*, in which she sings ballads written by the eighteenth-century Scottish noblewoman of the title.

Despite the depth of her knowledge of the music of Burns and other traditional sources, Jean Redpath facetiously calls herself "a musical illiterate." She never learned how to read music and believes it would be a drawback to her at this point. In her interview with Susan Wilson in the *Boston Globe* (January 20, 1983), she asserted: "I mean, if you're talkin' about a student of music, I immediately think of somebody who is heavily into the history of the notation, the arranging of. . . . And that's a closed book to me. I work with my ears and with the audience's ears. . . . You don't have to be able to read the musical notation or understand how to play the instrument if you just hang loose and let the stuff react."

Asked by Robert Sherman in an interview on radio station WQXR-FM in New York City whether she does any collecting of songs in the remote Scottish countryside, Miss Redpath responded: "Anywhere and everywhere I can get my hands or rather my ears on them. . . . I'm working with an oral tradition and its oral transmission. The material I'm most interested in has been passed on orally for generations, I think. I've just developed the muscle to take it in fast that way." The first to sing Burns's songs professionally in modern times, she described the process whereby she selects appropriate melodies from tapes made by Scottish dialect singers to fit the poet's lyrics. "I get a cassette in the mail with maybe fifty melodies and listen to that for a while and then write back and say, 'These are the thirty I'd like to work with for the next two records.'" After listening to the cassette at odd moments for several months, she masters the tunes through "brainwashing," as she puts it.

Describing her repertoire, as quoted in *Folk Music: More Than a Song*, Joan Redpath said: "I must know several hundred songs, and they span everything from bluegrass to 'Will You Love Me When I'm Old' to kids' songs to ghastly English translations of Italian opera to fifty-verse ballads in the Scottish tradition." Although she prefers to sing a cappella, for the sake of an audience unused to unaccompanied singing she will use a guitar, but with "the simplest possible accompaniment," because essentially she is "concerned with the song" and not how to dress it up or do variations of it." Jean Redpath has joined her voice with that of Lisa Neustadt of Watertown, Connecticut for three albums of traditional religious music with back-up by the Angel Band. These are *Angels Hovering 'Round* (1979), an album of American spirituals and gospel songs; *Shout for Joy* (1980), a collection of Christmas carols, and *Anywhere Is Home* (1981). When Miss Redpath sings with instrumental backing, she prefers the sounds of the violin, the cello, and the oboe.

In recent years Jean Redpath has visited the United States regularly from Scotland to sing traditional airs at celebrations of Robert Burns's birthday in January. She has been a frequent visitor to radio station WGBH-FM's "Morning Pro Musica" in Boston, of which her longtime friend Robert J. Lurtsema is host. She and Lurtsema are scheduled to lead a music tour of Scotland that is to depart from Boston in June 1984. Miss Redpath has also done some offbeat live commercials for the fictional "Bertha's Kitty Boutique" on Garrison Keillor's popular National Public Radio show, *The Prairie Home Companion*. Both on stage and in the classroom, Miss Redpath takes her role as an educator seriously. "I'm always aimin' to widen audiences' horizons with Burns, with any kind of Scottish image people may have, and with Scottish music and Scottish songs in general," she says. In her performances to capacity audiences at universities, art centers, clubs, and folk festivals, as far north as Newfoundland and as far south as Peru in the Western Hemisphere, as well as in other parts of the world, her object is to present what she believes is the true richness of the Scottish character.

Jean Redpath lives more or less "out of a suitcase" when she is not at her childhood home in Leven or at Stirling University. Described as "sprightly and salty," she stands five feet eight inches. According to her own account, her eyes are "gray-green," her hair is "salt and pepper," and her weight is "confidential." In addition to travel, she enjoys ornithology and photography, snapping pictures of wildlife and landscapes on both sides of the Atlantic. Asked how she manages the arduous round of teaching, recording, radio appearances, and touring, she rejoined, as quoted in the *Boston Globe* article: "Oh, it's at the expense of little things like sleepin' and eatin'. But it sure as hell beats boredom! There aren't enough days in the week. . . . If somebody all of a sudden said 'All right! the next six weeks are totally cleared,' within three days I'd have myself overscheduled again!"

References: N Y Times p49 N 15 '61 por, C p11 Ja 20 '80; Stereo Review 46:76 Je '81 por, 47:65+ My '82 por; Baggelaar, Kristin and Milton, Donald. Folk Music: More Than a Song (1976)

Richie, Lionel

1949(?)– Singer; songwriter. Address: b. c/o Motown Record Corp., 6255 Sunset Blvd., Los Angeles, Calif. 90028

Lionel Richie, the Motown Record Corporation's latest superstar, has been the prototype for a new breed of black popular vocalist, one that has been described by Nelson George in the *Village Voice* (November 1, 1983) as "singers who owe as much in vocal attack and material to MOR [middle of the road] and adult contemporary as to soul . . . voices that aren't based on clichéd reinterpretations of gospel music." Before going solo in 1982, Richie was the chief songwriter and lead vocalist with the Commodores, who sold more than 25 million albums worldwide over the previous nine years. With his gentle, usually country-flavored romantic ballads, rich in melody and direct in sentiment, and his soaring vocals, Richie has won a vast crossover audience. His first solo LP, *Lionel Richie* (1982), was the biggest-selling album in Motown history, and "Truly," a single from the LP, won him a Grammy for best male pop vocalist of 1982. Referring to the hit song from Richie's second solo album, *Can't Slow Down* (1983), Stephen Holden wrote in the *Atlantic* (May 1984): "Richie has no rough edges, and his cross-cultural party invitation, 'All Night Long,' involves a global harmony with a charm as dulcet as that of Harry Belafonte's 'Calypso.'"

Lionel B. Richie Jr. was born in Tuskegee, Alabama in 1949 or 1950, according to varying sources. His father, a retired Army captain who works as a systems analyst, and his mother, an elementary school principal, now live in Joliet, Illinois. Richie grew up in Tuskegee, in the home of his grandmother, Adlaide Foster, on the campus of Tuskegee Institute, the black college, where his late grandfather had been a colleague of the founder, Booker T. Washington, and where Mrs. Foster was an instructor in classical piano. In that environment, he was sheltered from any signs of racism, with the result that the real world outside came as something of a shock to him. "I think I got bitter later on," he told Steve Pond in an interview for *Rolling Stone* (March 3, 1983), "because I felt cheated when I found out that the world wasn't like they taught me it was. A lot of times when I'm writing, I try to introduce this world I was brought up to believe in—the world I haven't quite found yet."

Richie taught himself to play the piano by imitating his grandmother's playing. His uncle Bertram, a big-band hornman, gave him his first saxophone. It was many years, however, before he aspired to become a performer. "Before that, I was a music lover, a listener, period," he recalled in an interview with Lynn Van Matre, the pop music critic of the *Chicago Tribune* (December 12, 1982).

As a listener, Richie was influenced from his earliest years by the ballets and symphonies he attended at Tuskegee as well as his grandmother's playing "Bach and Beethoven all day." "I really didn't understand a lot of what I saw, or like a lot of it," he confessed to Liz Derringer when she interviewed him for the *New York Daily News* (October 11, 1981). "But I guess a lot of it rubbed off. Also I got the country flavor from living in Alabama. I never thought I'd be influenced to the point of writing it, but it's there. 'Three Times a Lady' comes from my classical background and of course my R&B background—that's the neighborhood." Other influences were gospel, the Motown sound of the Temptations and the Supremes, and, in his late adolescence, the recordings of such white rock 'n' roll artists as James Taylor and the groups Crosby, Stills and Nash and Cream.

Richie received all of his elementary and half of his secondary schooling in Tuskegee. After completing high school in Joliet, Illinois, he enrolled at Tuskegee Institute, in 1968, with the intention of becoming an Episcopal priest. He explained to Liz Derringer: "Most of my heroes when I was growing up were ministers—Bishop Murray, Bishop Carpenter, Father Jones. One of these guys played honky-tonk piano at a bar on Saturdays. This is a priest! So I really got another side of it. I felt real close to them. [But] after about maybe a semester at Tuskegee I realized that a minister in a church was not my thing. I remember the greatest advice that was given to me was, 'Sometimes God has a way of making you a corner preacher. You get to speak to the masses of people.' And even though I'm not wearing a collar and even though I'm not going to church every Sunday, when I stand onstage and sing, 'Zoom,' 'Just to be Close,' 'Easy,' 'Three Times A Lady,' 'Still,' and you watch the people going 'Yeah,' it's the sermon, so I'm fine."

Richie finally majored in economics and minored in accounting, with the idea of later going into law. Meanwhile, he had taken his tenor saxophone along to Tuskegee with the intention of learning how to play it. (All he knew were some James Brown riffs.) "That's right," he told Lynn Van Matre of the *Chicago Tribune*, "I hadn't a clue how to play when I first joined the Commodores there. Thomas McClary, the guitar player, asked if I wanted to play with this group at a school talent show, and I said sure. It wasn't until two years later that I told the rest of the Commodores that I was winging it in the beginning."

The Commodores were originally the Mystics, comprising McClary, on guitar, William ("Wak") King, on trumpet, and Richie. The three recruited three more: drummer Walter ("Clyde") Orange, bassist Ronald LaPread, and pianist Milan Williams, who disbanded his own group, the Jays, to join the Mystics. Unhappy with the name the Mystics, the six almost broke up arguing over such alternative cognomens as "The Fantastic Soulful Six" and "The Mighty Wonders." Liz Derringer asked Richie if it were true that "when you named yourselves the Commodores, you had elongated the name from commode?" Richie answered, with a laugh: "No, no, no. . . . We said, enough of this garbage. We opened up a dictionary, stuck a finger into the book and came up with the name 'Commodore.' But it was very close to commode, so that's always been our joke."

Richie sees a "strange" serendipity in his coming together with the Commodores because he "didn't plan any of this." "Everything just evolved from the fact that early on in life I found I was too small to play football, too short to play basketball, and too slow to run track." The Commodores' rise in the music business, on the other hand, was very carefully planned, in accordance with a strategy laid down in a 251-page thesis that Wak King wrote at

Tuskegee. In that thesis, King analyzed, as he later explained, "why the Beatles, Led Zeppelin, etc. could draw 20,000 people into an auditorium and it took nine R&B acts to get 4,000 people into a neighborhood theatre." "We took not only a musical approach, but a business approach from day one," King has said. "That's why we write the kind of music we write and make the types of business decisions we make. It wasn't just record the music and see what happens. Most of it was planned out." For one thing, the Commodores aimed at becoming "bigger than the Beatles." In an interview with Steve Bloom for the *New York Daily News* (November 9, 1980), Richie explained, "We really meant, we want to be *like* the Beatles . . . a household word, a musical legend." King interjected, "Plus the Beatles were not offensive, whereas the Rolling Stones brought a negative connotation. With them, it's a if-you-come-to-my-concert-don't-forget-to-bring-your-drugs kind of thing. The Beatles were clean-cut."

While studying at Tuskegee, the Commodores worked as entertainers weekends and summers. Benny Ashburn, a black New York City marketing consultant with no previous music-business experience, became their manager and obtained for them bookings at Small's Paradise in Harlem and the Cheetah, then a popular rock 'n' roll club in midtown Manhattan. At the Cheetah they met Suzanne DePasse, a booking agent who later became a vice-president of Motown Records. Through Miss DePasse, they auditioned as opening act for the Jackson Five's 1971 European tour, and with their tightly choreographed performance overcame the fierce competition in the auditions.

After their return from Europe, the Commodores signed a contract with Berry Gordy, the founder and president of Motown Records. "We thought we were going to revolutionize the music business. Come out with a new sound, you know, and kill them," Richie recalled in his interview with Lynn Van Matre of the *Chicago Tribune*. "Then we were given some advice, which was 'Before you go off and revolutionize the music business, take three steps back and get a following.' See, once you get a following, you can take it anywhere. You can go into new wave, heat wave, whatever."

During a two-year period of grooming and adjustment at Motown, the Commodores cut several unsuccessful singles while building up a following through tours by front-acting for the Jackson Five and others on tours. They finally found a compatible Motown producer/arranger in the person of James Anthony Carmichael, who has produced the Commodores' recordings ever since and who now produces Richie's solo albums and singles as well. "We needed someone to take what we had in its rough form and polish it up into a diamond," William King told Steve Bloom. "That's what Carmichael did."

Borrowing the words of James Taylor, Steve Bloom described the Commodores' rough form as a "churning urn of burning funk." Their first hits were hard-driving, discotheque-oriented rhythm and blues compositions representing for the most part a collective effort in which the members of the group took turns writing or cowriting songs. The very first was Milan Williams' instrumental "Machine Gun" (1974), the title cut on the group's first album. Another track on that LP, "Bump," became so popular that it gave its name to a dance. The group followed up those funk-rock successes with the thumping "party" hits "I Feel Satisfied," "Slippery When Wet," "Fancy Dancer" (cowritten by LaPread and Richie), and "Brickhouse," the funkiest and most popular of the lot, written by all of the Commodores and sung with elastic voice by Clyde Orange.

In concert, the Commodores were, as Nelson George recounted in the *Village Voice* (November 1, 1983), "great fun," with Richie and Orange exchanging lead vocals and LaPread, McClary, Williams, and King "leaping about with the raunch & roll vigor you expect from six Southern boys on a Saturday night." By 1976 the group was one of the most successful party bands in pop music, with three gold albums (500,000 copies sold) behind them and their first platinum LP (1 million copies sold) in the works. That success was achieved despite the risk of blandness inherent in a musical democracy. "Without the spiritual verbiage of Earth, Wind and Fire's Maurice White and the cosmic jive of P-Funk's George Clinton as media hooks," Nelson George reminisced, "the Commodores were the black equivalent of Journey or REO Speedwagon—dedicated professionals whose group identity obscured their individuality. . . . Richie never dominated the group the way White or Clinton did."

That situation was already beginning to change, however, by common agreement of the members of the group, who wanted to move away from the disco "fad," with its ephemeral "tunes," to ballads that could become standards. "Do you know any funk tunes that are standards?" Wak King rhetorically asked Steve Bloom in the *New York Daily News* interview. "They're here for three months and then you just have to write another." Richie added: "We wanted to write a musical résumé to show people there's more to the Commodores than just, 'Baby, baby, baby, baby.'"

Meanwhile, Richie was developing his skill at songwriting, taking lessons from the team of Holland, Dozier, and Holland and others at Motown. He recounted in the *Rolling Stone* interview with Steve Pond: "I started following producer and songwriter Norman Whitfield around, asking him to teach me how to write songs. I sat in on some Stevie Wonder sessions, and Stevie would sit there and sing 'da da da da' and then fill in the words. I said, 'Wait a minute, you mean all I gotta do is fill in the 'da da's'? When I found that out, the ball game was over."

The transition in the Commodores' style and the ascendancy of Richie as the group's increasingly sophisticated ballad composer and lead singer began unobtrusively, with Richie's slow-tempo romantic song "This Is Your Life" on the Commodores' 1975 album *Caught in the Act*. The fusion of country, soul, and middle-of-the-road in that ballad was carried forward in "Zoom," "Sweet Love," and the gold single "Just to be Close to You," in which Richie's voice, as described by Nelson George, "oozing with country melancholy, projected lyrics as sentimental and courtly as roses on the first date." The trend continued with the Southern-flavored "Easy," a gold single that became an MOR standard and helped give the Commodores their first platinum LP, *Commodores* (1977); and it culminated in the triple-platinum "Three Times a Lady," a tribute to Richie's wife, mother, and grandmother. In 1978 "Three Times a Lady" jumped from the top of the soul charts to the top of the country and pop categories in the United States. Internationally, it made number one in five countries and the top five in twenty-five countries. The Commodores were ranked the number-one R&B group in 1978 by the publications *Rolling Stone*, *Billboard*, and *Cashbox*. In addition, they finished third in the pop category in *Billboard*'s chart.

During 1978 the Commodores made a six-month tour, performing "Too Hot to Trot," "Funny Feelings," "I Like What You Do," and other songs in their repertoire in ninety-two dates across the country. In *Ebony* (May 1979) Ron Harris described Richie's spectacular entrance and what followed in the final performance of the tour, in Montgomery, Alabama: "Suddenly, as if out of nowhere, a white baby grand piano rises out of smoke from behind the stage and ascends towards the ceiling. A string-bean thin Richie is seated at the keyboard crooning 'Three Times a Lady.' Women squeal and temporarily the pace slows. But moments later it is up again. 'I Feel Sanctified.' For two hours the exhaustive musical assault continues. 'Just To Be Close To You,' 'Easy,' 'Say Yeah,' 'This Is Your Life.' Lights. Explosions. Cheers. Encores." In 1979 the Commodores signed a new, seven-year contract with Motown worth $20 million. They also contracted to do commercials for the Schlitz Brewing Company.

Richie's progress toward solo stardom was accelerated by his gold, number-one songs "Sail On" and "Still," included in the Commodores' 1979 triple-platinum album *Midnight Magic*. The 1980 LP *Heroes* included allusions to James Cleveland ("Jesus is Love"), Deodato, James Conley ("Got to be Together"), and Otis Redding ("An Old-Fashioned Love") as well as echoes of Bob Dylan, the group America, and the Isley Brothers. Richie's career outside the Commodores was launched with "Lady," written and produced for country-pop crossover king Kenny Rogers, the most popular male vocalist in the United States, in 1980. Remaining six weeks in the number-one spot nationally, the lachrymose "Lady" was the biggest single of Rogers' career. Four more songs by Richie were included on Rogers' platinum album *Share Your Love* (1981), produced by Richie. "Not since Gladys Knight and the Pips topped the charts with a string of country tunes in the mid-Seventies," Stephen Holden observed in *Rolling Stone* (October 15, 1981), "have country and soul blended together with this much commercial success."

While producing *Share Your Love*, Richie was working with the Commodores on their album *In the Pocket* (1981), generally regarded as their best since the 1977 *Commodores*. The LP included Richie's country love plaint "Oh No" and "Lady, You Bring Me Up." The latter, cowritten by Harold Hudson and Richie and coproduced and lead-sung by Richie, became the Commodores' first top-ten hit in two years. Also in 1981 Richie wrote and sang (with Diana Ross) "Endless Love," the title song of the motion picture. At one point during the last week of August 1981 Richie was connected as composer, performer, or producer with three of the ten best-selling singles: "Lady, You Bring Me Up," "Endless Love," and Kenny Rogers' "I Don't Need You," written by Rick Christian and produced by Richie.

Richie's decision to leave the Commodores to concentrate on his solo career was a difficult one for him to make, because the Commodores are, in his words, "not a group but a family." The decision jelled only after the family's "father-image," manager Benny Ashburn, died of a heart attack, in September 1982, and the success of Richie's first solo album, *Lionel Richie*, released just after Ashburn's death. Reviewing the LP in the *New York Daily News* (October 29, 1982), Hugh Wyat confessed to being "awed at both the singing and songwriting powers of Richie, who has the kind of stuff Joe Williams and Marvin Gaye are made of: musical majesty, as this album so emphatically demonstrates." The first single from *Lionel Richie*, "Truly," headed straight to the top of the charts and won Richie his first Grammy (after eleven nominations) for best male vocalist. Two more singles from the album made the top five: "You Are," cowritten with his wife, Brenda, and "My Love," on which Kenny Rogers sang harmony.

Lionel Richie was described by the recording artist as "a survey" of his past music "to let people know where [he] had been before taking them on a musical journey." The next step in that journey was *Can't Slow Down* (1983). One of that album's cuts, "All Night Long," released as a single six weeks before, was the number-three song in the United States by the time the LP was issued. Among the other tracks was "Penny Lover," written with Brenda Richie. With the exception of "Can't Slow Down," "All Night Long," and "Running With the Night," the themes were romantic, but only "Hello" was a ballad in the sentimental mode of Richie's previous work. That work was described by Stephen Holden in the *New York Times* (November 9, 1983) as "simple country ballads" inflected with "nineteenth-century Romantic feeling," songs bordering on "pure corn" although given "a compelling emotional immediacy" by Richie's "open-hearted sincerity." Most of Richie's songs on *Can't Slow Down* were diversified by collaboration with the studio keyboard virtuoso Greg Phillinganes and other Los Angeles professionals. The result was "a tour de force of contemporary studio craft," as Holden observed; along with the "much more sophisticated arrangements," Richie's voice came across as "noticeably more virile and confident, slipping comfortably into rhythmically complicated pop-funk settings." A video of "All Night Long" was included in the MTV playlist on cable television.

Backed by a seven-piece band and enhanced by lavish staging, Richie made his first tour as a solo artist in the fall of 1983, collecting screaming welcomes and generally rave reviews in cities across the United States. Reviewing his performance at Radio City Music Hall, Brian Chin of the *New York Post* (October 14, 1983) reported that Richie was "in fine form," rendering his songs and monologue reminiscences "with conviction and grace." "He also seemed to be developing a Richard Pryor-like panache when he began cutting up," Chin added. "In time, his stage presence could easily become as imposing as his songwriting."

Lionel Richie and his wife, Brenda (who is also his production assistant), divide their time between their home in Beverly Hills, California and Richie's old apartment in Tuskegee, where he has bought the whole apartment complex. His perennial returns to his quiet hometown and the people who have known him since childhood help to keep him sane and unspoiled by his success. Heeding advice given him by Dick Clark in 1974, he has made his motto, "Be humble and never put yourself higher than they [the public] are." When he was with the Commodores (all of whom still live in Tuskegee) he attributed the ability of the group's members to resist the normal pitfalls of stardom to three factors: "We get eight hours of sleep, three meals a day, and are from good southern families." Wary of getting "lost in the glamor," he tries to live simply in spite of his wealth, because he "doesn't ever want to get to where [he] can't walk into his kitchen in [his] bathrobe without passing eighteen folks" and because he "has found out that you can only drive one car at a time." In his case, the car is a Porsche. Within the Commodores, Richie was good-naturedly dubbed "Jack Benny" because of his frugality.

"I don't think there's much chance of me getting carried away anyway," he told Lynn Van Matre in the *Chicago Tribune* interview. "I'm basically a reserved person." On the other hand, he admitted to being "the biggest ham in the world," and he was known as one of the glibbest of the Commodores. (McClary and King were the other two talkative members of the group.) Still, he is "the shyest guy in the world," except when he is performing, "because you feed off the audience." One of Richie's long-term goals is to "set up a network of people" in the entertainment industry that will help deserving talent find a chance to display itself. "The only reason that I am where I am today," he explained to Liz Derringer of the *New York Daily News*, "is that somebody gave me a chance."

References: *Chicago Tribune* VI p5+ D 12 '82 pors; *Ebony* 34:62+ My '79 pors; *N Y Daily News* p8+ N 9 '80 pors, L p16 O 11 '81 pors; *Newsday* II p21 O 10 '82 por; *Rolling Stone* p50 O 13 '81 por, p41+ Mr 3 '83 pors; *Washington Post* C p1 Ag 1 '80 por; Nite, Norm N. *Rock On* vol 2 (1978)

Rivera, Chita

Jan. 23, 1933– Dancer; actress; singer. Address: b. c/o Armando del Rivero, Room 32D, 484 W. 43d St., New York City, N.Y. 10036

A generation of critics in the American musical theatre has exhausted a small thesaurus of pyrotechnical and electromagnetic metaphors in attempting to describe the galvanic energy of the song-and-dance actress Chita Rivera. Trained in classical ballet, the fiery Miss Rivera in 1955 emerged from the anonymity of Broadway choruses as one of the fresh comedic talents in the Off-Broadway show *Shoestring Revue* (1955). On Broadway she went on to create, among other roles, Anita in *West Side Story* (1957), Rose in *Bye Bye Birdie* (1960), Anyanka in *Bajour* (1964), Velma in *Chicago* (1975), and Anna in *The Rink* (1984). Of her Tony Award–winning performance as Anna, Richard Corliss wrote in *Time* (February 20, 1984): "Packing thirty years of Broadway savvy into the frame of a vivacious teenager, the fifty-one-year-old entertainer could by now sell a song to the deaf." In addition to her work on stage and on television, the musical-comedy veteran played Nickie in the movie version of *Sweet Charity* (1969), and she has logged some 100,000 miles with what is widely regarded as one of the best cabaret acts in show business.

The third of five children, Chita Rivera was born Dolores Conchita Figuero del Rivero in Washington, D.C. on January 23, 1933. Her father, who was Puerto Rican, played clarinet and saxophone with the United States Navy Band. He also sat in with Harry James's orchestra, and he played in the pit orchestra for the 1924-25 Broadway musical *Lady Be Good*. Her mother, Katherine (Anderson) del Rivero, who was of mixed Scots-Irish-Puerto Rican descent, went to work as a government clerk after the death of her husband, when Chita was seven. Mrs. Rivero herself died in 1983.

Conchita del Rivero was, in her words, "brought up very strictly, in the old-fashioned Latin way." She has described herself in childhood as a hyperenergetic tomboy who "could run faster than a whippet and beat all the boys." Her first stage experience was doing arabesques and splits in shows organized by her older brother, Julio, in the theatre he improvised in the basement of the Rivero home on Buchanan Street in Washington. Her younger brother Armando is now her manager.

Enrolled by her mother in singing, piano, and ballet classes, Conchita del Rivero quit the singing lessons after three sessions; she enjoyed piano playing the more she progressed at it, but it was dance that became her consuming passion. At the instigation of her ballet teacher, Doris Jones, she auditioned with George Balanchine and won a scholarship to Balanchine's School of American Ballet in New York City. While studying under Balanchine, she lived with the family of an uncle, Luciano Figuero, in the Bronx, where she attended Taft High School. She graduated from Taft in 1951.

In 1952 Miss del Rivero went along as moral support with a nervous girlfriend from the School of American Ballet to an open call for dancers for the national touring company of the Irving Berlin musical *Call Me Madam*, choreographed by Jerome Robbins. Her girlfriend was not hired, but she was. After spending ten months on the road in *Call Me Madam*, she returned to New York City to replace Onna White as a principal dancer in *Guys and Dolls*, and from that Broadway show she moved into the chorus of *Can-Can*.

Gwen Verdon, the star of *Can-Can*, encouraged Chita del Rivero to break out of chorus work and into singing and acting as well as dancing. The decisive push in that direction came from another *Can-Can* dancer, Dania Krupska, who was choreographing Ben Bagley's Off-Broadway *Shoestring Revue*. It was at Bagley's insistence that Conchita del Rivero changed her name, first to Chita O'Hara (for three days, until friends persuaded her otherwise) and finally to Chita Rivera. Of her four skits in the revue, the most popular was a takeoff of Marilyn Monroe auditioning with Mike Todd for a part in a film version of *The Brothers Karamazov*. "At its poorest it was good," Garrison P. Sherwood wrote of *Shoestring Revue* in Louis Kronenberger's *The Best Plays of 1954-55*, "and at

its best it was hilarious and delightful. Beatrice Arthur, Arte Johnson, Chita Rivera, and others went on to bigger if not better things even before the show closed."

Miss Rivera's "bigger thing" was the role of Fifi, one of the trio of French prostitutes in the short-lived Broadway show *Seventh Heaven*, a musical version of Austin Strong's saccharine play. Frank Quinn of the *New York Mirror* (May 27, 1955) called Miss Rivera "a gal of flashy, bold personality . . . a thrilling dancer who struts and slinks like a panther [and] catches the eye with her every movement." In 1955 she also toured with the Oldsmobile Industrial Show, and the following year she acted, sang, and danced the role of Rita Romano in the Broadway musical *Mr. Wonderful*.

Mr. Wonderful was essentially a vehicle for Sammy Davis Jr., but Chita Rivera's success in it brought her the major role of Anita in the landmark musical drama *West Side Story*, a contemporary variation on the Romeo and Juliet theme that was conceived by Jerome Robbins and written by Arthur Laurents (book), Leonard Bernstein (music), and Stephen Sondheim (lyrics). In that variation, Shakespeare's star-crossed lovers became the Puerto Rican girl Maria and the Polish-American boy Tony, caught in the crossfire of two street gangs, one Puerto Rican (the Sharks) and the other "American" (the Jets), on New York's Upper West Side. Shakespeare's Nurse became Anita (Miss Rivera), Maria's closest friend and the girlfriend of her brother, Bernardo, the leader of the Sharks. As Anita, Miss Rivera sang the poignant "A Boy Like That" (when Bernardo is killed in a gang fight); "I Have a Love," a duet with Maria (Carol Lawrence); and the song with which she was most identified, the rousing show-stopper "America," a sardonic comparison of the mainland United States with Puerto Rico.

Following its world premiere in Washington, D.C., the original production of *West Side Story*, directed and choreographed by Jerome Robbins, opened at the Winter Garden in New York City on September 26, 1957. It ran to critical raves for 732 performances and brought Chita Rivera her first nomination for an Antoinette Perry (Tony) Award. In the course of the run, Miss Rivera, who had married Anthony Mordente, a fellow cast member, became pregnant and dropped out of the cast. After the birth of their daughter, Lisa Angela Mordente (now herself an actress in the musical theatre and on television), she and her husband reprised their *West Side Story* roles in a 1958-1959 production of the musical in England, where bootleg recordings of the New York production had been selling for approximately fifteen dollars a copy. Although profits were less, the show was received even more enthusiastically in London than it had been in New York. "English audiences seem to recognize the fact that this is something new—the most thoroughly integrated musical show ever staged," Robert E. Griffith, one of the show's producers, explained to a reporter. "In New York, in the opinion of critics, the success of the show was based mostly on its dancing." Chita Rivera felt that her own performance had improved because she had learned to "mellow all those colors."

In the original, Tony Award–winning Broadway production of Bye Bye Birdie (1960–1961), an effervescent, affectionate spoof of teen-age mores that was directed and choreographed by Gower Champion, Miss Rivera starred opposite Dick Van Dyke as Rose Grant, a talent agency secretary who becomes involved in turning the loss of her agency's meal ticket (a rock 'n' roll singer named Conrad Birdie who is being drafted) into a promotional coup. (Her idea is the staging of a national farewell-kiss contest among swooning American adolescent girls.) In her solo "Spanish Rose" and such song-and-dance numbers as the dream ballet "How to Kill a Man" and "Shriners' Ballet" (in which she galvanized a staid stag banquet), Miss Rivera triumphed with New York critics and audiences, and she acquired her second Tony nomination. When the show was produced in England in 1961, her talent compensated for the loss of impact suffered by much of the American-oriented satire in the transatlantic crossing. British critics considered her to be Bye Bye Birdie's "greatest asset," an "adorable, irresistible musical star who radiates the rare qualities of stardom with every gesture, every inflection of her voice" and a "quality of parody and wit" that "makes her dancing so unique."

Typical of the British reviews of Bye Bye Birdie was the notice in the Guardian (May 25, 1961) by John Mapplebeck, who regarded the show as a throwback to the "smoothness, the bright toothpaste glamour, the sheer professionalism" of "the American musical as it was before the Bernstein revolution." At first, the casting of Miss Rivera in such a production seemed to Mapplebeck a "waste," as "pointless as setting a tigress amid chimps at a tea party." As it turned out, however, her very presence "somehow transmuted" the mere "competence" of the show into "brilliance." "So magnetic is her personality that we tend to forget the plot . . . and wait only for Miss Rivera to take the center of the stage."

Having become a favorite there, Chita Rivera returned to England in 1964 to do a television show and a benefit with the Beatles, the preeminent rock 'n' roll group of the day. Meanwhile she had been appearing frequently on American television since 1956. Her early television credits included guest shots on the variety shows of Ed Sullivan, Garry Moore, Sid Caesar, Dinah Shore, and Arthur Godfrey. She also did her first straight acting on television.

Zenda, a musical adaptation of The Prisoner of Zenda starring Miss Rivera and Alfred Drake, closed after pre-Broadway tryouts in San Francisco and Pasadena, California in 1963. Bajour, which ran on Broadway for seven months in 1964–1965, was a musical remarkable principally, as Otis L. Guernsey Jr. observed in The Best Plays of 1964–1965, "for the swing and sway of Chita Rivera" in the role of the scheming gypsy princess Anyanka, which brought the actress her third Tony

nomination. During the run of Bajour, Mayor Robert F. Wagner named Chita Rivera the official hostess of New York City's "World's Fair and Summer Festival Season."

Although "happiest when there's an orchestra pit in front" of her, and fearful of being "that close to all those strangers" and hating "to compete with alcohol," Chita Rivera put together a cabaret act with the help of lyricist Fred Ebb, composer John Kander, and choreographer Ron Field and took it on the road in January 1966. The act, in which she was supported by two women dancers, received generally good reviews ("charming and fiercely talented"; "a dazzling dancer"; "a very dramatic singer gifted with a fascinating raspy mezzo"), but she was glad to get back to the theatre, in summer stock performances as Linda Low in Flower Drum Song and as Jenny in Threepenny Opera.

In 1967 and 1968 Chita Rivera toured the United States and Canada as Charity, the dime-a-dance hostess with the golden heart in the national company of the 1966 Broadway hit Sweet Charity. In the motion-picture version released by Universal Pictures in February 1969, Shirley MacLaine had the title role and Chita Rivera was cast as her roommate, Nickie. She was unhappy with the appearance that director-choreographer Bob Fosse forced her to assume ("cheap," with "this ghastly white makeup") as Nickie, but Rex Reed, who panned the film in Women's Wear Daily (April 18, 1969), liked her "brassy" dancing, and Judith Crist of New York (April 7, 1969), in another otherwise negative review, hailed her as one of the "freshest and most gifted of song-and-dance newcomers to the screen."

That one experience in films confirmed Chita Rivera's respect for "the Broadway mentality," with its "dedication, hard work and the development of a craft," as opposed to "the Hollywood mentality, which is really a job . . . out of which sometimes comes fame." However, she liked California, with its wide-open spaces, especially as an environment for her daughter to grow up in, and she stayed in Los Angeles, making it her home for seven years.

In 1969 Chita Rivera was cast as the Spanish-Jewish mistress of Christopher Columbus in the Los Angeles Light Opera Company's still-born premiere production of Meredith Willson's 1491, which was, in Miss Rivera's words, "laughed . . . right out of California." Later in the same year, Harold Prince, the producer-director of the musical drama Zorba, which had just ended its first Broadway run, chose Miss Rivera to replace Maria Karnilova in the role of the narrator-oracle Hortense for the show's national tour (1969–1970). In the early 1970s she joined touring productions of Jacques Brel is Alive and Well and Living in Paris and Kiss Me Kate (with Hal Linden). During the same period she went "legitimate" for the first time, starring as Billy Dawn in a 1972 production of Born Yesterday in Philadelphia and as Serafina in a summer stock production of The Rose Tattoo in New Orleans. On television, she played next-door neighbor Connie Richardson in the situation comedy *The New Dick Van Dyke Show*, which ran on the CBS network from September 1973 to September 1974.

Chicago theatre critics were stunned by the intensity of Chita Rivera's performance as the Catholic divorcée in Oliver Hailey's *Father's Day*, which she did at the personal request of the author in 1974. It was "a very scary experience" for her, because of "the similarities between the part" and herself. (She and Anthony Mordente were divorcing.) Nevertheless, "the experience with *Father's Day* did a lot" for her, making her feel "much more secure as an actress, a dramatic actress."

A more club-wise Chita Rivera resumed her cabaret act, again created for her by Ebb, Kander, and Field, in January 1975. The new nightclub act, called "Chita Plus Two" (a reference to her male chorus), "exploded like a rocket" at the Grand Finale in New York City, as an "enchanted" Norma McLain Stoop reported in *After Dark* (March 1975), and the legendary film dancers Gene Kelly and Fred Astaire were in the opening-night audience when Miss Rivera took the act to Studio One in Los Angeles.

Miss Rivera returned to the Broadway stage in June 1975, costarring with Gwen Verdon and Jerry Ohrbach in the sinfully seductive Fosse/Ebb/Kander show *Chicago*, a wryly cynical "musical vaudeville" about corruption and vice in Chicago in the 1920s. As the sassy Velma Kelly, "the second most famous murderess in Cook County Jail," she drew thunderous ovations from audiences and critical descriptions like "sensational," "demonic," and "20,000 volts of untamed electricity." "Both the girls dance their hearts out . . . ," Clive Barnes wrote in his opening-night review in the *New York Times* (June 4, 1975). "Miss Verdon's voice, all candy innocence and yet somehow naughtily suggestive . . . , is perfectly matched by the strangulated tones of Miss Rivera's blasé worldliness." For her performance, Chita Rivera received her fourth Tony nomination.

Chicago ran for more than two years on Broadway, for a total of 898 performances. Halfway through the run, Chita Rivera left the cast to embark on a revised and expanded version of her nightclub act, which now included the number "Losing," an allusion to the Tony awards that eluded her. With her new act she toured the United States, Canada, and Europe into the 1980s. "Rivera is primarily a dancer," Curt Davis wrote of one performance in the *New York Post* (April 25, 1979), "but her singing has grown from an auxiliary talent to a primary one. Being able to sing while dancing demands great physical stamina, which she has, but she goes beyond that in quiet numbers to a dramatic depth that's surprising." In 1980 the National Academy of Concert and Cabaret Arts honored her with its award for best variety performance. Between 1972 and 1981 Miss Rivera was in the cast of four editions of the Milliken Breakfast Show, an industrial show sponsored by the fabric manufacturer.

Bring Back Birdie, the depressingly inadequate sequel to *Bye Bye Birdie*, closed after only four performances at the Martin Beck Theatre in March 1981, but Chita Rivera personally triumphed in the dance numbers "A Man Worth Fighting For" and "Well, I'm Not," and she earned her fifth Tony nomination. Even she, as the Queen, could not salvage the poor material in her next Broadway effort, *Merlin* (1983), a hybrid musical-magic show notable only for the illusions created by Doug Henning, the production's *raison d'être*. During the 1983–1984 television season she appeared in a production of the musical *Pippin* on the Showtime cable network.

It was specifically for Chita Rivera that John Kander and Fred Ebb, with the help of librettist Terrence McNally, wrote *The Rink*, set in a dilapidated roller-skating arena in a seedy amusement park "somewhere on the Eastern seaboard." In that musical, which opened at the Martin Beck Theatre on February 9, 1984, Miss Rivera was cast as Anna Antonelli, an Italian-American widow who decides to sell the family-owned rink to condominium developers. Liza Minelli was cast as her longestranged daughter, Angel, who bitterly opposes the demolition of the rink. The plot, with flashbacks, traces the mother-daughter conflict and its ultimate resolution. Critics generally agreed that the "banal," "catatonic," "tedious" book was redeemed by the musical's stars, especially Miss Rivera, who commanded the audience like "a lion tamer with a whip snap in her walk." "Miss Minelli's and Miss Rivera's performances are knowing and efficiently executed," the usually captious John Simon generously conceded in *New York* (February 20, 1984), "though Miss Rivera's is far more proficiently multifaceted."

For her performance in *The Rink* Miss Rivera finally won the Tony award for outstanding actress in a musical. Just before receiving it on June 3, 1984, she told Cindy Adams of the *New York Post* (June 4, 1984): "My mother passed away before *The Rink* opened. We were devoted. We were as one. I'm only an extension of my mother. I look like her. Think like her. Every step I do on that stage is for her. I'm dancing for her. If I win this Tony, I'm winning for her. For me this is all a master plan." Shortly after Stockard Channing replaced Liza Minelli in the role of Angel, *The Rink* closed, on August 4, 1984.

Chita Rivera, who lives in Westchester County, New York, has been linked romantically with several men since her divorce from Anthony Mordente, but she has never remarried. Besides watching her diet, she keeps in shape by swimming, playing tennis, bowling, and riding horseback, and she is reputedly expert at cooking and needlepoint. Short (five feet three inches) as well as lithe, with a swarthy complexion, tightly curled black hair, and a lean, high-cheekboned face, she is the first to acknowledge that she has never been "the ingénue or leading-lady type." With facetious self-deprecation, she has in interviews described her walk as "very definite," "this mug of mine" as one that requires her "to smile to look good," and her temperament as volatile ("I can't hide anything emotional"). "Not an aggressive planner," she "loathes the push and power one needs for that," but she is always "rarin' to go."

Others have described Miss Rivera as a hard-working perfectionist in her craft and, in her life, a "charming" person, good in conversation, "bountiful" in her loyalty and generosity to those around her, and "a toucher." The affection she enjoys among her peers was obvious in the response of the celebrity audience to her reception of the Tony Award in 1984. An active Democrat, she has participated in such political campaigns as those of

1972 presidential candidate George McGovern and former United States representative Bella Abzug. Her civic activities have included involvement in the "I Love a Clean New York" drive.

References: After Dark 8:66+ D '75 pors, 9:79+ N '76 pors; Dance Mag 39:32+ Ja '65 por, 59:40+ Ag '84; N Y Daily News V p13 S 18 '60 pors, III p5 O 31 '76; N Y Post p21 My 30 '65 por; N Y Times II p1+ My 29 '60 por, C p22 D 24 '81 por; Newsday II p5 Jl 20 '75, p4 F 5 '84; Biographical Encyclopedia & Who's Who of the American Theatre (1966); Notable Names in the American Theatre (1976); Who's Who in America, 1983-84; Who's Who in the Theatre, 1981

Rogers, Bernard W(illiam)

July 16, 1921- United States military officer; Supreme Allied Commander Europe, North Atlantic Treaty Organization

General Bernard W. Rogers, who became supreme Allied commander in Europe, or "SACEUR," in June 1979, has been commended by his colleagues for being "one of the more progressive thinkers in the army" and "an ideal combination of manager and combat leader." A West Point graduate and Rhodes Scholar, and a combat veteran of the Korean and Vietnam conflicts, Rogers won favorable publicity as commander of the 5th Infantry Division (Mechanized) in 1969-70 and as army chief of staff from 1976 to 1979, mainly because he instituted major reforms designed to make army training more meaningful for the common soldier and improved communications between officers and en-

listed personnel. As supreme Allied commander in Europe within the military structure of the North Atlantic Treaty Organization (NATO), Rogers has been a leading champion of "flexible response," making Western defenses less exclusively dependent on nuclear arms, while allowing the Allies a greater leeway in their response to aggression.

Bernard William Rogers was born on July 16, 1921 in Fairview, Kansas to William Henry and Lora (Haynes) Rogers. Many years later, Major General Dewitt C. Smith, the commandant of the Army War College, was quoted in the New York Times (March 6, 1979) as saying: "Deep down I think Bernie Rogers is still a small-town boy from the Midwest. He still talks about Kansas, and Kansas is still with him. There's a directness, a frankness, an understanding that little people count as well as big people. He still has his feet in the dirt, and he's proud of it."

After attending Kansas State College in 1939-40, Rogers received an appointment to the United States Military Academy at West Point, New York, where he was a track star and first captain of the corps of cadets. On graduating with a B.S. degree and a lieutenant's commission in 1943, he was assigned to serve as a platoon leader with the 70th Infantry Division at Camp Adair, Oregon until his reassignment to West Point in 1944. General Maxwell D. Taylor, who was at the time the superintendent at West Point, asked who was "the brightest and most promising" among the young officers stationed at West Point. Informed that it was "Bernie Rogers," he promptly appointed him to serve as his aide at the United States Military Academy. When General Mark Clark served as commander of the American forces in Austria in 1946-47, Rogers joined him as his aide.

In 1947 Rogers went to England to study politics, economics, and philosophy at Oxford University on a Rhodes scholarship. He obtained his B.A. degree from Oxford in 1950 and qualified for an M.A. degree in 1954. Meanwhile, during 1952, Rogers had served in Korea as commanding officer of the 3d battalion in the 9th infantry regiment of the 2d infantry division, earning a Bronze Star with V device. Then, in 1953–54 he was executive officer to the commander in chief of the Far East Command, and in 1954–55 he attended the Command and General Staff College for additional training. From 1956 to 1959 he served in the Pentagon as a staff officer and executive officer to the Army chief of staff; in 1959–60 he attended the Army War College at Carlisle Barracks, Pennsylvania; and during 1960–61 he was commanding officer of the first battle group of the 19th infantry division and chief of staff of the 24th infantry division, in Augsburg, West Germany.

From 1962 to 1966 Rogers served in the Pentagon as executive officer to General Maxwell D. Taylor, then the chairman of the Joint Chiefs of Staff, and from November 1966 until the summer of 1967 he saw combat duty in Vietnam as assistant commander of the 1st Infantry Division. In August 1967 Rogers—now a brigadier general—was named by President Lyndon B. Johnson to succeed Brigadier General Richard P. Scott as commandant of cadets at the United States Military Academy at West Point, and he remained at that post until 1969.

During 1969–70 Rogers served for a year as commander of the 5th Infantry Division (Mechanized) at Fort Carson, Colorado. While there, he instituted some well-publicized reforms that brought him criticism as well as praise. "It's very important today to provide the soldier with training he believes is meaningful," Rogers said, as quoted in the *New York Times* (November 2, 1970). "That means getting rid of make-work we've always had. I'm a nut on that one." Among other innovations, Rogers eliminated "kitchen police" duty, early morning formations and roll calls, and "G.I. parties" to scrub barracks for Saturday inspections. He established a junior officers' council and an enlisted men's council to air grievances and encourage suggestions, a racial harmony council to defuse race problems, a drug center to help active or potential narcotics addicts, and an on-post Greenwich Village–style coffee house. His innovations were credited with stimulating a substantial increase in reenlistments at Fort Carson.

As chief of legislative liaison in the office of the Secretary of the Army in 1971–72, Rogers earned the respect of key members of the House and Senate Armed Services committees. He then served as deputy chief of staff for personnel with the Department of the Army from 1972 to 1974, while the army was being converted into an all-volunteer force. In 1974 Rogers was promoted to four-star rank and was appointed commanding general of one of the army's top commands, the Army Forces Command at Fort McPherson, Georgia, which exercised authority over all army units in the United States. During his tenure in that post, Rogers had a confrontation with Senator William Proxmire, the nation's most vigilant critic of government waste. The senator had discovered in February 1976 that an army plane had been ordered on a "training mission" to deliver some of the general's personal effects. Rogers, who claimed to have been unaware of the alleged "training mission," prompt-

ly dismissed the officers who had arranged the flight and wrote out a check for $931.60 to the United States Treasury, to cover the cost. "General Rogers undoubtedly is not the first general or admiral involved in the personal use of an official aircraft," Proxmire later said on the Senate floor, "but he is the only general I know with the courage to say it was wrong and immediately take corrective action."

On July 28, 1976 President Gerald R. Ford appointed Rogers to succeed the retiring General Frederick C. Weyand as army chief of staff, making him the first of the occupants of the army's highest post in recent years who did not actually see World War II combat duty. Taking office in October of that year, Rogers remained as chief of staff following the inauguration of President Jimmy Carter in January 1977. During his three-year tenure, he concentrated much of his effort on enhancing the army's preparedness and on replenishing and updating its arsenal, which had been depleted by the Vietnam conflict. He also instituted reforms designed to improve communications between high-ranking officers and those of lower rank, both commissioned and enlisted, and he introduced a program of organizational effectiveness into the conduct of army personnel programs.

Agreeing with Secretary of Defense Harold Brown and Allied commanders in Europe, Rogers defended the existing all-volunteer army, while recognizing such problems as the prospect of future manpower shortages and a possible decline in the caliber of volunteers. The present volunteer, he said in mid-1977, was "more trainable," "better motivated," and less susceptible to desertion, crime, and narcotics addiction. Although he praised the role of women in the army, he rejected front-line combat duty for them: the prospect of "women with rifles and fixed bayonets holding a forward position" gave him "heartburn," he said. In a letter released in August 1978, Rogers called on base commanders to determine why black soldiers received "disproportionate numbers of punitive discharges," were "overrepresented in confinement facilities," and were generally "charged with more serious offenses" than white soldiers. He instructed commanders to "eliminate any discriminatory handling of soldiers" and to "use more imagination" in dealing with that "persistent problem area" while emphasizing that standards of discipline must be maintained.

Addressing a convention of Veterans of Foreign Wars that was held in Minneapolis, Minnesota in August 1977, Rogers pointed out that the main goal of the armed forces was to avoid war, since no one could emerge victorious in a nuclear conflict. To attain that goal, however, Rogers added that the United States must maintain a balance of nuclear forces with the Soviet Union, a high level of preparedness, and a willingness to apply force if needed. Although Rogers had previously felt that military conscription was unnecessary, he suggested in testimony before the manpower subcommittee of the Senate Armed Services Committee in

ROGERS

March 1979 that in order for the army to sustain its combat readiness in wartime, a limited draft might be necessary to supplement the all-volunteer force. He proposed that some 75,000 to 100,000 men be drafted each year for training in the combat arms and six years of standby service in the Individual Ready Reserve, and he also suggested that women be registered. His proposals for a limited draft were supported by all of the service chiefs but opposed by Army Secretary Clifford C. Alexander Jr., who maintained that a draft would be "unnecessary, unfair, and counterproductive."

In a meeting with the press in mid-June 1979, Rogers warned that during the early 1980s the United States would lag behind the Soviet Union in strategic nuclear capability and could be vulnerable to a Soviet "first strike" attack until about 1986, when the new powerful mobile multi-warhead MX missiles were scheduled to be employed. "There will be a time frame," Rogers said, "in which, in my opinion, we will have lost what I consider the level of strategic ability to insure essential equivalence." A few days later, Rogers revealed that the army had plans for a "quick-strike" contingency force of about 110,000 men to deal with crises in the Middle East and other areas outside of the jurisdiction of the North Atlantic Treaty Organization.

Effective June 29, 1979, General Bernard W. Rogers became supreme Allied commander in Europe, or SACEUR, of the sixteen-member North Atlantic Treaty Organization, a post consistently occupied by Americans since NATO was established in 1949 to provide a system of collective defense among Western nations. NATO has two other regional commands, Allied Command Atlantic and Allied Command Channel, headed by commanders who are known as "SACLANT" and "CINCHAN," respectively. Rogers had been nominated on February 28, 1979 by President Jimmy Carter, reportedly because he was basically apolitical and noncontroversial, unlike his predecessor, General Alexander M. Haig Jr., an outspoken critic of American policies involving NATO who was reported to entertain presidential ambitions. As SACEUR and as commander of all United States forces in Europe, Rogers took on authority over about 4 million troops, including some 300,000 Americans.

During his address to the annual assembly of NATO in Washington, D.C. in November 1979, Rogers noted that in the three decades of its existence the organization had succeeded in preserving peace with freedom in Europe, adding that the continued avoidance of conflict was contingent upon maintenance of an "essential equivalence" between the strength of the Western alliance and that of the Warsaw Pact. "One cannot help but to be impressed—perhaps depressed is the better word—by the folly, futility, and waste of war as a means of resolving man's problems," he observed. "But if there are to be no more wars, then our . . . alliance must be strong and prepared to stand up to the threat of the military power we face to the East."

To overcome the perceived lag in NATO's defenses behind those of the Warsaw Pact, Rogers called for modernization of its tactical nuclear forces, including the deployment of new intermediate range ballistic missiles. He also proposed that the United States develop the controversial neutron bomb which, he told an interviewer for *Reader's Digest* (December 1980), could "stop enemy tanks without endangering American soldiers," but he pointed out that the decision to produce it was "a political matter up to our political leaders." In early 1980 Rogers warned that Western Europe might be vulnerable to a surprise attack from the U.S.S.R. in the wake of the recent Soviet invasion of Afghanistan; that remark brought him censure from West Germany's Chancellor Helmut Schmidt, who maintained that the general's statement created unnecessary alarm. But Rogers won approval for his diplomacy in working out a compromise that enabled Greece, which had left the military wing of NATO in 1974 as a protest against Turkey's invasion of Cyprus, to renew its membership in the alliance in October 1980.

Remaining SACEUR after the inauguration of President Ronald Reagan in January 1981, Rogers devoted much of his effort in the early 1980s to implementing NATO's strategy of "flexible response." That strategy had prevailed since the abandonment of the strategy of "massive retaliation" in the 1960s. "Flexible response" is based, in Rogers' words, "not only on the possession of adequate forces, but also on maintaining flexibility in their planned employment so as to foster uncertainty in the mind of a potential aggressor as to the means by which NATO would respond to his aggression."

In keeping with the concept of "flexible response," Rogers proposed raising the nuclear threshold and lessening dependence on tactical nuclear armaments by building up conventional forces. Under Rogers' proposal, presented to Allied commanders in the fall of 1982, on the eve of the second round of strategic arms reduction talks with the Soviet Union in Geneva, conventional forces were to be equipped with innovative electronically guided missiles capable of knocking out "follow-on" Soviet bloc forces after an initial attack, thus lessening the need for nuclear weapons. To help meet the cost, Rogers proposed that the NATO powers increase their defense expenditures by some 4 percent annually. Although some criticized the Rogers proposal as being too costly, it was endorsed by NATO defense ministers in December 1982.

Rogers has expressed concern about a growing tendency toward "pacifism, neutralism, and unilateralism" that was on the rise in Europe, partly in response to the December 1979 decision by NATO's foreign and defense ministers to install 572 American-made Cruise and Pershing II intermediate-range missiles in Western Europe by 1983. The peace achieved by unilateral Western disarmament could, as he pointed out in *Foreign Affairs* (Summer 1982), be attained only "at an inevitably terrible cost as the burden of demands from the East became intolerable." In answer to some Americans, including congressmen, who were demanding the withdrawal of United States troops from Europe, Rogers asserted in October 1982 that the troops provided "the cement keeping the alliance together" and that Europeans might lose the will to resist Soviet domination if Americans withdrew.

On the other hand, Rogers criticized "those who argue that meaningful measures of arms control and reductions are unachievable given the record of intransigence by the Soviet Union." He noted that "the incentives for the Soviet Union to share the Western interest in such accords are growing," in that it is equally concerned with "avoiding the awesome destructiveness of nuclear war" and in that it could alleviate its domestic problems by diverting expenditures from the military to other sectors. He did not rule out the possible use of nuclear weapons if necessary "to retain the cohesiveness" of the NATO defense structure, as he indicated in late 1983. Such a decision, he said, would require consultation with NATO political leaders and would be carried out under procedures tested in war games by the alliance's military commanders.

At a news conference in West Germany in September 1984, Rogers called for new chemical weapons that would match those in the Warsaw Pact arsenals and provide the West with greater leverage in bargaining with the Soviet bloc. His views were at odds with those of West German Chancellor Helmut Kohl's center-right coalition, which shortly afterward introduced a resolution in the Bundestag calling for a global, verifiable ban on chemical weapons. Rogers pointed out, however, that chemical warfare should be resorted to only after consultation among the Allies under a formalized procedure like that involved in the use of nuclear weapons.

In addition to the Bronze Star with V device he earned in Korea, General Rogers holds the Distinguished Service Cross, the Defense Distinguished Service Medal, the Legion of Merit with four oak leaf clusters, the Distinguished Flying Cross with two oak leaf clusters, the Silver Star, and the Air Medal with thirty-five oak leaf clusters. He has written a number of articles as well as a monograph in the Vietnam Studies series entitled *Cedar Falls—Junction City: A Turning Point* (Department of the Army, 1974). Rogers is an honorary fellow of University College, Oxford University and a member of Phi Delta Theta, the Association of the United States Army, the Legion of Valor, the Council on Foreign Relations, the Association of American Rhodes Scholars, and the American Society of the French Legion of Honor.

Bernard W. Rogers was married on December 28, 1944 to Ann Ellen Jones of Hiawatha, Kansas. They have a son, Michael W. Rogers, an army officer, and two daughters, Diane and Susan. Associates have described Rogers variously, as temperamental, brilliant, complex, suave, poised, elitist, and dedicated to West Point tradition. According to one aide, quoted by Bernard Weinraub in the *New York Times* (March 6, 1979), Rogers "has a quick temper, and he's a quick forgiver. He's very intimidating because of his intelligence. He forgets nothing. But he has a sense of humor and is basically a very decent man." In trying to arrive at decisions, Rogers often asks associates whether a given course of action is good for NATO. His recreational activities include golf and reading. On social occasions he has sometimes been known to burst into song with his lilting tenor voice. Among his favorites is the Frank Sinatra hit "My Way."

References: *Chicago Tribune I* p18 Mr 11 '79 por; *N Y Times* p6 Mr 6 '79 por; *International Who's Who, 1984–85; Who's Who, 1984–85; Who's Who in America, 1984–85*

Rose, George

Feb. 19, 1920– Actor. Address: b. c/o International Creative Management, 40 W. 57th St., New York City, N.Y. 10019

Although he has been a New York City resident since 1961, George Rose is considered by many theatregoers to be the archetype of the British character actor. Resourceful and infinitely inventive, he learned his craft in the great English classical repertory companies, where he shared the stage with such luminaries as Sir Ralph Richardson and Sir Laurence Olivier. Equally at home in drama, comedy, and musicals, Rose has attributed his extraordinary versatility to "an interest that ranges widely over a number of things" and to "a solid belief in technique." Although he has scores of motion pictures and television productions to his credit, he is most in his element before an audience. "When I have a stage to go on, it's like putting a fish in water," the actor recently remarked, as quoted in the *New York Times* (September 9, 1983). "The more you work in the theatre the more you feel safer there than anywhere else."

George Walter Rose was born on February 19, 1920 in Bicester, a village about twelve miles north of Oxford, England. He is the only child of Eva Sarah (Rolfe) Rose and Walter John Alfred Rose, a butcher and farmer who practised what his son once called "the strictest kind of nineteenth-century Methodist conservatism." An indifferent student, George Rose received his elementary education locally, then went on to attend Oxford High School for Boys, where he "behaved in quite unspectacular fashion," as he puts it. After leaving school in 1936, Rose worked as a secretary to the bursar of Wadham College, Oxford University until he was, in his words, "drafted by Hitler" in 1940. He was discharged for medical reasons after three years of service.

Shortly after his demobilization, Rose, who hoped to become a cathedral organist, began attending classes at the Trinity College of Music in London. A few months later, in answer to an advertisement he had noticed on the school's bulletin board, he auditioned for and secured a part-time position as an offstage singer in Tyrone Guthrie's acclaimed production of *Peer Gynt* for the Old Vic Company, with Ralph Richardson in the title role and Laurence Olivier as the Button-molder. "To see them play on stage and control an audience, especially in comedy, impressed me tremendously," Rose told an interviewer in 1981. "It made me want to be involved in theatre more than anything else."

Rose therefore enrolled in 1944 at the Central School of Speech and Drama on a scholarship, while continuing to appear as a supernumerary in Old Vic productions. Throughout that turbulent period, which coincided with the worst of the V-1 and V-2 rocket attacks on the British capital, Rose also worked as an orderly at a central London hospital. "I was on the night shift, and I used to go from the theatre to . . . Middlesex Hospital," he told Jerry Tallmer in an interview for a *New York Post* (March 23, 1974) profile. "I cleaned large sections of it. Then I'd walk home to Belsize Park, in Hampstead. Then I'd go to school in the morning. And I was also studying music. You know what you can do when you're young."

On leaving drama school in 1945, Rose became a full-fledged member of the Old Vic Company. Over the next few years, he played a number of supporting or character roles, among them Sir Christopher Hatton in Richard Brinsley Sheridan's comedy of manners *The Critic*, Kastril in Ben Jonson's *The Alchemist*, Montfleury in *Cyrano de Bergerac*, Edmond Rostand's poetic drama, and Zemlyanika in Nikolai Gogol's *The Government Inspector*. He made his New York debut with the company in 1946, playing the role of Peto in a well-received production of *Henry IV, Part I*.

By the early 1950s, Rose was moving with ease between parts in contemporary plays in London's commercial West End and roles in classical repertory at the Shakespeare Memorial Theatre in Stratford-upon-Avon. His credits there included Lennox in *Macbeth*, Oswald in *King Lear*, Brabantio in *Othello*, Pompey in *Measure for Measure*, and Belarius in *Cymbeline*. An excellent comic actor, he was especially effective as Snug in *A Midsummer Night's Dream* and as Autolycus in *The Winter's Tale*, but it was as Dogberry, the ridiculously pompous constable in John Gielgud's celebrated production of *Much Ado About Nothing*, which finally reached New York in September 1959, that he established his reputation as a first-rate Shakespearean clown. "Mr. Rose's Dogberry makes it unnecessary for anyone to play the part again . . . ," Brooks Atkinson wrote in his *New York Times* (September 18, 1959) review of the Broadway opening of *Much Ado*. "Exuberant, full-voiced, grandly self-confident, Mr. Rose fractures the English language in the highest good humor, beaming benevolently on his watch and his masters."

Perhaps in an effort to avoid typecasting as a classical comedian, Rose also accepted a wide variety of roles in more contemporary plays. Among his West End assignments in the 1950s were the parts of the butler Humpage in John Whiting's fantasy *A Penny For a Song*, Nils Krogstad, the unscrupulous moneylender in Henrik Ibsen's *A Doll's House*, Creon in Christopher Logue's one-act *Antigone*, and Maitland, the paranoid manservant in Gielgud's extravagantly praised production of Enid Bagnold's offbeat comedy *The Chalk Garden*. Critics were especially taken with his interpretations of the unctuous Burgomaster in Friedrich Dürrenmatt's *The Visit* and as Bill Boanerges, the fatuous trade union cabinet minister in George Bernard Shaw's *The Apple Cart*. Rose relished the opportunity of working with Noel Coward in the revival of Shaw's political comedy, comparing the experience to "playing Broadway with Ethel Merman or the Lunts."

In January 1961 Rose took over from Leo McKern the part of The Common Man in Robert Bolt's smash hit *A Man for All Seasons*. A riveting historical drama, *A Man for All Seasons* starred Paul Scofield as Sir Thomas More, the Lord Chancellor to Henry VIII who was executed in 1534 for his refusal to swear allegiance to the king as head of the autonomous Church of England. In the virtuoso role of The Common Man, which required him to assume eight different guises (narrator, servant, boatman, innkeeper, steward, jailer, jury foreman, and executioner) Rose served as a kind of one-man Greek chorus, illuminating the action with witty observations about integrity, morality, and the human propensity to make compromises. When *A Man for All Seasons* opened in New York City in November 1961, it drew unanimous raves, with the critics lavishing praise on Bolt's literate script, Scofield's superb interpretation of the title role, and Rose's engaging portrayal of the timeless "common man"—the average citizen of all eras. John McMarten, the *New Yorker's* reviewer, rated Rose's contribution second only to Paul Scofield's. His colleagues apparently agreed, for the majority named Rose best supporting actor of the 1961–62 Broadway season in the trade newspaper *Variety's* annual poll of drama critics. Following the New York run, Rose toured the United States with the production for almost two years.

After *A Man for All Seasons* had run its course, Rose elected to settle permanently in New York City. "I was used to it here," he explained to a *New York Post* (April 3, 1976) reporter. "I didn't ever really intend emigrating, but I was sort of too lazy and too contented to move back." Not surprisingly, given his training and experience, Rose has had little trouble finding work on the Broadway stage, beginning in 1964 with John Gielgud's much ballyhooed production of *Hamlet,* starring Richard Burton. Staged as a "rehearsal piece," that tragedy drew a daunting number of unfavorable notices, but Rose's interpretation of the First Gravedigger was invariably singled out as one of the highlights of the evening. As George Oppenheimer observed in his review for *Newsday* (April 1, 1964), Rose's Gravedigger was "a comic of whom Shakespeare would have approved heartily." Later in the same year, Rose starred in William Hanley's *Slow Dance on the Killing Ground,* a brooding drama about three psychically scarred persons who meet by chance in a rundown Brooklyn candy store. The *New York Times's* Howard Taubman, who was enthusiastic about both the play and the cast, especially admired Rose's ability to fill his role of the close-mouthed, suspicious shop proprietor with the "pain and tension that suggests life."

In another fortunate pairing of actor and role, Rose received glowing reviews for his sensitive portrait of a disillusioned old soldier in *The Royal Hunt of the Sun,* Peter Shaffer's epic drama about the conquest of the Incaic Empire by the Spanish adventurer Francisco Pizarro. Reviewers were generally less impressed by the actor's performance in *Walking Happy,* a 1966 musical adaptation of Harold Brighouse's comedy *Hobson's Choice.* Critical commentary on the show ranged from "pleasant" to "ponderous," but most observers agreed that Rose's interpretation of Henry Hobson, the swaggering Lancashire boot merchant, was overdrawn. He was back on target in *Loot,* a knockabout farce by the British playwright Joe Orton that opened on Broadway in March 1968. Laced with macabre jokes about death, religion, marriage, and money, *Loot* was deemed vulgar by some reviewers and wickedly amusing by others, but even those who disliked the play applauded Rose's "unflappable comic finesse" in the part of Inspector Truscott, a corrupt, oafish Scotland Yard detective.

When the City Center Light Opera Company decided, in 1968, to mount a revival of the musical comedy classic *My Fair Lady,* George Rose was the obvious choice for the role of Alfred P. Doolittle, the roistering Cockney dustman, and, true to

form, he contributed what *New York Times* drama critic Richard F. Shepard called "a magnificently earthy performance," confidently barreling his way through such showstoppers as "With a Little Bit of Luck" and "Get Me To the Church on Time." He was equally commanding in *Canterbury Tales,* an undistinguished musical retelling of four of Chaucer's bawdier stories that was saved from oblivion by his virtuosic clowning in the role of The Steward. Rose's work in *Coco,* the Alan Jay Lerner–André Previn musical biography of the French couturière Gabrielle ("Coco") Chanel that starred Katharine Hepburn, was more low-keyed. The elaborately staged show, which opened in December 1969 to the biggest box-office advance in Broadway history, failed to impress many reviewers, some of whom complained about its forgettable score and lackluster direction. Among its strongest assets was Rose's well-rounded portrayal of Louis Greff, the designer's longtime friend and business associate. The actor was rewarded with a Tony Award nomination as best supporting actor in a musical.

Rose spent most of the early 1970s on the road, touring with the national companies of *Coco,* in 1971, and *Sleuth,* Anthony Shaffer's intricately plotted thriller about a detective novelist whose passion for game-playing ensnares him in a deadly duel of wits, from September 1972 until March 1973, and in a traveling production of Sigmund Romberg's operetta *The Student Prince,* in the summer of 1973. Between the completion of *Sleuth's* ninety-six-city bus-truck tour and the beginning of *The Student Prince* engagement, he spelled Patrick Macnee in the Broadway edition of *Sleuth.* Rose's only other New York appearance during the early 1970s was in *Wise Child,* Simon Gray's short-lived black comedy about an aging criminal on the run who masquerades as the mother of a young psychopath to elude the police. Critics greeted the production with a barrage of vituperation, reserving their few kind words for Rose's interpretation of the smirking proprietor of the seedy hotel in which the two felons take refuge.

One of the biggest hits of the 1974–75 Broadway season was *My Fat Friend,* Charles Lawrence's comedy featuring Lynn Redgrave as a self-conscious, overweight bookshop owner who struggles to slim down to impress the man of her dreams. Supervising her crash diet with martinet-like efficiency is Henry, a sharp-tongued homosexual played to perfection by George Rose. Clive Barnes, who reviewed *My Fat Friend* for the *New York Times* (April 1, 1974), thought Rose's flamboyant characterization was reason enough for seeing the show. "His naughtiness is irrepressible, and he spits his lines out with a sheer delight for his own cleverness, his face constantly bathed in a glow of self-congratulation," Barnes wrote, "although in fairness, Mr. Rose, a consummate actor, also portrays the role's few serious moments with convincing and touching sincerity." Joining the chorus of bravos, Rex Reed, Judith Crist, and Lance Morrow, among others, credited Rose with bringing the thinly plotted comedy alive. His achievement in *My Fat Friend* brought him a Drama Desk Award and a Tony nomination as best supporting actor in a play—a designation that Rose protested. "It simply wasn't a supporting role," he explained later, as quoted in the *New York Post* (April 3, 1976). "I don't think you can ask an actor to demote his achievements."

A reprise of his performance as Alfred P. Doolittle in a twentieth-anniversary Broadway revival of *My Fair Lady* netted Rose another Drama Desk Award and a 1976 Tony Award as best actor in a musical. In 1977 he signed on with the Brooklyn Academy of Music Theatre Company to play the title role in *Julius Caesar*, Almady, the aging matinee idol in Ferenc Molnar's romantic comedy *The Play's the Thing*, and perhaps most important, the plum cameo part of General Burgoyne in Shaw's *The Devil's Disciple*. In the opinion of virtually every New York critic, his skillfully modulated performance as the sardonic "Gentleman Johnny" in the last-named play was the production's greatest distinction. Returning to Broadway the following year in *The Kingfisher*, William Douglas Home's drawing-room comedy about a geriatric romance, Rose all but stole the show from his costars, Rex Harrison and Claudette Colbert. For his multilayered portrayal of the prissy and crochety valet Hawkins, he was honored with his third Drama Desk Award.

After a stint as Mr. Darling and Captain Hook in a 1979 revival of the musical *Peter Pan*, George Rose was tapped to play Major General Stanley in the New York Shakespeare Festival's production of Gilbert and Sullivan's *The Pirates of Penzance*. The role seemed tailor-made for Rose, but in his usual thoroughgoing manner, the actor prepared for his part by studying with a speech therapist, who made him recite his lines with a bone propped between his jaws. The unorthodox preparation paid off, for Rose's perfectly enunciated version of the tongue-twisting patter song "I Am the Very Model of a Modern Major General" regularly brought down the house. "This man is surely one of the comic treasures of the literate theatre," exulted Frank Rich of the *New York Times* in his review of the opening-night performance at the Delacorte Theatre in Central Park on July 29, 1980. Rose's "engaging" and "faultless" portrayal lost none of its spark when *Pirates* move to Broadway in January 1981, where it played to enthusiastic audiences for well over a year.

Rose's next venture, *Dance a Little Closer*, a lifeless musical version of Robert E. Sherwood's Pulitzer Prize–winning antiwar comedy *Idiot's Delight*, closed after one performance in May 1983, although Rose did what he could with his role of a tough-minded, pragmatic diplomat. He also acquitted himself well in the 1983 revival of the George S. Kaufman–Moss Hart comedy *You Can't Take It With You*, in which he played the flamboyant Russian ballet master Boris Kolenkhov, and as the sarcastic music critic Stephen Fauldgate, he contributed the "only enlivening performance," to

use Douglas Watts's words, to *Beethoven's Tenth*, Peter Ustinov's listless comedy that opened on April 14, 1984 and closed three weeks later.

Rose made his motion picture debut in 1952, as the Coachman in the British-made film version of Charles Dickens' *The Pickwick Papers*. He has since played character parts in over thirty movies, including *A Night to Remember* (United Artists, 1958), the documentary-style account of the sinking of the *Titanic*; the James Michener epic *Hawaii* (United Artists, 1966); the Elaine May comedy *A New Leaf* (Paramount, 1971); and most recently, the film edition of the Broadway production *The Pirates of Penzance*. Among his innumerable television credits are the roles of the butler Hacker in the short-lived *Beacon Hill*, CBS-TV's Americanized version of the British series *Upstairs, Downstairs*, and Loewy in NBC-TV's controversial miniseries *Holocaust*. He has also appeared in many *Hallmark Hall of Fame* productions. Rose has recorded Henry Fielding's novel *Tom Jones* in its entirety for the American Foundation for the Blind, and his sixty-plus recordings of adaptations of such literary classics as *Billy Budd*, *Wuthering Heights*, and *Three Men in a Boat* have been highly praised.

George Rose's appearance has changed little since Gilbert Millstein, writing in the *New York Times* (October 21, 1962), described him as having "contient brown eyes, a splayed nose bulwarked by an important upper lip and an appropriate chin—the whole set out in a broad face under a head of wiry hair." A self-described "compulsive collector" of phonograph records, he often spends his free time scouring second-hand record shops in search of rare recordings. In addition to listening to music, Rose's hobbies are reading and cooking. The actor shares his apartment in New York's Greenwich Village with several dogs and cats.

References: N Y *Daily News* p41 Ja 13 '81 por; N Y *Post* p33 Mr 23 '74 por, p13 Ap 3 '76 por; N Y *Times* II p5 O 21 '62; *Notable Names in the American Theatre* (1976); *Who's Who in the Theatre* (1981)

Sauvé, Jeanne
(sō vä´ zhan)

Apr. 26, 1922– Governor-General of Canada.
Address: b. Rideau Hall, Ottawa, Ontario,
Canada K1A OA1

Her Excellency the Right Honorable Jeanne Sauvé, who was invested as Canada's twenty-third governor-general on May 14, 1984, achieved that distinction as the culmination of a long public life marked by a cosmopolitan outlook and an understated commitment to liberal ideals. A product of the French Canadian cultural consciousness of recent decades, she first came to public attention as

Jeanne Sauvé

a bright, classy journalist involved in many reformist causes. When she moved directly into the political arena as a Liberal member of Parliament and three-time cabinet minister, her dexterous handling of national policy issues helped contribute to economic development and environmental protection. Her appointment as governor-general—a largely ceremonial but significant post—comes on the heels of her tumultuous term as Speaker of the House of Commons, so that it comes as no surprise that she has acknowledged her readiness for the "sense of serenity" the new job will bring. In short, Jeanne Sauvé is a creditable political survivor who confounds all ideological labels but makes very clear her dedication to Canada's welfare.

Jeanne Sauvé was born Jeanne Mathilde Benôit on April 26, 1922 in the small French-Ukrainian town of Prud'Homme, near Saskatoon in the central Canadian province of Saskatchewan. Her parents, Charles Albert Benôit, a building contractor, and Anna (Vaillant) Benôit, moved the family to Ottawa when Jeanne was three, and there they raised her and her two brothers and four sisters in a traditional Roman Catholic atmosphere. The father insisted upon a French-speaking household, Mrs. Sauvé has explained, as "his way of preserving our culture" in a predominantly English setting. She received her schooling at the Notre Dame du Rosaire Convent, where she consistently ranked at the top of her class. After finishing her secondary education, she attended the University of Ottawa for a time.

When she was twenty-one, Jeanne Benôit moved to Montreal, Quebec. That stay in the center of French culture in North America "was like freedom" to her, as she told Margaret Drury Gane in an interview for the *Toronto Globe and Mail Magazine* (June 5, 1976). Her language was spoken everywhere, she had no more feelings of rejection, and she felt as though she had come home. As national president from 1942 to 1947 of Jeunesse Etudiante Catholique (Young Catholic Students), a reformist group she had joined in Ottawa, she readily immersed herself in the political and intellectual life of a young Québécois generation eager to bring its influence to bear on Canada's national affairs. Among the talented members of Jeunesse Etudiante Catholique were Gérard Pelletier and Marc Lalonde, now Canada's ambassador to the United Nations and finance minister, respectively. Moreover, it is probable that Jeanne Sauvé first met Pierre Elliott Trudeau during that time, while he was studying law at the University of Montreal. Continuing her role as a student leader, she acted as a founding delegate in 1947 of La Fédération des Mouvements de Jeunesse du Québec (Federation of Quebec Youth Movements).

Another young Québécois whom she came to know in Montreal was Maurice Sauvé, then a student in economics. The two were married on September 24, 1948 and immediately set out to explore Europe together. In England for two years, Jeanne Sauvé taught French under the auspices of the London County Council; when the couple moved to France, she studied French civilization at the Université de Paris, obtaining her bachelor's degree in 1952, and she also worked in that city as an assistant to the director of UNESCO's youth section.

When Jeanne and Maurice Sauvé returned to Canada in 1952, they first worked as union organizers with the Canadian Federation of Labour. But Mrs. Sauvé soon embarked upon her own influential two-decade career as a bilingual broadcast journalist, interviewer, and commentator with the Canadian television network CBC, and she also appeared on Canada's CTV, Radio-Canada, and the United States networks NBC and CBS. Thanks to such Quebec programs as *Opinions*, which ran for seven years in the 1950s, the women's-issue show *A Million Women*, and an interview forum that she conducted for university students, she became a celebrity. "As a journalist, she was one of the best in the country—she was so alive," Charles Lynch, the Ottawa columnist, has recalled. And her talent as an interviewer received special praise. Joyce Fairbairn, who was for a time Jeanne Sauvé's reporting colleague, told Julianne Lebreche for *Chatelaine* magazine (October 1980) that she knew Mrs. Sauvé as "a first-rate interviewer. A model of poise and intelligence. . . . She could really bring people out." That warmth complemented what has been termed the "clear, sharp edge" of her commentaries, which demonstrated a certain radical outlook, particularly with regard to the political status of Canada's francophone, or French-speaking, minority. Applying her broadcasting ability to administrative know-how, from 1969 to 1972 Jeanne Sauvé was a director of the Montreal radio station CKAC and of Bushnell Communications, Ltd. From 1970 to 1972 she contributed editorial pieces to the *Montreal Star* and the *Toronto Star*.

While his wife covered public issues from the purview of the fifth estate, Maurice Sauvé in the 1950s and 1960s was taking an active part in Canadian politics. As public relations director for Quebec's Liberal party from 1958 to 1962, he played a crucial advisory role in the so-called "Quiet Revolution" of Jean Lesage, the province's prime minister from 1960 to 1966 who swept away many of Quebec's archaic political structures, instituted progressive social reforms, and tried to bring the previously isolated province into a parity of influence with English-speaking Canada. That same political sophistication and cultural pride informed the parliamentary term of Maurice Sauvé, who was sent to Ottawa by voters in the Montreal riding of Îles de la Madeleine in 1962 and retained his seat until 1968. As minister of forestry and rural development under Liberal prime minister Lester Pearson, Sauvé was seen as an enlightened, if sometimes controversial, force for change in Quebec's social and political life. He lost his riding in the same election that brought Liberal Pierre Elliot Trudeau into the prime minister's office.

Jeanne Sauvé resisted occasional charges that her own professional views would inevitably take their slant from Maurice Sauvé's. "Women are not appendages of men, so tied up with their interests that they cannot function as separate entities. It's an insulting implication," she told Margaret Drury Gane. She nevertheless paid close attention to Maurice Sauvé's successes and his eventual defeat, so that, when she accepted a Liberal party invitation to run on their ticket for a federal parliamentary seat in 1972, she "slipped into it quite easily," she has said, because his experience had made politics "natural" for her. With the electorate obviously agreeing, Mrs. Sauvé handily won the House of Commons seat in October of that year for the Montreal riding of Ahuntsic by 18,737 votes.

In an interview with Stanley McDowell of the *Toronto Globe and Mail* (November 28, 1972) shortly after her victory, Jeanne Sauvé interpreted the vote as a mandate "to make it possible for Quebeckers to relate to the federal government. And maybe because of the kind of reputation I have in the province, . . . the fact that I have come to politics will be meaningful for a lot of Quebec people." While she rejected such quasi-separatist Quebec slogans as "French power," she matter-of-factly stated her view that English-speaking Canadians had "not yet faced what it means to be a Canadian" in a bilingual country and expressed her hope that the cultural ramifications of that bilingual national character would soon be accepted. She interpreted the public mood as being concerned about unemployment and economic growth but asserted that, despite the belt-tightening atmosphere, new policies should be "directed to giving everybody a fair chance in society." Among the proposals she supported were correctives to past discrimination against women in public service and consideration of a guaranteed annual income program. During her first term in office, Jeanne Sauvé was one of only five women members of Parliament.

Within a month of her election Jeanne Sauvé was chosen by Prime Minister Trudeau as a cabinet member with the portfolio of minister of state for science and technology, becoming the first Quebec woman to serve in the nation's cabinet. That junior ministry, just two years old when she took the post, tested her political mettle, and she proved herself equal to the task. Over the next eighteen months Jeanne Sauvé sought international scientific cooperation agreements in trips to the Republic of China, Belgium, and France. Back home in Canada, she drew up policy on northern land development and, in July 1973, joined in presenting a major ocean development plan designed to encourage industrial exploitation of the suspected oil fields off Canada's coasts. That project seemed to have special urgency because of the OPEC oil embargo and the new competition for marine resources. Jeanne Sauvé was reelected as a member of Parliament in July 1974.

A former aide has observed that, as a cabinet minister, Jeanne Sauvé "always understood scientific things. She'd take information and, right away, would realize its application." That grasp of technically complex issues may have been a leading qualification for her next assignment in Pierre Trudeau's cabinet, as minister of environment. The thorniest problem facing her when she took that post in August 1974 concerned the Garrison Diversion Unit, a proposed North Dakota irrigation project that would divert water from the Missouri River into 250,000 acres of the state's farmland. Irrigation runoff would flow into the Red River and the Souris River, which run north across the United States–Canadian border into Manitoba Province. Long on the drawing board, the Garrison Unit was fiercely challenged by environmental groups and by the Canadian government as well, which foresaw damaging ecological effects. Although joint studies and negotiations were already underway, Jeanne Sauvé adopted a hard line in opposition, arguing that pollution and salinity levels would be unacceptable and that the importation of new riparian species into the Souris River would destroy its native wildlife. (In 1984 the United States Congress finally gave up on the twenty-year-old plan and began a search for a better one.)

In a related effort, Jeanne Sauvé helped to obtain from the United States an assent to abide by the joint Great Lakes Water Quality Agreement, under which it would construct purification facilities by the end of 1975. When plans for extending the Vancouver, British Columbia airport into the city's harbor area were announced, she supported the commercial and environmental concerns of salmon fishermen in that region.

Although Jeanne Sauvé was recognized as a strong, well-organized administrator during her tenure in those two ministries, some observers who had expected her to emerge as an outspoken firebrand for Québécois or women's causes were disappointed with her performance. In Ottawa she underplayed the critical flair that she had exhibited as a journalist and practised instead a discreet diplomacy with members of both sides of the House of Commons that distanced her from cliques and intramural disputes. Her special assistant, Pierre Nadeau, once described her technique of politicking: "You can kill your opponent and win. You can maim him and win. You can also charm him and win. . . . Obviously, for a negotiator, confrontation is distasteful as well as ineffective. The minister is a mediator, a negotiator."

Despite their varied readings of Jeanne Sauvé's parliamentary acumen, most observers concurred that her powers were at their height as cabinet minister of communications, the post she took in December 1975 in a reshuffling move by Prime Minister Trudeau. She walked into the thick of a jurisdictional dispute between Quebec and Ottawa over cable television regulation, with Quebec asserting that its provincial authority overrode federal controls. That claim, made in the spirit of leftist aspirations for Quebec "sovereignty," simmered unresolved into 1977, when the province's communications minister, Louis O'Neill, engaged his federal counterpart in political battle for control of nearly *all* telecommunications systems. Minister Sauvé voiced her willingness to negotiate the delegation of certain regulatory powers to Quebec—and to the other provinces, along similar terms—but, echoing a recent Supreme Court decision, she refused to cede the locus of authority to it. In her opinion, federal regulation was "absolutely necessary to maintain an effective and efficient system of telecommunications across Canada." That decision held, but the intransigence of the Quebec administration during that time prompted Jeanne Sauvé to remark that its leaders apparently did "not want to live within the constitution."

In less controversial communications policies, Jeanne Sauvé oversaw federal funding to launch Telidon, the Canadian videotext system linked to computer information banks; facilitated the introduction of subscription television; and secured greater resources for domestic satellite research and development. She received high marks for the "foresight" of those directives and for her view, as one department official put it, that "high-tech could push us out of our economic wasteland." Exercising her negotiating skills, in 1978 she started to work out a compromise with broadcasters in the northern United States who were angered by new Canadian legislation that discouraged Canadian advertisers from buying air-time on their stations. That same year she advised the secretary of state for external affairs on relations with the French-speaking world.

In May 1979 Pierre Trudeau's eleven-year tenure as prime minister ended with the general election that thrust the Progressive Conservatives, led by Joe Clark, into power. Ranking Liberals left their cabinet seats, but Jeanne Sauvé's constituents demonstrated their confidence by returning her to Parliament in the election. Then, when the Progressive Conservatives received a no-confidence vote that December, a new vote was scheduled for February 1980, and the Liberals regained their majority. Immediately prime minister–designate Trudeau offered Jeanne Sauvé the post of Speaker of the House of Commons for the new legislative session, set to begin that April. The non-partisan Speaker chairs the parliamentary debate and decides points of order; amid the honored British-style melée called "legislative deliberation," that seemingly sedate task has been compared to the plight of the bear in a bear pit. It was reported that, on receiving the summons from Trudeau, Jeanne Sauvé exclaimed, "Oh no, not that!" After pondering for twenty-four hours, she accepted the new role, and became the first woman Speaker in the history of the House.

Her stint as House Speaker did indeed prove to be the most trying three-and-a-half years of Jeanne Sauvé's career. Groping her way through the labyrinth of parliamentary rules and more familiar with the Privy Council than with the House floor, she struggled to memorize the names of her 281 colleagues and their ridings and to recognize for debate equal numbers from all parties. But complaints about her uneven acknowledgements extended even to Liberal backbenchers, who once sent to the Speaker's chair a set of opera glasses to heighten her awareness of them. She supervised the heated debate on Canada's new constitution in 1981–82 unscathed, but fared less well in the "bell-ringing incident" of March 1982, when Progressive Conservative MPs refused the call to vote on a Liberal energy bill for fifteen days, thereby bringing Parliament to a virtual halt. Jeanne Sauvé insisted she had no procedural instruments with which to break the deadlock, and the affair marked a low in public prestige for both the Speaker and the House as a whole. No reservations, however, were heard about her streamlining of the Commons' creaky internal operations, in which she cut deadwood from the staff and set account books in order. Jeanne Sauvé's memories of the period are not fond: "It was a very lonely job. . . . You grow to live without friendship and hope it will come back when your term is over."

The governor-general of Canada, who is appointed at the prime minister's recommendation for a five-year term, is the official representative of Queen Elizabeth II of England. The formal duties of the post require frequent travel throughout Canada, since the governor-general signs federal proclamations, receives ambassadors, bestows merit awards, opens sessions of Parliament on the advice of the prime minister, and informs the Queen on the state of the nation. In another first for Canadian women, Jeanne Sauvé was named in December 1983 to replace Governor-General Edward Schreyer, with the benediction of statesmen and citizens of all political persuasions. After an unspecified illness delayed her investiture some four months, she was sworn in at a full-dress ceremony of state on Parliament Hill in Ottawa on May 14, 1984. Among the governor-general's several titles are commander-in-chief, keeper of the great seal, and chancellor of the order of Canada.

"Despite our varied ethnic and racial origins," Governor-General Sauvé declared in her investiture speech, "we are Canadians determined to carry on the building of a great nation." She invited her countrymen to "set an example for the world by a deep involvement in global reconstruction . . . whose final objective is peace" and to "set out on a voyage of discovery and find the real meaning of the human journey." She praised Canada's hard-won prosperity and its promising young people, ending with the lines from the Book of Ecclesiastes: " . . . as the governor is, so will be the inhabitants of his city." Jeanne Sauvé maintains a large personal staff and official residences at the Rideau Hall estate in Ottawa and inside The Citadel in Quebec City. In two early official acts, she presented fifty-three military decorations and proclaimed a constitutional amendment protecting the rights of native peoples.

On Prime Minister Trudeau's resignation on June 30, 1984, the governor-general invited John N. Turner, the new Liberal party leader, to form a new government, and she dissolved Parliament several days later at Turner's request, setting the September 1984 elections which brought the Pro-gressive Conservatives, led by Brian Mulroney, into power. Later that month Jeanne Sauvé formally welcomed Pope John Paul II on his first visit to Canada.

Jeanne Sauvé is a petite woman whose snow-white coiffure and elegant beauty have evoked comparisons to the *grande dames* of Paris. She and her husband, Maurice, who now works as a corporate director, make their home in the outskirts of Montreal. The couple have one son, Jean-François, whose career is in banking. A supporter of the arts, Jeanne Sauvé has found time over the years to serve such groups as the Fédération des Auteurs des Artistes du Canada and the Union des Artistes. She is an honorary fellow of the Royal Architectural Institute of Canada and holds honorary degrees from the universities of New Brunswick and Calgary.

References: Chatelaine p48+ O '80 pors; Toronto Globe and Mail p1 Mr 1 '80 por, p4 D 24 '83 por; Toronto Globe and Mail mag p4+ Je 5 '76 pors; Macleans 97:8+ Ja 9 '84 pors; N Y Times p3 D 23 '83 por; Canadian Who's Who, 1983; International Who's Who, 1984–85

Sayles, John

Sept. 28, 1950– Writer; film director. Address: h. c/o Little, Brown & Co., Inc., 34 Beacon St., Boston, Mass. 02106

Although still in his early thirties, John Sayles has already accomplished more than most creative people achieve in a lifetime. His distinctive prose style and accurate ear for dialects have won him two O. Henry short-story awards and critical accolades for his novels, *Pride of the Bimbos* and *Union Dues*, but he is more widely known as the scriptwriter and director of such low-budget, offbeat films as *Return of the Secaucus Seven* and *Lianna*. Awarded the lucrative MacArthur Foundation prize in 1983, the multitalented author, actor, and filmmaker shows no signs of having scaled the summit of his career, and he is currently working on a number of promising ventures in writing and directing.

John Thomas Sayles was born on September 28, 1950 in Schenectady, New York to Donald John Sayles, a school administrator, and Mary (Rausch) Sayles, a teacher. Although he earned good grades in school and liked to write stories, often based on such popular television shows of the time as *The Untouchables*, for the delectation of himself and his friends, he had a more consuming interest in sports. At Mount Pleasant High School in Schenectady, Sayles earned letters in basketball, baseball, track, and football. As he later recalled in an article in the *New York Times Book Review* (September 6, 1981), "I never thought about being a writer as I grew up; a writer wasn't something to be. An

outfielder was something to be. Most of what I know about style I learned from Roberto Clemente."

Rejected by the United States Army in 1968 because of a missing vertebra, Sayles enrolled at Williams College in Massachusetts as a psychology major. Sayles, however, seemed more interested in extracurricular activities than in psychology and once quipped in an interview that he "majored in intramural sports and foreign movies." As an undergraduate, Sayles acted in school plays and in summer stock; he became fascinated with film through the foreign-film classes of Charles Thomas Samuels; and inspired by Nelson Algren's novel *Somebody in Boots*, he gradually came to realize that writing, which he still practiced as a pastime, might be a way of earning a living. When he graduated from Williams College in 1972, he was equipped to face the outside world with a one-thousand page, unpublished novel and, to use his words, an "utterly useless" bachelor's degree.

After graduation, Sayles took a variety of jobs to support himself, working as an orderly in a nursing home in Albany, as a day laborer in Atlanta, and as a meat packer in a Boston sausage factory. He also began to submit his work to magazines. For two years he received only rejection slips, but in 1975 his fortunes changed when his short story "I-80 Nebraska, M.490–M.205," appeared in the May issue of the *Atlantic* and won an O. Henry short-story award. Later, Peggy Yntema, an editor at the Atlantic Monthly Press, contacted him with the request that he either cut or expand "Men," a fifty-page story he had sent in. Sayles had just been laid off from his job at the sausage factory. Living on his $48-a-week unemployment insurance check, "[his] first and last grant for the arts," he spent twenty-seven weeks expanding "Men" into *Pride of the Bimbos* (Little, Brown, 1975), a rite-of-passage novel whose main characters are five men who play comic exhibition baseball games in drag. Although critics cited his occasional lapses in dialogue from dialect to formal English and his far-fetched plot as weaknesses, almost all reviewers praised Sayles's "deadly accurate ear" for dialects and agreed with Joseph McLellan's assessment in the *Washington Post's Book World* (August 24, 1975): "All the images pull together in this book with a smoothness that would do credit to a tenth novel. It is written with wit, style, irony and thematic depth."

Sayles continued to write over the next two years, and three of his short stories—"Breed," "Golden State," and "Hoop"—appeared in issues of the *Atlantic*. In 1977 "Breed" won an O. Henry award and was included in that year's *Best American Short Stories*. Several of his stories were included in anthologies, and when *The Anarchists' Convention*, his collection of fifteen short stories, was published by Little, Brown in 1979, it was warmly praised by most reviewers. In *Union Dues* (Little, Brown, 1977), his second novel, Sayles traces the journey of the runaway Hobie McNatt from a bleak coal-mining region in West Virginia to a radical commune in Boston, where his miner-father makes a fruitless search for his son. Although Sayles occasionally overemphasized the ironies inherent in his subject matter, his deft development of character, authentic depiction of the blue-collar world, flair for capturing ethnic speech, and evenhanded treatment of varying political viewpoints earned high marks from the critics. *Union Dues* was the only novel that year that was nominated for both the National Book Award and the National Book Critics' Circle Award.

Union Dues had been sold through a literary agency that had connections with the Hollywood film industry. An avid moviegoer, Sayles was so eager to try his hand at writing screenplays and directing that when the West Coast branch of the agency agreed to represent him on the strength of what he had already published and his script about the 1919 Chicago Black Sox bribery scandal, he promptly moved to Santa Barbara. Before long he was hired by Roger Corman to revise the script for the science-fiction thriller *Piranha* (New World Pictures, 1978), which Corman wanted to resemble *Jaws*, Universal Pictures' 1975 blockbuster. "My whole job," Sayles has recalled, "was to contrive a reason why people, once they hear there are piranhas in the river, don't just stay out of the river but end up getting eaten. That's basically what they paid me $10,000 for. The film came out well and made lots of money for them." Sayles also had a small role in *Piranha*.

Sayles wrote two other screenplays for New World Pictures: the commercially successful *Battle Beyond the Stars* (1980), a science-fiction version of the 1954 Kurasawa classic *The Seven Samurai* relocated in outer space, and *The Lady in Red* (1979), about the gangster John Dillinger's mistress. Sayles had intended it to be "a very political film," but by the time the film was made, he has said, "most of the scenes that explained why things happened were gone, and so what was left were the scenes where people shot each other." It was the only film scripted by Sayles for Corman that failed to make money in the United States. "It's done well in Europe," Sayles has pointed out. "Over there, they think gangsters still roam the streets of Chicago." Two other screenplays by Sayles—"Night Skies," written for Steven Spielberg, and "Terror of the Loch Ness," for MGM—never reached the stage of production.

Although Sayles enjoyed scriptwriting, he was unhappy about the fact that much of what he wrote often never appeared on the screen, as in the case of *The Lady in Red*, because of budget cuts, time constraints, or arbitrary studio preferences. "I didn't realize how political filmmaking is, . . . " Sayles explained in an interview for *Cineaste* (Winter 1980–81), "that you start out with something you want, but you're going to have to do other things just to get the money and get it made. You can be God in a novel, but the best you can be in a film is an enlightened despot, sometimes even less than that, depending on how much control the studio has." He therefore decided to make a film independently as a display piece to persuade studios to hire him as a feature-film director, with greater control over the material.

With only $40,000 (money he had saved from scriptwriting and the royalties from his novels), Sayles filmed *Return of the Secaucus Seven* in only twenty-five days in 1978 with non-union actors he knew from either Williams College or the Eastern Slope Playhouse in New Hampshire, paying them only $80 a week with the promise of more if he made a profit. Because of his cramped budget and lack of technical expertise, Sayles, who also appeared in the film, leaned heavily on dialogue to develop his characters and advance the story line, keeping expensive camera movements—and consequently action scenes—to a minimum. "I did what I knew I could do best," he explained in the *Cineaste* interview. "Sometimes a line of dialogue can save you a lot of shots that look great but don't tell you much. . . . My main emphasis is making films about people. I'm not interested in cinematic art."

The characters in the low-keyed *Return of the Secaucus Seven*, based on a group of young people Sayles had met in Boston in the mid-1970s, were "issue-oriented" demonstrators in the 1960s who had once been arrested on trumped-up charges in Secaucus, New Jersey on the way to a protest march on the Pentagon. Now turning thirty, they meet for a reunion in a farmhouse in New Hampshire and over the course of the weekend find themselves facing the responsibilities of adulthood and decisions about marriage, family, and education that their parents had made as teenagers. First shown in 1980 at the Filmex festival in Hollywood and the New Directors/New Films series in New York City before being released for a commercial run, *Secaucus* elicited nearly unanimous praise. Gary Arnold in his review for the *Washington Post* (January 28, 1981) recommended it as "a witty, affectionate and thoroughly modern comedy of manners," and in *Newsweek* (September 22, 1980) Jack Kroll was equally enthusiastic: "You feel as if you're eavesdropping on real people in real places with real relationships talking real talk. . . . [The actors] achieve that rare thing in movies, a true ensemble performance." *Time*, the *Boston Globe*, and the *Los Angeles Times* voted *Secaucus* among the ten best films of the year, and Sayles won the Los Angeles Film Critics award for best screenplay and a 1981 Oscar nomination in that category. As a result of *Secaucus'* success, Sayles was immediately offered a contract by Warner Brothers to direct "Blood of the Lamb," his screenplay about two men who infiltrate a fundamentalist religious sect. The film has not yet been released.

Although Sayles filmed *Secaucus* within his $40,000 budget, he needed an additional $20,000 to rent an editing machine and to pay for lab costs. To raise the extra capital, he once again turned to freelance writing, completing three scripts in one year. *Perfect Match* (CBS, 1980), a made-for-television movie, featured Colleen Dewhurst as a woman in need of a bone-marrow transplant who must find the daughter she long ago gave up for adoption. Because it was pitted against *Jaws* and *The End* in the same time slot it did not win as large a percentage of the television audience as Sayles thought it deserved. *The Howling* (Avco-Embassy, 1981), a screenplay cowritten with Terence H. Winkless, was no more successful. Although in his review in the *Chicago Tribune* (April 14, 1981) Larry Kart commended that parody of werewolf films for its "wry, satirical touches" and "remarkable" special effects, Vincent Canby panned it in the *New York*

Times (March 13, 1981) as only "a horror-hoot for people who think the height of eroticism is watching people in raccoon coats and bad tempers making love." The critics worked up more enthusiasm, however, for *Alligator* (Alpha, 1981), a witty sci-fi thriller about Ramon, a baby alligator that is flushed into the sewer system of a midwestern city and grows into an immense, predatory monster on his twelve-year diet of hormone-treated lab animals, toxic wastes, and other contaminants. Although Sayles's intention of having Ramon "[eat his] way through the whole socio-economic system" was diluted by heavy-handed editing, reviewers thought *Alligator's* "breezy suspense plot" and "snappy sense of humor" saved it from being yet another routine horror film.

With *Lianna* (United Artists Classics, 1983), Sayles turned once again to independent filmmaking. He had written the screenplay in 1978, but it was only after the success of *Return of the Secaucus Seven* and a three-and-a-half year fundraising campaign that he was able to secure the $300,000 he needed to film it. Its controversial subject matter—lesbianism—may have been partly responsible for the hesitancy of potential backers. Lianna, unhappily married to a philandering college professor, falls in love with Ruth, her childpsychology instructor, allows herself to be seduced, and then leaves her husband and two children to live with her lover. Ruth, however, wants to be more discreet about their affair and is not ready for any commitment. Without the support of her family or lover, Lianna must come to terms with her lesbianism and newfound independence on her own. According to Sayles, who also acted in the film, *Lianna* "is about changing, more than anything else. It's about where do we go from here."

Critics reached no consensus in their evaluations of *Lianna*. Gary Arnold dismissed it as a "rather shallow plunge into topicality" in his review for the *Washington Post* (February 25, 1983), and other critics were annoyed by what they regarded as its "gawkiness" and home-movie quality, its archly clever dialogue, inept acting, and the "klutziness of [Sayles's] direction." But in *Variety* (January 26, 1983), Sayles was praised for his unschmaltzy treatment of a sensitive subject and for his "finely honed dialog—emerging largely as a progression of ear-perfect conversations that unfold with a naturalism that makes the heroine's conflicts intensely credible." Also extolling its realism, Vincent Canby concluded in his *New York Times* review (January 19, 1983) that *Lianna* "so effectively simulates the manner and temper of ordinary lives that there is a danger that people will not recognize the very real art by which it was created."

Baby, It's You (Paramount), also a 1983 release, was the first Sayles film with major studio backing. Set in Trenton, New Jersey in the mid-1960s, it follows the ill-fated romance of Jill Rosen, the preppy daughter of a Jewish doctor, and Albert ("Sheik") Capadilupo, the somewhat delinquent son of an Italian garbageman. When Jill leaves for Sarah

Lawrence College to study acting and Sheik heads to Miami to become the next Frank Sinatra, the differences in their social classes finally drive a wedge between them. *Baby, It's You* was based on a story by the film's coproducer Amy Robinson, but Sayles detected marked similarities between it and his own experiences. As he explained to Steve Lawson in his article for the *New York Times Magazine* (April 17, 1983), both Trenton and his own hometown are largely "industrial towns— Schenectady has the big G.E. plant—and you can see where the divisions take root. When you come back home after graduation, the guys you'd been friends with might be collecting your garbage. In a funny way, high school's the last bastion of democracy."

Filmed on a comparatively modest $3-million budget, *Baby, It's You* generally scored a hit with the critics. Stanley Kauffmann derided it as a dull treatment of a conventional story in his *New Republic* review (May 2, 1983), but Joy Gould Boyum of the *Wall Street Journal* (April 8, 1983) praised the film's "strikingly authentic texture" and Sayles's "insights into the shifting nature of class." Writing in *Time* (April 18, 1983), Richard Corliss concluded, "Sayles is, as always, wise and fair to his mismatched characters. His movies look as if they were made by a fly on the wall that had an advanced degree in psychology."

Sayles has not been equally successful as a playwright. In 1981 he directed his two one-act plays—*New Hope for the Dead* and *Turnbuckle*—at the Boat Basin Theatre in New York City. According to Frank Rich in his review for the *New York Times* (July 8, 1981), they were "fairly amateurish in both craft and substance," and his characters—menial boxing-match employees in *New Hope* and a teacher-turned-professional wrestler in *Turnbuckle*—seemed "like warmed-over versions of the sentimental losers who populated television dramas of the 1950s." Patricia O'Haire, writing in the *New York Daily News* (July 9, 1981), while complimenting the acting in both plays, concurred: "There are too many holes—especially in 'Turnbuckle'—where the drama slips through and what is left is just not satisfying enough."

In January 1983 Sayles received one of the annual "genius" awards from the John D. and Catherine T. MacArthur Foundation, which grants him $30,000 a year, tax free, for five years. His pace has not slackened even though his financial security is now guaranteed. He is currently working on a variety of projects, including a novel about Cuban exiles in Miami called "Los Gusanos"; adaptations of three Grace Paley short stories for cable TV; and an adaptation of Jean Auel's best-selling novels *Clan of the Cave Bear* and *The Valley of Horses* for NBC. His most recent film, *The Brother From Another Planet*, was released in 1984. His film projects include "Matewan," about a conflict between mineworkers and mine owners in Virginia in 1920, and a screenplay for John Frankenheimer.

Describing the method behind his success, Sayles wrote in his *New York Times Book Review* article: "It doesn't matter to me if I'm writing by hand or on a typewriter, whether I'm alone or with other people, or what time of day it is. Once I start getting my head into a story, everything else sort of drops away. . . . Writing isn't easy, but it beats working for a living."

John Sayles, who stands six feet four inches tall and has unruly blond hair, lives in Hoboken, New Jersey with his companion of ten years, Maggie Renzi, whom he met at Williams College. Miss Renzi coproduced and acted in *Return of the Secaucus Seven* and *Lianna*. Unspoiled by success and, according to Steve Lawson, "uninterested in cigarettes, drugs, or alcohol," Sayles is an atypical celebrity, who continues to ride the bus from Hoboken to Manhattan where his production offices are located.

References: N Y Times C p9 Mr 6 '81 por; N Y Times Bk Rev p3+ S 6 '81 por; N Y Times Mag p109+ Ap 17 '83 por; Washington Post p3 Ja 28 '81 por; Who's Who in America, 1984-85

Schapiro, Meyer

Sept. 23, 1904– Art historian. Address: b. c/o George Braziller, Inc., 1 Park Ave., New York City, N.Y. 10016; h. 279 W. 4th St., New York City, N.Y. 10014

The polymathic Meyer Schapiro, professor emeritus of art history at Columbia University, has pervasively influenced two generations of artists, scholars, critics, curators, and dealers. "All of us built on his lectures; everybody who's around now got his or her ideas from Meyer," Professor Milton Brown of the City University of New York has testified. "The things he said in class in the early '30s have become common parlance." Schapiro, who taught at Columbia from 1928 to 1973, is best known for his revisionist view of Romanesque art, a view expounded in the essays collected in *Romanesque Art* (1977), the first volume of his *Selected Papers*, and for his pioneer academic championing of the "spontaneous sensibility" in modern art, the subject of the second volume of his papers, *Modern Art: 19th and 20th Centuries* (1978). When the last-named book won for Schapiro the Mitchell prize for outstanding writing on art history in English, Sir John Pope-Hennessy, the chairman of the Mitchell Prize jury, said: "If a census were taken of the living critics who have exercised a formative influence on our attitude to the art of the immediate past, it would be generally conceded that the most original and most influential was Professor Meyer Schapiro." *Late Antique, Early Christian and Mediaeval Art* (1979), the third volume of Schapiro's *Selected Papers*, won the National Book Critics Award. A fourth volume, "The Theory and Philosophy of Art," is in the planning stage.

One of five children (two of whom died early), Meyer Schapiro was born Meir Schapiro in Siauliai, Lithuania in what is now the Soviet Union on September 23, 1904. His mother was Fanny (Adelman) Schapiro, an Orthodox Jew, and his father was Nathan Menachem Schapiro, a descendant of Talmudic scholars. In late adolescence Nathan Schapiro abandoned the Orthodox tradition in which he had been raised and came under the influence of the Jewish Socialist Bund and the Haskala, the Eastern European "enlightenment" movement embracing Western secular learning.

Nathan Schapiro had worked as a bookkeeper before his marriage. Seeking a better life for his family, he immigrated alone in 1906 to the United States, where he obtained a job teaching Hebrew at the Yitzcak Elchanan Yeshiva on New York City's Lower East Side. In 1907, having saved enough money for the multiple transatlantic fare, he sent for his family, and it was during their immigration processing on Ellis Island that three-year-old Meir Schapiro's first name was changed to Meyer.

The Schapiros settled first in Williamsburg and then in Brownsville, Brooklyn. Nathan Schapiro became a prosperous paper-and-twine jobber, but he remained at heart always more the intellectual than the businessman, interested in literary Hebrew although not in its revival as a living language. The reading material in the Schapiro household included secular Bible studies, books on language and Darwinian theory, and such publications as the socialist *Call* and the *Jewish Daily Forward*. The prevailing language in the home was Yiddish.

Both his father and mother encouraged Meyer Schapiro's wide range of interests, from sports and electrical gadgetry to Hebrew, reading, developing photographs, and drawing. Schapiro began to draw in elementary school (P.S. 84 in Brooklyn). He was the only child in an evening art class at the Hebrew Educational Society settlement house in Brownsville taught by the painter and etcher John Sloan, the well-known member of the Ashcan School of social realism. Later, when in high school, he attended classes taught by Frank Mura at the Brooklyn Museum.

At Boys High School in Brooklyn, Meyer Schapiro did well in all of his subjects, but he received his highest grades in mathematics and Latin. During his high school years he attended Marxist lectures on anthropology, economics, and literature at the Young Peoples Socialist League. From the age of thirteen he worked summers, as a Western Union delivery boy, a warehouse packer, an electrical supply assembler, and an adjustments clerk at Macy's department store.

By skipping grades, Meyer Schapiro graduated from high school in 1920, at the age of fifteen. In September 1920 he entered Columbia College on a Pulitzer scholarship—as his brother Morris had done the previous year—and a Regents scholarship as well. Confident in math, languages, and writing but not sure that his skill in art could ever warrant a career in that field, he chose an undergraduate curriculum that included Latin, living languages, mathematics, ancient and modern literature, anthropology, philosophy, and art history. While he became more and more attracted to art history because it engaged his "sense of the deep connections of art with the totality of culture," he was unhappy with the classes in the subject offered at Columbia at the time, which he regarded as "snap" courses "given by men who had never really conducted investigations after writing their Ph.D. theses." In a 1927 memoir quoted by Helen Epstein in *Artnews* (May 1983), the poet and English professor Mark Van Doren described Schapiro as a Columbia student who "glowed—in his thick curly black hair, in his eager white cheeks, . . . in his darkly rolling eyes," in his "passionate . . . positively beautiful face," and in his intellectual "passion." "I heard now and then that his instructors often resented his knowledge, which they felt was intruded without cause during class discussions," Van Doren wrote. "I am sure, however, that his was the best of causes—a passion to know and make known."

In 1924 Schapiro took his B.A. degree at Columbia with honors in art history and philosophy. For his graduate work he considered going into anthropology—where Franz Boas would have been his mentor—or architecture, but he decided against those options as being less able to "satisfy [his] love of learning as well as [his] love of art." He applied for admission to the prestigious department of art history at Princeton University, but he was rejected there. (He suspects that there was "a Jewish factor" in the rejection.) So, with mixed feelings, he continued on into graduate art history at Columbia.

As a graduate student Schapiro had the good fortune to come under the guidance of the medieval scholar Ernest DeWald, who had moved from Princeton to Columbia. The reading that influenced the development of his point of view as an art historian included the works of Emmanuel Löwy, Roger Fry, and A. Kingsley Porter. The writers who most influenced him, however, were the German-speaking scholars, such as Wilhelm Vöge and Alois Riegl, who combined a close scrutiny of individual works of art with a broad synthetic viewpoint in relating forms to stages in the development of art. Using a dictionary and his family background in Yiddish to gain a mastery of German, he read the works of those scholars in the original, beginning with Vöge's book on the emergence of the monumental style in the eleventh and twelfth centuries. From Riegl, Schapiro came to see in the changes in art through the ages a process of development similar to the individual's growth in perception, which moves from the flat mode of seeing objects in early childhood "to visualizing them in deep space and in light and learning how objects change their appearance according to our mode of perception."

For the subject of his doctoral dissertation Schapiro chose the cloister and portal of Moissac, an abbey near Toulouse, France built in approximately 1100 A.D.—the middle of the Romanesque period in architecture and art, so-called to indicate the transition from the Roman to the Gothic style. Viewed as naive, unrealistic precursors of perfect Gothic art, the sculptures at Moissac were generally treated as crude archeological oddities until 1922, when Emile Mâle in his *L'Art religieux du XIIe Siècle en France* pronounced them "the very inception of the modern tradition of plastic art."

The on-site research in France necessary for Schapiro's dissertation was made possible by a fellowship from the Carnegie Corporation in 1926 and 1927. His research included the study of other Romanesque architecture and art, including illuminated manuscripts of the period, and of medieval church history, literature, theology, and liturgy. What attracted Schapiro to Romanesque sculpture was the challenge of explaining a great historical change. For 500 years there had been very little monumental stone sculpture in Western Europe, and then suddenly, in the eleventh century, artists and artisans in France, Spain, and Italy began to build great churches covered with stone figures and carved ornaments, many of which were "masterpieces" in Schapiro's judgment. "You can see," he pointed out to Helen Epstein, "almost year by year how the style changes from an archaic one to a more naturalistic and more complex one."

In his dissertation on Moissac, Schapiro tried to make clear not only the inventiveness of the medieval sculptors in contributing both to the expression of a subject and to the architectural order of a tympanum, pillar, capital, or frieze, but also their "search for increasingly more articulated naturalistic forms." He showed how the art at Moissac developed from early works that are "rather flat and uniform in their surface" and "often symmetrical" to later sculpture that is "more intricate and more intensively expressive."

The dissertation on Moissac was accepted in fulfillment of Schapiro's final Ph.D. requirement at Columbia in 1929. When part of the dissertation was published in the *Art Bulletin* two years later, it established Schapiro's reputation in the art community immediately and resoundingly. "Before Meyer," the medieval and Renaissance scholar John Plummer, a former student of Schapiro's, has observed, "most studies viewed Romanesque sculpture as . . . antiquarian artifacts belonging to a national heritage . . . as illustrations of religious themes characteristic of the period . . . or as a network of art historical influences. . . . Meyer treated a set of Romanesque sculptures for the first time as art rather than as documents."

In 1928, the year he became a lecturer in art history at Columbia, Schapiro married Dr. Lillian Milgram, a pediatrician. In the 1930s, Schapiro and Dr. Milgram's home in Greenwich Village became a salon for the radical left, and Schapiro became active in politics for the first time, writing for the *Marxist Quarterly*, the *New Masses*, the *Nation*, and the *Partisan Review* and voting for socialist and Communist candidates. With Stalin's ruthless purge of the Soviet Communist party and his non-aggression pact with Hitler in the late 1930s, Schapiro, like many others, became disillusioned with Communism. In 1940 he was prominent in organizing a secession of artists, critics, and academics from the Communist-dominated American Arts Congress and in forming the rival Federation of Modern Painters and Sculptors to "promote the welfare of free, progressive art in America," but he never took part in the bitter recrimination so rife among radicals and ex-radicals. The novelist Saul Bellow, who met Schapiro in Greenwich Village in the 1940s, recalled, as quoted by Helen Epstein: "Meyer never took part in any of the quarrels and backbiting and vendettas. . . . He was the one person in the Village against whom no one had anything terrible to say."

Schapiro became an assistant professor at Columbia in 1936, an associate professor in 1946, a full professor in 1952, and a university professor, with the privilege of choosing his own courses to teach, in 1965. He also lectured at New York University from 1932 to 1936 and at the New School for Social Research from 1938 to 1952. Writing in the *New York Times* (May 17, 1981), Anatole Broyard recalled his first course under Schapiro, at the New School in 1951: "I saw a simply dressed, classically handsome man with a transcendent expression on his face. Like the angel in paintings of the Annunciation, he had the air of someone bringing astonishing news. And he did. Talking about Cézanne, he observed that before him, European landscape paintings always had a point of entry, a plane where the viewer could 'walk' into the picture. But some Cézanne landscapes were abstracted out of their context like an aerial photograph. You could enter them only by leaping. . . . When Van Gogh loaded his pigment, we were told, this was a frantic grasping at tangibility by a man who felt that he was falling out of the real."

No reading of Schapiro's evenly paced, workmanlike, precise prose can convey the spellbinding effect of his eloquence on the lecture platform. According to Anatole Broyard, "Mr. Schapiro was so fluent, hardly ever pausing for a word or a formulation, that it was as if he heard voices." In his memoirs about the old *Partisan Review* circle, *The Truants* (1982), William Barrett recalled Schapiro's "need to pour himself out to a listener [in] a smooth and foaming flood, almost ecstatic in self-surrender to its own eloquence."

The painter Wolf Kahn, who audited Schapiro's course at Columbia in 1951, found him to be that rarest of art historians, one "who really turns painters on" with the sense he gives that art is the central activity, "tying Matisse in with psychology and other artists with mathematics and perception." Recalling the 1930s for Helen Epstein in *Artnews*, Milton Brown said: "Most people then taught the Impressionists, for example, in terms of color theory. Meyer saw them besides as celebrating the positive aspects of French social life and culture, the leisure activities of the bourgeoisie. A great deal of what was being taught was formalist. . . . With Meyer, art became an intellectual experience that grew out of a social context."

Among the students inspired by Schapiro were a legion of contemporary artists, including Allan Kaprow, Roberto Echaurren Matta, Robert Motherwell, and Lucas Samaras, and a virtual who's who of current art scholars, critics, and curators. Outside the classroom, it was Schapiro who, in 1935, took Fernand Léger to the basement of the Morgan Library and showed him the manuscript illuminations of the medieval Spanish monk Beatus that inspired the bold, wide bands of color Léger subsequently used in his work.

For half a century Schapiro was "the most famous art historian who never wrote a book," as Henri Zerner observed in his review of the paperback *Words and Pictures* (Mouton, 1973), which was not so much a book as a short illustrated lecture on the semiotics of the pictorial art in medieval Bibles and other Christian manuscripts. Likewise, *Vincent Van Gogh* (Abrams, 1950) and *Paul Cézanne* (Abrams, 1952) were not books by Schapiro but folios with introductory monographs by him. Partly because of his own apparent reluctance to have his dynamic lectures frozen in print, and his expressed reluctance to republish papers in which he saw "imperfections, inconsistencies, and unclear formulations," his admirers had to circulate his work as best they could in various *samizdat* forms, from photostats in the instance of the 1937 essay "The Nature of Abstract Art" to photocopies in that of the 1957 article "The Liberating Quality of Avant-Garde Art." In the latter he defended abstract art against allegations that it was an otherwise meaningless reflection of social illness and chaos. "Paintings and sculptures . . . ," he pointed out, "are the last hand-made personal objects within our culture." Midway between those two essays, in a 1950 essay on the 1913 Armory Show, Schapiro observed that, given the bleak political atmosphere of the time, modernist artists, denied "the chance to paint works of broad human content for a larger audience, works comparable in scope to those of antiquity or the Middle Ages . . . have no alternative but to cultivate in their art the only or surest realms of freedom—the interior world of their fancies, sensations, and feelings, and the medium itself."

Finally, in 1977, George Braziller, Inc., the New York publishing house prized for its art books, launched Schapiro's *Selected Papers*, a series of volumes bringing together his scattered essays and distillations of his lectures and thus making possible for the first time an appreciation of the full measure of his achievement. The first volume was *Romanesque Art* (1977), consisting of eight articles, including part of the dissertation on Moissac and an essay on the transition from Mozarabic to Romanesque in the abbey church of Silos, Spain. The thesis underlying all of the essays was explicitly stated in the first, "On the Aesthetic Attitude in Romanesque Art," written in 1947. In that essay Schapiro confronted head-on the once prevailing notion that medieval art was a product of a pious communal effort in which anonymous artists or artisans were satisfied solely with humble fulfillment of their organic roles out of dedication to God. A dubious Schapiro had observed in his 1939 essay "The Sculptures of Souillac" (also included in this volume) that one of the carvings at the French abbey was "a passionate *drôlerie* . . . corresponding to the role of violence at this point in the history of feudal society." By 1947 such intuitive observations had developed into the general view that "by the eleventh and twelfth centuries there had emerged in Western Europe within church art a new sphere of artistic creation without religious content and imbued with the values of spontaneity, individual fantasy, delight in color and movement, and the expression of feeling that anticipate modern art."

The nineteenth-century art historians who discerned intimations of modernism in the Romanesque style still judged that style by a standard of symmetry or stylized asymmetry borrowed from antique, high Renaissance, or Gothic art—what Schapiro saw to be a "mechanical Platonism." Measured against that standard, Romanesque art was, as Dan Hofstadter observed in *Commentary* (August 1980), "always found odd, at worst falling from the antique, at best striving toward the Gothic." Rejecting that prejudice, Schapiro showed that the sculptors' departures from natural shapes had, in his words, "a common character which is intimately bound up with the harmonious formal structure of the works" and is "subordinate to an essentially dynamic expressive end."

The second volume in the Braziller series, *Modern Art: 19th and 20th Centuries* (1978), consisted of a previously unpublished 1971 lecture on Mondrian and thirteen articles previously published over a forty-five-year period. The articles included pieces on Courbet, Seurat, Chagall, and Picasso in addition to the essays on Van Gogh and Cézanne and those on abstract art in general and the abstract painting of Arshile Gorky in particular. The first paper in *Modern Art* was, appropriately, "The Apples of Cézanne: An Essay on the Meaning of Still Life," perhaps Schapiro's best-known piece. Nowhere more than in Cézanne's "heroism" in an art "without rhetoric and convention" is there an example of the continuity through historically changing artistic vocabularies of the "spontaneous sensibility" that Schapiro looks for.

In her review of *Modern Art: 19th and 20th Centuries* in *Art in America* (March/April 1979), Linda Nochlin summed up Schapiro's major beliefs as an art historian: "his rejection of either metaphysical cant or formalist empiricism as ways of dealing with modern art; his insistence that formal choices are always rooted in larger systems of value which in turn are historically conditioned; his refusal to accept coarse historical determinism or simple alternation theories that purport to explain the genesis of modern styles; and his vision of modernism, beginning with Impressionism, as an assertion of personal freedom in the face of the increasing oppressiveness and depersonalization of individual life brought about by capitalist institutions." If "the dialectic is materialist, . . . concerned not with abstractions but with concrete historical and social situations, with vividly described objects and the specific subconditions of praxis in the art world itself," the approach is "fiercely joyous," in the tradition of Talmudic argumentation, and "profoundly moral," in its assumptions about the importance of the artist's inner experience and individualized expression "in an increasingly mechanized world." Regarding the "grandeur" and "seriousness" of Schapiro's reach, his scorn for the destructive irrationality of Dada and Surrealism and the "camp" sensibility of Pop Art, for "the whole realm of anti-art," Linda Nochlin rated his "powerful exclusivity of judgment and attention" as one of his "greatest sources of strength . . . and appeal: his is the brilliant certitude of the existence of a great tradition of modern achievement, rooted in the most profound moral value of Western civilization: personal freedom."

Late Antique, Early Christian and Mediaeval Art (1979), the third volume of Schapiro's *Selected Papers*, offered twenty-two articles on subjects ranging from a fourth-century illuminated calendar to a fifteenth-century altarpiece. Reviewing the first three volumes in the *American Scholar* (Winter 1980/81), Hilton Kramer voiced a minority opinion in challenging what Kramer considered Schapiro's sacrosanct secularist debunking of Romanesque religious symbolism and the contradiction of that revisionism with his "psychoanalytic" de-aestheticizing of modernist artists. "Why," Kramer asked, "is so much importance attached to what Schapiro calls the 'strong current of aestheticism in the culture of the twelfth century' while the stronger and far more explicit current of aestheticism in the late nineteenth- and twentieth-century art remains relegated to a place of almost marginal significance?" Kramer saw in the *Selected Papers*

an unresolved conflict "between the aesthete and the ideologue that sooner or later will have to be faced if their author is to be taken seriously as a significant analyst of our artistic heritage."

Meyer Schapiro and Dr. Lillian Milgram have a daughter, Miriam Schapiro Grosof, and a son, Ernest. In addition to their home in Greenwich Village, Schapiro and his wife have a house in rural Vermont, where they spend their summers. The Vermont house is the subject of many of Schapiro's paintings. Other subjects he has captured on paper or on canvas include landscapes and seascapes, including New York harbor, and portraits of his wife and his friends, including the late Whittaker Chambers, the controversial turncoat Communist spy to whom Schapiro, unlike most of his fellows on the political left, personally remained loyal to the end. As for his own politics, he told Helen Epstein for the two-part 1983 *Artnews* profile that he has "put behind [him] certain attitudes and expectations" of the socialism of his youth, "but others remain." With the proceeds from the sale of works donated by a number of American and European artists, a university professorship has been established at Columbia in Schapiro's name.

References: Art in America 67:29+ Mr/Ap '79 por; *Artnews* 72:59+ Summer '73 por, 82:60+ My '83 pors, 82:84+ Summer '83 pors; *Contemporary Authors* vols 97–100 (1981); *Who's Who in America*, 1984–85.

Schygulla, Hanna

(she-gōō´ lä)

Dec. 25, 1943– Actress. Address: b. c/o Robert Lantz, 888 7th Ave., New York City, N.Y. 10106; c/o Georges Beaume, 3 Quai Malaquais, Paris 75006, France

In a rags-to-riches story that in some respects parallels her country's rise from the ruins of World War II, the actress Hanna Schygulla emerged from a poverty-stricken childhood in war-ravaged Germany to attain international stardom. Her years of professional collaboration with the late avant-garde actor-director Rainer Werner Fassbinder produced a body of work staggering in volume and stunning in originality. As her stature as an actress was enhanced, so in general was the substance of her characters. She has molded her roles with finely tuned sensitivity to the complexity of human nature, while demonstrating a shrewd grasp of her character's placement within a film. Perhaps the purest example of her perceptiveness was her virtuoso presentation of the title role in Fassbinder's *The Marriage of Maria Braun*, a performance that earned her worldwide acclaim.

Hanna Schygulla was born on Christmas Day of 1943 in Katowice, Silesia, in what was then German-occupied Poland, to Joseph Schygulla, a lum-

Hanna Schygulla

ber merchant, and Antonie (Mzyk) Schygulla. Her father, who was at the time an infantryman in the German army, was captured in Italy by American forces and held as a prisoner of war until 1948. When Hanna was two, she and her mother were swept up in the wave of uprooted refugees surging through war-torn Germany. They settled in Munich but were so poor that for a time mother and daughter lived in a freight car on an unused section of track outside the city. Their fortunes improved after the father rejoined them. In an interview in *Vanity Fair* (January 1984), Miss Schygulla told Gideon Bachmann that even as she was growing up she held "some sort of special position." Her "funny name," as well as her abundance of energy, determination, audacity, and disregard for rules brought her much attention. "As a child I usually got to where I wanted to get," she recalled. Her early film idols were Brigitte Bardot and Marilyn Monroe.

On completing her secondary education at a Gymnasium in Munich, Hanna Schygulla worked for a time as an au pair girl in Paris, then returned to Munich, where she began her university studies in Germanic and Romance philology in 1964 with the ambition of becoming a high school teacher. "I studied hard when I was at the university," Miss Schygulla told Kevin Thomas of the *Los Angeles Times* (November 28, 1979). "I came from a very modest background." Her parents, she recalled, had to sacrifice to send her there.

One day Miss Schygulla accompanied a friend to an acting class at the Fridi-Leophard Studio in Munich, where she met Rainer Werner Fassbinder. By 1967 they were acting together in the Munich Action Theater. Miss Schygulla's first stage performance was in the title role of Sophocles' *Antigone*. "From the very first rehearsal,"

Fassbinder once said, "she became my star." After Fassbinder broke away to form an "antitheatre" performance group geared toward eradicating the conventional barriers between actors and audience, Miss Schygulla was recruited to replace an actress who had been accidentally stabbed and was left paralyzed. "I had been going with the intellect, studying to be a teacher, but I hadn't been satisfied," Hanna Schygulla told Kevin Thomas in explaining her decision to make acting her career. "It was becoming less and less spontaneous for me and increasingly uncomfortable. I wanted something more *sensual.*"

Starting in an old barroom, the ten-member troupe staged classics updated by Fassbinder. At first the main critical response was beery laughter from the student audiences, who reveled in the irreverence and bawdy spontaneity with which those hallowed works were presented. The Antitheater's satirical adaptation of Goethe's *Iphigenie auf Taurus* inspired the director Jean-Marie Straub to film the Fassbinder players. The result, the twenty-three-minute *Der Bräutigam, die Komödiantin und der Zuhälter* (1968; The Bridegroom, the Comedienne, and the Pimp), featuring Miss Schygulla, was not widely seen nor highly acclaimed, nor even widely reviewed.

Undaunted, Fassbinder wrote and directed his first full-length film, *Liebe ist kälter als der Tod* (Antitheater, 1969; Love Is Colder than Death), in which Miss Schygulla played a small-time gangster's inamorata. Its premiere at the 1969 Berlin Film Festival failed to arouse much enthusiasm but the pairing of the talented, prolific director and the versatile young actress set a precedent that endured through nearly half of the more than forty films that Fassbinder directed from 1969 until his death in 1982.

In Fassbinder's second feature film for Antitheater, *Katzelmacher* (1969)—the title is a pejorative Bavarian term for immigrant workers —the director played Jorgos, a Greek laborer harassed by the German bourgeois community into which he moved, while Hanna Schygulla was Marie, the girl who befriended him. The film received critical acclaim in West Germany, where it won for Fassbinder the 1969 West German Film Critics Prize and the Federal Film Prize. But when it was released in the United States by New Yorker Films some years later, it inspired little interest.

For the next few years, Hanna Schygulla starred in a nearly uninterrupted stream of Fassbinder films, many of them about alienated Germans trapped in meaningless lives, in which she portrayed a wide-ranging variety of character types. The single constant factor in her screen personas was the evocative complexity with which she endowed them. With each new release, Fassbinder's legend as a New Wave *Wunderkind* and Hanna Schygulla's as one of Germany's most accomplished actresses grew.

Among the Fassbinder Antitheater films in which Hanna Schygulla appeared in 1969 were *Götter der Pest* (Gods of the Plague), a gangster melodrama, and *Warum läuft Herr R. Amok?* (Why Does Mr. R. Run Amuck?), about the banality of middle-class life. In 1970 Miss Schygulla was featured in Fassbinder's *Rio das Mortes*, about a treasure hunt in South America; *Die Niklashauser Fahrt* (The Niklashausen Journey), an allegory set in fifteenth-century Germany; *Whity*, a tongue-in-cheek melodrama with the American South as its background; *Warnung vor einer heiligen Nutte* (Beware of a Holy Whore), a film about filmmaking; the made-for-television *Kaffeehaus* (Coffee House); and *Pioniere in Ingolstadt* (Recruits in Ingolstadt), Fassbinder's adaptation of Marieluise Fleisser's play about Bavarian small-town life, which was the final production of the Antitheater.

In *Händler der vier Jahreszeiten* (Tango, 1971; *Merchant of Four Seasons*, New Yorker Films, 1972), which deals with a fruit peddler whose frustrations lead him to drink himself to death, Hanna Schygulla played Erna, the sister of the protagonist, in a performance that brought her critical praise. She also appeared in several of Fassbinder's made-for-television productions, including *Bremer Freiheit* (1972), about a woman who destroys the oppressive men in her life; *Wildwechsel* (1972), released by New Yorker Films as *Jailbait*, a melodrama about teenage love; and *Acht Stunden sind kein Tag* (1972–73; Eight Hours Are Not a Day), an upbeat, popular five-episode series about a working-class family. In the feature film *Die bitteren Tränen der Petra von Kant* (Tango, 1972; *The Bitter Tears of Petra von Kant*, New Yorker Films, 1973), based on Fassbinder's play about lesbian entanglements, Hanna Schygulla appears in the role of Karin, who abandons her lesbian lover to return to her husband. It received mixed reviews from critics who saw it at the New York Film Festival.

In addition to working for Fassbinder, Hanna Schygulla also appeared occasionally in films by other directors, including Peter Fleischmann's *Jagdszenen aus Niederbayern* (1969; Hunting Scenes from Lower Bavaria), and Volker Schlöndorff's adaptation of Bertolt Brecht's *Baal*. Others include Reinhold Hauff's *Matthias Kneissl* (1970) and *Das Haus am Meer* (1971; House by the Sea); Franz J. Spieker's *Kuckucksei im Gangsternest* (1970; Cuckoo's Egg in a Gangster's Nest); Peter Lilienthal's *Jacob von Günten* (1971); Wim Wenders' *Falsche Bewegung* (1974; *Wrong Move*), an updating of Goethe's classic *Wilhelm Meister's Apprenticeship*; Vojtech Jasny's *Ansichten eines Clowns* (1975; Views of a Clown) and *Heimkehr des alten Herrn* (1977; Return of the Old Gentleman); Gaudenz Meili's *Der Stumme* (1975; The Mute); Claus Peter Witt's television series *Die Dämonen* (1977; The Demons); George Moorse's *Aussagen nach einer Verhaftung* (1978; Testimonies After an Arrest); and Marianne Lüdtke's *Die grosse Flatter* (1978). She has also appeared in theatrical productions of the Münchner Kammerspiele and other ensembles.

In the title role of Fassbinder's *Fontane Effi Briest* (Tango, 1974; *Effi Briest*, New Yorker Films, 1977), shown at the 1974 Berlin Film Festival, Hanna Schygulla seemed finally to have come into her own as an actress. The movie was adapted from Theodor Fontane's 1894 German novel about a naive young beauty who, after being married off to an older man by her ambitious mother, comes to a tragic end as a consequence of her brief affair with a handsome, rakish young officer. Miss Schygulla was "enchanting" and "stunning" as Effi, according to Vincent Canby of the *New York Times* (June 16, 1977). "The performances are admirable, rising to the top with Hanna Schygulla's pathetic Effi," Archer Winsten wrote in the *New York Post* (June 17, 1977). And Robert Martin of the *Toronto Globe and Mail* (January 4, 1978) wrote: "The film is essentially Hanna Schygulla's and she is splendid. . . . " But though *Effi Briest* promised to bring Hanna Schygulla her breakthrough to international stardom, it actually signaled a temporary halt in her acting career.

After years of her almost nonstop marathon with Fassbinder, Hanna Schygulla took what she called a sabbatical. Although she denied rumors of conflict between herself and the director, she later conceded to John Gruen during an interview for the *New York Times* (October 23, 1983): "I had to save my sanity. . . . I owe my career to him. But he was possessed—demonic." During her absence from the screen, she studied yoga and meditation, became a vegetarian, worked with the Rudolf Steiner School children's theatre, painted, and traveled, at one point hitchhiking with a friend from coast to coast through the United States for three months. She also stayed for a time in the German countryside with friends, and videotaped herself as she enacted her dreams.

If her temporary defection from the screen was barely noticed in the film world, Hanna Schygulla's return, in the Fassbinder masterpiece *Die Ehe der Maria Braun* (Albatros Film, 1979; *The Marriage of Maria Braun*, New Yorker Films, 1979), made international headlines. Her richly layered performance in the title role, which had previously been turned down by Romy Schneider, inspired comparison by the Hollywood media with Anna Karina, Giulietta Masina, Marlene Dietrich, Jean Harlow, Joan Crawford, and Stéphane Audran. To those comparisons she testily retorted: "You are always the new so and so. You are never yourself in Hollywood." The performance earned her the 1979 Berlin Film Festival's Silver Bear, the German Gold Filmband, and Italy's David di Donatello award for best actress.

In that allegory of postwar West Germany's "economic miracle," Hanna Schygulla played a war bride who applied sex and shrewdness to pave her way to prosperity before the film reached its literally explosive climax. Hanna Schygulla was responsible for the delicate ambiguity of the final scene. "I want always to bring something enigmatic to a role, so people can fill in," she told an interviewer for *Vogue* (February 1980). Filmed over a period of four weeks, *Maria Braun* was Fassbinder's first international commercial success. Hanna Schygulla's acting was singled out for special praise. Andrew Sarris wrote in the *Village Voice* (October 15, 1979): "The beating heart of the film is all Schygulla's," and Vincent Canby, in his review in the *New York Times* (October 14, 1979), called her performance "splendid and mysterious," while Rob Baker concluded in New York's *Soho Weekly News* (November 1, 1979): "Schygulla is not just a star, but a superstar, a giant."

Fassbinder's next project with Hanna Schygulla, *Die dritte Generation* (Tango/Project, 1979; *The Third Generation*, New Yorker Films, 1979), dealt with a group of young, middle-class terrorists. Some critics panned it as heavy-handed, muddled, and silly, but others congratulated Fassbinder for confronting a difficult subject with comprehension and ironic humor and praised the performances of Miss Schygulla and the other cast members.

Fassbinder's fifteen-hour television adaptation of Alfred Döblin's epic 1929 novel, *Berlin Alexanderplatz* (TeleCulture, 1980), featured Hanna Schygulla as Eva, a high-priced prostitute, whose friendship with the ex-convict anti-hero, Franz Bieberkopf, is an important motif in the star-studded miniseries. Released in New York City in 1983, three years after it was telecast in Germany, and a year after Fassbinder's untimely and tragic death, it astounded American audiences with its sheer size, and critics responded warmly to its direction and acting. "The viewer surrenders . . . to Schygulla, with her wicked-witch profile and wicked, witty mouth," Richard Corliss wrote in *Time* (August 15, 1983).

By that time, movie offers had begun to pour in from Hollywood, including the title role in Alan J. Pakula's *Sophie's Choice*—which later went to Meryl Streep—but Miss Schygulla turned them all down, fearing that she would become typecast in superficial roles. "I can only act when I feel there are hidden depths in a part and where I am personally involved," she told an interviewer for the *Hamburger Abendblatt*, as quoted in the *German Tribune* (April 20, 1980). "I don't want to be just a doll being rigged out in different costumes all the time."

In her next collaboration with Fassbinder, *Lili Marleen* (Roxy, 1981; United Artists, 1981), Hanna Schygulla starred as Willie, a cabaret singer modeled on Lale Andersen, whose song "Lili Marleen" became a hit with both German and Allied troops during World War II. The idea for the film was suggested by the German movie magnate Luggi Waldleitner to Miss Schygulla, who was intrigued by the opportunity to be the centerpiece of a lavish, glossy movie with worldwide distribution, and she agreed to star in it on the condition that Fassbinder would direct it. Fassbinder received a budget of $5 million, reportedly the highest in West German movie history. The film, which Miss Schygulla described as a "Nazi fairy tale," was a box-office success in West Germany, but it failed to win over the critics. In the United States, Rex Reed, in his syndicated column for the *New York Daily News* (July 11, 1981), outdid Spiro Agnew's alliteration in calling it "a sophomoric cinematic strudel of supreme silliness," and Charles Michener in *Newsweek* (August 10, 1981) panned it as "a voluptuous exercise in kitsch." Others were more favorably impressed. According to Andrew Sarris, writing in the *Village Voice* (July 8, 1981), Miss Schygulla and Giancarlo Giannini—who was seen as her Swiss-Jewish lover—"play the romantic leads mythologically rather than psychologically or ideologically. But it is a subtly nuanced mythology that is achieved. . . . "

Lili Marleen turned out to be Hanna Schygulla's last movie for Fassbinder. On June 10, 1982 the brilliant filmmaker was found dead, apparently from an overdose of drugs and alcohol. "Who is going to take us to our limits now?" Miss Schygulla cried out during a memorial service. Later, describing the director to Gideon Bachmann in *Vanity Fair* (January 1984), the actress said, "He was the master of irritation . . . , but then something would come along that was incredibly human, or simple. It was this mixture which produced a dynamic reaction in the spectator."

Among the films that Hanna Schygulla had made with other directors over the years, few received more than passing notice internationally until Volker Schlöndorff's *Die Fälschung* (Bioskop Film, 1981; *Circle of Deceit*, United Artists, 1982). Shot on location in Beirut, the film was lauded for its verisimilitude, and Miss Schygulla won praise for her creditable performance as Arianne, the tough-minded German widow of a Lebanese businessman, who has an affair with a German reporter disillusioned with his marriage and career. An equally turbulent but more remote period served as the backdrop in Ettore Scola's *La Nuit de Varennes* (Opera/Gaumont, 1982; Triumph), set in the French Revolution, in which Miss Schygulla played Countess Sophie, a member of the entourage of Louis XVI, who is fleeing Paris for Varennes. Critics heaped superlatives on the film and hailed Hanna Schygulla's performance as magnificent, beguiling, and mysterious.

According to an article in the *Hamburger Abendblatt* that was quoted in the *German Tribune* (January 10, 1982), the French director Jean-Luc Godard was reported to have been so fascinated by his private vision of Hanna Schygulla's "red-gold locks softly reflected by the setting sun in the evening wind" that he was determined to "find a story to fit it." The result was *Passion* (Sara/Sonimage Films, 1982; United Artists, 1983), a movie about moviemaking shown at the 1982 Cannes Film Festival and the 1983 New York Film Festival that was praised by Godard's fans and lambasted by others.

Hanna Schygulla's expressed desire to "portray taboo-breakers" was fulfilled in the Italian director Marco Ferreri's *Storia di Piera* (Faso Films, 1983), in which she played the free-spirited Eugenia, who helped to bring about the sexual initiation of her daughter Piera. "Miss Schygulla is as beautiful and mysterious as ever, even when the material seems simply to be muddled," Vincent Canby wrote in the *New York Times* (September 24, 1983). The performance brought her the prize for best actress at the 1983 Cannes Film Festival.

Hanna Schygulla's friend and former fellow actress Margarethe von Trotta directed her in *Heller Wahn* (Bioskop Film, 1983; Sheer Madness), which was shown at the 1983 Berlin Film Festival. But Hanna Schygulla found the role of Olga, a professor of women's literature who befriends Ruth, a suicidal former teacher, too staid for her liking. "I'm definitely not made for bourgeois parts," she told an interviewer for *Vogue* (December 1983). "I like roles that are illogical, chaotic, ambiguous." Her next part was that of Paulina, a German woman who fell in love with a Polish prisoner during World War II, in Andrej Wadja's *Eine Liebe in Deutschland* (1983), based on a novel by Rolf Hochhuth. Its presentation as *A Love in Germany* at the 1984 New York Film Festival at Lincoln Center prompted Vincent Canby to comment in the *New York Times* (October 7, 1984) that Miss Schygulla had "at long last become one of the great European film actresses of our era, comparable only to Jeanne Moreau. . . ."

Miss Schygulla's predilection for the complex has consistently set her apart. Her projection on screen of the various facets of a character results in a layered translucence, a magical image of shifting hues that verges on iridescence. But off the screen she looks, in the words of Jay Scott of the *Toronto Globe and Mail* (October 16, 1979), "very

much like the exceptionally non-mysterioso Hayley Mills and sounds very much like the guileless young women who wore flowers in their hair and listened to the music of Jimi Hendrix a long, long time ago."

According to a description of Hanna Schygulla by Roger Greenspun in the *New York Times* (October 9, 1972), "Her lips are cherry red, and when she smiles, they uncover even rows of pearly teeth. Beneath the soft swirls of her upswept blonde hair, her face all but radiates perfection. She is supernaturally beautiful." Of medium height, Hanna Schygulla has what Gideon Bachmann in *Vanity Fair* called a "bittersweet siren smile," and she speaks in a soft, musical voice. Preferring solitude to an active social life—perhaps that is one reason why she has never married—she lives in Paris but keeps an apartment near Munich, to which she hopes to return when she finds the West German political climate less stifling to the arts. "For me," she told John Gruen, "fearlessness and vision are what filmmaking is all about."

References: N Y Times p19+ O 23 '83 por; Vanity Fair p90+ Ja '84 pors; Vogue p240+ F '80 pors; Hanna Schygulla: Bilder aus Filmen von Rainer Werner Fassbinder (1981); Who's Who in Germany (1982–83)

Shepherd, Jean (Parker)

July 26, 1925(?)– Humorist. Address: b. c/o Leigh Brown, R.D. 1, Box 28, Washington, N.J. 07882

The multimedia performer and writer Jean Shepherd is a quintessentially American humorist in the Midwestern tradition of Mark Twain and George Ade. A fluent storyteller with a maverick wit, an elliptical imagination, and a gimlet eye for the authenticating detail of *trivia mundi*, Shepherd spins fables loosely drawn in part from his own rites of passage in "the great inverted bowl of darkness" that is Middle America. His purpose is twofold: to put the rituals of everyday life in the United States in the perspective of a pathetically futile human condition at which "you might as well laugh; there's little else you can do about it"; and to preserve the way of life of "the great unrecorded," so that future generations reading the literature of the twentieth century will not "think everyone was artistic, rich, and living in Westchester."

As an innovative, free-form raconteur on radio station WOR in New York for two decades, beginning in 1956, Shepherd attracted an immense cult following up and down the eastern seaboard with his mocking jabs at the fads and foibles of Americana generally and in particular for the elaborate monologues in which he created what Marshall McLuhan called "a nightly novel." That following has grown through syndication, recordings, and personal appearances, especially on college cam-

© 1984 Fred W. McDarragh

puses; through *Wanda Hickey's Night of Golden Memories* (1972) and the other best-selling books in which Shepherd has translated his episodic "novel" into print; through the critically acclaimed PBS television dramatizations of his stories, including *Phantom of the Open Hearth* (1976), the PBS travelogue/monologue series *Jean Shepherd's*

America (1969-71); and through the theatrical feature A Christmas Story (1983), co-adapted by Shepherd from one of his stories, which was the top-grossing motion picture during the 1983 holiday season.

As Leigh Brown, Shepherd's agent, producer, and wife, told John Kronenberger of the New York Times (June 6, 1971), "Jean doesn't like to talk about his personal life. He thinks it has nothing to do with his work." It is certain that Shepherd's birthday is July 26, but the year of his birth is elusive, ranging in published estimates from 1923 to 1929. The elder son of Jean P. and Anne (Heinrichs) Shepherd, he was born in Chicago, Illinois, where his father was an office manager for Borden Dairies and where his younger brother, Randy, would become an employee of the same company.

Shepherd grew up within commuting distance of Chicago, in Hammond, Indiana, the "tough and mean" industrial city that he fictionalizes as "Hohman" in his stories about the childhood and adolescence of "Ralph Parker." As Hohman, Hammond is universalized to represent, according to Shepherd, "Industrial Town America . . . Newark, Gary, Detroit . . . kind of like Faulkner used his mythical county to represent the South." He told Kristy Montee of the Fort Lauderdale News and Sun-Sentinel (March 14, 1976): "Don't think it's not authentic—but it's not memoirs. . . . All the characters are amalgams of people I've known and the 'I' in my books is not really me but a fictional guy, a sort of ultimate New Yorker—who is based on all the New Yorkers I've known who have come from the Midwest."

Yet Shepherd's relatively plotless vignettes are so intimate and ring so true it is difficult to believe he did not experience them. Among the vignettes is a recollection of the winter trek to school: "Kids plodded . . . through forty-five-mile-an-hour gales, tilting forward like tiny furred radiator ornaments, moving stiffly over the barren clattering ground with only the faint glint of two eyes peering out of a mound of moving clothing. . . . All were painfully plodding toward the Warren G. Harding School, miles away over the tundra [for the purpose of receiving] geography lessons involving the exports of Peru." It was not until the end of the third month of first grade that Shepherd's young hero "became dimly aware of a curse that would follow" him throughout his life. "Along with Martin Perlmutter, Schwartz, Chester Wocziewski, Helen Weathers and poor old Zynzmeister, I was a member of the Alphabetical Ghetto, forever doomed by the fateful first letter of our last names to squat restlessly, hopelessly, at the very end of every line known to man, fearfully aware that whatever the authorities were passing out, they would run out of goodies by the time they got to us."

Other vignettes of the Hoosier childhood and adolescence of Ralph Parker include his striking out on blind dates; his trial-by-prom; his fishing in fetid ponds and cleaning carpies on the back porch; men drinking boilermakers; his mother going to bank night at the movies during the Depres-

sion to get Pearlean dinnerware; his listening to the radio serial Little Orphan Annie with secret decoder ring in hand; and the Bumpuses, "a tightly knit band of total slobs" who moved in next door with 745 blue-ticked dogs, all named Big Blue or Big Red, "with the exception of seventeen named Luke."

Shepherd's fictionalized, hyperbolic recollections of childhood in the '30s and '40s are antinostalgic, as he pointed out to Faye Hammel of Cue (January 14, 1961): "Childhood seems good in retrospect because we were not yet aware of the basic truth: that we're all losers, that we're destined to die and death is a defeat." Like James Thurber and the other great humorists who came out of the Midwest, Shepherd's worldview has been conditioned by the Calvinist tenet that "we are all sinners." He told Miss Hammel: "I can't see real humor as coming from anywhere but this Midwestern tradition. Certainly, it couldn't come out of the Catholic or Jewish ethic. . . . The Protestant [is] told only one thing: things will be better if he straightens up. And he knows he's not going to straighten up."

During adolescence, Shepherd worked as a mail boy in a steel mill, and he began his radio career when he was sixteen, doing weekly sportscasts for the local radio station in Hammond, a job he got because, as he explained to Stewart Pinkerton Jr. of the Wall Street Journal (December 8, 1971), he "played high school football and was a ham radio operator." That job led to juvenile roles on network radio in Chicago, including the part of Billy Fairchild in the serial Jack Armstrong, the All-American Boy. During World War II he served in the United States Army Signal Corps, installing radar equipment. (Out of his Army experience came the grist for such revolt-against-authority stories as that of the recruit who, bored with calisthenic drills, walks off into a swamp, leading fifty others with him.) After the war, on the GI Bill, he studied acting at the Goodman Theater School in Chicago and engineering and psychology at Indiana University. In 1949 he left Indiana University, without a degree, to take a job at radio station WSAI in Cincinnati, Ohio. From WSAI he soon moved to station KYW in Philadelphia. After a year at KYW, he returned to Cincinnati to join the staff of a larger station there, WLW. In addition to his radio chores at WLW, he hosted a popular late-night comedy show, Rear Bumper, on WLW-TV.

Rear Bumper attracted the attention of Steve Allen, the original host of NBC's Tonight show. In 1955, when Allen was preparing to leave the late-night network show, he recommended Shepherd as his replacement. Shepherd was brought to New York, but the NBC job never worked out and he went to WOR-AM instead and began his twenty-one year association with that radio station.

Shepherd's first WOR programs were in short early-evening slots, but he was soon moved to longer midnight and pre-dawn shifts, where he found his natural audience, reflected in the title he gave his show, Night People, a group he has defined as "the nonbelievers who didn't completely like Ike and weren't completely convinced Adlai [Stevenson] was a savior." WOR's 50,000-watt signal carried Shepherd's voice to a metropolitan area audience of 66,000 and beyond, to twenty-seven states, as far north as Canada, and as far south as Bermuda. Listeners were alerted to the imminent arrival of that voice by the staccato trumpet call of Eduard Strauss's galloping "Banfrei" overture, Shepherd's theme. Without a script, but with a centerpiece story he had been mulling over for days, Shepherd would launch into a rambling chat, punctuated with conspiratorial whispers, infectious cackles, and explosive laughs. Sometimes he would play "The Sheik of Araby" on the kazoo, adding percussion by thumping his skull with his knuckles.

The early problems between Shepherd and the WOR management stemmed partly from his irreverent handling of commercials. After plugging Sweetheart soap, which was not a sponsor, he was suspended, but the suspension was rescinded after Shepherd's fans held protest rallies and the grateful soap company actually became a sponsor. In other breaches of broadcasting orthodoxy, Shepherd exhorted his listeners to importune bookstores with requests for a nonexistent book, *I, Libertine,* and to "hurl invective." In the latter ploy, which probably inspired the climatic scene in Paddy Chayefsky's 1976 screenplay *Network,* Shepherd would advise his listeners to put their radios in their windows and turn up the volume in order to inundate "the entire eastern half of the United States" with such shouts as "Excelsior, you fatheads!," "OK, drop the tools, we've got you covered!," and "Oh my God, this is fantastic!" If legend is correct, the last-mentioned exclamation, booming forth from radios at a girls school in New Jersey, sent housemothers on a room-by-room search for a priapic male intruder.

The heart of each program, however, was the yarn that almost invariably began, "I'm a kid, see. . . . " In his *New York Times* article John Kronenberger recalled, "If there was ever a voice to hypnotize a fourteen-year-old, it was Ol' Shep's: familiar but not condescending, sharing (it seemed) confidences with masculine camaraderie; constantly interrupting itself in a stream-of-consciousness more properly described as a torrent; now exploding into bursts of maniacal laughter, now subsiding into low chuckles that hinted (but never delivered) a fantastic dirty joke."

Shepherd's first book was *The America of George Ade* (Putnam, 1961), selections of Ade's fables, short stories, and essays that he edited, with an introduction. In the book of fiction *In God We Trust,* subtitled *All Others Pay Cash* (Doubleday, 1966), Ralph Parker, now a writer, returns to Hohman and reminisces with his boyhood chum, Flick. "Like his radio work," Bob Micklin wrote of the novel in *Newsday* (December 10, 1966), "it is fascinating in its total recall of the most minute details of adolescence." When *In God We Trust* appeared on the *New York Times* best-seller list, Shepherd had to call the newspaper to ask that the book be moved from the nonfiction to the fiction column.

Shepherd's most popular story, "Wanda Hickey's Night of Golden Memories," told of a prom date that turned into a fiasco. First published in *Playboy,* it was brought together with seven other *Playboy* stories by Shepherd in *Wanda Hickey's Night of Golden Memories and Other Disasters* (Doubleday, 1971), a book, like *In God We Trust,* apparently regarded by Shepherd to be not so much a collection as a "novel of sorts," a "succession" of "mysterious open-ended occurrences." Among its episodes were "Scut Farkas and the Murderous Maria," a tale with almost sinister supernatural overtones about an epic game of battling tops in which Shepherd's protagonist stalemates the school bully; "Daphne Bigelow and the Spine-Chilling Saga of the Snail-encrusted Tinfoil Noose," in which the young hero lands a date with the most desirable girl in school, a blueblood, and painfully discovers the reality of the barriers of social class; and "The Star-crossed Romance of Josephine Cosnowski," in which Shepherd's schoolboy alter ego's romantic illusions about Polish girls from East Chicago lead him to the brink of entrapment in a Roman Catholic early marriage.

The humorous pieces in *The Ferrari in the Bedroom* (Dodd, Mead, 1972) were original to that book, with the exception of three that first appeared in *Car and Driver* and one that first appeared in *National Lampoon.* In his introduction Shepherd explained that it had its genesis in newspaper and magazine items and ads that he had accumulated over the years, a "Vast File of Dynamic Trivia [the redemption of clichés by capitalization is a trick Shepherd picked up from George Ade] that should "be preserved for future generations so that one day they will know How It Really Was."

The trivia items became fantasies that Shepherd, in his words, "sat watching in the fetid, chewing-gum-littered theatre of[his] mind." Among the targets of those fantasies were poverty chic, a category including affluent leftist folk singers; automation and anti–drunk driving crusades (a combination resulting in the invention of the driverless car); the reversal of sex roles; and the oppressiveness of contemporary urban life.

Many of Shepherd's stories are mental flashbacks triggered by contemporary urban situations that disturb or bemuse the mature narrator. *A Fistful of Fig Newtons* (Doubleday, 1983) began with the protagonist stuck in rush-hour traffic on the New Jersey side of the Lincoln Tunnel. The sight of a car full of beer-swigging male college students ahead of him initiated the segue into the book's title episode, "A Fistful of Fig Newtons, or The Shootout in Room 303," a recollection of a college dormitory party with dire consequences. The slow journey through the tunnel sparked stories about a childhood summer at Camp Nobba-WaWa-Nockee, about misadventures in the Signal Corps; and about another disastrous date. To many Shepherd aficionados, the most enjoyable parts of *A Fistful of Fig Newtons* were the author's unstructured musings on American culture, especially that aspect he calls "the Utopia Complex . . . a sad, hopeless dream." As Shepherd (or his alter ego) exits the Lincoln Tunnel, he bellows his favorite W. C. Fields quotation: "Judas priest, what a gallimaufry!"

Reviewing *A Fistful of Fig Newtons* in the *New York Times* (February 28, 1982), Martin A. Jackson, a fan from childhood, recalled how Shepherd, "a radical in the best sense of the word . . . switched on bulbs in the heads of a whole generation by simply explaining America" to them. "I still think of him as a matchless radio artist, but he's a fine writer, too. . . . What Jean Shepherd does is cover absurdities and make us look cleanly at our own times. It's no easy trick." *A Fistful of Fig Newtons*, written in "the juicy vernacular that Jean Shepherd has made his own," confirmed Jackson in his view. "Shepherd understands the first requirement of the humorist: affection for his subject. . . . His wit is a kindly inside needling, a fond reminiscing about the embarrassing moments and quirky habits of people we've all grown up with."

In the late 1950s and early 1960s Shepherd starred in numerous Off-Broadway productions, presided over jazz concerts sponsored by the *Village Voice* (for which he was then writing), and began doing standup nightclub gigs and one-man stage shows. Some of his radio material was rendered visual on *Inside Jean Shepherd*, a show he hosted over WOR-TV during the 1960-61 television season. The following season he played a character in the soap opera *From These Roots* and did regular segments on the *Today* show. In 1962-63 on WCAU-TV in Philadelphia he conducted an off-beat interview show.

Jean Shepherd's America, aired by the Public Broadcasting Service for three seasons beginning in 1969, was a highly personalized guided tour of the United States. Accompanied by a backpack camera crew, Shepherd drove from the Florida Everglades to Nome, Alaska and across the country, discovering in "the perpetual swish of the windshield wipers . . . the sound track of our lives." Viewing the series as "an antidote to Bicentennialism," critics noted Shepherd's preoccupation with "childhood, derring-do, escape, animals, perpetual motion, male camaraderie" and were reminded of "Natty Bumpo, Ishmael, Huck Finn, Nick Adams."

The success of *Jean Shepherd's America* led to a second public television series, *Shepherd's Pie*. Later, PBS broadcast two full-length plays by Shepherd, *Phantom of the Open Hearth* (1976) based on the Wanda Hickey story, and *The Great American Fourth of July Picnic* (1982). *The Star-Crossed Romance of Josephine Cosnowski* is scheduled for airing in 1984, and new episodes of *Jean Shepherd's America* are being taped. Shepherd has also written the script for a made-for-television motion picture for the ABC network. That film, the pilot for a possible situation comedy, has been completed but is yet to be shown. Shepherd co-wrote and narrated (off camera) the theatrical feature film *A Christmas Story* (MGM-United Artists, 1983), the title of which he dislikes. (He wanted "Satan's Revenge.") That picture received mixed reviews but was a commercial hit, outgrossing *Terms of Endearment* at the box office during its first weeks of distribution, in November and December 1983. Based on "Red Ryder Nails the Cleveland Street Kid," one of the stories in *In God We Trust*, the film is about a Parker family Christmas gone awry.

Jean Shepherd is a stocky, robust man with blue-gray eyes, pleasant, regular features, mobility of facial expression, and a flat Midwestern voice. His customary wardrobe is so casual that it borders on the eccentric. Shepherd is a photographer, a pen-and-ink artist, an amateur radio operator, a collector of nineteenth-century religious art, an expert at a wide range of gadgetry, a private pilot, and a sports car buff. He has done print and electronic media commercials for sports cars as well as other products. He lives in an apartment in Manhattan and on three acres he owns in rural Washington, New Jersey, where he likes to fish. In addition, he summers in a cabin he owns in Portland, Maine and winters in a condominium in Fort Lauderdale, Florida. The humorist's first marriage, to a University of Cincinnati graduate, was brief. His second, to the actress Lois Nettleton in 1961, broke up after six years. In March 1977 he married Leigh Brown, his agent, his producer, and the amanuensis to whom he dictates his stories, articles, and books.

References: Chicago Tribune I p12+ Ap 21 '82; N Y Post mag p3 Je 23 '62 por, p29 D 8 '64 por; Realist p1+ O '60 por; Toronto Globe and Mail p17 N 18 '83 por; Contemporary Authors vols 77–80 (1979)

Silber, John R(obert)

Aug. 15, 1926– President, Boston University. Address: b. 147 Bay State Rd., Boston, Mass. 02215; h. 132 Carlton St., Brookline, Mass. 02146

One of the twelve distinguished citizens chosen by President Ronald Reagan on July 19, 1983 to make up the National Bipartisan Commission on Central America, which is headed by former Secretary of State Henry A. Kissinger, is Dr. John R. Silber, the president of Boston University. A philosopher and writer as well as university president, Silber is no stranger to the type of public debate that the Commission's report has generated, nor to the intellectual discipline and global viewpoint such an assignment demands. Dispute and conflict have sometimes marked his tenure at Boston University, along with his insistence on the highest standards of academic excellence in the finest traditions of Western humanism. A writer for *People* (June 2, 1980) summed up the complexities of Silber's reputation as follows: "Among faculty members and students alike, opinion is bitterly divided as to

John R. Silber

whether Silber is a colossus who has rescued BU from mediocrity or a megalomaniac who has shattered its spirit. He is far and away the most controversial college executive in the country today."

John Robert Silber was born on August 15, 1926 in San Antonio, Texas, the younger of two sons of Paul G. Silber, a German-American architect, and Jewell (Joslin) Silber, a schoolteacher. The family was well off until the stock market crash of 1929, but even during the privations of the Depression years an atmosphere of civility and cultural distinction prevailed in the household. John Silber was a diligent student both at the local public schools and at the Presbyterian Sunday school that he attended.

Early in life, John Silber had to face the fact that his right arm ends just below the elbow. It was not, however, the physical handicap that proved to be his most trying ordeal but the social attitudes of his peers, especially in elementary school where he was nicknamed "One-Armed Pete" and had to defend himself in constant fights. Some of his critics see the embattled child persisting in Silber's aggressive stance toward confrontations. "In some sense, John Silber never stopped fighting on the playground," Nora Ephron observed in a September 1977 *Esquire* article about him.

Silber's lifelong interest in philosophy and theology was first evident in his youthful intention to become a Protestant minister. After he graduated in 1947 from Trinity University in San Antonio *summa cum laude* in fine arts and philosophy, he attended Yale Divinity School for a year. Changing his career plans, he decided to concentrate on philosophy rather than theology and obtained his M.A. degree from Yale University in 1952 and his Ph.D. degree in 1956.

In 1957 Silber returned to his home state to become an assistant professor of philosophy at the University of Texas in Austin. A specialist in the philosophy of Immanuel Kant, he was promoted to full professor and department chairman in 1962 and to dean of the College of Arts and Sciences in 1967. The students in Silber's classes remember him as a demanding and probing teacher who used the Socratic method of instruction, relentlessly questioning them, constantly pushing them forward.

In those Austin years, John R. Silber gained a reputation as an outspoken liberal because of his chairmanship of the Texas Society to Abolish Capital Punishment and his defense of a young black woman who was refused an opportunity to sing in the school opera. Yet his philosophical training inclined him to adopt an attitude of political caution and to avoid "simplistic" solutions. For example, in a May 1968 symposium of the American Philosophical Association, Western Division, on "Philosophers and Public Policy," Silber argued against Noam Chomsky's blanket indictment of the Vietnam War. "In a world of this degree of moral complexity, simple moral answers and moral certainty are things of the past," Silber said. He added: "I predict that the day will come when intellectuals will be ashamed of having either asserted or applauded the statement that we Americans 'are simply without rival today as an agent of international criminal violence.'" And Silber made his disapproval of student protests quite clear that same turbulent year, criticizing the administration of Columbia University for adopting too mild a response in the face of disruptive demonstrations.

By July 1970 Silber's moderate liberalism and his controversial conduct as dean, including the appointment of twenty-two new department heads within less than three years, had met with the disapproval of the newly appointed University of Texas chancellor, Dr. Charles A. LeMaistre, and the conservative Board of Regents, headed by Frank C. Erwin, Jr. He was dismissed from his post as dean. A writer for *Time* (August 10, 1970), referring to Silber as "one of the country's leading philosophers," reported that he was "a target because of his liberalism, aggressiveness and potential candidacy for the U.T. presidency." Silber found himself thrust into the national spotlight.

As it happened, Silber's dismissal coincided with an impasse that had been reached by the members of a committee at Boston University, who were searching for a candidate for the university presidency following the sudden resignation in January 1971 of Dr. Arland Christ-Janer. The search committee had been working since February at the task of finding possible candidates for the leadership of the 23,000-student campus, but after making an exhaustive search they were turned down by their first candidate, Dr. John H. Knowles, the head of Massachusetts General Hospital. Silber's liberal and scholarly reputation and his aggressive administrative skills made him an immediately attractive alternative.

Silber's attitude when he went for an interview with the search committee in October seemed as much that of an interrogator as that of a candidate. He quickly summed up the dilemma confronting Boston University, a large private institution forced to compete with the state-sponsored University of Massachusetts and with Harvard University and the Massachusetts Institute of Technology across the Charles River. According to Silber, Boston University had to chart an independent course for itself. Impatient with mediocrity, he propounded an educational philosophy grounded in a classical, broad view of the importance of learning, reasoned discourse, and academic eminence.

Making no effort to ingratiate himself, in his first meeting with the search committee Silber seemed blunt and even antagonistic. As Edward Kern described the interview in a *Life* article entitled "Quest for a Silver Unicorn" (June 4, 1971), the members of the committee at first "couldn't decide whether they were more enthralled with his brains or appalled by his lack of social grace." He made no secret of his disdain for student radicals, nor for the level of faculty appointments at Boston University, but his concern for undergraduate education and his conception of interdisciplinary study in relation to the needs of the Boston community provided a much needed sense of direction for the troubled school. In November the committee recommended to the board of trustees that Silber be chosen for the post.

But John R. Silber set certain conditions for his acceptance of the appointment. Concerned with the pressing need to raise money to hire high-quality faculty, he wanted the freedom to speculate with Boston University's $12 million endowment, and he wanted the trustees to approve his plan to hire some thirty new faculty members right away (aiming eventually for 200), to the tune of an immediate $1.5 million deficit. To the surprise of many observers, the trustees accepted Silber's conditions.

The new president's inaugural address, "The Pollution of Time," contrasted sharply with the first press conference he had held following his appointment, when his comments had been marked by a forthright discussion of Boston University's "very grave" financial situation and by his serving notice of his intention to "enter into a dialogue with the mayor and the governor about whether it is not reasonable for the state and city to provide support" for Boston University. For his inaugural address Silber chose to display his classical, philosophic side rather than his hard-line pragmatism. Opening with a quotation from W. B. Yeats's "The Second Coming"—"Things fall apart; the center cannot hold"—Silber decried contemporary society's creation of an "instant culture," with its concomitant loss of a sense of history and with an atomization of learning. To many listeners he sounded like a conservative rather than like the liberal they had been led to expect.

But Silber escapes easy categorization. During his first year at Boston University, a writer for the *Christian Science Monitor* (November 22, 1971) called him a "university radical" who was "shaking up 'the system' as surely as the most committed of his radical undergraduates." Even before his inauguration, Silber hired twelve distinguished new faculty members from Yale, Princeton, and London University, among other places, to begin immediate implementation of his goals of making Boston University top-rated in teaching standards and of restoring an integrated and meaningful coherence to undergraduate education.

The new course that Silber wanted to chart for Boston University soon brought him into conflict with some of the established members of its faculty. His drive to hire new talent met with resistance from some department chairmen, who felt that Silber was behaving in an autocratic manner without seeking their consultation. He clashed also with students, especially with members of the undergraduate newspaper the *Daily Free Press*. Those tensions came to a head in March 1972 when Silber called in the local police to break up a student demonstration against Marine recruitment on campus. The statement that Silber issued to the press on that occasion reflected his philosophy of law. Invoking the names of Socrates, Gandhi, Martin Luther King, and Henry David Thoreau, Silber argued that though those men chose to violate a law, they nevertheless recognized the legal right of the community to punish them for their transgressions. Nothing seemed more deplorable to them than a state of anarchy.

The next few years brought continued tension and controversy to the Boston University campus, with Silber striving for excellence and financial stability and some faculty members and students objecting to what they saw as the "tyranny" of his "autocratic" rule. Faculty members began in 1974 to organize for a union. The following year members of the Boston University faculty voted to affiliate with the American Association of University Professors (AAUP).

Nothing clashed so fundamentally with Silber's philosophy of education and his view of the university as an environment steeped in learning and fostering talent as the idea of a faculty union. "When faculty members start seeing themselves as mass men and women to be judged by mass uniform standards," he once commented, "when merit is thrown out the window, when across-the-board raises are emphasized, and when protection of each person's job, not the maximum protection of the institution, is emphasized, maintaining and even improving quality are truly achievements." The Boston University administration refused to negotiate with the AAUP and challenged the election in a lawsuit.

In the interim period while the suit was in the courts, the battle between Silber and the faculty continued to be waged on other terrain. In April 1976 ten out of the university's fifteen deans called for Silber's resignation. The faculty senate supported that demand by a vote of 377 to 117, but the members of the board of trustees unanimously voted their confidence in Silber, and he stayed on. By the time the Federal Court of Appeals decided in favor of the AAUP and the two sides sat down to negotiate in 1978, other controversies were roiling the university administration. A student newspaper charged Silber with selling admissions to the law and medical schools, and students protested hefty tuition hikes. Silber's critics contended that if a person openly disagreed with the administration he courted the possibility of being fired, and the Civil Liberties Union of Massachusetts sued Boston University on the issue of freedom of speech.

In April 1979, after the breakdown of contract negotiations, the Boston University faculty went out on strike. That strike was soon settled, but when clerical workers struck the following fall and some faculty members refused to cross their picket lines, the Silber administration charged five of them with "gross neglect of duty" and moved to discipline them under the "no strike" provision of the new labor contract. Faculty members throughout the Boston area mobilized in protest against what the M.I.T. professor and Nobel laureate Salvador Luria called "the latest in a pattern of attacks upon civil liberties." Within a month, more than 600 faculty members at Boston-area institutions had signed a petition calling for Silber's ouster, and by the end of the year over 2,000 professors had joined the nationwide petition drive. On December 18 the Boston University faculty voted 457½ to 215½ for Silber's dismissal.

Faculty hopes for negotiating a third contract were dashed on June 29, 1984, when Judge George S. McInerny ruled that members of the Boston University chapter of the AAUP were barred from engaging in collective bargaining under federal law, on the ground that faculty members are "supervisors" and "managers." Some observers were convinced that McInery's ruling would bring about the quietus of faculty unionization at private colleges and universities in the United States.

Nonetheless it was not only the Boston University Board of Trustees that remained staunchly pro-Silber. A nationwide favorable response to Silber's stance emerged after he was interviewed in January 1980 on the CBS-TV show 60 Minutes. In a wide-ranging interview for Educational Record (Spring 1980), Silber reflected on that response as evidence of the American citizenry's desire to see traditional values restored to education, a gratifying sign to Silber, who had never abandoned his advocacy of tradition, order, excellence, and a natural aristocracy of talent. In articles for the New York Times and for such magazines as Encounter, Harper's, and Atlantic, as well as in many speeches including the bicentennial July 4, 1976 Oration before the Municipal Authorities of Boston, Silber consistently stressed the pitfalls of a false egalitarianism that lowers standards and the need for maintaining the university as a marketplace of open inquiry, free of the "ideological license" of prevailing political winds.

It is Silber's love for the life of the mind—he often quotes Socrates' dictum that "the unexamined life is not worth living"—and his determination to make the university viable in the contemporary world that has led to what others sometimes view as a single-minded fanaticism in his pursuit of objectives at Boston University. The results testify to the wisdom of his course: the average scholastic aptitude scores of Boston University freshmen have risen though they have fallen nationally; the university has been operating on a balanced budget; money from external grants and contracts has nearly tripled; and many distinguished scholars have joined the faculty, including the internationally known writer Elie Wiesel, who has tendered the president the following tribute: "Silber is absolutely brilliant. He is a strong man who knows what he wants—excellence."

John R. Silber continues to speak out on many issues of public concern, including his advocacy of the creation of a "Tuition Advance Fund" (a federal loan system for higher education with the IRS as the eventual collection agency), the continuing crisis in American high schools, and the need for more stringent government enforcement of the draft registration law. At the same time, he has maintained his scholarly work, editing Works in Continental Philosophy and serving as associate editor of Kant-Studien. Over the years he has published widely in the field of philosophy of law and ethics on such topics as "The Ethical Significance of Kant's Religion" and "Human Action and the Language of Volition." He has received many grants and awards, is a member of a host of scholarly associations, and was one of the founding members of the board of directors of the National Association of Independent Colleges and Universities. In 1984 Silber served on President Reagan's commission on Central America, headed by Henry A. Kissinger. Its report was submitted on January 12, 1984.

Silber's marriage to his wife, Kathryn Underwood, dates back to his student days at Trinity University where they met as debating partners. They were married on July 12, 1947. The couple have seven children and live in the three-story French Renaissance house that is the official home of Boston University presidents. Silber gets up every workday at 6:30 A.M. to begin his fourteen-hour schedule with stretches and sit-ups. In his rare periods of relaxation, he goes either to Squam Lake in New Hampshire or to New York City for a round of museums, concerts, and theatre. Short and wiry, Silber has sandy-colored hair, a square jaw, blue eyes, and the springy step of an athlete. He speaks in a resonant voice, with a Texas accent.

Silber admits that the internecine battles and tensions at Boston University have been personally taxing but adds that he finds the excitement and importance of his work more than compensate for any emotional drain. "I think one really sees the lines of force within the culture on a miniature scale in the college as in no other institution in our society," he told an interviewer for the Educational

Record. "As a philosopher, I find it interesting just as a laboratory, seeing these forces at work."

References: Educ Rec 61:18+ Spring '80 por; Esquire 88:76+ S '77 por; Life 70:55+ Je 4 '71 por; People 13:82+ Je 2 '80 por; Sat Rev 7:16+ Mr 15 '80; Who's Who in America, 1984-85

Smuin, Michael

Oct. 13, 1938– Choreographer. Address: b. c/o The San Francisco Ballet, 455 Franklin St., San Francisco, Calif. 94102

"Ballet is entertainment," Michael Smuin, the choreographer and a winner of the 1983 *Dance* magazine award, said several years ago in an interview for *Horizon*. "It must make you laugh, cry, think . . . , but it must entertain you." A former character dancer known for his technical agility and mercurial stage presence, Smuin has created some twenty-five ballets over as many years, and he has rarely failed to entertain his audiences. Some of his dramatic ballets—*Romeo and Juliet*, *The Tempest*, and *A Song for Dead Warriors*—have enjoyed what one writer called an "almost hysterical" public response.

Like Roland Petit and Maurice Béjart, with whom he is occasionally compared, Smuin is a consummate showman, with a showman's instinctual theatrical flair, but his eclectic choreography is fundamentally American, firmly rooted in the traditions of the dance halls and the Broadway stage. Smuin's choreography for and direction of the musical *Sophisticated Ladies*, his only Broadway venture to date, won him two 1981 Tony

Award nominations and an Outer Critics Circle Award. As the codirector, with Lew Christensen, of the San Francisco Ballet since 1973, Smuin has helped to restore that troupe to its preeminent position as the oldest classical company in the United States.

Michael Smuin was born in the university town of Missoula, Montana on October 13, 1938. Perhaps because his parents were active in the local community theatre group, Smuin had always dreamed of a career as a performer, but it was not until he saw the celebrated American dancer Leon Danielian's virtuosic interpretation of the showpiece Blue Bird pas de deux, in a touring production by the Ballets Russes de Monte Carlo in the mid-1940s, that he became an "instant convert," in his words, to ballet. "I was captivated, enchanted, and bewitched," he has recalled, as quoted in *Dance* magazine (September 1983). "After the performance, I would dance all over the house the minute someone would turn the radio on." Shortly after that, he enrolled in ballet and tap classes at Pauline Ellis' dancing school, paying for his tuition by taking odd jobs.

As a teenager, Smuin supplemented his dance training with gymnastics lessons. A member of his high school's tumbling team, he also earned a spot on the boxing squad and won two local bantamweight titles. But his athletic achievements did not deflect him from his artistic goals, and when he was sixteen, he auditioned for and won a scholarship to the University of Utah's dance department. Moving to Salt Lake City, he secured a part-time job and arranged to complete his high school education while taking ballet classes from Willam Christensen, the chairman and master teacher of the university's ballet school. Smuin's training at the school also included character dancing, fencing, music, and acting classes and regular appearances in the university's annual summer musical productions and in Christensen's Utah Ballet recitals.

After seeing Smuin dance in a Utah Ballet production in 1957, Willam Christensen's brother Lew, the artistic director of the San Francisco Ballet, asked the promising young dancer to join the California troupe. Smuin accepted with alacrity, and a few months later, he made his company debut, performing the Tarantella in Lew Christensen's *Emperor Norton*. Rising rapidly through the ranks to the position of principal dancer, Smuin took on a wide variety of roles. By all accounts, he was happiest in parts that required unusual speed, agility, and buoyant elevation, such as the Truck Driver in *Filling Station*, the Bandit in *Con Amore*, and the Joker in *Jest of Cards*, in which he scored a spectacular personal success.

Encouraged by Lew Christensen, Smuin decided in 1959 to try his hand at choreography. His first effort—*Vivaldi Concerto*, which he created for the regional Bay Area Ballet—revealed a "definite aptitude" for dance composition, according to local reviewers. The following year, during the San Francisco Ballet's summer break, he organized

Ballet 1960, a workshop group comprised of sixteen temporarily unemployed dancers that presented experimental pieces by fledgling choreographers. Among the works offered were Smuin's humorous *Accent, Symphony in Jazz,* and *Session,* which was performed to the accompaniment of conga drums. The season was so well received by audiences and critics alike that the workshop became an annual San Francisco Ballet event. In recognition of his accomplishments, Smuin was named, in 1961, company ballet master and special assistant to Christensen.

In an effort to extend his range both as a performer and a choreographer, Smuin took a leave of absence from the San Francisco Ballet in 1962 and went to New York City. As he indicated to Laura Leivick in an interview for *Dance* magazine (February 1983), he had hoped to work with George Balanchine, the peerless choreographer who then headed the New York City Ballet, but much to his disappointment, City Ballet had no openings at the time for a *demi-caractère* dancer. Smuin soon found work, however, as a dancer in the chorus of the hit Broadway musical comedy *Little Me.* When that engagement ended, he and his wife, the ballerina Paula Tracy, put together a specialty dance act that he has described as "disguised ballet." Billed as Michael and Paula, the pair performed with considerable success on televised variety shows and in nightclubs and cabarets throughout the United States and Europe for three years, with Smuin taking an occasional month off to accept a choreographic commission.

In 1966 Smuin joined American Ballet Theatre as a member of the corps de ballet. Two years later, he was promoted to the rank of principal. The company's large and varied repertory afforded the dancer an unusual opportunity to display his versatility as well as his extraordinary virtuosity. Such guaranteed crowd pleasers as Sir Frederick Ashton's *Les Patineurs* and Jerome Robbins' irresistible *Fancy Free* showed off his dazzling technique to good advantage, but it was in character parts, among them the comical Peruvian Traveler in *Gaité Parisienne* and Dr. Coppelius, the eccentric toymaker in *Coppélia,* that he came into his own. He was perhaps most effective in the title roles of Michel Fokine's masterpiece *Petrouchka* and of *Billy the Kid,* Eugene Loring's stylized folk ballet, both of which he interpreted in an unorthodox manner. His Billy the Kid, for instance, was uncommonly cold and humorless, "almost more a Chicago hood than a Western gunman," according to *New York Times* dance critic Clive Barnes.

Another congenial role was the Soldier in *The Catherine Wheel,* a series of duets derived from Arthur Schnitzler's play about amorous infidelities that Smuin himself had choreographed for American Ballet Theatre in 1967. Emboldened by the favorable public response to *The Catherine Wheel,* he created over the next few years the ballets *Gartenfest* (Mozart), an airy, Balanchinian exercise in pure dance; *The Eternal Idol* (Chopin), a sensuous, neoromantic pas de deux inspired by Rodin's sculptures; *Schubertiade* (Schubert), a sparkling entertainment reminiscent of Balanchine's *Liebeslieder Walzer;* and *Pulcinella Variations* (Stravinsky), a playful abstraction of the *commèdia dell'arte* form. The nimble wit, choreographic ingenuity, and flamboyant showmanship that are the hallmarks of Smuin's ballets are present to a certain degree in each of those early works, but they are perhaps most evident in *Pulcinella Variations.* "There are all manner of movement inventions in this new *Pulcinella,* including pretty patterns and funny ones, bursts of physical prowess, and such chuckle-making capers as a human treadmill in which an ensemble of men rolling across the stage carry a girl, lying on her stomach like a giddy odalisque, from one side of the stage to the other," veteran dance critic Walter Terry observed in the *Saturday Review* (August 10, 1968) after the ballet's premiere.

In early 1973 Smuin left American Ballet Theatre to return to the San Francisco Ballet, as its associate artistic director. "Ballet Theatre had become a luxury to me," he explained to Herbert Kupferberg in an interview for *Dance News* (March 1973). "I was well-paid. I didn't work all that hard. . . . I got a little self-satisfied, which is dangerous. The creative process gets stagnant. I just felt I couldn't function creatively as I thought I should in Ballet Theatre, and that it was time for me to make a change."

Rejoining the San Francisco Ballet in time for its 1973–74 season, Smuin energetically set out to rebuild the artistically moribund and debt-ridden company. His new productions—among them a sumptuous, full-length *Cinderella,* which he choreographed with his codirector, Lew Christensen, following Prokofiev's libretto; *Mother Blues,* an exuberant fusion of funky popular dances with classical and modern idioms set to William Russo's "Three Pieces for Blues Band and Orchestra"; and the lyrical love duet *Harp Concerto* (Reinecke)— refreshed the stale repertory and revived flagging ticket sales. The long-standing financial troubles, however, were not so easily cured, and in mid-1974, the company faced bankruptcy. With Smuin's encouragement, the dancers organized a "Save Our Ballet" campaign. To draw attention to their plight, company members performed their daily barre exercises in department-store windows and tutu-clad ballerinas took to the streets to sell buttons, T-shirts, and used, autographed pointe shoes. As a publicity stunt, Smuin entered a tricycle race with a chimpanzee. Their collective efforts aroused the interest of San Franciscans, who contributed funds and responded enthusiastically to the new subscription-ticket campaign, and attracted attention and support, including grants from the National Endowment for the Arts, the Ford Foundation, and the Andrew W. Mellon Foundation, among other philanthropic organizations. Perhaps most important, the Save Our Ballet Campaign evolved into a comprehensive five-year plan that succeeded in putting the company on its feet by the end of the decade.

In those first five years of Smuin's stewardship, the San Francisco Ballet staged seventy new productions, including revivals and the company premieres of works by Sir Frederick Ashton, John Cranko, Jerome Robbins, John Butler, Doris Humphrey, and others. Among the most popular additions to the repertory were several new ballets by Smuin himself: *Q. a. V.* (Quattro a Verdi), a daredevil display piece for a quartet of dancers; *Medea* (Barber), an ingenious one-act retelling of Euripides' tragedy; *Shinjū*, a kabuki-style dance-drama about the suicide of a pair of star-crossed lovers set to a percussive original score by Paul Seiko Chihara; *Mozart's C Minor Mass*, which Smuin has described as an "uninhibited physical celebration of Mozart's music"; *Songs of Mahler*, a series of romantic vignettes designed to showcase the particular talents of individual dancers; and a full-length *Romeo and Juliet*.

Smuin's *Romeo and Juliet* was the unquestioned hit of the San Francisco Ballet's 1975–76 season. Created on a shoestring $100,000 budget, the ballet relied for its impact not on lavish sets and costumes, but on the emotional power of Prokofiev's music, rich characterizations, and innumerable telling details—a mother emerging from a street fight cradling the limp body of her child in her arms; Mercutio's kinswoman taking up the sword of her slain comrade and boldly attacking Tybalt; Lady Capulet keening over Tybalt's corpse. "There is no theatrical suspense in *Romeo and Juliet*," Smuin explained to Olga Maynard, as quoted in *After Dark* magazine (August 1976). "We know they are doomed. I wanted my ballet to show that, under the circumstances, their end is inevitable."

More than any other choreographer's, Smuin's version of *Romeo and Juliet* underlines that inevitability by using choreography and dramatic embellishments to play up the contrast between the rapturous innocence of the young lovers and the vulgarity, adultery, and hypocrisy of Renaissance society. Although many reviewers were as impressed by the theatrical staging as by the choreography, most found something to admire, singling out for special praise the impassioned, Bolshoi-style duets of Romeo and Juliet and the tour de force solos of Mercutio, in which Smuin employed quick, precisely articulated beats "as if they were witty conversational punctuations," to quote *Dance* magazine's Irene Oppenheim. A perennial public favorite, *Romeo and Juliet* was the first three-act classical ballet to be presented over public television by the PBS series *Dance in America*, in 1978.

As soon as he completed work on *Romeo and Juliet*, Smuin began contemplating a second Shakespearean ballet. He considered several plays, including *King Lear* and *The Merchant of Venice*, but he eventually settled on *The Tempest* because its fantastical subject matter and its elaborate masque seemed especially suitable for balletic translation. Collaborating closely with composer Paul Seiko Chihara, who contributed the pastiche Purcellian score, and with Tony Walton and Willa Kim, the designers of, respectively, the imaginative sets and costumes, Smuin was something of a Prospero himself, as he conjured up the first full-length American classical ballet created from scratch. Constructed after the nineteenth-century style of Petipa, the ballet has at its heart a full act of colorful divertissements (Prospero's masque), but instead of the traditional classical vocabulary, Smuin playfully introduced such contemporary dance forms as the beguine, tango, and blues—an innovation not all critics found to their liking.

Balletgoers, however, were invariably enchanted, and when *The Tempest* opened at the War Memorial Opera House in San Francisco in May 1980, they wildly cheered the cheekily incongruous divertissements and the spectacular special effects, among them a flying Ariel and an onstage shipwreck. On the whole, reviewers were less enthusiastic, many contending that the theatrical razzle-dazzle frequently overwhelmed what was essentially "workmanlike," to use Stephanie von Buchau's word, choreography. Out-of-towners finally got a chance to see *The Tempest* on March 1981, when it was televised nationwide on *Dance in America*. The production earned three Emmy Award nominations, including one for outstanding achievement in choreography.

Smuin's choreographic inventions propelled the development of the San Francisco Ballet, and by the early 1980s, the company was widely regarded as one of the finest classical troupes in the United States. Among its strengths is the finely tuned ensemble work of its dancers, more than 70 percent of them products of the company school. Because of the artistic fulfillment that comes from frequent performances and the relative security of a forty-four-week contract, there is little turnover in the nonranked company. "We had to build satisfying careers for our dancers," Smuin explained, as quoted in the *San Diego* (California) *Union* (January 27, 1980). "That was the only way we could get rid of their itch for New York. And we had to build repertoire that would challenge our dancers and hold our audiences." To that end, Smuin often visited the European dance capitals to search out new works, and in recent years he annexed to the San Francisco Ballet's extensive repertory Jiri Kylian's *Forgotten Land*, Maurice Béjart's *Firebird*, and Robert North and Wayne Sleep's *David and Goliath*, among other things. Like his mentor, Lew Christensen, Smuin also encouraged company members to choreograph, and the repertory now includes ballets by dancers Robert Gladstein, Tomm Ruud, John McFall, Kirk Peterson, and Jerome Weiss.

Smuin's own contributions to the San Francisco Ballet in the late 1970s and early 1980s ranged from such conventional pieces as the neoclassic *Mozart Piano Concerto No. 21* and the glittering showpiece *Duettino* (Verdi) to the enormously popular dance revues *Stravinsky Piano Pieces* and *To the Beatles*, both of which shrewdly mixed contemporary and classical vocabularies. "I'm intrigued with giving the idiom of classical dance an American accent by trying to infuse ballet with the rhythm, speed, and syncopation of American popular culture," the choreographer explained in his speech accepting the 1983 *Dance* magazine award. "Not to undermine the tradition, but to extend it, to realize that the only true tradition is a living one." With the stunning multimedia dance-drama *A Song for Dead Warriors* (Charles Fox), which traces the life of a young American Indian from his birth to his violent death and, in so doing, reflects on the tragic history of his people, Smuin immeasurably extended the boundaries of contemporary dance. The ballet, which was televised by PBS as an entry in its 1983-84 *Dance in America* series, earned him an Emmy Award for best choreography. His most recent exploration into multimedia work is *Romanze*, an unabashedly romantic duet made in collaboration with the filmmaker Francis Ford Coppola.

Although he was actively involved in all aspects of company planning, Smuin took time off from his managerial responsibilities in 1981 to rescue a Broadway-bound musical that was floundering in its out-of-town tryouts. Called in at the last minute, he discarded the ponderous book, trimmed, restaged, and rechoreographed some three dozen numbers, and turned *Sophisticated Ladies*, which had begun its life as a musical history of Duke Ellington's career, into a splashy, opulent revue. Starring Judith Jamison, Gregory Hines, and Hinton Battle, *Sophisticated Ladies* opened at the Lunt-Fontanne Theatre in New York City on March 1, 1981 to generally favorable notices, although a few critics, most notably the *New York Post*'s Clive Barnes and Stanley Kauffmann, writing in the *Saturday Review*, complained that it was little more than "a handsomely tarted-up band show," as Barnes put it in his opening night commentary. Responding to their criticisms, Smuin told Robert W. Larkin of *Newsday* (March 12, 1981), "I never pretended it was a musical like *South Pacific*. Ninety percent of the show is Ellington's music. The rest is decoration."

Michael Smuin is a short, compact man with a leonine head, widely-spaced green eyes, and thick, wavy black hair tinged with gray. A compulsive worker, he appears to have boundless energy and what one interviewer described as "a terrier's ferocity." "I like to prepare and study, rehearse, edit, solve problems," he said, as quoted in *Dance* magazine (February 1983). "There is something selfish, maybe, about my pleasure in rehearsing the dancers and collaborating with composers, designers, lighting designers. I'm interested right up through dress rehearsal. But I hate the moment of giving up a work to the public for the first time. . . . After the premiere, I may like a ballet again, but it's not mine." Smuin served a three-year term on the National Endowment for the Arts's dance advisory panel and, in 1980, he traveled to the People's Republic of China as a member of the first official United States Dance Study Team. He and his wife, Paula, have one son, Shane.

References: *Ballet* N 2:16+ O '80 por; *Dance* 36:50+ O '62 pors, 40:18+ Ag '66 pors, 50:42+ My '76 pors, 52:67+ N '78, 57:52+ F '83 por; *Concise Oxford Dictionary of Ballet*, 2d ed (1982); *Who's Who in America*, 1982-83

Strawberry, Darryl

Mar. 12, 1962- Baseball player. Address: b. New York Mets, Shea Stadium, Roosevelt Ave. and 126th St., Flushing, N.Y. 11368

To baseball's lowly New York Mets, finishing last in the east division of the National League in 1983 was not a novel experience. This time, however, the club emerged from its customary losing season with an unaccustomed sanguinity. The chief reason for the hopefulness was one man, the celebrated rookie right fielder Darryl Strawberry. Called up from the minors in May 1983, the lean and lanky lefthanded power hitter suffered the criticism of disappointed fans and the press for almost two months while he painfully "learned the league," as he put it. Then he surged, hitting over .300 during the last half of the season, accumulating season totals of twenty-five home runs and seventy-four runs-batted-in, and becoming the National League Rookie of the Year. Before the beginning of the 1984 season, Strawberry's teammate and friend Mookie Wilson told a reporter: "One thing we had to convince Darryl of last year was that no one guy can do it by himself. He knows that now. He's more relaxed about things. But we all feel pressure for this team to do better. . . . This year, if the young pitchers come on, we should be better—a lot better. At least competitive. The next year, though, '85, watch out for us."

The third of five children, Darryl Strawberry was born in the Crenshaw district of Los Angeles on March 12, 1962. His father is Henry Strawberry, a postal worker who once played semipro baseball, and his mother is Ruby Strawberry, a telephone company circuit designer. He has two older brothers, Michael and Ronnie, and two younger sisters, Regina and Michelle. Michael was briefly a minor-league outfielder in the Los Angeles Dodgers' system.

When Darryl was thirteen his parents separated, and they ultimately divorced. After the separation, Ruby Strawberry raised her children single-handedly. "I don't mean to brag," she told Fred Kerber of the *New York Daily News* (May 22, 1983), "but Darryl is very much like me. It takes a lot to get me upset. I tried to instill that attitude in my children. I always talked a lot with Darryl. I told him to go to school, get a good education and have faith in God. The Lord's been watching over us because we had our tough times. But we pulled through." Darryl was "never any trouble," according to Mrs. Strawberry. A "very private person," remarkably immune to peer pressure, he "knew what he wanted and what he didn't want." When he spent time with other children, "if they started to become involved in mischief, he just walked away."

Strawberry had the good fortune to come under the guidance of a succession of surrogate fathers. The first was John Moseley, a neighbor, who was an assistant baseball coach at Compton (California) College. "Mr. Moseley taught me everything I know about the game," Strawberry said in an interview with William Nack of *Sports Illustrated* (April 23, 1984). "I heard it first from him." Nack quoted Moseley: "Darryl was never a guy to mess around with girls. Baseball is all Darryl talked about. He was a baseball fanatic." In early adolescence Strawberry was moody and rebellious, carrying, in his own words, "a bad attitude around" with him. That attitude was partly exorcised by Brooks Hurst, the baseball coach at Crenshaw High School, who benched Strawberry for lack of effort for most of his sophomore season. Strawberry now considers the benching "the best thing that happened" to him.

Playing right field and doing some pitching, Strawberry had a .371 batting average and hit four home runs in his junior year. As a senior he batted .400 and had five home runs, eighteen runs-batted-in, and, on the mound, a 4–1 record. With his power at the plate and his strong arm in the field, he became the most sought-after schoolboy player in the country. "He was so skinny he was almost frail," Harry Minor, the scout for the New York Mets, recalled when interviewed by John Feinstein for *Inside Sports* (March 1984). "He was gangly and crude, but one look at him and you knew he was an athlete. He moved like an athlete. It was just a matter of time."

Playing forward, Strawberry also starred in basketball at Crenshaw High School. As his graduation neared, he received scholarship offers from Arizona State and Oklahoma State universities, both of which gave him the option of either basketball or baseball. The latter was his decided preference, however, and the major leagues were his goal. Inundated with offers from American and National League clubs, he turned the screening of the offers over to his mother, who in turn enlisted the services of Richie Bry, a St. Louis agent who represents more than 100 professional baseball and football players. Touted as "the black Ted Williams," Strawberry was the overall number-one pick in the 1980 free-agent draft. He signed with the New York Mets for $600 a month and a $200,-000 bonus, the largest signing bonus in the major leagues in twenty years.

On July 13, 1980 Strawberry reported to the Mets' Appalachian League rookie club at Kingsport, Tennessee. In his debut at the plate in Kingsport, Strawberry singled, but he managed only two hits in his next forty-four at-bats. Lonely and homesick, he called his mother every day, collect. "He was so pitiful," Ruby Strawberry recounted to William Nack of *Sports Illustrated*. Adjusting somewhat, Strawberry finished the season at Kingsport with a .268 batting average, five home runs, and twenty runs-batted-in.

Moving up to Class A ball at Lynchburg, Virginia, Strawberry again had trouble gaining momentum. "His work habits on the field weren't real good the first third of the season," Gene Dusan recalled in his interview with William Nack. "Then he started pushing himself and concentrating." Again, with Dusan's encouragement and help, he improved as the season progressed, finishing with a .255 batting average, thirteen home runs, and seventy-eight RBIs. He also had thirty-one stolen bases, twenty-six more than the previous year. Harry Minor, who had rated Strawberry "a four or five on a scale of eight for speed" when he scouted him, explained the great improvement to John Feinstein: "In Lynchburg, they started letting him run on his own, and he changed his running style. He had this slow-gaited kind of style in high school and his first year in pro ball. At Lynchburg, he showed the kind of speed he really had. He can steal fifty bases in the major leagues some day."

While Strawberry was finding himself in pro ball, some in the Mets' front office wondered if they had not gambled too heavily on him, but the management generally maintained faith in his potential, partly because Strawberry himself never lost his confidence. He knew that he had "to get used to professional pitching" and that it was "just a matter of time" until he did so. He finally began performing up to expectation in 1982 at Jackson, Mississippi in the Double A Texas League, where Gene Dusan was again his manager. That year he hit .283, with thirty-four home runs and ninety-seven RBIs, and stole forty-five bases, and he was named Most Valuable Player in the league. After the season he conceded to a reporter that he still had to cut down on his strikeouts (145 in 129 games at Jackson) and improve against lefthanders. "But you'll notice that while my strikeout total may be high," he pointed out, "I also walk a lot and I hit for average." His 100 walks topped the Texas League and his 123 hits led the Jackson club.

Playing winter ball for the La Guaira club near Caracas, Venezuela following the 1982 regular season, Strawberry hit .303 and led the Venezuelan League with a .564 slugging average. Doing so well in Venezuela made him feel that he was "capable of playing at any level of baseball." The New York media felt likewise, and thumped for Strawberry's promotion to the parent club in 1983. The media had a strong argument. The New York team had declined from the "Miracle Mets" of the late 1960s and early 1970s to become mired in the lower regions of the National League East in the late 1970s. During several turnovers of management, disastrous trades were made, leaving the team desperately in need of a firebrand, a need underlined by the Mets' 68–94 record in 1982.

Frank Cashen, the general manager of the Mets, however, thought it would be unfair to call Strawberry up to the majors without giving him some Triple A experience. That remained Cashen's conviction even when Strawberry was leading the Mets in hitting during spring training in 1983. Accordingly, Strawberry began the 1983 season at Tidewater, Virginia in the AAA International League. One month into the season, Cashen changed his mind, for two reasons. One was Strawberry's .333 average at Tidewater. The other was more compelling: the Mets were off to a 6–15 start. On May 4, 1983 Cashen called Strawberry to the rescue.

Strawberry's ballyhooed arrival in New York was anticlimaxed by a poor start and a protracted slump. His first National League game, on May 6, 1983, was a baptism of fire administered by the dreaded Mario Soto of the Cincinnati Reds, the master of a bewildering mixture of changeup and hopping fastball. Strawberry struck out in his first three times at bat and popped up in his fourth and final time. He remained hitless through seven additional at-bats in the week following, and in his first month in the majors he hit safely only fourteen times out of eighty-seven. "I was thinking about how I was doing instead of just having fun," he later realized. "The thing is that I love to play baseball, and when you're given what I've been given by the man upstairs, you've got to just let it happen."

On June 5, 1983, when his average stood at .161, Strawberry was benched, and he remained out of the lineup until June 26. During that twenty-one-day hiatus he received the concentrated guidance of Jim Frey, now the manager of the Chicago Cubs, who was then the Mets' batting coach. Strawberry developed a more aggressive attitude under Frey, who taught him to go for power without worrying about strikeouts, to plan special strategies against particular pitchers, and not to let the pitchers get ahead of him in counts.

Returning to the lineup, a more relaxed Strawberry batted .313 over the last fifty-four games of the 1983 season, bringing his final average to .257.

His other 1983 statistics included nineteen stolen bases; twenty-six home runs, a record for both a Met lefthander and a Met rookie; seventy-four RBIs, another club record for a rookie; a .512 slugging percentage, the highest in the team's history; and a home-run ratio of one for every 16.1 times at bat, the second-best in the National League. There was also an improvement in Strawberry's fielding, which had previously been too cautious. The only negative statistic was his 128 strikeouts in 420 at-bats. By a landslide, the Baseball Writers Association of America voted him National League Rookie of the Year. He was the third player and first non-pitcher in Met history to be so honored.

In January 1984 Richie Bry negotiated for Strawberry a new contract including a base annual pay of $200,000 and incentives that could yield $40,000 more. In addition to his income from the Mets, Strawberry will almost certainly earn considerable sums from endorsements and other commercial projects that Bry is carefully seeking out for him. "I am of the philosophy," the agent told Jane Gross in an interview for the *New York Times Magazine* (February 26, 1984), "that you're better off waiting for the big one . . . rather than prostituting yourself with $2,000 deals at car dealers and local pizza parlors."

The attention given Strawberry by the press, enormous from the spring of 1983 on, had become a major threat to his privacy by the spring of 1984. While management, trying to protect him from the pressure of too much publicity, remained somewhat restrained in its public assessments of Strawberry, his teammates openly joined in the media's adulation. The veteran catcher Ron Hodges told reporters that he had never before known a player "who can do everything that well." John Stearns, the Met catcher reduced to pinch-runner by injuries, said, "If Darryl works hard . . . he can be one of the all-time greats in this game. And if he doesn't . . . he'll be just another great player."

During spring training in 1984 Strawberry's teammates good-naturedly dubbed him "Captain Straw," an allusion to his expressed aspiration to become team leader. "Leadership? Yeah, I think I can provide some," Strawberry told John Lombardi of the *New York Daily News* (April 1, 1984). "No, I don't think the other guys resent me sayin' it. I'm gonna lead by example and not put so much pressure on myself as I did last year. . . . Like I know now that it's okay for a long-ball hitter to strike out more than it is for a smaller guy, whose job is to get on base a lot."

All winter long, Strawberry looked forward to April 2, the opening day of the 1984 season. In Cincinnati on that day the opposing pitcher was Mario Soto, the perpetrator of the humiliation suffered by Strawberry in his major league debut the year before. On this occasion Strawberry wreaked sweet revenge, clouting Soto's third pitch into the second deck of Riverside Stadium, a distance of 450 feet. Emulating the press, which has had a field day punning on Strawberry's last name, the Mets' promotion department came up with "Strawberry

Sundae," a Shea Stadium celebration staged in honor of Strawberry on Sunday, April 29, 1984. On that occasion, 28,562 fans ate free ice cream, gave Strawberry a standing ovation as he received his 1983 Rookie of the Year plaque, and watched the Mets beat the Philadelphia Phillies, 6–2. That win brought the Mets' record for the season to 12–8, putting the team in a tie for first place in the National League East with the Chicago Cubs. In a ten-game streak that began nine games earlier, Strawberry batted .389, with two homers and nine RBIs. Subsequently, his streaks of success were interspersed with prolonged lapses, and he finished the season batting .251. Among his other 1984 statistics were twenty-seven doubles, four triples, twenty-six home runs, and ninety-seven runs-batted-in. The Mets ended in second place in the National League East, behind the Chicago Cubs.

Darryl Strawberry, who is six feet six inches tall and weighs 195 pounds, lifts weights to add sinew to his lean, hard frame and the long arms that give his smooth, looping swing so much of its power.

With his towering height, handsome face, confident bearing, dazzling smile, deep baritone voice, natty wardrobe, and polished manner, Strawberry is every inch the superstar in his public appearances, and he intends to improve his delivery as a public speaker by taking voice and communications classes.

In private, Strawberry is an unaffected homebody. Avoiding the celebrity social circuit, he spends his time during the off-season close to his mother in Los Angeles and fiancée, Lisa Andrews, in Pasadena, where Miss Andrews is a loan coordinator for a bank. According to published reports, the two plan to marry in January 1985. During baseball seasons, Strawberry has been living in hotels near Shea Stadium, but he is looking for a house on the water on Long Island's North Shore. He is also planning to buy a new home for his mother.

References: Inside Sports 6:26+ Mr '84 pors; N Y Daily News p6 / Ap 1 '84 pors; N Y Times Mag p16+ F 26 '84 pors; Sports Illus 60:32+ Ap 23 '84 pors

Tandy, Jessica

June 7, 1909– Actress. Address: b. 63–23 Carlton St., Rego Park, N.Y. 11374

NOTE: This biography supersedes the article that appeared in *Current Biography* in 1956.

Since making her professional acting debut in 1927, Jessica Tandy has played over one hundred and fifty roles on stage, in films, and on television. After emigrating from England to the United States in 1940, Miss Tandy established herself as a formidable dramatic actress with her indelible portrayal of the emotionally unhinged Blanche DuBois in the original production of *A Streetcar Named Desire*. She continues to astound critics and audiences with her inexhaustible reserve of creativity and her subtly nuanced acting, often displayed in tandem with her equally eminent husband, Hume Cronyn. Although the couple occasionally appear in films, they always return to their first love, the stage, where their most recent performances—in *Foxfire* and *The Gin Game*—won them critical acclaim in the United States and abroad.

Jessica Tandy was born in London, England on June 7, 1909, the third child and only daughter of Harry and Jessie Helen (Horspool) Tandy. As a child, she attended Dame Alice Owen's Girls' School in London. Because Jessica's father, who was involved in the manufacture and sale of rope, died of cancer when she was twelve, her mother had to teach night school and take clerical jobs to supplement her earnings as headmistress at a school for retarded children. Despite their straitened circumstances, Mrs. Tandy nurtured a sense of ambition in Jessica and her brothers, Michael and Tully. She introduced them to literary classics, took them to plays, pantomimes, and museums, and during Christmas holidays in their five-room flat in northeast London, the children staged family theatricals, directed by Michael.

By the time she was a teenager, Jessica Tandy had resolved to be an actress. Her mother "endorsed the stage as a dignified way for [her] to break out of [her] bleak life," as Miss Tandy recounted to Timothy White in an interview for the *New York Times Magazine* (December 26, 1982). A drama instructor tutored her on Saturdays, and she took evening courses in Shakespeare for two years. Determined to acquire as thorough a grounding as possible in her chosen profession, she began three years of dramatic training at London's Ben Greet Academy of Acting in 1924.

At eighteen, Jessica Tandy made her professional debut on November 22, 1927 in the Soho district of London at a small backroom theatre called Playroom Six as Sara Manderson in The Manderson Girls. Her role demanded five elegant costumes, which she was required to provide out of her salary of two pounds a week. Too poor to buy them readymade, she sewed them herself. The following year she joined the Birmingham Repertory Company, where she was entrusted with several roles before touring for six months as the ingenue Lydia Blake in Eden Phillpotts' Yellow Sands. On February 21, 1929 she made her London debut at the Court Theatre as Lena Jackson in The Rumour, but it was her acclaimed portrayal of Manuela in Children in Uniform, which began its run on October 7, 1932, that established Miss Tandy as a gifted actress. Roles in over two dozen contemporary plays during the next decade added luster to her reputation.

Nevertheless, Jessica Tandy most relished classical theatre, especially Shakespeare. First appearing as Olivia in a 1930 Oxford University Dramatic Society presentation of Twelfth Night, she returned to that play three times as Viola, most notably in Tyrone Guthrie's production that opened on February 23, 1937 at London's Old Vic and featured Laurence Olivier as Sir Toby Belch. In April of that year, she again performed at the Old Vic with Olivier in Guthrie's production of Henry V. Although during the 1930s she added to her repertoire the roles of Cressida in Troilus and Cressida, Titania in A Midsummer Night's Dream, and Anne Page in The Merry Wives of Windsor, perhaps her most memorable Shakespearean performance was in John Gielgud's 1934 production of Hamlet at the New Theatre in London, in which her Ophelia perfectly complemented Gielgud's legendary interpretation of the title role. But after again sharing the Old Vic stage with Gielgud in 1940 as Cordelia in King Lear and as Miranda in The Tempest, Miss Tandy did not take on another Shakespearean role until 1961, when she was cast as both Cassandra in Troilus and Cressida and as Lady Macbeth at the American Shakespeare Festival in Stratford, Connecticut. She portrayed Gertrude in a 1963 production of Hamlet for the inaugural season of the Tyrone Guthrie Theatre in Minneapolis, Minnesota, and in 1976, appearing for the first time at the Stratford Festival in Ontario, Canada, she performed in A Midsummer Night's Dream, alternating in the roles of Hippolyta and Titania.

Spurred by the outbreak of World War II, her divorce from the actor Jack Hawkins after eight years of marriage, the need to support their six-year-old daughter, Susan, and the lure of jobs in the Hollywood movie industry, Jessica Tandy emigrated from England in 1940 with ten pounds in her pocket and settled permanently in the United States.

(She became a naturalized citizen in 1954.) Her many triumphs on the British stage and her experience on Broadway in such short-lived theatrical offerings as The Matriarch (1930), in which she had made her New York debut, as well as in the more successful The White Steed (1939), helped her to land roles in several minor Broadway plays during her first two years in New York. Nevertheless, before her marriage in 1942 to the actor Hume Cronyn, Jessica Tandy had to struggle to make ends meet. At one point when she had lost all her savings—one hundred dollars—and had no immediate offers of employment, she came close to abandoning her career. "That was a tough time," she admitted to Chris Chase in an interview for the New York Times (March 24, 1974). "It mattered terribly that I should make a living, and I couldn't." "I got to that stage," she continued, "where I felt I'd made it up, I never could act, I didn't act well, I'd lost it."

Her prospects brightened somewhat after the Cronyns moved to Hollywood and she was given a five-year contract with Twentieth Century-Fox. However, her first American film, The Seventh Cross (1944), a melodrama about the anti-Nazi underground movement that starred Spencer Tracy, was produced by MGM, the studio with which Hume Cronyn was a contract player. Acting for the first time with her husband, she contributed an "emotionally devastating" performance as his nettlesome wife in that movie. After playing bit parts in several more motion pictures—The Valley of Decision (MGM, 1945), The Green Years (MGM, 1947), and the controversial Forever Amber (Twentieth Century-Fox, 1947)—she won a leading role in Universal-International Pictures' A Woman's Vengeance (1948), Aldous Huxley's screen adaptation of his short story "The Gioconda Smile."

"But there came a point when I felt that I just had to act in a play again," Miss Tandy observed in her interview with Roy Newquist in Showcase (Morrow, 1966). Although she was still under contract with Twentieth Century-Fox, in 1946 Hume Cronyn directed her in Portrait of a Madonna, one of several one-act dramas by the struggling young playwright Tennessee Williams that he had optioned over the years. Her sensitive characterization of the neurotic Miss Collins in that production at the Las Palmas Theatre in Los Angeles met with warm critical approval. More important, it convinced Williams to cast her as Blanche DuBois in the now classic Broadway production of A Streetcar Named Desire, which opened at the Ethel Barrymore Theatre on December 3, 1947 under the direction of Elia Kazan. Playing opposite Marlon Brando as her brutish brother-in-law, Stanley Kowalski, and Kim Hunter as her sister Stella, Miss Tandy created a sensation among critics and theatregoers with her acute portrayal of the faded Southern belle who loses her sanity when her façade of grandeur and gentility is breached by Kowalski. In his appraisal of the play's première for the New York Times (December 4, 1947), Brooks Atkinson marveled at her "almost incredibly true" performance. "For it does seem almost incredible," he asserted, "that she could understand such an elusive part so thoroughly and that she can convey it with so many shades and impulses that are accurate, revealing and true." *Streetcar* ran for over two years on Broadway before beginning a national tour and won both a Pulitzer Prize and the New York Drama Critics Circle Award. Jessica Tandy garnered her first Antoinette Perry (Tony) Award and the Twelfth Night Club Award, but for the 1951 film version her role went to Vivien Leigh, the star of the London production.

In spite of that disappointment, playing Blanche changed her life, as she explained to Samuel G. Freedman in a *New York Times* interview (November 27, 1983), since it brought her back to the theatre. Offered only insignificant parts since her emigration from England, she had felt "rather unused." "*Streetcar*," she told Freedman, "gave me back the challenge, and the challenge has never left."

Although her Blanche DuBois certified Jessica Tandy as a superb dramatic actress, she did not act in another Tennessee Williams play for over two decades, in order to avoid being typecast. She next annexed a Williams character to her repertoire in 1970 in the Lincoln Center Repertory Theatre revival of his atypical, phantasmagoric *Camino Real*. A *Time* reviewer (January 19, 1970) applauded her rendering of the aging, tragic courtesan Marguerite Gautier in "the authentic Williams tone of defeated gentility, of the violated heart, abusive in self-judgment and terribly tarnished by the world yet untarnished in spirit," but like most critics he had serious reservations about the production, which closed on February 21 after fifty-two performances.

In the somewhat more successful revival of *The Glass Menagerie*, which opened at the Eugene O'Neill Theatre on December 1, 1983, Miss Tandy turned in a distinctive performance in one of the foremost roles in American drama as the quixotic Amanda Wingfield of Tennessee Williams' Depression-era "memory play." Studiously avoiding a replication of either Laurette Taylor's noteworthy portrayal of Amanda Wingfield in the original 1945 mounting, which she clearly remembered, or her own interpretations of Williams' other tragic heroines, she evinced a "sympathetic understanding of a woman whose comic but tiresome affectations are in fact part of the life-support system that enables Amanda to survive," as John Beaufort observed in the *Christian Science Monitor* (December 7, 1983). Moreover, in his review for the *New Republic* (January 9–16, 1984), Robert Brustein maintained that Jessica Tandy's personal attributes enriched her characterization: "Because she possesses quiet elegance, regal dignity, and genuine faded beauty, her affectations of shabby gentility seem more authentic than were perhaps intended by the author." Despite the virtuosity of Miss Tandy's magnificent star turn, the production itself received less enthusiastic notices and closed in mid-February 1984.

After her extensive tour in *A Streetcar Named Desire*, Miss Tandy essayed another neurotic searching for happiness in the title role of Samson Raphaelson's *Hilda Crane*. Hume Cronyn directed her in *Hilda Crane*, but after its run ended on New Year's Eve of 1950 the couple wanted to act together once again. Rather than waiting to be offered roles in an appropriate vehicle, the Cronyns generated their own work. The first of the productions they introduced over the next decade was *The Fourposter*, Jan de Hartog's two-character comedy, in which the interplay between Cronyn as Michael and Jessica Tandy as his wife Agnes made that hilarious history of a thirty-five-year marriage one of the biggest hits on Broadway after it opened at the Ethel Barrymore Theatre on October 24, 1951 for a run of 632 performances. When the New York City Center staged a revival in January 1955, critics were even more extravagant in their praise of the Cronyns' performances.

Following their 1953 tour in *The Fourposter*, the Cronyns signed on at low salaries as charter members of the newly formed Off-Broadway Phoenix Theatre and starred in its first production, Sidney Howard's *Madam, Will You Walk*, which opened on December 1, 1953. That play folded after only forty-two performances, and during the next decade their other collaborative efforts—*The Honeys* (1955), *A Day by the Sea* (1955), *The Man in the Dog Suit* (1958), *Triple Play* (1959), *Big Fish, Little Fish* (1962), and *The Physicists* (1964)—fared no better in spite of uniformly complimentary notices for Jessica Tandy and Hume Cronyn.

Once again performing on her own, Jessica Tandy evoked lavish praise from theatre critics for her role in Peter Shaffer's *Five Finger Exercise*, which opened under Sir John Gielgud's direction on December 2, 1959 at the Music Box Theatre. As the wealthy, snobbish Louise Harrington, whose strained relationships with her too-dependent son and uncultured husband are brought to a deadly climax through the presence of her daughter's tutor, she riveted audiences with a characterization that Brooks Atkinson applauded as "brilliant" in the *New York Times* (December 13, 1959) and George Oppenheimer, writing in *Newsday* (December 9, 1959), considered her "finest" since Blanche DuBois. The New York Drama League awarded her its Delia Austrian Medal for her performance, and the London-originated play, which began a seven-month tour after 337 Broadway performances, was chosen the best foreign play of the season by the Drama Critics Circle.

Edward Albee's *A Delicate Balance*, which opened its 132-performance run at the Martin Beck on September 22, 1966, provided Jessica Tandy with her next award-winning role. Agnes and Tobias, a complacent suburban couple played by Miss Tandy and Hume Cronyn, are forced to reevaluate their marriage and other relationships when their best friends, suddenly terrified by an overwhelming sense of meaninglessness, Agnes' alcoholic sister, and their daughter, just divorced for the fourth time, come for comfort and refuge.

Voicing the consensus, Variety (September 29, 1966) praised her "expertly dimensioned and poised portrayal of the quietly domineering wife." Miss Tandy received the 1966 Leland Powers Honor award for her part in the Pulitzer Prize–winning drama, but neither her bravura performance nor Gielgud's direction could salvage her next Albee venture, All Over, which closed on May 1, 1971 after only forty-two performances at the Martin Beck Theatre.

Before opening in All Over, in January 1971 Jessica Tandy agreed to replace Dandy Nichols in Home, a play by David Storey that is set in an unidentified institution or asylum. Featuring Gielgud and Sir Ralph Richardson, Home had won high praise during its London run, and appearing at Broadway's Morosco Theater as the dour Marjorie, a fellow resident of the institution, she perfectly complemented the other high-powered performers. Marjorie was "the furthest thing from [her] that could possibly be," Miss Tandy told Chris Chase in the New York Times interview, but she had been delighted to accept the challenge. "If you go on doing what you know you can do, and what you've done before," she explained, "it would be dull."

At the Samuel Beckett Festival at Lincoln Center in late 1972, Jessica Tandy undertook two more challenging roles. As Winnie in the ironically titled Happy Days, she was trapped from the waist down in a sand dune in the first act, and up to her neck in the second, but continued to babble her reminiscences to her husband Willie, played by Cronyn. Her Winnie won her a Drama Desk award. In the tantalizing world première of Not I on November 22, 1972, she became the disembodied Mouth, a pair of brightly painted lips framed in a tiny circle of light on a black stage that delivered a twenty-three minute, breathless stream-of-consciousness litany of anguish to a silent cowled figure. Miss Tandy received an Obie and another Drama Desk award for her performance and took the play on a tour of Eastern universities, but she was relieved to relinquish the role because she found the import of the words to be "terrifying."

The Cronyns' next Broadway venture was Noel Coward in Two Keys, an engaging production of two plays by the master of sophisticated wit that ran for 140 performances at the Ethel Barrymore Theater in 1974. Miss Tandy was impeccable as the blue-haired and bitchy social climber Anna-Mary Conklin in the curtain-raiser, Come into the Garden, Maud, and as the sympathetic but abused Hilde Latymer in A Song at Twilight. Again going her separate way, Jessica Tandy took on the intimidating role of Mary Tyrone in Eugene O'Neill's autobiographical Long Day's Journey Into Night, which the playwright once described as "old sorrow, written in tears and blood." Performing opposite William Hutt under Robin Phillips' direction, she gave a masterful performance at the Theatre London in Ontario, Canada. Turning once more to comedy, she portrayed the mother in Andrew Davies' Rose, which starred Glenda Jackson as a maverick British schoolteacher. Although she appeared in only two scenes, John Simon attested in New York magazine (April 6, 1981) that Jessica Tandy was "an unalloyed delight," "the most lovable of irritating mothers," and the "most plausible" reason for seeing the play. Rose closed at the Cort Theater on May 23, 1981 after sixty-eight performances, but for her touching characterization Miss Tandy netted a Tony nomination for best supporting actress.

Involved since the 1960s in the burgeoning regional theatre movement, Jessica Tandy and Hume Cronyn have often appeared at the Tyrone Guthrie Theater in Minneapolis, the Stratford (Connecticut) American Shakespeare Festival, the Shaw Festival at Niagara on the Lake, and the Stratford Festival in Ontario, Canada. While visiting regional theatres across the United States, the Cronyns chanced upon The Gin Game by D. L. Coburn, then an unknown, first-time playwright, during its première in March 1977 at the Actors Theater of Louisville, Kentucky. Directed by Mike Nichols, the Cronyns brought the two-character dark comedy, which traces the deterioration of a budding friendship between lonely oldsters into a vicious tug-of-war at a welfare nursing home, to Broadway's John Golden Theater on October 6, 1977. The clever device of a series of gin games lays bare some unpleasant truths about themselves that rigid Fonsia Dorsey and cantankerous Weller Martin have long refused to confront. A few critics found flaws in the script, but all praised the marvelous interplay of the stars, which Jack Kroll lauded in Newsweek (October 17, 1977) as "professionalism raised to the level of incandescence." Miss Tandy earned a quartet of honors—the Drama Desk Award (1977-78), her second Tony Award (1978), the Los Angeles Drama Critics Circle Award (1979), and Chicago's Sarah Siddons Award (1979). Racking up a total of more than 800 performances, the Cronyns took The Gin Game, which won a 1978 Pulitzer Prize, to Moscow, Leningrad, and London, where it was taped live in June 1980 and aired on public television in the United States on March 6, 1984.

From time to time, the Cronyns have given poetry and prose readings on tour, as in Face to Face (1954) and The Many Faces of Love (1974). While preparing for the latter, Cronyn asked their friend Susan Cooper to contribute some material about love. She sent him the opening chapters of the first Foxfire book—a collection of reminiscences and anecdotes gathered by Appalachian schoolchildren, including an old woman's account of her love for the land. Intrigued, he decided to collaborate with Miss Cooper on a play built on Foxfire. Tried out at the 1980 Stratford Festival, Foxfire opened on Broadway at the Ethel Barrymore Theatre on November 11, 1982. Most reviewers liked its gentle affirmation of traditional values, though some complained that the play had more theme than plot, but Jessica Tandy's performance as Annie Nations was extolled by audiences and critics alike. She portrayed an American primitive—a self-sufficient seventy-nine-year-old widow and mother who converses with the ghost of her ornery husband,

Hector, played by Cronyn. For her "outstanding achievement" in *Foxfire*, Miss Tandy was voted a Drama Desk Award and her third Tony. In his review of the play for the *New York Times* (November 12, 1982), Frank Rich wrote: "Everything this actress does is so pure and right that only poets, not theatre critics, should be allowed to write about her." She earned equally glowing reviews for her portrayal of the aged spinster and feminist Miss Birdseye in the film adaptation of Henry James's novel *The Bostonians* (Rank and Rediffusion, 1984).

In describing the offstage persona of the petite (five feet four inches tall), silver-haired, ageless Jessica Tandy, Robin Reif wrote in *Dial* (March 1984): "There's a precision about her looks, but the direct blue eyes, the luminous skin, and the still-sensuous mouth create an impression of delicate poise rather than severity." As part of her technique, Jessica Tandy looks for ways to go from one contradiction, crosscurrent, or ambiguity in a character to the other—sometimes in the same sentence. "That's what makes acting absolutely fascinating to me," she maintains, "because I think that's what people *are*."

When exhausted by acting stints, the Cronyns used to escape to a small island in the Bahamas once called Children's Bay Cay, which they bought from the British Crown in 1945. In 1980 they sold the island and now maintain a home in a suite in Manhattan's Wyndham Hotel, not too far from the theatre district. To the much-repeated query about the marital longevity of the Cronyns, who have remained together for forty-two years, Miss Tandy told Michael Kernan in an interview for the *Washington Post* (December 23, 1982), "The reason we can live and work together is that in no way do we threaten each other. We're safe: I can't play him, and he can't play me. That's basic." Both Jessica Tandy and Hume Cronyn, who were inducted into the Theater Hall of Fame in 1979, intend to keep on performing "as long as [they] can stand."

References: L A Times Calendar p1+ Mr 25 '84 por; Newsday II p4+ Ja 2 '83 pors; N Y Daily News (Leisure section) p3+ D 5 '82 pors; N Y Times II p1+ Mr 24 '74 por; N Y Times Mag p20+ D 26 '82 por; Playbill 2:6+ N '83 pors; Washington Post D p1 D 23 '82 pors; Newquist, Roy. Showcase (1966); Who's Who, 1984-85; Who's Who in the Theatre (1981)

Tobin, James

Mar. 5, 1918- Economist, educator. Address: b. Dept. of Economics, Yale University, Box 2125 Yale Station, New Haven, Conn. 06520; h. 117 Alden Ave., New Haven, Conn. 06515

When the 1981 Nobel Memorial Prize for Economic Science was awarded to James Tobin, the Sterling Professor of Economics at Yale University, the enthusiasm with which many of Tobin's fellow economists greeted the announcement was prompted by more than their respect for his scholarly contributions to economic research and theory over the years. Although the Swedish Academy of Sciences makes its awards on the basis of scientific merit rather than political or policy implications, the fact that Tobin, following John Maynard Keynes, is a key defender of government intervention in economics, unlike the "supply siders" and "monetarists" who came to power in Washington with the Reagan presidency, was not lost on the press. Nonetheless, so monumental have been Tobin's contributions that no one, whether liberal or conservative, could dispute the justice of the award.

Tobin's contributions include the "Portfolio Selection Theory," an analysis of investment behavior that emphasizes the complexity of factors involved, since investors do not invariably seek the highest rate of return on their investment but balance the rate of return with security; and the "Q factor," a concept representing the ratio of market value to replacement cost of a firm that helps ex-

plain the state of financial markets. Repudiating doctrines that make governmental restraint a priority, without regard to social consequences, he believes that achievement of national goals requires the flexible allocation of resources between the private *and* public sectors. That vision, Tobin has remarked, concerns him both as a "citizen, a political animal, as well as a professional economist." Writing for *Newsday* (October 18, 1981), Robert

Reno called Tobin "one of the renaissance men of twentieth century economics," "a man who conveys an immense sense of modesty that tends to camouflage his immense sense of outrage . . . an improbable champion of Keynesian, interventionist, redistributive, egalitarian economics in its darkest hour."

James Tobin was born on March 5, 1918 in Champaign, Illinois, the son of Louis Michael Tobin, the publicity director for athletics at the University of Illinois, and Margaret (Anketell Edgerton) Tobin, a social worker. His father was an avid reader who stimulated the intellectual curiosity of both his sons, James and Roger. As a child of the Great Depression, James Tobin discovered that its bleak realities turned his intellectual interests in the direction of economics. "The economic problems of the United States and the entire world were obvious to anyone growing up in that period," Tobin recalled in an interview with Jean W. Ross for *Contemporary Authors*. "It was natural for aware people . . . to be very much concerned about economic matters." It seemed to Tobin that economics had the virtue of combining the intellectual challenge of mathematics with "social relevance and real world importance."

In 1935 Tobin graduated from University High School in Urbana, Illinois, where his extracurricular activities had included basketball, dramatics, and editing the school yearbook. At Harvard, which he entered on a national scholarship, he majored in economics and was active in student government, basketball, and yearbook. During his early years as a Harvard undergraduate, the initial impact of the recent publication of John Maynard Keynes's *The General Theory of Employment, Interest, and Money* (1936) was being felt in American academic circles. In that pathbreaking work, Keynes outlined what came to be called the "Keynesian revolution" or the "new economics," a doctrine that went against established laissez-faire orthodoxy by advocating government intervention in the economy through fiscal and monetary policies, to achieve economic growth and full employment.

At that time Tobin had not yet studied economics, and when his tutor gave him Keynes's book to read, it constituted his introduction to the field in general, and to what would become his own line of research in particular. In 1939 he received his A.B. degree from Harvard *summa cum laude*, with membership in Phi Beta Kappa. His other honors included a Shaw Traveling Fellowship. He obtained his M.A. degree in economics from Harvard in 1940.

In 1941 Tobin entered government service as a junior economist, working first with the Office of Price Administration and then with the Civilian Supply and War Production Board. At the time of the attack on Pearl Harbor in December 1941, he decided to join the United States Navy and entered the officers training program at Columbia University. Another member of that same naval officers training class was Herman Wouk, who later be-

came celebrated for writing *The Caine Mutiny*. Tobin, apparently, was the inspiration for one of Wouk's characters in that novel, a midshipman named Tobit, whom he described as "mandarin-like . . . with a domed forehead, measured quiet speech, and a mind like a sponge . . . ahead of the field by a spacious percentage." Tobin served four years on the *U.S.S. Kearny*, and by the end of the war, he was second in command of the ship.

As a teaching fellow, Tobin returned to Harvard in 1946 and received his Ph.D. degree in economics the following year, after submitting a thesis on "The Theoretical and Statistical Study of Consumption Function." From 1947 to 1950 he was a junior fellow of the Harvard Society of Fellows, with time out in 1949–1950 for a brief association with the Department of Applied Economics at Cambridge University in England. In 1950 Tobin was appointed associate professor of economics at Yale University; he was promoted to full professor in 1955 and was given the chair of Sterling Professor of Economics, which he still holds, in 1957. Those early years of Tobin's work already saw him making seminal contributions to the field, developing the work of Keynes and correcting what he regarded as some of the shortcomings of the Keynesian framework. (Tobin's view is that "pure Keynes" tends to inflation and overheating of the economy.) He served as associate editor of *Econometrica* from 1951 to 1953, and was an American editor of the *Review of Economic Studies* from 1952 to 1954.

In 1955 James Tobin received the American Economic Association's John Bates Clark Medal, awarded to "that American economist under the age of forty who is judged to have made a significant contribution to economic thought and knowledge." That year, the Cowles Foundation for Research in Economics, which is dedicated to relating economic theory to mathematical and statistical studies, moved from the University of Chicago to Yale, where Tobin became its director.

Tobin's flourishing academic career and his neo-Keynesian perspective led him to enter the arena of public debate on government economic policy. For the January 1961 issue of *Challenge* magazine, for example, he wrote an article that criticized the Federal Reserve Board's tight monetary practices, arguing that they would frustrate attempts by the new Kennedy administration to create higher levels of employment and production. So little did Tobin himself regard that article as a personal move towards a more active role in the public arena that he was on his way, following its publication, to a quiet scholarly year at the University of California when he received a call from President John F. Kennedy, asking him to serve as one of the three members of the President's Council of Economic Advisers. At first Tobin resisted, since he wanted to remain in academic life. "Mr. President," he reportedly said, "I am what you might call an ivory tower economist." "That's all right, professor," JFK replied. "I am what you might call an ivory tower president."

Tobin's presence on the Council of Economic Advisers, along with that of Kermit Gordon and chairman Walter Heller, brought a new dimension to the American political and economic scene. When the Council issued its first Report to the President, in January 1962, Joseph A. Loftus wrote in the *New York Times* (January 23, 1962): "Not in some years have professional economists, in a state paper, measured the economy in the human terms found today in the report of the Council of Economic Advisers. . . . Talking about people in an economic report, and not just statistics, may draw some criticism. Still the council members believe they have met the most exacting standards of their profession."

In an interview conducted the previous summer with Harry Schwartz of the *New York Times* editorial board, which was published in the *New York Times Magazine* (July 23, 1961), the three Council members had spelled out their policy as targeted towards the attainment of full employment and a faster growth rate, together with increased competition and a more vigorous enforcement of antitrust laws. The 1962 report advocated increased investments in science and technology, plants and equipment, and education and training, as the policy needed to achieve economic growth and rising productivity, which it called "the foundation of the country's leadership of the free world."

James Tobin's active and occasionally controversial role on the Council encompassed everything from speaking to the research and economic staffs of AFL-CIO unions, where he advised against cost-of-living clauses in wage contracts, to meeting with Valéry Giscard d'Estaing, then finance minister of France, in an effort to determine why that country had fared so well economically in the postwar years. One of his particular concerns was a push for international monetary reform, an issue taken up by President Kennedy in June 1963, after Tobin's resignation from the Council and return to Yale the previous September. Kennedy had accepted Tobin's resignation with "deep and sincere regret," writing him that he had "convincingly demonstrated that the ivory tower can produce public servants of remarkable effectiveness."

In 1963 Tobin evaluated his tenure in the Kennedy administration in an article he wrote for *Ventures*, the magazine of the Yale Graduate School. Concentrating on the larger issue of the role of the academic economist in government service, he concluded that professional advisers to the president need not be "coldly scientific and nonpolitical"; nor need they offer "purely 'objective' diagnoses and recommendations." To Tobin, it seemed only natural that the president seek advice from those academicians who share the objectives of his administration. In his opinion, following a stint of government service the economist "will return to his university . . . with a new sense of research priorities and with an enriched agenda of problems for himself, his colleagues, and his students."

That Tobin had, indeed, returned with an "enriched agenda" is evident from the wide-ranging scope of his writings and research in the following years, during which he wrote with a pronounced liberal stance on matters of public concern and policy. In an article for the *New Republic* (October 24, 1964), for example, he attacked Barry Goldwater's presidential campaign for raising the "phony issue" of the growing size of the federal government. "Goldwater won't touch the amounts spent for national defense . . . ," Tobin commented. "[His] axe will fall . . . on those politically vulnerable federal programs, e.g., foreign economic aid, the Peace Corps, the antipoverty package, the support of science and arts, national parks, forests and lands—which attest, however feebly, that America is still capable of compassion, foresight, and taste."

Lyndon B. Johnson's defeat of Goldwater in the presidential election failed to blunt Tobin's critical edge. Testifying before the Joint Economic Committee of Congress in February 1967, he warned that the administration, which sanctioned deficit financing as the Vietnam war escalated, was moving in the direction of accepting a rise in unemployment, and asserted, "We can do better than this." In his article for the quarterly *Daedalus* (Fall 1965), entitled "On Improving the Economic Status of the Negro," Tobin urged that the federal government direct its fiscal and monetary policies towards the goal of achieving full employment, as the most effective means of assuring general economic prosperity and the best guarantee of lifting black Americans from poverty.

On the occasion of his assumption of the presidency of the American Economic Association late in 1970, Tobin emphasized the need for permanent wage and price controls. In his opinion, such a controlled economy, with the federal government acting on the advice of professional economists, could bring about the end of full-fledged recession. It was with that goal in mind that Tobin, in 1972, lent his talents to the ill-fated presidential campaign of George S. McGovern, joining the economic coterie around McGovern that a writer for *Time* (July 17, 1972) dubbed the "McGovernomics men," with Tobin standing out as "the group's intellectual giant." One of the most controversial planks in McGovern's platform was an income redistribution plan, largely fashioned by Tobin, who had earlier spelled out his program of a national system of income guarantees and supplements in an article entitled "Raising the Incomes of the Poor," in *Agenda for the Nation* (Brookings Institution, 1968). In it Tobin had written: "Perhaps someday a national administration will muster the courage to ask the American people to tax themselves for social justice and domestic tranquillity."

James Tobin's huge output includes journal articles, contributions to dozens of collections edited by others, and several books of his own, including his three-volume *Essays in Economics*, of which Vol. I is *Macroeconomics* (North-Holland Publishing, 1971); Vol. II is *Consumption and*

TREVOR

Econometrics (North-Holland, 1975); and Vol. III is *Theory and Policy* (MIT Press, 1982). His *The New Economics, One Decade Older* (Princeton Univ. Pr., 1974) deals with the decline of the "new economics" doctrine of the Kennedy administration, which he had helped to shape, once the Vietnam war began to eliminate other priorities.

In announcing their bestowal of the 1981 Nobel Memorial Prize for Economic Science to James Tobin, the members of the Nobel committee maintained that his work had "unquestionably inspired substantial research during the 1970s on the effect of monetary policy, the implications of government budget deficits, and stabilization policy in general." With characteristic modesty, Tobin concluded his acceptance speech in Stockholm, Sweden with the statement: "I would like to think of the institution of this prize not as a celebration of [economics'] achieved status as science but as encouragement of the scientific spirit of economic inquiry at its best."

Although Tobin graciously refused to deliver a polemic against Reaganomics at the press conference held on October 13, 1981, the day of the Nobel Committee's announcement, within a week he was continuing the criticism of the Reagan administration's economic policies that he had mounted since its inception. At an October 16, 1981 address to the Sesquicentennial Conference at New York University he traced the history of American economic policy since the Great Depression, noting that while many global, external factors could explain the phenomenon of "stagflation" in the United States in the late 1970s, the Reagan adminstration attributed economic problems solely to the activist government policies of the postwar decades. Far from being any "revolution," Tobin claimed, Reaganomics represents a counterrevolution: "The old doctrines and policies, new forty years ago, are discredited, replaced by new doctrines and policies, old forty years ago." He concluded: "The purely monetary cure for inflation could hold down the economy for half a decade. . . . The 'new federalism' . . . will have devastating effects on . . . the poor. Meanwhile the tax cuts will be widening the gulf between the living standards of the rich and those of the poor, without the promised compensation in the conquest of stagflation. In the end, I think, a democratic polity will not tolerate in its government and central bank an economic strategy of indifference to the real state of the economy."

Such a vision had shaped Tobin's work from the beginning, and promises to do so in the future. William Parker, head of graduate work in economics at Yale, had characterized Tobin as "sort of an old Roman citizen" with "a real sense of civic duty and virtue." Over the years, Tobin has consistently served as a consultant for government and private agencies, including the Federal Reserve System, the United States Treasury, the Congressional Budget Office, and the Ford Foundation. He was chairman of New Haven's City Plan Commission in 1967–1970, a member of the New York City Commission on Inflation and Economic Welfare in 1969–1970, and chairman of the Committee to Study Puerto Rico's Finances, 1974–1975.

James Tobin has received honorary degrees from several universities. He was visiting lecturer at the University of Essex (1966), the University of Nairobi (1972–73), and the University of Helsinki (1978). He is a member of the National Academy of Sciences, the American Philosophical Society, the American Academy of Arts and Sciences, and a Fellow of the American Statistical Association. One journalist, William D. Marbach of *Newsweek* (October 26, 1981), has described him as "a kindhearted man with an Irish twinkle in his eyes and a fondness for rumpled tweed jackets." Tobin enjoys lunching with the students in his undergraduate courses, and he takes great pride in his teaching. He was married on September 14, 1946 to Elizabeth Fay Ringo, and the couple have four children: Margaret, Louis, Hugh, and Roger. For recreation, Tobin enjoys riding his bicycle, playing tennis, skiing, sailing, canoeing, fishing, playing chess, and watching baseball.

References: *N Y Times* D p1+ O 14 '81 por; *Newsday* p76 O 18 '81 por; *Newsweek* p62 O 26 '81 por; *Washington Post* p1+ O 14 '81 por; *Yale Alumni Magazine and Journal* p4+ D '81 por; *American Men of Science* (1968); *Contemporary Authors new rev vol 5* (1981); *Who's Who, 1984–85*

Trevor, William

May 24, 1928– Irish writer. Address: h. "Shobrooke Mill," Crediton, Devon, England

Often with dark and subtle humor and by indirection William Trevor reticently uncovers in short stories, novels, and plays much that is unsuspected in the everyday life of English and Irish cities and villages. Sometimes decency and courage emerge from concealed recesses, but more frequently he flushes out pretension, sadness, and evil in working-class and middle-class mores. From his first important novel, *The Old Boys*, in 1964 to *Fools of Fortune* in 1983, Trevor has maintained a continuity of thematic preoccupations—chiefly with domestic and other private relationships—that is paralleled in his short stories. Lately he has expanded his range to include Irish religious and political controversies. V. S. Pritchett, to whom other critics have compared Trevor as a master of the short story, regards him as "one of the finest short-story writers at present writing in the Anglo-Irish modes." In England most of his work has been published by the Bodley Head and in the United States, by the Viking Press.

"If anyone asks why I write gloomy novels, they need only know that my father came from the South and my mother from the North," William Trevor said in an interview for the *Guardian* (No-

William Trevor

vember 3, 1971), referring both to the split within his native Ireland and the theme of personal isolation that pervades his fiction. He was born William Trevor Cox on May 24, 1928 in Mitchelstown, County Cork to Protestant parents James William and Gertrude (Davison) Cox. The family included two other children, another son and a daughter. Both of Trevor's grandfathers were farmers. His father's work as a bank manager required frequent moves for the family from one provincial town to another, including Skibbereen, Tipperary, and Maryborough.

Beginning with a convent school in Youghal, Trevor attended more than a dozen different schools, among them the Tate School in Wexford, Sanford Park School in Dublin, and St. Columba's College in the County Dublin mountains. In 1946 he graduated from St. Columba's, where he had been a prefect, or student officer, and entered Trinity College in Dublin, which awarded him a B.A. degree in history in 1950. At St. Columba's he had become interested in sculpture, and during his university years his work in carving and modeling had been exhibited in Dublin.

To earn a living, Trevor taught history for two years, from 1950 to 1952, in Armagh, Northern Ireland. When, in 1952, he obtained a post as art teacher at Rugby in England, he was able to give more time to sculpture. He won the Irish section of the Unknown Political Prisoner sculpture competition in 1953 and later a commission to do relief carvings for All Saints Church in Braunston, near Rugby. Moving to Somerset in 1956, he continued working as a church sculptor, taught art part-time in a school in Taunton, and had one-man exhibitions in Dublin and Bath.

Largely because of economic pressures, Trevor took a job in 1960 as a copywriter with an advertis-

ing agency in London. By that time he had embarked upon a literary career, with the publication in 1958 of a novel, A Standard of Behaviour (Hutchinson). His childhood love of reading and teenage interest in the techniques of putting together mystery stories had led him to believe that someday he would become a writer. But sculpture had for many years apparently satisfied his creative drive. As he began to dislike the increasingly abstract direction of his art, however, he turned to writing as a means of expressing his involvement with humanity. To avoid publishing under the name he had become known by as a sculptor, William Trevor Cox, he adopted William Trevor as a pseudonym. His two artistic pursuits are not unrelated, as he explained in an interview for Publishers Weekly (October 28, 1983): "There's a way in which you think as a sculptor. You see things in the round. . . . And I've found that I still think like that when I'm writing. I'm still obsessed by form and pattern—the actual shape of things, the shape of a novel or the shape of a short story."

Admittedly written mainly for profit, A Standard of Behaviour is an unimpressive picaresque work. As Jay L. Halio and Paul Binding pointed out, however, in British Novelists Since 1960 (1983), "Even in the disregarded first novel with its ironic title . . . , we can see the characters and themes that will continue to interest Trevor throughout his career so far: misfits and charlatans, lost love, the gloom of loneliness and alienation." From the beginning Trevor's preferred literary form was the short story rather than the novel, and it was in his early short stories, some of which appeared in the Transatlantic Review, that he began to develop his distinctive low-key style. The stories came to the attention of executives at the Bodley Head, who urged him to write a novel.

In his infrequent discussions of his fiction Trevor has spoken of himself as a novelist who writes out of a sense of curiosity about people and circumstances. That curiosity sometimes impels him to speculate about the strange, or what he does not know from his own experience, such as what it is like to be an elderly person or a woman. The title characters of his second novel, The Old Boys (1964), are eight octogenarians, members of the committee of the Old Boys' Association of their public school, whose reunion to consider the election of a new chairman kindles old rivalries and rancors. Through his exploration of the way the past impinges on the present, a theme to which he returned in later fiction, Trevor brings off a cutting indictment of British public schools. His painful but also comic depiction of the impairments, indignities, pretensions, and childishness of his genteel elderly men is achieved in part by a mannered dialogue that some reviewers attributed to the influence of Ivy Compton-Burnett. But according to W. L. Webb in the Guardian (May 1, 1965), the stylized archaic diction that Trevor's characters apply to even the most trivial topic "surely has its roots in the old-fashioned idioms and speech habits of his boyhood. (His own conversation retains strong traces of them.)"

Originality was, in fact, one of the most highly praised qualities of *The Old Boys* and no doubt contributed to Trevor's winning of the Hawthornden Prize in 1965. His talent for dialogue facilitated his adaptation of the novel as a television play, presented on the BBC in 1965, and later as a stage play, which had a limited run at the Mermaid Theatre in London in 1971 and later toured the provinces. After reading *The Old Boys*, Alastair Sim commissioned Trevor to write *The Elephant's Foot*, a play about the preparation of an estranged elderly couple for a Christmas reunion with their children. It opened in Nottingham in the spring of 1966 and also enjoyed a provincial tour. As a dramatist, again, Trevor owed much of his effectiveness to his dialogue, with its peculiar juxtaposition of elegant and colloquial language.

Southwest suburban London, the locale of the residential hotel in *The Old Boys*, is also the home of the establishment that gave Trevor the title for his next novel, *The Boarding-House* (1965). To the sly and dubiously saintly Mr. Bird it is a "great institution," filled with his handpicked assortment of solitary misfits in need of comfort. He wills the boarding-house to two of his tenants, odious Nurse Clock and larcenous Mr. Studdy, a feuding pair who on his death connive to replace their fellow residents with older, more easily exploitable boarders. The "marvelous facility for macabre invention" that a reviewer for the London *Times Literary Supplement* (May 6, 1965) admired in *The Boarding-House* became a hallmark of much of Trevor's work.

Thanks to the success of his novels, Trevor was able to quit work in the advertising agency in about 1965 and move to a rural area of Devon. But, aside from making an occasional excursion to Dublin and elsewhere, he continued for a time to write about the London suburbs so familiar to him. In *The Love Department* (1966; 1967) the inexperienced Edward Blakeston-Smith, on assignment from the love department of a mass magazine, tries to track down a sex pervert, Septimus Tuam, in a farcical pursuit through Wimbledon. A "fey atmosphere" and Trevor's archness in telling his story seemed to Karl Miller of the *New Statesman* (September 23, 1966) to owe something to Muriel Spark.

The female mind is the alien region, comparable to that of old age, that Trevor investigated in his next three novels. Mrs. Ivy Eckdorf of *Mrs. Eckdorf in O'Neill's Hotel* (1969; 1970) is a well-known Munich photographer determined to capture with her camera the past and present character of the once-plush O'Neill's Hotel in Dublin, now a decrepit haven for drunks and oddballs. Her professionalism dissolves into madness as she comes to share the fantasies and pretensions that shield the hotel's occupants from their misery. Another intruder into a darkly bizarre world, the title character of *Miss Gomez and the Brethren* (1971) is an orphan from Jamaica, a former prostitute, and a convert to the Brethren of the Way who releases her religious fervor on a community of unfortu-

nates and eccentrics in London's Crow Street, SW 17, an area about to be destroyed by bulldozers in the interests of "development."

In *Elizabeth Alone* (1973; 1974) a divorced middle-aged woman, Elizabeth Aidallbery, becomes a patient, along with three other women, in a ward of the Cheltenham Street Women's Hospital in London. Trevor, who once said that his fiction results from a "relentless pursuit of the truth," usually portrays individuals who prefer their safe daydreams to truth. But every now and then one of them breaks through the insulation of delusion and tries to open the eyes of others. A patient that Elizabeth meets at the hospital, Miss Samson, facially disfigured from birth, undergoes an agonizing loss of faith. Her recognition of the loneliness and frustration in the lives of the other patients arouses a compassion that she insists upon transmitting to Elizabeth. Referring to the affirmation reached in the novel, the reviewer for the London *Times Literary Supplement* (October 26, 1973) wrote, "The stance of compassion which is adopted finally in *Elizabeth Alone* can now be seen to be implicit in all Mr. Trevor's best work. It give him a place as a writer capable of handling the human comedy instead of merely manipulating comic human beings."

With the same acuity that Trevor had exhibited in probing the thoughts and feelings of the aged and of women, he explored the minds of psychopaths in *The Children of Dynmouth* (1976; 1977) and *Other People's Worlds* (1980; 1981). The pivotal character of the former is fifteen-year-old unloved and amoral Timothy Gedge, who whiles away his time by spying on the residents of the Dorset resort town of Dynmouth. He plans to win attention by performing in a spring fete, and when he threatens to blackmail several respectable citizens to get props for his act, they are forced to accept painful awarenesses about themselves. Joyce Carol Oates, who has proved her own proficiency in the Gothic novel, praised *The Children of Dynmouth* in the *New York Times Book Review* (April 17, 1977) as "a small masterpiece of understatement [that] manages to give life to a surprising variety of people, linking them together in the rhythms of a community as well as in the more urgent rhythms of suspenseful narrative. It is a sensitive and honorable achievement, a work of rare compassion." Equally disparate are the characters of the also chilling *Other People's Worlds*—an illegitimate and illiterate teenage daughter, senile parents in a nursing home, and a pure-hearted widow, among others—whose lives are intersected by their love or hatred for Francis Tyte, a small-time egotistical actor. So extreme is his distortion of reality that he imagines the persons he exploits to be his persecutors.

Reviewing *Other People's Worlds* for *Encounter* (November 1980), Penelope Lively noted that "one of William Trevor's strengths has always been the portrayal of the banality of evil." Characters are more important than events in Trevor's fiction, but evil does not invariably stem from malicious intentions of crippled personalities. "I am interested in people who are not necessarily the victims of other people, but simply the victims of circumstances, as they are in *Fools of Fortune* [1983]. I'm interested in the sadness of fate, the things that just happen to people," he told Amanda Smith in the *Publishers Weekly* interview. The only one of Trevor's novels so far that deals directly with Anglo-Irish hostility, *Fools of Fortune* shows how the centuries-old conflict foredooms the relationship between Anglo-Irish Willie Quinton, heir to the Kilneagh estate in County Cork, and his beloved English cousin Marianne. Inescapability from the past brings revenge, murder, alcoholism, suicide, and madness. But Trevor leavens his chronicle of grief and violence with comic episodes, lyrical interludes, a flavoring of Yeatsian romanticism, and his characteristic final muted note of affirmation.

Coinciding with the publication of *Fools of Fortune* was that of *The Stories of William Trevor* (Penguin, 1983), a gathering of all the short stories contained in his five collections: *The Day We Got Drunk on Cake* (1967; 1968), *The Ballroom of Romance* (1972), *Angels at the Ritz* (1975; 1976), *Lovers of Their Time* (1978), and *Beyond the Pale* (1981; 1982). The stories had earlier appeared in the *Transatlantic Review, London Magazine, Encounter, Antioch Review, New Yorker,* and *Atlantic Monthly,* among other magazines. They have been widely anthologized.

Trevor's compressed, lean prose and his penchant for oblique understatement are particularly appropriate to the economical short story form, which, like poetry, can deliver multiplicity of meaning. In his review of *Angels at the Ritz* Robert Nye observed in the *Christian Science Monitor* (June 16, 1976), "Each of his stories is like a poem, an incident, an experience, a situation which he has captured in words and drawn out to just the length it will tolerably sustain." Recalling that Graham Greene had considered *Angels at the Ritz* the best collection of stories since James Joyce's *Dubliners* (1914), Ted Solotaroff commented in the *New York Times Book Review* (February 21, 1982), "Both Trevor and the early Joyce are geniuses at presenting a seemingly ordinary life as it is, socially, psychologically, morally, and then revealing the force of these conditions in the threatened individual's moment of resistance to them. This is the deeper realism: accurate observation turning into moral vision."

Like his early novels, many stories in Trevor's first collection deal with elderly people in southwest London, while some of his more recent stories—the superb "Attracta" of *Lovers of Their Time,* for instance—are, like his latest novel, devoted to Anglo-Irish relationships. His continued partiality to the vulnerable, especially the elderly, is evident in "Broken Homes," also included in *Lovers of Their Time,* an excruciating story about an aged widow who is perfectly contented with her modest flat until a schoolteacher insists upon sending in youngsters from broken homes to redecorate

it. In "The Blue Dress," which appears in *Beyond the Pale,* he proves that he has retained his touch for the macabre.

Most of the characters in the stories of the ironically titled *Lovers of Their Time* suffer from nostalgia, an affliction they share with the men and women in every period of Trevor's work. Marriage and the home, which from the beginning of his writing have accommodated the hidden lives of his seemingly transparent individuals and the human disposition to make do, prevail in two of his latest stories, "Running Away" (*Atlantic,* April 1984) and "Bodily Secrets" (*Encounter,* May 1984). Henrietta, the former wife of a college professor who had discarded her for a young hippie, raises to herself the question of having run away when she returns reluctantly from Italy to resume her domestic responsibilities at the end of his affair. In "Bodily Secrets" a well-to-do widow with concealments of her own marries a man who had confessed to her alone that he spends his weekends away in Dublin in homosexual escapades.

One of the reasons that Trevor is much better known in England than in the United States is that he has developed many of his stories into short plays for British radio and television. Although the one-act play is not popular on the stage, during 1972 two of his plays were produced in London, "A Night with Mrs. da Tanka" and "Going Home," and during 1973 theatregoers saw three plays, "A Perfect Relationship," "The 57th Saturday," and "Marriages." *Scenes from an Album* was produced in Dublin in 1981.

In recent years, while maintaining a home in Devon, Trevor has been living and working for the most part in Italy. An Italian residence creates for him the distance he desires from the places he writes about in England and Ireland. A product, in part, of his new perspective is his first nonfiction book, the splendidly illustrated *A Writer's Ireland* (Thames and Hudson; Viking, 1984), a chronological literary expedition that abounds in quotations from well-known and lesser-known Irish writers. "This book is not an academic investigation of either Irish literature or the inspiration of landscape," Trevor explained in his introduction. "It is a writer's journey, a tour of places which other writers have felt affection for also, or have known excitement or alarm in."

Among William Trevor's honors are the Whitbread Award (for *The Children of Dynmouth*), the Allied Irish Bank Prize, the Heinemann Award, the Irish Community Prize, and the Royal Society of Literature Award. He is a member of the Irish Academy of Letters and a Commander, Order of the British Empire. On August 26, 1952 Trevor married Jane Ryan. Their two sons are Patrick and Dominic. Trevor's recreational interests include motion pictures, traveling, gardening, and walking. He has little contact with other writers and does not often talk about his work, but in his *Publishers Weekly* conversation he disclosed, "What interests me most about writing is the relationship between you and the unknown reader and the sort of link you have with that person, the way in which that person actually picks up something which isn't in the story. . . . It's not in any way a personal one. It's purely people on the same sort of wavelength."

References: Guardian p7 My 1 '65 por, p10 N 3 '71 por; Pub W 224:80+ O 28 '83 por; British Novelists Since 1960. Dictionary of Literary Biography vol 14 (1983); Contemporary Authors new rev vol 4 (1981); Contemporary Dramatists (1982); Contemporary Novelists (1976); International Who's Who, 1984–85; Who's Who, 1984–85; World Authors: 1950–1970 (1975)

Trump, Donald J(ohn)

1946– Real estate developer. Address: b. Trump Organization, 725 5th Ave., New York City, N.Y. 10022

It has been said of Donald J. Trump, president of the billion-dollar Trump Organization, that not since the days of William Zeckendorf Sr. has any real estate developer attracted so much public attention in New York City at such an early age. Since the mid-1970s Trump has become one of Manhattan's most grandiose and controversial builders. A major step in his rise to eminence in the high-rolling world of real estate developers was his success in persuading the city to build its multimillion-dollar convention center on the West 34th Street site on which he had been awarded the option after its original owner, the Penn Central Company, went into bankruptcy. About that time, Trump bought the Commodore Hotel, which had also been owned by Penn Central, and turned it

into the "classy and glassy" Grand Hyatt Hotel. But perhaps his best-known project is the Trump Tower, built at a cost estimated at $200 million, next to Tiffany's on Fifth Avenue, where stores are rented for as much as $500 a square foot and where "a top-of-the-line" two-bedroom apartment can be had for $2.25 millon. Trump, who considers building as his "art form," has variously been called a "megalomaniac," a "visionary," and so superb a salesman that "he could sell sand to the Arabs and refrigerators to the Eskimos."

Donald John Trump was born in 1946 in a twenty-three-room house in the exclusive Jamaica Estates in Queens, New York City, one of the five children of Fred C. and Mary Trump. His oldest brother, Fred, Jr., died a few years ago; his younger brother, Robert, is an executive vice-president of the Trump Organization; his sister Maryanne Trump Barry is a federal judge in Trenton, New Jersey; another sister, Elizabeth, is an administrative assistant with the Chase Manhattan Bank. Donald Trump's interest in his father's real estate business was already evident when as a small boy he would glue all the toy blocks he could find together into one giant skyscraper. Later, along with his brothers, he spent summers working at Trump construction sites or rent collection offices.

His father, a man of Swedish Protestant stock, had been so young when he started his real estate business in 1923 that he needed his mother's signature to validate leases. From the family's minister, the Rev. Norman Vincent Peale, Donald Trump learned about the power of positive thinking. "The mind can overcome any obstacle," he has said. "I never think of the negative." The household in which Trump grew up was by his father's admission competitive, for Fred Trump trained his offspring so that they would "know how to make a buck." Donald, he recalled, "was a pretty rough fellow when he was small."

Seeking to curb his son's wildness, Fred Trump shipped him off to the New York Military Academy in Cornwall-on-Hudson. There, Donald Trump was elected captain of the baseball team and captain of a student regiment. "He was a real leader," Colonel Theodore Dobias, his baseball coach, has recalled. "He was even a good enough firstbaseman that the White Sox sent a scout to look at him." After graduation and a stint at Fordham University, Trump entered the Wharton School of Finance at the University of Pennsylvania but found that college bored him because his real estate courses emphasized single family houses rather than major projects. "Donald always used to talk about changing the Manhattan skyline," one of his college friends has said. In November 1964, during his freshman year at Wharton, Trump attended the ceremonies for the opening of the Verrazano-Narrows Bridge and observed that while all the politicians who had opposed the bridge were being applauded, Othmar H. Ammann, the eighty-five-year-old engineer who designed it, was being ignored. "I realized then and there, that if you let people treat you how they want, you'll be made a fool," Trump told Howard Blum of the *New York Times* (August 26, 1980). "I realized then and there something I would never forget: I don't want to be made anybody's sucker." While studying at Wharton, Donald Trump helped his father to negotiate real estate transactions. He graduated in 1968 with a B.A. degree in economics, at the head of his class.

At the time of his graduation, Trump was uncertain about his career plans. "The first thing I did when I got out of college," he told Robert Masello, as quoted in *Town & Country* (September 1983), "was to analyze the current economic climate and think about just what business I wanted to go into." He seriously considered entering the oil business, but he eventually decided to join his father at the Trump Organization, which in those days built middle-income apartment houses in Brooklyn, Queens, and Staten Island. "I learned a lot about real estate just through osmosis from my father," he has recalled, "but what really made it appeal to me as a career was the creativity involved."

Donald Trump's job was the refinancing of many of the company's 5,000 apartment units, and he helped parlay them into the 25,000 apartments that the Trump Organization eventually owned. "I gave Donald free rein," Fred Trump told Owen Moritz, as quoted in the *New York Daily News Magazine* (August 10, 1980). "He has great vision, and everything he touches seems to turn to gold." Donald Trump's maxim, which he later applied so profitably, was "location, location, location." His major source of inspiration was William Zeckendorf, the real estate giant of the late 1950s. But Trump's life-style at the time was not that of a staid entrepreneur. He frequented such New York celebrity haunts as Elaine's and Regine's, dressed fastidiously as always, and one woman, as quoted in *New York* (November 17, 1980), remembers him as a "kind of fringe member of the social crowd."

In October 1973 the United States Justice Department brought suit against the Trump Organization, charging it with discriminatory renting practices against blacks, but Trump vehemently denied the charge. "Five to 10 percent of our units are rented to blacks in the city," he said. "But we won't sign leases with welfare clients unless they have guaranteed income levels, because otherwise, everyone immediately starts leaving the building." Trump later signed an agreement providing open-housing opportunities for minority groups. It was in about 1973 that the Trump Organization turned its attention to Manhattan, a move that Donald Trump saw as pivotal to his company's stake in the city's future.

Following the 1974 election of Hugh L. Carey, to whose gubernatorial campaign the Trump Organization had contributed generously, Donald Trump hired Louise M. Sunshine, the former chairman of Carey's campaign finance committee, who as a lobbyist became a key member of the Trump Organization's staff. After the Penn Central railroad went into bankruptcy, Trump moved to secure options on its Hudson River railroad yards and on its fifty-nine-year-old Commodore Hotel. Aided, accord-

ing to New York City Councilman Henry J. Stern, by his ties with Governor Carey and bolstered by the lobbying efforts of Mrs. Sunshine, Trump was able to persuade officials of the financially strapped city in concert with state authorities to agree to build the New York convention center on the site of the defunct Penn Central railroad yards. Trump claimed to have received a $500,000 commission plus $88,000 in expenses for the sale of the West 34th Street site to the Urban Development Corporation. He asserted that he would have dispensed with the commission if officials had agreed to name the center for his father.

Peter Solomon, former deputy mayor for economic development, has recalled that Trump at first maintained that he was entitled to a $4,400,000 commission, but it was finally decided after reading the terms of the original Penn Central contract with the developer that he merited no more than $500,000. "But what really got me," Solomon has said, "was his bravado. I think it was fantastic. It was unbelievable. He almost got us to name the convention center after his father in return for something he never really had to give away. I guess he just thought we would never read the fine print or, by the time we did, the deal to name the building after his father would have been set." Meanwhile, the convention center had become bogged down in huge cost overruns, but Trump's offer to take charge, without payment, of the completion of the project was not accepted.

When Donald Trump proposed in 1976 to buy the Commodore with the intention of renovating it, the hotel had been losing some $1.5 million a year and had not paid any taxes to the city for several years. Fred Trump disapproved of the purchase, saying, "This is like trying to buy a ticket on the Titanic." But Donald Trump, unperturbed by the Commodore's losses and the parlous condition of the city's finances, worked out a fifty-fifty joint venture with the Hyatt Corporation and then proceeded to negotiate a forty-year tax abatement by the city—the first of its kind ever granted to a commercial property. Hotel expert Bjorn Hanson of the accounting firm of Laventhol & Horwath estimated the value of the tax break at about $45 million. "Clearly the city could have gotten a better deal," Deputy Mayor Robert F. Wagner, Jr., has said. "But Donald Trump made his deal at a time when the city was desperate for development. Also, he had the vision to have picked the Commodore site when he did. You've got to remember when Trump bought the Commodore, East 42nd Street was going downhill, and nobody was building hotels in New York."

The Hyatt deal, made with the crucial backing of Mayor Abraham D. Beame, who like Carey had been a recipient of Trump campaign contributions, was rather intricate. After buying the Commodore from Penn Central for $10 million, Trump then sold it to the Urban Development Corporation for $1 with the stipulation that he and his family and partners would run the hotel for ninety-nine years, while the city would receive revenues based upon the Hyatt's profitability. At the end of the ninety-nine-year lease, the property would revert to the city. Completed in the summer of 1980, the Grand Hyatt has some 1,400 rooms, a presidential suite renting at $2,000 a night, a ballroom, a shopping arcade, and five restaurants. Its construction earned Trump the designation of the "William Zeckendorf of bad times."

In February 1979, about four years after first learning from a highly placed contact whom he had met through the resourceful Louise Sunshine that the lease for the Fifth Avenue site of the Bonwit Teller department store might be available, Trump acquired it for $10 million as the location of his planned apartment complex, the Trump Tower. It was a site he coveted because of its proximity to the exclusive Tiffany & Company. "If you go to Paris, if you go to Duluth," Trump has said, "the best location is called the 'Tiffany location.' That is a standard real estate phrase." The Genesco Company, which owned the Bonwit Teller store, had turned down previous Trump offers for the lease, but when a new chairman of the board took office in 1979, the company agreed to sell. Trump lined up the necessary credit from the Chase Manhattan Bank and went into a "roughly fifty-fifty" partnership with the Equitable Life Assurance Society, which owned the land under Bonwit and which had provided mortgage financing for the Hyatt deal. When the city turned down Trump's request for a residential tax abatement under section 421-A of its real property law, claiming that the law was intended to encourage low- and middle-income rather than luxury housing, the builder, represented by attorney Roy Cohn, took the city to court. After losing his case in the state Supreme Court Appellate Division, Trump was awarded a $50,-000,000 tax abatement by the Court of Appeals.

Further controversy was stirred up when Trump, after pledging the Bonwit building's art deco frieze and geometrically intricate grillwork to the Metropolitan Museum of Art on condition that the financial and logistical problems of removal would not be prohibitive, decided to have the artwork jackhammered instead. A New York Times editorial called the demolition "a memorable version of cashflow calculations outweighing public sensibilities." Trump, in turn, called the artwork "junk," and maintained that its removal intact might have endangered pedestrians.

The Trump Tower, which opened for occupancy in 1982, is the tallest and most expensive reinforced concrete structure in New York City. Among its residents are such highly solvent celebrities as Sophia Loren, Johnny Carson, and David Merrick. Its atrium, which the New York Times architecture critic Paul Goldberger praised as "warm, luxurious, and even exhilarating," features such shops as Asprey's of London and Charles Jourdan—whose rent for the first year was reportedly $1 million. Trump once said reflectively, "I'll be thirty-six years old when Trump Tower opens, and I'll have done everything I can do, and sometimes I think, maybe it was a mistake to have raced through it all so fast."

But Trump showed no signs of slowing down. One of his more profitable transactions was his purchase in 1980 of the Barbizon-Plaza Hotel and an adjacent apartment house for about $13 million. By 1983 the property was reported to have increased nearly tenfold in market value. Continuing to provoke controversy, in 1982 Trump made himself unpopular with tenants of a building he owned on Central Park South by offering to shelter some of the city's homeless in its fourteen vacant apartments. The tenants of the rent-controlled building contended that Trump was trying to drive them out in order to erect a new high-rise project, and the city turned down his offer. Meanwhile, he had been completing work on the Trump Plaza, a $125 million cooperative apartment complex on East 61st Street scheduled for occupancy in 1984. And the $250 million Harrah's hotel-casino Atlantic City, which Trump has been building in partnership with Holiday Inn, will reportedly rank as the resort's largest gaming palace when it opens in 1984. Trump moved into the sports world in September 1983 by buying the New Jersey Generals of the United States Football League from Oklahoma oilman J. Walter Duncan and former Generals coach Chuck Fairbanks for an estimated $10 million, and he reportedly has tried to lure Miami Dolphin "supercoach" Don Shula to the Generals with an offer of $1 million a year. "We expect within two or three years to have virtual parity with the NFL," he has said optimistically. And, according to friends, he would like someday to head his own television network.

Among other projects, Trump hopes to build a 1,940-foot structure that is to be the tallest building in the world, on a Manhattan landfill near the South Street Seaport. He would also like to construct a domed sports stadium in New York City, and he has indicated an interest in buying into the controversial Lincoln West development on Manhattan's West Side. But his plans for a sixty-story "Trump Castle" with a drawbridge and moat, on Manhattan's Madison Avenue, were abandoned in April 1984 when Trump and his project partner, the Prudential insurance company, decided that it was more profitable to sell the site.

The Trump Organization, of which Donald J. Trump is president, is an umbrella organization for the Trump family assets, with more than a dozen subsidiaries. Owned entirely by Donald Trump are Trump Enterprises, Inc.; the Trump Corporation; the Trump Development Company; Wembly Realty, Inc.; the Park South Company; the Land Corporation of California; and the now inactive Gold Company. In partnership with others, Donald Trump owns the Trump-Equitable Fifth Avenue Company, Regency-Lexington Partners, the Seashore Corporation of Atlantic City, and Trump Plaza: The East 61st Street Company. Other subsidiaries, owned by the Trump family, are Trump Equities, Inc.; Trump Management, Inc.; and the Trump Construction Company.

In 1975 Donald J. Trump took time out to date Ivana Winkelmayr, a fashion model and former

Olympic skier, who grew up in Czechoslovakia. They met at a party in Montreal where, it is said, Trump fell immediately in love with her, and they were married within a year in a ceremony performed by Dr. Norman Vincent Peale. Not the jet set couple they can easily afford to be, the Trumps are said to live fairly quiet lives in their triplex atop the Trump Tower, often spending weekends at their country home in southwestern Connecticut. Trump has made Ivana an executive vice-president in charge of design of the Trump Organization. The Trumps, who have a son, Donald, and a daughter, Ivanka, became parents for the third time in early 1984.

Donald Trump is six feet two inches tall, weighs 190 pounds, and has sandy hair and blue eyes. He neither drinks nor smokes and is, according to his wife, "a very good golfer, with only a three handicap." Although on the state and local levels Trump has backed Democrats like Hugh Carey, Abraham Beame, and Edward Koch, he supported Ronald Reagan in the 1980 presidential campaign and has made several social visits to the White House.

Trump serves as cochairman of the Vietnam Veterans Memorial Commission. Concerned about the prospect of a nuclear holocaust, he has said that he would like to negotiate arms control agreements with the Soviet Union. "Negotiation is an art," he told William E. Geist, as quoted in the *New York Times Magazine* (April 8, 1984), "and I have a gift for it."

References: N Y Daily News Mag p10+ Ag 10 '80 por; N Y Times p4+ N 1 '76 pors, B p1+ Ag 26 '80 pors, III p1+ Ag 7 '83 por; NY Times Mag p28+ Ap 8 '84 pors; New York 13:26+ N 17 '80 pors; Sports Illus 60:53+ F 13 '84 por; Town & Country 137:202+ S '83 pors; Wall St J p1+ Ja 14 '82 por

John Sotomayer/The New York Times

Tully, Alice

Sept. 11, 1902– Music patron. Address: b. c/o Alice Tully Hall, 1941 Broadway, New York City, N.Y. 10023

New York City's stellar music patron, Alice Tully embodies the traditional nineteenth-century ideal of untouted private philanthropy and arts patronage. A former dramatic soprano herself, she is the donor of Alice Tully Hall, the chamber music recital hall in the Lincoln Center for the Performing Arts that Donal Henahan of the *New York Times* has extolled as "the most satisfactory place to experience music at Lincoln Center, both visually and acoustically." Miss Tully played an active role in the planning of the hall and in the formation of its resident company, the Chamber Music Society of Lincoln Center. As Mark A. Schubart, the director of the Lincoln Center Institute, remarked in an interview in 1976, "She is a professional in the arts and brings to her philanthropy not only generosity, but a real understanding of what she is helping."

The older of the two daughters of William J. Tully, a lawyer and two-term New York state senator, Alice Bigelow Tully was born on September 11, 1902, in Corning, New York. Her maternal grandfather, Amory Houghton Jr., founded the Corning Glass Works. Other relatives include the late Alanson B. Houghton, an uncle who served as the United States ambassador to Germany and to Great Britain in the 1920s, and Katharine Hepburn, who is a second cousin. Alice Tully spent her earliest years in Corning, but in 1908 she moved with her family to New York City, where her father became the general solicitor for the Metropolitan Life Insurance Company. As befitted her background of wealth and social position, she received her elementary and secondary education at, respectively, Mrs. J. D. Randall MacIvor's School in New York City and the Westover School in Middlebury, Connecticut. Although she had taken piano lessons as a child, Miss Tully, by her own admission, was not exposed to much music until she was in her mid-teens. The turning point in her life was a piano recital by Josef Hofmann. "When I came out of that concert, I knew that music was where my future was going to be," she recalled in an interview with Harold C. Schonberg of the *New York Times* (October 24, 1982). From then on, she was an avid concertgoer. By the time she was seventeen, she had decided to become a professional singer. "That wasn't what my family had in mind for me," she told Schonberg. "I was the first one to break away from their routine. . . . It was a shock to my parents. On the other hand, they seemed glad that I had a purpose in life."

After taking private singing lessons in New York City for three years, Alice Tully went to Paris in 1923, accompanied by a chaperone, to continue her vocal training. Eventually she was joined there by her younger sister, Marion, and by her parents, who rented an apartment on the Ile Saint-Louis. In the midst of the artistic ferment of Paris in the 1920's, Miss Tully led what she has described as "a cloistered existence." "I existed only for music and my voice," she told one reporter. For seven years she studied under Jean Périer, the renowned tenor who created the role of Pelléas in Debussy's opera Pelléas et Mélisande. She was also a pupil of the voice teachers Thérèse Leschetizky and Miguel Fontecha. Her instructor for stage work was Georges Wague, the leading mime of the Paris Opéra and a professor at the Conservatoire. In Wague's mise en scène classes, she learned more than thirty operatic roles.

Alice Tully made her professional debut in 1927 in a concert with the Pasdeloup Orchestra at the Salle Gaveau in Paris. As she performed in subsequent concerts and recitals around the Continent, she stored up details of the acoustical properties and physical arrangements of the concert halls that she found to be especially congenial to artist and listener alike. Many years later, she would call upon those recollections in planning her own hall. Miss Tully included in her eclectic, carefully planned programs songs, some of them "neglected gems," by Gluck, Haydn, Wolf, Mahler, Franck, Ravel, and Richard Strauss, among others, as well as a number of pieces by contemporary English and American composers, but she was, by all accounts, most successful as an interpreter of French art songs, especially those of Debussy and Satie. In reviewing her New York City debut as a recitalist, at Town Hall on November 28, 1936, the New York Times music critic applauded the manner in which she "deftly envisaged the varied contrasting moods" of Debussy's "De Soir." "It was songs of this sort, where not much power was demanded of the voice and where it remained mainly in the middle and lower registers," he wrote, "that Miss Tully made her best effects."

In later recitals at Town Hall and throughout the United States, the soprano earned high marks for her readings of dramatic songs. "Miss Tully is one of those attractive personalities who manage to live their music so convincingly that its great emotional values are vividly underscored," Edward Barry observed in the Chicago Tribune (January 12, 1937). "She casts a real spell over an audience and succeeds in communicating her own fervor and her own sense of the importance of the songs." In addition to giving song recitals, Miss Tully appeared in opera productions "whenever [she] got the chance, which was rare," as she admitted to Donal Henahan of the New York Times (March 14, 1977). "When I was young," she went on, "they didn't want American singers here [in the United States],

and they didn't want them in Europe, either. It was terribly difficult." Among her operatic credits were appearances as Santuzza—by her own estimation, her "best part"—in Cavalleria Rusticana with the Salmaggi Opera in New York City in 1933 and the title role in Carmen at the Manhattan Opera House two years later.

Throughout the 1930s, Alice Tully divided her time between the United States and Europe, but at the outbreak of World War II, she settled in New York City, where she continued her professional career. Having become enamored of airplanes during her many transatlantic trips, she took flying lessons in her spare time and eventually acquired a single-engine pilot's license. After the United States entered the war, she flew submarine patrols for the Civil Air Patrol for a time, then, thinking she would be "of more use," served as a Red Cross nurse's aide at the French Hospital in New York City from 1942 until the end of the war. Although she occasionally sang for friends at small private parties, Alice Tully never again performed professionally. "Time," she explained to one reporter, had "caught up with my voice." Looking back on her fourteen-year career, she told Harold Schonberg, "It may not have been the biggest career, but it was a good one. I was always concerned with the best in music, and I think I had something individual to offer. It was an honorable career."

Since the late 1940s, Miss Tully has quietly devoted herself to diverse philanthropic activities. She finally emerged from anonymity in 1966 as the major donor of funds for a concert hall, especially designed for the performance of chamber music, in the Lincoln Center for the Performing Arts complex on Manhattan's Upper West Side. Her involvement with the project had begun some eight years earlier, when her cousin, Arthur Houghton Jr., the chairman of Corning Glass Works and a founder of Lincoln Center, asked her to contribute to the construction of the proposed recital hall. She readily agreed, on the condition that her gift, which covered most of the cost of the $4.5-million facililty, was to be anonymous. John D. Rockefeller 3d eventually persuaded the reluctant Miss Tully to allow the new hall to be named in her honor. Although she was not in on the initial planning, Alice Tully made what she has called the "creature comforts" of the hall a personal project. "If my name was going to be on it, I wanted it to be good," she explained to Robert Jones of the New York Sunday News (March 13, 1977). "I was happy with the acoustics, but the walls originally looked like a cigar box and the seats were a screaming orange-red." To provide a "serene" and "tranquil" setting for the appreciation of chamber music, she insisted on a more restful color scheme and on extra legroom between the rows of seats so that concertgoers with long legs—like herself—could "stretch out" in comfort.

Designed by the architects Pietro Belluschi and Catalan & Westermann, in collaboration with Heinrich Keilholz, an acoustician, Alice Tully Hall occupies the entire main floor of the east side of the

Juilliard School of Music building at the north end of the Lincoln Center complex. At once grand and intimate, the handsome recital chamber, which seats a total of 1,096 music lovers, has ribbed basswood walls, a beige ceiling, plum wall-to-wall carpeting, and muted raspberry red upholstered chairs set in curved, widely spaced rows without inner aisles. A small balcony holds 100 persons and six side boxes another fifty. As Henry W. Simon observed in an article for *High Fidelity/Musical America* (December 1969), "The effect is neither solemn nor showy but rather one of quiet, decent civility. Just right, that is, for the reception of the most quiet, decent, and often profoundest form of music—chamber music." Another welcome feature was the spacious size of the lobby—the only one in the city, Simon pointed out, that is large and airy enough to accommodate comfortably the entire audience during intermissions.

Alice Tully Hall was formally opened on September 11, 1969, its donor's birthday, with a gala inaugural concert by its resident company, the Chamber Music Society of Lincoln Center, which Miss Tully had helped to form. The program, featuring Bach's Trio Sonata in C, Schumann's "Dichterliebe," and Schubert's String Quintet in C, performed by violinists Pinchas Zukerman and James Buswell, cellists Pierre Fournier and Leslie Parnas, violist Walter Trampler, and harpsichordist Charles Wadsworth, who also serves as the company's artistic director, and guest artist Hermann Prey, the German baritone, provided an ideal test of the auditorium's acoustics. As Harold C. Schonberg reported in the *New York Times* (September 12, 1969), the hall produced "a nice, clear . . . modern sound. That is, clarity rather than warmth is its main characteristic. . . . Everybody walked out content, knowing that New York now has a fine new hall designed primarily for chamber music that really works." Alice Tully Hall can also be adapted for dance performances, orchestral concerts, and for such film showings as the annual New York Film Festival.

In its first season, the virtues of Alice Tully Hall lured away from historic Town Hall such popular attractions as the Clarion Music Society, the Music from Marlboro series, and the Bach Aria Group. Also moving to Tully Hall were the Little Orchestra Society, the Juilliard Orchestra, and the New York Pro Musica. One of the highlights of the inaugural season was the world premiere of Riccardo Malipiero's "Serenata per Alice Tully," which Clarion Concerts had commissioned to honor the music patron. The twelve-tone chamber music composition "juxtaposes disparate musical elements in a unified musical whole," artfully suggesting, in the view of *New York Times* music critic Allen Hughes, the variety of music performed at the hall. Over the next few years, Tully Hall was the setting for the world premieres of several pieces dedicated to Alice Tully, including the delightful vocal trio "A Round for Alice," composed by William Schuman, the president emeritus of the Juilliard School of Music, and two works by Gian-Carlo

Menotti—"Cantilene e Scherzo," a quintet for harp and strings commissioned by the Chamber Music Society, and "Nocturne" for soprano, string quartet, and harp, which was written in celebration of her eightieth birthday. The vocal soloist for the first performance of "Nocturne" was Marvis Martin, a young protégée of Miss Tully's.

Having overseen the creation of the perfect concert hall, Alice Tully turned her attention to providing the perfect organ for it. On her frequent trips to Europe in the late 1960s, she spent much of her time looking at and listening to different organs. She even sent an emissary behind the Iron Curtain to examine Bach's organ in the St. Thomas-Kirche in Leipzig. "Choosing an organ is like choosing an orchestra," she explained, as quoted in *Town and Country* (December 1976). "We wanted it flexible: suitable for Baroque music, French repertoire, Bach, and contemporary compositions." The commission was finally awarded to the Theodore Kuhn Company of Männedorf, Switzerland. Under the direction of Dr. Friedrich Jakob, the company's master craftsmen constructed a massive organ, with 4,192 pipes and sixty-one stops—the number of stops in Bach's organ—capable of producing sixty-one different tone qualities. After hearing the instrument in a dedication recital by the French organist André Marchal on April 9, 1975, Allen Hughes pronounced it to be "the best in New York and one of the best in the country." Experts have estimated the undisclosed cost of the organ to be well over $250,000.

With her encompassing devotion to music, Alice Tully has long lent her time and efforts to many musical organizations. Chairman of the board of the Chamber Music Society of Lincoln Center since its inception, she sits on the boards of directors of the Juilliard School of Music, the Philharmonic Symphony Society of New York Inc., the Metropolitan Opera, and Lincoln Center for the Performing Arts Inc. She is also vice-president of Festival Foundation (Spoleto, Italy), honorary board chairman of the New School of Music in Philadelphia, Pennsylvania, and chairman of the concert committee of the Pierpont Morgan Library. Named an honorary trustee of the Metropolitan Museum in 1979, she continues to serve on the museum's visiting committee of the department of musical instruments.

Alice Tully took on additional responsibilities as a member of the international council of the Museum of Modern Art, the advisory council for the Notre Dame University Art Gallery, and the board of trustees of the International Exhibition Foundation. New York University has benefited from her services as a trustee and advisory council member of its Institute of Fine Arts, an advisory board member of its Maison Française, and an associate member of its Medical Center board. Reaffirming her ties to France, Miss Tully has been active in the Alliance Française since the 1940s. She was awarded the Ordre Nationale du Mérite by the French government in 1968. Her manifold concerns extend to the Humane Society, wildlife preservation groups, and the Save the Children Federation, of which she has been a director. "Most of the time she sits very quietly and listens," Mrs. John D. Rockefeller 3d, who is on many of the same boards, has said. "But if she has strong feelings about something, she speaks out: very tactfully, but with a good deal of certainty."

A tall, slim woman with a regal bearing and a gracious manner, Alice Tully was once described by Donal Henahan as "the portrait of a lady come to life, the American heiress stepping out of a Henry James novel." She seldom grants interviews, but on those rare occasions she delights in reminiscing about her professional career and in commenting on the current classical music scene. In a recent interview with Harold Schonberg, for instance, she bemoaned the drop in the popularity of song recitals, a decline she attributed to the harmful effect of jet-paced international careers on the vocal chords. "We have a great many wonderful voices," she said, as quoted in the New York Times (October 24, 1982), "but the pace! The fatigue! Today Dallas, tomorrow New York, the next day where else? I blame it on greedy managers and, yes, on greedy singers, too. Voices are not allowed to develop naturally. They all try to be dramatic singers, and it usually doesn't work. Singers won't spend enough time with their teachers, with their art." When asked to name her favorite singers, she unhesitatingly listed sopranos Lotte Lehmann, Kirsten Flagstad, and Margarete Matzenauer, Hugues-Adhémar Cuénod, the Swiss tenor, baritones Heinrich Schlusnus and Pierre Bernac, and Enrico Caruso, the "greatest voice of all."

Miss Tully, who has never married, lives in a spacious apartment occupying the entire twenty-seventh floor of a building overlooking Central Park. Her living room is filled with vases of fresh flowers and metal or ceramic animals, mostly lions. She attends nearly every concert at Alice Tully Hall, and while she lives within walking distance of Lincoln Center, she usually arrives at the theatre in a chauffeured Rolls-Royce. After the performance, she often hosts a late-night dinner party at her apartment. For her guests' comfort and convenience, she customarily provides transportation home in a rented fleet of Rollses and Bentleys.

Among the many awards and honors Alice Tully has received for her good works are citations for her contribution to music from the National Association for American Composers and Conductors and from the Third Street Music School Settlement in New York City. Miss Tully recently served as the honorary cosponsor of the seventy-fifth anniversary of the latter institution, a model for some fifty settlement music schools in the United States and Canada. Sigma Alpha Iota, the international music fraternity, awarded her honorary membership in 1970, and, four years later, inducted her into the elite Circle of Fifteen, which numbers among its members Marian Anderson, the singer, and Sarah Caldwell, the opera director and conductor.

The venerable National Arts Club of New York presented Miss Tully with a special citation in 1975, and in 1976 New York University awarded her the Gallatin Medal for "contributions of lasting significance to society." Other awards include a Golden Apple Trophy from Cue magazine for service to New York City, in 1977, and the Handel Medallion, the city of New York's highest cultural award, in 1970. Pace University presented her with an honorary doctor of humane letters degree in 1973, and the New England Conservatory of Music conferred an honorary Doctor of Music degree on her in 1974.

References: Hi Fi 19:MA4+ S '69; N Y Sunday News Mag p26+ Ap 24 '77; N Y Times p50 My 10 '66 por, p50 S 11 '69 por, p37 Mr 14 '77 por, II p1+ O 24 '82 por; Town and Country 130:128+ D '76

Turner, John (Napier)

June 7, 1929– Former Prime Minister of Canada; leader of the Canadian Liberal party. Address: b. House of Commons, Ottawa, Ontario, Canada; h. 435 Russell Hill Rd., Toronto, Ontario, Canada

On June 16, 1984 John Turner succeeded Pierre Elliott Trudeau as the leader of Canada's Liberal party, and on the final day of that month he became Canada's seventeenth prime minister. Less than two weeks later, Turner called a general election for September 4. On that day Canadian voters handed the Liberals a resounding defeat, making Turner's tenure as prime minister one of the shortest in their nation's history. A moderate Liberal, somewhat to the political right of Trudeau, Turner does not greatly differ in his outlook from Progressive Conservative leader Brian Mulroney, a relatively liberal Tory, who succeeded him as prime minister on September 17, 1984. Both are generally well disposed to the United States, and both emphasize a need for fiscal responsibility tempered by social compassion.

John Napier Turner was born on June 7, 1929 in Richmond, Surrey, England to Leonard and Phyllis (Gregory) Turner. His father, a British journalist who wrote for *Punch*, died in 1931. His mother, a native of Rossland, British Columbia and the daughter of a miner, had remained in England after going there on a scholarship at the London School of Economics. She returned to Canada with John and his younger sister, Brenda, in 1932, after the early deaths of her husband and another of their three children. To support her family, Mrs. Turner took a job on the tariff board in Ottawa. During World War II she was administrator of oils and fats on the War Prices and Trade Board in the government of Prime Minister Mackenzie King, and in the 1960s she served as chancellor of the University of British Columbia. In 1945 she married Frank Ross, a Scottish-born Vancouver industrialist, who was active in the Liberal party and served from 1955 to 1960 in the ceremonial post of lieutenant governor of British Columbia.

Although Turner spent his early years in modest circumstances, his mother managed to send him to prestigious private schools in Ottawa, such as St. Patrick's College and Ashbury College. At sixteen he entered the University of British Columbia, where he studied political science, played ice hockey, and ran for the track team, winning national championships in sprinting. Only the physical impairment caused by an automobile accident kept him off the Canadian Olympic team in 1948.

After graduating with a B.A. degree and winning honors in political science in 1949, Turner went to Oxford University on a Rhodes Scholarship, earning a B.A. degree in jurisprudence in 1951 and a B.C.L. in 1952. He toured Europe as a member of a combined Oxford-Cambridge track team, studied French civil law at the Sorbonne in Paris in 1952-53, and was admitted to the English bar, Gray's Inn, in 1953, before embarking on his legal career in Canada. Later, in 1957, Oxford University granted him an M.A. degree.

Admitted to the Quebec bar in 1954, Turner joined the Montreal law firm of Stikeman, Elliott and began quietly to build his professional reputation as a corporate attorney. He gained some public notice when he became friends with Great Britain's Princess Margaret at a ball given by Lieutenant Governor Ross in honor of her visit to British Columbia in 1958, resulting in unsubstantiated rumors of a transatlantic romance.

By 1960 Turner had become a member of the Liberal party, and he soon turned his attention toward politics. In 1962 he ran for the Canadian House of Commons from the Montreal riding of St. Lawrence-St. George and defeated the incumbent, Egan Chambers, a promising young member of the Progressive Conservative party and a friend of the family. According to Chambers, Turner "got *la jeunesse dorée* [the gilded youth] very much out to work for him . . . the fashionable cocktail party circuit . . . ."

Turner, who spent his first years in the House of Commons as a backbencher, won reelection in 1963 and again two years later. Then, in December 1965, Prime Minister Lester B. Pearson named him minister without portfolio. In April 1967 Turner was appointed registrar general, and in December of that year he became Canada's first minister of consumer and corporate affairs. When Pearson announced his intention to resign, Turner declared himself a candidate for his party's leadership, but finished a distant third with 195 votes at the Ottawa convention that in April 1968 chose Pierre Elliott Trudeau as the new Liberal chief. When Trudeau became prime minister after the conclave, he added the post of solicitor general to his former rival's responsibilities.

Turner lost his Montreal riding through redistricting in 1968, but in the Liberals' general election triumph in June of that year he was returned to Parliament from the safely Liberal district of Ottawa-Carleton. From July 1968 until January 1972 Turner served as minister of justice and attorney general in the Trudeau cabinet. Turner's insistence on appointing the best available lawyers to the bench, his efforts to set up a framework for systematic review of Canadian law, and his reform of the bail law earned him the reputation as the best minister of justice since confederation. Moreover, Turner was responsible for guiding through the Parliament the important Official Languages Act of 1969, which mandated the creation of bilingual federal facilities in any Canadian district with either a French or an English minority amounting to 10 percent of its population. During the "October crisis" of 1970 in which the Trudeau government, in response to terrorist attacks and kidnappings by Quebec separatists, suspended many civil liberties, Turner vigorously defended the government's policies in public, but he was believed to have had personal reservations about the program and reportedly worked to minimize the amount of time that the repressive War Measures Act was kept in force.

In January 1972 Turner became Trudeau's minister of finance, a post that he held through a difficult period in which Canada suffered from budget deficits and a combination of rising unemployment and inflation. To resolve the problems, Turner advocated spending restraints, reductions in personal and corporate income taxes, and the adoption of voluntary wage and price controls. During his tenure at the finance ministry Turner also served as the chairman of the policy-making board of the International Monetary Fund and displayed prescience in anticipating the troubles that Third World nations were soon to experience in paying their debts to the West.

By 1975 Turner seemed to have reached a new peak in his influence, having become a favorite of the business community, of Liberal party workers, and of his colleagues in Parliament. Then, on September 10 of that year, during a private meeting with Prime Minister Trudeau, he suddenly resigned as minister of finance for what he said were personal reasons. But later he attributed the decision to Trudeau's reluctance to support his efforts to negotiate voluntary wage-and-price restraints.

Commentators have suggested that Turner did not at first expect Trudeau to take his intention to resign seriously, but had hoped instead to be assured of more support for his battle against inflation, or to be made deputy prime minister, or perhaps to be promised eventual succession to the Liberal party leadership. But Trudeau took him at his word, and when he offered to appoint him a judge or senator, the still young and ambitious Turner had no choice except to resign rather than accept such an honorific position, which would have marked him as a politician in eclipse.

Turner left the Canadian Parliament in February 1976 to become senior partner with Bill Macdonald in the Toronto law firm of McMillan, Binch, where he devoted much of his effort to the general planning of major business deals involving corporations and governments. During his eight-year tenure, McMillan, Binch grew into one of Toronto's leading law firms. Turner also earned seats on the boards of directors of at least a dozen major firms, including Bechtel Canada, Canadian Pacific, and the Seagram Company.

Turner generally avoided public involvement in politics during his years with McMillan, Binch. He showed no interest in vying for power after the Progressive Conservative leader Joe Clark briefly replaced Trudeau in the prime ministership in 1979, and he took no overt action in his own behalf as Trudeau's popularity faded after 1980. Nevertheless, he remained a force in Canadian politics. According to Christina McCall-Newman, the author of *Grits: An Intimate History of the Liberal Party* (1983), Turner was, in the eyes of many, "the prince-in-exile, the once and future contender for the Liberal crown." He continued to speak out occasionally on such matters as the need for budgetary restraint. During the late 1970s he produced a newsletter for corporate clients, in which he sometimes attacked the policies of leading officials, including Jean Chrétien, who later became his chief rival for leadership of the Liberals. He also kept in touch with a network of political contacts centered on the so-called "195 Club" of loyalists who had stayed with him through the final ballot at the 1968 convention.

By September 1983 popular support for the Liberals had plummeted to a record low of 23 percent. Rather than risk almost certain defeat in the national elections that had to be held by the spring of 1985, Prime Minister Trudeau gave official notice on February 29, 1984 that he would resign as leader of his party. On March 16 Turner stepped before the microphones at the Chateau Laurier hotel in Ottawa to announce his candidacy for the Liberal party leadership. "I believe that I have the experience for the job, and the toughness to govern tempered with compassion," he declared.

Some observers predicted that the campaign, which pitted Turner against six other contenders, would be a "coronation." His separation from Trudeau, who had become increasingly unpopular, seemed to have enhanced his own popularity. But his candidacy had its liabilities as well as its advantages. His campaigning style was said to be awkward; his election staff proved inefficient; and his position as frontrunner made him the target of intense attention from the media. Moreover, Turner was personally less popular within the Liberal party than his rival, Energy Minister Jean Chrétien. Some Liberals criticized Turner for "quitting" in 1975, and he was weak among the women and youths who would control half of the seats at the party's leadership convention.

Turner's campaign for the leadership focused on economic issues. He declared his intention to reduce the Canadian deficit through a program of spending restraints, more efficient social programs, higher revenues, and perhaps increased taxes. At the same time, he identified unemployment rather than inflation as the country's "major economic and social problem," and he promised to achieve his goals without reducing support for education, medicare, or health services. Turner aimed his economic appeal especially at the West, where the Liberals controlled only two out of eighty ridings. He called for decentralization of banking facilities, increased oil exploration, improved transportation, a review of agricultural policies, and new emphasis on gaining markets in Asia and the Pacific.

Other contenders for the party leadership complained that Turner was offering "vapid generalities" and a Canadian version of "Reaganomics." He was also under fire for his approach to the nation's sensitive language issue. His suggestion that the dispute raging in Manitoba over the entrenchment of French language rights in the constitution would be best settled at the provincial level brought him strong criticism, as did his statement that he favored "in principle" Quebec's Bill 101 to make French the only official language in that province. Turner's positions reflected his desire to deemphasize the power of the central government, but his apparent rejection of the Liberal party's commitment to the rights of language minorities created such a furor that he had quickly to issue clarifications of his views.

At the Liberal party's convention, which opened at the Ottawa civic center on June 14, 1984, Turner reached out for support to his party's blocs of minorities, women, youths, and farmers. He received a boost when External Affairs Minister Allan MacEachen symbolically announced his support by joining the candidate in his box. On the first ballot, Turner received 1,593 votes, just 125 fewer than the number needed for victory, while Chrétien, his nearest rival, polled 1,067. After an abortive attempt by his opponents to organize a "stop Turner" movement, Turner scored an easy victory on the second ballot, taking 1,862 votes to Chrétien's 1,368.

On June 30, 1984, the day after Canada's thirty-second Parliament went into recess, Pierre Elliott

Trudeau submitted his resignation as prime minister to Governor General Jeanne Sauvé, who promptly invited Turner to form a new government and to be sworn in with his cabinet. The twenty-eight ministers around Turner were eight fewer than those who formed Trudeau's inner circle, but most of them had served in the prime minister's cabinet. Turner did not feel that he had the popular mandate to make wholesale changes, and he treated his accession to the prime ministership as the establishment of a caretaker government.

Some political commentators thought that Turner would wait until late autumn for the general election, so that his administration could establish its own identity and recruit a full slate of candidates to run in the western ridings. But strong considerations weighed in favor of an early election. According to opinion polls, Turner's victory had moved the Liberals ahead of the Progressive Conservatives by a margin of 48 to 39 percent, and many party members were eager to hold the election before an anticipated economic downturn. Moreover, Turner did not relish the thought of attempting to direct the government from the gallery of the House of Commons, where, as a minister without a seat, he would have had to take his place on September 10, when the Parliament reopened.

On July 6, 1984 Turner quietly left Canada for a weekend trip to England where he met with Queen Elizabeth II and Prime Minister Margaret Thatcher. At Turner's request the monarch agreed to delay until late October her visit to Canada, originally scheduled for July, thereby opening the possibility for a summer political campaign. On July 9 Turner asked Governor General Sauvé to dissolve the Parliament and set the national election for September 4. He announced that he would not run for a safe seat in Ontario as originally planned, but would attempt to oust the Progressive Conservative incumbent from the more challenging Vancouver Quadra riding, one of Canada's wealthiest constituencies. The subsequent decision by Turner's Tory counterpart, Brian Mulroney, to give up his safe Nova Scotia seat and to challenge a Liberal incumbent in his native riding of Manicouagan, Quebec set up a situation in which both leaders were risking possible defeat to make inroads in regions where their parties had been notoriously weak.

Turner opened his campaign with a series of blunders. His selection early in July of seventeen members of Parliament for lucrative patronage appointments, in accordance with a written pledge extracted from him by Trudeau, was seen by constitutional experts as ill-advised. Soon after that, Turner was sharply criticized for widely publicized incidents in which he publicly patted the derrières of two leading female Liberal politicians. The prime minister's efforts to excuse his actions as the impulsive gestures of a "tactile politician" did little to enhance his image. Finally, Turner's reputation for competence suffered when he incorrectly alleged that the western province of Manitoba was losing population.

Later in the campaign Turner drew favorable attention for his proposal to spend $1 billion to fight unemployment among the young and for his appointment of Senator Keith Davey, a skilled political manipulator known as "the rainmaker," as his campaign manager. Nevertheless, the prime minister continued to slip in the opinion polls, especially after he fared poorly in televised debates with Mulroney and the New Democratic candidate Edward Broadbent.

On September 4, 1984 the Liberal party suffered its worst defeat in Canada's history. Of the 282 seats in the House of Commons, the Progressive Conservatives won 211, while the Liberals had their representation reduced from 135 to forty, with the New Democratic party receiving thirty seats. Turner relinquished the prime ministership on September 17, 1984, when Brian Mulroney was sworn in to head the new Progressive Conservative government. Dismissing demands by some Liberals that he be replaced as party leader, Turner pledged himself shortly after the election to "the task of rebuilding the Liberal party."

John Turner has remarked that he sees politics and public life as "a high and noble calling" which presents the opportunity "to repay what one [has] been given." With his plan to help rebuild the spirit and structure of the Liberal party, he expects to continue his role in public service.

Canada's Liberal party leader is a strikingly handsome man noted for his trim physique, brilliant blue eyes, silver hair, and elegant attire. He is said to be a warm and thoughtful person who delights in the achievements of his friends. Turner often uses slang, a habit that some commentators attribute to his lack of ease among strangers. He shares with his opponent Mulroney a fondness for the telephone and a dislike of written communication. Turner favors "masculine cuisine," such as steak and french fries, and Chivas Regal whiskey. He plays the piano, is fond of skiing, tennis, and squash, and takes his family on a canoeing vacation in northern Canada each year.

John Napier Turner has been married since May 11, 1963 to Geills McCrae Kilgour, the daughter of an insurance executive from Winnipeg. Mrs. Turner, an accomplished photographer, met her husband in 1958, when she was a student at McGill University. Turner is a devout Catholic, but his wife retains her Anglican affiliation. The Turners have four children, Elizabeth, Michael, David, and Andrew.

References: Macleans 84:19+ My '71 pors, 97:36+ Mr 12 '84 pors, 97:10+ Mr 26 '84 pors, 97:12+ Je 25 '84 pors; Toronto Globe and Mail p1+ My 26 '84 pors, L p1+ Je 18 '84 pors; Canadian Who's Who, 1982; International Who's Who, 1984–85; Who's Who, 1984–85

TURNER

Turner, Tina

*Nov. 25, 1940(?)- Singer. Address: b. c/o Agency
for the Performing Arts, Inc., 888 7th Ave., New
York City, N.Y. 10106; c/o Capitol Records, 1370
Ave. of the Americas, New York City, N.Y.
10019*

Singing professionally since 1956, when she joined
Ike Turner and the Kings of Rhythm in a black juke
joint in St. Louis, Missouri, Tina Turner has powerfully influenced the whole texture of contemporary rock and soul music. A seminal "crossover"
group, the Ike and Tina Turner Revue first brought
their irresistibly danceable blend of wailing blues,
raw soul, and hip-shaking rock 'n' roll to the attention of white audiences in the late 1960s and enjoyed world-wide fame in the 1970s. Miss Turner's
songs of love's sorrows and pleasures, delivered in
a voice that combines Otis Redding's husky break
and James Brown's growl with some of Aretha
Franklin's soaring cadences, went to the heart of
1960s sensibility; her volcanic and erotic stage performance, which has spawned would-be
"raunch-and-roll" imitators, was a definitive musical "happening." She broke with Ike Turner in 1976
and has since then toured on her own. Having im-
printed the genre for a generation of popular musicians, in her 1984 solo album *Private Dancer* Tina
Turner retains the passsionate vocal rhythms of an
authentic rock 'n' roller who, in the words of one
reviewer, "has come through the fire, cognizant in
the ways of the world, her spirit undefeated."

The daughter of a cotton plantation manager
and his wife, Tina Turner was born Anna Mae Bullock on November 25, 1940 in the country borough
of Nutbush, near Brownsville, Tennessee. (Her
year of birth is listed in some sources as early as
1938 and as late as 1941.) She has described the

borough's ambience in her own composition
"Nutbush City Limits" (1973): "Church house/Gin
house . . . Schoolhouse/Out-house . . . Just a
one-horse town . . . Better watch what you're putting down." In her large family even the young
children shared the field work, and Anna Mae
quickly learned to hate it. Displaying her musical
instinct precociously, as a schoolgirl she sang everything from ballads and operatic selections in
class talent shows, to gospel hymns in a Sanctified
Church choir and "the low-down dirty" blues—her
favorite even then—with rhythm bands at picnics.
"And I've always danced," Tina Turner told David
Thomas, as quoted in his article for the British publication *The Face* (January 1984). "I never had any
training. I just danced." She dreamed of one day
transcending the lot of poor rural blacks, as Cheryl
Lavin reported in a *Chicago Tribune* profile (January 30, 1983): "I had an image in my head of how
a star was—somebody with a star on the door and
a lot of chiffon dresses. I wanted that." She admitted to Miss Lavin that she did not like herself very
much as a child.

Following her parents' divorce when she was
eleven, Anna Mae Bullock moved in with her
grandmother. She and her sister Ailene joined
their mother in St. Louis after the grandmother
died in the mid-1950s, and the teen-age girls began
to frequent such local rhythm-and-blues night
spots as the Club Manhattan, where, in 1956, they
met Ike Turner and his band, the Kings of Rhythm.
After "about a year" of coaxing on her part, one
night she was allowed to take the microphone and
belt out a B. B. King blues number with the group.
Her soulful expressiveness was immediately apparent. "When Ike heard me," Carl Arrington
quotes Tina Turner as saying in an article for
People (December 7, 1981), "he said, 'My God!' He
couldn't believe that voice coming out of this frail
little body." Soon after, she joined the band for occasional engagements, using the name "Little
Anna." Meanwhile she worked days at a St. Louis
hospital.

Already a seasoned producer and performer
when he teamed up with young Anna Mae Bullock, the Mississippi-born Ike Turner had traveled
the South's black-music circuit with the Kings of
Rhythm for several years, sharing bills with seminal early blues artists like Johnny Ace, Howlin'
Wolf, and B. B. King. By all accounts, Turner's
combination of management ability—it is reported
that he formed his first band at age eleven—and
musical sense served him well during the ferment
in black music in the 1950s, when the electrified instruments and faster rhythms of urban black musicians were translating the rural blues sound into
the beat that would become rock 'n' roll. A "hot" regional band in those days, the Kings of Rhythm had
recorded at least one single, Jackie Brenston's
"Rocket 88" (1951), which was a "race record" hit
on black radio stations.

When the scheduled vocalist failed to appear for
a recording session with the Kings of Rhythm in
1959, Anna Mae Bullock filled in at the last mo-

ment. The resulting cut for the Sue record label, Ike Turner's "Fool in Love" (1960), sold 800,000 copies in the rhythm-and-blues market and remained on *Billboard's* Hot 100 chart for thirteen weeks. The group's transformation into its slicker, star-class form rapidly followed. Turner chose for his lead singer the name Tina, and later they married; a female dance-and-vocal backup trio, dubbed the Ikettes, joined the act; the instrumental section expanded to comprise trombone, trumpet, two saxophones, two guitars, drums, and organ; and thus, as the Ike and Tina Turner Revue, the troupe embarked on cross-country tours. With Ike Turner's musical composition and scoring adapted to Miss Turner's passionate, wailing delivery, and her own choreography designed to highlight her energetically seductive stage persona, the Revue won renown on the rhythm-and-blues circuit, showcasing the roots of rock 'n' roll, in the words of Irwin Stambler, with the "sounds of the ghetto, raucousness of low-down blues, plaintiveness of country blues, and a gospel fervor." Tina Turner's soul-drenched quaking, pleading, and shaking while she sang, as she once put it, "Baptist and blues" transformed the "chitlin'-belt" auditoriums and ghetto nightclubs that welcomed them into revival meetings flavored as much with a sexual as an evangelical message. Eighteen performances a week, for a reported fee of $450 per night, were not unusual for the ambitious Revue at that time.

The Turners, who continued to record for the Sue label, hit the rhythm-and-blues singles charts in 1961 with "It's Gonna Work Out Fine," "I Pity the Fool," and "I Idolize You" and the following year with "Poor Fool" and "Tra La La La La." Considered by the music industry to have great potential, the Revue produced several albums in the mid-1960s, at first for Warner Brothers and later for the Liberty label and its parent company, United Artists. The group's single recordings in the late 1960s, such as "I've Been Lovin' You Too Long," "Bold Soul Sister," and "The Hunter," were produced by Blue Thumb. By 1969, the Ike and Tina Turner Revue had fifteen albums and sixty singles to its credit.

Mainstream stardom in the United States long eluded the Ike and Tina Turner Revue because, as Ike Turner explained for an *Ebony* profile (May 1971), "The black radio stations kept telling [him], 'It's too pop,' and the white stations claimed it was 'too rhythm and blues.'" In Great Britain, however, the Revue's sound provoked considerable excitement, as was the case for a number of black performers in the mid-1960s. When the group's single "River Deep, Mountain High," produced by rock 'n' roll wizard Phil Spector and featuring, in the words of Jon Pareles, Tina Turner's "hurricane alto," was released by London Records in 1966, it jumped straight to the top of the British pop charts and held the number-one spot for many weeks. (Spector later called that cut his "masterpiece.") A stint as the opening act for the Rolling Stones, a preeminent British rock group of the period, on a European tour that year proved to be the turning

point for the Revue. "The whole world was changing in '66, remember?" Miss Turner observed to Michael T. Leech in an interview for *After Dark* (December 1971). "I knew the world was going to be different, and us too." During the long tour, the Ike and Tina Turner Revue purveyed its brand of overdrive rhythm-and-blues to wild acclaim, while its members gradually absorbed some of the techniques of white rock bands. By the time the group hit the United States, again with the Rolling Stones, later in the decade, it had evolved into the most explosive rock 'n' roll band white concertgoers had ever seen—"They didn't know what it was, but they liked it," Miss Turner has recalled—and Tina Turner was widely acknowledged to be the "grittiest, most sensual female soul singer around."

The Ike and Tina Turner Revue presented a concert act of seemingly spontaneous ecstasy. It was, in fact, meticulously rehearsed. After the band played several rhythm-and-blues numbers to warm up the house, Ike Turner, looking cool and gaunt with his helmet of slicked-down hair and wearing, typically, a double-breasted yellow-green suit, came onstage and picked up the bass line on his guitar. Joined by the provocatively strutting Ikettes, the Revue increased the musical tension until Tina Turner, in the shortest of miniskirts, pounced onstage, as one observer wrote, "in midscream with both legs pumping, hips grinding, long mane whirling, [with] her mouth wrapped around some of the sexiest sounds ever set to music." In such manner, she worked her way through rock and soul standards like the Beatles' "Help" and "With a Little Help from My Friends," the Rolling Stones' "Honky Tonk Woman," Aretha Franklin's "Respect," and Sly and the Family Stone's "I Want to Take You Higher." Concert reviewers competed to find words adequate to convey Miss Turner's kinetic, erotic performance, describing her as a "voodoo doctor's fetish object flung down hard" and a springing "tiger" whose face was "a mask of sensuality."

Miss Turner explained her style of musical interpretation in her introduction to the Revue's single "Proud Mary" (1970), which was first recorded by the group Creedence Clearwater Revival. "We never, ever, do *nothin'* nice and easy," she intones as the song begins. "So we're gonna do it nice—and *rough.*" That rough yet insistently melodic hard-rock sound took the Ike and Tina Turner Revue to engagements in Japan, Africa, and other spots around the world in the early 1970s, including some of the most prestigious concert halls and music festivals in the United States. Millions of rock 'n' roll devotees who failed to catch the Revue live were treated to Tina Turner's pseudo-orgasmic performance of the number "I've Been Lovin' You Too Long" in *Gimme Shelter* (Cinema V, 1971), the Maysles brothers' documentary film of the Rolling Stones' 1969 United States tour. Although none of the Revue's albums, such as *Workin' Together* (Liberty, 1970), *Blues Roots* (United Artists, 1972), *Nutbush City Limits* (UA, 1973), and *The Gospel According to Ike and Tina* (UA, 1974), reached the gold record mark, they were prized for their effervescent synthesis of major trends in black- and white-oriented popular music. In 1971 the Ike and Tina Turner Revue won a Grammy Award for best rhythm-and-blues vocal by a group for their recording of "Proud Mary."

Television appearances on late-night talk shows and variety programs hosted by Ed Sullivan, Pearl Bailey, Andy Williams, and others further confirmed the Turners' arrival as certified superstars. (That hard-won recognition from Middle America led one commentator to theorize that "the new consciousness may be upon us.") Ike and Tina Turner kept a sumptuous home, equipped with a recording studio and Ike Turner's personally designed furniture shaped like musical instruments, in a Los Angeles suburb, and they drove the most expensive cars. Some music critics suggested that the couple's conspicuous commercial success threatened to overwhelm the gutsy vitality of their music with "cellophane packaging," but the pair nevertheless commanded enormous respect from their colleagues in the rock music profession. Janis Joplin, for example, considered Tina Turner the best performer in the business, and Mick Jagger of the Rolling Stones credited her with teaching him how to dance on the concert stage.

Although Tina Turner was the visible and audible dynamo of the Revue's success, behind the scenes Ike Turner engineered every facet of the group's act, picking the songs, directing the band, producing the records, and managing the money. Miss Turner's earnings, it was said, were less a salary than an "allowance." His reputation was that of a brilliant but severe taskmaster, and, as Miss Turner has recalled, by the early 1970s their marriage was irreparably strained. Striking out on her own professionally, she released the solo albums Let Me Touch Your Mind (1972), Tina Turns the Country On (1974), and, following her much-praised appearance as the wild "Acid Queen" in the motion-picture rock-opera Tommy (Columbia, 1975), Acid Queen (United Artists, 1975).

Throughout the early 1970s, Miss Turner continued to tour with the Revue, but meanwhile her perspective on her career and her life had matured. She had learned the professional ropes from her husband, but then, as she explained to Cheryl Lavin, "There was no room to grow." Under Ike Turner's omnipresent direction, she had come to see herself as a "shadow." "I was living a life of death," she went on. "I didn't exist." She had been considering a split for some time when, in Dallas, Texas in July 1976, Turner physically beat her shortly after their arrival there for a concert date. Later that day she left the tour and Ike Turner and flew to Los Angeles with a ticket bought by a friend. She had only a few cents and a credit card in her pocket, but, she told Carl Arrington, "I felt proud. I felt strong. I felt like Martin Luther King."

In an interview with Marion Collings of the New York Daily News, (June 1, 1984) Tina Turner described the immediate aftermath of the breakup: "I stopped. I rented a house and second-hand furniture. . . . At night, I'd look at the stars in the sky instead of at concert lights. It was a year before I could even think of going back to work." Fending for herself for the first time in her life, she was slapped with lawsuits because she had walked off a nationwide tour, and she faced her husband's anger. The eventual divorce settlement in 1978 left her, she has claimed, with little to show except her "peace of mind."

Tina Turner rebuilt her career slowly, at first taking on advisers and producers who proved "disastrous." A 1978 solo album, Rough (United Artists), sparked little commercial or critical attention, and record companies interested in new wave or disco music deemed her material out-of-date. Miss Turner performed outside the country and, in the United States, concentrated on dates at hotels or small clubs, where she experimented with a slick new show that featured a five-piece band and two backup singers. "I never stopped touring," she pointed out to Carolyn Martin in an interview for Rockamerica's Videofile (July 1984), "but as far as the press were concerned it was 'Tina what? Tina who?'" When she appeared in New York City in early 1981 after a five-year absence, pop music critics acknowledged Tina Turner's rock 'n' roll credentials and the theatrical success of her "jungle Aphrodite" characterization, but some agreed with Stephen Holden that her "music suffer[ed] for the sake of that image." "[Miss Turner] pushes her powerful voice to a screeching frenzy that is a caricature . . . ," Holden wrote in his review for the New York Times (May 14, 1981). "The set has gusto but no subtlety."

Confidently impervious to any attempts to dismiss her and irrepressibly hard-working, Tina Turner was the special guest artist with the Rolling Stones on their sold-out United States tour in 1981. Young audiences for whom the Ike and Tina Turner Revue was a grand legend rediscovered her roiling musical intensity and up-front sexual appeal, laced with a knowing good humor. Other major concert bookings followed. Signing on new managers, Miss Turner developed a repertoire that adhered more closely to its blues-roots sound while incorporating synthesized and reggae-influenced music. Stephen Holden withdrew his reservations about Miss Turner's style when he reviewed her 1983 performance at the Ritz in New York City for the New York Times (January 30, 1983). "The material she picks," he wrote, "invariably supports [her pushing] her large coarse voice with its frayed edges close to its physical limits. . . . [The song] Proud Mary's central image of a great riverboat has become an exhilarating metaphor for Miss Turner's staying power, and her sprinting hard-rock version of it was magnificent." Her recent appearances have included an internationally televised show with pop-rocker Rod Stewart at the Los Angeles Forum in 1981; a record-breaking European tour in 1983–84; and special-guest billing with the singer Lionel Richie on his 1984 United States tour.

Tina Turner's LP Private Dancer (Capitol, 1984), headed solidly for a gold record as of late 1984, drew unanimous high marks from critics, who hailed the "startling scope," "scratchy, luscious sensitivity," and "lucid center inside her raspy coloratura" demonstrated in her diverse offerings. Produced by several contemporary British arrangers, among them Martyn Ware and Greg Walsh of Heaven 17, the album features her interpretation of David Bowie's future-shock ballad "1984," a tear-your-heart-out version of Ann Peebles' "I Can't Stand the Rain," and an upbeat rendering of Al Green's "Let's Stay Together." The last-named song, along with her "What's Love Got to Do With It?", was a number-one single hit for weeks in 1984. Stephen Holden, writing in the New York Times (August 26, 1984), judged Private Dancer, with its "innovative fusion of old-fashioned soul singing and new wave synth-pop," to be a "landmark . . . in the evolution of soul-pop music."

A lanky, curvaceously proportioned woman who proudly flaunts her "great legs," Tina Turner has a tawny gold complexion ("the same color as her voice," according to one interviewer), and a mobile, handsome face. When not on the road, she lives alone at her home in Sherman Oaks, California, where her frequent solitary pursuit—reading in occult subjects—belies her semi-manic stage image. "That's my act. That's not who I am. I consider myself a very balanced person," she has said. An adherent since about 1970 of Nichiren Shoshu Buddhism, she chants every day, and she credits that practice with making her "stronger" and revealing "the power of the self." The four sons she raised, Craig, Ike Jr., Michael, and Ronald, now live on their own. Among other projects Tina Turner is planning for the future is a movie role with Mel Gibson in a sequel to the Australian film The Road Warrior.

References: After Dark 4:31+ D '71 pors; Chicago Tribune XII p1+ Ja 30 '83 pors; Dial p31+ Jl 84 pors; Ebony 26:88+ My '71 pors, 37:66+ Je '82 pors; N Y Times II p22 Ag 26 '84 por; Newsweek 74:92+ N 3 '69 por, 104:76 S 10 '84 por; People 16:100+ D 7 '81 pors; Jahn, Michael. Rock (1973); Roxon, Lillian. Rock Encyclopedia (1971); Stambler, Irwin. Encyclopedia of Pop, Rock, and Soul (1974); Who's Who in America, 1982–83

Updike, John (Hoyer)

Mar. 18, 1932– Writer. Address: b. c/o Alfred A. Knopf Inc., 201 E. 50th St., New York City, N.Y. 10022; h. Beverly Farms, Mass. 01915

NOTE: This biography supersedes the article that appeared in Current Biography in 1966.

Best known as the author of Rabbit, Run (1960) and as a chronicler of suburban angst, John Updike has established himself as one of America's most eminent men of letters, a legatee of the tradition of Edmund Wilson. An extraordinarily prolific writer, Updike has produced eleven novels, nine volumes of short stories, four major poetry collections, and innumerable essays and book reviews. His coruscating prose style and penchant for detailing every aspect of his characters' lives—including their gonadal tribulations and sometimes sordid sexual adventures—have won him a large and faithful readership but have also irritated some reviewers who consider his work to be all dazzling surface and no substance. Undeterred by his critics, Updike still produces at least one book a year, and as two of his more recent novels—The Coup (1978) and The Witches of Eastwick (1984)—demonstrate, he has not yet reached the outer limits of what seems to be an inexhaustible talent.

John Hoyer Updike, the only child of Wesley Russell Updike, a high school mathematics teacher, and Linda Grace (Hoyer) Updike, was born on March 18, 1932 in Shillington, Pennsylvania, a community he would later use as his model for the fictional town of Olinger. His parents had lived in Shillington since his father lost his job as a tele-

phone-cable splicer early in the Depression, but in 1945, no longer able to afford their large home, the Updikes moved, with John's maternal grandparents, to a stone farmhouse eleven miles away.

As a child, John Updike suffered from hay fever, psoriasis, and a stammer. He took refuge in such private pleasures as drawing and writing. Although he once considered becoming a cartoonist like the New Yorker's James Thurber and Saul Steinberg, by the age of eighteen he was hoping to pursue a writing career. He has admitted that his mother's literary ambitions (her novel *Enchantment* was published by Houghton Mifflin in 1971) may have sparked his own literary aspirations, but another factor was his somewhat solitary childhood. "I'm sure," he explained to Helen Dudar in an interview for *Newsday* (November 28, 1978), "that my capacity to fantasize and to make coherent fantasies, to have the patience to sit down day after day and to whittle a fantasy out of paper, all that relates to being an only child." While attending Shillington High School from 1946 to 1950, he contributed regularly to its newspaper, "The Chatterbox," and submitted his work, with little success, to minor magazines as well as to the redoubtable *New Yorker*.

After graduating from high school, Updike was given a scholarship to attend Harvard College, where he majored in English, took a few art courses, and headed the staff of the *Harvard Lampoon*. In Cambridge, Updike met Mary Entwistle Pennington, a Radcliffe undergraduate, and they were married on June 26, 1953. The following year, he received both an A.B. degree, *summa cum laude*, and a one-year Knox fellowship to study painting at the Ruskin School of Drawing and Fine Arts at Oxford University. During that year in England, Mrs. E. B. White, an editor at the *New Yorker*, offered him a position at that magazine, which had begun to publish some of his light verse. He accepted, and returning to the United States with his family in 1955, he settled in Manhattan.

"Since boyhood," Updike once wrote, "I had wanted to live in New York. I had wanted to work for the magazine that I now did work for." But in spite of his initial contentment and the praise he earned for his light verse, his vignettes in the "Talk of the Town" section, and his short stories, he soon grew restless. "New York," he realized, "was not going to help me unpack my shadowy message." So while still contributing on a freelance basis to the *New Yorker*, in 1957 he moved to Ipswich, a small Massachusetts town near Boston, which provided a more congenial atmosphere for his writing.

Updike's first volume, *The Carpentered Hen and Other Tame Creatures*, a collection of fifty-five poems, most of which had appeared in the *New Yorker*, was published in 1958 by Harper and Row. (Knopf published most of his later books.) Anticipating the majority opinion, an advance reader for the Kirkus book service applauded Updike's "bent for word usage," "exercise of ideas, spontaneity, and a pleasant type of ingenuity," and especially recommended his witty verse reminiscent of Ogden Nash. But Donald J. Greiner in his book *The Other John Updike: Poems/Short Stories/Prose/Play* (Ohio Univ. Pr., 1981) has cautioned that the obvious humor "masks serious intent, and the reader does a double-take after his initial grin as he determines the point of attack." The sixty pieces in *Telephone Poles and Other Poems* (1963), his second poetry collection, evoked much of same response from reviewers, who warmly praised it; many years later, Donald J.

Greiner described it as "Updike's homage to the world in which small things are infinitely fine and the daily cycle is forever."

Updike again displayed his "Chekhovian flair for the rendering of the everyday event," as Evelyn Geller described it in the *Wilson Library Bulletin* (September 1961), in *The Same Door* (1959), a collection of sixteen short stories that originally appeared in the *New Yorker*. Although like other critics, A. C. Spectorsky, writing in the *Saturday Review* (August 22, 1959), was impressed by the "exciting brilliance" of the stories and their "lean and lapidary" prose, Richard H. Rupp voiced the opposition's view in a *Sewanee Review* article (Autumn 1967), in which he took Updike to task for his "restless, exhaustive exploration of minute physical detail"—quickly becoming an Updike trademark—that realistically depicted the characters' surroundings but failed to develop their "capacity to feel and make us feel."

Updike shifted his focus somewhat in *The Poorhouse Fair* (1959), his first novel. Centering on the annual one-day fair staged by the elderly residents of a local poorhouse, it explores the mounting tensions between those old people, who are carefully shut away from the mainstream of society except on that single day of the year, and Mr. Connor, the prefect of the home, whose utopian vision of a future free of want and suffering blinds him to the present needs of those in his care: a sense of dignity and of belonging. Interpreted by most critics as a thinly disguised attack on the welfare state, *The Poorhouse Fair* drew widely divergent responses: some reviewers admired his taut, carefully constructed prose, while others criticized his emotionally chilly style and self-conscious fascination with language at the expense of substance. Nevertheless, *The Poorhouse Fair* won the 1960 Rosenthal Foundation Award of the National Institute of Arts and Letters and established Updike as an exceptionally promising young man of letters.

Set in 1959 in the fictional town of Brewer, Pennsylvania, *Rabbit, Run* (1960), Updike's second novel, explores more deeply than his earlier works the vapid world of suburbia and the protracted adolescence of some male members of the American middle class. Harry ("Rabbit") Angstrom, a twenty-six-year-old husband and father, yearns for the excitement of his days as a high school basketball star and the meaning that his status as an athlete gave to his life. Propelled by fears of responsibility and aging, by his insignificant job, and by his unhappy marriage to the alcoholic Janice, who is pregnant with their second child, Rabbit runs away. He then has an affair with a young woman named Ruth, whom he also impregnates and abandons, but he fails to exorcise his anxiety and confusion. Yet Angstrom's vague sense of his own worth and of some intrinsic importance in life sustains him, even when his baby daughter drowns while being bathed by his drunken wife. The novel's clinically explicit sexual encounters repelled some reviewers, while others found his characters uninvolving and his story pointless. But David Boroff, writing in the *New York Times Book Review* (November 6, 1960), voiced a majority opinion when he called *Rabbit, Run* "a tender and discerning study of the desperate and the hungering in our midst."

An older and paunchier but still hungering Harry Angstrom reappears in *Rabbit Redux* (1971). Set in Brewer in 1969, it finds Rabbit back home and still besieged by problems: his own malaise, mirrored in the general unrest in the United States, and a still-shaky marriage that has been further weakened by his wife's infidelity. *Rabbit Redux* was panned by most critics, who considered its topicality intrusive and its technique heavy-handed.

John Updike more successfully assimilated current events into the latest installment in the series, *Rabbit Is Rich* (1981). He also transformed sex—a pervasive element in his work—from "a subject for anguished mulling" into the genuine "stuff of lives," as Roger Sale pointed out in the *New York Times Book Review* (September 27, 1981). Middleaged Rabbit, now reasonably content in his marriage and the proud manager of his deceased father-in-law's Toyota dealership, has finally come to terms with his daughter's accidental death and, more or less, with his own mortality. For *Rabbit Is Rich* Updike was honored in 1981 with the National Book Critics Circle Award, and in 1982 with the American Book Award and the Pulitzer Prize. Updike plans to write the fourth—and final—volume of his Angstrom cycle before the end of the 1980s.

Although the mediocre, rather bland Harry Angstrom, an *homme moyen sensuel*, seems to be the very personification of "middleness," the Rabbit trilogy transcends the simple fictional treatment of three decades of life in Middle America. Updike once remarked that his books grow out of the existence of "insolvable problems." Rabbit Angstrom, for instance, struggles to reconcile the irreconcilable: his own relentless "individual wants"—immortality, wealth, sexual gratification, unbounded freedom—and the constraints that society and his own human finiteness impose on him. In a comment that applies to the entire trilogy, Updike explained that *Rabbit, Run* is "about the bouncing, the oscillating back and forth between these two kinds of urgencies until, eventually, one just gets tired and wears out and dies, and that's the end of the problem." Some critics read theological meanings into Rabbit's quest for a solution to his dilemma, but in his *New York Times Book Review* article Roger Sale discerned another purpose. Roughly Updike's age and a lifetime resident of a fictionalized Shillington, Rabbit Angstrom could be the author's *doppelgänger*, "the one who didn't leave Shillington, go to Harvard, become a dazzling novelist." In an interview with Curt Suplee for the *Washington Post* (September 27, 1981) Updike admitted that "Harry was invented as sort of a real alter-ego." In light of that, the trilogy might be Updike's version of Henry James's "The Jolly Corner": an exploration of what might have been.

Originally conceived as a "contrasting companion" to *Rabbit, Run*, *The Centaur* (1963), set in Pennsylvania in the 1940s, infuses the story of a father and son relationship with mythological overtones. George Caldwell, an unassuming teacher at Olinger High School, suggests the wise centaur Chiron, an instructor of heroes, and his teenage son Peter resembles Prometheus, to whom Chiron surrendered his immortality in order to escape the pain of a wound. Through George Caldwell's dying, Peter learns to appreciate the worth of his father's life and values, but on yet another level the book is another "portrait of the artist as a young man." Some critics found its mythology obtrusive, but most rated *The Centaur* highly, and when the book won the National Book Award for fiction the citation praised it as "a courageous and brilliant account of a conflict in gifts between an inarticulate American father and his highly articulate son."

Cherished personal experiences permeate *The Centaur*, which Updike has described as "a monument, however inadequate," to his father. The nineteen short stories in *Pigeon Feathers* (1962) also drew on autobiographical elements—Updike's Pennsylvania boyhood, his marriage, and his parenthood—but were less hospitably received than *The Centaur*. Expressing the critical consensus in the *New Republic* (May 14, 1962), J. M. Edelstein complained that "stunning and moving as these stories are, they leave me troubled. My impressions, though of beauty, of real ideas, and of a major talent, are also of things unsaid and of a sureness that smacks of slickness." Despite similar criticisms of his "flashy" and self-conscious prose style, *Of the Farm* (1965), the last volume in that informal chronicle of his early life, was widely acclaimed. In it, Joey Robinson brings his new wife and stepson to visit his widowed mother, a strong-willed woman (reminiscent of Linda Updike) who still lives on the farm where he grew up. Writing in the *New York Times Book Review* (November 14, 1965), Peter Buitenhuis had special praise for Updike's insightful and carefully rendered portrayal of the tensions among the various characters and his refusal to solve their problems neatly at the end. "This novel," he concluded, "is, very clearly and very completely, a small masterpiece."

With *Couples* (1968), Updike charted what for him was new territory as he delineated the licentiousness of ten couples in the Boston suburb of Tarbox (a town modeled after Ipswich), and the complications and implications of life in America's "post-Pill paradise." A few reviewers dismissed it as merely a steamy "sex novel," and R. F. Clayton warned in *Library Journal* (March 15, 1968) that some readers would "gag with disgust at the excruciatingly detailed varieties of sexual play" depicted in the novel. Nevertheless, like other critics, Clayton recommended *Couples* as a trenchant metaphorical treatment of "the moral disease which is eating at the soft vitals of the American middle class." Paula and Nick Backscheider added in *Modern Fiction Studies* (Spring 1974) that for Piet Hanema and the other characters sex is, though subconsciously, a search for meaning or God and a means of denying, at least temporarily, their ever growing fear of their own mortality.

Despite his impressive literary output, awards, and complimentary reviews, Updike felt that the literary establishment had shunted him aside in favor of such prominent Jewish writers as Saul Bellow, Bernard Malamud, Philip Roth, and J. D. Salinger. "Out of that unease," he explained to Paul Gray in a *Time* (October 18, 1982) cover story on him, "I created Henry Bech to show that I was really a Jewish writer also." In the two short story collections *Bech: A Book* (1970) and *Bech is Back* (1982), Henry Bech, the antithesis of his productive, athletic, WASP creator, narrates his own rise from a once successful writer suffering from a creative block of thirteen years' duration to the celebrity author of a new best-seller, and his personal, professional, and sexual misadventures along the way. Viewed as self-indulgent and boring by some, the stories were warmly received by most reviewers, and Updike continued his *jeu d'esprit* in several articles in which he is "interviewed" by Bech himself.

With the riotous *A Month of Sundays* (1975), Updike returned to his scrutiny of the "post-Pill paradise." Through the Reverend Thomas Marshfield's narrative of his adulterous adventures, recorded during a month's enforced retreat at a rest home, Updike created, according to Rosemary Dinnage in the London *Times Literary Supplement* (July 4, 1975), "a hilariously solemn theological farce, knotted with puns, exploding with allusions, reverberating with camp blasphemies." *Marry Me: A Romance* (1976) is a more serious treatment of adultery, in which the two principles—Jerry Conant and Sally Mathias—are torn between their desire to marry and their unwillingness to hurt their present spouses and families. Most critics were dissatisfied with the novel, but in the *Wall Street Journal* (December 7, 1976) Edmund Fuller described it as "poignantly amusing, keenly observant, in capturing the terrible sadnesses in marriages in crisis."

Those "terrible sadnesses" as well as some joys form the core of *Too Far to Go: The Maples Stories* (Fawcett, 1979), a collection of seventeen stories mostly culled from the *New Yorker*. It chronicles the slow dissolution of Joan and Richard Maple's marriage, a union that, not surprisingly, closely resembles that of the Updikes. The Maples, too, moved from New York to a town near Boston, had four children, suffered through repeated quarrels and reconciliations, and ended two decades of marriage with an amicable divorce. (Mary and John Updike were divorced in 1977.) "They are the most civilized stories imaginable," Paul Theroux commented in the *New York Times Book Review* (April 8, 1979), "and because of this the most tender." Updike's other major short story collections are *The Music School* (1966), *Museums and Women* (1972), and *Problems and Other Stories* (1979).

Inspired by his 1973 Fulbright lectureship in Africa, *The Coup* (1978) represented a radical departure in subject matter and setting from the typical Updike novel. Colonel Hakim Félix Ellelloû, the American-educated black leader of the African nation of Kush, is the protagonist and narrator of the novel, which relates his struggle to hold onto his power in his drought-stricken land and to understand himself. Although comic in tone, *The Coup* also derides the often misguided attempts by the United States government to win over emerging nations through various forms of aid. Like many of his colleagues, Robert Towers was disappointed by Updike's caricatures of the Americans and by "the narcissistic, self-intoxicating element" in his prose style, but in the *New York Times Book Review* (December 10, 1978) he hailed Ellelloû as "an extraordinary tour-de-force of a character" and *The Coup* as, finally, "a rich, surprising, and often funny novel."

Updike again broke new ground in *The Witches of Eastwick* (1984) by relating his story from a feminine perspective. Its three central characters, all liberated women, discover that they have acquired magical powers after divorcing their husbands. Their cosy little coven is disrupted when the satanic Darryl Van Horne seduces the three witches and then betrays them by marrying a younger woman. Their spells, at first more impish than evil, then take a decidedly malevolent turn before they accept their defeat and conjure up new husbands to comfort them. Interpreted by some as an antifeminist tract and panned by Jonathan Yardley in the *Washington Post* (May 13, 1984) as "mere cleverness and contrivance," the novel nevertheless beguiled most critics. Despite some reservations, Paul Gray contended in *Time* (May 7, 1984) that it "manifests most of Updike's virtues; it is witty, ironic, engrossing and punctuated by transports of spectacular prose."

In spite of his successes as a novelist and short story writer, Updike has not restricted himself to those genres. In *Midpoint* (1969) and *Tossing and Turning* (1977), two favorably reviewed books of poetry, he deals with both a wide range of personal experiences and the more abstract topics of love, death, and the sexual revolution. He has also written essays, book reviews, sketches, and speeches, many of which were reprinted in *Assorted Prose* (1965) and *Picked-Up Pieces* (1975). *Hugging the Shore* (1983), his most recent collection of prose, generated virtually unanimous praise for the luster of his style and awe at the range and depth of his analyses. In the *Christian Science Monitor* (October 3, 1983), Bruce Allen wrote that "there cannot be serious disagreement over [Updike's] emergent status as one of our finest literary critics. *Hugging the Shore* bristles with erudition, energy, and (quietly asserted) high seriousness; it is also one of the year's most entertaining books." The author's other works include several children's books and *Buchanan Dying*, an unsuccessful closet drama based on the life of President James Buchanan that was published in 1974 and produced in Lancaster, Pennsylvania two years later.

John Updike now lives and works in a large seaside home about twenty-five miles north of Boston. His many honors include membership in the

American Academy of Arts and Sciences. He has four children from his first marriage: Elizabeth, David, Michael, and Miranda. On September 30, 1977 he married Martha R. Bernhard. Reasonably content with his new life, he acknowledged in the *Time* magazine cover story: "I've had a generous share of the good things, money, prizes. I lack for nothing. What I would like to do in the time I have left is deliver my best self."

References: *N Y Times Mag p60+ D 10 '78 pors; Newsday A p4+ N 28 '78 por; Time 120:72+ O 18 '82 pors; Washington Post F p1+ S 27 '81 por; Contemporary Authors new rev vol 4 (1981); International Who's Who, 1984–85; Who's Who in America, 1984–85*

Vadim, Roger

(vä-dēm′ ro-zhā′)

Jan. 26, 1928– French motion picture director; scenarist. Address: b. c/o Avco Embassy Pictures Corp., 956 Seward St., Los Angeles, Calif. 90038

The controversial French filmmaker Roger Vadim, while lauded by many cinéastes for his technical craftsmanship, striking color imagery, and decorative elegance, is dismissed by some as a superficial voyeur in his own glossy seraglio. Vadim, however, has secured for himself a place in cinema history that even his severest critics cannot gainsay: with his first, spectacular directorial effort, *Et Dieux créa la Femme/ And God Created Woman* (1956), "the free story of a free girl," he sexually liberated the cinema, and the honesty and great international success of the film opened the way for the "new

wave" in French filmmaking. It was in *Et Dieu créa la Femme* that Vadim transformed his first wife, Brigitte Bardot, into the world's most famous "sex kitten," and in such subsequent films as *Les Liaisons dangereuses, La Ronde,* and *Barbarella* he made the rest of his succession of wives (Annette Stroyberg and Jane Fonda) and lovers (including Catherine Deneuve) into sex symbols. His pioneering screen erotica, while anti-puritanical and anti-hypocritical, was stylistically mannered, delicate, and essentially romantic, and it seems tame in comparison with much of the sex-oriented fare that has come in recent years through the floodgates he helped to open. Vadim found "pleasure" in battling the censors, but now that the battle is won and the enemy routed, the resultant pornography "saddens" him with its lack of "taste and personal approach," and he says he may turn his hand away from sexual themes, to science fiction, which has always interested him.

Roger Vadim is the professional name of Roger Vadim Plemiannikov. He was born at 83 Rue du Cardinale-Lemoine on Montagne Sainte-Geneviève in Paris, France at ten o'clock on the evening of January 26, 1928. His father was Igor Plemiannikov, a White Russian émigré who became a French citizen and a vice-consul in the French foreign service. His mother was Marie-Antoinette Plemiannikov, a French photographer. He and his younger sister, Hélène, spent their earliest years in consulates in Poland, Egypt, and Turkey (where they were briefly kidnaped by anti-French militants) and in a house in the Savoy Alps.

It was at the breakfast table in the Plemiannikovs' Alpine home one morning in July 1937 that Vadim began "to pay for all the unearned happiness [he] had enjoyed since the cradle." In his autobiography, *Memoirs du diable* (Editions Stock, 1975; translated as *Memoirs of the Devil,* Harcourt Brace Jovanovich, 1977), he recounts how his father, "so young and so kind," suffered cardiac arrest, slumping forward, "his face falling into his bowl of coffee" and becoming "sheet-white." His sister "burst out laughing," but he "knew from the very first instant . . . that it was over." "I aged more in that instant than I have ever aged since."

Because Igor Plemiannikov had forgotten to pay the last installment on his life insurance policy, his survivors were reduced from "a privileged life" to living on Marie-Antoinette Plemiannikov's pension, "a third of the wages of a post office clerk." They became hand-to-mouth nomads, trekking about France, often on foot, seeking refuge—never very successfully—with relatives, doing migrant labor, and, in the case of the children, getting piecemeal schooling. The five years of German occupation during World War II were "a brutal experience" for Vadim, but, "being a child . . . not conditioned by . . . the habits of peacetime," he was less affected by the "fear, hunger, and omnipresent death" than by a sense of "passionate adventure."

In 1943 the Plemiannikovs moved back to the Alps, where the mother rented a farmhouse in the ski resort town of Col des Gets at a modest price and turned it into a hostel. She did so for two reasons. One was to obtain extra ration vouchers to help feed her family, which had been expanded to include an adopted younger son, Jessie. The other was to provide a refuge for Jews, fugitive members of the Resistance, and people escaping forced labor in Germany. The first outlaw to find sanctuary with the Plemiannikovs was Gérald Hanning, an architect and close colleague of Le Corbusier, wanted by the occupation authorities as a suspected agent for British intelligence. Madame Plemiannikov and Hanning, ten years her junior, fell in love and were married in the Gets town hall on December 12, 1943. Vadim found in his stepfather "a good companion and teacher," one who introduced him to avant-garde architecture, town planning, and art. Above all, he taught him the lesson that would imbue all of his work in film: "That it was a weakness to take oneself too seriously, but a sign of strength to take what one was doing seriously." Many of the other fugitives were transients, mostly Jews, whom Vadim, an excellent skier, would escort across the mountains into Switzerland under cover of night.

When the Nazis and the Vichy militiamen moved into Col de Gets for the savage "Sunday of reprisals" in 1944, the Plemiannikov-Hannings, alerted by local gendarmes, fled, first to Grenoble, where Le Corbusier arranged lodging for them, and finally to Paris. They arrived in the French capital in time to witness the arrival of General Leclerc's tanks, the vanguard of the American and Free French forces that liberated the city, turning the streets, in Vadim's description, into "a great exuberant pageant in which all Parisians took part, wearing their joy like a costume . . . giddy with wine and freedom."

Wise beyond his years, Vadim came of age sexually and artistically during the intoxicating summer of liberation and the heady postwar years, "the hour of hope" following five years of "suffocation." He captured the exhilaration of that time in his transparently autobiographical novel The Hungry Angel (Atheneum, 1983), about a youth in a hurry to begin a new life. The reviewer for Publishers Weekly (September 9, 1983) described the novel as "sensitive, at times touching, and at times quite funny."

Abandoning early plans to follow in his father's diplomatic footsteps, Vadim enrolled in Charles Dullin's drama school at the Théâtre Sarah Bernhardt in Paris when he was sixteen. "I think it was his mother's idea that he should become an actor," Annette Stroyberg once told a reporter. "He was so bad." Through his sister, who was working as an extra on Petrus, Vadim met the director of that film, Marc Allégret. He served his apprenticeship in filmmaking as an assistant to and scenarist for Allégret, at the Francoeur Studios for nine years beginning in 1947. Allégret introduced him to the intellectual elite of Saint-Germain-des-Près, including Colette, Jean Genet, and André Gide (who nicknamed him "Shambles").

One day in 1949 Marc Allégret noticed a photograph in Elle, the women's magazine, of Brigitte Bardot, the sixteen-year-old daughter of petit bourgeois parents, presented as an example of beautiful French young womanhood. At Allégret's suggestion, Vadim met the Bardots and maneuvered Brigitte into her motion-picture career. After he complied with the demands of her parents that he convert to Roman Catholicism (he had been raised Orthodox) and get a respectable job (he became a journalist with the magazine Paris Match, briefly), he and Miss Bardot were married in December 1952.

While writing dialogue for several unspectacular motion pictures that Mlle. Bardot made for Allégret, Vadim was preparing for his coup—the molding of his wife into "the unattainable dream of every married man." That blow was struck with Et Dieu créa la Femme (1956), the story of one Juliette (Mlle. Bardot), a wanton Riviera beach nymph, directed by Vadim, produced by Raoul J. Lévy, and cowritten by the two. Shot on location in Saint-Tropez in Cinemascope and luscious Eastman color pastels, the movie single-mindedly showcased the bikini-clad charms of its provocative heroine as she perambulated from the bed of her husband, Michel (Jean-Louis Tintignant), to that of her brother-in-law, Antoine (Christian Marquand), and back again.

In 1957 Et Dieu créa la Femme was released in English-speaking countries by Kingsley International under the title And God Created Woman, with the promotional trail line, "But the devil gave shape to Bardot." Primed by the free advance publicity provided by French censors, the film was critically controversial but a box-office blockbuster internationally, especially in the United States. It opened the way for the nouvelle vague not only by its commercial success outside of France but also by its erotic frankness, a departure from the stagnant "boulevard" tradition. That tradition offered what François Truffaut has described as "cinematographic lies about love," trivializing it as smirking comedy or farce so as not to embarrass the consciences of secretly prurient audiences or disguising it as medical, legal, or social "case histories." "All one has to do to save appearances and throw the idiotic censors off the track is to show someone in a white tunic in front of a hospital," Truffaut wrote in reviewing Et Dieu créa la Femme shortly after its release. "Vadim didn't want to hide behind such hypocritical procedures; he bet on realism and life, with no cynicism or provocation, and he won. . . . The film is not perfect but Brigitte Bardot is magnificent; for the first time she is completely herself. . . . She is directed affectionately, like a pet animal, as Jean Renoir directed Catherine Hessling in Nana. There is no vulgarity, no failure of taste. . . . Et Dieu créa la Femme, an intimate film, a notebook film, reveals a new French director who is more personal than Boisrond, Boisol, Carbonnaux, and Joffé—and more gifted." Vadim's one major defect was "to remove himself from the carnal aspect in favor of an insidious, hence less pure eroticism: a show of panties, positions composed for the camera, a sea-drenched dress, the heroine's anti-social aggressiveness, and so on."

The scandal that hovered over *Et Dieu créa la Femme* in the late 1950s is difficult to understand in light of the pornography that has since rushed through the cinematic floodgates that its eroticism helped to open. "It was not because Bardot was naked or shown making love (she wasn't), but because of the attitude she portrayed," Vadim told Suzanne Lowry in an interview for the *Guardian* (September 17, 1976). "It was the first time on the screen that a woman was shown as really free on a sexual level, with none of the guilt attached to nudity or carnal pleasure. It was the same kind of freedom a boy might have. This disturbed some people."

The second film Vadim directed was a thriller set in Venice in winter, *Sait-on Jamais* (1957), released in English under two titles, *No Sun in Venice* and *When the Devil Drives*. Armand Thirard, the photography director of *Et Dieu créa la Femme*, again contributed to what Roy Armes in *The Personal Style* (1966), the second volume of his *French Cinema Since 1946*, called Vadim's "considerable technical mastery." Armes described Vadim's handling of the plot as "limp . . . in contrast to the sex scenes," which featured Françoise Arnoul.

In an interview with Kathleen Halton for the *Washington Post* (December 14, 1964), Vadim said he thought his first two films were "modern . . . a little in advance." "After that I didn't have any ideas of my own, so I used other people's. One or two of those films were interesting, the others were not." One of the failures was *Les Bijoutiers du Clair de Lune/The Night Heaven Fell* (1958), a Bardot vehicle based on Albert Visalie's novel. *Les Liaisons dangereuses* (1959), an updating of Pierre Choderlos de Laclos' shocking 1782 novel about a depraved couple (Gérard Philipe and Jeanne Moreau) who get their comeuppance, was an enormous *succès de scandale*, thanks partly to censorship problems over nude scenes by Vadim's second wife, Annette Stroyberg. (Vadim and Bardot had been divorced in December 1957.)

Miss Stroyberg played an unlikely, placid vampire in *Et Mourir de Plaisir/Blood and Roses* (1960) —an arty, elegant fantasy loosely based on Sheridan Le Fanu's novel *Carmilla*—a film distinguished by the color photography of Claude Renoir. At the request of Brigitte Bardot, who starred as a cover girl in love with her photographer in *La Bride sur le Cou/Please Not Now* (1961), Vadim completed the directing of that film, which had been begun by Jean Aurel. The following year he contributed the episode "L'Orgeuil"/"Pride" to *Les Sept Péchés Capitaux/Seven Capital Sins*. *Le Repos de Guerrier/Love on a Pillow* (1963), another Bardot vehicle, was an unsuccessful attempt to recoup the personal style of *Et Dieu créa la Femme*.

Vadim and Miss Stroyberg were divorced in 1961. Catherine Deneuve, Vadim's third "fiancee" (but never his wife) made her film debut in *Le Vice et la Vertu/Vice and Virtue* (1963), a lurid adaptation of the Marquis de Sade's *Justine*, set in a Nazi brothel in occupied France. *Château en Suède* (1964), adapted from Françoise Sagan's stage comedy, was an attempt at zaniness about as successful as the English translation of its title: *Nutty, Naughty Chateau*. "He [Vadim] is surrounded by yes-men and has no time to cultivate his intelligence," Jacques Doniol-Valcroze observed to Kathleen Halton in 1964. "His talent as a designer is shown in *Château en Suède*, but in my opinion this decorative talent is all that's left."

A new stage in Vadim's career coincided with his association with the American actress Jane Fonda, whom he met in 1963 and married in 1965 and from whom he was divorced in 1970. Many critics regarded as ill-advised Vadim's first vehicle for his third wife, *La Ronde* (1964), a remake of Max Ophuls' classic, which they found "leaden" and "tedious" despite a script by Jean Anouilh and photography by Henri Decaë. To Roy Armes, Vadim's "glossy" way of dealing with his sexual themes was epitomized in the final scene of *La Ronde*: "In a shadowy garden lit by strategically placed candles, a beautiful blonde in a long white evening dress dances alone to the strains of a lush romantic melody, played by an invisible orchestra."

In *La Curée/The Game Is Over* (1966), Vadim's free adaptation of Émile Zola's novel, Miss Fonda, playing the young bride of an aging billionaire widower, seduces her stepson—to her ruin. Miss Fonda came to feel that Vadim was pushing her screen image as a sex symbol to the point of degradation, and the last straw seems to have been his casting of her as the space maiden who drives even machines mad with lust in the kinky science-fiction burlesque *Barbarella*. The movie was an international box-office success, and many critics loved it, but it probably contributed to the dismantling of the Vadim-Fonda ménage, in 1971. Before leaving Vadim, Miss Fonda, with her brother, Peter, played in "Metzengerstein," Vadim's contribution to *Spirits of the Dead*, an Edgar Allan Poe trilogy released by American International in 1969.

During the waning period of their marriage, Vadim and Miss Fonda moved to California. There, Vadim made for Metro-Goldwyn-Mayer the satirical black comedy–mystery *Pretty Maids All in a Row* (1971), in which Rock Hudson was cast against type, as a solid, charming American high school guidance counselor who regretfully murders the girl students he seduces when they threaten to expose him. Some critics compared the film favorably to Noel Black's *Pretty Poison* (1968). Others found it "disgusting," "embarrassingly unfunny," and "silly but enjoyable."

Brigitte Bardot and Vadim reunited professionally for the making of *Si Don Juan Etait une Femme/If Don Juan Were a Woman* (1973), the plot of which was implicit in the title, given a Lesbian twist. Vadim's *Night Games*, made in the United States and released by Avco Embassy Pictures in 1981, starred newcomer Cindy Pickett as a Bel Air, California housewife who does not sleep with her husband because she was once raped and the memory of the assault prevents her from having sex with "ordinary men." A male house guest solves her problem by appearing for secret evening trysts disguised as a large bird. In *La Jeune Fille Assassinée/Charlotte* (1975), written by Vadim on the basis of an actual case he was familiar with, he himself played the role of a writer researching the brutal murder of a beautiful young model (Sirpa Lane), the daughter of an influential Parisian. When his investigation reveals, in flashbacks, that the murder was an act mutually agreed upon beforehand by two game-playing perverts, a nymphomaniac and a necrophiliac (the latter a German with high family connections), he decides to drop his project.

Since his divorce from Jane Fonda, Vadim has had two romantic liaisons, the first with Catherine Schneider, a French heiress, and the second with Ann Biderman, a Hollywood screenwriter. He has four children, a daughter each by Annette Stroyberg and Jane Fonda, and a son each by Catherine Deneuve and Catherine Schneider. A devoted father, he shares custody of his children. As a husband and lover, he has been careful never to indulge in verbal acrimony, because "you never forget ugly words," and he remains on amicable terms with his ex-partners. Afraid ever since childhood of being alone, and expecially of sleeping alone, he makes sure that his abodes swarm with guests. When friends are sick or in trouble, he is loyally at their side.

Roger Vadim is tall, sinewy, and still rather slim, despite an incipient double chin. His dark hair is graying and thinning, his hazel eyes are nearsighted, and his clothes are either elegant or studiedly informal. Confessing that he is "shy, but trained not to show it" and "not liberated," the nervously restless, chain-smoking Vadim projects a vulnerability that enhances his natural charm.

A leftist, Vadim was the one—he says—who "taught Jane [Fonda]" her politics, although she "went too far." He chose to make films about sex rather than politics partly because the censorship in France will let you "go further" with the former than the latter. According to his friend Christian Marquand, Vadim is "always escaping . . . always trying to recover his childhood, which he makes the subject matter of his movies." Other friends say that the "psychic powers" he discovered in himself as a child "still frighten him" and that the fright contributes to his escape into such vigorous recreations as water skiing, auto racing, and boating. Among his sedentary recreations is the painting of surrealistic pictures inspired by his dreams. He speaks Turkish and Russian as well as fluent French and English. Having what he calls "a Russian sense of time," he carries through life's crises the thought, "If the moment is wrong, time will right it." Vadim currently lives with Ann Biderman in Santa Monica, California.

References: *Guardian* p9 Ap 7 '73 por, p9 S 17 '76 por; *N Y Times* p 11 S 6 '70 por; *Washington Post* C p1+ Jl 19 '75 por; Thomson, David. *A Biographical Dictionary of Film* (1976); Vadim, Roger. *Memoirs of the Devil* (1976)

Vogel, Hans-Jochen

(fō´gəl hans yô´кən)

Feb. 3, 1926– West German political leader. Address: b. c/o Bundeshaus, 5300 Bonn 1, Federal Republic of Germany

After being in power for some thirteen years, the Social Democratic party of the Federal Republic of Germany was defeated in October 1982 by a vote of no confidence that ended the chancellorship of Helmut Schmidt. The man chosen to pick up the party's standard was Hans-Jochen Vogel, who had served with distinction as chief mayor of Munich and later as federal minister of housing and minister of justice, and whose brief tenure as governing mayor of West Berlin in 1981 helped to bring some measure of stability to that beleaguered city. Originally identified with the right wing of the Social Democratic party, he eventually acquired a reputation as a mediator and conciliator among the party's divergent elements. Although in the national elections of March 6, 1983 Vogel did not succeed in his efforts to defeat the incumbent Christian Democratic chancellor, Helmut Kohl, he was regarded by many observers as the best hope for restoring the morale of the Social Democratic party in his role as leader of the opposition in the Bundestag.

Hans-Jochen Vogel was born on February 3, 1926 in the city of Göttingen in Lower Saxony, where his father, Dr. Hermann Vogel, was a university lecturer in the agrarian sciences. His mother seems to have been the major influence on his life and that of his younger brother, Bernhard Vogel—who in 1976 succeeded Helmut Kohl as the Christian Democratic minister president of the state of Rhineland-Palatinate. An assertive woman, she so inspired her sons to achieve excellence in their studies that as a gymnasium student in Göttingen and Giessen, Hans-Jochen Vogel usually headed his class. As was mandatory under the Nazi regime, Vogel joined the Hitler Youth in his teens. Inducted into the German army in 1943, he served as a noncommissioned officer in Italy but was wounded in a battle near Bologna and taken prisoner.

After the war, Vogel was briefly employed as a transport worker until the reopening of the German universities in 1946 enabled him to study law at Marburg and Munich. In 1948 he passed his preliminary law examination, and in January 1949 he became a Referendar, or junior barrister, in the Bavarian town of Miesbach. Meanwhile, as a student he had attended meetings of the various political parties that had sprung up in postwar Germany without being particularly impressed by any of them. Then, in the summer of 1949, he heard Kurt Schumacher and other Social Democratic leaders speak at Rosenheim and was so inspired by their ideas of social reform within a democratic framework that in 1950 he became a member of the Social Democratic party.

Vogel qualified, magna cum laude, in 1950 for his doctor of jurisprudence degree with a dissertation dealing with penal law involved in resistance to government authority. The following year he completed his final Bavarian state law examination, in first place among 374 candidates. From February 1952 until 1954 he was assessor, or legal assistant, in the Bavarian ministry of justice, earning the title of Regierungsrat, or government counsel. After serving in 1954–55 as Amtsgerichtsrat, or district court counsel, in Traunstein, Vogel was chosen by Bavaria's Social Democratic minister president, Wilhelm Hoegner, to join the staff of the Bavarian state chancellery. Assigned the task of revising and updating some eighty volumes of the obsolescent Bavarian civil code, he succeeded in reducing them to five volumes. Although he was invited by Willy Brandt, then the mayor of West Berlin, to join his administration, Vogel decided instead to run as a candidate for the Munich city council, and after his election in May 1958 he became head of its legal section.

In October 1959 Vogel was chosen by a Social Democratic conference of delegates as candidate in the forthcoming Bavarian local elections to succeed Thomas Wimmer, the retiring Oberbürgermeister, or chief mayor, of Munich. Elected on March 27, 1960 with 64.3 percent of the vote, he became, at thirty-four, the youngest chief mayor of a major European city at the time. Aware of the "crisis of the big cities," which he viewed as a "human problem of the first order," Vogel soon became one of West Germany's best-known public officials and a leading spokesman for the needs and aspirations of its urban centers. As chief executive of West Germany's third-largest city, he concentrated his efforts on improving the quality of life of Munich's more than one million residents. Among other projects, Vogel promoted the construction of some 400 kilometers of new city streets, 175,000 residential apartments, a modern underground mass-transit system, and a pedestrian mall extending over several blocks near the civic center. In April 1965 he visited Rome, where he convinced officials of the International Olympics Committee to designate Munich as the site of the 1972 Olympic games. His popularity during his first term as chief mayor was evidenced by the fact that in March 1966 he was reelected for a second six-year term by 77.9 percent of Munich's voters.

During the second half of his tenure as Munich's chief mayor, Vogel devoted much of his energy to preparations for the 1972 Olympics along with a vast urban renewal project that was badly needed to cope with the city's annual population growth of some 40,000 people. Subsidized by the West German federal and Bavarian state governments and by fund-raising enterprises, the construction of the Olympic games complex required the city's taxpayers to spend only a fraction of the cost, and in Vogel's view, its benefits gave Munich a head start of some twenty years in coping with its problems. "The city's investment has turned a municipal wasteland into a permanent recreation area," Vogel told John M. Goshko of the Washington Post (August 13, 1972).

In the early 1970s Vogel came more and more into conflict with the left wing of the badly divided Bavarian Social Democratic party organization, especially with its Young Socialist faction, and he warned of what he saw as a process of erosion within the party. In his opinion, the left failed to provide answers for the pressing demands of the day and would, in the long run, hinder the party in its attempts to appeal to voters. Criticized by fellow party members for his alleged authoritarianism and self-righteousness, he abandoned plans to run for a third term as Munich's chief mayor, but despite strong opposition, he was elected chairman of the Bavarian Social Democratic party organization for a five-year term in May 1972.

On expiration of his mayoral term in June 1972, shortly before the opening of the Olympics, Vogel—who had been a member of the federal executive of the Social Democratic party since 1970—moved to Bonn, where he was named to the party's presidium in August. Elected to the federal Bundestag in November 1972, he was appointed the following month to the post of minister of regional planning, housing, and urban development in Chancellor Willy Brandt's coalition cabinet of Social Democrats and Free Democrats. Applying the expertise he had gained as chief mayor of Munich and as president of the Standing Conference of

Town Councils, he campaigned for reforms in real estate laws with the aim of improving living conditions for city dwellers and small homeowners while curbing professional land speculators. Determined to have enough funds from tax revenues available for his ministry's budget, Vogel occasionally clashed with Finance Minister Helmut Schmidt, the "strong man" in the Brandt cabinet.

After the resignation of Willy Brandt in May 1974, Helmut Schmidt, the new chancellor, appointed Vogel to the post of minister of justice. In that post, Vogel promoted, among other measures, liberalization of legislation concerning divorce and abortion, successfully campaigned to remove the statute of limitations for the prosecution of Nazi war criminals, took action to curb resurgent Nazi activity, and won praise for his firm but judicious handling of outbreaks of extreme leftist terrorism in the late 1970s. Within the Social Democratic party organization, Vogel gradually made his peace with the left wing, and as a member of the party's commission on fundamental principles, he acquired a solid understanding of Social Democratic history and theory. By 1980 Vogel was viewed as a likely successor to Schmidt in the chancellorship.

When in January 1981 a financial scandal in West Berlin forced its governing mayor, Dietrich Stobbe, and his Social Democratic–Free Democratic coalition Senate to resign, Vogel was chosen by Social Democratic leaders in Bonn to step in and try to repair the damage to the party's reputation. The scandal, involving the loss of some $57 million in guaranteed credits extended by the city to a construction firm that went bankrupt, was attributed to negligence and possible collusion on the part of some of Stobbe's top aides. Vogel resigned as justice minister from the Bonn cabinet on January 22, 1981 to accept the challenge in Berlin because, in his words, he recognized "the city's importance to our republic and to peace in Europe." On the following day, the city's parliament—by a vote of seventy-three to sixty, with two abstentions—elected Vogel as interim governing mayor, pending new elections.

Taking office with a newly reorganized Senate, Vogel immediately set out to deal with the city's most urgent problems, including its severe housing shortage, which had recently touched off violent protests by tens of thousands of youths and had given rise to a militant squatters' movement occupying scores of vacated buildings. "The foremost problem is to end violence and start talking," Vogel said after appointing a team of aides to open talks with the alienated youths. He often stayed at his desk at the Schöneberg Rathaus until well beyond midnight and toured the city to talk with Berliners from all walks of life. Ordering police not to evict the squatters by force, he tried to grant them legal status as tenants of the buildings they occupied and made some $10 million available for a program to enable them to repair their houses.

But despite his best efforts during his 100 days as governing mayor, Vogel failed to keep his party in power in West Berlin. In the election of May 10, 1981—called two years ahead of schedule at the insistence of the opposition Christian Democrats— the Social Democrats lost control of West Berlin's city hall for the first time since 1954. They did, however, prevent the Christian Democrats from gaining an absolute majority since they obtained an estimable 38.4 percent of the popular vote. After the election, Vogel remained in West Berlin as leader of the parliamentary opposition.

On October 1, 1982 the Social Democratic party was forced into opposition on the West German national scene by a 256 to 235 vote of no confidence in the Bundestag that replaced Chancellor Helmut Schmidt with Christian Democratic leader Helmut Kohl. Two weeks earlier, the Free Democrats had defected from the coalition they had formed with the Social Democrats, depriving the Schmidt government of a parliamentary majority. The government's downfall was attributed to a variety of factors, notably the deteriorating economic situation and the Social Democrats' unwillingness to cut social expenditures as much as the Free Democrats demanded to cope with the growing deficit. Within the Social Democratic party there were rifts over economic policy, the projected deployment by NATO of American nuclear missiles on West German soil, and the party's relationship with the emerging "Green" environmentalist and antinuclear political movement.

After Schmidt announced his intention to step down for health and political reasons, the Social Democratic party executive in Bonn, on October 29, 1982, unanimously nominated Vogel as the party's candidate for chancellor in forthcoming elections, scheduled for March 1983. Although the current Bundestag's four-year term was not due to expire until the fall of 1984, Kohl moved up the election date to obtain an early confirmation by the voters for his new Christian Democratic–Free Democratic government. Vogel's eighteen months in West Berlin had enhanced his reputation, and he was widely regarded as the man who could unite the Social Democratic party's disparate elements of workers, intellectuals, and youth.

Considered by some observers as the most crucial in West Germany since the end of World War II, the election campaign was conducted primarily on economic and defense issues. Campaigning under the slogan "In German Interests," Vogel made as many as five or six speeches a day in town squares and auditoriums across the country and cultivated an image of competence and respectability for his party. In response to Kohl's free-market, private-investment views and his criticism of the Social Democrats' deficit spending policies, he called for increased taxes for high-income groups, a shorter work week, extended labor participation in the management of industries, a reform in the Common Market's agricultural policies, and a $3.5-billion government investment program to stimulate consumer spending and create hundreds of thousands of jobs, mainly in the areas of ecology and production of energy.

Vogel's visits to both Washington and Moscow in January 1983 established the Social Democrats as the party that could bridge the gap between East and West. He denied charges by his opponents that he was Moscow's candidate and affirmed his party's loyalty to NATO, but rejected Kohl's policy of unconditional acceptance of the Atlantic Alliance's 1979 decision to deploy American-made Cruise and Pershing II intermediate-range missiles in West Germany if Soviet-American arms negotiations in Geneva failed to produce an agreement. Calling for American concessions to the U.S.S.R., he declared that a Social Democratic government would accept the new weapons "only under extreme circumstances" and appealed to the voters for a mandate "to do everything possible to make the stationing of more missiles superfluous!"

Toward the Green party, which appeared for the first time to have prospects of obtaining at least 5 percent of the popular vote—the minimum required for Bundestag representation—Vogel took an ambivalent position. While opposing their demands for unconditional rejection of nuclear missiles, he tried to siphon off votes from the Greens by taking a firm environmentalist stand and by exhorting voters to listen to the "good questions" of the Greens but not necessarily to their answers. Although he did not go so far as to consider the Greens as potential coalition partners, he left the door open for possible future cooperation.

As the election neared, the campaign was marred by mudslinging. In late February, the sensationalist *Bild am Sonntag*, a mass-circulation weekly owned by the right-wing Axel Springer newspaper chain, published an article alleging that as a member of the Hitler Youth, Vogel had been "something like an extended arm" of Nazi propaganda chief Joseph Goebbels. Vogel and the Social Democratic party promptly filed a libel suit against the newspaper. Some 125 journalists employed by the Springer interests then issued a statement disassociating themselves from the article.

As had been predicted in public opinion polls, the elections of March 6, 1983 marked a defeat for Vogel and the Social Democrats. Of the 39.3 million votes cast, the Social Democrats received 38.2 percent, a reduction from the 42.9 percent they had won in 1980, while their Bundestag representation was reduced from 218 to 193 seats. On the other hand, Kohl's Christian Democratic Union and its Bavarian ally, the Christian Social Union, headed by Franz-Josef Strauss, together increased their share of the popular vote from 44.5 percent to 48.8 percent and their parliamentary representation from 226 to 244 seats. The Free Democrats received 6.9 percent of the vote and thirty-four seats, while the Green party's share was 5.6 percent of the vote and twenty-seven seats.

The election result, which was welcomed by President Ronald Reagan in Washington, D.C. and by Prime Minister Margaret Thatcher in London, was attributed by political observers to the opinion among voters that Kohl's policies were more realistic, while Vogel's views were utopian. After con-

gratulating Kohl, Vogel promised that his party would be one of "constructive opposition." Entering the new Bundestag as representative of a West Berlin constituency, Vogel formally became leader of the parliamentary opposition on March 8, 1983 and, with an eight-member "shadow" cabinet, embarked on the task of trying to revitalize the defeated Social Democratic party. At a special Social Democratic party congress in Cologne in November 1983, at which the party, by a vote of 383 to fourteen, adopted a resolution opposing deployment of the new missiles by NATO, Vogel accused the Kohl government of pushing through deployment "against the wishes of the overwhelming majority of our people."

In an effort to promote a compromise between NATO and the U.S.S.R. on the question of nuclear armaments in Europe, and to help bring about a resumption of the stalled Geneva arms control talks, Vogel conferred with United States officials in Washington, D.C. in February 1984 and assured them of his party's loyalty to NATO. The following month he headed a Social Democratic delegation to Moscow and held cordial talks with Communist party General Secretary Konstantin U. Chernenko, but without positive results.

Among the distinctions that Vogel has earned over the years are the German Federal Republic's great Bundesverdienstkreuz, the Bavarian Verdienstorden, and the rank of honorary commander of the Order of the British Empire. His published works include the books *Städte im Wandel* (Cities in Transition, 1971), *Die Amtskette; Meine 12 Münchener Jahre* (The Chain of Administration; My 12 Years in Munich, 1972), and *Reale Reformen; Beiträge zu einer Gesellschaftspolitik der Neuen Mitte* (Real Reforms; Contributions to a Social Policy of the New Center, 1973).

Hans-Jochen Vogel was first married in 1951, to Ilse Leisnering. From that marriage, which ended in divorce in 1970, he has a son, Bernd, and two daughters, Sabine and Bärbel. In 1973 he married Lieselotte (Biersack) Sonnenholzer, who has two daughters from her previous marriage and holds a degree in Germanic studies. Gray-haired, over six feet tall, and of sturdy build, Vogel wears neatly tailored suits and horn-rimmed glasses that give him a somewhat owlish appearance. Known to his associates as a compulsive worker and a fanatic for punctuality, he is also noted for his sense of humor and his humanist philosophy. He is a Roman Catholic. His recreations include mountaineering, swimming, and reading history. Vogel's favorite historic figure is Nicholas von der Flüe, a religious hermit and former landowner who saved the Swiss Confederation by an impassioned plea for unity at the diet of Stans in 1481 and was canonized in 1872.

References: Der Spiegel 37:30+ F 7 '83 pors; German Tribune p5 N 14 '82 por; London Sunday Times p20 F 13 '83 por; N Y Times A p3 N 3 '82 por, A p10 F 15 '83; International Who's Who, 1984–85; Wer ist Wer? (1983); Who's Who in Germany (1980)

Wagner, Robert

Feb. 10, 1930- Actor. Address: b. c/o William Morris Agency, 151 El Camino Beverly Blvd., Beverly Hills, Calif. 90212

"When I first went under contract," actor Robert Wagner once told an interviewer, "I was one of 150 kids. None of the others got anywhere." Wagner, the product of a massive publicity buildup by the motion picture studio Twentieth Century-Fox, has endured. After some fifteen films in which he played what he called "pretty boy" roles, Wagner surprised critics and audiences with his highly professional performance as a self-aggrandizing jet pilot in the 1958 movie *The Hunters*. He has since parlayed his matinee-idol looks and debonair charm into three hit television series, *It Takes a Thief*, *Switch*, and most recently, *Hart to Hart*.

The son of a well-to-do steel company executive, Robert John Wagner Jr.—"R.J." to his friends—was born in Detroit, Michigan on February 10, 1930. When he was about nine, he moved with his family to Los Angeles, California, where he completed his elementary education in a succession of local private schools, including the Black-Foxe Military Institute and the Harvard School. Wagner, who by his own account was a "romantic kid," read a great deal as a child, especially the adventure stories of Robert Louis Stevenson and Zane Grey, but he spent most of his time at the movies. "I used to try to jump over the wall of the Fox studios and watch 'em make pictures," the actor admitted to Edith Efron years later in an interview for a *TV Guide* (June 29, 1978) profile. A summer job as a caddy at an exclusive Bel-Air golf club, where he rubbed elbows with such stars as Clark Gable, Fred Astaire, Alan Ladd, and Randolph Scott, heightened his interest in filmmaking,

and by his mid-teens, he had set his sights on a movie career.

Following his graduation from high school in 1948, Wagner made the rounds of the motion picture casting offices. Although his acting experience was limited to small roles in schoolboy productions, he landed a bit part in *The Happy Years* (MGM, 1950), an adaptation of Owen Johnson's delightful stories about a mischievous youngster's adventures at a boys' school in the 1890s. Shortly after he completed work on the film, the fledgling actor was spotted in a Beverly Hills cafe by a talent agent. A few weeks later, the twenty-year-old Wagner was under contract to Twentieth Century-Fox as a $75-a-week extra. His early assignments at the studio included making more than 100 screen tests "with every pretty girl some producer or executive thought would be screen material," as he recalled in an interview for the *New York Mirror* (August 7, 1960). "It was terrific experience," he went on. "I listened and observed as the girls were coached, and it was priceless help."

Wagner was among the last of the untrained but physically attractive young actors—Tony Curtis and Rock Hudson were others—to be launched as new motion picture stars on a wave of studio-generated publicity. It proved to be a mixed blessing. "Darryl Zanuck brought me in as a sort of young Tyrone Power," Wagner told Roderick Mann of the *New York World Telegram and Sun* (September 17, 1962). "But he resigned, and I was left there with a tennis racket in one hand and a beach ball in the other. And they never let me grow up. . . . During the first five years I was under contract there they'd just say: 'Report to such-and-such a set tomorrow,' and I'd clock in and draw my costume and get on with it. All I usually knew was the director's name. Sometimes not even that. And there'd always be one or two kids standing about who looked just like me. That was to show I was replaceable."

Twentieth Century-Fox executives officially introduced Robert Wagner to moviegoers in *The Halls of Montezuma* (1951), a blood-and-thunder account of the United States Marines' heroic exploits in World War II. Wagner's contribution to the film, which starred Richard Widmark, went largely unnoticed by the critics, but it was a box-office success, as was Wagner's next movie, *The Frogmen* (1951), a wartime adventure graphically recounting the operations of the United States Navy's underwater demolition teams. The actor's third film credit in 1951 was a supporting role in the frothy domestic comedy *Let's Make It Legal*, starring Claudette Colbert and McDonald Carey.

Ironically, it was a one-minute scene toward the end of the lachrymose biopic *With a Song in My Heart* (1952), the true story of singer Jane Froman's comeback after she was crippled in an airplane crash, that finally thrust Wagner into the spotlight. In his review of April 12, 1952, the *Washington Post*'s Richard L. Coe dismissed the movie as "the most pretentious hogwash in some weeks," but he tempered his diatribe with praise for "several appealing moments near the end when a nerve-shattered soldier to whom the singer had once addressed 'Embraceable You' in a stateside nightclub reappears in a German hospital. . . . One Robert Wagner plays the scene with quiet force."

In some subsequent films, Wagner was required to do little more than look handsome and clean-cut, but he was gradually entrusted with meatier roles, and he often turned in memorable performances, most notably in John Ford's remake of the World War I adventure *What Price Glory?* (1952) and *Titanic* (1953), a melodrama about the last hours aboard the doomed luxury liner that struck an iceberg and sank on its maiden voyage in 1912. Wagner got his first billing as the reckless and charming Tony Petrakis in *Beneath the Twelve-Mile Reef* (1953), a hackneyed drama about the rivalry between Greek immigrant sponge fishermen off the coast of Florida, in which the actors took a back seat to the stunning underwater photography. The actor fared only slightly better in his next outing, *Prince Valiant* (1954), a lavish cinematization of the popular comic strip that drew mixed notices from the critics. Some responded favorably to the film's swashbuckling energy and to Wagner's dashing athleticism as the eponymous hero; others, among them the *New Yorker's* John McCarten, complained about its feeble script and primitive acting. McCarten, in particular, took Wagner to task for reciting his lines "in a vacant monotone" and for failing to flesh out his character.

The year 1954 also saw the release of *Broken Lance*, a well received western that Wagner later described as "the only film" out of the thirty-odd movies he made for Twentieth Century-Fox that he was "really proud of." The story of Matt Devereaux, a strong-willed cattle baron played by veteran actor Spencer Tracy, and his four quarrelsome sons, *Broken Lance* had the advantages of a solid script, spectacular scenery, and vigorous direction by Edward Dmytryk. Although the movie critic for the *New York Times*, in his review of July 30, 1954, felt that Wagner, as the half-breed Joe, Devereaux's devoted youngest son, was "simply a handsome but strangely juvenile vaquero given to sullen posturing," *Variety's* reviewer considered the actor's portrayal to be "his best work yet." Spencer Tracy was also impressed by Wagner's performance—so impressed, in fact, that he specifically requested his young colleague for the role of his larcenous younger brother in *The Mountain* (1956), Paramount's film version of Henri Troyat's novel about a grizzled alpinist's attempt to guide a rescue party to the site of an airplane crash on the icy peak that had repeatedly defeated him in previous climbs. The lion's share of the critical praise went to Tracy, as the aged mountaineer; Wagner's performance was generally dismissed as "needlessly unpleasant," and "too unrelievedly evil." Wagner redeemed himself to an extent with his credible interpretation of the impetuous, swaggering title character in *The True Story of Jesse James* (1957).

One of the most talked-about young actors of the late 1950s, Robert Wagner was regularly featured in such fan magazines as *Photoplay* and *Modern Screen*, where he was invariably touted as the "most promising actor," the "fastest rising star," or the "brightest new face" on the Hollywood scene. Few stories captured the moviegoing public's imagination as completely as Wagner's highly publicized romance with Natalie Wood, a former child star who had successfully made the transition to leading lady. When Wagner and Miss Wood were married on December 28,1957, their union was ballyhooed by gossip columnists as one of the glittering screen matches of the century. Wagner himself credited the marriage with helping him shed what he has called his "one-dimensional boy" image. "For the first time I began to see myself as a mature guy," he explained, as quoted in the *New York Herald Tribune* (August 25, 1958), "and I began to get confidence in myself, probably because there was someone else who cared whether I sank or swam."

Wagner's transformation from self-conscious juvenile to a poised leading man was perhaps first evident in his impressive portrayal of a brash, hotshot fighter pilot in the rousing adventure *The Hunters* (1958). "Robert Wagner never had it so good," exulted Irene Thirer in her review for the *New York Post* (August 27, 1958). "He gives a glib, flip performance . . . which, at last, stamps him as a player of distinction." Several less successful efforts followed, including stints as a song-and-dance man in *Say One for Me* (1959), a contrived and undistinguished musical, and a trumpet player in the cliché-ridden soap opera *All the Fine Young Cannibals* (MGM, 1960), the only theatrical film in which he and Natalie Wood costarred.

The early 1960s were years of readjustment for Wagner. Maintaining that it was time he made his own decisions "about parts and scripts," he announced the end of his long association with Twentieth Century-Fox shortly after the release of *All the Fine Young Cannibals*. A few months later, in 1962, his celebrated marriage with Natalie Wood ended, a casualty of excessive publicity and conflicting careers, according to Hollywood insiders. Wagner's breakthrough as a free agent came with the release of *The War Lover* (Columbia, 1962), the film version of John Hersey's penetrating character study of a reckless pilot. Overcoming the handicap of a muddled script, he turned in such a well-rounded performance in a supporting role that Richard L. Coe of the *Washington Post and Times Herald* was prompted to observe, in his review of November 10, 1962, "Robert Wagner seems to be making strides as an actor." Eagerly accepting the chance to work with Academy Award–winners Frederic March, Sophia Loren, and Maximilian Schell and the legendary Italian director Vittorio de Sica, Wagner journeyed to Rome late in 1962 to make *The Condemned of Altona* (Twentieth Century-Fox, 1963), de Sica's retelling of Jean-Paul Sartre's brooding play about a powerful German shipping family that profitably served a succession of governments, including the Third Reich. Although the critical consensus was that Wagner was out of his depth as the liberal-minded younger son, the actor was unperturbed. "I took a salary cut to do [the film] because I knew I'd learn," he explained to Roberta Brandes Gratz of the New York Post (December 7, 1968), "and I did learn."

On his return to the United States in 1963, Wagner costarred with David Niven and Peter Sellers in the slapstick comedy hit The Pink Panther (United Artists, 1964), the first in what was to become a highly profitable series featuring the bumbling French detective Inspector Clouseau. Wagner also scored in Harper (Warner Brothers, 1966), a Paul Newman vehicle about a cynical private detective's search for a wealthy Californian. The New York Times's Bosley Crowther, who was unimpressed by the film, nevertheless considered Wagner's performance as the neurotic private pilot for the missing man to be "excellent for type and atmosphere." Over the next few years, Robert Wagner received star billing in several lightweight but mildly diverting motion pictures, including Banning (Universal, 1967), The Biggest Bundle of Them All (MGM, 1968), Don't Just Stand There (Universal, 1968), and Winning (Universal, 1969).

Making the jump to television, Wagner hesitantly agreed, in 1967, to star in It Takes a Thief, an adventure series reminiscent of the popular Mission: Impossible and The Man From U.N.C.L.E. Wagner played the role of Alexander Mundy, a suave professional thief who is paroled from prison on the condition that he use his expertise as a cat burglar in the service of the S.I.A., a fictional government counterespionage agency. A midseason replacement in ABC-TV's 1967-68 prime-time schedule, It Takes a Thief earned consistently above-average ratings, from its debut in January 1968 until its cancellation two-and-a-half years later.

With the success of It Takes a Thief, Wagner's services were suddenly in demand by television producers eager to cash in on his increasingly recognizable name and face. In the early 1970s Wagner appeared in a number of made-for-television movies, among them The Cable Car Mystery, Killer By Night, Madame Sin, and The Affair, a bittersweet love story in which he appeared opposite Natalie Wood, whom he had remarried in July 1972. The pair were also teamed as Brick and Maggie in an acclaimed 1976 television production of Tennessee Williams' Cat on a Hot Tin Roof. Sir Laurence Olivier, who not only played the patriarch Big Daddy, but also supervised the filming, had personally requested the Wagners for the younger leads.

In 1975 Robert Wagner was recruited to costar in Switch, a CBS-TV crime series about a former con man (Wagner) and a former policeman (Eddie Albert) who team up as private investigators. Wagner and Albert brought to their roles their own individual brands of charm, and despite a lukewarm critical reception, the series enjoyed a respectable three-year run, from September 1975 to September 1978. Occasionally Wagner took time out from his television work to make a theatrical film, such as the World War II melodrama Midway (Universal, 1976) and The Towering Inferno (Twentieth Century-Fox, 1974), a multimillion-dollar disaster epic with a huge international cast headed by Paul Newman and Steve McQueen.

Hart to Hart, the most successful of Wagner's regularly scheduled series, made its debut in September 1979. Based on a 1970 concept by Sidney Sheldon, the best-selling novelist, the project was resurrected by producers Aaron Spelling and Leonard Goldberg with Wagner in mind. Scriptwriter Tom Mankiewicz refined Sheldon's original concept into a stylish comedy-love story about an urbane self-made millionaire and his journalist wife whose passion for amateur sleuthing involves them in jet-setting murder and intrigue. Although Wagner denied that the show was an updated version of the popular William Powell–Myrna Loy Thin Man film series of the 1930s, he acknowledged that the affectionate, bantering marriage relationship so central to the success of the Thin Man movies was equally vital to the success of Hart to Hart. Accordingly, he selected Stefanie Powers, with whom he had worked in an episode of It Takes a Thief, to play the part of Jennifer. "Her style is perfect for me," he explained, as quoted in the New York Daily News (September 20, 1979). Wagner also sought out the gravel-voiced veteran actor Lionel Stander to play the role of Max, the Harts's friend and chauffeur.

The breezy interplay between the two stars and a hefty budget that allowed for on-location filming in exotic spots were key ingredients in Hart to Hart's popularity. TV Guide critic Robert Mackenzie, who described Hart to Hart as "ABC's nicely timed dabble in the tradition of married sleuths," noted in his review of December 6, 1979 that Wagner and Miss Powers "quip and banter, drive zippy cars, have a dog, solve crimes and frequently nibble on each other's ears. I not only like the idea, I like them." Having run its course after five seasons, Hart to Hart was axed by the network in the spring of 1984.

Still boyishly handsome, Robert Wagner stands six feet tall and usually weighs around 165 pounds. He has blue eyes, light brown hair, and a dazzling smile. A natural athlete and sportsman, he excels at horseback riding, water skiing, boating, and sports-car racing, and he is a licensed pilot. He also plays golf and tennis. His preferred indoor recreation is reading. The harmony of Wagner's personal and professional life ended on November 29, 1981, when Natalie Wood died in a drowning accident. Devastated, Wagner resumed the psychotherapy he had begun years earlier at Miss Wood's urging. Attempting to put his life back together, Wagner sold the Beverly Hills house that he and Miss Wood had shared and moved to a secluded ranch-style home in West Los Angeles with his daughters Kate, from his 1963 marriage to Marion Marshall, the actress, that ended in divorce; Natasha, Miss Wood's child, from her marriage to

British producer Richard Gregson; and Courtney, Wagner and Miss Wood's only child together.

References: Good H 179:60+ Ag '74 pors; McCall's 110:84+ S '83 pors; N Y Post p33 D 7 '68 por; People 20:96+ Jl 4 '83 pors; Sat Eve Post 251:82+ Mr '79 pors; TV Guide 16:26+ Je 29 '68 por, 27:32+ N 3 '79 por; Who's Who in America, 1984–85; Who's Who on Television (1982)

Walcott, Derek (Alton)

Jan. 23, 1930– Poet; playwright. Address: b. c/o Farrar, Straus & Giroux, 19 Union Square West, New York City, N.Y. 10003

The West Indian poet and playwright Derek Walcott, a master of Caribbean patois, also "possesses English more deeply and sonorously than most of the English themselves," as the Irish poet Seamus Heaney has observed. Another fellow poet, Robert Graves, has seen in Walcott's work "a closer understanding of [the English language's] inner magic than most (if not any) of his English-born contemporaries." Seven volumes of Walcott's work have been published in the United States, where the poet spends half of each year conducting a poetry workshop at Boston University. Of the seventh, the long sequence titled Midsummer (Farrar, Straus & Giroux, 1984), James Atlas has written: "Walcott's latest poems . . . meditate with grim intensity on the same themes that have animated his work for more than twenty years: the plight of the perpetual outsider, the black, the citizen of an island haunted by its colonial past, and his ambivalent love for that island."

Unlike his poetry, with its carefully honed rhetoric, Walcott's one-act plays are loosely structured, spontaneously cadenced folk allegories, written mostly in mixtures of Creole and native English dialects and originally intended for Caribbean audiences with little previous contact with live drama. They include O Babylon!, a folk drama in modified Rastafarian dialect, and The Dream on Monkey Mountain, which the author has described as a play about "the West Indian search for identity and the damage that the colonial spirit has done to the soul."

Derek Alton Walcott, now a resident of Trinidad, is of mixed African, Dutch, and English descent, with white grandfathers on both sides of the family. He and his twin brother, Roderick, a poet, were born on January 23, 1930 in Castries on the West Indian island of St. Lucia, then a British dependency and now an independent member of the Commonwealth. "The people there [in St. Lucia]," he told a "Talk of the Town" interviewer for the New Yorker (June 26, 1971), "speak the same Creole that people do in Haiti; we learn English in school almost as a foreign language, and perhaps that makes us value English the more. Islands are great places to live in because the sea is close and there is the elemental feeling of things that are bigger than you are."

Both of Walcott's parents were schoolteachers. In addition, his father, Warwick Walcott, was a watercolor painter and his mother, Alix Walcott, "loved to act," as the poet has recalled. The father died when Derek was one, as Walcott related in the New Yorker interview, and he and his brother and older sister "grew up with a terrific mother in a house full of books." He described St. Lucia to the interviewer as "a very green, misty island, which always has a low cloud hanging over the mountaintops," so that "when you come down by plane, you break through the mist, and it's as if you were entering some kind of prehistoric Eden." The strong visual element in Walcott's poetry was fostered in part by his boyhood practice of painting landscapes of a countryside where "the thick green hills boiled all day with their broad-leaved, volcanic vegetation." However, as he pointed out to James Atlas in an interview for the New York Times Magazine (May 23, 1982), he does not think that he has ever adequately "conveyed the elation" he felt "over the bounty, the beauty of being in a place like St. Lucia."

In school, Walcott told Atlas, "cultivated colonials of easy graces" presented poetry to him as "living speech," and he became "infatuated" with the style of the great poets in the English literary tradition. Like "every child all over the Empire," he was raised to be "Civic Britannica." "When we sang Kipling's hymn in church on Sundays, that very hymn was being sung by people of all colors all over the world." He would later sum up the pros and cons of the colonial predicament in his patois line, "We was in chains, but chains made us unite."

In 1948, when he was eighteen, Walcott, with his mother's encouragement, began privately to publish slim books of poetry—three in all—conveying such experiences as "the fierce, barbarous, unchristened blaze of the tropical morning." After graduating from St. Mary's College in St. Lucia, Walcott went on scholarship to the University of the West Indies in Kingston, Jamaica, where he majored in French, Latin, and Spanish. While an undergraduate, he wrote his first play, *Henri Christophe: A Chronicle*, which was produced in St. Lucia in 1950, and his second, *Henri Dernier*, a play for radio.

After taking his B.A. degree in 1953, Walcott taught at St. Mary's College, his alma mater, at Boys Secondary School in Grenada, and at Kingston College in Jamaica. Meanwhile, he wrote art and literary criticism for the *Trinidad Guardian* and feature articles for the Jamaican publication *Public Opinion*. His plays *Ione* and *Sea at Dauphin* were produced in Trinidad in 1954. *Sea at Dauphin* is about an old fisherman who commits suicide when he is superannuated and about the crew that takes on a boy as his replacement. It depicts the sea as a "white man" God's "spit on Dauphin people" and the hard life of those who wrest a bare subsistence from it as an endless circle of despair. The government of Trinidad commissioned Walcott to write an epic pageant to mark the first convocation of the abortive West Indian Federal Parliament, and the result was *Drums and Colours*, produced in Trinidad in 1958. Also produced in Trinidad that year was Walcott's *Ti-Jean and His Brothers*, a metaphysical verse based on a Trinidad folk fable. In the play Lucifer sets out to capture the souls of three brothers, and he succeeds until he meets more than his match in the youngest of the three.

On a Rockefeller Foundation grant in New York in 1957 and 1958, Walcott attended José Quintero's directing classes and the rehearsals of the Phoenix Theatre's repertory company. On returning to the West Indies, he founded his own company, the Trinidad Theatre Workshop. The first play in the troupe's repertoire was Walcott's *Malcochon*, in which six characters speaking a blend of French Creole and West Indian English dialect exemplify six different views of God and justice and at the same time reveal their common frail humanity. First produced in St. Lucia in 1959, *Malcochon* was staged in London the following year under the title *Six in the Rain*. Finding little support for his theatre workshop in the Caribbean, Walcott optioned his later plays to Joseph Papp, the director of the Public Theatre in New York City.

The first collection of poetry in Walcott's definitive canon was *In a Green Night* (Jonathan Cape, 1962). Critics hailed it as a landmark in Caribbean literature in English, in which the previous notable achievements (aside from Edward Braithwaite's Creole dialect verse) were in prose. Reading it was, to use Walcott's own phrase, "like entering a Renoir," a painting in verse described by P. N. Furbank in *The Listener* (July 5, 1962) as "full of summery melancholy, fresh and stinging colours, luscious melody, and intense awareness of place." "His joyful appreciation of the immediate physical world," Furbank pointed out, "serves to focus the other things he has to say, to give substance to conflicting loyalties. He uses a metaphysic of natural mutability and renewal—the 'green yet ageing orange tree' of Marvell's Bermudas—to come to terms with the immutable historic wrongs [done] his people." While "intensely and innocently literary," echoing Villon, and Dante, Catullus, and the metaphysicals, his poems have "immense freshness and verve." Looking back at *In a Green Night* in his essay on Walcott in *Contemporary Poets* (1981), Louis James commented on the "combination of virtuosity with control," the "sure sense of tone and nuance," and the "delight in the sensuous and dramatic vitality of words." Braving the risk of "artificiality," James wrote, Walcott used a comparatively "standard English" form in order to overcome the "formidable difficulties" of finding "an authentic voice" for expressing his complex, often ambiguous attitudes "without the support of a vital tradition of Caribbean poetry in English behind him."

Reviewing Walcott's *Selected Poems* (Farrar, Straus, 1964) in the *New York Times Book Review* (December 31, 1964), Robert Mazzocco detected an "itch to be impressive" in many of the "orotund, mellifluously spun lines" that set the poet apart from his English-born contemporaries, "most of whom in the manner of the Movement write wry, inelegant miniatures, the new emblem of the Welfare State." "Walcott has special gifts . . . not much evident in younger poets, whether English or American: his textures are musical, he has a painter's eye, his craftmanship is adventurous, and his moral or imaginative responses aren't shabby. . . . When these qualities triumph . . . then the full force of his personality, the personality of *place*, the troubled beauty of his Antillean land, comes strikingly to the surface."

Walcott continued to probe personal isolation and regional identity in surges of scenic delight balanced with descriptions of degradation in the poems of *The Castaway* (Jonathan Cape, 1965), which won the Royal Society of Literature award. The title poem of *The Gulf* (Jonathan Cape, 1969; Farrar, Straus, 1970) is a meditation on racial violence that seemed to Roy Fuller, writing in *London* (November 1969), to be "entirely successful, a poem of vision and compassion, with just the right amount of concrete detail to make effective the rhetoric and imaginative use of vocabulary that have always been Walcott's strength." In the *American Poetry Review* (May/June 1978), Valerie Trueblood described the verse in *The Gulf* as "lonely, fiery work" in which "the rage" that had been there all along for the looking in Walcott's poetry "is tougher now." She singled out the poem "Negatives," which opens with a television scene of the invasion of Biafra, with "corpses sprawled on the white glare," as in a photographic negative. "The emotion in this poem . . . is, first, the uncomfortable pity of the TV watcher. . . . It is also the sorrow of one poet speaking to another [the Biafran Christopher Okigbo]—a political and visionary one, young, dead . . . who was often accused of not being 'native' enough in his verse. Finally, it is the anguish of a particular man, a West Indian descendant of Africans, who does not take the deaths in the poem impersonally."

Among Walcott's plays, the best-received was *The Dream on Monkey Mountain,* first produced by the Eugene O'Neill Memorial Foundation in Waterford, Connecticut in 1969 and staged Off Broadway the following year. The protagonist of that poetic drama is an old charcoal burner named Makak who comes down from his hut on the mountain to sell his wares in town, gets drunk, and lands in jail, where he hallucinates about being the king of a united Africa. "Makak is an extreme representation of what colonialism can do to a man— he is reduced to an almost animal-like state of degradation," the playwright explained to the *New Yorker* interviewer. "When he dreams that he is king of united Africa, I am saying that some sort of spiritual return to Africa can be made, but it may not be necessary. The romanticized, pastoral vision of Africa that many black people hold can be an escape from the reality around us. In the West Indies, where all the races live and work together, we have the beginnings of a great and unique society. The problem is to recognize our African origins but not to romanticize them. . . . [Makak] thought he was going to an Africa where man could be primal and communal. Instead, it's back to original sin, with the tribes killing one another."

Walcott's play *In a Fine Castle,* produced in Los Angeles in 1972, is, in the author's words, "the story of a bourgeois French Creole family who live in one of Port of Spain's elaborate Victorian mansions" that "deals with the contrast between carnival and revolution." "Trinidad is a society where carnival is regarded as a serious matter and revolution as fun. It's the ambiguity of this view that makes life there so interesting." *The Charlatan,* a richly textured musical fantasy with a calypso beat, set in carnival time, dramatizes such matters as realistic social conscience, love, cultural mores, and contrasting unorthodoxies, personified, for example, in a white voodoo doctor and a black M.D. It was produced in Los Angeles in 1974. *Remembrance,* about a Port of Prince father and his two sons, one a martyred revolutionary and the other an impoverished artist, was produced in New York in 1979. *Pantomime,* set in a gazebo on a cliff in Tobago, was staged in Washington, D.C. in 1981. Among Walcott's other plays are *The Mulatto's Orgy* and *On the Right Hand of God the Father.* Their reception in the United States would undoubtedly be more enthusiastic were it not for the white caricaturing there of black folk themes in the past.

In his autobiographical book-length poem *Another Life* (Jonathan Cape, 1973; Farrar, Straus, 1973), Walcott looks back on his childhood and his magical rites of poetic passage as part of a Caribbean way of life that is sealed off "in a bell jar." Writing in the *New York Times Book Review* (May 6, 1973), George Lamming explained: "The increasing

pressures of race and politics in Caribbean society always threaten to put such a writer on trial. Walcott is not popular among a later generation of cultural nationalists who, in his view, have sought to turn white mythology on its head by discovering in blackness a new aristocracy of skin. [His] turbulent meditation on the dilemma of his time . . . is a formidable achievement."

The emotional tenor of the forty-six poems in *Sea Grapes* (Farrar, Straus & Giroux, 1976), ranging from erudite and tender to desperate and bitter, is summed up in the concluding line of the title poem: "The classics can console. But not enough." That poem treats such important Walcott themes as the wanderer, home, "the ancient war between obsession and responsibility," and the elusiveness of peace. In one scene the poet contemplates London where birds fly indiscriminately over the descendants of slaves and slave-holders alike and an "involuntary bell" of compassion tolls "for everything even in London / heart of our history, original sin." The moving narrative poems in *The Star-Apple Kingdom* (Farrar, Straus & Giroux, 1980)— including one tracing the odyssey of a poor mulatto sailor, a fugitive from Trinidad—were mostly meditations on power relationships in the history of slavery and imperialism and in current developments between the industrialized countries and the Third World.

The long sequence titled, not entirely ironically, *The Fortunate Traveler* (Farrar, Straus & Giroux, 1982) reflects the poet's international peregrinations—mostly between the West Indies and the United States—and expresses a linguistic as well as a geographical dislocation. In the poem "North and South" Walcott writes: "I accept my function / as a provincial elegist at the end of an empire, / a single, circling satellite," and in the quatrains of "Sea Change" he juxtaposes images ("light rain and governments falling") to convey the picture of political trouble in a tourist's paradise.

Walcott, long a self-described "divided child," torn between "the stuffed dark nightingale of Keats" and the "virginal unpainted world," has exacerbated his predicament with his new apprenticeship to the American vernacular and the style of such poets as Robert Lowell. Reviewing *The Fortunate Traveler* in the *New York Review of Books* (March 4, 1982), Helen Vendler traced the poet's spiritual odyssey back to the early, often unhappy disjunction between his concern with the black colonial predicament and "his harmonious pentameters, his lyrical allusions, his stately rhymes, and his Yeatsian meditations." Now, she pointed out, he is "not only the colonial but also the exile and, in his returns to the West Indies, the prodigal son." A poet more completely in exile, Joseph Brodsky (in whose apartment Walcott often stays when visiting New York City), in an essay in the *New York Review of Books* (November 10, 1983) described the West Indies as "the place discovered by Columbus, colonized by the British, and immortalized by Walcott." As thus immortalized, Brodsky wrote, "the West Indies is that realm which once, in its innocence of history, mistook for 'a light at the end of a tunnel / the lantern of a caravel' and paid for that dearly: it was a light at the tunnel's entrance."

Thrice married and twice divorced, Walcott has a son by his first wife and two daughters by his second. His present wife is Norline Metivier, a Trinidadian actress and dancer. In Trinidad, the Walcotts make their home in the Hotel Normandie, on the outskirts of Port of Spain. In Massachusetts, they live in a condominium in the Boston suburb of Brookline. In addition to Boston University, Walcott has taught or lectured at Harvard, Columbia, Yale, and Rutgers universities. He regularly gives readings on American college campuses, and he often flies to cities where his plays are being staged in order to supervise the productions, of which two recent ones were *Beef, No Chicken*, at the Yale Repertory Theatre, and *The Isle Is Full of Noises*, in Hartford. Walcott's chief source of income besides teaching and reading has been grants, the major one being a tax-free $250,000 MacArthur Foundation award. Among the many honors his poetry has drawn is the National Writers Prize of the Welsh Arts Council.

Derek Alton Walcott is tall, lithe and muscular in his physique, and casually neat in his wardrobe, which is typified by chino trousers, turtleneck sweaters, and open-neck flannel shirts. He has a

"gaiety about him, a love of banter," according to James Atlas—"only the subject is always poetry." Atlas described Walcott's consciously personal and intense teaching style: "He radiates a certain energetic poise, a relaxed vigilance. Striding back and forth before a blackboard, he moves with an actor's grace. His discourse has a tense edge to it, a sense of pressure; what he is looking for, he reminds the class, is 'vehemence'—that quality so visible in his own work."

In readings, according to Atlas, Walcott chain-smokes as he declaims his poetry "with high-strung fervor." Occasionally he reverts to histrionics, but his pose as "an obsessed and self-destructive figure" is "laced with irony." Atlas described a declamation by Walcott of "The Star-Apple Kingdom": "He intoned the long, densely eloquent lines in a melodic vibrato that had nothing theatrical about it. The poem's rhetorical intensity seemed utterly natural, speech harnessed to meter. One could hear the syncopated rhythms of calypso and the sonorous cadences of Walcott's English masters in every line."

References: N Y Times p2 Ag 21 '79 por; N Y Times Mag p32+ My 23 '82 por; New Yorker 47:30+ Je 26 '71; N Y Rev of Books 30:39+ N 10 '83; Contemporary Authors vols 89-92 (1980); Contemporary Poets (1981)

Walker, Alice

Feb. 9, 1944- Writer; social activist. Address: b. c/o Wendy Weil, Julian Bach Literary Agency, 747 Third Ave., New York City, N.Y. 10017.

Alice Walker is not only an essayist, poet, and award-winning novelist and short-story writer but also a social activist and an ardent "womanist"—that is, a black feminist. Although some reviewers have faulted her work for its unflattering portrayal of men, her ability to capture dialect and to evoke life in the rural South and the passionate intensity of her social concerns, as demonstrated in such books as *Revolutionary Petunias*, a collection of poems, and her Pulitzer Prize–winning novel, *The Color Purple*, have prompted many critics to rank Alice Walker among the best of contemporary American writers.

Alice Malsenior Walker was born on February 9, 1944 in Eatonton, Georgia, the youngest of the eight children of Willie Lee and Minnie Tallulah (Grant) Walker. Her father, who was "wonderful at math [but] a terrible farmer," to use her words, earned only $300 a year from sharecropping and dairy farming, while her mother, who helped him in the fields, supplemented the family income by working as a maid. Although she was deeply influenced by both her parents, Alice Walker especially admired her mother. "I grew up believing that there was nothing, literally nothing, my mother

couldn't do once she set her mind to it . . . ," she told Jacqueline Trescott during an interview for the *Washington Post* (August 8, 1976). "So in a way when the . . . women's movement happened, I was really delighted because I felt they were trying to go where my mother was and where I always assumed I would go." Her parents were also storytellers, and at the age of eight Alice began to record those stories and some poems of her own in a notebook. But since sharing a three- or four-room home with nine other people allowed her little of the quiet and solitude she needed to write, she spent a lot of time outdoors, roaming the fields to find some privacy.

In 1952 Alice Walker was accidentally wounded in the eye by a shot from a BB gun fired by one of her brothers. Because they had no access to a car, the Walkers were unable to take their daughter to a hospital for immediate treatment, and when they finally brought her to a doctor a week later, she was permanently blind in that eye. A disfiguring layer of scar tissue formed over it, rendering the previously outgoing child self-conscious and painfully shy. Stared at and sometimes taunted, she felt like an outcast and turned for solace to reading and to poetry writing. Although when she was fourteen the scar tissue was removed—and she subsequently became valedictorian and was voted most popular girl and queen of her senior class—she came to realize that her traumatic injury had had some value: it allowed her to begin "really to see people and things, really to notice relationships and to learn to be patient enough to care about how they turned out." Because of the accident, she became eligible for and won a scholarship for handicapped students to attend Spelman College, a black women's college in Atlanta, beginning in 1961. Her neighbors raised the $75 for her bus fare to the state capital.

Already powerfully moved by what she had learned of the civil-rights movement on television, at Spelman Miss Walker came under the influence of the radical historians Staughton Lynd and Howard Zinn and soon became involved in civil rights demonstrations in downtown Atlanta. Zinn's dismissal in her sophomore year for being overly sympathetic to the demonstrators and Spelman's restrictive rules in general led her to accept a scholarship offer from Sarah Lawrence, the exclusive but progressive women's college in Bronxville, New York.

In the summer of 1964, Alice Walker traveled around Africa in search of a "spiritual home," as Gloria Steinem phrased it in an interview with her for Ms. (June, 1982). When she returned to Sarah Lawrence in the fall, she was pregnant and for a time she contemplated suicide. Then she decided to have an abortion. Almost all of the poems in Once, her first volume of poetry, were written in the week immediately after the abortion. Barely pausing to eat or sleep, she wrote poems about Africa, suicide, love, and civil-rights activism and slipped batches of them as they were completed under the door of her teacher, Muriel Rukeyser, the well-known poet. Impressed by her poems, Miss Rukeyser showed them to her agent, who in turn gave them to Hiram Haydn, an editor at Harcourt Brace Jovanovich. Although Haydn quickly accepted the poems, Once was not published by Harcourt Brace until 1968. Writing in Poetry (Feb-

ruary 1971), Lisel Mueller lavished praise on Once, complimenting the "sensitive, spirited, and intelligent" young author on her spare but insightful poetry. "Feeling is channeled into a style that is direct and sharp, honest speech pared down to essentials. Her poems are like pencil sketches which are all graven outline: no shaded areas, no embellishments. Wit and tenderness combine into humanity."

After receiving her B.A. degree from Sarah Lawrence in 1965, Miss Walker canvassed voters in Liberty County, Georgia, later worked in New York City's Welfare Department (a job she "couldn't stand"), and wrote at night. When she won her first writing fellowship in 1966, she at first planned to use it to move to Senegal, West Africa. Instead she spent the summer in Mississippi "to be in the heart of the civil-rights movement," helping people who had been taken off the welfare rolls or thrown off their farms for registering to vote. While there she met Melvyn Rosenman Leventhal, a young Jewish civil rights lawyer. She and Leventhal lived together contentedly for a year in New York City but were married on March 17, 1967 because they felt it would otherwise be impossible, given the greater bias against interracial relationships outside of marriage, to continue their political work. And, as she explained to Gloria Steinem for the Ms. interview, "we could challenge the laws against intermarriage at the same time. . . . Love, politics, work—it was a mighty coming together."

While they were living in New York City in a studio apartment over Washington Square Park, Alice Walker's first published essay, "The Civil Rights Movement: What Good Was It?," an impassioned declaration of her commitment to the cause, appeared in the American Scholar (August 1967) and won the $300 first prize in its annual essay contest. "To Hell With Dying," her best-known and first-published short story, celebrating the love and loyalty of a young girl for a dying old man, also appeared that year.

In September 1967, the Leventhals moved to Mississippi, becoming the first legally married interracial couple in Jackson. There Leventhal sued racist real-estate dealers and fought to desegregate the state's schools while his wife served briefly as a black-history consultant to Friends of the Children of Mississippi (a Head Start program) and as a writer-in-residence at Jackson State College in 1968–69 and at Tougaloo (Mississippi) College in 1970–71.

Although she "atrophied," according to her husband, during their seven-year residence in Jackson, Alice Walker's literary career advanced considerably. Her first novel, The Third Life of Grange Copeland, which she wrote on a fellowship at the MacDowell Colony in New Hampshire in 1967, was published by Harcourt Brace in 1970. Beginning in the 1920s, the novel tells the story of Grange Copeland, a black tenant farmer in the South who deserts his wife and his son, Brownfield, for the promise of the North—a life that, in time, he finds even more degrading. Years later he returns to the South a mellower and wiser man, only to discover Brownfield repeating his mistakes by viciously abusing his wife and his daughter, Ruth. When Brownfield goes to prison for murdering his wife, Grange takes custody of Ruth. Through his granddaughter, he is given a chance to rectify the errors he made in raising his own child, and their mutual love gives him his "third life." But when the still angry and violent Brownfield tries to reclaim Ruth after his release from prison, the conflict between father and son results in the death of both men.

The critical response to *The Third Life of Grange Copeland* was mixed. Like most reviewers, Robert Coles, writing in the *New Yorker* (February 27, 1971), applauded her skill in developing characters, but found fault with her analysis of them. In her appraisal for *Saturday Review* (August 22, 1970), Josephine Hendin observed that Miss Walker "never probes the impact of poverty on Brownfield's inner life, or the psychic starvation that makes him so unable to love. . . . [She] disappoints by explaining Grange's conversion in political clichés [and her] solution ignores the depth and force of the loveless agony she describes."

To be close to her lecturing commitments in literature at both Wellesley College and the University of Massachusetts (Boston) in 1972–73, Alice Walker moved to Massachusetts, where she spent a year and a half. Her "escape" from Mississippi, which had "just about driven [her] around the bend," her enforced separation from her husband, who had to remain in Jackson to continue his work, and the death of her father made 1973 a traumatic year for the author. That year also saw the publication of three more books by her. *Revolutionary Petunias and Other Poems* (Harcourt Brace), like *Once*, earned high marks from the critics. Writing in *Parnassus: Poetry in Review* (Spring–Summer 1976), Darwin Turner had high praise for its use of "plain, unaffected diction" and its revelations of "human behavior and emotion" but found that "some phrases border[ed] on the banal." A reviewer for *Choice* (September 1973) noted that Alice Walker's "poetry is strongly narrative and compelling. One reads in order to follow the narrative thread, and the thread never gets gnarled or monotonous." *Revolutionary Petunias* was nominated for a National Book Award and won the Lillian Smith Award of the Southern Regional Council.

Alice Walker's *In Love and Trouble: Stories of Black Women* (Harcourt Brace), her first collection of short fiction, also captured a prestigious prize: the Richard and Hinda Rosenthal Award from the American Institute of Arts and Letters. Most of the thirteen stories, each of which has a black woman as its protagonist, had already been published, but assembling them in a single volume underlined the intensity of Miss Walker's concern for the lives of black women, especially those who are poor, uneducated, and Southern. The author's skill at "getting inside the minds of the confused, the ignorant, [and] the inward-turning character" was singled

out for special praise by J. H. Bryant in his review for the *Nation* (November 12, 1973). Writing in the *New York Times Book Review* (March 17, 1974), Mel Watkins was equally enthusiastic: "These stories are perceptive miniatures, snapshots, that capture their subjects at crucial and revealing moments. In this collection, Miss Walker is moving without being maudlin, ironic without being [gimmicky]." Written for children, *Langston Hughes: American Poet* (Crowell), her biography of the "poet laureate of the Negro race"—a man whom she greatly admires and who has had a lasting influence on her own writing and political attitudes—was also published in 1973.

Melvyn Leventhal and Alice Walker moved back to New York City in 1974. There she accepted a position as contributing editor for *Ms.* magazine, completed work on her second novel, *Meridian* (Harcourt Brace, 1976), and published her third book of poems, *Goodnight, Willie Lee, I'll See You in the Morning* (Dial, 1979). She somehow also managed to find time to edit an anthology of the writings of Zora Neale Hurston, the Harlem Renaissance writer and folklorist who was in many ways Miss Walker's role model, entitled *I Love Myself When I'm Laughing . . . and then Again When I Am Looking Mean and Impressive* (Feminist Press, 1979).

Often praised as one of the finest novels to come out of the civil-rights movement, *Meridian* is concerned with the explosive tensions and permanent impact of that movement on the lives of three young people—a black woman, Meridian Hill, whose refusal to say she will kill, as well as die, for the Revolution causes her to be thrown out of a radical political cell in New York; Truman Held, a black male activist and sometime lover of Meridian's who becomes an artist as the movement fades; and their friend Lynne Rabinowitz, a Jewish civil-rights worker whom Held eventually marries.

In recommending *Meridian* in *Newsweek* (May 31, 1976), Margo Jefferson wrote that Alice Walker is "both ruthless and tender. Her eye for hypocrisy is painfully sharp, . . . [and] her eye for eccentricities and subtleties of character is equally astute." On the other hand, in *Commonweal* (April 29, 1977) Gordon Burnside criticized Miss Walker's characterization of Meridian Hill because in her total selflessness and dedication to the cause of civil rights she becomes a "disappearing central character." Although Burnside considered *Meridian* "a failure as a novel," he valued it as "an extremely interesting historical document" that transports its readers to "the Movement's very heart."

Alice Walker's second collection of short fiction, *You Can't Keep a Good Woman Down* (Harcourt Brace, 1981), dealt with characters from a wider social spectrum than those that had figured in her earlier *In Love and Trouble*. In her evaluation for the *New York Times Book Review* (May 21, 1981), Katha Pollitt made a charge often leveled against Alice Walker's work: she found the stories to be "too partisan." "The black woman," she observed, "is *always* the most sympathetic character." But Miss Walker makes no attempt to hide her "womanist" (a term she coined for "black feminist or feminist of color") bias. As she explained to Barbara A. Bannon in an interview for *Publishers Weekly* (August 31, 1970): "The black woman is one of America's greatest heroes. . . . She has been oppressed beyond recognition. Her men have actually encouraged this oppression and insisted on it."

In *The Color Purple,* her third novel, Alice Walker again focused on the cruel domination of black men over black women, this time using the time-honored epistolary technique. *The Color Purple* spans about thirty years in the life of Celie, a Southern black woman. When she was a teenager her stepfather beat her and raped her repeatedly, gave away the two children she bore him, and forced her into a loveless marriage with a widower who beat her for no other reason than "she my wife." Through her relationship with other women—mainly with Shug Avery, a dazzlingly vital blues singer who moves in with Celie and her husband as his mistress but also becomes Celie's lover—she transcends her degrading circumstances and is transformed and redeemed.

The letters in *The Color Purple* are couched in a language that Alice Walker calls black folk English, which resembles dialect (a term she rejects as condescending) but is far easier to read and more musical. Most of them are written by Celie to God, but some are addressed to Celie from her sister Nettie, a missionary in Africa, and after Celie finds a cache of letters from Nettie that her husband has hidden for years, there are a few from Celie to Nettie.

Reviewers acclaimed *The Color Purple,* and Peter S. Prescott pronounced it in *Newsweek* (June 21, 1982) to be "an American novel of permanent importance." Even those critics troubled by its feminist slant or weaknesses in plot and structure congratulated Alice Walker on her eloquent use of black folk English. For example, Robert Towers, writing in the *New York Review of Books* (August 12, 1982), admired "the conversion, in Celie's letters, of a subliterate dialect into a medium of remarkable expressiveness, color, and poignancy. . . . N[o] other novelist . . . has so successfully tapped the poetic resources of the idiom." *The Color Purple* was nominated for the National Book Critics Circle award, won both an American Book Award and the Pulitzer Prize for fiction, and remained on the *New York Times* list of best-sellers for over twenty-five weeks. Warner Brothers bought the movie rights for $350,000.

In several interviews Alice Walker has discussed the composition of *The Color Purple,* mentioning her conversations with and visits from Celie and the other characters. Nevertheless, writing is not a mystical experience for her but a process of "total concentration" that allows her to create her fictional world. "If you're silent for a long time," she explained to Gloria Steinem, "people just arrive in your mind." In 1978, with a retainer from *Ms.* to work as a long-distance editor,

she moved from Brooklyn to California in search of that salutary silence.

In 1983, *In Search of Our Mothers' Gardens: Womanist Prose,* a collection of Alice Walker's essays that were written between 1966 and 1982, was published by Harcourt Brace. Some deal with politics or literature, but almost all contain biographical material, including an account of her depression and abortion during her senior year in college. Although she considered deleting some material she now finds embarrassing, she decided against it. "It's my life, and I really respect it. If there are flaws, that's the way it was," she has said. Her most recent publication is *Horses Make a Landscape More Beautiful* (Harcourt Brace, 1984), her fourth collection of poetry.

Alice Walker is quiet, soft-spoken, and petite. She has won many honors, including a National Endowment for the Arts grant in 1969, a Radcliffe Institute fellowship in 1971-73, and a Guggenheim award in 1978. Divorced from Melvyn Leventhal in 1976, she shares custody of their daughter, Rebecca Grant, with him. She now lives in San Francisco and spends much of her time with her "cherished companion," Robert Allen, a political writer and editor of the *Black Scholar.* Still a social activist, she has recently become involved with the antinuclear movement. When asked by one interviewer why she writes, the author explained: "I'm really paying homage to people I love, the people who are thought to be dumb and backward but who were the ones who first taught me to see beauty."

References: *Ms.* 10:35+ Je '82 por; *N Y Times* p13 Ap 16 '83 por; *N Y Times Mag* p24+ Ju 8 '84 pors; *Washington Post* G p1+ Ag 8 '76 por, E p1+ O 15 '82 por; *Contemporary Authors* new rev vol 9 (1983); Walker, Alice. *In Search of Our Mothers' Gardens: Womanist Prose* (1983); *Who's Who in America,* 1984-85

Washington, Harold

Apr. 15, 1922– Mayor of Chicago. Address: b. City Hall, 121 N. LaSalle St., Chicago, Ill. 60602

The election of Harold Washington in April 1983 as the first black mayor of Chicago, the second largest city in the United States, was a major political event for both that city and the country. It threatened the long-standing rule of Chicago's Democratic machine because Washington won the Democratic primary and the general election as a largely anti-organization independent, though he had won reluctant party support in some quarters. His victory was also expected to encourage blacks throughout the nation to register to vote. For Washington, his triumph meant that he had overnight become a major black leader and a power in the Democratic party. Yet, although not previously well-known, Washington has a solid political back-

Harold Washington

ground of sixteen years in the Illinois legislature and two years in the United States House of Representatives, in both of which he consistently supported liberal causes, focusing on civil rights issues.

Harold Washington was born in Chicago, Illinois on April 15, 1922, one of eleven children of Roy L. Washington and Bertha (Jones) Washington. His father was a Methodist minister, a lawyer, and a Democratic precinct captain on Chicago's predominantly black South Side at a time when most local blacks were Republicans. As a boy, Harold Washington ran errands for the Democratic organization, making political contacts that would later prove useful. A promising athlete, he won the city's high school championship in 120-meter high hurdles in 1939, and he also was an amateur middleweight boxer. After graduating from Du Sable High School, Washington entered the Army Air Force. Stationed in the Pacific, he was decorated with the Mariannas Campaign Ribbon.

After the war Washington attended Roosevelt University in Chicago where he studied political science and economics and won election to the office of senior class president in 1949, despite the fact that his class was only 5 percent black. After receiving his B.A. degree that year, he enrolled at Northwestern University Law School, which granted him a J.D. degree in 1952. When his father died in 1954, Washington took over as captain of his precinct. He served as an assistant city prosecutor from 1954 to 1958 and from 1960 to 1964 worked as an arbitrator for the Illinois Industrial Commission. Meanwhile, he had established a private law practice.

From 1965 through 1976 Washington served for six terms in the Illinois House of Representatives and from 1977 through 1980 he was a member of the state Senate, acquiring a reputation as an innovative legislator and eloquent orator. He drafted bills to strenghten Illinois' Fair Employment Practices Commission, to make Martin Luther King Jr.'s birthday a state holiday, to protect witnesses to crimes, and to help poor and elderly consumers. Having for years pressed for adoption of legislation setting aside funds for minority contractors, Washington finally won passage in 1979, and in 1980 he guided through both houses a bill establishing a Department of Human Rights. Washington was also a founder of the Illinois legislature's Black Caucus. On eleven occasions his colleagues voted him one of the ten best state legislators.

At first, Washington loyally supported Chicago's formidable Democratic machine, but he began to distance himself from the organization in the early 1970s over the issue of police brutality against local blacks, and in 1977 he broke with the machine completely because of its refusal to share power with independent blacks. Washington ran in the special 1977 mayoral election necessitated by the death of Chicago's longtime chief executive and Democratic political boss, Richard J. Daley. Machine candidate Michael Bilandic won the race, with Washington finishing a distant third, garnering only 11 percent of the vote.

Turning the tables on the machine three years later, Washington handily defeated the organization candidate in the party's First District United States congressional primary on the city's South Side and then easily scored a victory over his Republican opponent in the 92 percent black district, the most impoverished in all of Illinois. As a liberal Democrat, Washington was a consistent opponent of President Ronald Reagan's social service cuts and increases in military spending. According to *Congressional Quarterly Almanac*, Washington tied as the fifth most frequent House Democratic opponent of Reagan policies on key roll call votes in 1982, and he helped put together the coalition that preserved the key features of the 1965 Voting Rights Act against administration attempts to weaken it.

Approached in the summer of 1982 about running again for mayor of Chicago, Washington expressed reluctance because he preferred to stay in Congress, but political developments in the black community soon changed his mind. In 1979 many blacks had backed the successful reform mayoral candidacy of Jane Byrne in the Democratic primary because they believed that the Daley machine had not given blacks their fair share of city patronage jobs, private-sector neighborhood jobs, and municipal services. When Jane Byrne quickly made her peace with the organization, the feeling of deprivation in the black community persisted. The upshot was a grass-roots voter registration campaign that added some 100,000 blacks to the voting rolls by the November 1982 election, with the result that blacks constituted 40 percent of Chicago's 1.6 million registered voters, roughly equivalent to their proportion of the city's population. Moreover, some 70 percent of registered blacks voted in November. Those impressive figures convinced Washington of the viability of a black candidacy, and a few days after the election he agreed to run in the Democratic mayoral primary scheduled for February 22, 1983.

Waging his primary campaign in the face of serious disadvantages, Washington entered the race considerably later than his two rivals, Mayor Jane Byrne and Richard A. Daley, state's attorney for Cook County and son of the former mayor. Outside of the black community he was far less known than his opponents and had far less campaign money to spend than the other two candidates. While Byrne spent about $10 million and Daley approximately $2 million, Washington was believed to have spent less than $750,000. He therefore had to restrict his television advertising to the last week of the campaign.

Washington was able to overcome those obstacles by waging an effective campaign among Chicago's increasingly unified, assertive, and sophisticated black electorate. His forceful and often charismatic style, as exhibited on black-oriented radio stations, engendered great enthusiasm within the black community for his candidacy, especially when he focused his campaign on issues important to that constituency. He pledged to do away with the Democratic machine's patronage system, promised to establish a civilian review board to hear complaints against the police department, and also proposed a variety of economic and job programs vital to a black population with a 20 percent unemployment rate. Finally, his clear superiority as an orator and wit over his opponents during four televised debates helped establish the credibility of his candidacy.

Scoring an upset primary victory, Washington received 36.3 percent of the vote to Jane Byrne's 33.5 percent and Daley's 29.8 percent. The key to his success was the record primary turnout of 69 percent of eligible black voters, who gave him 82 percent of their votes, while white voters split their votes almost evenly between Byrne and Daley. Although Washington carried only nineteen wards to Jane Byrne's twenty-two, his pluralities were overwhelming: three-to-one or four-to-one margins in the black wards.

Normally, the Democratic nomination was tantamount to election since Chicago's feeble Republican party had not elected a mayor since 1927, but Washington captured less than 10 percent of the white and Hispanic primary votes, a figure he clearly had to improve upon in the April 12 general election. That seemed a difficult task since racial prejudices ran deep in Chicago, a city of insular communities that was once cited by an official of the United States Civil Rights Commission as "the most segregated city in the nation." There was widespread fear, especially in the white ethnic wards of the Northwest and Southwest Sides, that a victory on the part of Washington would give blacks control of the city.

Many observers felt that Washington did not do an effective job of allaying white fears. In his primary night victory statement he said, as quoted by Mitchell Locin and Thomas Schilling of the *Chicago Tribune* (February 24, 1983): "I assure you that in the months leading up to the general election, our campaign will reach out to all the citizens of this city. . . . Our determination is to unify this city." But in the same statement, he repeated his racially oriented refrain, "It's our turn." Early in the campaign he asserted that the Chicago-based civil rights leader Jesse Jackson, who was widely disliked by whites, would not play a role in a Harold Washington administration, but in March he indicated that a "race war" might erupt if he did not win. Meanwhile refusing to, as he put it, "grovel" before white Democratic ward committeemen for support, he argued that the organization should automatically back the nominee and threatened reprisals against committeemen who withheld their support.

By the end of March it was clear that Washington was failing in his attempt to make the election a referendum on Reagan administration policies and that instead race had become the campaign's central issue, to his detriment. Although on March 24 the Cook County Democratic organization officially endorsed Washington, eight white ward committeemen openly backed his Republican opponent, Bernard Epton, many more worked covertly for the Republican nominee, and most of the remainder did little in Washington's behalf. A poll taken during the last week of March showed that a twenty-eight-point Washington lead in midmonth had shrunk to twelve points, although that diminished lead held steady for the last few weeks before the election.

The legal difficulties of Harold Washington haunted his campaign. In his speeches and commercials, Epton stressed that his opponent was suspended from the Illinois bar from 1970 to 1976 for failing to perform work for several of his clients and that in 1972 he served 33 days in jail for not filing federal income tax returns for four years. (He owed the not exactly monumental amount of $508.05.) For conservative ethnic whites, those problems provided a socially acceptable reason for voting against a black candidate; white liberals most likely to vote for him were disturbed by Washington's record.

Fearful that a Washington loss would damage its standing among blacks across the country, the national Democratic party gave him more backing than any other mayoral candidate had ever received, despite initial coolness on the part of its leading figures. Although the Democratic National Committee contributed $90,000 to Washington's campaign, created a Chicago task force, and pressured Chicago Democratic leaders to back the party's nominee, and though Democrats from around the country campaigned for him, those outside efforts were believed to have generated more resentment than support for him within the parochial world of Chicago politics.

During the last two weeks of the campaign, the tide against Harold Washington seemed to turn. On

March 27, he was verbally abused by an angry crowd when attending a church with Walter Mondale on the mostly white Northwest Side, and William Zimmerman, Washington's media adviser, believed that the unseemly behavior of the crowd forced many voters to face the consequences of their racism, causing them to draw back "from a line they didn't want to cross." At about the same time, the Epton campaign itself came under fire for the blatantly racist "Before It's Too Late" slogan on its television commercials, and a week before the election the slogan was dropped. Most important, during the last days of the race Washington campaigned sixteen hours a day, concentrating on the affluent, liberal north lakefront wards and the Hispanic neighborhoods where he was most likely to get nonblack votes.

When in the April 12 general election a record 82 percent of Chicago's 1.8 million registered voters went to the polls, Harold Washington received 667,000 votes to Bernard Epton's 622,000 votes for a victory margin of 3.3 percent, and he won virtually all of the black votes. Also essential to his victory was his 19 percent of the white vote, most of which came from the six North Shore liberal lakefront wards, where he got 42 percent, and his almost 60 percent of the Hispanic vote.

The election of Washington was an event of national importance since it was expected to increase black voter registration throughout the country and it immediately established him as one of the country's most important black leaders. During his first few months as mayor, Washington made several trips around the nation, receiving exuberant welcomes in black communities as he urged their members to register and vote. Michael Steed, executive director of the Democratic National Committee, told Douglas Frantz of the Chicago Tribune (April 17, 1983): "I think he is going to take a very active role nationally. I cannot see the '84 presidential election going by without the national party seeking his advice and counsel."

In the meantime, back at home Mayor Washington faced grave problems following his April 29 inauguration, including an $80 million deficit for the city's fiscal budget. At the first meeting of the newly elected city council on May 2, which was reported nationally, Washington had the support of only twenty-one aldermen out of fifty, consisting of the council's sixteen blacks and five independent whites. That enabled the twenty-nine machine-oriented members led by Alderman Edward Vrdolyak, the Cook County Democratic chairman, to reorganize the council so as to solidify their control over the body. The number of black committee chairmen was reduced from eight to three, and machine loyalists were placed in control of all but three of the council's committees, including such important panels as zoning, police and fire, finance, and cable television. Determined to retain the power and financial rewards, legal and illegal, that organization aldermen had traditionally obtained through their control of the council and its key committees, the majority also adopted rule changes eliminating the mayor's control over the flow of ordinances in the council.

Unlike Jane Byrne, Washington refused to retreat from his promises of reform in the face of the machine's power. He was able to hold the council to a standstill by use of his veto, which the council majority did not have the necessary two-thirds vote to override, his initiative power in budgetary matters, his appointive power, and his authority to withhold funding from council committees. In an interview with David Axelrod, Monroe Anderson, and Tim Franklin of the Chicago Tribune (August 7, 1983), Washington said: "I guess a lot of the [aldermen] . . . think that I'll give in and Vrdolyak and I can sit down and divide [the spoils]. That's bull." Confident of ultimate victory, he told the interviewers, "I'm going to run them all the way into Lake Michigan with this reform."

Even while Washington and the Vrdolyak forces were stalemated during the spring and summer of 1983, the Mayor was able to introduce some important reforms. In May he reached an agreement in federal court limiting political appointments to 1,259 out of a 42,000-person city work force (previously, the number had been limited to 500). Two months later, he issued an executive order giving the public far greater access to city records, secured passage of an ordinance requiring more public hearings on the budget, and transferred funds from City Hall salaries to neighborhood projects.

Toward the end of the summer of 1983 it appeared that the city council majority was beginning to recognize the need to work with the Mayor. When Washington announced on August 23 his nomination of Fred Rice to be Chicago's first black police commissioner, no objection was heard from the council. Following a long dispute, the mayor and city council agreed on August 31 on a compromise plan for balancing Chicago's troubled budget. The first part called for the cancellation of some property tax cuts, which Vrdolyak's forces had adamantly opposed; the second part called for the layoff of hundreds of city workers. The machine forces had contended that only temporary furloughs were needed.

Although the Chicago city government continued to be riven by racial polarization and ridden with machine politics during 1984, Washington could be credited with some successes as a reform mayor. He gave his support to a court order designed to rid the city of the last vestiges of patronage; encouraged city employees to unionize; reduced the staggering budget deficit inherited from the previous administration; and cut down the size of garbage crews from four men to three. His most important achievement was his hiring of many more women, blacks, and Hispanics for top posts, though such appointments further soured the mood in some quarters. Even Washington's severest critics had to concede that under his regime, Chicago found itself more solvent than it had been under the dispensation of Jane Byrne.

Harold Washington has long been engaged to marry Chicago schoolteacher Mary Ella Smith. He was divorced twenty-eight years ago following ten years of a childless marriage. Although he is a workaholic, Washington needs so little sleep that he has adequate time for recreation. He reads a great deal, favoring biographies, and is an enthusiastic jogger. A private man, Washington's idea of the perfect evening is talking with a circle of close friends. Not long before the mayoral primary, he moved from the South Side to an apartment in the more well-to-do Hyde Park section of Chicago.

References: Chicago Tribune II p1+ F 13 '83 por; Almanac of American Politics, 1982 por; Who's Who in American Politics, 1984-85

Weir, Peter

(wēr)

Aug. 21, 1944- Australian motion picture director. Address: b. c/o Australian Film Commission, 8 West St., North Sydney, N.S.W. 2060, Australia

Peter Weir is probably the best-known Australian motion-picture director this side of the Pacific. Although he has only six feature films to his credit, among them the hauntingly beautiful *Picnic at Hanging Rock* and *The Last Wave*, an unnerving apocalyptic parable, Weir has been compared by film critics to the late Alfred Hitchcock for his ability to imbue the banalities of mundane life with unspeakable terror. "Everything is built on the real and ordinary, but there's chaos underneath," he explained in a *Washington Post* (February 4, 1979) interview. "We try to protect ourselves from the mystery, but it's all around, just waiting to reveal

itself and terrorize us. The ironic thing about movies is that you can use this highly sophisticated technology to restore the sense of mystery that an industrialized urban society tends to obscure. It's a mechanical process with an uncanny power of emotional suggestion."

Peter Lindsay Weir was born in Sydney, Australia on August 21, 1944, one of the three children of Lindsay Weir, a prosperous real estate broker, and his wife, Peggy (Barnsley) Weir. Reared in what he has described as "a classic sort of middle-class home" in a seacoast suburb of Sydney, he had, by his own account, a "wonderful childhood." He remembers with special fondness his father's nightly bedtime stories—interminable cliffhangers about the adventures of Black Bart, Captain Blood, and other swashbuckling heroes—and his own solitary war games, played with matchstick soldiers. As a boy, Weir was "absolutely obsessed with war." "I . . . think that the great horror and evil, the monstrous crimes that go back to the First World War, are still in the air," he explained to Stephen Farber in an interview for *New West* magazine (November 19, 1977). "And certain people somehow receive this guilt. At least that's what happened with me. I collected pictures of mutilated bodies along with more normal things like Spitfires and tanks. I went to all the war movies. . . . It was some ancient impulse working through me. Somewhere in that area lies the deep well that I've drawn from in my films."

After attending the Scots College, a private boys' grammar school in Sydney, and Vaucluse Boys' High School, Weir went on to the University of Sydney, intending to become a criminal lawyer, but finding the course work not to his liking, he left the university after several semesters and went to work for his father's real estate firm. By 1965 he had earned enough in commissions to finance a trip to Europe. During the five-week ocean voyage, he and a few friends amused themselves by putting together a comedy revue, which they called *Bilgewater*, for the entertainment of the other passengers and the ship's crew. Weir returned home some eighteen months later "totally changed" and, as he told Gary Arnold of the *Washington Post* (February 4, 1979), determined to pursue his "crazy idea that no career could be more appealing than a career in show biz."

To that end, Weir took a job as a stagehand at ATN-7, a Sydney television station, and, in his spare time, appeared with his friend Grahame Bond, a writer and comedian, in satiric stage revues similar to the BBC-TV series *Monty Python's Flying Circus*. Occasionally, he and other ATN employees used the station's cameras and production facilities to make short films. Weir's first effort was *Count Vim's Last Exercise*, an exuberant but somewhat slapdash comedy that was the highlight of the ATN employees' Christmas party in 1967. Encouraged by his colleagues' favorable response, he followed up with *The Life and Times of the Rev. Buck Shotte*, a thirty-minute spoof of religious cults that eventually earned him a Young Filmmakers Award and a promotion to a directing job at ATN. Outraged when he was denied a raise in salary to go along with his increased responsibility, Weir resigned from the station's staff early in 1969.

A few months later, the Commonwealth Film Unit, which made documentaries for the government, hired Peter Weir as a director, but since very few motion pictures were then being produced, he usually worked instead as a production assistant or cameraman, although he was paid a director's salary. About a year later, Weir finally got the chance to go professional when he was given the assignment of directing "Michael," the opening segment of the trilogy Three to Go, a feature film showcasing the work of the film unit's young directors. "Michael," starring Matthew Burton as a straitlaced office worker who is gradually drawn into the hippie subculture of the 1960s, was, in the view of many critics, the least successful of the three episodes, but it was nonetheless awarded the 1970 Grand Prix by the Australian Film Institute. While continuing to work for the Commonwealth Film Unit, Weir, with financial assistance from the newly formed Experimental Film Fund, moonlighted on an original short feature called Homesdale. The movie, which he has fittingly described as a "horror-comedy" about a remote country resort where guests are encouraged to act out their fantasies, won him a second consecutive Grand Prix at the Australian Film Institute's annual awards ceremony in 1971.

Having discharged his contractual obligations to the Commonwealth Film Unit, now known as Film Australia, with the production of the documentaries Incredible Floridas (1972) and What Ever Happened to Green Valley? (1973), Weir began shooting his first full-length feature film in October 1973. Adapted from his own unpublished short story, The Cars That Ate Paris is a surreal comedy about the enterprising citizens of a declining outback town who, with what Weir has called "true pioneering spirit," revive their community's flagging economy by luring unwary motorists into carefully staged accidents and then pillaging their wrecked automobiles for spare parts and other salable items. Given its world premiere at the Sydney Film Festival in June 1974, The Cars That Ate Paris was an immediate hit with the critics. Among the most enthusiastic was Bob Ellis, who ranked the film, "in its sheer watchability," above "any other Australian film of recent years," except for Ted Kotcheff's Wake in Fright. Peter Weir "has a directness of presentation, wholly uncontaminated by the smallest hint of coyness, that on certain occasions . . . catches the breath . . . ," Ellis wrote in the monthly Nation Review. "The climax, an automotive grande bouffe of Boschian proportions, purges and numbs the psyche as thoroughly as anything this side of Straw Dogs." Despite its critical acclaim, the film failed at the box office in Australia and, later (in a considerably recut and redubbed version called The Cars That Ate People), in the United States.

While he was in the midst of post-production work on The Cars That Ate Paris, Peter Weir was approached by Patricia Lovell, the actress and television personality, about making a film version of Joan Lindsay's best-selling book Picnic at Hanging Rock. Miss Lovell, who greatly admired Homesdale, thought that the young director's sure handling of suspenseful psychological dramas was perfectly suited to the unsettling turn-of-the-century tale (which may or may not be based on an actual incident) about the mysterious disappearance of several adolescent schoolgirls and their teacher during a Valentine's Day outing at a sacred aboriginal site in 1900. Fascinated by the story, Weir joined forces with Miss Lovell and with Hal and Jim McElroy, the producers of The Cars That Ate Paris, to set up, in January 1975, Picnic Productions. One month later, he was shooting on location at Hanging Rock, an unusual volcanic formation in South Australia. "What intrigued me about the Lindsay book was that there was no solution," Weir told Diane Jacobs in an interview for the New York Times (January 14, 1979). "I think it really did happen, and I made the film in that spirit. But more important, I think that this sort of thing does happen every day. People do disappear."

It was Weir's careful attention to what Diane Jacobs called the "conceptual underpinnings"—in this case, the idea of "the unfathomable lurking just beyond the pedestrian"—that endowed Picnic at Hanging Rock (1975) with its hypnotic appeal. As Tom Allen observed in the Village Voice (February 26, 1979), shortly after the movie's American premiere, in Weir's hands, "the enigma alone and the manner of posing the questions become the content and style of the film." Contributing to the eerie atmosphere were the ethereal beauty of the young girls and the exoticism of the Australian bush country itself, photographed in lyrical soft focus by Russell Boyd, who was rewarded with a British Academy Award for best cinematography in 1976. Both a critical and a commercial success, Picnic at Hanging Rock was unaccountably ignored by the judges of the 1976 Australian Film Institute Awards, but Weir took some consolation in the film's three Sammy awards, for best picture, best director, and best art director.

The phenomenal success of Picnic at Hanging Rock brought Weir dozens of offers, but no project interested him as much as a plot outline he had developed several years earlier, about a contemporary man's encounter with what the director has called "other forms of perception." The idea grew out of Weir's own experience with paranormality while he was poking around some Roman ruins in Tunisia in 1971. He described the curious incident to David Stratton in an interview for Stratton's book The Last New Wave: The Australian Film Revival (1980): "I was suddenly seized with this strange feeling I was going to find something, I even saw what I was going to see. And there it was, on the ground, a carving of a child's head. I brought it home and I thought about it for ages afterwards. What was that experience? Why did I see the head in my mind before I saw it in actuality? And then I started to think, what if a very rational person—a lawyer, say—had the same experience? How would he cope with it? And that was the beginning of The Last Wave."

In The Last Wave (1977), David Burton, a liberal white corporate attorney (played by Richard Chamberlain), is inexplicably called upon to defend a group of aborigines accused of murdering a member of their tribe. Drawn to the group's leader (portrayed by the aboriginal actor Gulpilil), whom he has recognized as the ominous figure in his recurrent nightmare, and to the mystical abstractions of aboriginal culture, Burton embarks on a personal search "for a spiritual life, for holiness, and for the lost fear . . . of life," as Weir put it. To prepare himself mentally for shooting The Last Wave, the director immersed himself in tribal lore and traditions. "The film became as much an odyssey for me as it was for the central character . . . ," he told David Stratton. "I felt that whatever it was I was dealing with in that film I never understood; nor will I; nor, perhaps, should I. I can't see things the way they [the aborigines] saw them, but I became so close to something—it was a curious experience of using film as a means to discovery."

Before releasing The Last Wave in Australia, Weir entered it in several international motion picture competitions, including the Teheran Film Festival, where it won the top prize "for the bold originality of its depiction of a cultural confrontation through which modern man's increasing detachment from his collective unconscious is revealed." Although Australian critics generally felt that The Last Wave suffered in comparison to Picnic at Hanging Rock, their American counterparts were more favorably disposed to the film. Most of them viewed it as a virtuosic exercise in pure cinema—an "excursion into the realm of purely visual storytelling in which forms and correspondences mean far more than words," as David Sterritt observed in his Christian Science Monitor (January 19, 1979) review.

Both Picnic at Hanging Rock and The Last Wave had been partly financed by the South Australian Film Corporation, and in 1977 that organization agreed to back Weir's production of a motion picture about the so-called Gallipoli campaign, the blundered World War I battle to take control of the Dardanelles that resulted in the slaughter of thousands of Australians. During one of several extended delays in preproduction work, Weir passed the time by making a feature film for the TCN-9 television network. Plumber, a black comedy about an insolent and incompetent plumber who disrupts the lives of an academic couple by dismantling their bathroom, won Weir two Sammy awards, for best original teleplay and best television production of 1979. It was subsequently released in the United States as a theatrical motion picture by Cinema Ventures.

In the meantime, the South Australian Film Corporation had withdrawn from the Gallipoli project. Undeterred, Weir secured funding from Associat-

ed R & R Films, the Robert Stigwood–Rupert Murdoch production company, and subsequently made arrangements with Paramount Pictures to distribute the film abroad. Having decided to tell the story of the rout from the perspective of the ordinary soldier, Weir and his scriptwriter, David Williamson, talked to dozens of World War I veterans before creating their central characters—Archy (Mark Lee), the patriotic idealist, and Frank (Mel Gibson), the cocky realist, the "new Australian." Gallipoli (1981) follows the two friends from their first encounter at a provincial track meet through their enlistment and training in the Australian light cavalry to their participation in the disastrous campaign.

Gallipoli swept the Australian Film Institute awards for 1981, taking top honors in nine categories. Despite mixed notices, it set house records during its first weekend at the Baronet Theatre in New York City and went on to draw sizable audiences in movie houses across the United States. Some critics complained that the film's sentimentality and visual beauty diluted its effectiveness as an antiwar statement, turning it instead into what the Washington Post's Gary Arnold called a "dovish Art Object"; others, most notably Jack Kroll, contended that Weir had dealt "with the horrors of World War I with something of the same blend of power and lyricism that marked the work of the soldier-poets like Wilfred Owen and Siegfried Sassoon." Gallipoli "is Weir's best film . . . ," Kroll concluded in his Newsweek (September 7, 1981) review, "an absorbing film and a moving lament for a brave and betrayed generation."

Because the worldwide box-office success of Gallipoli made Peter Weir a bankable international director, it was comparatively easy for him to persuade executives of MGM/UA Entertainment Co. to put up the money for his next venture, the film version of C. J. Koch's novel The Year of Living Dangerously. It was the first time an Australian feature film had been fully financed by a major American motion picture studio. Attracted to Koch's novel because of its "tentative awareness of Australians' being in fact Asian" rather than European, Weir deliberately constructed his film as "an Indonesian shadow play, all light and darkness, good and evil, left and right," as he explained to Dale Pollock in an interview for Newsday (September 7, 1981).

The complicated plot of The Year of Living Dangerously centers around Guy Hamilton, an ambitious Australian journalist on his first overseas assignment. In his eagerness to scoop his fellow reporters, he allows himself to be drawn into events leading up to the ouster, in 1965, of Indonesian president Sukarno by Billy Kwan, the mysterious Australasian dwarf he has hired as his cameraman. Weir chose Mel Gibson for the role of Hamilton, Sigourney Weaver as Jill Bryant, Hamilton's love interest, and in what proved to be an inspired bit of casting, the diminutive stage actress Linda Hunt as Billy Kwan.

Weir, who prefers to shoot his motion pictures on location because of the close and constant relationship between cast and crew, began filming *The Year of Living Dangerously* in the Philippines, but work on the production was repeatedly disrupted by threats of violence from Moslem militants, whose ire may have been sparked by rumors that the picture was anti-Moslem. Worn down by the continual intimidation, Weir finally packed up and returned to Australia, where he completed the film without further incident. Despite the excellent performances of the leading players, especially Miss Hunt, who received the 1984 Academy Award as best supporting actress, *The Year of Living Dangerously* generally failed to impress the critics, largely because its "baffling" and "incoherent" narrative raised expectations that it failed to fulfill.

Once described as a "deceptively cherubic-looking choirboy," Peter Weir is tall and slim, with a thatch of dark blond hair and mesmerizing eyes. Never a movie buff, he began to study the recognized classics of filmmaking only recently. He especially admires the works of Stanley Kubrick and Nicolas Roeg. His recreations also include reading (he enjoys the detective stories of Sir Arthur Conan Doyle for "those personal details") and sculpting. Weir lives with his wife of eight years, the former Wendy Stites, and their two children, Lindsay and Peggy, in a house near the sea, on the Barranjoey Peninsula north of Sydney.

References: N Y Times II p17+ Ja 14 '79 por; Washington Post H p1+ F 4 '79 por; International Who's Who, 1983–84; Stratton, David. The Last New Wave (1981); Who's Who, 1984–85; Who's Who in Australia, 1983

Wenders, Wim

(ven´dûrz vim)

Aug. 14, 1945– German motion picture director. Address: b. Constantin-Film, Albert-Rosshaupter-Str. 73, 8000 München 70, Federal Republic of Germany; b. Gray City, Inc., 853 Broadway, New York City, N.Y. 10003

"Film is the art of seeing," Wim Wenders said in an interview in 1977. "I want to help people to see again." Perhaps the most visually oriented of the younger German motion picture directors, Wenders, who made his living as a professional artist before turning his hand to filmmaking in 1967, brings to his work a painter's eye for composition and for the unusual, telling detail. He has been widely praised for his haunting visual representations of the aimlessness and superficiality of contemporary urban life, especially in the United States, but his recurrent themes, rooted as they are in the tradition of the nineteenth-century *Bildungsroman*, are quintessentially German. He was the first filmmaker of his generation to address the question of what it meant to be German in a postwar society dominated by American culture. The winner of the International Critics' Prize at the Cannes Film Festival in 1976 for *Im Lauf der Zeit/ In the Course of Time*, Wenders took the top award—the Golden Palm—at the 1984 festival for his most recent film, *Paris, Texas*. He is the first West German to win the Golden Palm without having to share the honor with another director, as Volker Schlöndorff had to do in 1979 with Francis Ford Coppola.

The son of a surgeon, Wilhelm Wenders was born in Düsseldorf, an industrial city in the Ruhr Valley of West Germany, on August 14, 1945. Wenders' preoccupation with the impact of American culture on the German psyche stems from his childhood during the Allied occupation following World War II. As he explained to Jan Dawson in an interview for Dawson's *Wim Wenders* (1976), "The need to forget twenty years created a hole, and [the German] people tried to cover this . . . by assimilating American culture. . . . The fact that U.S. imperialism was so effective over here was highly favored by the Germans' own difficulties with their past. One way of forgetting it, and one way of regression, was to accept the American imperialism. . . . We covered it with chewing gum. And Polaroid pictures."

Wenders attended a "very old-fashioned," to use his words, Catholic parochial school, and for a time he contemplated entering the priesthood, but his ecclesiastical ambitions disappeared when he discovered, in his early teens, the forbidden joys of pinball machines, rock 'n' roll, and American movies. "The first thing which was really important to me was sitting, listening to Chuck Berry on a jukebox, in a place where I was not allowed to go," he told Terry Curtis Fox, who interviewed him for the *Village Voice* (October 3, 1977). "When I listened to rock 'n' roll over the Armed Forces Radio Network, it was a culture which was not approved of by my father's generation. I even had to hide my first Elvis Presley records. I saw thirty or forty [Howard] Hawks and [John] Ford films before I saw any European movies."

In 1963 Wenders entered college as a premed student. Finding medicine not to his liking, he switched to philosophy a year later, but that subject, too, failed to hold his attention. Throughout that period, he devoted more of his time to painting than to studying. Finally, in 1966, he dropped out of college and moved to Paris, where he learned the art of etching as an apprentice in Johnny Friedlaender's studio. Wenders spent his evenings at the Cinémathèque, watching one movie after another. Preferring what he has called the "physical approach" of American and British directors to the more "intellectual approach" of their Continental counterparts, he was especially taken with the films of Anthony Mann, Nicholas Ray, Alfred Hitchcock, and Sam Fuller. It was during his year in Paris that Wenders decided to pursue a career in filmmaking, primarily because it was, in his words, "a little bit of everything that I wanted."

Wenders returned to Germany in September 1967 and enrolled at the newly established Hochschule für Fernsehen und Film in Munich. To his dismay, the curriculum emphasized art history and literature rather than actual filmmaking, and he attended classes only sporadically, but he is nonetheless the only major young German director to have had formal training in cinematography. During his three years at the Hochschule, Wenders wrote movie reviews for *Filmkritik*, a monthly cinema magazine, and for the daily newspaper *Süddeutsche Zeitung* and made seven films—six plotless, "experimental" short subjects and a feature.

The first of Wim Wenders' short films, *Schauplätze/Locations* (1967), has been lost, except for the two takes—shots of railroad tracks and a passing train—that form the opening and closing scenes of *Same Player Shoots Again* (1968), which takes its title from pinball. *Silver City* (1969), at twenty-five minutes the longest of his short films, consists entirely of three-minute views from various apartment windows. Both *3 Amerikanische LPs/3 American LPs* (1969) and *Alabama: 2000 Light Years* (1969) were constructed around contemporary American pop music. In fact, as John Sandford pointed out in his book *The New German Cinema* (1980), Wenders' only short film without American references is *Polizeifilm/Police Film* (1970), a comic work describing the tactics used by the Munich police to control student protesters at a street demonstration in 1968. The filmmaker has described his 145-minute feature *Summer in the City* (1971), about an ex-convict trying to make a fresh start, as "a documentary about the end of the sixties" reflecting "a longing for bet-

ter times." Some sources say the film constituted his thesis for a degree in cinematography.

Shortly after leaving the Hochschule, Wenders and fourteen other promising young filmmakers founded the Filmverlag der Autoren to produce and distribute their films. One of the cooperative's first releases was *Die Angst des Tormanns beim Elfmeter/The Goalie's Anxiety at the Penalty Kick* (1972), based on the existential novel by the avant-garde Austrian playwright Peter Handke. *The Goalie's Anxiety at the Penalty Kick* is about a former professional soccer player who picks up a cinema cashier, murders her, then wanders aimlessly around the city, waiting for the police to arrest him. Both a Kafkaesque portrait of an alienated individual and a nail-biting thriller, it resembles Wenders' student films in its saturation with American imagery—rock music, pinball machines, jukeboxes, American currency, and homesick American tourists.

Der Scharlachrote Buchstabe/The Scarlet Letter, an adaptation of Nathaniel Hawthorne's classic tale of spiritual conflict in colonial New England, which he made for German television in 1973, is, in Wenders' opinion, his least satisfying work. While initially drawn to the idea of the Puritans as transplanted Europeans in the strange, wild land that was seventeenth-century America, Wenders came to feel restricted by the period costumes and artificial sets. "You can't improvise with the past . . . ," he explained to Jan Dawson. "And of course Puritans had no pinball machines. So I lost interest." He went on to admit that he did not, "either at the beginning or the end, have any feelings" for the victimized central character, Hester Prynne. Still, *The Scarlet Letter* clearly bears Wenders' stamp in its depiction of Hester's sense of isolation in a repressive, male-dominated society.

Impressed by the performance of seven-year-old Yella Rottländer, who played Hester Prynne's daughter, Wenders wrote *Alice in den Städten/Alice in the Cities* (1974) with the young actress in mind. The first in a trilogy of what the director has called his "road movies," *Alice in the Cities* follows the title character and Philip Winter, the restless, burned-out German photojournalist who had befriended her in the United States, as they travel around northern Germany searching for the little girl's grandmother. On its commercial American release in 1977 (it had been shown previously in the United States at the 1974 New York Film Festival), *Alice in the Cities* was dismissed by some critics as being little more than "an unsatisfying, avant-garde version" of the 1973 American film *Paper Moon*, to quote Frank Rich. Yet even Rich, in his review for the *New York Post* (April 29, 1977), conceded that Wenders had "the ability to make us look at the world through fresh eyes." Rich found the director's perspective on life in the United States, especially as revealed in still photographs—"of Florida beaches, empty hotel rooms, superhighways"—taken by Winter, to be unusually perceptive.

"Shooting *Alice in the Cities* myself was an experience after which I felt much closer to the European cinema," Wenders told Rob Baker in an interview for the *Soho Weekly News* (October 13, 1977). "I started seeing myself as much more a German or European director. I realized the American cinema was something I couldn't reproduce—it needed a totally different education, a totally different attitude toward everything." As if to underline his newfound German sensibility, he chose as his point of departure for his next film, *Falsche Bewegung/Wrong Move* (1975), Goethe's *Wilhelm Meisters Lehrjahre*. In Peter Handke's updated, free adaption of the classic *Bildungsroman* about a young man's search for spiritual growth and self-knowledge, the protagonist, an aspiring writer, sets out on a journey around Germany, hoping to find in his native land the inspiration that will exorcise his chronic writer's block. Along the way, he encounters modern-day reincarnations of Goethe's characters, but unlike Goethe's hero, Wenders' Wilhelm fails in his quest. Alone at the end, he wonders if he has "missed something" and is "still constantly missing something, with every new movement."

Although *Wrong Move* was hailed by German film critics, with *Der Spiegel's* Siegfried Schober going so far as to call it "one of the most important German films since Lubitsch, Lang, and Murnau," moviegoers, in Germany and elsewhere, responded more favorably to *Im Lauf der Zeit/In the Course of Time* (1976). Retitled *Kings of the Road* for its release abroad, the film was at least partly inspired by Walker Evans' stark photographs of rural poverty in the United States during the Depression. In Wenders' long, bleak tale, two chance travel companions, an itinerant motion picture projectionist-repairman and a runaway husband (played by Wenders regulars Rüdiger Vogler and Hanns Zischler), travel the back country roads of the economically depressed eastern fringes of West Germany in a battered converted moving van, following the projectionist's route from one small town to another. Wenders had roughed out a story line beforehand, but he frequently improvised on the spot in order to incorporate what he has called "*trouvailles*"—unexpected incidents—into his film.

The open-ended documentary style of *Kings of the Road* clearly reflects Wenders' debt to the director Yasujiro Ozu, his "only master," whose sublime craftsmanship and naturalistic approach illuminated Japanese domestic life in motion pictures of exquisite technical simplicity. Critics also saw in *Kings of the Road* traces of the Hollywood western, particularly Ford's *Two Rode Together*, and of the contemporary "buddy movie" about male bonding. Yet in Wenders' view, the American film most akin thematically to his three road movies—*Alice in the Cities, Wrong Move*, and *Kings of the Road*—is Bob Rafelson's *Five Easy Pieces*, starring Jack Nicholson as a prodigal pianist who, as Wenders put it, "just move[s] away from things that get bad." For Wenders' characters, however, hitting the road is more than a way to escape from a dreary routine; it is an "entirely phenomenological" experience. "Everyone's senses are more aware when they're traveling and in a new situation . . . ," the director explained to Jan Dawson. "Sometimes I think the emotion in my films comes only from the motion: it's not created by the characters. . . . The people in my films don't actually change much, if at all, but nevertheless constantly maintain the idea [that they are capable of change]."

Wenders' biggest success in the United States to date is *Der Amerikanische Freund/The American Friend* (1977), a slick, existential thriller, which, at $1.2 million, cost more than his previous five features combined. Based on Patricia Highsmith's suspense novels *Ripley's Game* and *Ripley Under Ground*, the film centers on the relationship between Jonathan Zimmermann, a small-businessman who is dying of leukemia, and his "American friend," Tom Ripley, a smooth-talking con artist who persuades him to kill a professional rival. As several critics observed, the tangled and, at times, incomprehensible plot of *The American Friend* is ultimately less important than its stunning visual images. "The glory of this study in blue and red . . . is its ability to transform each image into an immediate emotional statement . . . ," Terry Curtis Fox wrote in the *Village Voice* (October 3, 1977). "Watching *The American Friend* is like hearing a particularly potent piece of rock 'n' roll for the first time: even when the words aren't clear you are captured by the power of the nuance, content to leave literal clarity to future listenings (or, in this case, viewings)."

The conflict between narrative and cinematic image was equally apparent in *Hammett* (1982), Wenders' first American production and the first of his projects not to be photographed by Robby Müller, the cinematographer, or distributed by Filmverlag der Autoren. Drawn to the novels of Dashiell Hammett because of his sharp eye for the seamy underside of American society's upper echelons, Wenders agreed to direct the Zoetrope Studios' production of Joe Gores's mystery *Hammett: A Novel* (1975). In it, Hammett puts aside a revision of *The Dain Curse* to team up with his old Pinkerton partner in an investigation of murder and municipal corruption in San Francisco's Chinatown in 1928. But Wenders envisioned *Hammett* as being more than a detective story. "It is about somebody's imagination, a biography of this man's imagination—how he invented his writing and his characters and his kind of stories," the filmmaker insisted, as quoted in the *Aquarian* (March 2, 1983), a weekly devoted to the performing arts.

The disappointing critical reception that greeted the release of the intensely atmospheric, multilayered *Hammett* was the last in a long series of frustrations connected with its production. Wenders and Francis Ford Coppola, the head of Zoetrope Studios, had begun work on the film in 1978, but artistic differences over the script (Coppola ordered several rewrites) and various technical and logistical problems held up production for months. During one prolonged delay, Wenders returned to Europe to make *Der Stand der Dinge/The State of Things* (1982), a "horror-comedy," to use his description, which he wrote, cast, financed, and filmed in a matter of weeks. Widely interpreted as a fictional treatment of Wenders' ongoing troubles with Coppola, the film chronicles the trials and tribulations of an arty European director left stranded on location, without enough funds to complete his picture, by a Hollywood producer. *The State of Things* took the top award at the Venice Film Festival in 1982 and, the following year, captured West Germany's National Film Prize, which is given annually by the Ministry of the Interior.

The *Hammett* period was a watershed for Wenders, for it was during those years that he extended his concern with the effect of biculturalism on interpersonal communication to include an examination of the creative process itself. The loose structure of *Lightning Over Water* (1981), a rather self-conscious dramatized "documentary-within-a-documentary" about the last days of director Nicholas Ray, who died of cancer in 1979, derives from Wenders' preference for what he has called the "distilled improvisation" method of filmmaking—a method that, in his words, "allows you to take a character as the center of your film, and not the story." That the method is sometimes less than entirely successful is attested to by some of the characters in *Lightning Over Water*, who conceded on film that the improvised narrative was occasionally compromised by the obtrusiveness of the cameras. The final version of the film, which included footage from Ray's cinéma-vérité melodrama *The Lusty Men* and from his uncompleted work "You Can't Go Home Again," was appreciated more by the cognoscenti than the general public and fared poorly at the box office.

Interpersonal relationships, especially between men, have long been a favorite subject of Wenders'. In *Paris, Texas* (1984), which he wrote in collaboration with the Pulitzer Prize-winning American playwright Sam Shepard, he explored for the first time a woman's development and the relationship between the woman and her husband, who has recently returned to his family after a long absence. "Most movies about men and women describe relationships as a total disaster, or they describe them as if love can overcome everything," Wenders explained to Melinda Camber Porter in an interview for the London *Times*, as quoted in the *World Press Review* (March 1984). "I felt that this film should make an effort to show not a solution, not a utopia, but just some sort of transcendence or reverse order of things, where everything could be done again." When *Paris, Texas* was shown at the Cannes Film Festival in May 1984, critics especially admired Wenders' evocative depictions of the vast expanses of the American Southwest and the neon-lit enclaves of motels and truck-stop diners that dot America's highways.

A tall, gangly man with light brown hair, Wim Wenders is a "self-confessed pessimist" who exudes Beethovenian gravity. Little is known about his private life. Separated since 1982 from Ronee Blakely, the American actress and singer-songwriter whom he had married in August 1979, he makes his home in New York City, the headquarters of Gray City, Inc., the independent production and distribution company he formed in 1981 with producer Chris Sievernich. The company, whose first release was *Lightning Over Water*, has acquired the rights to Wenders' earlier German-made features from A. J. Bauer Films, and it has also marketed his most recent short films—*Reverse Angle: NYC March '82, Chambre 666*, and *Tokyo*. To encourage young, independent filmmakers, Wenders has produced a number of motion pictures, including Peter Przygodda's *Born to Diesel* (1978), Christopher Petit's *Radio On* (1979), and *The Left Handed Woman* (1978), a domestic film noir by Peter Handke. As for himself, Wenders told Melinda Camber Porter, "I do not know what I would have done had I not become a filmmaker. Not only do I measure my life through the ten movies that I have made so far, but also the changes that I have undergone personally have all been reinforced by the films I make."

References: *Christian Sci Mon* p19 Ja 15 '79 por; *Cinema* 216:22+ D '76 pors; *Films in Review* 34:355+ Je/Jl '83 por; *Wide Angle* 2:73+ no. 4 '78 pors; Dawson, Jan. *Wim Wenders* (1976); *International Motion Picture Almanac, 1984*; Sandford, John. *The New German Cinema* (1980); *Wer ist Wer?* (1983)

White, Robert E(dward)

Sept. 21, 1926– Former U.S. ambassador to El Salvador. Address: b. c/o Simmons College, 300 The Fenway, Boston, Mass. 02115

Robert White, the career diplomat who was chosen by President Jimmy Carter in 1980 for an emergency assignment as U.S. ambassador to El Salvador, has emerged as one of the most knowledgeable and persistent critics of President Ronald Reagan's policies toward Central America. Currently the Visiting Warburg Professor of International Relations at Simmons College in Boston, White, who was forced out of the Foreign Service by the new Reagan administration in 1981, has continued to speak out on the issues that were the focus of his professional life for a quarter century. He has questioned the American government's apparently increasing emphasis on military rather than political solutions to the insurgency in El Salvador, and he has condemned Washington's rapprochement with Roberto d'Aubuisson, who is the head of Salvador's far-right Nationalist Republican Alliance and the opponent of centrist José Napoleón Duarte, who

Robert E. White

won the run-off election for the presidency of that country in May 1984. During sworn testimony that he gave before the subcommittee on the Western Hemisphere of the House Foreign Affairs Committee in February 1984, White charged that the Reagan administration has covered up important documents supplied by him three years ago that prove d'Aubuisson guilty of the assassination of Archbishop Oscar Arnulfo Romero in 1980 and identify six wealthy Salvadorans living in Miami as the financiers of the right-wing "death squads" responsible for 80 percent of the 47,000 political murders committed in El Salvador since 1979.

Robert Edward White was born on September 21, 1926 in Stoneham, Massachusetts to Edward V. and Emily G. (McGuire) White. He served overseas in the United States Navy from 1944 to 1946. After the war, White matriculated at St. Michael's, a Roman Catholic college in Winooski, Vermont. He earned a B.A. degree in 1952 and spent the following academic year in England as a Fulbright scholar at the University of Bristol. In 1954, White received a master's degree from the Fletcher School of Law and Diplomacy at Tufts University.

White worked in the private sector until he joined the Foreign Service in August 1955. His initial assignments in the State Department were as an international economist, foreign affairs officer, and information specialist. He received his first overseas post in July 1958, when he became vice-consul at the American consulate in Hong Kong. In the following June, he took the position of second secretary at the U.S. embassy in Ottawa, Ontario, Canada, but returned to Washington in September 1961 to assume new responsibilities as departmental foreign affairs officer.

Robert E. White's long involvement in Latin American diplomacy began in June 1963 when the State Department assigned him to the Consulate General in Guayaquil, Ecuador as deputy principal officer. He served there for two years before he was appointed the chief of the political section in Tegucigalpa, Honduras. Although from 1968 to 1970 he was temporarily detached from the Foreign Service to serve as deputy director (1968–69) and later director (1969–70) of the Latin American regional office of the Peace Corps, he returned to the diplomatic corps as deputy chief of mission at the U.S. embassy in Managua, Nicarauga. He took over the same position two years later at the American embassy in Bogotá, Colombia.

After completing his assignment in Colombia in 1975, White became Washington's deputy representative to the Organization of American States (OAS). His performance in that new post was controversial. At the General Assembly of the OAS held in Santiago, Chile in June 1976, White introduced in behalf of the United States and four other nations a strong appeal calling on the member states to "strengthen respect for human rights," and he also explicitly criticized the host government for its violations of those rights. When the State Department, allegedly at the instigation of Secretary of State Henry Kissinger, later reprimanded White for his actions, the American representative threatened to resign "unless immediate action [was] taken to restore [his] professional standing." The reprimand was withdrawn, and in February 1976 White used the occasion of an inter-American conference on education, science, and culture, which was held in Uruguay, to repeat his call for greater respect for human rights within the Western Hemisphere.

The victory of Jimmy Carter in the November 1976 presidential election led to a noticeable shift toward making the defense of human rights a key theme in American foreign policy. Not surprisingly, Robert White found the new political climate congenial, and in October 1977 Carter named him the American ambassador to Paraguay. In his new assignment, White earned the reputation of being one of the "activist" American envoys dispatched to Latin America by the Carter administration. He and several other career diplomats extended the traditional role of American ambassadors by speaking out in favor of moderate reform and maintaining political contacts with the leadership of responsible opposition groups in Latin America. Host governments did not always appreciate the change, and ambassadors were often accused by those countries of interfering in their internal affairs. Washington, however, encouraged the strong stand its representatives took, especially on matters related to human rights. According to a State Department official, "Perhaps more than ambassadors anywhere else in the world, they are implementing policy." In July 1978, for example, after Domingo Laino, the vice-president of Paraguay's Authentic Radical Liberal party, was arrested for issuing an anti-government statement in Washington, D.C., White expressed America's deep concern to Foreign Minister Alberto Nogues and was accused by the government of being meddlesome for doing so. And in July 1979 White joined a group of Congressmen in urging the Asunción government to seek out and extradite Dr. Josef Mengele, known as the "angel of death," who had fled to Paraguay after World War II and taken citizenship there to escape prosecution for his involvement in the torture and killing of thousands of people during genetic experiments at Auschwitz.

In February 1980, President Carter nominated White to be the American ambassador to El Salvador where, on October 15, 1979, junior officers in the Army had overthrown the dictatorial government of President Carlos Humberto Romero. The Carter administration had given its tacit support to the coup in the hope that the politically moderate four-man junta that took power would initiate much-needed reforms such as land redistribution to undercut popular support for the leftist guerrillas, who were fomenting a Nicaragua-style, that is, a Marxist-Leninist, revolution in El Salvador. As a spur in that direction, the administration closely tied its program of financial and military aid to demonstrable progress in land reform and the curtailment of human rights abuses.

A staunch supporter of President Carter's policies in Central America, Ambassador White, like Carter, entertained no illusions about the guerrillas' intentions. Although he conceded in his article for the New York Times Magazine (July 18, 1982) that the "left constituted a vital and authentic popular force," he maintained that the extremist, Marxist-Leninist leaders of the leftist movement were determined to undermine American influence and democracy in the region. As a result, he seconded the administration's opinion that "there was only one realistic way to deal with that: arrive at a negotiated solution that would prevent a guerrilla victory and augment the power of the democratic left." Conservative Republicans in the U.S. Congress, however, opposed any concessions to the left, and Senator Jesse Helms of North Carolina labeled Carter's ambassadorial nominee as a "leftist" and "dangerous ideologue" who supported "murky proposals to turn El Salvador's economic system toward socialism." Helms managed to delay confirmation of White's appointment for six weeks, but on March 5, 1980 the full Senate approved the president's selection by a margin of 71–17.

Once in El Salvador, White tried to keep the government on the path to reform. He supported the junta's actions to convert all land holdings over 1,500 acres into producer cooperatives and to nationalize private banks in order to democratize access to credit. He also encouraged plans to give 150,000 sharecroppers title to the lands that they tilled and to redistribute the rich coffee lands of between 250 and 1,500 acres. White hoped that those programs would alleviate the suffering caused by what he described as "the most skewed system of income distribution in the hemisphere," and thus dilute the revolutionary zeal of the poor.

But because that system had been perpetuated by an elite corps of El Salvador's wealthy, according to White, those measures generated enormous resistance among the plutocrats. Following the overthrow of the Humberto government, which they had supported, and the introduction of the junta's reforms, the ultraconservatives resorted to a combination of terrorism and political maneuvering to regain the power they had held, with the support of the military, since 1932. Rightist "death squads" assassinated hundreds of opposition leaders, union leaders, and suspected leftist sympathizers every month. On March 24, 1980, just two week after White's arrival in San Salvador, right-wing gunmen murdered Archbishop Oscar Arnulfo Romero as the social-activist priest celebrated Mass. And during 1980, some landowners and industrialists also sponsored two abortive coups, both led by Roberto d'Aubuisson. An army officer who was cashiered for his abuses of human rights, d'Aubuisson has also been repeatedly linked to the death squads and has been accused by White of ordering the archbishop's murder. In addition, he founded in 1981 and was the presidential candidate of ARENA (the Spanish acronym of the Nationalist Republican Alliance party), the political arm of the ultraconservatives.

His fears of the left notwithstanding, White believed that the real threat to El Salvador's survival lay on the right. According to the ambassador, the "anachronistic power structure" in place before the 1979 coup had constituted "one of the most selfish oligarchies the world has ever seen," and the inequities produced by it had sown the seeds of revolution. White predicted in an interview for U.S. News & World Report (January 26, 1981) that if the extreme right returned to power and subverted the reforms sponsored by the junta "El Salvador would lose the important support it now enjoys in many progressive countries of Europe and Latin America. The violence would increase. Leftist forces would be spiritually and materially strengthened by new recruits who would have abandoned hope for a moderate solution. You would have a resurgence of the battle between the two extremes."

Ambassador White himself became a target of the rightists. Believing that he had pressured the authorities into briefly detaining d'Aubuisson and eight others on suspicion of plotting against the junta, armed rightist demonstrators besieged the envoy's residence on May 10, 1980. Using loudspeakers, they denounced White as a Communist and demanded an end to interference by the United States in El Salvador's domestic affairs. Finally, on May 12, White and his deputy chief of mission, Mark Dion, were able to break through the barricades in an armored Cadillac while Marine guards scattered the demonstrators with tear gas. Later that day, four men fired submachine guns at the American Embassy in San Salvador. Nevertheless, he continued to put pressure for reform on the government of José Napoleón Duarte, who became the leading figure in the junta after joining it in March 1980. White developed confidence in Duarte, a civilian and political moderate who had been tortured and forced into exile by the military after winning the presidential election in 1972 and who, in the ambassador's view, had "honest-to-God democratic credentials." His optimism, however, was soon tested when on December 4 four American Catholic churchwomen, considered leftist because of their social work among the poor, were found murdered. White, who was one of the first people to arrive at the grave where the corpses had been hidden, was furious, and his anger was tempered only by the announcement of a political shakeup that made Duarte president of the junta on December 13.

Ronald Reagan's victory in the 1980 presidential election marked the beginning of the end of Robert E. White's tenure in El Salvador. Even before his election, Reagan had made it abundantly clear that he considered the violence in Central America to have been instigated and supported by Cuba and the Soviet Union rather than to have been brought about by internal tensions, and he disparaged President Carter's policy of linking aid to the issue of human rights. The President-elect advocated increased aid to the military in El Salvador to help it defeat the left while buttressing right-wing elements. Early in December, Reagan's transition team issued a report that called for the replacement of sixty ambassadors, including White, and that specifically criticized envoys who functioned "in the capacity of social reformers and advocates of new theories of social change." White accused the transition team of "malice and stupidity" and claimed that it had "totally undermined [his] authority and [his] effectiveness at the very time the United States needs the most leverage."

Shortly after President Reagan's inauguration, Secretary of State Alexander M. Haig called White to Washington for consultations. According to the ambassador, Haig assured him that he had done an "excellent job," and that his analyses had been "exactly right," but that changes nevertheless had to be made. On February 1, 1981, Haig relieved White of his duties in El Salvador. Apparently the ambassador had gone too far in publicly questioning the new administration's intention to emphasize military aid to El Salvador and in accusing the State Department of permitting a coverup of the murder of the Catholic missionaries. White expected to receive another assignment, but none was forthcoming. According to sources in the Reagan administration, Haig personally decided to force the ambassador out of the Foreign Service, and later in February White received notice that he was being "automatically retired" in accordance with a statute for releasing ambassadors for whom there were no further duties. White, who was only the tenth ambassador to be so separated under the law, remarked that the renowned Cold War expert, George F. Kennan, had suffered the same fate. "So with Kennan," he said, "I'm in pretty good company."

Since his dismissal, White has continued to criticize the Reagan administration's definition of and solutions for the problems of El Salvador. In his opinion, the Salvadoran revolution is "home-grown" and the military represents "the problem, not the solution." The former ambassador has also described the election that was held in El Salvador on March 28, 1982—as a direct result of pressure from the Reagan administration—as "a distortion of the democratic process." The voters were given numbered ballots, which they had to place in transparent boxes, and no candidates to the left of Duarte's centrist Christian Democrats were allowed to run. According to White, the surprise of the election "was not that the rightist candidates won 60 percent of the vote but that they did not win even more."

White believes that Washington compounded the problems caused by the 1982 election, which drove Duarte from office, by using its influence to have Alvaro Alfredo Magaña, an independent conservative, rather than the leading vote-getter, d'Aubuisson, installed as president. D'Aubuisson had vowed to end the turmoil in El Salvador in six months—an impossible promise to keep, according to White—and if he had been allowed to take office his failure to fulfill his campaign pledge might have undermined his influence and paved the way for his replacement by non-Marxist moderates. Instead, under the ineffectual Magaña, the rightists and military consolidated their position and stepped into the power vacuum. The moderates have been driven toward the guerrillas for whom, in White's judgment, victory has become inevitable. According to the former envoy, the best hope at present is for the government to deal with the guerrillas before the latter have no incentive to make concessions. Successful negotiations could keep pluralism and democracy alive by dividing power among the various factions in the country.

However, the credibility of White's assertions about the situation in El Salvador was considerably weakened in early 1984. When Arturo Muyshondt, a wealthy Salvadoran whom White had not only called a "madman" and "scum" but also accused of helping to bankroll the death squads, filed a $10-million libel suit against him and in March petitioned Congress to strip him of the life-long title of ambassador, White admitted that the first name may have been misspelled and so "[his] statement may have named Arturo Muyshondt erroneously." Later that month, the New York Times reported that the Salvadoran security-police officer whom White had put forth as an informant against the death squads had actually been promised $50,000 by White and other critics of the Reagan administration's policies in El Salvador to speak out against the President's tactics in public and before Congress. White denied that he took part in the financing or that he did more than assure certain congressmen that the Salvadoran was, to quote the Washington Post (March 28, 1984), "in a position to know the things he alleged."

On June 4, 1955 Robert E. White married Mary Anne Cahill. They have five children: Christopher Cahill, Kevin McGuire, Claire Elizabeth, Mary

Louise, and Laura Cary. A Roman Catholic, White received an honorary doctorate in humane letters in 1978 from St. Michael's College, his alma mater. He serves on the board of directors of the American School in Honduras and is a member of the American Foreign Service Association and of the Society for International Development. White has also been a senior associate of the Carnegie Endowment for International Peace.

References: N Y Times p3 Je 11 '77 por; American Catholic Who's Who, 1980–81; Biographic Register of the Department of State, 1974; Who's Who in American Politics, 1977–78; Who's Who in the World, 1982–83

Wilder, Billy

June 22, 1906– Motion picture director; writer; producer. Address: b. c/o Equitable Investment Corporation, 6253 Hollywood Blvd., Los Angeles, Calif. 90028

NOTE: This biography supersedes the article that appeared in Current Biography in 1951.

Described in Film Comment (May–June 1982) as "romantic and cynic, lover of Old World farce conventions and practitioner of New World verismo," Billy Wilder is one of Hollywood's great directors, producers, and screenwriters, with over fifty films and six Academy Awards to his credit. His films range from stark melodrama, like Double Indemnity (1944), The Lost Weekend (1945), and Sunset Boulevard (1950), to antic farce, such as The Seven Year Itch (1955) and Some Like It Hot

(1959), and satiric comedy, like A Foreign Affair (1948) and The Apartment (1960), in which he dissects human foibles with razor-sharp wit. In the words of his biographer Maurice Zolotow, Billy Wilder is "the very heart and soul of the film industry."

Billy Wilder was born Samuel Wilder on June 22, 1906 in the town of Sucha in Galicia, a section of Poland that was then part of the Austro-Hungarian Empire. His father, Max Wilder, who died in 1926, ran a chain of railway cafes, imported watches, and operated a trout hatchery. His mother, Eugenia (Baldinger) Wilder (some sources give her maiden name as Dittler), who died at Auschwitz during World War II, had spent several years in the United States in her youth. She nicknamed her younger son Billy because of her fascination with the legendary American hero Buffalo Bill. Wilder has a brother, Wilhelm, born in 1905, who under the name W. Lee Wilder produced Hollywood films in the 1950s.

During his childhood, Wilder spent much of his time in the gaming rooms of hotels, became adept at billiards and cards and learned "many things about human nature—none of them favorable." At the Realgymnasium in Vienna, where the family moved in 1914, he was mainly interested in sports and rebelled against the rigid pedagogy but did well in history, languages, and literature. As a teenager, he became addicted to American jazz and dancing, Ernst Lubitsch films, and Westerns.

Wilder attended the University of Vienna's pre-law program for three months in the fall of 1924. He then obtained a job with the newspaper Die Stunde writing interviews, crime and sports stories, and hard-hitting personality profiles. Once, in a single day, he interviewed Arthur Schnitzler, Richard Strauss, and Alfred Adler and made an unsuccessful attempt to obtain an interview with Sigmund Freud. According to Maurice Zolotow, Wilder's discovery about that time that his flapper girlfriend was a prostitute became a major source of his sour cynicism and of the ambivalent image of women seen in his films.

In 1926 Wilder's interests led him to a publicity job with the American jazz bandleader Paul Whiteman in Berlin. Remaining there, he obtained work as a writer for the popular Berliner Zeitung am Mittag, or "B.Z.," and for such publications as Nachtausgabe, Börsenkurier, Tempo, and the cultural journal Querschnitt. He also ghostwrote dozens of scenarios for silent films. For a time, Wilder worked as a hired hotel dance partner, or Eintänzer, for older women, an experience he wrote about in a B.Z. exposé on the Berlin gigolo scene. An important influence on Wilder during his Berlin period was the Romanisches Café, a bohemian haunt frequented by such celebrities as Bertolt Brecht, Thomas Mann, George Grosz, Fritz Lang, Hermann Hesse, and Erich Maria Remarque.

In 1929 Wilder collaborated with Fred Zinnemann and others in making the film Menschen am Sonntag (People on Sunday). The bawdy verité romance, or "street symphony," shot in Wannsee park on the outskirts of Berlin, depicts the fleeting escape that four strangers share for a day. It resulted in jobs for the collaborators with the mammoth film production combine Universum Film Aktien Gesellschaft (UFA). Of Wilder's twelve UFA credits as a scenario writer for comedies, operettas, and romantic thrillers, the best known was the popular *Emil und die Detektive* (1931; Emil and the Detectives), based on Erich Kästner's classic children's novel. But for a Jew with left-wing sympathies, it soon became apparent that the UFA studios, controlled by the pro-Nazi industrialist Alfred Hugenberg, and Germany itself, held little promise. In March 1933, a week after the German Reichstag fire, Wilder fled to Paris.

In Paris, Wilder directed his first film, *Mauvaise Graine* (1933; Bad Seed), a juvenile crime thriller starring Danielle Darrieux. Then, in December 1933, Columbia Pictures producer Joe May cabled Wilder that he had accepted his script for *Pam-Pam*, a "musical strudel" about counterfeiters and a runaway girl, and offered him a six-month Hollywood contract at $150 a week.

Reaching Los Angeles early in 1934, Wilder was one of a growing colony of European émigrés in Hollywood, among them Peter Lorre, with whom he shared living quarters for a time. Wilder followed Joe May to Twentieth Century-Fox, where he received his first American screen credit for co-adapting the Jerome Kern musical *Music in the Air* (1934), starring Gloria Swanson. Wilder next wrote the scenario for *Lottery Lover* (1935), a B melodrama set in Paris, and contributed to the script of *Under Pressure*. Then, with Hy Kraft he wrote *Champagne Waltz* (Paramount, 1937), a Vienna-based comedy about a bandleader courting a prima donna. As a result, Paramount offered Wilder a $250-a-week contract, marking the beginning of his seventeen years with that studio.

Wilder's first project after he joined Paramount was *Rhythm on the River*, a Bing Crosby vehicle, but its release was delayed until 1940. Meanwhile, the studio paired Wilder's "vulgar energy" with the refined dialogue of Charles Brackett, a former theatre critic for the *New Yorker*. Their sometimes stormy twelve-year partnership began with the spicy but tasteful comedy *Bluebeard's Eighth Wife* (1938), starring Claudette Colbert and Gary Cooper. It was directed by Ernst Lubitsch, whom Wilder regards as his mentor.

After collaborating on Paramount's *What a Life* (1939), an adolescent romance, and *Midnight* (1939), a Mitchell Leisen comedy starring Claudette Colbert as a Bronx Cinderella in Paris, Brackett and Wilder wrote *Ninotchka* (MGM, 1939), Lubitsch's classic comedy hit about a Soviet commissar (Greta Garbo) who undergoes a political conversion under the romantic influence of a Paris playboy (Melvin Douglas). Although that good-natured lampoon of Communism caused some controversy at a time when many Hollywood directors, writers, and actors held pro-Soviet sympathies, it brought the writers their first Oscar nominations. In 1939 Wilder became a United States citizen.

Back at Paramount, Wilder and Brackett wrote the scenario for Leisen's *Arise My Love* (1940), a romance set in the Spanish Civil War, and *Hold Back the Dawn* (1941), based on a story by Ketti Frings. The latter concerns an American schoolteacher (Olivia de Havilland) vacationing in Mexico, who is seduced into marriage by a Romanian gigolo (Charles Boyer). The *New York Times*'s Bosley Crowther (October 2, 1941) found it "an amazingly poignant picture." But Wilder, infuriated by Leisen's last-minute script changes to accommodate Boyer, swore to have directorial control over the films he worked on in the future. The final films he wrote but did not direct were Sam Spiegel's all-star *Tales of Manhattan* (Twentieth Century-Fox, 1942), based on a script he had written earlier for UFA, and Sam Goldwyn's *Ball of Fire* (RKO, 1942), coauthored by Brackett, directed by Howard Hawks, and costarring Barbara Stanwyck and Gary Cooper, about a stripper pursued by gangsters who finds refuge with a group of professors.

Wilder's American directorial debut—with Brackett as cowriter and producer—was *The Major and the Minor* (RKO, 1942), in which an Army major (Ray Milland) shares his Pullman compartment with a young woman (Ginger Rogers) who disguises herself as a twelve-year-old in order to be able to travel at half-fare. It was followed by the mildly successful comedy-melodrama *Five Graves to Cairo* (Paramount, 1943), in which an English soldier (Franchot Tone) is disguised as a waiter in a Libyan oasis hotel so that he can discover the location of German supply dumps from General Erwin Rommel (Erich von Stroheim).

Wilder's next film was *Double Indemnity* (Paramount, 1944), adapted from James M. Cain's novel about duplicity, greed, and coldblooded murder among members of Southern California's upper middle class. The story so disgusted Brackett that the mystery author Raymond Chandler stood in for him as cowriter. Innovatively shot on location, the *film noir* has a "vibrantly malignant" Barbara Stanwyck scheming with a "blithe prig" of an insurance agent (Fred MacMurray) to murder her husband and thus enable her to collect on a double indemnity policy. A cool claims investigator (Edward G. Robinson) looks on as the schemers' "pitilessly developed" relationship dissolves. Howard Barnes, reviewing *Double Indemnity* in the *New York Herald Tribune* (September 7, 1944) noted that with this film Wilder proved himself to be "one of the really first-rate directors."

Brackett returned as cowriter for *The Lost Weekend* (Paramount, 1945), based on Charles Jackson's best-seller about an alcoholic. The film's bleak drama and documentary expressionism riveted audiences and critics alike. Despite covert efforts by the liquor industry to suppress it, *The Lost Weekend* earned four Academy Awards. In addition to winning top honors as best picture, it garnered for its star, Ray Milland, the best actor award and brought Wilder two Oscars, as cowriter and director. It also received the Cannes Film Festival's first Grand Prix.

Invited by Elmer Davis, head of the Office of War Information, to join the United States Army's Psychological Warfare Division for help in its denazification program, Wilder spent six months in Germany in 1945 with the rank of colonel, taking part in the restructuring of the UFA-dominated motion picture industry and of German radio facilities. Back in Hollywood, he directed, and cowrote with Brackett, *The Emperor Waltz* (Paramount, 1948), an opulent semi-operetta in Technicolor about a brash Yankee phonograph salesman (Bing Crosby) romancing a straitlaced countess (Joan Fontaine) in Emperor Franz Josef's court.

Wilder's cynicism came to a head with the comedy *A Foreign Affair* (Paramount, 1948), a grim portrayal of American occupation soldiers involved in bombed-out Berlin's *demimonde*. It features a triangle consisting of a crusading Iowa Republican Congresswoman (Jean Arthur), a magnificently sleazy cabaret singer (Marlene Dietrich) who had been a Nazi's mistress, and her current lover, an American officer (John Lund). But though the film was denounced in Congress and by the Defense Department, and United States government pressure played a part in its withdrawal from circulation at a time when the Cold War was escalating, critics welcomed its satiric humor. And Maurice Zolotow has called it "still one of the best political pictures ever made in Hollywood."

Wilder's "mordant and haunting" *Sunset Boulevard* (Paramount, 1950) depicts an aging silent screen star (Gloria Swanson) with delusions of a comeback, living in a rotting Hollywood palace attended by her butler and ex-husband (Erich von Stroheim). It is narrated in flashback by a cynical screenwriter (William Holden) whose dead body is seen floating in the swimming pool at the beginning of the film. Like *Double Indemnity*, *Sunset Boulevard* focuses on the escalating tension between predatory partners. Widely regarded as the best film ever made about the Hollywood mystique, it contrasts the modern film industry with Gloria Swanson's mummified silent screen aura and is punctuated by epigrams, including one that is perhaps Wilder's most famous and prophetic line: "I am big. It's the pictures that got small." *Sunset Boulevard* was nominated for six Oscars and won three, including one for the writing team of Wilder, Brackett, and D. M. Marshman Jr. It was Wilder's last collaboration with Brackett.

Wilder made his debut as a producer with *Ace in the Hole* (Paramount, 1951; later retitled *The Big Carnival*), which he also directed. He collaborated on the script with Lesser Samuels and Walter Newman. The film stars Kirk Douglas as an unscrupulous reporter who seizes on the plight of a man trapped in a New Mexico cave by creating a media spectacle out of the hamstrung rescue effort. But although it won honors at the Venice Film Festival and received on Oscar nomination for screenwriting, it was a critical and commercial failure.

For his next production, Wilder filmed the play *Stalag 17*, which he had bought from its Broadway producers for $50,000. It stars William Holden as a hustler and confidence man running a black market operation for his fellow inmates in a World War II German prisoner-of-war camp. The successful 1953 Paramount production earned Holden an Academy Award as best actor and brought Wilder an Oscar nomination as best director. Then, with Ernest Lehman, Wilder adapted *Sabrina* (Paramount, 1954) from Samuel Taylor's Broadway hit, with Humphrey Bogart as an aging executive who falls under Audrey Hepburn's elfin spell even though his plan had been merely to divert her from his playboy brother (William Holden). Wilder parted company with Paramount Pictures in 1954 after one of its executives insisted on toning down the anti-Nazism in a new dubbed version of *Stalag 17* destined for the West German market.

Wilder's first independent work was the comedy hit *The Seven Year Itch* (1955), a George Axelrod play, which he adapted for Twentieth Century-Fox with the playwright and coproduced with Charles K. Feldman. Filmed in CinemaScope, it depicts a guilt-ridden husband (Tom Ewell) contemplating mischief with his ingenuously alluring neighbor (Marilyn Monroe) during his wife's absence. At the same time, Wilder was working with Wendell Mayes and Charles Lederer on a Warner Brothers production of *The Spirit of St. Louis* (1957), an adaptation of Charles A. Lindbergh's autobiography, starring James Stewart and narrated by him. But the film encountered production problems and took a financial loss when it was released in its botched version.

With *Love in the Afternoon* (Allied Artists, 1957), a Lubitsch-like charade, Wilder began a twenty-five-year partnership with the screenwriter I. A. L. Diamond. Based on Claude Anet's novel *Ariane*, the film features a winsome young cellist (Audrey Hepburn) wooed in Paris by an aging philanderer (Gary Cooper) who is being investigated by her detective father (Maurice Chevalier) and hunted by the jealous husband of one of his conquests. Wilder's next film, *Witness for the Prosecution* (United Artists, 1958), which he wrote with Harry Kurnitz as a tribute to Alfred Hitchcock, was the unexpected hit of the year. It marked the beginning of his sixteen-year relationship with the newly formed Mirisch Brothers' production company. Based on Agatha Christie's courtroom stage drama, it features an icy German war bride (Marlene Dietrich) who testifies against her husband (Tyrone Power), accused of a rich widow's murder but ably defended by a feisty barrister at Old Bailey (Charles Laughton).

Some Like It Hot (1959), inspired by a 1932 UFA film written by Robert Thoeren, was a huge box-office success. Set in 1929, it features two jazz musicians (Jack Lemmon and Tony Curtis) on the lam from a Chicago mob, who masquerade as members of an all-girl band of which Marilyn Monroe is the vocalist. Romantic difficulties ensue when Curtis as "Josephine" falls for Miss Monroe and Lemmon as "Daphne" is courted by a harebrained million-aire (Joe E. Brown). During the filming, Wilder had problems with the temperamental Monroe, leading to a highly publicized splenetic exchange with her husband, Arthur Miller. Described in *Variety* (February 25, 1959) as "a gay romp that knows just when to draw back before crossing the line to the vulgar," *Some Like It Hot* earned an Academy Award for costume design and five other Oscar nominations, including two for Wilder as cowriter and director.

Described by Maurice Zolotow as a "satiric masterpiece of upward mobility through corporate pandering," Wilder's *The Apartment* (United Artists, 1960) is about a lowly clerk (Jack Lemmon) who hopes to advance his career by lending his apartment to his bosses for their extramarital assignations. Shirley MacLaine costars as the jilted girl whom Lemmon wins at the end. Although the film was panned by some critics for its sordid aspects, it was generally well received. Bosley Crowther, for example, of the *New York Times* praised it for its adherence to a "line of extremely sophisticated balancing between cynicism and sentiment, between irony and pity, that has run through most of the best American comedies." *The Apartment* earned for its creator three Academy Awards, as writer, as director, and as producer of the year's best film.

After scrapping his plans to make a Marx Brothers comedy, Wilder devoted himself to filming the headlong farce *One, Two, Three* (United Artists, 1961), set in post-World War II Berlin. Based on a 1926 play by Ferenc Molnár, it stars James Cagney as a local representative of the Coca-Cola company who unsuccessfully tries to prevent his superior's empty-headed daughter from marrying a hippy-type East Berlin Communist. Although some critics, notably Pauline Kael and Andrew Sarris, deplored what they saw as the film's lack of good taste, others sang its praises, with Arthur M. Schlesinger Jr. going so far as to call it "an irresistible evocation of the mood of Mark Twain." Wilder next cowrote, produced, and directed *Irma La Douce* (United Artists, 1963), which became a major box-office success. Adapted from Alexandre Breffort's French hit musical, it deals with a Parisian prostitute (Shirley MacLaine) and her policeman boyfriend (Jack Lemmon), who monopolizes her attention at night by disguising himself as a wealthy English lord.

In accordance with his maxim that "the only pictures worth making are the ones that are playing with fire," Wilder adapted Anna Bonacci's play *L'Ora della Fantasia* into the film *Kiss Me, Stupid* (United Artists, 1964). It concerns a wife (Felicia Farr) and a prostitute (Kim Novak) who trade places for a night after the former's jealous but ambitious husband (Ray Walston) offers her to a lecherous entertainer (Dean Martin) as part of a business deal. Lambasted in reviews as "squalid," "smutty," "sordid," "coarse," and in "cheery bad taste," *Kiss Me, Stupid* had the dubious distinction of being condemned by the Roman Catholic Church's Legion of Decency.

In December 1964 the Museum of Modern Art in New York City presented a sixteen-film, thirty-five-year retrospective of Wilder's work. Similar showings were later held in Paris, Berlin, and Los Angeles. Nevertheless, Wilder's popularity declined in the 1960s as sexual inhibitions relaxed, blunting the edge of his satire and leading him at times to adopt less subtle antics for younger audiences.

After spending a year in Switzerland, where he wrote material for the James Bond spoof *Casino Royale* (Columbia, 1967) and viewed many new films, Wilder produced, cowrote, and directed *The Fortune Cookie* (United Artists 1966; released in Great Britain as *Meet Whiplash Willie*). The story of a television sports cameraman (Jack Lemmon) whose lawyer brother-in-law (Walter Matthau) persuades him to fake injuries and sue for a million dollars after a minor accident, it was seen by some critics as a sharp satire on sleazy American mores, and it earned Matthau an Oscar as best supporting actor.

Wilder then worked in London on the satirical *The Private Life of Sherlock Holmes* (United Artists, 1970) with I. A. L. Diamond, Harry Kurnitz, and playwright John Mortimer. The film depicts Holmes (Robert Stephens) as an inept, troubled cocaine addict who, with his partner Dr. Watson (Colin Blakely), becomes involved in international intrigue. His next work, the farce *Avanti!* (United Artists, 1972), adapted from a play by Samuel Taylor and filmed in Italy, had to do with an American executive (Jack Lemmon) who is romantically involved with the daughter (Juliet Mills) of the Englishwoman with whom his late father carried on annual vacation trysts for years until both were killed in a car crash.

For *The Front Page* (Universal, 1974), Wilder and Diamond rewrote the 1928 Ben Hecht–Charles MacArthur comedy about Chicago journalists. Directed by Wilder and produced by Paul Monash, it stars Walter Matthau as an unscrupulous editor and Jack Lemmon as his star reporter. For all its limitations, *The Front Page* was a box-office success and brought Wilder a contract with Universal Pictures. But Universal dropped its contract in 1976, when presented with Wilder's most personal script, *Fedora* (United Artist, 1978), based on a story in Thomas Tryon's book *Crowned Heads*. Financed by West German tax-shelter money and filmed in Munich, Paris, and Corfu, it was cowritten by Wilder and Diamond and directed by Wilder. Like *Sunset Boulevard*, it is, in the words of David Ansen of *Newsweek* (April 23, 1979), a "barbed disquisition on the subjects of stardom, vanity, mythmaking, and death." The story is narrated in a long flashback by William Holden in the role of a second-rate film producer who seeks the ageless Garboesque recluse Fedora (Marthe Keller) and learns her secret.

Wilder's most recent film, with himself as director and Diamond as his cowriter, was *Buddy, Buddy* (MGM, 1981), adapted from a play by Francis Veber. It costars Walter Matthau as a hit man for the mob and Jack Lemmon as a would-be suicide who befriends him. Described by Stephen Farber in the *New York Times* (December 6, 1981) as "the blackest of black comedies," it failed to inspire enthusiasm from critics and audiences.

In May 1982 Wilder was honored by the Film Society of Lincoln Center at a star-studded gala celebration in recognition of his work, spanning half a century. According to Michiko Kakutani, writing in the *New York Times* (May 4, 1982), after completing *Buddy Buddy* Wilder and Diamond still met each morning at their office, "rejecting ideas, narrowing the choices of what to do next." Emphatically waving aside all thoughts of retirement, Wilder said: "As far as I'm concerned, this ball game is not over. . . . There are still a few hits left in me."

In May 1936 Billy Wilder married Judith Coppicus Iribe, a member of an old California family. From that marriage, which ended in divorce in 1947, he has a daughter, Victoria (Mrs. Tony Set-

tember), and a grandchild. With his second wife, the former starlet and singer Audrey Young, whom he married in June 1949, Wilder makes his home in an elegant Hollywood apartment filled with part of his modern art collection, one of the largest in private hands in the world. Formerly red-haired, the cherubic, baldish Wilder typically is in "opulent casual dress." Speaking "with a curious blend of Austrian formality and American slang," the self-styled master storyteller is, in the words of Aljean Harmetz of the *New York Times* (June 29, 1979), "jovial, clever, acerbic, peremptory, crafting his sentences with sophisticated eye and razor tongue."

References: Dick, Bernard. *Billy Wilder* (1980); Katz, Ephraim. *Film Encyclopedia* (1979); Masden, Axel. *Billy Wilder* (1968); Seidman, Steve. *The Film Career of Billy Wilder* (1977); Zolotow, Maurice. *Billy Wilder in Hollywood* (1977)

Williams, Billy Dee

April 6, 1937– Actor. Address: b. c/o Star Direction, 605 N. Oakhurst Drive, Beverly Hills, Calif. 90210

Steering clear of what is known in show business as "blaxploitation" typecasting, Billy Dee Williams has established for himself the stage, screen, and television persona of a debonair romantic hero whose magnetism transcends race. A tall, athletically built man with a roguish smile, melodic voice, and panther-like gait, Williams has been accumu-

lating theatrical credits since childhood. His first love, however, was painting, and he did not begin to pursue acting singlemindedly until he attracted attention with his touching portrayal of the sailor lover of the heroine in the original Broadway production of *A Taste of Honey* (1960–61). After a decade in the doldrums, Williams's career blasted starward with his role as the dying football player's best friend in the made-for-television hit film *Brian's Song* (1971), and he achieved matinee-idol status as the husband of Billie Holiday in the screen biography *Lady Sings the Blues* (1972), produced by Berry Gordy and starring Diana Ross.

Williams later starred in the Gordy screen productions *Mahogany* (1975) and *The Bingo Long Traveling All-Stars and Motor Kings* (1976). For younger audiences, the most memorable of his later screen portrayals was that of the jive-talking Lando Calrissian, the opportunistic but valiant space pirate who switches to the good side in the intergalactic adventure fantasies *The Empire Strikes Back* (1980) and *Return of the Jedi* (1983), the second and third box-office blockbusters in George Lucas' ongoing *Star Wars* saga. His made-for-TV starring vehicles have ranged from *The Scott Joplin Story* (1976) to the comedy *Christmas Lilies of the Field* (1979) and the comedy-adventure detective film *Shooting Stars* (1983).

Billy Dee Williams and his twin sister, Loretta, were born on April 6, 1937 in Harlem, New York City, where they grew up on West 110th Street. Their Texas-born father, William December Williams, worked at three jobs—cook, janitor, and maintenance man. Their mother, Loretta Anne Williams, an immigrant from the island of Montserrat in the West Indies, was an opera singer *manqué* who worked as an elevator operator at the Lyceum Theatre on Broadway. With both parents working, the West Indian maternal grandmother played an important role in raising the twins. Taught to "surmount [their] surroundings," and imbued with "an interest in education and culture," Williams and his sister "were always painting" in childhood, as the actor recalled in an interview with Judy Klemesrud for the *New York Times* (September 19, 1976). "I played ball and hung out with the guys on the street, but unlike my friends, I was always stepping in and out [of street life]." Although the father was a Baptist, the children were raised as Methodists. Loretta Williams became a portrait painter, and Billy Dee Williams, a shy, withdrawn, overweight boy, originally planned to become a fashion illustrator. With that in mind, he attended the High School of Music and Art, at 135th Street and Convent Avenue in Manhattan, and then, on scholarship, the School of Fine Arts in the National Academy of Design, on Fifth Avenue.

Meanwhile, Williams had begun acting at age seven, when the producer Max Gordon spotted him keeping his mother company in the elevator at the Lyceum Theatre and gave him a walk-on role as a page in Kurt Weill's musical *The Firebrand of Florence*, starring Lotte Lenya. At the High School of Music and Art, Williams was encouraged in acting by the director John Stix. "Looking back, I feel I was destined to act, though I never consciously went after it," he told Roberta Plutzik when she interviewed him for *After Dark* (June 1980). "But I remember when I was a very chubby twelve-year-old boy watching my friends get all the girls. I bragged that one day I'd be Rudolph Valentino."

While Williams was studying at the National Academy of Design, a serendipitous encounter with a CBS casting director led to bit parts in the television religious series *Lamp Unto My Feet* and *Look Up and Live* and other TV shows. "When I needed money for paint and canvases," he told Lois Armstrong of *People* (July 7, 1980), "I would do some TV work." Concurrently with his art studies, he studied the Stanislavsky "Method" of natural acting under Sidney Poitier and Paul Mann at the Actors Workshop in Harlem. At the movies, he paid close attention to another Method actor, Marlon Brando, and he studied how Clark Gable, Humphrey Bogart, and other stars "made love to women on the screen."

Williams made his motion picture debut auspiciously, giving what critics assessed to be a "vivid," "firm" performance as Josh Quincy, the frightened, hostile young patient of the dedicated old Jewish Brooklyn slum doctor (Paul Muni) in *The Last Angry Man* (Columbia, 1959). His first young-adult role on Broadway was that of the Harlem street gang leader Duke Curtis in *The Cool World* (1960), a sensitive portrayal that failed to save the play, which alienated critics with its raw exposure of black juvenile delinquency and closed after two performances.

In the first American production of Shelagh Delaney's drama *A Taste of Honey*, set in a grim Lancashire industrial slum, Williams played with delicate grace the roving black sailor who has a brief affair with the lonely young heroine (Joan Plowright) and leaves her pregnant. The play ran on Broadway from October 1960 to September 1961, won the New York Drama Critics' 1961 award for best foreign play, and drew for Williams notices ("could not be more right," "lightfooted as a dancer") that persuaded him to put aside his paints and brushes for good.

Much less successfully, Williams was cast in the satiric fantasy *The Blue Boy is Black* as a gullible fellow servant in a white household who is betrayed—along with the household—by a ruthlessly ambitious black maid (Cicely Tyson). That play ran Off Broadway for twenty-three performances in 1963. The two-year gap between *A Taste of Honey* and *The Blue Boy is Black* was indicative of the problem Williams, a self-described "mongrel . . . always too dark for white roles or too light for black parts," had getting roles in the race-conscious 1960s.

Discouraged by his "minority" problem as well as the failure of his first two marriages, Williams fell into a protracted psychological and emotional depression. In 1964, when he was at his "lowest ebb," he recalls, he met a white woman named Rachel, a spiritual "master" who "gave" him "a rebirth." Living with him for a year, Rachel introduced him to consciousness expansion through meditation and the mind-altering drug LSD and to the mystical philosophy of P. D. Ouspensky and G. I. Gurdjieff—in sum, to "the connection between the political, the moral, and the spiritual." He told Judy Klemesrud: "She helped me understand those things, through Eastern philosophy and Western philosophy, everything from Buddhism to Jung. She was my first teacher. She was an ex-addict and an ex-prostitute who had gone through so much, and she pulled herself out of it, and helped me, too."

In 1967 Williams returned to Broadway for four months as the replacement for Robert Hooks opposite Leslie Uggams in the musical *Hallelujah, Baby!* Off Broadway, he was in productions of *The Firebugs* (1968), *Ceremonies in Dark Old Men* (1969), and *Slow Dance on the Killing Ground* (1970). He had a small part, as the lost-and-found clerk, in the motion picture *The Out-of-Towners* (Paramount, 1970). In the film *The Final Comedown* (New World, 1972), written, produced, and directed by Oscar Williams, he played the protagonist, Johnny Johnson, a gentle young black man who, radicalized by social injustice, leads an armed urban rebellion and dies in a shootout with police. Critics were grateful for the dynamism that Williams and his supporting cast managed to inject into *The Final Comedown's* "pretentious," "amateurish," and declamatory script.

Williams' big break came when Lou Gossett Jr., who was slated to costar in the made-for-television movie *Brian's Song* (1971), was injured playing basketball. Replacing Gossett in the poignant ABC production about the death from cancer of Chicago Bears football player Brian Piccolo, Williams gave a persuasive, deeply affecting portrayal of Gale

Sayers, Piccolo's teammate and friend. Seen by an estimated audience of 55 million, *Brian's Song* was one of the highest rated TV movies of 1971, and Williams was nominated for an Emmy for his part in it. In another made-for-TV picture, Truman Capote's *The Glass House* (1972), Williams played a rebellious convict.

Sensing "the great charisma" Williams possessed, despite his "cocky and condescending" attitude, Berry Gordy, the Motown Productions mogul, signed the actor to a seven-year motion picture contract guaranteeing him from $100,000 to $200,-000 a year. Publicizing Williams as "the black Clark Gable," Gordy cast him opposite Diana Ross in *Lady Sings the Blues* (Paramount, 1972), the story of the late drug-addicted jazz singer Billie Holiday (Miss Ross). If the film was, as it seemed, calculated to make Williams a star, it succeeded. As Louis McKay, the unstable singer's steadfast third husband, Williams became a suave and sophisticated sex symbol overnight, as 8,000 letters a week from female fans of all races attested.

Williams followed up his role in *Lady Sings the Blues* with that of a federal agent turned vigilante to avenge his daughter's death by drug overdose in *Hit!* (Paramount, 1973), an international dope-ring caper film. In the police melodrama *The Take* (Columbia, 1974) he starred as an amoral cop who extorts payoffs with one hand and busts the crime syndicate with the other. Berry Gordy again brought Williams and Diana Ross together in *Mahogany* (Paramount, 1975), the story of Tracy (Miss Ross), a poor black young woman from the South Side of Chicago who becomes a fashion model and designer. After rising to the top of the international world of *haute couture*, Tracy renounces all for love, returning to the ghetto to help her boyfriend, Brian (Williams), a dedicated civil rights worker, run for Congress. The film, Gordy's first directorial effort, was panned by critics as a "cheap," "superficial" recycling of old Hollywood "tinsel." The critics nonetheless found Williams "agreeable," demonstrating in some scenes "a flair for comedy" that showed up the sentiments of the rest of the picture.

The last feature film that Williams made for Berry Gordy was the surprise hit of the summer of 1976, *The Bingo Long Traveling All-Stars and Motor Kings* (Universal), the seriocomic epic of a barnstorming black baseball team in the days before the major leagues were integrated. In that picture, he portrayed the wily eponymous pitcher, a character loosely modeled on the legendary Satchel Paige; James Earl Jones played his slugging catcher; and Richard Pryor turned in an inventive performance as a teammate who is dangerously facetious in his flouting of Jim Crow protocol. Writing in the *Washington Post* (July 16, 1976), Gary Arnold described the film's stars as a "dynamic trio," a "winning combination." For Arnold, the movie itself, in which "the Stepin Fetchit sort of put-on is perceived for the ironic survival technique it was," set a "new standard of success for movies about black Americans."

Williams—who once said that he "really believe[s]" that he is "surrounded by fantastic spirits that guide" him—was supernaturally "directed" to return to the stage as Martin Luther King Jr. in *I Have a Dream*, billed as "an evening of theatre and music based on the words" of the martyred civil rights leader. In preparing for the role, Williams watched television clips and listened to recordings of King's speeches and sermons in order to "capture the essence and spirit of the man" rather than to impersonate him. His muted performance impressed critics with its taste and sincerity when *I Have a Dream* toured the United States in the spring and summer of 1976 and ran for ten weeks on Broadway in the fall of the same year.

In the made-for-television movie *The Scott Joplin Story* (NBC, 1976), Berry Gordy's first TV production, Williams played the ragtime turn-of-the-century pianist and composer. Williams made no films for Gordy during the remaining two years of his Motown contract. His next major role was that of Homer Smith, the black journeyman carpenter who ambivalently comes to the aid of a community of German nuns in the Arizona badlands in *Christmas Lilies of the Field* (NBC, 1979), a made-for-television sequel to the 1963 feature film *Lilies of the Field*, in which Sidney Poitier, as Smith, had a clash of wills with the mother superior. As the reviewer for *Variety* (December 19, 1979) observed, Williams' "strongly etched performance" breathed "a lot of life into the leisurely storyline" and compensated for "the saccharine content of the plot."

In a sidekick role too sketchy for his talent, Williams teamed with Sylvester Stallone in *Nighthawks* (Universal, 1981), a shallow thriller about two New York City undercover policemen (Stallone and Williams) hunting down an international terrorist. As Lando Calrissian, the maverick chief of the Cloud City of Bespin, he turned against the evil Empire and joined the good Rebel forces in *The Empire Strikes Back* (Twentieth Century-Fox, 1980), the sequel to George Lucas' space fantasy *Star Wars*, set "a long time ago in a galaxy far, far away." He continued to swagger effectively in that supporting role in *Return of the Jedi* (Twentieth Century-Fox, 1983), which fared less well than its predecessors with reviewers but did even better at the box office, setting a first-week gross record of $43.3 million.

Parker Stevenson and Billy Dee Williams starred as a salt-and-pepper team of actors-turned-detectives in *Shooting Stars* (ABC, 1983), a seriocomic made-for-television police movie that gave Williams a chance to put a tongue in the cheek of his ultra-cool image. As he told a reporter, he likes "doing heroes . . . who run through life, trip over doors, but make it anyway." Also in 1983, Williams played a Georgia police chief in the last segment of the CBS miniseries *The Chiefs*. In the fall of 1984 Williams joined the cast of the ABC network's weekly prime-time soap opera *Dynasty* as Brady Lloyd, a recording industry executive married to Dominique Deveraux (Diahann Carroll). Back on the big screen, he played a cop tracking down a homicidal maniac in mid-Manhattan's sleazy porn world in *Fear City* (1984), a Zupnik-Curtis production.

Essential to Williams's glamorous screen image are his dazzling smile and his natty attire, in which the fashionable is given a rakish touch by the angle of his hat brim and his unbuttoned shirt collar. The almond-eyed, 177-pound-six-footer has what Lynn Norment in *Ebony* (January 1981) described as a "sexy voice" and "curly . . . silky" hair. In explaining to Miss Norment that he keeps his hair carefully "relaxed" not to be "ostentatious" but rather to be "more versatile," he pointed out that his "films have always been in [the] direction" of the "colorless." In other interviews he has said that he considers himself not a "black actor" but an "international person," albeit a "minority" one, "an alien being in a world that doesn't accept" him. "We don't need black and white labels," he said on one occasion. "Today the word 'black' is accepted, but that will have to change too." To expand his range of options as an actor, Williams has formed his own production company in partnership with a businessman friend, Gary Judas.

Miss Norment found Williams to be "egotistical but not abrasive," "long-winded and philosophical but not boring," and "charming and flirtatious but not offensive"—a "serious, contemplative man . . . serious about his family and his privacy." Williams lives quietly in a four-bedroom ranch-style house in Laurel Canyon in the Hollywood Hills with his wife of twelve years, the former Teruko Nakagami, a Japanese-American, a tranquilizing influence without whom, he says, he would be "running around like a crazy person." Williams' laid-back manner belies, he confesses, "lots of turmoil inside." He releases tension and keeps in athletic trim by daily workouts in a gym, by swimming, by meditating, and by painting and sketching. Many of his oils, pastels, and charcoal drawings are portraits of his wife and his friends, including Richard Pryor.

The Williamses have an eleven-year-old daughter, Hanako; in addition, Mrs. Williams has a grown daughter, Miyako, by her previous marriage to the musician Wayne Shorter, and Williams has a grown son, Corey, from his first marriage, to Audrey Sellers. There were no offspring from the actor's second marriage, to Marlene Clark. As he told Charles L. Sanders in the 1983 *Ebony* interview, a large measure of his motivation for leading "a disciplined life" comes from his desire "to be part of preparing [his] kids for the new world." "Mediocrity became rampant in the '60s," he explained, "and a lot of unprepared people were given jobs and opportunities. But that's all over now; you've got to have a special skill; you have to be prepared for the twenty-first century."

References: *After Dark* 13:53+ Je '80 pors; *Ebony* 29:54+ Ap '74 pors, 36:31+ Ja '81 pors, 38:126+ Je '83 pors; *N Y Daily News* mag p13+ S 26 '76 por; *N Y Times* II p3+ S 19 '76 por; *Newsday* II p3+ Ap 26 '81 pors; *People* 14:82+ Jl 7 '80 pors; *Time* 108:64 Ag 23 '76 por; *Washington Post* p9+ D 27 '75 por; *Who's Who in America, 1984-85*

Williams, Vanessa

Mar. 18, 1963– Former beauty contest winner; musician. Address: h. Millwood, N.Y. 10546

Soon after Vanessa Williams was crowned as Miss America 1984, she received a telephone call from President Ronald Reagan at the White House, who assured her, "Your selection is not only a wonderful thing for you, it's a wonderful thing for our nation." Reagan was of course referring to the fact that Miss Williams is the first black woman in the sixty-two-year history of the Miss America pageant to be awarded the top prize—a distinction that some black leaders compared to that of Jackie Robinson, who broke major league baseball's color barrier. The comparison was apt, for Miss Williams, like Robinson, is a talented and determined individual who resists stereotyping. Gifted, ambitious, and refreshingly candid, she was, in the words of one observer, "perhaps the least wimpy winner to walk down the runway in Atlantic City in years—and the least predictable."

Just how unpredictable Vanessa Williams can be was demonstrated in July 1984, when it was discovered that she had posed for explicitly sexual nude photos with another woman while serving as a receptionist at the TEC Model Registry in Mount Kisco, New York in the summer of 1982. The photos were published in the September 1984 issue of *Penthouse*, one of the raunchier "skin" magazines, and set an all-time sales record for the publication.

After flustered members of the pageant executive committee asked Miss Williams to step down in order to preserve the pristine image of Miss America, she reluctantly yielded on July 23. Although she wanted to hold on to her title, she felt that doing so might cause "potential harm" to the pageant and create a "deep, deep division." The first Miss America to abdicate in the history of the pageant, she was succeeded by Suzette Charles, the first runner-up.

Vanessa Williams was born in New York City on March 18, 1963 to Milton and Helen Williams. At that time her family lived in the borough of the Bronx, but a year later they moved to Millwood (population 2,500), a predominantly white and middle-class enclave thirty-five miles north of New York City in Westchester County. Her mother teaches singing in the public schools of Ossining, New York, and her father teaches music in the public schools of Elmsford, New York. In interviews Vanessa Williams has often referred to the "values" that her parents "instilled" in her.

In keeping with a family agreement that she and her younger brother, Christopher, study music and other performing arts until the age of fifteen, Vanessa was subjected to a taxing training schedule even as a child. She studied French horn for nine years, piano for five years, melophone for fourteen years, dancing for six years, and acting, marching band, and modelling for six years. Small wonder that Milton Williams once had to coax his daughter back inside the house after she briefly ran away to the woods of their backyard in protest. He told a New York Times reporter (September 19, 1983), "We were not concerned about her becoming a professional musician. We wanted her to have as many options as possible. It gives her a great sense of freedom."

Although Vanessa Williams endured some racial taunts in school, she had to deal with the problem on her own because, as Milton Williams has explained, "She had to live in school herself. . . . We could not come there to resolve problems." Independence was also encouraged in other areas: the Williams children had to help pay for half of any special treats such as dress-up clothes. Although their parents bought them, they could not be used until Vanessa and Christopher earned enough to pay for them.

On the strength of her obvious talents, Vanessa Williams became a star performer at Horace Greeley High School in Chappaqua, New York. She performed in plays and musicals, sang in the school choir, and played the French horn in both the school band and the orchestra. In addition, she joined the All-State Women's Choir and the All-County Orchestra and traveled with the orchestra on exchange trips to Miami, Boston, Caracas, Venezuela, and Nassau, the Bahamas. While still in high school she entered her first pageant, a talent program sponsored by the fraternal order of the Masons, finishing fourth in the national competition, and she was also a drama finalist in the presidential scholars program. In 1981 she enrolled at Syracuse University, where she majored in musical theatre. One indication of her growing celebrity was the notation next to her picture in her high school yearbook, which read, "See you on Broadway."

Vanessa Williams' interest in the Miss America pageant was aroused in the spring of 1983, when the executive director of the Miss America Greater Syracuse Pageant—who had seen her in a school show—approached her as a possible contestant. At first she resisted, since she intended to spend the summer performing in an Equity production of Cyrano de Bergerac on the Syracuse campus, followed by a stint in the Broadway show Mighty Fine Music. The Equity show was canceled, however, and Miss Williams was free to enter the beauty contest, which she won in April 1983. Advancing to the Miss New York State pageant, she became the first black woman to take that title, after she captivated the judges and the audience with her rousing, pop-jazz rendition of "Happy Days Are Here Again." And in an all-important seven-minute interview with the judges, she deftly fielded questions regarding Central America, astrology, her choice of music and dance as a career, and her opinion of Harold Washington, Chicago's first black mayor.

Although she had previously viewed beauty pageants as "exploitative meat shows," Vanessa Williams entered the Miss America preliminaries because, as she explained to a New York Daily News (September 18, 1983) reporter, "Fifty percent of the contest is based on talent." She added, "In the swimsuit competition, they want to see if you're poised and taking care of your body. And in the evening-gown segment, you get a chance to make a little speech and let the audience know something about you." Miss Williams also wanted the exposure, believing it would help further her theatrical ambitions, and she admitted that the pageant's top prizes (a $25,000 scholarship and some $100,000 in personal appearance fees) were also powerful lures.

When she discussed her chances of being crowned Miss America, Vanessa Williams conceded, "It's a long shot," perhaps remembering that the Miss America contest, which originated in 1921, officially barred minority entrants for thirty years. The first black contestant, Cheryl Browne, who competed as Miss Iowa, did not enter until 1970, and since then, only two black women have become finalists, though Lencola Sullivan, who as Miss Arkansas finished as fourth runner-up in 1980, staunchly insists that she had "as good a chance as anyone." Nevertheless, in 1983 minority participation in the pageant was still such a novelty that a good deal of press attention was focused on the unprecedented number of no fewer than four black candidates: Vanessa Williams, Suzette Charles of New Jersey, Deneen Graham of North Carolina, and Amy Elizabeth Keys of Maryland. The four women were asked to pose together so often that they began to joke about it, and the question that Miss Williams remembers being asked most often was what it felt like to have a chance to become the first black Miss America. In answer to one such query, she responded, "Ideally, a black Miss America could be a role model for all young women in America, not just minorities."

From the start of the Miss America pageant—held, as always, in Atlantic City, New Jersey in mid-September—Miss Williams was patently a favorite. On the first night of the judging, Wednesday, September 14, 1983, she won the swimsuit competition, and two nights later she ranked first in the talent competition, reprising the "Happy Days Are Here Again" number that had helped her capture the New York State title. Her dynamic singing style reminds some listeners of Barbra Streisand's, though she prefers to compare herself to Lena Horne. "I'm a stylistic singer," she explains. "I don't have the legitimate voice, like an operatic singer, or a jazz singer who slides in and out of every note."

The next night, September 17, before a nationwide television audience, Vanessa Williams was crowned Miss America, narrowly edging past Suzette Charles, who is also black—an occurrence that the eight-member all-white panel of judges dismissed as a mere coincidence. Miss Williams, too, discounted speculation that she won her title because of reverse bias. "I don't think they chose me because I'm black and it's time for a black Miss America," she insisted. "They chose me because they thought I could do the job."

Despite her later annoyance that "people and the press aren't focusing on me as a person, they're focusing on my being black," Vanessa Williams nevertheless expressed the hope that "being Miss America and the first black woman to hold the title will help open doors for blacks, Puerto Ricans, whoever." Many black leaders agreed. The Reverend Joseph E. Lowery, president of the Southern Christian Leadership Conference, observed that it took too long for the Miss America pageant to "recognize that intelligence and talent and beauty are not exclusive properties of any racial or ethnic group." And Shirley Chisholm, the former United States congresswoman from Brooklyn, noted that though some blacks might be tempted to discount the importance of Vanessa Williams' victory, her triumph was "not trivial because it shows in a sense that the country, for whatever the motivation might be, seems to be trying to move toward a more equalitarian set of circumstances."

Other black activists, particularly members of the Congress of Racial Equality (CORE), had a different point of view. Pointing to Vanessa Williams' straight hair, light skin, and middle-class suburban background, CORE spokesmen charged that she was not a representative product of the black community. Stung by those observations and angered that she should be expected to fit into any stereotypical mold, Miss Williams replied, "It makes me furious that some people believe that." Her anger peaked when a black reporter asked her if she thought she would have won if her skin had been darker. "Why can't a black be supportive?" she

asked another interviewer. "Can't I get credit for anything?" In another interview she tried to settle the issue by declaring, "Just because I have lighter skin and lighter hair doesn't mean I am any less a person. I am not more pro-white or pro-black."

Still, the racial issue did not disappear, and its ugly side surfaced soon after the pageant when Vanessa Williams began to receive hate mail. One Los Angeles letter writer threatened to throw acid in her face because she is black. As a result, when she visited Los Angeles she was virtually confined to her room, and armed guards accompanied her when she appeared on television's *Hour Magazine*. For the most part, however, her personal appearances continued at a hectic pace—with no cancellations because of her race. Far from causing consternation among those who traditionally play host to Miss America, her status as the first black woman to hold the title made her the most sought-after pageant winner in the history of that venerable American institution. Usually accompanied by a female traveling companion, Miss Williams remained on a relentless year-long daily schedule that kept her on the go from seven in the morning until at least eleven at night.

Once a defiant symbol of racial segregation, Governor George C. Wallace helped roll out the red carpet for her when she toured the state of Alabama. She gave away pens in Chicago, sang in the aisles of a department store in Cleveland, and demonstrated the art of making corsages at a Corpus Christi, Texas grocery store. At one point, exhausted despite a daily regimen of megadoses of multivitamins, Miss Williams lamented: "I haven't seen my family, I haven't seen my friends, and I haven't been able to talk to anyone, really." She added, however, that her strength was increasing every day because of "an abundance of energy from people."

But her reign was not devoid of glamorous moments. Vanessa Williams dined at the White House, a first for a Miss America, performed with Bob Hope at Syracuse University, fed the octogenarian George Burns a piece of ceremonial birthday cake, appeared with the Guy Lombardo Band on New Year's Eve and with Lionel Hampton at a UN reception, and made several television appearances, including a cameo role in a segment of the series *Love Boat*. Establishing other precedents, she was the first Miss America to be interviewed at the National Press Club in Washington, D.C. and the first to attend the National Black Mayors' Conference.

A registered political Independent who describes herself as "sometimes liberal, sometimes conservative, depending on the issues," Vanessa Williams has endorsed the Equal Rights Amendment but has expressed reservations regarding the legalization of marijuana. It has been her unwillingness to duck controversial issues that has set her apart from previous title-holders. Despite the fact that she comes from what she describes as a "deeply religious" Catholic home, she believes that abortion is "a right women should have. It should be there for women to use, but I don't think everyone should use it." She bases her stance on her conviction that "there are too many useless deaths and child abuses." Although she also favors birth control because "it's essential for preventing abortion," she holds no brief for "the rhythm method." When reporters began to solicit her views on an increasing number of issues, she announced, "It's difficult to develop overnight opinions on things I haven't even researched." She also began reminding her indefatigable questioners that she was only twenty years old and "just human."

It was perhaps the human, vulnerable quality that prompted such feminists as Gloria Steinem and Susan Brownmiller and such black leaders as Jesse Jackson and Benjamin Hooks to rally to the defense of Vanessa Williams when the scandal about her compromising nude photos broke like an unexpected summer storm in July 1984. Her family was also supportive during her ordeal, backing her contention that she had not signed a model release, though Tom Chiapel, the photographer, and Bob Guccione, the publisher of *Penthouse*, and his lawyer, insisted that she had done so.

In her defense, Miss Williams maintained that Chiapel had assured her that the photos would be shown only in silhouette and would never be published. On September 8, 1984 Vanessa Williams filed papers in the state Supreme Court in White Plains, New York, for a suit against Chiapel.

Vanessa Williams stands five feet six inches tall and weighs 110 pounds. She has catlike green eyes, a tawny complexion, wavy, gold-streaked brown hair, and a dazzling smile. Refusing to discuss her private life, she has, however, revealed that for the past four years she dated a Syracuse University student who is majoring in finance. On other aspects of her life she has not hesitated to speak out, making no effort to hide what she calls her "invigorating kind of personality." Conceding that she is "a very controversial person," she insists that she wants "to be distinctive" and to be remembered "as interesting."

References: *Chicago Tribune* I p20 N 23 '83 por; *Jet* p12+ O 10 '83 pors; *N Y Times* p1+ S 19 '83 por, B p1+ Ap 3 '84 pors; *Newsday* p4+ S 19 '83 pors, II p4+ Ja 14 '84 pors; *People* 20:34+ O 3 '83 pors, 20:65 D 26 '83 pors; *Redbook* 161:74+ F '84 pors; *Time* 122:10+ O 17 '83 pors; *Washington Post* B p1 S 19 '83 pors, C p1 S 20 '83 por

Winfield, Dave

Oct. 3, 1951– Baseball player. Address: b. New York Yankees, River Ave. and E. 161st St., Bronx, N.Y. 10451

When David M. Winfield left the University of Minnesota in 1973, he was a multi-threat natural athlete of such potential that professional teams in three sports drafted him. He opted for baseball—specifically the San Diego Padres of the National League. After "eight years of mediocracy" (his agent's phrase) as an outfielder in San Diego, Winfield jumped leagues to sign with "a winner," the New York Yankees, who gave him not only the most lucrative contract in the history of sports but also a star-class showcase for his prowess. With his size (six feet six, 220 pounds) and speed, Winfield the outfielder foils home runs with leaping catches that only a man of his height and body control could make. It is at the plate, however, that he is most feared. Always a powerful batter, he used to describe himself as "a wrist hitter, a line-drive hitter." Ironically, since arriving in Yankee Stadium (the structure of which is not conducive to homers by righthanders), Winfield has developed into a slugger. Going into the 1984 season, his major league career statistics include 1,514 games played, a .283 batting average, 254 doubles, fifty-six triples, 236 home runs, and 961 runs batted in. Winfield puts at least as much energy into his work with the David M. Winfield Foundation, a charitable foundation serving underprivileged youth, as he does into baseball.

David Mark Winfield was born on October 3, 1951 in St. Paul, Minnesota. Three years later his father, Frank Winfield, a dining-car waiter on the Great Northern Railroad, and his mother, Arline, separated. From that time on, David and his older brother, Steve, were raised by their mother—who took a job as an aide in the audiovisual department of the St. Paul public school system—with the assistance of their grandmother, who lived down the street. "Considering that we grew up in a broken home," Winfield recalled in an interview with Don Freeman for *Sport* (December 1975), "we had a happy childhood because of the love and affection our mother gave us." Another contributing factor in Winfield's happy childhood was Bill Peterson, the director of the Oxford Playground (now the Jimmy Lee Playground), only half a block from the Winfield home. "Bill Peterson was a white man in the black community," Winfield told Freeman, "but he gave more to that community than anyone I know. To me, at different times, he was coach, friend, father, all rolled into one."

The Winfield brothers were introduced to basketball as well as baseball at the Oxford Playground, but baseball was their favorite sport. A year ahead of Dave in school, Steve drifted away from baseball when, as a freshman at the University of Minnesota, he became active in the civil rights movement. (Steve now coaches amateur teams, works in the physical education department of the university, and helps run the David M. Winfield Foundation.) Dave was "a very slow starter but also a very fast learner," according to Jim Fritsche, the baseball and basketball coach at Central High School in St. Paul, as quoted by Howard Liss in *Picture Story of Dave Winfield* (1982). He did not try out for the high school baseball team until his junior year—when he grew four or five inches almost overnight and began to tower over his classmates—and he "didn't make an impression on anyone in basketball until his senior year." That year he was All-City and All-State in both basketball (where his forte was rebounding) and baseball (where his best position was pitcher). When he graduated, the Boston Red Sox offered to sign him. After conferring with his mother and brother, he rejected the offer, because he knew he would be assigned to a minor league team to gain experience and he had heard how black players were sometimes treated in the boondocks.

Instead, Winfield went on scholarship to the University of Minnesota, where he had difficulty settling down at first. During the summer following his freshman year he was arrested as an accomplice in the theft of a snowblower from a Minneapolis hardware store. "My mother came to the jail and there were tears in her eyes . . . ," he told Don Freeman in the *Sport* interview. "I pledged to my mother that I would never do anything like that again, ever. I was lucky. They let me go. But I was on probation the rest of my time in college. I feel that shame burning through me again, just by telling the story now for print. But I do it so that kids can know what a terrible feeling it is to do something so stupid and wrong and how awful it is to hurt someone who has loved you and cared for you."

Buckling down to his studies (political science and Afro-American history and culture), Winfield maintained a B average over the next three years and left college just a few credits short of a degree. In his sophomore year he made the varsity baseball team as a pitcher and won eight out of eleven games. An injury to his right arm in his junior year forced him off the mound, and he finished that season alternating between left field and first base. Playing semi-pro ball as a pinch-hitter with the Fairbanks Gold Panners in the Alaskan League that summer, he began to exhibit his potential as a power hitter. "When he came back to us," George Thomas, the current University of Minnesota coach (he was then assistant to Dick Siebert) recalled in an interview with Steve Goldstein of the *New York Daily News* (December 21, 1980) "he was a more developed ballplayer."

As a pitcher-outfielder (and team captain) in his senior year at the university, Winfield won thirteen games, lost one, struck out 109 opposing batters, hit .385, and had nine home runs, thirty-three RBIs, and a 2.74 earned run average. He was voted the most valuable player in the National Collegiate Athletic Association tournament and named to the college All-American baseball team. In basketball, he moved from an intramural team up to the varsity in his junior year, when, subbing for Ron Benhagen (who had been suspended for contributing to a game-related riot), he averaged eleven points and six rebounds a game in the final eleven games. The Minnesota Gophers finished the season 21–4 and won the Big Ten basketball championship. With Benhagen back in the lineup, Winfield spent most of the next basketball season, his last, on the bench, but when he did play he was brilliant at rebounding and forward defense.

In the 1973 professional draft Winfield was chosen by four pro teams in three sports. In baseball, the San Diego Padres wanted him. In basketball, both the Atlanta Hawks and the Utah Stars drafted him. Although he had never played football in high school or college, he was also drafted by the Minnesota Vikings of the National Football League, because the Vikings thought that his size, speed, and agility would make him a good receiver. Having always aimed at becoming a major league baseball player, Winfield chose to go with the Padres, at a salary of $18,000 and a bonus of $50,000. Although he had made his high school and college reputation chiefly as a pitcher, the Padres perceived him as "an everyday player." "He has more physical tools than any free agent we ever signed," Peter Bavasi, the San Diego general manager, commented. "He can do the five things you look for in a player with superior potential: run, throw, field, hit for average, and hit with power."

Winfield remembers his first months in San Diego as "the hardest" in his life. "I didn't know anything about the National League," he told Ron Fimrite of *Sports Illustrated* (July 9, 1979). "I was seeing pitches I'd never seen before. I was playing in a ball park the size of an airport. I'd get my legs all tangled up in the outfield. I was holding my hands too low on the bat. I was hitching my swing, overstriding, overswinging. I'd been a pitcher. Now I was an outfielder. I was thrown into a sink-or-swim situation. I learned to swim the hard way."

Not being pennant contenders, the Padres could afford to allow Winfield to learn on the job, at his own pace. Although the San Diego front office tended to regard him exclusively as a power hitter, he decided he "was going to be a line-drive hitter." Accordingly, he learned to hit to all fields and developed into one of the best line-drive batters in either league. He also learned how to concentrate and how to motivate himself for sustained performance. Winfield's early seasons with the Padres consistently began in glory and ended in prolonged slumps—until he learned "total concentration." "Two years ago," he explained to Ron Fimrite in 1979, "I resolved the technical part of hitting. Last year I resolved the mental part. . . . Now I know how to hit .300." In 1978, the first year he rose above the .200's, his batting average was .308, and he duplicated that figure in 1979. The following year, however, he slipped back down to .276. During his last four years with the Padres he averaged .292, twenty-six homers, ninety-nine runs batted in, and 159 games a season. He batted .364 in four All-Star appearances, won two Gold Gloves, and led the National League in total bases once, with 333 in 1979.

Meanwhile, Winfield had acquired as friend, adviser, and agent one Albert S. Frohman, a former big-band pianist and kosher food caterer from Brooklyn. It was the shrewd, fatherly Frohman who negotiated Winfield's pay raises in San Diego (culminating in a four-year, $1.4-million contract) and who instilled in him the conviction that his competitive fire was going to waste in the service of a chronic loser like San Diego and that he would receive the respect he deserved only in the context of a winning team. It was possible for him to move to such a team under the terms of the 1976 rule revoking the old "reserve clause" in major league contracts. Under the reserve clause, a player became the property of the team he signed with and could not go to another team unless he was traded or sold. Under the new rule, a team has control over a player for only six years. At the end of that time, he may agree to continue playing for the team, or he may become a free agent, go through the re-entry draft, and sign with another club.

The team that appealed to Winfield was the New York Yankees, for four reasons: George Steinbrenner, the principal owner of the Yankees, was known to be a high-rolling spender for talent; the Yankees were perennial pennant contenders; New York was a city that could offer him a future in business outside of baseball; and it was a city where his programs for underprivileged children would have an ample clientele. For his part, George Steinbrenner was told by his scouts and other advisers that Winfield was "a premier player" of yet unfulfilled potential, worth gambling on as someone who might help the Yankees regain the American League pennant, which they had last won in 1978. Winfield would fill the gap left in the New York lineup by the death of Thurman Munson, bringing righthanded power to a team lopsided with lefthanders, and his speed might help to rev up the Yankees' sluggish base running.

In a series of crafty moves—beginning with a salary demand that San Diego had to refuse—Frohman maneuvered Winfield through the re-entry draft and into a contract with the Yankees, signed on December 15, 1980. The record-breaking ten-year pact, with cost of living escalators, was for $23,906,134. With a signing bonus of $1 million, the total came to almost $25 million. Even without the escalators, Winfield was assured of more than $15 million. Half of each year's cost-of-living increase would be contributed to the David M. Winfield Foundation.

In going to the Yankees, Winfield had to make several adjustments. The most obvious was accepting in stride the pressure of expectation that came with the signing of his elephantine contract. Another was moving from right field—then covered for the Yankees by Reggie Jackson—to left field. The most difficult was the adjustment he had to make in his swing because of "Death Valley," the Yankee Stadium's vast (430 feet) center-left center expanse, which has robbed righthanded sluggers of home runs for generations. "Pitchers say, we'll throw up in your zone in Yankee Stadium," he remarked to a reporter, "[we'll] let you hit it here. So I got to adjust my swing for base hits here." Partly because of "Death Valley," the Yankees did not expect home-run histrionics from him, just complete ballplaying. "We can't expect him to be a Reggie [Jackson]," George Steinbrenner said. "But he is a hell of an athlete, a good man on the club."

In his first season with the Yankees, Winfield helped to carry the team to its thirty-third American League pennant with club-leading statistics in hits, total bases, and game-winning runs batted in. His sixty-eight RBIs ranked fifth in the league, his .294 batting average was second on the team, and his thirteen home runs were only two behind lefthanders Jackson and Graig Nettles. Between seasons, Winfield poured most of his energy into the David M. Winfield Foundation, which he had founded in San Diego in 1977. Among the foundation's projects in San Diego was the David M. Winfield Pavilion, a block of seats in the stadium reserved for underprivileged children with tickets paid for by Winfield. (He continued to dispense free tickets to poor young people after his move to Yankee Stadium.) At Christmas 1981 the foundation treated 10,000 New York families to turkey dinners and distributed 25,000 toys. In the New York area it also made grants to hospitals, sponsored physical fitness, nutrition, and medical checkup programs, and gave college scholarships to several outstanding but needy high school graduates annually. In 1982 Winfield brought suit against George Steinbrenner, charging that the latter had defaulted on a contracted second payment to the foundation.

With the departure of Reggie Jackson to the California Angels in 1982, Winfield was moved into the cleanup spot in the Yankee lineup. Using a coiled, bent-over stance at the plate to decrease the strike zone, he exhibited a new aggressiveness, slugging his way out of Jackson's shadow. He finished second in the league in slugging percentage (.560) and third in home runs (thirty-seven), the best such figures for a Yankee righthander since Joe DiMaggio. In addition, he led the Yankees in RBIs (106) and game-winning RBIs (fifteen). For all that, the Yankees finished fifth in the American League East, with a 79–83 record.

After a four-way tie for first place in the American League East in 1983, the Yankees finished third, with a 91–71 record. Winfield was fifth in the league in home runs, with thirty-two, third in RBIs, with 161, second in game-winning RBIs, with twenty-one, and seventh in slugging percentage, with .513. He made his seventh consecutive All-Star appearance, and in August he made baseball history of a bizarre sort when a ball he threw in Toronto struck and killed a seagull, an endangered species in Canada. He was arrested, but charges were dropped and Toronto city administrator Paul V. Godfrey apologized for "a day in the life of Toronto sports we'd like to forget."

In 1984 the Yankees finished in third place in the American League East and Winfield had the second best batting average in the league, .340, just behind the .343 of Don Mattingly, also of the Yankees. Hitting thirty-four doubles, four triples, and nineteen home runs, he had a slugging average of .515, and he drove in 100 runs, thirteen of them game-winners.

With his contagious open smile, cool Dave Winfield exudes an untroubled joy in playing baseball, even under pressure, and he attributes much of his success as an athlete to his ability to "separate your home from your work." He describes himself as "easy going . . . but if something's unjust . . . watch out!" Interviewers report him to be soft-spoken, articulate, intelligent, politely reserved but affable, "an easy man to like."

A bachelor who has been dating the same "main lady" for many years, Winfield shies away from New York City night life, except for Broadway shows. At home he watches a selective few television programs, including The Jeffersons and Wall Street Week, and pursues his hobby of photography. On outdoor vacations, he enjoys fishing. He personally decorated his homes in Teaneck, New Jersey and St. Paul, Minnesota, and he designs his own clothes for custom-making by his tailors. He does not smoke or drink, and he describes himself as "very conservative"—"I'm not square, but I don't blow money." Of his philanthropic work he has said: "The reason I do this, and nobody seems to understand, is that I never got where I am by myself. I had a lot of people helping me. Now I want to return that favor and help the kids."

References: N Y Daily News p107+ D 21 '80 pors; N Y Times V p3 Je 1 '75 por, C p14 D 16 '80 por; N Y Times Mag p25+ Mr 29 '81 pors; Newsday p14+ Jl 11 '82 pors; Sport 61:69+ D '75 pors; Sports Ill 51:33+ Jl 9 '79 pors, 54:22+ Ja 5 '81 pors; Time 116:43 D 29 '80 por; Liss, Howard. Picture Story of Dave Winfield (1982); Who's Who in America, 1984–85

Winger, Debra

1955– Actress. Address: b. c/o Paramount Pictures Corp., 1 Gulf & Western Plaza, New York City, N.Y. 10023

At the April 1984 Academy Award ceremonies, actress Shirley MacLaine spoke of "the turbulent brilliance of Debra Winger," referring to her costar and fellow Oscar nominee for best actress award in the film Terms of Endearment (1983). During the relatively brief period that she has been on the Hollywood scene, Miss Winger has given several masterful performances, notably in Urban Cowboy (1980) and An Officer and a Gentleman (1982). In those and other films she presented a unique persona, distinguished by a gravelly voice that can be strangely touching, a gamine-like appearance that can be forlorn or rough-and-tumble or coolly elegant, and an intensity and passion that heighten the reality of her performances. Director James L. Brooks once said of Debra Winger: "She has one of the best minds I've ever come across. Working with her is like studying for a college exam with the best student in the class."

Of Hungarian-Jewish descent, Mary Debra Winger was born in Cleveland, Ohio in 1955, the youngest of three children in a close-knit family that included a brother, now a school principal, and a sister, who is a secretary. Her father, Robert Winger, is general manager of a kosher frozen food business, and her mother, Ruth Winger, worked as an office manager after the family moved to Van Nuys in the San Fernando Valley of Southern California about 1961. "I never understood women's liberation, because I never knew what my mother had to be liberated from. . . . So I never knew why women were so angry," Debra Winger told Gene Siskel in an interview in the Chicago Tribune

(November 27, 1983). In school she appeared in several plays, but at home she received no inspiration to make acting her career, nor did the film director George Cukor, whom she met through her father when she was fourteen, give her any encouragement in that direction. According to her own account, she was nurtured as a "Jewish-American Princess," but she was too energetic and independent to fit into such a role.

During her summer vacation visits to her Orthodox Jewish maternal grandparents in Cleveland, Debra Winger often heard talk about Israel that whetted her interest in the Jewish state. Consequently, after graduation from high school in 1971 and a brief sojourn in Europe, she went to Israel, where she lived and worked on a kibbutz and applied for citizenship. But three months of rigorous military training with the Israeli army made her change her mind, and soon she was back in the United States studying sociology and criminology at California State University at Northridge.

On New Year's Eve 1973, while working in her spare time at the Magic Mountain amusement park, Debra Winger was thrown from a moving truck and almost died of a cerebral hemorrhage. The accident left her partly paralyzed and blind in one eye for several months. She has attributed her desire to act and, in the words of Don Chase of *Newsday* (December 11, 1983), "her need to give herself over fully to every experience," to her brush with death, which gave her an entirely new perspective on life. "Poetically, I look at my accident as a huge hunk of grace, which propelled me into doing what I wanted to do," she told an interviewer for *People* (September 1, 1980).

Dropping out of the university one year short of graduation, Debra Winger studied for three years with the actor Michael V. Gazzo and appeared in some repertory theater productions in the San Fernando Valley. Her early television acting assignments included commercials for such companies as Metropolitan Life Insurance, American Dairy Milk, McDonald's, and Burger King, and she was featured in the television film *Special Olympics*. She also made some guest appearances on such programs as *Police Woman*, and she was briefly seen in a featured role, as Drusilla, the Wonder Girl, Lynda Carter's younger sister, in ABC-TV's *Wonder Woman*. Her first Hollywood film appearance, in a minor role in *Thank God It's Friday* (Columbia, 1978), a showcase for disco performers, received little notice from critics. But her performance in the small role of Melanie, in *French Postcards* (Paramount, 1979), a comedy about American students in Paris, prompted Gary Arnold in the *Washington Post* (November 9, 1979) to refer to her "sexual charm and vitality" and to note that she was the only one in the cast who recalled "the sort of individuality and humor that informed *all* the young characters in *American Graffiti*."

Debra Winger won out over some 200 other aspirants to star opposite John Travolta in director James Bridges' blue-collar romantic melodrama *Urban Cowboy* (Paramount, 1980), filmed on loca-

tion at Gilley's, a huge honky-tonk bar on the outskirts of Houston. To prepare for the role of Sissy—described by Vincent Canby in the *New York Times* (June 11, 1980) as the "tough, sweet, intuitively intelligent young woman" whom the hero marries—Miss Winger practiced drinking tequila with beer chasers at Gilley's and undertook an exercise routine to build up her muscles.

A highlight of *Urban Cowboy* is the scene in which Debra Winger rides a mechanical bucking bull that had been set up in Gilley's bar, apparently to rechannel the energy of patrons from the potential violence in the atmosphere. The point made by Sissy's ride is that despite the "macho" symbol of the bull, a woman can ride it as successfully as a man. In the words of Andrew Sarris in his *Village Voice* review (June 24, 1980), Debra Winger's "audaciously suggestive ride . . . was easily the erotic high point of the movie." She herself felt emotionally "raw and naked" in that scene and was embarrassed when critics referred to its sexuality. "I had worked so hard on it gymnastically, I never intended for it to be sexual," she told Gene Siskel. "All I thought was that I was making [Travolta] jealous by how good I was on the bull." Although many reviews of *Urban Cowboy* were negative, critics singled out Debra Winger for special praise, and her costar, John Travolta, as quoted in *People* magazine (September 1, 1980), described her as being "very, very sexy and sensuous, and funny and smart."

Debra Winger's next film was *Cannery Row* (MGM/United Artists, 1982), writer-director David S. Ward's adaptation of John Steinbeck's novel of the title and its sequel, *Sweet Thursday*, about life in the shabby waterfront district of Monterey, California. As Suzy, a reluctant bordello girl—a role originally intended for Raquel Welch—Miss Winger was cast opposite Nick Nolte, who played Doc, a marine biologist and former baseball player with a troubled past. The film was generally panned, but again Debra Winger's notices were mostly favorable. *Variety*'s critic (February 3, 1982) acclaimed her "winning personality and great cracking voice"; Pamela Kessler in the *Washington Post* (February 12, 1982) found her to be a "delightful comedienne"; and Richard Schickel in *Time* (February 15, 1982) called her "the best thing in a bad movie."

Although Debra Winger has been called temperamental—according to Liz Smith in the *New York Daily News* (June 16, 1981), she lost out on *Raiders of the Lost Ark* because she was "too big for her blue jeans to read for Steven Spielberg and George Lucas"—she was given an extraordinary chance to display her talents in the romantic drama *An Officer and a Gentleman* (Paramount, 1982), directed by Taylor Hackford. As Paula Pokrifki, a Polish-American paper-mill worker, Miss Winger was cast opposite Richard Gere, who played the role of a cocky but emotionally undernourished young cadet struggling to make the grade at a naval aviation officer candidate school under the tutelage of a tough drill instructor. Her sense of concurrent sexuality and sensitivity came together in that film even more stunningly than before.

David Ansen in Newsweek (August 2, 1982) viewed her as "one of those rare actresses who seems to open herself totally to the camera"; and Rex Reed in his syndicated column (New York Daily News, July 28, 1982) called the film "a miracle" and "the sleeper of the year" and found Miss Winger's portrayal of Paula to be "heartbreaking, three-dimensional, seedily lyrical." According to Janet Maslin, writing in the New York Times (July 28, 1982), "Miss Winger . . . has such emotional immediacy that she positively glows. [Her] face is so open and so changeable, that she makes Paula's feelings as apparent and as affecting as they can be." There was even a critical comparison by Andrew Sarris of the Village Voice (August 10, 1982) of Debra Winger and Richard Gere in this old-fashioned romance with evoked memories of Jean Harlow and Clark Gable. But despite the rapturous reviews, Debra Winger was not happy about An Officer and a Gentleman. Her nude scene with Gere made her "uncomfortable," and she felt that some crucial scenes were deleted from the film in the editing. "I can never be totally pleased because it's not the full performance I gave," she told Gene Siskel.

After reading the script for Terms of Endearment (Paramount, 1983), about a sometimes volatile, sometimes tender mother-daughter relationship spanning thirty years, Debra Winger persuaded director James L. Brooks to cast her as Emma Horton, the ill-starred daughter. In the film, Emma is more passive than active. But although she is essentially the foil of an overly possessive mother—played by Shirley MacLaine—the story is an extraordinarily touching one, and Miss Winger won accolades for the honesty and sensitivity of her performance. "The work of MacLaine and Winger is so natural and so transparent that it seems effortless," Don Chase wrote in Newsday (December 11, 1983). According to David Ansen in Newsweek (November 21, 1983), Debra Winger is "the mortar that holds all the parts together. . . . Once again [she] reaffirms her uncanny capacity for total immersion in a part. There's something fearlessly direct about her acting." And Rita Kemply observed in the Washington Post (November 26, 1983): "Her Emma is steadfastly goodnatured, tolerant; she lives a small life on a grand scale. She's shimmering, glorious, vibrant." The performance earned for Debra Winger an award for best actress of 1983 from the National Society of Film Critics. She was also nominated for an Oscar in that category from the Academy of Motion Picture Arts and Sciences, but the award went to Shirley MacLaine.

James Bridges, who had directed Debra Winger in Urban Cowboy, wrote the film Mike's Murder (Warner Brothers, 1984) especially for her. Completed a year before its release, the picture was refilmed to eliminate some of its excessive violence. In Mike's Murder she played Betty, a "nice girl" drawn into the sleazy drug culture of the Los Angeles underworld following the murder of her boyfriend. According to Bridges, her role as Betty was more challenging than her role as Emma had been, because "it's quieter, on a small, ordinary person scale." But Vincent Canby writing in the New York Times (March 9, 1984) felt that "she had no role to play" but exists only "as a token female in a narrative primarily concerned with male hustling and drugs." And although the critic for Newsday (March 9, 1984) appreciated Debra Winger's "dark beauty, expressive face and graceful presence," he dismissed the film as "a slick, run-of-the-mill" suspense thriller.

Although she in not universally hailed as a classic beauty, and her voice was once compared in People (December 26, 1983) to "five pounds of walnuts being cracked underwater," Debra Winger's versatility as an actress is well established. It was precisely the quality of her voice that once brought her an unpublicized part in Steven Spielberg's science fiction hit E.T. (Universal, 1982). Her voice was one of two that were electronically mixed to create the sound of the extraterrestrial creature of the title.

Jack Nicholson, who appeared with Debra Winger in Terms of Endearment, has said of her, as quoted in People (December 26, 1983): "She's a metamorphic actress. I think she's a great actress—a genius." Her approach to a role is what she calls "hanging out," steeping herself in the environment of the film, or conducting what Don Chase of Newsday has called "emotional research."

Debra Winger remains close to her parents. She is fond of the poems of E. E. Cummings and writes poetry, but not for publication. She makes her home at Malibu, California, and also has a cabin in New Mexico. She enjoys driving her BMW car at high speed, often accompanied by her German shepherd dog Pete. In 1984 she stumped with Senator Gary Hart in Ohio to help him in his bid for the Democratic presidential nomination. Although she has said that she has no plans for marriage, Debra Winger had been romantically linked, among others, with Robert Kerrey, Nebraska's bachelor governor, whom she met while filming Terms of Endearment on location, and who, in her words, is "absolutely someone important" in her life. He presented her at the time with an honorary membership in the "Nebraska Navy."

Although she is a comparative newcomer to the acting profession, Debra Winger's originality and style have already had an influence on other performers. In a review in Newsweek (March 5, 1984) of a television production of Tennessee Williams' A Streetcar Named Desire, critic Harry F. Waters wrote that Beverly D'Angelo in the role of Stella "projected the unabashed lustiness of Debra Winger." And Pauline Kael wrote in the New Yorker (August 2, 1982): "Debra Winger has the vividness of those we call 'born' performers. She makes you feel that there's something humming inside her."

References: Chicago Tribune XVII p14+ N 27 '83 pors; People 14:84+ S 1 '80 pors, 20:25+ D 26 '83 por, 21:85+ F 6 '84 pors; Newsday II p4 D 11 '83 pors; Newsweek 102:91+ N 21 '83 pors; Washington Post B p1+ D 13 '83 por; International Motion Picture Almanac, 1984

Zhao Ziyang

(jou dzē-yäng´)

Nov. 1919(?)- Prime Minister of the People's Republic of China. Address: b. c/o State Council, Beijing, People's Republic of China

Zhao Ziyang, whose cross-country tour of the United States in January 1984 marked the high-water point in recent American-Chinese relations, has emerged as a major international leader since his accession to the prime ministership of the People's Republic of China in 1980. Yet only seventeen years ago, during the Cultural Revolution, Zhao, who was then a provincial party leader, was derided by the radical Red Guards as a capitalist stooge and subsequently purged. His remarkable political renascence exemplifies the new pragmatism of China under Deng Xiaoping, who came to power after Mao Zedong's death in 1976. The best-known of a small group of comparatively young technocrats whom Christopher Wren, writing in the New York Times (January 10, 1984), has described as being "willing to bend the constraints of traditional Marxist ideology to make things work," Zhao has pursued as prime minister the same bold policy of economic modernization that distinguished his administration of Sichuan Province in the mid-1970s. Although Zhao himself is a popular political fig-

ure—observers have frequently compared him to the beloved Zhou Enlai—his revisionist policies have met with strong resistance from Maoist radicals and only cautious acceptance from wary bureaucrats, whose reluctance to support fully any new government policies could kill the prime minister's innovative reforms by the so-called "death of a thousand slices," that is, by slow, relentless incompetence, according to the Sinologist Kenneth Lieberthal.

Zhao Ziyang was born in the central Chinese province of Henan in November 1919, the son of a well-to-do grain merchant and landlord. (Some sources give his year of birth as 1918 or 1921.) By the standards of the majority of the revolutionary leaders of the People's Republic of China, he is well-educated, having attended secondary schools in Kaifeng and Wuhan, where he first became attracted to the then-outlawed Communist Youth League. Zhao officially joined the league in 1932, and six years later, he became a full-fledged member of the Communist party.

During the Second Sino-Japanese War (1937–45) and the subsequent civil war between the Communists and the Kuomintang, the Nationalist party led by Chiang Kai-shek, Zhao served as a local party official in a Communist-held area of central China. After the Communist victory and the establishment of the People's Republic of China in 1949, he was sent to Guangdong, the southern province adjacent to Hong Kong, to oversee the redistribution of land from the so-called "exploiting classes" to the peasant farmers. Over the next few years, he became something of an expert on agricultural reform and wrote a number of articles on the subject. He also served for a time as the Communist party representative for the major daily newspaper in Guangzhou, the provincial capital of Guangdong. Rising steadily in the party hierarchy, he was named first secretary of the Guangdong Province Communist party in 1965. Zhao was one of a handful of government officials to be appointed to a top provincial post without having first become a member of the Chinese Communist party's central committee.

Then, in the mid-1960s, Zhao's career, like those of many other progressive party officials, ran afoul of a turbulent upheaval in Beijing politics. After the Great Leap Forward, the ambitious nationwide agricultural modernization scheme based on "people's communes" that Mao introduced in the late 1950s, failed to improve the country's economic situation, Liu Shaoqi and Deng Xiaoping introduced a more moderate economic program. To correct the mistakes of the Great Leap Forward and spur agricultural production, Deng increased the size of the farmers' private plots and offered material rewards for individual enterprise. But the Maoists, who felt that Deng and his fellow revisionists sacrificed ideological principles to economic growth, reasserted the need for radical reform in the mid-1960s, and Liu and Deng were eventually purged for being "capitalist roaders." As the so-called Cultural Revolution, the radicals' attempt to proletarianize party thinking, gained momentum, millions of soldiers, workers, and students organized in cadres called Red Guards and set about ridding the provincial party organizations of Liu and Deng's supporters.

Zhao Ziyang attended at least one Red Guard rally, at which he reportedly called on the demonstrators "to expose and repudiate" Deng Xiaoping for trying to subvert proletarian rule and reinstate capitalism. Within a few months, however, Zhao himself fell victim to the Red Guards' zeal. In February 1967, he was paraded through the streets of Guangzhou in a dunce cap and denounced as a "counterrevolutionary," a "revisionist," and a "stinking remnant of the landlord class" for allegedly advocating material incentives and putting production before politics. Forced to renounce the moderate economic policies instituted by Liu and Deng in a degrading public self-criticism, Zhao was summarily dismissed from his posts. At the age of forty-four, he seemed to have come to the end of his political career.

With agricultural and industrial production at a standstill because of the destructive rampages of the Red Guards, the Cultural Revolution gradually lost popular support. Seeing radical reform as a threat to China's survival, a more centrist element in the Communist party, led by Prime Minister Zhou Enlai, took control in the early 1970s, and many Cultural Revolution pariahs reappeared in positions of importance. Probably because of his ties to senior officials who had survived the purges, Zhao Ziyang was among the first to be rehabilitated. After serving briefly as party secretary in Inner Mongolia, he resumed his duties as a party functionary in Guangdong Province in 1972. Over the next few years, he rose through the ranks from vice-chairman of the Guangdong Revolutionary Committee to first secretary of the Guangdong Province Communist party. As first secretary, he helped to oust the radicals who had been responsible for his political humiliation.

Late in 1975, Zhao was appointed first secretary of the Sichuan Province Communist party. The most populous and formerly the richest province in China, Sichuan was then on the brink of disaster because of prolonged political upheavals. Shortages were so severe that some peasants reportedly resorted to selling their daughters in exchange for additional food ration coupons. Using the same material incentives that Liu and Deng had employed so successfully in the early 1960s, Zhao quickly restored the Sichuan economy. Among other things, he allowed factories to set prices and to retain part of their profits to invest in new enterprises, expanded the amount of farmland set aside for private plots to 15 percent of all arable land, revived peasant markets, and experimented with tax incentives. Within three years, industrial production was up an astonishing 81 percent and agricultural output 25 percent. According to Newsweek (September 22, 1980), grateful peasants hailed their savior in public rallies with chants of "For grain to soothe your hunger pangs, seek Zhao Ziyang."

Zhao's remarkable achievements in Sichuan brought him to the attention of Deputy Prime Minister Deng Xiaoping, who had emerged as the dominant figure in the Chinese leadership after Mao's death in 1976. Zhao's pragmatic administration of the Sichuan province was exactly the sort of economic policy management that Deng wanted to foster in post-Mao China: peaceful and productive. In recognition of Zhao's efforts, Deng rapidly promoted the provincial administrator, making him a nonvoting member of the Politburo in 1977 and a full member in 1979. Eventually, Deng called Zhao to Beijing and named him, in April 1980, deputy prime minister in charge of the government's daily operations.

Five months later, at the annual meeting of the National People's Congress, China's nominal parliament, Deng engineered a bloodless purge of the government's top leadership that resulted in the resignations of a number of very elderly and/or Maoist officials, including Prime Minister Hua Guofeng, Mao's designated successor, and masterminded Zhao Ziyang's succession to the prime ministership. (Hua retained his party posts until 1982, when he was ousted from the ruling Politburo.) Zhao was reappointed to a new five-year term as prime minister on June 18, 1983.

The 1980 shakeup that thrust Zhao into power marked a significant change in Chinese politics. Repudiating Mao's radical brand of Sino-Marxism, Deng and Zhao set out to transform China into what Zhao described, in a public speech at a Beijing banquet honoring Robert Muldoon, the visiting prime minister of New Zealand, on September 11, 1980, as "a modernized, highly democratic and civilized socialist state" by the year 2000. To that end, the two leaders endorsed revisionist economic policies similar to those of Yugoslavia and Hungary. "The defect of management in China is that state control is too tight," Zhao explained, as quoted in the New York Times (September 8, 1980). "It does not provide for enthusiasm for the enterprises." In his view, China "should accept any structure, system, policy and measure that can promote the development of productive forces" within the Marxist bounds of state ownership of the means of production. "We must not bind ourselves as silkworms do within cocoons."

Putting his theory to the test, Zhao concentrated on reviving China's moribund economy, primarily by extending to the nation at large the program of "material incentives" he had used to such advantage in Sichuan. In 1980 alone he approved granting some self-management to nearly 7,000 state-owned industrial enterprises. Among other things, they were allowed to set their own production goals, sell their products, and keep a share of their surplus profits. The following year, however, he was forced to scrap his ambitious plans to modernize China's heavy industry, mainly because they overtaxed the country's underdeveloped resources. Instead he focused on stepping up agricultural production and developing light industry and textile manufacturing.

The bold five-year plan covering 1981 through 1985 that Zhao made public on November 30, 1982 stressed higher productivity, increased profitability, and "real growth" at the "safe and appropriate" annual rate of 4 to 5 percent. As he explained in his report to the National People's Congress, more rapid development would seriously undermine the country's economic and political stability. To make the socialist economy more efficient and, at the same time, increase government revenues, he introduced such traditional elements of capitalism as taxes, interest rates, and floating prices. Additional free-market economic incentives were announced on October 20, 1984 at a meeting of the Communist party Central Committee. The new measures, which restrict government control, are intended to give greater independence to more than a million state-owned business enterprises.

Another of the new prime minister's domestic goals was to streamline the government's "bloated overlapping administrative structure," to use his words. Citing the problems created by too many competing decision makers in the top-heavy Chinese bureaucracy, Zhao announced in March 1982 a plan to trim some 200,000 people—about one-third of the government's personnel—from the payroll by, among other things, telescoping twelve ministries into six, reducing the number of state councils from ninety-eight to fifty-two, and slashing ministerial and departmental staffs. He also encouraged aging bureaucrats to retire on comfortable pensions and, for the first time in Chinese history, set a mandatory retirement age for top-level civil servants. "In carrying out this profound revolution, we mean to reform that part of the state administration that is incompatible with the requirements of economic, cultural, and political work," Zhao told a meeting of the standing committee of the National People's Congress on March 2, 1982. "We are not making a revolution against persons." According to the official press, however, there were two specific targets: corrupt, self-indulgent officials and Maoist radicals, many of whom were originally recruited for their ideological beliefs rather than their technical expertise.

A third vital component of Zhao's modernization program was the expansion of trade and scientific and cultural exchanges with Western nations, particularly the United States. Since 1979, when formal diplomatic relations were established, trade between the two countries has increased tenfold, making the People's Republic of China the United States' most important socialist trading partner. Zhao has vigorously promoted Western trade with and investment in China as a way of rapidly acquiring advanced technology and management skills. Under his administration, American companies have been encouraged to invest in the development of China's natural resources, and the Chinese government has invested in American meatpacking, personal computer, and metals industries. China is also financially involved in a forestry project on the Solomon Islands and in fisheries in Sri Lanka and recently began negotiating possible investments in Canadian mining and wood pulp manufacturing.

The Chinese leadership's commitment to modernization has put an end to the confrontation-style diplomacy of the militant 1960s, and Zhao's foreign policy has been generally conciliatory toward the West. The 1980 election of Ronald Reagan, an outspoken proponent of the so-called "two Chinas" policy, to the presidency of the United States caused some initial strain, but since the August 17, 1982 joint communiqué in which the United States reaffirmed its acceptance of the Beijing government as "the sole legal government of China" and pledged to "reduce gradually" its arms sales to Taiwan, relations have improved. Despite continuing weapons sales, most Western political analysts agree that by 1984 the economic relationship between the United States and the People's Republic of China was strong enough to withstand differences of opinion on the future of Taiwan.

During a visit to the United States in January 1984, however, Zhao emphasized the importance of the Taiwan issue as "the principal obstacle to the growth of Chinese-U.S. relations." In a speech to the Foreign Policy Association and the National Committee on United States–China Relations in New York City on January 17, 1984, Zhao outlined his government's policy regarding Taiwan and guaranteed that under any reunification agreement, Taiwan's government and economic system would "remain unchanged." "I believe everybody will agree that on these reasonable terms it will not be difficult to bring about China's peaceful reunification if there is no foreign interference . . . ," he said. "We are seeking a peaceful settlement of the Taiwan question in good faith. But we cannot make a commitment to any foreign country that only peaceful means will be used in solving the Taiwan issue, because this is China's internal affair and within China's sovereign rights."

On other foreign policy fronts, Zhao moved quickly to stabilize relationships with China's neighbors, particularly the Soviet Union, with whom China shares a long and vulnerable border. Eager to strengthen ties with other developing nations, he publicly expressed China's "friendly feelings" toward the peoples of Eastern Europe and, in 1983, he made a month-long, ten-nation tour of Africa. During the tour, Zhao, as an expression of China's good faith, canceled a $100 million debt owed by Zaire since 1973 and promised to help the government of Kenya construct a new sports complex in Nairobi. In September 1984 the Chinese government concluded discussions with Great Britain regarding the future of Hong Kong, a British Crown Colony, after the expiration of the current lease in 1997. As Zhao had indicated in an earlier interview for the New York Times (January 17, 1984), the agreement allows Hong Kong to keep its social and economic system for fifty years after the restoration of Chinese sovereignty.

When in October 1983 the Chinese government mounted a crusade against the "spiritual pollution" of Western ideas and those "liberals" who embraced them, some Westerners feared a return to the intense antiforeignism of the Cultural Revolution, but experienced China watchers saw the crackdown as a calculated ploy by Deng and Zhao to mollify Maoists and forestall left-wing criticism of their revisionist economic policies. The drive against Western "evils," which had been diluted to such a degree that it was virtually meaningless, was officially halted in January 1984, just before Zhao's sixteen-day North American tour. During the prime minister's visit to Washington, he and President Reagan signed a new agreement on industrial cooperation, renewed an existing accord on technological and scientific exchanges, and laid the groundwork for future agreements in specific areas of research and development, such as off-shore oil exploration. During President Reagan's reciprocal visit to China three months later the two leaders initialed a nuclear-power pact and an accord designed to encourage American businessmen to help develop China's industrial base.

Making up for his lack of prior diplomatic experience, Zhao Ziyang has proved himself to be a good student of statecraft. Unlike the folksy, tobacco-chewing Deng, he projects an urbane, cultivated image in his well-cut Western suits and silk shirts. "The man is a mandarin," one American diplomat observed, as quoted in the *Washington Post* (January 10, 1984). "There's no spittoon in evidence around him." The first high-ranking Chinese official to wear Western dress in public since before the Cultural Revolution, Zhao explained in a press conference during his trip that he had adopted the garb not only as an ideological statement but also because he found it "more comfortable." At home, however, Zhao has carefully cultivated a reputation as an honest, hard-working man of simple tastes. On one occasion, according to an anecdote popular among Sichuan residents, a group of party officials arrived in a limousine to take him to an official banquet, only to find him waiting patiently in line with a group of workers to buy a bowl of noodles.

A man of medium height and stocky build, Zhao Ziyang has wavy, graying black hair, brown eyes, and rather delicate features. Western diplomats and journalists have found him to be cheerful, witty, and candid. Although he often works long into the night, he habitually arises at dawn to jog for about forty minutes. Little is known of Zhao's personal life. His wife, Liang Baiqi, was a Party functionary in Guangdong Province before their marriage. They reportedly have four sons, at least one of them an army officer, and one daughter. Zhao lives in an official residence at Zhongnanhai.

References: N Y Times p8 Ap 25 '80 por, p1 S 8 '80 por, p7 Ja 10 '84; Newsweek 96:45 S 22 '80 por; Washington Post p13 S 6 '80 por, p1+ Ja 10 '84; International Who's Who, 1984–85; International Year Book and Statesmen's Who's Who, 1984; Who's Who in the People's Republic of China (1981)

Photo Credits

OBITUARIES

ADAMS, ANSEL (EASTON) Feb. 20, 1902–Apr. 22, 1984 Photographer; conservationist; helped to establish photography as art form; renowned for sharply detailed, panoramic photos of the American West; cofounder of influential "Group f/64" (1932–34); among many exhibitions worldwide, had one-man show at An American Place (1936) and retrospectives at Metropolitan Museum of Art (1974) and Museum of Modern Art (1979) in New York; author of seven portfolios and thirty books, including *Yosemite* (1960) and *Images: 1923–74* (1975); director of Sierra Club (1934–71); among many honors, awarded Sierra Club's Muir Medal (1963) and Presidential Medal of Freedom (1980); died near Carmel, California. See *Current Biography* (May) 1977.

Obituary N Y Times B p6 Ap 24 '84

ALBRIGHT, IVAN (LE LORRAINE) Feb. 20, 1897–Nov. 18, 1983 Artist; known for meticulous, ironic "magic realism" with which he conjured an alarming nether world; painted dynamic still lifes in which objects, viewed from multiple and conflicting vantages, are, as he said, "at war"; in his portraits, depicted obsession, decay, and decrepitude; worked for a decade on the funereal *The Door* and two decades on the startlingly chaotic *The Window*; with his twin brother, Malvin Marr Albright, did the canvases showing the moral degeneration of the title character in the film *The Picture of Dorian Gray* (1945); died in Woodstock, Vermont. See *Current Biography* (December) 1969.

Obituary N Y Times p31 N 19 '83

ALSTON, WALTER (EMMONS) Dec. 1, 1911–Oct. 1, 1984 Baseball manager; was mentor of National League's Dodgers, first in Brooklyn and later in Los Angeles, for twenty-three years beginning in 1954; guided club to seven league pennants and four world championships; died in Oxford, Ohio. See *Current Biography* (June) 1954.

Obituary N Y Times p29 O 2 '84

ANDROPOV, YURI (VLADIMIROVICH) June 15, 1914–Feb. 9, 1984 General Secretary of Communist party, USSR, whose long public absences because of illness beclouded his short term as premier; rose from post as regional chief to become secretary of Central Committee of Communist party (1957–67); as chairman (1967–82) of KGB, Soviet internal and external security force, improved its intelligence network and aided policy-making in Czechoslovakian invasion (1968), Cuban presence in Angola (mid-1970s), Afghanistan invasion (1979), and military crackdown in Poland; member of Politburo (1967–) and its ten-man Secretariat (1982–); outmaneuvered other contenders for succession on death of premier Leonid I. Brezhnev in November 1982, announcing intention to improve domestic economic productivity and relations with China and the West; offered arms reduction proposals that met with skepticism from NATO and Reagan administration, thus contributing to new escalation in arms race; died in Moscow. See *Current Biography* (May) 1983.

Obituary N Y Times p1+ F 11 '84

ARON, RAYMOND (CLAUDE FERDINAND) Mar. 14, 1905–Oct. 17, 1983 Author; journalist; university professor; one of France's most distinguished scholars and commentators on world affairs; was variously described as a conservative or a liberal in the tradition of Alexis de Tocqueville; professor at Sorbonne (1955–68) and Collège de France (from 1970); editorial writer for conservative Paris daily *Le Figaro* (1947–77); columnist for weekly *L'Express* (from 1977); author of *The Century of Total War* (1954), *The Opium of the Intellectuals* (1957), *Peace and War* (1967), *In Defense of Decadent Europe* (1979), and other books. See *Current Biography* (June) 1954.

Obituary N Y Times D p31 O 18 '83

ASTIN, ALLEN V(ARLEY) June 12, 1904–Feb. 4, 1984 United States government official; physicist; during World War II, assisted in development of top secret and highly effective "proximity fuse" weaponry; as director of National Bureau of Standards (1952–69) successfully rode out national political controversy over bureau's ban on a battery additive (1953), oversaw developments in electronic, meteorological, and guided missile technology; in retirement, served in posts for National Academy of Sciences and Department of State; won France's Legion of Honor and other awards for his research; died in Bethesda, Maryland. See *Current Biography* (May) 1956.

Obituary N Y Times D p22 F 9 '84

ATKINSON, (JUSTIN) BROOKS Nov. 28, 1894–Jan. 13, 1984 Theatre critic; journalist; joined *New York Times* as editor of *Book Review* (1922–25); as *Times* drama critic (1925–42, 1946–60), earned respect for objective, candid reviews of over 3,000 opening-night performances; championed Off-Broadway theatre; was catalyst in careers of producer Joseph Papp, actors George C. Scott, Geraldine Page, among others, and one of first supporters of works of Eugene O'Neill; wrote "Critic at Large" column for *Times* (1960–65); Brooks Atkinson Theatre named in his honor (1960); elected to Theatre Hall of Fame and Museum (1972); wrote many books; won 1947 Pulitzer Prize for reporting on Soviet Union; died in Huntsville, Alabama. See *Current Biography* (February) 1961.

Obituary N Y Times p1+ Ja 15 '84

BAINTON, ROLAND H(ERBERT) Mar. 30, 1894–Feb. 13, 1984 Theologian; educator; writer; ordained minister of Congregationalist Church in 1927; joined faculty of Yale Divinity School in 1920 as instructor in New Testament; held Titus Street Professorship of Ecclesiastical History there from 1936 till retirement in 1962; leading authority on Reformation and Martin Luther; wrote thirty-two books, including award-winning *Here I Stand; A Life of Martin Luther* (1950), which sold over 1.2 million copies, and *The Reformation of the Sixteenth Century* (1952); died in New Haven, Connecticut. See *Current Biography* (June) 1962.

Obituary N Y Times D p26 F 14 '84

BARZINI, LUIGI (GIORGIO, JR.) Dec. 21, 1908–Mar. 30, 1984 Italian author; journalist; politician; best known for urbane and often amusing essays and books revealing America to Italians and vice-versa; after college education in United States, became acclaimed roving international correspondent for Milan daily *Corriere della Sera*; during World War II was forced into exile by Mussolini as anti-fascist; in 1953 published first American book, the friendly but critical *Americans Are Alone in the World*, his translation of his Italian original; riled many compatriots with his witty, best-selling cultural history *The Italians*, an account of self-defeating individualism; also wrote, among numerous other works, best-seller *The Europeans* and play *I Disarmati* (1957); was member of Italian parliament (1958–72); died in Rome, Italy. See *Current Biography* (July) 1972.

Obituary N Y Times p38 Ap 1 '84

BASIE, COUNT Aug. 21, 1906–Apr. 26, 1984 Band leader; revolutionized jazz with smooth, driving rhythm and spare keyboard style; studied with Fats Waller; pianist with Walter Page's Blue Devils (1928–29) and Bennie Moten's big band (1929–35); formed own band in 1935; with larger band, won popularity after bookings at Chicago's Grand Terrace and New York's Roseland Ballroom and Famous Door in 1935–36; one of most influential big band leaders of 1930s and 1940s, played with such jazz greats as Benny Goodman and Duke Ellington; among many hits, recorded "One O'Clock Jump," "L'il Darlin'," and "April in Paris"; honors include 1982 Black Music Association gala tribute and 1981 Kennedy Center performing arts achievement award; died in Hollywood, Florida. See *Current Biography* (June) 1942.

Obituary N Y Times p1+ Ap 27 '84

BERLINGUER, ENRICO May 25, 1922–June 11, 1984 General Secretary of Italian Communist party (PCI), from 1972 until his death; as an architect of "Eurocommunism," asserted high degree of independence from Soviet Union; rejected violent revolution while supporting parliamentary democracy, mixed economy, and membership in EEC and NATO; joined Communist party in 1943 and rose through its ranks as protégé of Palmiro Togliatti; failed in 1976 to bring PCI to power through his proposed "historic compromise" with Christian Democrats and other parties, but was granted a formal consultative role; died in Padua, Italy. See *Current Biography* (July) 1976.

Obituary N Y Times p1+ Je 12 '84

BETJEMAN, SIR JOHN Aug. 28, 1906–May 19, 1984 British poet; author; merged love of architecture and conservation interests in many books celebrating England, among them *Vintage London* (1942) and *A Pictorial History of English Architecture* (1972); best known for humorous, often satiric verses in traditional meters and rhyme schemes; for such poetry collections as *A Few Late Chrysanthemums* (1954) and verse autobiography *Summoned by Bells* (1960) won Queen's Gold Medal for Poetry (1960); was named Companion of Literature by Royal Society of Literature (1968); knighted in 1969; named poet laureate of England in 1972; died in Trebetherick, Cornwall, England. See *Current Biography* (March) 1973.

Obituary N Y Times p40 My 20 '84

BIDDLE, KATHERINE GARRISON CHAPIN Sept. 4, 1890–Dec. 30, 1978 Widow of former attorney general Francis Biddle; poet, whose works first appeared in late 1920s in *Yale Review*, *Scribner's*, *Harper's*, and other magazines; published collections of poems, including *Outside the World* (1930), *Time Has No Shadow* (1936), and *The Other Journey* (1959); won plaudits for her ballad poems set to music, especially *Plain-Chant for America*; died after long illness in Devon, Pennsylvania. See *Current Biography* (October) 1943.

Obituary N Y Times p24 Ja 2 '78

BOLES, PAUL DARCY Mar. 5, 1919–May 4, 1984 Writer; limned small-town American life in such novels as *The Beggars in the Sun* (1954), *Glenport, Illinois* (1956), and *Deadline* (1957); received Friends of American Writers Award for novel *Parton's Island* (1959) and Indiana Writers Conference Award for short-story collection *A Million Guitars* (1968); was cleared of plagiarism charges brought against him by writer Hazel Cartin in lawsuit concerning novel *The Limner* (1975); died in Atlanta, Georgia. See *Current Biography* (Yearbook) 1956.

Obituary N Y Times p44 My 6 '84

BOYLSTON, HELEN DORE Apr. 4, 1895–Sept. 30, 1984 Author; drew partly on own experience as nurse to create "Sue Barton" series of vocational novels for girls (1936–52); also wrote "Carol Page" series (1941–46), dealing with acting, World War I diary *Sister* (1927), biography *Clara Barton* (1955), and, with Rose W. Lane, journal *Travels with Zenobia: Paris to Albania by Model T Ford* (1983); died in Trumbull, Connecticut. See *Current Biography* (July) 1942.

Obituary N Y Times D p17 O 5 '84

BRADY, WILLIAM T(HOMAS) Mar. 12, 1896–May 18, 1984 Business executive; rose steadily at Corn Products Refining Company (now CPC International) from student trainee in 1919 to president and chief executive officer in 1956; expanded company's foreign holdings; added Skippy peanut butter, Hellman's mayonnaise, and Knorr soups to company's list of basic corn syrup and starch products through canny mergers and acquisitions; during his tenure, company ranked second only to General Foods in volume of food processed; chairman of board, 1960–64; died in Beverly Hills, California. See *Current Biography* (January) 1961.

Obituary N Y Times D p15 My 21 '84

BRANDT, BILL 1904–Dec. 20, 1983 British photographer; noted for poetic intuition; after working for surrealist photographer Man Ray in Paris, returned to London in 1931 and began documenting various levels of British social life with candid photos, many on assignment for British, French, or American publications; after World War II, concentrated on British landscapes, portraits of artists, and female nudes; presented his works in many exhibitions, including retrospectives at New York City's Museum of Modern Art (1969) and at the opening of the National Centre of Photography in Bath, England (1981), and in such books as his *The Land* (1975), *Shadow of Light* (1977), and *Nudes 1945-1980* (1980); died in London. See *Current Biography* (August) 1981.

Obituary N Y Times B p12 D 22 '83

BRETT, GEORGE P(LATT), JR. Dec. 9, 1893–Feb. 11, 1984 Publisher; after succeeding his father to presidency of Macmillan Co. in 1931, expanded company's trade department branch offices, diversified publications, and added to its list of authors such luminaries as Vachel Lindsay, Jack London, Winston Churchill, and Edgar Lee Masters; in 1936 published Margaret Mitchell's novel *Gone With the Wind,* which has sold over twenty-one million copies; after retirement in 1958, was board chairman for two years; on several occasions, accepted publishing-related assignments from U.S. Department of State; died in Southport, Connecticut. See *Current Biography* (December) 1948.

Obituary N Y Times D p29 F 16 '84

BRINTON, HOWARD H(AINES) July 24, 1884–Apr. 9, 1973 Educator; writer; director of Quaker-sponsored Pendle Hill Graduate School for Religious and Social Study in Wallingford, Pennsylvania (1936–52); represented American Friends Service Committee in Germany (1919–20) and Japan (1952–54); author of *The Mystic Will* (1930), *Quaker Education in Theory and Practice* (1940), *The Religious Philosophy of Quakerism* (1973), and other books. See *Current Biography* (July) 1949.

Obituary Contemporary Authors new rev vol 3 (1902)

BRISTOW, GWEN Sept. 16, 1903–Aug. 16, 1980 Writer; journalist; reporter for *New Orleans Times-Picayune* (1925–34); author of historical fiction, including *Deep Summer* (1937), *The Handsome Road* (1938), and *This Side of Glory* (1940), which were compiled in the volume *Plantation Trilogy* (1962); with her husband, Bruce Manning, wrote *The Invisible Host* (1930) and other mystery novels; died in New Orleans. See *Current Biography* (Yearbook) 1940.

Obituary Contemporary Authors vol 102 (1981)

BROWER, CHARLES (HENDRICKSON) Nov. 13, 1901–July 23, 1984 Advertising executive; after working his way up from copywriter, was president (1957–64), chief executive officer (1964–67) and chairman (1964–70) of Batten, Barton, Durstine & Osborn, one of the largest ad agencies in the United States; died in Brielle, New Jersey. See *Current Biography* (February) 1965.

Obituary N Y Times B p8 Jl 26 '84

BUNKER, ELLSWORTH May 11, 1894–Sept. 27, 1984 United States diplomat; executive in sugar industry (1927–66); ambassador to Argentina (1951), Italy (1952–53), India (1956–61), and Nepal (1956–59); mediated disputes between Netherlands and Indonesia (1962) and between Egypt and Saudi Arabia (1963); as representative to Organization of American States (1964–66), promoted establishment of moderate civilian government in Dominican Republic; ambassador to South Vietnam during key years of United States in-

volvement there (1967–73); chief negotiator of Panama Canal treaties (1973–78); died at Brattleboro (Vermont) Memorial Hospital. See *Current Biography* (March) 1978.

Obituary N Y Times p9 S 29 '84

BURTON, RICHARD Nov. 10, 1925–Aug. 5, 1984 Welsh-born actor; one of Great Britain's most distinguished Shakespearean performers, noted for commanding stage presence and cello-like timbre; won acclaim for Broadway performances in *Hamlet, Camelot,* and *Equus;* appeared in over fifty British or American motion pictures, including *My Cousin Rachel* (1952), *Look Back in Anger* (1959), and *The Night of the Iguana* (1964); nominated seven times for Academy Awards; weathered two tempestuous marriages with Elizabeth Taylor, with whom he costarred in such films as *Cleopatra* (1962), *Who's Afraid of Virginia Woolf?* (1966), and *The Taming of the Shrew* (1967), and in Broadway production of *Private Lives* (1983); also appeared in television dramas; died in Geneva, Switzerland. See *Current Biography* (December) 1960.

Obituary N Y Times p1+ Ag 6 '84

CAPOTE, TRUMAN Sept. 30, 1924–Aug. 26, 1984 Author; one of leading American writers of post–World War II period; noted for lucidity and elegant prose; wrote thirteen books, including novels *Other Voices, Other Rooms* (1948) and *The Grass Harp* (1951) and collections of short fiction *A Tree of Night* (1949) and *Breakfast at Tiffany's* (1958); pioneered genre of "nonfiction novel" with *In Cold Blood* (1966), a meticulously researched account of a Kansas mass murder, and collaborated on script of its film adaptation (1967); adapted several of his short stories, including the autobiographical "A Christmas Memory," for television; collaborated on script for John Huston film *Beat the Devil* (1954); wrote book for Broadway musical *House of Flowers* (1954); died in Los Angeles. See *Current Biography* (March) 1968.

Obituary N Y Times C p16 Ag 27 '84

CARTER, (BESSIE) LILLIAN Aug. 15, 1898–October 30, 1983 Mother of Jimmy Carter, thirty-ninth president of the United States, and grande dame of Plains, Georgia; with her unaffected manner, refreshing candor, and independent ways, was a darling of the press, which referred to her, as she requested, as "Miss Lillian"; worked for decades as registered nurse and served as Peace Corps volunteer in India for two years (1966–68); stumped the hustings in Jimmy Carter's state and national political campaigns and represented him abroad on numerous occasions; died in Americus, Georgia. See *Current Biography* (January) 1978.

Obituary N Y Times A p1+ O 31 '83

CHAGLA, MAHOMED ALI CURRIM Sept. 30, 1900–Feb. 26, 1981 Indian diplomat and jurist; junior judge (1941–47) and chief justice (1947–58) of High Court in Bombay; championed social legislation and civil liberties; among other diplomatic duties, served as ambassador to United States (1958–61) and high commissioner to Great Britain (1962–63); minister of education (1963–66) and of external affairs (1966–67); won National UNESCO Award for Distinguished Service to Human Rights (1978); died in Bombay, India. See *Current Biography* (June) 1959.

Obituary N Y Times Biographical Service 12:146 F 27 '81

CHAPMAN, ALBERT K(INKADE) May 31, 1890–Aug. 27, 1984 Business executive; joined Eastman Kodak Company during World War I as United States Army Air Corps officer heading a project to develop an aerial camera and film; president (1952–1960) and board vice-chairman (1960–62) of Eastman Kodak; chairman of the board from 1962 until his retirement in 1967; died in Rochester, New York. See *Current Biography* (September) 1952.

Obituary N Y Times D p22 Ag 29 '84

CHAPMAN, CHARLES F(REDERIC) Jan 4, 1881–Mar. 21, 1976 Editor; writer; known as "No. 1 yachtsman" of United States; author of standard instruction book *Piloting, Seamanship and Small Boat Handling* (1926), which sold over 2 million copies in fifty-one editions; joined editorial staff of *Motor Boating* magazine and served as its editor, publisher, and vice-president before his retirement in 1969; was also a vice-president of Hearst Corporation; founded United States Power Squadrons (1914); organized National Outboard Racing Commission (1927) and served as its national secretary; navigator for Garfield Arthur ("Gar") Wood on several races between speedboats and railroads in 1920s; died in Essex, Connecticut. See *Current Biography* (May) 1958.

Obituary N Y Times p34 Mr 23 '76

CHARLOT, JEAN Feb. 8, 1898–Mar. 20, 1979 French-born painter; muralist; first gained recognition in Mexico during 1920s, working with Diego Rivera and others in Mexican mural movement; executed *Fall of Tenochtitlán* (1922), said to be first contemporary fresco in Western Hemisphere; taught at Columbia, Yale, and other universities and colleges; author of book *Art From the Mayans to Disney* (1939); died at his home in Honolulu, Hawaii. See *Current Biography* (September) 1945.

Obituary N Y Times B p5 Mr 23 '79

CHURCH, FRANK (FORRESTER) July 25, 1924–Apr. 7, 1984 United States Democratic Senator from Idaho (1956–81); lawyer; as member (1959–81) and chairman (1979–81) of Senate Foreign Relations Committee, pressed for nuclear test ban treaty with USSR and against further bombing and troop commitment in Southeast Asia; chaired Select Committee on Intelligence during 1975–76 probes of illegal activities of CIA and FBI that led to curb of such abuses; backed liberal legislation favoring civil and equal rights, social programs, conservation, and water rights for Idaho; practiced international law at firm of Whitman & Ransom (1981–84); died in Bethesda, Maryland. See *Current Biography* (March) 1978.

Obituary N Y Times p44 Ap 8 '84

CLARK, MARK W(AYNE) May 1, 1896–Apr. 17, 1984 United States Army lieutenant general; as one of top five U.S. commanders in World War II European theatre, led secret mission to Algiers that facilitated invasion of North Africa; as commander of Fifth Army, directed invasion of Italy, controversial Rapido River battle, and 1944 capture of Rome; forced May 2, 1945 German surrender in the Italian Alps; as UN commander and commander in chief of U.S. Far East command (1952–53), signed Korean armistice; retired in 1953; president of The Citadel (1954–65); received Distinguished Service Medal (1942), Distinguished Service Cross for Heroism (1945), and Italy's Grand Cross of Order of Merit (1975); died in Charleston, South Carolina. See *Current Biography* (November) 1950.

Obituary N Y Times B p7 Ap 18 '84

CORTÁZAR, JULIO Aug. 26, 1914–Feb. 12, 1984 Avant-garde Argentine writer known for his imaginative, intellectual, metaphysical fiction in the tradition of Jorge Luis Borges; after President Juan Perón's election in 1946, quit post at University of Buenos Aires and had lived in exile in Paris since 1951; accepted French citizenry in 1981; collections of short stories include *Bestiary* (1951), *Story of Cronopios and Famas* (1962), and *End of the Game* (1956); among his best-known novels are *The Winners* (1960), *Hopscotch* (1963), and *Book of Manuel* (1973); vocal supporter of revolutions in Cuba and Nicaragua; won Rubén Darío Order from Nicaragua in 1983 and Prix Médicis in 1974; died in Paris. See *Current Biography* (February) 1974.

Obituary N Y Times D p11 F 13 '84

CRONIN, JOE Oct. 12, 1906–Sept. 7, 1984 Baseball player; manager; executive; began career as major-league shortstop with Washington Nationals in 1928; was player-manager with Nationals from 1932 to 1934 and with Boston Red Sox from 1935 to 1945; after year as non-playing field manager, in 1948 became Boston's general manager, a position he held for eleven years; elected to Baseball Hall of Fame in 1956; served as president of American League from 1959 to 1973; died in Osterville, Massachusetts. See *Current Biography* (March) 1965.

Obituary N Y Times p7 S 8 '84

DART, JUSTIN W(HITLOCK) Aug. 7, 1907–Jan. 26, 1984 Business executive; rapidly advanced from job as stock clerk at Walgreen Company in 1929 to general manager and director of its 375-drugstore chain (1939–41); president of United Drug subsidiary Liggett Drug Company (1941–43) and later president and director of United Drug (1946–75); renamed business Rexall Drug in 1946 and Dart Industries in 1969; chairman and chief executive officer of Dart (1966–80); chairman of executive committee and director of Dart & Kraft, Inc. (1980–84); a "kingmaker" in California Republican politics, was an adviser in President Ronald Reagan's "kitchen cabinet"; died in Los Angeles, California. See *Current Biography* (November) 1946.

Obituary N Y Times B p4 Ja 27 '84

DOLIN, ANTON July 27, 1904–Nov. 25, 1983 Dancer; choreographer; a leading authority on classic ballet; as member of Serge Diaghilev's Ballets Russes (1921–29), became first internationally renowned British ballet star; guest dancer with Vic-Wells Ballet (1931–35); cofounder and director (1935–38) of Markova-Dolin Ballet; ballet master and premier dancer of New York's Ballet Theater (1940–46); cofounder and principal male dancer of London's Festival Ballet (1950–61); author of several books, including memoirs; was knighted in 1981; died in Paris, France. See *Current Biography* (January) 1946.

Obituary N Y Times p44 N 27 '83

DREW, GEORGE A(LEXANDER) May 7, 1894–Jan. 4, 1973 Canadian political leader; author; elected leader of Conservative party in Ontario in 1938, was sent to provincial legislature the following year; when Liberals lost power in 1943, formed new provincial government, serving as prime minister until 1948; national leader of Conservative party, 1948–56; ambassador with Canadian High Commission to London, 1957–64; as Ontario premier, championed primacy of provincial jurisdiction within Canadian federation; wrote on World War I, armaments trade, and fiscal policy; died in Toronto. See *Current Biography* (December) 1948.

Obituary N Y Times p39 Ja 5 '73

ECKSTEIN, OTTO Aug. 1, 1927–Mar. 22, 1984 German-born economist; United States citizen since 1945; joined Harvard University faculty in 1955, promoted to full professor of economics in 1963; consultant to government agencies and such major companies as RAND Corp. (1957–64); as member of Council of Economic Advisers (1964–66) under President Lyndon B. Johnson, helped establish wage-price guidelines and develop Great Society programs; cofounder and president (1968–81) of Data Resources Inc., leading computer-based economic forecasting firm; died in Boston, Massachusetts. See *Current Biography* (February) 1967.

Obituary N Y Times D p15 Mr 23 '84

EGAN, WILLIAM ALLEN Oct. 8, 1914–May 6, 1984 First governor of Alaska (1959–67, 1971–75); as member of territorial House of Representatives (1941–43, 1947–56), sponsored bill proposing statehood for Alaska that finally passed in 1946; led constitutional convention in 1956 and was architect of state charter; elected "senator" during convention, lobbied Congress to approve Alaskan statehood; immediately after Alaska became forty-ninth state on January 3, 1959, was inaugurated governor; died in Anchorage, Alaska. See *Current Biography* (September) 1959.

Obituary N Y Times B p6 My 8 '84

ERNST, JIMMY June 24, 1920–Feb. 6, 1984 German-born painter; son of surrealistic painter Max Ernst; joined Brooklyn College's Department of Design in 1951; promoted to professor in 1963; an abstractionist, began in 1943 to exhibit such works as *Stillness* that used broad areas of colors often intersected by lines or grids; is represented in permanent collections of Whitney Museum of Art, Metropolitan Museum of Art, and Solomon R. Guggenheim Museum in New York City, the Corcoran Gallery in Washington, D.C., and the Chicago Institute of Art, among others; held Guggenheim fellowship in 1951; was elected to American Academy and Institute of Arts and Letters in 1983; became United States citizen in 1952. See *Current Biography* (March) 1966.

Obituary N Y Times D p24 F 7 '84

FAGERHOLM, KARL-AUGUST Dec. 31, 1901–May 22, 1984 Finnish government official; barber (1917–23); chairman of Finnish Barbers Trade Union (1920–23); chairman (1930–42) and honorary chairman since 1943 of Shopworkers Union; Social Democratic member of Parliament (1930–66); elected speaker of the Diet four times (1945–48, 1950–56, 1959–61, 1965–66); minister of social affairs (1937–43, 1944); since 1952, director-general of state alcohol monopoly; during three terms as prime minister (1948–50, 1956–57, 1958–59), was steadfast proponent of conciliation and Nordic cooperation in face of unrelenting pressures from USSR; died in Helsinki, Finland. See *Current Biography* (October) 1948.

Obituary N Y Times B p10 My 23 '84

FARRAR, MARGARET (PETHERBRIDGE) Mar. 23, 1897–June 11, 1984 Crossword-puzzle editor; by upgrading language and style, was instrumental in transforming newspaper space filler into enduring, intellectually challenging national pastime; began career in 1920 at *New York World*, which had published the first modern word-square game (the creation of Edward Wynne) seven years before; was first crossword-puzzle editor for *New York Times*, from 1942 to 1969; compiled 134 collections of puzzles; also edited mystery books for Farrar, Straus & Giroux, the publishing company cofounded by her husband, the late John C. Farrar. See *Current Biography* (June) 1955.

Obituary N Y Times D p27 Je 12 '84

FARRINGTON, (MARY) ELIZABETH PRUETT May 30, 1898–July 21, 1984 Delegate to United States Congress from Territory of Hawaii (1954–56), succeeding her late husband, Joseph R. Farrington; a leading advocate of Hawaiian statehood; president and director (1957–61) of family-owned *Honolulu Star-Bulletin* and *Hilo Tribune-Herald*; president of Hawaiian Broadcasting System (1960–61); president of National Federation of Women's Republican Clubs (1949–53); died in Honolulu. See *Current Biography* (June) 1955.

Obituary N Y Times p16 Jl 23 '84

FEINSINGER, NATHAN P(AUL) Sept. 20, 1902–Nov. 2, 1983 Labor mediator; lawyer; after forty-four years at University of Wisconsin, retired in 1973 as emeritus professor of law; founded Center for Teaching and Research in Dispute Settlement at the university in 1967; served as mediator of national disputes for War Labor Relations Board (1942–45) and as chairman of Wage Stabilization Board (1951–52); helped to settle labor disputes in steel, transit, automobile, and communications industries; died in Glenwood Springs, Colorado. See *Current Biography* (May) 1952.

Obituary N Y Times B p14 N 4 '83

FELD, IRVIN May 9, 1918–Sept. 6, 1984 Show business impresario; chairman and chief operating officer, Ringling Brothers Barnum & Bailey Circus; as musical entrepreneur in 1940s, pioneered staging of pop concerts in stadiums and other large arenas; later produced shows featuring, among others, Bill Haley, Fats Domino, and Paul Anka (whom he discovered) and arranged bookings for such high-priced performers as Frank Sinatra and Nat King Cole; managed Ringling circus since 1957 and, to save it from folding, bought it twice, in 1967 and 1982; died in Venice, California. See *Current Biography* (February) 1979.

Obituary N Y Times p7 S 8 '84

FOX, ROBERT J(OHN) Apr. 18, 1930–Apr. 27, 1984 Roman Catholic priest; social worker; as coordinator of New York archdiocese's Spanish Community Action project in 1960s, initiated programs aimed at raising quality of life and easing tensions in eight New York City slum neighborhoods and creating "an air of celebration of the city"; continued his work for inner-city human renewal while serving as assistant pastor of St. Paul's Church in Spanish Harlem; died in Manhattan. See *Current Biography* (May) 1970.

Obituary N Y Times B p8 Ap 30 '84

GALLUP, GEORGE (HORACE) Nov. 18, 1901–July 26, 1984 Public opinion statistician; pioneered in techniques of scientific public opinion sampling; founder (1935) and chairman of American Institute of Public Opinion, or Gallup Poll, based in Princeton, New Jersey, which gained international prominence after correctly predicting victory for Franklin D. Roosevelt in 1936 presidential election; board chairman of Gallup Organization Inc., founded in 1958 to conduct market research; taught journalism at Drake, Northwestern, and Columbia universities; research director at Young & Rubicam advertising agency (1932–47); author of *The Pulse of Democracy* (1940) and other books; died near Lake Thun, Switzerland. See *Current Biography* (December) 1952.

Obituary N Y Times p1+ Jl 28 '84

GANDHI, INDIRA (PRIYADARSHINI NEHRU) Nov. 19, 1917–Oct. 31, 1984 Prime Minister of India (1966–77, 1980–84); dominant Indian political figure for about two decades; joined all-India Congress party in 1938; served as its president in 1959–60; formed breakaway Indian National Congress (I) in 1978; official hostess for her father, Prime Minister Jawaharlal Nehru (1947–64); as prime minister, instituted major reforms, including strong population control program; was criticized for authoritarian rule, especially under state of emergency (1975–77), and for such acts as raid on Sikh Golden Temple in Amritsar (1984); was assassinated near her home in New Delhi, reportedly by Sikh extremist members of her own security guard. See *Current Biography* (June) 1966.

Obituary N Y Times A p1+, p20+ N 1 '84

GILES, BARNEY McKINNEY Sept. 13, 1892–May 6, 1984 United States Army officer, retired; was a pilot in World War I; as deputy commander and chief of staff of Army Air Forces during World War II, advanced his idea of importance of fighter protection for bombers; retired in rank of lieutenant-general in 1946; died in San Antonio, Texas. See *Current Biography* (July) 1944.

Obituary N Y Times B p22 My 10 '84

GOBBI, TITO Oct. 24, 1915–Mar. 5, 1984 Italian baritone; was renowned for skilled character portrayals, especially that of Scarpia in *Tosca*; made debut as Belcore in *l'Elisir d'Amore* at La Scala in 1942; performed throughout Europe and U.S. in such varied parts as title roles in Mozart's *Don Giovanni* and Alban Berg's *Wozzeck*; directed operas at Lyric Opera of Chicago and Metropolitan Opera Company and Juilliard American Opera Center in New York City; died in Rome, Italy. See *Current Biography* (January) 1957.

Obituary N Y Times B p10 Mr 6 '84

GOODRICH, FRANCES 1891(?)–Jan. 29, 1984 Writer; in collaboration with her husband, Albert Hackett, adapted numerous stage- and screenplays; for their theatrical adaptation of *The Diary of Anne Frank*, won Pulitzer Prize, Tony award, and a New York Drama Critics Circle award for 1955–56 season; entered show business as stage actress in 1916, and teamed up with Hackett in 1930; among other screenplays, wrote *The Thin Man* (1934); *Easter Parade* (1948); *It's a Wonderful Life* (1946); *Father of the Bride* (1950); *Seven Brides for Seven Brothers* (1954); and screen version of *The Diary of Anne Frank* (1959); died in New York City. See *Current Biography* (October) 1956.

Obituary N Y Times B p6 Ja 31 '84

GOUDGE, ELIZABETH Apr. 24, 1900–Apr. 1, 1984 British author; wrote novels, short stories, and plays, many of them historical romances lovingly set in English countryside and other places familiar to her; was best known for novel *Green Dolphin Street* (1944), story of two young women from the Channel islands wooing the same man in nineteenth-century New Zealand, which was made into 1947 MGM motion picture; died at her home near Henley-on-Thames, England. See *Current Biography* (September) 1940.

Obituary N Y Times B p6 Ap 27 '84

HARRIS, SIR ARTHUR TRAVERS Apr. 13, 1892–Apr. 5, 1984 Marshal of British Royal Air Force; with Royal Flying Corps during World War I, served in Africa and led anti-zeppelin defenses of London and raids in France; was appointed to Air Ministry in 1933; during World War II, planned and directed saturation night raids on German industrial cities, climaxing with the fire-bombing of Dresden that destroyed the city and killed 50,000 civilians; engaged in rancorous public dispute with advocates of precision daytime bombing; died in Goring-on-Thames, England. See *Current Biography* (September) 1942.

Obituary N Y Times p32 Ap 7 '84

HELLMAN, LILLIAN June 20, 1905(?)–June 30, 1984 Playwright; as motion-picture scenarist, adapted many of her own plays to the screen; in Hollywood in early 1930s, met detective-story writer Dashiell Hammett, with whom she lived on and off for thirty-one years and under whose stern coaching she honed her craft;

achieved initial Broadway success with *The Children's Hour* (1934), intense drama about two slandered women schoolteachers; later contributed to the contemporary theatrical repertory the plays *Watch on the Rhine* (1941), about an heroic anti-Nazi German, and three bristling indictments of greed, hypocrisy, and decadence in a wealthy Southern family resembling Miss Hellman's own maternal forebears: *The Little Foxes* (1939), *Another Part of the Forest* (1946), and *Toys in the Attic* (1960); was blacklisted for leftist loyalties throughout 1950s; wrote three books of memoirs, one of which, *Pentimento* (1974), inspired 1977 film *Julia*; died near her summer home in Martha's Vineyard, Massachusetts. See *Current Biography* (June) 1960.

Obituary N Y Times p1+ Jl 1 '84

HOGBEN, LANCELOT (THOMAS) Dec. 9, 1895–Aug. 22, 1975 Scientist; author; known for *Mathematics for the Million* (1936), *Science for the Citizen*, and other brightly written works making weighty scientific subjects meaningful and entertaining to lay reader; politically, was progressive "scientific humanist" who advocated elimination of poverty and illiteracy through global socialism; taught at McGill University in Canada and, later, at University of Cape Town in South Africa; died in Wrexham, Wales. See *Current Biography* (December) 1941.

Obituary N Y Times p24 Ag 23 '75

HOLYOAKE, SIR KEITH J(ACKA) Feb. 11, 1904–Dec. 8, 1983 Prime minister of New Zealand (1957; 1960 72); governor general (1077–80); member of Parliament (1932–77) and of right-of-center National party; occupied executive posts in a number of agricultural organizations; served as minister of agriculture (1949–57) and in other cabinet posts; as prime minister, supported United States military involvement in Vietnam and was faced with threatened loss of agricultural export markets on Great Britain's entry into Common Market; was created a Knight of the Order of the Garter (1980); died in Wellington, New Zealand. See *Current Biography* (February) 1963.

Obituary N Y Times p33 D 9 '83

HUNSAKER, JEROME C(LARKE) Aug. 26, 1886–Sept. 10, 1984 Aeronautical engineer; professor emeritus, Massachusetts Institute of Technology; founded first American college course in aeronautics at M.I.T. in 1914; supervised design, construction, and procurement of United States Navy aircraft in World War I; later designed *Shenandoah*, first large United States airship, and light carrier-based airplanes as well as methods of launching and deck-landing such planes; for Bell Laboratories, developed communications systems for aircraft, and for Goodyear-Zeppelin Corporation, gas-proof fabric for dirigibles; died in Boston, Massachusetts. See *Current Biography* (October) 1942.

Obituary N Y Times B p6 S 12 '84

HURD, PETER Feb. 22, 1904–July 9, 1984 Artist; noted for landscapes, portraits, and scenes of ranch life of his native Southwestern United States, executed in egg tempera, watercolor, or lithography; student of painter N. C. Wyeth, who became his father-in-law; artist-correspondent for *Life* magazine during World War II; executed official commissioned portrait of Lyndon B. Johnson (1967) that was rejected by him and later acquired by Smithsonian Institution; also worked as book illustrator and executed public works projects, including mural for post office in Dallas, Texas (1938); died in Roswell, New Mexico. See *Current Biography* (October) 1957.

Obituary N Y Times B p6 Jl 10 '84

JOHNSON, CROCKETT Oct. 20, 1906–July 11, 1975 Cartoonist; creator of comic strip *Barnaby* (1941–62), about a five-year-old boy and his portly, cigar-smoking, pink-winged fairy godfather, Mr. O'Malley, which appeared in the now defunct New York tabloid *PM* and other publications; also created weekly cartoon feature *The Little Man With the Eyes* (1940–43) for *Collier's* magazine; author and illustrator of over a dozen children's books, including *Harold's Fairy Tale* (1950), painted mathematical abstractions in oils; died in Norwalk, Connecticut. See *Current Biography* (December) 1943.

Obituary N Y Times p38 Jl 13 '75

JONES, MARVIN Feb. 26, 1886–Mar. 4, 1976 United States Democratic Representative from Texas (1917–41); as chairman of House Committee on Agriculture (1931–40) and a close adviser to President Franklin D. Roosevelt and Secretary of Agriculture Henry A. Wallace, helped to draft key New Deal farm legislation; president of UN conference on food and agriculture (1943); United States food administrator (1943–45); chief justice of United States Court of Claims (1947–64). See *Current Biography* (August) 1943.

Obituary N Y Times p28 Mr 6 '76

KANE, HARNETT T(HOMAS) Nov. 8, 1910–Sept. 4, 1984 Author of two dozen books, mainly about the American South, including *Louisiana Hayride* (1941), an exposé of political corruption in his home state; *New Orleans Woman* (1946), a biographical novel; and *Natchez on the Mississippi* (1947), a historical study; also contributed to *National Geographic Magazine*, *Saturday Review*, and other publications; received two Rosenwald Regional Fellowships; died in New Orleans. See *Current Biography* (Yearbook) 1947.

Obituary N Y Times B p5 S 14 '84

KAPITSA, PYOTR L(EONIDOVICH) July 8, 1894–Apr. 8, 1984 Soviet physicist; during his years in Britain (1921–34), studied under atomic physics pioneer Lord Ernest Rutherford; developed groundbreaking methods for liquefying helium, intensifying magnetic fields, and liquefying air in industry at low cost; named director of USSR's Institute of Physical Problems in 1934, dismissed in 1946, perhaps for refusal to work on atom bomb, but reinstated as director in 1955, serving there till death; outspoken advocate of freedom in scientific pursuits; honors include Stalin Prizes (1941, 1943), Hero of Socialist Labor Awards (1945, 1974), and 1978 Nobel Prize for lifetime's work; fellow of British Royal Society and USSR's Academy of Sciences; died in Moscow. See *Current Biography* (October) 1955.

Obituary N Y Times B p11 Ap 11 '84

KASTLER, ALFRED May 3, 1902–Jan. 7, 1984 French physicist; educator; taught physics at French lycées and universities before becoming assistant (1941–45) and later full professor (1945–68) at École Normale Supérieure in Paris and director of its physics lab; director of research, Centre National de la Recherche Scientifique (1968–72); awarded 1966 Nobel Prize in physics for discovery and development of optical methods for studying Hertzian resonance in atoms, which led to development of the laser; peace activist since World War II; was made Chevalier de la Légion d'Honneur (1952) and was elected to French Academy of Sciences (1964); died at Bandol on the French Riviera. See *Current Biography* (December) 1967.

Obituary N Y Times p 28 Ja 8 '84

KEIGHLEY, WILLIAM Aug. 4, 1889–June 24, 1984 Theatre and film director; actor; toured in Ben Greet's Shakespearean repertory company (1905–08) and acted on Broadway (1915–23) before directing such plays as *The Perfect Alibi* (1928) and *Penny Arcade* (1930); under contract to Warner Bros., directed first film *Easy To Love* in 1934; other films include *Each Dawn We Die* (1939), *The Man Who Came to Dinner* (1941), and *Street With No Name* (1948); as head of Army Air Corps film division during World War II, made training films and directed "Target for Today," among other duties; in 1945, replaced Cecil B. De Mille as host of Lux Radio Theater; awarded Army Air Force's Legion of Merit (1945). See *Current Biography* (November) 1948.

Obituary N Y Times B p8 Je 26 '84

KIRKPATRICK, RALPH June 10, 1911–Apr. 13, 1984 Harpsichordist; musicologist; contributed to revival of interest in harpsichord and reevaluation of baroque music; began playing concert tours of Europe and America in 1930s; mastered repertoire that included the keyboard works of Mozart, Handel, Purcell, Rameau, and Couperin; was best known for his performances of Domenico Scarlatti and Johann Sebastian Bach; recorded Bach's entire canon for clavier; wrote definitive critical biography *Domenico Scarlatti* (1953); died at his home in Guilford, Connecticut. See *Current Biography* (September) 1971.

Obituary N Y Times B p10 Ap 16 '84

KITCHELL, IVA Mar. 31, 1908–Nov. 19, 1983 Dancer; won international fame as dance comedian, impersonating great dancers and satirizing classical ballet as well as modern dance; began career at fourteen with Chicago Opera Ballet, later toured vaudeville circuit and became featured dancer at New York's Radio City Music Hall; toured Europe in 1938 and South America during 1950s; gave first of several Carnegie Hall programs of dance pantomimes and parodies in 1948; also appeared at Jacob's Pillow dance festivals and in nightclubs and cabarets; after retirement from stage in 1961, taught ballet at her Huntington, Long Island studio; died in Ormond Beach, Florida. See *Current Biography* (December) 1951.

Obituary N Y Times D p20 N 21 '83

KLEIN, JULIUS Sept. 5, 1901–Apr. 6, 1984 Army officer; editor for Hearst Newspapers (1926–33); executive at R.K.O. (1934–39); as lieutenant colonel, led 10,000 troops in South Pacific and Philippines in 1943; National Guard commanding officer (1948–51); promoted to brigadier general of line in National Guard in 1950; retired as major general in 1966; with Chancellor Konrad Adenauer, worked to speed up payments to relatives of Jews killed under Nazis; national commander of Jewish War Veterans (1947–48); founder and chairman (1947–84) of public relations firm; honors include many medals for bravery in Philippines, Bronze Star, French Legion of Honor, Fighters for State of Israel medal; died in Chicago, Illinois. See *Current Biography* (July) 1948.

Obituary N Y Times D p14 Ap 9 '84

KNOPF, ALFRED A. Sept. 12, 1892–Aug. 11, 1984 Publisher; noted for excellence of the more than 5,000 books he published under Borzoi imprint during half-century career, including works of sixteen Nobel laureates and twenty-six Pulitzer Prize winners; founder (1915), president (1918–57), board chairman (1957–72), and chairman emeritus (from 1972) of Alfred A. Knopf, Inc., which became a subsidiary of Random House in 1966; publisher of *American Mercury* magazine (1924–34); received many honors, including outstanding service award of National Parks Centennial Commission (1972) and Francis Parkman silver medal (1974); died at his home in Purchase, New York. See *Current Biography* (November) 1966.

Obituary N Y Times p1+ Ag 12 '84

KRASNER, LEE Oct. 27, 1908–June 19, 1984 Painter; with her husband, the late Jackson Pollock, and other first-generation action painters of the New York School, founded abstract expressionism, the dominant movement in American art in the late 1940s and the 1950s; a master of line and color, created multivalent canvases at once pensive and fiercely energetic, characterized by bold, often bulbous shapes on dynamic fields, suggesting the rhythms of nature; received full independent recognition belatedly, especially through the recent Lee Krasner retrospective at the Museum of Fine Arts, Houston; died in New York City. See *Current Biography* (March) 1974.

Obituary N Y Times D p23 Je 21 '84

KROC, RAY(MOND) A. Oct. 5, 1902–Jan. 14, 1984 Restaurateur; salesman; and later Midwestern sales manager for Lily-Tulip Cup Co. (1923–41); exclusive sales agent for "Mult-A-Mixer," machine that mixed five milkshakes simultaneously (1941–55); in Chicago in 1955 founded McDonald's hamburger franchise, which grew to multibillion-dollar, 2,500-store chain by 1973; chairman (1968–77) and later senior chairman (1977–84) of McDonald's board of directors; owner of San Diego Padres baseball team (1974–79); contributed generously to charities through his Kroc Foundation; died in San Diego. See *Current Biography* (March) 1973.

Obituary N Y Times p28 Ja 15 '84

KUTCHUK, (MUSTAFA) FAZIL 1906–Jan. 15, 1984 Vice-president of Cyprus; Turkish-Cypriot leader;

physician; editor and owner of *Halkin Sesi*, Turkish-language daily paper (1941-60); formed National Political party in 1944; chairman of Evcaf High Council (1956-60); elected vice-president of Cyprus in 1960 when island gained independence from Britain; forced out of office in 1963 when bipartite government collapsed but retained title until he retired from politics in 1971; died in London, England. See *Current Biography* (February) 1961.

Obituary N Y Times D p12 Ja 16 '84

LLEWELLYN, RICHARD Dec. 8, 1906-Nov. 30, 1983 Welsh author; playwright; journalist; film scenarist; best known for first novel, *How Green Was My Valley* (1940), story about hard life of Welsh miners that became international best-seller and was made into Oscar-winning film and television miniseries; subsequently wrote, among other works, novel *None But the Lonely Heart* (1943; complete version, 1969) and three novels chronicling further adventures of Huw, youthful hero of *How Green Was My Valley*; died in Dublin, Ireland. See *Current Biography* (April) 1940.

Obituary N Y Times B p10 D 2 '83

LOSEY, JOSEPH Jan. 14, 1909-June 22, 1984 Motion picture director; master of elegant cinematic gestures disclosing human weakness, spiritual depravity, and the ambiguities in interpersonal and individual-societal conflicts; began career on Broadway and in Hollywood; blacklisted as leftist, moved to England in 1952; became a *Cahiers du Cinéma* cult hero with his early British films; earned international acclaim with his screen collaborations with the writer Harold Pinter, including *The Servant* (1963), *Accident* (1966); and *The Go-Between* (1971); died at his home in London. See *Current Biography* (December) 1969.

Obituary N Y Times p29 Je 23 '84

MACHITO, Feb. 16, 1909-Apr. 15, 1984 Cuban band leader; immigrated to United States in 1937; as leader and male vocalist of Afro-Cubans band, brought Latin beat to jazz and traditional dance music; collaborated with such jazz greats as Charlie Parker, Buddy Rich, Flip Phillips, and Dizzy Gillespie on many records, including "Afro-Cuban Jazz Suite" (1949) and LP *Afro-Cuban Jazz Moods* (1977); began touring extensively with Afro-Cubans band in 1950s, first in United States, then in Europe, Japan, Central and South America; among sixty LPs, recorded 1982 Grammy-winning *Machito and His Salsa Big Band* and two albums nominated for Grammys; died in London, England. See *Current Biography* (February) 1983.

Obituary N Y Times p20 Ap 17 '84

MALIK, ADAM July 22, 1917-Sept. 5, 1984 Indonesian statesman; took part in struggle that led to independence of Indonesia from Dutch rule after World War II; fell into disfavor with President Sukarno and was jailed (1947) but was later rehabilitated; ambassador to U.S.S.R. and Poland (1959-62); minister of commerce (1963-65); minister of foreign affairs (1966-77); helped to found Association of South East Asian Nations (1967); president of United Nations General Assembly (1971-72); vice-president of Indonesia

(1978-83); died at his home in Bandung, Indonesia. See *Current Biography* (November) 1970.

Obituary N Y Times B p5 S 6 '84

MASON, JAMES May 15, 1909-July 27, 1984 British-born actor, noted for portrayals of suave aristocrats and romantic villains; beginning in 1935, acted in over 100 British or American films, including *The Man in Grey* (1943), *The Seventh Veil* (1945), *Odd Man Out* (1947), *Five Fingers* (1952), *North by Northwest* (1959), and *The Boys From Brazil* (1979); portrayed General Erwin Rommel in *The Desert Fox* (1951), Brutus in *Julius Caesar* (1953), and Humbert Humbert in *Lolita* (1962); was nominated for Academy Awards for performances in *A Star Is Born* (1955), *Georgy Girl* (1966), and *The Verdict* (1982); was awarded British film industry's Golden Seal (1977); also appeared in British and American theatre and on television; died in Lausanne, Switzerland. See *Current Biography* (May) 1947.

Obituary N Y Times p8 Jl 28 '84

MAYS, BENJAMIN E[LIJAH) Aug. 1, 1895-Mar. 28, 1984 Educator; civil rights proponent; Baptist minister; was dean of Howard University's Divinity School (1934-40), president of Morehouse College (1940-67), and member of Board of Education in Atlanta, Georgia (1967-81); a conciliator in struggle for equal rights for blacks, opposed extreme militants and inspired Martin Luther King Jr., who called him "my spiritual mentor"; was elected first black vice-president of Federal Council of Churches of Christ in America in 1944; was coauthor of *The Negro's Church* (1933) and author of numerous civil-rights articles and an autobiography, *Born to Rebel* (1971); died in Atlanta. See *Current Biography* (May) 1945.

Obituary N Y Times D p23 Mr 29 '84

McBRIDE, LLOYD Mar. 9, 1916-Nov. 6, 1983 President of United Steelworkers of America (1977-83); elected president of USWA Local 1295 in 1937; rose through ranks to become a staff representative (1946), a subdistrict director (1958), and director (1965) of District 34 in Missouri; between 1965 and 1977, increased district's membership by 33 percent; as president of USWA, maintained predecessor I. W. Abel's no-strike policy in labor disputes; member of board of directors of American Arbitration Association and of executive council of AFL-CIO; died in Whitehall, Pennsylvania. See *Current Biography* (February) 1978.

Obituary N Y Times D p19 N 7 '83

McFARLAND, ERNEST W[ILLIAM) Oct. 9, 1894-June 9, 1984 United States Senator from Arizona (1941-53); as senator and later Senate majority leader (1951-53), worked to consolidate international communications and was instrumental in creation of special Presidential Communications Policy Board in 1950; also supported Central Arizona Project for Colorado River aqueduct and aid to veterans; governor of Arizona (1955-60); Arizona State Supreme Court judge (1964-67) and chief justice (1967-71) until retirement; wrote autobiography *Mac* (1979); died in Phoenix, Arizona. See *Current Biography* (January) 1951.

Obituary N Y Times p44 Je 10 '84

McGANNON, DONALD H(ENRY) Sept. 9, 1920–May 23, 1984 Broadcasting executive; practiced law from 1947 to 1951; joining DuMont Television Network in 1951, became general manager and assistant director (1952–55); as president of Westinghouse Broadcasting Corp. (1955–), emphasized educational and cultural programming, banned cigarette ads, and in 1965 established first all-news radio station (WINS); successfully lobbied FCC for Prime Time Access Rule to return thirty minutes of evening air time to local stations; to encourage employment of minorities, set up Employment Clearing House in 1965; died in Chester, Connecticut. See *Current Biography* (February) 1971.

Obituary N Y Times B p18 My 24 '84

MERCER, MABEL Feb. 3, 1900–Apr. 20, 1984 British-born singer; began singing in 1914 in family's music-hall act; during 1920s and 1930s, performed in such famous Paris clubs as Bricktop's, Le Grand Duke, and Chez Florence; after becoming United States citizen in 1952, sang in many New York City nightclubs including Bricktop's (1941–61); distinctive style of emphasizing lyrics and phrasing rather than music and rhythm influenced Frank Sinatra, Billie Holiday, Lena Horne, and Johnny Mathis, among others; starred in BBC-TV film "Miss Mercer in Mayfair" (1977); honors include first annual *Stereo Review* Award of Merit (1973)—now renamed Mabel Mercer Award—and Presidential Medal of Freedom (1983); died in Pittsfield, Massachusetts. See *Current Biography* (February) 1973.

Obituary N Y Times p24 Ap 21 '84

MERMAN, ETHEL Jan. 16, 1909(?)–Feb 15, 1984 Singer; actress; fifty-year legend of stage, radio, and screen whose untrained belting voice, flawless diction, and brassy delivery won acclaim from composers, critics, and audiences; began Broadway career when she brought the house down with a sustained high note in "I Got Rhythm" in the Gershwin musical *Girl Crazy*; entered motion pictures with *We're Not Dressing* (1934) and began weekly radio program in 1935; by 1959 had starred in thirteen musical stage hits, including *Anything Goes* (1934), *Annie Get Your Gun* (1946), and *Gypsy* (1959); motion picture credits include *There's No Business Like Show Business* (1954) and *It's a Mad, Mad, Mad, Mad World* (1963); made last major appearance at Carnegie Hall benefit concert in 1982; died in New York City. See *Current Biography* (May) 1955.

Obituary N Y Times p1+ F 16 '84

MIRÓ, JOAN Apr. 20, 1893–Dec. 25, 1983 Spanish artist; surrealist painter who drew much of his inspiration from nature; was noted for his use of basic bright colors and his playful wit; played major role in the imaginative life of the twentieth century, exercising important influence on such American abstract expressionists as Jackson Pollock, Mark Rothko, and Robert Motherwell; for many years, beginning in 1919, divided his time between Paris and a farm in Montroig, near Barcelona; produced scores of murals for public buildings in London, Paris, New York, and other cities; also created sculptures, stage designs, mosaics, and tapestries; died at his home in Palma, Majorca. See *Current Biography* (November) 1973.

Obituary N Y Times p1+ D 26 '83

MOODY, JOSEPH E(UGENE) Dec. 18, 1903–May 22, 1984 Coal association executive; in 1942, served in federal Office of Production Management and War Manpower Commission; won high praise for work as personnel and labor-relations director at various corporations (1937–47); as president of Southern Coal Producers Association (1947–68), represented more than 350 companies in strained labor-contract negotiations with United Mine Workers of America; president of National Bituminous Coal Operators Association (1968–73); died in Cape Cod, Massachusetts. See *Current Biography* (December) 1948.

Obituary N Y Times D p17 My 25 '84

MOTLEY, ARTHUR H(ARRISON) Aug. 22, 1900–May 30, 1984 Publisher; business leader; his flair for resuscitating flagging publishing ventures helped him advance from post of salesman (1928) at Crowell-Collier Publishing Company to become publisher (1941–46) of its *American Magazine*; as president (1946–70) of *Parade*, the syndicated Sunday magazine supplement, oversaw a five-fold increase in circulation to ten million; in cooperation with Marshall Plan, advised Europeans on business strategies after World War II; vice-president (1958–60) and president (1960–61) of Chamber of Commerce of United States; died in Palm Springs, California. See *Current Biography* (January) 1961.

Obituary N Y Times p21 Je 1 '84

NIEMÖLLER, (FRIEDRICH GUSTAV EMIL) MARTIN Jan. 14, 1892–Mar. 6, 1984 German Protestant minister; evolved from early right-wing nationalist to leader of church's opposition to Hitler and, in 1950s and 1960s, West Germany's foremost pacifist and foe of nuclear armament; was interned in concentration camps from 1937 to 1945; after his release, worked to reunite fragmented German Protestantism; in 1960s served as president of World Council of Churches; was awarded USSR's Lenin Peace Prize (1967) and West Germany's Grand Cross of Merit (1971); wrote many social, political, and theological articles and books; died in Wiesbaden, West Germany. See *Current Biography* (March) 1965.

Obituary N Y Times p1+ Mr 8 '84

O'BRIEN, PAT Nov. 11, 1899–Oct. 15, 1983 Actor; comedian; prototype of congenial, rugged Irish American, noted for portrayals of priests, policemen, or soldiers in many of the more than 100 motion pictures in which he appeared, including *Angels With Dirty Faces* (1938), *The Fighting 69th* (1940), *Fighting Father Dunne* (1948), and *The Last Hurrah* (1958); was perhaps best known for his performance as legendary Notre Dame football coach in *Knute Rockne—All-American* (1940), co-starring Ronald Reagan as George Gipp; also appeared in Broadway plays and on television; died in Santa Monica, California. See *Current Biography* (March) 1966.

Obituary N Y Times p36 O 16 '83

ODISHAW, HUGH Oct. 13, 1916–Mar. 4, 1984 Scientific administrator; educator; as executive secretary of division of physical sciences of National Academy of Sciences, directed American participation in International Geophysical Year (1957-58), mammoth world-wide exploration of earth and its environment as interrelated physical systems; remained executive director of IGY World Data Center A until 1972; was dean of college of earth sciences at University of Arizona at Tucson from 1972 until his death; died at university's medical center. See *Current Biography* (February) 1971.

Obituary N Y Times B p11 Mr 6 '84

OWINGS, NATHANIEL A(LEXANDER) Feb. 5, 1903-June 13, 1984 Architect; urban planner; conservationist; promising "to build only in the vernacular of our age," in 1936 formed partnership with Louis Skidmore that became inventive architectural firm of Skidmore, Owings & Merrill, top-ranking winner of design awards; presided over or was "catalyst" (his word) in more than $3 billion worth of construction, including the wartime secret atomic city in Oak Ridge, Tennessee and the United States Air Force Academy in addition to Manhattan's Lever House and the other skyscrapers that were his firm's specialty; wrote *The American Aesthetic* (1969); died at his home in Santa Fe, New Mexico. See *Current Biography* (May) 1971.

Obituary N Y Times B p18 Je 14 '84

PARTCH, VIRGIL F(RANKLIN) Oct. 17, 1916-Aug. 10, 1984 Cartoonist; noted for drawings, signed "VIP," presenting people in preposterous situations; perhaps best known for "Big George" cartoons, distributed to daily press by News America Syndicate; contributed to *New Yorker, Saturday Evening Post,* and other magazines; published several collections of his work, including *Water on the Brain* (1945) and *VIP's Quips* (1975); died with his wife in automobile accident north of Los Angeles. See *Current Biography* (July) 1946.

Obituary N Y Times D p9 Ag 13 '84

PERKINS, CARL D(EWEY) Oct. 15, 1912-Aug. 3, 1984 United States representative from Kentucky (1949-84); lawyer; a classic liberal in the New Deal tradition; succeeded Adam Clayton Powell Jr. in 1967 as chairman of the Education and Labor Committee of the House of Representatives; guided through Congress such social measures as federal aid to schools, financial assistance for college students, a school lunch program, coal mine safety provisions, and measures benefiting labor; devoted much of his energy in recent years to combating President Ronald Reagan's proposed budget cuts; died in Lexington, Kentucky. See *Current Biography* (February) 1968.

Obituary N Y Times p28 Ag 4 '84

PERKINS, DEXTER June 20, 1889-May 12, 1984 Historian; educator; during almost forty-year career at University of Rochester, promoted from assistant professor (1915) to full professor and department chairman (1925-54); on retirement, became first John L. Senior Professor of American Civilization at Cornell University (1954-59); expert on U.S. diplomatic history, wrote seventeen books, including several on Monroe Doctrine; official American historian at San Francisco Security Conference (1945) that led to establishment of United Nations; presided over Salzburg (Austria) Seminar in American Studies (1950-61);

wrote memoirs *Yield of the Years* (1969); died in Rochester, New York. See *Current Biography* (January) 1958.

Obituary N Y Times D p26 My 16 '84

PETERSON, (FREDERICK) VAL(DEMAR ERASTUS) July 18, 1903-Oct. 16, 1983 Republican Governor of Nebraska (1947-53); administrative assistant to President Dwight D. Eisenhower (1953); federal civil defense administrator (1953-57); ambassador to Denmark (1957-61) and to Finland (1969-73); administrator of J. M. McDonald Foundation (1961-65); distinguished professor of political science and public affairs at Wayne State College in Nebraska (from 1973); died in Dodge County, Nebraska. See *Current Biography* (June) 1949.

Obituary N Y Times D p31 O 18 '83

PIDGEON, WALTER Sept. 23, 1898-Sept. 25, 1984 Actor; remembered for aura of staunch integrity and tweedy urbanity he brought to screen, especially in *Mrs. Miniver* (1942) and subsequent motion pictures he made with Greer Garson; began career in vaudeville and musical comedy, and later returned to Broadway in straight roles; made some 100 films, beginning with silents and including *Man Hunt* (1941), *How Green Was My Valley* (1941), and *Advise and Consent* (1962); died in Santa Monica, California. See *Current Biography* (September) 1942.

Obituary N Y Times D p0 S 20 '84

POWELL, WILLIAM July 29, 1892-Mar. 5, 1984 Actor; began career in vaudeville and in over two hundred plays; typecast as villain in such silent films as *Sherlock Holmes* (1921) and *Beau Geste* (1926); with advent of "talkies," starred as dapper, sophisticated, and witty leading man opposite Carole Lombard, Hedy Lamarr, Jean Harlow, among others; with costar Myrna Loy, won renown for role as retired detective Nick Charles in six *Thin Man* films (1934-47) based on Dashiell Hammett mysteries; other notable parts include leads in *The Great Ziegfeld* (1936) and *Life With Father* (1947) and last role, as doctor in *Mister Roberts* (1955); nominated for three Oscars as best actor; died in Palm Springs, California. See *Current Biography* (October) 1947.

Obituary N Y Times B p11 Mr 6 '84

PRIESTLEY, J(OHN) B(OYNTON) Sept. 13, 1894-Aug. 14, 1984 British writer; published over 100 books, including fiction, drama, and essays; depicted British personality through pungently humorous character sketches; helped to popularize long novel with his best-selling 250,000-word *The Good Companions* (1929), which was made into a play; also wrote such novels as *Lost Empires* (1965) and *The Image Men* (1969), as well as hit plays like *Dangerous Corner* (1932), *An Inspector Calls* (1945), and *The Linden Tree* (1947), and the autobiographical volume *Instead of the Trees* (1977); delegate to UNESCO conferences (1946-47); helped to found Committee for Nuclear Disarmament; rejected knighthood and peerage but accepted Great Britain's Order of Merit (1977); died at Stratford-upon-Avon. See *Current Biography* (May) 1976.

Obituary N Y Times p1+ Ag 16 '84

RAHNER, KARL Mar. 5, 1904-Mar. 30, 1984 German Catholic theologian; Jesuit priest; since 1936, was professor of dogmatic theology and philosophy of religion at succession of Jesuit colleges and universities in Austria and West Germany; propounded controversial "theology of liberation," applying theology to worldwide social and political problems, in over 4,000 books and articles, including such major works as *Spirit in the World* (1939; 1966); served as adviser at Vatican Council II; appointed in 1969 by Pope Paul VI to commission studying post-Vatican Council II theological trends; died in Innsbruck. See *Current Biography* (July) 1970.

Obituary N Y Times D p13 Ap 2 '84

RENAULT, MARY Sept. 4, 1905-Dec. 13, 1983 British-born author, whose real name was Mary Challans; known for her scholarly reconstruction of life in ancient Greece in such novels as *The Last of the Wine* (1956), *The King Must Die* (1958), *The Bull From the Sea* (1962), and her trilogy on Alexander the Great, of which the last volume was *Funeral Games* (1981); also wrote several novels with contemporary themes, including *Return to Night* (1946), her first American best-seller; as resident of South Africa since end of World War II, spoke out against apartheid and censorship laws; died in Cape Town. See *Current Biography* (January) 1959.

Obituary N Y Times B p5 D 14 '83

ROBINSON, JOHN (ARTHUR THOMAS) June 15, 1919-Dec. 5, 1983 Anglican prelate; provoked controversy with his challenges to established theology of the Church of England, questioning such concepts as the virgin birth and the divinity of Christ; was fellow and dean at Clare College, Cambridge University (1951-59), examining chaplain to Archbishop of Canterbury (1953-59), Bishop Suffragan of Woolwich (1959-69), lecturer in theology at Trinity College, Cambridge (from 1969), and author of *Honest to God* (1963) and other works; died at his home in Yorkshire, England. See *Current Biography* (February) 1965.

Obituary N Y Times D p23 D 7 '83

ROBITZEK, EDWARD H(EINRICH) Dec. 12, 1912-Feb. 20, 1984 Physician; lung specialist; began thirty-three year association with Sea View Hospital and Home on Staten Island, New York City in 1940; was director of medicine (1954-61) and director of medical services (1961-73) at Sea View; with colleagues, developed revolutionary drug isoniazid to treat resistant cases of tuberculosis in 1950s; was private practitioner in Staten Island until 1975 and attending physician at Sailors Snug Harbor there until 1976; won Albert and Mary Lasker Foundation Award for his tuberculosis research in 1955; died in Berlin, Maryland. See *Current Biography* (December) 1953.

Obituary N Y Times p38 F 26 '84

ROBSON, DAME FLORA Mar. 28, 1902-July 7, 1984 One of Great Britain's most distinguished actresses; appeared in some sixty motion pictures and over 100 plays, in England and the United States, during career spanning half a century; won acclaim for motion picture portrayal of Queen Elizabeth II in *Fire Over England* (1937) and performances in supporting roles in such films as *Wuthering Heights* (1939) and *Saratoga Trunk* (1945); on stage, performed with distinction in such roles as Lady Macbeth (1933), Abbie in *Desire Under the Elms* (1931), and Ellen Creed in *Ladies in Retirement* (1940); was created a Dame Commander of the Order of the British Empire in 1960; died in Brighton, England. See *Current Biography* (January) 1951.

Obituary N Y Times p22 Jl 8 '84

ROTHA, PAUL June 3, 1907-Mar.(?) 1984 British documentary film producer; director; scriptwriter; painter; designer; art critic; among many touching socially oriented documentaries, made several for UNESCO, over a hundred for British Ministry of Information during World War II, and such later films as *The Life of Adolf Hitler* (1961) and *The Silent Raid* (1963); was head of BBC documentary film department (1953-55); with publication of first of many highly respected film histories, *Celluloid; The Film Today* (1931), established himself as a foremost film historian; won gold medals at Venice and Brussels film festivals and several British Film Academy awards; died in Wallingford, Oxfordshire, England. See *Current Biography* (April) 1957.

Obituary Guardian p19 Mr 13 '84

ROTHSCHILD, LOUIS S(AMUEL) Mar. 29, 1900-Sept. 1, 1984 United States government official; business executive; began career in various positions with family-owned department-store chain Rothschild and Sons, of which he became president in 1942; in administration of President Dwight D. Eisenhower in 1950s served in Department of Commerce as undersecretary for transportation and chairman of Federal Maritime Commission; later ran private investment business in Washington; died in Washington, D.C. See *Current Biography* (December) 1957.

Obituary N Y Times D p18 S 4 '84

SANANIKONE, PHOUI Sept. 6, 1903-Dec. 4, 1983 Prime minister of Laos (1950-51; 1958-59); served several times as foreign minister during 1950s; also served as president of Chamber of Deputies (1948-50; 1960-74) and president of nationalist group Rassemblement du Peuple Lao (1962-74); after Communist takeover in Laos, went into exile in France and was sentenced to death in absentia by Laotian government (1975); formed Laotian government in exile (1978); died in Paris, France. See *Current Biography* (September) 1959.

Obituary N Y Times B p23 D 12 '83

SARGEANT, HOWLAND H(ILL) July 13, 1911- Feb. 29, 1984 United States government official; propagandist and promoter of cultural exchange; joined Department of State in 1947; as deputy assistant secretary for public affairs, oversaw operations of Voice of America and other government information services; led United States delegations to UNESCO annual general conferences, 1950-52; appointed assistant secretary for public affairs by President Harry S. Truman, 1952-53; president and trustee of Radio Liberty, 1954-74; since 1980, director of Harkness Foundation, sponsor of British Commonwealth exchange students coming to United States; died in New York City. See *Current Biography* (December) 1952.

Obituary N Y Times B p5 Mr '52

SAVITCH, JESSICA 1947–Oct. 23, 1983 Broadcast journalist; worked as researcher, reporter, and anchor for CBS affiliates (1970–77); as reporter for NBC (1977–83), was congressional correspondent, covered 1978 and 1980 elections, and appeared regularly on *Today* and *Meet the Press*; as one of first women to anchor evening newscasts, anchored one-minute *NBC News Digest*, NBC weekend nightly news, and PBS documentary series *Frontline*; won Alfred I. Dupont–Columbia University award for local broadcasting, Clarion Award, and four Emmys; died in auto accident in Bucks County, Pennsylvania. See *Current Biography* (January) 1983.

Obituary N Y Times D p34 O 25 '83

SCHACHT, AL(EXANDER) Nov. 12, 1894–July 14, 1984 Baseball player; comedian; restaurateur; pitched for Washington Senators (1919–21) and minor league teams and coached for a time; forced by sore arm to cut short baseball career, teamed up with Nick Altrock to provide comic entertainment for fans before games, becoming known as "Clown Prince of Baseball"; entertained American servicemen overseas during World War II; wrote several books, including autobiographical *Clowning Through Baseball* (1941); died in Waterbury, Connecticut. See *Current Biography* (May) 1946.

Obituary N Y Times B p11 Jl 16 '84

SCHNEIDER, ALAN Dec. 12, 1917–May 3, 1984 Russian-born director; profoundly influenced course of avant-garde in American theatre; was attracted to "unexplored territory," a theatrical terrain that he charted with fidelity to script and concern for "inner reality"; directed first United States productions of Samuel Beckett's plays and many of Harold Pinter's; was a primary director of works of Edward Albee; helped to pioneer an appreciation of Bertolt Brecht; described his "basic interest" as "the intense theatricality" that "unites Brecht and Beckett and Albee"; died of injuries sustained when he was struck by motorcyclist in London, where he was in process of staging James Duff's *War at Home*. See *Current Biography* (December) 1969.

Obituary N Y Times p1+ My 4 '84

SCHWARTZ, ARTHUR Nov. 25, 1900–Sept. 4 1984 Composer; in collaboration with various lyricists, most notably Howard Dietz, created some of the loveliest and most haunting songs in the American musical theatre, sophisticated compositions marked by warmth as well as wit and melodic inventiveness; for revues and musical comedies in early 1930s, wrote, among other songs, the standards "I See Your Face Before Me," "Dancing in the Dark," "You and the Night and Music," and "Something to Remember You By"; later wrote the scores for several Hollywood musicals in addition to such Broadway shows as *By the Beautiful Sea* (1954), with Dorothy Fields, and *The Gay Life* (1961), with Dietz; died in Kintersville, Pennsylvania.

See *Current Biography* (November) 1979.

Obituary Newsday p35 S 5 '84

SHAW, IRWIN Feb. 27, 1913–May 16, 1984 Prolific author; playwright; gained national recognition with antiwar one-act *Bury the Dead* (1936), first of seven stage plays; with short stories such as "The Girls in Their Summer Dresses" and "Sailor Off the Bremen," published in the *New Yorker* in 1930s, influenced new generation of writers with direct style, strong characterizations; wrote a dozen highly popular novels, of which World War II drama *The Young Lions* (1948) remained public favorite and became star-vehicle motion picture (1958); wrote screenplays and radio scripts; has fourteen million copies of novels and story collections in print in twenty-five languages; remembered for seemingly effortless, intricately plotted prose; died in Davos, Switzerland. See *Current Biography* (October) 1942.

Obituary N Y Times B p19 My 17 '84

SHEHAN, LAWRENCE (JOSEPH), CARDINAL Mar. 18, 1898–Aug. 26, 1984 Roman Catholic prelate; bishop of Bridgeport, Connecticut (1953–61); archbishop of Baltimore from 1961 until his retirement in 1974; a staunch opponent of racial discrimination and United States military involvement in Vietnam, and a champion of reconciliation of Roman Catholicism with other faiths; took part in March on Washington led by Rev. Martin Luther King Jr. in 1963; as a member of Vatican Secretariat for the Promotion of Christian Unity, helped to repair relations between Roman Catholic and Eastern Orthodox churches; was elevated by Pope Paul VI to Cardinal in 1965; died in Baltimore. See *Current Biography* (October) 1965.

Obituary N Y Times B p7 Ag 28 '84

SHOLOKHOV, MIKHAIL A(LEKSANDROVICH) May 24, 1905–Feb. 21, 1984 Russian writer; a longtime member of the Soviet Communist party, was elected to its Central Committee in 1961; the best-known of his novels, *And Quiet Flows the Don*, a four-volume work about civil war and revolution as experienced by the inhabitants of a Cossack village, enjoyed worldwide success; an apologist for the Soviet system in much of his later work; won Nobel Prize for Literature in 1965; awarded Stalin Prize in 1941 and Order of Lenin three times; died in Veshenskaya in Rostov region of Russia. See *Current Biography* (February) 1960.

Obituary N Y Times D p21 F 22 '84

SMITH, CARLETON Feb. 19, 1910–May 28, 1984 Foundation official; musicologist; instructor at DePaul University, Chicago in economics and trade (1928–34); music editor for *Esquire* (1934–42); during 1940s, advised government and private corporations on financial and public relations; as director of National Arts Foundation (1947–), launched cultural exchange projects; for recovery of priceless composers' manuscripts in post–World War II Europe, received Finnish and Austrian decorations; through NAF, worked to establish American prizes in artistic fields not covered by Nobel prizes; originator of prestigious Pritzker Prize in architecture; died in Long Island, New York. See *Current Biography* (April) 1961.

Obituary N Y Times p21 Je 1 '84

SOUVANNA PHOUMA, PRINCE OF LAOS Oct. 7, 1901–Jan. 10, 1984 Prime Minister of Laos; French-trained engineer; held engineering posts for Public Works Service of Indo-China (1931–51); served as president of National Assembly (1960); as five-time prime minister of Laos (1951–54, 1956–57, 1957–58, 1960–62, 1962–75), strove to maintain Laotian non-aligned status; ousted in 1975 by Pathet Lao, led by his half-brother Prince Souphanouvong, which then abolished monarchy and formed People's Democratic Republic of Laos; ambassador to France (1958–59) and to Italy; became adviser to Laotian government in 1976; died in Vientiane, Laos. See *Current Biography* (November) 1962.

Obituary N Y Times D p19 Ja 11 '84

STUART, JESSE Aug. 8, 1907–Feb. 17, 1984 Author; folk poet; one of America's most honored and most prolific regionalist writers; based his work, including his short stories, novels like *Trees of Heaven* (1940), and his autobiography, *Beyond Dark Hills* (1938), on life in Greenup County, Kentucky; best-known for his collection of poems, *Man With A Bull-Tongue Plow* (1934), and *Taps for Private Tussie* (1943); named poet laureate of Kentucky in 1954; obtained Guggenheim fellowship in 1937; won Academy of American Poets prize in 1961; died in Ironton, Ohio. See *Current Biography* (August) 1940.

Obituary N Y Times D p6 F 20 '84

TAYLOR, GLEN H(EARST) Apr. 12, 1904–Apr. 28, 1984 United States Senator from Idaho (1945–51); during 1920s and 1930s, worked first as traveling stage actor and later as "Crooning Cowboy"; as Senator, outspoken proponent of pacifist measures and more power for United Nations; bolted Democratic party in 1948 for unsuccessful run with Henry A. Wallace as vice-presidential candidate of Progressive party; after losing Senate seat in 1950, founded Taylor Topper Inc., wig manufacturing company; died in Burlingame, California. See *Current Biography* (October) 1947.

Obituary N Y Times p13 My 5 '84

THOMAS, CHARLES S(PARKS) Sept. 28, 1897–Oct. 17, 1983 Secretary of the Navy (1954–56); businessman; among other posts in business, was president of the retail concern Foreman & Clark, Inc. (1937–53), Trans World Airlines (1958–), and Irvine Co. (1960–66), California's largest land developer; during World War II as civilian assistant to secretary of navy, set up inventory control and logistics programs and procured aircraft; returning to government, served as undersecretary of navy and assistant secretary of defense (1953) before appointed secretary of navy; received Distinguished Civilian Service Award (1945) and Presidential Medal for Merit (1947); died in Corona del Mar, California. See *Current Biography* (December) 1954.

Obituary N Y Times D p27 O 20 '83

TOURÉ, (AHMED) SEKOU Jan. 9, 1922–Mar. 26, 1984 President of Guinea; prominent Third World spokesman; in 1940s was labor organizer with connections to French Communist labor federation; turning to politics, helped found African Democratic Rally party in 1946; in 1950s, served in legislative assembly, was secretary general of Guinea Democratic party, mayor of Conakry, and representative to French National Assembly; a brilliant orator and politician, persuaded his countrymen to vote for independence from France in 1958; as prime minister (1958–72) and president (1958–84), ruled with heavy hand domestically and leaned to USSR internationally; died during heart surgery in Cleveland, Ohio. See *Current Biography* (June) 1959.

Obituary N Y Times A p6 Mr 28 '84

TSARAPKIN, SEMYON K(ONSTANTINOVICH) 1906–1984 Envoy extraordinary and plenipotentiary and member of collegium, Ministry of Foreign Affairs, Union of Soviet Socialist Republics; as diplomat in United States during World World II, participated in formative meetings of the United Nations; was Soviet deputy representative in UN Security Council from 1949 to 1954; served in USSR's embassy in Bonn, West Germany for five years beginning in 1966; was roving ambassador from 1971 until his death, announced by press agency Tass on September 19, 1984. See *Current Biography* (June) 1960.

Obituary N Y Times B p22 S 20 '84

TUBB, ERNEST Feb. 9, 1914–Sept. 6, 1984 Singer; songwriter; musician; one of country music's legendary personalities; popularly known as the "Texas Troubadour"; introduced raucous "honky-tonk" sound, which became a trademark of country music; helped to establish Nashville, Tennessee as a country music recording center; wrote over 150 songs, including the all-time hit "Walking the Floor Over You," which sold over a million records, and such other country classics as "Try Me One More Time" and "You Nearly Lose Your Mind"; performed regularly at Nashville's Grand Ole Opry from 1942 to 1982; was elected to Country Music Hall of Fame in 1965; died in Nashville. See *Current Biography* (October) 1983.

Obituary N Y Times p16 S 7 '84

UNDERHILL, RUTH M(URRAY) Aug. 22, 1884–Aug. 15, 1984 Anthropologist; author; educator; a leading authority on the culture of American Indians, especially of the Southwest, among whom she found the serenity of her own Quaker background; wrote nineteen books, including *Autobiography of a Papago Woman* (1936), *Red Man's America* (1953), *The Navajos* (1956), and *Red Man's Religion* (1965); died at her Denver, Colorado home. See *Current Biography* (February) 1954.

Obituary N Y Daily News p36 Ag 17 '84

VOORHIS, (HORACE) JERRY Apr. 6, 1901–Sept. 11, 1984 Former liberal Democratic United States representative from California; in 1946, after five terms in Congress, was unseated by Richard Nixon, who was then launching the political career that would take him to the presidency; never again sought public office, but remained active in local politics and for twenty years headed the Cooperative League of the U.S.A.; died in Claremont, California. See *Current Biography* (August) 1941.

Obituary N Y Times B p6 S 12 '84

WADSWORTH, JAMES J(EREMIAH) June 12, 1905–Mar. 13, 1984 Government official; New York State assemblyman (1931–41); assistant manager of industrial relations at Curtiss-Wright Corp. (1941–45); during 1940s held several defense-related federal posts; as acting deputy administrator of civil defense for National Security Resources Board (1950–53), was instrumental in drafting or implementing many now-standard civil-defense plans; as deputy representative (1953–60) and later head (1960) of U.S. delegation to UN, helped negotiate partial ban on nuclear weapons; was member of Federal Communications Commission from 1965 to 1970; at his own expense published autobiography The Silver Spoon in 1980; died in Rochester, N. Y. See Current Biography (June) 1956.

Obituary N Y Times B p12 Mr 15 '84

WALLACE, LILA (BELL) ACHESON Dec. 25, 1889–May 8, 1984 Editor; publisher; with husband De Witt Wallace, launched Reader's Digest in 1922 with first issue of 5,000 copies; by 1984, had largest circulation of any magazine, printing 30 million copies in seventeen languages; art collection included works by Manet, Cézanne, Gauguin, Matisse, and other modern masters; during lifetime contributed over $60 million to philanthropies and hospitals as well as to Metropolitan Museum of Art in New York City and other cultural concerns; many honors include presidential Medal of Freedom (1972); died in Mount Kisco, New York. See Current Biography (May) 1956.

Obituary N Y Times p1 My 9 '84

WARING, FRED June 9, 1900–July 29, 1984 Orchestra and choral leader; one of last giants of Big Band era; catered to mainstream of American musical taste; led his Pennsylvanians from early 1920s until 1981, when he gave his farewell concert at President Ronald Reagan's inaugural festivities; composed some 200 songs; made first all-musical film, Syncopation (1929) with Pennsylvanians, who also became first orchestra to have own television show (1949); performed regularly at White House during presidency of Dwight D. Eisenhower; received Congressional Gold Medal from President Reagan (1983); invented "Waring Blendor," a food-processing device; died at State College, Pennsylvania. See Current Biography (September) 1940.

Obituary N Y Times p18 Jl 30 '84

WEST, JESSAMYN July 18, 1902–Feb. 23, 1984 Writer; while recovering from tuberculosis, began writing short stories based on her Quaker ancestors who farmed in Indiana; published stories and poems with similar subject in Harper's, Atlantic Monthly, and The New Yorker, among other magazines; with The Friendly Persuasion (1945), her first collection of short stories, gained critical success; with its film adaptation (1956), won award at Cannes festival and an Academy Award nomination; also wrote Cress Delahanty (1953), Leafy Rivers (1967), Massacre at Fall Creek (1975), and Double Discovery (1980), a memoir; died in Napa, California, where she had lived for many years. See Current Biography (August) 1977.

Obituary N Y Times p10 F 25 '84

WILLSON, MEREDITH May 18, 1902–June 15, 1984 Composer; lyricist; flutist with John Philip Sousa's band (1923–24); composed The Missions of California (1940) and other symphonies as well as film scores for Charlie Chaplin's The Great Dictator (1940) and Lillian Hellman's The Little Foxes (1941); among other radio shows, hosted The Big Show with Tallulah Bankhead in early 1950s and wrote its theme song "May the Good Lord Bless and Keep You"; best known for hit Broadway musical The Music Man (1957), which won Tony and Drama Critics Circle awards and included such classics as "76 Trombones"; his other musicals were The Unsinkable Molly Brown (1960) and Here's Love (1963); died in Santa Monica, California. See Current Biography (June) 1958.

Obituary N Y Times p24 Je 17 '84

WILSON, PETER (CECIL) Mar. 8, 1913–June 3, 1984 British art auctioneer; businessman; after brief stint as journalist for Reuters, in 1936 joined auction house of Sotheby & Co. in London as porter in furniture department; as company chairman (1958–80), engineered Sotheby's expansion into $575-million-per-year, preeminent international auction house through sales of art from collections of King Farouk, Jakob Goldschmidt, and others, and through acquisition in 1964 of Parke-Bernet auction house in New York City; named honorary company president for life in 1980; made Commander of British Empire in 1970; died in Paris, France. See Current Biography (February) 1968.

Obituary N Y Times D p27 Je 5 '84

WINCHELL, CONSTANCE M(ABEL) Nov. 2, 1896–May 21, 1983 Librarian; after working for University of Michigan library and American Library in Paris, joined reference staff of Columbia University Library in 1925 and served as reference librarian there from 1941 until her retirement in 1962; compiled seventh and eighth editions of American Library Association's Guide to Reference Books (1951; 1967) as well as supplements to the guide; was awarded American Library Association's Isadore Gilbert Mudge citation (1960); died in New Paltz, New York. See Current Biography (June) 1967.

Obituary N Y Times p24 My 25 '83

WISE, JAMES DeCAMP Oct. 7, 1898–Jan. 7, 1984 Business executive; lawyer; corporate counsel to business firms (1925–1945); as member of board of directors (1939–67), president (1945–61), and chairman (1956–61) of Bigelow-Sanford Carpet Company, pioneered introduction of synthetic fibers into carpets and modernized its techniques of production; received Distinguished Civilian Service award (1947) for role as special assistant to undersecretary of navy during World War II; served as a director of Federal Reserve Bank of New York (1959–64); died in New York City. See Current Biography (April) 1954.

Obituary N Y Times B p12 Ja 12 '84

WOODSON, CARTER G(ODWIN) Dec. 19, 1875–Apr. 3, 1950 Educator; editor; visionary black historian who rose from poverty in post-Civil War South and received Ph.D. degree from Harvard University (1912); sought recovery of black experience in the United

States and Africa with such books as *A Century of Negro Migration* (1918), *History of the Negro Church* (1921), *Negro Makers of History* (1928), and *The African Background Outlined* (1936); in 1915 founded Association for the Study of Negro Life and History; edited *Journal of Negro History* (from 1915) and *Negro History Bulletin* (from 1937); served on faculties of Howard University and West Virginia State College; died in Washington, D.C. See *Current Biography* (Yearbook) 1944.

Obituary Who's Who in Colored America (1950)

WRIGHT, LOUIS B(OOKER) Mar. 1, 1899–Feb. 26, 1984 Director of Folger Shakespeare Library (1948–68); during 1926–48, was faculty member at eight universities, including University of North Carolina (1926–32); as member of permanent research group at Henry E. Huntington Library (1932–48), pursued interest in English Renaissance and colonial America, helped develop research group program, and expanded reference collection; advisory board member (1942–71) and later chairman of board (1950–71) of Guggenheim Foundation; historical consultant to National Geographic Society since 1971; among many books on historical subjects, wrote *Shakespeare for Everyman* (1964); died in Chevy Chase, Maryland. See *Current Biography* (November) 1950.

Obituary N Y Times D p27 F 28 '84

WU, K(UO) C(HENG) Oct. 21, 1903–June 6, 1984 Nationalist Chinese official; educator; won recognition as skillful administrator during terms as mayor of Hankou (1932–38), Chongqing (1939–41), and Shanghai (1945–49) and governor of Taiwan (1949–53); minister without portfolio in Chiang Kai-shek's Nationalist government (1950–54); after Chiang's forces fled mainland China in 1954, resigned from government to protest its abandonment of democracy and immigrated to United States; subsequently taught at Armstrong State College in Georgia; died in Savannah, Georgia. See *Current Biography* (February) 1953.

Obituary N Y Times D p22 Je 7 '84

YADIN, YIGAEL Mar. 21, 1917–June 28, 1984 Israeli archaeologist; as Haganah's chief of operations during Arab-Israeli War in 1948, captured large Egyptian force and brought food and arms to beseiged Jerusalem through knowledge of ancient Roman roads and Israeli military tactics; made army chief of staff and Israel's youngest general in 1949; retired in 1952; returning to archaeology, discovered Old Testament scroll fragments; during 1960s, excavated Masada and Hazor and discovered letters by Simon Bar Kochba dating from second century; formed new Democratic Movement for Change party in 1977; deputy prime minister (1977–81); died in Hadera, Israel. See *Current Biography* (February) 1966.

Obituary N Y Times B p16 Je 29 '84

ZABLOCKI, CLEMENT J(OHN) Nov. 18, 1912–Dec. 3, 1983 United States Democratic Representative from Wisconsin (1949–83); chairman of House Foreign Affairs Committee (1977–83); was noted as a moderate and master of compromise; helped to guide Congress toward a more active role in foreign policy; initially was a staunch supporter of United States military involvement in Vietnam, but later helped to draft War Powers Act (1973), restricting president's war-making powers; during administration of President Ronald Reagan, tried to promote bipartisan foreign policy, but differed with president on approach to nuclear arms control and other issues; died at Capitol Hill Hospital in Washington, D.C. See *Current Biography* (June) 1983.

Obituary N Y Times p52 D 4 '83

BIOGRAPHICAL REFERENCES

Almanac of American Politics, 1984

American Architects Directory, 1970

American Catholic Who's Who, 1978

American Medical Directory, 1979

American Men and Women of Science (1982)

Asia Who's Who (1960)

Biographical Directory of Librarians in the United States and Canada (1970)

Biographical Directory of the American Congress, 1774–1971 (1971)

Biographical Directory of the USSR (1958)

Biographical Encyclopaedia & Who's Who of the American Theatre (1966)

Biographical Encyclopedia of Pakistan, 1971–72

Biographical Encyclopedia of Scientists (1981)

Burke's Peerage, Baronetage, and Knightage, 1970

Canadian Who's Who, 1982

Celebrity Register (1973)

Chi è? (1961)

China Yearbook, 1982

Chujoy, A., and Manchester, P. W., eds. Dance Encyclopedia (1967)

Concise Biographical Dictionary of Singers (1969)

Concise Oxford Dictionary of Ballet (1982)

Congressional Directory, 1981

Congressional Quarterly Almanac, 1982

Contemporary Artists (1983)

Contemporary Authors (1962–83)

Contemporary Dramatists (1977)

Contemporary Literary Critics (1977)

Contemporary Novelists (1982)

Contemporary Poets (1980)

Contemporary Poets of the English Language (1970)

Debrett's Peerage and Baronetage (1980)

Dictionary of Contemporary American Artists (1982)

Dictionary of International Biography (1975–82)

Dictionary of Latin American and Caribbean Biography (1971)

Dictionnaire de biographie française (1964)

Directory of American Judges (1955)

Directory of American Scholars (1974)

Directory of British Scientists, 1966–67

Directory of Medical Specialists, 1983–84

Encyclopedia of Pop, Rock and Soul (1977)

Ewen, D., ed, Composers of Today (1936); Living Musicians (1940; First Supplement 1957); Men and Women Who Make Music (1949); American Composers Today (1949); European Composers Today (1954); The New Book of Modern Composers (1961); Popular American Composers (1962; First Supplement, 1972); Composers Since 1900 (1969); Musicians Since 1900 (1970)

Far East and Australasia, 1984–85

Feather, Leonard. Encyclopedia of Jazz (1984); Encyclopedia of Jazz in the Sixties (1966)

Filmgoer's Companion (1977)

Football Register, 1984

Foremost Women in Communications (1970)

Grove's Dictionary of Music and Musicians (1955)

Hindustan Year Book and Who's Who, 1963

Hvem er Hvem? 1973

International Authors and Writers Who's Who, 1982

International Motion Picture Almanac, 1984

International Television Almanac, 1984

International Who's Who, 1984–85

International Who's Who in Art and Antiques, 1976

International Who's Who in Music, 1980

International Who's Who in Poetry (1974–75)

International Who's Who of the Arab World (1978)

International Year Book and Statesmen's Who's Who, 1984

Japan Biographical Encyclopedia & Who's Who, 1964–65

Jews in the World of Science (1956)

Junior Book of Authors (1951)

Katz, E. Film Encyclopedia (1982)

Kelly's Handbook to the Titled, Landed and Official Classes, 1964

Kleine Slavische Biographie (1958)

Kraks Bla Bog, 1964

Kürschners Deutscher Gelehrten-Kalender, 1970

Leaders in Education (1974)

Leaders in Electronics (1979)

Leaders in Profile (1975)

Martindale-Hubbell Law Directory, 1979

McGraw-Hill Encyclopedia of World Biography (1973)

McGraw-Hill Encyclopedia of World Drama (1984)

McGraw-Hill Modern Scientists and Engineers (1980)

Middle East and North Africa, 1978–79

More Junior Authors (1963)

Nalanda Year-Book and Who's Who in India and Pakistan, 1958

National Cyclopaedia of American Biography (1926–84)

New Century Cyclopedia of Names (1954)

New Grove Dictionary of Music and Musicians (1980)

Nordness, Lee, ed. Art USA Now (1963)

Notable Australians (1978)

Notable Names in the American Theatre (1976)

Nouveau Dictionnaire National des Contemporains (1968)

Official Baseball Register, 1981

Official Catholic Directory, 1976

Oxford Companion to Film (1976)

Panorama Biografico degli Italiani d'Oggi (1956)

Political Profiles (1976–79)

Politics in America (1984)

Poor's Register of Directors and Executives, 1974

Prominent Personalities in the USSR (1968)

Quién es Quién en la Argentina, 1968-69

Quién es Quién en Venezuela, Panama, Ecuador, Colombia, 1956

Robinson, Donald. 100 Most Important People in the World Today (1972)

Slonimsky, Nicolas. Baker's Biographical Dictionary of Musicians (1978)

Something About the Author (1971-84)

Third Book of Junior Authors (1972)

Thomas, S. Men of Space (1960-68)

Thompson, K. A. Dictionary of Twentieth-Century Composers (1973)

Thompson, O., ed. International Cyclopedia of Music and Musicians, 1975

Thomson, D. Biographical Dictionary of Film (1981)

Twentieth Century Authors (1942; First Supplement, 1955)

Two Hundred Contemporary Authors (1969)

Vem är Det, 1973

Webster's Biographical Dictionary (1971)

Wer ist Wer? (1983)

Who is Who in Music (1951)

Who's Who, 1984-85

Who's Who among Black Americans, 1980-81

Who's Who in Advertising (1963)

Who's Who in Africa, 1973

Who's Who in America, 1984-85

Who's Who in American Art (1984)

Who's Who in American Education, 1967-68

Who's Who in American Politics, 1983-84

Who's Who in Art (1982-83)

Who's Who in Australia, 1980

Who's Who in Austria, 1971-72

Who's Who in Baseball, 1971

Who's Who in Belgium (1962)

Who's Who in California, 1983

Who's Who in Canada, 1984-85

Who's Who in Chicago and Illinois (1950)

Who's Who in Colored America, 1950

Who's Who in Communist China (1969)

Who's Who in Engineering, 1982

Who's Who in Finance and Industry, 1983-84

Who's Who in France, 1983-84

Who's Who in France (Paris), 1953-54

Who's Who in Germany (1980)

Who's Who in Hollywood, 1900-1976

Who's Who in Israel, 1981-82

Who's Who in Italy, 1957-58

Who's Who in Labor, 1976

Who's Who in Latin America Pts 1-7 (1945-71)

Who's Who in Library and Information Services (1982)

Who's Who in Malaysia, 1983

Who's Who in Music, 1969

Who's Who in New York, 1960

Who's Who in New Zealand (1968)

Who's Who in Opera, 1976

Who's Who in Philosophy (1969)

Who's Who in Professional Baseball (1973)

Who's Who in Publishing (1971)

Who's Who in Railroading in North America (1959)

Who's Who in Rock Music (1982)

Who's Who in Saudi Arabia, 1978-79

Who's Who in Space, 1966-67

Who's Who in Spain, 1965

Who's Who in Switzerland, 1982-83

Who's Who in the Arab World, 1984

Who's Who in the East, 1983-84

Who's Who in the Midwest, 1984-85

Who's Who in the Netherlands, 1962-63

Who's Who in the People's Republic of China (1981)

Who's Who in the South and Southwest, 1984-85

Who's Who in the Theatre (1981)

Who's Who in the United Nations (1975)

Who's Who in the USSR, 1972

Who's Who in the West, 1984-85

Who's Who in Western Europe (1981)

Who's Who in the World, 1980-81

Who's Who in World Aviation and Astronautics (1958)

Who's Who in World Jewry (1978)

Who's Who of American Women, 1983-84

Who's Who of British Engineers, 1980-81

Who's Who of British Scientists, 1980-81

Who's Who of Jazz (1985)

Who's Who of Rhodesia, Mauritius, Central and East Africa, 1965

Who's Who of Southern Africa, 1982

Who's Who on Television (1982)

Wie is Dat? (1956)

Women Lawyers in the United States (1957)

World Artists: 1950-1980 (1984)

World Authors: 1950-1970 (1975)

World Authors: 1970-75 (1980)

World Biography (1954)

World Who's Who in Science (1968)

World's Who's Who of Women (1983)

Writers Directory (1984-86)

PERIODICALS AND NEWSPAPERS CONSULTED

ALA Bul—American Library Association Bulletin
After Dark
Am Artist—American Artist
Am Libs—American Libraries
Am Scholar—American Scholar
Am Sociol R—American Sociological Review
America
Américas
Arch Forum—Architectural Forum (disc.)
Arch Rec—Architectural Record
Archaeology
Art & Artists
Artforum
Art N Artnews
Arts
Arts & Arch—Arts & Architecture
Atlan—Atlantic Monthly
Aviation W—Aviation Week and Space Technology

Ballet N—Ballet News
Barron's
Biog N—Biography News (disc.)
Book-of-the-Month Club N
  Book of the Month Club News
Book World
Broadcasting
Bsns W—Business Week

Cath World—Catholic World
Chicago Tribune
Christian Sci Mon—Christian Science Monitor
Columbia J R—Columbia Journalism Review
Commonweal
Cong Digest—Congressional Digest
Cong Q—Congressional Quarterly Weekly Report
Cosmo—Cosmopolitan
Crawdaddy
Cue (now incorporated into New York)
Cur Hist—Current History
Cur World Leaders—Current World Leaders

Dance & Dancers
Dance Mag—Dance Magazine
Discover

Ebony
Ed & Pub—Editor & Publisher
Encounter
Esquire

Facts on File
Family Circle
Films & Filming
For Affairs—Foreign Affairs

For Policy Bul—Foreign Policy Bulletin
Forbes
Fortune

Geo
German Tribune
Good H—Good Housekeeping
Guardian

Harper's
Hi Fi—High Fidelity
Hi Fi/Stereo R—Hi/Fi Stereo Review
Holiday
Horizon

Illus Lond N—Illustrated London News
Intellectual Digest—(disc.)
International Herald Tribune

Ladies Home J—Ladies' Home Journal
Le Monde
Lib J—Library Journal
Life
London Observer
Look—(disc.)
Los Angeles Times

McCall's
Macleans—Maclean's
Mlle—Mademoiselle
Modern Maturity
Ms
Mus Am—Musical America
Mus Courier—Musical Courier (disc.)
Mus Mod Art—Museum of Modern Art Bulletin

N Y Daily News
N Y Herald Tribune Bk R
  —New York Herald Tribune Book Review (disc.)
N Y Post
N Y Rev of Books—New York Review of Books
N Y Sunday News
N Y Times
N Y Times Bk R—New York Times Book Review
N Y Times Mag—New York Times Magazine
N Y World-Telegram—New York World-Telegram and Sun (disc.)
N Y World Journal Tribune—(disc.)
Nat Geog Mag—National Geographic Magazine
Nat R—National Review
Nation
Nations Bsns—Nation's Business
Nature
New Leader

New Repub—New Republic
New Statesm—New Statesman
New Times—(disc.)
New York
New Yorker
Newsday
Newsweek

Omni
Opera N—Opera News

Parade
Penthouse
People
Philadelphia Inquirer
Playbill
Playboy
Plays & Players
Pop Sci—Popular Science Monthly
Psych Today—Psychology Today
Pub W—Publishers Weekly

Read Digest—Reader's Digest
Redbook
Reporter—The Reporter (disc.)
Rolling Stone

Sat Eve Post—Saturday Evening Post
Sat R—Saturday Review (disc.)
Sci Am—Scientific American
Sci Mo—Scientific Monthly
Sci N L—Science News Letter
Science
Smithsonian
Spec—Spectator
Spiegel—Der Spiegel
Sport
Sports Illus—Sports Illustrated
Sr Schol—Senior Scholastic

Time
Times—London Times
Times Lit Sup—London Times Literary Supplement
Toronto Globe and Mail
TV Guide

U N Rev—United Nations Review
U S News—U.S. News & World Report

Variety
Village Voice
Vogue

Wall St J—Wall Street Journal
Washington M—Washington Monthly
Washington Post
Wilson Lib Bul—Wilson Library Bulletin

Yale R—Yale Review

CLASSIFICATION BY PROFESSION—1984

ART
Callahan, Harry M.
Castelli, Leo
de Kooning, Willem
Golub, Leon
Komar, Vitaly
Melamid, Aleksandr
Morley, Malcolm A.
Schapiro, Meyer

ASTRONAUTICS
Bluford, Guion S., Jr.

BUSINESS
Attenborough, Richard
Cunningham, Mary
Houseman, John
King, Don
Naisbitt, John
Trump, Donald J.

DANCE
Andersen, Ib
Brooks, Louise
Childs, Lucinda
Rivera, Chita
Smuin, Michael

DIPLOMACY
Botha, Roelof F.
White, Robert E.

EDUCATION
Boorstin, Daniel J.
Bruner, Jerome
Callahan, Harry M.
Campbell, Joseph
Carver, Raymond
Hall, Donald
Hatfield, Mark O.
Johanson, Donald C.
Kelman, Charles D.
Kennedy, Donald
Le Roy Ladurie, Emmanuel
Mayr, Ernst

Medvedev, Roy
Norman, Marsha
Paterno, Joe
Phillips, William
Ponnamperuma, Cyril
Redpath, Jean
Schapiro, Meyer
Silber, John R.
Tobin, James
Walker, Alice

FINANCE
Cunningham, Mary

GOVERNMENT AND POLITICS, FOREIGN
Alfonsín, Raúl
Botha, Roelof F.
Chernenko, Konstantin U.
Craxi, Bettino
Ershad, Hussain Muhammad
Evren, Kenan
FitzGerald, Garret
Jayewardene, J. R.
Kelly, Petra
Kinnock, Neil
Machel, Samora Moises
Mandela, Nelson
Mintoff, Dom
Mulroney, Brian
Ortega, Daniel
Price, George
Sauvé, Jeanne
Turner, John
Vogel, Hans-Jochen
Zhao Ziyang

GOVERNMENT AND POLITICS, U.S.
Bird, Rose E.
Boorstin, Daniel J.
Conable, Barber B.
Ferraro, Geraldine A.
Hatfield, Mark O.
Kennedy, Donald

McFarlane, Robert C.
Pendleton, Clarence M., Jr.
Rangel, Charles B.
Rogers, Bernard W.
Tobin, James
Washington, Harold
White, Robert E.

INDUSTRY
Cunningham, Mary

INTERNATIONAL RELATIONS
Rogers, Bernard W.

JOURNALISM
Adler, Renata
Hersh, Seymour
James, Clive
Koppel, Ted
Naisbitt, John
Sauvé, Jeanne

LABOR
Lawe, John

LAW
Bird, Rose E.
Conable, Barber B.
Ferraro, Geraldine A.
Jayewardene, J. R.
Mandela, Nelson
Mulroney, Brian
Rangel, Charles B.
Vogel, Hans-Jochen

LIBRARY SERVICE
Boorstin, Daniel J.

LITERATURE
Adler, Renata
Atwood, Margaret
Bly, Robert
Calvino, Italo
Caro, Robert A.
Carver, Raymond

Deighton, Len
Fierstein, Harvey
Hall, Donald
James, Clive
McGinniss, Joe
McMurtry, Larry
Quennell, Peter
Sayles, John
Shepherd, Jean
Trevor, William
Updike, John
Vadim, Roger
Walcott, Derek
Walker, Alice

MEDICINE
Kelman, Charles D.

MILITARY
Bluford, Guion S., Jr.
Evren, Kenan
O'Connor, John J.
Ortega, Daniel
Rogers, Bernard W.

MOTION PICTURES
Attenborough, Richard
Brooks, Louise
Childs, Lucinda
Cleese, John
Close, Glenn
Collins, Joan
Cross, Ben
Ford, Harrison
Gibson, Mel
Gielgud, John
Hirsch, Judd
Houseman, John
Irons, Jeremy
Kinski, Nastassja
Laurents, Arthur
McKellen, Ian
Peters, Bernadette
Rivera, Chita
Rose, George
Sayles, John
Schygulla, Hanna
Shepherd, Jean
Tandy, Jessica
Vadim, Roger
Wagner, Robert
Weir, Peter
Wenders, Wim

Wilder, Billy
Williams, Billy Dee
Winger, Debra

MUSIC
Ax, Emanuel
Battle, Kathleen
Craft, Robert
Iglesias, Julio
Kelman, Charles D.
Loudon, Dorothy
MacDermot, Galt
Marsalis, Wynton
Peters, Bernadette
Rawls, Lou
Redpath, Jean
Richie, Lionel
Tully, Alice
Turner, Tina
Williams, Vanessa

NONFICTION
Atwood, Margaret
Boorstin, Daniel J.
Bruner, Jerome
Campbell, Joseph
Caro, Robert A.
Cleese, John
Collins, Joan
Craft, Robert
Cunningham, Mary
Deighton, Len
Gielgud, John
Hall, Donald
Hatfield, Mark O.
Hersh, Seymour
James, Clive
Le Roy Ladurie, Emmanuel
McGinniss, Joe
Medvedev, Roy
Naisbitt, John
Schapiro, Meyer
Shepherd, Jean
Trevor, William
Updike, John
Vadim, Roger
Walker, Alice

OTHER CLASSIFICATIONS
Williams, Vanessa

PHILANTHROPY
Tully, Alice

Winfield, Dave

PSYCHOLOGY
Bruner, Jerome

PUBLISHING
Calvino, Italo
Phillips, William

RADIO
Houseman, John
Iglesias, Julio
Koppel, Ted
Laurents, Arthur
Sauvé, Jeanne
Shepherd, Jean

RELIGION
Kolvenbach, Peter-Hans
Lustiger, Jean-Marie
O'Connor, John J.

SCIENCE
Bluford, Guion S., Jr.
Hawking, Stephen W.
Johanson, Donald C.
Kelman, Charles D.
Kennedy, Donald
Mayr, Ernst
McClintock, Barbara
Ponnamperuma, Cyril

SOCIAL ACTIVISM
Kelly, Petra
Mandela, Nelson
Medvedev, Roy
Walker, Alice

SOCIAL SCIENCES
Boorstin, Daniel J.
Bruner, Jerome
Campbell, Joseph
Johanson, Donald C.
Le Roy Ladurie, Emmanuel
Medvedev, Roy
Naisbitt, John
Tobin, James

SPORTS
Gossage, Rich
King, Don
Lendl, Ivan
Lewis, Carl
Louganis, Greg

Morgan, Joe
Nettles, Graig
Paterno, Joe
Strawberry, Darryl
Trump, Donald J.
Winfield, Dave

TELEVISION
Cleese, John
Close, Glenn
Collins, Joan
Cross, Ben
Gielgud, John
Hall, Donald
Hirsch, John
Hirsch, Judd
Houseman, John
Iglesias, Julio
Irons, Jeremy
James, Clive
Koppel, Ted
McKellen, Ian

Norman, Marsha
Peters, Bernadette
Rawls, Lou
Rose, George
Sauvé, Jeanne
Sayles, John
Schygulla, Hanna
Shepherd, Jean
Tandy, Jessica
Wagner, Robert
Weir, Peter
Williams, Billy Dee

THEATRE
Attenborough, Richard
Brooks, Louise
Childs, Lucinda
Close, Glenn
Collins, Joan
Cross, Ben
Fierstein, Harvey
Gibson, Mel

Gielgud, John
Hirsch, John
Hirsch, Judd
Houseman, John
Irons, Jeremy
Laurents, Arthur
Loudon, Dorothy
MacDermot, Galt
McKellen, Ian
Norman, Marsha
Peters, Bernadette
Rivera, Chita
Rose, George
Sayles, John
Schygulla, Hanna
Smuin, Michael
Tandy, Jessica
Walcott, Derek
Williams, Billy Dee

CUMULATED INDEX—1981–1984

For the index to 1940–1970 biographies, see
Current Biography Cumulative Index 1940–1970.
For the index to 1971–1980 biographies, see the 1980 yearbook.

Boylston, Helen Dore obit Nov 84
Bradbury, Ray Jul 82
Bradford, Robert F(iske) obit May 83
Bradley, Bill Sep 82
Bradley, Omar N(elson) obit May 81
Bradley, William W(arren) See Bradley, Bill
Bradshaw, Thornton F(rederick) Jun 82
Brady, William T(homas) obit Jul 84
Brandt, Bill Aug 81 obit Feb 84
Brett, George Jul 81
Brett, George P(latt), Jr. obit May 84
Breuer, Marcel (Lajos) obit Aug 81
Brezhnev, Leonid I(lyich) obit Jan 83
Brinton, Howard H(aines) obit Yrbk 84 (died Apr 73)
Bristow, Gwen obit Yrbk 84 (died Aug 80)
Brodsky, Joseph (Alexandrovich) Jul 82
Brokaw, Tom May 81
Brooks, Louise Apr 84
Brower, Charles (Hendrickson) obit Nov 84
Brown, Charles L(ee, Jr.) Sep 81
Brown, Sterling (Allen) Aug 82
Brundtland, Gro Harlem Nov 81
Bruner, Jerome (Seymour) Oct 84
Bryant, Paul W(illiam) obit Mar 83
Buckley, William F(rank) Jr. Oct 82
Buckmaster, Henrietta obit Jun 83
Bugas, John S(tephen) obit Feb 83
Bunker, Ellsworth obit Nov 84
Buñuel, Luis obit Sep 83
Burton, Richard obit Sep 84
Buscaglia, (Felice) Leo(nardo) Oct 83
Bush, George (Herbert Walker) Sep 83
Butler, Richard Austen See Butler of Saffron Walden, R.A.B., Baron obit
Butler of Saffron Walden, Richard Austen Butler, Baron obit May 82
Byrne, John Keyes See Leonard, Hugh

Cabot, John M(oors) obit Apr 81
Caetano, Marcello (José) obit Jan 81

Caldicott, Helen Oct 83
Callahan, Harry M(orey) Nov 84
Calvino, Italo Feb 84
Calvo Sotelo (y Bustelo), Leopoldo Aug 81
Campbell, Earl Apr 83
Campbell, Joseph Jun 84
Cámpora, Héctor José obit Feb 81
Canetti, Elias Jan 83
Canham, Erwin D(ain) obit Feb 82
Capote, Truman obit Oct 84
Carlino, Lewis John May 83
Carlisle, Kitty See Hart, Kitty Carlisle
Carlucci, Frank (Charles 3d) Oct 81
Carmichael, Hoagy obit Feb 82
Caro, Anthony Nov 81
Caro, Robert A. Jan 84
Carroll, John A(lbert) obit Oct 83
Carroll, Vinnette Sep 83
Carson, Johnny Apr 82
Carter, Betty Mar 82
Carter, (William) Hodding 3d Aug 81
Carter, (Bessie) Lillian obit Jan 84
Carver, Raymond Feb 84
Cary, William L(ucius) obit Apr 83
Case, Clifford P(hilip) obit Apr 82
Castelli, Leo Aug 84
Catledge, Turner obit Jul 83
Celler, Emanuel obit Mar 81
Chagla, Mahomed Ali Currim obit Jan 84
Chaikin, Joseph Jul 81
Chapin, Katherine Garrison See Biddle, K. G. C. obit
Chapman, Albert K(inkade) obit Yrbk 84
Chapman, Charles F(rederic) obit Yrbk 84 (died Mar 76)
Charles, Prince of Belgium obit Jul 83
Charlot, Jean obit Yrbk 84 (died Mar 79)
Chase, Mary (Coyle) obit Jan 82
Chayefsky, Paddy obit Sep 81
Cheever, John obit Aug 82
Chernenko, Konstantin U(stinovich) Aug 84
Chicago, Judy Feb 81
Childs, Lucinda Apr 84
Christopher, Warren M(inor) Jun 81
Chuikov, Vasili (Ivanovitch) obit May 82
Chun Doo Hwan Mar 81
Church, Frank (Forrester) obit May 84

Church, Sam(uel Morgan), Jr. Oct 81
Churchill, Sarah obit Jan 83
Cimino, Michael Jan 81
Citrine of Wembley, Walter McLennan Citrine, Ist Baron obit Apr 83
Clair, René obit May 81
Clark, Lord Kenneth (Mackenzie) obit Jul 83
Clark, Mark W(ayne) obit Jun 84
Clark, William P(atrick) Jul 82
Clausen, A(lden) W(inship) Nov 81
Clavell, James Oct 81
Cleese, John Jan 84
Close, Charles See Close, Chuck
Close, Chuck Jul 83
Close, Glenn Nov 84
Cody, John Patrick Cardinal obit Jun 82
Cohen, Benjamin V(ictor) obit Oct 83
Cohen, William S(ebastian) Apr 82
Coleman, Lonnie (William) obit Oct 82
Collins, Joan Jan 84
Conable, Barber B., Jr. Jul 84
Conley, Eugene obit Feb 82
Connelly, Marc obit Feb 81
Conway, Tim Apr 81
Cook, Donald C(larence) obit Feb 82
Cooke, Terence J(ames) Cardinal obit Nov 83
Coon, Carleton S(tevens) obit Jul 81
Corcoran, Thomas Gardiner obit Feb 82
Corman, Roger Feb 83
Cortázar, Julio obit Apr 84
Cossiga, Francesco Jan 81
Costello, Elvis Sep 83
Cotrubas, Ileana Oct 81
Cowles, John obit Apr 83
Cowles, Virginia (Spencer) obit Nov 83
Cox, Allyn obit Jan 83
Cox, William Trevor See Trevor, William
Craft, Robert Mar 84
Craxi, Bettino Feb 84
Crick, Francis Mar 83
Crisler, Herbert Orin obit Oct 82
Cronin, A(rchibald) J(oseph) obit Mar 81
Cronin, Joe obit Nov 84
Crosby, John (O'Hea) Nov 81
Cross, Ben Aug 84
Crowther, (F.) Bosley obit Apr 81
Cruyff, Johan Nov 81
Cruz, Celia Jul 83
Cukor, George obit Mar 83
Cullberg, Birgit Nov 82

Cunningham, Sir Alan (Gordon) obit Apr 83
Cunningham, Mary (Elizabeth) Nov 84
Cuomo, Mario (Matthew) Aug 83
Curran, Joseph E(dwin) obit Oct 81
Curzon, Clifford obit Oct 82

Dacre of Glanton, Baron, See Trevor-Roper, H. R.
Dalai Lama Jun 82
Dale, Jim Jul 81
D'Amato, Alfonse Sep 83
Daniels, Jonathan (Worth) obit Jan 82
Dannay, Frederic obit Oct 82
Danner, Blythe Jan 81
Dart, Justin W(hitlock) obit Mar 84
D'Aubuisson, Roberto Jul 83
Dausset, Jean May 81
Davis, Andrew May 83
Davis, James C(urran) obit Feb 82
Davis, Peter (Frank) Feb 83
Day, Dorothy obit Jan 81
Dayan, Moshe obit Jan 82
Dean, William F(rishe) obit Oct 81
Debray, (Jules) Régis Jun 82
Debus, Kurt H(einrich) obit Nov 83
Decker, Mary Oct 83
Decter, Midge Apr 82
Deighton, Len Sep 84
De Kooning, Elaine (Marie Catharine) Jul 82
De Kooning, Willem Sep 84
De La Madrid (Hurtado), Miguel Apr 83
Del Tredici, David Mar 83
De Montebello, (Guy-)Philippe (Lannes) Apr 81
Dempsey, Jack obit Jul 83
Dempsey, William Harrison See Dempsey, Jack obit
Densen-Gerber, Judianne Nov 83
Denton, Jeremiah A(ndrew) Jr. May 82
De Palma, Brian Sep 82
De Rochemont, Richard (Guertis) obit Sept 82
Deukmejian, (Courken) George, Jr. Jun 83
Dewey, Charles S(chuveldt) obit Feb 81
Dial, Morse G(rant) obit Jan 83
Diamond, Neil May 81
Diana, Princess of Wales Jan 83
Dickinson, Angie Feb 81
Dietz, Howard obit Sep 83
Dillard, Annie Jan 83
Dingell, John D(avid) Jr. Aug 83

DiSalle, Michael V(incent) obit Nov 81
Dodds, Harold W(illis) obit Jan 81
Dodge, Cleveland E(arl) obit Feb 83
Doe, Samuel K(anyon) May 81
Doenitz, Karl obit Feb 81
Dole, Elizabeth Hanford Jun 83
Dolin, Anton obit Jan 84
Domenici, Pete V(ichi) Jun 82
Donovan, Raymond J(ames) Jan 82
Dorticós (Torrado), Osvaldo obit Aug 83
Douglas, Donald W(ills) obit Mar 81
Douglas, Melvyn obit Sep 81
Drabble, Margaret May 81
Drew, George A(lexander) obit May 84
Druckman, Jacob May 81
Drummond, (James) Roscoe obit Nov 83
Duarte (Fuentes), José Napoleón Sep 81
Dubinsky, David obit Jan 83
Dubos, René J(ules) obit Apr 82
Dunne, John Gregory Jun 82
Durant, Will(iam James) obit Jan 82

Eckstein, Gustav obit Nov 81
Eckstein, Otto obit May 84
Edwards, Blake Jan 83
Edwards, (W.) Don(lon) Mar 83
Edwards, James B(urrows) Nov 82
Edwards, Joan obit Oct 81
Egan, William Allen obit Jul 84
Elizabeth, Queen Mother of Great Britain Aug 81
Emerson, Faye obit May 83
Ernst, Jimmy obit Apr 84
Ershad, Hussain Muhammad Nov 84
Ethridge, Mark (Foster) obit Jun 81
Evans, Luther H(arris) obit Feb 82
Evren, Kenan Apr 84

Fagerholm, Karl-August obit Jul 84
Fagg, Fred D(ow) Jr. obit Jan 82
Falwell, Jerry Jan 81
Farrar, Margaret (Petherbridge) obit Aug 84
Farrington, (Mary) Elizabeth Pruett obit Sep 84
Fassbinder, Rainer Werner obit Aug 82

Feinsinger, Nathan P(aul) obit Jan 84
Feld, Irvin obit Nov 84
Feldstein, Martin (Stuart) May 83
Ferguson, Homer obit Mar 83
Ferraro, Geraldine A(nne) Sep 84
Fielding, Temple (Hornaday) obit Jul 83
Fierstein, Harvey Feb 84
Fisher, M(ary) F(rances) K(ennedy) Sep 83
Fisher, Welthy (Blakesley Honsinger) obit Feb 81
Fisk, James Brown obit Oct 81
Fitzgerald, Albert J. obit Jul 82
Fitzgerald, Ed obit Jun 82
FitzGerald, Garret Aug 84
Fitzsimmons, Frank E(dward) obit Jul 81
Florinsky, Michael T(imofeevich) obit Jan 82
Folon, Jean-Michel Feb 81
Fonda, Henry obit Sep 82
Fontanne, Lynn obit Sep 83
Foot, Michael (Mackintosh) May 81
Ford, Harrison Sep 84
Fortas, Abe obit May 82
Foster, Jodie Jun 81
Fox, Carol obit Sep 81
Fox, Robert J(ohn) obit Jun 84
Fox, Virgil (Keel) obit Jan 81
Francis, Dick Aug 81
Fraser of North Cape, Bruce Austin Fraser, 1st Baron obit Apr 81
Frederika (Louise), Consort of Paul I, King of the Hellenes obit Apr 81
Frei (Montalva), Eduardo obit Mar 82
Freud, Anna obit Mar 83
Frings, Ketti (Hartley) obit Apr 81
Frisch, Karl von obit Yrbk 83 (died Jun 82)
Frye, (Herman) Northrop Aug 83
Fuller, R(ichard) Buckminster (Jr.) obit Aug 83

Gajdusek, D(aniel) Carleton Jun 81
Gallup, George (Horace) obit Sep 84
Galtieri, Leopoldo (Fortunato) Aug 82
Gandhi, Indira (Priyadarshini Nehru) obit Yrbk 84
Gardner, John (Champlin, Jr.) obit Nov 82
Garroway, Dave obit Sep 82
Garth, David Jan 81
Gates, Thomas S(overeign), Jr. obit May 83
Gemayel, Amin Mar 83

Gerbner, George Aug 83
Gershwin, Ira obit Oct 83
Giauque, William F(rancis) obit May 82
Gibb, Barry Sep 81
Gibson, Mel Apr 84
Gibson, William Jul 83
Gielgud, John Feb 84
Gilder, George Oct 81
Giles, Barney McKinney obit Aug 84
Gimbel, Peter (Robin) Jan 82
Giroux, Robert Nov 82
Glass, Philip Mar 81
Glemp, Jozef Sep 82
Gobbi, Tito obit May 84
Godfrey, Arthur obit May 83
Godunov, Alexander Feb 83
Golden, Harry (Lewis) obit Nov 81
Goldmann, Nahum obit Oct 82
Golub, Leon (Albert) Aug 84
Gomulka, Wladyslaw obit Oct 82
Goodrich, Frances obit Apr 84
Gordon, Mary (Catherine) Nov 81
Gorin, Igor obit Jun 82
Gorsuch, Anne (McGill) Sep 82
Gosden, Freeman F(isher) obit Feb 83
Gossage, Rich Aug 84
Goudge, Elizabeth obit Aug 84
Gould, Glenn obit Nov 82
Gould, Stephen Jay Sep 82
Grace, Princess of Monaco obit Nov 82
Gramm, Donald obit Jul 83
Grass, Günter (Wilhelm) Jul 83
Grasso, Ella T(ambussi) obit Mar 81
Graves, Nancy (Stevenson) May 81
Gray, Gordon obit Feb 83
Gray, Simon (James Holliday) Jun 83
Gretzky, Wayne, Feb 82
Gribble, Harry Wagstaff (Graham-) obit Apr 81
Griffin, (Samuel) Marvin obit Aug 82
Grillo, Frank Raúl See Machito
Grosvenor, Melville Bell obit Jun 82
Gruenther, Alfred M(aximilian) obit Jul 83
Grumman, Leroy R(andle) obit Jan 83
Guare, John Aug 82
Guinness, Alec Mar 81
Guthrie, Arlo Feb 82

Habib, Philip C(harles) Sep 81
Hagerty, James C. obit Jun 81
Hall, Donald (Andrew) May 84

Hall, Joyce C(lyde) obit Jan 83
Hallstein, Walter obit May 82
Handler, Philip obit Feb 82
Handy, Thomas T(roy) obit Jun 82
Hanks, Nancy obit Mar 83
Hanna, William Jul 83
Hanson, Duane (Elwood) Oct 83
Hanson, Howard obit Apr 81
Harburg, E(dgar) Y(ipsel) obit Apr 81
Hardwick, Elizabeth Feb 81
Hare, David Aug 83
Harkness, Rebekah (West) obit Sep 82
Harrar, J(acob) George obit Jun 82
Harrell, Lynn Feb 83
Harris, Sir Arthur Travers obit May 84
Harrison, Wallace K(irkman) obit Jan 82
Harry, Debbie Nov 81
Hart, Kitty Carlisle Oct 82
Hartman, David Jun 81
Hatch, Orrin G(rant) Aug 82
Hatfield, Mark O(dom) Mar 84
Hauge, Gabriel (Sylfest) obit Sep 81
Haughey, Charles J(ames) Feb 81
Hawke, Bob Aug 83
Hawke, Robert James Lee See Hawke, Bob
Hawking, Stephen W(illiam) May 84
Hawkins, Augustus F(reeman) Feb 83
Hays, (Lawrence) Brooks obit Jan 82
Head, Edith obit Jan 82
Heaney, Seamus (Justin) Jan 82
Hearns, Thomas Mar 83
Hearst, Patricia (Campbell) Aug 82
Heckler, Margaret M(ary O'Shaughnessy) Aug 83
Heinz, (Henry) John, (3d) Apr 81
Hellman, Lillian obit Aug 84
Henley, Beth Feb 83
Hersh, Seymour (Myron) Mar 84
Hesburgh, Theodore M(artin) Jul 82
Hicks, Granville obit Aug 82
Hildebrand, Joel H(enry) obit Jul 83
Hill, Benny Feb 83
Hillenkoetter, Roscoe H(enry) obit Aug 82
Hines, Earl (Kenneth) obit Jun 83
Hines, Fatha See Hines, Earl (Kenneth) obit
Hirsch, John (Stephen) Apr 84
Hirsch, Judd Mar 84

Hirshhorn, Joseph H(erman) obit Oct 81
Hoagland, Edward (Morley) Sept 82
Hoffa, James R(iddle) obit Mar 83
Hoffer, Eric obit Jul 83
Hoffman, Abbie Apr 81
Hoffman, Anna M(arie) Rosenberg obit Jul 83
Hogben, Lancelot (Thomas) obit Jan 84
Holden, William obit Jan 82
Holliday, Jennifer Jun 83
Hollings, Ernest F(rederick) Jul 82
Holloway, Stanley obit Mar 82
Holmes, Larry Aug 81
Holt, John (Caldwell) Jun 81
Holyoake, Keith J(acka) obit Feb 84
Hope, Stanley C. obit Oct 82
Horner, H(orace) Mansfield obit Jul 83
Hosmer, (Chester) Craig obit Mar 83
Houghton, Amory obit Apr 81
Houseman, John Apr 84
Howard, Elston (Gene) obit Feb 81
Hu Yaobang Nov 83
Hughes, Barnard Sep 81
Hughes, Emmet John obit Nov 82
Hunsaker, Jerome C(larke) obit Nov 84
Huppert, Isabelle Nov 81
Hurd, Peter obit Sep 84
Hurt, John Jan 82
Hussein, Saddam (al-Tikriti) Sep 81
Huston, John Mar 81

Idris Senussi I, King of Libya obit Jul 83
Idriss Senussi I, King of Libya See Idris Senussi I, King of Libya obit
Iglesias, Julio Jun 84
Ilg, Frances L(illian) obit Sep 81
Illia, Arturo (Umberto) obit Mar 83
Irons, Jeremy Aug 84
Ivory, James Jul 81

Jackson, Henry M(artin) obit Oct 83
Jackson, Michael Nov 83
Jacobi, Derek May 81
James, Clive (Vivian Leopold) Nov 84
James, Harry obit Aug 83
Jaruzelski, Wojciech (Witold) Mar 82
Jaworski, Leon obit Feb 83
Jayewardene, J(unius) R(ichard) Jan 84

Jenkins, Ray H(oward) obit Feb 81

Jenkins, Roy (Harris) Oct 82

Jennings, Peter (Charles) Nov 83

Jennings, Waylon Apr 82

Jensen, Jackie obit Oct 82

Jessel, George (Albert) obit Jul 81

Jobs, Steven (Paul) Mar 83

Johanson, Donald C(arl) Feb 84

John, Tommy Oct 81

Johnson, Crockett obit Jan 84

Johnson, Earvin Jan 82

Johnson, Harold K(eith) obit Nov 83

Johnson, Magic See Johnson, Earvin Jan 82

Johnson, Pamela Hansford obit Aug 81

Jones, Carolyn obit Sep 83

Jones, David C(harles) Jul 82

Jones, James R(obert) Oct 81

Jones, Marvin obit Jan 84

Julia, Raul Sep 82

Kahn, Herman obit Aug 83

Kaiser, Edgar F(osburgh) obit Feb 82

Kane, Harnett T(homas) obit Yrbk 84

Kania, Stanislaw Jun 81

Kapitsa, Pyotr L(conidovich) obit May 84

Kapitza, Peter L(eonidovich) See Kapitsa, P. L. obit

Karmal, Babrak Mar 81

Kassebaum, Nancy Landon Feb 82

Kastler, Alfred obit Mar 84

Kaufman, Henry Aug 81

Kay, Hershy obit Feb 82

Keighley, William obit Aug 84

Kelly, Grace See Grace, Princess of Monaco obit

Kelly, Petra (Karin) Mar 84

Kelman, Charles D(avid) Jun 84

Kemper, James S(cott) obit Nov 81

Kennedy, Donald Jul 84

Khalid, King of Saudi Arabia obit Aug 82

Kieran, John (Francis) obit Feb 82

King, Don Jun 84

King, Stephen Oct 81

Kingman, Dave Mar 82

Kingsley, Ben Nov 83

Kinnock, Neil (Gordon) Apr 84

Kinski, Nastassja Jun 84

Kintner, Robert E(dmonds) obit Feb 81

Kirkpatrick, Jeane (Duane) J(ordan) Jul 81

Kirkpatrick, Ralph obit Aug 84

Kistiakowsky, George B(ogdan) obit Feb 83

Kitaj, R(onald) B(rooks) Apr 82

Kitchell, Iva obit Jan 84

Klein, Julius obit May 84

Kline, Nathan S(chellenberg) obit May 83

Knight, John S(hively) obit Aug 81

Knopf, Alfred A. obit Oct 84

Koestler, Arthur obit Apr 83

Koivisto, Mauno (Henrik) Sep 82

Kolff, Willem Johan May 83

Kolvenbach, Peter-Hans May 84

Komar, Vitaly, and Melamid, Aleksandr Oct 84

Koop, C(harles) Everett Sep 83

Koppel, Ted Jul 84

Kosygin, Aleksei N(ikolayevich) obit Feb 81

Krantz, Judith May 82

Krasner, Lee obit Aug 84

Krebs, Sir Hans obit Feb 82

Kroc, Ray(mond) A. obit Mar 84

Kucuk, Fazil See Kutchuk, (M.) F. obit

Kundera, Milan Mar 83

Kuralt, Charles Jul 81

Kutchuk, (Mustafa) Fazil obit Mar 84

Kylian, Jiri Sep 82

Ladurie, Emmanuel Le Roy See Le Roy Ladurie, E.

Laffer, Arthur (Betz) Feb 82

Lagerfeld, Karl Jan 82

LaMarsh, Judy obit Jan 81

Land, Edwin H(erbert) Mar 81

Lang, Jack Aug 83

Lange, Jessica May 83

Lansing, Sherry (Lee) May 81

Laughlin, James May 82

Laurents, Arthur Nov 84

Lawe, John (Edward) Jan 84

Lebowitz, Fran(ces Ann) Mar 82

Leboyer, Frédérick Jul 82

Léger, Jules obit Jan 81

Le Guin, Ursula K(roeber) Jan 83

Lehrer, Tom Jul 82

Lelouch, Claude Nov 82

Lendl, Ivan Sep 84

Lennon, John obit Feb 81

Lennox-Boyd, Lord Alan T(indal) obit May 83

Lenya, Lotte obit Jan 82

Leonard, Hugh Apr 83

Leonard, Ray See Leonard, Sugar Ray

Leonard, Sugar Ray Feb 81

Leopold III, King of the Belgians obit Nov 83

Le Roy Ladurie, Emmanuel (Bernard) Jul 84

Lesage, Jean obit Feb 81

LeSourd, Catherine Marshall See Marshall, S.C.W. obit

Levi, Julian (Edwin) obit Apr 82

Levin, Meyer obit Sep 81

Lewis, Carl Nov 84

Lewis, Drew Feb 82

Liberman, Evsei (Grigorevich) obit May 83

Liebman, Max obit Sep 81

Lilienthal, David E(li) obit Mar 81

Limann, Hilla Jun 81

Link, Edwin (Albert) obit Yrbk 83 (died Sep 81)

Littlejohn, Robert McG(owan) obit Jul 82

Llewellyn, Richard obit Jan 84

Lloyd Webber, Andrew Jun 82

Lockridge, Richard obit Oct 82

Loeb, William obit Nov 81

Longo, Luigi obit Jan 81

Loos, Anita obit Oct 81

Loquasto, Santo Jun 81

Loring, Eugene obit Oct 82

Losey, Joseph obit Aug 84

Loudon, Dorothy Jun 84

Louganis, Greg Oct 84

Louis, Joe obit Jun 81

Love, Iris (Cornelia) Aug 82

Lowery, Joseph E. Nov 82

Lucas, Martha B. See Pate, M. B. L. obit

Ludlum, Robert Nov 82

Luns, Joseph M(arie) A(ntoine) H(ubert) Apr 82

Lustiger, Jean-Marie Feb 84

Lynd, Staughton (Craig) May 83

Lynde, Paul (Edward) obit Feb 82

Ma, Yo-Yo Jul 82

MacDermot, Galt Jul 84

Macdonald, Dwight obit Mar 83

MacDonald, Malcolm (John) obit Mar 81

Macdonald, Ross obit Sep 83

MacEachen, Allan J(oseph) Apr 83

Machel, Samora Moises Mar 84

Machito Feb 83 obit Jun 84

Mackay, John A(lexander) obit Aug 83

MacLeish, Archibald obit Jun 82

Malik, Adam obit Nov 84

Mandela, Nelson (Rolihlahla) Jan 84

Mandrell, Barbara Aug 82

Marsalis, Wynton Oct 84

Marshall, (Sarah) Catherine (Wood) obit May 83

Mason, James obit Sep 84

Mason, Marsha Apr 81

Massey, Raymond obit Sep 83
Mauroy, Pierre Jun 82
Mayr, Ernst Nov 84
Mays, Benjamin E(lijah) obit May 84
Mazey, Emil obit Nov 83
McBride, Lloyd obit Jan 84
McCabe, Thomas B(ayard) obit Jul 82
McCain, John S(idney), Jr. obit Jun 81
McCall, Tom (Lawson) obit Mar 83
McClintock, Barbara Mar 84
McColough, C(harles) Peter Jan 81
McCormack, John W(illiam) obit Jan 81
McCullough, Colleen Apr 82
McFadden, Mary Apr 83
McFarland, Ernest W(illiam) obit Aug 84
McFarlane, Robert C(arl) May 84
McGannon, Donald H(enry) obit Jul 84
McGinniss, Joe Jan 84
McKellen, Ian Jan 84
McLean, Robert obit Feb 81
McLuhan, (Herbert) Marshall obit Feb 81
McMurtry, Larry (Jeff) Jun 84
McPhee, John (Angus) Oct 82
McQueen, Steve obit Jan 81
McRae, Carmen Apr 83
Mearns, David C(hambers) obit Jul 81
Medeiros, Humberto S(ousa) obit Nov 83
Medvedev, Roy (Aleksandr) Sep 84
Meese, Edwin, 3d Sep 81
Melamid, Aleksandr See Komar, V.
Mendès-France, Pierre obit Jan 83
Mengistu Haile Mariam Jul 81
Mennin, Peter obit Aug 83
Menon, K(umara) P(admanbha) S(ivasankara) obit Yrbk 83 (died Nov 82)
Mercer, Mabel obit Jun 84
Merman, Ethel obit Apr 84
Merrill, James (Ingram) Aug 81
Michals, Duane (Steven) Apr 81
Michel, Robert H(enry) Sep 81
Mifune, Toshiro Jun 81
Millar, Kenneth See Macdonald, R. obit
Miller, Irving obit Feb 81
Miller, William E(dward) obit Aug 83
Milosz, Czeslaw Oct 81
Miner, Worthington (C.) obit Mar 83
Mintoff, Dom Mar 84
Miró, Joan obit Feb 84

Mitterrand, François (Maurice) Oct 82)
Monaco, Mario del obit Jan 83
Monk, Thelonious obit Apr 82
Montale, Eugenio obit Nov 81
Montana, Joe Sep 83
Montebello, (Guy-)Philippe (Lannes) de See De Montebello, Philippe
Montgomery, Robert obit Nov 81
Moody, Joseph E(ugene) obit Jul 84
Moon, Sun Myung Mar 83
Moore, Dudley Jun 82
Morgan, Joe Sep 84
Morganfield, McKinley See Waters, Muddy
Morley, Malcolm A. Jun 84
Morris, Wright (Marion) May 82
Morrison, Philip Jul 81
Mortimer, John (Clifford) Apr 83
Morton, Thruston B(allard) obit Oct 82
Moses, Robert obit Sep 81
Mosley, Sir Oswald (Ernald) obit Feb 81
Motley, Arthur H(arrison) obit Jul 84
Mubarak, (Mohamed) Hosni Apr 82
Mudd, Roger (Harrison) Jan 81
Mueller, R(euben) H(erbert) obit Sep 82
Mulroney, (Martin) Brian Apr 84
Mumford, L(awrence) Quincy obit Jan 83
Murphy, Charles S(prings) obit Oct 83
Murphy, Eddie Nov 83
Murray, Anne Jan 82
Myer, Dillon S(eymour) obit Jan 83

Naisbitt, John Nov 84
Nakasone, Yasuhiro Jun 83
Navon, Yitzhak May 82
Nearing, Scott obit Oct 83
Nelligan, Kate Jul 83
Nesbitt, Cathleen (Mary) obit Sep 82
Nettles, Graig Jul 84
Neumann, Emanuel obit Jan 81
Newell, Homer E(dward), Jr. obit Sep 83
Newman, Randy Oct 82
Nicholson, Ben obit Apr 82
Nicolson, Marjorie Hope obit Jun 81
Niemöller, (Friedrich Gustav Emil) Martin obit May 84
Niven, David obit Sep 83
Noel-Baker, Philip J(ohn) obit Mar 83

Nofziger, Lyn Jan 83
Norman, Marsha May 84
Northrop, John K(nudsen) obit Apr 81
Nozick, Robert Jun 82

Obote, (Apollo) Milton Apr 81
Obraztsova, Elena Feb 83
O'Brien, Leo W(illiam) obit Jul 82
O'Brien, Pat obit Jan 84
Ochsner, (Edward William) Alton obit Nov 81
O'Connor, John J(oseph) Jun 84
O'Connor, Sandra Day Jan 82
Odishaw, Hugh obit Jun 84
O'Hara, Mary obit Jan 81
Oliver, James A(rthur) obit May 82
Olson, Harry F(erdinand) obit Jun 82
O'Neil, James F(rancis) obit Sep 81
Orff, Carl obit May 82
Ortega, Daniel Oct 84
Osborn, Frederick (Henry) obit Mar 81
O'Shea, Milo Jun 82
Ovandia Candia, Alfredo obit Mar 82
Owings, Nathaniel A(lexander) obit Aug 84
Oz, Amos Jul 83
Ozick, Cynthia Aug 83

Packwood, Bob Jan 81
Padover, Saul K(ussiel) obit Apr 81
Paige, Leroy (Robert) obit Aug 82
Paik, Nam June Mar 83
Papandreou, Andreas (George) Apr 83
Parker, Buddy obit Jun 82
Parsons, Harriet (Oettinger) obit Mar 83
Partch, Virgil F(ranklin) obit Oct 84
Pate, Martha B. Lucas obit Jul 83
Paterno, Joe Feb 84
Pauley, Edwin W(endell) obit Sep 81
Paxton, Tom Sep 82
Payne, (Pierre Stephen) Robert obit Apr 83
Pella, Giuseppe obit Aug 81
Pelletier, Wilfrid obit Jun 82
Pelli, Cesar Apr 83
Peltz, Mary Ellis (Opdycke) obit Jan 82
Pendleton, Clarence M(cLane), Jr. Sep 84
Pepper, Claude (Denson) Jan 83
Perahia, Murray Mar 82

Pérez de Cuéllar, Javier Aug 82

Pérez Esquivel, Adolfo Mar 81

Perkins, Carl D(ewey) obit Sep 84

Perkins, Dexter obit Jul 84

Perlman, Alfred E(dward) obit Jul 83

Perry, Gaylord Nov 82

Peters, Bernadette Sep 84

Peterson, Oscar Oct 83

Peterson, (Frederick) Val(demar Erastus) obit Jan 84

Phillips, William Oct 84

Pidgeon, Walter obit Nov 84

Pierce, Samuel Riley, Jr. Nov 82

Piñero, Miguel Nov 83

Plunkett, Jim Feb 82

Podgorny, Nikolai (Viktorovich) obit Mar 83

Ponnamperuma, Cyril (Andrew) Apr 84

Ponnelle, Jean-Pierre Mar 83

Popkin, Zelda obit Jul 83

Potok, Chaim May 83

Powell, William obit May 84

Presser, Jackie Sep 83

Pressler, Larry Oct 83

Price, Byron obit Sep 81

Price, George (Cadle) Aug 84

Priestley, J(ohn) B(oynton) obit Oct 84

Primrose, William obit July 82

Putnam, Ashley Mar 82

Pym, Francis (Leslie) Sep 82

Quennell, Peter (Courtney) May 84

Quimby, Edith H(inkley) obit Mar 83

Rafferty, Max(well Lewis, Jr.) obit Aug 82

Rahner, Karl obit May 84

Rambert, Marie Feb 81 obit Aug 82

Ramey, Samuel Jul 81

Rand, Ayn May 82 obit May 82

Rangel, Charles B(ernard) Mar 84

Rauschning, Hermann obit Apr 83

Rawlings, Jerry (John) Jun 82

Rawls, Lou Mar 84

Reagan, Nancy May 82

Reagan, Ronald (Wilson) Nov 82

Reddy, N(eelam) Sanjiva Mar 81

Redford, Robert Mar 82

Redpath, Jean Feb 84

Reeve, Christopher May 82

Regan, Donald T(homas) Nov 81

Reichelderfer, F(rancis) W(ilton) obit Mar 83

Renault, Mary obit Feb 84

Rexroth, Kenneth Apr 81 obit Aug 82

Richardson, Sir Ralph obit Nov 83

Richie, Lionel Jul 84

Riddleberger, James W(illiams) obit Jan 83

Ride, Sally K(risten) Oct 83

Riley, Bridget (Louise) Sep 81

Rios Montt, José Efraín May 83

Ritter, Bruce Jun 83

Rivera, Chita Oct 84

Rivlin, Alice M(itchell) Oct 82

Roa (y García), Raúl obit Sep 82

Robarts, John P(armenter) obit Jan 83

Robinson, John (Arthur Thomas) obit Feb 84

Robinson, M(aurice) R(ichard) obit May 82

Robison, Paula May 82

Robitzek, Edward H(einrich) obit May 84

Robson, Dame Flora obit Sep 84

Rodgers, Bill Aug 82

Rogers, Bernard W(illiam) Oct 84

Rogers, Kenny Jan 81

Rogers, Roy Oct 83

Rogge, O(etje) John obit Jun 81

Romano, Umberto obit Nov 82

Rooney, Andy Jul 82

Root, Waverley (Lewis) obit Jan 83

Rose, George Sep 84

Rosen, Samuel obit Jan 82

Rosenberg, Anna M(arie) See Hoffman, A.M.R. obit

Rostenkowski, Dan(iel D.) Jan 82

Roszak, Theodore obit Oct 81

Roszak, Theodore Apr 82

Roth, William V(ictor), Jr. Apr 83

Rotha, Paul obit May 84

Rothschild, Louis S(amuel) obit Oct 84

Rouse, James W(ilson) Feb 82

Rubinstein, Artur obit Mar 83

Rukeyser, Louis Feb 83

Russell, Mark Mar 81

Ryan, T(ubal) Claude obit Nov 82

Sadat, Anwar (el-) obit Nov 81

Salazar, Alberto May 83

Salisbury, Harrison E(vans) Jan 82

Sananikone, Phoui obit Feb 84

Sanders, Harland obit Feb 81

Sanders, Marlene Feb 81

Sanger, Frederick Jul 81

Sargeant, Howland H(ill) obit Apr 84

Saroyan, William obit Jul 81

Sarton, May May 82

Sauvé, Jeanne Aug 84

Savitch, Jessica Jan 83 obit Mar 84

Sayles, John Feb 84

Schacht, Al(exander) obit Sep 84

Schapiro, Meyer Jul 84

Schaufuss, Peter May 82

Schillebeeckx, Edward Jun 83

Schlöndorff, Volker Aug 83

Schnabel, Julian Nov 83

Schneerson, Menachem Mendel Sep 83

Schneider, Alan obit Jun 84

Schneider, Romy obit Jul 82

Schrader, Paul Aug 81

Schreyer, Edward Richard Feb 81

Schwartz, Arthur obit Oct 84

Schygulla, Hanna Jul 84

Scott, Hazel (Dorothy) obit Nov 81

Seaga, Edward (Phillip George) Apr 81

Seghers, Anna obit Jul 83

Seifert, Elizabeth obit Oct 83

Selleck, Tom Nov 83

Selye, Hans (Hugo Bruno) Jan 81 obit Jan 83

Sert, José Luis obit May 83

Sert, Josep Lluis See Sert, José Luis obit

Seymour, Whitney North obit Jul 83

Shamir, Yitzhak Feb 83

Sharon, Ariel Apr 81

Shaw, Irwin obit Jul 84

Sheed, Frank (Joseph) Sep 81 obit Jan 82

Sheed, Wilfrid Aug 81

Shehan, Lawrence (Joseph), Cardinal obit Oct 84

Shehu, Mehmet obit Feb 82

Shepherd, Jean (Parker) Apr 84

Shera, Jesse H(auk) obit Jun 82

Shields, Brooke Oct 82

Sholokhov, Mikhail A(leksandrovich) obit Apr 84

Shoup, David M(onroe) obit Mar 83

Sidney, Sylvia Oct 81

Silber, John R(obert) Feb 84

Sills, Beverly Feb 82

Simmons, Richard May 82

Sinclair, Adelaide Helen Grant Macdonald See Sinclair, Mrs. D. B. obit

Sinclair, Mrs. D. B. obit Jan 83

Slezak, Walter obit Jun 83

Slick, Grace Apr 82

Sliwa, Curtis Feb 83

Smith, Carleton obit Jul 84

Smith, James H(opkins), Jr. obit Feb 83
Smith, Red obit Feb 82
Smith, William French Jan 82
Smuin, Michael Oct 84
Sneider, Vern obit Jun 81
Soames, (Arthur) Christopher (John), Baron of Fletching Aug 81
Sobhuza II, King of Swaziland Mar 82 obit Oct 82
Soong Ching-ling. See Sun Yat-sen, Mme. obit
Souvanna Phouma, Prince of Laos obit Mar 84
Sovern, Michael I(ra) Feb 81
Sowell, Thomas Jul 81
Soyer, Isaac obit Sep 81
Speer, Albert obit Oct 81
Spiegelman, Sol(omon) obit Mar 83
Spillane, Mickey Sep 81
St. George, Katharine (Delano Price Collier) obit Jul 83
Stankiewicz, Richard (Peter) obit May 83
Stein, Jules (Caesar) obit Jun 81
Steiner, (Francis) George Oct 83
Stenmark, Ingemar Apr 82
Stevens, Robert T(en Broeck) obit Mar 83
Stever, H(orton) Guyford Jan 81
Stigler, George J(oseph) Jul 83
Stockman, David (Alan) Aug 81
Stoddard, George D(insmore) obit Feb 82
Strasberg, Lee obit Apr 82
Strawberry, Darryl Jun 84
Stroessner, Alfredo Mar 81
Struble, Arthur D(ewey) obit Jul 83
Stuart, Jesse obit Apr 84
Stutz, Geraldine (Veronica) May 83
Styne, Jule May 83
Sullivan, John L(awrence) obit Oct 82
Sun Myung Moon See Moon, S. M.
Sun Yat-sen, Mme. obit Jul 81
Sunay, Cevdet obit Aug 82
Suslov, Mikhail A(ndreye-vich) obit Mar 82
Sutherland, Donald Feb 81
Suzuki, Zenko Jan 81
Swanson, Gloria obit May 83
Syberberg, Hans Jürgen Apr 83

Tabb, Mary Decker See Deck-er, Mary
Taft, Charles P(helps, 2d) obit Aug 83
Talvela, Martti Oct 83

Tandy, Jessica Aug 84
Tati, Jacques obit Jan 83
Taylor, A(lan) J(ohn) P(ercivale) Nov 83
Taylor, Glen H(earst) obit Jul 84
Teague, Olin E(arl) obit Apr 81
Teale, Edwin Way obit Jan 81
Teller, Edward Nov 83
Tennstedt, Klaus Sep 83
Theorell, (Axel) Hugo (Teodor) obit Oct 82
Thomas, Charles Allen obit May 82
Thomas, Charles S(parks) obit Jan 84
Thomas, D(onald) M(ichael) Nov 83
Thomas, Franklin A(ugustine) Oct 81
Thomas, Lowell (Jackson) obit Oct 81
Thompson, Hunter S(tockton) Mar 81
Thompson, Paul See Rotha, Paul obit
Thornton, Charles B(ates) obit Jan 82
Thurman, Howard obit Jun 81
Tiegs, Cheryl Nov 82
Tiger, Lionel Jan 81
Timerman, Jacobo Nov 81
Tinker, Grant A. Mar 82
Tobin, James Oct 84
Todd, Richard May 82
Tomasson, Helgi Apr 82
Tormé, Mel Mar 83
Torrijos Herrera, Omar obit Sep 81
Tors, Ivan (Lawrence) obit Aug 83
Touré, (Ahmed) Sekou obit May 84
Townshend, Peter Aug 83
Trevor, William Sep 84
Trevor-Roper, H(ugh) R(edwald) Sep 83
Trippe, Juan T(erry) obit May 81
Truman, Bess (Wallace) See Truman, Mrs. Harry S obit
Truman, Mrs. Harry S obit Jan 83
Trump, Donald J(ohn) Feb 84
Tsarapkin, Semyon K(onstantinovich) obit Nov 84
Tsongas, Paul E(fthemios) Jul 81
Tubb, Ernest Oct 83 obit Oct 84
Tuck, William M(unford) obit Aug 83
Tully, Alice Jan 84
Tune, Tommy Jan 83
Turner, John (Napier) Nov 84
Turner, Tina Nov 84
Twining, Nathan F(arragut) obit May 82

Tworkov, Jack obit Oct 82
Tyler, Anne Jun 81

Umberto II, King of Italy obit May 83
Underhill, Ruth M(urray) obit Oct 84
Updike, John (Hoyer) Oct 84
Urey, Harold C(layton) obit Mar 81
Urrutia Lleo, Manuel obit Aug 81

Vadim, Roger Jan 84
Vagnozzi, Egidio Cardinal obit Feb 81
Valenzuela, Fernando Oct 82
Van den Haag, Ernest Oct 83
Vaughan, Harry H(awkins) obit Jul 81
Vera-Ellen obit Oct 81
Vidal, Gore Jun 83
Vidor, King obit Jan 83
Viguerie, Richard A(rt) Jan 83
Vinson, Carl obit Jul 81
Vogel, Hans-Jochen Jan 84
Von Zell, Harry obit Jan 82
Voorhis, (Horace) Jerry obit Nov 84
Vorster, Balthazar Johannes obit Nov 83

Wadsworth, James J(eremiah) obit May 84
Wagner, Robert Jun 84
Waitz, Grete Apr 81
Wajda, Andrzej Jul 82
Walcott, Derek (Alton) Apr 84
Walesa, Lech Apr 81
Walker, Alice Mar 84
Wallace, DeWitt obit May 81
Wallace, Lila (Bell) Acheson obit Jul 84
Wallenstein, Alfred obit Mar 83
Walton, Sir William Turner obit May 83
Wang Shih-chieh obit Jun 81
Ward, Barbara (Mary) obit Jul 81
Waring, Fred obit Sep 84
Warren, Harry obit Nov 81
Washington, Harold Feb 84
Waters, Muddy May 81 obit Jun 83
Watt, James G(aius) Jan 82
Watts, Heather May 83
Weaver, Earl Feb 83
Webb, Jack obit Mar 83
Webber, Andrew Lloyd See Lloyd Webber, A.
Wechsberg, Joseph obit Jun 83
Weidenbaum, Murray L(ew) Mar 82
Weidlein, Edward R(ay) obit Nov 83
Weinberg, Robert A(llan) Jun 83

Weir, Peter Aug 84
Weiss, Peter obit Jul 82
Wenders, Wim Jul 84
Wertham, Fredric obit Jan 82
West, Jessamyn obit Apr 84
West, Mae obit Jan 81
West, Dame Rebecca obit May 83
Weston, (Theodore) Brett Feb 82
White, Robert E(dward) May 84
Whitehead, Don(ald Ford) obit Mar 81
Whitney, John Hay obit Apr 82
Wilder, Alec obit Feb 81
Wilder, Billy Oct 84
Wilkins, Roy obit Oct 81
Will, George F(rederick) Sep 81
Williams, Billy Dee Apr 84
Williams, Eric (Eustace) obit May 81
Williams, Gluyas obit Apr 82
Williams, John Jul 83
Williams, John Bell obit May 83
Williams, Mary Lou obit Jul 81
Williams, Paul Jun 83

Williams, Tennessee obit Apr 83
Williams, Vanessa May 84
Wills, Garry Jun 82
Willson, Meredith obit Aug 84
Wilson, Carroll Louis obit Mar 83
Wilson, Kenneth G(eddes) Sep 83
Wilson, Peter (Cecil) obit Aug 84
Winchell, Constance M(abel) obit Sep 84
Winfield, Dave Jan 84
Winger, Debra Jul 84
Wise, James DeCamp obit Apr 84
Wood, John Apr 83
Wood, Natalie obit Jan 82
Woods, Donald Feb 82
Woods, George D(avid) obit Oct 82
Woodson, Carter G(odwin) obit Yrbk 84 (died Apr 50)
Wright, Louis B(ooker) obit Jun 84
Wu, K(uo) C(heng) obit Aug 84
Wurf, Jerry obit Feb 82
Wyeth, Andrew (Newell) Nov 81

Wyler, William obit Sep 81
Wyman, Thomas H(unt) Jun 83
Wyszynski, Stefan Cardinal obit Jul 81

Yadin, Yigael obit Aug 84
Yankelovich, Daniel Mar 82
Yeh, George K(ung-)C(hao) obit Jan 82
Yost, Charles W(oodruff) obit Jul 81
Young, Milton R(uben) obit Jul 83
Yourcenar, Maguerite Nov 82
Yukawa, Hideki obit Nov 81

Zablocki, Clement J(ohn) Jun 83 obit Jan 84
Zhao Ziyang Jun 84
Ziaur Rahman Jun 81 obit Jul 81
Zulli, Floyd, Jr. obit Jan 81
Zworykin, Vladimir K(osma) obit Sep 82